NOTABLE
TWENTIETH-CENTURY
SCIENTISTS

NOTABLE
TWENTIETH-CENTURY
SCIENTISTS

VOLUME 3 L-R

Emily J. McMurray, Editor

Jane Kelly Kosek and Roger M. Valade III, Associate Editors

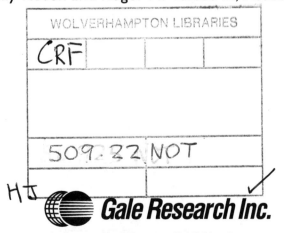

 Gale Research Inc.

An International Thomson Publishing Company

I(T)P

NEW YORK • LONDON • BONN • BOSTON • DETROIT • MADRID
MELBOURNE • MEXICO CITY • PARIS • SINGAPORE • TOKYO
TORONTO • WASHINGTON • ALBANY NY • BELMONT CA • CINCINNATI OH

Editor
Emily J. McMurray

Production Editor
Donna Olendorf

Associate Editors
Joanna Brod
Pamela S. Dear
Kathleen J. Edgar
Marie Ellavich
David M. Galens
Jeff Hill
Denise E. Kasinec
Thomas F. McMahon
Jane Kelly Kosek
Mark F. Mikula
Mary L. Onorato
Scot Peacock
Terrie M. Rooney
Deborah A. Stanley
Aarti Dhawan Stephens
Brandon Trenz
Roger M. Valade III
Polly A. Vedder
Thomas Wiloch

Assistant Editors
John Jorgenson
Margaret Mazurkiewicz
Geri J. Speace
Linda Tidrick
Kathleen Wilson

Senior Editor
James G. Lesniak

Picture Permissions Supervisor
Margaret A. Chamberlain

Picture Permissions Assistant
Susan Brohman

Front Matter Design
Paul Lewon

Art Director
Cynthia Baldwin

Cover Design
Mark Howell

Copyright © 1995
Gale Research Inc.
835 Penobscot Building
Detroit, MI 48226-4094

All rights reserved including the right of reproduction in whole or in part in any form.

ISBN 0-8103-9181-3 (Set)
ISBN 0-8103-9184-8 (Volume 3)

Printed in the United States of America.
Published simultaneously in the United Kingdom by Gale Research International Limited (An affiliated company of Gale Research Inc.)

I(T)P™ Gale Research Inc., an International Thomson Publishing Company.
ITP logo is a trademark under license.

Library of Congress Cataloging-in-Publication Data

Notable twentieth century scientists / Emily J. McMurray, editor.
    p. cm.
    Includes bibliographical references and index
    ISBN 0-8103-9181-3 (set)
    1. Scientists—Biography—Dictionaries. 2. Engineers-
-Biography—Dictionaries. I. McMurray, Emily J., 1959- .
Q141.N73 1995
509.2′2—dc20
  [B]   94-5263
                                          CIP

10 9 8 7 6 5 4 3 2 1

Contents

Introduction vii

Advisory Board xi

Contributors xii

Photo Credits xiii

Entry List xv

Chronology xxiii

Author Listings

    Volume 1: A-E 1

    Volume 2: F-K 607

    Volume 3: L-R 1153

    Volume 4: S-Z 1749

Selected Biographical Sources 2307

Field of Specialization Index 2309

Gender Index 2325

Nationality/Ethnicity Index 2333

Subject Index 2345

Introduction

Over the past several years, Gale Research Inc. has received numerous requests from librarians for a source providing biographies of scientists. *Notable Twentieth-Century Scientists* has been designed specifically to fill that niche. The four-volume set provides students, educators, librarians, researchers, and general readers with an affordable and comprehensive source of biographical information on approximately 1,300 scientists active in this century in all of the natural, physical, and applied sciences, including the traditionally studied subjects of astronomy, biology, botany, chemistry, earth science, mathematics, medicine, physics, technology, and zoology, as well as the more recently established and as yet sparsely covered fields of computer science, ecology, engineering, and environmental science. International in scope, *Notable Twentieth-Century Scientists* coverage ranges from the well-known scientific giants of the early century to contemporary scientists working at the cutting edge of discovery and knowledge.

Superior Coverage of Women, Minority and Non-Western Scientists

Addressing the growing interest in and demand for biographical information on women, minority and non-Western scientists, *Notable Twentieth-Century Scientists* also seeks to bring to light the achievements of more than 225 women scientists, almost 150 Asian American, African American, Hispanic American, and Native American scientists, and nearly 75 scientists from countries outside North America and Western Europe. The scarcity of published information on scientists representing these groups became evident during the compilation of this volume; as a result, information for many of the sketches on these listees has been obtained through telephone interviews and correspondence with the scientists themselves or with their universities, companies, laboratories, or families.

Though we have made every attempt to include key figures, we make no claim to having isolated the "most notable" women, minority, or non-Western scientists—an impossible goal. We are pleased that the majority of the biographies we wanted to feature are included; however, time constraints, space limitations, and research and interview availability prevented us from listing more scientists deserving of inclusion. Our hope is that in presenting these entries, we are providing a basis for future research on the lives and contributions of these important and historically marginalized segments of the scientific community.

Inclusion Criteria

A preliminary list of scientists was compiled from a wide variety of sources, including established reference works such as the *Dictionary of Scientific Biography,* history of science indexes, science periodicals, awards lists, and suggestions from organizations and associations. The advisory board, made up of librarians, academics, and individuals from scientific associations, evaluated the names and made suggestions for inclusion. Final selection of names to include was made by the editors on the basis of the following criteria:

- Discoveries, inventions, overall contributions, influence, and/or impact on scientific progress in the twentieth century
- Receipt of a major science award; all Nobel Prize winners in Physics, Chemistry, and Physiology or Medicine are found here, as are selected recipients of numerous other awards, including the Fields Medal (mathematics), Albert Lasker awards (medicine), the Tyler Prize (environmental science), the National Medal of Science, and the National Medal of Technology
- Involvement or influence in education, organizational leadership, or public policy
- Familiarity to the general public
- Notable "first" achievements, including degrees earned, positions held, or organizations founded; several listees involved in the first space flights are also included

Entries Provide Easy Access to Information

Entries are arranged alphabetically by surname. The typical *Notable Twentieth-Century Scientists* entry provides the following information:

- **Entry head**—offers an at-a-glance information: name, birth/death dates, nationality and primary field(s) of specialization.

- **Biographical essay**—ranges from 400 to 2500 words and provides basic biographical information [including date and place of birth, parents names and occupations, name(s) of spouse(s) and children, educational background and degrees earned, career positions, awards and honors earned] and scientific endeavors and achievements explained in prose accessible to high school students and readers without a scientific background. Intratextual headings within the essays highlight the significant events in the listee's life and career, allowing readers to find information they seek quickly and easily. In addition, **bold-faced** names in entries direct readers to entries on scientists' colleagues, predecessors, or contemporaries also found in *Notable Twentieth-Century Scientists*.

- **Selected Writings** by the Scientist section—lists representative publications, including important papers, textbooks, research works, autobiographies, lectures, etc.

- **Sources** section—provides citations of biographies, interviews, periodicals, obituaries, and other sources about the listee for readers seeking additional information.

Indexes Provide Numerous Points of Access

In addition to the complete list of scientists found at the beginning of each volume, readers seeking the names of additional individuals of a given country, heritage, gender, or profession can consult the following indexes at the end of volume 4 for additional listings:

- **Field of Specialization Index**—groups listees according to the scientific fields to which they have contributed
- **Gender Index**—provides lists of the women and men covered
- **Nationality/Ethnicity Index**—arranges listees by country of birth and/or citizenship and/or ethnic heritage
- Comprehensive **Subject Index**—provides volume and page references for scientists and scientific terms used in the text. Includes cross references.

Photos

Individuals in *Notable Twentieth-Century Scientists* come to life in the 394 photos of the scientists.

Acknowledgments

The editors would like to thank, in addition to the advisory board, the following individuals for their assistance with various aspects of the production of *Notable Twentieth-Century Scientists*: Bruce Seely, Secretary of the Society for the History of Technology and Professor at Michigan Technological University, Houghton, Michigan for his assistance in identifying notable engineers; Nancy Anderson, librarian at University of Illinois at Urbana Champaign Mathematics Library for assistance with mathematicians; Arthur Norberg, former director of the Charles Babbage Institute Center for the History of Information Processing at the University of Minnesota, Minneapolis, for assistance with computer scientists; and Kathleen Prestwidge for much assistance in identifying and providing information about minority and women scientists. Special acknowledgment is also due to Jim Kamp and Roger Valade for their technical assistance and to Denise Kasinec for her administrative assistance in the preparation of these volumes.

Advisory Board

Russell Aiuto
Senior Project Officer, Council of Independent Colleges
Former Director of the Scope, Sequence and Coordination of Secondary School
Science program, National Science Teachers Association
Washington, DC

Stephen G. Brush
Professor, Department of History and Institute for
Physical Science & Technology
University of Maryland, College Park

Nancy Bard
Head Reference Librarian,
Thomas Jefferson High School for Science and Technology
Alexandria, Virginia

James E. Bobick
Head, Science and Technology Department
The Carnegie Library of Pittsburgh
Pittsburgh, Pennsylvania

Michael J. Boersma
Science Exhibit Developer, Museum of Science and Industry
Chicago, Illinois

Catherine Jay Didion
Executive Director, Association for Women in Science
Washington, DC

Kathleen J. Prestwidge
Professor Emerita, Bronx Community College
Flushing, New York

Lewis Pyenson
Professeur titulaire, Department of History, University of Montreal
Quebec, Canada

Robin N. Sinn
Head Reference Librarian, Academy of Natural Science
Philadelphia, Pennsylvania

John Sweeney
Head of Science and Technology Information Service
British Library Science Reference and Information Service
London, England

Contributors

Russell Aiuto, Ethan E. Allen, Julie Anderson, Olga K. Anderson, Denise Adams Arnold, Nancy E. Bard, Dorothy Barnhouse, Jeffery Bass, Matthew A. Bille, Maurice Bleifeld, Michael Boersma, Barbara A. Branca, Hovey Brock, Valerie Brown, Leonard C. Bruno, Raymond E. Bullock, Marjorie Burgess, Gerard J. Buskes, Joseph Cain, Jill Carpenter, Dennis W. Cheek, Kim A. Cheek, Tom Chen, Miyoko Chu, Jane Stewart Cook, Kelly Otter Cooper, G. Scott Crawford, Tom Crawford, Karin Deck, Margaret DiCanio, Mindi Dickstein, Rowan L. Dordick, John Henry Dreyfuss, Thomas Drucker, Kala Dwarakanath, Marianne Fedunkiw, Martin R. Feldman, Eliseo Fernandez, George A. Ferrance, Jerome P. Ferrance, William T. Fletcher, David N. Ford, Karyn Hede George, Chris Hables Gray, Loretta Hall, Betsy Hanson, Robert M. Hawthorne, Jr., Elizabeth Henry, T. A. Heppenheimer, Frank Hertle, J. D. Hunley, Roger Jaffe, Jessica Jahiel, Jeanne Spriter James, J. Sydney Jones, D. George Joseph, Mark J. Kaiser, Lee Katterman, Sandra Katzman, Janet Kieffer Kelley, Evelyn B. Kelly, Karen S. Kelly, James Klockow, Susan E. Kolmer, Geeta Kothari, Jennifer Kramer, Marc Kusinitz, Roger D. Launius, Penelope Lawbaugh, Benedict A. Leerburger, Jeanne M. Lesinski, Linda Lewin, John E. Little, Pamela O. Long, C. D. Lord, Laura Mangan-Grenier, Gail B. C. Marsella, Liz Marshall, Renee D. Mastrocco, Patricia M. McAdams, William M. McBride, Mike McClure, Avril McDonald, Christopher McGrail, Kimberlyn McGrail, Donald J. McGraw, William J. McPeak, Carla Mecoli-Kamp, Leslie Mertz, Robert Messer, Philip Metcalfe, Fei Fei Wang Metzler, George A. Milite, Carol L. Moberg, Sally M. Moite, Patrick Moore, Paula M. Morin, M. C. Nagel, Margo Nash, Laura Newman, David E. Newton, F. C. Nicholson, Joan Oleck, Donna Olshansky, Nicholas Pease, Daniel Pendick, David Petechuk, Tom K. Phares, Devera Pine, Karl Preuss, Rayma Prince, Barbara J. Proujan, Amy M. Punke, Lewis Pyenson, Susan Sheets Pyenson, Jeff Raines, Mary Raum, Leslie Reinherz, Jordan P. Richman, Vita Richman, Francis Rogers, Terrie M. Romano, Daniel Rooney, Shari Rudavsky, Kathy Sammis, Karen Sands, Neeraja Sankaran, Joel Schwarz, Philip Duhan Segal, Alan R. Shepherd, Joel Simon, Michael Sims, Julian A. Smith, Linda Wasmer Smith, Lawrence Souder, Dorothy Spencer, John Spizzirri, David Sprinkle, Darwin H. Stapleton, Sharon F. Suer, Maureen L. Tan, Peter H. Taylor, Melinda Jardon Thach, Sebastian Thaler, R. F. Trimble, Cynthia Washam, Wallace Mack White, C. A. Williams, Katherine Williams, Nicholas S. Williamson, Philip K. Wilson, Rodolfo A. Windhausen, Karen Wilhelm, Karen Withem, Alexandra Witze, Cathleen M. Zucco.

Photo Credits

Photographs appearing in *Notable Twentieth-Century Scientists* were received from the following sources:

AP/Wide World Photos: **pp. 1, 31, 36, 38, 45, 48, 75, 98, 108, 112, 129, 150, 166, 169, 172, 174, 186, 192, 195, 198, 202, 203, 207, 211, 219, 221, 231, 234, 241, 278, 285, 295, 297, 299, 310, 313, 315, 321, 322, 326, 331, 341, 344, 348, 358, 373, 377, 388, 390, 397, 401, 402, 414, 417, 424, 434, 437, 441, 456, 476, 481, 484, 496, 503, 507, 516, 518, 529, 539, 541, 544, 550, 556, 565, 568, 573, 597, 613, 624, 628, 649, 657, 660, 668, 671, 675, 685, 702, 707, 709, 713, 722, 725, 744, 746, 756, 761, 763, 768, 771, 774, 778, 803, 806, 833, 835, 842, 853, 855, 877, 885, 890, 900, 932, 939, 949, 951, 959, 970, 986, 990, 1023, 1045, 1057, 1060, 1062, 1084, 1090, 1125, 1134, 1137, 1160, 1163, 1172, 1184, 1185, 1188, 1191, 1202, 1203, 1206, 1211, 1216, 1219, 1234, 1236, 1240, 1246, 1253, 1261, 1271, 1281, 1284, 1313, 1339, 1346, 1354, 1357, 1386, 1392, 1405, 1410, 1414, 1420, 1429, 1436, 1444, 1455, 1465, 1475, 1483, 1493, 1499, 1507, 1513, 1516, 1525, 1536, 1549, 1568, 1573, 1591, 1600, 1618, 1643, 1654, 1666, 1678, 1680, 1683, 1714, 1720, 1724, 1733, 1741, 1751, 1762, 1767, 1777, 1781, 1800, 1802, 1803, 1808, 1818, 1832, 1849, 1865, 1877, 1891, 1894, 1898, 1908, 1917, 1961, 1970, 1975, 2005, 2016, 2029, 2034, 2039, 2041, 2049, 2064, 2072, 2101, 2106, 2112, 2122, 2125, 2128, 2153, 2158, 2161, 2168, 2170, 2176, 2200, 2208, 2227, 2236, 2245, 2266, 2273, 2302, 2305;** The Bettmann Archive: **pp. 12, 426, 739, 925, 1037;** Courtesy of Keiiti Aki: **p. 14;** UPI/Bettmann: **pp. 58, 511, 546, 583, 751, 945, 1003, 1016;** Courtesy of Francisco Jose Ayala: **p. 80;** UPI/Bettmann Newsphotos: **pp. 83;** Archive Photos: **pp. 102, 523, 1040, 1210, 1769, 1990, 2132, 2276;** Courtesy of George Keith Batchelor: **pp. 124;** Photograph by Ingbert Gruttner, Courtesy of Arnold Beckman: **pp. 131;** Courtesy of Robert Arbuckle Berner: **p. 160;** Courtesy of Yvonne Brill: **p. 255;** Courtesy of Lester Brown: **p. 266;** Courtesy of Glenn W. Burton: **p. 283;** Courtesy of John R. Cairns: **p. 291;** The Granger Collection, New York: **pp. 304, 469, 652, 655, 1050, 1086, 1168, 1480, 1588, 1754, 1796, 2019, 2054;** New York University Medical Center Archives: **p. 355;** Courtesy of Stanley N. Cohen: **p. 379;** Courtesy of Rita R. Colwell: **p. 386;** Courtesy of Francisco Dallmeier: **p. 445;** Courtesy of Michael Ellis DeBakey: **p. 466;** Courtesy of Dennis Jack: **p. 489;** Courtesy of Nance K. Dicciani: **p. 495;** Courtesy of Theodor O. Diener: **p. 499;** Courtesy of Edsgar Dijkstra: **p. 501;** Archive/DPA: **pp. 513, 839, 1958;** Courtesy of Mildred Dresselhaus: **p. 521;** Courtesy of Cecile Hoover Edwards: **p. 559;** Courtesy of Helen T. Edwards: **p. 561;** Courtesy of the estate of Philo T. Farnsworth: **p. 609;** Courtesy of Lloyd Ferguson: **p. 622;** Courtesy of Solomon Fuller: **p. 710;** Courtesy of William Gates: **p. 733;** Courtesy of Adele Jean Goldberg: **p. 781;** Courtesy of Mary L. Good: **p. 796;** © Michael K. Nichols/Magnum Photos: **p. 798;** Courtesy of Govindjee: **p. 809;** Courtesy of Evelyn Granville: **p. 812;** Photograph by Washington University Photographic Services, Courtesy of Viktor Hamburger: **p. 851;** Courtesy of Wesley L. Harris, Sr.: **p. 868;** Courtesy of William Hewlett: **p. 918;** Photograph by Bradford Bachrach, Courtesy of Gladys Hobby: **p. 935;** Archive/Express Newspapers: **pp. 937, 961;** Courtesy of Phillip G. Hubbard: **p. 967;** Courtesy of Russell Hulse: **p. 978;** Courtesy of Keiichi Itakura: **p. 998;** Courtesy of Frank B. Jewett: **p. 1021;** Courtesy of Barbara Crawford Johnson: **p. 1026;** Courtesy of Marvin M. Johnson: **p. 1032;** Courtesy of Harold S. Johnston: **p. 1036;** Courtesy of Yuet Wai Kan: **p. 1056;** Courtesy of Motoo Kimura: **p. 1097;** Courtesy of Georges Köhler: **p. 1117;** Courtesy of Thomas E. Kurtz: **p. 1147;** Courtesy of Raymond Kurzweil: **p. 1149;** Mary Evans Picture Library: **pp. 1178, 1462, 1637, 1829, 2027, 2119, 2138, 2250;** The Granger Collection: **p. 1197, 1640, 1737;** Courtesy of Susan E. Leeman: **p. 1213;** Courtesy of Carroll Leevy: **p. 1214;** © Leonard Freed/Magnum Photos: **p. 1222;** Courtesy of Aldo Leopold: **p. 1226;** Courtesy of Julian H. Lewis: **p. 1239;** Courtesy of Irene D. Long: **p. 1270;** © Dennis Stock/Magnum Photos: **p. 1277;** Courtesy of Stanford University Visual Services: **p. 1350;** Courtesy of Evangelia Micheli-Tzanakou: **p. 1370;** Courtesy of Elizabeth and James Miller: **p. 1376;** Courtesy of Stanley L. Miller: **p. 1379;** Courtesy of Beatrice Mintz: **p. 1394;** Courtesy of Russell Mittermeier: **p. 1397;** Courtesy of Robert N. Noyce: **p. 1491;** Courtesy of NASA: **p. 1497;** Courtesy of David Packard: **p. 1523;** Courtesy of Jennie Patrick: **p. 1535;** Brown Brothers, Sterling, Pa.: **pp. 1542, 1708, 1871, 1998,**

2193, 2213, 2222; © Bruce Davidson/Magnum Photos: **p. 1545;** Courtesy of Irene C. Peden: **p. 1559;** Courtesy of the estate of Edith Peterson: **p. 1578;** Photo by Charles Harrington/Cornell University Photography, Courtesy of David Pimentel: **p. 1583;** Courtesy of Al Qöyawayma: **p. 1627;** Courtesy of Elsa Reichmanis: **p. 1661;** Courtesy of Juan C. Romero: **p. 1707;** Courtesy of Mary Ross: **p. 1711;** Courtesy of Stanley Runcorn: **p. 1727;** Archive/Nordick: **p. 1730;** Courtesy of Carl Sagan: **p. 1758;** Courtesy of Pedro A. Sanchez: **p. 1774;** Courtesy of Brookhaven National Laboratory: **p. 1785;** Photograph by Burgdorf Fotografi, Courtesy of Mogens Schou: **p. 1792;** Courtesy of Mary M. Shaw: **p. 1823;** Courtesy of Isadore M. Singer: **p. 1852;** Courtesy of Michael Smith: **p. 1868;** Courtesy of Chauncey Starr: **p. 1904;** Courtesy of Walter S. Sutton: **p. 1950;** Photograph by Robert P. Matthews, Courtesy of Joseph Taylor, Jr.: **p. 1980;** Courtesy of Stuart Taylor: **p. 1984;** Courtesy of Edward Teller: **p. 1987;** Topham/The Imageworks: **p. 2002;** Courtesy of Sheila E. Widnall: **p. 2184;** Courtesy of Richard Wilstatter: **p. 2219;** Photograph by John Sholtis, Courtesy of Norton Zinder: **p. 2297.**

Entry List

A

Abelson, Philip Hauge
Adams, Roger
Adams, Walter Sydney
Adamson, Joy
Adrian, Edgar Douglas
Ahlfors, Lars V.
Aiken, Howard
Aki, Keiiti
Alcala, Jose
Alcorn, George Edward
Alder, Kurt
Aleksandrov, Pavel S.
Alexander, Archie Alphonso
Alexander, Hattie
Alexanderson, Ernst F. W.
Alfvén, Hannes Olof Gösta
Alikhanov, Abram Isaakovich
Allen, Jr., William E.
Altman, Sidney
Alvarez, Luis
Alvariño, Angeles
Amdahl, Gene M.
Ames, Bruce N.
Ammann, Othmar Hermann
Anders, Edward
Andersen, Dorothy
Anderson, Carl David
Anderson, Gloria L.
Anderson, Philip Warren
Anderson, W. French
Anfinsen, Christian Boehmer
Appleton, Edward
Arber, Agnes
Arber, Werner
Armstrong, Edwin Howard
Armstrong, Neil
Arrhenius, Svante August
Artin, Emil
Astbury, William
Aston, Francis W.
Atanasoff, John
Atiyah, Michael Francis
Auerbach, Charlotte
Avery, Oswald Theodore
Axelrod, Julius
Ayala, Francisco J.

Ayrton, Hertha

B

Baade, Walter
Bachrach, Howard L.
Backus, John
Baeyer, Johann Friedrich Wilhelm
   Adolf von
Baez, Albert V.
Bailey, Florence Merriam
Baird, John Logie
Baker, Alan
Baker, Sara Josephine
Baltimore, David
Banach, Stefan
Banks, Harvey Washington
Banting, Frederick G.
Bárány, Robert
Barber, Jr., Jesse B.
Bardeen, John
Barkla, Charles Glover
Barnard, Christiaan Neethling
Barnes, William Harry
Barr, Murray Llewellyn
Bartlett, Neil
Barton, Derek H. R.
Bascom, Florence
Basov, Nikolai
Batchelor, George
Bateson, William
Bayliss, William Maddock
Beadle, George Wells
Beckman, Arnold
Becquerel, Antoine-Henri
Bednorz, J. Georg
Begay, Fred
Behring, Emil von
Békésy, Georg von
Bell, Gordon
Bell Burnell, Jocelyn Susan
Beltrán, Enrique
Benacerraf, Baruj
Benzer, Seymour
Berg, Paul
Berger, Hans
Bergius, Friedrich

Bergström, Sune Karl
Berkowitz, Joan B.
Bernays, Paul
Berner, Robert A.
Bernstein, Dorothy Lewis
Berry, Leonidas Harris
Bers, Lipman
Best, Charles Herbert
Bethe, Hans
Bhabha, Homi Jehangir
Binnig, Gerd
Birkhoff, George David
Bishop, Alfred A.
Bishop, J. Michael
Bishop, Katharine Scott
Bjerknes, Jacob
Bjerknes, Vilhelm
Black, Davidson
Black, James
Blackburn, Elizabeth H.
Blackett, Patrick Maynard Stuart
Blackwell, David
Bloch, Felix
Bloch, Konrad
Blodgett, Katharine Burr
Bloembergen, Nicolaas
Bluford, Guion S.
Blumberg, Baruch Samuel
Bohr, Aage
Bohr, Niels
Bolin, Bert
Bondi, Hermann
Booker, Walter M.
Bordet, Jules
Borel, Émile
Borlaug, Norman
Born, Max
Bosch, Karl
Bose, Satyendranath
Bothe, Walther
Bott, Raoul
Bovet, Daniel
Bowie, William
Boyer, Herbert W.
Boykin, Otis
Brady, St. Elmo
Bragg, William Henry
Bragg, William Lawrence

Branson, Herman
Brattain, Walter Houser
Braun, Karl Ferdinand
Breit, Gregory
Brenner, Sydney
Bressani, Ricardo
Bridgman, Percy Williams
Brill, Yvonne Claeys
Bronk, Detlev Wulf
Brønsted, Johannes Nicolaus
Brooks, Ronald E.
Brouwer, Luitzen Egbertus Jan
Brown, Herbert C.
Brown, Lester R.
Brown, Michael S.
Brown, Rachel Fuller
Browne, Marjorie Lee
Bucher, Walter Herman
Buchner, Eduard
Bullard, Edward
Bundy, Robert F.
Burbidge, E. Margaret
Burbidge, Geoffrey
Burnet, Frank Macfarlane
Burton, Glenn W.
Bush, Vannevar
Butenandt, Adolf

Cairns, Jr., John
Calderón, Alberto P.
Caldicott, Helen
Callender, Clive O.
Calvin, Melvin
Cambra, Jessie G.
Canady, Alexa I.
Cannon, Annie Jump
Cantor, Georg
Cardona, Manuel
Cardozo, W. Warrick
Cardús, David
Carlson, Chester
Carothers, Wallace Hume
Carrel, Alexis
Carrier, Willis
Carruthers, George R.
Carson, Benjamin S.
Carson, Rachel
Carver, George Washington
Castro, George
Cech, Thomas R.
Chadwick, James
Chain, Ernst Boris
Chamberlain, Owen
Chamberlin, Thomas Chrowder
Chance, Britton
Chandrasekhar, Subrahmanyan
Chang, Min-Chueh
Chargaff, Erwin

Charpak, Georges
Chaudhari, Praveen
Cherenkov, Pavel A.
Chestnut, Harold
Chew, Geoffrey Foucar
Child, Charles Manning
Chinn, May Edward
Cho, Alfred Y.
Chu, Paul Ching-Wu
Church, Alonzo
Clarke, Edith
Claude, Albert
Claude, Georges
Clay, Jacob
Clay-Jolles, Tettje Clasina
Cloud, Preston
Cobb, Jewel Plummer
Cobb, William Montague
Cockcroft, John D.
Cohen, Paul
Cohen, Stanley
Cohen, Stanley N.
Cohn, Mildred
Cohn, Zanvil
Colmenares, Margarita
Colwell, Rita R.
Commoner, Barry
Compton, Arthur Holly
Conway, Lynn Ann
Conwell, Esther Marly
Cooke, Lloyd M.
Coolidge, William D.
Cooper, Leon
Corey, Elias James
Cori, Carl Ferdinand
Cori, Gerty T.
Cormack, Allan M.
Cornforth, John
Coulomb, Jean
Courant, Richard
Cournand, André F.
Cousteau, Jacques
Cowings, Patricia S.
Cox, Elbert Frank
Cox, Geraldine V.
Cox, Gertrude Mary
Cram, Donald J.
Cray, Seymour
Crick, Francis
Cronin, James W.
Crosby, Elizabeth Caroline
Crosthwait Jr., David Nelson
Curie, Marie
Curie, Pierre

Dale, Henry Hallett
Dalén, Nils
Dallmeier, Francisco

Dalrymple, G. Brent
Daly, Marie M.
Daly, Reginald Aldworth
Dam, Henrik
Daniels, Walter T.
Dantzig, George Bernard
Darden, Christine
Dart, Raymond A.
Dausset, Jean
Davis, Margaret B.
Davis, Marguerite
Davis, Jr., Raymond
Davisson, Clinton
DeBakey, Michael Ellis
de Broglie, Louis Victor
Debye, Peter
de Duvé, Christian
de Forest, Lee
de Gennes, Pierre-Gilles
Dehmelt, Hans
Deisenhofer, Johann
Delbrück, Max
Deligné, Pierre
Dennis, Jack B.
de Sitter, Willem
d'Hérelle, Félix
Diaz, Henry F.
Dicciani, Nance K.
Diels, Otto
Diener, Theodor Otto
Dijkstra, Edsger W.
Dirac, Paul
Djerassi, Carl
Dobzhansky, Theodosius
Doisy, Edward A.
Dole, Vincent P.
Domagk, Gerhard
Donaldson, Simon
Douglas, Donald W.
Draper, Charles Stark
Dresselhaus, Mildred S.
Drew, Charles R.
Drucker, Daniel Charles
Dubois, Eugène
Dubos, René
Dulbecco, Renato
Durand, William F.
Durrell, Gerald
du Vigneaud, Vincent
Dyson, Freeman J.

Earle, Sylvia A.
Eccles, John C.
Eckert, J. Presper
Eddington, Arthur Stanley
Edelman, Gerald M.
Edgerton, Harold
Edinger, Tilly

Edison, Thomas Alva
Edwards, Cecile Hoover
Edwards, Helen T.
Ehrenfest, Paul
Ehrenfest-Afanaseva, Tatiana
Ehrlich, Paul
Ehrlich, Paul R.
Eigen, Manfred
Eijkman, Christiaan
Einstein, Albert
Einthoven, Willem
Eisner, Thomas
Eldredge, Niles
Elion, Gertrude Belle
El-Sayed, Mostafa Amr
Elton, Charles
Emerson, Gladys Anderson
Enders, John F.
Engler, Adolph Gustav Heinrich
Enskog, David
Erlanger, Joseph
Ernst, Richard R.
Esaki, Leo
Esau, Katherine
Estrin, Thelma
Euler, Ulf von
Euler-Chelpin, Hans von
Evans, Alice
Evans, James C.

Faber, Sandra M.
Farnsworth, Philo T.
Farquhar, Marilyn G.
Farr, Wanda K.
Fauci, Anthony S.
Favaloro, René Geronimo
Fedoroff, Nina V.
Feigenbaum, Edward A.
Feigenbaum, Mitchell
Fell, Honor Bridget
Ferguson, Lloyd N.
Fermi, Enrico
Fersman, Aleksandr Evgenievich
Feynman, Richard P.
Fibiger, Johannes
Fieser, Louis
Fieser, Mary Peters
Fischer, Edmond H.
Fischer, Emil
Fischer, Ernst Otto
Fischer, Hans
Fisher, Elizabeth F.
Fisher, Ronald A.
Fitch, Val Logsdon
Fitzroy, Nancy D.
Fleming, Alexander
Fleming, John Ambrose
Flexner, Simon

Florey, Howard Walter
Flory, Paul
Flügge-Lotz, Irmgard
Fokker, Anthony H. G.
Forbush, Scott Ellsworth
Ford, Henry
Forrester, Jay W.
Forssmann, Werner
Fossey, Dian
Fowler, William A.
Fox, Sidney W.
Fraenkel, Abraham Adolf
Fraenkel-Conrat, Heinz
Franck, James
Frank, Il'ya
Franklin, Rosalind Elsie
Fraser-Reid, Bertram Oliver
Fréchet, Maurice
Freedman, Michael H.
Frenkel, Yakov Ilyich
Friedman, Jerome
Friedmann, Aleksandr A.
Friend, Charlotte
Frisch, Karl von
Frisch, Otto Robert
Fujita, Tetsuya Theodore
Fukui, Kenichi
Fuller, Solomon

Gabor, Dennis
Gadgil, Madhav
Gadgil, Sulochana
Gagarin, Yuri A.
Gajdusek, D. Carleton
Gallo, Robert C.
Gamow, George
Gardner, Julia Anna
Garrod, Archibald
Gasser, Herbert Spencer
Gates, Bill
Gates, Jr., Sylvester James
Gaviola, Enrique
Gayle, Helene Doris
Geiger, Hans
Geiringer, Hilda
Geller, Margaret Joan
Gell-Mann, Murray
Ghiorso, Albert
Giacconi, Riccardo
Giaever, Ivar
Giauque, William F.
Gibbs, William Francis
Giblett, Eloise R.
Gilbert, Walter
Gilbreth, Frank
Gilbreth, Lillian
Glaser, Donald
Glashow, Sheldon Lee

Glenn, Jr., John H.
Goddard, Robert H.
Gödel, Kurt Friedrich
Goeppert-Mayer, Maria
Goethals, George W.
Gold, Thomas
Goldberg, Adele
Goldmark, Peter Carl
Goldring, Winifred
Goldschmidt, Richard B.
Goldschmidt, Victor
Goldstein, Avram
Goldstein, Joseph L.
Golgi, Camillo
Good, Mary L.
Goodall, Jane
Goudsmit, Samuel A.
Gould, Stephen Jay
Gourdine, Meredith Charles
Gourneau, Dwight
Govindjee
Granit, Ragnar Arthur
Granville, Evelyn Boyd
Greatbatch, Wilson
Greenewalt, Crawford H.
Griffith, Frederick
Grignard, François Auguste Victor
Gross, Carol
Grothendieck, Alexander
Groves, Leslie Richard
Guillaume, Charles-Edouard
Guillemin, Roger
Gullstrand, Allvar
Gutenberg, Beno
Guth, Alan
Gutierrez, Orlando A.

H

Haagen-Smit, A. J.
Haber, Fritz
Hadamard, Jacques
Hahn, Otto
Haldane, John Burdon Sanderson
Hale, George Ellery
Hall, Lloyd Augustus
Hamburger, Viktor
Hamilton, Alice
Hanafusa, Hidesaburo
Hannah, Marc R.
Hansen, James
Harden, Arthur
Hardy, Alister C.
Hardy, Godfrey Harold
Hardy, Harriet
Harmon, E'lise F.
Harris, Cyril
Harris, Wesley L.
Hartline, Haldan Keffer
Hassel, Odd

Hauptman, Herbert A.
Hausdorff, Felix
Hawking, Stephen
Hawkins, W. Lincoln
Haworth, Walter
Hay, Elizabeth D.
Hazen, Elizabeth Lee
Healy, Bernadine
Heimlich, Henry Jay
Heinkel, Ernst
Heisenberg, Werner Karl
Hench, Philip Showalter
Henderson, Cornelius Langston
Henry, John Edward
Henry, Warren Elliott
Herschbach, Dudley R.
Hershey, Alfred Day
Hertz, Gustav
Hertzsprung, Ejnar
Herzberg, Gerhard
Herzenberg, Caroline L.
Hess, Harry Hammond
Hess, Victor
Hess, Walter Rudolf
Hevesy, Georg von
Hewish, Antony
Hewlett, William
Heymans, Corneille Jean-François
Heyrovský, Jaroslav
Hicks, Beatrice
Hilbert, David
Hill, Archibald V.
Hill, Henry A.
Hinshelwood, Cyril N.
Hinton, William Augustus
Hitchings, George H.
Hobby, Gladys Lounsbury
Hodgkin, Alan Lloyd
Hodgkin, Dorothy Crowfoot
Hoffmann, Roald
Hofstadter, Robert
Hogg, Helen Sawyer
Holley, Robert William
Holmes, Arthur
Hopkins, Frederick Gowland
Hopper, Grace
Horn, Michael Hastings
Horstmann, Dorothy Millicent
Houdry, Eugene
Hounsfield, Godfrey
Houssay, Bernardo
Hoyle, Fred
Hrdlička, Aleš
Huang, Alice Shih-hou
Hubbard, Philip G.
Hubbert, M. King
Hubble, Edwin
Hubel, David H.
Huber, Robert
Huggins, Charles B.
Hulse, Russell A.
Humason, Milton L.

Hunsaker, Jerome C.
Hutchinson, G. Evelyn
Huxley, Andrew Fielding
Huxley, Julian
Hyde, Ida H.
Hyman, Libbie Henrietta

Imes, Elmer Samuel
Ioffe, Abram F.
Isaacs, Alick
Itakura, Keiichi
Iverson, F. Kenneth

Jackson, Shirley Ann
Jacob, François
Jansky, Karl
Janzen, Dan
Jarvik, Robert K.
Jason, Robert S.
Jeffreys, Harold
Jeffries, Zay
Jemison, Mae C.
Jensen, J. Hans D.
Jerne, Niels K.
Jewett, Frank Baldwin
Jobs, Steven
Johannsen, Wilhelm Ludvig
Johnson, Barbara Crawford
Johnson, Clarence L.
Johnson, Jr., John B.
Johnson, Joseph Lealand
Johnson, Katherine Coleman
  Goble
Johnson, Marvin M.
Johnson, Virginia E.
Johnston, Harold S.
Joliot-Curie, Frédéric
Joliot-Curie, Irène
Jones, Fred
Jones, Mary Ellen
Josephson, Brian D.
Julian, Percy Lavon
Juran, Joseph M.
Just, Ernest Everett

Kamerlingh Onnes, Heike
Kan, Yuet Wai
Kapitsa, Pyotr
Kapitza, Pyotor Leonidovich
  See Kapitsa, Pyotr
Karle, Isabella
Karle, Jerome

Karlin, Samuel
Karrer, Paul
Kastler, Alfred
Kates, Robert W.
Kato, Tosio
Katz, Bernard
Katz, Donald L.
Kay, Alan C.
Keith, Arthur
Kelsey, Frances Oldham
Kemeny, John G.
Kendall, Edward C.
Kendall, Henry W.
Kendrew, John
Kettering, Charles Franklin
Kettlewell, Bernard
Khorana, Har Gobind
Khush, Gurdev S.
Kilburn, Thomas M.
Kilby, Jack St. Clair
Kimura, Motoo
Kinoshita, Toichiro
Kinsey, Alfred
Kirouac, Conrad
  See Marie-Victorin, Frère
Kishimoto, Tadamitsu
Kistiakowsky, George B.
Kittrell, Flemmie Pansy
Klug, Aaron
Knopf, Eleanora Bliss
Knudsen, William Claire
Knuth, Donald E.
Koch, Robert
Kocher, Theodor
Kodaira, Kunihiko
Kohler, Georges
Kolff, Willem Johan
Kolmogorov, Andrey Nikolayevich
Kolthoff, Izaak Maurits
Konishi, Masakazu
Kornberg, Arthur
Korolyov, Sergei
Kossel, Albrecht
Kountz, Samuel L.
Krebs, Edwin G.
Krebs, Hans Adolf
Krim, Mathilde
Krogh, August
Kuhlmann-Wilsdorf, Doris
Kuhn, Richard
Kuiper, Gerard Peter
Kurchatov, Igor
Kurtz, Thomas Eugene
Kurzweil, Raymond
Kusch, Polycarp

Ladd-Franklin, Christine
Lamb, Jr., Willis E.
Lancaster, Cleo

Lancefield, Rebecca Craighill
Land, Edwin H.
Landau, Lev Davidovich
Landsberg, Helmut F.
Landsteiner, Karl
Langevin, Paul
Langmuir, Irving
Latimer, Lewis H.
Lattes, C. M. G.
Laub, Jakob Johann
Laue, Max von
Lauterbur, Paul C.
Laveran, Alphonse
Lawless, Theodore K.
Lawrence, Ernest Orlando
Leakey, Louis
Leakey, Mary
Leakey, Richard E.
Leavitt, Henrietta
Le Beau, Désirée
Lebesgue, Henri
Le Cadet, Georges
Leder, Philip
Lederberg, Joshua
Lederman, Leon Max
Lee, Raphael C.
Lee, Tsung-Dao
Lee, Yuan T.
Leeman, Susan E.
Leevy, Carroll
Leffall, Jr., LaSalle D.
Lehmann, Inge
Lehn, Jean-Marie
Leloir, Luis F.
Lemaître, Georges
Lenard, Philipp E. A. von
Leopold, Aldo
Leopold, Estella Bergere
Leopold, Luna
Lester, Jr., William Alexander
Levi-Civita, Tullio
Levi-Montalcini, Rita
Lewis, Gilbert Newton
Lewis, Julian Herman
Lewis, Warren K.
Li, Ching Chun
Li, Choh Hao
Libby, Willard F.
Liepmann, Hans Wolfgang
Lillie, Frank Rattray
Lim, Robert K. S.
Lin, Chia-Chiao
Lipmann, Fritz
Lippmann, Gabriel
Lipscomb, Jr., William Nunn
Little, Arthur D.
Lizhi, Fang
Lloyd, Ruth Smith
Loeb, Jacques
Loewi, Otto
Logan, Myra A.
London, Fritz

Long, Irene D.
Lonsdale, Kathleen
Lord Rayleigh
    See Strutt, John William
Lorentz, Hendrik Antoon
Lorenz, Edward N.
Lorenz, Konrad
Lovelock, James E.
Luria, Salvador Edward
Lwoff, André
Lynen, Feodor
Lynk, Miles Vandahurst

M

Maathai, Wangari
MacArthur, Robert H.
Macdonald, Eleanor Josephine
MacDonald, Gordon
MacGill, Elsie Gregory
Mac Lane, Saunders
MacLeod, Colin Munro
Macleod, John James Rickard
Maillart, Robert
Maiman, Theodore
Maloney, Arnold Hamilton
Mandelbrot, Benoit B.
Mandel'shtam, Leonid Isaakovich
Manton, Sidnie Milana
Marchbanks, Jr., Vance H.
Marconi, Guglielmo
Marcus, Rudolph A.
Margulis, Gregori Aleksandrovitch
Margulis, Lynn
Marie-Victorin, Frère
Markov, Andrei Andreevich
Martin, A. J. P.
Massevitch, Alla G.
Massey, Walter E.
Massie, Samuel P.
Masters, William Howell
Matthews, Alva T.
Matuyama, Motonori
Mauchly, John William
Maunder, Annie Russell
Maury, Antonia
Maury, Carlotta Joaquina
Maynard Smith, John
Mayr, Ernst
McAfee, Walter S.
McCarthy, John
McCarty, Maclyn
McClintock, Barbara
McCollum, Elmer Verner
McConnell, Harden
McMillan, Edwin M.
Medawar, Peter Brian
Meitner, Lise
Mendenhall, Dorothy Reed
Merrifield, R. Bruce

Meselson, Matthew
Metchnikoff, Élie
Meyerhof, Otto
Michel, Hartmut
Micheli-Tzanakou, Evangelia
Michelson, Albert
Midgley, Jr., Thomas
Miller, Elizabeth C. and James A.
Miller, Stanley Lloyd
Millikan, Robert A.
Milne, Edward Arthur
Milnor, John
Milstein, César
Minkowski, Hermann
Minkowski, Rudolph
Minot, George Richards
Minsky, Marvin
Mintz, Beatrice
Mitchell, Peter D.
Mittermeier, Russell
Mohorovičić, Andrija
Moissan, Henri
Molina, Mario
Moniz, Egas
Monod, Jacques Lucien
Montagnier, Luc
Moore, Charlotte E.
Moore, Raymond Cecil
Moore, Ruth
Moore, Stanford
Morawetz, Cathleen Synge
Morgan, Arthur E.
Morgan, Garrett A.
Morgan, Thomas Hunt
Mori, Shigefumi
Morley, Edward Williams
Morrison, Philip
Moseley, Henry Gwyn Jeffreys
Mössbauer, Rudolf
Mott, Nevill Francis
Mottelson, Ben R.
Moulton, Forest Ray
Muller, Hermann Joseph
Müller, K. Alex
Müller, Paul
Mulliken, Robert S.
Mullis, Kary
Munk, Walter
Murphy, William P.
Murray, Joseph E.

N

Nabrit, Samuel Milton
Nagata, Takesi
Nambu, Yoichiro
Nathans, Daniel
Natta, Giulio
Neal, Homer Alfred
Néel, Louis

Neher, Erwin
Nernst, Walther
Neufeld, Elizabeth F.
Newell, Allen
Newell, Norman Dennis
Nice, Margaret Morse
Nichols, Roberta J.
Nicolle, Charles J. H.
Nier, Alfred O. C.
Nirenberg, Marshall Warren
Nishizawa, Jun-ichi
Nishizuka, Yasutomi
Noble, G. K.
Noddack, Ida Tacke
Noether, Emmy
Noguchi, Hideyo
Nomura, Masayasu
Norrish, Ronald G. W.
Northrop, John Howard
Novikov, Sergei
Noyce, Robert

Oberth, Hermann
Ocampo, Adriana C.
Ochoa, Ellen
Ochoa, Severo
Odum, Eugene Pleasants
Odum, Howard T.
Ogilvie, Ida H.
Olden, Kenneth
Oldham, Richard Dixon
Onnes, Heike Kamerlingh
    See Kamerlingh Onnes, Heike
Onsager, Lars
Oort, Jan Hendrik
Oparin, Aleksandr Ivanovich
Oppenheimer, J. Robert
Osborn, Mary J.
Osterbrock, Donald E.
Ostwald, Friedrich Wilhelm

Packard, David
Palade, George
Panajiotatou, Angeliki
Panofsky, Wolfgang K. H.
Papanicolaou, George
Pardue, Mary Lou
Parker, Charles Stewart
Parsons, John T.
Patrick, Jennie R.
Patrick, Ruth
Patterson, Claire
Patterson, Frederick Douglass
Paul, Wolfgang

Pauli, Wolfgang
Pauling, Linus
Pavlov, Ivan Petrovich
Payne-Gaposchkin, Cecilia
Peano, Giuseppe
Pearson, Karl
Peden, Irene Carswell
Pedersen, Charles John
Pellier, Laurence Delisle
Pennington, Mary Engle
Penrose, Roger
Penzias, Arno
Perey, Marguerite
Perrin, Jean Baptiste
Pert, Candace B.
Perutz, Max
Péter, Rózsa
Petermann, Mary Locke
Peterson, Edith R.
Piasecki, Frank
Piccard, Auguste
Pimentel, David
Pinchot, Gifford
Pincus, Gregory Goodwin
Planck, Max
Pogue, William Reid
Poincaré, Jules Henri
Poindexter, Hildrus A.
Polanyi, John C.
Polubarinova-Kochina, Pelageya
    Yakovlevna
Pólya, George
Ponnamperuma, Cyril
Porter, George
Porter, Rodney
Poulsen, Valdemar
Pound, Robert
Powell, Cecil Frank
Powless, David
Prandtl, Ludwig
Pregl, Fritz
Prelog, Vladimir
Pressman, Ada I.
Prichard, Diana García
Prigogine, Ilya
Prokhorov, Aleksandr
Punnett, R. C.
Purcell, Edward Mills

Qöyawayma, Alfred H.
Quarterman, Lloyd Albert
Quimby, Edith H.
Quinland, William Samuel

Rabi, I. I.

Rainwater, James
Ramalingaswami, Vulimiri
Raman, C. V.
Ramanujan, S. I.
Ramart-Lucas, Pauline
Ramey, Estelle R.
Ramón y Cajal, Santiago
Ramsay, William
Ramsey, Frank Plumpton
Ramsey, Norman Foster
Randoin, Lucie
Rao, C. N. R.
Ratner, Sarah
Ray, Dixy Lee
Rayleigh, Lord
    See Strutt, John William
Reber, Grote
Reddy, Raj
Reed, Walter
Rees, Mina S.
Reichmanis, Elsa
Reichstein, Tadeus
Reid, Lonnie
Reines, Frederick
Revelle, Roger
Richards, Jr., Dickinson Woodruff
Richards, Ellen Swallow
Richards, Theodore William
Richardson, Lewis Fry
Richardson, Owen W.
Richet, Charles Robert
Richter, Burton
Richter, Charles F.
Rickover, Hyman G.
Ride, Sally
Rigas, Harriett B.
Risi, Joseph
Ritchie, Dennis
Robbins, Frederick
Roberts, Lawrence
Roberts, Richard J.
Robinson, Julia
Robinson, Robert
Rock, John
Rockwell, Mabel M.
Roelofs, Wendell L.
Rogers, Marguerite M.
Rohrer, Heinrich
Roman, Nancy Grace
Romer, Alfred Sherwood
Romero, Juan Carlos
Röntgen, Wilhelm Conrad
Ross, Mary G.
Ross, Ronald
Rossby, Carl-Gustaf
Rothschild, Miriam
Rous, Peyton
Rowland, F. Sherwood
Rowley, Janet D.
Rubbia, Carlo
Rubin, Vera Cooper
Runcorn, S. K.

Ruska, Ernst
Russell, Bertrand
Russell, Elizabeth Shull
Russell, Frederick Stratten
Russell, Henry Norris
Russell, Loris Shano
Rutherford, Ernest
Ružička, Leopold
Ryle, Martin

Sabatier, Paul
Sabin, Albert
Sabin, Florence Rena
Sagan, Carl
Sager, Ruth
Sakharov, Andrei
Sakmann, Bert
Salam, Abdus
Salk, Jonas
Samuelsson, Bengt
Sanchez, David A.
Sanchez, Pedro A.
Sandage, Allan R.
Sanger, Frederick
Satcher, David
Schaller, George
Schally, Andrew V.
Scharff Goldhaber, Gertrude
Scharrer, Berta
Schawlow, Arthur L.
Schneider, Stephen H.
Schou, Mogens
Schrieffer, J. Robert
Schrödinger, Erwin
Schultes, Richard Evans
Schwartz, Melvin
Schwinger, Julian
Seaborg, Glenn T.
Segrè, Emilio
Seibert, Florence B.
Seitz, Frederick
Semenov, Nikolai N.
Serre, Jean-Pierre
Shannon, Claude
Shapiro, Irwin
Shapley, Harlow
Sharp, Phillip A.
Sharp, Robert Phillip
Shaw, Mary
Sheldrake, Rupert
Shepard, Jr., Alan B.
Sherrington, Charles Scott
Shockley, Dolores Cooper
Shockley, William
Shoemaker, Eugene M.
Shokalsky, Yuly Mikhaylovich
Shtokman, Vladimir Borisovich
Shurney, Robert E.

Siegbahn, Kai M.
Siegbahn, Karl M. G.
Sikorsky, Igor I.
Simon, Dorothy Martin
Simon, Herbert A.
Simpson, George Gaylord
Singer, I. M.
Singer, Maxine
Sioui, Richard H.
Sitterly, Charlotte Moore
    See Moore, Charlotte E.
Skoog, Folke Karl
Slater, John Clarke
Slipher, Vesto M.
Slye, Maud
Smale, Stephen
Smith, Hamilton O.
Smith, Michael
Snell, George Davis
Soddy, Frederick
Solberg, Halvor
Solomon, Susan
Sommerfeld, Arnold
Sommerville, Duncan McLaren
    Young
Sorensen, Charles E.
Sørensen, Søren Peter Lauritz
Spaeth, Mary
Sparling, Rebecca H.
Spedding, Frank Harold
Spemann, Hans
Sperry, Elmer
Sperry, Roger W.
Spitzer, Jr., Lyman
Stahl, Franklin W.
Stanley, Wendell Meredith
Stark, Johannes
Starling, Ernest H.
Starr, Chauncey
Starzl, Thomas
Staudinger, Hermann
Stefanik, Milan Ratislav
Stein, William Howard
Steinberger, Jack
Steinman, David B.
Steinmetz, Charles P.
Steptoe, Patrick
Stern, Otto
Stevens, Nettie Maria
Stever, H. Guyford
Steward, Frederick Campion
Stewart, Thomas Dale
Stibitz, George R.
Stock, Alfred
Stoll, Alice M.
Stommel, Henry
Størmer, Fredrik
Strassmann, Fritz
Straus, Jr., William Levi
Strutt, John William
Strutt, Robert
Stubbe, JoAnne

Sturtevant, A. H.
Sumner, James B.
Suomi, Verner E.
Sutherland, Earl
Sutherland, Ivan
Sutton, Walter Stanborough
Svedberg, Theodor
Swaminathan, M. S.
Synge, Richard
Szent-Györgyi, Albert
Szilard, Leo

Tamm, Igor
Tan Jiazhen
Tapia, Richard A.
Tarski, Alfred
Tatum, Edward Lawrie
Taube, Henry
Taussig, Helen Brooke
Taylor, Frederick Winslow
Taylor, Jr., Joseph H.
Taylor, Moddie
Taylor, Richard E.
Taylor, Stuart
Telkes, Maria
Teller, Edward
Temin, Howard
Tereshkova, Valentina
Terman, Frederick
Terzaghi, Karl
Tesla, Nikola
Tesoro, Giuliana Cavaglieri
Tharp, Marie
Theiler, Max
Theorell, Axel Hugo Teodor
Thom, René Frédéric
Thomas, E. Donnall
Thomas, Martha Jane Bergin
Thompson, D'Arcy Wentworth
Thompson, Kenneth
Thomson, George Paget
Thomson, J. J.
Thurston, William
Tien, Ping King
Tildon, J. Tyson
Timoshenko, Stephen P.
Tinbergen, Nikolaas
Ting, Samuel C. C.
Tiselius, Arne
Tizard, Henry
Todd, Alexander
Tombaugh, Clyde W.
Tomonaga, Sin-Itiro
Tonegawa, Susumu
Townes, Charles H.
Trotter, Mildred
Trump, John G.
Tsao, George T.

Tsiolkovsky, Konstantin
Tsui, Daniel Chee
Tswett, Mikhail
Turing, Alan
Turner, Charles Henry
Tuve, Merle A.

U

Uhlenbeck, George
Uhlenbeck, Karen
Urey, Harold
Uyeda, Seiya

V

Vallois, Henri-Victor
Van Allen, James
Van de Graaff, Robert J.
van der Meer, Simon
van der Waals, Johannes Diderik
van der Wal, Laurel
Vane, John R.
van Straten, Florence W.
Van Vleck, John
Varmus, Harold E.
Vassy, Arlette
Veksler, V. I.
Vernadsky, Vladímir Ivanovich
Virtanen, Artturi Ilmari
Vollenweider, Richard
Volterra, Vito
von Braun, Wernher
von Kármán, Theodore
von Klitzing, Klaus
von Mises, Richard
von Neumann, John
Voûte, Joan George Erardus
  Gijsbert
Vries, Hugo de

W

Waelsch, Salome
Wagner-Jauregg, Julius
Waksman, Selman
Wald, George
Wallach, Otto
Walton, Ernest
Wang, An
Wang, James C.
Wankel, Felix
Warburg, Otto
Washington, Warren M.
Watkins, Jr., Levi
Watson, James D.
Watson-Watt, Robert
Weber-van Bosse, Anne Antoinette

Weertman, Julia
Wegener, Alfred
Weidenreich, Franz
Weil, André
Weinberg, Robert A.
Weinberg, Steven
Weinberg, Wilhelm
Weizsäcker, Carl F. Von
Weller, Thomas
Went, Frits
Werner, Alfred
West, Harold Dadford
Wetherill, George West
Wexler, Nancy
Weyl, Hermann
Wheeler, John Archibald
Whinnery, John R.
Whipple, Fred Lawrence
Whipple, George Hoyt
White, Augustus
White, Gilbert Fowler
Whitehead, Alfred North
Whittaker, Robert Harding
Whittle, Frank
Wickenden, William E.
Widnall, Sheila E.
Wiechert, Emil
Wieland, Heinrich
Wien, Wilhelm
Wiener, Alexander
Wiener, Norbert
Wiesel, Torsten
Wigglesworth, Vincent
Wigner, Eugene Paul
Wiles, Andrew J.
Wilkes, Maurice
Wilkins, Jr., J. Ernest
Wilkins, Maurice Hugh Frederick
Wilkinson, Geoffrey
Williams, Anna W.
Williams, Daniel Hale
Williams, Frederic C.
Williams, O. S.
Williamson, James S.
Willstätter, Richard
Wilson, C. T. R.
Wilson, Edmund Beecher
Wilson, Edward O.
Wilson, J. Tuzo
Wilson, Kenneth G.
Wilson, Robert R.
Wilson, Robert Woodrow
Windaus, Adolf
Wirth, Niklaus
Witkin, Evelyn Maisel
Witten, Edward
Wittig, Georg
Wolman, Abel
Wood, Harland G.
Woodland, Joseph
Woodward, Robert B.
Woodwell, George M.

Wozniak, Stephen
Wright, Almroth Edward
Wright, Jane Cooke
Wright, Louis Tompkins
Wright, Sewall
Wright, Wilbur and Orville
Wu, Chien-Shiung
Wu, Y. C. L. Susan

X

Xie Xide

Y

Yalow, Rosalyn Sussman
Yang, Chen Ning
Yau, Shing-Tung
Young, Grace Chisholm
Young, J. Z.
Yukawa, Hideki

Z

Zadeh, Lotfi Asker
Zeeman, E. C.
Zeeman, Pieter
Zel'dovich, Yakov Borisovich
Zen, E-an
Zernike, Frits
Ziegler, Karl
Zinder, Norton
Zinsser, Hans
Zsigmondy, Richard
Zuse, Konrad
Zworykin, Vladimir

Chronology of Scientific Advancement

1895 Scottish physicist *C. T. R. Wilson* invents the cloud chamber

French physicist *Jean Baptiste Perrin* confirms the nature of cathode rays

1896 American agricultural chemist *George Washington Carver* begins work at the Tuskegee Institute

1897 English physicist *J. J. Thomson* discovers the electron

1898 Polish-born French radiation chemist *Marie Curie* and French physicist *Pierre Curie* discover polonium and radium

1900 German physicist *Max Planck* develops Planck's Constant

1901 Austrian American immunologist *Karl Landsteiner* discovers A, B, and O blood types

German geneticist *Wilhelm Weinberg* outlines the "difference method" in his first important paper on heredity

1902 English geneticist *William Bateson* translates Austrian botanist Gregor Mendel's work

1903 Polish-born French radiation chemist *Marie Curie* becomes the first woman to be awarded the Nobel Prize

German chemist *Otto Diels* isolates molecular structure of cholesterol

1904 English electrical engineer *John Ambrose Fleming* develops the Fleming Valve

Russian physiologist *Ivan Petrovich Pavlov* receives the Nobel Prize for digestion research

1905 German-born American physicist *Albert Einstein* publishes the theory of relativity

German chemist *Fritz Haber* publishes *Thermodynamics of Technical Gas Reactions*

German chemist *Walther Nernst*'s research leads to the Third Law of Thermodynamics

1906 Danish physical chemist *Johannes Nicolaus Brønsted* publishes his first paper on affinity

English neurophysiologist *Charles Scott Sherrington* publishes *The Integrative Action of the Nervous System*

1907 Prussian-born American physicist *Albert Michelson* becomes the first American to receive the Nobel Prize for physics

1908 American astrophysicist *George Ellery Hale* discovers magnetic fields in sunspots

1909 German bacteriologist and immunologist *Paul Ehrlich* discovers a cure for syphilis

American engineer and inventor *Charles Franklin Kettering* successfully tests the first prototype of the electric automobile starter

1910 English American mathematician *Alfred North Whitehead* and English mathematician and philosopher *Bertrand Russell* publish the first volume of *Principia Mathematica*

American engineer and inventor *Lee De Forest* attempts the first live broadcast of radio

New Zealand-born English physicist *Ernest Rutherford* postulates the modern concept of the atom

1911 English mathematician *Godfrey Harold Hardy* begins his collaboration with J. E. Littlewood

Polish-born French radiation chemist *Marie Curie* becomes the first scientist to win a second Nobel Prize

1912 Danish physicist *Niels Bohr* develops a new theory of atomic structure

Austrian physicist *Victor Hess* discovers cosmic rays

English biochemist *Frederick Gowland Hopkins* publishes a groundbreaking work illustrating the nutritional importance of vitamins

German physicist *Max von Laue* discovers X-ray diffraction

Austrian physicist *Lise Meitner* becomes the first woman professor in Germany

German meteorologist and geophysicist *Alfred Wegener* proposes the theory of continental drift

1913 German bacteriologist and immunologist *Paul Ehrlich* gives an address explaining the future of chemotherapy

English physicist *Henry Gwyn Jeffreys Moseley* discovers atomic number

French physicist *Jean Baptiste Perrin* verifies German-born American physicist *Albert Einstein*'s calculations of Brownian Motion

American astronomer and astrophysicist *Henry Norris Russell* publishes Hertzsprung-Russell diagram

Russian-born American aeronautical engineer *Igor I. Sikorsky* designs *Ilya Mourometz* bomber

German chemist *Richard Willstätter* and Arthur Stoll publish their first studies of chlorophyll

American geneticist *A. H. Sturtevant* develops gene mapping

1916 American chemist and physicist *Irving Langmuir* receives a patent for an energy-efficient, longer-lasting tungsten filament light bulb

American geneticist and embryologist *Thomas Hunt Morgan* publishes *A Critique of the Theory of Evolution*

German theoretical physicist *Arnold Sommerfeld* reworks Danish physicist *Niels Bohr*'s atomic theory

American anatomist *Florence Rena Sabin* publishes *The Origin and Development of the Lymphatic System*

1918 Danish physical chemist *Johannes Nicolaus Brønsted* publishes his thirteenth paper on affinity

1919 New Zealand-born English physicist *Ernest Rutherford* determines that alpha particles can split atoms

1920 American astronomer *Harlow Shapley* convinces the scientific community that the Milky Way is much larger than originally thought and the Earth's solar system is not its center

1921 Canadian physiologist *Frederick G. Banting* and Canadian physiologist *Charles Herbert Best* discover insulin

1923 Danish physical chemist *Johannes Nicolaus Brønsted* redefines acids and bases

English astronomer *Arthur Stanley Eddington* publishes *Mathematical Theory of Relativity*

American astronomer *Edwin Hubble* confirms the existence of galaxies outside the Milky Way

American physicist *Robert A. Millikan* begins his study of cosmic rays

1924   French theoretical physicist *Louis Victor de Broglie* publishes findings on wave mechanics

English astronomer *Arthur Stanley Eddington* determines the mass-luminosity law

1925   German-born American physicist *James Franck* and German physicist *Gustav Hertz* prove Danish physicist *Niels Bohr*'s theory of the quantum atom

Italian-born American physicist *Enrico Fermi* publishes a paper explaining Austro-Hungarian-born Swiss physicist *Wolfgang Pauli*'s exclusion principle

English statistician and geneticist *Ronald A. Fisher* publishes *Statistical Methods for Research Workers*

1926   German-born English physicist *Max Born* explains the wave function

American physicist and rocket pioneer *Robert H. Goddard* launches the first liquid-propellant rocket

American geneticist *Hermann Joseph Muller* confirms that X rays greatly increase the mutation rate in *Drosophila*

Austrian physicist *Erwin Schrödinger* publishes his wave equation

1927   American physicist *Arthur Holly Compton* receives the Nobel Prize for X-ray research

English physiologist *Henry Hallett Dale* identifies the chemical mediator involved in the transmission of nerve impulses

German chemist *Otto Diels* develops a successful dehydrogenating process

German physicist *Werner Karl Heisenberg* develops the Uncertainty Principle

Belgian astronomer *Georges Lemaître* formulates the big bang theory

Hungarian American mathematical physicist *Eugene Paul Wigner* develops the law of the conservation of parity

American astronomer *Edwin Hubble* puts together the theory of the expanding universe, or Hubble's Law

1928   German chemist *Otto Diels* and German chemist *Kurt Alder* develop the Diels-Alder Reaction

Scottish bacteriologist *Alexander Fleming* discovers penicillin

Austro-Hungarian-born German physicist *Hermann Oberth* publishes a book explaining the basic principles of space flight

Indian physicist *C. V. Raman* discovers the Raman Effect

1929   American physicist *Robert Van de Graaff* constructs the first working model of his particle accelerator

Danish astronomer *Ejnar Hertzsprung* receives the Gold Medal Award for calculating the first intergalactic distance

Norwegian American chemist *Lars Onsager* develops the Law of Reciprocal Relations

German-born American mathematician *Hermann Weyl* develops a mathematical theory for the neutrino

Russian-born American physicist and engineer *Vladimir Zworykin* files his first patent for color television

1930   English statistician and geneticist *Ronald A. Fisher* publishes *The Genetical Theory of Natural Selection*

Austrian-born American mathematician *Kurt Friedrich Gödel* proves the incompleteness theorem

Austro-Hungarian-born Swiss physicist *Wolfgang Pauli* proposes the existence of the neutrino

1931   American engineer *Vannevar Bush* develops the differential analyzer with colleagues

American chemist *Wallace Hume Carothers* founds the synthetic rubber manufacturing industry with his research

South African-born American virologist *Max Theiler*'s research leads to the production of the first yellow-fever vaccine

German biochemist *Otto Warburg* establishes the Kaiser Wilhelm Institute for Cell Physiology

1932

English atomic physicist *John Cockcroft* and Irish experimental physicist *Ernest Walton* split the atom

American physicist *Carl David Anderson* discovers the positron

English-born Indian physiologist and geneticist *John Burdon Sanderson Haldane* publishes *The Causes of Evolution*

American physicist *Ernest Orlando Lawrence* develops the cyclotron and disintegrates a lithium nucleus

1933

Canadian-born American biologist and bacteriologist *Oswald Theodore Avery* identifies DNA as the basis of heredity

English physicist *Paul Adrien Maurice Dirac* wins the Nobel Prize for his work on the wave equation

Italian-born American physicist *Enrico Fermi* proposes his beta decay theory

German inventor *Felix Wankel* successfully operates the first internal combustion, rotary engine

1934

French nuclear physicist *Frédéric Joliot-Curie* and French chemist and physicist *Irène Joliot-Curie* discover artificial radioactivity

American inventor *Edwin H. Land* develops a commercial method to polarize light

New Zealand-born English physicist *Ernest Rutherford* achieves the first fusion reaction

American chemist and physicist *Harold Urey* receives the Nobel Prize in chemistry for his discovery of deuterium, or heavy hydrogen

1935

American seismologist *Charles F. Richter* and German American seismologist *Beno Gutenberg* develop the Richter(-Gutenberg) Scale

English physicist *James Chadwick* receives the Nobel Prize for the discovery of the neutron

1936

German experimental physicist *Hans Geiger* perfects the Geiger-Mueller Counter

Russian biochemist *Aleksandr Ivanovich Oparin* publishes his origin of life theory

English mathematician *Alan Turing* publishes a paper detailing a machine that would serve as a model for the first working computer

1937

Russian-born American biologist *Theodosius Dobzhansky* writes *Genetics and the Origin of Species*

Australian English pathologist *Howard Walter Florey* discovers the growth potential of polymeric chains

German-born English biochemist *Hans Adolf Krebs* identifies the workings of the Krebs Cycle

Hungarian American biochemist and molecular biologist *Albert Szent-Gyorgyi* receives the Nobel Prize for isolating vitamin C

1938

German chemist *Otto Hahn*, Austrian physicist *Lise Meitner*, and German chemist *Fritz Strassmann* discover nuclear fission

American physicist *Carl David Anderson* discovers the meson

1939

Swiss-born American physicist *Felix Bloch* measures the neutron's magnetic movement

American chemist *Wallace Hume Carothers* founds the synthetic fiber industry with his research

French-born American microbiologist and ecologist *René Dubos* discovers tyrothricin

American chemist *Linus Pauling* develops the theory of complimentarity

Russian-born American aeronautical engineer *Igor I. Sikorsky* flies the first single-rotor helicopter

1940

American physicist and inventor *Chester Carlson* receives a patent for his photocopying method

English experimental physicist *George Paget Thomson* forms the Maud Committee

Russian-born American microbiologist *Selman Waksman* develops streptomycin

1941

German-born English biochemist *Ernst Boris Chain* and Australian English pathologist *Howard Walter Florey* isolate penicillin

German-born American physicist *Hans Bethe* develops the Bethe Coupler

American biochemist *Fritz Lipmann* publishes "Metabolic Generation and Utilization of Phosphate Bond Energy"

1942

Hungarian American physicist and biophysicist *Leo Szilard* and Italian-born American physicist *Enrico Fermi* set up the first nuclear chain reaction

German-born American biologist *Ernst Mayr* proposes the theory of geographic speciation

American physicist *J. Robert Oppenheimer* becomes the director of the Manhattan Project

1943

German-born American molecular biologist *Max Delbrück* and Italian-born American molecular biologist *Salvador Edward Luria* publish a milestone paper regarded as the beginning of bacterial genetics

English physicist *James Chadwick* leads the British contingent of the Manhattan Project

French oceanographer *Jacques-Yves Cousteau* patents the Aqualung

Italian-born American molecular biologist *Salvador Edward Luria* devises the fluctuation test

1944

German American rocket engineer *Wernher Von Braun* fires the first fully operational V-2 rocket

Austrian-born American biochemist *Erwin Chargaff* discovers the genetic role of DNA

American nuclear chemist *Glenn T. Seaborg* successfully isolates large amounts of plutonium and develops the actinide concept

American paleontologist *George Gaylord Simpson* publishes *Tempo and Mode in Evolution*

1945

English physicist *James Chadwick* witnesses the first atomic bomb test

American biochemist *Fritz Lipmann* discovers coenzyme A

Hungarian American mathematician *Johann Von Neumann* publishes a report containing the first written description of the stored-program concept

American chemist *Linus Pauling* determines the cause of sickle-cell anemia

Austrian physicist *Erwin Schrödinger* publishes *What Is Life?*

1946

American geneticist *Joshua Lederberg* and American biochemist *Edward Lawrie Tatum* show that bacteria may reproduce sexually

English zoologist *Julian Huxley* becomes the first director-general of UNESCO

1947

French oceanographer *Jacques-Yves Cousteau* breaks the free diving record using his Aqualung

Hungarian-born English physicist *Dennis Gabor* discovers holography

American inventor *Edwin H. Land* demonstrates the first instant camera

American mathematician *Norbert Wiener* creates the study of cybernetics

1948

American physicist *John Bardeen* develops the transistor

American chemist *Melvin Calvin* begins research on photosynthesis

Russian-born American physicist *George Gamow* publishes "Alpha-Beta-Gamma" paper

American zoologist and sex researcher *Alfred Kinsey* publishes *Sexual Behavior in the Human Male*

American biochemist *Wendell Meredith Stanley*

receives Presidential Certificate of Merit for developing an influenza vaccine

Swedish chemist *Arne Tiselius* receives the Nobel Prize for research in electrophoresis

1949 Hungarian-born American physicist *Edward Teller* begins developing the hydrogen bomb

American astronomer *Fred Lawrence Whipple* suggests the "dirty snowball" comet model

1950 American geneticist *Barbara McClintock* publishes the discovery of genetic transposition

1951 American chemist *Katharine Burr Blodgett* receives the Garvan Medal for women chemists

American biologist *Gregory Goodwin Pincus* begins work on the antifertility steroid the "pill"

Dutch-born English zoologist and ethologist *Nikolaas Tinbergen* publishes *The Study of Instinct*

1952 German-born American astronomer *Walter Baade* presents new measurements of the universe

French-born American microbiologist and ecologist *René Dubos* publishes a book linking tuberculosis with certain environmental conditions

American microbiologist *Alfred Day Hershey* conducts the "Blender Experiment" to demonstrate that DNA is the genetic material of life

Italian-born American molecular biologist *Salvador Edward Luria* discovers the phenomenon known as restriction and modification

American microbiologist *Jonas Salk* develops the first polio vaccine

English chemist *Alexander Todd* establishes the structure of flavin adenine dinucleotide (FAD)

1953 Russian theoretical physicist *Andrei Sakharov* and Russian physicist *Igor Tamm* develop the first Soviet hydrogen bomb

English molecular biologist *Francis Crick* and American molecular biologist *James D. Watson* develop the Watson-Crick model of DNA

English molecular biologist *Rosalind Elsie Franklin* provides evidence of DNA's double-helical structure

American physicist *Murray Gell-Mann* publishes a paper explaining the strangeness principle

American zoologist and sex researcher *Alfred Kinsey* publishes *Sexual Behavior in the Human Female*

French microbiologist *André Lwoff* proposes that "inducible lysogenic bacteria" can test cancerous and noncancerous cell activity

English biologist *Peter Brian Medawar* proves acquired immunological tolerance

American chemist *Stanley Lloyd Miller* publishes "A Production of Amino Acids under Possible Primitive Earth Conditions"

Austrian-born English crystallographer and biochemist *Max Perutz* develops method of isomorphous replacement

1955 English chemist *Alexander Todd* and English chemist and crystallographer *Dorothy Crowfoot Hodgkin* determine the structure of vitamin B12

American biochemist *Sidney W. Fox* begins identifying properties of microspheres

American microbiologist *Jonas Salk*'s polio vaccine pronounced safe and ninety-percent effective

English biochemist *Frederick Sanger* determines the total structure of the insulin molecule

1956 American biochemist *Stanley Cohen* extracts NGF from a mouse tumor

American experimental physicist *Leon Max Lederman* helps discover the "long-lived neutral kaon"

1957 American biochemist *Arthur Kornberg* and Spanish biochemist *Severo Ochoa* use DNA polymerase to synthesize DNA molecules

1958
American physicist *James Van Allen* discovers Van Allen radiation belts

American geneticist *George Wells Beadle* receives the Nobel Prize for the One Gene, One Enzyme Theory

American population biologist *Paul R. Ehrlich* makes his first statement regarding the problem of overpopulation

German physicist *Rudolf Mössbauer* discovers recoilless gamma ray release

1959
American computer scientist *Grace Hopper* develops the COBOL computer language

German physicist *Rudolf Mössbauer* uses the Mössbauer Effect to test the theory of relativity

1960
English physicist and biochemist *John Kendrew* and Austrian-born English crystallographer and biochemist *Max Perutz* formulate the first three-dimensional structure of the protein myoglobin

American Chemist *Willard F. Libby* receives the Nobel Prize for his development of radiocarbon dating

Russian-born American virologist *Albert Sabin*'s oral polio vaccine is approved for manufacture in the United States

1961
French biologists *François Jacob* and *Jacques Monod* discover messenger ribonucleic acid (mRNA)

American chemist *Melvin Calvin* receives the Nobel Prize in his chemistry for research on photosynthesis

American biochemist *Marshall Warren Nirenberg* cracks the genetic code

1962
American marine biologist *Rachel Carson* publishes *Silent Spring*

Russian theoretical physicist *Lev Davidovich Landau* receives the Nobel Prize for his research into theories of condensed matter

Hungarian-born American physicist *Edward Teller* becomes the first advocate of an "active defense system" to shoot down enemy missiles

New Zealand-born English biophysicist *Maurice Hugh Frederick Wilkins* shows the helical structure of RNA

1963
German American physicist *Maria Goeppert-Mayer* becomes the first woman to receive the Nobel Prize for theoretical physics

American chemist *Linus Pauling* becomes the only person to receive two unshared Nobel Prizes

1964
American psychobiologist *Roger W. Sperry* publishes the findings of his split-brain studies

1965
American geneticist *A. H. Sturtevant* publishes *The History of Genetics*

1967
English astrophysicist *Antony Hewish* and Irish astronomer *Jocelyn Susan Bell Burnell* discover pulsars

South African heart surgeon *Christiaan Neethling Barnard* performs the first human heart transplant

American primatologist *Dian Fossey* establishes a permanent research camp in Rwanda

1968
American physicist *Luis Alvarez* wins the Nobel Prize for his bubble chamber work

1969
American astronaut *Neil Armstrong* becomes the first man to walk on the moon

1970
Indian-born American biochemist *Har Gobind Khorana* synthesizes the first artificial DNA

American biologist *Lynn Margulis* publishes *Origins of Life*

1971
English ethologist *Jane Goodall* publishes *In the Shadow of Man*

1972
American evolutionary biologist *Stephen Jay Gould* and American paleontologist *Niles*

Eldredge introduce the concept of punctuated equilibrium

American physicist *John Bardeen* develops the BCS theory of superconductivity

American inventor *Edwin H. Land* reveals the first instant color camera

1973 American radio engineer *Karl Jansky* receives the honor of having the Jansky unit adopted as the unit of measure of radiowave intensity

Austrian zoologist and ethologist *Konrad Lorenz* receives the Nobel Prize for his behavioral research

American biochemist and geneticist *Maxine Singer* warns the public of gene-splicing risks

1974 English astrophysicist *Antony Hewish* receives the first Nobel Prize awarded to an astrophysicist

1975 French oceanographer *Jacques-Yves Cousteau* sees his Cousteau Society membership reach 120,000

American zoologist *Edward O. Wilson* publishes *Sociobiology: The New Synthesis*

1976 American computer engineer *Seymour Cray* introduces the CRAY-1 supercomputer

1977 Russian-born Belgian chemist *Ilya Prigogine* receives the Nobel Prize in chemistry for his work on nonequilibrium thermodynamics

1980 American biochemist *Paul Berg* receives the Nobel Prize for the biochemistry of nucleic acids

1981 American virologist *Robert C. Gallo* develops a blood test for the AIDS virus and discovers human T-cell leukemia virus

1982 American astronaut and physicist *Sally Ride* becomes the first American woman in space

1983 Indian-born American astrophysicist and applied mathematician *Subrahmanyan Chandrasekhar* receives the Nobel Prize for research on aged stars

American primatologist *Dian Fossey* publishes *Gorillas in the Mist*

French virologist *Luc Montagnier* discovers the human immunodeficiency virus (HIV)

American astronomer and exobiologist *Carl Sagan* publishes an article with others suggesting the possibility of a "nuclear winter"

1986 American physicist *Richard P. Feynman* explains why the space shuttle *Challenger* exploded

1987 Chinese American physicist *Paul Ching-Wu Chu* leads a team that discovers a method for higher temperature superconductivity

1987 American molecular biologist *Walter Gilbert* begins the human genome project to map DNA

1988 English theoretical physicist *Stephen Hawking* publishes *A Brief History of Time: From the Big Bang to Black Holes*

English pharmacologist *James Black* receives the Nobel Prize for his heart and ulcer medication work

1989 German-born American physicist *Hans Dehmelt* and German physicist *Wolfgang Paul* share the Nobel Prize for devising ion traps

1990 American physicists *Jerome Friedman, Henry W. Kendall,* and *Richard E. Taylor* are awarded the Nobel Prize for confirming the existence of quarks

American surgeon *Joseph E. Murray* receives the Nobel Prize for performing the first human kidney transplant

1991 German physician and cell physiologist *Bert Sakmann* and German biophysicist *Erwin Neher*

are awarded the Nobel Prize for inventing the patch clamp technique

 English biochemist *Richard J. Roberts* and American biologist *Phillip A. Sharp* share the Nobel Prize for their research on DNA structure

American astrophysicists *Russell A. Hulse* and *Joseph H. Taylor, Jr.* receive the Nobel Prize for their work on binary pulsars

NOTABLE
TWENTIETH-CENTURY
SCIENTISTS

Christine Ladd-Franklin
1847-1930
American logician and psychologist

Christine Ladd-Franklin made fundamental contributions to the scientific understanding of color vision and to syllogistic reasoning (deductive reasoning) and symbolic notation in logic. Although official policies of her era excluded women from advanced studies and academic positions at major universities, Ladd-Franklin studied logic and mathematics at Johns Hopkins University, researched color vision at universities in Göttingen and Berlin, and went on to lecture in psychology and logic at Johns Hopkins and Columbia University. Throughout her career she was an outspoken and effective campaigner for opening graduate programs and academic employment to women.

Christine Ladd was born in Windsor, Connecticut, on December 1, 1847. Her parents were Eliphalet Ladd, a New York merchant, and Augusta (Niles) Ladd. Her relatives included William Ladd, who founded the American Peace Society, and John Milton Niles, a former postmaster-general of the United States. Ladd-Franklin grew up in Connecticut and New York. At the age of twelve, after the death of her mother, Ladd-Franklin went to stay with her father's family in Portsmouth, New Hampshire. She graduated as valedictorian of her class from Wesleyan Academy in Wilbraham, Massachusetts, in 1865 and attended Vassar College, where she studied mathematics. Ladd-Franklin received her A.B. from Vassar in 1869 and spent the next nine years teaching secondary school. During this period, she wrote articles on mathematics for the *Educational Times,* an English publication.

When Ladd-Franklin sought to attend lectures in mathematics at the recently established Johns Hopkins University, she was admitted by the English mathematician J. J. Sylvester, who knew of her work. She also attended the lectures of logician Charles Sanders Peirce and of mathematics professor William Story. Ladd-Franklin studied at Johns Hopkins from 1878 to 1882. Sylvester persuaded the mathematics department to grant Ladd a $500 annual fellowship, which was renewed for three years. Her Ph.D. thesis, entitled "The Algebra of Logic," was published in 1883 in Peirce's *Studies in Logic by Members of the*

Johns Hopkins University. In this work, Ladd proposed that logical statements could be analyzed more easily for validity when presented in the form of "inconsistent triads," which she later called "antilogisms," than when expressed as classical syllogisms. An antilogism comprises "three statements that are together incompatible." One example given by Ladd-Franklin in "The Antilogism," *Mind,* 1928, is "It is impossible that any of these measures should be idiotic, for none of them is unnecessary, and nothing that is necessary is idiotic." Her work was praised in its time, and Eugene Shen wrote in *Mind,* 1927, "No scheme in logic is more beautiful than that based on the eight propositions of Dr. Ladd-Franklin."

An Authority on Color Vision

Ladd-Franklin turned to investigations of vision in the 1880s and began publishing articles on this subject in 1887. During a visit to Europe in 1891 and 1892, she studied Ewald Herwig's theory of color perception with G. E. Müller in Göttingen and did experiments in Müller's laboratory. She also attended lectures by the mathematician Felix Klein. Ladd-Franklin went on to visit Berlin, where she worked in the laboratory of Hermann von Helmholtz and attended lectures by Arthur König on Helmholtz's theory of color vision. Herwig believed that color perception arises from three opposing pairs of basic colors, while Helmholtz maintained that all the colors the eye sees can be generated from three basic colors-red, green, and blue. Ladd-Franklin synthesized these ideas, proposing her own color theory, which she presented to the International Congress of Psychology in London in 1892. She claimed that color vision had evolved from light (white) sensitivity by the addition of differentiation between yellow and blue light, followed by the separation of the yellow sensitivity into the perception of red and green. Consequently, yellow and white as well as blue, red and green, are perceived as basic colors. After a period of controversy, Ladd-Franklin's ideas were accepted by psychologists for many years.

An associate editor of *Baldwin's Dictionary of Philosophy and Psychology* in 1901 and 1902, Ladd-Franklin resumed lecturing in logic and psychology at Johns Hopkins from 1904 to 1909. In 1914 she became a lecturer at Columbia, where she continued teaching until 1927, when she was nearly eighty years old. In the late twenties, she investigated the visual phenomenon of "blue arcs," which she believed showed that active nerve fibers emit a faint light. A collection of her major works on vision was published as *Colour and Colour Theories* in 1929.

Opening Closed Doors

Ladd-Franklin's professional career was shaped by the restrictions placed on women scientists and scholars in the late nineteenth and early twentieth centuries. She studied mathematics instead of physics because university laboratories did not admit women, and mathematics did not require laboratory work. Like other women, Ladd-Franklin was a "special student" at Johns Hopkins, a status outside normal admissions. When she completed her graduate work in 1882, the university would not grant her a degree. The situation was similar during her visit to Germany, where Ladd-Franklin was only allowed auditor status, and Müller delivered lectures to her privately. Even Ladd-Franklin's teaching positions at Johns Hopkins and Columbia were temporary, not permanent, appointments. One of the greatest disappointments of her career was suffered in 1914 when a leading group of experimental psychologists refused her request to attend their meeting on color vision at Columbia. Ladd-Franklin, a leading authority on the subject, gained admittance only by having one of the members take her as his guest. Johns Hopkins awarded its first doctorate to a woman in 1893, and officially began to admit women in 1907. In 1926, the school awarded Ladd-Franklin the Ph.D. in mathematics that she had earned in 1882.

Ladd-Franklin and other women in academic fields devised strategies to open American doctoral programs to women. The Association of Collegiate Alumnae, predecessor of the American Organization of University Women, was formed in 1881. Ladd-Franklin proposed that the ACA start a fellowship for study overseas. The $500 fellowship that was established in 1890 helped American women gain entrance to lectures and later to earn doctoral degrees at German universities. Once women had been admitted abroad, it became easier to persuade American graduate schools to accept them also. From 1900 to 1917, Ladd-Franklin administered the Sarah Berliner fellowship, which supported new women doctorates in research. She hoped to persuade graduate schools to take the fellows into their faculty, since there was no cost to the school. This program did help women establish academic careers, but most worked at women's colleges. The scholarship did not fulfill Ladd-Franklin's goal of placing women in academic positions at coeducational schools.

Christine Ladd married Fabian Franklin, a member of the mathematics faculty at Johns Hopkins, on August 24, 1882. The couple had two children, of whom only one, Margaret, survived into adulthood. In 1895 Franklin became a journalist, and the family later moved to New York when he became an associate editor of the *New York Evening Post*. In addition to her scholarly work and articles about women's education, Ladd-Franklin published opinions on many subjects. In letters to the editors of the *New York Times* during World War I, she objected to tight collars for soldiers and advocated calling citizens of the United States "Usonians." Ladd-Franklin died of pneumonia in New York City on March 5, 1930.

SELECTED WRITINGS BY LADD-FRANKLIN:

Books

"On the Algebra of Logic," *Studies in Logic by Members of the Johns Hopkins University,* edited by C. S. Peirce, Little, Brown, 1883, pp. 17–71.
Colour and Colour Theories, Harcourt, Brace, 1929.

Periodicals

"Some Proposed Reforms in Common Logic," *Mind,* Volume 15, 1890, pp. 75–88.
"Women and Letters," *New York Times,* December 13, 1921, p. 18.
"Women and Economics," *New York Times,* May 28, 1924, p. 22.
"The Antilogism," *Mind,* Volume 37, 1928, pp. 532–34.

SOURCES:

Books

Ogilvie, Marilyn Bailey, "Christine Ladd-Franklin," *Women in Science,* Massachusetts Institute of Technology, 1986, pp. 116–17.
Rossiter, Margaret W., *Women Scientists in America,* Johns Hopkins University Press, 1982.

Periodicals

Church, Alonzo, "A Bibliography of Symbolic Logic," *Journal of Symbolic Logic,* December, 1936, p. 138.
"Dr. Ladd-Franklin, Educator, 82, Dies," *New York Times,* March 6, 1930, p. 23.
Shen, Eugene, "The Ladd-Franklin Formula in Logic: The Antilogism," *Mind,* Volume 37, 1927, pp. 54–60.
"To Restore Ideal at Johns Hopkins," *New York Times,* February 23, 1926, p. 12.
Venn, J., "Studies in Logic," *Mind,* Volume 8, 1883, p. 594–603.

—Sketch by Sally M. Moite

Willis E. Lamb, Jr.
1913-
American physicist

The period between 1913 and 1928 marked a revolutionary era during which a number of fundamental new concepts about atomic structure were developed. Two decades after **Paul Dirac** published a modified form of the Schrödinger wave equation that explained essentially all of the then-known empirical data on atomic structure, Willis E. Lamb, Jr. observed a behavior in hydrogen atoms that violated one of Dirac's predictions about atomic structure. That behavior, now known as the Lamb shift, involves an infinitesimal difference in energy levels between two electron orbitals in the hydrogen atom. Although the difference is very small, it is sufficient to have raised questions about Dirac's theory. The resolution of those questions by **Richard P. Feynman**, **Julian Schwinger**, and **Sin-Itiro Tomonaga** some years later eventually led to the development of a whole new field of physics, quantum electrodynamics. For his discovery of this phenomenon, Lamb was awarded a share of the 1955 Nobel Prize in physics.

Willis Eugene Lamb, Jr., was born in Los Angeles on July 12, 1913. His mother, the former Marie Helen Metcalf, was a teacher, and his father, Willis Eugene Lamb, Sr., was an electrical engineer. After graduating from Los Angeles High School in 1930, Lamb enrolled at the University of California at Berkeley. He majored in chemistry and earned his B.S. in 1934. He then remained at Berkeley for his graduate research. After completing his doctoral research in physics under the direction of **J. Robert Oppenheimer**, Lamb was awarded his Ph.D. in 1938. His thesis dealt with the electromagnetic properties of nuclear particles.

Lamb's first academic appointment was in the fall of 1938 as instructor of physics at Columbia University. Over the next thirteen years, he was promoted to assistant professor, associate professor, and finally, in 1948, full professor. Between 1943 and 1952, Lamb was also associated with the Columbia Radiation Laboratory, where he was engaged in a variety of military research projects, primarily for the Army Signal Corps, the Office of Naval Research, and the Office of Scientific Research and Development. Much of this work had to do with radar and microwave radiation, providing Lamb with experience that was to become invaluable in his later studies.

Discovers the "Lamb Shift"

With his wartime obligations completed, Lamb returned to his own research in 1946. That research involved analysis of the hyperfine structure of the hydrogen spectrum. In the early 1940s, the dominant theory of atomic structure was that proposed by Paul Dirac in 1928. Dirac's theory, in turn, had evolved out of the earlier work of **Niels Bohr**, **Erwin Schrödinger**, **Max Born**, **Werner Heisenberg**, and a number of others. With regard to the hydrogen atom, Dirac predicted the existence of three energy states, the first two of which would be degenerate, that is, identical.

The energy states of an atom are investigated by bombarding the atom with an external source of radiation. Electrons in the atom are excited by the radiation and move briefly to a higher energy level. When they return to their ground state, they reemit radiation in a form that can be detected as spectral lines. When energy is emitted from two electron orbitals with nearly equal energies, the spectral lines are closely spaced and may appear to form a single line. Close observation may reveal, however, that a line that at first seems to be a singlet actually has detailed, or hyperfine, structure, consisting of two or more very slightly spaced lines. This indicates a slight difference in the energy levels of the two electron orbitals.

Lamb set out to test Dirac's theory about the degeneracy of the first two energy states of hydrogen. Because the difference between two closely-spaced energy states was known to be very small (if it existed at all), Lamb had recourse to the highly precise microwave spectroscopy techniques with which he had become familiar in his war research. Working with R. C. Retherford (first his graduate student and later his colleague at Columbia), Lamb was able to show that a very small difference exists between the first two energy levels. That difference has now become known as the Lamb shift.

The Lamb shift has had a profound effect on atomic theory. The inability of the Dirac theory to explain or predict this phenomenon caused scientists to begin a fundamental reassessment of their view of atomic structure. Out of that reassessment has come an entirely new approach to the interaction of matter and energy, known as quantum electrodynamics. Harvard's Dr. **Norman Ramsey** later described Lamb's research in the December 1953 issue of the *Proceedings of the American Academy of Arts and Sciences* as Lamb's "most important experiment and, indeed, one of the most significant of all postwar experiments."

In 1951, Lamb accepted an appointment as professor of physics at Stanford University, a post he held for five years. During that period, he also spent a year as Loeb Lecturer in physics at Harvard (1953–54). In 1956, Lamb left Stanford to accept an appointment as fellow at New College and Wykeham Professor of Physics at Oxford University. He returned to the United States in 1962 to become Henry Ford II Professor of Physics at Yale University and then, in 1972, J. Willard Gibbs Professor of Physics at Yale. Two years later, Lamb left Yale to accept a position as professor of physics and optical sciences at the University of Arizona. During the years since his Columbia research, Lamb has worked on a variety of topics, including the fine structure of the helium atom, beta decay, theories of nuclear structure, laser theory, cosmic ray showers, and magnetron theory and design.

In addition to his 1955 Nobel Prize, Lamb has been awarded honorary degrees by the University of Pennsylvania (1953), Yeshiva University (1964), and Gustavus Adolphus College (1975). He married Ursula Schaefer, a professor of history, on June 5, 1939.

SELECTED WRITINGS BY LAMB:

Books

(With M. Sargent and M. O. Scully) *Laser Physics,* Addison-Wesley, 1974.

Periodicals

(With Robert C. Retherford) "Fine Structure of the Hydrogen Atom by a Microwave Method," *Physical Review,* Volume 72, 1947, pp. 241–43.

(With Miriam Skinner) "The Fine Structure of Singly Ionized Helium," *Physical Review,* Volume 78, 1950, pp. 539–50.

SOURCES:

Books

McGraw-Hill Modern Scientists and Engineers, Volume 2, McGraw-Hill, 1980, pp. 200–201.
Wasson, Tyler, editor, *Nobel Prize Winners,* Wilson, 1987, pp. 589–90.
Weber, Robert L., *Pioneers of Science: Nobel Prize Winners in Physics,* American Institute of Physics, 1980, pp. 155–56.

Periodicals

Newsweek, September 29, 1947.
New York Times, November 3, 1955.
Proceedings of the American Academy of Arts and Sciences, December, 1953.

—*Sketch by David E. Newton*

Cleo Lancaster
1948-
American biologist

Cleo Lancaster is recognized as a pioneer in the field of prostaglandin cytoprotection—the cellular protection of the gastric lining by the use of hormone-like fatty acids—leading to new ulcer therapies.

Lancaster was born in Edgecomb County, North Carolina, on December 10, 1948, the daughter of Robert, a truck driver, and Elizabeth B. Lancaster, a farmer and cook. Growing up in an agricultural area, Lancaster came into daily contact with nature. "Farming influenced my appreciation and fascination for living things," she remarked in an interview with J. Sydney Jones. "The farm animals we prepared for food taught me comparative anatomy which prevented me from being repulsed in anatomy or physiology classes." She attended local grammar and high schools, where she first gained an appreciation for biology from one of her teachers, and upon graduation attended Elizabeth City State University in North Carolina, initially planning to become a biology teacher. By her third year in college, however, Lancaster had decided to seek a career in research. As she told Jones, "I decided to pursue a career in research as opposed to teaching because I wanted the challenge of discovery. . . . Research allowed you to go as far as your talents could take you."

Lancaster earned a B.S. in biology in 1971, and upon graduation became a research assistant in radiation genetics for the Brookhaven National Laboratory in Upton, New York, for the summer. In the fall of 1971 she went to work for Upjohn Company in Kalamazoo, Michigan, as a research associate in gastrointestinal (GI) or ulcer research. While at Upjohn, she also enrolled in graduate school at Western Michigan University, graduating with an M.S. in biomedical science in 1979.

Prostaglandin Research Breaks New Ground

At Upjohn, Lancaster has been primarily involved with developing experimental models of such gastrointestinal diseases as ulcers, diarrhea, pancreatitis, and colitis, in order to discover natural or synthetic chemicals that could treat such conditions. Between 1971 and 1974 she researched the ulcer-causing effects of nicotine, linking smoking to duodenal ulcers in humans. She has also done work on the reduced irritant effects of ibuprofen versus aspirin, as well as the ulcer-causing effect of both a steroid used in organ transplant patients and of alcohol when taken in conjunction with aspirin. By far Lancaster's most important research was accomplished between 1971 and 1991, revealing the cytoprotective properties of prostaglandins, a substance initially found in semen and thought to be produced in the prostate gland, though it is now recognized that these fatty acids are produced in many parts of the body. Prostaglandins stimulate muscle contraction, function with the autonomic and central nervous systems, and can be used to inhibit gastric acid secretion. Lancaster's research showed that prostaglandins stimulate mucus/bicarbonate production and increase the cell resistance of the stomach lining, thus preventing ulcers. Working with Upjohn colleague André Robert, Lancaster developed two new-use patents: one for a treatment of pancreatitis, and the second for the treatment of ulcers with oxamate derivatives, an asthma preparation. She has also helped to develop surgical techniques for the research of gastric secretion.

In 1989 Lancaster became a research associate in Upjohn's Safety Pharmacology group, where she is responsible for the evaluation of new drugs and their effects on the GI tract. She is a member of the New York Academy of Science and has won the Upjohn Laboratory Special Recognition award as well as the Mary McLeod Bethune Award for Science and Technology. In her free time, Lancaster collects decorative glass, teaches a Saturday science class for seventh graders, reads, and fishes.

SELECTED WRITINGS BY LANCASTER:

Periodicals

(With others) "Cysteamine-Induced Duodenal Ulcers: A New Model to Test Antiulcer Agents," *Digestion,* Volume 11, 1974, pp. 199–214.

(With André Robert) "Intestinal Lesions Produced by Prednisolone: Prevention (Cytoprotection) by 16, 16-Dimethyl Prostaglandin E$_2$," *American Journal of Physiology,* December, 1978, pp. E703-E708.

(With others) "Cytoprotection by Prostaglandins in Rats: Prevention of Gastric Necrosis Produced by Alcohol, HCl, NaOH, Hypertonic NaCl and Thermal Injury," *Gastroenterology,* Volume 77, 1979, pp. 433–443.

(With others) "Mild Irritants Prevent Gastric Necrosis through 'Adaptive Cytoprotection' Mediated by Prostaglandins," *American Journal of Physiology,* July, 1983, pp. G113-G121.

"Prevention by Prostaglandins of Caerulein-Induced Pancreatitis in Rats," *Laboratory Investigation,* May, 1989, pp. 677–691.

(With others) "Interleukin–1 Is Cytoprotective, Antisecretory, Stimulates PEG2 Synthesis by the Stomach, and Retards Gastric Emptying," *Life Sciences,* Volume 48, 1991, pp. 123–134.

SOURCES:

Periodicals

"Cleo Lancaster, Senior Research Biologist, the Upjohn Company," *Journal of the NTA,* spring, 1992, p. 39.

Other

Lancaster, Cleo, interview with J. Sydney Jones conducted January 18, 1994.

—*Sketch by J. Sydney Jones*

Rebecca Craighill Lancefield
1895-1981
American bacteriologist

Rebecca Craighill Lancefield is known throughout the world for the system she developed to classify the bacterium streptococcus. Her colleagues called her laboratory at the Rockefeller Institute for Medical Research (now Rockefeller University) "the Scotland Yard of streptococcal mysteries." During a research career that spanned six decades, she meticulously identified over fifty types of this bacteria. She used her knowledge of this large, diverse bacterial family to learn about pathogenesis and immunity of its afflictions, ranging from sore throats, rheumatic fever and scarlet fever to heart and kidney disease. The Lancefield system remains a key to the medical understanding of streptococcal diseases.

Born Rebecca Craighill on January 5, 1895, in Fort Wadsworth on Staten Island in New York on January 5, 1895, she was the third of six daughters. Her mother, Mary Montague Byram, married William Edward Craighill, a career army officer in the Army Corps of Engineers who had graduated from West Point. Lancefield received a bachelor's degree in 1916 from Wellesley College, after changing her major from English to zoology. Two years later, she earned a master's degree from Columbia University, where she pursued bacteriology in the laboratory of **Hans Zinsser**. Immediately on graduating from Columbia, she formed two lifelong partnerships. She married Donald Lancefield, who had been a classmate of hers in a genetics class. And she was hired by the Rockefeller Institute to help bacteriologists **Oswald Avery** and Alphonse Dochez, whose expertise on pneumococcus was then being applied to a different bacterium. This was during World War I, and the project at Rockefeller was to discover whether distinct types of streptococci could be isolated from soldiers in a Texas epidemic so that a serum might be produced to prevent infection. The scientists employed the same serological techniques that Avery had used to distinguish types of pneumococci. Within a year, Avery, Dochez, and Lancefield had published a major report which described four types of streptococci. This was Lancefield's first paper.

Lancefield and her husband took a short hiatus to teach in his home state at the University of Oregon, then returned to New York. Lancefield worked simultaneously on a Ph.D. at Columbia and on rheumatic fever studies at the Rockefeller Institute in the laboratory of Homer Swift, and her husband joined the Columbia University faculty in biology. Before World War I, physicians had suspected that a streptococcus caused rheumatic fever. But scientists, including Swift, had not been able to recover a specific organism from patients. Nor could they reproduce the disease in animals using patient cultures. Lancefield's first project with Swift, which was also her doctoral work, showed that the alpha-hemolytic class of streptococcus, also called green or viridans, was not the cause of rheumatic fever.

Develops Classification of Streptococci

As a result of her work with Swift, Lancefield decided that a more basic approach to rheumatic fever was needed. So she began sorting out types among the disease-causing class, the beta-hemolytic streptococci. She used serological techniques while continuing to benefit from Avery's advice. Her major tool for classifying the bacteria was the precipitin test. This involved mixing soluble type-specific antigens, or substances used to stimulate immune responses, with antisera (types of serum containing antibodies) to give visible precipitates. Precipitates are the separations of a substance, in this case bacteria, from liquid in a solution—the serum—in order to make it possible to study the bacteria on its own.

Lancefield soon recovered two surface antigens from these streptococci. One was a polysaccharide, or carbohydrate, called the C substance. This complex sugar molecule is a major component of the cell wall in all streptococci. She could further subdivide its dissimilar compositions into groups and she designated the groups by the letters A through O. The most common species causing human disease, Streptococcus pyogenes, were placed in group A. Among the group A streptococci, Lancefield found another antigen and determined it was a protein, called M for its matt appearance in colony formations. Because of differences in M protein composition, Lancefield was able to subdivide group A streptococci into types. During her career, she identified over fifty types, and

since her death in 1981 bacteriologists have identified thirty more.

Lancefield's classification converged with another typing system devised by **Frederick Griffith** in England. His typing was based on a slide agglutination method, in which the bacteria in the serum collects into clumps when an antibody is introduced. For five years the two scientists exchanged samples and information across the Atlantic Ocean, verifying each other's types, until Griffith's tragic death during the bombing of London in 1940. Ultimately, Lancefield's system, based on the M types, was chosen as the standard for classifying group A streptococci.

In further studies on the M protein, Lancefield revealed this antigen is responsible for the bacteria's virulence because it inhibits phagocytosis, thus keeping the white blood cells from engulfing the streptococci. This finding came as a surprise, because Avery had discovered that virulence in the pneumococcus was due to a polysaccharide, not a protein. Lancefield went on to show the M antigen is also the one that elicits protective immune reactions.

Researches Pathogenesis and Immunity of Streptococci

Lancefield continued to group and type strep organisms sent from laboratories around the world. Until the end of her life, her painstaking investigations helped unravel the complexity and diversity of these bacteria. Lancefield's colleague **Maclyn McCarty**, told contributor Carol L. Moberg that Lancefield was "never satisfied with quick answers," and her success came from a determination to stick with scientific problems for a long time. Her thoroughness, he added, was a significant factor in her small but substantial bibliography of nearly sixty papers.

Once her system of classification was in place, however, Lancefield returned to her original quest to elucidate connections between the bacteria's constituents and the baffling nature of streptococcal diseases. She found that a single serotype of group A can cause a variety of streptococcal diseases. This evidence reversed a long-standing belief that every disease must be caused by a specific microbe. Also, because the M protein is type-specific, she found that acquired immunity to one group A serotype could not protect against infections caused by others in group A.

From her laboratory at Rockefeller Hospital, Lancefield could follow patient records for very long periods. She conducted a study which determined that once immunity is acquired to a serotype, it can last up to thirty years. This particular study revealed the unusual finding that high titers, or concentrations, of antibody persist in the absence of antigen. In the case of rheumatic fever, Lancefield illustrated how someone can suffer recurrent attacks, because each one is caused by a different serotype.

In other studies, Lancefield focused on antigens. She and Gertrude Perlmann purified the M protein in the 1950s. Twenty years later she developed a more conservative test for typing it and continued characterizing other group A protein antigens designated T and R. Ten years after her official retirement, she made a vital contribution on the group B streptococci. She clarified the role of their polysaccharides in virulence and showed how protein antigens on their surface also played a protective role. During the 1970s, an increasingly high-rate of infants were being born with group B meningitis, and her work laid the basis for the medical response to this problem.

During World War II, Lancefield had performed special duties on the Streptococcal Diseases Commission of the Armed Forces Epidemiological Board. Her task involved identifying strains and providing antisera for epidemics of scarlet and rheumatic fever among soldiers in military camps. After the commission dissolved, her colleagues in the "Strep Club" created the Lancefield Society in 1977, which continues to hold regular international meetings on advances in streptococcal research.

An associate member at Rockefeller when Maclyn °McCarty took over Swift's laboratory in 1946, Lancefield became a full member and professor in 1958 and emeritus professor in 1965. While her career and achievements took place in a field dominated by men, Lewis Wannamaker in *American Society for Microbiology News* quotes Lancefield as being "annoyed by any special feeling about women in science." In *Profiles of Pioneer Women Scientists,* Elizabeth O'Hern cites Lancefield as saying that women "sometimes expect too much." Nevertheless, most recognition for Lancefield came near her retirement. In 1961, she was the first woman elected president of the American Association of Immunologists, and in 1970 she was one of few women elected to the National Academy of Sciences. Other honors included the T. Duckett Jones Memorial Award in 1960, the American Heart Association Achievement Award in 1964, the New York Academy of Medicine Medal in 1973, and honorary degrees from Rockefeller University in 1973 and Wellesley College in 1976.

In addition to her career as a scientist, Lancefield had one daughter. Lancefield was devoted to research and preferred not to go on lecture tours or attend scientific meetings. Rockefeller's laboratories were not air-conditioned and her main diversion was leaving them during the summer and spending the entire season in Woods Hole, Massachusetts. There she enjoyed tennis and swimming with her family, which eventually included two grandsons. Official retirement did not change her lifestyle. She drove to her Rockefeller laboratory from her home in Dougla-

ston, Long Island, every working day until she broke her hip in November 1980. She died of complications from this injury on March 3, 1981, at the age of eighty-six. Her husband Donald died the following August.

The pathogenesis of rheumatic fever still eludes scientists, and antibiotics have not eliminated streptococcal diseases. Yet the legacy of Lancefield's system and its fundamental links to disease remain and a vaccine against several group A streptococci is being developed in her former laboratory at Rockefeller University by Vincent A. Fischetti.

SELECTED WRITINGS BY LANCEFIELD:

Periodicals

(With O. T. Avery and A. R. Dochez) "Studies on the Biology of Streptococcus. I. Antigenic Relationships between Strains of *Streptococcus haemolyticus,*" *Journal of Experimental Medicine,* Volume 30, 1919, pp. 179–213.
"The Antigenic Complex of *Streptococcus haemolyticus,*" *Journal of Experimental Medicine,* a series of five reports, Volume 47, 1928, pp. 91–103, 469–480, 481–491, 843–855, 857–875.
"The Serological Differentiation of Human and Other Groups of Hemolytic Streptococci," *Journal of Experimental Medicine,* Volume 57, 1933, pp. 571–595.
"Specific Relationship of Cell Composition to Biological Activity of Hemolytic Streptococci," *The Harvey Lectures, 1940–1941,* series 36, 1941, pp. 251–290.
(With M. McCarty and W. N. Everly) "Multiple Mouse-protective Antibodies Directed Against Group B Streptococci. Special Reference to Antibodies Effective Against Protein Antigens," *Journal of Experimental Medicine,* Volume 142, 1975, pp. 165–179.

SOURCES:

Books

O'Hern, E. M., *Profiles of Pioneer Women Scientists,* Acropolis Books, 1985, pp. 69–78.

Periodicals

McCarty, M., "Rebecca Craighill Lancefield," *Biographical Memoirs, National Academy of Sciences,* Volume 57, 1987, pp. 226–246.
Schwartz, J. N., "Mrs. L.," *Research Profiles,* summer, 1990, pp. 1–6.

Wannamaker, L., "Rebecca Craighill Lancefield," *American Society for Microbiology News,* Volume 47, 1981, pp. 555–558.

Other

McCarty, Maclyn, interview with Carol L. Moberg conducted on February 9, 1994.

—*Sketch by Carol L. Moberg*

Edwin H. Land
1909-1991
American inventor

Edwin H. Land

Edwin H. Land was the driving force behind the Polaroid Corporation's engineering and marketing successes. He was the first to figure out how to manufacture practical and useful polarized screens during the 1930s, and he produced revolutionary optics for the military during World War II. But it was the development of the instant camera that made his company famous, and he was able to dominate the instant-photography market with cameras that first produced pictures in sepia tones, then in black and white, and finally in color. One who routinely discarded conventional wisdom, Land believed that market research was not necessary; he claimed that any invention would sell if people believed it was something they could not live without.

An only child, Edwin Land was born to Martha F. and Harry Land on May 7, 1909, in Bridgeport, Connecticut. His father ran a salvage and scrap metal business; the family was well-off and Land had a comfortable upbringing. In his youth he dreamed of being an inventor and idolized Michael Faraday, **Thomas Alva Edison**, and Alexander Graham Bell. Even as a boy, Land was very interested in polarized light. He entered Harvard at age seventeen in 1926. While walking along Broadway in New York City that same year, he was overwhelmed by the glare from headlights and store signs that shone in his eyes. Land perceived safety hazards in all that glare, and he determined that polarized lights could reduce it. He left Harvard at the end of the school year to pursue this idea and did not return for three years.

Land's parents provided an allowance that enabled him to stay in New York and work on this idea. He studied at the New York Public Library and even found a laboratory at Columbia University whose window was habitually unlocked. He would climb in at night and conduct various experiments. During this

period Land met Helen Maislen, a graduate of Smith College who began assisting him in his research. They were married in 1929, and Land returned to Harvard that same year. This time the university provided him with a laboratory to conduct his research.

Develops a Commercial Method to Polarize Light

It had been known since the eighteenth century that certain kinds of crystals could affect the direction of light waves. In his effort to develop a method for polarizing light, Land was searching for a crystal that could not only reduce glare but was stable and economical enough to be produced commercially. He conceived of the idea of two plates which would absorb the light waves that were not wanted and transmit those that were. He then succeeded in aligning millions of microscopic iodine crystals in one direction, thus creating the first polarizer. As Mark Olshaker wrote in the *Instant Image:* "Land's singular achievement was in discovering a way to synthesize a sheet material that could align light waves in the desirable planes of vibration. The invention was a combined achievement of chemistry and optics." Land presented a paper on his discovery at a physics colloquium at Harvard in February, 1932. In June he left the university, one semester short of a degree, and never returned.

With a Harvard graduate student named George Wheelwright, who had been one of his teachers, Land formed Land-Wheelwright Laboratories, Inc. in June of 1932. The two men worked on developing methods of manufacturing polarized sheets made of crystals trapped in nitrocellulose. On November 30, 1934, Eastman Kodak gave Land-Wheelwright an order for ten thousand dollars worth of polarizing filters. Kodak wanted a polarizer laminated between two sheets of optical glass, but neither Land nor Wheelwright had any idea how to manufacture such an item. Nonetheless, they accepted the order—a decision typical of the way Land would work in the future. Their persistence paid off, and Land-Wheelwright Laboratories invented what they dubbed "Polaroid," with which they fulfilled their contract with Eastman Kodak.

Land had a flair for the dramatic which he put to good use in marketing his inventions. For example, when he was trying to sell his polarizers for use as sunglasses, he rented a room at a hotel and invited executives from the American Optical Company to meet him there. The late afternoon sun produced a glare on the windowsill; Land put a fishbowl there and the glare rendered the goldfish inside it invisible. When the executives arrived, Land handed them each a sheet of polarizer and they were able to see the fish instantly. Land told them that from now on their sunglasses should be made with polarized glass, and the company bought the idea.

Land gave his first press conference on polarization on January 30, 1936, at the Waldorf Astoria Hotel. He repeated it for the National Academy of Sciences and the New York Museum of Science soon after that. The press coverage Land expected from this last presentation was overshadowed by the abdication of King Edward VIII in England. But his sales ability once again came through. On August 10, 1937, a group of investors, impressed with Land-Wheelwright's accomplishments, put up 375,000 dollars to fund the Polaroid Corporation. Furthermore, they gave Land controlling interest in the company.

With the money Land purchased some competing patents on polarization and decided that the 1939 New York World's Fair would be an excellent way to demonstrate to automakers and the American public the virtues of polarized headlights. Chrysler rented Polaroid space in one of its booths, and Land played a three-dimensional movie he had invented which graphically illustrated how much improved polarized headlights were. The twelve-minute film was well-received by the public; 150,000 people saw it in its first two months, but Detroit never bought Land's system. Polaroid nevertheless enjoyed good success with its Polaroid Day Glasses and the dual polarized windows they installed on Union Pacific's Copper King rail cars. By January of 1940 the company had about 240 employees, and it moved from Boston to Cambridge.

Achieves Growth During World War II

Early in 1941 the Navy invited companies to bid on a contract to develop an altitude finder. Before the other companies even replied, Polaroid invented the item and presented it to the Navy. During the war, Polaroid provided the Army and Navy with various types of goggles, as well as improved gunsights for Sherman tanks. Land drove the company hard, convinced that the Allies' only hope of winning lay in the superiority of the science behind the effort. To this end, he invented "vectography," a system that took three-dimensional photographs. Such photos were invaluable in reconnaissance efforts, especially when camouflage was employed by the enemy. Polaroid also worked on the guided missile program known as the SX–70 or "Project Dove." The company's work was deemed valuable enough for them to have won four Navy "E" pennants for excellence.

Two of Land's employees, **Robert B. Woodward** and William E. Doering, solved a critical problem for the Allies. With the Japanese controlling Java, and thus the world supply of cinchona trees, quinine—the only cure known for malaria—was unavailable. Woodward and Doering synthesized quinine and Polaroid waived the royalties from this synthetic compound and gave them to the government with no commercial limitations. Woodward later won the 1965 Nobel Prize in chemistry for synthesizing cortisone.

Invents Instant Photography

By 1943 Land had a three-year-old daughter named Jennifer. While vacationing in Santa Fe just before Christmas, Land's daughter asked him why they could not see the pictures they had taken during the day. Land recalled his reaction to this question, as quoted in the *New York Times:* "As I walked around that charming town I undertook the task of solving the puzzle she had set me. Within the hour, the camera, the film, and the physical chemistry became so clear to me." Several years of intense work at Polaroid followed, and on February 21, 1947, Land demonstrated his instant camera at the winter meeting of the Optical Society of America. Although the images were in sepia, public reaction was so enthusiastic that Polaroid came under much pressure to manufacture the camera quickly even though they did not yet have the capability to do it. The camera also had another revolutionary feature: it linked aperture size and shutter speed, which eliminated much of the guesswork in using the camera.

In addition to his consumer products, Land also developed a new optical system for the Sloan-Kettering Cancer Institute in 1948 that enabled scientists to observe living human cells in their natural color. Near the end of 1953 he also invented a microscope that used light invisible to the human eye for illumination.

Both of these inventions were a great aid in cancer research. In 1954 President Eisenhower appointed Land the head of an intelligence committee to study how to prevent a future attack like the one at Pearl Harbor. Land's recommendation to Eisenhower was to establish a system of aerial reconnaissance; this was the beginning of the U2 spy plane project, which carried several Polaroid developments on board.

In 1952 Polaroid introduced true black-and-white film for their instant camera. But unlike the sepia prints which held their images very well, the black-and-white ones faded over time. Land pressed his company to find a solution, which they did in only four weeks. Yet he was not happy with it, since it required swabbing the photo after pulling it from the camera; Land wanted his instant camera to require only one step. In addition, research continued simultaneously to develop an instant camera that produced color photos. Land even had his own private laboratory where he did much work on this.

It was not until April of 1972 that Land was finally able to reveal to the public a long-time dream brought to reality: the SX–70 instant color camera. The introduction of color had meant overcoming a host of technological obstacles. His achievement was recognized with the October 27, 1972, cover of *Life* magazine, which showed Land taking pictures of children from behind his SX–70.

Land was awarded the Hood Medal from the Royal Photographic Society in London in 1935. He was named one of America's Modern Pioneers by the National Association of Manufacturers on February 27, 1940. On December 6, 1963, Land received the Presidential Medal of Freedom, awarded by Lyndon Johnson less than three weeks after John F. Kennedy's assassination. In 1967, Land received the National Medal of Science, which was again presented by President Johnson. In February 1977 Land was inducted into the Inventor's Hall of Fame by the American patent office. All told, Land received 533 patents.

Land also started an inner city program for disadvantaged blacks during the 1960s, as well as the Rowland Foundation in 1965. Land later founded the Rowland Institute for Science. His financial gifts to various institutions, such as the Massachusetts Institute of Technology (MIT) and Harvard University, were always anonymous. He was a visiting professor at MIT, a member of Harvard's visiting committees for astronomy, chemistry, and physics, and a fellow at MIT's School for Advanced Study. Land received an honorary doctorate from Harvard in 1957, and others from such notable institutions as Yale, Tufts, Columbia University, Loyola, and Washington University. In 1951 Land was elected President of the American Academy of Arts and Sciences and served for two

years. Land retired in August of 1982, and died March 1, 1991, of undisclosed causes.

SELECTED WRITINGS BY LAND:

Books

Generation of Greatness: The Idea of a University in an Age of Science, MIT Press, 1975.

Periodicals

"Vectographs: Images in Terms of Vectorial Inequality and Their Application in Three-Dimensional Representation," *Journal of the Optical Society of America,* June, 1940.
"A New One-Step Photographic Process," *Journal of the Optical Society of America,* February, 1947.
(With L. W. Chubb, Jr.) "Polarized Light for Auto Headlights. Part II," *Traffic Engineering,* July, 1950.
"Some Aspects of the Development of Sheer Polarizers," *Journal of the Optical Society of America,* December, 1951.
"Thinking Ahead: Patents and New Enterprises," *Harvard Business Review,* September/October, 1959.
"The Retinex Theory of Color Vision," *Scientific American,* December, 1977.

SOURCES:

Books

Olshaker, Mark, *The Instant Image,* Stein & Day, 1978.
Wensberg, Peter C., *Land's Polaroid,* Houghton, 1987.

Periodicals

Berg, Howard C., "Edwin H. Land," *Physics Today,* April, 1992, p. 106.
Pace, Eric, "Edwin H. Land, Dies at 81; Invented Polaroid Camera," *New York Times,* March 2, 1991.

—*Sketch by Susan E. Kolmer*

Lev Davidovich Landau
1908-1968
Russian theoretical physicist

Lev Davidovich Landau was one of the twentieth century's finest theoretical physicists. Known as the last of the "Universalists," Landau was most remarkable for the breadth of his erudition and for his ability to move with ease between the various branches of physics. His *Collected Papers* record the scope of his interests—which included everything from low-temperature physics to the symmetry of space—and the exactitude with which he approached every challenge. Landau was a teacher no less than he was a theoretician; the towering standards that he set for himself were conveyed to his students at the School of Landau, many of whom later achieved recognition in their own right. Landau's work was widely and repeatedly recognized as evidenced by the copious honors bestowed upon him, most notably, the 1962 Nobel Prize in physics "for his pioneering theories concerning condensed matter, especially liquid helium." Landau was born on January 22, 1908, in Baku on the Caspian Sea. Now the capital of Azerbaijan, Landau's hometown was, at that time, part of the Soviet Union. His parents were educated and well-to-do Russians; his father was a petroleum engineer at one of Baku's oil fields, his mother, independent and educated far beyond the standards for women of that time. She became, first, a midwife, before going on to become a physician, working during the First World War as a field doctor and later as a teacher. One of Landau's biographers, Anna Livanova, writes in *Landau: A Great Physicist and Teacher* that "it may have been her example that gave Landau the foundation of his own versatility, his calling as both scientist and teacher." Lev also had a sister, Sofia, some years his senior, who became a chemical engineer.

Although he would later deny that he had been a child prodigy, he demonstrated that he was advanced at an early age when he finished school at age thirteen. He thought to study maths and physics, subjects which he loved, but his parents decided to send him, with his sister, for a year to an economics college since he was still very young. In 1922, he enrolled in the University of Baku in the faculties of maths and physics and of chemistry.

In 1924, Landau transferred to the University of Leningrad to enroll in its department of physics. There, he attended classes twice weekly and spent the rest of the time pursuing his own lines of research and "dreaming formulae." While still an undergraduate, in 1926, Landau also became a supernumerary graduate student at Leningrad's Physicotechnical Institute.

Lev Davidovich Landau

That same year, his first scientific paper, "On the Theory of the Spectra of Diatomic Molecules," was published to considerable interest.

Upon graduating from the university the following year, he joined the Physicotechnical Institute as a fully fledged graduate student. This was where he first came into contact with a group of other theoreticians and with "big physics," as the new quantum mechanics was known. He avidly read scientific papers written by the leading lights of nuclear physics, which enabled him to keep abreast of developments in Western Europe, the heartland of the new physics. Characteristic of him then and throughout his life was his extraordinary critical sense and his complete independence of thought. A paper published by him in 1927, when he was still only nineteen, on "The Damping Problem in Wave Mechanics," amply demonstrated that he was far from run of the mill. It was the first time that anyone had described the quantum state of systems with the aid of the density matrices. It was during this period that Landau was given the nickname by which he would always be known, becoming "Dau" to his teachers, fellow students, pupils, and to himself.

Meets Cream of Nuclear Physicists during European Trip

In 1929, Landau made his first trip abroad. Over a period of eighteen months, he visited Switzerland, Germany, Denmark, England, Belgium, and Holland, meeting all the great physicists of the day with the exception of the one that he, perhaps, admired the most and was most often compared to: **Enrico Fermi**. Landau called Fermi "the second last of the Universalists"; after the Italian's death, Landau became, in his own words, "the last of the universal physicists," according to Livanova in her biography of the scientist.

The bulk of his time was spent in Copenhagen at **Niels Bohr**'s Institute of Theoretical Physics, regarded by many as the mecca of physicists. Surrounded by the top names in the field, including **Wolfgang Pauli**, **George Gamow**, **Werner Karl Heisenberg**, **Felix Bloch**, and **Paul Ehrenfest**, Landau was far from daunted and proved himself a match of the greatest minds. Indeed, it was noted of him that he was mentally more agile than almost any of his contemporaries, being the first to solve a problem, often in the most unconventional way. In this, he was aided by his powerful grasp of mathematics, which he considered the first tool of the theoretician. The only regret he was heard to voice during this period was that he had not been born sooner. "All the nice girls have been snapped up and married, and all the nice problems have been solved. I don't really like any of those that are left," he remarked during a meeting in Berlin at the close of 1929, according to Livanova. By 1930, when Landau came to Denmark, the basics of quantum mechanics had already been figured out. Nonetheless, he subsequently managed to find enough unsolved problems to keep him busy throughout his life.

Bohr influenced Landau more than any other physicist. The Russian often said of his Danish mentor that he was his only teacher. Their relationship was mutually respectful and lifelong. "The success of the school of theoretical physics which Landau subsequently founded in the Soviet Union undoubtedly owed much to Bohr's example," said the Russian scientist **Pyotr Kapitsa**, according to Livanova. Dau and Kapitsa would later work together.

In Cambridge, Landau worked with the New Zealand-born Cavendish professor, **Ernest Rutherford**. Here, he met for the first time his fellow Russian, Kapitsa, and developed his theory of the diamagnetism of metals. This predicted the occurrence of unusual magnetic properties of free electrons in metals.

In Zurich, he worked with the German physicist Wolfgang Pauli, to whom he was frequently compared for the sharp tongues and critical faculties they had in common. In Zurich, too, he wrote two important and well received papers with the German physicist Rudolf Peirels, one of which pertained to relativistic quantum theory.

Begins Teaching at Kharkov

Returning to Leningrad in 1931, he determined to begin teaching, as well as to continue his own work. First, he worked closely with Matvey Bronstein at the Physicotechnical Institute, before moving to Ukraine in 1932 to head the Theoretical Institute at its then capital, Kharkov. Here, finally, Landau was able to realize his wish to teach. Kharkov was where Landau devised his first "theoretical minimum" program in physics for members of the institute staff and began work on his magnum opus, the *Course of Theoretical Physics,* which remains, long after Landau's death, the bible of theoretical physics. These volumes, covering the spectra of the field, testify, perhaps more than anything else Landau produced, to his genius. Of them, one of his pupils at Kharkov remarked, "It is Landau's true memorial. He alone could have created it; no other person. Books more striking than these will never be written, no matter what the subject," wrote Livanova. Another commented, "If there is no answer there, it will not be found anywhere." The course was co-written with one of Landau's favorite pupils, Evgeny Lifshitz, for Landau could not bear to write.

The theoretical minimum was an examination, with nine component parts, covering all of theoretical physics, including the necessary maths. It was Landau's conception of the minimum a theoretician should know before he would accept him as a pupil. Just how unusual it was can be gauged by the fact that the traditional approach is to view physics as a series of specialities. Not Landau. For him, physics was an indivisible whole, and anyone serious about studying under him had to prove that they, like him, were capable of moving with ease between the various branches. It was a challenge that few were up to: between 1933 and 1961, just forty-three people passed the examination, which was open to anyone who cared to tackle it.

Landau's unusual approach was seen, too, in the theoretical seminars which he introduced at Kharkov. These, too, covered the gamut of theoretical physics, an approach unheard of then or since. Landau was an active participant at these seminars; invariably, he knew more than anyone else there. "Landau knew everything because he was interested in everything," recalled Alexander Kompaneets, one of Landau's pupils, in Livanova's biography. Kompaneets, who incidentally placed first in the list of physicists who had passed the theoretical minimum, also noted: "There will not soon be another theoretical physicist with such erudition."

Investigates Low-Temperature Physics

In 1935, he accepted the chair of General Physics at the University of Kharkov. In addition to his administrative and teaching duties, he took a close interest in the groundbreaking work on low-temperature physics which was being carried out at the university. Landau's angle was the behavior of matter at low temperatures. He published four papers on the topic during this period (out of a total of seventeen on a wide range of subjects). Even with this heavy workload, Landau found time for leisure pursuits: tennis, reading, movies, and fraternizing with his wide circle of friends. He was preoccupied, also, by his recent acquaintance with Kora Drobantseva, a food engineer at a chocolate factory. They married in 1937 and had one son, Igor, who went on to become an experimental physicist.

Landau and Kora moved to Moscow in 1937, where Kapitsa had invited him to head the theoretical division at the Institute of Physical Problems. Here, Landau felt completely at home. He continued working on a range of theoretical problems, being interrupted only briefly during the Second World War when the Institute was evacuated to Kazan. There, Landau devised theories and made calculations of the processes governing the efficiency of armaments and published three papers on the detonation of explosives. For his war-related work, he was made a Hero of Socialist Labour in 1945.

When the war ended, Landau resumed his work on superfluidity. He succeeded in explaining various properties of liquid helium–4 mathematically; for instance, he explained why the element flows without friction below a temperature of 2 degrees Kelvin and has a thermal conductivity 800 times greater than copper at room temperature. This work laid the groundwork for later research into superconductivity, that is, the complete disappearance of electrical resistance in certain metals at temperatures near absolute zero. He forecast that sound would travel at two speeds in liquid helium; at that of a familiar pressure wave and at that of a temperature wave. This theory was experimentally verified in 1944 by the Russian scientist, Vasily Peshkov. Landau also continued to work for the government's nuclear weapons program.

In 1945, Landau investigated shock waves for the engineering company of the Soviet Army. The following year, he turned his attention to the oscillation of plasmas. He predicted that the isotope helium–3 would show unique properties at a temperature near absolute zero on the Kelvin scale, including a wave propagation called "zero sound" and sudden spinning.

Landau received many honors during his lifetime, including The State Prize three times and the Lenin Prize once. He was twice awarded the Order of Lenin, was elected an honorary member of the British Institute of Physics and Physical Society, a foreign member of the Royal Society of London, a member of the U.S. National Academy of Sciences, and a member of the Danish and Netherlands Royal Academies of Sciences. He received the Max Planck Medal, the Fritz London Prize, and the Nobel Prize in physics.

Landau's career was brought to a tragic and abrupt halt on January 7, 1962, when he was involved in a car crash. The base of his skull, ribs, and pelvic bones were broken, and for six weeks the doctors struggled to save his life as he slipped in and out of a coma. He survived, but was so badly injured that he could never work again.

Bedridden, Landau Wins 1962 Nobel Prize

Landau was still confined to his bed when it was announced that he had won the 1962 Nobel Prize in physics for his groundbreaking research into theories of condensed matter, especially liquid helium. As he was not well enough to travel to Stockholm, his wife and son accepted the award on his behalf. He spent the remaining years of his life battling his injuries until he died on April 1, 1968, after surgery to repair an intestinal blockage. He was sixty years old.

SELECTED WRITINGS BY LANDAU:

Books

Lectures on Nuclear Theory, Consultants Bureau, 1958.
Theory of Elasticity, Pergamon, 1959.
Electrodynamics of Continuous Media, Pergamon, 1960.
Mechanics, Pergamon, 1960.
Quantum Mechanics, Pergamon, 1960.
Statistical Physics, Pergamon, 1960.
What is Relativity?, Basic Books, 1961.
Collected Papers of L. D. Landau, Gordon & Breach, 1965.
A Shorter Course on Theoretical Physics, Pergamon, 1972.
The Classical Theory of Fields, Pergamon, 1980.

SOURCES:

Books

Biographical Memoirs of Fellows of the Royal Society, Volume 15, Royal Society (London), 1969.
Dorozynski, Alexander, *The Man They Wouldn't Let Die,* Macmillan, 1965.
Livanova, Anna, *Landau, A Great Physicist and Teacher,* Pergamon, 1980.
Weber, Robert L., *Pioneers of Science: Nobel Prize Winners in Physics,* The Institute of Physics, 1980.

—Sketch by Avril McDonald

Helmut E. Landsberg
1906-1985
German-born American meteorologist

For his extensive work in the field, Helmut E. Landsberg has been called the father of modern climatology. During his studies he documented how the growth of cities could alter local climate, and he strove to understand how weather, in turn, affects human health. Described by colleagues as a visionary, he was concerned with ideas ranging from the climate of one's bed to global warming. Landsberg held numerous university and government posts, ushering the United States Weather Bureau into the computer age and founding a program in meteorology at the University of Maryland.

Helmut Erich Landsberg was a man of small stature, with what some colleagues called an infectious enthusiasm. An only child, he was born on February 9, 1906, in Frankfurt-am-Main, Germany. Landsberg's interest in health can be traced back to his family's influence. His father, Georg Julius Landsberg, was a physician. His mother, Klara Judith Zedner Landsberg, was a homemaker. During his childhood, Landsberg witnessed air raids and food shortages in conjunction with World War I. As a college student at the University of Frankfurt, Landsberg studied earth sciences and took a special interest in earthquakes. He stayed on to write his Ph.D. thesis, comparing two instruments (seismographs) that measured earthquakes. After earning his degree in 1930, Landsberg spent four years in the Taunus Hills supervising an observatory for meteorology and seismology. Although he continued to publish papers on earthquakes, Landsberg's attention began to shift upward, to the atmosphere.

Based on work done at the Taunus Observatory, Landsberg later published significant findings on the importance of microscopic dust particles in air pollution. He also issued the first quantitative study of how these minute particles could be inhaled, calculating that some ninety million of them could be retained in the lungs. Landsberg was deeply conscious of the need to control air pollution. "If regular inspection of drinking water is regarded as indispensable, why not regular inspection of the air we breathe?" he said to the *New York Times* in 1937. After Landsberg immigrated to the United States and became a naturalized citizen, he helped formulate air pollution legislation for President Harry Truman's Air Pollution Committee in 1949.

It was only a casual comment that had brought Landsberg to the United States initially. He had mentioned to a former professor his desire to learn English, and asked to be informed of any job openings in the United States. Upon the professor's recommendation, Pennsylvania State College (later Pennsylvania State University) offered the young Landsberg $1,800 to teach geophysics as an assistant professor for one year. Landsberg packed up his books in 1934 and came to the United States, where the rest of his career in meteorology unfolded.

Issues Landmark Book on Climatology

At Penn State, Landsberg taught the first seminar offered in the United States on bioclimatic problems. He initiated a new climatological and geophysical station on campus, building many of the instruments himself. His stay at Penn State lasted for seven years. Landsberg kept busy in the laboratories and classrooms; he also took his work, literally, to bed. He measured changing temperatures in bed throughout the night to study its micro-climate. Although some thought he was joking, he reasoned that since people spend at least one-third of their lives asleep, they should know if their bed's climate is truly comfortable. Landsberg's book, *Physical Climatology,* published in 1941, was taken quite seriously, by contrast. It was the first English-language work of its kind, explaining how to use sophisticated statistics to study climate and helping bolster the field as a quantitative physical science.

In 1941, the Swedish-American meteorologist **Carl-Gustaf Rossby** invited Landsberg to come to the University of Chicago as an associate professor of meteorology. Landsberg spent three years there, studying wind flow off Lake Michigan and investigating sand dune formation. Landsberg also trained young cadets how to use meteorological instruments for the United States Army Air Corps. During World War II, military strategists consulted him on climatological conditions in Europe. After the war, President Harry Truman's senior science adviser, **Vannevar Bush**, appointed Landsberg to head the Committee on Geophysical Sciences, later the Committee on Geophysics and Geography of the Joint Research and Development Board. From 1949 to 1951 Landsberg helped re-establish communication with scientists from Germany and Japan—countries opposing the Allied Forces during World War II. He also fostered scholarly exchange between universities and government groups. Landsberg then moved on to head the Geophysics Research Directorate of the United States Air Force from 1951 to 1954. He coordinated atmospheric research at seven laboratories to improve forecasting and understanding of the atmosphere's circulation. Appointed as the director of the U.S. Weather Bureau's Office of Climatology from 1954 to 1965, Landsberg introduced computer methods and compiled information on climate for the *National Atlas of the United States of America.* From 1965 to 1967 he directed the Environmental Data Service.

Landsberg retired from the government in 1967 to return to academics. At that time, a demand for government meteorologists existed, but few schools in the Washington, D.C., area offered training. Landsberg helped establish a program in meteorology at the University of Maryland. As a research professor there, he encouraged his students to address problems of acid rain before they became a political issue. He also initiated a novel study, tracking climate changes in Columbia, Maryland, as it rapidly grew from a tiny town to a city.

The University of Maryland made Landsberg professor emeritus after he retired in 1974. He continued to guide students as well as to publish papers. During his retirement, committee members often consulted him about where to place power plants and how to detect carbon dioxide. Landsberg had long been involved in the debate over whether increasing carbon dioxide levels were causing global warming. He had looked back at weather records worldwide, seeking evidence. Although wary about the potential for global warming, Landsberg, in later years, seemed to doubt that the human influence on carbon dioxide levels had a significant impact on a global scale.

Throughout his career, Landsberg contributed to a diverse range of topics. He was fascinated by climatic trends whether they seemed linked to ocean currents or the varying energy output of the sun. His colleagues described him as having an encyclopedic knowledge and a thirst for reading in several languages. He was acknowledged for the interest he took in the interactions between climate and human health, from aches and pains before the approach of a storm, to mood swings and the influence of weather on the timing of births and deaths.

During his lifetime, he made major contributions to the World Meteorological Organization, and acted as president of the Commission for Climatology, beginning in 1969, and served for the maximum eight years. Landsberg participated in other committees, including the American Geophysical Union of which he was president from 1968 to 1970. The Union awarded him its William Bowie Medal for outstanding contributions to fundamental geophysics and for unselfish cooperation in research in 1978. Upon acceptance of the award, he credited his success to the help of his colleagues and students, as well as his wife, A. Frances Simpson. The couple had one son, Bruce Simpson.

Landsberg also published three books and more than three hundred articles and papers during his career. He was editor-in-chief of the *World Survey of Climatology* for more than twenty years. Always looking beyond his own work, he encouraged international cooperation in research. In 1985, Landsberg was one of nineteen scientists honored by President Ronald Reagan with the National Medal of Science,

the highest civilian award for achievement in science given in the United States. On December 6 of that same year, while attending the ninth session of the World Meteorological Organization Commission for Climatology in Geneva, Switzerland, Landsberg died of a sudden heart attack.

SELECTED WRITINGS BY LANDSBERG:

Books

Physical Climatology, Gray Publishing, 1941, 2nd edition, 1956.
Weather and Health, Doubleday, 1969.
The Urban Climate, Academic Press, 1981.
Reconstruction of Past Climates, Wiley, 1983.

Periodicals

"Comfortable Living Depends on Microclimate," *Weatherwise,* February, 1950, pp. 7–10.
"Weather, Climate, and You," *Weatherwise,* October, 1986, pp. 248–253.

SOURCES:

Books

Baer, F., N. L. Canfield, and J. M. Mitchell, *Climate in Human Perspective: A Tribute to Helmut E. Landsberg,* Kluwer Academic Publishers, 1991.

Periodicals

Mitchell, Murray J., "Helmut Landsberg: Climatologist Extraordinary," *Weatherwise,* October, 1986, pp. 254–261.
New York Times, January 3, 1937.
Sullivan, Walter, "Two Climate Experts Decry Predictions of Disasters," *New York Times,* February 22, 1976, p. 48.

—*Sketch by Miyoko Chu*

Karl Landsteiner
1868-1943
Austrian American immunologist

Karl Landsteiner was one of the first scientists to study the physical processes of immunity. He is best known for his identification and characterization of the human blood groups, A, B, and O, but his

Karl Landsteiner

contributions spanned many areas of immunology, bacteriology and pathology over a prolific forty-year career. Landsteiner identified the agents responsible for immune reactions, examined the interaction of antigens and antibodies, and studied allergic reactions in experimental animals. He determined the viral cause of poliomyelitis with research that laid the foundation for the eventual development of a polio vaccine. He also discovered that some simple chemicals, when linked to proteins, produced an immune response. Near the end of his career in 1940, he and the immunologist Philip Levine discovered the Rh factor, which helped save the lives of many fetuses with mismatched Rh factor from their mothers. For his work identifying the human blood groups, he was awarded the Nobel Prize for medicine in 1930.

Born June 14, 1868, Landsteiner was the only child of Dr. Leopold Landsteiner, a famous Viennese journalist, and Fanny Hess Landsteiner. Leopold Landsteiner was the Paris correspondent for several German newspapers and the founder of the daily *Presse,* an influential liberal newspaper. The family lived in Baden bei Wien, an upper-middle-class suburb of Vienna. Karl was six years old when his father suffered a massive heart attack and died. Karl was placed under the guardianship of a family friend, but remained extremely close to his mother.

In 1885, when he was seventeen, Landsteiner passed the entrance examination for medical school at the University of Vienna, where early in his training he expressed enthusiasm for the study of chemistry. He took a year off from school at the age of twenty for his obligatory military service. When he was twenty-one, Landsteiner and his mother converted from Judaism to Catholicism and Karl was christened Karl Otto Landsteiner. Landsteiner graduated from medical school at the age of 23 and immediately began advanced studies in the field of organic chemistry, working in the research laboratory of his mentor, Ernst Ludwig. In Ludwig's laboratory Landsteiner's interest in chemistry blossomed into a passion for approaching medical problems through a chemist's eye.

For the next ten years, Landsteiner worked in a number of laboratories in Europe, studying under some of the most celebrated chemists of the day: **Emil Fischer**, a celebrated protein chemist who subsequently won the Nobel Prize for chemistry in 1902, in Wurzburg; Eugen von Bamberger in Munich; and Arthur Hantzsch and Roland Scholl in Zurich. Landsteiner published many journal articles with these famous scientists. The knowledge he gained about organic chemistry during these formative years guided him throughout his career. The nature of antibodies began to interest him while he was serving as an assistant to Max von Gruber in the Department of Hygiene at the University of Vienna from 1896 to 1897. During this time Landsteiner published his first article on the subject of bacteriology and serology, the study of blood. He had found a subject that was to occupy his entire scientific career.

Discovers Blood Types

Landsteiner moved to Vienna's Institute of Pathology in 1897, where he was hired to perform autopsies. He continued to study immunology and the mysteries of blood on his own time. In 1900, Landsteiner wrote a paper in which he described the agglutination of blood that occurs when one person's blood is brought into contact with that of another. He suggested that the phenomenon was not a pathology, as was the prevalent thought at the time, but was due to the unique nature of the individual's blood. In 1901, Landsteiner demonstrated that the blood serum of some people could clump the blood of others. From his observations he devised the idea of mutually incompatible blood groups. He placed blood types into three groups: A, B, and C (later referred to as O). Two of his colleagues subsequently added a fourth group, AB.

In 1907 the first successful transfusions were achieved by Dr. Reuben Ottenberg of Mt. Sinai Hospital, New York, guided by Landsteiner's work. Landsteiner's accomplishment saved many lives on the battlefields of World War I, where transfusion of compatible blood was first performed on a large scale. In 1902 Landsteiner was appointed as a full member of the Imperial Society of Physicians in Vienna. That same year he presented a lecture, together with Max Richter of the Vienna University Institute of Forensic Medicine, in which the two reported a new method of typing dried blood stains to help solve crimes in which blood stains are left at the scene.

In 1908 Landsteiner took charge of the department of pathology at the Wilhelmina Hospital in Vienna. His tenure at the hospital lasted twelve years, until March of 1920. During this time, Landsteiner was at the height of his career and produced fifty-two papers on serological immunity, thirty-three on bacteriology and six on pathological anatomy. He was among the first to dissociate antigens, which stimulate the production of immune responses known as antibodies, from the antibodies themselves. Landsteiner was also among the first to purify antibodies, and his purification techniques are still used today for some applications in immunology.

Landsteiner also collaborated with Ernest Finger, the head of Vienna's Clinic for Venereal Diseases and Dermatology. In 1905, Landsteiner and Finger successfully transferred the venereal disease syphilis from humans to apes. The result was that researchers had an animal model in which to study the disease. In 1906, Landsteiner and Viktor Mucha, a scientist from the Chemical Institute at Finger's clinic, developed the technique of dark-field microscopy to identify and study the microorganisms that cause syphilis.

Works Toward Polio Vaccine

One day in 1908 the body of a young polio victim was brought in for autopsy. Landsteiner took a portion of the boy's spinal column and injected it into the spinal canal of several species of experimental animals, including rabbits, guinea-pigs, mice and monkeys. Only the monkeys contracted the disease. Landsteiner reported the results of the experiment, conducted with Erwin Popper, an assistant at the Wilhelmina Hospital.

It had generally been accepted that polio was caused by a microorganism, but previous experiments by other researchers had failed to isolate a causative agent, which was presumed to be a bacterium. Because monkeys were hard to come by in Vienna, Landsteiner went to Paris to collaborate with a Romanian bacteriologist, Constantin Levaditi of the Pasteur Institute. Working together, the two were able to trace poliomyelitis to a virus, describe the manner of its transmission, time its incubation phase, and show how it could be neutralized in the laboratory when mixed with the serum of a convalescing patient. In 1912 Landsteiner said that the development of a vaccine against poliomyelitis might prove difficult but was certainly possible. The first successful intravenous polio vaccine, developed by **Jonas Salk**, wasn't administered until 1955.

Landsteiner kept a grueling work schedule that allowed little time for social activity. He was serving at a war hospital in 1916 when, at the age of 48, he married Leopoldine Helene Wlasto. Helene bore a son christened Ernst Karl on April 8, 1917. After the war, Landsteiner's Austria was in chaos, with extreme shortages of food and fuel. He accepted a position as chief dissector in a small Catholic hospital in The Hague, Netherlands. There, from 1919 to 1922, he performed routine laboratory tests on urine and blood. Nevertheless, he managed to publish twelve papers on different aspects of immunology. It was during this time that Landsteiner began working on the concept of haptens, small molecular weight chemicals such as fats or sugars, that determine the specificity of antigen-antibody reactions when combined with a protein "carrier." He combined haptens of known structure with well-characterized proteins such as albumin, and showed that small changes in the hapten could affect antibody production. He developed methods to show that it is possible to sensitize animals to chemicals that cause contact dermatitis (inflammation of the skin) in humans, demonstrating that contact dermatitis is caused by an antigen-antibody reaction. This work launched Landsteiner into a study of the phenomenon of allergic reactions.

Post-War Europe Prompts Move to United States

In 1922, Landsteiner accepted a position at the Rockefeller Institute in New York. Throughout the 1920s Landsteiner worked on the problems of immunity and allergy. He discovered new blood groups: M, N and P, refining the work he had begun 20 years before. Soon after Landsteiner and his collaborator, Philip Levine, published the work in 1927, the types began to be used in paternity suits.

The Landsteiner family spent their summers in an isolated house on Nantucket that reminded Landsteiner of his Scheveningen home in the Netherlands. Landsteiner developed a profound dislike for his growing celebrity as the world's foremost authority on the mechanisms of immunity. He never got used to the noise and crowds of New York City, confessing to friends that he wished he could lock his family away when he was not home. Despite these problems, he became a United States citizen in 1929. Always shunning publicity, even avoiding offers to give public seminars, Landsteiner was stunned when he was besieged by reporters in 1930, upon the news that he had won the Nobel Prize.

In his Nobel lecture, Landsteiner gave an account of his work on individual differences in human blood, describing the differences in blood between different species and among individuals of the same species. This theory is accepted as fact today but was at odds with prevailing thought when Landsteiner began his work. In 1936 Landsteiner summed up his life's work in what was to become a medical classic: *Die Spezifität der serologischen Reaktionen,* which was later revised and published in English, under the title *The Specificity of Serological Reactions.*

Landsteiner officially retired in 1939, at the age of seventy-one, but went on working. With Levine and **Alexander Wiener** he discovered another blood factor, labeled the Rh factor, for Rhesus monkeys, in which the factor was first discovered. The Rh factor was shown to be responsible for the dreaded infant disease, erythroblastosis fetalis, which occurs when mother and fetus have incompatible blood types and the fetus is injured by the mother's antibodies. During his later years, Landsteiner formed a friendship with **Linus Pauling**, the American biochemist who won the Nobel Prize in chemistry in 1954. Their discussions led Pauling to apply his knowledge to immunology and to contribute a chapter to the revised edition of Landsteiner's book, *The Specificity of Serological Reactions.*

Landsteiner was said to worry incessantly and was overcome toward the end of his life with fear that the Nazis would take over the civilized world. He began to fear for his family's lives. Something of a scandal developed when he tried to prevent publication of his Jewish descent. Later his fear of fascism was surpassed by the discovery that Helene had a malignant thyroid tumor. On June 14, 1943, Landsteiner celebrated his seventy-fifth birthday with his wife, Helene, and his son, who had completed medical school and was a practicing physician. On June 24, Landsteiner had just sent off the final revision of the manuscript for his book, when he was seized by a coronary obstruction. He died two days later on Saturday, June 26, 1943. Helene died the same year on Christmas day. Upon his death, tributes were published around the world, but no mention of his death was published in his native Austria or Germany until 1947, after the war and the defeat of Nazism.

SELECTED WRITINGS BY LANDSTEINER:

Books

Die Spezifität der serologischen Reaktionen, Julius Springer, 1933, revised and translated as *The Specificity of Serological Reactions,* Ernest K. Landsteiner), 1945.

SOURCES:

Books

Speiser, Paul P., *Karl Landsteiner,* Bruder Hollinek Wiener Neudorf, 1975.

Periodicals

Bendiner, Elmer, "Karl Landsteiner: Dissector of the Blood," *Hospital Practice,* March 30, 1991, pp. 93–104.

Heidelberger, Michael, "Karl Landsteiner," *Biographical Memoirs,* Volume 40, Columbia University Press, 1969, pp. 176–210.

—*Sketch by Karyn Hede George*

Paul Langevin
1872-1946
French physicist

During his tenure as professor of physics at the Sorbonne in Paris, Paul Langevin conducted important research involving the production and use of ultrasound, research that he adapted to military applications during World War II. Langevin was a critical figure in introducing and explaining physicist **Albert Einstein's** theory of relativity to his French colleagues. He was also widely known and highly respected as an activist for peace and an advocate for social justice.

Langevin was born in Paris on January 23, 1872. His father was Victor Langevin, an appraiser-verifier. Young Langevin enjoyed study and was consistently first in his class throughout both his elementary and secondary education. The latter was completed at the École Municipale de Physique et Chimie, where chemist **Pierre Curie** oversaw Langevin's laboratory work.

In 1891, Langevin enrolled at the Sorbonne. While attending classes there, he also worked as a private tutor. Two years later, he passed the entrance examination for the École Normale Supérieure but did not enroll until 1894 because of a year's service in the French army. In 1897, Langevin placed first in a competition for a one-year scholarship to Cambridge University. There, he worked under physicist **J. J. Thomson** at the Cavendish Laboratory at Cambridge on the ionizing effects of radiation and the properties of gaseous ions.

After completing his year in England, Langevin returned to Paris, where he worked with physicist **Jean Baptiste Perrin** at the École Normale Supérieure and then with Pierre Curie at the Sorbonne. Langevin received his Ph.D. from the Sorbonne in 1902. Throughout this period, his main interests were the ionizing effects of radiation and the ionization of gases, but he also spent some time working with the Curies during their work on radioactivity.

Langevin's first academic appointments were teaching posts at the Collège de France and, simultaneously, at the École Municipale de Physique et Chimie (from 1904) and the École Nationale Supérieure de Jeunes Filles (from 1906). In 1909, he became professor of physics at the Sorbonne, a post he was to hold for three decades. Langevin married in 1898 and had four children, two of whom became physicists.

Studies Relativity and Magnetic Phenomena

Among the broad range of topics that occupied Langevin during the period from 1904 to 1909, two in particular stand out. The first is his work on relativity theory. He developed a number of fundamental concepts in this area independent of Einstein's work. Einstein later acknowledged Langevin's work in this field in his essay "Paul Langevin in Memoriam." "It appears to me," Einstein wrote, "as a foregone conclusion that he would have developed the Special Theory of Relativity, had that not been done elsewhere." Instead, Langevin became the spokesperson and interpreter for Einstein's theory in the French scientific community.

Langevin was more successful in another area, the phenomenon of paramagnetic and diamagnetic materials. These terms refer to substances that are weakly attracted to and repelled by, respectively, a magnetic field. Langevin explained these phenomena by assuming that they are caused by the magnetic field produced as an electron orbits an atomic nucleus, along with the interaction between that field and some external magnetic force. In addition, Langevin was able to explain how paramagnetic and diamagnetic susceptibility vary inversely with temperature, a fact that had been observed experimentally in 1895 by Pierre Curie.

Research on Ultrasonics Leads to Important Applications

During his years at the Sorbonne, Langevin turned his attention to another phenomenon, the production and use of ultrasonic sound (sound waves a frequency above the range of human hearing). In the 1880s, Pierre Curie had discovered the piezoelectric effect, the vibration of a crystal that occurs when an electric potential is applied across the face of the crystal. Langevin found that he could modify Curie's research design so as to obtain microwave signals (shorter electromagnetic waves) from the vibrating crystal.

The value of this discovery was that microwaves are more efficient tools for the detection of objects than are sound waves. As World War II approached, Langevin began to see the possibility of using microwaves for the underwater detection of submarines. Although his invention was not perfected until after the war had ended, the principle on which it was based is still used in sonar and other detection systems.

In addition to his fame as a scientist, Langevin became known as a great humanitarian. He fought vigorously for many social causes and, during World War II, was imprisoned by the Vichy regime for his opposition to fascism. After the war, Langevin remained active in a number of educational and political reform movements. His good friend and professional colleague, J. D. Bernal, wrote in the June 14, 1947 issue of *Nature* that Langevin "will be remembered in France and throughout the world even more as a man and as a citizen than as a scientific investigator. From his early scientific days, he realized the obligation of the man of science to fight for justice." Langevin died in Paris on December 19, 1946, after a brief illness.

SELECTED WRITINGS BY LANGEVIN:

Periodicals

"L'évolution de l'espace et du temps," *Scientia*, Volume 10, 1905, p. 1171.
"Magnétisme et théorie des électrons," *Annales de chimie et de physique,* Volume 5, 1905, p. 70.
(With M. Ishimoto) "Utilisation des phénomènes piézo-électriques pour la mesure de l'intensité des son en valeur absolue," *Journal de physique,* Volume 4, 1923, p. 539.

SOURCES:

Books

Einstein, Albert, *Out of My Later Years,* Philosophical Library, 1950, pp. 558–59.

Article

Bernal, J. D., "Prof. Paul Langevin, For. Mem. R.S. (1872–1946)," *Nature,* June 14, 1947, pp. 798–99.

—*Sketch by David E. Newton*

Irving Langmuir
1881-1957
American chemist and physicist

Irving Langmuir was a renowned chemist, physicist, and industrial researcher who worked at the General Electric Company for more than forty years. In addition to developing important improvements to the light bulb and other devices, he made significant contributions to the understanding of chemical forces and reactions that occur at the boundaries between different substances. For his work in this field of research, known as surface chemistry, Langmuir received the 1932 Nobel Prize for chemistry. He was only the second American—and the first scientist employed as an industrial researcher—to attain such an honor.

Langmuir, the third of four sons, was born on January 31, 1881, in Brooklyn, New York, to Charles Langmuir, an insurance executive of Scottish descent, and Sadie Comings Langmuir, the daughter of an anatomy professor and a descendant, on her mother's side of the family, of settlers who came to America on the Mayflower. Langmuir received part of his secondary-school education in France, where his father had been posted for several years. In 1903, Langmuir completed his baccalaureate degree in metallurgical engineering at the Columbia University School of Mines, where he had studied chemistry, physics, and mathematics with equal interest. Thereafter, Langmuir went to the University of Göttingen in Germany to pursue his postgraduate degree. There he studied under noted physical chemist and future Nobel laureate **Walther Nernst**. Langmuir wrote his doctoral dissertation on the chemical reactions between a glowing platinum wire and hot gases at low pressure; this research formed the foundation for later work at the General Electric Company (GE). Upon returning to the United States in 1906, Langmuir taught chemistry at the Stevens Institute of Technology in Hoboken, New Jersey.

Seeks Opportunity at GE Research Laboratory

By 1909, Langmuir had become dissatisfied with the lack of research opportunities at the Stevens Institute and applied for a summer job at the GE research laboratory in Schenectady, New York. He began his career with GE at a time when the laboratory gave its professional scientists the freedom to pursue personal research interests whether or not they related to company goals. Langmuir, who valued professional and financial success as well as scientific inquiry and accomplishment, was well suited for work at GE, and his summer position stretched into a

Irving Langmuir

lifelong career. He became known among his colleagues for his analytical mind, creativity, ambition, and excellent research skills.

Langmuir's first assignment at the laboratory was to help perfect a new type of electric lamp (light bulb), one that used a tungsten metal wire as a light emitter instead of the more fragile carbon filament pioneered by **Thomas Edison** and others. Scientists at the time thought that the tungsten filament would work best if a vacuum were created in the glass bulb. Over time, however, the tungsten filament became brittle when set aglow by electric current; it also blackened the inside of the bulb. Langmuir began to study the problem, and within four years, he found that the lamp's lifetime and efficiency could be improved greatly by filling the bulb with a mixture of inert gases (nitrogen and argon, for example) and by using a coiled filament. The result was a more energy-efficient and longer-lasting light bulb, for which Langmuir received a patent in 1916. The new light bulb design was extremely profitable for GE and saved its customers millions of dollars on their electric bills.

Early in his tenure at GE, Langmuir also studied vacuum tubes, which were becoming increasingly important to developments in radio broadcasting and the control of electrical power—innovations that would revolutionize society in Langmuir's lifetime. His research led him to invent an enhanced vacuum pump that was one hundred-fold more powerful than any existing vacuum pump. The new pump greatly improved the manufacture of vacuum tubes and was widely used by industry. Langmuir's other technical contributions include a hydrogen welding torch, an improved electric stove, and a new kind of gauge for measuring gas concentrations.

In later years at GE, Langmuir continued his research in several other important areas. He developed theories explaining chemical reactions of gases at high temperature and low pressure. He also devised useful explanations about the structure of the atom. Langmuir's studies of electricity's effects on gases prompted him to coin the term "plasma" for the unstable mixture produced when gases are charged with large amounts of electricity. Langmuir's plasma research paved the way for scientific progress in physics, astrophysics, and thermonuclear fusion (atomic reactions used in nuclear weapons and energy).

Work in Surface Chemistry Leads to Nobel Prize

Langmuir's most acclaimed work was perhaps in the field of surface chemistry. He studied and defined principles of adsorption, the phenomenon he observed in the tendency of gas molecules to cling in a single layer to surfaces of liquids or solids, and in the behavior of thin films of oil on the surfaces of liquids. Langmuir's body of experimental techniques and theories had applications in many fields, including biology, chemistry, and optics. For his contributions in surface chemistry, Langmuir won the Nobel Prize in 1932. In that same year he became assistant director of the GE laboratory, the position he held until he retired in 1950.

Beginning in 1938, Langmuir increasingly turned his attention to atmospheric science and meteorology, lifelong interests he pursued even after his retirement. During World War II, he investigated methods of aircraft de-icing and invented a machine to produce smoke screens that would shield troops from enemy observation. Later, as head of Cirrus, a joint program of the United States Army Signal Corps, the Navy, and the Air Force, Langmuir helped develop ways of seeding clouds with dry ice and silver iodide to make rain and snow.

Langmuir married Marion Mersereau in 1912 and adopted two children, Kenneth and Barbara. In his leisure time, he hiked, sailed, and piloted his own plane, once observing a solar eclipse from an altitude of nine thousand feet. His interest in the world extended well beyond the realm of atoms and molecules to mountain climbing and classical music. In 1935 he ran (unsuccessfully) for a seat on the city council of Schenectady, New York. He actively supported wilderness conservation and control of atomic energy. Achieving celebrity in his own time, Langmuir was also a popular public speaker. He received numerous awards and medals, fifteen honor-

ary degrees, and sixty-three patents. He wrote more than two hundred scientific papers and reports from 1906 to 1956, and since 1985, his name has been honored as the title of the American Chemical Society's journal of surfaces and colloids. Upon his death from a heart attack in Massachusetts on August 16, 1957, the *New York Times* ran his obituary on the front page.

SELECTED WRITINGS BY LANGMUIR:

Books

The Collected Works of Irving Langmuir, 12 volumes, C. G. Smits, 1960–62.

SOURCES:

Books

Hughes, Thomas P., *American Genesis: A Century of Invention,* Viking-Penguin, 1989.

Periodicals

Reich, Leonard S., "Irving Langmuir and the Pursuit of Science and Technology in the Corporate Environment," *Technology and Culture,* October, 1983, pp. 199–221.
Wise, George, "A New Role for Professional Scientists in Industry: Industrial Research at General Electric, 1900–1916," *Technology and Culture,* winter, 1980, pp. 408–429.

—*Sketch by Daniel Pendick*

Lewis H. Latimer
1848-1928
American inventor, draftsperson, and engineer

Despite his lack of any formal education, Lewis H. Latimer, the son of an escaped slave, became a member of **Thomas Alva Edison**'s research team and made several outstanding contributions to the development and commercialization of the electric light. Latimer was a self-taught draftsman who began as an office boy and rose to become chief draftsman for both the General Electric and Westinghouse companies.

Lewis Howard Latimer was born in Chelsea, Massachusetts, on September 4, 1848. His father, George A. Latimer, had been a slave in Virginia and had escaped to Boston; some years after he gained his freedom there, his former owner, James B. Gray, came to Boston to reclaim him. Latimer's case was taken up by abolitionists such as William Lloyd Garrison and Frederick Douglass who raised the necessary four hundred dollars to purchase Latimer's freedom. The Latimer case was the first of several famous Boston fugitive cases, after which Massachusetts passed a personal liberty law forbidding state officers from participating in the tracking down of fugitive slaves. George Latimer deserted the family when Lewis was ten years old, forcing the boy to leave school and take a job to help support his mother, Rebecca (Smith) Latimer, and her other four children.

Becomes A Self-Taught Draftsman

By 1864, Latimer had turned sixteen and the Civil War had begun. He enlisted in the Union navy and served as a "landsman" on the gunboat *U.S.S. Massasoit*. Eventually, he became a lieutenant in the 4th Battalion of the Massachusetts Volunteer Militia. After receiving an honorable discharge in 1865, Latimer returned to Boston and accepted a job as an office boy in the patent firm of Crosby and Gould. It was there that Latimer first became interested in the craft of mechanical drawing, and he soon began to teach himself the art. Patent applications required that very detailed and accurate drawings be submitted, and Latimer was so fascinated by this craft that he saved his money to buy second-hand drafting tools and learned how to use them from library textbooks. After studying every night after work, Latimer felt he was ready to ask his employers for permission to make the drawings for a invention; once they saw how skilled he was, they promoted him to the position of junior draftsman.

In ten years' time, Latimer had been promoted to chief draftsman for Crosby and Gould. In this position he was responsible for perfecting the final drawings that decided the success or failure of patent applications. One of the firm's clients was Alexander Graham Bell, and it fell to Latimer to execute the drawings for Bell's historic invention, the telephone; in 1876, Bell received his patent. Three years later, Latimer left Crosby and Gould to join the United States Electric Lighting Company. This new firm was the brainchild of American inventor and entrepreneur Hiram S. Maxim, and was to be one of the first to enter the new and rapidly expanding field of electric lighting. Thomas Edison had just invented the first electric incandescent lamp, and Maxim was determined to improve upon Edison's invention and take the lead (which he did with Latimer's help). By 1882, Latimer had invented an improved carbon filament that lasted longer at high temperatures; in addition,

he devised a cheaper method of making the filaments. The new light was called the "Maxim lamp" and was to be used in railroad stations throughout the United States, Canada, and other countries.

Begins Long Career At General Electric

While Maxim was attempting to seize world leadership in electricity away from Edison, Latimer left him in 1882 and joined the Olmstead Electric Light and Power Company of New York where he could continue his experimentation on improved filaments. Staying there for only two years, Latimer then joined one of Edison's companies, the Excelsior Electric Company, in 1884. There Latimer worked as a draftsman and engineer and was able to continue his pioneering electrical research. Upon joining Edison, Latimer no longer switched companies; when Excelsior was later incorporated into the Edison General Electric Company—which became known simply as GE—Latimer became one of its key members.

The electric light industry by the end of the 1880s was in a state of chaos and contention as the federal courts were asked to resolve scores of suits involving patent rights for incandescent lighting. One of the most significant legal contests involved Edison and the combined rival forces of Westinghouse and Thompson-Houston. The legal issue centered on Edison's 1880 invention of the carbon filament lamp, the challenger being the United States Electric Lighting Company, a Westinghouse subsidiary and Latimer's old employer. Latimer's value to Edison became immediately clear, since it was he who had received some of the patents that were now being used to challenge Edison. Latimer found himself in the unique position of being able to help his present employer discredit the originality of his own early designs. To accomplish this, Latimer was promoted to the company's legal department and began what would prove a career as an expert witness. His testimony aided Edison in eventually overcoming all challenges, and Latimer would continue as an expert witness in many of the other related trials that ensued. He remained with General Electric until 1912, when his expertise as a witness was no longer needed.

As a man of many talents, Latimer did not simply retire when he left General Electric at age sixty-four. He worked as an independent electrical and mechanical engineer for another sixteen years and taught mechanical drawing to immigrants at the Henry Street Settlement in New York City. Latimer also loved to write and in 1925 his friends and family published his *Poems of Love and Life*. Writing was nothing new to Latimer, however, since in 1890 he had written a groundbreaking book on electric lighting, *Incandescent Electric Lighting: A Practical Description of the Edison System*. Latimer's curiosity and probing mind led him to art and music as well, but his primary interest remained invention. This impulse was exhibited as early as 1874 when he received a patent for an improved railroad car water closet (toilet) while working for Crosby and Gould. Later Latimer also obtained patents for such varied devices as an apparatus for cooling and disinfecting, a rack for hats, coats, and umbrellas that locked, and a new device for supporting books.

When Latimer died in Flushing, New York, on December 11, 1928, he left behind his wife, Mary Wilson (Lewis) Latimer (whom he married on December 10, 1873), and two children, Louise Rebecca and Emma Jeanette. He had been a member of such diverse organizations as the New York Electrical Society, the Grand Army of the Republic, and the Negro Society for Historical Research. Most significantly, Latimer was the only African American member of the famous team of inventors called the "Edison Pioneers." On May 10, 1968, the Lewis H. Latimer public school in New York City was named for him, dedicated to honor the memory of a man who had worked in the background but whose inventiveness and perseverance made him a key figure in the history of electric lighting.

SELECTED WRITINGS BY LATIMER:

Books

Incandescent Electric Lighting: A Guide for Lighting Engineers, Van Nostrand, 1890.

SOURCES:

Books

Bigelow, Barbara Carlisle, editor, *Contemporary Black Biography,* Volume 4, Gale, 1993, pp. 148–150.
Hayden, Robert C., *Eight Black American Inventors,* Addison-Wesley, 1972, pp. 78–92.
Klein, Aaron E., *The Hidden Contributors: Black Scientists and Inventors in America,* Doubleday, 1971, pp. 97–108.
Logan, Rayford W., and Michael R. Winston, editors, *Dictionary of American Negro Biography,* Norton, 1982, pp. 385–386.

—Sketch by Leonard C. Bruno

C. M. G. Lattes
1924-
Brazilian physicist

Brazilian physicist C. M. G. Lattes, in collaboration with several other researchers, discovered that in cosmic rays, which consist of mesons and protons, two types of mesons exist. They also determined that mesons can be produced under laboratory conditions. This feat of making matter from energy, in a certain respect, was considered by other scientists to be essential in studying how matter is held together.

Cesare Mansueto Giulio Lattes was born July 11, 1924, in Curitiba, Brazil. He was the older of one of two sons of Giuseppe, a São Paulo bank manager, and Lina (Maroni) Lattes. He graduated from the Instituto Medio Dante Alighieri in 1939, and went on to earn his master's degree in 1943 from the University of São Paulo, where he would take the position of third assistant professor of physics, becoming first professor in 1948.

While a university student, Lattes became interested in nuclear physics through the work of his professors, Giuseppe P. S. Occhialini and G. Wataghin. When Occhialini went to the University of Bristol in 1946 and 1947 to conduct research on cosmic rays, he took Lattes with him to serve as a research assistant. In April 1947, Occhialini, Lattes, and **Cecil Frank Powell** of Bristol went to the Bolivian Andes. They spent three months on Mount Chacaltaya exposing photographic plates to cosmic rays, which are strongest at high elevations, and discovered that there are two types of mesons in cosmic rays, lighter and heavier mesons. While the heavier mesons with a positive charge were eventually disintegrated, the heavier mesons with a negative charge were sometimes attracted to the protons, the other component of cosmic rays, causing the protons to fly apart in a star-shaped pattern which the scientists observed using the photographs.

In 1948, Lattes was named a consultant to the Radiation Laboratory at the University of California at Berkeley under a Rockefeller Foundation National Research Fellowship. He worked with physicist Eugene Gardner, who had been using photographic plates to study the disintegration of atoms. Lattes and Gardner used a cyclotron to shoot a stream of alpha particles at a thin layer of carbon, near which photographic plates were set up. The first plate, Lattes recognized, showed a similar pattern to that which he, Occhialini and Powell found on the plates they exposed on the mountaintop—but at a far greater density. Gardner and Lattes had succeeded in producing mesons in the laboratory at the rate of one hundred million times as many per second than were observed on the mountain.

Further study allowed the men to determine that the meson's mass was equal to approximately three hundred and thirteen electrons. Announced on March 8, 1948, their work has since helped scientists study the forces that hold matter together. Lattes, with others, also utilized the photographic plate method to examine the radioactive element samarium.

Lattes married math student Marta Siqueira Netto on January 20, 1948. That year he also received an honorary degree from the University of São Paulo.

SELECTED WRITINGS BY LATTES:

Periodicals

"On the Abundance of Nuclei in the Universe," *Physical Review,* March, 1946.

SOURCES:

Books

Current Biography Yearbook, H. W. Wilson, 1949, p. 342–344.

—*Sketch by F. C. Nicholson*

Jakob Johann Laub
1882-1962
Austrian Polish Argentine physicist and diplomat

Jakob Johann Laub was the first of **Albert Einstein**'s scientific collaborators and a staunch defender of relativity. His work contributed in significant measure to the widespread acceptance of the theory of relativity in the early decades of the twentieth century. Laub did research on electron physics, atmospheric electricity and radiation, but his work was not widely recognized in the scientific community, in part perhaps because he spent more than twenty years as a diplomat for Argentina in the middle of his career.

Laub was born in Rzeszów, Galicia, a part of partitioned Poland then belonging to Austria. His father, Abraham (or Adolf) Laub, was the manager of an estate near the German border. His mother was

Anna Schoenborn-Banur. During his life, Laub several times attempted to mask his heritage: at birth his name was spelled Jakub, as a young man Jakob, and at death Jacobo; in his early twenties he also renounced Judaism, the religion of his birth, and became a nominal Catholic; and in the 1920s he announced that he had been born in Jägerndorf, Silesia—not Rzeszów. These mutations reflect Laub's professional trajectory which, although striking, was shared by a large number of early twentieth-century scientists.

After attending classical secondary school in Rzeszów, Laub studied briefly at the universities of Cracow and Vienna before entering the University of Göttingen as a student of mathematics and physics. There, taking courses and seminars with mathematicians **David Hilbert** and **Hermann Minkowski**, he became interested in the theory of electrons, which was then the rage among mathematical physicists and which directly preceded Einstein's formulation of the special theory of relativity as an explanation of subatomic phenomena. Laub turned to experiment, and in 1905 he decided to study with Wilhelm Wien at the University of Würzburg. (It was usual then for students to move freely among German-language universities.) Laub's doctoral dissertation, completed under Wien and published in 1907, concerned the phenomenon of secondary cathode-ray emission. At his oral defense in 1906, he referred to Einstein's special relativity, as Wien (co-editor of the *Annalen der Physik,* the journal in which the theory had first appeared) had recommended to him in 1905. Wien and Laub were among the very first physicists to appreciate the implications of Einstein's work. Laub remained at Würzburg for several years, pursuing post-doctoral work related to relativity.

Collaboration with Einstein

By 1908 Einstein had still not received a university appointment and was employed as a patent clerk at Berne. Laub took the unusual step of writing, in February of that year, to ask if he could study relativity with Einstein. The two physicists got along well. They published two papers and a note criticizing Minkowski's formulation of electromagnetic force and suggesting an experiment to decide between Einstein's relativity and the electron theory of Dutch physicist **Hendrik Lorentz**. These were Einstein's first published scientific collaborations.

At Einstein's urging Laub accepted an assistantship with physicist Philipp E. A. von Lenard at the University of Heidelberg in 1909. Lenard, however, was jealous of Einstein's revolutionary interpretation of the photoelectric effect, as he had won a Nobel prize in 1905 for his own non-Einsteinian interpretation of the effect. Lenard wanted Laub to measure the density of the electromagnetic ether, the imagined universal medium for light propagation. Einstein's work, however, had made it clear that light does not require a medium, and there were no other reasons to suppose that an electromagnetic ether fills the universe. Laub, a convinced Einsteinian, concentrated his efforts instead on publishing a masterful survey of the experimental evidence for relativity in 1910. The publication intensely displeased Lenard, who drove Laub to find another position. Laub declined an assistant professorship at the University of Illinois, accepting instead a professorship of geophysics and theoretical physics at the University of La Plata, in Argentina. He quickly married his fiancee Ruth Elisa Wendt (daughter of a professor of English at the University of Hamburg) and in 1911 left for La Plata (the marriage was registered a second time in Buenos Aires, in 1914).

University politics in Argentina again deprived Laub of tranquility. His administrative superior, American astronomer William Joseph Hussey, did not like Laub's independent turn of mind. In 1914 Laub left La Plata for a professorship of physics in nearby Buenos Aires at the national normal school, the Instituto Nacional del Profesorado Secundario. There, for the rest of the decade, he taught and published on experimental electron physics. He spent the Argentine summers in Madrid, working with physicist Blas Cabrera and associating with physiologist Santiago Ramón y Cajal. At this time he was active as a left-wing socialist, collaborating with Rudolf Grossmann, a respected scholar at Hamburg, who published communist political ideas under the pseudonym Pierre Ramus.

Diplomatic Career

In 1920 Laub joined the Argentine diplomatic corps, having become an Argentine citizen in 1915. Except for interruptions due to the Argentine revolution of Felix Uriburu (1928–1930) and the Second World War (1943–1947), he spent the rest of his life in Europe. He was posted at consulates in Munich, Breslau, Hamburg, and finally Warsaw, where he was the ranking Argentine diplomat at the time of the German and Soviet invasion. By this time he lived alone (Ruth had divorced him in Argentina around 1928), on occasion sending money to support his former wife and daughter Mercedes, who had both returned to live in Germany. In the late 1930s Laub used diplomatic connections to obtain travel permits for Ruth to go to New York and then to China. With the collapse of Poland, Laub was tranferred to the Argentine consulate in Zurich and then, in 1943, to Argentina. There he continued research on a long-standing interest, atmospheric electricity.

In 1947, after his official retirement from the Argentine diplomatic service, Laub went to live in Fribourg, Switzerland. There he collaborated with

Friedrich Dessauer at the physics institute of the local university, again on atmospheric electricity and radiation. With Juan Domingo Perón's accession to power in Argentina, however, the value of Laub's retirement pension plummeted. By 1960 Laub was destitute and in need of money to pay for operations to arrest cancer of his hands, probably a result of his early experimental work. He tried unsuccessfully to obtain royalties for patent work on high-frequency transmission that he had carried out in the 1930s for the German postal and telephone monopoly in Breslau and for the Berlin company of C. Lorenz. He sold his unique and extensive scientific correspondence with Albert Einstein, among other luminaries. Jakob Laub, who had worked closely with a handful of Nobel laureates on a wide variety of problems, died in Fribourg in poverty and obscurity in 1962.

SELECTED WRITINGS BY LAUB:

Periodicals

(With Walther Knoche) "Meteorologische und Luftelektrische Messungen während der totalen Sonnenfinsternis am 10. Oktober 1912 auf der Facenda Boa Vista bei Christina, Brasilien," *Terrestrial Magnetism and Atmospheric Electricity,* Volume 21, 1916, pp. 117–204.
"¿Qué son espacio y tiempo?" *Revista de filosofía,* Volume 5, 1919, pp. 386–405.
"Algunas observaciones aeroeléctricas en los territorios nacionales de Rio Negro y Neuquén," *Revista,* Volume 22, 1925, pp. 205–234.
"Über Schwankungen atmosphärischer Ionen und ihrer biologischen Wirkung," *Bulletin der Schweizerischen Akademie der medizinischen Wissenschaft,* Volume 16, 1960, pp. 292–304.

SOURCES:

Books

Pyenson, Lewis, *Cultural Imperialism and Exact Sciences: German Expansion Overseas, 1900–1930,* Peter Lang, 1985, pp. 163–228.
Pyenson, Lewis, *The Young Einstein: The Advent of Relativity,* Adam Hilger, 1985, pp. 215–246.
Stachel, John, et al., *The Collected Papers of Albert Einstein,* Volume 2: *The Swiss Years: Writings, 1900–1909,* Princeton University Press, 1989, pp. 503–535.

Periodicals

Budischin, F., "Entwicklung und Ausbau des hochfrequenten Drahtfunks in Deutschland," *Fernmeldetechnische Zeitschrift,* Volume 1, 1948, 201–202.

Pyenson, "Silver Horizon: A Note on the Later Career of the Physicist-Diplomat Jakob Laub," *Jahrbuch für Geschichte von Staat, Wirtschaft und Gesellschaft Lateinamerikas,* Volume 25, 1988, 757–766.

—Sketch by Lewis Pyenson

Max von Laue

Max von Laue
1879-1960
German physicist

Max von Laue distinguished himself early in his career with the discovery of X-ray diffraction, a process which is now used to examine the structure of crystals and has been widely used in research of proteins and other organic substances. The experiment also proved the wavelength of X rays. **Albert Einstein** viewed Laue's work as one of the greatest discoveries in physics. Laue was awarded the Nobel Prize in physics in 1914, at the age of thirty-five. He subsequently enjoyed a long career, distinguished not only by his contributions to physics but also by his willingness to oppose the Nazi regime in his native Germany.

Laue was born on October 9, 1879, in Pfaffendorf, Germany, near Koblenz, to Julius Laue, a civil official of the Prussian military court system, and the former Minna Zerrenner. The family name was changed to von Laue when his father was raised to hereditary nobility in 1913. Due to his father's profession, Laue's family moved often during his childhood, requiring him to attend many different schools. He began to show a marked interest in physics by the age of twelve. His mother arranged visits for him to Urania, a science society in Berlin that exhibited working models of various types of scientific machinery accompanied by explanatory demonstrations. Laue graduated from the Protestant gymnasium in Strasbourg in 1898. He then studied at the University of Strasbourg while simultaneously completing his one year of compulsory military service.

In the fall of 1899 Laue transferred to the University of Göttingen and ultimately to the University of Berlin, where he studied under Nobel laureate **Max Planck**. Laue graduated with highest honors in July of 1903, earning a Ph.D. in physics. For his doctoral dissertation he studied the theory of light interference among parallel plates located in the same plane. This included a complicated discussion of the interaction between intersecting light waves which destroy or reinforce each other, depending on their relative phases. Laue spent the next two years at the University of Göttingen as a postdoctoral student. At the end of that time he passed the examination to teach in the gymnasiums.

In 1905, Laue was invited to become Planck's assistant at the Institute for Theoretical Physics in Berlin. While working together, he and Planck established a friendship that was to last a lifetime. Laue remained at the institute until 1909, pursuing Planck's idea of applying the concept of entropy (the second law of thermodynamics which states that all closed systems become increasingly disordered) to radiation fields. In 1906 he also began work at the University of Berlin as a privatdocent, an unsalaried lecturer whose sole income derived from students who chose to attend his lectures.

Laue left Berlin in 1909 for the University of Munich, where he joined the physics faculty under **Arnold Sommerfeld**. There he lectured on optics and thermodynamics as a privatdocent. He was one of the early proponents of Einstein's theory of relativity, at a time when many in the field of physics remained skeptical. As early as 1907 Laue was working on a mathematical proof for relativity drawn from his work in optics; when coupled with the famous Michaelson-Morley experiment, this proof was instrumental in convincing physicists of the theory's validity. Laue published one of the first monographs on relativity in 1911.

Discovers X-Ray Diffraction

It was while in Munich that Laue made his most significant discovery. Since **Wilhelm Conrad Röntgen** had discovered X rays in 1895, no one had been able to conclusively determine if they were very short electromagnetic waves. This was widely supposed but unproven, and in 1912 Laue took up this question. At the same time, he was writing a chapter on wave optics for an encyclopedia of mathematics in which he had to express mathematically how diffraction affected light waves. While he was thinking about the length of X rays and the physics of diffraction, Laue began a series of discussions with a colleague regarding the behavior of light waves in a crystal, whose internal physical structure was also a matter of some dispute. The discussion started Laue thinking about the possibility of using a pure crystal which could be exposed to X rays. The resulting diffraction of light energy through the crystal could provide a means to measure the wavelength of X rays.

On April 21, 1912, Walter Friedrich and Paul Knipping began an experiment in Sommerfeld's laboratory, exposing a copper sulfate crystal to X rays. This produced a pattern of dark points on a photographic plate behind the crystal—which is now known as a Laue diagram in honor of Laue's insightful speculations. The difficulty then was to deduce how to calculate the wavelengths of the X rays. As Laue was walking home after seeing the photographs, it suddenly struck him that his understanding of the mathematics of diffraction in optical gratings, which he had concurrently been examining, could be applied with some variations in this new context. Laue then worked out the calculations which related the diagram to the positions of atoms within the crystal and to X-ray wavelength. Another, much clearer set of photographs a few weeks later proved to the group's satisfaction that Laue's new equations were exactly correct. It was now possible to use X rays to determine indirectly but precisely the structure of crystals and to use crystals to determine the wavelengths of X rays.

For his discovery of X–ray diffraction, Laue was awarded the Nobel Prize for physics in 1914. In his presentation speech, quoted in *Reality and Scientific Truth,* G. D. Granqvist of the Royal Swedish Academy of Sciences said, "proof was thus established that these light waves are of very small wavelengths. However, this discovery also resulted in the most important discoveries in the field of crystallography. . . . It is now possible to determine the position of atoms in crystals, and much important knowledge has been gained in this connection." Of the discovery, Jacob Bronowski wrote in *The Ascent of Man* that it "was a double stroke of ingenuity, for it was the first proof that atoms are real, and also the first proof that X rays are electromagnetic waves."

Laue was a theoretical physicist and as such did not concern himself with studying the structure of individual substances. That he left to others, such as **William Henry Bragg** and **William Lawrence Bragg** who went on to make substantial contributions to crystallography by building upon Laue's work. X-ray diffraction and X-ray spectroscopy have since revealed the molecular structures of penicillin, amino acids, and many other crystalline structures as nature yielded many secrets to these new techniques of the laboratory. Laue, however, continued to work on the theoretical aspects of X-ray diffraction and spectroscopy.

Laue was appointed an associate professor at the University of Zurich in 1912. Two years later he became a full professor at Frankfurt. He spent much of World War I working with **Wilhelm Wien** at the University of Würzburg on the development of vacuum tubes to improve telephone and wireless communication. In 1919, Laue returned to the University of Berlin as a professor of physics, where he once again was able to work with Planck. Laue was awarded the Max Planck Medal by the German Physical Society in 1932, perhaps the highest scientific honor in Germany at the time. During the 1930s, he contributed to Walther Meissner's theoretical work on superconductivity, a phenomenon where electrical resistance within materials completely disappears at absolute zero.

The rise to power of dictator Adolf Hitler's Nazi regime in 1933 brought significant changes to the administration of German science. Laue was one of only a few scientists who publicly opposed the Nazis's dismissal of Einstein, who was Jewish, as director of the Kaiser Wilhelm Institute for Physics. At a meeting of the German Physical Society on September 18, 1933, Laue likened the Nazi rejection of relativity, based on their ideological objection to its origination from a Jew, to the rejection of Galileo's ideas in the seventeenth century by the Catholic Church. Although Einstein was not reinstated, Laue achieved some measure of success in his opposition of the Nazis. In December 1933, he led the move to block the admission of Johannes Stark, a Hitler lackey, to the Prussian Academy. Even though Laue met with some government censure during World War II, he was allowed to continue his work. During the war, he became the spokesperson for the physicists after the appointment of Stark to the presidency of the German Research Association. He continued to write to Einstein at the Institute for Advanced Study at Princeton University throughout the war, doing so at great personal risk and with a rather cavalier attitude. When asked why he persisted despite the risks he replied, as quoted in *Reality and Scientific Truth:* "They are so stupid, these people who check and censor my mail. I just write 'Professor Albert, Fine Hall, Princeton, USA,' and it arrives." He later said,

"The regime seems prepared to provide some entertainment for me."

Even though Laue had not worked in the German uranium project he was nonetheless arrested with the other German scientists after the war and taken to England. They were kept at Huntingdon near London for six months, and not even their guards were permitted to know their names. Laue was allowed to return to Germany in 1946, and he became instrumental in the rebuilding of German science. It always saddened him that many German scientists did not return to Germany after the war. In 1950, at the age of seventy-one, he became the director of the Fritz Haber Institute of Physical Chemistry in Berlin-Dahlem. He held this post until 1959 when he was named director emeritus.

Laue had married Magdalene Degen on October 6, 1910. They had two children, a son and a daughter. He enjoyed mountain climbing, sailing, listening to classical music, and fast driving. On April 8, 1960, as he was hurrying to yet another scientific meeting at age eighty-one, Laue's automobile collided with a motorcycle. On April 23, he died from injuries sustained in the accident; he was buried in Göttingen near Planck and **Walther Nernst**. Many throughout the world mourned the man who had contributed so much to theoretical physics and a lived a life of high moral principles. A younger colleague who had studied under Laue remarked, as quoted in *Reality and Scientific Truth:* "I know his ethical ideas were on a very high level. His consciousness that whatever he did was just and right, and his judgment of right or wrong, were very definite."

SELECTED WRITINGS BY LAUE:

Books

History of Physics, translation by Ralph Oesper, Academic Press, 1950.

Theory of Superconductivity, translation by Lothar Meyer and William Band, Academic Press, 1952.

Gesammelte Schriften und Vortrage, (title means "Collected Writings and Lectures"), 3 volumes, Brunswick, 1961.

"My Development As a Physicist: An Autobiography," *Fifty Years of X-Ray Diffraction,* edited by Peter Paul Ewald, N.V.A. Obsthoek's Uitgeversmaatschappij, 1962, pp. 278–307.

SOURCES:

Books

Biographical Memoirs of Fellows of the Royal Society, Volume 6, Royal Society (London), 1960, pp. 135–56.

Frisch, O. R., F. A. Paneth, F. Laves, and P. Rosbaud, editors, *Trends in Atomic Physics: Essays Dedicated to Lise Meitner, Otto Hahn, Max von Laue on the Occasion of Their 80th Birthday,* Interscience Publishers, 1959.

Rosenthal-Schneider, Ilse, *Reality and Scientific Truth: Discussions with Einstein, von Laue, and Planck,* Wayne State University Press, 1980.

Segre, Emilio, *From X-Rays to Quarks: Modern Physicists and Their Discoveries,* W. H. Freeman, 1980.

Wasson, Tyler, editor, *Nobel Prize Winners, An H. W. Wilson Biographical Dictionary,* H. W. Wilson, 1987.

Periodicals

Forman, Paul, "The Discovery of the Diffraction of X-Rays by Crystals," *Archive for History of Exact Sciences,* Volume 6, 1969, pp. 38–71.

—*Sketch by Dennis W. and Kim A. Cheek*

Paul C. Lauterbur
1929-
American chemist

Paul C. Lauterbur invented and developed the use of nuclear magnetic resonance (NMR) to create images of organs and other tissues in the human body. Magnetic resonance imaging (MRI), as it is also called, has become an important tool in modern medicine as it offers a method for looking at soft tissues in the body without the use of X rays or surgery.

Paul Christian Lauterbur was born on May 6, 1929, in Sidney, Ohio, to Edward Joseph Lauterbur, a mechanical engineer, and Gertrude Wagner Lauterbur, a homemaker. The oldest of three children, Paul's brother, Edward Jospeh II, died at the age of sixteen. He also has a younger sister, Margaret McDonough.

In an interview with Lee Katterman, Lauterbur said that he spent his entire childhood in Sidney, Ohio. He was interested in all kinds of science, and he credits an aunt, Anna Pauline Lauterbur, a schoolteacher, as an important resource in helping him satisfy his curiosity. He attended the Case Institute of Technology (now part of Case Western Reserve University) in Cleveland, where he majored in chemistry. After graduating from Case Institute in 1951,

Lauterbur moved to Pittsburgh where he joined a research group at the Mellon Institute. He pursued his interest in organosilicon chemistry, the study of organic compounds primarily composed of carbon, hydrogen, and silicon. The Mellon Institute was affiliated with the University of Pittsburgh, so in addition to his research Lauterbur began to take graduate classes on a part-time basis.

In 1953 Lauterbur was drafted into the U.S. Army and assigned to the service's Army Chemical Center Medical Laboratories in Edgewood, Maryland. For the next two years, he helped establish the army's first nuclear magnetic resonance spectroscopy laboratory. NMR machines, only recently available from commercial sources, were proving to be valuable tools for determining the structure of chemical compounds. In nuclear magnetic resonance spectroscopy, a chemical compound is exposed to a magnetic field and a radio signal. Certain atoms in the compound, such as hydrogen, carbon 13, and fluorine 19, then absorb energy in patterns that provide information about the arrangement of these atoms.

After his stint in the army, Lauterbur returned to the Mellon Institute in 1955 on the condition that it buy an NMR machine. He organized an NMR laboratory at the institute and continued his research on organosilicon chemistry and the refinement of NMR as an analytical tool. He also took more classes and in 1962 received a Ph.D. in chemistry from the University of Pittsburgh. In 1963 Lauterbur moved to New York to become an associate professor of chemistry at the State University of New York (SUNY) at Stony Brook. By now, he was concentrating his research on NMR studies, refining ways that the information obtained using this tool could be used to interpret the structure of chemical compounds. Lauterbur spent the 1969–70 school year on a sabbatical at Stanford University in California. The same year Lauterbur was promoted to professor of chemistry at SUNY, Stony Brook.

Uses NMR to Peer Inside the Body

Lauterbur said in the interview with Katterman that the idea to use nuclear magnetic resonance to create images came to him during the summer of 1971. Until this time, NMR primarily had been applied to studying molecular structures of individual chemical compounds or simple mixtures. The typical output from an NMR spectrograph was graphical data that required interpretation to help deduce chemical structures. Lauterbur determined that NMR technology could be used to peer inside the human body and produce images that might be used to distinguish tissues or to spot abnormalities representing the early stages of illness. He coined the word *zeugmatography* to describe the use of NMR for making images. Lauterbur wanted to distinguish his method of image

formation and the physics underlying it from other techniques, such as those using X rays, based on other physical properties and principles. Although he first thought of NMR imaging in 1971, his idea did not appear in scientific literature until 1973 after various patent applications could be filed.

Initially Lauterbur spent time confirming that NMR could be used to make images that were reliable and reproducible. He had to make sure that the magnets necessary for whole body studies could be made. Lauterbur also undertook many experiments testing NMR imaging of biological and nonbiological systems. Lauterbur said there were many skeptics of his proposal at first. Some scientists claimed his ideas violated established physical principles. Others said that while the physics might be right, the technique would never be practical. Still others suggested that the medical profession would never accept the new technology. And Lauterbur remembers many rejected grant applications. "Fortunately a few were funded," he told Katterman, and through it all, he remained confident. "Once I thought of it," he said of NMR imaging, "it was clear it would work. I just had to work out the details." After spending some fourteen years developing the idea at the Stony Brook campus, Lauterbur joined the faculty of the University of Illinois at Urbana-Champaign where he continued his work.

At about the same time that Lauterbur was working on his new NMR techniques, other scientists were developing computerized tomography (CT) scanning, the use of multiple X-ray images to create pictures of two-dimensional "slices" of the body, and this process reached practical use in hospitals ahead of Lauterbur's NMR method. In an interview with the *Chicago Tribune* in 1990, Lauterbur said that the effect of CT technology had a mixed impact on his own research. "The precedent with X rays had both a negative and positive effect on our work," said Lauterbur. "It was negative in that people looked at CT and asked why we need another expensive imaging medium. A lot of analysts and companies said that. But it was positive in persuading people that a big, expensive medical technology could be worthwhile."

Once it was introduced, magnetic resonance imaging—as Lauterbur's NMR technique is now called—quickly gained wide acceptance as a tool for medical diagnosis. MRI is especially good for contrasting different types of soft tissue clustered together, such as a tumor embedded in healthy brain tissue. It also has the potential for the study of biological function, such as following metabolism in the brain or other organs. Lauterbur and others have been working on a type of microscopy based on nuclear magnetic resonance that may be able to produce images of individual cells in tissue. With this technique, it is becoming possible to look inside thick, opaque tissues or other materials and see structural details that cannot be seen by light microscopy.

Lauterbur has received many awards recognizing his work with NMR. In 1984 he received the prestigious Albert Lasker Clinical Medical Research Award. The following year the General Motors Cancer Research Foundation presented Lauterbur with the Charles F. Kettering Prize, which comes with a $100,000 award and a gold medal. In 1988 he was awarded the National Medal of Science and in 1989 the National Medal of Technology. In 1990 Lauterbur became the first recipient of the Bower Award, a $290,000 prize given by the Franklin Institute of Philadelphia. Lauterbur has received honorary degrees from Carnegie-Mellon University in Pittsburgh, l'Université de L'Etat à Liège in Belgium, and Nicolaus Copernicus Medical School in Kraków, Poland.

Lauterbur married M. Joan Dawson in 1984 and has one child, Mary Elise, from the marriage. He also has two children, Daniel and Sharyn, from a previous marriage to Rose Mary Caputo.

SELECTED WRITINGS BY LAUTERBUR:

Periodicals

"Image Formation by Induced Local Interactions: Examples Employing Nuclear Magnetic Resonance," *Nature,* Volume 242, 1973, p. 190.
(With Thomas F. Budinger) "Nuclear Magnetic Resonance Technology for Medical Studies," *Science,* Volume 226, 1984, pp. 288–298.
"NMR Imaging in Biomedicine," *Cell Biophysics,* Volume 9, 1986, pp. 211–214.

SOURCES:

Periodicals

Van, Jon, "U. of I. Scientist Wins Prize for Alternative to X-Rays," *Chicago Tribune,* September 19, 1990, pp. A1, A7.

Other

Lauterbur, Paul, interview with Lee Katterman conducted January 4, 1994.

—*Sketch by Lee Katterman*

Alphonse Laveran
1845-1922
French biologist

Alphonse Laveran was a French army physician who took advantage of his period of service in Algeria to study malaria, a disease known since ancient times and common in tropical and subtropical areas. Using very primitive technology, he discovered and ultimately proved that malaria was caused by a minute animal parasite; he also suggested, though he did not himself prove, that the parasite was transmitted to human beings by some species of mosquito. He later went on to study other diseases caused by parasites. For the work he did in this field throughout his career, he was awarded the Nobel Prize in medicine in 1907.

Charles Louis Alphonse Laveran was born on June 18, 1845, into a military family in Paris. He was the second child and only son of Louis-Theodore Laveran, a career military physician, and Marie-Louise Anselme Guénard de la Tour Laveran. When Laveran was five years old, he went with his parents to Algeria, where his father was stationed. His father was his first teacher, and after the family returned to Paris in 1856, Laveran received his secondary education at the College Sainte-Barbe and the Lycée Louis-le-Grand. In 1863, he entered the military medical school at Strasbourg, which his father had also attended; Laveran graduated in 1867. He joined the military medical service following graduation and saw active duty during the Franco-Prussian War of 1870–1871. It was at this time that he first witnessed the ravages which diseases can cause in an army at war. In 1874, he won by competitive examination an appointment to a professorship earlier held by his father at the École du Val-de-Grace, a military medical school in Paris. This was a temporary appointment, and at its conclusion in 1878 he was sent to the military hospital at Bône (now Annaba) in Algeria.

Discovers the Malaria Protozoan

It was while at Bône that Laveran began a careful study of malaria, common in many parts of Algeria, in an effort to learn its cause. He set up a small laboratory and with the primitive, low-powered microscope available to him, he spent much time examining blood samples from malaria patients both living and deceased. His studies were briefly interrupted when he was transferred to Biskra, Algeria, where malaria was rare, but they were resumed when he moved on to Constantine, also in Algeria. There, on November 6, 1880, he first observed under the microscope circular and cylindrical bodies which had moving filaments, or flagella. This confirmed his earlier suspicion that malaria was caused by living animal cells, minute single-celled creatures called protozoa, which acted as parasites in the human body. The particular protozoan which Laveran had discovered to be the cause of malaria later came to be called plasmodium.

Laveran's discovery was presented to the Academy of Medicine in Paris on November 23, 1880. A second paper, based upon further research, was published by the Société Médicale des Hopitaux on December 24 of that year. In 1881, Laveran published a brief monograph, *Nature parasitaire des accidents de l'impaludisme,* which provided more details of his findings. Laveran's conclusions were not immediately accepted by other scientists studying malaria. His microscopic research proved difficult to replicate. Moreover, in the wake of the discoveries of the German scientist **Robert Koch** and others, it was widely assumed at the time that bacteria were the causes of most diseases, including malaria.

Laveran, however, continued his research, examining the blood of hundreds of malaria patients, both in Algeria and in Italy. By 1884, in a personal microscopic demonstration, he was able to persuade Louis Pasteur that his theory was correct. Other noted scientists such as William Osler were convinced during the course of the 1880s. Also in 1884, Laveran published a book, *Traité des fièvres palustres avec la description des microbes du paludisme,* which summarized all of his research on malaria. In this work, he revealed his suspicion that the malaria protozoa were nurtured and transmitted to human beings by some species of mosquito. It remained for the British physician, **Ronald Ross**, working in India in the late 1890s, to prove that the malaria parasite was indeed transmitted by the Anopheles mosquito.

Laveran returned to Paris from Algeria in 1883 and became professor of military hygiene at the École du Val-de-Grace in 1884. He married Sophie Marie Pidancet in 1885; they had no children. When his professorship came to an end in 1894, he was offered only temporary administrative positions at the military hospitals at Lille and at Nantes. Angry because he was not offered a post at a military laboratory where he could continue his research, he resigned from the military medical service in December of 1896 and accepted a position at the Pasteur Institute in Paris. There he pursued his research for the rest of his life.

Expands Research to Other Disease-Causing Parasites

Laveran's demonstration that protozoa, as well as bacteria, could be the causes of disease in both human beings and animals led many other researchers into the field. Laveran himself did much significant work on disease-causing parasites. He was especially concerned with the trypanosome family of protozoa, one of which is the cause of the disease trypanosomiasis, or African sleeping sickness, transmitted by the tsetse fly. He also studied the trypanosome responsible for another tropical disease, kala azar, or dumdum fever,. He was awarded the Nobel Prize in 1907 for his work on all disease-causing protozoa. He used half of the prize money to establish a laboratory for research on tropical diseases at the Pasteur Institute.

Laveran was honored with membership in the French Academy of Sciences in 1901. The French government made him a Commander of the Legion of Honor in 1912. During World War I he served on several committees concerned with preserving the health of French soldiers, and he served as president of the Academy of Medicine in 1920. He died after a short illness on May 18, 1922.

SELECTED WRITINGS BY LAVERAN:

Books

Nature parasitaire des accidents de l'impaludisme. Description d'un nouveau parasite trouvé dans le sang des malades atteints de fièvre palustre, Bailliere, 1881.
Traité des fièvres palustres avec la description des microbes du paludisme, O. Doin, 1884.

Periodicals

"Protozoa as Causes of Disease: Nobel Lecture, December 11, 1907," *Nobel Lectures: Physiology or Medicine, 1901–1921,* Elsevier, 1967, pp. 264–271.

SOURCES:

Books

Fox, Daniel M., Marcia Meldrum, and Ira Rezak, editors, *Nobel Laureates in Medicine or Physiology: A Biographical Dictionary,* Garland, 1990, pp. 343–347.
Gillispie, Charles Coulson, editor, *Dictionary of Scientific Biography,* Scribner, 1973, Volume 8, pp. 65–66.
Magill, Frank N., editor, *The Nobel Prize Winners: Physiology or Medicine,* Salem Press, 1991, Volume 1, pp. 99–105.
Walker, M. E. M., *Pioneers of Public Health,* Books for Libraries Press, 1968, pp. 206–217.
Wasson, Tyler, editor, *Nobel Prize Winners,* H. W. Wilson, 1987, pp. 601–603.

Periodicals

Manson-Bahr, Philip, "The Story of Malaria: The Drama and the Actors," *International Review of Tropical Medicine,* Volume 2, 1963, pp. 329–390.

Smith, Dale C., and Lorraine B. Sanford, "Laveran's Germ: The Reception and Use of a Medical Discovery," *American Journal of Tropical Medical Hygiene,* Volume 34, 1985, pp. 2–20.

—Sketch by John E. Little

Theodore K. Lawless

Theodore K. Lawless
1892-1971
American dermatologist

Theodore K. Lawless was a pioneer in developing treatments for the early stages of syphilis and established dermatological treatment programs for arsenic-damaged skin. In the course of his long career, he built a private practice in the heart of Chicago's African American community that became one of the most prestigious skin clinics of its day. Honored worldwide for his work, Lawless amassed wealth through his business ventures and furthered the causes of health and African American education with monetary donations.

Theodore Kenneth Lawless was born on December 6, 1892, in Thibodaux, Louisiana, the son of Alfred Lawless, a minister, and Harriet (Dunn) Lawless. In 1914 he received his A.B. degree from Talladega College in Alabama. After attending the University of Kansas from 1914 to 1916, he began studying medicine at the Northwestern University School of Medicine, from which he received his M.D. in 1919. It was during this time that he focussed on a career in dermatology, becoming a fellow in dermatology and syphilology at Massachusetts General Hospital from 1920 to 1921 while also studying at both Columbia University and Harvard University. During the early 1920s, Lawless studied abroad at some of the most prestigious centers of dermatology in Europe.

Upon returning to America, Lawless began his private practice in Chicago, developing the largest dermatology clinic in the city. He also accepted a teaching post at Northwestern in 1924 and set up the University's first clinical laboratory. Throughout the 1920s and 1930s, Lawless not only kept up his practice but also taught and conducted dermatological research. He investigated and developed a diagnosis

for sporotrichosis, a fungal disease that produces subcutaneous and lymphoid ulcerated lesions, and did important work in syphilis research. Lawless pioneered the use of electrically-induced fever as a therapy for the early stages of syphilis, a disease that was incurable before the advent of penicillin. He also researched leaks that occurred during injections of arsenical drugs, which were another method of treating syphilis at the time. If some of the arsenical preparation leaked out during injection, as frequently happened, tissues surrounding the vein where the injection was being made would be damaged. Lawless developed a treatment for such accidental leaks.

In 1941, Lawless resigned from his position at Northwestern University after having been assigned no students to teach, apparently in an incident inspired by racism. He concentrated on his private practice and became extremely successful both in his practice and in various investment businesses into which he entered. Lawless donated a research laboratory to Chicago's Provident Hospital and money to African American colleges in the American south. He was also active in international affairs, helping to establish a dermatology clinic at the Beilinson Hospital Center in Israel, which was named after him. During World War II, he served with the U.S. Chemical Warfare Board, as well on an advisory committee on venereal disease.

Lawless, who never married, continued to research in his later years. He was also a respected and tireless instructor whose dermatology lectures at Cook County Hospital were eagerly attended by medical students. Lawless was honored by many organizations for his research and philanthropy. Among other awards, he received the Harmon Award in 1929 for outstanding medical work and the National Association for the Advancement of Colored People's Spingarn Medal in 1954. He was also a fellow of the American Medical Association, associate examiner in dermatology for the National Board of Medical Examiners, president of the board of trustees of Dillard University, and Diplomate of the American Board of Dermatology. Lawless died in on May 1, 1971, in Chicago.

SELECTED WRITINGS BY LAWLESS:

Periodicals

(With Elizabeth J. Ward) "The Diagnosis of Sporotrichosis," *Archives of Dermatology and Syphilology,* Volume 22, 1930, pp. 381–388.
"Treatment of Accidental Perivascular Injections of Arsphenamine or Neoarsphenamine," *Journal of Laboratory and Clinical Medicine,* Volume 16, 1931, p. 1910.
(With Clarence A. Neymann and S. L. Osborne) "The Treatment of Early Syphilis with Electropyrexia," *Journal of the American Medical Association,*Volume 107, 1936, pp. 194–199.

SOURCES:

Periodicals

Cobb, W. Montague, "Theodore Kenneth Lawless," *Journal of the National Medical Association,* Volume 62, No. 4, 1970, pp. 310–312.

—*Sketch by J. Sydney Jones*

Ernest Orlando Lawrence
1901-1958
American physicist

Known as the youngest physics professor at the University of California at Berkeley, Ernest Orlando Lawrence played a major role in the development of nuclear physics. From 1936 until his death he

Ernest Orlando Lawrence

was director of the Radiation Laboratory at Berkeley, where he invented the cyclotron, a device that accelerates the speed of nuclear particles. The invention of the cyclotron inaugurated a new era in the study of nuclear physics, and for this achievement he was awarded the 1939 Nobel Prize in physics. At Lawrence's laboratory several radioactive isotopes were discovered; one of these was plutonium, an element essential to the development of the atomic bomb. Lawrence played an active role in the research on nuclear weapons both during and after World War II, and he remained a strong advocate of increasing America's nuclear arsenal.

Lawrence was born in Canton, South Dakota on August 8, 1901, the eldest son of Carl Gustav Lawrence and Gunda Jacobson Lawrence. Both parents were of Norwegian ancestry; his mother was a teacher, and his father was a state superintendent of public education who then became president of a teacher's college. Lawrence completed public school in South Dakota at age sixteen; he began college at Saint Olaf's in Minnesota and then transferred to the University of South Dakota, from which he graduated with a B.S. in 1922. His gift for physics had become apparent, and he went on to earn a master's degree in 1923 at the University of Minnesota. He then followed his physics professor, W. F. G. Swann, first to the University of Chicago and then to Yale, where in 1925 Lawrence completed his doctorate. His dissertation was on the photoelectric effect, a phenomenon that occurs when certain electrons give off light energy as they change their position around the nucleus of an atom. By this time he had met such notable physicists as **Albert Michelson** and **Niels Bohr** and had gained a reputation for being an innovative experimenter.

Lawrence left Yale in 1928 for a job at the University of California at Berkeley, which was then a little known state school. But the seeds for growth in the field of nuclear physics were sown with the hiring of Lawrence and his contemporary, **J. Robert Oppenheimer**. Berkeley was soon to be a center for nuclear research equal to any other in the world. In 1930, a mere two years later, Lawrence became a full professor at just twenty-nine years of age. While at Yale Lawrence had met his future wife, Mary Kimberly Blumer, who was the daughter of the dean of Yale's medical faculty. Molly, as she was called, was just sixteen at the time. They were married in 1932, and she joined him in California. They would have two sons and four daughters.

Develops the Cyclotron

At Berkeley, Lawrence became interested in the nucleus, or center, of atoms. In particular, he was curious about what kinds of reactions would occur if protons, the positively charged particles in the nucleus, were given high energy levels. He had read about a Norwegian engineer who had built a device which accelerated nuclei in a straight line, but it had failed to impart enough power to cause nuclear reactions. With graduate students Niels E. Edlefsen and M. Stanley Livingston, Lawrence developed a circular, rather than linear, accelerator. The particle accelerator had the shape of a flat circular can cut in two. When particles such as protons were placed in the center of the can, a magnetic field forced them to travel in a circular path. Each time a particle went by, the magnetic field pushed it again. All of these small pushes increased the speed of the particle as it spiraled toward the rim of the can. When it approached the rim, the particle was made to hit a target—a nucleus. The result would be to disintegrate or "smash" the nucleus. Lawrence called the device a cyclotron and he and his team began to improve on it. They were fortunate enough to convince the Federal Telegraph Company to donate a huge eighty-ton magnet that was no longer in use. With this magnet, and a bigger cyclotron chamber, Lawrence could impart a great deal of energy onto particles, measured in millions of electron volts.

The cyclotron ushered in a new era of experimentation in high-energy physics. In 1932, Lawrence and his team were able to disintegrate a lithium nucleus. As they smashed other nuclei, they were able to measure how much energy is needed to bind the nucleus of an atom together. In other experiments they bombarded other elements to obtain radioactive isotopes of carbon, iodine and uranium. With his

younger brother John Lawrence, who was also at Berkeley, Lawrence looked for medical uses for radioisotopes; one development was using them as tracers to study metabolism, an application which is still important today. In 1936, at age thirty-five, Lawrence became the director of the Radiation Laboratory at Berkeley. In 1939, with the importance of the cyclotron proven, he received the Nobel Prize. He had already been the recipient of the Comstock Prize of the National Academy of Sciences and the Royal Society's Hughes Medal.

Participates in the Development of the Atomic Bomb

During World War II, the Radiation Laboratory, with Lawrence at the helm, played an important role in developing the atomic bomb. Urged on by German refugees who feared that the Nazis might produce an atomic weapon first, his laboratory worked to obtain the most useful materials for nuclear fission. When nuclear fission occurs, the nucleus of some radioactive elements disintegrates, releasing a great deal of energy. Research was done at Berkeley to find a way to separate uranium, and the technique was then used on a larger scale at the laboratory at Oak Ridge, Tennessee, which provided the uranium 235 for the atomic bomb that was eventually dropped on Hiroshima. While Lawrence remained at the Radiation Laboratory, **J. Robert Oppenheimer** went to direct the laboratory at Los Alamos, New Mexico where the first bomb was made.

After the dropping of two fission bombs on Hiroshima and Nagasaki, resulting in destruction and loss of life never seen before in human history, there was a division in the ranks of the world's nuclear physicists. In the postwar era, Oppenheimer and others became convinced that the development of further nuclear weapons should cease in the interest of humanity. But Lawrence believed in continuing this work. He argued that it was in the interest of the United States to build even more powerful weapons, such as the hydrogen or thermonuclear bomb. The rift between these two men came to a head when Oppenheimer appeared before a Congressional hearing and subsequently lost his security clearance. The opinion of the government and the public at the time supported Lawrence's advocacy of nuclear buildup.

Lawrence and Hungarian-born physicist **Edward Teller** founded a second radiation laboratory in Livermore, California, for research on nuclear weapons. Bigger and better accelerators were created that could boost nuclear particles with energy measured in billions of electron volts; thus was born a powerful accelerator known as the bevatron. Lawrence's visions for physics laboratories on a grand scale set the stage for the particle accelerators built in the suburbs of New York and Chicago—Brookhaven National Laboratory on Long Island and Fermilab in Geneva, Illinois. He also influenced the creation of an accelerator at CERN (Centre Européen pour la Recherche Nucléaire) in Switzerland. Each laboratory was set up with an international team of physicists, in much the same way the Radiation Laboratory had been.

During the 1950s, Lawrence oversaw operations in the nuclear research laboratories he had helped to fashion. His original cyclotron had been superseded by newer and faster ones designed by other scientists, but he continued to show his inventiveness, both in nuclear physics and in applied physics. He even designed a novel type of color television picture tube. In 1957 he was awarded the Fermi Award, the highest honor in physics in the United States. Lawrence was also busy as a government consultant on nuclear-energy issues for the Eisenhower administration. In the summer of 1958 he attended a conference in Geneva on the possibility of detecting violations of nuclear test agreements, but, ill and weary from recurrent ulcerative colitis, he flew home for an operation. He did not survive and died on August 27, 1958.

In 1961, the transuranium element 103 was discovered at Berkeley and was named lawrencium in his honor. The Lawrence Hall of Science at the University is a museum and research center dedicated to improving science education. The Radiation Laboratory is now known as the Lawrence Berkeley Laboratory, and the facilities in Livermore, California are now called the Lawrence Livermore Laboratory.

SELECTED WRITINGS BY LAWRENCE:

Periodicals

"The Photoelectric Effect in Potassium Vapour as a Function of the Frequency of Light," *Philosophical Magazine,* Volume 12, 1925, pp. 345–59.

(With M. S. Livingstone and M. G. White) "Disintegration of Lithium by Swiftly Moving Protons," *Physical Review,* Volume 42, 1932, pp. 150–151.

(With John H. Lawrence and Paul C. Aebersold) "Comparative Effects of X-Rays and Neutrons on Normal and Tumor Tissue," *Proceedings of the National Academy of Sciences,* Volume 22, 1936, pp. 543–557.

Books

"High Energy Physics," *Science in Progress,* edited by G. A. Baitsell, Yale University Press, 1949.

SOURCES:

Books

Childs, Herbert, *An American Genius: The Life of Ernest Lawrence,* Dutton, 1968.
Gillespie, C. C., editor, *Dictionary of Scientific Biography,* Scribner, 1970.

Periodicals

Alvarez, Luis W., *Biographical Memoirs, National Academy of Science,* Volume 41, 1970, pp. 251–294.
Livingston, M. Stanley, "History of the Cyclotron (Part I)," *Physics Today,* Volume 12, October 1959, pp. 18–23.

—Sketch by Barbara A. Branca

Louis Leakey
1903-1972
African-born English paleontologist and anthropologist

A pioneer in the field of paleoanthropology—the study of early humans and prehumans through both their fossilized remains and the cultural artifacts (mostly stone tools) they left behind—Louis Leakey helped change the prevailing view of humankind's origins. Along with other paleoanthropologists, he sought clues to, among other mysteries, how and when modern humans and apes split off from a common ancestor, and the identification of the point at which a creature appeared on the earth who can accurately be given the designation "human."

Louis Seymour Bazett Leakey was born on August 7, 1903, in Kabete, Kenya. His parents, Mary Bazett (d. 1948) and Harry Leakey (1868–1940) were Church of England missionaries at the Church Missionary Society, Kabete, Kenya. Louis spent his childhood in the mission, where he learned the Kikuyu language and customs (he later compiled a Kikuyu grammar book). As a child, while pursuing his interest in ornithology—the study of birds—he often found stone tools washed out of the soil by the heavy rains, which Leakey believed were of prehistoric origin. Stone tools were primary evidence of the presence of humans at a particular site, as toolmaking was believed at the time to be practiced only by humans and was, along with an erect posture, one of the chief characteristics used to differentiate humans

Louis Leakey

from nonhumans. Scientists at the time, however, did not consider East Africa a likely site for finding evidence of early humans; the discovery of *Pithecanthropus* in Java in 1894 (the so-called Java Man, now considered to be an example of *Homo erectus*) had led scientists to assume that Asia was the continent from which human forms had spread.

The Search for Africa's Oldest Hominid

Shortly after the end of World War I, Leakey was sent to a public school in Weymouth, England, and later attended St. John's College, Cambridge. Suffering from severe headaches resulting from a sports injury, he took a year off from his studies and joined a fossil-hunting expedition to Tanganyika (now Tanzania). This experience, combined with his studies in anthropology at Cambridge (culminating in a degree in 1926), led Leakey to devote his time to the search for the origins of humanity, which he believed would be found in Africa. Anatomist and anthropologist **Raymond A. Dart**'s discovery of early human remains in South Africa was the first concrete evidence that this view was correct. Leakey's next expedition was to northwest Kenya, near Lakes Nakuru and Naivasha, where he uncovered materials from the Late Stone Age; at Kariandusi he discovered a 200,000-year-old hand ax.

In 1928 Leakey married Henrietta Wilfrida Avern, with whom he had two children: Priscilla, born in 1930, and Colin, born in 1933; the couple was

divorced in the mid–1930s. In 1931 Leakey made his first trip to Olduvai Gorge—a 350-mile ravine in Tanzania—the site that was to be his richest source of human remains. He had been discouraged from excavating at Olduvai by Hans Reck, a German paleontologist who had fruitlessly sought evidence of prehistoric humans there. Leakey's first discoveries at that site consisted of both animal fossils, important in the attempts to date the particular stratum (or layer of earth) in which they were found, and, significantly, flint tools. These tools, dated to approximately one million years ago, were conclusive evidence of the presence of hominids—a family of erect primate mammals that use only two feet for locomotion—in Africa at that early date; it was not until 1959, however, that the first fossilized hominid remains were found there.

In 1932, near Lake Victoria, Leakey found remains of *Homo sapiens* (modern man), the so-called Kanjera skulls (dated to 100,000 years ago) and Kanam jaw (dated to 500,000 years ago); Leakey's claims for the antiquity of this jaw made it a controversial find among other paleontologists, and Leakey hoped he would find other, independent, evidence for the existence of *Homo sapiens* from an even earlier period—the Lower Pleistocene.

In the mid–1930s, a short time after his divorce from Wilfrida, Leakey married his second wife, Mary Douglas Nicol; she was to make some of the most significant discoveries of Leakey's team's research. The couple eventually had three children: Philip, Jonathan, and **Richard E. Leakey**. During the 1930s, Leakey also became interested in the study of the Paleolithic period in Britain, both regarding human remains and geology, and he and **Mary Leakey** carried out excavations at Clacton in southeast England.

Until the end of the 1930s, Leakey concentrated on the discovery of stone tools as evidence of human habitation; after this period he devoted more time to the unearthing of human and prehuman fossils. His expeditions to Rusinga Island, at the mouth of the Kavirondo Gulf in Kenya, during the 1930s and early 1940s produced a large number of finds, especially of remains of Miocene apes. One of these apes, which Leakey named *Proconsul africanus,* had a jaw lacking in the so-called simian shelf that normally characterized the jaws of apes; this was evidence that *Proconsul* represented a stage in the progression from ancient apes to humans. In 1948 Mary Leakey found a nearly complete *Proconsul* skull, the first fossil ape skull ever unearthed; this was followed by the unearthing of several more *Proconsul* remains.

Louis Leakey began his first regular excavations at Olduvai Gorge in 1952; however, the Mau Mau (an anti-white secret society) uprising in Kenya in the early 1950s disrupted his paleontological work and induced him to write *Mau Mau and the Kikuyu*, in an effort to explain the rebellion from the perspective of a European with an insider's knowledge of the Kikuyu. A second work, *Defeating Mau Mau*, followed in 1954.

During the late 1950s, the Leakeys continued their work at Olduvai. In 1959, while Louis was recuperating from an illness, Mary Leakey found substantial fragments of a hominid skull that resembled the robust australopithecines—African hominids possessing small brains and near-human dentition—found in South Africa earlier in the century. Louis Leakey, who quickly reported the find to the journal *Nature,* suggested that this represented a new genus, which he named *Zinjanthropus boisei*, the genus name meaning "East African man," and the species name commemorating Charles Boise, one of Leakey's benefactors. This species, now called *Australopithecus boisei,* was later believed by Leakey to have been an evolutionary dead end, existing contemporaneously with *Homo* rather than representing an earlier developmental stage.

In 1961, at Fort Ternan, Leakey's team located fragments of a jaw that Leakey believed were from a hitherto unknown genus and species of ape, one he designated as *Kenyapithecus wickeri,* and which he believed was a link between ancient apes and humans, dating from fourteen million years ago; it therefore represented the earliest hominid. In 1967, however, an older skull, one that had been found two decades earlier on Rusinga Island and which Leakey had originally given the name *Ramapithecus africanus,* was found to have hominid-like lower dentition; he renamed it *Kenyapithecus africanus,* and Leakey believed it was an even earlier hominid than *Kenyapithecus wickeri.* Leakey's theories about the place of these Lower Miocene fossil apes in human evolution have been among his most widely disputed.

The Discovery of *Homo Habilis*

During the early 1960s, a member of Leakey's team found fragments of the hand, foot, and leg bones of two individuals, in a site near where *Zinjanthropus* had been found, but in a slightly lower and, apparently, slightly older layer. These bones appeared to be of a creature more like modern humans than *Zinjanthropus,* possibly a species of *Homo* that lived at approximately the same time, with a larger brain and the ability to walk fully upright. As a result of the newly developed potassium-argon dating method, it was discovered that the bed from which these bones had come was 1.75 million years old. The bones were, apparently, the evidence for which Leakey had been searching for years: skeletal remains of *Homo* from the Lower Pleistocene. Leakey designated the creature whose remains these were as *Homo habilis* ("man with ability"), a creature who walked upright and had

dentition resembling that of modern humans, hands capable of toolmaking, and a large cranial capacity. Leakey saw this hominid as a direct ancestor of *Homo erectus* and modern humans. Not unexpectedly, Leakey was attacked by other scholars, as this identification of the fragments moved the origins of the genus *Homo* back substantially further in time. Some scholars felt that the new remains were those of australopithecines, if relatively advanced ones, rather than very early examples of *Homo.*

His Last Years

Health problems during the 1960s curtailed Leakey's field work; it was at this time that his Centre for Prehistory and Paleontology in Nairobi became the springboard for the careers of such paleontologists as **Jane Goodall** and **Dian Fossey** in the study of nonhuman primates. A request came in 1964 from the Israeli government for assistance with the technical as well as the fundraising aspects involved in the excavation of an early Pleistocene site at Ubeidiya. This produced evidence of human habitation dating back 700,000 years, the earliest such find outside Africa.

During the 1960s, others, including Mary Leakey and the Leakeys' son Richard, made significant finds in East Africa; Leakey turned his attention to the investigation of a problem that had intrigued him since his college days: the determination of when humans had reached the North American continent. Concentrating his investigation in the Calico Hills in the Mojave Desert, California, he sought evidence in the form of stone tools of the presence of early humans, as he had done in East Africa. The discovery of some pieces of chalcedony (translucent quartz) that resembled manufactured tools in sediment dated from 50,000 to 100,000 years old stirred an immediate controversy; at that time, scientists believed that humans had settled in North America approximately 20,000 years ago. Many archaeologists, including Mary Leakey, criticized Leakey's California methodology—and his interpretations of the finds—as scientifically unsound, but Leakey, still charismatic and persuasive, was successful in obtaining funding from the National Geographic Society and, later, several other sources. Human remains were not found in conjunction with the supposed stone tools, and many scientists have not accepted these "artifacts" as anything other than rocks.

Shortly before Louis Leakey's death, Richard Leakey showed his father a skull he had recently found near Lake Rudolf (now Lake Turkana) in Kenya. This skull, removed from a deposit dated to 2.9 million years ago, had a cranial capacity of approximately 800 cubic centimeters, putting it within the range of *Homo* and apparently vindicating Leakey's long-held belief in the extreme antiquity of that genus; it also appeared to substantiate Leakey's interpretation of the Kanam jaw. Leakey died of a heart attack in early October, 1972, in London.

A Controversial Career

Some scientists have questioned Leakey's interpretations of his discoveries. Other scholars have pointed out that two of the most important finds associated with him were actually made by Mary Leakey, but became widely known when they were interpreted and publicized by him; Leakey had even encouraged criticism through his tendency to publicize his somewhat sensationalistic theories before they had been sufficiently tested. Critics have cited both his tendency toward hyperbole and his penchant for claiming that his finds were the "oldest," the "first," the "most significant"; in a 1965 *National Geographic* article, for example, Melvin M. Payne pointed out that Leakey, at a Washington, D.C., press conference, claimed that his discovery of *Homo habilis* had made all previous scholarship on early humans obsolete. Leakey has also been criticized for his eagerness to create new genera and species for new finds, rather than trying to fit them into existing categories. Leakey, however, recognized the value of publicity for the fundraising efforts necessary for his expeditions. He was known as an ambitious man, with a penchant for stubbornly adhering to his interpretations, and he used the force of his personality to communicate his various finds and the subsequent theories he devised to scholars and the general public.

Leakey's response to criticism was that scientists have trouble divesting themselves of their own theories in the light of new evidence. "Theories on prehistory and early man constantly change as new evidence comes to light," Leakey remarked, as quoted by Payne in *National Geographic*. "A single find such as *Homo habilis* can upset long-held—and reluctantly discarded—concepts. A paucity of human fossil material and the necessity for filling in blank spaces extending through hundreds of thousands of years all contribute to a divergence of interpretations. But this is all we have to work with; we must make the best of it within the limited range of our present knowledge and experience." Much of the controversy derives from the lack of consensus among scientists about what defines "human"; to what extent are toolmaking, dentition, cranial capacity, and an upright posture defining characteristics, as Leakey asserted?

Louis Leakey's significance revolves around the ways in which he changed views of early human development. He pushed back the date when the first humans appeared to a time earlier than had been believed on the basis of previous research. He showed that human evolution began in Africa rather than Asia, as had been maintained. In addition, he created research facilities in Africa and stimulated explora-

tions in related fields, such as primatology (the study of primates). His work is notable as well for the sheer number of finds—not only of the remains of apes and humans, but also of the plant and animal species that comprised the ecosystems in which they lived. These finds of Leakey and his team filled numerous gaps in scientific knowledge of the evolution of human forms. They provided clues to the links between prehuman, apelike primates, and early humans, and demonstrated that human evolution may have followed more than one parallel path, one of which led to modern humans, rather than a single line, as earlier scientists had maintained.

SELECTED WRITINGS BY LOUIS LEAKEY:

Books

The Stone Age Cultures of Kenya Colony, Cambridge University Press, 1931, new edition, F. Cass, 1971.

Adam's Ancestors: An Up-to-Date Outline of What Is Known about the Origin of Man, Methuen, 1934, 4th edition published as *Adam's Ancestors: An Up-to-Date Outline of the Old Stone Age (Palaeolithic) and What Is Known about Man's Origin and Evolution,* 1953, Harper, 1960.

The Stone Age Races of Kenya, Oxford University Press, 1935, 2nd edition, Anthropological Publishing, 1970.

Stone Age Africa: An Outline of Prehistory in Africa, illustrated by wife Mary Leakey, Oxford University Press, 1936, reprinted, Negro Universities Press, 1970.

White African: An Early Autobiography, Hodder & Stoughton, 1937, reprinted with a new introduction by author, Ballantine Books, 1973.

(With M. Leakey) *Some String Figures from North East Angola* (booklet), [Lisboa, Portugal], 1949.

(With M. Leakey) *Excavations at the Njoro River Cave: Stone Age Cremated Burials in Kenya Colony,* Clarendon Press, 1950.

Mau Mau and the Kikuyu, Methuen, 1952, Day, 1954.

Defeating Mau Mau, Methuen, 1954.

First Lessons in Kikuyu, East African Literature Bureau, 1959.

The Progress and Evolution of Man in Africa, Oxford University Press, 1961.

(With Vanne Morris Goodall) *Unveiling Man's Origins: Ten Decades of Thought about Human Evolution,* Schenkman, 1969.

By the Evidence: Memoirs, 1932–1951, Harcourt, 1974.

The Southern Kikuyu Before 1903, three volumes, Academic Press, 1977.

SOURCES:

Books

Cole, Sonia, *Leakey's Luck: The Life of Louis Seymour Bazett Leakey, 1903–1972,* Harcourt, 1975.

Isaac, Glynn, and Elizabeth R. McCown, editors, *Human Origins: Louis Leakey and the East African Evidence,* Benjamin-Cummings, 1976.

Johanson, Donald C., and Maitland A. Edey, *Lucy: The Beginnings of Humankind,* Simon & Schuster, 1981.

Leakey, Mary, *Disclosing the Past,* Doubleday, 1984.

Leakey, Richard, *One Life: An Autobiography,* Salem House, 1984.

Malatesta, Anne, and Ronald Friedland, *The White Kikuyu: Louis S. B. Leakey,* McGraw-Hill, 1978.

Periodicals

Payne, Melvin M., "The Leakeys of Africa: Family in Search of Prehistoric Man," *National Geographic,* February, 1965, pp. 194–231.

—*Sketch by Michael Sims*

Mary Leakey

Mary Leakey
1913-
English paleontologist and anthropologist

For many years Mary Leakey lived in the shadow of her husband, **Louis Leakey,** whose reputation, coupled with the prejudices of the time, led him to be credited with some of his wife's discoveries in the field of early human archaeology. Yet she has established a substantial reputation in her own right and has come to be recognized as one of the most important paleoanthropologists of the twentieth century. It was Mary Leakey who was responsible for some of the most important discoveries made by Louis Leakey's team. Although her close association with Louis Leakey's work on Paleolithic sites at Olduvai Gorge—a 350-mile ravine in Tanzania—has led to her being considered a specialist in that particular area and period, she has in fact worked on excavations dating from as early as the Miocene Age (an era dating to approximately 18 million years ago) to those as recent as the Iron Age of a few thousand years ago.

Developing an Interest in Archaeology

Mary Leakey was born Mary Douglas Nicol on February 6, 1913, in London. Her mother was Cecilia Frere, the great-granddaughter of John Frere, who had discovered prehistoric stone tools at Hoxne, Suffolk, England, in 1797. Her father was Erskine Nicol, a painter who himself was the son of an artist, and who had a deep interest in Egyptian archaeology. When Mary was a child, her family made frequent trips to southwestern France, where her father took her to see the Upper Paleolithic cave paintings. She and her father became friends with Elie Peyrony, the curator of the local museum, and there she was exposed to the vast collection of flint tools dating from that period of human prehistory. She was also allowed to accompany Peyrony on his excavations, though the archaeological work was not conducted in what would now be considered a scientific way—artifacts were removed from the site without careful study of the place in the earth where each had been found, obscuring valuable data that could be used in dating the artifact and analyzing its context. On a later trip, in 1925, she was taken to Paleolithic caves by the Abbé Lémozi of France, parish priest of Cabrerets, who had written papers on cave art. After her father's death in 1926, Mary Nicol was taken to Stonehenge and Avebury in England, where she began to learn about the archaeological activity in that country and, after meeting the archaeologist Dorothy Liddell, to realize the possibility of archaeology as a career for a woman.

By 1930 Mary Nicol had undertaken coursework in geology and archaeology at the University of London and had participated in a few excavations in order to obtain field experience. One of her lecturers, R. E. M. Wheeler, offered her the opportunity to join his party excavating St. Albans, England, the ancient Roman site of Verulamium; although she only remained at that site for a few days, finding the work there poorly organized, she began her career in earnest shortly thereafter, excavating Neolithic (early Stone Age) sites in Henbury, Devon, where she worked between 1930 and 1934. Her main area of expertise was stone tools, and she was exceptionally skilled at making drawings of them. During the 1930s Mary met Louis Leakey, who was to become her husband. Leakey was by this time well known because of his finds of early human remains in East Africa; it was at Mary and Louis's first meeting that he asked her to help him with the illustrations for his 1934 book, *Adam's Ancestors: An Up-to-Date Outline of What Is Known about the Origin of Man.*

In 1934 Mary Nicol and Louis Leakey worked at an excavation in Clacton, England, where the skull of a hominid—a family of erect primate mammals that use only two feet for locomotion—had recently been found and where Louis was investigating Paleolithic geology as well as fauna and human remains. The excavation led to Mary Leakey's first publication, a 1937 report in the *Proceedings of the Prehistoric Society.*

Excavating at Olduvai Gorge

By this time, Louis Leakey had decided that Mary should join him on his next expedition to Olduvai Gorge in Tanganyika (now Tanzania), which he believed to be the most promising site for discovering early Paleolithic human remains. On the journey to Olduvai, Mary stopped briefly in South Africa, where she spent a few weeks with an archaeological team and learned more about the scientific approach to excavation, studying each find *in situ*—paying close attention to the details of the geological and faunal material surrounding each artifact. This knowledge was to assist her in her later work at Olduvai and elsewhere.

At Olduvai, among her earliest discoveries were fragments of a human skull; these were some of the first such remains found at the site, and it would be twenty years before any others would be found there. Mary Nicol and Louis Leakey returned to England. Leakey's divorce from his first wife was made final in the mid–1930s, and he and Mary Nicol were then married; the couple returned to Kenya in January of 1937. Over the next few years, the Leakeys excavated Neolithic and Iron Age sites at Hyrax Hill, Njoro River Cave, and the Naivasha Railway Rock Shelter,

which yielded a large number of human remains and artifacts.

During World War II, the Leakeys began to excavate at Olorgasailie, southwest of Nairobi, but because of the complicated geology of that site, the dating of material found there was difficult. It did prove to be a rich source of material, however; in 1942 Mary Leakey uncovered hundreds, possibly thousands, of hand axes there. Her first major discovery in the field of prehuman fossils was that of most of the skull of a *Proconsul africanus* on Rusinga Island, in Lake Victoria, Kenya, in 1948. *Proconsul* was believed by some paleontologists to be a common ancestor of apes and humans, an animal whose descendants developed into two branches on the evolutionary tree: the *Pongidae* (great apes) and the *Hominidae* (who eventually evolved into true humans). *Proconsul* lived during the Miocene Age, approximately 18 million years ago. This was the first time a fossil ape skull had ever been found—only a small number have been found since—and the Leakeys hoped that this would be the ancestral hominid that paleontologists had sought for decades. The absence of a "simian shelf," a reinforcement of the jaw found in modern apes, is one of the features of *Proconsul* that led the Leakeys to infer that this was a direct ancestor of modern humans. *Proconsul* is now generally believed to be a species of *Dryopithecus,* closer to apes than to humans.

Discovering "Dear Boy": *Zinjanthropus*

Many of the finds at Olduvai were primitive stone hand axes, evidence of human habitation; it was not known, however, who had made them. Mary's concentration had been on the discovery of such tools, while Louis's goal had been to learn who had made them, in the hope that the date for the appearance of toolmaking hominids could be moved back to an earlier point. In 1959 Mary unearthed part of the jaw of an early hominid she designated *Zinjanthropus* (meaning "East African Man") and whom she referred to as "Dear Boy"; the early hominid is now considered to be a species of *Australopithecus*—apparently related to the two kinds of australopithecine found in South Africa, *Australopithecus africanus* and *Australopithecus robustus*—and given the species designation *boisei* in honor of Louis Leakey's sponsor Charles Boise. By means of potassium-argon dating, recently developed, it was determined that the fragment was 1.75 million years old, and this realization pushed back the date for the appearance of hominids in Africa. Despite the importance of this find, however, Louis Leakey was slightly disappointed, as he had hoped that the excavations would unearth not another australopithecine, but an example of *Homo* living at that early date. He was seeking evidence for his theory that more than one hominid form lived at Olduvai at the same time; these forms were the australopithecines, who eventually died out, and some early form of *Homo,* which survived—owing to toolmaking ability and larger cranial capacity—to evolve into *Homo erectus* and, eventually, the modern human. Leakey hoped that Mary Leakey's find would prove that *Homo* existed at that early level of Olduvai. The discovery he awaited did not come until the early 1960s, with the identification of a skull found by their son Jonathan Leakey that Louis designated as *Homo habilis* ("man with ability"). He believed this to be the true early human responsible for making the tools found at the site.

Working on Her Own

In her autobiography, *Disclosing the Past,* released in 1984, Mary Leakey reveals that her professional and personal relationship with Louis Leakey had begun to deteriorate by 1968. As she increasingly began to lead the Olduvai research on her own, and as she developed a reputation in her own right through her numerous publications of research results, she believes that her husband began to feel threatened. Louis Leakey had been spending a vast amount of his time in fundraising and administrative matters, while Mary was able to concentrate on field work. As Louis began to seek recognition in new areas, most notably in excavations seeking evidence of early humans in California, Mary stepped up her work at Olduvai, and the breach between them widened. She became critical of his interpretations of his California finds, viewing them as evidence of a decline in his scientific rigor. During these years at Olduvai, Mary made numerous new discoveries, including the first *Homo erectus* pelvis to be found. Mary Leakey continued her work after Louis Leakey's death in 1972. From 1975 she concentrated on Laetoli, Tanzania, which was a site earlier than the oldest beds at Olduvai. She knew that the lava above the Laetoli beds was dated to 2.4 million years ago, and the beds themselves were therefore even older; in contrast, the oldest beds at Olduvai were two million years old. Potassium-argon dating has since shown the upper beds at Laetoli to be approximately 3.5 million years old. In 1978 members of her team found two trails of hominid footprints in volcanic ash dated to approximately 3.5 million years ago; the form of the footprints gave evidence that these hominids walked upright, thus moving the date for the development of an upright posture back significantly earlier than previously believed. Mary Leakey considers these footprints to be among the most significant finds with which she has been associated.

In the late 1960s Mary Leakey received an honorary doctorate from the University of the Witwatersrand in South Africa, an honor she accepted only after university officials had spoken out against apartheid. Among her other honorary degrees are a D.S.Sc. from Yale University and a D.Sc. from the University of Chicago. She received an honorary D.Litt. from Oxford University in 1981. She has also received the Gold Medal of the Society of Women Geographers.

Louis Leakey was sometimes faulted for being too quick to interpret the finds of his team and for his propensity for developing sensationalistic, publicity-attracting theories. In recent years Mary Leakey has been critical of the conclusions reached by her husband—as well as by some others—but she has not added her own interpretations to the mix. Instead, she has always been more concerned with the act of discovery itself; she has written that it is more important for her to continue the task of uncovering early human remains to provide the pieces of the puzzle than it is to speculate and develop her own interpretations. Her legacy lies in the vast amount of material she and her team have unearthed; she leaves it to future scholars to deduce its meaning.

SELECTED WRITINGS BY MARY LEAKEY:

Books

(Illustrator) Louis Leakey, *Stone Age Africa: An Outline of Prehistory in Africa,* Oxford University Press, 1936, reprinted, Negro Universities Press, 1970.

(With husband, Louis Leakey) *Some String Figures from North East Angola* (booklet), [Lisboa, Portugal], 1949.

(With L. Leakey) *Excavations at the Njoro River Cave: Stone Age Cremated Burials in Kenya Colony,* Clarendon Press, 1950.

Olduvai Gorge, Volume III: *Excavation in Beds I and II, 1960–63,* foreword by J. D. Clark, Cambridge University Press, 1971.

Olduvai Gorge: My Search for Early Man, Collins, 1979.

Africa's Vanishing Art: The Rock Paintings of Tanzania, Doubleday, 1983.

Disclosing the Past: An Autobiography, Doubleday, 1984.

SOURCES:

Books

Cole, Sonia, *Leakey's Luck: The Life of Louis Seymour Bazett Leakey, 1903–1972,* Harcourt, 1975.

Isaac, Glynn, and Elizabeth R. McCown, editors, *Human Origins: Louis Leakey and the East African Evidence,* Benjamin-Cummings, 1976.

Johanson, Donald C., and Maitland A. Edey, *Lucy: The Beginnings of Humankind,* Simon & Schuster, 1981.

Leakey, Louis, *By the Evidence: Memoirs, 1932–1951,* Harcourt, 1974.

Leakey, Richard, *One Life: An Autobiography,* Salem House, 1984.

Malatesta, Anne, and Ronald Friedland, *The White Kikuyu: Louis S. B. Leakey,* McGraw-Hill, 1978.

Moore, Ruth E., *Man, Time, and Fossils: The Story of Evolution,* Knopf, 1961.

Reader, John, *Missing Links,* Little, Brown, 1981.

Periodicals

Payne, Melvin M., "The Leakeys of Africa: Family in Search of Prehistoric Man," *National Geographic,* February, 1965, pp. 194–231.

—*Sketch by Michael Sims*

Richard E. Leakey
1944-

African-born English paleontologist and anthropologist

The son of paleoanthropologists **Mary Leakey** and **Louis Leakey**, Richard Erskine Frere Leakey was born on December 19, 1944, in Nairobi, Kenya. Continuing the work of his parents, Leakey has pushed the date for the appearance of the first true humans back even further than they had, to nearly three million years ago. This represents nearly a doubling of the previous estimates. Leakey also has found more evidence to support his father's still controversial theory that there were at least two parallel branches of human evolution, of which only one was successful. The abundance of human fossils uncovered by Richard Leakey's team has provided an enormous number of clues as to how the various fossil remains fit into the puzzle of human evolution. The team's finds have also helped to answer, if only speculatively, some basic questions: When did modern human's ancestors split off from the ancient apes? On what continent did this take place? At what point did they develop the characteristics now considered as defining human attributes? What is the relationship among and the chronology of the various genera and species of the fossil remains that have been found?

The Commencement of a Career in Paleontology

While accompanying his parents on an excavation at Kanjera near Lake Victoria at the age of six, Richard Leakey made his first discovery of fossilized animal remains, part of an extinct variety of giant pig. Richard Leakey, however, was determined not to "ride upon his parents' shoulders," as Mary Leakey wrote in her autobiography, *Disclosing the Past.* Several years later, as a young teenager in the early 1960s, Richard demonstrated a talent for trapping wildlife, which prompted him to drop out of high school to lead photographic safaris in Kenya. His paleontological career began in 1963, when he led a team of paleontologists to a fossil-bearing area near Lake Natron in Tanganyika (now Tanzania), a site that was later dated to approximately 1.4 million years ago. A member of the team discovered the jaw of an early hominid—a member of the family of erect primate mammals that use only two feet for locomotion—called an *Australopithecus boisei* (then named *Zinjanthropus*).) This was the first discovery of a complete *Australopithecus* lower jaw and the only *Australopithecus* skull fragment found since Mary Leakey's landmark discovery in 1959. Jaws provide essential clues about the nature of a hominid, both in terms of its structural similarity to other species and, if teeth are present, its diet. Richard Leakey spent the next few years occupied with more excavations, the most important result of which was the discovery of a nearly complete fossil elephant.

In 1964 Richard married Margaret Cropper, who had been a member of his father's team at Olduvai the year before. It was at this time that he became associated with his father's Centre for Prehistory and Paleontology in Nairobi. In 1968, at the age of twenty-three, he became administrative director of the National Museum of Kenya.

While his parents had mined with great success the fossil-rich Olduvai Gorge, Richard Leakey concentrated his efforts in northern Kenya and southern Ethiopia. In 1967 he served as the leader of an expedition to the Omo Delta area of southern Ethiopia, a trip financed by the National Geographic Society. In a site dated to approximately 150,000 years ago, members of his team located portions of two fossilized human skulls believed to be from examples of *Homo sapiens,* or modern humans. While the prevailing view at the time was that *Homo sapiens* emerged around 60,000 years ago, these skulls were dated at 130,000 years old.

The Excavation of Koobi Fora

While on an airplane trip, Richard Leakey flew over the eastern portion of Lake Rudolf (now Lake Turkana) on the Ethiopia-Kenya border, and he noticed from the air what appeared to be ancient lake sediments, a kind of terrain that he felt looked promising as an excavation site. He used his next National Geographic Society grant to explore this area. The region was Koobi Fora, a site that was to become Richard Leakey's most important area for excavation. At Koobi Fora his team uncovered more than four hundred hominid fossils and an abundance of stone tools, such tools being a primary indication of the presence of early humans. Subsequent excavations near the Omo River in Kenya, from 1968, unearthed more examples of early humans, the first found being another *Australopithecus* lower jaw fragment. At the area of Koobi Fora known as the KBS tuff (tuff being volcanic ash; KBS standing for the Kay Behrensmeyer Site, after a member of the team) stone tools were found. Preliminary dating of the site placed the area at 2.6 million years ago; subsequent tests over the following few years determined the now generally accepted age of 1.89 million years.

In July of 1969, Richard Leakey came across a virtually complete *Australopithecus boisei* skull—lacking only the teeth and lower jaw—lying in a river bed. A few days later a member of the team located another hominid skull nearby, comprising the back and base of the cranium. The following year brought the discovery of many more fossil hominid remains, at the rate of nearly two per week. Among the most important finds was the first hominid femur to be found in Kenya, which was soon followed by several more. It was at about this time that Leakey obtained a divorce from his first wife, and in October of 1970, he married Meave Gillian Epps, who had been on the 1969 expedition.

The Discovery of "Skull 1470"

In 1972, Richard Leakey's team uncovered a skull that appeared to be similar to the one identified by his father and called *Homo habilis* ("man with ability"). This was the early human that Louis Leakey maintained had achieved the toolmaking skills that precipitated the development of a larger brain capacity and led to the development of the modern human—*Homo sapiens*. This skull was more complete and apparently somewhat older than the one Louis Leakey had found and was thus the earliest example of the species *Homo* yet discovered. They labeled the new skull, which was found below the KBS tuff, "Skull 1470," and this proved to among Richard Leakey's most significant discoveries. The fragments consisted of small pieces of all sides of the cranium, and, unusually, the facial bones, enough to permit a reasonably complete reconstruction. Larger than the skulls found in 1969 and 1970, this example had approximately twice the cranial capacity of *Australopithecus* and more than half that of a modern human—nearly 800 cubic centimeters. At the time, Leakey believed the fragments to be 2.9 million years old (although a more recent dating of the site would place them at less than 2 million years old). Basing his

theory in part on these data, Leakey developed the view that these early hominids may have lived as early as 2.5 or even 3.5 million years ago and gave evidence to the theory that *Homo habilis* was not a descendant of the australopithecines, but a contemporary.

By the late 1960s, relations between Richard Leakey and his father had become strained, partly because of real or imagined competition within the administrative structure of the Centre for Prehistory, and partly because of some divergences in methodology and interpretation. Shortly before Louis Leakey's death, however, the discovery of Skull 1470 by Richard Leakey's team allowed Richard to present his father with apparent corroboration of one of his central theories.

Richard Leakey did not make his theories of human evolution public until 1974. At this time, scientists were still grappling with Louis Leakey's interpretation of his findings that there had been at least two parallel lines of human evolution, only one of which led to modern humans. After Louis Leakey's death, Richard Leakey reported that, based on new finds, he believed that hominids diversified between 3 and 3.5 million years ago. Various lines of australopithecines and *Homo* coexisted, with only one line, *Homo,* surviving. The australopithecines and *Homo* shared a common ancestor; *Australopithecus* was not ancestral to *Homo*. As did his father, Leakey believes that *Homo* developed in Africa, and it was *Homo erectus* who, approximately 1.5 million years ago, developed the technological capacity to begin the spread of humans beyond their African origins. In Richard Leakey's scheme, *Homo habilis* developed into *Homo erectus,* who in turn developed into *Homo sapiens,* the present-day human.

As new finds are made, new questions arise. Are newly discovered variants proof of a plurality of species, or do they give evidence of greater variety within the species that have already been identified? To what extent is sexual dimorphism responsible for the apparent differences in the fossils? In some scientific circles, the discovery of fossil remains at Hadar in Ethiopia by archaeologist Donald Carl Johanson and others, along with the more recent revised dating of Skull 1470, cast some doubt on Leakey's theory in general and on his interpretation of *Homo habilis* in particular. Johanson believed that the fossils he found at Hadar and the fossils Mary Leakey found at Laetoli in Tanzania, and which she classified as *Homo habilis,* were actually all australopithecines; he termed them *Australopithecus afarensis* and claimed that this species is the common ancestor of both the later australopithecines and *Homo*. Richard Leakey has rejected this argument, contending that the australopithecines were not ancestral to *Homo* and that an earlier common ancestor would be found, possibly among the fossils found by Mary Leakey at Laetoli.

The year 1975 brought another significant find by Leakey's team at Koobi Fora: the team found what was apparently the skull of a *Homo erectus,* according to Louis Leakey's theory a descendent of *Homo habilis* and probably dating to 1.5 million years ago. This skull, labeled "3733," represents the earliest known evidence for *Homo erectus* in Africa.

The Excavation of Turkana Boy

Richard Leakey began to suffer from health problems during the 1970s, and in 1979 he was diagnosed with a serious kidney malfunction. Later that year he underwent a kidney transplant operation, his younger brother Philip being the donor. During his recuperation Richard completed his autobiography, *One Life,* which was released in 1984, and following his recovery, he renewed his search for the origins of the human species. The summer of 1984 brought another major discovery: the so-called Turkana boy, a nearly complete skeleton of a *Homo erectus,* missing little but the hands and feet, and offering, for the first time, the opportunity to view many bones of this species. It was shortly after the unearthing of Turkana boy—whose skeletal remains indicate that he was a twelve-year-old youngster who stood approximately five-and-a-half feet tall—that the puzzle of human evolution became even more complicated. The discovery of a new skull, called the Black Skull, with an *Australopithecus boisei* face but a cranium that was quite apelike, introduced yet another complication, possibly a fourth branch in the evolutionary tree.

SELECTED WRITINGS BY LEAKEY:

Books

(Contributor and editor) *Fossil Vertebrates of Africa,* Academic Press, 1969.
(Editor with others and contributor) *Earliest Man and Environments in the Lake Rudolf Basin: Stratigraphy, Palaeoecology, and Evolution,* Chicago University Press, 1976.
(With Roger Lewin) *Origins: What New Discoveries Reveal about the Emergence of Our Species and Its Possible Future,* Dutton, 1977.
(With Roger Lewin) *People of the Lake: Mankind and Its Beginnings,* Doubleday, 1978.
(Editor with wife Meave G. Leakey) *Koobi Fora Research Project,* Volume I: *The Fossil Hominids and an Introduction to Their Context, 1968–1974,* Clarendon, 1978.
(Editor with Glynn Isaac) *Human Ancestors: Readings from "Scientific American,"* W. H. Freeman, 1979.

(Editor and author of introduction) Charles Darwin, *The Illustrated Origin of Species,* Hill & Wang, 1979.
The Making of Mankind, Dutton, 1981.
One Life: An Autobiography, Salem House, 1984.
(With Roger Lewin) *Origins Reconsidered: In Search of What Makes Us Human,* Doubleday, 1992.

Periodicals

"Skull 1470," *National Geographic,* June, 1973, pp. 819–829.
"Further Evidence of the Lower Pleisticene Hominids from East Rudolf, Northern Kenya," *Nature,* Volume 278, 1974, pp. 653–656.

SOURCES:

Books

Cole, Sonia, *Leakey's Luck: The Life of Louis Seymour Bazett Leakey, 1903–1972,* Harcourt, 1975.
Johanson, Donald C., and Maitland A. Edey, *Lucy: The Beginnings of Humankind,* Simon & Schuster, 1981.
Leakey, Mary, *Disclosing the Past: An Autobiography,* Doubleday, 1984.
Reader, John, *Missing Links,* Little, Brown, 1981.

Periodicals

Payne, Melvin M., "The Leakeys of Africa: Family in Search of Prehistoric Man," *National Geographic,* February, 1965, pp. 194–231.

—*Sketch by Michael Sims*

Henrietta Leavitt
1868-1921
American astronomer

Henrietta Leavitt's most famous discovery was the "period-luminosity" relation for variable stars (those changing in brightness), an important method of obtaining distances to far-off galaxies. She also identified 2400 new variable stars and established brightness scales that helped other astronomers with their own observations.

Henrietta Leavitt

Henrietta Swan Leavitt was born in Lancaster, Massachusetts, on July 4, 1868, to Henrietta Swan Kendrick and George Roswell Leavitt, a Congregationalist minister who had a parish in Cambridge. After attending public school in Cambridge, Leavitt moved with her family to Cleveland, Ohio, where she attended Oberlin College from 1885 to 1888. She switched, however, to the Society for the Collegiate Instruction of Women (now Radcliffe College) in 1892. During her senior year, she took an astronomy course, which fired her interest in the subject. After receiving an A.B. from Radcliffe in 1892, Leavitt took another astronomy course, then spent a number of years home because of an illness that left her severely deaf. After some traveling, Leavitt volunteered as a research assistant at Harvard College Observatory in 1895, and was appointed to the permanent staff in 1902 by the astronomer Edward Pickering at a salary of thirty cents an hour. Leavitt worked at Harvard from 1902 until her death. While Pickering gave Leavitt little chance to do theoretical work, she became chief of the photographic photometry department at the observatory.

Establishes Scale of Star Brightnesses

In 1907 Pickering asked Leavitt to establish a "north polar sequence" of star brightnesses to serve as a standard for the entire sky. This standard was desirable because the photographic process in astronomy was complex—the brightness of star images on film was not proportional to their actual brightness, and each telescope gave different results for different color stars. Once determined, brightnesses could be estimated by comparing one star with another, rather than referring to photographic images. Leavitt used 299 plates from thirteen telescopes, and compared stars ranging from the fourth to the twenty-first magnitude in brightness (each increasing unit of magnitude corresponds to a reduction in brightness by a factor of 2.512 on a logarithmic scale). The results were published in the *Annals of Harvard College Observatory.* In 1913 Leavitt's system was adopted by the International Committee on Photographic Magnitudes. She made this work a lifelong project, and established brightness sequences for 108 areas in the sky. When Pickering developed forty-eight "Harvard standard regions" in the sky, Leavitt derived secondary brightness standards for them. These were used as international standards until superseded by improved methods.

Discovers Period-Luminosity Relation

Leavitt discovered 2400 new variable stars, about half those known at the time. Most notably, she studied photographs of the Magellanic Clouds (the Milky Way's two companion galaxies) taken at Harvard's observatory in Arequipo, Peru. Of the 1800 variable stars Leavitt detected on the Magellanic Cloud pictures, some were Cepheid variables, whose change in brightness is extremely regular. (Cepheids were named after the first star of this type to be discovered, Delta Cephei.) In 1908 Leavitt found that the brighter the Cepheid was overall, the longer it took to change its magnitude. Leavitt reasoned that since the Cepheids in the Magellanic Clouds were nearly all the same distance from Earth, their periods were related to their light output: the longer the period of pulsation, the brighter the star. By 1912 Leavitt had proven that Cepheids' apparent brightness increased linearly with the logarithm of their periods. That year, she published a table of the length of twenty-five Cepheid periods—ranging from 1.253 days to 127 days, with an average of 5 days—and their apparent brightness.

Before this period-luminosity relation had been established, cosmic distances could only be determined out to about 100 light-years. With it, however, distances of out to ten million light-years could be calculated. The intrinsic brightness of a Cepheid could now be gotten directly from a measure of its period, and this allowed the distance to be calculated. Astronomer **Ejnar Hertzsprung** adapted the period-luminosity relation so it could determine the actual distance of stars from Earth. Hertzsprung and astronomer **Harlow Shapley** found that the Magellanic Clouds were in the range of 100,000 light-years from Earth—an astonishing and unexpectedly high value. Leavitt was not aware as she worked that the Magellanic Clouds lay outside our own Galaxy.

Leavitt died of cancer December 21, 1921, in Cambridge. During her lifetime she had little opportunity to give free rein to her intellect, but her talents did not go unnoticed. According to *Women of Science,* her colleague Margaret Harwood described her as possessing the best mind at the observatory, and contemporary astronomer **Cecilia Payne-Gaposchkin** said Leavitt was the most brilliant woman at Harvard.

SELECTED WRITINGS BY LEAVITT:

Periodicals

"1,777 Variables in the Magellanic Clouds," *Annals of Harvard College Observatory,* Volume 60, number 4, 1908, pp. 87–108.

"Ten Variable Stars of the Algol Type," *Annals of Harvard College Observatory,* Volume 60, number 5, 1908, pp. 109–146.

SOURCES:

Books

Kass-Simon, G., and P. Farnes, editors, *Women of Science,* Indiana University Press, 1990.

Ogilvie, M. B., *Women in Science,* MIT Press, 1986.

—*Sketch by Sebastian Thaler*

Désirée Le Beau
1907-1993
Austro-Hungarian-born American chemist

Désirée Le Beau was an early pioneer in what is known today as rubber recycling. A colloid chemist (one concerned with substances made up of tiny insoluble, nondiffusable particles suspended in a medium of different matter), she developed methods of reclaiming natural and synthetic rubbers, primarily from old tires, to be used to produce new products, and held several patents for these processes. Le Beau made significant strides in this field during World War II, when American rubber sources were unavailable due to the conflict.

Leaves Wartime Europe for U.S.

Born to Phillip and Lucy Le Beau in Teschen, Austria-Hungary (now Poland), on February 14, 1907, Le Beau worked briefly in Paris before Hitler's aggressions in Europe prompted her to relocate to the United States. Le Beau's lifelong career began as a college fluke, when she inadvertently sat down in the chemistry laboratory instead of her intended pharmacy laboratory. By the time she realized the mistake, she knew she wanted to study chemistry. Le Beau first completed undergraduate studies at the University of Vienna, then earned her Ph.D. in chemistry in 1931 from the University of Graz in Austria, where she minored in physics and mathematics.

In 1932 Le Beau accepted a position with the Austro-American Rubber Works in Vienna. She then moved to Paris in 1935 to join the Société de Progrès Technique as a consultant. The following year, she came to the United States and filled a post as Research Chemist with Dewey & Almy Chemical Company in Massachusetts. From 1940 to 1945, Le Beau served as a Research Associate at Massachusetts Institute of Technology's Department of Chemical Engineering and Division of Industrial Cooperation. In 1945, she was appointed Director of Research at Midwest Rubber Reclaiming Company in Illinois, the world's largest independent reclaiming company at the time, where she studied the structures of natural and synthetic rubbers and clays. There, Le Beau developed a tie pad for railroads using reclaimed rubber. One of her patents was for this process, which she developed in 1958. She also held patents for a method of producing reclaimed rubber in particulate form (formed of tiny separate particles), and for methods of reclaiming using certain amines and acids. In 1950 she was named a Currie lecturer at Pennsylvania State College.

Le Beau married Henry W. Meyer on August 6, 1955. In addition to her contributions in science, Le Beau spoke English, French, German, Swedish and Latin. She embraced as hobbies music, interior decorating, swimming and horseback riding. Her many honors included the 1959 Society of Women Engineers Achievement Award for "her significant contributions to the field of rubber reclamation." Le Beau was also the first woman to chair the American Chemical Society's Division of Colloid Chemistry, as well as the first woman to chair the Society's St. Louis section. She was elected a Fellow of the American Institute of Chemists, and she authored numerous publications on reclamation.

SELECTED WRITINGS BY LE BEAU:

Books

"Reclaiming of Elastomers," in Jerome Alexander's *Colloid Chemistry,* Volume 7, Reinhold Publishing, 1950, pp. 569–597.

Periodicals

"Basic Reactions Occurring During Reclaiming of Rubber I," *Rubber Chemistry and Technology* 21, 1948, p. 895.

"Reclaiming Agents for Rubber: Solvent Naphtha I," *Rubber Age,* October, 1950.

SOURCES:

Periodicals

Society of Women Engineers Newsletter, June, 1959, pp. 1, 3.

　　　　　　　—*Sketch by Karen Withem*

Henri Lebesgue
1875-1941
French mathematician

In the first decade of the twentieth century, Henri Lebesgue developed a new approach to integral calculus in order to overcome the restrictions of previous theories. At that time, integration was used to calculate the area under a curve, but if the curve was discontinuous the theory was difficult to apply and left some questions unanswered. Lebesgue's theory of integration circumvented the problems caused by these discontinuities and was compatible with other basic mathematical operations.

Henri Léon Lebesgue was born in Beauvais, France, on June 28, 1875. His father was a typographical worker, and his mother was an elementary school teacher. He entered the École Normale Supérieure in 1894 and quickly demonstrated mathematical talent along with an irreverent attitude that gave him the tendency to ignore subjects that did not interest him. For instance, he passed his chemistry course only by mumbling his answers to the examiner who was hard of hearing. Even in mathematics he graduated third in his class in 1879. Nevertheless, his questioning of the traditional methods of mathematics was the basis for his reexamination of the concepts of length, area, and volume. He stayed on to work in the library for two years after his graduation in 1879.

Lebesgue inherited the solid foundation for the theory of calculus that was laid by the mathematical giants of the nineteenth century. Karl Friedrich Gauss, Augustin Louis Cauchy, Niels Henrik Abel, and others of this period had introduced rigorous definitions of convergence, limit, and continuity. They had also formulated a precise definition of the integral, one of the two central concepts of calculus. Just as addition gives the total of a finite set of numbers, the integral pertains to the limiting case of the sum of a quantity that varies at every one of an infinite set of points. Such a quantity is described mathematically by a function, and integration of a function can represent the area bounded by a curve, the total work done by a variable force, the distance a planet travels in its elliptical orbit around the sun, among other possibilities. Cauchy's definition of the integral applied to functions that were continuous, that is, curves without any jumps. It could also handle a finite number of discontinuities, points where jumps occurred.

In 1854 Georg Bernhard Riemann introduced an extension of the concept of integration which found its way into most calculus books. Unfortunately, the Riemann integral was unsatisfactory for dealing with some sequences of functions. Even if the sequence of functions approached a limit and each function in the sequence was continuous, the limit might not be a function that could be handled by Riemann integration. The problem was to find a definition for integration that would be compatible with taking the limit of a sequence of functions.

Builds upon Previously Established Theories

Lebesgue was influenced by the work of René Baire (another recent graduate of the École Normale Supérieure) and **Émile Borel**. By 1898, when Lebesgue published his first results, Baire had formulated an insightful theory of discontinuous functions. In that same year Borel published a theory of measure that generalized the concepts of area to new types of regions obtained as limits.

Lebesgue taught at the Lycée Central in Nancy from 1899 to 1902. During that time he developed the ideas for his doctoral thesis at the Sorbonne. The work, "Intégrale, longueur, aire," extended Borel's theory of measure, defined the integral geometrically and analytically, and established nearly all the basic properties of integration. J. C. Burkill notes in the obituary of Lebesgue for the *Journal of the London Mathematical Society:* "It cannot be doubted that this dissertation is one of the finest which any mathematician has ever written."

Lebesgue's consideration of discontinuous curves and nonsmooth surfaces was shocking to some of his contemporaries. Camille Jordan cautioned Lebesgue that he should not expect other scholars to appreciate his work. Fortunately, the usefulness of his new ideas quickly overcame any resistance, and Lebesgue received a university appointment as maître des conférences at Rennes in 1902. During his first year he gave lectures for the Cours Peccot at the Collège de France on his new integral and the next year on its application to trigonometric series. Lebesgue published these lectures in the series of tracts edited by Borel and was the first author in this series of monographs other than Borel himself. He gave a thorough exposition of the historical background of the problems leading up to the properties an integral should satisfy, including the compatibility with the limit of a sequence of functions.

In 1906 Lebesgue left Rennes to become chargé de cours for the faculty of sciences, and later a professor, at Poitiers. In 1910 he was maître des conférences at the Sorbonne, and in 1921 he became professor at the Collège de France. Among his many prizes and honors was his election to the Académie des Sciences in 1922. By that time Lebesgue had nearly ninety publications on measure theory, integration, geometry, and related topics. Although his ideas were ignored at the great centers of mathematics such as Göttingen, his integral was presented to undergraduates at Rice Institute as early as 1914, and served as an inspiration to the founders of the Polish schools of mathematics at Lvov and Warsaw in 1919.

During the last twenty years of his life, Lebesgue's work became widely known, and his approach to integration evolved as a standard tool of analysis. Lebesgue himself began to concentrate more on the historical and pedagogical issues associated with his work. He believed that mathematicians should work from the problems that motivate theory and resist being bound to tradition. He felt that mathematical education should follow this same principle. He freely used the words "deception" and "hypocrisy" to describe the lack of connection between students' natural intuition of numbers and geometry and the manner in which these subjects were taught. In "Sur le mesure des grandeurs," Lebesgue complained about teaching of mathematics: "An infinite amount of talent has been expended on little perfections of detail. We must now attempt an overhaul of the whole structure."

Lebesgue died in Paris on July 26, 1941. Even during the last months of his terminal illness, he continued his course on geometrical constructions at the Collège de France and dictated a book on conic sections. He was survived by his wife, mother, a son, and a daughter. His view of mathematics can be summed up in the concluding words of "Sur le développement de la notion d'intégrale": "A generalization made not for the vain pleasure of generalizing but in order to solve previously existing problems is always a fruitful generalization. This is proved abundantly by the variety of applications of the ideas that we have just examined."

SELECTED WRITINGS BY LEBESGUE:

Books

Leçons sur l'intégration et la recherche des fonctions primitives, [Paris], 1904.
Leçons sur les séries trigonométriques, [Paris], 1906.
Notice sur les travaux scientifiques de M. Henri Lebesgue, [Toulouse], 1922.
Measure and the Integral, Holden-Day, 1966.

Periodicals

"Intégrale, longueur, aire," *Annali di Mathematica,* Volume 7, 1902, pp. 231–359.
"Sur le développement de la notion d'intégrale," *Matematiska Tidskrift,* 1926, pp. 54–74.
"Sur le mesure des grandeurs," *l'Enseignement Mathématique,* Volume 31, 1931.

SOURCES:

Books

Hawkins, Thomas, *Lebesgue's Theory of Integration,* University of Wisconsin Press, 1970.

Periodicals

Burkill, J. C., "Henri Lebesgue," *Journal of the London Mathematical Society,* Volume 19, 1944, pp. 56–64.
Denjoy, A., L. Felix, and P. Montel, "Henri Lebesgue, le savant, le professeur, l'homme," *l'Enseignement Mathematique,* 1957.
Kac, Mark, "Henri Lebesgue et l'Ecole Mathematique Polonaise: apercu et souvenirs," *l'Enseignement Mathematique,* Volume 21, 1975, pp. 111–114.

—*Sketch by Robert Messer and Tom Chen*

Georges Le Cadet
1864-1935
French astronomer and meteorologist

Georges Le Cadet rose from modest circumstances to direct France's principal observatory, Phu-liên, in Vietnam. He focused his attention on inventorying rainfall and climatological data in French Indochina. Like many French physicists and astronomers in the tropics, he was interested in the special characteristics of tropical meteorology. Le Cadet studied atmospheric electricity, proposing a mechanism for tropical lightning that focused on vertical circulation of air masses. His qualitative explanations conformed to French meteorological style during the early years of the twentieth century.

Georges Henri Pierre Le Cadet was born in Lyons, France, to a servant and a chambermaid. He attended the Ecole de la Martinière, a well-known technical school in his native city. Beginning at age fifteen, Le Cadet worked in the Lyons Observatory at Saint-Genis Laval as a technician. He slowly ascended the academic ladder, first in fine arts and then in astronomy. In 1898 he completed a doctorate on atmospheric electricity. As part of his research, he became passionately interested in balloon ascents. An associate astronomer at the Lyons Observatory who received several local honors, Le Cadet was considered for being the successor of the Phu-liên Observatory, near Hanoi. At that time, he already had a grasp on Mandarin Chinese—a form of the Chinese language. In 1906 he became interim director of the observatory, which had been constructed over the preceding seven years and was intended to serve as France's naval observatory in the Far East. Le Cadet's directorship became permanent after three years, and he guided the observatory's fortunes until 1927.

While at Phu-liên, Le Cadet came to an important conclusion about atmospheric electricity during a typhoon—a tropical storm found in the western North Pacific that produces strong winds rotating about a center of low atmospheric pressure. At that time, it was questioned why typhoons generally did not produce electrical discharges. Le Cadet found that discharges were usually the result of a vortex —fluid swirling with a center that forms a vacuum—horizontal to the earth; typhoons produce vertical vortices, which corresponds with the lack of discharges. During the first third of the twentieth century, no one in the exact sciences in greater France commanded a larger staff than Le Cadet at the Phu-liên Observatory.

SELECTED WRITINGS BY LE CADET:

Books

Observation de l'éclipse de soleil du 14 janvier 1907, [Hanoi], 1907.
Etude du champ électrique de l'atmosphère, [Paris], 1908.

SOURCES:

Books

Pyenson, Lewis, *Civilizing Mission: Exact Sciences and French Overseas Expansion, 1830–1940,* Johns Hopkins University Press, 1993, p. 79–81.

Periodicals

Lagrula, Joanny Philippe, "Georges Le Cadet," *L'astronomie,* Volume 49, 1935, p. 385–389.

—*Sketch by Lewis Pyenson*

Philip Leder
1934-
American geneticist

Philip Leder is best known for his work in mapping the genetic code and discovering the role antibodies play in causing cancer. He was among the first to clone the mammalian gene globin, and his later research focused on determining the genetic basis of cancer in hopes of contributing to its prevention and cure.

The only child of George and Jacqueline Bourke Leder, Leder was born on November 19, 1934, in Washington, DC. His father was a self-employed merchant, and his mother was a homemaker. He attended public school in Arlington, Virginia, and high school in Washington, DC, before enrolling at Harvard College. In 1956 he received a B.S. *cum laude* in biochemistry and went on to study medicine at Harvard Medical School where he graduated in 1960.

Leder completed his internship and residency at the University of Minnesota in Minneapolis. In 1962 he enlisted in the public health service branch of the coast guard rather than be drafted into the army. He served at the National Institutes of Health (NIH) in Bethesda, Maryland, and it was there that he became interested in genetics. "I was a physician but I really loved doing science," he told Marianne P. Fedunkiw in an interview. "In the 1960s genetics was a formal field. It was so fascinating; it opened an entirely new chapter—you might call it molecular genetics—and I grew up with the field."

During his three years at NIH, Leder sought to understand the genetic code, the arrangement of proteins in deoxyribonucleic and ribonucleic acids (DNA and RNA) that all living organisms share. Along with his colleague, biochemist **Marshall Warren Nirenberg**, he used a simple test to determine the coding potential of nucleotides, the building blocks of genes. In 1965 he showed that the nucleotides worked in groups of as few as three and further demonstrated how to match the code-word to its corresponding amino acid, a necessary component of proteins. "The

Philip Leder

content but not the order was known then, and we didn't know whether the order of the bases mattered," Leder told Fedunkiw. He left NIH in 1965 to spend a year as a visiting scientist at the Weizmann Institute in Rehovot, Israel. There he carried on his protein synthesis work, using it to understand gene regulation.

When he returned to NIH in 1966 he became research medical officer in the biosynthesis section of the laboratory of biochemistry at the National Cancer Institute. He also served as chairman of the graduate program in the department of biochemistry from 1968 to 1973. In 1969 he moved to the National Institute of Child Health and Human Development (NICHD) branch of the NIH, where he was named head of the section on molecular genetics in the laboratory of molecular genetics. From 1972 until 1980 Leder served as chief of the laboratory.

Work on Antibodies Leads to Gene Cloning

Leder's research interests shifted in the 1970s to understanding the genetic basis for the multitude of antibodies (proteins formulated to provide immunity from harmful substances) and examining the structure of mammalian genes and the possibility of cloning (producing identical copies) them. His work on antibodies sought to explain how an individual is capable of synthesizing hundreds of millions of different antibodies. In 1976 Leder devised the first NIH-approved system to clone gene fragments. This was first used successfully on the mammalian gene,

globin, in 1977. His research showed that certain coding sequences and gene structures were interrupted by precursor-messenger RNA. At that point in Leder's research, introns and exons—components of mammalian genes—were not understood; it was not known yet that the introns, a particular series of nucleotides, are edited out of the sequence during transcription of RNA. Leder's work later demonstrated how the split structure is edited. He continued to concentrate on this area of genetics until the early 1980s.

In the 1980s Leder began to investigate the genetic basis of cancer through the use of mice bred to carry cancer-causing genes. He devised a way of introducing specific oncogenes—those genes with the potential to cause other cells to become cancerous—into the mice, and he showed how a particular oncogene, c-myc, leads to cancer. Other experiments studied the cancerous results when mice with one type of oncogene were bred with mice containing another oncogene. "I hope yet to make a substantive contribution to the understanding of breast cancer and if not its prevention then its treatment," Leder told Fedunkiw. Since 1980 he has been the John Emory Andrus Professor of Genetics and chairman of the department of genetics at Harvard Medical School. In 1986 Leder accepted the position of senior investigator at the Howard Hughes Medical Institute at the Harvard Medical School.

In recognition of his achievements Leder was awarded the Richard Lounsberry Award by the National Academy of Sciences in 1981. In 1987 he received the Albert Lasker Medical Research Award, and President Bush presented Leder with the National Medal of Science in 1989. He has also received honorary doctorates from Yale University, Mount Sinai Medical Center in New York, and the University of Guelph, Ontario, Canada. Leder married Aya Leder in 1959. Aya Leder herself is a molecular geneticist at Harvard Medical School and co-author of a number of papers with her husband. They have three children. Of his outside interests, Leder has said, "My hobby is my work."

SELECTED WRITINGS BY LEDER:

Periodicals

(With M. W. Nirenberg) "RNA Codewords and Protein Synthesis. I. The Effect of Trinucleotides Upon Binding of sRNA to Ribosomes," *Science,* Volume 145, 1964, pp. 1399–1407.

(With J. G. Seidman, A. Leder, M. H. Edgell, et al.) "Multiple Related Mouse Immunoglobulin Variable Region Genes Identified by Cloning and Sequence Analysis," *Proceedings of the National Academy of Sciences USA,* Volume 75, 1978, pp. 3881–3885.

(With J. G. Seidman) "The Arrangement and Re-arrangement of Antibody Genes," *Nature,* Volume 276, 1978, pp. 790–795.

(With T. Stewart and P. K. Pattengale) "Spontaneous Mammary Adenocarcinomas in Transgenic Mice the Carry and Express MTV/myc Fusion Genes," *Cell,* Volume 38, 1984, pp. 627–637.

SOURCES:

Leder, Philip, interview with Marianne P. Fedunkiw conducted December 22, 1993.

—Sketch by Marianne P. Fedunkiw

Joshua Lederberg

Joshua Lederberg
1925-
American geneticist

Joshua Lederberg is a Nobel Prize-winning American geneticist whose pioneering work on genetic recombination in bacteria helped propel the field of molecular genetics into the forefront of biological and medical research. In 1946, Lederberg, working with **Edward Lawrie Tatum**, showed that bacteria may reproduce sexually, disproving the widely held theory that bacteria were asexual. The two scientists' discovery also substantiated that bacteria possess genetic systems comparable to those of higher organisms, thus providing a new repertoire for scientists to study the genetic basis of life.

Continuing with his work in bacteria, Lederberg also discovered the phenomena of genetic conjugation and transduction—or the transfer of either the entire complement of chromosomes or chromosome fragments, respectively—from cell to cell. In his work on conjugation and transduction, Lederberg became the first scientist to manipulate genetic material, which had far-reaching implications for subsequent efforts in genetic engineering and gene therapy. In addition to his laboratory research, Lederberg lectured widely on the complex relationship between science and society and served as a scientific adviser on biological warfare to the World Health Organization.

Lederberg was born in Montclair, New Jersey, on May 23, 1925. His father, Zwi Hirsch Lederberg, was a rabbi; his mother, Esther Goldenbaum, had emigrated from Palestine two years before Lederberg was born. Lederberg's parents moved to New York City,

eventually settling in the Washington Heights district. Lederberg attended the city's public schools, where, as he wrote in the book *The Excitement and Fascination of Science: Reflections of Eminent Scientists,* he was a precocious youth whose inquiring mind was nurtured by "a cadre of devoted and sympathetic teachers." At Stuyvesant High School (which specialized in science education), Lederberg first encountered other youths who could compete with him intellectually. Through a program known as the American Institute Science Laboratory, Lederberg was given the opportunity to conduct original research in a laboratory after school hours and on weekends. Here he pursued his interest in biology, working in cytochemistry, or the chemistry of cells. A voracious reader, Lederberg was influenced early on by science-oriented writers such as Bernard Jaffe, Paul de Kruif, and H. G. Wells. For a Bar Mitzvah present he received Meyer Bodansky's *Introduction to Physiological Chemistry,* and on his sixteenth birthday, **E. B. Wilson**'s *The Cell in Development and Heredity.*

After graduating from high school in 1941, Lederberg entered Columbia University as a premedical student. He received a tuition scholarship from the Hayden Trust, which, coupled with his living at home and commuting to school, made it financially possible for him to attend college. Although his undergraduate studies focused on zoology, Lederberg also received a foundation in humanistic studies under Lionel Trilling, James Gutman, and others. Lederberg's work in zoology was fostered by H. Burr

Steinbach, who helped Lederberg get space in a histology lab to pursue his own research. This early undergraduate research included an interest in the cytophysiology of mitosis in plants and the uses of genetic analysis in cell biology. In 1942, Lederberg met Francis Ryan, whose work in the biochemical genetics of *Neurospora* was Lederberg's first opportunity to see significant scientific research as it occurred. Lederberg graduated with a B.A. with honors in 1944 at the age of nineteen.

At the age of seventeen, Lederberg had enlisted in the United States Navy V–12 college training program, which featured a condensed pre-med and medical curriculum to produce medical officers for the armed services during World War II. While an undergraduate he also was assigned duty at the U.S. Naval Hospital at St. Albans in Long Island. He began his medical courses at the Columbia College of Physicians and Surgeons in 1944, but left after two years to study under Edward L. Tatum in the microbiology department at Yale University.

Embarks on Nobel Prize-winning Research

In spring of 1945 Ryan had suggested that Lederberg ask Tatum—who had made substantial contributions to biochemical genetics—if Lederberg could work in Tatum's lab at Yale. Lederberg was interested in natural recombination; and Tatum, working with **George W. Beadle**, had done pioneering investigations proving that the DNA (deoxyribonucleic acid) of *Neurospora* (a genus of fungi) played a fundamental role in many of the chemical reactions in *Neurospora* cells. While Lederberg helped Tatum continue his studies of *Neurospora,* the two proceeded to embark on a more tenuous line of research, studying *Escherichia coli* (a bacterium that lives in the gastrointestinal tract) for evidence of genetic inheritance. At the international Cold Spring Harbor Symposium of 1946, Lederberg and Tatum were graciously granted additional time to talk about their *E. Coli* research in addition to the *Neurospora* studies. The scientists' announcement that they had discovered sexual or genetic recombination in the bacterium was met with keen interest by an audience that included the leading molecular biologists and geneticists in the world. The prevailing theory among biologists of the time was that bacteria reproduced asexually by cells essentially splitting, creating two cells with a complete set of chromosomes (threadlike structures in the cell nucleus that carry genetic information). Lederberg and Tatum had found evidence that some strains of *E. coli* pass on hereditary material cell to cell. They found that a conjugation of two cells produced a cell that subsequently began dividing into offspring cells. These offspring showed that they inherited traits from each of the parent strains.

In *The Excitement and Fascination of Science,* Lederberg recalled the intense scrutiny this discovery came under at the Cold Spring Harbor Symposium. **André Lwoff** suggested that perhaps what they had found was a cross-feeding of nutrients between the cells. But in general at that meeting and a second one the following year, Lederberg found the giants of genetics, such as **Jacques Monod**, **Salvador E. Luria**, and Lwoff, to be supportive of and interested in his research. Lederberg also received requests for *E. coli* cultures by others who wanted to investigate his findings.

Lederberg's interest in basic research began to draw him further and further away from pursuing a medical career. In 1947 while at Yale he received an offer from the University of Wisconsin to become an assistant professor of genetics with a focus on the new field of microbial genetics. Although only two years away from receiving his M.D. degree, Lederberg viewed his return to medical school in *The Excitement and Fascination of Science* as a "grave (if not total) interruption of research at its most exciting stage." His prospective appointment at Wisconsin was met with some skepticism concerning his youth (he was only twenty-two) and his yet-to-be fully-accepted research. More troubling personally were references to his character and his Jewish heritage. But the strong support of senior colleagues at Wisconsin and Yale prevailed. Lederberg accepted the position at Wisconsin (receiving his Ph.D. degree from Yale in 1948) and spent a fruitful and satisfying decade there. He never regretted abandoning his medical training, although he noted his later honorary medical degrees from Tufts University and the University of Turin as being among his most valued.

Lederberg continued to make groundbreaking discoveries at Wisconsin and firmly established himself as one of the most promising young intellects in the burgeoning field of genetics. By perfecting a method to isolate mutant bacteria species using ultraviolet light, Lederberg was able to prove the long-held theory that genetic mutations occurred spontaneously. He found he could "mate" two strains of bacteria—one resistant to penicillin and the other to streptomycin—and produce a bacteria resistant to both antibiotics. He also found that he could manipulate a virus's virulence.

Working with graduate student **Norton Zinder**, Lederberg discovered genetic transduction, which involves the transfer only of hereditary fragments of information between cells as opposed to complete chromosomal replication (conjugation). Lederberg went on to breed unique strains of viruses. Although these strains promised to reveal much about the nature of viruses in hopes of one day controlling them, they also posed a clear threat in terms of creating harmful biochemical substances. At the time, the practical aspect of Lederberg's work was hard to evaluate. The Nobel Prize Committee, however recognized the significance of his contributions to genetics and, in 1958, awarded him the Nobel Prize in physiology or medicine for the bacterial and viral research that provided a new line of investigations of viral diseases and cancer. Lederberg shared the prize with Beadle and Tatum. Lederberg's work in genetics eventually proved to be one of the foundations of gene mapping, which eventually led to efforts to genetically treat disease and identify those at risk of developing certain diseases.

Addresses Role of Science in Society

A brilliant laboratory scientist and technician, Lederberg was also concerned with the role of science in society and the far-reaching effects of scientific discoveries, particularly in genetics. In a Pan American Health Organization/World Health Organization lecture in biomedical sciences called "Health in the World Tomorrow," Lederberg acknowledged concerns of the public, and even some scientists, over the newfound ability to tamper with the genetic code of life. But he was more concerned with the many ethical questions that would arise over the inevitable successes the advancing fields of microbiology and genetics were ushering in. Lederberg saw the biological revolution as "a philosophical one" that was to bring a "new depth of scientific understanding about the nature of life." He foresaw advancements in the treatment of cancer, organ transplants, and geriatric medicine as presenting a whole new set of ethical and social problems, such as the availability and allocation of expensive health-care resources.

Although Lederberg had a profound faith in science, he was not so confident of scientists' ability to rationally communicate the ramifications of their work. In *Man and His Future,* he lamented the "archaic clumsiness of our basic mechanisms of communication. Man's dilemma," he said, "is the discrepancy between the size of his population and the complexity of his institutions, on one hand, and his individual feebleness, measured as a data input rate of no more than fifty bits per second."

Lederberg was also interested in the study of biochemical life outside of earth and coined the term *exobiology* to refer to such studies. Along with physicist Dean B. Cowie, he expressed concern in *Science* over the possible contamination of biological life on other planets from microbes carried by human spacecraft. He was also a consultant to the U.S. Viking space missions to the planet Mars.

Lederberg's career included an appointment as chairman of the new genetics department at Stanford University in 1958. In 1978 he was appointed president of Rockefeller University. Working with his first wife, Esther Zimmer, a former student of Tatum's whom Lederberg married in 1946, Lederberg investi-

gated the role of bacterial enzymes in sugar metabolism. He also discovered that penicillin's ability to kill bacteria was due to its preventing synthesis of the bacteria's cell walls. Among Lederberg's many honors were the Eli Lilly Award for outstanding work by a scientist under thirty-five years of age and the Alexander Hamilton Medal of Columbia University. After divorcing his first wife, Lederberg married Marguerite Stein Kirsch in 1968, with whom he had two children, a daughter and a son.

While Lederberg recognized the intense competition that sometimes arises among modern-era scientists, he described his own personal scientific dealings as congenial. "The shared interests of scientists in the pursuit of a universal truth," said Lederberg in *The Excitement and Fascination of Science,* "remain among the rare bonds that can transcend bitter personal, national, ethnic, and sectarian rivalries."

SELECTED WRITINGS BY LEDERBERG:

Books

Papers in Microbial Genetics: Bacteria and Bacterial Viruses, University of Wisconsin Press, 1951.
(With others) *Man and His Future,* Little, Brown, 1963, pp. 263–273.
"Health in the World of Tomorrow," *Third PAHO/WHO Lecture on the Biomedical Sciences, PAHO/WHO Scientific Publication no. 175,* 1968, pp. 5–15.
(With others) *The Excitement and Fascination of Science: Reflections by Eminent Scientists,* Volume 3, Part 1, Rockefeller University, 1990, pp. 893–915.

Periodicals

(With Dean B. Cowie) *Science,* June 27, 1958, pp. 1473–1475.

SOURCES:

Books

McGraw-Hill Modern Men of Science, McGraw-Hill, 1966, pp. 290–291.
Nobel Prize Winners, H. W. Wilson, 1987, pp. 611–613.

—Sketch by David Petechuk

Leon Max Lederman
1922-
American experimental physicist

Leon Max Lederman, physicist, educator, and advocate for basic research, has spent his scientific career designing experiments and devices for unlocking the structure of the atom. During the heyday of physics research at Columbia University in New York City, Lederman participated in pioneering experiments that proved the existence of a new kind of neutrino—a subatomic particle not observed previously. These experiments also established a new technique for probing physical phenomena involving the "weak" nuclear force, one of the three fundamental forces that rule the atom. For this work, Lederman shared in the 1988 Nobel Prize for physics.

Lederman, son of Russian immigrants Morris Lederman and Minna Rosenberg, was born on July 15, 1922, in New York City, where his father operated a laundry. Lederman pursued his undergraduate education at the City College of New York, earning a baccalaureate degree in chemistry in 1943. After serving three years in the U.S. Army, Lederman enrolled at Columbia University in New York City to study physics. He began his doctoral research in 1948, designing a special instrument to study subatomic particles produced by a new atom-smasher (the synchrocyclotron accelerator) then under construction at Columbia's Nevis Laboratories in Irvington, New York. In 1950, while still a graduate student, Lederman and physicist John Tinlot made special modifications to the Nevis accelerator, transforming the machine into a significantly more powerful research tool. In his doctoral research, Lederman used the new Columbia accelerator to measure the lifetimes of two different kinds of pions, a type of meson or fundamental particle that the machine produced in abundance. Lederman received his Ph.D. in 1951 and held various teaching and research positions at Columbia University until 1989.

Conducts Subatomic Particle Research

A handful of experiments Lederman participated in during the 1950s proved especially significant. In 1956, he helped discover a new particle, the "long-lived neutral kaon." From 1959 to 1962 Lederman and his colleagues **Melvin Schwartz** and **Jack Steinberger** conducted research on subatomic particles for which they were later awarded the Nobel Prize in physics. The scientists used the accelerator at Brookhaven National Laboratories in Upton, New York, to find a previously unobserved particle—the muon neutrino. Notoriously elusive creatures, neutrinos are

Leon Max Lederman

difficult to study because they have no electric charge and no detectable mass.

In the experiments, the scientists fired a beam of protons at a block of beryllium metal, producing a blast of subatomic debris, including neutrinos. A forty-foot-thick barrier of steel plates culled from a battleship in the process of demolition absorbed all particles but the neutrinos. After eight months of shooting protons, the scientists found that some fifty-six neutrinos had betrayed their existence in the accelerator's ten-ton particle detector, the result of two different kinds of interactions involving the weak force, a fundamental physical force responsible for particle decay processes in radioactivity. One of the particles, the electron neutrino, had been known to physicists already. But the scientists also found the elusive muon neutrino, produced only during high-energy collisions.

This result provided a key theoretical insight, laying the cornerstone for the standard model of the atom: that there are two kinds of neutrinos, one intimately associated with electrons and the other with muons. But just as important, the celebrated "two-neutrino experiment" marked the first time anyone had artificially created a beam of neutrinos in the laboratory. The neutrino-beam technique, adopted at accelerator laboratories around the world, made possible subsequent experiments probing the weak nuclear force, which operates at short range and governs certain kinds of radioactive decay. Importantly, neutrino collisions produce only interactions involving the weak force.

A leader in the particle-physics community, Lederman served as an administrator at research institutions organized around the giant particle accelerators that came to dominate high-energy physics in the postwar era. From 1962 to 1979, he headed Columbia's Nevis Laboratories. During these years he was involved with original research much of his time. From 1976 to 1977, for instance, he participated in the discovery of a new, massive particle—the upsilon —that belonged to an entirely new grouping of subatomic particles. For this, Lederman shared the 1982 Wolf Prize, awarded by Israel, with colleague Martin Perl.

Then, from 1979 to 1989, Lederman directed the Fermi National Accelerator Laboratory (Fermilab) in Batavia, Illinois. Throughout his career, Lederman's research has remained centered on experiments and advanced equipment. It is not surprising, then, that in 1982 Lederman challenged his colleagues in the physics world to commit themselves to constructing the most powerful accelerator ever conceived—later christened the Superconducting Super Collider (SSC). Lederman and others argue that the giant SSC, designed to smash particles into each other at high energies, was needed to further explore the fundamental structure of matter.

Lederman played a significant role in advancing his field far enough that a large, next-generation accelerator like the SSC has become necessary to both confirm and extend existing theories. Lederman's work, done in collaboration with other researchers, helped to unveil a number of new subatomic particles. These discoveries enabled theorists to construct a "standard model" of the atom, listing the hierarchy of quarks and leptons thought to make up all matter in the universe.

After the Nobel Prize

Recognition for Lederman's research at Columbia University came in 1988, when he and former colleagues Schwartz and Steinberger were awarded the Nobel Prize in physics for the research on neutrinos they conducted from 1959 to 1962. After receiving the prize, Lederman ended his tenure as director of Fermilab, retaining the title of emeritus director. Concerned with the level of understanding and appreciation of science in the United States, Lederman returned to teaching in 1989, accepting a professorship at the University of Chicago. There he taught an undergraduate course popularly known as "physics for poets." Following his 1992 retirement from the University of Chicago, Lederman became a professor at the Illinois Institute of Technology in Chicago, teaching first-year physics.

In 1945, Lederman married Florence Gordon, with whom he had three children, Rena, Jesse, and Heidi. He later married Ellen Carr in 1981. A member of the National Academy of Sciences, Lederman served as president of the American Association for the Advancement of Science from 1990 to 1991. He has received numerous honorary degrees and awards, including the National Medal of Science in 1965. He has coauthored over two hundred scientific papers.

SELECTED WRITINGS BY LEDERMAN:

Books

(With David Schramm) *From Quarks to the Cosmos,* W. H. Freeman, 1989.
(With Dick Teresi) *The God Particle,* Houghton Mifflin, 1993.

Periodicals

"1986 Richtmyer Lecture: Unification, Grand Unification, and the Unity of Physics," *American Journal of Physics,* Volume 54, 1986, pp. 594–600.
"Observations in Particle Physics from Two Neutrinos to the Standard Model," *Science,* Volume 244, 1989, pp. 664–672.

SOURCES:

Books

Weinberg, Steven, *Dreams of a Final Theory,* Pantheon Books, 1992.

Periodicals

Peterson, Ivars, "Particles of History," *Science News,* Volume 142, 1992, pp. 174–175.
Thomsen, Dietrick E., "The Prairie Home Accelerator," *Science News,* Volume 133, 1988, pp. 10–11.

Other

Lederman, Leon M., interview with Daniel Pendick conducted June 8, 1993.

—Sketch by Daniel A. Pendick

Raphael C. Lee
1949-

American biomedical engineer and plastic surgeon

Plastic surgeon Raphael C. Lee, who holds both a medical degree and a Ph.D. in electrical engineering, is a leading expert in the treatment of victims of high-voltage electrical shocks. He has done pathbreaking research on the effects of electricity on living tissue, and has used his education and expertise to develop new methods for the treatment of scars and burns. In 1981, he was one of the first recipients of a grant from the John D. and Catherine T. MacArthur Foundation, and he used part of the prize money to establish a laboratory that combined research in both the biological and the physical sciences. He has taught medicine at Harvard and electrical engineering at the Massachusetts Institute of Technology and is now a professor in both biomechanics and plastic and reconstructive surgery at the University of Chicago.

Lee was born in Sumter, South Carolina, on October 29, 1949. He became interested in physics as a teenager when he chanced upon a physics book, though there was only one such course available to him in high school. At the University of South Carolina, Lee majored in electrical engineering. He developed a keen interest in lasers and their applications to medicine, and it was this interest that led him to apply to medical school.

In 1975, Lee completed a joint program in medicine and engineering: He received a master's degree in engineering from Drexel University and a doctor of medicine degree from Temple University. He did his residency at the University of Chicago, and during this time he received his Ph.D. in electrical engineering from the Massachusetts Institute of Technology. Lee did his plastic surgery residency at the Massachusetts General Hospital in Boston, and beginning in 1983 he taught at Harvard Medical School and served as an electrical engineering research scientist at MIT.

Observes Victims of Electrical Trauma

In 1981, Lee was awarded a grant from the MacArthur Foundation. "I must have been a controversial choice," he told *Hemispheres* magazine. "Some people must have thought, 'Why give money to a surgeon?'" But the grant, which lasted until 1986, enabled him to pursue his own directions in medical research, and it was during what he calls "the MacArthur years" that he first began to examine the effects of electricity on living tissue.

The victims of electrical trauma, such as utility workers who come into contact with high-voltage electrical lines, suffer wounds that often resemble burns. Before Lee began his research, it had long been held that the damage done by electrical shock was primarily thermal in nature: tissue was burned because the electricity generated heat as it passed through the body. But Lee believed that many of the consequences of electrical trauma could not be explained as thermal effects; muscle tissue can continue to break down days and weeks after the accident, and victims also suffer damage to their organs and other complications, including cataracts and paralysis, after long periods of time have elapsed. Acute infections are common and almost three-quarters of those who suffer high-voltage electrical trauma have at least one limb amputated.

Discovers Electrical Trauma Causes Cell Damage

In 1986, Lee was able to establish that many of the complicated effects of exposure to high-voltage electricity were not the result of heat. He and members of his team devised an experiment in which muscle cells were subjected to electricity at short intervals; the application of electricity in this way prevented the accumulation of heat that occurred in a typical electrical shock but duplicated the strength of the electrical current. Lee and his colleagues were thus able to separate the effects of heat from the effects of electrical energy, and they discovered that muscle cells still suffered extensive damage. After several years of further research, they were able to establish why high-voltage electrical trauma is so severe. Electrical currents damage the outer membrane of cells, actually perforating it, in a phenomenon known as electroporation. This perforation of the membrane disrupts the complex chemistry of the cell, leading to the destabilization and deterioration of tissue.

In 1989, Lee returned to the University of Chicago, where he received a dual appointment in the department of plastic and reconstructive surgery and in the Biomechanics Group of the Department of Organismal Anatomy and Biology. In the research laboratory he directed there, Lee worked on discovering a technique for treating electrical trauma victims by resealing the perforations in the membranes of their cells. "Most of the clinicians who were established in burn research were very skeptical that this could be done," Lee told the *University of Chicago Magazine.* "No one had even tried it. It seemed farfetched." There are certain materials called surfactants which can form a layer or sheet of molecules that resembles cell membrane in important respects. By 1992, Lee and his research team had discovered several polymers which can initiate the sealing of cell membranes. One of these was poloxamer 188, which, after a series of successful applications to rats in the laboratory, has been scheduled for experimental trials on humans in 1994.

The University of Chicago has recently established an electrical trauma program, of which Lee is the director. The unit has specially equipped intensive-care rooms and an extensive transportation system so that victims of high-voltage electric shock can be airlifted from anywhere in the United States to the unit within six hours. The results of Lee's research may be also applicable to chemical burns, ionizing radiation, and some thermal injuries, as well as cardiac and brain cells damaged by a heart attack or stroke. The concept of opening and closing pores may also have some applications to gene therapy, allowing the pores of a cells to be closed after a gene has been inserted.

In 1981 Lee was named a Coller Surgical Society Traveling Scholar. In 1985, he was listed as one of "American's 100 Brightest Young Scientists" by *Science Digest,* and he was also named a Searle Scholar. He won the American college of Surgeons Schering Scholarship in 1987. In 1988 he received the James Barrett Brown Award from the American Association of Plastic Surgeons for "advancing knowledge in the field of Plastic Surgery." Lee is married and has two children.

SELECTED WRITINGS BY LEE:

Periodicals

(With K. J. McLeod and H. P. Erlich) "Frequency Dependence of Electrical Field Modulation of Fribroblast Protein Synthesis" *Science,* Volume 236, 1987, pp. 1465–1469.

(With D. C. Gaylor and K. Prakah-Asante) "Role of Cell Membrane Rupture in the Pathogenesis of Electrical Trauma," *Journal of Surgical Residency,*Volume 44, 1988, pp. 670–682.

(With L. P. River, F. S. Pan, L. Ji, and R. L. Wollmann) "Surfactant-Induced Sealing of Electropermeablized Skeletal Muscle Membranes *in vivo,*" *Proceedings of the National Academy of Science,* Volume 89, 1992, pp. 4524–4528.

SOURCES:

Periodicals

"Breakthrough in Electrical Burn Treatment," *Electric Power Research Institute Journal,* September, 1992, pp. 16–21.

Easton, John, "The Hole Truth," *University of Chicago Magazine,* December, 1991, pp. 16–19.

Penney, Cynthia, "Genius Grants," *Hemispheres,* October, 1992, pp. 72–75.

—Sketch by Margo Nash

Tsung-Dao Lee
1926-
Chinese American physicist

Tsung-Dao Lee and his colleague physicist **Chen Ning Yang** developed the revolutionary theory that the unusual behavior of the K-meson (a subatomic particle) is a result of its violating a supposedly inviolable law of nature, conservation of parity, which defines the basic symmetry of nature. A few months after their theory had been announced, fellow physicist **Chien-Shiung Wu** obtained experimental confirmation of their remarkable discovery. For their work, Lee and Yang were awarded the 1957 Nobel Prize in physics.

Lee was born in Shanghai, China, on November 24, 1926. He was the third of six children born to Tsing-Kong Lee, a businessman, and Ming-Chang Chang. Lee attended the Kiangsi Middle School in Kanchow and, after graduation, entered the National Chekian University in Kweichow. After the invasion of Japanese troops in 1945, Lee fled to the south, where he continued his studies at the National Southwest Associated University in Kunming.

Immigrates to the United States

In 1946, Lee was presented with an unusual opportunity. One of his teachers at Kunming was the theoretical physicist Ta-You Wu. When Wu decided to return to the United States (where he had worked toward his Ph.D. degree), he invited Lee to accompany him. Lee accepted the offer, but found himself in a somewhat peculiar position. He had not yet received his bachelor's degree and found that only one American university would accept him for graduate study without a degree. He therefore decided to enroll in that institution, the University of Chicago.

At Chicago, Lee selected a topic in astrophysics for his doctoral research. Working under physicist **Enrico Fermi**, he completed that research and was awarded his Ph.D. in 1950 for his dissertation, on the hydrogen content of white dwarf stars. While at Chicago, Lee also renewed his friendship with physicist Chen Ning Yang. Lee and Yang had been acquaintances at Kunming, but they became very

Tsung-Dao Lee

close friends after both reached the United States. They were separated in 1950 when Lee went to the Yerkes Astronomical Observatory at Lake Geneva, Wisconsin, and Yang went to the Institute for Advanced Studies at Princeton University. Lee then spent the next year (1950–51) as a research associate at the University of California at Berkeley. The two friends were reunited in 1951, however, when Lee accepted an appointment at the Institute for Advanced Studies.

Discussions with Yang Lead to Revolutionary Theory

Lee's departure from Princeton in 1953 for a post as assistant professor of physics at Columbia University seems to have had little effect on his collaboration with Yang. The two worked out a schedule that allowed them to continue meeting once a week, either in New York City or in Princeton. By the spring of 1956, these regular meetings had begun to focus on a particularly interesting subject, a subatomic particle known as the K-meson. Discovered only a few years earlier, the K-meson puzzled physicists because it appeared to be a single particle that decayed in two different ways. The decay schemes were so different that physicists had become convinced that two distinct forms of the K-meson existed, forms they called the tau meson and theta meson.

The single difference between these two mesons was that one form had even parity and the other form

had odd parity. The term parity refers to the theory that the laws of nature are not biased in any particular direction. That is, if one has two sets of interactions that are mirror images of each other, the physical laws describing those interactions are identical. This concept is known as the conservation of parity, a concept long held by physicists.

The problem that Lee and Yang attacked was that vast amounts of experimental evidence suggested that the theta and tau mesons were one and the same particle. The only contrary evidence was that the two mesons had opposite parity and, therefore, supposedly could not be identical. During an intense three-week period of work in the spring of 1956, Lee and Yang solved this puzzle. Their solution was to suggest, simply enough, that in some types of reactions, parity is not conserved. The beta decay of the (one and only) K-meson was such a reaction. They then devised a series of experiments by which their theory could be tested. The fundamental elements in the Lee-Yang theory were announced in a paper sent to the *Physical Review* on June 22, 1956 and later given the title, "Question of Parity Conservation in Weak Interactions."

About six months later, the experiments suggested by Lee and Yang were carried out by one of their colleagues, Chien-Shiung Wu, first at Columbia and then at the National Bureau of Standards. The experiments confirmed the Lee-Yang prediction in every respect. Less than a year later, the two theorists were awarded the 1957 Nobel Prize in physics for their work.

After promotions to associate professor (1955) and professor (1956) at Columbia, Lee returned to the Institute for Advanced Studies in 1960 for three years. He then was appointed Enrico Fermi Professor of Physics at Columbia in 1963. In 1984, he was made University Professor at Columbia. Beginning in 1981, Lee held appointments as honorary professor at a number of Chinese universities, including the University of Science and Technology (1981), Jinan University (1982), Fudan University (1982), Quinghua University (1984), Peking University (1985), Nanjing University (1985), and Zhejiang University (1988). He married Hui-Chung Chin (also known as Jeanette) on June 3, 1950, while they were both students at Chicago. The Lees have two sons, James and Stephen.

SELECTED WRITINGS BY LEE:

Books

Particle Physics and Introduction to Field Theory, Harwood Academic Press, 1981.
T.D. Lee: Selected Papers, Birkhausen, 1987.

Periodicals

(With Chen Ning Yang) "Question of Parity Conservation in Weak Interactions," *Physical Review,* Volume 104, 1956, pp. 254–58.

SOURCES:

Books

Crease, Robert P., and Charles C. Mann, *The Second Creation,* Macmillan, 1986, pp. 205–7.
McGraw-Hill Modern Scientists and Engineers, Volume 2, McGraw-Hill, 1980, pp. 215–16.
Nobel Prize Winners, H. W. Wilson, 1987, pp. 615–17.
Weber, Robert L., *Pioneers of Science: Nobel Prize Winners in Physics,* American Institute of Physics, 1980, pp. 167–68.

Periodicals

Bernstein, Jeremy, "A Question of Parity," *New Yorker,* May 12, 1962, pp. 49ff.

—*Sketch by David E. Newton*

Yuan T. Lee

Yuan T. Lee
1936-
Chinese-born American chemist

Yuan T. Lee, a professor of chemistry at the University of California, shared the 1986 Nobel Prize in chemistry with **Dudley Herschbach** and **John C. Polanyi** for their work in the field of chemical kinetics, also called reaction dynamics. Herschbach and Lee worked together on their study of what happens when individual particles of matter collide and chemically change. Lee's major contribution to the prize-winning effort was to improve the instruments. Before Lee worked on the apparatus, Herschbach's research was very limited in scope. With the changes Lee made, the equipment could be used to study almost any chemical change. The new apparatus is so useful it is described as a "universal" machine, and a laboratory "workhorse" by colleagues at the University of California.

Yuan Tseh Lee was born in Hsinchu, Taiwan, on November 29, 1936. Lee's father was an artist and art teacher; his mother taught elementary school. When the Japanese occupied Taiwan during World War II,

the people of Hsinchu were sent to live in the mountains; there Lee could not go to school. After the war he finished elementary school. Lee graduated from Hsinchu High School in 1955. His academic standing was so high that he won admission to the National Taiwan University without taking an entrance examination. Lee majored in chemistry at the University. He was influenced by a biography of **Marie Curie**. Lee received his B.S. in 1959. Two years later he earned a M.S. degree from the National Tsinghua University. In 1962 Lee attended the University of California at Berkeley. He married Bernice Chinli Wu, a childhood acquaintance, in 1963. They have three children, a daughter and two sons. In 1968 Lee moved to the University of Chicago as an assistant professor. He became an associate professor in 1971, and a full professor in 1973. The next year he returned to the University of California at Berkeley as a professor of chemistry. He continued his research at the Lawrence Berkeley Laboratory. In 1974 Lee also became a United States citizen.

Ingenuity Overcomes Technical Difficulties

Lee received his Ph.D. in 1965 from the University of California at Berkeley, then stayed on as a postdoctoral student for a year and a half. He designed and constructed the apparatus needed to facilitate his research into the reaction that occurs when a stream of neutral hydrogen atoms collides with a stream of positively charged nitrogen ions.

Since 1963 Herschbach had been doing similar research at Harvard, but he did not have the apparatus he needed for very sophisticated experiments. In 1967 Herschbach invited Lee to join him. In less than a year at Harvard, Lee succeeded in designing the intricate universal crossed-molecular-beam apparatus that would provide the means for Herschbach's research. Herschbach's experiments were not entirely new. Physicists had used streams of colliding subatomic particles to study the nature of matter for many years. But he was the first to explore chemical reactions in depth by this method. With Lee's contribution they could analyze the results of collisions between individual particles to determine the products and the energy of the products in detail never before possible. Herschbach had tried hot wire detectors but only a certain few reactions could be evaluated by this method. Lee adapted a very sensitive mass spectrometer as a detector to replace the hot wire. A mass spectrometer has a slit which allows particles of different mass to be sorted and detected electronically as the slit is moved across a field of bombarding product particles. The product particles are what result when the molecular beams cross paths and collide. The results of scanning the products are recorded. With the sophisticated, specially adapted spectrometer, not only were the results better from each test reaction, but many more reactions could now be studied.

Lee was awarded the Ernest Orlando Lawrence Memorial Award of the United States Energy Research and Development Agency in 1981. Two years later he received an award from the Atomic Energy Commission. In 1986 he received the Peter Debye Award from the American Chemical Society, the National Medal of Science from the National Science Foundation, and shared the Nobel Prize in chemistry with Herschbach and Polanyi "for their contributions concerning the dynamics of elementary chemical processes." The citation for the Nobel Prize describes the method used by Herschbach and Lee as "one of the most important advances within the field of reaction dynamics." Lee is described as a modest, quiet person, extremely talented and deeply committed to his research. A colleague at the University of California says Lee "combines two qualities rarely found in the same scientist: brilliance and attention to detail." He adds, Lee is "the kind of guy who comes into the lab at midnight to see how things are going." Herschbach describes Lee as "the Mozart of physical chemistry" because he has "a precise touch" when he is at work in the laboratory. In his presentation at the Nobel award, Lee said that "the experimental investigation of elementary chemical reactions is presently a very exciting period. . . . In the remaining years of the twentieth century, there is no doubt that the experimental investigation of the dynamics and mechanics of elementary chemical reactions will play a very important role."

SELECTED WRITINGS BY LEE:

Periodicals

"Molecular Beam Studies of Elementary Chemical Processes," *Science,* May 15, 1987, pp. 793–98.

SOURCES:

Periodicals

Peterson, I., "Chemistry: Probing Reaction Dynamics," *Science News,* October 25, 1986, p. 262.
Waldrop, M. Mitchell, "The 1986 Nobel Prize in Chemistry," *Science*, November 7, 1986, pp. 673-74.

—*Sketch by M. C. Nagel*

Susan E. Leeman
1930-
American neuroendocrinologist

Susan E. Leeman is known for her work with substance P and neurotensin, peptides that help govern the functioning of the nervous, endocrine and immune systems. As a result of this research, Leeman is considered one of the founders of the field of neuroendocrinology, and was the first woman elected to the Physiology and Pharmacology section of the National Academy of Sciences.

Leeman was born Susan Epstein on May 9, 1930, in Chicago, Illinois, to Dora G. Epstein, a graduate of Hunter College, and Samuel Epstein, a graduate of City College of New York and a prominent metallurgist. After attending public school, Leeman enrolled in Goucher College, where she received her B.A. in physiology in 1951. After college, Leeman's science career was slow in starting. "When I graduated it was in the 1950s, and women weren't supposed to do anything," Leeman told contributor Devera Pine in an interview. "I worked in New York for a while and studied philosophy. But I decided that was too hard and that I probably should go measure something."

Leeman began that quest to "measure something" by applying to graduate school at Radcliffe College in the Division of Medical Sciences at Harvard Medical School. It was here that Leeman first

Susan E. Leeman

became interested in neuroendocrinology. For her thesis, she searched for a test to measure the corticotropin releasing factor (CRF). Leeman earned her Master's in medical science in 1954 and a Ph.D. in physiology in 1958. From 1958 to 1959, she was an instructor in the school's physiology department. Leeman had three children from a 1957 marriage. She was subsequently divorced.

From Harvard Medical School, Leeman moved on to Brandeis University, serving as a postdoctoral fellow in the neurochemistry training program from 1959 to 1962. She remained at Brandeis until 1971, becoming, in turn, a senior research associate, adjunct assistant professor, and assistant research professor in the Graduate Department of Biochemistry.

Isolates Substance P

During these years, Leeman continued work on corticotropin, a hormone used in the treatment of rheumatoid arthritis and rheumatic fever. In fact, it was while she was trying to purify corticotropin that Leeman made a chance finding that would determine the direction of her scientific career: she instead found a peptide that could stimulate the secretion of saliva. That chemical turned out to be substance P, which had been discovered in the 1930s, but had never been isolated. Leeman and her colleagues isolated and characterized the peptide.

Substance P is a transmitter that has many functions in the body. It is distributed throughout both the central and peripheral nervous systems and the spinal cord. Substance P is important in neuro-immune interactions and seems to play a role in inflammatory responses. During her work with substance P, Leeman discovered another peptide, neurotensin, which is involved in relaxation and contraction of the blood vessels. She and her colleagues isolated it and determined its amino acid sequence. Neurotensin is found in both the central nervous system and the gastrointestinal tract. It may be involved in psychiatric disorders and, possibly, regulation of the menstrual cycle.

Leeman continued and expanded her work on substance P and neurotensin throughout her professional career. From 1972 to 1980 she was assistant professor and then associate professor of physiology at Harvard Medical School. She served as professor of physiology at the University of Massachusetts Medical School from 1980 to 1982, and as director of the university's interdepartmental neuroscience program from 1984 to 1992. In 1992 Leeman became a professor of pharmacology and experimental therapeutics at Boston University School of Medicine. For her ground-breaking work, Leeman received many awards. In the 1960s she received the Research Career Development Award from the National Institutes of Health. In 1991 she became the first woman elected to the Physiology and Pharmacology Section of the National Academy of Sciences. In 1993, Eli Lilly and Company awarded her the 1993 Excellence in Science Award, citing Leeman as one of the founding scientists of neuroendocrinology.

SELECTED WRITINGS BY LEEMAN:

Periodicals

"The isolation of a new hypotensive peptide, neurotensin, from bovine hypothalami," with R. E. Carraway, *Journal of Biological Chemistry,* 248, 1973, pp. 6854–6861.
"Isolation of a sialagogic peptide from bovine hypothalamic tissue and its characterization as substance P," with M. M. Chang, *Journal of Biological Chemistry,* 245, 1970, pp. 4784–4790.

SOURCES:

"BUSM professor receives Excellence in Science Award," Boston University School of Medicine press release, April 9, 1993.
Leeman, Susan E., interviews with Devera Pine conducted February 4 and February 7, 1994.

—Sketch by Devera Pine

Carroll Leevy
1920-
American physician and nutritionist

A researcher, teacher, and administrator, Carroll Leevy established the first clinic in the world for alcoholics with liver disease. Internationally recognized for his research, Leevy defined alcoholic liver disease as an immune reaction to the effects of alcohol.

Born on October 13, 1920, in Columbia, South Carolina, to Isaac and Mary Leevy, Carroll Moton Leevy received his undergraduate degree at Fisk University in Nashville, Tennessee. He attended the University of Michigan Medical School, receiving his medical degree in 1944. Leevy began his postdoctoral training at the Jersey City Medical Center, serving first as intern, then as resident and chief resident physician from 1944 to 1948. He had two post doctoral fellowships, one at Banting-Best Institute of Medical Research at the University of Toronto, in 1952, and the other at Thorndike Memorial Laboratory at Harvard Medical School, from 1958 to 1959. During this same time, 1948 to 1959, Leevy was also the director of clinical investigation and the outpatient department at Jersey City Medical Center. During the latter of his two military services, he was staff officer and assistant chief of medicine at the U.S. Naval Hospital in St. Albans from 1954 to 1956.

Beginning in 1957, Leevy began teaching at the New Jersey Medical School (now affiliated with the University of Medicine and Dentistry of New Jersey), starting as associate professor of medicine. From 1975 to 1991 he was chair of the department of medicine and physician-in-chief of the University Hospital, and, in 1990, he was appointed director of the New Jersey Medical School Liver Center. In addition, in 1984, Leevy became the scientific director of the Sammy Davis, Jr. National Liver Institute.

Leevy estimated that he taught 3,160 graduates at New Jersey Medical School between 1960 and 1993. Between 1947 and 1993, he estimated that he trained more than 3,500 physicians in internal medicine, and more than 200 graduate physicians in the specialty of hepatology, nutrition, and gastroenterology.

Work Experience Prompts Liver Research and Establishment of Clinic

Leevy's experiences as an intern and resident at the Jersey City Medical Center pointed him toward researching alcoholic liver disease, he told Devera Pine in an interview. "We had huge numbers of cases

Carroll Leevy

in the Jersey Medical Center. That was the beginning," he said. "We had no good diagnostic and therapeutic measures for liver disease. People would come in and they would bleed, have fluid retention, and would die."

The overwhelming number of people with liver disease prompted Leevy to establish the first clinic for alcoholic liver disease in the Jersey Medical Center in 1948. "We helped develop and implement current methods of treatment," he told Pine. Leevy also began investigating the mechanisms of liver disease. He and his colleagues found that alcoholic liver disease is due to an immunologic reaction to a breakdown product of alcohol. Leevy considers this his most important contribution as a researcher. In addition, Leevy helped develop a technique to evaluate the liver's ability to repair itself. The technique can evaluate the effectiveness of various drugs in treating liver disease.

Throughout the course of his career, Leevy served on both national and international advisory panels. He was a member of the National Digestive Disease Advisory Board, the National Commission on Digestive Diseases, the Ad Hoc Committee on Liver Centers, and the Clinical Cancer Training Committee, all under the auspices of the National Institutes of Health (NIH). He was a consultant in gastroenterology and hepatology to the U.S. Food and Drug Administration, and a member of the World Health Organization's Committee on Chronic Liver

Disease. The honors he was awarded included the Distinguished Service Award, in 1991, from the American Association for the Study of Liver Diseases, and the Robert H. Williams Distinguished Chair of Medicine Award, in 1991, from the Association of Professors of Medicine.

In addition to being a member of many professional organizations, Leevy served as president of the American Association for the Study of Liver Diseases from 1967 to 1968. He was both vice chair and chair of the program committee, section on gastroenterology, of the American Medical Association.

Leevy lectured and wrote extensively, publishing books and more than 500 research papers related to his field. He received grants from the NIH, the Veterans Administration, and National Aeronautics and Space Association (NASA) for his research. Furthermore, Leevy holds two patents: one for a process and apparatus for evaluating liver disease; the other for a type of monoclonal antibody. In 1956 he married Ruth Barboza and subsequently had two daughters.

SELECTED WRITINGS BY LEEVY:

Books

Practical Diagnosis and Treatment of Liver Disease, Hoeber-Harper, 1957.
Liver Regeneration in Man, Charles C. Thomas, 1973.

Periodicals

(With R. Zetterman) "Immunologic Reactivity and Alcoholic Liver Disease," *Bulletin of the New York Academy of Medicine,* Volume 51, 1975, p.533.
(With C. B. Leevy) "Liver Disease of the Alcoholic," *Gastroenterology,* Volume 105, 1993, p.734.

SOURCES:

Leevy, Carroll, interview with Devera Pine conducted January 25, 1994.

—*Sketch by Devera Pine*

LaSalle D. Leffall, Jr.
1930-
American surgical oncologist

Surgical oncologist LaSalle D. Leffall, Jr. has worked to focus attention on the problem of high cancer death rates among minorities, especially African Americans. As the first black president of the American Cancer Society and as an educator at Howard University, Leffall has dedicated his career to educating both the medical profession and the lay public about cancer risks for minorities.

Leffall, the son of Martha (Jordan) Lefall and LaSalle Leffall, Sr., was born in Tallahassee, Florida, on May 22, 1930. He attended public school and was the valedictorian of his high school class, graduating in 1945. In 1948, he received a B.S., summa cum laude, from Florida A & M University. From there, Leffall enrolled in Howard University College of Medicine. Again, he achieved academic excellence, graduating first in his class and receiving his M.D. degree in 1952. Leffall's formal medical education continued for the next seven years. He was an intern at Homer G. Phillips Hospital in St. Louis and assistant resident in surgery at both D.C. General Hospital and Freedmen's Hospital, both in Washington, D.C. From 1957 to 1959, Leffall was a senior fellow in cancer surgery at Memorial Sloan-Kettering Cancer Center in New York. He decided to study at Sloan-Kettering because of the new frontiers posed by cancer surgery, Leffall stated in an interview with Devera Pine for *Notable Twentieth-Century Scientists.* "I thought surgery was the most dynamic field," he recalled. "Memorial Sloan-Kettering was using some of the most exciting techniques."

After one year as Chief of General Surgery in the U.S. Army Hospital in Munich (1960 to 1961), Leffall turned to a career in education, becoming an assistant professor at Howard University in 1962. Leffall continued at Howard, serving as assistant dean of the College of Medicine from 1964 to 1970. In 1970, he was appointed professor and chair of the Department of Surgery. "I have a very strong feeling for Howard University. If I had not been accepted there, I wouldn't be a physician and surgeon today," he said in his interview. "When I came along in 1948, predominantly white medical schools rarely accepted blacks." As a researcher, Leffall has focused on clinical studies of cancer of the breast, colorectum, head and neck. He has published more than 116 articles in various professional journals and forums.

In addition to his careers in medicine and education, Leffall has led an active professional life. Leffall became a diplomate of the American Board of

LaSalle D. Leffall, Jr.

Surgery in 1958 and a fellow of the American College of Surgeons in 1964. He was a consultant to the National Cancer Institute beginning in 1972 and a consultant to Walter Reed Army Medical Center beginning in 1971. In 1978 he became the first black president of the American Cancer Society. He used this national forum to emphasize the problems of cancer in minorities, holding the first conference on cancer among black Americans in February of 1979. "I have tried to point out the problems of lack of access to care and the increased death rate," he told Pine. In 1980, President Carter appointed him to a six-year term as a member of the National Cancer Advisory Board.

Leffall has lectured extensively and has served as visiting professor at more than 200 medical institutions. He has received many awards, including the St. George Medal and Citation, the highest divisional award of the American Cancer Society, and the Distinguished Volunteer Service Award from the Secretary of the U.S. Department of Health and Human Services. In 1987, M.D. Anderson Hospital and Tumor Institute in Houston established the Biennial LaSalle D. Leffall Jr. Award. Though Leffall told Pine that he was grateful for all the awards, he said he considers the ones he received from his students over the years "first among equals." In fact, along with his medical career, Leffall considers his teaching one of his most important accomplishments. The role of a teacher, he said, is "to inspire, to instruct, to stimulate, to stretch the imagination and

to expand the aspirations of others. It's an honor to be a teacher."

Leffall married Ruth McWilliams in 1956; the couple had one son.

SELECTED WRITINGS BY LEFFALL:

Books

"Claude H. Organ, Jr., M.D.," "The Howard University Department of Surgery and Freedman's Hospital," "Surgical Leaders and Role Models," *A Century of Black Surgeons, The U.S.A. Experience,* Transcript Press, 1987.

Periodicals

"Alarming Increase of the Cancer Mortality in the U.S. Black Population (1950–1967)," *Cancer,* April 1973, pp 736–768.

"Health Status of Black Americans," *The State of Black America,* National Urban League, Inc., 1990, p. 121.

"Access to Surgical Care in the Inner Cities: One Provider's Perspective," *Bulletin, American College of Surgeons,* April 1993, pp. 15–19.

SOURCES:

Other

Leffall, LaSalle D., Jr., interview with Devera Pine conducted February 3, 1994.

—Sketch by Devera Pine

Inge Lehmann
1888-1993
Danish geophysicist

Trained as a mathematician and an actuary, Danish geophysicist Inge Lehmann used painstaking analyses, measurements and observations of shock waves generated by earthquakes to propose in 1936 that the earth had a solid inner core. Throughout her long career which extended far beyond her official retirement in 1953, Lehmann conducted research in Europe and North America and was active in international scientific organizations including serving as the first president and a founder of the European Seismological Federation.

Lehmann was one of two daughters born to Alfred Georg Ludvig Lehmann, a University of Copenhagen professor of psychology, and Ida Sophie Torsleff. She was born on May 13, 1888. As a child, she attended and graduated from the first coeducational school in Denmark, an institution founded and run by Hanna Adler, the aunt of future Nobel Prize-winning physicist **Niels Bohr**. She began her university education by studying mathematics at the University of Copenhagen from 1907 to 1910. She continued her mathematical studies the following year at Cambridge University in England before returning to Denmark, where she worked as an actuary from 1912 to 1918. She also continued her formal education. In 1920 she earned her masters degree in mathematics from the University of Copenhagen and later studied mathematics at the University of Hamburg. In 1925 she began her career in seismology as a member of the Royal Danish Geodetic Institute and helped install the first seismographs at her Copenhagen office. "I was thrilled by the idea that these instruments could help us to explore the interior of the earth, and I began to read about it," she was quoted in a 1982 article published in the *Journal of Geological Education*. Lehmann later helped establish seismograph stations in Denmark and Greenland.

After further study with seismologists in France, Germany, Belgium and the Netherlands and after earning a master of science degree in geodesy from the University of Copenhagen in 1928, Lehmann was named chief of the Royal Danish Geodetic Institute. In that position, which she held until her retirement in 1953, she was Denmark's only seismologist for more than two decades. She was responsible for supervising the Denmark's seismology program, overseeing the operation of the seismograph stations in Denmark and Greenland and preparing the institute's bulletins.

Discovers Inner Core of the Earth

Despite this heavy work load, Lehmann still found time to explore scientific research. In 1936 she published her most significant finding, the discovery of the earth's inner core, under the simple title of "P." The letter P stood for three types of waves generated by Pacific earthquakes that Lehmann had been carefully observing through the planet for ten years. By studying the shock waves generated by earthquakes, recorded on seismographs as travel-time curves, she theorized that the earth has a smaller solid inner core. Within a few years, work by other scientists, including **Harold Jeffreys** and **Beno Gutenberg**, substantiated her findings.

Lehmann continued her research well after her retirement in 1953, exploring the nature of the planet's interior in Denmark, in Canada at the Dominion Observatory in Ottawa and in the United States at the University of California at Berkeley, the California Institute of Technology, and the Lamont Doherty Earth Observatory at Columbia University. She was a named a fellow of both the Royal Society of London and Edinburgh and was named to the Royal Danish Academy of Science and Letters and the Deutsche Geophysikalische Gesellschaft. In 1971 she was awarded the William Bowie Medal of the American Geophysical Union in recognition of her "outstanding contributions to fundamental geophysics and unselfish cooperation in research." She was also awarded honorary doctorates by the University of Copenhagen and Columbia University.

Lehmann remained single throughout her long and productive life. Her interests were not restricted to science. She was concerned with the poor in her native Denmark and the plight of European refugees. Travel in conjunction with her work also afforded her frequent opportunities to pursue two of her hobbies—visiting art galleries throughout Europe and the United States and the outdoors. Lehmann enjoyed hiking, mountain climbing and skiing. She died in 1993 at the age of 105.

SELECTED WRITINGS BY LEHMANN:

Periodicals

"P'," *Travaux Scientifiques,* Volume 14, 1936.

SOURCES:

Books

Bolt, Bruce A., *Inside the Earth,* W. H. Freeman, 1982, pp. 18–21.
Current Biography Yearbook, 1962, H. W. Wilson, 1962, pp. 250–252.

Periodicals

Rossbacher, Lisa A., "The Geologic Column," *Geotimes,* August, 1993, pp. 36.
EOS Transactions, American Geophysical Union, July, 1971, pp. 537–38.
Journal of Geological Education, Volume 30, 1982, pp. 291–92.

—*Sketch by Joel Schwarz*

Jean-Marie Lehn
1939-
French chemist

Jean-Marie Lehn shared the 1987 Nobel Prize in chemistry for his contributions to the field of supramolecular or host-guest chemistry, particularly for his development of the crown ethers known as a cryptands and his work on synthesizing artificial enzymes. His work in this area has numerous applications in medicine and industry and in chemical and biochemical research.

Jean-Marie Pierre Lehn was born to Pierre and Marie (Salomon) Lehn on September 30, 1939, in Rosheim, in the Alsace region of northeastern France. His father had an unusual career combination as both a baker and an organist. After completing a diverse curriculum of chemistry, classics, and philosophy at the Collège Freppel in 1957, Lehn continued his studies at the University of Strasbourg, where his attention was turned to organic chemistry by Guy Ourisson, one of his professors.

After earning his bachelor's degree in 1960, Lehn joined Ourisson as a researcher at the National Center for Scientific Research (CNRS) in France. During his six-year tenure there, he researched the chemical and physical properties of the enzymes used to synthesize vitamin A, and spent a year in the United States as a visiting professor at Harvard University, working with **Roald Hoffmann** on quantum mechanics and with **R. B. Woodward** on the composition of vitamin B12. He received his Ph.D. from the University of Strasbourg in 1963.

Lehn returned to the University of Strasbourg as an assistant professor of chemistry in 1966. By this time, he had already begun studies of the human nervous system in order to determine biological and chemical relationships within the human body and was making great strides in the area of physical organic chemistry. It was during this period that he coined the term "supramolecular chemistry," later called "host-guest chemistry." Lehn defined supramolecular chemistry as a process whereby molecules recognize one another and selectively connect or bond, though the movement occurs quickly and the structural bonding is not permanent. In 1969, Lehn accepted an associate professorship at the Université Louis Pasteur, which became a full professorship in 1970.

International Acclaim for Work in Supramolecular Chemistry

Several years earlier, the American chemist **Charles John Pedersen** had published the results of his research on molecules known as ethers, in which carbon and oxygen atoms are strung together to form a crown-like shape. He referred to these molecules as crown ethers. Pedersen's work in the early 1960s was quite astounding because it enabled him to achieve so many practical applications in his laboratory. The shape of the crown ether, he found, allowed it easily to capture, or bind with, a metal ion. By altering the ring of atoms, he could create designer crown ether molecules, or hosts, to capture specific ions, or guests.

Lehn expanded upon Pedersen's work by showing that crown ethers could be made three-dimensional by adding layers. The molecule now formed a cavity, or crypt, that increased the number of contact points to which the metal ions could adhere, thus making the crown ether more selective with regard to the type of molecule it would capture. Lehn called these structures cryptands. They resembled, he said, chemical "locks" that only particular molecular "keys" would fit. Concurrently, another American chemist, **Donald J. Cram**, was reporting significant findings in molecular selectivity. Cram and Lehn both discovered techniques for synthesizing crown ether molecules into artificial enzymes. Lehn, Pedersen and Cram shared the 1987 Nobel Prize in chemistry for their work in "elucidating mechanisms of molecular recognition, which are fundamental to enzymic catalysis, regulation, and transport." Through their combined efforts, they have made it possible to create synthetically molecules and enzymes with enormous pharmacological and research applications; one enzyme developed by Lehn, for instance, binds with the neurotransmitter acetylcholine. Because of this research, scientists have the capability of "caging" certain toxic materials, thus either rendering them harmless or making them easier to extract from soil or water. Host-guest chemistry is also useful in the purification of metals.

In 1965, Lehn married Sylvie Lederer, with whom he had two sons, David and Mathias. In addition to listening to music and traveling, Lehn enjoys playing the piano, carrying on the musical tradition of his father. In 1979, Lehn moved to Paris, where he became a professor of chemistry and chair of chemistry of molecular interactions at the Collège de France. Director of the laboratories in both Strasbourg and Paris, he has traveled internationally as a visiting professor and has received a number of awards, including the Paracelsus Prize in 1982, the von Humboldt Prize in 1983, and the Vermeil Medal of Paris in 1989, in addition to the Nobel Prize. He was made chevalier of the Ordre National du Mérite in 1976, chevalier of the Légion d'Honneur in 1983, and officer of the Légion d'Honneur in 1988. Lehn is recognized internationally for his work and has published numerous papers and chapters in books on the subject. He continues to build a distinguished career in chemistry.

SELECTED WRITINGS BY LEHN:

Books

Preparative Organic Chemistry, Springer-Verlag, 1982.

(Editor with C. W. Rees), *Molecular Semiconductors: Photoelectrical Properties and Solar Cells,* by J. Simon and J. J. André, Springer-Verlag, 1985.

(With B. Dietrich and P. Viout), *Macrocyclic Chemistry: Aspects of Organic and Inorganic Supramolecular Chemistry,* VCH, 1993.

SOURCES:

Books

Nobel Prize Winners, 1987–1991 Supplement, H. W. Wilson Co., 1992.

Periodicals

"Chemistry in the Image of Biology," *Science,* Volume 238, October, 1987, pp. 611–12.

"Chemistry Prize for Makers of Macromolecules," *Nature,* Volume 329, October 22, 1987, p. 662.

"Chemistry," *Scientific American,* Volume 257, December, 1987, p. 46.

"Winners of Nobels in Chemistry and Physics," *The New York Times Biographical Service,* Volume 18, number 7, October, 1987, p. 1042.

—*Sketch by Amy M. Punke*

Luis F. Leloir
1906-1987
French-born Argentine biochemist

Luis F. Leloir began a career in medicine but found himself drawn to the relatively more tractable problems posed by biochemistry. His early research involved investigations of fatty acids in the liver, which led to the discovery of antihypertensives. In a subsquent search for the "missing link" in the conversion of carbohydrates in the body into energy, Leloir discovered a group of substances called sugar nucleotides, which allowed him and others to determine the precise mechanism of energy conversion.

Luis F. Leloir

Leloir also discovered glycogen, which is synthesized along with nucleotides and is the major store of energy in animal cells. Leloir's work with sugar nucleotides won him the Nobel Prize in chemistry in 1970.

Luis Federico Leloir was born on September 6, 1906, in Paris, France. Leloir's grandparents on both sides were immigrants to Argentina from France and Spain. When they moved to Argentina they invested in land, which turned to considerable profit as cattle and crops took on great importance in Argentine industry. This money would serve Leloir well later, as it would allow him to follow a career solely in scientific research at a time when such opportunities were very scarce in Argentina.

Leloir's parents, Federico and Hortensia Aguirre Leloir, were in France in 1906 only for a visit, and returned to their home in Buenos Aires, Argentina, when Leloir was two years old. Federico Leloir was educated as a lawyer, though he never practiced in that field. The younger Leloir grew up in a house filled with books on a variety of topics. Later in his life Leloir maintained there was no specific reason for his foray into the field of science, as it was clearly not a family tradition. He described himself as ill-suited to a career in music, sports, politics, or law, but acknowledged that he had a tremendous capacity for teamwork. Leloir completed his primary and secondary education in Buenos Aires, and then enrolled at the University of Buenos Aires to study medicine. He graduated with a medical degree in 1932, followed by employment in the hospital of the university as an intern. He found medicine somewhat limited in terms of the treatment options available at the time, and had no confidence in his own ability to diagnose and treat his patients.

He decided to try a position in research at the Institute of Physiology, still at the university, to help develop new options in treatment for physicians and to work on a Ph.D. degree. He worked under **Bernardo Houssay**, a Nobel winner in 1947 in the area of adrenal gland research, and consequently developed an interest in biochemistry. His doctoral thesis was written on the influence of the adrenal glands on carbohydrate metabolism, and his thesis won the annual prize of the faculty for best thesis. Leloir's relationship with Houssay would last the rest of Houssay's life, and Leloir described him as an intellectual inspiration.

In 1936 Leloir left Argentina to spend a year in Cambridge, England, conducting postdoctoral work in enzyme research at the Biochemical Laboratory of Cambridge University. He then returned to Buenos Aires and began research on breakdown of fatty acids in the liver. Eventually, his work led to a collaborative discovery of the peptide hypertensin, so named by this group because of its vasoconstrictive action. Vasoconstriction is the constriction of blood vessels, which causes high blood pressure or hypertension. Another group of scientists at Eli Lilly, a pharmaceutical company in Indianapolis, made a similar discovery around the same time, and named their peptide angiotensin. Both groups used these different names for the same peptide for several years, fighting over which it should be called, until finally a compromise was reached. Today the peptide is known as angiotensin. Later, in 1946, Leloir and his group issued a book based on their research findings in this area called *Renal Hypertension*.

Seeks Research Opportunities in the United States

Though averse to political involvement, Leloir was affected by the Argentine government's decision in 1943 to dismiss Houssay from his position at the university. Houssay had innocently signed a letter that was interpreted as antigovernment, and the country's politics at the time were in a state of upheaval. Many others at the university resigned their positions in support of Houssay, and Leloir decided it would be a good time for him to work abroad. He had married Amelie Zuberbuhler in 1943; together they left for the United States with no positions secured. After a short time in New York City, the Leloirs settled in St. Louis, Missouri, where Leloir worked as a research assistant in a biochemistry laboratory at Washington University. Later he moved to the Enzyme Research Laboratory of the College of Physi-

cians and Surgeons of Columbia University in New York.

In 1945 Leloir returned to Argentina to work again under Houssay, who had been reinstated at the university. Leloir, though, had begun to hatch a plan to start a private research institute, and slowly began gathering the necessary team. Houssay was eventually removed from his post again, this time for being "over age," but Leloir had his team assembled, and finally received backing from Jaime Campomar. The owner of a textile firm, Campomar had expressed an interest to Houssay in sponsoring a research institute specifically in the area of biochemistry. Thus the Institute for Biochemical Investigations was begun.

The future of Leloir's institute was in question after Campomar died in 1957. In a bit of a last-ditch effort, Leloir applied to the National Institutes of Health in the United States for funding, and to his surprise obtained it. The institute continued to receive monies from the NIH for several years until rules for granting money to foreign applicants were changed. In 1958 the government of Argentina offered assistance as well, giving the institute a former girls' school for a new home. Further financial backing came a short while later after the formation of the Argentine National Research Council, and the institute became associated with the faculty of the University of Buenos Aires.

Scientists at this time were familiar with the idea that carbohydrates are broken down by the body into simpler sugars for energy. Beginning in the late 1940s, Leloir believed there was a "missing link" in the understanding of this process, and set out to find it. What he eventually discovered was a group of substances, now known as sugar nucleotides, that are responsible for the conversion into energy of sugars stored in the body. The discovery of these substances helped Leloir, among others, to determine specifically the process of carbohydrate conversion into energy. Leloir also found that a complex sugar called glycogen is synthesized with these sugar nucleotides, stored in the liver and muscles, and then broken down by the body into simpler glucose as energy is needed.

For his work with sugar nucleotides, Leloir was awarded the Nobel Prize in chemistry in 1970. He was only the third Argentine to receive the Nobel in any field, and the first in the area of chemistry. He instantly became a national hero, and was later honored as the subject on a postage stamp. Leloir was somewhat leery of the Nobel, telling *Newsweek* that his prize money would be spent on further research, "if I'm ever allowed to work again in the peace and quiet that I'm used to."

Leloir played a major role in the establishment of the Argentine Society for Biochemical Research as well as the Panamerican Association of Biochemical Sciences. Among his memberships were the National

Academy of Sciences (United States) and the American Academy of Arts and Sciences. He was elected to membership in the Royal Society of London in 1972, and to the French Academy of Sciences in 1978. In addition to the Nobel, he received prizes and honors from universities all over the globe, including the Gairdner Foundation Award in 1966 and honorary degrees from the Universities of Paris, Granada (Spain), and Tucumán (Argentina). In 1971 he was keynote speaker at a biochemistry symposium held in his honor.

Leloir was known to be courteous and accessible. He has been given credit for performing major scientific research with limited funding. He often used homemade apparatus and gadgets, and encouraged inventions for use in his laboratory. In one instance Leloir constructed makeshift gutters out of waterproof cardboard to protect the library in his research laboratory from a leaky roof. Leloir died on December 2, 1987, in Buenos Aires, leaving his wife, one daughter, and several grandchildren.

SELECTED WRITINGS BY LELOIR:

Books

(With Eduardo Braun-Menendez, Juan Carlos Fasciolo, and others) *Renal Hypertension,* translated by Lewis Dexter, C. C. Thomas, 1946.

Periodicals

(With J. M. Muñoz) "Fatty Acid Oxidation in the Liver," *Biochemistry Journal,* Volume 33, 1939, pp. 734–741.
"Far away and Long Ago," *Annual Review of Biochemistry,* Volume 52, 1983, pp. 1–15.

SOURCES:

Books

Glycosidic Linkage, Academic Press, 1972.
McGraw-Hill Modern Scientists and Engineers, McGraw-Hill, 1980.

Periodicals

Cabib, Enrico, "Research on Sugar Nucleotides Brings Honor to Argentinian Biochemist," *Science,* November 6, 1970.
"Divide and Honor," *Newsweek,* November 9, 1970, p. 100.
Paladini, Alejandro C., "Luis Federico Leloir," *FASEB Journal,* September, 1988, pp. 2751–2752.

"Plasmas, Magnets, and Sugars," *Time,* November 9, 1970.

—Sketch by Kimberlyn McGrail

Georges Lemaître
1894-1966
Belgian astronomer

Both a Catholic priest and a mathematical physicist, Georges Édouard Lemaître originated the "big bang" theory of the creation or evolution of the universe. The theory began with his deduction that if galaxies in the universe are now moving away from each other, they must once have been closer together. Lemaître proposed that all matter in the universe was once contained in what he called a "primeval atom" before being scattered, and radically changed, by a massive explosion. The theory has been called the greatest achievement of modern cosmology.

Lemaître was born July 17, 1894, in Charleroi, Belgium, into a deeply religious family. His father, Joseph Lemaître, had received a law degree but chose a career as a glassblower; after a fire, however, he moved to Brussels where he returned to practicing law. His mother was Marguerite Lannoy Lemaître. When he was only nine years old, Lemaître had already decided to become both a priest and a scientist. "There was nothing dramatic about it," he told the *New York Times Magazine.* "I was a good student, especially so in the dull, hard subjects like mathematics and fascinated with the smattering of knowledge I picked up in elementary school. So I naturally followed my bent ... exactly at the same time, in the same month as I remember it, I made up my mind to become a priest." Lemaître did not see a contradiction between these ambitions: "I was interested in truth from the standpoint of salvation, you see, as well as truth from the standpoint of scientific certainty." He entered the University of Lovain but he did not study physics; he graduated as a mining engineer in 1914.

When World War I broke out, Lemaître joined the Belgian Army and became an artillery officer. While in the army, he read *Electricite et optique* by **Henri Poincaré**, and the book made him reconsider his career as an engineer. At the end of the war, Lemaître returned to Louvain to study physics and mathematics. He finished his master's thesis, on the approximation of several real variables, in 1920.

Georges Lemaître

After receiving his master's degree, he studied for a time toward his doctorate, and then entered the seminary at Mailines, Belgium, in October 1920. He was ordained as a Roman Catholic priest in 1923. After his ordination, Lemaître won several fellowships that allowed him to study abroad. He spent 1924 studying solar physics at Cambridge University, where he first met and worked with astronomer **Arthur Eddington**. In 1925, Lemaître went to the United States, where he studied at Harvard University and the Massachusetts Institute of Technology (MIT). He focused his studies on the application of **Albert Einstein**'s theory of relativity to astronomy, and he received his doctorate from MIT in 1927. Lemaître than returned to Belgium to join the faculty at the University of Louvain.

During his time in England and the United States, Lemaître met and worked with some of the great astronomers of his time. Besides Eddington, he became acquainted with **Edwin Hubble**, **Harlow Shapley**, and **Vesto M. Slipher**. Slipher had been measuring the radial velocities of galaxies since 1912 and found that most seemed to be moving away from the Milky Way, our own galaxy. Hubble, too, observed that galaxies were moving away from each other. (In 1929, he would formulate Hubble's law, which states that the distance to a galaxy and the velocity at which is moving away are directly related.) Shapley, who like Hubble worked at the Mount Wilson Observatory in California, determined the size of the Milky Way and the sun's position within it.

These advances in astronomy, as well as others, contributed to Lemaître's examination of the theory of relativity.

Formulates the Big Bang Theory

One of the components of Einstein's original theory of relativity was the proposition that the universe was static and unchanging and yet could collapse if disturbed. He based this idea on a series of mathematical calculations, which he would later retract, calling them the "biggest blunder" of his career. But before Einstein realized his mistake, Lemaître had already begun to question the idea of a static universe, partly on the basis of what he had learned from the observations of American and English astronomers. In 1927 Lemaître published a paper entitled, "A Homogeneous Universe of Constant Mass and Increasing Radiation, Taking Account of the Radial Velocity of Extragalactic Nebulae." Lemaître argued that if all the galaxies in the universe were speeding away from each other, they had to have been at some point in the past closer together. He envisioned the matter and energy of the universe to have been wrapped up tightly in what he called a primeval atom. He pictured this "atom," or "egg" to be about thirty times the size of the sun but immeasurably dense.

Between twenty billion to sixty billion years ago, he believed, the egg burst in an explosion which threw matter and energy off in all directions. The expansion that began with this explosion continued until the universe was about a billion light-years wide. To explain the expansion, Lemaître postulated the existence of what he called cosmical repulsion. An antithesis to gravity, he speculated that cosmical repulsion grew stronger as objects became more distant from each other and thus kept the universe's expansion going. As a result of this explosion, Lemaître believed, the original density of matter had been reduced so greatly that simple atoms like hydrogen had been able to form larger, more complex atoms. In *Revue des Questions Scientifiques,* Lemaître wrote: "The atom world broke up into fragments, each fragment into still smaller pieces. . . . The evolution of the world can be compared to a display of fireworks that had just ended: some few red wisps, ashes, and smoke. Standing on a cooled cinder, we see the slow fading of the suns, and we try to recall the vanished brilliance of the origin of the worlds."

Lemaître did not realize that **Aleksandr Friedmann**, a Russian meteorologist and mathematician, had challenged Einstein's assumption of a static universe five years earlier. Friedmann pointed out that Einstein had erred in the calculations he used to devise his static universe, and he reached much the same conclusion Lemaître did about the origins of the universe. The work of Friedmann and Lemaître greatly simplified the calculations necessary for the theory of relativity, and Friedmann is considered a cofounder of the big bang theory.

When first published, Lemaître's theory was considered fantastic; the *New York Times* called it "highly romantic." It did, however, catch the eye and imagination of the great astronomer Eddington, whom Lemaître had met during his time at Cambridge. Eddington arranged for the paper to be published in the *Monthly Notices of the Royal Astronomical Society* in 1931. In December 1932, Lemaître explained his view of the development of the universe in a lecture at Mount Wilson Observatory in California. Einstein was in the audience. When Lemaître concluded, as quoted in *Catholic World*, Einstein stood up and said: "This is the most beautiful and satisfactory explanation of creation to which I have ever listened." The two theorists afterward developed a profound admiration for each other. Dutch astronomer **Willem de Sitter**, who had his own theory that held the universe was expansive but empty, concurred with Einstein: "There can be not the slightest doubt that Lemaître's theory is essentially true, and must be accepted as a very real and important step toward a better understanding of Nature."

Despite such praise, Lemaître's original theory lacked sufficient mathematical backing for widespread acceptance. Discoveries of cosmic rays during the early 1930s did lend weight to the theory, but it was not until 1946 when **George Gamow** provided much of the mathematical backing the original work had lacked, that the theory was taken seriously by most physicists. Gamow examined the big bang from just before it began, in theory, to just after it ended. He abandoned Lemaître's idea of cosmical repulsion and argued that the force of the initial explosion alone would be enough to make the universe continue to expand.

But in 1948, **Hermann Bondi** and **Thomas Gold** of Cambridge University suggested that there had been no bang, no creation event whatsoever. In what came to be known as the steady-state theory, Bondi and Gold argued that the universe had always existed and had never really changed. As galaxies moved out of our range of observation, new galaxies formed in the spaces in between, so the number of galaxies in view remained fairly constant. Among the supporters of the steady state theory was the astronomer **Fred Hoyle**, who did much to refine and popularize it.

The two theories remained rivals throughout the 1950s and on into the 1960s, but results from the use of radio astronomy effectively disproved the steady-state theory. Because light can take so long to travel across the great distances in space, what astronomers on earth study is actually light from stars as they existed thousands of millions of years ago. Using radio astronomy, **Martin Ryle** at Cambridge University showed that the distribution of distant galaxies is not the same as those closer to the earth in space and time, thus proving that the universe is changing. In 1965, the detection of cosmic microwave background radiation presented strong evidence that there had been a period of time when the universe was hot and dense—as it would have been immediately after the big bang. Although other theories continue to arise as scientists attempt to explain the beginning of the universe, Lemaître's theory with its attendant modifications is still the most widely accepted.

After 1927, Lemaître served as a professor of astrophysics at the University of Louvain, teaching and conducting research. Throughout his career he continued to refine his theory, but he also investigated such subjects as the three-body problem, calculating machines, and cosmic rays. He remained, throughout his life, active in the Catholic Church. He saw no conflict between his scientific work and his religious beliefs. He once said, as quoted in the *New York Times:* "All problems in life can be solved either by religion or science, but not by both combined." In an interview with the *New York Times Magazine,* he put much of the blame for the perception of a conflict on scientists: "Once scientists can grasp that the Bible does not purport to be a textbook of science, the old controversy between religion and science vanishes." He acknowledged, however, this is more difficult for some branches of science to do than others, but physicists and astronomers "have been religious men, with a few exceptions. The deeper they penetrated into the mystery of the universe, the deeper was their conviction that the power behind the stars and behind the electrons of atoms was one of law and goodness."

Lemaître was awarded the Prix Francqui in 1934. Einstein was one of his sponsors, and Eddington was among the judges. In 1935, Villanova University presented him with the Mendel Medal. That year, he also received an honorary degree from McGill University in Montreal. Lemaître died in Louvain, Belgium, on June 20, 1966. He was seventy-one years old. At the time of his death he was president of the Pontifical Academy of Sciences in Rome.

SELECTED WRITINGS BY LEMAÎTRE:

Books

A Homogeneous Universe of Constant Mass and Increasing Radiation, Taking Account of the Radial Velocity of Extragalactic Nebulae, 1927.
The Primeval Atom, Van Nostrand, 1950.

Periodicals

"The Big Bang Theory," *Monthly Notices of the Royal Astronomical Society,*1931.

SOURCES:

Books

Gamow, George, *The Creation of the Universe,* Viking Press, 1961.

Hartmann, William K., *Astronomy: The Cosmic Journey,* Wadsworth, 1987.

Jastrow, Robert, *God and the Astronomers,* Norton, 1978.

Moore, Patrick, *History of Astronomy,* Oldbourne, 1983.

Moore, *The Picture History of Astronomy,* Grossett & Dunlap, 1973.

Rival Theories of Cosmology, Oxford University Press, 1960.

Silk, James, *The Big Bang,* W. H. Freeman, 1980, pp. 20–26.

Periodicals

Aikman, Duncan, "Lemaître Follows Two Paths to Truth," *New York Times Magazine,* February 19, 1933, pp. 3, 18.

Cevasco, George A., "The Universe and Abbé Lemaître," *Catholic World,* June 1951, pp. 184–88.

"Earth's Age Given As 2 Billion Years," *New York Times,* July 24, 1933, p. 16.

"Finds No Conflict of Science, Religion," *New York Times,* December 11, 1932.

Physics Today, September, 1966, pp. 119–20.

Revue des Questions Scientifiques, November, 1931.

—*Sketch by F. C. Nicholson*

Philipp E. A. von Lenard
1862-1947

Hungarian-born German physicist

Philipp E. A. von Lenard was a brilliant experimental physicist who made important contributions to the study of the photoelectric effect, the characterization of cathode rays, the nature of phosphorescence, ionization potentials, and other phenomena. He was awarded the 1905 Nobel Prize in physics primarily for his work on cathode rays. He taught and carried on research at a number of German universities, including Heidelberg, Bonn, Breslau, and Kiel, as well as at the Technische Hochschule in Aachen. In spite of his gifts as an experimentalist, Lenard is also remembered as an anti-Semite and enthusiastic proponent of National Socialism. His unwillingness to embrace many of the new developments in science taking place in the 1920s and 1930s is thought to be at least partially due to his political feelings that these ideas were false pronouncements from "Jewish science." By the end of his life, Lenard had lost the personal respect and professional esteem of the great majority of his colleagues in the scientific community.

Philipp Eduard Anton von Lenard was born on June 7, 1862 in Pressburg, Hungary, now Bratislava, Slovakia. His father was Philipp von Lenard, a prosperous wine merchant, and his mother, the former Antonia Baumann. Young Philipp was expected to take over his father's business, but was not enthusiastic about that prospect. He attended technical universities in Budapest and Hungary, and spent a year working for his father before a trip to Germany rekindled his desire to study science. After attending the lectures of German chemist Robert Bunsen, Lenard decided to study physics at the University of Heidelberg in Germany, in the winter of 1883. He remained there for four semesters, spending two more semesters at the University of Berlin before returning to Heidelberg, where he received a doctorate with high honors in 1886.

Takes Posts at Heidelberg, Bonn, Breslau, Aachen, and Kiel

Lenard was asked to stay on at Heidelberg as assistant to his former teacher, Georg Quincke. During his three years in that position, Lenard began research on phosphorescence, a topic that was to occupy him off and on for the next four decades. He was later to discover that phosphorescence occurs as a result of impurities in a material and that it attains some maximum intensity for a given concentration of impurity. After leaving Heidelberg in 1890, Lenard visited England where he worked at the electromagnetic and engineering laboratories of the City and Guilds of the London Central Institution. He soon came to dislike the English, however, and left after six months to take a post at the University of Breslau. After only one semester there, he accepted an appointment as an assistant to Heinrich Hertz at the University of Bonn, where he began to experiment with cathode rays.

When Hertz died unexpectedly in 1894 at the age of thirty-six, Lenard became responsible for publishing Hertz's mammoth three-volume work *Gesammelte Werke,* interrupting his own research. He continued this task when he moved back to the University of Breslau in 1894 to become associate professor of physics. Once more, he remained at Breslau only briefly before taking consecutive posts at the Technische Hochschule in Aachen (1895–96) and the University of Heidelberg (1896–98). Finally, in

1898, he was appointed professor of physics and director of the physics laboratory at the University of Kiel, where he would remain for nine years.

Makes Important Discoveries about Cathode Rays and the Photoelectric Effect

In the years prior to 1914, Lenard made his most important scientific discoveries, particularly those relating to his studies of cathode rays and the photoelectric effect. Research on the former had been inspired by William Crookes's 1879 discovery of cathode rays, beams of charged particles produced during the discharge of electricity in vacuum tubes. Lenard was interested (as were other researchers) in finding a way to study cathode rays outside of vacuum tubes. Based on Hertz' discovery that cathode rays could permeate thin metal sheets, Lenard found, in 1892, that cathode rays can be made to pass out of a vacuum tube through a thin aluminum window. Using this arrangement, Lenard was able to make a number of observations regarding the properties of cathode rays.

As a result of these studies, Lenard came to the conclusion that matter—and, therefore, the atoms of which matter consists—is largely empty space. He suggested that an atom consists of neutral pairs of dynamids, one positively charged and the other negatively charged. Though incorrect, this concept presaged the nuclear model of the atom developed by **Ernest Rutherford** a decade later. It was for his work on cathode rays that Lenard was awarded the 1905 Nobel Prize in physics.

During the same period, Lenard also studied the photoelectric effect, the phenomenon that occurs when a beam of light strikes a metal plate, resulting in the emission of electrons from the plate. Lenard made the interesting discovery that the velocity of electrons emitted during this process was effected by the wavelength of the incident light, and that an increase in that light's intensity increased the number of electrons emitted, but not their speed. He was unable to explain this result, an anomaly unpredictable with the laws of classical physics. In fact, it was not until **Albert Einstein** applied the principles of quantum theory to this phenomenon that Lenard's results were correctly interpreted, an accomplishment that won for Einstein the 1921 Nobel Prize in physics.

Lenard was an enormously complex individual about whom a great deal has been written. He experienced a number of personal disillusionments, as when he failed to discover X rays only a short time before his countryman, **Wilhelm Conrad Röntgen**, did so. This disappointment was especially hard on Lenard since he had made substantial contributions to the theoretical and experimental aspects of Röntgen's discovery, contributions that Röntgen never acknowledged.

As Lenard grew older, he began to develop profound anti-Semitic feelings. In his unpublished autobiography, for example, quoted in Alan D. Beyerchen's *Scientists under Hitler: Politics and the Physics Community in the Third Reich,* Lenard describes the theory of relativity as "a Jewish fraud, which one could have suspected from the first with more racial knowledge than was then disseminated, since its originator Einstein was a Jew." Ultimately, Lenard rejected the traditional notion that science is an international activity that transcends national boundaries. Instead, he wrote in his textbook on experimental physics, *Deutsche Physik* (German Physics), "In reality, science, like everything man produces, is racially determined, determined by blood."

Before long, Lenard became one of the leaders of Aryan physics, an attempt to keep science pure of Jewish and other foreign influences, and he enthusiastically supported Adolf Hitler and his political agenda. When Hitler was named chancellor in 1933, Lenard wrote to him, offering his skills as a scientific advisor while pointing out how badly the nation's university system needed cleansing of Jewish influences.

In the decade after Hitler's ascent to power, Lenard was constantly involved in power struggles aimed at gaining control of the nation's scientific establishment, though, in his early seventies by then, he was probably too old to make many substantive contributions to the Nazi regime. In addition, he was defeated at nearly every turn by less able, lesser known scientific figures with more important contacts to inner circles of Nazi politics. Instead, he was given a number of awards and honorary appointments, such as the Eagle Shield of the Reich and election to the Executive Committee of the German Research Association. He survived the war, but was expelled from his post at the University of Heidelberg by Allied officials in 1945. After this disgrace, he settled in the village of Messelhausen, close to Heidelberg, where he died on May 20, 1947. Lenard had been married in 1897 to Katherine Schlehner. The one child of whom we know, Werner, died in February 1922, due to malnutrition brought on by wartime conditions in World War I.

SELECTED WRITINGS BY LENARD:

Books

Über Kathodensthralen, J. A. Barth, 1906.
Über Äther und Materie, C. Winter, 1911.
Über Relativitatsprinzip, Äther, Gravitation, S. Hirzel, 1920.
Grosse Naturforscher: Eine Geschichte der Naturforschung in Lebensbeschreibungen, Münich, 1929.

SOURCES:

Books

Beyerchen, Alan D., *Scientists under Hitler: Politics and the Physics Community in the Third Reich,* Yale University Press, 1977, pp. 79–102.

Heathcote, Niels H. de V., *Nobel Prize Winners in Physics, 1901–1950,* Henry Schuman, 1953, pp. 34–40.

Nobel Prize Winners, H. W. Wilson, 1987, pp. 620–623.

Weber, Robert L., *Pioneers of Science: Nobel Prize Winners in Physics,* American Institute of Physics, 1980, pp. 26–28.

—*Sketch by David E. Newton*

Aldo Leopold

Aldo Leopold
1886-1948
American conservationist

Aldo Leopold was an early environmentalist who laid the groundwork for many of the conservation laws and policies in place today. His 1933 book, *Game Management,* has guided generations of biologists in protecting North America's wildlife. Leopold's collection of essays, published posthumously in 1949 as *A Sand County Almanac, and Sketches Here and There,* presents his thoughts and ideas about nature and the interdependency of life.

Born in Burlington, Iowa, on January 11, 1886, Leopold developed an early appreciation for the outdoors from his father, Carl Leopold. As a boy, Leopold learned how to hunt and read tracks left by wild animals, a practice he continued throughout his life and passed on to his wildlife management students. Leopold's father also introduced him to the writings of the American authors Henry David Thoreau, Jack London, Stewart Edward White, and Ernest Thompson Seton. His mother, Clara Starker Leopold, was a homemaker who instilled in her son a taste for literature, philosophy, and poetry.

Leopold graduated from Yale University's Sheffield Scientific School in 1908, then studied for a year at Yale's newly-founded school of forestry. The school espoused the conservation philosophy of **Gifford Pinchot**, a Yale graduate and benefactor who in 1898 had become the chief of the United States Department of Agriculture's Division of Forestry (a forerunner to the United States Forest Service). Pinchot supported what is known as the utilitarian approach to conservation—a view which held that people have the right to use natural resources wisely—and he believed that forests should not be set aside as reserves but maintained to produce timber indefinitely. Like his Yale colleagues, Leopold accepted Pinchot's philosophy, but he kept his mind open to insights that in a few years would pit him against the Forest Service chief.

In 1909, Leopold went to work for the Forest Service as a ranger in a district that included territories which are now the states of New Mexico and Arizona. He climbed the ranks quickly, becoming deputy supervisor and then supervisor of Carson National Forest, then assistant district forester at Albuquerque, New Mexico, in 1913. While in New Mexico, Leopold met Estella Bergere, a somewhat shy, slim, athletic woman from Santa Fe who shared his love for the outdoors. They were married in Santa Fe on October 9, 1912. All five of their children would eventually follow Leopold to careers in science.

Promotes Controversial Conservation Ethic

The conservation ethic that defined Leopold's career began to take shape as early as 1915, in a game handbook he wrote for forest rangers and officers. Leopold believed that the preservation of nature had an intrinsic value, both ethical and aesthetic. His ideas contrasted with conventional thinking of the day; Pinchot's philosophy of "wise use" and other conservation theories viewed the value of game and nature itself as purely economic.

That same year, Leopold organized Albuquerque sportsmen interested in protecting wildlife into a game protection association. To reach the members, he established a newsletter called *The Pine Cone.* Leopold became secretary of the New Mexico Game Protection Association in 1916, and he gave the organization a powerful voice in state politics. The issue he emphasized most strongly during his tenure was the protection of big game, which he believed could be facilitated by taking the choice of a state game warden away from politicians. Big game was disappearing, he argued, because the warden failed to enforce game laws. The issue became so popular that both New Mexico gubernatorial candidates pledged their support for it. The winner, Ezequiel de Baca, later broke his promise and appointed an inept game warden, but he died before his candidate could be confirmed. His successor appointed the association's choice.

In the summer of 1918, Leopold organized a conference to promote the draining of the Rio Grande to cultivate farmland. Years later, however, he viewed wetlands drainage in a different light, considering it destructive to wildlife habitat. Leopold remained politically active throughout his career, although not as strongly as during his years in Albuquerque.

Leopold's innovative ideas about conservation nearly cost him his job as assistant district forester in charge of operations in Albuquerque. Yet he ignored the opposition and launched a vigorous campaign to preserve large, ecologically sound regions. He promoted his philosophy in a series of articles directed at different audiences—sportsmen, fellow foresters, citizen conservationists, economists, and the general public.

Persuades Government to Designate First Wilderness Reserve

His conservation campaign eventually succeeded. In 1924, the United States Forest Service set aside a half million acres of the Gila Wilderness in New Mexico; this was the first officially designated wilderness reserve on federal land. That same year, Leopold left field work to become the associate director of the United States Forest Products Laboratory in Madison, Wisconsin. Leopold left the Forest Service in 1928 to become a private forestry and wildlife consultant. In 1931, he was awarded *Outdoor Life*'s gold medal for his conservation efforts, an award which is given annually to one conservationist from the east and another from the west.

Leopold brought his famous "conservation ethic" to the forefront in 1933, with the publication of *Game Management,* considered to be his most impor-tant work. Here, Leopold argued that people should see the environment as a community for all life and not as an economic commodity to be exploited. His arguments for a conservation ethic influenced the development of several federal wildlife conservation laws during his lifetime, including the 1934 Fish and Wildlife Coordination Act. But his ideas had their greatest influences two and three decades after his death, as national concern about the environment increased. His work shaped the landmark 1969 National Environmental Policy Act, which required the federal government to consider the environmental impact of its development plans. The Endangered Species Act of 1973 is also indebted to Leopold's teachings; this act recognized the need to conserve the ecosystem of endangered plants and animals. Other acts influenced by Leopold include the Forest and Rangelands Renewable Resources Planning Act of 1974, the National Forest Management Act of 1976, and the Federal Land Policy and Management Act of 1976. All of these focused on preserving ecosystems, rather than individual species.

Appointed First Professor of Wildlife Management

In 1933, the same year *Game Management* was published, the University of Wisconsin hired Leopold to fill the first professorship in wildlife management ever created at a university. It was a position Leopold held until his death. Leopold and his students developed the "inversity principle," which holds that the average production of a breeding population decreases as the number of individuals increases. He particularly appreciated the skills textbooks could not teach and tried to instill in his students the ability to "read the landscape" and "read sign" of wild creatures. One of Leopold's former students, Robert A. McCabe, recalled in *Science* that Leopold "had a way of looking at a landscape and telling you its history and its future fifty years hence."

From his academic post, Leopold played a leading role in several environmental organizations. In 1934, he was named to President Franklin D. Roosevelt's Special Committee on Wild Life Restoration. He became a director of the Audubon Society the following year, as well as a founder of the Wilderness Society. In 1947, Leopold was elected honorary vice president of the American Forestry Association and president of the Ecological Society of America. That same year, the newly formed Conservation Foundation appointed Leopold to its advisory council.

In 1934, Leopold bought an abandoned farm on the Wisconsin River (fifty miles north of Madison) where he wrote a series of poetic essays, inspired by the seasonal changes in the wildlife. Eventually, the essays would be collected and published after Leopold's death as *A Sand County Almanac* in 1949.

Month by month, Leopold recorded his observations of nature's ways in his simple, non-scientific prose.

It was on his farmland that Leopold died of a heart attack on April 21, 1948, while battling a brush fire at a neighbor's farm. He was put to rest where his life had begun, in Burlington, Iowa, overlooking the Mississippi River.

SELECTED WRITINGS BY LEOPOLD:

Books

Game Management, Scribner's, 1933.
A Sand County Almanac, and Sketches Here and There, Oxford University Press, 1949.

Periodicals

"The River of the Mother of God," *Wilderness*, Spring, 1991, pp. 19–26.

SOURCES:

Books

Meine, Curt, *Aldo Leopold, His Life and Work*, The University of Wisconsin Press, 1988.
Seed, John, and others, *Thinking Like a Mountain: Toward a Council of All Beings*, New Society Publishers, 1988.

Periodicals

Carter, Luther J., "The Leopolds: A Family of Naturalists," *Science*, March 7, 1980, pp. 1051–1055.

—*Sketch by Cynthia Washam*

Estella Bergere Leopold
1927-

American paleoecologist

Estella Bergere Leopold has never seen most of the plants she studies; they died millions of years ago. But Leopold has discovered what they looked like, how they were nourished, and how they reproduced, just by looking at the fossils of their spores,

seeds, and leaves. The American scientist is known as one of the leading authorities on paleoecology, the study of prehistoric organisms and their environments. In an interview with contributor Cynthia Washam, Leopold explained her work: "We compare assemblages of pollen and spores as they appear on the landscape today with those we find in rocks for a particular time period, and try to get the idea of the landscape and climate represented by the fossils. The fossils are probably the most important evidence of environments of the past. You put all this together and get a picture of past landscapes."

Studying landscapes to recreate their pasts is something Leopold has been doing since childhood. Although she was born in Madison, Wisconsin, on January 8, 1927, her most cherished memories are of the weekends spent on the family farm fifty miles north of her home. There, the budding scientist learned to "read signs" of wildlife from her father, the famous writer and conservationist, **Aldo Leopold**. The elder Leopold preserved his memories of the farm for generations of naturalists through his popular book, *A Sand County Almanac*.

Leopold also taught his children the value of conservation. Much of their time at the farm was spent planting tree seedlings and restoring an old corn field back to the tall-grass prairie it was meant to be. Leopold's mother, Estella Bergere Leopold, was a homemaker who shared her husband's love for the outdoors. All five of the Leopold children pursued careers in science. Estella and brothers Starker and Luna achieved an American record when all three were elected to the prestigious National Academy of Sciences.

Leopold earned her bachelor's degree in botany in 1948 at the University of Wisconsin at Madison, where her father had taught wildlife management. Two years later, she received her master's degree in botany from the University of California at Berkeley. She had been accepted into the doctoral program at the University of California at Los Angeles, but changed her plans when she heard that the professors there were particularly hard on female students. A colleague persuaded her to study at Yale, where she was welcomed by **George Evelyn Hutchinson** and other acclaimed ecologists. Although she was the only female graduate studying science, Leopold felt comfortable at Yale. There, the young botanist developed her interest in paleoecology while studying ice-age environments in Connecticut. Leopold earned her Ph.D. in 1955. Her dream was to teach, but she felt intimidated by the male competition and settled for the security of government work.

Discovered Patterns of Evolution in Rocky Mountain Fossils

She had a distinguished, twenty-one-year career as a research paleobiologist for the U.S. Geological

Survey in Denver, Colorado. There, Leopold dug into the strata of the Rocky Mountains to reconstruct the evolution of forests over the past 60 million years. Her research revealed that patterns of evolution were influenced by changes in landscape and climate. Extinction and evolution are highest in the middle of the continent, where seasonal climate changes are greatest, Leopold concluded. Coastal areas, with their more moderate climates, are able to sustain older species, such as the giant redwood. Leopold earned several grants and awards for her work, including National Science Foundation Travel Grants to Spain, Poland, England, and the former Soviet Union. In 1974 she was honored for her research by election to the National Academy of Sciences.

Like her late father, Leopold championed conservation. She served on the national boards of the Environmental Defense Fund, the National Audubon Society, and The Nature Conservancy and Friends of the Earth. The Colorado Wildlife Federation in 1969 named her Conservationist of the Year. Seven years later, she received the Keep Colorado Beautiful award.

In 1967 Leopold finally realized her dream of teaching, when she was hired as an adjunct professor at the University of Colorado. She held that position until 1976, when she retired from the U.S. Geological Survey to direct the Quaternary Research Center at the University of Washington in Seattle. She stepped down from that post in 1982 and has remained with the university as a professor of botany. Leopold taught several botany, forestry, and paleoecology courses while continuing her research on past environments. In 1984 she was chosen as a fellow of the Geological Society of America. She earned fellowship to the American Association for the Advancement of Science in 1980 and 1986 and was elected to the American Academy of Arts and Sciences in 1992.

In 1976 Leopold took up an avocation in editing as associate editor of the scholarly journal, *Quaternary Research.* She left that post in 1983, but has remained on the editorial board ever since. In 1990 she joined the editorial board of *Quaternary International.* By 1994, Leopold was considering retirement. She hoped to spend her retirement years as her father had, writing about what she has learned in a style laymen would understand and enjoy. "I want to write a book," she told contributor Washam, "*The Origin of Modern Flora.*"

SELECTED WRITINGS BY LEOPOLD:

Books

"Ecological Requirements of the Wilderness Act," in *Wilderness and the Quality of Life,* Sierra Club Books, 1969.

Periodicals

"Abrupt Uplift within the Past 1700 Years at Southern Puget Sound, Washington," *Science,* December 4, 1992, p. 1611–23.

SOURCES:

Books

Bellamy, David, *Bellamy's New World,* British Broadcasting Corporation, 1983.
Bostick, P.E., "Paleoecology," *Magill's Survey of Science,* Volume 5, Salem Press, 1991, pp. 2037–43.
Leopold, Aldo, *A Sand County Almanac,* original edition, 1949, Oxford University Press, 1966.
McGraw-Hill Encyclopedia of Science & Technology, Volume 13, McGraw-Hill Book Company, 1987, pp. 37–44.

Other

Leopold, Estella B., interview with Cynthia Washam conducted January 18, 1994.

—Sketch by Cynthia Washam

Luna Leopold
1915-
American geologist, hydrologist, and meteorologist

Luna Leopold is the foremost authority in the field of hydrology, but his scientific education also includes the study of botany and climatology. Leopold is considered to be one of the first scientists to be educated in the field of environmental conservation, and his career has been distinguished by his active influence in scientific ethics and public policy in the conservation field. His special area of expertise has been the study of the formation and flow of rivers. Leopold is professor emeritus of geology and landscape architecture at the University of California at Berkeley. Previously, he was Chief Hydrologist and then Senior Research Hydrologist with the U.S. Geological Survey. He was also the first hydrologist to be elected to the National Academy of Sciences, and he has served as President of the Geological Society of America.

Luna Bergere Leopold was born in Albuquerque, New Mexico, on October 8, 1915, to Aldo Leopold and Estella Bergere. Aldo Leopold was a professor and one of the advocates of early environmentalism in the United States. Leopold obtained a B.S. degree in civil engineering at the University of California in 1936. He then spent a year studying at the University of Wisconsin, where he explored such subjects as botany, ecology, geology and climatology. After a year with the United States Soil Conservation Service in Albuquerque, he enrolled at Harvard University for a year of graduate studies in geology in 1937.

Leopold then returned to work with the Soil Conservation Service for four more years. Following a year with the U.S. Army Corps of Engineers, Leopold became a United States Army private. He achieved the rank of second lieutenant and was an officer instructor for cadets in meteorology, which he taught while completing his M.A. in physics-meteorology. He received the degree in 1944. Leopold then fulfilled an assignment by the Air Force as commanding officer of the Research Weather Station at the University of California at Los Angeles, studying the meteorological facets of air pollution in the Los Angeles area. In 1946 Leopold made a brief excursion into what would later become the primary focus of his career, starting up a research laboratory for the study of sediment in western rivers with the United States Bureau of Reclamation.

In 1947 Leopold began his only journey into private enterprise, working as chief research meteorologist for the Pineapple Research Institute and the Hawaiian Sugar Planters Association Experiment Station in Honolulu. During his tenure there, he developed a short-range weather forecasting capability for the sugar and pineapple industries. Leopold continued his research on the hydrology of New Mexico and Arizona while in Hawaii, which prompted a colleague at Harvard to invite Leopold to finish his doctoral studies at the university. He received his Ph.D in geology from Harvard in 1950.

Develops Theory of Stream Hydraulics

Leopold's long relationship with the U.S. Geological Survey began in 1950, when he joined the staff as a senior engineer. He was promoted to Chief Hydraulic Engineer in 1956, and in 1960 he became Chief Hydrologist. Six years later, he was promoted to the position of Senior Research Hydrologist. Almost immediately upon joining the Geological Survey, Leopold's study of the flow of streams intensified, and he developed a theory of the hydraulics of river flow under evolving conditions of climate, vegetation and runoff. He used his interdisciplinary background to quantify the development of stream channels, defining the relationship between channel size parameters and sediment load within a river. Scientific opinion at

the time held that the path of a stream is determined by its sediment load. Leopold's theory, now widely accepted, proposed that the water of a river or stream will seek to travel through the landscape along a path that involves the smallest and most uniform expenditure of energy possible. In his words, "A river's course is a sequence of curves that lessens its erosive force." Geology, soil, vegetation, and climate all play a role in determining what the "ideal" course of a river would be. Although Leopold conceded that there are no rivers that had "achieved" this goal of minimal, most uniform energy expenditure, he said that all rivers work their way towards the best possible path. Leopold also found that the wavelength of the meanders (that is, the tightness of the curves) of a river running through a relatively flat landscape correlated strongly with the river's width. Leopold wrote a landmark paper in which he compared the pattern of tree branches to that of river flows.

Involvement with Environmental Movement

During his years at the Geological Survey, Leopold became increasingly concerned with resource management in the United States. He had been an active member of the Sierra Club for a long time, but in 1968 he accepted a seat on the Board of Directors of that organization. He advocated reform in the federal resource administration and pushed for a reorganization of the proliferating public agencies which oversee water use, deploring their dissociation from one another and their indebtedness to special interest groups, including agribusiness.

In 1973 Leopold left the Geological Survey to become professor of geology and landscape architecture at the University of California at Berkeley, where he is now emeritus professor. Since then he has worked to sway public opinion on environmental issues. In a lecture delivered to the Water, Science and Technology Board of the U.S. National Academy of Sciences in 1990, Leopold said his conservation ethics were based upon "the unwritten gut feeling that the resources of the planet and the nation are worthy of husbandry—indeed, are essential to our long-term well-being." He noted in the same lecture that another central environmental concern is equity, "a dedication to fairness, a desire to consider various interests and treat all with some measure of equality. We see all around us a shocking lack of evenhandedness, the pressure of special interests, and the bending under that pressure."

Leopold maintains that policy decisions in the area of water management and conservation must preserve "the integrity of the hydrologic continuum" and the effective operation of drainage basins to maintain a balance among the geological processes that support the environment. He is critical of the unchecked use of water for irrigation, which accounts for some eighty to ninety percent of total water use, citing Geological Survey findings that water loss due to seepage amounts to as much as one third of water actually used in agriculture. He also deplores the fact that one third to one half of all irrigated land is used for surplus crops. Leopold points out that present agricultural practices are not sustainable, since they are destroying or depleting renewable resources. He calls for stronger pro-conservation leadership from government, improvement of water engineering practices, and the need to develop an ethical perspective from which the scientific community, as well as government, should work.

The honors and recognition received by Leopold include the Kirk Bryan Award of the Geological Society of America (1958); the Veth Medal of the Royal Netherlands Geographical Society (1963); the Cullum Medal of the American Geographical Society (1965); the Distinguished Service Medal of the U.S. Department of the Interior (1960); and the Rockefeller Public Service Award (1966). In addition to being elected to the National Academy of Sciences, Leopold was elected to the American Academy of Arts and Sciences in 1969, and the American Philosophical Society in 1971. He served as president of the Geological Society of America in 1972. Leopold authored and coauthored several books on geomorphology and water and environmental planning, as well as publishing well over a hundred scientific papers. Leopold married Carolyn Clugston in 1940 and had a son and a daughter with her. He was divorced in 1973 and married Barbara Beck Nelson the same year.

SELECTED WRITINGS BY LEOPOLD:

Books

(With Thomas Maddock, Jr.) *The Flood Control Controversy,* Ronald, 1954.
(With W. B. Langbein) *A Primer on Water,* U.S. Government Printing Office, 1960, enlarged edition by Leopold published as *Water: a Primer,* W. H. Freeman, 1974.
(Editor) *Round River: From the Journals of Aldo Leopold,* Oxford University Press, 1972.
(With Thomas Dunne) *Water in Environmental Planning,* W. H. Freeman, 1978.

Periodicals

"Ethos, Equity and the Water Resource—The 1990 Abel Wolman Distinguished Lecture," *Environment,* March, 1990, pp. 17–41.

SOURCES:

Books

National Leaders of American Conservation, Smithsonian Institution Press, 1985.

　　　　　　　　　　　　—Sketch by Karen Withem

William Alexander Lester, Jr.
1937-
American chemist

William Alexander Lester, Jr. has had a distinguished career in research, teaching, and administration. As the associate dean of the University of California at Berkeley's College of Chemistry as well as faculty senior scientist at Lawrence Berkeley Laboratory, he has long been at the forefront of molecular collision theory—a field which seeks to explain and predict the essential properties of individual molecules and their effects on each other. Developing the computational methods to accomplish this has also involved him in the most current issues surrounding high-performance computing. Lester has also directed and organized the nation's first unified effort at conducting research in chemistry using computational methods.

Lester was born in Chicago, Illinois, on April 24, 1937, to William and Elizabeth Clark Lester. He received his bachelor's degree in chemistry from the University of Chicago in 1958 and his master's degree in chemistry from the university a year later. For a year he did postgraduate work at Washington University in St. Louis, Missouri, but received his Ph.D. in chemistry in 1964 from the Catholic University of America in Washington, DC. Lester began his professional career as a theoretical physical chemist at the National Bureau of Standards in 1961. In 1964 he became research associate and assistant director of the Theoretical Chemistry Institute of the University of Wisconsin, Madison. In 1968 Lester joined the staff of the IBM Research Laboratory at San Jose, California, and conducted research in quantum chemistry and molecular collisions. His studies on molecular collisions helped to explain such everyday phenomena as combustion, sound propagation, and atmospheric reactions. This research also provided the basis for understanding in microscopic detail the chemical reactions that take place during those processes. In 1975 Lester moved to Yorktown Heights, New York, to join the IBM T.J. Watson Research

Center, where he became director of research on the planning staff of the vice president. A year later he returned to California to manage the molecular interactions group at the IBM laboratory in San Jose.

In 1978 Lester was chosen to be the director of the National Resource for Computation in Chemistry (NRCC). Located at the University of California's Lawrence Berkeley Laboratory, this new unit was dedicated to the development of new computational methods for chemists. He also assumed the position of associate director and senior staff scientist at the Lawrence Berkeley Laboratory that year. In 1981 he became professor of chemistry at the University of California, Berkeley, and faculty senior scientist at the Materials and Molecular Research Division at Lawrence. When he became associate dean of the College of Chemistry at Berkeley in 1991, he remained as faculty senior scientist at Lawrence.

In addition to his research, Lester has edited the proceedings of a major conference and served on the editorial board of the *Journal of Physical Chemistry* (1979–1981), *International Journal of Quantum Chemistry* (1979–1987), *Journal of Computational Chemistry* (1980–1987), and *Computer Physics Communications* (1981–1986). Besides extensive service on governmental advisory committees and national and international panels, he chaired the Gordon Conference on Atomic and Molecular Interactions in 1978. In 1993 he became a member of the National Science Foundation's Blue Ribbon Panel on High Performance Computing.

Among the many honors and awards Lester has received is the IBM Outstanding Contribution Award in 1974. He also received the Percy L. Julian Award in Pure or Applied Research in 1979 and the Outstanding Teacher Award in 1986, both given by the National Organization of Black Chemists and Chemical Engineers; he also won the Catholic University of America Alumni Achievement Award in Science in 1983. He is a fellow of the American Association for the Advancement of Science, the American Physical Society, and a member of the American Chemical Society. He married Rochelle Diane Reed in 1959; they have two children.

SELECTED WRITINGS BY LESTER:

Books

(Editor) *Proceedings of the Conference on Potential Energy Surfaces in Chemistry,* 1971.

SOURCES:

Books

Sammons, Vivian O., *Blacks in Science and Medicine,* Hemisphere Publishing, 1990, p. 152.

—*Sketch by Leonard C. Bruno*

Tullio Levi-Civita
1873-1941
Italian mathematician

Tullio Levi-Civita's research spanned the gap between pure and applied mathematics. He and his colleagues recognized the importance of **Albert Einstein**'s theories of relativity almost immediately after their publication in 1905; in turn they provided the mathematical tools for the extension to the general theory of relativity. Levi-Civita and his mentor Gregorio Ricci-Curbastro had been working on an "absolute" differential calculus, leading to a paper in 1900 that provided an essential part of the mathematical language of relativity. A 1915 correspondence between Levi-Civita and Einstein led to Levi-Civita's extension of the notion of parallel lines to curved space and to Einstein's ten gravitational field equations.

Levi-Civita was born in Padua, Italy, on March 29, 1873. From his mother and father, Bice Lattis and Giaccomo Levi-Civita, he inherited both wealth and politically liberal tendencies. Giaccomo's career as a lawyer led him to serve for a number of years as mayor of Padua, and in 1908 he became a senator of the Kingdom of Italy. Although he encouraged his son to enter the legal profession, he never opposed Tullio's desire to follow his interests in mathematics and physics.

Levi-Civita was an outstanding student at the Ginnasio-Liceo Tito Livio in Padua. After his graduation in 1890, he spent four years studying mathematics at the University of Padua. He began writing mathematical papers as an undergraduate, and his first publication was in 1893. In 1895 he became resident professor at the teachers' college of the Faculty of Science at Pavia. Three years later he was elected to the chair of mechanics at the University of Padua. When the Austrian offensive in the fall of 1917 led university officials to close the school, Levi-Civita took a position in Rome where he continued his teaching and research for another twenty years.

Although Levi-Civita is mostly known for his work in applied mathematics, his early work pertained to geometry and analytic number theory. In 1895 he began focusing his mathematical interest on solving problems of physics. He and his colleague Gregorio Ricci-Curbastro became intrigued with the geometry of curved surfaces, which they called "absolute differential geometry," where "absolute" referred to the surface itself, not its position in space. Together they published an article in 1901 on the subject entitled "Methodes de calcul differentiel absolu et leurs applications."

The 1915 Epistolary Controversy

Albert Einstein found Ricci's and Levi-Civitas' paper useful for describing his general theory of relativity. In her article "The Italian Mathematicians of Relativity," Judith Goodstein translates Einstein's reaction to reading their work: "[I]n all my life I have never before labored at all as hard, and ... I have become imbued with a great respect for mathematics, the subtle parts of which, in my innocence, I had till now regarded as pure luxury. Compared with this problem, the original theory of relativity is child's play." Einstein's respect for Levi-Civita is evident in a series of letters the scientists wrote to each other in early 1915. Levi-Civita gradually convinced Einstein of a crucial weakness in his original formulation of gravitational field equations. This correspondence led Einstein to discover the correct equations by the end of that year.

Levi-Civita's greatest contribution to the field of mathematics was his concept of parallel displacement. The notion of parallel lines had been familiar since Euclid, but Levi-Civita's method, published in 1917, allowed the notion to be extended to the curved space called for by general relativity. This enabled physicists to develop a unified representation of gravitational and electromagnetic fields within the theory of relativity.

Levi-Civita made several direct contributions to the theory of relativity. In a series of papers published from 1917 to 1919, he and his students investigated rotational systems in a gravitational field. Even an erroneous result in 1937 led to a revived interest in the study of how two objects affect one another's motion under the laws of relativity. He also attempted to reconcile the two main theories of twentieth-century physics, quantum mechanics and the relativistic theory of gravitational fields.

Levi-Civita was a popular teacher and lecturer. He kept detailed files of his extensive correspondence with colleagues and former students throughout the world. He loved to travel and enjoyed attending international conferences. He married a former student, Libera Trevesani, in 1914. Levi-Civita also enjoyed mountain-climbing until his poor eyesight forced him to give up this activity. He continued to take long bicycle rides in the mountains, even when he was past the age of sixty.

Levi-Civita was strongly opposed to the rise of fascism in Italy, and for many years his international prominence protected him from persecution. However, the 1938 anti-Jewish laws in Italy forced him to leave his position in Rome. Although he received offers of asylum from many countries, his health had deteriorated, and severe heart trouble prevented him from traveling. Levi-Civita suffered a stroke near the end of 1941 and died on December 29, 1941.

SELECTED WRITINGS BY LEVI-CIVITA:

Books

Opere mathematiche. Memorie e note, four volumes, [Bologna], 1954–1960.

Periodicals

(With Gregorio Ricci-Curbastro) "Methodes de calcul differentiel absolu et leurs applications," *Math. Ann.,* 54, 1901, pp. 125–201.
"Nozione di parallelismo in una varieta qualunque e conseguente specificazione della curvatura reimanniana," *Rend. Circ. Mat. Palermo,* 42, 1917, pp. 173–215.

SOURCES:

Books

Howard, Don, and John Stachel, editors, *Einstein and the History of General Relativity,* Birkhauser, 1989.

Periodicals

Goodstein, Judith R., "The Italian Mathematicians of Relativity," *Centarus,* Volume 26, 1982–83, pp. 241–261.
Hodge, W. Volume D., "Tullio Levi-Civita," *Journal of the London Mathematical Society,* Volume 18, 1943, pp. 107–114.

—*Sketch by Robert Messer*

Rita Levi-Montalcini
1909-
Italian-born American neurobiologist

Rita Levi-Montalcini is recognized for her pioneering research on nerve cell growth. During the 1950's she discovered a protein in the nervous system, which she named the nerve growth factor (NGF). Her subsequent collaboration with biochemist **Stanley Cohen** at Washington University in St. Louis, Missouri, led to the isolation of that substance. Later applications of their work have proven useful in the study of several disorders, including Alzheimer's disease, cancer, and birth defects. Levi-Montalcini's and Cohen's work was recognized in 1986 when they were jointly awarded the Nobel Prize for physiology

Rita Levi-Montalcini

or medicine. Levi-Montalcini became the fourth woman to receive the Nobel in that field.

Levi-Montalcini, the third of four children of Adamo Levi and Adele Montalcini, was born into an upper-middle-class Jewish family in Turin, Italy, in 1909. She grew up in a traditional family and was steered by her father to pursue an education at an all-girls' high school that prepared young women for marriage. She graduated from high school when she was eighteen, having demonstrated exceptional intellectual ability, but was unable to enter a university because of the limited education that had been offered to her. Levi-Montalcini was uncertain what she wanted to do with her life (though she was certain she did not want to marry and have children), and it wasn't until three years later, when her beloved governess was stricken with cancer, that she decided to become a doctor.

After having convinced her father she wanted to enter medical school, Levi-Montalcini passed the entrance exams with distinction. She enrolled in the Turin School of Medicine in 1930, where she studied under Dr. Giuseppe Levi, a well-known histologist and embryologist who introduced Levi-Montalcini to research on the nervous system. She graduated from medical school in 1936 and became Levi's research assistant. With the rise of Fascism in the late 1930's, Jews were restricted from academic positions as well as the medical profession, and Levi-Montalcini was forced to resign from her academic and clinical posts

in 1938. The following year, she accepted a position at the Neurological Institute in Brussels, where she worked until the Nazi invasion in 1939 precipitated her return to Italy.

Conducts Research in Hiding

Upon returning to Italy, she took up residence in Turin with her family. Restrictions imposed upon Jews had increased during her absence, and Levi-Montalcini was forced to set up a private laboratory in her bedroom. Again working with Levi, who had also been banned from his academic post, Levi-Montalcini began researching the nervous system of chicken embryos. In a memoir published in *Women Scientists: The Road to Liberation,* Levi-Montalcini recalls, "Looking back to that period I wonder how I could have found so much interest in, and devoted myself with such enthusiasm to, the study of a small neuroembryological problem, when all the values I cherished were being crushed, and the triumphant advance of the Germans all over Europe seemed to herald the end of Western civilization. The answer may be found in the well-known refusal of human beings to accept reality at its face value, whether this be the fate of the individual, of a country, or of the human race." Her research at the time, in fact, laid the groundwork for her discovery of NGF.

By 1942 the Allied bombing of Turin forced Levi-Montalcini and her family to move to the countryside, where she continued experimentation on chicken embryos to study the mechanisms of nerve cell differentiation, or the specialization of nerve cells. Contrary to previous studies conducted by the respected neuroembryologist **Viktor Hamburger**, who theorized that nerve cells reached their destinations because they were directed by the organs to which they grew, Levi-Montalcini hypothesized that a specific nutrient was essential for nerve growth. When Nazi troops invaded northern Italy in 1943, Levi-Montalcini was again forced to relocate, this time to Florence, where she remained for the duration of the war under an assumed name. Following the liberation of Florence in 1944, Levi-Montalcini worked as a doctor in a refugee camp, and, when northern Italy was liberated the following year, she resumed her post as research assistant to Levi in Turin. Hamburger, who was interested in a paper Levi-Montalcini had published on her wartime experiments, contacted her in 1946, inviting her to fill a visiting research position at Washington University in St. Louis. This temporary position ultimately lasted over three decades.

Fortuitous Collaborations Yield Results

Levi-Montalcini's early work at Washington University concerned further experimentation on the growth processes of chicken embryos in which she observed a migratory sequence of nerve cells. Her observations validated her theory on the existence of a "trophic factor," which provided the essential nutrients for nerve cell differentiation. In 1950 she began studying mouse tumors that had been grafted onto chicken embryos, and which Elmer Bueker had earlier demonstrated were capable of eliciting a proliferation of nerve cells. After repeating Bueker's results, Levi-Montalcini reached a different conclusion. Instead of maintaining that the nerve cells proliferated in response to the presence of the tumor, she deduced that the nerve cells grew out of the tumor and that, thus, the tumor released a substance that elicited the growth. Traveling to Rio de Janeiro in 1952, Levi-Montalcini further tested her hypothesis using tissue cell cultures. Her tissue culture experiments regarding the presence of a substance in the tumor proved highly successful. However, there remained the important step of isolating this substance, which she called "the nerve-growth promoting agent" and later labled nerve growth factor . Upon returning to Washington University, Levi-Montalcini began working with American biochemist Stanley Cohen between 1953 and 1959. During that time, they extracted NGF from snake venom and the salivary glands of male mice. Through these experiments, Cohen was able to determine the chemical structure of NGF, as well as produce NGF antibodies. Levi-Montalcini maintained her interest in the research of NGF; and, when she returned to italy in 1961, she established a laboratory at the Higher Institute of Health in Rome to perform joint NGF research with colleagues at Washington University.

A Lifetime of Accomplishments Is Recognized

By 1969 Levi-Montalcini established and served as director of the Institute of Cell Biology of the Italian National Research Council in Rome. Working six months out of the year at the Institute of Cell Biology and the other six months at Washington University, Levi-Montalcini maintained labs in Rome and St. Louis until 1977, at which time she resumed full-time residence in Italy. During this time she received numerous awards for her work, including becoming the tenth woman to be elected to the National Academy of Sciences in 1968. Despite her success, Levi-Montalcini was the only director of a laboratory conducting NGF research for many years. Later researchers, realizing the significance of understanding the growth of nerve fibers in treating degenerative diseases, have continued the work that Levi-Montalcini began in the late 1930s.

Levi-Montalcini remains active in the scientific community, upholding status as professor emeritus at Washington University since 1977, as well as contributing greatly to scientic studies and programs in her native country. Since winning the Nobel Prize in 1986, she was appointed president of the Italian Multiple Sclerosis Association and also became the first woman to attain membership to the Pontifical Academy of Sciences in Rome. In 1987 she was awarded the National Medal of Science, the highest honor among American scientists.

Keeping abreast with current scientific trends, Levi-Montalcini conducts further research at the Institute of Cell Biology in Rome, focusing on the importance of NGF in the immune and endocrine systems. Additionally, with her twin sister, who is an artist, Levi-Montalcini has established educational youth programs that provide counseling and grants for teenagers interested in the arts or sciences. Recognized not only for her astute intuitive mind and her dedication to fully understanding the mechanisms of NGF, Levi-Montalcini, frequently described by her congenial manner and wit, has influenced three generations of scientists during her own lifetime.

SELECTED WRITINGS BY LEVI-MONTALCINI:

Books

"Reflections on a Scientific Adventure," in *Women Scientists: The Road to Liberation,* edited by Derek Richter, Macmillan Press, 1982, pp. 99–117.
(Editor with Pietro Calissano) *Molecular Aspects of Neurobioloay,* Springer-Verlag, 1986.
In Praise of Imperfection: My Life and Work, Basic Books, 1988.

Periodicals

"The Nerve Growth Factor," *Scientific American,* June, 1979, pp. 68–77.
"The Nerve Growth Factor 35 Years Later," *Science,* Volume 237, 1987, pp. 1154–61.

SOURCES:

Periodicals

Holloway, Marguerite, "Finding the Good in the Bad," *Scientific American,* January, 1993, pp. 32, 36.
Levine, Joe, "Lives of Spirit and Dedication," *Time,* October 27, 1986, pp. 66–8.
Marx, Jean L., "The 1986 Nobel Prize for Physiology or Medicine," *Science,* October 31, 1986, pp. 543–44.
Randall, Frederika, "The Heart and Mind of a Genius," *Vogue,* March, 1987, pp. 480, 536.
Schmeck, Harold M., Jr., "Two Pioneers in Growth of Cells Win Nobel Prize," *New York Times,* October 14, 1986, pp. Al, C3.

Suro, Roberto, "Unraveler of Mysteries," *New York Times,* October 14, 1986, p. C3.

—*Sketch by Elizabeth Henry*

Gilbert Newton Lewis
1875-1946
American chemist

Gilbert Newton Lewis

Gilbert Newton Lewis is best known for his theory on the natures of acids and bases, as well as for his explanation of chemical bonding. However, he also made successful contributions to thermodynamics (a branch of physics concerned with the properties of heat), photochemistry, and isotope separation, which is the sorting of a mixture of isotopes—or a species of an element with the identical atomic number but different atomic mass—into its respective isotopic constituents. In addition, his "electron dot" structures have provided a visual model for how molecules hold together.

Lewis's ideas about chemical bonding are still among the first theories taught to beginning chemistry students. When Lewis began his career, theories of energy and energy flow (thermodynamics) were almost never applied to practical chemical problems. His efforts made considerable progress toward finding ways of integrating thermodynamic principles into real chemical systems. Lewis helped to revolutionize chemical education in the United States, making it more investigative and analytical rather than simply descriptive.

Lewis was born on October 23, 1875, in Weymouth, Massachusetts, to Francis Wesley and Mary Burr (White) Lewis. His early education was informal and private; he learned to read while still very young and was educated at home until age thirteen, when he enrolled in a prep school affiliated with the University of Nebraska. J. H. Hildebrand noted in the *Annual Review of Physical Chemistry* that Lewis regarded his unusual schooling as "an advantage that ... occurred frequently in the careers of distinguished men, that of having 'escaped some of the ordinary processes of formal education.'" In 1894 Lewis transferred from the University of Nebraska to Harvard University, where he received a B.S. degree in chemistry two years later. He continued his studies at Harvard—pursuing his Ph.D. in chemistry under the direction of **Theodore William Richards**—while teaching part time at the Phillips Academy in Andover, Massachusetts. He received his doctorate in 1899, at the age of

twenty-four. His Ph.D. thesis, "Some Electrochemical and Thermochemical Relations of Zinc and Cadmium Amalgams," formed the basis of his first scientific publication.

In the following years, Lewis taught at Harvard, did postdoctoral work in Germany with chemists **Wilhelm Ostwald** and **Walther Nernst**, and spent a year in the Philippines working for the Bureau of Science in Manila. It was during these years that Lewis began thinking about many of his most important contributions to chemical theory. While in Germany, Lewis made the acquaintance of **Albert Einstein**, and he later published several papers on Einstein's theories, although his work in this field met with indifferent success. Distressed by the rigidity of thought at Harvard, Lewis moved to the Massachusetts Institute of Technology in 1905 as an associate professor. In the research group of chemist Arthur Amos Noyes, he reached full professor status, becoming acting director of research less than five years later, a remarkable achievement in such a short period of time. In 1912, Lewis moved to California to take the position of dean in the College of Chemistry at the University of California, Berkeley, where he remained for the rest of his working life, except for a decorated tour of duty with the Army Chemical Warfare Service in France during World War I.

Reshapes Methods for Teaching Physical Chemistry

At Berkeley, Lewis established himself as a motivating force for both researchers and students.

Although too nervous in front of large groups to teach much himself, he influenced the entire process of chemical education. He redesigned the chemistry curriculum to include the teaching of thermodynamic principles. His textbook *Thermodynamics and the Free Energy of Chemical Substances,* coauthored with Merle Randall and published in 1923, was widely studied by generations of pupils. In order to attract more students to the discipline, Lewis paid particular attention to the education of first-year students, involving them in research early in their studies. He gave his colleagues great freedom of choice in their research projects and insisted on a broad base of chemical knowledge rather than rigid specialization. He encouraged discussion and debate among all of his colleagues and students (an unusual practice at that time), demanded that the university provide adequate money for facilities and equipment, and gradually built one of the best chemistry programs in the world. Nearly three hundred Ph.D. degrees in chemistry were awarded at Berkeley during Lewis's tenure, and several of the department's graduate students, including **Glenn Seaborg, Willard Libby,** and **Melvin Calvin,** eventually won Nobel Prizes.

Revolutionizes Chemical Research in Thermodynamics

A cornerstone of thermodynamics is a quantity called *free energy,* a mathematical combination of several energy-related characteristics of a system. Free energy tells the chemist how likely a reaction is to occur, how complete an individual chemical reaction is likely to be, and how much work must go into or come out of the reacting system in order to accomplish the reaction. Until Lewis began working in the area, however, the theory was entirely mathematical; very little actual measured data existed to enable practical calculation of this important quantity for real reactions. While at the Massachusetts Institute of Technology, Lewis began meticulous work measuring the free energy values associated with several chemical processes, both organic and inorganic. Between 1913 and 1923, he and his frequent collaborator Merle Randall published several papers and a book on free energy, in which they summarized virtually all the known data on the subject. Lewis also showed how this free energy data could be applied to many different problems in chemistry. For example, he formulated the concept of *activity,* which, because it relied on thermodynamic principles in addition to chemical concentration, better explained the behavior of reactions occurring in solution.

Proposes a Theory of Chemical Bonding

By the time Lewis began thinking about chemical bonding, the electron had been discovered and was believed to participate in bonding. The periodic table was largely laid out, and repeating properties had been observed to occur every eight elements. Several different ideas had been advanced to explain how atoms hooked together to make molecules, but none of them were entirely satisfactory. Lewis had been thinking about the relationship between the eight membered rows on the periodic table in relation to the number of electrons for some time, but it was not until 1916 that he formally proposed his theory of bonding.

Atoms, according to the theory Lewis proposed, have eight electrons around them on the outside. These eight electrons occupy the corners of a cube. When bonding occurs, particularly between atoms which do not have a full complement of eight electrons, the pooled electrons from both atoms pair up, with a pair shared between the bonding atoms. Sharing pairs of electrons enables each atom in a molecule to obtain the greatest stability. He symbolized these pairs with dots, a convention still used today.

No one took this theory seriously when Lewis first proposed it, but in 1919 the noted chemist **Irving Langmuir** further developed Lewis's idea about an octet of electrons conferring the greatest stability. Langmuir was more persistent and articulate in convincing the chemical community that the theory was important, and so it was for a time called the Lewis-Langmuir electron dot theory. Lewis took issue with the compound name, feeling that he had originated the theory, but historians largely agree that Langmuir made important contributions and that the theory would have languished even longer had it not been for his activism on its behalf. In 1923, Lewis published a book on the theory, *Valence and the Structure of Atoms and Molecules.*

Pursues Research in Other Areas

In 1933, after a decade of frustration in his areas of interest, Lewis abruptly started working on a completely new subject, isotope separation. The identity of an element depends not on its atomic weight, but rather on the number of protons in the atom's nucleus. Isotopes are differently weighted forms of a single element; most separation science depends on exploiting the differences in chemical reactions of different elements, but isotopes of the same element are very difficult to separate because their chemistry is identical. Lewis, working with the isotopes of hydrogen, managed to prepare nearly pure water containing only the deuterium isotope of hydrogen. This is the so-called "heavy water" important in nuclear reaction research. This was his major contribution to this area, however; his subsequent investigations on isotopes were largely unsuccessful.

In his 1923 book on valence, Lewis had successfully applied his chemical bonding theory to acids and bases, but once again it had received little notice. At that time, chemists thought that acids must have a hydrogen ion to donate and that a base must be able to receive a hydrogen ion. They were at a loss, however, to explain acidic behavior in compounds that possessed no donatable hydrogen. In 1938, Lewis gave a lecture at Philadelphia's Franklin Institute in which he insisted that this obstacle could be removed by defining an acid as any electron-pair recipient and a base as any electron-pair donor. These definitions cover almost all chemicals in any reaction, including hydrogen ion transfers, and are still used today.

The last years of his life found Lewis engaged in the study of photochemistry—the interaction of light energy with chemical compounds to cause reactions. As with most of his other areas of interest, Lewis had begun to investigate light and color early in his career, but his most solid published work occurred later. He collaborated with the respected chemist Melvin Calvin on a review paper concerning photochemistry, and he then experimented in the areas of fluorescence and phosphorescence. Eventually, he began to connect these experiments with the rapidly developing field of quantum mechanics, once again combining theory and practice as he had done with thermodynamics and chemical reactions decades earlier. Lewis's interests outside of chemistry included economics and prehistoric glaciation in the Americas; his last paper, published posthumously, concerned the thermodynamics of ice ages. He officially retired in 1941, although he continued his scientific work until his death from a heart attack in his Berkeley laboratory on March 23, 1946. He left behind his wife, Mary Hinckley Sheldon Lewis, whom he had married in 1912, and three children. His two sons followed him to careers in chemistry.

SELECTED WRITINGS BY LEWIS:

Books

(With Merle Randall) *Thermodynamics and the Free Energy of Chemical Substances,* McGraw, 1923.
Valence and the Structure of Atoms and Molecules, Chemical Catalog Company, 1923.

Periodicals

"The Atom and the Molecule," *Journal of the American Chemical Society,* Volume 38, 1916, pp. 762–785.
(With Merle Randall) "The Activity Coefficient of Strong Electrolytes," *Journal of the American Chemical Society,* Volume 43, 1921, pp. 1112–1154.

SOURCES:

Periodicals

Hildebrand, J. H., "Fifty Years of Physical Chemistry in Berkeley," *Annual Review of Physical Chemistry,* Volume 14, 1963, p. 1.
Saltzman, M. D., "Benzene and the Triumph of the Octet Theory," *Journal of Chemical Education,* Volume 51, August, 1974, p. 498.
Tiernan, N. F., "Gilbert Newton Lewis and the Amazing Electron Dots," *Journal of Chemical Education,* Volume 62, July, 1985, p. 569.

—*Sketch by Gail B. C. Marsella*

Julian Herman Lewis
1891-1989
American physiologist and pathologist

Julian Herman Lewis was the first African American to receive a Ph.D. in physiology at the University of Chicago. His early research in immunology was followed by investigations into a wide range of scientific fields, among them anthropology, pathology, physiology, tuberculosis research, and psychology. In addition, he became interested in the biological status of African Americans and made a detailed study of their ancestry in Africa, which he published in his book *The Biology of the Negro.*

Lewis was born in Shawneetown, Illinois, on May 26, 1891, to John Calhoun Lewis and Cordelia O. Scott Lewis, both of whom were public school teachers. His father had been born into slavery and had later attended Berea College, where he had met his wife. Although the college had been set up to educate newly freed slaves after the Civil War, by the time young Julian was ready to enter a new state law had been passed excluding Negroes, and he was sent to the University of Illinois, instead. Here, as one of the few blacks at the college, he had to deal with a degree of discrimination and social exclusion; Richard Bardolph relates in his book *The Negro Vanguard* that when Lewis was elected captain of his ROTC unit, the dean had him transferred to a specially created ceremonial office to "prevent possible trouble." He nevertheless excelled in his classes and graduated Phi Beta Kappa in 1911. A year later, he received an M.A., and then studied at the University of Chicago, where he was awarded a Ph.D. in physiology in 1915. The same year, his dissertation on the role of lipids in immunity was published in the *Journal of Infectious*

Julian Herman Lewis

Diseases, for which he received the Ricketts Prize. In 1917, Lewis received his medical degree from Rush Medical College and obtained an appointment to the department of pathology at the University of Chicago. He would rise the position of associate professor, serving there until 1943.

In 1926, Lewis was among the first to be awarded the new John Simon Guggenheim Fellowship for study abroad and conducted research at the University of Basel, Switzerland. Throughout the years, he presented papers at many scientific conferences, and his work received coverage in such publications as *Life* and *Time.* During World War II, he participated in a government-sponsored research project to investigate the possibility of using beef plasma as a substitute for human blood.

Combining his interests in his field and in his ancestry, Lewis delved into the history of African Americans in relationship to their anatomy, their physiological characteristics, and their responses to a variety of diseases. In 1942, he published the results of his investigations in *The Biology of the Negro,* which he wrote with a grant-in-aid from the Julius Rosenwald Fund. So well documented was the book's objective analysis of the subject that it cited well over a thousand references in the scientific literature. A book review in the *Journal of the National Medical Association* called it "a fair, impartial, scientific and masterly study and analysis of racial characteristics, likenesses and differences, with special reference to the Negro," and added: "It is noteworthy that the author has failed to discover any fundamental evidence to show that the Negro is biologically inferior to other groups in the genus *Homo.*"

Lewis married Eva Overton in 1918, and they had three children, Gloria Julienne, Julian Herman, Jr., and John Overton. Lewis was a member of many scientific societies, including the Society for Experimental Pathology, the American Association of Immunologists, and the American Association of Pathologists and Bacteriologists. In recognition of his outstanding career, he was awarded the Benjamin Rush Medal in 1971. In his later years, he served as director of the pathology department at Our Lady of Mercy Hospital in Dyer, Indiana, a position he held until his death on March 6, 1989, just short of his ninety-eighth birthday.

SELECTED WRITINGS BY LEWIS:

Books

The Biology of the Negro, University of Chicago Press, 1942.

Periodicals

"Lipids in Immunity. The Absorption of Substances Injected Subcutaneously and the Inhibitory Action of Heterologous Protein Mixtures on Anaphylaxis," *Journal of Infectious Diseases,* July, 1915.

(With Deborah A. Henderson), "The Racial Distribution of Isohemagglutinin Groups," *Journal of the American Medical Association,* October 21, 1922.

(With Theodore R. Sarbin), "Studies of Psychosomatics," *Psychosomatic Medicine,* April, 1943.

SOURCES:

Books

Bardolph, Richard, *The Negro Vanguard,* Negro Universities Press, 1959, p. 188.
Sammons, Vivian O., *Blacks in Science and Medicine,* Hemisphere Publishing, 1990, p. 153.

Periodicals

"Age Regression," *Life Magazine,* November 30, 1942, pp. 86, 88.
Review of *The Biology of the Negro, Journal of the National Medical Association,* July, 1942.

Other

Correspondence and telephone conversations with son, Julian H. Lewis, Jr., January, 1994.

—Sketch by Maurice Bleifeld

Warren K. Lewis
1882-1975
American chemical engineer

Warren K. Lewis played a major role in establishing chemical engineering as a distinct discipline. A textbook that he coauthored with two colleagues—*Principles of Chemical Engineering*—was published in 1923 and quickly emerged as a landmark in the development of this field. Lewis also applied his methods to problems of petroleum refining, working as a consultant to Standard Oil of New Jersey (now Exxon Corporation). His work paved the way for industrial-scale production of high-octane gasolines. These boosted the performance of automobile engines and brought major advantage to Allied air power during World War II. He also was recognized as an influential educator, molding a generation of industry and academic leaders at Massachusetts Institute of Technology (MIT). In 1966 he won the John Fritz Medal, an engineering award whose prior recipients included George Westinghouse, **Thomas Alva Edison**, **Orville Wright**, and Alexander Graham Bell.

Warren Kendall Lewis was born on August 21, 1882, near Laurel, Delaware. His parents, Henry Clay and Martha Ellen (Kinder) Lewis, were farmers, and Lewis at first expected to pursue this career; however, he wanted to attend college as well. The local high school offered only three years of instruction, but he received strong encouragement from a cousin who taught English in Newton, Massachusetts. Lewis transferred to a high school in Newton for his fourth year, entering nearby MIT in 1901. He received an S.B. in chemical engineering in 1905 and then left for Germany, earning a Ph.D. in chemistry from the University of Breslau in 1908.

Returning to the United States, Lewis swiftly climbed the academic ladder at MIT, rising from assistant professor of chemistry in 1910 to full professor of chemical engineering in 1914. He then broadened his experience by working as a consultant to the Goodyear Tire and Rubber Company from 1916 to 1920. At Goodyear, Lewis's contributions were far-reaching. The company faced a wartime shortage of naphtha—a volatile liquid hydrocarbon mixture used as a solvent. He eased this shortage by showing how to distill commercial gasoline, which was in ready supply, to obtain this product, and he further developed a method of improving solvent recovery. Then, ranging beyond conventions of industrial chemistry, Lewis addressed the fundamental nature of rubber itself by studying its macromolecules (very large molecules.) He also demonstrated relations between these macromolecules and similar ones

Warren K. Lewis

found in other materials, including leather and cellulose.

Builds New Foundations for Chemical Engineering

Prior to World War I, the chemical industry was already well-established in Britain, Germany, and the United States. It was producing large quantities of sulfuric acid, alkali, high explosives, petroleum distillates, and early forms of chemical fertilizer. Industrial chemists also were reaching into new areas: saccharine, rayon, early plastics such as celluloid and Bakelite. However, in pursuing new initiatives, the dominant theme was experiment and empiricism, rather than reliance on underlying principles. Each major process existed largely as an industry in its own right; an engineer who had experience in sulfuric acid would not qualify for employment in an alkali plant. At the time, a chemical engineer was essentially a mechanical engineer who had learned chemistry and stood ready to design chemical process plants. However, a British chemist, George E. Davis, was advocating a broader approach. Rather than focus on processes separately, he argued that specific processes were built up from basic, individual operations, many of which were common to the production of a variety of products. For instance, the alcohol and petroleum-distillate industries were separate and distinct, but both relied on distillation, which in turn demanded such elementary operations as evaporation and condensation (which purify the liquid). These, he maintained, deserved study in their own right, to be applied as needed in future processes that would require distillation.

At MIT, Davis's message drew strong support from W. H. Walker, Lewis's mentor. In 1907 Walker had revised the chemical engineering curriculum, strengthening its emphasis on chemistry and on engineering principles; he also worked closely with **Arthur D. Little**, a consulting chemist. In 1915 Little coined the term "unit operations" to describe Davis's basic processes. The way was now open to reestablish chemical engineering on new foundations; these would feature unit operations, to be regarded as building blocks in constructing industrial processes. In turn, the chemical engineer would study these operations using mathematics, treating them quantitatively rather than through empiricism, or through experiment and observation. In 1920 Walker and Lewis, together with their colleague W. H. McAdams, developed this approach in systematic fashion by writing the manuscript that would reach print in 1923 as their textbook, *Principles of Chemical Engineering*.

Its effect was explosive. A host of universities set up new chemical engineering departments or strengthened existing ones in the wake of the book's publication. It marked the coming-of-age of chemical engineering, for this field now held a body of material that was all its own and that it could treat quantitatively. Henceforth, chemical-process design could seek the rigor and precision of the design of engines in mechanical engineering, as well as the subtlety and versatility of circuit design in electrical engineering, and Lewis already was in the forefront in applying this new power.

Develops Processes for High-Octane Gasolines

Lewis's new field of activity lay in the petroleum industry. The field was producing straight-run gasolines, distilled directly from crude oil, but was living with large inefficiencies in the refinery processes. As a consultant with Standard Oil of New Jersey, Lewis introduced to the industry concepts drawn from alcohol distillation, and the new principles of fractional distillation—or the separation of components of a mixture from one another—quickly led to fractionating columns of greatly increased efficiency. In 1951 a contributor to *Fortune* magazine noted that "in the twenties Lewis transformed fractional distillation, *the* basic refinery process, from a black art into a science."

This work was closely related to another topic: the production of high-octane fuels. Such fuels are essential for high-performance engines. These engines demand high compression of the fuel-air mix within their cylinders, yet this compression tends to produce knocking, a sudden detonation. To control knocking is essential; it robs an engine of power and can

actually damage its parts. In turn, high-octane fuels avoid knock, permitting successful achievement of high compression. Tetraethyl lead, added in small quantities to conventional gasolines, gave useful boosts in their octane rating. But to go farther, and in particular to reach 100-octane, it was necessary to subject these gasolines to chemical reforming. France's **Eugene Houdry** introduced the use of catalysts in this process, with the first plant using Houdry's process opening in 1936, but yields proved to be unsteady, while the process itself was quite inefficient. The reason was that the catalyst rapidly collected carbon, which fouled its operation. Houdry's plant was therefore clumsy to operate, demanding frequent interruptions to regenerate the catalyst by burning off the carbon.

At Standard Oil, Lewis's colleagues sought to improve this process by using a powdered catalyst, whisking it swiftly between chambers for production and for regeneration. Early work produced nothing of direct industrial value, but these results led Lewis to pursue an entirely new approach. A finely-powdered catalyst could form a dense mixture with vaporized petroleum, with the chemical reaction releasing heat and producing intense turbulence. The turbulence, in turn, would keep the powder well mixed and prevent it from settling out. This mix then would act as a fluid, readily flowing between the two chambers to permit quick regeneration. Working with his colleague Edwin R. Gilliland, Lewis developed this technology, called the fluidized-bed technique, which became available just as the United States was entering World War II. It was quickly applied on a massive scale. As a result, Allied aircraft flew with 100-octane fuel, outperforming their German counterparts that had to make do with 87-octane. After the war, low-cost, high-octane fuels sparked a surge in commercial aviation. The influence of the high-octane fuels also reached consumers, for two gallons of 1950-vintage automobile gasoline could do the work of three gallons from 1925.

Wins Distinction As a Teacher

Through all these developments, Lewis saw himself primarily as a teacher. He had become head of MIT's Department of Chemical Engineering in 1920 but returned to his professorship in 1929, so he could devote more time to his students. In turn, a number of them went on to provide leadership in the industry. They included Gilliland, who played a key role in developing the fluidized bed and later served as a member of the President's Science Advisory Committee. Another was Eger Murphree, who headed the research-and-development arm of what is now Exxon. **Crawford Greenewalt** built the main nuclear reactors of the Manhattan Project, and became president of Du Pont. Walter G. Whitman served as science advisor to the State Department. Bradley Dewey and Per

Frolich became presidents of the American Chemical Society.

In the classroom, Lewis adopted an adversarial style, often asking questions for which the obvious answer was wrong. He would upset a student by acting bombastic and overbearing, then encourage the student to resolve the issue by using logic. He approached his students with genuine personal interest and held a sense of history, which he used to provide examples that illustrated his points. Lewis also cherished great literature and maintained a strong religious conviction. In 1950, *Life* magazine conducted a survey of student leaders, who chose Lewis as one of America's eight greatest university teachers. Among the other honors Lewis received throughout his career are the 1947 Priestly Medal, the 1949 Gold Medal of the American Institute of Chemists, the 1957 Industrial and Engineering Chemistry Award of the American Chemical Society, and the 1958 Founders Award of the American Institute of Chemical Engineers.

In 1909 Lewis married Rosalind Kenway. They had four children: Warren Jr., Henry Clay, Rosalind, and Mary. Lewis became professor emeritus in 1948 but took the post of lecturer so that he could continue teaching. Twenty years later he was still going to his office regularly, though by then he was in his mideighties. He died on March 9, 1975, in Plymouth, Massachusetts.

SELECTED WRITINGS BY LEWIS:

Books

(With W. H. Walker and W. H. McAdams) *Principles of Chemical Engineering,* McGraw-Hill, 1923.

SOURCES:

Books

Furter, William F., editor, *History of Chemical Engineering,* American Chemical Society, 1980.

Periodicals

McFadyen, Aubrey D., "Warren K. Lewis," *Chemical and Engineering News,* September 29, 1947, pp. 2814, 2865.
"Tomorrow's Oil," *Fortune,* November, 1951, pp. 140–149.

—*Sketch by T. A. Heppenheimer*

Ching Chun Li
1912-
Chinese-born American biostatistician and population geneticist

Ching Chun Li, known as C. C., is a world-renowned biostatistician and population geneticist who influenced the course of modern medical research with his innovative techniques. As the chief biostatistician for a chemotherapy study funded by the National Institute of Health in the 1950s, Li instituted the practice of random and "blind" testing in clinical trials. He and a colleague introduced the "singles method" in segregation analysis that presented a faster, more accurate way of tracing genetic defects along the family line. Li has published more than 150 research articles and ten books, including *Population Genetics,* which led the field for more than twenty years. Among other elected positions in various international science societies, Li served as president of the American Society for Human Genetics in 1961, and was named Pittsburgh Statistician of the year in 1970. Motivated by scientific integrity, Li advocated teaching social scientists the phenomenon and consequences of gene segregation, and refused to entertain ideas on the impact of racial differences on intelligence.

C. C. Li was born in Tientsin, China, on October 27, 1912. His early education took place at the same British missionary school that his father, a business man and biblical scholar, had attended. He played soccer, captained the basketball team and was elected president of the student government. From 1932 to 1936 Li attended the University of Nanking; there he first learned genetics, plant breeding, and field experiment design and analysis. In 1937, he attended Cornell University's College of Agriculture and studied plant breeding, genetics and biometry under Professor H. H. Love. Influenced greatly by **Theodosius Dobzhansky**'s 1937 book, *Genetics and the Origin of Species,* Li devoted the rest of his life to the study of population genetics.

Upon completion of his Ph.D. from Cornell in 1940, Li spent a year studying mathematics in postdoctoral positions at the University of Chicago, Columbia University and North Carolina State University. While he was in Chicago, Li met Clara Lem, and they were married in September, 1941.

Li and his wife spent the next nine months journeying to China through the war zones of World War II. They took boats through bomb-ridden waters, were stranded in Hong Kong, endured starvation, and completed a thirty-eight day walk from Japanese-occupied Kowloon to Kweilin in Free China. Because of the war, Li was not able to reach his father in Chungking, nor his mother in Shanghai. They stayed with Li's brother in Kweilin, where their son Jeff was born, and there Li taught at the Agricultural College of the National Kwangsi University. In the summer of 1943, the trio set out to visit Li's father in Chungking; en route, tragedy struck as Jeff became sick with dysentery and died. For the next three years, Li taught at the University of Nanking at Chengtu. When the war ended in 1945, Clara flew to Shanghai to meet Li's mother for the first time, and gave birth to their second child, Carol. In 1946, Li became professor and chairman of Peking University's Department of Agronomy, and began writing his first book, *Population Genetics.*

Persecution in China

The next four years left indelible impressions on Li's life. During this time the Chinese Communist Party, led by Mao Zedong, followed the direction of the Soviet Union which had adopted, as doctrine, the beliefs of geneticist Trofim Denisovich Lysenko, who has been described as the greatest charlatan of the 20th century. Lysenkoism asserted that controlled environmental influences could produce particular traits that could then be inherited by following generations. (Li later claimed that Lysenkoism had no scientific basis, offering as an example the Chinese tradition of binding women's feet; while this tradition had been practiced for hundreds of years, Chinese women continued to give birth to babies with normal feet.)

The Chinese government tried to coerce Li into deserting Mendelian genetics by asserting that Li did not understand Lysenkoism, but Li responded by translating Lysenko's texts into Chinese. Though forced to resign from the University of Peking in 1950, the government was still not satisfied, and tried to denounce him on political grounds. Their tactic was to get one of Li's workers to accuse him of criticizing communism; however, everyone refused.

Although remorseful of leaving his parents and country, Li decided to escape to the United States to obtain the intellectual freedom necessary to carry on his research. In a *Health Sciences Review* article Li once said, "Many people have a professional life—publish papers, create controversies and enemies—but it is my fight against Lysenkoism that was the turning point in my life."

Li made his way to the United States with the help of a brother in Hong Kong and of several American scientists—particularly Nobel prize-winner **Herman Joseph Muller**, to whom Li later paid tribute by naming another son Steven Muller Li. In 1951, Li accepted a position at the University of Pittsburgh, where he became a professor of biometry in 1960 and served as the head of the Department of Biostatistics

and Human Genetics from 1969 to 1975. In 1975, Li was named University Professor, the highest rank conferred by the university. For the next two years he served on the Congressional commission for the control of Huntington's Disease. He also became interested in the field of inclusion probabilities in parentage testing, often used to determine the outcome of paternal law suits. In molecular population genetics, Li and his colleagues have made important contributions to the understanding of similarities of the DNA profiles between two individuals. They have also calculated the probability of a perfect match in DNA profiles of a random pair of individuals in homogeneous or heterogeneous populations. In whatever area Li focused attention, he made original contributions that advanced scientific method and human understanding.

SELECTED WRITINGS BY LI:

Books

Population Genetics, University of Chicago Press, 1955.
Human Genetics, Principles and Methods, McGraw, 1961.
Introduction to Experimental Statistics, McGraw, 1964.
Path Analysis, A Primer, Boxwood Press, 1975.
Analysis of Unbalanced Data: A Pre-program Introduction, Cambridge University Press, 1982.

Periodicals

"The Correlation Between Parents and Offspring in a Random Mating Population," *American Journal of Human Genetics,* Volume 6, 1954, pp. 383–86.
"A Clinical Study of the Comparative Effect of Nitrogen Mustard and DON in Patients with Bronchogenic Carcinoma, Hodgkins Disease, Lymphosarcoma, and Melanoma," *Journal of the National Cancer Institute,* Volume 22, 1959, pp. 433–39.
"The Diminishing Jaw of Civilized People," *American Journal of Human Genetics,* Volume 13, 1961, pp. 1–8.
"Path Coefficients and Derivatives," *Biometrische Zeitschrift,* Volume 17, 1975, pp. 213–15.
(With S. Mazumdar and R. Bryce), "Correspondence Between a Linear Restriction and a Generalized Inverse in Linear Model Analysis," *American Statistician,* Volume 34, number 2, 1980, pp. 103–05.
(With A. Chakravarti), "Estimating the Prior Probability of Paternity from the Results of Exclusion Tests," *Forensic Science International,* Volume 24, 1984, pp. 143–47.

(With D. E. Weeks and A. Chakravarti), "Similarity of DNA Fingerprints Due to Chance and Relatedness," *Human Heredity,* Volume 43, No. 1, 1993, pp. 45–52.

SOURCES:

Periodicals

Petechuk, David A., "The Life and Times of C. C. Li", *Health Sciences Review,* October, 1989.
Speiss, Elliot B., "Ching Chun Li, Courageous Scholar of Population Genetics, Human Genetics, and Biostatistics: A Living History Essay," *American Journal of Medical Genetics,* Volume 16, 1983, pp. 603–30.

—Sketch by Karin Deck

Choh Hao Li
1913-1987
Chinese-born American biochemist

Choh Hao Li is credited with isolating and purifying eight of the ten different hormones manufactured in the front portion, or adenohypophysis, of the pituitary gland. The pituitary is the pea-sized governing gland which is located at the base of the brain, and it manufactures hormones responsible for metabolism, reproduction, growth, and maturation. One of these is adrenocorticotropin (ACTH), an adrenal booster used in the treatment of arthritis. Another is somatotropin, or human growth hormone (HGH), which has proven particularly effective on children whose growth has slowed or stopped because of hypopituitary problems. Li was director of the Hormone Research Laboratory of the University of California at Berkeley, and he received the Lasker Award for Basic Medical Research in 1962.

Li was born in Canton, China, on April 21, 1913, to Mewching Tsui and Kan-chi Li. His father was an industrialist with a high-school education, but Li's parents made sure their eleven children received college educations. Li attended Pui-Ying Middle School in Canton, where he developed a curiosity about nature at an early age. He continued his studies at the University of Nanking, earning his B.S. degree in chemistry there in 1933, and he stayed for two years as a chemistry instructor.

Li came to the United States in 1935 to study chemistry at the University of California. Because the chemistry department there had never heard of the University of Nanking, he was initially admitted on a six-month probationary period. But they were impressed with his work, and he was allowed to stay. He earned his Ph.D. in chemistry in 1938, supporting himself by teaching Chinese to children in Chinatown, and he was immediately appointed research associate with experimental biologist Herbert M. Evans at the Institute of Experimental Biology. He would remain at the University of California for the rest of his career.

Begins Pituitary Hormone Research

In 1938, Li first began research on the adenohypophysis of the pituitary gland. With Evans and Miriam E. Simpson, he made his first significant contribution to pituitary hormone research in 1940, when he isolated the interstitial cell-stimulating hormone (ICSH) from sheep glands and pig glands. ICSH is a fertility hormone which controls ovulation in women and the production of sperm in men. This hormone is the basis for modern oral contraceptives. In 1950, Li was appointed director of the Hormone Research Laboratory, part of the University of California's School of Medicine. He continued his investigations of pituitary hormones, isolating and identifying them and attempting to develop methods to synthesize them.

By 1953, Li and his colleagues isolated and purified the adrenocorticotropic hormone (ACTH). This hormone regulates the adrenal cortex, which produces sex hormones as well as hormones that govern metabolic functions; it also produces adrenaline. Li found that an injection of ACTH can stimulate the cortex to increase the secretion of cortisone and that it was therefore as effective as cortisone itself in treating arthritis. But it was not until many years later, in 1973, that he managed to synthesize it. In 1956, Li and his associates isolated and purified human growth hormone (HGH), though determining its structure took them until 1966. This accomplishment has important applications in medicine, as the hormone can stimulate human growth and has been used with cases of hyperpituitary dwarves to help them achieve a normal size. But HGH can also be beneficial to sex hormones, the production of antibodies, and the healing of wounds, and has been proven effective in reducing blood cholesterol levels, developing breast tissue, and increasing the milk of nursing mothers; in addition, it can affect diabetes, obesity, and giantism. In 1992, the National Institute on Aging initiated studies to determine whether HGH can actually reverse or slow the aging process.

Discovers Beta-endorphin

In 1978 Li discovered beta-endorphin, a substance produced in the brain that acts as a painkiller. This discovery initiated a number of investigations into new treatments for pain. In addition to its morphine-like characteristics, beta-endorphin can exert behavioral effects on both animals and humans when it is administered intravenously. Li was also the first to synthesize growth factor 1, which has important resemblances to insulin.

Li was the recipient of many prestigious awards for his contributions to medical research. Among them were the Ciba Award from the Endocrine Society, which he received in 1947. He was also awarded the Emory Prize of the American Academy of Arts and Sciences, and the Lasker Award for Basic Medical Research, which Mrs. Lyndon B. Johnson presented to him in 1962. He received the Scientific Achievement Award from the American Medical Association in 1970, the National Award from the American Cancer Society in 1971, and the Nichols Medal in 1979.

Li married Annie Lu on October 1, 1938; they had a son and two daughters. Li died on November 28, 1987 at age seventy-four.

SELECTED WRITINGS BY LI:

Books

(Editor) *Hormonal Proteins and Peptides,* 13 volumes, Academic Press, 1973–1987.

SOURCES:

Books

McGraw-Hill Modern Scientists and Engineers, McGraw-Hill, 1980, pp. 228–229.
Robinson, Donald, *The Miracle Finders,* David McKay Company, 1976.

Periodicals

"Dr. Choh Hao Li, Biochemist; Synthesized Hormone for Growth," *New York Times,* December 1, 1987, p. D27.

—Sketch by Janet Kieffer Kelley

Willard F. Libby
1908-1980
American chemist

Chemist Willard F. Libby developed the radiocarbon dating technique used to determine the age of organic materials. With applications in numerous branches of science, including archaeology, geology, and geophysics, radiocarbon dating has been used to ascertain the ages of both ancient artifacts and geological events, such as the end of the Ice Age. In 1960, Libby received the Nobel Prize for his radiocarbon dating work. During World War II, Libby worked on the Manhattan Project to develop an atomic bomb and was a member of the Atomic Energy Commission for several years in the 1950s. An outspoken scientist during the Cold War between the U.S. and the former Soviet Union, Libby advocated that every home have a fallout shelter in case of nuclear war. Opposed to bans against nuclear weapons testing, Libby was considered by some to be a pawn for a federal administration that wished to continue the arms race. Libby, however, was a strong proponent of the progress of science, which he believed resulted in more benefits than detriments for the human race.

Willard Frank Libby was born to Ora Edward and Eva May Libby on December 17, 1908, on a farm in Grand Valley, Colorado. In 1913, the family, which included Libby and his two brothers and two sisters, moved to an apple ranch north of San Francisco, California, near Sebastopol, where Libby received his grammar school education. A large boy who would eventually grow to be six-feet three-inches tall, Libby developed his legendary stamina while working on the farm. He played tackle for his high school football team and was called "Wild Bill," a nickname used by some throughout Libby's life. After graduating from high school in 1926, Libby enrolled at the University of California, Berkeley. He made money for college by building apple boxes, earning one cent for each box and sometimes $100 in a week. "I was the fastest box maker in Sonoma County," he told Theodore Berland, who interviewed Libby for his book *The Scientific Life.*

Although Libby was interested in English literature and history, he felt obligated to seek a more lucrative career and entered college to become a mining engineer. By his junior year, however, Libby became interested in chemistry, spurred on by the discussions of his boarding house roommates, who were graduate students in chemistry. Libby took on an heavy course load, focusing on mathematics, physics, and chemistry. After receiving his B.S. in chemistry in 1931, he entered graduate school at Berkeley and studied under the American physical chemist **Gilbert**

Willard F. Libby

Newton Lewis and Wendell Latimer, who were pioneering the physical chemistry field.

During graduate school, Libby built the United States' first Geiger-Muller tube for detecting radioactivity, which results from the spontaneous disintegration of an atom's nucleus. Libby refined the mechanism in order to detect minute amounts of radioactivity in elements not previously thought to be radioactive, including samarium. Libby continued to make his own Geiger counters throughout his life, claiming that they were much more sensitive than those manufactured for the open market.

Libby received his Ph.D. in 1933 and was appointed an instructor in chemistry at Berkeley. After the Japanese bombed Pearl Harbor in 1941, Libby, who was on a year sabbatical as a Guggenheim Fellow at Princeton University, joined a group of scientists in Chicago, Illinois, to work on the Manhattan Project, a government-sponsored effort to develop an atomic bomb. During this time, he worked with American chemist and physicist **Harold Urey** at Columbia University on gaseous diffusion techniques for the separation of uranium isotopes (isotopes are different forms of the same element having the same atomic number but a different number of protons). After the war, he accepted an appointment as a professor of chemistry at the University of Chicago and began to conduct research at the Institute of Nuclear Studies.

Embarks on Nobel Prize-winning Research

In 1939, scientists at New York University had sent radiation counters attached to balloons into the earth's upper atmosphere and discovered that neutron showers were created by cosmic rays hitting atoms. Further evidence indicated that these neutrons were absorbed by nitrogen, which then decayed into radioactive carbon–14. In addition, two of Libby's former students, Samuel Ruben and Martin Kamen, made radioactive carbon–14 in the laboratory for the first time. They used a cyclotron (a circular device that accelerates charged particles by means of an alternating electric field in a constant magnetic field) to bombard normal carbon–12 with neutrons, causing it to decay into carbon–14.

Intrigued by these discoveries, Libby hypothesized that radioactive carbon–14 in the atmosphere was oxidized to carbon dioxide. He further theorized that, since plants absorb carbon dioxide through photosynthesis, all plants should contain minute, measurable amounts of carbon–14. Finally, since all living organisms digest plant life (either directly or indirectly), all animals should also contain measurable amounts of carbon–14. In effect, all plants, animals, or carbon-containing products of life should be slightly radioactive.

Working with Aristide von Grosse, who had built a complicated device that separated different carbons by weight, and graduate student Ernest C. Anderson, Libby was successful in isolating radiocarbon in nature, specifically in methane produced by the decomposition of organic matter. Working on the assumption that carbon–14 was created at a constant rate and remained in a molecule until an organism's death, Libby thought that he should be able to determine how much time had elapsed since the organism's death by measuring the half-life of the remaining radiocarbon isotopes. (Half-life is a measurement of how long it takes a substance to lose half its radioactivity.) In the case of radiocarbon, Libby's former student Kamen had determined that carbon–14's half-life was 5,370 years. So, in approximately 5,000 years, half of the radiocarbon is gone; in another 5,000 years, half of the remaining radiocarbon decays, and so on. Using this mathematical calculation, Libby proposed that he could determine the age of organisms that had died as many as 30,000 years ago.

Since a diffusion column such as von Grosse's was extremely expensive to operate, Libby and Anderson decided to use a relatively inexpensive Geiger counter to build a device that was extremely sensitive to the radiation of a chosen sample. First, they eliminated 99% of the background radiation that occurs naturally in the environment with eight-inch thick iron walls to shield the counter. They then used a unique chemical process to burn the sample they were studying into pure carbon lampblack, which was then placed on the inner walls of a Geiger counter's sensing tube.

Libby first tested his device on tree samples, since their ages could be determined by counting their rings. Next, Libby gathered tree and plant specimens from around the world and discovered no significant differences in normal age-related radiocarbon distribution. When Libby first attempted to date historical artifacts, however, he found his device was several hundred years off. He soon realized that he needed to use at least several ounces of a material for accurate dating. From the Chicago Museum of Natural History, Libby and Anderson obtained a sample of a wooden funerary boat recovered from the tomb of the Egyptian King Sesostris III. The boat's age was 3,750 years; Libby's counter estimated it to be 3,261 years, only a 3.5% difference. Libby spent the next several years refining his technique and testing it on historically significant—and sometimes unusual—objects, such as prehistoric sloth dung from Chile, the parchment wrappings of the Dead Sea Scrolls, and charcoal from a campsite fire at Stonehenge, England. Libby saw his new dating technique as a way of combining the physical and historical sciences. For example, using wood samples from forests once buried by glaciers, Libby determined that the Ice Age had ended 10,000 to 11,000 years ago, 15,000 years later than geologists had previously believed. Moving on to man-made artifacts from North America and Europe (such as a primitive sandal from Oregon and charcoal specimens from various campsites), Libby dispelled the notion of an Old and New World, proving that the oldest dated human settlements around the world began in approximately the same era. For many years after Libby's discovery of radiocarbon dating, the journal *Science* published the results of dating studies by Libby and other scientists from around the world. In 1960, Libby was awarded the Nobel Prize in chemistry for his work in developing radiocarbon dating. In his acceptance speech, as quoted in *Nobel Prize Winners,* Libby noted that radiocarbon dating "may indeed help roll back the pages of history and reveal to mankind something more about his ancestors, and in this way, perhaps about his future." Further progress in radiocarbon dating techniques extended its range to approximately 70,000 years.

In related work, Libby had shown in 1946 that cosmic rays produced tritium, or hydrogen–3, which is also weakly radioactive and has a half-life of 12 years. This radioactive form of hydrogen combines with oxygen to produce radioactive water. As a result, when the U.S. tested the Castle hydrogen bomb in 1954, Libby used the doubled amount of tritium in the atmosphere to date various sources of water, deduce the water-circulation patterns in the U.S., and determine the mixing of oceanic waters. He also used the method to date the ages of wine, since grapes absorb rain water.

Enters the Political Arena

In 1954, U.S. President Dwight D. Eisenhower appointed Libby to the Atomic Energy Commission (AEC). Although he continued to teach graduate students at Chicago, Libby drastically reduced his research efforts and plunged vigorously into his new duties. Previously a member of the commission's General Advisory Committee, which developed commission policy, Libby was already acquainted with the inner workings of the commission. He soon found himself embroiled in the nuclear fallout problem. Upon a recommendation by the Rand Corporation in 1953, Libby formed and directed Project Sunshine and became the first person to measure nuclear fallout in everything from dust, soil, and rain to human bone.

As a member of the AEC, Libby testified before the U.S. Congress and wrote articles about nuclear fallout. He noted that all humans are exposed to a certain amount of natural radiation in sources such as drinking water. He went on to point out that the combination of the body's natural radioactivity, cosmic radiation, and the natural radioactivity of the earth's surface was more hazardous than fallout resulting from nuclear testing. Libby believed, and most scientists concurred, that the effects of nuclear fallout on human genetics were minimal.

Many scientists, however, thought that Libby was merely a "yes man" for the federal administration. In reply, Libby often responded to what he considered misguided thinking. He once wrote to the French physician and author Albert Schweitzer, who had publicly declared that future generations would probably suffer from fallout, that he doubted whether Schweitzer was aware of the most recent data on the subject and that nuclear testing was necessary for the defense effort and the free world's survival. Even after Libby resigned from the AEC in 1959 to resume his scientific studies, he continued to argue with zeal about the necessity for nuclear testing. He also urged the nation's industrial community to employ isotopes in factories and on farms and was a member of the international Atoms for Peace project that supported nuclear energy production for non-military purposes. Libby's experiences in Washington, DC, convinced him that more scientists needed to be in positions of political power and not just advisers. As a result, he was pleased when U.S. President John F. Kennedy appointed **Glenn T. Seaborg**, a nuclear chemist, chair of the AEC in 1961.

Returns to Academia

After retiring from the AEC, Libby took a position in the chemistry department at the University of California, Los Angeles (UCLA), largely due to his first wife's desire to live in California again. Libby had married Leonor Lucinda Hickey in 1940, and the couple had twin daughters. When the family moved to their new home in Bel-Air, California, Libby proceeded to build his own fallout shelter, using sandbags and railroad ties, for approximately $30. During the Cold War, Libby believed that every home should have a fallout shelter in case of nuclear war and wrote a series of articles for the Associated Press news service proposing this necessity. According to Berland, Libby once complained, after hearing a physician say that perhaps it would have been better if scientists had never discovered the power of the atom, that the only way to stop such inevitable discoveries was to "kill all the scientists." He went on to tell Berland that physicians would then have to "go back to witchcraft" for treating people.

In 1962, Libby received a joint appointment as director of the Institute of Geophysics and Planetary Physics. He believed that the new frontier in science was outer space and said that the U.S. must support a large space exploration program in order to prevent the Soviets from controlling outer space, which would probably enable them to rule the world.

Libby and his wife Leonor divorced in 1966. Libby later married Leona Woods Marshall, a professor of environmental engineering at UCLA. He retired in 1976 and died in Los Angeles on September 8, 1980, from complications suffered during a bout of pneumonia.

SELECTED WRITINGS BY LIBBY:

Books

Radiocarbon Dating, University of Chicago Press, 1952, second edition, 1955.

SOURCES:

Books

Berland, Theodore, *The Scientific Life,* Coward-McCann, 1962.
Nobel Prize Winners, H. W. Wilson, 1987.

—*Sketch by David Petechuk*

Hans Wolfgang Liepmann
1914-
German-born American aerospace engineer

Hans Wolfgang Liepmann, in over half a century of research and teaching at the California Institute of Technology, made major contributions to making high-speed flight of aircraft, missiles, and spacecraft practical by enhancing our understanding of the forces acting on such vehicles. Under his tutelage, dozens of students have earned their doctorates and gone on to join their professor as leaders in aerodynamic research.

Born in Berlin, Germany, on July 3, 1914, Hans Wolfgang Leopold Edmund Eugen Victor Liepmann was a well-traveled young man before he came to the United States. His father, Dr. Wilhelm Liepmann, was a German obstetrician who married Emma J. Leser. Their son's interest in science developed very early. As a child, he even tried building his own rockets, an endeavor his parents emphatically terminated when one rocket caused an explosion in his bedroom. After high school, Liepmann served a year as an apprentice, then followed his family to Istanbul, Turkey, when his father was appointed a professor at Istanbul University. The younger Liepmann studied there and then in Prague before moving on to Switzerland, where he earned his doctorate in physics and mathematics from the University of Zurich in 1938. He spent another year as a research fellow at the university before the eminent **Theodore von Kármán** invited him to join the Guggenheim Aeronautical Laboratory at the California Institute of Technology (Caltech) in Pasadena. He would become director of this facility in 1972. Liepmann moved permanently to the United States and later became a citizen.

He remained affiliated with Caltech throughout his professional life. He became a full professor in 1949 and has held two prestigious endowed chairs as the Charles Lee Powell Professor of Fluid Mechanics and Thermodynamics and, beginning in 1983, the Theodore von Kármán Professor of Aeronautics. Liepmann's own name now adorns such a position: a donation from the Boeing Company enabled Caltech to establish the Hans W. Liepmann Professorship in Aeronautics.

Makes Contributions to Research and Education

Liepmann's most outstanding contributions came with his work in gas dynamics, the effects of shock waves and buffeting on aircraft, and the control of laminar turbulence, which concerns the uneven movement of fluids—such as fuel—during flight. All these highly technical subjects deal with the interaction between an airframe and the environment through which it moves and are therefore vital to an understanding of high-speed flight, a subject Liepmann worked on during World War II. Knowledge of these various elements is vital to designing an aircraft or spacecraft that will be controllable. After the war, Liepmann applied his research to the Douglas X–3, one of the first supersonic experimental jets. He also participated in a 1945 study by scientists from Douglas Aircraft and the RAND research institute that gave an early endorsement to the feasibility of orbiting an artificial satellite. In addition to his association with Douglas Aircraft, Liepmann was a consultant at various times for two other aerospace giants, Boeing and TRW. He was on several technical committees of the National Advisory Committee on Aeronautics and its successor, the National Aeronautics and Space Administration. Liepmann was appointed to advisory panels of the U.S. Air Force, including the MX Panel during the development of that missile, and the North Atlantic Treaty Organization. He also served two terms on the National Academy of Engineering's Aeronautics and Space Engineering board. To Liepmann, these connections with government and industry were a way to apply his research in practical areas and obtain feedback to guide further research. His contributions were recognized often, one example being the American Physical Society's presentation of its Fluid Dynamics Prize to Liepmann in 1980.

Liepmann was proudest of his achievements as a teacher. He co-authored two textbooks and created a graduate course in gas dynamics. The textbooks became widely used standards and were translated into several languages, including Russian. He guided over fifty students to their Ph.D.s, one notable example being George Solomon, who went on to head aerospace giant TRW. Eleven of Liepmann's pupils became members of the prestigious National Academy of Engineering. Liepmann also received Caltech's undergraduate teaching award in 1986. Liepmann's reputation was international, and overseas accolades came from the Indian Academy of Sciences, the German Society for Aeronautics, and the Max Planck Institute in Gottingen, Germany, which made him an honorary fellow. In 1985, Liepmann became the Theodore von Kármán Professor of Aeronautics, Emeritus. He continued to lecture, investigate, and add to his list of over forty published professional papers and articles. His later work included probing the phenomena involved in turbulent mixing of fluids, the dynamics of liquid helium, and the laws of thermodynamics. In 1986, he received America's highest scientific honor, the National Medal of Science. The citation honored his "invaluable contributions to the physical sciences and engineering and their impact on national defense," noting that his work "contributed to high-speed flight, understanding

aircraft buffeting, new methods for efficient combustion, and a new generation of chemical lasers."

Liepmann married Dietlind Goldschmidt, holder of a doctorate in classical archaeology, in 1954. The couple raised her two sons from a previous marriage and had two of their own, Till and Dorian, who both earned doctorates in engineering themselves. After Dietlind passed away in 1990, Liepmann spent much of his spare time at his home in La Canada-Flintridge, near Caltech, reading and pursuing his longstanding interest in Islamic history as well as enjoying himself by playing tennis. He also accepted an occasional lecture invitation and continued contributing to various research projects, working partly from his home via computer. The honors for Liepmann's lifetime of work continued, capped in September, 1993, by the U.S. Department of Commerce's National Medal of Technology. This was given both for his research and for his "devotion to the education of the world's leaders in aeronautics."

SELECTED WRITINGS BY LIEPMANN:

Books

(With A. Puckett) *Introduction to Aerodynamics of a Compressible Fluid,* Wiley, 1947.
(With A. Roshko) *Elements of Gasdynamics,* Wiley, 1957.

Periodicals

American Scientist, March-April, 1979, pp. 221–228.
Journal of Fluid Mechanics, 1982, pp. 187–200.

SOURCES:

Periodicals

Physics Today, October, 1980, p. 83; July, 1986, pp. 77–78.

Other

Braden, Paul, Hans W. Liepmann, U.S. Department of Commerce, interview with Matthew A. Bille, August 16, 1993.
Cheetham, Karen, Hans W. Liepmann, California Institute of Technology, interview with Matthew A. Bille, August 23, 1993.
"Presentation of the National Medal of Science," U.S. Department of Commerce press release, March 12, 1986.

—Sketch by Matthew A. Bille

Frank Rattray Lillie
1870-1947
Canadian-born American biologist

Frank Rattray Lillie was both an internationally-acclaimed biologist and one of the founders of the Woods Hole Oceanographic Institute at Woods Hole, Massachusetts. It was while at Woods Hole that Lillie's work in embryology and zoology helped make that institution's Marine Biological Laboratory a premier research facility. Perhaps most famous for his work on sex hormones, Lillie was also lauded for his research in morphology, the study of animal and plant structures. Over the course of his career at Woods Hole, Lillie acted as director of the Marine Biological Laboratory and president of the Oceanographic Institute. For his work at the Institute, Lillie received the Agassiz Medal of the National Academy of Sciences in 1940. Lillie was the first person to serve as president of the National Academy of Sciences and chairman of the National Research Council at the same time.

An only child, Lillie was born on June 27, 1870, in Toronto, Canada, to George Waddell Lillie, an accountant and partner in a pharmaceutical firm, and Emily Ann Rattray Lillie, the daughter of a Scottish tobacco merchant who eventually became a Congregational minister. A mediocre grammar and high school student, Lillie was considered a "late bloomer." It was only after a friend introduced him to the world of insects and fossils during his senior year in high school that Lillie recognized his true calling: natural science studies.

When Lillie entered the University of Toronto, his original goal was to become a minister. He made the natural sciences his major because he had become convinced that science posed a threat to religion. Years later— after he had become a scientist himself—Lillie attempted to reconcile science and religion. "The constant discoveries of new animals and plants and of the principles of their reproduction . . . all profoundly affected the intellectual milieu and the outlook on society, philosophy, and religion," he wrote in *The Woods Hole Marine Biological Laboratory.* Eventually, Lillie met R. Ramsey Wright, who both introduced the budding scientist to embryology and recommended his placement as a research fellow at the Marine Biological Laboratory and Clark University.

Rises to Prominence in the Academic World

In 1892, Lillie moved to the University of Chicago as a fellow in morphology, getting his doctorate in zoology in 1894. Under the guidance of newly-appointed department chairman C. O. Whitman, Lillie wrote his dissertation on the cell lineage of the freshwater mussel, an effort that won him acclaim as a promising investigator. After teaching zoology for five years at the University of Michigan, Lillie spent a year as professor of biology at Vassar College. He returned to the University of Chicago in 1900, steadily climbing the professorial ladder to eventually become dean of biological sciences in 1931 and emeritus professor in 1935. Lillie's administrative tenure was noted for the chairman's emphasis on democratic structures and the enhancement of undergraduate programs.

Lillie's association with Woods Hole began rather inauspiciously. When Lillie first visited the Marine Biological Laboratory, it was housed in one small building. Over the years, Lillie's efforts both in the lab and at fundraising helped the institute—and its reputation—grow. Every summer, after a year spent teaching and doing laboratory research, Lillie returned to Woods Hole to work in the woodland setting, following the motto of the scientist Louis Agassiz, "Study nature not books." While teaching at various universities and researching at Woods Hole, Lillie developed his theories about the physiology of fertilization from work with the annelid Nereis and the sea urchins Arbacia and Strongylocentrotus which he plucked from nearby ponds; Lillie also studied marine eggs taken from local waters. The advantage of using these subjects, the scientist wrote in *The Woods Hole Marine Biology Laboratory,* is that "some of these eggs are glass-like in transparency. With the microscope, the fascinating life-histories of many species can be studied in the living condition from the beginning."

Develops Fertilization Theories

During the first two decades of his career, Lillie concentrated on studying the fertilization and early development of invertebrate eggs. He focused on cell division, using a light microscope to explore the chemical and physical properties that determine an embryo's early development, ultimately concluding that the study of microscopic cell components was vital to understanding overall structural organization. In 1914, Lillie turned his microscope on mammals. The opportunity to study a pair of calf fetuses occurred when the manager of Lillie's cattle farm sent the researcher a pair of calf fetuses. Lillie's research—which developed from analyzing this pair and subsequent cattle twins—introduced biologists to the nature, origin, and action of sex hormones when such knowledge was inchoate, at best; it also lead to Lillie's theory of the freemartin, the term applied to the development of a sterile genetic female twin. Lillie's study of bovine twins eventually led the scientist to work with colleagues on the isolation, chemical analysis, and synthesis of sex hormones. This research was followed by Lillie's isolation—with F. C. Koch at the University of Chicago—of the first known androgens, or male sex hormones. That finding, in turn, led to greater understanding of the role of sex hormones in animal behavior.

Lillie's life outside the laboratory was also very busy. Shortly after receiving his doctorate, he met and married Frances Crane, a young woman who had been his embryology student at Woods Hole. The couple had five daughters and one son; they later adopted three more boys. Over the years, several universities bestowed honorary degrees upon Lillie for his contributions to science, including the University of Toronto, Yale University, and Johns Hopkins University. Lillie died in Chicago on November 5, 1947.

SELECTED WRITINGS BY LILLIE:

Books

Development of the Chick: An Introduction to Embryology, Holt, 1908, revised as *Lillie's Development of the Chick,* H.L. Hamilton, 1952.
The Woods Hole Marine Biological Laboratory, University of Chicago Press, 1944.

SOURCES:

Periodicals

Moore, C. R., "Frank Rattray Lillie, 1870–1947," *Science,* Number 107, 1948, pp. 33–35.
Willier, B. H., "Frank Rattray Lillie," *Anatomical Record,* Number 100, 1948, pp. 407–410.

—*Sketch by Rayma Prince*

Robert K. S. Lim
1897-1969
Singaporean-born American physician and physiologist

Robert K. S. Lim earned an international reputation for his studies of gastrointestinal physiology and the central nervous system. He expanded his early studies, which had employed some of Russian physiologist **Ivan Petrovich Pavlov**'s technically-demanding experimental techniques, by exploring the relationship between gastric juice and blood. He later conducted studies on the neurophysiology of pain (with particular attention to how aspirin works) and persuaded his colleagues of the utility of employing dogs in neurophysiological research. He is credited with establishing Western physiology in China and with significantly improving the quality of medical care in the Chinese army during the 1930s and 1940s.

Robert Kho-seng Lim was born on October 15, 1897, in Singapore, the eldest son of Lim Boon-kang, an eminent physician and graduate of the University of Edinburgh. Lim was sent to Scotland for his education at a young age, and he decided to attend the world-famous medical school at Edinburgh University. A successful student, Lim graduated in 1919 with bachelors degrees in medicine and chemistry. In medical school at Edinburgh, he worked with the physiologist Edward A. Sharpey-Schafer, under whose guidance he received a Ph.D. in 1920. He taught physiology to medical students there for the next four years; many of them, like Lim, were veterans of World War I. He then left for the United States, where he embarked on further post-graduate studies with Julius Carlson and Andrew Ivy at the University of Chicago.

Having married Margaret Torrance in Scotland in 1920, Lim arrived in China in 1924 to continue his work in physiology at the Peking Union Medical College, where he was appointed professor and department chair, the youngest person and the first Chinese to fill these positions. Even though he was more fluent in English than in Chinese, he soon became an enormously popular teacher and a motive force in the early development of the college. Lim helped to found the Chinese Physiological Society in 1926, became its first chairman, and also served as president of the Chinese Medical Association.

With the opening of hostilities in the Sino-Japanese War in 1931, Lim's intense patriotism led him into the area of military medicine, where he became renowned for his organizational skills. This sideline—soon to become his consuming passion—led him to form what would eventually become the Chinese Red Cross Medical Relief Corps. Having drastically improved sanitation and the quality of medical care in the Chinese army, he later supplied medical support to U.S. General Joseph Stillwell's Chinese Expeditionary Force, beginning in 1942. Subsequently Chiang Kai-shek appointed him surgeon general of the medical services of the Chinese army, with special responsibility for organizing post-war health programs. For his wartime efforts, the United States government honored Lim with the Legion of Merit and with the Medal of Freedom.

After the communist victory in mainland China, Lim resigned his position as surgeon general in 1948, and returned to research in physiology. He moved to the United States, receiving appointments at the

University of Illinois, Creighton University, and, finally, at the Miles Medical Science Research Laboratories in Indiana. Lim maintained his ties with his homeland, however, serving the American Bureau for Medical Aid to China (ABMAC) in a number of capacities for more than twenty years.

During his long career, Lim served as the managing editor of the *Chinese Journal of Physiology,* to which he contributed many papers. Among his scientific honors and professional memberships, Lim was elected a fellow of the Royal Society of Edinburgh in 1923. He became a foreign associate member of the National Academy of Sciences in 1942, which elected him a regular member in 1955, when he became a citizen of the United States. He died of cancer of the esophagus at the home of his son James in Kingston, Jamaica, on July 8, 1969. Lim survived his first wife, by whom he also had a daughter, Effie. He was survived by his second wife, Tsing-Ying Tsang.

SELECTED WRITINGS BY LIM:

Books

(With H. C. Chang, T. P. Feng, and others) *Outline of Physiology,* [Peking], 1935.
(With C. N. Liu and R. L. Moffitt) *A Stereotaxic Atlas of the Dog's Brain,* [Springfield, Ill.], 1960.

Periodicals

(With A. C. Ivy and J. E. McCarthy) "Contributions to the Physiology of Gastric Section, II. Intestinal Phase of Gastric Secretion," *Journal of Experimental Physiology,* Volume 15, 1925, pp. 55–68.
(With M. H. Pindell and others) "The Experimental Evaluation of Sedative Agents in Animals," *Ann. of the New York Academy of Science,* Volume 64, 1956, pp. 667–78.

SOURCES:

Books

Bowers, John Z., *Western Medicine in a Chinese Palace: Peking Union Medical College, 1917–1951,* Josiah Macy, Jr., Foundation, 1972.
Davenport, Horace, "Robert Kho-seng Lim," *Biographical Memoirs of the National Academy of Sciences,* Volume 51, 1980, pp. 281–306.

Periodicals

"Robert Kho-seng Lim, Ph.D.," *ABMAC Bulletin,* Volume 30, July, August, 1969, pp. 1–4.

—*Sketch by Susan Sheets Pyenson*

Chia-Chiao Lin
1916-
Chinese-born American mathematician and astronomer

Born in Fukien, China, on July 7, 1916, the son of Kai and Y. T. Lin, Chia-Chiao Lin pursued his undergraduate studies at the National Tsing Hua University in China, receiving a B.Sc. in 1937. He was awarded a master's degree in applied mathematics from the University of Toronto in 1941 and a Ph.D. in aeronautics from the California Institute of Technology in 1944. A former student of **Theodore von Kármán** whose varied background includes mathematics, aeronautics, and fluid mechanics, Lin's work has contributed to multiple disciplines within the scientific community, as well as to government and industry. His importance lies in his use of mathematical modeling to create new formal tools for theoretical investigation in a number of sciences, including meteorology, oceanography, astrophysics, chemical engineering, and planetary sciences.

Following early work on fluid mechanics, Lin turned to a concentration on the hydrodynamics of superfluid helium and, later, on astrophysics. It was his work in this latter field that led to his development of the density wave theory of the spiral structure of galaxies, which provided an answer to one of the most long-standing puzzles in astronomy. This theory attempts to explain the formation of galaxies, their shapes (elliptical, normal spiral, barred spiral, etc.), and their luminosity.

Scientists had long recognized that the shapes of galaxies appeared to have a certain regularity—a regularity that could be governed by wave phenomena. The density wave theory was developed to explain these patterns and to analyze their dynamical implications; such implications include star formation, which the theory explains as being triggered by galactic shocks induced by a low-amplitude density wave pattern. The density wave theory also classifies spiral galaxies by associating specific shapes with particular wave patterns, or "modes"; according to Lin, normal spiral modes and barred spiral modes correspond to normal spiral galaxies and transition barred galaxies and some barred spiral galaxies. Lin's theory has since been confirmed by a wealth of observational data and has provided a model for applying theoretical mathematics and physics—often in conjunction with computer science—to other disciplines.

Lin has been instrumental in the exchange of information between scientists in the United States and China and has organized trips by Chinese scientists to the United States. He has served as an advisor to the Chinese government on issues involving education and as an educational consultant for applied mathematics groups. He is a member of the National Academy of Science's Committee on Support of Research in the Mathematical Sciences; he served as the president of the Society for Industrial and Applied Mathematics and the chairman of the Committee on Applied Mathematics of the American Mathematical Society.

After a two-year stint as assistant and later associate professor of applied mathematics at Brown University, Lin took a position at Massachusetts Institute of Technology as professor of applied mathematics in 1947; he is now professor emeritus. He has also worked at Jet Propulsion Laboratories, and has served as a consultant to a number of industries. Lin married Shou-Ling Liang in 1946; they have one daughter.

SELECTED WRITINGS BY LIN:

Books

The Theory of Hydrodynamic Stability, Cambridge University Press, 1955.
Selected papers of C. C. Lin (two volumes), World Scientific Publishing, 1987.

Periodicals

(With W. H. Reid) "Turbulent Flow, Theoretical Aspects," *Handbuch der Physik-Encyclopedia of Physics,* Volume 8, number 2, 1963.
(With Frank H. Shu) "On the Spiral Structure of Disk Galaxies," *Astrophysical Journal,* number 140, 1964, pp. 646–655.
(With Shu) "On the Spiral Structure of Galaxies II: Outline of a Theory of Density Waves," *Proceedings of the National Academy of Sciences* number 55, 1966, pp. 229–234.

—*Sketch by Michael Sims*

Fritz Lipmann
1899-1986

Prussian-born American biochemist

Fritz Lipmann was one of the leading architects of the golden age of biochemistry. His landmark paper, "Metabolic Generation and Utilization of Phosphate Bond Energy," published in 1941, laid the foundation for biochemical research over the next

Fritz Lipmann

three decades, clearly defining such concepts as group potential and the role of group transfer in biosynthesis. Most biochemists clearly recognized that Lipmann had revealed the basis for the relationship between metabolic energy production and its use, providing the first coherent picture of how living organisms operate. His discovery in 1945 of coenzyme A (CoA), which occurs in all living cells and is a key element in the metabolism of carbohydrates, fats, and some amino acids, earned him the 1953 Nobel Prize in physiology or medicine. Lipmann also conducted groundbreaking research in protein synthesis. Lipmann was an instinctual researcher with a knack for seeing the broader picture. Lacking the talent or inclination for self-promotion, he struggled early in his career before establishing himself in the world of biochemistry.

Fritz Albert Lipmann was born on June 12, 1899, in Königsberg, the capital of East Prussia (now Kaliningrad, Russia). The son of Leopold, a lawyer, and Gertrud Lachmanski, Lipmann grew up in a happy and cultured surroundings and fondly remembered the peaceful years at the turn of the century. He counted his only brother Heinz, who would pursue the arts as opposed to science, as one of the two people who most influenced him in his formative years. The other was Siegfried (Friedel) Sebba, a painter who would remain his friend for life. From these two, he first learned to appreciate the arts, an avenue of interest that he used to escape the confines and pressures of his laboratory investigations.

Early on, Lipmann demonstrated a diffidence in academic pursuit that would belie his future success. He admitted that he was never very good at school, even when he reached the university. After graduating from the gymnasium, Lipmann decided to pursue a career in medicine, largely due to the influence of an uncle who was a pediatrician and one of his boyhood heroes. In 1917 he enrolled in the University of Königsberg but had his medical studies interrupted in 1918 as he was called to the medical service during World War I. Serving near the front during the last days of the war, he first learned to exert authority and never forgot the grim experience of severely wounded men receiving bad care.

In 1919 he was discharged from the army and went to study medicine in Munich and Berlin. Lipmann's brother was a literature student in Munich, and Lipmann became involved with his brother's circle of artistic friends while he lived in Schwabing, which Lipmann called the Greenwich Village of the city at that time. Throughout his life he maintained fond memories of Berlin. He eventually returned to Königsberg to complete his studies and obtained his medical degree from Berlin in 1922. Even though he cared about patients, Lipmann became more intrigued by what went on inside the human body. This interest was further cultivated when during his practical year of medical studies he worked in the pathology department in a Berlin hospital and took a three-month course in modern biochemistry taught by Peter Rona. At the same time, Lipmann was troubled by his concerns over the ethics of profiting from providing necessary medical services. The final turning point came when he went to the University of Amsterdam on a half-year stipend to study pharmacology. There, he first became versed in biochemical problems and the working of a biological laboratory. He left Amsterdam bent on a new career as a researcher.

Returning to Königsberg, Lipmann, who had no money, lived with his parents while he studied chemistry in the university for the next three years. Looking for a laboratory to do research in for his thesis, he chose to work with biochemist **Otto Meyerhof**, whose physiological investigations focused on the muscle. For the most part, Lipmann worked on inhibition of glycolysis (the breakdown of glucose by enzymes) by fluoride in muscle contraction and did his doctoral dissertation on metabolic fluoride effects. During this time in Berlin, Lipmann met many of the era's great biochemists, including Karl Lohmann, who discovered adenosine triphosphate (ATP—a compound that provides the chemical energy necessary for a host of chemical reactions in the cell) and taught Lipmann about phosphate ester chemistry, which was to play an important role in Lipmann's later research. Lipmann also met his eventual lifelong companion while attending one of the masked balls popular at

that time. Freda Hall, an American-born German and an artist, would become his wife.

Over the next ten years, Lipmann continued with a varied but not very lucrative research career. In *The Roots of Modern Biochemistry,* Freda remembered her husband as a very "unusual young man" who "seemed to be certain of a goal" but "had no position, no prospects, and it did not seem to trouble him." Although he was interested in his work, Freda recalled that "at no time was Fritz the obsessed scientist without other interests. He always had time for fun," which included tennis matches, bicycle races, and the theater.

Lipmann spent a short time in Heidelberg when Meyerhof moved his laboratory there but then returned to Berlin and worked with Albert Fischer on tissue culturing and the study of metabolism as a method to measure cell growth. But soon uniformed followers of Hitler began to appear in the streets of Berlin; both Lipmann and Freda had unpleasant encounters, and once Lipmann was beaten up. Realizing that they would soon have to leave Germany, Lipmann, through Fischer's intervention, received an offer to work at the Rockefeller Foundation (now Rockefeller University). Before leaving for the United States, Lipmann and Freda Hall were married on June 21, 1931. As it turned out, Freda's birth in Ohio made her an American citizen, thus greatly reducing obstacles to immigration. At the Rockefeller Foundation, Lipmann worked in the laboratory of chemist Phoebus Aaron Theodor Levene, who had conducted research on the egg yolk protein, which he called vitellinic acid, and found that it contained 10 percent bound phosphate (that is, phosphate strongly attached to other substances). Lipmann's interest in this protein, which served as food for growing animal tissues, led him to isolate serine phosphate from an egg protein.

At the end of the summer of 1932, Lipmann and his wife returned to Europe to work with Fischer, who was now in the Biological Institute of the Carlsberg Foundation in Copenhagen, Denmark. Free to pursue his own scientific interests, Lipmann delved into the mechanism of fermentation and glycolysis and eventually cell energy transformation. In the course of these studies, Lipmann found that pyruvate oxidation (a reaction that involves the loss of electrons) yielded ATP. Lohmann, who first discovered ATP, had also found that creatine phosphate provides the muscle with energy through ATP. Further work led Lipmann to the discovery of acetyl phosphate and the recognition that this phosphate was the intermediate of pyruvate oxidation. A discovery that Lipmann said was his most impressive work and had motivated all his subsequent research.

Writes Groundbreaking Essay

Despite his belief in his work, Lipmann had still to make his mark in research. In his book, *Wander-*

ings of a Biochemist, Lipmann would remember his efforts at the institute and throughout that decade as a time of personal scientific development that set the stage for his later discoveries. "In the Freudian sense," said Lipmann, "all that I did later was subconsciously mapped out there; it started to mature between 1930 and 1940 and was more elaborately realized from then on."

But before Lipmann could piece together his formula for the foundation of how organisms produce energy, once again the rise of the Nazis forced him and his wife to flee to the United States; they were nearly penniless. Fortunately, Lipmann acquired a research fellowship in the biochemistry department of Cornell University Medical College. His work with pyruvate oxidation and ATP had germinated and set him on a series of investigations that led to his theories of phosphate bond energy and energy-rich phosphate bond energy. During a vacation on Lake Iroquois in Vermont, Lipmann began his essay "Metabolic Generation and Utilization of Phosphate Bond Energy," in which he introduced the squiggle (~) to represent energy-rich phosphate, a symbol subsequently used by other researchers to denote energy-rich metabolic linkages. In this essay, Lipmann also first proposed the notion of group potential and the role of group transfer in biosynthesis.

This essay was the turning point in Lipmann's career. Prior to its publication, Lipmann had contributed disparate pieces to the puzzle of biosynthesis, but through his natural scientific instinct and the ability to see the broader picture, he had now laid the foundation for the basis of how living organisms function. Although his essay covered a wide range of topics, including carbamyl phosphate and the synthesis of sulfate esters, his elucidation of the role of ATP in group activation (such as amino acids in the synthesis of proteins), foretold the use of ATP in the biosynthesis of macromolecules (large molecules). In more general terms, he identified a link between generation of metabolic energy and its utilization. A prime example of ATP's role in energy transmission was the transfer of phosphor potential from ATP to provide the energy needed for muscles to contract.

Despite the growing acknowledgement that Lipmann had written a groundbreaking paper in biochemistry, he soon found himself without a solid job prospect when Dean Burk, whose lab Lipmann worked in, left for the National Institutes of Health. Burk was reluctant to take Lipmann with him because of Lipmann's lack of interest in Burk's cancer research. While Lipmann's renown had grown, he had also antagonized other researchers, especially by his insistence that the term "bond energy" had been misused and his replacement of the term with "group potential" to refer to the capacity of a biochemical bond to carry potential energy for synthesis. It also took many years for the squiggle to be fully accepted

as a way to denote energy-carrying bonds. Fortunately, Lipmann gained an unusual appointment in the Department of Surgery at the Massachusetts General Hospital through the support of a Ciba Foundation fellowship. "This was really one of the lucky breaks in my life," Lipmann recalled in his autobiography. Soon he received growing support from the Commonwealth Fund as more and more people began to recognize the importance of his work. Building upon his group transfer concept, Lipmann delved into the nature of the metabolically active acetate, which had been postulated as an "active" intermediary in group activation. In 1945, working with a potent enzyme from pigeon liver extract as an assay system for acetyl transfer in animal tissue, Lipmann and colleagues at Massachusetts General Hospital discovered Coenzyme A (CoA), the "A" standing for the activation of acetate. (Coenzymes are organic substances that can attach themselves to and supplement specified proteins to form active enzyme systems.) Eventually, CoA would be shown to occur in all living cells as an essential component in the metabolism of carbohydrates, fats, and certain amino acids. In 1953 Lipmann received the Nobel Prize in physiology or medicine for his discovery specifically of the acetyl-carrying CoA, which is formed as an intermediate in metabolism and active as a coenzyme in biological acetylations. (Lipmann shared the prize with his old colleague and friend, **Hans Krebs**, from Berlin.) Although proud of the Nobel Prize, Lipmann often stated that he believed his earlier work on the theory of group transfer was more deserving.

In 1957 Lipmann once again found himself at the Rockefeller Institute, twenty-five years after his first appointment there. Lipmann was to spend the next thirty years at the institute, primarily working on the analysis of protein biosynthesis. He and his colleagues contributed greatly to our understanding of the mechanisms of the elongation step of protein synthesis (stepwise addition of single amino acids to the primary protein structure).

A Productive Career

Lipmann's productive career included 516 publications between 1924 and 1985. His 1944 paper on acetyl phosphate is a citation classic, having been cited in other works more than seven hundred times. His work on high-energy phosphate bonds and group transfer discoveries propelled biochemistry to the forefront of physiological research for nearly three decades. In addition to the Nobel Prize, Lipmann received the National Medal of Science in 1966 and was elected a foreign member of the Royal Society in London.

In 1959 the Lipmanns, who had a son Stephen Hall, bought a country home with Fritz's Nobel Prize money. Although his wife described him essentially as a city person, Lipmann enjoyed the country and often strolled the twenty acres of woods that surrounded his home with his Australian terrier, Pogo, named after the satiric comic strip character popular in the 1960s and 1970s. A private man who avoided political and social issues, Lipmann did, however, sign the Nobel laureate public appeal letters seeking prohibition of the hydrogen bomb and asking for freedom for the Polish Worker's Union. Lipmann's talent for writing was evident in the easy-to-follow and informative format of his scientific essays and in his autobiography. Still, he was given to preoccupation, and a colleague fondly recalled Lipmann once combing an auditorium after a lecture in search of his shoes, which he had left behind in going to the podium.

Lipmann's unique ability to see the entire scientific picture set him apart from many of his contemporaries. Interestingly, this ability also translated into his noted penchant for spotting four-leaf clovers almost anywhere. He kept them in books, manuscripts, and wallets, perhaps reflecting his own estimation that he had been fortunate in a life and career that allowed him to follow his instincts so successfully.

Despite failing strength, Lipmann continued to work until he suffered a stroke on July 17, 1986, and died seven days later. "One evening I heard him say: I can't function anymore," recalled Freda Hall in *The Roots of Modern Biochemistry*, "and that was that." Lipmann's ashes were scattered along his walking path in the woods that surrounded his home.

SELECTED WRITINGS BY LIPMANN:

Books

Wanderings of a Biochemist, Wiley-Interscience, 1971.

Periodicals

"Metabolic Generation and Utilization of Phosphate Bond Energy," *Advances in Enzymology*, Volume 1, 1941.
"A Long Life in Times of Great Upheaval," *Annual Review of Biochemistry*, Volume 53, 1984.

SOURCES:

Books

Lipmann Symposium: Energy, Regulation, and Biosynthesis in Molecular Biology, Walter de Gruyter, 1974.

McGraw-Hill Modern Men of Science, McGraw-Hill, 1966.
The Roots of Modern Biochemistry, Walter de Gruyter, 1988.

—*Sketch by David Petechuk*

Gabriel Lippmann
1845-1921
French physicist

Gabriel Lippmann had a distinguished career as an inventor, theoretician and academic. At the Faculty of Sciences, a laboratory in Paris, France, he became professor of mathematical physics in 1883, a professor of experimental physics in 1886, and, later, director of the laboratory. He stayed active in this position, overseeing the laboratory's incorporation into the Sorbonne, until he died at sea on July 13, 1921. A member of the French Academy of Sciences and the Bureau des Longitudes, he was elected in 1908 as a Foreign Member of the Royal Society of London. Even before he had finished his doctorate in 1875, he embarked on a lifetime of publishing papers and the creation of measuring instruments to accompany research and observation in physics, astronomy, and seismology. Lippmann is most often remembered, however, for developing an early process of color photography. It was for this achievement that he received the 1908 Nobel Prize for physics.

Born in Hollerich, Luxemburg, on August 16, 1845, to French parents, Gabriel Jonas Lippmann began his education at home. When he was thirteen, his family settled in Paris, where he entered the Lycée Napoléon. After ten years he attended the Ecole Normale. During this time, he assisted with the publication of the *Annales de Chimie et de Physique* by summarizing German articles. In this manner he learned of recent discoveries in electricity. In 1873 he traveled, as part of a scientific mission, to Germany, where, at Heidelberg, he worked in physicist Gustav Kirchhoff's laboratory. There, Wilhelm Kühne, a professor of physiology, showed him an experiment in which a drop of mercury, covered with diluted sulfuric acid, contracted when touched with a piece of iron wire—only to recover its original shape when the wire was removed. Lippmann theorized that the wire had somehow changed the tiny electrical current between the acid and the mercury, causing it to ball up. He obtained permission to systemically confirm his supposition with experiments in Kirchhoff's laboratory.

Creates the Capillary Electrometer and Pursues Its Theoretical Implications

Lippmann's investigations resulted in an 1873 publication that theoretically described the mercury phenomenon that Kühne had shown him as well as the device he developed from it, the capillary electrometer. This instrument, which came into wide use before the advent of solid-state electronics, could measure electrical currents as small as 1/1,000 of a volt. Its elegant design consisted of a narrow tube (or capillary), pitched at a slight horizontal angle, containing mercury covered with diluted acid. Any change in the electric charge between the two liquids caused a ripple at their interface to move up the tube. As a result of Lippmann's work on the capillary electrometer, the Sorbonne awarded him a doctorate in 1875.

In 1876 Lippmann published a paper showing that it was possible to reverse the electro-magnetic phenomenon he had investigated in 1873. Returning to the experiment of mercury covered with acid, he demonstrated that altering the shape of the mercury by mechanical means, somehow squeezing it together, had an impact on the electrical field between the mercury and the acid. To demonstrate definitively the reversibility of the two processes, Lippmann devised an engine based on the principles of his capillary electrometer. This engine turned when electrified and produced electricity when turned mechanically. Lippmann built upon the earlier work of French engineer Sadi Carnot. In 1824 Carnot demonstrated, with a reversible heat engine, the thermodynamic principle that there exists an inverse (or opposing) and measurable relationship between heat and force. Following this reasoning, Lippmann established a more general theorem which he published in 1881. It states that given any phenomenon, the reverse phenomenon also exists and that one can calculate its degree of change.

Advances Observational Methods in Astronomy and Seismology

Lippmann made important innovations in observation for physics, such as introducing high-speed photographs to record the behavior of pendulums. Not content to confine his efforts to one field, he also modernized observational instruments in astronomy and seismology. His most notable upgrade was a device called the coelostat. Using a mirror attached to a machine that reproduced the axis and rotation of the earth, the coelostat insured that whole regions of the sky, rather than a single star, could be photographed without registering any motion. By increasing the area to be recorded, it improved on an earlier device, the siderostat. Lippmann created another instrument related to the coelostat, called the uranograph. This device produced a photographic map of the sky with its longitudes automatically imprinted on it. Lippmann also devised a method for measuring longitudinal differences between observatories through radio and photography. In his contributions to the field of seismology, Lippmann proposed using telegraphic signals for the early detection of earthquakes as well as for measuring how quickly they traveled. In addition, he suggested a seismograph that would record seismic waves while taking into account the earth's acceleration.

Wins 1908 Nobel Prize in Physics for Color Photography

The achievement that won Lippmann his widest recognition, and the 1908 Nobel Prize in physics, was his perfection of a photographic process with relatively permanent color. As early as the beginning of the nineteenth century, its was widely known that moist silver chloride could reproduce the colors of the spectrum. In 1848, Edmond Becquerel managed to reproduce colored objects on a silver plate covered with a layer of silver chloride. Unfortunately, Becquerel had no way of fixing the colors, which faded rapidly. In 1890, Otto Weiner confirmed, through an experiment, that Becquerel's phenomenon was the result of "interference" - light waves trapped at different levels in the layer of silver chloride.

In 1891 Lippmann published a method where a transparent plate with a layer of silver nitrate, gelatin, and potassium bromide in emulsion was placed, emulsion-side-down, in a holder with mercury in it. During exposure, which in the initial experiments lasted fifteen minutes, light waves became fixed in the emulsion after repeatedly bouncing off the mercury, faithfully reproducing the colors in nature. After the plate was developed, the colors, seen in reflected light, were permanent. Although it presented a significant leap forward at the time, Lippmann's method proved impractical. There was no way to create copies and the exposure time, although later reduced to a minute, was still too long to suit the needs of mass production.

Lippmann married Mademoiselle Cherbuliez in 1888, their union producing no children. There is little public information regarding his personal life. What he is known for is his body of work, which is considered ingenious and progressive. Rather than the antiquated photographic process for which he received the Nobel Prize, however, many scientists believe Lippmann's real contributions to science lay in his work with the capillary electrometer and his theoretical papers.

SOURCES:

Books

Dictionary of Scientific Biography, Volume VII, Scribner's, 1970, pp. 387–88.

Heathcote, Niels H., editor, *Nobel Prize Winners in Physics 1901–1950,* Schuman, 1953, pp. 65–69.

Periodicals

Turner, H. H., "Some Notes on the Use and Adjustment of the Coelostat", *Monthly Notices of the Royal Society,* Volume 56, 1896, p. 408.

—*Sketch by Hovey Brock*

William Nunn Lipscomb, Jr.
1919-
American physical chemist

William Nunn Lipscomb, Jr. worked in several of the subdivisions of chemistry in his career, but was awarded the 1976 Nobel Prize in chemistry for his studies of chemical bonding in boron compounds, particularly the boron hydrides. These materials break some of the conventional rules of chemistry, and Lipscomb's theories have expanded chemists' understanding of how atoms can be bonded to one another.

Lipscomb was born on December 9, 1919, to William and Edna (Porter) Lipscomb. He grew up in Lexington, Kentucky, after his family had moved there from Cleveland, Ohio, when he was a year old. He graduated from the University of Kentucky with a degree in chemistry in 1941. After serving with the United States Office of Scientific Research and Development during World War II, he finished his doctorate in physical chemistry at the California Institute of Technology in 1946. His thesis advisor was the distinguished Nobel Laureate **Linus Pauling**. Lipscomb taught for several years at the University of Minnesota, and in 1959 moved to Harvard University, where he spent the rest of his working life.

Explores the Enigma of Boranes

The bonding in boranes—a compound consisting of boron and hydrogen—had puzzled chemists ever since the German chemist **Alfred Stock** had synthesized them. (Boranes do not normally occur in nature; they are purely man-made compounds.) Normally, chemists expect a bond to consist of two electrons located between two atoms; this is standard bonding theory, originally advanced by American chemist **Gilbert Newton Lewis**. Additionally, they expect most atoms to be stable if their outer electron shells contain eight electrons, in either bonded or non-bonded pairs. Boranes do not appear to possess sufficient outer-shell electrons to conform to either of these ideas, and are thus classified as "electron deficient" compounds. Several scientists, including Pauling himself, had tried to explain electron deficiency, but none of the theories proved satisfactory. H. C. °Longuet-Higgins had advanced the theory that hydrogen could be linked to two boron atoms, forming a "three-center" bond with hydrogen bridging the two borons.

Lipscomb and his co-workers Bryce Crawford, Jr., and W. H. Eberhardt expanded on this idea in 1954 when they suggested in the *Journal of Chemical Physics* that, in addition to the three-center bond, a regular covalent bond could hold boron and hydrogen atoms together under certain circumstances. Each bond still consisted of two electrons, but the covalent link was made possible because more than two atoms regarded themselves as bonded by the two electrons. Depending on the boron compound, the three atoms linked by the single bond might be three borons, or two borons and a hydrogen. Lipscomb knew how radical this idea was; his 1954 paper with Crawford and Eberhardt stated, "We have even ventured a few predictions, knowing that if we must join the ranks of boron hydride predictors later proved wrong, we shall be in the best of company."

Lipscomb's research also expanded the understanding of the unusual shape of large boron molecules. Because of the three-center bonds, these molecules fold up into basket or cage-like structures that are chemically very stable. (Chemical stability does not occur in the smaller boranes, however, which are volatile, reactive, and occasionally explosive). Lipscomb's contributions to the structure determination and molecular orbital theories of these molecules allowed the planned synthesis of many more of them, including boron combined with other elements. Carboranes, for example, are boron cages with carbon embedded in the structure; they are used in the manufacture of highly stable polymers that resist both heat and chemicals. Many other elements are now known to make stable cage structures, but Lipscomb's elucidation of boron chemistry laid much of the groundwork for later discoveries.

Undertakes Protein Research

Later in his career, Lipscomb worked on biochemical problems, particularly the structure determination of proteins. As in his boron work, he used the technique of X-ray diffraction in his investigations. A success in this area was his determination of the structure of carboxypeptidase A, a digestive enzyme and an enormous molecule with a molecular weight of 34,400. He next worked on the enzyme trans-carbamylase, which is involved in the synthesis of nucleic acids in the body.

In 1976 Lipscomb was awarded the Nobel Prize in chemistry for his work on the chemical bonding in boron compounds. Russell N. Grimes, writing in *Science,* noted that theories advanced by Lipscomb had been utilized in regard to many elements, "but it is fair to say that it all began with boron hydrides— and it is here that Lipscomb's powerful insight and creative imagination have been so effectively felt." In addition to the Nobel Prize, Lipscomb has garnered many other awards, among them the George Ledlie Prize of Harvard University and the Distinguished Service Award of the American Chemical Society.

Lipscomb married Mary Adele in 1944; the couple had a son and a daughter, but were divorced in 1983. Lipscomb married Jean Evans, a lettering artist, soon afterwards. A well-read and enthusiastic individual, affectionately called "Colonel" by his associates, Lipscomb is also an excellent musician. His particular interest is chamber music, and he has played clarinet in chamber groups with professionals. Russell Grimes wrote in *Science* that "the dominant personal characteristics of Professor Lipscomb have been an unfailing scientific imagination, a refusal to accept the limitations imposed by current dogma, an ability to perceive relationships often missed by others, and above all, a delight in the intellectual challenge of uncovering scientific truth."

SELECTED WRITINGS BY LIPSCOMB:

Books

Boron Hydrides, W. A. Benjamin, 1963.
(With G. R. Eaton) *NMR Studies of Boron Hydrides and Related Compounds,* W. A. Benjamin, 1969.

Periodicals

(With Bryce Crawford and W. H. Eberhardt) *Journal of Chemical Physics,* 1954.

SOURCES:

Books

Nobel Prize Winners: An H. W. Wilson Biographical Dictionary, H. W. Wilson Company, 1987, p. 638.

Periodicals

Grimes, Russell N., "The 1976 Nobel Prize for Chemistry," *Science,* November 12, 1976, p. 709.

—*Sketch by Gail B. C. Marsella*

Arthur D. Little
1863-1935
American chemical engineer

Arthur D. Little was an influential chemical engineer and entrepreneur who is widely considered the father of industrial research. He made his most significant contributions to the chemistry of paper making, revolutionizing the industry in the United States. He founded Arthur D. Little, Inc. for chemical engineering and built it into an enormously influential international industrial management and consulting firm. He invented processes for tanning leather, producing artificial silk, and manufacturing various petroleum products. He was an eloquent speaker and writer who was widely published and in great demand. During his lifetime he was granted numerous patents and awarded a long list of honors, degrees, and medals.

Born December 15, 1863, in Boston, Arthur Dehon Little was the first of Thomas and Amelia Hixson Little's four sons. His mother had emigrated from England, and his father had served as an artillery captain and been wounded during the American Civil War. Little was named for Arthur Dehon, a Civil War hero and close friend of his father's. After the war, the family moved to Portland, Maine, where Little was enrolled in the public schools. As a schoolboy, he entered a Harvard contest for the best essay on animals and vegetation along the Atlantic coast and won second prize. At age twelve, he and friend invested in their first chemistry equipment, purchasing a test tube, some sulfuric acid, and iron scraps. The next year, he installed a more extensive chemical laboratory in his parent's basement. By high school, his parents decided his unique intellectual abilities would benefit from a different school, and they moved to New York City so could attend the Berkeley School.

In 1881, Little enrolled at the Massachusetts Institute of Technology; he majored in chemistry, though he had a strong interest in journalism and in 1881 founded a student newspaper, the *Tech,* with three other undergraduates. During the summer of 1882, he studied paper making in Amherst, Massachusetts. By 1884, however, his family was no longer able to afford tuition at M.I.T., and he left without a degree. He began working at the Richmond Paper Company in Rumford, Rhode Island—the first American mill to use a sulfite process for wood-pulp production. After six weeks on the job Little, then twenty-one years old, became superintendent of the plant when the Swedish and German scientists to whom he was apprenticed both quit after an argument. Little demonstrated his uncommon management and engineering abilities when he devised and later patented a wood-pulp digester that greatly speeded the work of the sulfite plant. Later, he set up other sulfite plants and became a leading authority on paper making.

Forms Pioneering Industrial Research Firm

On October 1, 1886, Little and Roger B. Griffin formed a chemical engineering partnership with about $2,500 in capital, specializing in paper-making technology. Later the firm, which pioneered in industrial research, earned its income by analyzing the content of goods like sugar, metal ores, spices, ground nut shells, drinking water, and other chemicals. Tragically, Griffin died following a laboratory accident in 1893. In 1909, after a partnership with William H. Walker, Little reorganized the firm as Arthur D. Little, Inc. In 1921, Little envisioned a great chemical industry based on petroleum products like ethylene, butylene, and propylene. He began a pilot petroleum plant in Boston but was unable to keep it afloat. The plant was sold to Standard Oil of New Jersey. In keeping with his reputation as an industrial visionary, Little also foresaw the rise of the motion picture in the early 1900s.

Arthur D. Little, Inc. became known as a company that employed a diverse group of highly educated scientists and engineers that could solve almost any problem. In fact, Little once took it upon himself and his company to make a silk purse from sows' ears. He ordered from a Chicago meat packer 100 pounds of sows' ears rendered into ten pounds of glue and turned the glue into gelatin with the addition of small amounts of acetone and chrome alum. The mixture was then filtered under pressure and forced through a finely perforated spinneret. The resulting fine gelatin strands were dried and then softened by bathing in a glycerin solution. At that point the silky strands were woven into two purses of different colors. Conversation pieces more than practical items, the purses were widely displayed at trade shows and other promotional events.

Little was an advocate of industrial chemical research at a time when the vast majority of industrialists held chemistry in low esteem. He once wrote, "Research serves to make building-stones out of stumbling blocks." Arthur D. Little, Inc. went on to become one of the largest industrial research labs in the United States, and the firm eventually grew into an international industrial consulting firm; it specialized in marketing, energy, manufacturing, information, and environmental consulting and employed over 2,500 people with yearly corporate earnings of nearly $300 million.

In 1893, Little demonstrated the Schultz processes for chrome tanning, which revolutionized the leather industry. In 1895, he was granted a patent for making cellulose acetate filters for incandescent lamps. He patented processes for the production of artificial silk, also known as rayon, in 1894, but sold the rights at auction for $2,500 after encountering financial difficulties. By 1928, worldwide production of the material was estimated at nearly 266 million pounds and the market worth at over $81 million. In 1906, he was asked by the U.S. Forest Service to investigate novel sources for wood pulp, and his study led eventually to the establishment of the U.S. Forest Products Laboratory in Madison, Wisconsin. In 1911, Little and his staff were called upon by the young General Motors to analyze and test automobile components. In 1916, he was asked by Lord Shaughnessy, the president of the Canadian Pacific Railway, to assemble a survey of Canada's natural resources. Within seven months, Little and his assistants had produced 165 reports on various resources from wood to petroleum, which served as the basis for the Canadian government's Honorary Advisory Council for Scientific and Industrial Research.

During World War I, Little dedicated his chemical and engineering knowledge to the war effort. He was in charge of special research efforts for the Signal Corps and the Chemical Warfare Service. He worked on the development of airplane dopes (preparations used to strengthen and protect the cloth surfaces of airplane wings), acetone, and chemical filters in gas masks. His contribution to the development of the activated charcoal gas mask helped save thousands of lives during World War I, and by 1918 there was an A.D. Little Unit in the Chemical Development Section of the Research Division of the Chemical Warfare Service.

Little traveled abroad on many occasions and was a member of the Boston social establishment. He was president of the American Chemical Society from 1912 to 1914. He was named president of the Institute of Chemical Engineers in 1919. Little was president of the Society of Chemical Industry from 1928 to 1929 and was awarded their Perkin Medal. He received honorary degrees from the University of Pittsburgh, Manchester University in England, Tufts University, Columbia University, and Rutgers University. For some time he served as a member of the visiting committee on the department of chemistry at Harvard, and in 1905 he strongly and successfully advised against a merger of M.I.T. with Harvard.

Life-long Association with M.I.T.

Little lectured on paper making from 1893 through 1916 at M.I.T. and was a life member of the M.I.T. Corporation. By 1915, he was chair of the visiting committee for the departments of chemistry and chemical engineering and that same year he convinced M.I.T. president Richard C. Maclaurin to create a school for chemical engineering. Little and

Maclaurin looked for funding, and in June it came in the form of a $300,000 check from George Eastman of Kodak. By 1919, the M.I.T. School of Chemical Engineering was in operation. In 1921, Little was named president of the M.I.T. Alumni Association.

On January 22, 1922, Little married Henriette Rogers Anthony. Little and his wife never had children, but they adopted his fifteen-year-old nephew, Royal. Little's adopted son went on to be very influential in the affairs of Arthur D. Little, Inc., becoming a highly successful businessman who was widely cited as the founder of the modern business conglomerate. Little himself was a man of deep and broad knowledge on many subjects, who throughout his life retained his humility despite his innumerable successes and awards. He died on August 1, 1935, in Northeast Harbor, Maine, at the age of seventy-one.

SELECTED WRITINGS BY LITTLE:

Books

(With R. B. Griffin) *Chemistry of Paper Making,* H. Lockwood, 1894.
Handwriting on the Wall; A Chemist's Interpretation (essays), Little, Brown, 1928.

SOURCES:

Books

Dictionary of American Biography, Scribner, 1944, pp. 500–501.
Kahn, E. J., *The Problem Solvers: A History of Arthur D. Little, Inc.,* Little, Brown, 1986.

—*Sketch by John Henry Dreyfuss*

Fang Lizhi
1936-

Chinese astrophysicist

Fang Lizhi is an astrophysicist and political dissident who has spent most of his career in mainland China. Trained as a solid-state physicist, he later became involved in cosmology, a branch of astronomy concerned with space and time theory. In 1972 he published a paper on the big bang theory, previously a forbidden topic in China. An outspoken advocate for human rights and intellectual freedom

Fang Lizhi

since his days as a student, Lizhi sought political asylum at the United States Embassy after the 1989 Tiananmen Square massacre in Beijing, China. He relocated to the United States in 1990 and joined the Institute for Advanced Study in Princeton, New Jersey.

The son of a postal clerk, Fang Lizhi was born on February 12, 1936, in Hangzhou, China, to Fang Chengpu and Shi Peiji. Lizhi grew up in a politically unstable era in China, as power shifted from Japanese control first to the Nationalists and then to the Communists. At sixteen, Lizhi entered Beijing University to study theoretical and nuclear physics. He gained membership in the elite Chinese Communist Party (CCP) before graduating with highest distinction in 1956. He did graduate work in nuclear reactor theory at the Institute of Modern Physics Research.

But his academic success did not stop him from speaking out, and he called for democracy and freedom of expression while still a student. With Mao Zedong as China's leader, Marxist ideology pervaded politics, culture, and even science. Lizhi objected to the oppressive Marxist influence on physics, and in 1956 when Mao invited commentary from intellectuals, Lizhi promptly called for educational reform and academic freedom. After many academics had spoken their minds, thousands were imprisoned in labor camps; Lizhi was expelled from the CCP, but he was still allowed to help organize a new physics department at the University of Science and Technology (Keda) in Beijing. He taught electromagnetics and quantum mechanics and studied solid-state and laser physics. Lizhi married physicist Li Shuxian in 1961; the couple has two sons.

During China's Cultural Revolution (1966–1976), Mao sought to purge society of Western and traditional Chinese influences. Many intellectuals were punished for their beliefs, and in 1966 Lizhi endured a year of solitary confinement. He was then sent to Anhui Province to work in the mines and on the railroad until 1969. During this time he read Lev Landau's *Classical Theory of Fields* which led him to abandon solid-state physics for cosmology. In 1969, Lizhi was sent to teach astrophysics at a new branch of Keda in Hefei; he began writing again while he was there, but his articles were published under a pseudonym because of the political climate.

At the time Lizhi began studying astrophysics, publications about cosmology had been forbidden by the CCP. This prohibition, in place since 1949, was lifted in 1972, and Lizhi and others published an article on the big bang theory. The article was immediately condemned by the Communists because it contradicted the Marxist claim that the universe was infinite, but Lizhi and his colleagues were not punished. He continued his work throughout the 1970s in a gradually improving academic and political climate. In 1978, he was readmitted to the CCP and he won China's National Award for Science and Technology. At Keda he became the university's youngest full professor. He was allowed to travel and spent six months at Cambridge University in England. In 1985 he won the International Gravity Foundation Prize in the United States for a paper he had written with Humitako Sato on quasars and the history of the universe. Lizhi spent part of 1986 at Princeton's Institute for Advanced Study.

Lizhi has spent much of his career in astrophysics conducting theoretical research on the shape of the universe. He has been particularly concerned with topology, a mathematical discipline concerned with geometric point sets. Lizhi has likened cosmology to archaeology, because it reconstructs the history of the universe from physical evidence such as light that has been travelling for millions of years, cosmic background radiation, and the relationship between matter and antimatter. Lizhi has used topology to speculate on the shape the universe might have taken in the first fraction of a second after the big bang. His question is, as Hans Christian von Baeyer put it in *The Sciences,* whether the universe is "a ball or a doughnut," and his theoretical work in this area could help improve the scientific understanding of the future as well as the history of the universe—in particular, whether the universe will continue to expand or whether gravity will eventually begin to pull it back together again.

Despite offers from many foreign universities and research institutions, Lizhi remained in China throughout the 1980s out of a strong sense of obligation. "The democracies have many astrophysicists," he is quoted as saying in *Current Biography Yearbook,* "and China not so many. I love China . . . I want to stay where I can both have an impact on science and help to import democracy." In 1984 Lizhi was appointed vice president of Keda. Lizhi and Guan Weiyan, Keda's president, drafted a plan to increase the power of the faculty and to foster freedom of speech on campus. They invited foreign visitors and encouraged students to study abroad, which was then consistent with national policy. Lizhi began to campaign throughout China for freedom of expression, but in 1986 a student campaign for democratic reforms turned into a series of large demonstrations in Beijing. Though they had actually discouraged the marches, Lizhi and Weiyan were blamed by the CCP for the activities. Lizhi was reassigned to a research position at the Beijing Observatory and in 1987 he was again expelled from the party.

Because of his long-standing role in encouraging democracy and promoting human rights, Lizhi was revered by the intellectual community in China. Although he played no role in the student demonstrations in Beijing's Tiananmen Square in 1989 and made no statements in support of them, the CCP considered Lizhi one of the perpetrators. On June 5, 1989, the day after troops massacred students in Tiananmen Square, Lizhi and his wife sought refuge in the United States Embassy in Beijing. They remained there for thirteen months, receiving permission to leave the country only after intense diplomatic pressure from the United States. In the summer of 1990 he was a visiting researcher at Cambridge University, where his family joined him, and he then accepted a position at the Institute for Advanced Study.

In 1991, Lizhi published in English an anthology of political and philosophical essays. The University of Arizona hired him as associate professor of physics in 1992. Maintaining his loyalty to China, Lizhi has expressed hope for progress in human rights there. Although he was a passionate spokesperson for greater political and personal freedom, he considered his role not that of a politician but that of a scientist and a person of conscience. In addition to his other honors, Lizhi received the Robert F. Kennedy Memorial Human Rights Award in 1989.

SELECTED WRITINGS BY LIZHI:

Books

(With J. Ruffini) *Cosmology of the Early Universe,* Taylor & Francis, 1985.

Bringing Down the Great Wall: Writings on Science, Culture, and Democracy in China, Knopf, 1991.

Periodicals

"A Chinese Tom Paine Speaks Out on Democracy," *Washington Post,* January 18, 1987, p. C1.
"Human Rights Must Be Part of New China," *Los Angeles Times,* April 13, 1989, p. 7.
"The Chinese People Must Participate in a Universe of Rights," *Los Angeles Times,* November 26, 1989.
"First Word," *Omni,* March, 1990, p. 8.

SOURCES:

Books

Current Biography Yearbook 1989, H.W. Wilson, 1989, pp. 173–177.
Newsmakers, Gale, 1988.

Periodicals

Aikman, David, "Interview: The Science of Human Rights," *Time,* August 20, 1990, pp. 12–15.
Brown, William, "A Dissident View on Life, the Universe and Democracy," *New Scientist,* July 21, 1990, p. 19.
Von Baeyer, Hans Christian, "Fang's Universe," *The Sciences,* March/April, 1991, pp. 10–12.
Williams, James H., "Fang Lizhi's Expanding Universe," *China Quarterly,* September, 1990, pp. 459–484.

—*Sketch by Miyoko Chu*

Ruth Smith Lloyd
1917-

American anatomist

Ruth Smith Lloyd was the first African American woman to earn a Ph.D. in anatomy. Lloyd, who spent a large portion of her teaching career at Howard University, specialized in issues surrounding fertility as well as research on the female sex cycle and the relation of sex hormones to growth.

Ruth Smith Lloyd was born in Washington, DC, on January 25, 1917. The youngest of three girls born to Mary Elizabeth Smith and Bradley Donald Smith, Lloyd graduated from Dunbar High School in Washington and went on to receive her A.B. from Mt. Holyoke College in 1937. At this point, Lloyd planned to study zoology and then begin teaching at the high school level. However, after she attained her master's degree at Howard University, her professors encouraged her to work towards an advanced degree in anatomy. Her mentor at Howard recommended specifically that she study at Western Reserve University, and it was there that she began her serious studies in anatomy. In 1941 Lloyd earned her Ph.D. in anatomy, thus becoming the first African American woman to achieve that goal.

While studying at Western Reserve, Lloyd worked in the school's fertility laboratories, which kept colonies of monkeys. Lloyd would eventually concentrate her research and teaching efforst in the field of endocrinology and medical genetics. In 1941 she took a position at the Howard University college of medicine as an assistant in physiology. After a brief period, during which she taught zoology at Hampton Institute, Lloyd took time to begin raising her family. In 1939 she married a physician, Sterling M. Lloyd, with whom she would have three children.

In 1942, Lloyd returned to Howard University, where she remained for the rest of her professional career. That same year she was promoted to an instructor, and by 1958 she was an assistant professor of anatomy. Soon afterward, she became an associate professor at Howard's graduate school, where she remained until her retirement. Lloyd, who now lives in her native Washington, DC, said in an interview with Leonard C. Bruno that even upon reflection, she is unimpressed with her unique accomplishments. She sees little that is unusual or remarkable about her story, and described herself to Bruno as an average person with a normal life.

SOURCES:

Lloyd, Ruth S., interview with Leonard C. Bruno conducted January 6, 1994.

—*Sketch by Leonard C. Bruno*

Jacques Loeb
1859-1924
German-born American physiologist

Jacques Loeb intended to be a philosopher. As a young man growing up in Germany, he was interested in the question of will—more specifically, whether freedom of the will existed. Spurred by the work of Schopenhauer and Nietzsche, Loeb was determined to show that free will did not exist. Philosophy, however, fell by the wayside at college, to be replaced by science, and Loeb went on to become one of the foremost proponents of mechanistic conceptions in biology and physiology. His work on animal tropism—automatic movements determined by physical stimuli such as light or gravity—and his researches in sea urchin parthenogenesis in an attempt to explain biological processes in terms of chemical agents earned him the reputation as a scientist who was not afraid to take moral and ethical stands, making him something of a household name at the turn of the twentieth century. Though sponsored for the Nobel Prize on a score of occasions by fellow scientists around the world, Loeb never won that prestigious prize, although his work did establish the use of objective experimental factors in the analysis of behavior.

Born on April 7, 1859, in Mayen, Germany, Jacques Loeb was the first son of Benedict Loeb, a prosperous Jewish businessman, and Barbara Isay Loeb. His father was an ardent francophile and engendered in his son a love for the classics of eighteenth-century thought—the rationalism of which would go on to shape Loeb's life. A younger brother, Leo, became a doctor, emigrated to the United States, and helped to develop a number of approaches toward the study of cancer.

Loeb's parents died when he was still a teenager. Orphaned, he first accepted a position in his uncle's bank in Berlin, but shortly returned to school, graduating with a classical education from the Askanische Gymnasium, and setting his course for the University of Berlin and a career in philosophy. Loeb had already established the path of his life's work: to determine if free will existed. Initially he felt he could unravel this conundrum through the study of philosophy, but he was soon disabused of this notion, disappointed in the "wordmongers" that were teaching him. In 1880 he set a new course, this time enrolling at Strasbourg to study science in an effort to localize function in the brain. He received an M.D. in 1884, writing his thesis on blindness caused by injury to the cerebral cortex. But still this did not get to the heart of his investigation into free will.

Plant Tropism Gains Loeb's Interest

In 1886 Loeb became an assistant to Adolf Fick, the professor of physiology at the University of Würzburg, and it was during his two years at this university that he also became fast friends with the researcher Julius von Sachs. It was a happy combination, for Fick was a powerful proponent of the application of physics to biology and medicine, and von Sachs introduced Loeb to his work on plant tropism. Loeb saw his path clearly now: to show that lower animals were every bit as affected by external stimuli such as light and gravity as were plants, thereby proving that animals had no free will. In short, he was postulating the importance of mechanistic influences on behavior, and this in a time when mechanism—such as demonstrated in **Ivan Petrovich Pavlov**'s work on reflexes—was just coming into vogue. By 1888 Loeb was publishing articles on animal tropism, showing how certain caterpillars just emerging from their cocoons will climb to the tips of branches to feed—not out of mysterious instinct, but because they are following the light. Through an ingenious series of experiments, Loeb thought that he had solved his question of free will once and for all, eliciting simply by outside stimulus of light or heat any number of given animal movements. He even suggested that such complicated structures as ethics and morals were merely the products of tropism combinations.

His conclusions soon came under harsh criticism, especially by the American biologist Herbert Spencer Jennings. Jennings proved that many of Loeb's supposed tropic responses in animals were in fact the result of avoidance responses in the animals he was testing, and later researchers such as Morgan and Thorndike went on to more fully disprove the theory of animal tropism for the broad majority of animals. Yet Loeb had managed in his experiments to question the nature of instinct, thereby bringing mechanistic conceptions to the very forefront of any discussion on behavior.

Loeb continued his researches at the University of Strasbourg as well as at the Naples biological station from 1889 to 1890. It was while he was at the latter institution that he came under the influence of group of inspired American cytologists and embryologists and became interested in the field of development mechanics, or the stimuli needed for parthenogenesis (reproduction without fertilization, or "virgin birth") to begin. He began to wonder whether spermatozoa were in fact necessary for the cell to begin segmentation. This was a logical extension of his work on animal tropism, discovering whether or not the activation of the egg could be explained as a series of chemical reactions. He would spend the next ten years searching for that explanation.

Meanwhile, Loeb had met and fallen in love with an American, Anne Leonard, who had just received her doctorate in philology from the University of Zurich. The couple was married in the spring of 1890, and by late 1891 they had moved to the United States, Loeb accepting a teaching post at Bryn Mawr, Pennsylvania. They had three children together, two of whom also became scientists.

Proceeds with Studies on Parthenogenesis

Loeb accepted a position at the University of Chicago in 1892 and remained there for the next ten years, teaching summer courses in physiology at Woods Hole, Massachusetts. He continued the research begun in Naples, testing his hypothesis that salts acted upon living organisms by combining their ions with protoplasm. Loeb devised an experimental setting in which he immersed fertilized sea urchin eggs into water whose osmotic pressure had been increased by the addition of sodium chloride. Then, replacing the eggs in ordinary salt water, he observed that they started to undergo segmentation.

By 1899 Loeb had used this technique to raise larvae from unfertilized eggs, creating artificial parthenogenesis. The popular press made much of this at the time, speculating that perhaps males could be done away with all together. Because of the media attention, as well as his uncompromising socialist stance, Loeb's name was well known in America and he became acquainted with such social reformers as Thorsten Veblen, H. L. Mencken, and Sinclair Lewis.

In 1902, Loeb went to the University of California at Berkeley where he stayed until 1910, continuing summer work at the marine lab in Pacific Grove, California. Feeling increasingly cut off from contact with his fellow scientists, Loeb accepted a position at the Rockefeller Institute for Medical research in New York city (now Rockefeller University), where he remained from 1910 until his death. He was a critic of the First World War and was especially disappointed in the fact that German socialists were supporting the war effort. By the end of the war, his research had taken a new direction into proteins, making important contributions to the theory of their nature as colloids (substances consisting of microscopic particles suspended in a gelatin). He died on February 11, 1924, in Hamilton, Bermuda, working up to the end. His legacy remains not only in his more than 400 publications but also in the very practice of his discipline: the pioneer of objective analysis of behavior, Loeb turned its study into the rigorously experimental science it is today.

SELECTED WRITINGS BY LOEB:

Books

The Mechanistic Conception of Life, University of Chicago Press, 1912.

Forced Movements, Tropisms, and Animal Conduct, Lippincott, 1918.

SOURCES:

Books

Dictionary of Scientific Biography, Scribner's, 1973, pp. 445–446.
Fleming, Donald, "Introduction," in *The Mechanistic Conception of Life,* by Jacques Loeb, Belknap Press, 1964, pp. vii-xii.

Periodicals

De Kruif, Paul H., "Jacques Loeb, the Mechanist," *Harper's Monthly Magazine,* Volume 146, 1922–1923, pp. 181–190.
Kobelt, Nina, "Jacques Loeb Bibliography," *Journal of General Physiology,* Volume 8, 1928, lxiii-xcii.
Osterhout, W. J. V., "Jacques Loeb," *Journal of General Physiology,* Volume 8, 1928, pp. ix-lix.

—*Sketch by J. Sydney Jones*

Otto Loewi
1873-1961
German-born American pharmacologist and physiologist

Otto Loewi (pronounced *lō–ee*) made important early discoveries about how nerve impulses are transmitted. He found that nerve transmissions depend both on electrical stimulation and certain chemical substances produced by nerve cells. For this discovery he shared the 1936 Nobel Prize for Physiology or Medicine with **Henry Hallett Dale**, a British scientist who showed that chemical transmissions of nerve impulses take place in the voluntary, as well as the involuntary, nervous system.

Loewi was born in Frankfurt am Main, Germany, on June 3, 1873, the son of Jakob Loewi, a wealthy Jewish wine merchant, and Anna Willstadter Loewi. As a young man, Loewi wanted to be an art historian, but he was dissuaded from pursuing this career by his parents, who urged him to study medicine instead. Although he had done poorly in mathematics and physics at the Frankfurt Gymnasium, he took their advice and in 1891 entered the University of Strasbourg to study medicine. He was fortunate at Strasbourg; there were many excellent teachers and researchers there who developed his interest in biology and physiology. Loewi received his medical degree in 1896.

After graduation Loewi briefly visited Italy, and then returned to Germany for more training in chemistry and experimental methods. During this period, he also worked in the tuberculosis and pneumonia wards at the City Hospital of Frankfurt, where he was discouraged from continuing with clinical medicine because of high death rates. Instead, he turned his attention to an academic career in scientific research, and in 1898 he joined the department of pharmacology at the University of Marburg, first with an assistantship and then as a lecturer.

Begins Research on Nerve Impulses

By 1902, Loewi had published the results of his scientific research at Marburg. His work dealt with the functioning of the kidneys and the effects on these organs of substances that increase the production of urine, known as diuretics. In 1903, along with other researchers including Henry Hallett Dale, Loewi began to consider the chemical transmission of nerve impulses. The hormone adrenaline and the chemical muscarine had already been identified as possible nerve transmitters by several English physiologists. In 1905, Loewi followed Hans Meyer, under whom he had worked at Marburg, to the University of Vienna. 1905 was the same year he met Gulda Goldschmiedt, the daughter of a chemistry professor, in Switzerland, and he married her the following year. They would have four children.

At the University of Vienna, Loewi concentrated on the effects of adrenaline and noradrenaline on diabetes and blood pressure. He also studied the response of the heart to the stimulation of the vagus nerve, one of the main cranial nerves in the autonomic system. In 1909, he was appointed to the University of Graz as a professor of pharmacology, where he remained until the German occupation of Austria in 1938.

By 1921, fifteen years after the idea of chemical transmission of nerve impulses had first been proposed by the English physiologists, scientists had still not discovered definite evidence of the existence of a chemical transmitter within the nervous system. At this time, Loewi was fully engaged in the search for such evidence, and one night he had a dream for the design of an experiment that would determine the existence of a chemical transmitter. He jotted down some notes from the dream, still half asleep, but when he awoke the next morning he could not read his scrawl. The next night at three o'clock the idea

returned to him; this time he immediately went to his laboratory.

For this pathbreaking experiment, Loewi used two hearts from frogs. He removed the vagus nerve from the first heart, and he stimulated the same nerve in the second one. After stimulating the nerve in the second heart, he removed some fluid and injected it into the heart without the vagus nerve. He observed that the rate of this heart slowed as if the vagus nerve had been stimulated. Then he stimulated the heart with the vagus nerve so it would beat faster. He again removed fluid and injected it into the heart without the vagus nerve. Its rate increased as if it had been stimulated directly by the missing nerve.

Loewi had established the role chemicals play in the transmission of nerve impulses, but he was not sure at first what these chemicals were. He called one "vagus substance" and the other "accelerator substance." Over the next fifteen years, Loewi, along with his colleagues, published a number of papers on the results of his initial experiment. What he had called vagus substance was identified as acetylcholine in 1926; other transmitters were later identified. In 1936, Loewi identified adrenaline as one of the sympathetic nervous system transmitters and noradrenaline as the most important one. Henry Hallett Dale shared the 1936 Nobel Prize with Loewi for his discovery of chemical transmitters in the voluntary nervous system.

After the German occupation of Austria in 1938, Loewi was only allowed to leave because he turned over his Nobel Prize money to the Nazis. His family was also able to escape, and they joined him in New York City in 1940. He became a United States citizen in 1946. He spent the rest of his life writing articles, delivering lectures, and writing his memoirs. He died on December 25, 1961, at the age of eighty-eight in New York City.

SELECTED WRITINGS BY LOEWI:

Books

The Secretion of the Urine, 1917.
From the Workshop of Discovery, 1953.

Periodicals

"The Humoral Transmission of Nervous Impulse," *Harvey Lectures,* Volume 28, 1934, pp. 218–233.
"The Ferrier Lecture on Problems Connected with the Principle of Humoral Transmission of Nervous Impulses," *Proceedings of the Royal Society,* Volume 118B, 1935, pp. 299–316.

"The Edward Gamaliel Janeway Lectures: Aspects of the Transmission of Nervous Impulse," *Journal of the Mount Sinai Hospital,* Volume 12, 1945, pp. 803–816, 851–865.

SOURCES:

Books

A Biographical Dictionary of Scientists, Wiley, 1982, pp. 337–338.

Biographical Memoirs of Fellows of the Royal Society, Volume 8, Royal Society (London), 1962, pp. 67–89.

Dictionary of Scientific Biography, Scribner, 1973, Volume 8, pp. 451–456.

Nobel Prize Winners, H. W. Wilson, 1987, pp. 640–642.

—Sketch by Jordan P. Richman

Myra A. Logan
1908-1977
American physician and surgeon

Myra A. Logan fulfilled the image of the selfless, humanitarian doctor, practicing medicine to serve the community rather than simply to earn money. An urbane, modest person who never lost sight of her civic responsibilities, she is thought to be the first African American woman elected a fellow of the American College of Surgeons, and was the first woman to perform open heart surgery. Additionally, her research on antibiotics and breast cancer saved countless lives.

Myra Adele Logan was born in 1908 in Tuskegee, Alabama, the eighth child of Warren and Adella Hunt Logan. She enjoyed a relatively privileged upbringing, for her father was a trustee and treasurer of the prestigious Tuskegee Institute and her mother was a noted activist in health care and the suffrage movement. Booker T. Washington was a neighbor. Education and optimism were in the air of the Logan household, as was an interest in health care: in addition to her mother, Logan also had an aunt and sister who were or became involved in health matters, and her brother, Arthur, as well as a brother-in-law, was a physician. Logan attended Atlanta University in Georgia, graduating with a B.A. in 1927 as valedictorian of her class. She went north for graduate studies, taking her M.S. in psychology from Columbia University in New York. After working for a time on a YWCA staff in Connecticut, Logan finally made up her mind to study medicine, winning the first Walter Gray Crump $10,000 four-year scholarship to New York Medical College. She graduated in 1933 and interned as well as served her residency at Harlem Hospital in New York.

Sets Out on Career as Surgeon and Researcher

Her years at Harlem Hospital in the emergency room and riding ambulance as a young internee prepared Logan well for her future career in surgery. She not only delivered babies on the way to the hospital, but also repaired numerous stab wounds to the heart. Remaining at Harlem Hospital, she became an associate surgeon there, and was also a visiting surgeon at Sydenham Hospital. In 1943 she became the first woman to perform open heart surgery, in the ninth operation of its kind anywhere in the world. She also became interested in the then-new antibiotic drugs, researching aureomycin and other drugs and publishing her results in *Archives of Surgery* and *Journal of American Medical Surgery.* In the 1960s, Logan began to work on breast cancer, developing a slower X-ray process that could detect more accurately differences in the density of tissue and thus help discover tumors much earlier. In addition to maintaining a private practice, she was also a charter member of one of the first group practices in the nation, the Upper Manhattan Medical Group of the Health Insurance Plan, a concept that houses physicians of various specialties under one roof and that is the norm today.

Logan found time in her busy schedule to stay committed to social issues. Early in her career, she was a member of the New York State Committee on Discrimination, but resigned in protest in 1944 when Governor Dewey ignored the anti-discrimination legislation the committee had proposed. She was also active in Planned Parenthood as well as the National Association for the Advancement of Colored People (NAACP), and after her retirement in 1970 she served on the New York State Workmen's Compensation Board. Her myriad medical and civic achievements led to her election to the American College of Surgeons.

Logan married the well known painter Charles Alston in 1943. The couple had no children, devoting their lives to professional pursuits. She was a lover of music and a fine classical pianist. She also enjoyed the theater and reading. Myra Adele Logan died at Mount Sinai Hospital in New York on January 13, 1977, of lung cancer at the age of 68. Her husband, Charles Alston, died only a few months later.

SOURCES:

Books

Black Women in America—An Historical Approach, Carlson Publishing, 1993, p. 731.

Haber, Louis, *Women Pioneers of Science,* Harcourt, 1979, pp. 97–104.

Sammons, Vivian Ovelton, *Blacks in Science and Medicine,* Hemisphere Publishing, 1990, p. 156.

Periodicals

Flint, Peter B., "Dr. Myra Logan, 68; Physician in Harlem," *New York Times Biography Service,* January 15, 1977, pp. 100–101.

Journal of the National Medical Association, July, 1977, p. 527.

—*Sketch by J. Sydney Jones*

Fritz London
1900-1954
German American physicist

Fritz London discovered practical applications of quantum mechanics and is known primarily for his work with the explanation of the covalent bond in hydrogen. His theories regarding superconductivity and superfluids were also important contributions to the development of these areas of science. Fritz Wolfgang London was born on March 7, 1900, in Breslau, Germany (now Wroclaw, Poland). He was the elder of two sons born to Luise (Hamburger) and Franz London, who taught mathematics at the University of Breslau as well as at the University of Bonn. Fritz London received a classical education in high school, and his university studies followed the same pattern. He attended the universities of Bonn, Frankfurt, and Munich, receiving his Ph.D. in philosophy from Munich in 1921; his dissertation involved a study of symbolic logic. In the four-year period following his graduation, London taught at various secondary schools in Germany and continued to study and write about philosophy. He then decided to pursue a new field of interest—theoretical physics—and returned to Munich to study under German theoretical physicist **Arnold Sommerfeld.**

Applies Quantum Theory to the Hydrogen Molecule

One of the first topics on which London worked at Munich was the hydrogen molecule. He was interested in the question of whether or not modern quantum mechanics could provide an explanation for the covalent bond—the chemical bond involving shared electrons—that holds two hydrogen atoms together in a hydrogen molecule. That task became the model for much of London's subsequent work.

Until the 1930s, quantum mechanics, or wave mechanics, had been regarded as a totally sufficient system—in fact, the only correct system—for dealing with atomic-scale particles and their interactions with energy. The practical application was much less clear, and London began to explore the ways in which quantum principles could be used to explain visible phenomena. His research into the hydrogen molecule in the late 1920s, along with German physicist Walter Heitler, is recognized for advancing the existing knowledge of chemical bonding. In his 1954 introduction to London's second volume of *Superfluids,* Felix Bloch described the duo's success with the hydrogen molecule as an illustration of "the direct connection between pure quantum phenomena and some of the most striking facts of chemistry." In 1927 London and Heitler published a paper detailing the results of their analysis.

After this triumph, London continued to work on similar problems, looking for the applications of quantum theory to various types of chemical reactions and to the nature of forces between two molecules. Most of his work was brought together in a book on molecular theory scheduled to be published by the German firm of Springer. By the time the manuscript reached the publisher, however, London had left Germany, and Springer refused to honor its contract. Although London continued to work on the book in English translation, it never appeared in print.

Investigates Superconductivity and Superfluidity

In 1932 London turned his energies toward a new topic: superconductivity, or the complete disappearance of electrical resistance in a substance, seen particularly at low temperatures. That topic was one his younger brother Heinz London had selected for his doctoral research at the University of Breslau. Over the next few years, the London brothers worked together to develop a new theory of superconductivity. In the course of their research, they found that an extremely thin outer layer in the superconducting material contains the electrical current. A key element in their studies was a new perspective on the subject provided by the 1933 discovery by W. Meissner and R. Ochsenfeld that superconducting materials tend to expel a magnetic field within it prior to cooling. Bloch, in his introduction to volume two of London's *Superfluids,* called the Londons' 1934 paper on superconductivity "a decisive step forward by indicating the direction in which a solution [to the problem of superconductivity] has to be sought."

London's work on superconductivity seemed to lead naturally to a related topic: superfluidity. First described by the Russian physicist **Pyotr Kapitsa** in the late 1930s and early 1940s, superfluidity is the tendency of a fluid to flow without resistance, much as electrons flow without resistance in a superconductor. Liquid helium below the temperature of 2.19 K, for example, may flow upward along the sides of a container and pass through tiny cracks that would be impervious, or impenetrable, to other liquids. London spent a large fraction of the last two decades of his life trying to solve that challenge. The result of that effort was the monumental two-volume work *Superfluids,* the second part of which was published after his death.

London's research work was interrupted in the 1930s by the rise of Nazi dictator Adolf Hitler in Germany. Both London and his brother left Germany in 1933 for England, where they both accepted appointments at Oxford University's Clarendon Laboratory. Fritz then spent two years at the Institut Henri Poincaré in Paris before taking a job as professor of theoretical chemistry at Duke University in North Carolina. He remained at Duke until his death of a heart attack in Durham, North Carolina, on March 30, 1954. He was survived by his wife, the former Edith Caspary, an artist, and their two children.

SELECTED WRITINGS BY LONDON:

Books

Superfluids, Wiley, Volume 1, 1950, Volume 2, introduction by Felix Bloch, 1954.

SOURCES:

Books

Gillispie, Charles Coulson, editor, *Dictionary of Scientific Biography,* Volume 8, Scribner's, 1975, pp. 473–479.

—Sketch by David E. Newton

Irene D. Long
1951-
American aerospace medicine physician

Irene D. Long, the first black female chief of the Occupational Medicine and Environmental Health Office at the National Aerospace Agency (NASA), is one of the highest-ranking professional women at the center. She is responsible for overseeing that the health and welfare of workers is not compromised before, during, or after a space craft launch (a program so comprehensive that it has been used as a model at other worksites). Long's career in aerospace medicine also involves support to the Johnson Space Center's collection of medical data on the condition of astronauts, including the effects of space on an individual's physiology and the consequences of weightlessness.

Irene Duhart Long, the second of two children, was born November 16, 1951, in Cleveland, Ohio, to Andrew Duhart, a steelworker, and Heloweise Davis Duhart, who taught adult education. At the age of nine, fascinated by reports of the space program that she saw on television, Long informed her parents that she was going to have a career in aerospace medicine. Gearing her education toward fulfilling her childhood dream, she graduated from high school, enrolled at Northwestern University, and received her baccalaureate degree in biology in 1973. Long then attended the St. Louis School of Medicine, eventually obtaining a doctorate of medicine degree. Following residency training in general surgery at Ohio's Cleveland Clinic and Mt. Sinai Hospital (in Cleveland), Long enrolled in the Wright State University school of medicine and earned a master's degree in aerospace medicine.

Childhood Dream Realized

After completing the third year of the residency program at Ames Research Center in Mountain View, California, Long realized her childhood dream in 1982 by joining the staff at NASA's Kennedy Space Center in Florida. As the Chief of the Occupational Medicine and Environmental Health Office, she works with a team of physicians to provide medical services to the astronauts in emergency cases such as an aborted mission. Additionally, she and her office assures that the health of eighteen thousand workers, civil servants, and contractors at the Kennedy Space Center is not compromised. Her office is also responsible for administering physicals to employees to ensure that they are healthy and can satisfactorily perform any physical requirements necessary in their jobs.

Irene D. Long

Long oversees the inspections of workspaces around the center to protect employees from exposure to various hazards such as toxic chemicals, fire, and decompression—all possibilities when a space craft is launched. In addition, she coordinates efforts between multidisciplinary teams—including personnel from the Department of Defense, environmental health agencies, and the astronaut office—which work together to stage successful launches, as well as prepare for emergency situations.

Besides carrying out these duties, Long is also an author. In a landmark paper, she showed that people with sickle-cell trait—a condition different from the disease—should not be prohibited from flying. She determined that the lower oxygen level does not cause their red blood cells to sickle, which can be an extremely painful ailment.

One of the programs Long is proudest of helping to create is the Space Life Sciences Training Program. The program's goal is to encourage minorities and female college students to become interested and take part in science, particularly space life sciences. Participants spend six weeks at the Kennedy Space Center where they learn about space physiology in plants, animals and humans, experiment development, and teamwork concepts. Long, whose hobbies outside of her work include making various craft items and collecting antiques, resides in Florida.

SELECTED WRITINGS BY LONG:

Periodicals

"Sickle Cell Trait and Aviation," *Aviation, Space and Environmental Medicine,* October, 1982, pp. 1021–1029.
(With Jeffrey K. Myers, David A. Tipton, and Daniel Woodard) "Emergency Medical Operations at Kennedy Space Center in Support of Space Shuttle," *Journal of the Florida Medical Association,* August, 1992, pp. 557–561.
(With Emmett B. Ferguson, Paul Humbert, and Tipton) "Health Services at the Kennedy Space Center," *Journal of the Florida Medical Association,* August, 1992, pp. 562–564.

SOURCES:

Periodicals

Ebony, September, 1984, pp. 61–64.

Other

Long, Irene D., interview with Barbara Proujan conducted January 12, 1994.

—Sketch by Barbara Proujan

Kathleen Lonsdale
1903-1971
Irish-born English crystallographer

Kathleen Lonsdale was an early pioneer of X-ray crystallography, a field primarily concerned with studying the shapes of organic and inorganic molecules. In 1929, she was the first to prove experimentally that the hexamethylbenzene crystal, an unusual form of the aromatic compound, was both hexagonal and flat in shape. In 1931, she was the first to use Fourier analysis to illustrate the structure of hexachlorobenzene, an even more difficult organic structure to analyze.

In 1945, Lonsdale was the first woman, along with microbiologist Marjory Stephenson, admitted as a fellow to the Royal Society. She was the first female professor at University College, London, the first woman named president of the International Union of Crystallography, and the first woman to hold the post of president of the British Association for the

Kathleen Lonsdale

Advancement of Science. She accepted her achievements as a pioneering woman scientist with characteristic humility. In 1966, the "lonsdaleite," a rare form of meteoric diamond, was named for her. According to the *Journal of Chemical Education,* upon learning that Clifford Frondel at Harvard University had suggested the name, she wrote to him: "It makes me feel both proud and rather humble that it shall be called lonsdaleite. Certainly the name seems appropriate since the mineral only occurs in very small quantities (perhaps rare would be too flattering) and is generally rather mixed up!"

Lonsdale was born January 28, 1903 in Newbridge, Ireland, a small town south of Dublin. She was the youngest of ten children born to Jessie Cameron Yardley and Harry Frederick Yardley, who was postmaster for the British garrison stationed there. Her father was a heavy drinker, and in 1908, when Kathleen was five years old, her parents were separated. Her mother moved the family moved to Seven Kings, England, a small town east of London. Growing up in England, Kathleen won a scholarship to attend County High School for Girls in Ilford. At the age of 16, she enrolled in Bedford College for Women in London, where in 1922 she received a B.S. in mathematics and physics. She graduated at the head of her class, receiving the highest marks in ten years, and among her oral examiners was **William Henry Bragg**, the 1915 Nobel Laureate in Physics. He was so impressed with her academic performance that he invited her to work with him and a team of scientists using X-ray technology to explore the crystal structure of organic compounds.

Lonsdale worked with Bragg from 1922 to 1927, first at University College, London, and then at the Royal Institution. During these years she also completed her research for a master's thesis on the structure of succinic acid and related compounds; she published it in 1924, with collaborator **William Thomas Astbury**, as a theory of space groups that included tables for 230 such groups and mathematical descriptions of crystal symmetries.

Continues Work on the Structure of Crystals

On August 27, 1927, she married Thomas Lonsdale, who was a fellow student of hers. They moved from London to Leeds, where her husband worked for the British Silk Research Association by day and completed his doctoral dissertation on the torsional strengths of metals by night. Lonsdale worked at the University of Leeds, studying the structure of hexamethylbenzene, and in 1929 she produced the first proof of its hexagonal, planar shape. Her discovery was made independently of her colleagues' work in London, and it was supported by Bragg even though it contradicted his own theory that the compound had a "puckered" shape.

In 1930, the Lonsdales returned to London, where her husband had found a permanent post at the Testing Station of the Experimental Roads Department in the Ministry of Transport at Harmondsworth. Between 1929 and 1934, Lonsdale gave birth to their three children; she worked at home during this period, developing formulae for the structure factor tables. These formulas were published in 1936 as "Simplified Structure Factor and Electron Density Formulae for the 230 Space-Groups of Mathematical Crystallography." For the study of ethane derivatives contained in this book, Lonsdale received her doctorate of science.

In 1934, Lonsdale returned to the Royal Institution, where she would work with Bragg until his death in 1942. Upon her return, however, she found that no X-ray equipment was available. Forced to make do with a large electromagnet, Lonsdale undertook experimental work that eventually proved the difference between sigma and pi electronic orbitals, thus establishing the existence of molecular orbitals. She then turned her attentions to the field of thermal vibrations, finding that divergent X-ray beams could be used to measure the distance between carbonatoms.

Lonsdale was made a fellow of the Royal Society in 1945, and in 1946 she founded her own crystallography department at University College, London. In 1949, Lonsdale was named professor of chemistry at the college, her first permanent academic post following years of living from one grant to the next. During these years, she wrote a popular textbook, *Crystals and X-Rays* (1948), and served as editor-in-chief of the first three volumes of the *International X-Ray Tables* (1952, 1959, and 1962). In 1949, Lonsdale began working with South African scientist Judith Grenville-Wells (later Milledge), eventually collaborating with her on a study of diamonds, as well as on studies of minerals at high temperatures and high pressures, and how solid state reactions work. Milledge later became executor of Lonsdale's literary estate. In the 1960s, Lonsdale became fascinated with body stones (in lectures, she was fond of exhibiting an X ray of a bladder stone from Napoleon III), and she undertook extensive chemical and demographic studies of the subject. She retired from University College in 1968.

Lonsdale and her husband were committed pacifists. They became Quakers in 1936 and together worked toward world peace, as well as prison reform. During World War II, she and her husband gave shelter to refugees, and in 1943 Lonsdale spent a month in jail for refusing to register for war duties and then refusing to pay a fine of two pounds. In 1956, she wrote a book in reaction to extensive nuclear testing by the United States, the Soviet Union, and Great Britain. Entitled *Is Peace Possible?*, the book explored the relationship between world peace and world population needs, as viewed through her own experience as the youngest of ten children. Lonsdale was against nuclear weapons of any kind, and she worked tirelessly for world peace.

In 1956, just a day after the first of her ten grandchildren was born, Lonsdale was named a Dame Commander of the Order of the British Empire, and in 1957 she received the Davy Medal of the Royal Society. In 1966, she became the first female president of the International Union of Crystallography, and in 1968 the first woman to hold the post of president of the British Association for the Advancement of Science. Following her husband's retirement from the Ministry of Transport, the Lonsdales moved to Bexhill-on-Sea. On April 1, 1971, she died of cancer in London.

SELECTED WRITINGS BY LONSDALE:

Books

Simplified Structure Factor and Electron Density Formulae for the 230 Space-Groups of Mathematical Crystallography, G. Bell and Sons, 1936.
Crystals and X-Rays, G. Bell and Sons, 1948.
(With N. F. M. Henry) *International Tables for X-Ray Crystallography,* Kynoch Press, Volume 1, 1952, Volume 2, 1959, Volume 3, 1962.
Removing the Causes of War (Swarthmore Lectures), Allen & Unwin, 1953.

Is Peace Possible?, Penguin Books, 1957. (With J. Kasper) *International Tables for X-Ray Crystallography,* Volume 2, Kynoch Press, 1959.
(With C. H. MacGillavry and G. D. Reich) *International Tables for X-Ray Crystallography,* Volume 3, Kynoch Press, 1962.
I Believe (Arthur Stanley Eddington Memorial Lecture), Cambridge University Press, 1964.
(With others) *The University, Technology, and Society,* Heriot-Watt University, 1968.

Periodicals

(With William Thomas Astbury) "Tabulated Data for the Examination of the 230 Space-groups by Homogenous X-Rays," *Philosophical Transactions of the Royal Society,* Volume 224A, 1924, pp. 221–257.
"The Structure of the Benzene Ring in $C6(CH3)6$," *Proceedings of the Royal Society,* Volume 123A, 1929, pp. 494–515.
"Diamonds, Natural and Artificial," *Nature London,* Volume 153, **1944**, **pp.** 669–672.
"Human Stones," *Scientific American,* Volume 219, 1968, pp. 104–111.

SOURCES:

Books

Biographical Memoirs of Fellows of the Royal Society, Volume 21, Royal Society (London), 1975, pp. 447–489.
Kass-Simon, G. and P. Farnes, editors, *Women of Science,* Indiana University Press, 1990, pp. 355–359.

Periodicals

Julian, Maureen M., "Profiles in Chemistry: Dame Kathleen Lonsdale (1903–1971)," *Journal of Chemical Education,* Volume 59, November, 1982, pp. 965–966.
Mason, Joan, "The Admission of the First Women to the Royal Society of London," *Notes and Records of the Royal Society of London,* Volume 46, 1992, pp. 279–300.

—Sketch by Mindi Dickstein

Hendrik Antoon Lorentz
1853-1928
Dutch physicist

Hendrick Antoon Lorentz was widely regarded as the world's leading theoretical physicist at the end of the nineteenth century and the beginning of the twentieth. His earliest work dealt with optical phenomena, but by 1892 he had begun to develop one of the concepts for which he is most famous, the electron theory. Based on the presumed existence of tiny charged particles in matter, this theory explained a number of well-known physical phenomena. In 1902 Lorentz received the Nobel Prize in Physics for his work on the interaction of radiation and matter; he shared the award with **Pieter Zeeman**. In the first decade of the twentieth century, Lorentz worked on the effect of motion on the properties of a particle, foreshadowing some of the fundamental concepts that were later to become part of **Albert Einstein**'s theory of relativity.

Hendrik Antoon Lorentz was born in Arnhem in the Netherlands, on July 18, 1853. His father was Gerrit Frederik Lorentz, owner of a nursery; his mother, Geertruida van Ginkel Lorentz, died when Lorentz was four years old, and five years later his father was married for a second time, to Luberta Hupkes. Lorentz attended primary and secondary schools in Arnhem, and while he showed a special interest in the sciences, he did well in all subjects. In 1870, Lorentz entered the University of Leiden, where he studied physics and mathematics. He became especially interested in the lectures of Frederick Kaiser, a professor of astronomy, and Pieter Leonhard Rijke, the university's only professor of physics. Lorentz passed his candidate's examination (approximately equivalent to a bachelors degree) in November 1871, only eighteen months after entering the university.

Lorentz returned to Arnhem to prepare for his doctoral examination. Over the next two years he supported himself by teaching in the local high school; he passed the examination *summa cum laude* in 1873. He then began his doctoral research on the theory of reflection and refraction, an aspect of electromagnetic theory that James Clerk Maxwell had left unsolved in his earlier studies of the subject. Lorentz was awarded his Ph.D. in 1875 for his thesis, "The Theory of Reflection and Refraction of Light."

Lorentz remained in Arnhem for four years after receiving his doctorate, continuing to teach high school and trying to decide the future direction of his career. He was uncertain as to whether he should focus on mathematics or physics. That choice was made even more difficult in 1877 when he was offered a chair in mathematics at the University of Utrecht and a chair in theoretical physics at the University of Leiden. The position at Leiden was the first in theoretical physics created in the Netherlands and one of the first in the world. Lorentz chose physics, not only establishing his own future but that of the field of theoretical physics over the next half century.

During his first few years at Leiden, Lorentz concentrated on the study of optical phenomena. One of his accomplishments during this period was the discovery of a formula relating the density of a substance to its index of refraction. That formula is now known as the Lorentz-Lorenz equation in honor of his work and that of the Danish physicist Ludwig Lorenz, who made the same discovery almost simultaneously.

Develops Theory of Electrons and Lorentz Transformations

In the early 1890s, Lorentz began work on one of his most important theoretical contributions, commonly known as his theory of electrons. Electrons had not yet been discovered, so the term is somewhat misleading; Lorentz posited the existence of tiny, charged particles to explain a number of physical phenomena, and these particles had properties very similar to those of the electron that was discovered by J. J. Thomas in 1897. Lorentz argued, for example, that electromagnetic radiation is produced by the vibration of the tiny charged particles, and this has turned out to be true of electrons.

An important consequence of Lorentz's electron theory was the prediction that spectral lines would be split if the source of light from which they came was placed within a strong magnetic field. Spectral lines are an optical phenomenon, and they occur when the light from a gas flame is split into different colors. Lorentz hypothesized that the presence of the magnetic field would alter the motion of the charged particles which produced the spectral lines, causing them to shift positions. Lorentz's theory was confirmed by a series of experiments conducted in 1896 by Lorentz's younger colleague at Leiden, **Pieter Zeeman**. For their discovery and explanation of the splitting of spectral lines, Lorentz and Zeeman were jointly awarded the 1902 Nobel Prize in physics.

In the last decade of the nineteenth century, Lorentz began to do more work in electrodynamics. One of the foundations of electrodynamic theory at the time was the posited existence of a substance called aether (or ether). The existence of aether was thought necessary to explain a number of physical phenomena, such as light waves, and it was believed to fill all space. In 1887, **Albert Michelson** and **Edward W. Morley** performed a classic experiment which failed to find any evidence for the existence of aether. In his own studies of electromagnetic phenomena, Lorentz had found it necessary to postulate the existence of an aether, so he was troubled by the results of the Michelson-Morley experiment.

Lorentz decided that one way to explain the Michelson-Morley results was to assume that objects traveling through the aether (in which he continued to believe) underwent a shortening in length in the direction in which they were moving. He derived a formula that predicted an amount of shortening that would exactly account for the failure of Michelson and Morley to find any evidence of the motion of light through the aether. At almost the same time, Irish physicist George Francis FitzGerald postulated a formula identical to that of Lorentz's. According to the Lorentz-FitzGerald transformation, the length of a body contracts by a factor of the square root of 1 - v^2/c^2 as it moves through the aether (v equals velocity and c is the speed of light). Lorentz also calculated that the mass of a particle would increase by the same factor. The Lorentz-FitzGerald transformation was later found by **Albert Einstein** to be a necessary consequence of the theory of relativity.

During his long tenure at Leiden, Lorentz had an enormous influence on the development of modern physics. That influence resulted not only from his own research and writing, but also from the students he trained and the professional organizations with which he became involved. In 1912, however, he resigned from his post at Leiden to become director of the Teyler's Stichting Museum in Haarlem, Netherlands. In his new job at Haarlem, Lorentz had his own, well-equipped laboratory, a facility that he had been promised for decades—though never received—at Leiden. During his eleven-year tenure in Haarlem, Lorentz continued to teach at Leiden once a week and in 1919 became involved in the Dutch effort to reclaim land from the Zuider Zee. He was also very interested in science education in the Netherlands and served on the government board of education from 1919 until 1926.

Lorentz was held in high esteem by his professional colleagues and was offered a number of important positions in professional organizations. From 1911 to 1927, for example, he was chair of the International Solvay Congress in Physics. He also served as president of the physics section of the Royal Netherlands Academy of Sciences and Letters from 1909 to 1921. In 1923 he was elected as one of the seven members of the International Commission on Intellectual Cooperation of the League of Nations, becoming president of the group two years later. Among his many awards and honors were the 1908 Rumford Medal and the 1918 Copley Medal from the Royal Society. Lorentz was married in 1881 to Aletta Catherina Kaiser, a niece of his astronomy professor at Leiden. The couple had three children. Lorentz was

still active in physics when he died in Haarlem on February 4, 1928.

SELECTED WRITINGS BY LORENTZ:

Books

Lectures on Theoretical Physics, 8 volumes, Macmillan, 1927–1931.
H. A. Lorentz, Collected Papers, 9 volumes, M. Nijhof, 1934–1939.

SOURCES:

Books

De Haas-Lorentz, Geertruida, editor, *H. A. Lorentz: Impressions of Life and Work,* North-Holland, 1957.
Gillispie, C. C., editor, *Dictionary of Scientific Biography,* Volume 8, Scribner's, 1975, pp. 487–500.
Magill, Frank N., editor, *The Nobel Prize Winners: Physics,* Volume 1, Salem Press, 1989, pp. 35–42
Wasson, Tyler, editor, *Nobel Prize Winners,* H. W. Wilson, 1987, pp. 642–45.
Weber, Robert L., *Pioneers of Science: Nobel Prize Winners in Physics,* American Institute of Physics, 1980, pp. 12–13.

Periodicals

McCormmach, Russell, "H. A. Lorentz and the Electromagnetic View of Nature," *Isis,* winter, 1970, 495–97.
Nersessian, Nancy, "Why Wasn't Lorentz Einstein?" *Centaurus,* Volume 29, 1986, pp. 205–42.

—*Sketch by David E. Newton*

Edward N. Lorenz
1917-
American meteorologist

Edward N. Lorenz stands as one of the central figures in the development of the theoretical basis of numerical weather and atmospheric predictability and general atmospheric circulation energy theory. He is also considered the originator of fundamental chaotic system theory. His conceptualization of chaotic dynamical systems is particularly noteworthy in that it lends itself to applications in mathematics and the social sciences as well as the physical sciences.

Edward Norton Lorenz was born in West Hartford, Connecticut, on May 23, 1917. His earlier schooling culminated with his graduation from Dartmouth College with an A.B. in 1938, and Harvard University with an A.M. in 1940, followed by a M.S. in 1943 and Sc.D. in 1948 from the Massachusetts Institute of Technology (MIT). After a brief stint as mathematics instructor at Harvard (1941–1942), Lorenz joined the U.S. Army Air Corp, serving as a weather forecaster from 1942 to 1946. In 1948 Lorenz married Jane Loban; they had three children.

In 1946 Lorenz began his academic meteorology career with a research staff position in the department of meteorology at MIT (1946–1955). He had been schooled under the influence of **Carl-Gustaf Rossby**, who had collaborated in the formulation of the Bergen school of meteorology, founded by meteorologist **Vilhelm Bjerknes** in Norway during the era of World War I. Rossby had started the first modern school of meteorology in the western hemisphere at MIT in 1928. Stressing a physical-dynamical interpretation of atmospheric movement, the Bergen group provided the first systematic model of both a new theoretical and practical meteorology, initializing dynamic meteorology and synoptic meteorological forecasting, respectively. Rossby's work centered on the sinusoidal wave-like patterns of motion in the upper atmosphere and their relation to forecast weather, and he played an important role in the work of the United States Weather Bureau and in military forecasting. The critical importance of an understanding of weather predictability for aviation technology and logistics had been dramatically demonstrated during World War II.

Early Career

In 1950 Lorenz's own special interest in atmospheric general circulation began to appear in his research at MIT and in articles in the *Journal of Meteorology*. He concentrated in particular on the atmospheric energy balance, as in the studies of poleward atmospheric angular momemtum (a circular force operating on the atmosphere and brought on by the rotation of the earth), eddy momentum flux (lower atmosphere frictional effect), and transport of atmospheric heat flux. In 1951 he was a visiting scientist at the Lowell Observatory at Harvard and further enriched his research connections with a visiting associate co-professorship (1954–1955) at the University of California at Los Angeles. There meteorologist **Jacob Bjerknes**, then the principal exponent of the Bergen meteorology, was involved in upper-air current research in relation to weather forecasting. This was part of a joint research effort between UCLA and MIT in statistical weather prediction (MIT Statistical Forecasting Project). Lorenz was involved in work on the theoretical basis of dynamic and statistical systems, as well as general circulation modeling, which was reflected in his mid–1950s publications.

By the end of the forecasting project (1959), Lorenz had been promoted from an assistant to associate professor. By then, he had started looking at nonlinearity (occurring when system output is not directly proportional to system input) versus linear predictability (system output is directly proportional to system input) in relation to long-term weather forecasting. At about the same time Lorenz was also looking at atmospheric energy in relation to numerical weather prediction via the use of the high-speed computer for weather forecasting. MIT's involvement with computer-aided forecasting had developed with the addition of the meteorologist Jule Gregory Charney to the faculty in 1956. At the Princeton Institute for Advanced Study, Charney had worked out a set of dynamic forecasting equations, including the basic differential equations of atmospheric motion. Lorenz began working on a series of simplified general circulation equations as a determining basis for computer-aided modeling of atmospheric flow.

Develops Determinate Chaos Model

Lorenz formulated a numerical computer model programmed to solve twelve simultaneously simplified dynamic equations of general atmospheric motion and used them in interpreting a physical simulation of atmospheric motion. These so-called dishpan experiments used a cylindrical pan heated on the edge and rotated at the center to simulate atmospheric circulation and were first carried out by D. Fultz in 1950. By varying the temperature gradient or changing the rate of rotation of the pan, Lorenz was able to create a realistic simulation of the transitions of seasonal zonal flow patterns. Most importantly, the zonal breakdown patterns that simulated frontal dynamics of the northern hemisphere atmosphere could be observed.

Lorenz had already proposed an explanation of what is called two regime flow in such experiments in 1953. He attempted to use his system of equations to determine the predictability of general hydrodynamic flow as simulated in the dishpan. His model, it turned out, was very sensitive to initial conditions imposed on the parameters (quantities specifying the state of the environment of flow or other process) of his simplified equations. Lorenz discovered that this variability sometimes led to widely divergent, physically chaotic, results. Convinced that the data and the computer were not the source of these apparently random results, he suspected that weather prediction might be limited and began analyzing the physics of chaotic behavior in nature.

The phenomenon of chaos, to be understood as nonlinear systems in the natural world, had been largely ignored by scientists before the calculating density of the computer became available. Developments in the study of predictability had thus far seemed to point to definite, regular correlations between modern theoretical physical structures and nature. But that is not the case. Lorenz's computer calculation experiments had hinted at the subtle complexity of the chaos phenomenon in the nonlinear characteristics of atmospheric flow. Following hydrodynamic mathematics, Lorenz proceeded to develop the simplest model of heat flux as it applies to fluids and came up with his three classic autonomous nonlinear ordinary differential equations. Plotting solutions to these equations, Lorenz found that the results continually trace out a regular double spiral configuration, a butterfly shape, that never repeats over the same trace.

This congruence of data plots was dubbed the "attractor" (also the "Lorenz attractor"). The pattern Lorenz had discovered was a graphic representation of the phenomenon known as "period doubling," which is now defined as one of the transitional states from regularity to the irregular and complex physical motion of chaos. The equations provided a mathematical definition for atmospheric nonlinear motion, which is called turbulence, and other advanced stages of instability. The implications of nonlinear characteristics apply to a wide range of natural phenomena, leading to the conclusion that chaos is determinate and not a random phenomenon. Lorenz presented these findings in his 1963 classic article "Deterministic Nonperiodic Flow," which initiated the theoretical study of chaos as a general phenomenon characteristic of many physical processes that display not only the familiar attractor but other characteristic scenarios when parameters go beyond certain values.

Integrating the chaotic theory factor into his general circulation and numerical prediction research, Lorenz continued many studies on the range of atmospheric predictability and the role of the chaos phenomenon in determining weather and climate in general. Progress in weather forecasting reflected the growth of computer sophistication with more realistic multi-level models of the atmosphere. These advances, however, also curtailed the hopes of earlier meteorologists, who had anticipated extending reliable forecasting to the longer term. Lorenz's research resulted in several papers dealing with the limits of atmospheric modeling and forecasting the weather. This work resulted in the conclusion that the weather is fundamentally unpredictable beyond a two-to-three-week period in general.

Lorenz's innovative contributions to atmospheric circulation, numerical modeling, and chaos theories garnered him visiting research positions at the Norwegian Meteorological Institute in Oslo (1962); the National Center for Atmospheric Research in Boulder, Colorado (1973–1974); and the European Centre for Medium Range Weather Forecasting (1981–1982). Along with several honorary memberships and degrees, Lorenz has received many awards for his seminal work, including the Rossby Research Medal (American Meteorological Society, 1969), the Symons Memorial Medal (Royal Meteorological Society, 1973), and the Kyoto Prize (1991). In 1992 Lorenz was the first recipient of the American Geophysical Union's Revelle Medal for his achievements in understanding atmospheric processes and determining climate. Since 1987 Lorenz has been professor emeritus in the Department of Earth, Atmospheric, and Planetary Sciences of the Massachusetts Institute of Technology.

SELECTED WRITINGS BY LORENZ:

Books

The Nature and Theory of the General Circulation of the Atmosphere, World Meteorological Organization, 1967.

Periodicals

"Deterministic Nonperiodic Flow," *Journal of Atmospheric Science,* Volume 20, 1963, pp.130–141.

"The Growth of Errors in Prediction," *Turbulence and Predictability in Geophysical Fluid Dynamics and Climate Dynamics,* Soc. Italiana di Fisica, Bologna, Italy, pp. 243–265.

SOURCES:

Books

Gleick, James, *Chaos: Making a New Science,* Viking, 1987.

Hyun Kim, Jong and John Stringer, *Applied Chaos,* John Wiley & Sons, 1992.

—Sketch by William J. McPeak

Konrad Lorenz
1903-1989
Austrian zoologist and ethologist

Konrad Lorenz played a lead role in forging the field of ethology, the comparative study of animal behavior, and helped regain the stature of observation as a recognized and respected scientific method. Along the way, his observations—particularly of greylag geese—led to important discoveries in animal behavior. Perhaps his most influential determination was that behavior, like physical traits, evolves by natural selection. In one of his many books, *On Aggression,* he wrote, "Historians will have to face the fact that natural selection determined the evolution of cultures in the same manner as it did that of species." In 1973, he and two other ethologists jointly accepted the Nobel Prize for physiology or medicine for their behavioral research. Born on November 7, 1903, in Vienna, Austria, Lorenz was the younger of two sons born to Adolf Lorenz and his wife and assistant, Emma Lecher. His father was an orthopedic surgeon whose new hip-joint operation brought him renown on both sides of the Atlantic Ocean. The young Konrad Lorenz received his schooling in Vienna at a private elementary school and at the Schottengymnasium, one of the city's best secondary schools. But his love of animals began outside of school, primarily at the family's summer home in Altenberg, Austria. Lorenz's parents indulged his interests, allowing him to have many pets as a youth. His interests became more grounded in science when he read about Charles Darwin's evolutionary theory at the age of 10.

Although Lorenz had an apparent interest in animals, his father insisted he study medicine. In 1922, Lorenz began premedical training at Columbia University in New York but returned early to Austria to continue the program at the University of Vienna. Despite his medical studies, Lorenz found time to informally study animals. He also kept a detailed diary of the activities of his pet bird Jock, a jackdaw. In 1927, his career as an animal behaviorist was launched when an ornithological journal printed his jackdaw diary. During the following year, he received an M.D. degree from the University of Vienna and became an assistant to a professor at the anatomical institute there. Lorenz recalled that period in his 1982 book *The Foundations of Ethology:* "When studying at the university under the Viennese anatomist, Ferdinand Hochstetter, and after I had become thoroughly conversant with the methodology and procedure of phylogenetic (evolutionary) comparison, it became immediately clear that the methods employed in comparative morphology were just as

Konrad Lorenz

applicable to the behavior of the many species of fish and birds I knew so thoroughly, thanks to the early onset of my love for animals." His interests led him to study zoology at the University of Vienna, and in 1933, Lorenz earned his Ph.D. in that field.

Spends "Goose Summers" in Altenberg

Lorenz then turned to animal behavior research for several years. It was during this time, 1935–38, that Lorenz developed the theories for which he is best known. He spent what he called his "goose summers" at the Altenberg home, concentrating on the behavior of greylag geese and confirming many hypotheses that he had formed while observing his pet birds. In his later book *The Year of the Greylag Goose,* Lorenz explains that he studied greylag geese for "many reasons, but the most important is that greylag geese exhibit a family existence that is analogous in many significant ways to human family life." While working with the geese, Lorenz developed the concept of imprinting. Imprinting occurs in many species, most noticeably in geese and ducks, when—within a short, genetically set time frame—an animal will accept a foster mother in the place of its biological mother, even if that foster mother is a different species. Lorenz raised goslings which, deprived of their parents and confronted instead with Lorenz, accepted him and attached themselves to him as they normally would to their mother. Lorenz has often been photographed in Altenberg walking down a path or rowing across the water with a string of goslings following, single-file, behind him. He similarly found that mallard ducks would imprint on him, but only when he quacked and presented a shortened version of himself by squatting. While he enjoyed his close contact with animals, it did present some awkward situations. On one occasion, while walking his ducklings, which were hidden in the tall grass behind him, he stopped quacking for a minute and looked up from his squatted position to see a group of tourists quizzically watching from beyond the fence.

In addition he and **Nikolaas Tinbergen,** future Nobel Prize cowinner, developed the concept of the innate releasing mechanism. Lorenz found that animals have instinctive behavior patterns, or fixed-action patterns, that remain dormant until a specific event triggers the animal to exhibit this behavior for the first time. The fixed-action pattern is a specific, ordered series of behaviors, such as the fighting and surrender postures used by many animals. He emphasized that these fixed-action patterns are not learned but are genetically programmed. The stimulus is called the "releaser," and the nervous system structure that responds to the stimulus and prompts the instinctive behavior is the innate releasing mechanism.

In *The Foundations of Ethology,* Lorenz explained that animals have an "innate schoolmarm" that reinforces useful behavior and checks harmful behavior through a feedback apparatus. "Whenever a modification of an organ, as well as of a behavior pattern, proves to be adaptive to a particular environmental circumstance, this also proves incontrovertibly that information about this circumstance must have been 'fed into' the organism." This information can take one of two routes: learning, or genetic programming.

Lorenz later devised a hydraulic model to explain an animal's motivation to perform fixed-action patterns. In this model, he explained that energy for a specific action accumulates either until a stimulus occurs or until so much energy has built up that the animal displays the fixed-action pattern spontaneously. He witnessed the spontaneous performance of a fixed-action pattern first when, as a boy, he watched his pet starling suddenly fly off its perch to the ceiling of the room, snap at the air in the same way it would snap at an insect, then return to beat the "insect" on the perch, and finally swallow.

These exciting years for Lorenz did not go without controversy. He wrote a paper, "Disorders Caused by the Domestication of Species-Specific Behavior," which some critics felt contained a strong Nazi flavor in its word choice. While Lorenz repeatedly condemned Nazi ideology, many still believed the paper reflected a pro-Nazi stance; he had to weather many criticisms.

Tells of His Life with Animals

While the research continued, Lorenz accepted an appointment in 1937 as lecturer in comparative anatomy and animal psychology at the University of Vienna. In 1940, he became professor of psychology at the University of Konigsberg in Germany but a year later answered the call to serve in the German Army. In 1944, Lorenz was captured by the Russians and sent to a prison camp. It was not until 1948 that he was released. Upon his return, Lorenz went back to the University of Vienna before accepting a small stipend from the Max Planck Society for the Advancement of Science to resume his studies at Altenberg. By 1952, Lorenz had published a popular book *King Solomon's Ring,* an account of animal behavior presented in easily understood terminology. Included in the book are many of his often-humorous experiences with his study subjects. The book also includes a collection of his illustrations. As he writes in the book: "Without supernatural assistance, our fellow creatures can tell us the most beautiful stories and that means *true* stories, because the truth about nature is always far more beautiful even than what our great poets sing of it, and they are the only real magicians that exist."

Lorenz writes that he was prompted to pen *King Solomon's Ring* by an occasion when his assistant and friend Dr. Alfred Seitz and he were working on a film about the greylag geese. Seitz was trying to call in some ducklings and accidentally used the language of the geese. When he realized his error, Seitz apologized to the ducklings before switching to their quacking. Lorenz recalls in the book, "it was at that very moment that the thought of writing a book first crossed my mind. There was nobody to appreciate the joke, Alfred being far too preoccupied with his work. I wanted to tell it to somebody and so it occurred to me to tell it to everybody."

In 1955, with the increased support of the Max Planck society, Lorenz, ethologist Gustav Kramer, and physiologist Erich von Holst established and then codirected the Institute for Behavioral Physiology in Seewiesen, Bavaria, near Munich. During the ensuing years at Seewiesen, Lorenz again drew attention, this time for the analogies he drew between human and animal behavior—which many scientists felt were improper—and his continuing work on instinct. The latter work gave further support to ethologists who believed that the innate behavior patterns found in animals evolved through natural selection, just as anatomical and physiological characters evolved. This drew arguments from many animal psychologists who contended that all behavior is learned.

Following the deaths of codirectors von Holst and Kramer, Lorenz became the sole director of the Seewiesen institute in 1961. In 1966, Lorenz again faced some controversy with his book *On Aggression.*

In the book, Lorenz describes aggression as "the fighting instinct in beast and man which is directed against members of same species." He writes that this instinct aids the survival of both the individual and the species, in the latter case by giving the stronger males the better mating opportunities and territories. The book goes on to state that animals—particularly animals that can inflict severe damage to one another with sharp canines or horns—will use rank, territory, or evolved instinctual behavior patterns to avoid actual violence and fatalities. Lorenz says only humans purposefully kill each other—a fact that he attributes to the developement of artificial weapons outpacing the human evolution of killing inhibitions. Critics say the book's conclusions encourage the acceptance of violence in human behavior. *On Aggression* is an example of Lorenz's shift in the 1960s from solely animal behavior to include human social behavior.

Accepts Nobel Prize for Behavioral Research

In 1973, Lorenz, Tinbergen, and **Karl von Frisch,** who studied bee communication, jointly accepted the Nobel Prize for their behavioral research. In the same year, Lorenz retired from his position as director of the Seewiesen institute. He then returned to Altenberg where he continued writing and began directing the department of animal sociology at the Austrian Academy of Science. In addition, the Max Planck Society for the Promotion of Science set up a research station for him at his ancestral home in Altenberg. In 1978, Lorenz gave a more personal view of his work with his picturebook *The Year of the Greylag Goose.* As he begins the volume: "This is not a scientific book. It would be true to say that it grew out of the pleasure I take in my observations of living animals, but that is nothing unusual, since all my academic works have also originated in the same pleasure. The only way a scientist can make novel, unexpected discoveries is through observation free of any preconceived notions."

In 1927, the same year his career-launching diary was published, Lorenz married childhood friend Margarethe "Gretl" Gebhardt, a gynecologist. They had two daughters, Agnes and Dagmar, and a son, Thomas. Lorenz was 85 years old when he died Feb. 27, 1989 of kidney failure at his home in Altenburg, Austria.

SELECTED WRITINGS BY LORENZ:

Books

King Solomon's Ring, foreword by Julian Huxley, New American Library, 1952.
Evolution of Modification of Behavior, The University of Chicago Press, 1965.
On Aggression, translated by Marjorie Kerr Wilson, Harcourt, 1966.
The Year of the Greylag Goose, photographs by Sybille and Klaus Kalas, translated by Robert Martin, Harcourt, 1978.
The Foundations of Ethology, Springer-Verlag, 1981.

SOURCES:

Books

Evans, Richard I., *Konrad Lorenz: The Man and His Ideas,* Harcourt, 1975.
Nisbett, Alec, *Konrad Lorenz,* Harcourt, 1976.
Nobel Prize Winners, Wilson, 1987, pp. 645–47.

Periodicals

Time, March 13, 1989, p. B6.
Washington Post, March 1, 1989.

—*Sketch by Leslie Mertz*

James E. Lovelock
1919-
English climatologist and inventor

James E. Lovelock is an eclectic scientist whose work has spanned biology, chemistry, medicine, and physics. He has invented many devices, but he is best known as the proponent of the Gaia hypothesis—a theory which calls the earth a "single physiological system," an organism or something resembling one which regulates itself for the survival of life.

Lovelock was born on July 26, 1919, in the English village of Letchworth, Hertfordshire. His father, Thomas A. Lovelock, was a local art dealer, and his mother, the former Nellie A. E. March, served as a local official in the small town. Lovelock's early life was spent roaming country fields and hiking along the rolling Hertfordshire hills. He credits his father with his interest in nature, and he has described how his father would take him on long walks and point out various birds, insects, and plants. Lovelock has recalled that he "was brought up to believe that science was serious but not sacrosanct and that creative science required a sense of wonder and a sense of humor."

Lovelock was never enamored with schools or classrooms; he considered himself one of those "better able to teach ourselves heuristically than to be taught." After graduating in 1938 from the Strand School, a London secondary school, he enrolled at the University of London's Birkbeck college, where he took a series of evening courses. After several years of night school, Lovelock became a full-time student at the University of Manchester; he majored in chemistry, earning a B.S. degree in 1941. The advent of World War II interrupted his studies, and it wasn't until 1949 that he obtained a Ph.D. in medicine from the University of London. Lovelock also holds a Doctor of Science degree in biophysics from the University of London, which he earned in 1959. He married Helen M. Hyslop in 1942.

Patents an Electron Capture Detector and Other Inventions

During World War II, Lovelock was hired as a staff scientist with the National Institute for Medical Research (NIMR) in London, and he remained there for the next two decades. He became involved in a very large number of projects at NIMR, many of which were hampered by technical problems. It was the wide variety of technical problems he encountered in his work at the institute that led him to become an inventor. When he began investigating the effects of thawing and freezing on living tissue, for example, there was no diathermy machine (used to generate heat in tissue) that could be effectively used on living cells. He invented such a machine, and since then he has patented some sixty inventions—including a method for freezing bull sperm, a gauge for Scuba divers to monitor blood pressure, and other precision measuring instruments. In 1957, Lovelock invented a device known as an electron capture detector; about the size of a package of cigarettes, it was designed to measure the level of chemical contamination in the environment. **Rachel Carson** used this instrument to measure the level of pesticides in the environment and based her 1962 book, *Silent Spring,* on the results. Lovelock also used his electron capture detector to prove the presence of chlorofluorocarbons in the atmosphere, and his findings were a key factor in the developing understanding of global warming and the depletion of the ozone layer.

Develops Gaia Hypothesis

In 1961, Lovelock was hired by NASA to work with a group that was designing instruments and experiments to determine if life exists beyond Earth. He left England and moved to Houston with his family, which now consisted of two daughters and two sons. In Houston, he also accepted a position as professor of chemistry at the Baylor College of Medicine. For several years Lovelock shuttled from there to NASA's Jet Propulsion Laboratory in Pasadena, California. Although their yearning for their native soil led Lovelock and his family back to England after only two years, he still consulted with NASA at their facilities in both Texas and California.

It was during his NASA work with life in space that Lovelock developed his Gaia theory. In 1965, he and colleague Dian Hitchcock were at the Jet Propulsion Laboratory discussing the comparative atmospheres of Mars, Venus, and the earth. They noted that the atmospheres of Mars and Venus are close to equilibrium, whereas Earth's atmosphere is "in a deep state of disequilibrium." It was then, Lovelock remembers, that "I glimpsed Gaia.... An awesome thought came to me. The Earth's atmosphere was an extraordinary and unstable mixture of gases, yet I knew that it was constant in composition over quite long periods of time. Could it be that life on Earth not only made the atmosphere, but *regulated* it—keeping it at a constant composition, and at a level favorable for organisms?" An English neighbor of his, author William Golding, suggested several years later that he name his concept after the Greek goddess of the earth, Gaia.

Lovelock first published his hypotheses in a brief paper that appeared in a 1968 publication of the American Astronautical Society, but there was little reaction. The following year, however, Lovelock read another paper on his theory before a meeting on the origins of life in Princeton, New Jersey. This time the reaction was strongly negative; only University of Massachusetts biologist **Lynn Margulis**, who edited the paper, and Swedish chemist Lars Gunnar Sillen lent their support to this hypothesis.

In 1979, Lovelock responded to criticism from his scientific colleagues and published a more expanded version of his theory, *Gaia: A New Look at Life on Earth.* Although he has won many converts to Gaia, including a number of environmentalists, the theory remains extremely controversial in scientific circles. By claiming that the earth regulates itself to make the environment more hospitable to life, Lovelock seems to be proposing a theory that "runs counter to the laws of natural selection." Many scientists consider it absurd to claim, as he does, that the earth is a "superorganism." Lovelock himself is aware that his theory might have shortcomings, but he continues to defend its importance. In *Healing Gaia* (1991), he has written: "Gaia theory may be wholly or partially in error. To the real scientist this is not as important as how well the theory fits these criteria: Is it useful? Does it suggest interesting experiments? Does it explain puzzling data we have gathered? What are its predictions? Does it have a mathematical basis? Gaia gives positive answers to all of these questions and therefore surely merits consideration, not contumely, from scientists."

Lovelock lives in the small English community of St. Giles on the Heath, and now works in his own laboratory. Income from his many inventions allow him to avoid the bustle of big cities and large research facilities. His wife Helen died in 1989 and in 1991 he married the former Sandra J. Orchard. He is a fellow of the Royal Society, a Commander of the British Empire, and an Associate of the Royal Institute of Chemistry. From 1986 to 1990 he served as president of the Marine Biological Association.

SELECTED WRITINGS BY LOVELOCK:

Books

Gaia: A New Look at Life on Earth, Oxford University Press, 1979.
The Ages of Gaia, W. W. Norton and Co., 1988.
Healing Gaia, Crown Publications, 1991.

SOURCES:

Periodicals

Beardsley, Tim, "Gaia: The Smile Remains, But the Lady Vanishes," *Scientific American,* December, 1989, pp. 35–36.
"Gaia: The Veiled Goddess," *Economist,* December 22, 1990, pp. 101–107.
Wiley, John P., Jr., "The Gaia Hypothesis—That Life Creates the Conditions It Needs Has Its Day in Court; The Jury Is Out," *Smithsonian,* May, 1988, pp. 30–34.

—*Sketch by Benedict A. Leerburger*

Salvador Edward Luria

Salvador Edward Luria
1912-1991
Italian-born American molecular biologist

Salvador Edward Luria was one of the founders of molecular biology. His work in the early 1940s with a biological substance known as bacteriophage opened up new research areas in the fields of biochemistry, bacteriology, and virology, and had significant implications for genetic engineering. For his pioneering work in molecular biology and for making others aware of the scientific relevance of the bacteriophage, or bacterial virus, Luria shared the Nobel Prize in 1969.

Luria was born in Turin, Italy, on August 13, 1912, to David Luria and Ester Sacerdote. David Luria, a member of one of Turin's most influential Jewish families, was a trained accountant and managed a small printing business. In the 1920s, Luria (known as Salva to friends and family) attended Liceo d'Azeglio high school, one of Northern Italy's finest schools that also produced a number of future leaders of post-Fascist Italy. In 1929 he enrolled in medical school at the University of Turin, where he studied with nerve-tissue expert Giuseppe Levi, an eminent histologist and outspoken anti-Fascist. While in medical school, Luria befriended Ugo Fano, who gave Luria evening lessons in calculus and physics by means of astronomy.

Fano's influence made Luria reassess his medical career and consider a switch to the more personally appealing basic sciences. Despite his work in Levi's lab, Luria had little interest in his early mentor's discipline. "Histology was not for me," he later wrote in his autobiography *A Slot Machine, A Broken Test Tube: An Autobiography.* "And in medical school I found no other source of intellectual inspiration, nothing that appealed to a mind full of dreams of physics." He decided to pursue training in radiology, a specialty he believed would bridge the gap between medicine and physics. After receiving his medical degree summa cum laude in 1935, Luria joined a radiology department in Turin and signed up for a course. His sense of disappointment was profound; he found radiology the dullest of medical specialties.

At this rather low point in his professional life, Luria was drafted by the Italian Army—a fortuitous event that enabled him to delay his choice between medicine and science. Luria's three-year stint as a medical officer in the army proved that he was not cut out for a medical career. Medical decision making frightened him and made him overtly aware of the poor quality of his previous training. For Luria, the study of physics and calculus was more intriguing. After his discharge in 1937, he moved to Rome to complete his radiology training and study at the Physics Institute of the University of Rome, which was then under the direction of renowned physicist **Enrico Fermi**. While there, he was introduced to the new discipline of radiation biology and, more important, to the writings of the German physicist **Max Delbrück**, who had conceived the idea of the gene as a molecule. Luria later described the discovery of Delbrück's work as "the Holy Grail of biophysics."

Move to United States Propels Bacteriophage Study

In 1938, while sitting in a broken down trolley car on the streets of Rome, Luria struck up a conversation with Geo Rita, a microbiologist who shared his knowledge of a virus-like parasite of bacteria known as bacteriophage. Bacteriophage multiply rapidly and are easy to control experimentally. Luria believed that he could use bacteriophage to validate Delbrück's theories and, with Rita's help, set up a series of experiments employing it. Luria's notion that he was on to something was reinforced when he learned that Delbrück was also conducting experiments with bacteriophage.

At this point, world politics intervened. In 1938 Italian dictator Benito Mussolini issued the "Racial Manifesto," a document that more closely aligned Italy with Nazi Germany and increased anti-Semitism. Earlier that year, Luria had been awarded a fellowship for study in the United States with Delbrück at the University of California at Berkeley, but the offer was suddenly withdrawn without explanation. Luria then left Italy and traveled to France for a brief stay at the Radium Institute of Paris. In the spring of 1940, as the German Army approached Paris, Luria fled the city on a bicycle, traveling to Marseilles where he acquired an American visa. With the help of Enrico Fermi (who had also emigrated to the United States) and others, he obtained a position at Columbia University and continued his work. He finally corresponded with and met Delbrück, who agreed to conduct joint experimental work. The two spent the summer of 1941 at Columbia University's Biological Laboratory at Cold Spring Harbor on Long Island. Here, Luria was reunited with his old friend Fano.

A Guggenheim Fellowship in 1942–43 enabled Luria to work with Delbrück at Vanderbilt University. In 1943 he accepted a faculty position at Indiana University in Bloomington, where he taught bacteriology and virology. During this time, Luria continued his radiation biology experiments, using bacteriophage to study bacterial resistance to viruses. Radiation was known to cause mutations in bacteria, but the process or processes that triggered these mutations were still unknown. The major biochemists of the day believed that bacterial resistance was activated by an adaptive response—that the individual bacterium altered itself to avoid viral attack. Luria thought that this resistance was due to spontaneous mutation, a rapid genetic change that enabled a new bacteria strain to develop and survive. He struggled with this problem for years, knowing intuitively that spontaneous mutation had to be the cause of resistance.

While attending a faculty dance in Bloomington in February of 1943, Luria watched a man playing a slot machine. It occurred to him that the pattern of slot-machine returns was similar to what happens to mutant bacteria. Slot-machine returns fluctuate—sometimes the machine pays off in small increments, sometimes in large clusters. But the returns happen most often at random. Luria was certain that bacteria would obey the same mathematical principles of distribution. The morning after the dance, he set up an experimental test of his idea. Within a week, he had devised the fluctuation test, which supported the theory of spontaneous mutation. Luria believed he had achieved a major breakthrough in genetics and wrote a note to Max Delbrück explaining his experiment. Delbrück quickly supplied the mathematical analysis, and the two collaborated on a paper outlining the fluctuation test. According to Luria, "bacteria became overnight a choice organism for genetic research."

Although the idea of mutation had already been proposed by other scientists, Luria and Delbrück's fluctuation test paved the way for new technologies for measuring mutations. The technically unsophisticated test produced enough mathematical quandaries to keep biostatisticians busy for several decades. (In 1979 oncologists James Goldie and A. J. Goldman used the Luria and Delbrück analysis to develop a theory of explaining how cancer cells become resistant to chemotherapy.)

Soon after the fluctuation-test paper was published, Luria discovered that the bacteriophage also undergoes mutations. "Specifically, a bacteriophage culture will contain a few individuals that by mutation have become capable of attacking bacteria that are resistant to the normal phage," Luria later wrote. "This observation opened up another area of work, the field of genetics of bacteriophage, just as the fluctuation-test experiments had done for bacteria."

Around this same time, Luria began working with biologist **Alfred Day Hershey,** who was then studying bacteriophage at Washington University in St. Louis. Hershey, Delbrück, and Luria formed the nucleus of the so-called American Phage Group. The Phage Group agreed informally to conduct experiments using only certain strains of bacteriophage so that the geographically separated scientists could easily reproduce and validate each other's experiments and data. Luria accepted a new position as professor of bacteriology at the University of Illinois at Champaign-Urbana in 1950. In 1951 he completed his examination of bacterial and bacteriophage mutation, showing that during phage reproduction mutant phage clones develop spontaneously. This was the first example of reactivation of radiation-damaged cells. Luria hypothesized that the cells had undergone genetic recombination, sharing certain parts of their deoxyribonucleic acid (DNA). In 1952 he and graduate student Mary Human accidentally discovered the phenomenon now known as restriction and modification, in which sections of cellular DNA are broken apart and modified in an identifying way. This discovery paved the way for the future development and use of restriction enzymes—those that break double-stranded DNA into fragments at specific sites in the interior of the molecule. Restriction enzymes are vital to the modern genetic field of recombinant DNA (DNA prepared in the laboratory by breaking up and splicing together DNA from several different sources) technology.

The Post-Phage Era, Politics, and the Nobel Prize

In 1953 Luria was scheduled to speak at the annual meeting of the Society of General Microbiology in Oxford, England. Politics, however, once again intervened in his private life, this time in the form of American McCarthyism. Even though Luria had been a naturalized U.S. citizen since 1947, he was denied a travel visa because of his unpopular leftist political stands. Instead, his former student **James Watson**—who would later win the Nobel Prize for his work with DNA—presented Luria's paper on phage proteins.

During his post-Phage era, Luria concentrated on his teaching and administrative responsibilities. He was appointed professor and chairman of the Department of Microbiology at the Massachusetts Institute of Technology (MIT) in 1959. His research at MIT focused on colicins, a virulent protein that rapidly kills bacteria by disrupting normal cell functions. He and his colleagues studied this protein for more than a decade and contributed important new data on the biochemistry of bacterial cell membranes. Luria was named the Sedgwick Professor of Biology at MIT in 1964 and became a nonresident fellow of the Salk Institute in La Jolla, California, in 1965.

In 1969 Luria, Delbrück, and Hershey were awarded the Nobel Prize for Physiology or Medicine "for their discoveries concerning the replication mechanism and the genetic structure of viruses." Soon after winning this award, Luria was named Institute Professor of Biology at MIT. In 1974 he was appointed director of the MIT Center for Cancer Research, where he recruited such notable scientists as biochemist Phillips Robbins and Nobel laureate **David Baltimore**. Luria was also honored as Professor Emeritus at MIT.

Luria married psychologist Zella Hurwitz in 1945. Their son Daniel, a political economist, was born in 1948. Throughout his life, Luria had strong leftist sympathies and often described himself to his friends as a socialist. He was an early critic of America's involvement in Vietnam, of the size of the national defense budget, and of NASA's costly lunar program. He enjoyed political activism and aligned himself with a number of pacifist causes. In addition to his political activities, he was an amateur painter and sculptor and an avid reader of fiction and poetry. In his later years, he taught a world literatures course at MIT.

Throughout his career, Luria received numerous honors and awards, including the Lenghi Prize of the National Academy of Science of Italy (1965) and the Louisa Gross Hurwitz Prize of Columbia University (1965). His general audience book, *Life: The Unfinished Experiment,* won a National Book Award for Sciences in 1974. Luria died of a heart attack on February 6, 1991, at his longtime residence in Lexington, Massachusetts.

SELECTED WRITINGS BY LURIA:

Books

General Virology, Wiley and Company, 1953.
Life: The Unfinished Experiment, Charles Scribner's Sons, 1973.
36 Lectures in Biology, MIT Press, 1975.
A Slot Machine, A Broken Test Tube: An Autobiography, Harper & Row, 1984.

Periodicals

"Interference between Bacterial Viruses, *Archives of Biochemistry,* Volume 1, 1942, pp. 111–141.
"Mutations of Bacterial Viruses Affecting Their Host Range," *Genetics,* Volume 30, 1945, pp. 84–99.
"Reactivation of Inactivated Bacteriophage by Transfer of Self-Replicating Units," *Protocol of the National Academy of Sciences,* Volume 33, 1947, pp. 253–264.

"Host-Induced Modifications of Viruses," *Cold Spring Harbor Symposium on Quantitative Biology,* Volume 18, 1953, pp. 237–244.
"Colicins and the Energetics of Cell Membranes," *Scientific American,* Volume 233, 1975, pp. 30–37.

SOURCES:

Books

Cairns, J., Stent, G. S., and J. D. Watson, editors, *Phage and the Origins of Molecular Biology,* Cold Spring Harbor Laboratory of Quantitative Biology, 1966.

Periodicals

Bertani, G., "Salvador Edward Luria (1912–1991)," *Genetics,* Volume 131 (1), 1992, pp. 1–4.
Judson, H. F., "Salvador Edward Luria," *Lancet,* Volume 337, 1991, p. 606.

—*Sketch by Tom Crawford*

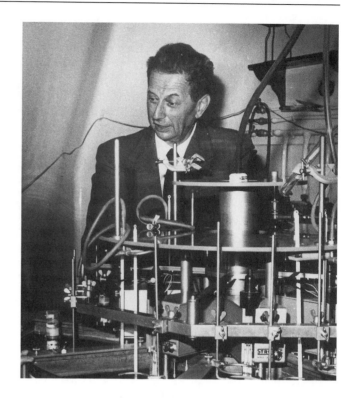

André Lwoff

André Lwoff
1902-

French microbiologist

André Lwoff is a French microbiologist whose seminal work in the genetic control of virus synthesis has helped guide successive generations of scientists toward a new outlook on cell physiology. Lwoff's primary contributions have come from his study of the biology of viruses, including the genetics of bacteria and the mechanisms of viral infection and replication. An erudite man who has painted and is well versed in philosophy and literature, Lwoff was one of the foremost teachers and mentors to guide a generation of scientists who would move biology to a new frontier. A lifelong resident of Paris, Lwoff, who is Jewish, was an active member of the French underground during World War II.

André Michel Lwoff was born in Ainay-le-Chateau, in central France, on May 8, 1902. His parents were Russian immigrants who had come to France in the late nineteenth century. His father, Solomon Lwoff, was a physician in a psychiatric hospital; his mother, Marie Siminovitch, was a sculptor. Although Lwoff—who early on loved to paint, listen to music,

and read—inherited his mother's artistic temperament, his interest in science was cultivated by his father, who often took the boy with him on his daily rounds. Lwoff spent most of his younger years in a rural community near Paris.

On the advice of his father, Lwoff attended the University of Paris (the Sorbonne) to study medicine, a field in which he could earn a comfortable living. But his real interest lay in his other major avenue of study, biology. Lwoff spent his summers at the Marine Biology Laboratory at Roscoff, in Britanny. He graduated with a bachelor's degree in the natural sciences in 1921 and, at the age of nineteen, became an assistant at the Pasteur Institute in Paris, working under microbiologists Édouard Chatton and Fèlix Mesnil. While conducting research part-time at the Institute, Lwoff continued to work toward his medical degree, which he received in 1927. He received his doctorate in natural science in 1932.

Lwoff's keen intellect was first applied to morphological studies of protozoa, one-celled animals that often live as parasites on other animals. Lwoff focused specifically on ciliates, which are covered with cilia (hair-like structures), and discovered a new species of ciliated protozoa. These studies eventually culminated in the discovery of the extranuclear inheritance characteristic of these organisms and earned Lwoff recognition as a leader in protozoology. Lwoff next turned his attention to an even simpler form of life, bacteria. The scientific community at that time primarily studied bacteria in terms of their role in putrification, fermentation, and the biological factors involved in disease. Lwoff, however, was more interested in the general biological properties of bacteria. Focusing on how such simple organisms get nutrition, he discovered how to produce chemically defined media for their growth—a discovery that led him to identify specific growth factors identified as vitamins.

Lwoff's discovery astounded the scientific community because it pointed to the bacterium as an organism much like higher organisms that need nutritional factors to grow and survive. Lwoff continued his research on vitamins, analyzing how vitamin deficiencies cause interruptions at certain points during metabolic processes. In 1936, in collaboration with his wife, Marguerite, whom he had married in 1925 and with whom he worked throughout his life, Lwoff published what was to become an extremely influential paper on how vitamins function as coenzymes, small molecules that help the larger enzyme molecules perform their catalytic functions. These discoveries revealed Lwoff's gifted intuitive approach to research and demonstrated the unity of biochemical action in all living things. In 1938, the Pasteur Institute made Lwoff the chief of a new program focusing on the emerging field of microbial physiology.

During the 1930s, Lwoff developed a friendship with Eugéne Wollman, a pioneer researcher of lysogenic bacteria, which have the hereditary power to produce bacteriophage, or bacterial viruses. In effect, these bacteriophage parasitize other bacteria and can cause bacterial lysis or cell destruction, which releases a host of bacteriophage particles, or phages. Initial interest in bacteriophages stemmed from scientists who thought it might be possible to use bacteriophages to fight specific diseases. Although this approach was, for the most part, ineffective, scientists were intrigued by the phenomenon since the appearance and disappearance of phages was highly unpredictable. Wollman, working with his wife, Elisabeth, had theorized that bacteriophages may be types of "lethal genes" that were reintroduced into the genetic makeup of an organism.

Active in French Resistance

By the early 1940s, however, lysogeny had become an area that was considered of little importance by the young school of American bacterial virologists and many others, who now focused their work on T strains of *Escherichia coli,* in which lysogeny did not occur. The advance of World War II further disrupted the study of lysogeny. The Wollmans, who were Jewish, were captured by the Gestapo in Paris in 1943 and sent to the notorious Auschwitz concentration camp in Poland, never to be heard from again. Lwoff, meanwhile, had joined a resistance group in France

that focused primarily on gathering intelligence for the Allies. He managed to escape capture when his underground network was destroyed by the Gestapo, who arrested many of Lwoff's compatriots. But Lwoff was soon involved in another underground network. He also hid American airmen in his apartment as they tried to make their way to unoccupied France after having being shot down over Nazi territory. After the war, Lwoff was awarded the Medaille de la Resistance and was made Commander Legion d'Honneur for his efforts in resisting the Nazi occupation of France.

At war's end, Lwoff chose to continue the work of his friends the Wollmans. At the time, scientists who still worked in the field of bacterial lysogeny said that the haphazard release of phages probably occurred because of one of two reasons: the release of phages either resulted from bacteria mutation that spontaneously created phages (virus particles), or that the lysogenic bacteria leaked the phages without bursting. Furthermore, **Félix d'Hérelle** had hypothesized that bacteria are resistant to phages released by other bacteria and only absorb the phage from like bacteria. He also theorized that cells in cultured lysogenic bacteria carry "free" phages on their surface, which further strengthen the phage-host association that render bacteria resistant to later viral destruction. He believed that the increase of phages in a lysogenic bacterial culture was due to a few susceptible, or phage-sensitive, bacteria.

Lwoff began working with a lysogenic strain of soil bacteria called *Bacillus megaterium* and a second strain of bacteriasusceptible to phage infection. Lwoff exhibited remarkable dexterity and skill in the extremely difficult procedure of growing individual bacteria in a microdrop and then fishing out the newly divided bacteria with a capillary pipette—only a few microns in diameter—without contaminating the specimen. He would then transfer the bacteria to a new noncontaminated medium. Although the approach was time-consuming and cumbersome, Lwoff was able to show that, contrary to D'Hérelle's theory, lysogenic bacteria could multiply for nineteen successive generations without the intervention of exogenous, or cell surface, phages. These successive generations were also lysogenic, which proved that lysogeny was a genetic trait. Lwoff's discoveries once again made lysogeny a viable area of study. Lwoff had also dispelled the notion that the host-virus relationship was one that always ended in morbidity, showing that the two could coexist.

Through his experiments, Lwoff also determined that lysogenic bacteria release the phages they produce by lysing, or breaking down, the cell. Still, Lwoff had not explained what actually took place during lysogeny. He did, however, go on to confirm Wollman's earlier finding that when the enzyme lysozyme was used to artificially break open lysogenic bacteria without affecting the phages, no phage particles could be found. He soon discovered what he called "prophages," which, unlike normal bacteriophages, were noninfectious. Furthermore, Lwoff discovered that the prophages acted as "bacterial genes" that integrated themselves into the chromosome of the host, where the genes are located. Reproduction of the phage particle was halted by a regulatory gene in the phage DNA.

Lwoff next theorized that some external environmental stimulus could interfere with the dormant merger of phage particles and host DNA and thus cause the production of bacteriophage. After months and months of experiments, Lwoff and his colleagues at the Pasteur Institute decided to irradiate the bacteria with ultraviolet light, which normally kills bacteria and bacteriophages. To their surprise, they found that ultraviolet light caused the phage to multiply and eventually destroy the bacterial cell. Lwoff would later note this discovery as one of the most thrilling of his scientific career. Further research showed that other stimuli, including chemicals that were known to cause cancers, could produce the same effect.

Lwoff's studies of lysogeny provided a viable model for a viral theory of cancer; and, in 1953, Lwoff proposed that "inducible lysogenic bacteria" might serve as a way of testing cancerous and noncancerous activity in cells. Although this proved difficult and engendered much debate over the possible viral origins of some cancers, Lwoff was correct in postulating that viruses' protein coats contain carcinogenic properties that can be activated by outside factors such as ultraviolet light. His research on lysogeny also led Lwoff to study poliomyelitis virus. He demonstrated that, unlike vaccine strains of the virus, some strains of the poliovirus were not affected by temperature fluctuations.

Wins Nobel Prize for Studies of Lysogeny

Lwoff was awarded the Nobel Prize for physiology or medicine in 1965 for his lysogeny studies. He shared the award with fellow Pasteur Institute scientists **Jacques Lucien Monod** and **François Jacob**. These three were the first French scientists to win the Nobel Prize in thirty years, and Lwoff and his fellow Nobel Prize winners were largely unknown in France until they received the award. But this was not the case in the United States, where Lwoff had traveled and conducted some of his most important scientific dialogues. Soon, many young scientists came from the U.S. to visit Lwoff and learn as much about his expertise in the field of microbiology as possible. They were also drawn to Lwoff because his line of research was fundamentally similar to that used in studying the genetic manipulation of microorganisms. Lwoff's influence was also enhanced because he spoke fluent English.

Unfortunately for many of his devotees, Lwoff was in no position to take them under his wing. His quarters in the attic of the Pasteur Institute were cramped and crowded with equipment. At the Institute, Lwoff was not obligated to teach and preferred to dedicate his time to his research. Even François Jacob had to plead with Lwoff on several occasions to work with him at the Institute. Despite this obstacle, many students and fellow scientists formed close relationships with Lwoff over the years. Lwoff had also helped Monod early in his career by allowing Monod to work with him in his laboratory at the Institute. In one series of studies, scientist Alice Audureau isolated a genus of bacterium taken from the gut of Lwoff; Monod eventually named the genus *Moraxella lwoffii* in Lwoff's honor.

In the book *Of Microbes and Life,* many of Lwoff's former students and colleagues contributed essays in celebration of the "fiftieth anniversary of [Lwoff's] immersion in biology." In the book, **Salvador Edward Luria** aptly described Lwoff's Renaissance nature, which made him so interesting to so many of his fellow scientists. "André Lwoff—scientist, painter, master of language, leader of one of the great schools of biology—is a prototype scientists-humanist, in whom the 'two cultures,' supposedly divergent and losing touch of each other, remain happily married." Lwoff was also noted for his marvelous sense of humor and enthusiasm, which, to the careful reader, would often shine through in even his most scientific papers. Lwoff retired from the Pasteur Institute in 1968 and became director of the Cancer Research Institute at Villejuif, near Paris, a position he held until 1972.

SELECTED WRITINGS BY LWOFF:

Books

L'Evolution Physiologique, Herman, 1944.
Problems of Morphogenesis in Ciliates, Wiley, 1950.
The Kinetosomes in Development, Reproduction, and Evolution, Wiley, 1950.
Biological Order, Massachusetts Institute of Technology Press, 1962.

Periodicals

"Lysogeny," *Bacteriological Reviews,* Volume 17, 1953, pp. 269–337.

SOURCES:

Books

Monod, Jacques, and Ernest Borek, *Of Microbes and Life,* Columbia University Press, 1971.

Periodicals

Stent, Gunther S., "1965 Nobel Laureates in Medicine or Physiology," *Science,* Volume 150, 1965, pp. 462–464.

—*Sketch by David Petechuk*

Feodor Lynen
1911-1979
German biochemist

Feodor Lynen was a well-respected biochemist whose work led to a better understanding of how cells make and use cholesterol and other materials necessary for life. His discovery of the structure of acetyl-coenzyme A led to a detailed description of the steps of several important life processes, including the metabolism of both cholesterol and fatty acids. Aside from influencing biochemistry, his work was also important to medicine because cholesterol was known to contribute to heart attacks, strokes, and other circulatory diseases. For his work on cholesterol and the fatty acid cycle, Lynen shared the 1964 Nobel Prize in medicine or physiology with German-American biochemist **Konrad Emil Bloch**.

Feodor Felix Konrad Lynen was born in Munich, Germany, on April 6, 1911, the seventh of eight children. His father, Wilhelm L. Lynen, was a professor of engineering at the Munich Technical University. His mother, Frieda (Prym) Lynen, cared for the family. Lynen showed an early interest in his older brother's chemistry experiments but remained undecided about his career throughout secondary school. He considered medicine and even thought of becoming a ski instructor. Ultimately, he enrolled in the Department of Chemistry at the University of Munich in 1930, where he studied with German chemist and Nobel laureate **Heinrich Wieland**. Wieland was Lynen's principal teacher both as an undergraduate and graduate student. On February 12, 1937, Lynen received his doctorate degree. Three months later, on May 17, he married Wieland's daughter, Eva, with whom he would have five children: Peter, Annemarie, Susanne, Eva-Marie, and Heinrich.

Upon his graduation, Lynen stayed at the University of Munich in a postdoctoral research position. In 1942, he was appointed a lecturer, and he became an associate professor in 1947. Throughout his years with the Tuniversity, where he stayed until his death, Lynen supervised the research of nearly ninety students, many of whom reached leading positions in academia or industry.

In the early 1940s, Germany entered into war against much of Europe and, eventually, the United States. Lynen, however, was exempt from both military service and work in Nazi paramilitary organizations because of a permanently damaged knee that resulted from a ski accident in 1932. The onset of World War II made it difficult to continue working in Munich and, in an effort to maintain his research, Lynen moved his lab to a small village, Schondorf on the Ammersee, about eighteen miles from Munich. In 1945, the University's Department of Chemistry in Munich was completely destroyed. In the chaotic aftermath of Germany's surrender, scientific research halted altogether. Lynen eventually continued his work at various lab facilities, but did not return to the rebuilt Department of Chemistry until 1949.

In the first years after the war, German scientists were spurned by their European and American colleagues. Only four German biochemists were invited to attend the First International Congress of Biochemistry held in Cambridge, England, in July of 1949. Lynen, one of the four, made an ideal good-will ambassador for Germany because of his good sense of humor and the fondness he had for parties. "I believe the problem of mankind is its lack of simple joys," Lynen is quoted as saying in *Current Biography Yearbook.* "I think one should drink for fun occasionally." His cheery nature and solid research drew many foreign scientists to Munich. His magnetic personality was formally recognized years later when, in 1975, he was chosen to serve as president of the Alexander von Humboldt Foundation, an institution devoted to fostering relations between Germany and the international scientific community.

During the 1940s, Lynen began studying how the living cell changes simple chemical compounds into sterols and lipids, complex molecules that the body needs to sustain life. The long sequence of steps and the roles various enzymes and vitamins played in this complicated metabolic process were not well understood. After World War II, Lynen began to publish his early findings. At the same time, he became aware of similar work being conducted in the United States by Bloch. Eventually, Lynen and Bloch began to correspond, sharing their preliminary discoveries with each other. By working in this manner, the scientists determined the sequence of thirty-six steps by which animal cells produce cholesterol.

Discovers Crucial Compound in Cholesterol Synthesis

One of the breakthroughs in the cholesterol synthesis work came in 1951 when Lynen published a paper describing the first step in the chain of reactions that resulted in the production of cholesterol. He had discovered that a compound known as acetyl-coenzyme A, which is formed when an acetate radical reacts with coenzyme A, was needed to begin the chemical chain reaction. For the first time, the chemical structure of acetyl-coenzyme A was described in accurate detail. By solving this complex biochemical problem, Lynen established his international reputation and created a new set of challenging biochemical problems. Determining the structure of acetyl-coenzyme A supplied Lynen with the discovery he needed to advance his research.

Lynen, who had remained an enthusiastic skier even after his 1932 accident, suffered a second serious ski injury at the end of 1951. (Although the second accident left him with a pronounced limp, Lynen continued to hike, swim, mountain climb, and ski.) During his rehabilitation, he contemplated how the structure and action of acetyl-coenzyme A made it a likely participant in other biochemical processes. Upon his return to the lab, Lynen began investigating the role of acetyl-coenzyme A in the biosynthesis of fatty acids and discovered that, as with cholesterol, this substance was the necessary first step. Lynen also investigated the catabolism of fatty acids, the chemical reactions that produce energy when fatty acids in foods are burned up to form carbon dioxide and water.

In 1953, Lynen was made full professor at the University of Munich. A year later, he was named director of the newly established Max Planck Institute for Cell Chemistry. At a time when other universities were attempting to coax Lynen away from Munich, this position ensured that he would stay.

In addition to elucidating the role of acetyl-coenzyme A, Lynen's research revealed the importance of many other chemicals in the body. One of the most significant of these was his work with the vitamin biotin. In the late 1950s, Lynen demonstrated that biotin was needed for the production of fat.

Receives Nobel Prize

Lynen and Bloch shared the Nobel Prize in medicine or physiology in 1964, largely because the Nobel Committee recognized the medical importance of their work. Medical authorities knew that an accumulation of cholesterol in the walls of arteries and in blood contributed to diseases of the circulatory system, including arteriosclerosis, heart attacks, and strokes. In its tribute to Lynen and Bloch, the Nobel Committee noted that a more complete understanding of the metabolism of sterols and fatty acids promised to reveal the possible role of cholesterol in heart disease. Any future research into the link between cholesterol and heart disease, the Nobel committee observed, would have to be based on the findings of Lynen and Bloch.

In 1972, Lynen moved to the Max Planck Institute for Biochemistry, which had just recently been founded. Between 1974 and 1976, Lynen was acting director of the Institute. He continued to oversee a lab at the University of Munich, however.

In 1976, on the occasion of his sixty-fifth birthday, more than eighty of Lynen's friends, students, and colleagues contributed essays to a book, *Die aktivierte Essigsäure und ihre Folgen,* in which they described their relationship with Lynen. They celebrated Lynen as a renowned scientist and a proud Bavarian. The author of over three hundred scholarly pieces, Lynen was also praised as a hard-working man who expected much of himself and his students. Six weeks after an aneurism operation, Lynen died on August 6, 1979.

SELECTED WRITINGS BY LYNEN:

Periodicals

"Life, Luck and Logic in Biochemical Research," *Perspectives in Biology and Medicine,* Volume 12, 1968–69, pp. 204–217.

SOURCES:

Books

Die aktivierte Essigsäure und ihre Folgen, edited by G. Hartmann, De Gruyter, 1976.
Biographical Memoirs of Fellows of the Royal Society, Volume 28, Royal Society (London), 1982.
Current Biography Yearbook, H. W. Wilson, 1967, pp. 263–65.

—*Sketch by Liz Marshall*

Miles Vandahurst Lynk
1871-1956
American physician and medical educator

In a long and distinguished career, Miles Vandahurst Lynk not only helped to create a medical school that trained hundreds of African Americans, but also founded, edited and published the first black medical journal and served as one of the prime movers in creating the National Medical Association for black physicians. Fine accomplishments for anyone, they seem all the more amazing when it is realized that Lynk was born to former slaves and was self-educated until the age of thirteen.

Lynk was born on June 3, 1871, in Brownsville, Tennessee, the son of John Henry and Mary Louise Lynk. Former slaves, Lynk's parents were farmers leading a basic life close to the land. But Lynk wanted, from an early age, to become a doctor. He was largely self-educated throughout his early years. As he reports in his autobiography, *Sixty Years of Medicine,* "I cultivated home study [and] literally attended 'Pine Knot College.'" So successful were his independent studies, that at age thirteen he passed his county's teacher's examination, but was too young to use the certificate he earned. He apprenticed for a time with a local Brownsville physician, J. C. Hairston, and then attended Meharry Medical College, graduating second in a class of thirteen in 1891. He practiced medicine in Jackson, Tennessee, until 1901.

Pursues Career as Publisher and Medical Educator

In 1892, fresh out of medical school, he began publishing *The Medical and Surgical Observer,* the first black medical journal in the nation. One of the first editions of that journal carried a plea for "an Association of medical men of color, national in character," to parallel the then all-white American Medical Association. In 1895, Lynk, along with Robert F. Boyd, was instrumental in starting the National Medical Association (NMA) in Atlanta, Georgia, an organization with thousands of members today and a well-respected journal.

Private practice, helping to found the NMA, and publishing a medical journal were not enough for Lynk. He pursued his studies even while practicing medicine, earning an M.S. from Walden University in Nashville in 1900, and a Bachelor of Laws degree from the University of West Tennessee in 1901. Around 1900, he and his wife, Beebe Steven (a chemist and pharmacist), mortgaged their house to follow another dream: establishing a medical college for African Americans at the University of West Tennessee, located first in Jackson and then in Memphis, Tennessee. Lynk served as its president and his wife taught pharmacy and chemistry. Always under-funded, the school finally closed in 1923, but not before graduating 266 students, ninety-eight of whom passed the state boards.

Lynk did not confine his activities solely to medical matters. A prolific writer, he also authored a how-to for public speaking and a history of African American soldiers in the Spanish-American War, as well as his own autobiography. Lynk married a second time, in 1949, to Ola Herin Moore, and in 1952 the NMA awarded him its Distinguished Service Medal for a lifetime of work in medicine and the advancement of African Americans. He died on December 29, 1956, in Memphis, Tennessee.

SELECTED WRITINGS BY LYNK:

Books

The Afro-American School Speaker and Gems of Literature for School Commencements Literary Circles, Debating Clubs, and Rhetoricals Generally, University of West Tennessee Press, 1911.
Sixty Years of Medicine: or, The Life and Times of Miles V. Lynk, Twentieth Century Press, 1951.
Black Troopers, or Daring Deeds of Negro Soldiers in the Spanish-American War, AMS Press, 1971.

SOURCES:

Books

Dictionary of American Medical Biography, Greenwood Press, 1984, p. 466.
Morais, Herbert M., *The History of the Negro in Medicine,* Publishers Co., 1967, pp. 63–68.
Sammons, Vivian Ovelton, *Blacks in Science and Medicine,* Hemisphere Publishing, 1990, pp. 157–58.

Periodicals

Journal of the National Medical Association, January, 1941, pp. 46–47; November, 1943, pp. 205–06; November, 1952, pp. 475–76; December, 1981, pp. 1219–25.

—*Sketch by J. Sydney Jones*

Wangari Maathai
1940-
Kenyan environmentalist

Wangari Maathai has a long string of firsts next to her name: she was the first woman in central or eastern Africa to hold an advanced degree; the first to become an assistant professor at the University of Nairobi; and the first to head a university department in Kenya. But Maathai's real work has been far from the cloistered halls of academia. Since the 1970s Maathai has gained much international support and fame for her grassroots Green Belt Movement, which has planted millions of trees in Africa since 1977. This movement, which has networked with other environmental groups across Africa and the world, have gained Maathai many honors, including the Right Livelihood Foundation's Goldman Environmental Prize in 1985. Yet, while Maathai's involvement with environmental as well as human rights issues have earned her worldwide respect, Maathai has been condemned by the Kenyan government as an instigator of protests and political unrest. A courageous, vital, and outspoken woman, Maathai blends the best of science and humanism in her work.

Maathai's respect for the environment, she has said repeatedly in interviews and public appearances, is part of her birth legacy. Born Wangari Muta Maathai, on April 1, 1940, she was the oldest daughter of subsistence farmers. Raised in Nyeri, Kenya, in the White Highlands, she could easily have been made to assume household responsibilities for her five siblings. Instead, her parents, on the behest of her older brother, sent her to school. A few years later, Maathai's teachers at the Loreto Limuru Girls School became instrumental in obtaining for her a scholarship that enabled her to continue her education in the United States at Mount St. Scholastica College in Kansas. She graduated with a B.S. in biology from her in 1964, going on to earn an M.S. from the University of Pittsburgh in 1965. Maathai's research at Pittsburgh later led to a position at the University of Nairobi in the department of veterinary medicine when she returned to her native Kenya in 1966. Although her male colleagues were slow to recognize her ability, by 1971 she had earned her doctorate from the University of Nairobi, became a lecturer, and later an assistant professor, and finally was promoted to become the head of the faculty of veterinary medicine.

Focuses on Environmental Concerns

Maathai's professional career was assured by these advances, and she married a Nairobi businessman, having three children with him. It was when her husband was running for parliament in the early 1970s that Maathai became actively involved in environmental and human rights concerns. Following an election promise, Maathai opened an agency that paid poor people to plant trees and shrubs so they could earn a rudimentary living. By 1977 this enterprise had become a national organization known as the Green Belt Movement, sponsored by many countries and environmental groups worldwide. The philosophy of the movement was simple. Since ninety percent of the African population depended on wood for fuel, the depleting number of trees was leading to a crisis situation. Women had to travel long distances to gather firewood, and even though food was available, the shortage of readily available fuel meant that they could not cook enough food to satisfy the family's needs. Because of this, nutritional deficiencies were developing among the population. Maathai saw a basic solution to this cycle: Plant more trees. The Green Belt movement helped the local population to do this by establishing nurseries which offered free seedlings for communities to plant and tend. The incentive was a small payment for every tree that was planted and preserved for more than three months by the villagers. Maathai's efforts to fight the deforestation of Kenya have proved incredibly successful over the years, resulting in the planting of over ten million native trees such as acacias, cedars, baobabs, and cotton trees. In addition to conserving the soil and ecology of the land, the Green Belt movement provides employment to 80,000 workers, and has won worldwide attention for Maathai. She has been richly honored for her efforts, and among her laurels are the Woman of the Year Award for both 1983 and 1989, the Windstar Award for the Environment, 1989, the prestigious Goldman Environmental Prize in 1991, the Africa Prize for Leadership, also in 1991, and the Jane Addams International Women's Leadership Award and the Edinburgh Medal, both in 1993.

Maathai's ideas, many of which oppose Kenyan traditions, have also led her to actively participate in her country's political arena. Because of her increasing notoriety, Maathai's husband initiated divorce proceedings against her in the early 1980s. Her opposition to the one-party government system in Kenya, beginning with her notable and vocal opposition to the construction of a 60-story office tower in Uhuru Park in Nairobi in 1989, has cost Maathai her freedom many times. For example, although she managed to stop the Uhuru Park construction, her opposition earned her the enmity of Kenya's president, Daniel arap Moi. And her subsequent increasing involvement with human rights issues has led her to be imprisoned many times. Despite governmental opposition, however, Maathai continues her work for Green Belt and lectures widely. Her message over the years has remained the same, and she firmly believes that one person can make a difference. "The Green Belt Movement is about hope," Maathai told Christopher Boyd in a 1992 *Chicago Tribune* interview. "It tells people they are responsible for their own lives . . . It raises an awareness that people can take control of their environment, which is the first step toward greater participation in society."

SELECTED WRITINGS BY MAATHAI:

Books

The Green Belt Movement: Sharing the Approach and the Experience, International Environmental Liaison Center, 1988.

Periodicals

"Foresters Without Diplomas," *Ms. Magazine,* March-April, 1991, p. 74.
"Kenya's Green Belt Movement," *UNESCO Courier,* March, 1992, p. 23.

SOURCES:

Books

Wallace, Aubrey, *Eco-Heroes: Twelve Tales of Environmental Victory,* Mercury House, 1993, pp. 1–21.

Periodicals

Boyd, Christopher, *Chicago Tribune,* January 5, 1992, p. VI 1.
Gennino, Angelo, "A Green Belt in Tree Defense," *American Forests,* September-October, 1990, p. 80.
"The Green Belt Movement," *Geographical Magazine,* April, 1990, p. 51.
Hultman, Tami, "Portrait of a Grass-Roots Activist," *Utne Reader,* November-December, 1992, pp. 86–87.

"Protectors of Forests Take Home the Prizes," *Wall Street Journal,* May 10, 1991, p. B1.
"Wangari Maathai, 'Afforestation of the Desert'," *The American Biology Teacher,* February, 1985, p. 76.
"Wangari Maathai: Empowering the Grassroots," *Africa Report,* November-December, 1990, p. 30.

—*Sketch by J. Sydney Jones*

Robert H. MacArthur
1930-1972
Canadian-born American biologist and ecologist

Few scientists have combined the skills of mathematics and biology to open new fields of knowledge the way Robert H. MacArthur did in his pioneering work in evolutionary ecology. Guided by a wide-ranging curiosity for all things natural, MacArthur had a special interest in birds and much of his work dealt primarily with bird populations. His conclusions, however, were not specific to ornithology but transformed both population biology and biogeography in general.

Robert Helmer MacArthur was born in Toronto, Ontario, Canada, on April 7, 1930, the youngest son of John Wood and Olive (Turner) MacArthur. While Robert spent his first seventeen years attending public schools in Toronto, his father shuttled between the University of Toronto and Marlboro College in Marlboro, Vermont, as a professor of genetics. Robert MacArthur graduated from high school in 1947 and immediately immigrated to the United States to attend Marlboro College. He received his undergraduate degree from Marlboro in 1951 and a master's degree in mathematics from Brown University in 1953. Upon receiving his doctorate in 1957 from Yale University under the direction of **G. Evelyn Hutchinson**, MacArthur headed for England to spend the following year studying ornithology with David Lack at Oxford University. When he returned to the United States in 1958, he was appointed Assistant Professor of Biology at the University of Pennsylvania.

Work on Frequency Distribution

As a doctoral student at Yale, MacArthur had already proposed an ecological theory that encompassed both his background as a mathematician and his growing knowledge as a naturalist. While at Pennsylvania, MacArthur developed a new approach to the frequency distribution of species. One of the problems confronting ecologists is measuring the numbers of a specific species within a geographic area—one cannot just assume that three crows in a ten-acre corn field means that in a 1000-acre field there will be three hundred crows. Much depends on the number of species occupying a habitat, species competition within the habitat, food supply, and other factors. MacArthur developed several ideas relating to the measurement of species within a known habitat, showing how large masses of empirical data relating to numbers of species could be processed in a single model by employing the principles of information theory. By taking the sum of the product of the frequencies of occurrences of a species and the logarithms of the frequencies, complex data could be addressed more easily.

The most well-known theory of frequency distribution MacArthur proposed in the late 1950s is the so-called broken stick model. This model had been suggested by MacArthur as one of three competing models of frequency distribution. He proposed that competing species divide up available habitat in a random fashion and without overlap, like the segments of a broken stick. In the 1960s, MacArthur noted that the theory was obsolete. The procedure of using competing explanations and theories simultaneously and comparing results, rather than relying on a single hypothesis, was also characteristic of MacArthur's later work.

In 1958, MacArthur initiated a detailed study of warblers in which he analyzed their niche division, or the way in which the different species will specialize to be best suited for a narrow ecological role in their common habitat. His work in this field earned him the Mercer Award of the Ecological Society of America. In the 1960s, he studied the so-called "species-packing problem." Different kinds of habitat support widely different numbers of species. A tropical rain forest habitat, for instance, supports a great many species, while arctic tundra supports relatively few. MacArthur proposed that the number of species crowding a given habitat correlates to niche breadth. The book *The Theory of Island Biogeography,* written with biodiversity expert **Edward O. Wilson** and published in 1967, applied these and other ideas to isolated habitats such as islands. The authors explained the species-packing problem in an evolutionary light, as an equilibrium between the rates at which new species arrive or develop and the extinction rates of species already present. These rates vary with the size of the habitat and its distance from other habitats.

In 1965 MacArthur left the University of Pennsylvania to accept a position at Princeton University.

Three years later, he was named Henry Fairfield Osborn Professor of Biology, a chair he held until his death. In 1971, MacArthur discovered that he suffered from a fatal disease and had only a few years to live. He decided to concentrate his efforts on encapsulating his many ideas in a single work. The result, *Geographic Ecology: Patterns in the Distribution of Species,* was published shortly before his death the following year. Besides a summation of work already done, *Geographic Ecology* was a prospectus of work still to be carried out in the field.

MacArthur was a Fellow of the American Academy of Arts and Science. He was also an Associate of the Smithsonian Tropical Research Institute, and a member of both the Ecological Society and the National Academy of Science. He married Elizabeth Bayles Whittemore in 1952; they had four children: Duncan, Alan, Donald, and Elizabeth. Robert MacArthur died of renal cancer in Princeton, New Jersey, on November 1, 1972, at the age of 42.

SELECTED WRITINGS BY MACARTHUR:

Books

(With Joseph H. Connell) *The Biology of Populations,* Wiley, 1966.
(With Edward O. Wilson) *The Theory of Island Biogeography,* Princeton University Press, 1967.
Geographic Ecology: Patterns in the Distribution of Species, Harper, 1972.

SOURCES:

Books

Gillispie, Charles Coulson, editor, *Dictionary of Scientific Biography,* Volumes 17–18, Supplement 2, Scribner, 1990.

—*Sketch by Benedict A. Leerburger*

Eleanor Josephine Macdonald
1906-
American epidemiologist

Eleanor Josephine Macdonald has been a pioneer in the field of cancer epidemiology. Over the course of forty years, she made several significant contributions to the understanding of cancer and was a strong advocate for early treatment of cancer symptoms. Macdonald was the first cancer epidemiologist; previously, epidemiologists had only researched communicable diseases. While working at the Massachusetts Department of Public Health, she was the first to precisely determine incidence rates for cancer. In Connecticut, Macdonald developed the first population-based cancer registry. Later, she proved that there is a connection between sunlight and malignant melanoma of the skin. Many of the cancer programs in existence today are due to her efforts, or are patterned after programs she developed.

Macdonald, the third of six children, was born on March 4, 1906, in West Somerville, Massachusetts, to Angus Alexander, an engineer of Scottish descent who worked for the American Telephone and Telegraph Company, and Catharine Boland Macdonald, a concert pianist of Anglo-Irish descent. She was educated at Radcliffe College and graduated with a degree in music and history of literature and English. She performed as a professional cellist for two years after graduation. Around this time, a physician friend of her father's requested her help writing a research paper; this work inspired her to become an epidemiologist.

Develops First Accurate Cancer Incidence Data and First Cancer Registry

Macdonald took a job with the Massachusetts Department of Public Health, beginning a series of studies on cancer, a subject which would become the focus of her lifetime's work. At the Massachusetts agency, the first cancer program in the country was set up. Here Macdonald studied the incidence of cancer and other chronic diseases occurring in people older than age 40. For a period of five years, she and her colleagues went house-to-house in Massachusetts seeking information on the residents' health. When she presented her results, the medical community hailed it as the first accurate calibration of cancer incidence in the country. Macdonald felt that although cancer was a pervasive problem, with early detection people would fare better. She collaborated with a group of physicians who went out to every one of the 355 communities in Massachusetts to raise people's awareness of cancer. The physicians provided outpatient diagnostic clinics and encouraged individuals to see a doctor when the symptoms of cancer first appeared. The physicians also explained cancer symptoms to community physicians who were unlikely to have seen many cancer patients. Coming to a doctor sooner enabled many people to have their cancer treated while it was still in an early stage and helped more people recover or live longer. Macdonald's approach to the problem of cancer made her the first epidemiologist in the cancer research field. She also approached the issue on another level, speaking about public health and cancer awareness on a radio

program that aired every week for a number of years. During this time, Massachusetts became the first state to have a cancer awareness week.

From 1940 to 1948, Macdonald worked for the Connecticut State Health Department. There she created a population-based cancer record registry and follow-up program for the state of Connecticut, the first such program in the world. Over a six-year period, she and a volunteer checked all hospital records for patients with cancer. They then traced each case to find what had become of the patients. They found 1,800 were still alive, although physicians who had treated them earlier had assumed they had died. "This was the beginning of follow-up for cancer patients," Macdonald commented in an interview for *NTCS*. Cancer registries that have been created since have used this system as a model. This aspect of her career was only a part of her work at the time. For about 10 years, Macdonald worked weekends to set up and run the statistical department at Memorial Sloane Kettering in New York, a hospital that specializes in cancer. In addition, she served as a consultant to the National Advisory Cancer Council in Washington, D.C.

Identifies Link between Exposure to Sun and Skin Cancer

Macdonald's next major opportunity to further her work arose when she was asked to set up and run the cancer epidemiology program at the University of Texas M. D. Anderson Hospital in Houston. Macdonald was made a full professor of epidemiology in 1948, a position she held for 45 years. In her years with the University of Texas, Macdonald created a pilot cancer registry and follow-up program in El Paso with data compiled from 1944 onward. This pioneering program was very comprehensive and included data from hospitals, clinics, laboratories, nursing homes, private group practices, and dermatologists' offices—places where cancer patients would have been seen. The study included follow-up in 56 counties for 23 years. This survey yielded the first cancer incidence data for Hispanics, which turned out to be lower than in whites. From her research, Macdonald determined that intense exposure to sunlight was linked directly to a rise in the occurrence of skin cancer, including melanoma. Part of her evidence was the fact that individuals who live closer to the equator have a higher incidence of skin cancer than those who live farther away.

Macdonald's work resulted in clinical trials to check the effectiveness of cancer treatments. She also helped to organize the first southwestern chemotherapy trials for leukemia patients. She stepped down from her position as professor in 1974, but has remained on call for the University of Texas M. D. Anderson Hospital. "It has been marvelous to be a pioneer. Everyone encouraged me in my work, and I did not feel that they discriminated against me because I was female," Macdonald stated in her interview. Macdonald was awarded the Myron Gordon award in 1973 for research into pigment cell growth in melanoma. That year she also won several other awards, including an Outstanding Service Award from the American Cancer Society. During her career, she was a member of the American Association for the Advancement of Science and the American Public Health Association; in 1946 she was elected a member of the American Association for Cancer Research. Now retired and living in Texas, she remains active by taking classes and pursuing her hobbies of playing the cello and writing.

SELECTED WRITINGS BY MACDONALD:

Books

(With Evelyn B. Heinze) *Epidemiology of Cancer in Texas: Incidence Analyzed by Type, Ethnic Group, and Geographic Location,* Raven Press (New York), 1978.
"Present Directions in the Epidemiology of Lung Cancer," in *Thoracic Oncology,* edited by N. C. Zhoi and H. C. Grillo, Raven Press (New York), 1983, pp. 1–22.

Periodicals

"Fundamentals of Epidemiology," *Radcliffe Quarterly,* February 1936, pp. 19–22.

SOURCES:

Macdonald, Eleanor J., interview with Barbara Proujan conducted on January 13, 1994.

—*Sketch by Barbara Proujan*

Gordon MacDonald
1929-
Mexican-born American geophysicist and climatologist

Trained as a geophysicist, Gordon MacDonald made major contributions to planetary science and did extensive research on the internal structure of the earth early in his career. Since the late 1960s, he has concentrated his efforts on climatology and atmospheric studies. Besides building a distinguished research and teaching record, MacDonald has become a leading spokesman on domestic and international environmental policy, particularly with respect to the issue of global warming.

The son of Gordon J. MacDonald and Josephine Bennett, Gordon James Fraser MacDonald was born on July 30, 1929, in Mexico, where his father, a Scotsman, was employed as an accountant at a metal refinery. MacDonald was enrolled in local schools until 1941, when the family relocated to the United States. MacDonald earned undergraduate and graduate degrees from Harvard University, culminating his studies there with a doctorate in geophysics in 1954. He taught at MIT for several years before taking a position at the University of California at Los Angeles in 1958. Until 1967, he served at UCLA as head of the Institute of Geophysics and Planetary Physics and of the Atmospheric Research Laboratory. He was also Chair of the Department of Planetary and Space Science.

Studies Origins of the Moon

MacDonald's early research focused primarily on the formation and early history of the moon. He studied tidal effects on both the moon and the earth in relation to the moon's orbit and rotation. He concluded that available theories concerning the moon's formation could not be valid. There are three earlier theories concerning the moon's formation. The oldest of these holds that the moon was formed of matter blown off the earth's crust, perhaps as a result of a major collision with another celestial body. Problems with this theory led to the hypothesis that the earth and the moon were formed at the same time from basically the same matter. A final theory seeks to explain differences between the materials that make up the earth and the moon and holds that the earth captured a celestial body, now called the moon, fully-formed, in its gravitational field. Considering his data on orbits, rotation and tidal effects, together with the age of the moon's surface, MacDonald proposed what is essentially a variant of the last of the three theories. His theory describes the origin of the moon as resulting from the coalescence of several earlier satellites which had been captured by the earth's gravitational field.

MacDonald also conducted research on the thermal properties of the interior of the earth. He studied the depth of the continents; the relationship between earthquakes and thermal phenomena; and viscosity and convection patterns in the earth's mantle, the region between core and crust that contains molten material. With **Walter Munk**, he published *The Rotation of the Earth: A Geophysical Discussion* in 1960. MacDonald was the recipient of the American Geophysical Union's 1965 James B. Macelwane

Award and was given the Man of Science Award in 1966.

In the 1960s, MacDonald also took on a number of different functions in public government. From 1965 to 1969 he was a member of the President's Science Advisory Council. MacDonald served as vice-president of research at the Institute for Defense Analyses in Washington, D.C., from 1967 to 1968 and then went on to the University of California at Santa Barbara. During these years, the primary focus of his research shifted to atmospheric studies. Before long, however, he was back in the nation's capital, this time as a member of President Nixon's Council on Environmental Quality, where he served from 1970 to 1972. In this capacity, he played an important role in formulating and implementing federal environmental legislation.

Describes Global Warming

MacDonald was full professor of environmental studies at Dartmouth College from 1972 to 1979. At that time he became an adjunct professor at Dartmouth to take up the position of Chief Scientist at the MITRE Corporation, a private scientific and engineering consulting firm. During his years at MITRE, he conducted research on deep-gas theories, on acoustic phenomena in the upper atmosphere, and on the effects of carbon dioxide in the atmosphere. He also developed an understanding of potential weather modification as a consequence of changes in atmospheric carbon dioxide content, often referred to as the greenhouse effect or global warming. His involvement with the formulation of public policy with respect to the environment deepened at this time. He continued his involvement with legislative issues as a member of the Board of Directors of the Environmental Law Institute from 1975 to 1984.

MacDonald ended his relationship with Dartmouth in 1984, when he accepted the position of Vice-President at MITRE in addition to continuing his duties as Chief Scientist there. Besides doing scientific research, MacDonald became more and more interested in issues of conflict resolution, as techniques of conflict resolution are essential to implementing environmental policy, whether on a global or local scale. In 1990, he returned to teaching, accepting a position at the University of California at San Diego as Professor of International Relations and Pacific Studies and as Director of the Environmental Policy Program. MacDonald has published a great many journal articles and monographs in the areas of geophysics, atmospheric studies, and environmental studies.

In 1960 MacDonald married Marcelline Kuglen; they had two sons, Gordon James and Michael, and a daughter, Maureen. MacDonald later married Betty Ann Kipniss, with whom he has a son, Bruce.

SELECTED WRITINGS BY MACDONALD:

Books

(With Walter Heinrich Munk) *The Rotation of the Earth: A Geophysical Discussion,* Cambridge University Press, 1960.
(Editor with L. Sertorio) *Global Climate and Ecosystem Change,* Plenum, 1990.

Periodicals

"Greenhouse Gases and Electric Power Resources," *Global Warming: A Northwest Perspective,* Pacific Northwest Laboratory, 1990.
"Overview of Global Atmospheric Change," *Global Atmospheric Change and Public Health,* Elsevier, 1990.

—Sketch by Jeanne M. Lesinski

Elsie Gregory MacGill
1908-1980
Canadian aeronautical engineer

Elsie Gregory MacGill overcame severe illness to become the first woman to design, build, and test an airplane. She was also the first woman named chief aeronautical engineer of a North American firm. During World War II, she transformed a railway boxcar plant into an aircraft factory that produced twenty-three Hawker Hurricane fighters per week. Active as a consultant and in aeronautics and women's organizations after the war, MacGill is remembered as an influential figure in Canadian industrial development.

MacGill was born in Vancouver, British Columbia, Canada, on March 27, 1908, the daughter of a barrister father and Helen Gregory MacGill, who was British Columbia's first woman judge of the juvenile court. Both her mother and grandmother were active suffragettes, and MacGill chronicled her mother's life in her book, *My Mother, the Judge.* As a girl, MacGill became interested in radio, which led her to study engineering at the University of Toronto. In 1927, she became the first woman to receive a degree there in electrical engineering.

MacGill then obtained a position with Austin Aircraft Company in Pontiac, Michigan, and during her employment attended graduate school at the University of Michigan. Weeks before her final examinations, she was stricken with polio, and paralysis left her unable to walk. From her hospital bed, MacGill completed her exams; she received the first master's degree in aeronautical engineering to be given to a woman by the university. MacGill returned home to Vancouver, where she earned the money to pay her hospital bills by writing articles on airplanes for popular magazines. While convalescing in a wheelchair, she designed a flying boat. After she had recovered enough to walk with crutches, MacGill completed two years of doctoral work on air currents at the Massachusetts Institute of Technology. She was then employed by the Fairchild Aircraft Company in Montreal, where she applied stress analysis to the structure of airplane wings and fuselages. As a result of these innovations, she was the first woman to read a paper before the Canadian Engineering Institute, and became its first woman member.

In 1937, MacGill joined the Canadian Car and Foundry Company as chief aeronautical engineer. Her first project was designing the "Maple Leaf Trainer II" plane for the Mexican Air Force. Overseeing the aircraft's construction and test flights before it was turned over to Mexico, she became the first woman in the world to design, build, and test a trainer plane.

Transforms Factory to Produce World War II Fighter Planes

MacGill's next endeavor was to begin Canadian production of the United Kingdom's 400-mile-per-hour Hawker Hurricane fighter planes. MacGill directed the conversion of a boxcar factory into a Hurricane plant. She was given 3,600 blueprints from England, and with those in hand, she began retooling the plant, adapting old machines and installing new ones. It took MacGill and 120 employees a year to convert the plant. Her staff included housewives, lumbermen, trappers, and fishermen. The factory began filling its first order in January 1940, producing forty of the planes. This was an especially difficult task because all of the plane's 25,000 parts had to be interchangeable with their British equivalents. MacGill accompanied the Hurricane to England to test the integrity of the plane's design. When a wing and a chunk of its body were exchanged with those of a British Hurricane, the fit was perfect. With the success of the first batch of aircraft, production was increased. By the spring of 1941, a staff of 4,500 was building twenty-three Hurricanes per week. At its peak, MacGill's workers numbered 5,600—700 of whom were women. The factory also produced the first "winterized" Hurricanes, equipped with skis, and with wing and tail de-icers. MacGill later became involved in the production of the Curtiss Wright SB2C Helldiver fighter planes, which were flown from U.S. Naval aircraft carriers.

MacGill began her own aeronautics consulting firm in Toronto in 1943. Following the war, she served as Canadian Technical Advisor to the United Nations Civil Aviation Organization, for which she also chaired the Stress Analysis Committee. She helped to draft international airworthiness regulations for the design and production of civilian aircraft. MacGill married E. J. Soulsby, a business executive, in 1943. Continuing in her family's feminist tradition, MacGill was an early advocate of equal pay for equal work. In 1967, she was appointed to the Royal Commission on the Status of Women. Of her trials and accomplishments, MacGill was quoted in *Women Can Be Engineers* as saying she that accepted "life's buffets and awards with equal thanks."

MacGill received many honors. She was the first female fellow of the Canadian Aeronautics and Space Institute, a fellow of the United Kingdom's Royal Society of Arts, and a fellow of the Royal Aeronautical Society. She was a member of the Engineering Institute of Canada, and its national councillor from 1965 to 1968. She was the first female member of the Association of Consulting Engineers of Canada. From 1962 to 1964, she served as national president of the Canadian Federation of Business and Professional Women's Clubs. MacGill received the 1953 Society of Women Engineers Achievement Award, the Order of Canada in 1971, and the Julian C. Smith Award from the Engineering Institute of Canada in 1973. She died in 1980.

SELECTED WRITINGS BY MACGILL:

Books

My Mother, the Judge, first published by Ryerson Press, reprinted, Stoddart Publishing, 1981.

SOURCES:

Books

Goff, Alice C., *Women Can Be Engineers,* Edwards Brothers, 1946, p. 45–49.

—Sketch by Karen Withem

Saunders Mac Lane
1909-
American mathematician

Saunders Mac Lane, a prolific American mathematician, expanded modern mathematical thinking with his work on cohomology theory and category theory, which he collaborated on with Samuel Eilenberg. Mac Lane was a believer in the interconnectedness of all the branches of mathematics, with rigor and abstraction being part of the framework with which one can view mathematics as a whole. His most significant contributions involved investigations of the algebraic aspects of various fields of geometry. The Mathematical Association of America awarded Mac Lane both the Chauvenet Prize (1941) and the Distinguished Professor Award (1976) for his service. In 1986 he received the Steele Prize from the American Mathematical Society in honor of his influential career.

Mac Lane was born in Norwich, Connecticut, on August 4, 1909, to Donald Bradford Mac Lane and Winifred Saunders Mac Lane, descendants of *Mayflower* settlers and the Scottish Macleans of Mull. Both his father and grandfather were congregational ministers, known for their liberal thinking. In 1924, when Mac Lane was fifteen, his father died, and the family moved to Leominster, Massachusetts, to live with his grandfather. Mac Lane credits his writing skill to a composition teacher at the high school in Leominster. Agreeing with his father's and grandfather's liberal views, Mac Lane wrote for the school newspaper on topics such as the need to end military spending.

In 1926, Mac Lane graduated from high school and went to Yale (an uncle paid his tuition), where he won the Barge Prize in a freshman mathematics competition. In the summer of 1929, Mac Lane's work at General Electric with scientists **Irving Langmuir** and **Katherine Blodgett** on the characteristics of filaments of tungsten resulted in his first published paper. He finished his undergraduate education at Yale in 1930, and then went to the University of Chicago on a fellowship. At Chicago he met Eliakim H. Moore, who had been one of the first Americans to embrace the noted German mathematician **David Hilbert**'s axiomatic (or postulational) approach to mathematics. It was this axiomatic method that held Mac Lane's attention; he would later do his dissertation on the role of logic and rigor in mathematics. In Chicago he met an economics student, Dorothy Jones, whom he married in 1933.

Mac Lane completed his master's degree in one year and then went to Göttingen, Germany, to work with a circle of mathematicians that had formed around Hilbert. Mac Lane attended lectures on noncommutative algebra given by **Emmy Noether**, who had a forceful, enthusiastic style that engaged students in the excitement of mathematics. Mac Lane adopted this style in his own teaching. He chose to study under **Paul Bernays** in logic. Unfortunately, at this time Germany was at the beginning of a decade of upheaval with the rise of the Nazi regime. The mathematics departments at Göttingen and other German universities experienced an exodus of faculty throughout the 1930s. Mac Lane's advisor Bernays was one of many Jews dismissed from the university. In order to finish before the department collapsed, Mac Lane took his examination in the summer of 1933 under **Hermann Weyl**. He had been writing his dissertation that spring, which was published the following year. Upon publication, he received his doctorate from Göttingen.

For the next five years Mac Lane held appointments at Yale as a Sterling Fellow, at Harvard as a Benjamin Pierce Instructor, and at the University of Chicago. Between 1935 and 1939 he published twenty-three papers in logic and valuation theory. The papers on valuation theory were influenced by the thought of Oystein Ore, who taught Mac Lane two algebra courses at Yale, and who continued to work with Mac Lane when he returned to Yale as a Sterling Fellow. Mac Lane made great advancements in the area of valuation theory; in one paper he proved a theorem known thereafter as Mac Lane's theorem. During his year in Chicago (1937–38), he and Dorothy had their first child, Gretchen. The next year he was hired as an assistant professor at Harvard, where he later became a full professor in 1946, staying there until 1947. In 1941 he took a one-year leave to teach at Yale, where their second child, Cynthia, was born.

Coauthors Modern Algebra Text

In the late 1930s, both Mac Lane and Garrett Birkhoff were teaching graduate algebra courses (Mac Lane at Harvard, Cornell, and Chicago, and Birkhoff at Harvard). They agreed to write a text for a standard graduate algebra course. Mac Lane had been using B. L. van der Waerden's text, which was based on lectures presented by **Emil Artin** and Emmy Noether at Göttingen, and a text written by a Chicago professor, Adrian Albert, which stressed linear algebra. Mac Lane was also influenced by a lecture given by Emil Artin on Galois theory when Artin had visited Chicago. The text Birkhoff and Mac Lane wrote incorporated all of these influences. It was first published in 1941, and has since gone through numerous editions. The book was a great success because it reflected the new connections between classical, axiomatic, and conceptual ideas about algebra, which mainly stemmed from the 1920s Göttingen school headed by Artin, Noether, and Hilbert.

Develops Cohomology Theory and Category Theory

In 1941, Mac Lane began a long and productive collaboration with Samuel Eilenberg on the interface between the field of geometry called topology (the classification of spaces under continuous deformations) and algebra (the manipulation of formulas according to rules). This was the beginning of cohomology theory, which uses algebraic groups to study the geometric properties of topological spaces, and homological algebra, which attempts to use algebra to compare topological spaces. Mac Lane and Birkhoff were also solidifying ideas that they both had about the universality of certain mathematical structures. In 1945, their first paper on categories was published. Category theory is in one sense an organization of mathematical objects, and in another a tool for gaining deeper understanding into each particular object. Eilenberg and Mac Lane set out to combine all the theories from the separate structures into one theory; as Mac Lane wrote in *The Mathematical Intelligencer* in 1988, "the true nature of mathematics is best represented as an elaborately connected network of formal ideas." This work was to occupy Mac Lane for the next forty years, and he published more than forty papers on these topics. In all, he published more than six books and one hundred research articles.

During World War II, Mac Lane took part in the war effort as director of the applied mathematics group at Columbia University. In 1947 he returned to Chicago as professor of mathematics, where he stayed until his retirement in 1982. In 1949 he was elected to the National Academy of Sciences, and in 1963 served as its vice president. He was also named the Max Mason Distinguished Professor in 1963 in Chicago. He has served as president of both the Mathematical Association of America (1953–54) and the American Mathematical Society (1973–74). Since retirement, Mac Lane has continued to influence the mathematical community. His research interests returned to the foundations of mathematics, on which he published a book in 1986. Mac Lane has also contributed regularly to the *Notices of the American Mathematical Society* and the *Mathematical Intelligencer* on the topics of the foundation of mathematics, the role of government in mathematics, and the directions both mathematics and the mathematical societies should be taking.

SELECTED WRITINGS BY MAC LANE:

Books

(With Garrett Birkhoff) *A Survey of Modern Algebra,* Macmillan, 1941.
Selected Papers, edited by I. Kaplansky, Springer-Verlag, 1979.

Periodicals

"The Health of Mathematics," *Mathematical Intelligencer,* Volume 5, number 4, 1983.
"Response to Steele Prize Award," *American Mathematical Society Notices,* Volume 34, number 2, 1987, pp. 229–231.
"Group Extensions for 45 Years," *Mathematical Intelligencer,* Volume 10, number 2, 1988, pp. 29–35.
(With Garrett Birkhoff) "*A Survey of Modern Algebra: The Fiftieth Anniversary of its Publication,*" *Mathematical Intelligencer,* Volume 14, number 1, 1992.

—Sketch by Karin Deck

Colin Munro MacLeod
1909-1972
Canadian-born American microbiologist

Colin Munro MacLeod is recognized as one of the founders of molecular biology for his research concerning the role of deoxyribonucleic acid (DNA) in bacteria. Along with his colleagues **Oswald Avery** and **Maclyn McCarty**, MacLeod conducted experiments on bacterial transformation which indicated that DNA was the active agent in the genetic transformation of bacterial cells. His earlier research focused on the causes of pneumonia and the development of serums to treat it. MacLeod later became chairman of the department of microbiology at New York University; he also worked with a number of government agencies and served as White House science advisor to President John F. Kennedy.

MacLeod, the fourth of eight children, was born on January 28, 1909, in Port Hastings, in the Canadian province of Nova Scotia. He was the son of John Charles MacLeod, a Scottish Presbyterian minister, and Lillian Munro MacLeod, a schoolteacher. During his childhood, MacLeod moved with his family first to Saskatchewan and then to Quebec. A very bright youth, he skipped several grades in elementary school and graduated from St. Francis College, a secondary school in Richmond, Quebec, at the age of fifteen. He was granted a scholarship to McGill University in Montreal but was required to wait a year for admission because of his age; during that time he taught elementary school. After two years of undergraduate work in McGill's premedical program, during which he became managing editor of the student newspaper and a member of the varsity ice hockey team, he entered the McGill University Medical School. He received his medical degree in 1932.

Following a two-year internship at the Montreal General Hospital, MacLeod moved to New York City and became a research assistant at the Rockefeller Institute for Medical Research. His research there, under the direction of Oswald Avery, focused on pneumonia and the pneumococcal infections which cause it. He examined the use of animal antiserums (liquid substances that contain proteins that guard against antigens) in the treatment of the disease. MacLeod also studied the use of sulfa drugs, synthetic substances that counteract bacteria, in treating pneumonia, as well as how pneumococci develop a resistance to sulfa drugs. He also worked on a mysterious substance then known as "C-reactive protein," which appeared in the blood of patients with acute infections.

Works on Bacterial Transformation and DNA

MacLeod's principal research interest at the Rockefeller Institute was the phenomenon known as bacterial transformation. First discovered by **Frederick Griffith** in 1928, this was a phenomenon in which live bacteria assumed some of the characteristics of dead bacteria. Avery had been fascinated with transformation for many years and believed that the phenomenon had broad implications for the science of biology. Thus, he and his associates, including MacLeod, conducted studies to determine how the bacterial transformation worked in pneumococcal cells.

The researchers' primary problem was determining the exact nature of the substance which would bring about a transformation. Previously, the transformation had been achieved only sporadically in the laboratory, and scientists were not able to collect enough of the transforming substance to determine its exact chemical nature. MacLeod made two essential contributions to this project: He isolated a strain of pneumococcus which could be consistently reproduced, and he developed an improved nutrient culture in which adequate quantities of the transforming substance could be collected for study.

By the time MacLeod left the Rockefeller Institute in 1941, he and Avery suspected that the vital substance in these transformations was DNA. A third scientist, Maclyn McCarty, confirmed their hypothesis. In 1944 MacLeod, Avery, and McCarty published "Studies of the Chemical Nature of the Substance Inducing Transformation of Pneumococcal Types: Induction of Transformation by a Deoxyribonucleic Acid Fraction Isolated from Pneumococcus Type III" in the *Journal of Experimental Medicine.* The article proposed that DNA was the material which brought about genetic transformation. Though the scientific community was slow to recognize the article's signifi-

cance, it was later hailed as the beginning of a revolution that led to the formation of molecular biology as a scientific discipline.

Influences Science as an Administrator

MacLeod married Elizabeth Randol in 1938; they eventually had one daughter. In 1941 he became a citizen of the United States and was appointed professor and chairman of the department of microbiology at the New York University School of Medicine, a position he held until 1956. At New York University he was instrumental in creating a combined program in which research-oriented students could acquire both an M.D. and a Ph.D. In 1956 he became professor of research medicine at the Medical School of the University of Pennsylvania. He returned to New York University in 1960 as professor of medicine and remained in that position until 1966.

From the time the United States entered World War II until the end of his life, MacLeod was a scientific advisor to the federal government. In 1941 he became director of the Commission on Pneumonia of the United States Army Epidemiological Board. Following the unification of the military services in 1949, he became president of the Armed Forces Epidemiological Board and served in that post until 1955. In the late 1950s he helped establish the Health Research Council for the City of New York and served as its chairman from 1960 to 1970. In 1963 President John F. Kennedy appointed him deputy director of the Office of Science and Technology in the Executive Office of the President; from this position he was responsible for many program and policy initiatives, most notably the United States/Japan Cooperative Program in the Medical Sciences.

In 1966 MacLeod became vice-president for Medical Affairs of the Commonwealth Fund, a philanthropic organization. He was honored by election to the National Academy of Sciences, the American Philosophical Society, and the American Academy of Arts and Sciences. MacLeod was en route from the United States to Dacca, Bangladesh, to visit a cholera laboratory when he died in his sleep in a hotel at the London airport on February 11, 1972. In an obituary in the *Yearbook of the American Philosophical Society,* Maclyn McCarty wrote of MacLeod's influence on younger scientists: "His insistence on rigorous principles in scientific research was not enforced by stern discipline but was conveyed with such good nature and patience that it was simply a part of the spirit of investigation in his laboratory."

SELECTED WRITINGS BY MACLEOD:

Periodicals

(With Oswald T. Avery and Maclyn McCarty) "Studies of the Chemical Nature of the Substance Inducing Transformation of Pneumococcal Types: Induction of Transformation by a Deoxyribonucleic Acid Fraction Isolated from Pneumococcus Type III," *Journal of Experimental Medicine,* February, 1944, pp. 137–157.

SOURCES:

Books

McCarty, Maclyn, *The Transforming Principle: Discovering that Genes Are Made of DNA,* Norton, 1985.

Periodicals

Austrian, Robert, "Colin Munro MacLeod, 1909–1972," *Journal of Infectious Diseases,* February, 1973, pp. 211–214.
"Colin MacLeod, a Microbiologist," *New York Times,* February 13, 1972, p. 62.
McCarty, Maclyn, "Colin Munro MacLeod (1909–1972)," *Yearbook of the American Philosophical Society: 1972,* 1973, pp. 222–230.
McDermott, Walsh, "Colin Munro MacLeod, January 28, 1909—February 11, 1972," *National Academy of Sciences, Biographical Memoirs,* 1983, pp. 182–219.

—Sketch by John E. Little

John James Rickard Macleod
1876-1935
Scottish physiologist

John James Rickard Macleod was a distinguished physiologist, teacher, and author who, together with Sir Frederick Grant Banting, discovered insulin, a drug to control diabetes. In 1923, both Macleod and Banting were awarded the Nobel Prize for physiology or medicine for their discovery. Macleod also studied respiratory problems. Early in his career he made important contributions to the understanding of caisson's disease, caused by rapid withdrawal from compressed atmosphere.

Macleod was born in Cluny, near Dunkeld, Scotland, on September 6, 1876, the son of the Reverend Robert Macleod. Soon after his birth, the family moved to Abderdeen. Macleod attended Aberdeen Grammar School and Aberdeen University. He went on to study medicine at Marischal College, where he graduated with honors in 1898 and was awarded the Matthews Duncan and Fife Jamieson Medals. With an Anderson traveling scholarship, Macleod continued his education at Leipzig's Physiology Institute where he studied biochemistry for a year. In 1900 he returned to London to become a demonstrator in physiology at the London Hospital Medical College, and the following year became a biochemistry lecturer there. The same year he was named a Mackinnon research scholar by the Royal Society. During this period, Macleod published his experiments on intracranial circulation and caisson's disease. In 1902 he attended Cambridge University and obtained a diploma in public health. Macleod journeyed to America in 1903 to become professor of physiology at Western Reserve University in Cleveland, where he stayed for 15 years. The same year he arrived at Western Reserve, his text, *Practical Physiology,* was published.

Turns His Attention to Metabolism

Macleod began his investigations into the human body's carbohydrate metabolism during his early years at Western Reserve, studying salt and urea metabolism. Studies of the breakdown of liver glycogen followed, and in 1913, he published *Diabetes: Its Physiological Pathology.* In 1918, Macleod went to the University of Toronto to become a professor of physiology and associate dean of the faculty of medicine. Macleod's major areas of interest at this time were the effects of oxygen excess and deprivation. He also studied respiration in animals whose brains had been removed or spines cut. During this period, he wrote *Physiology and Biochemistry in Modern Medicine.* The 1000-page book went through seven editions and became a standard text in the field.

In 1921 Macleod returned to his work on carbohydrate metabolism, comparing the blood-sugar level in normal animals with that of animals with their pancreas removed. At the time it was known that diabetes was caused by the failure of the pancreas to secrete a substance that regulates sugar metabolism, causing an abnormally high concentration of glucose in the blood and an excretion of sugar into the urine. It was also understood that the unidentified substance sped the passage of sugar in the form of glucose through the body to be oxidized as a source of energy or converted the sugar into glycogen for storage for later use as glucose. Macleod appointed **Frederick Grant Banting**, a Canadian orthopedic surgeon, to specifically investigate the function of a cluster of cells in the pancreas known as the islet of Langerhans. Macleod chose **Charles Herbert Best**, one of his senior medical students, to be Banting's chief laboratory assistant. Together the three men planned how they would separate the islet from the pancreas to isolate the substance secreted by the cell cluster. This substance, Macleod believed, was the sugar regulator they were seeking.

When Banting and Best tied the ducts of the pancreas so that it would atrophy, they were able to isolate a residue in the islet. They injected this extract into dogs and found that it did indeed lower blood glucose. The problem of how to obtain larger quantities of the extract, named insulin, remained. For help, Banting turned to James Bertram Collip, a young Canadian biochemist. Collip used pancreas glands bought from a butcher as a source of insulin. To demonstrate how safe the extract was, Banting and Best injected themselves with insulin. By January, 1922, they had begun clinical trials. A youngster named Leonard Thompson was the first diabetic to receive insulin injections. The results proved that the new treatment controlled the debilitating disease. Solving the final problem of making insulin therapy available to the general public, an American biochemist, John Jacob Abel, converted insulin into a crystalline form in 1926, so that it could be given in precise dosages. Today insulin is prepared from the pancreatic tissue of domestic animals.

The Nobel Prize committee acted with remarkable swiftness to recognize the achievement. Macleod and Banting were given the Nobel Prize in 1923, only a year after their discovery. Collip later noted that Macleod's outstanding position in the field of carbohydrate metabolism had made it appropriate and fortunate that the discovery of insulin had been made in his laboratory. Macleod, for his part, maintained that it was only through team work that insulin could be isolated. He shared his prize money with Collip, while Banting divided his with Best.

In 1928 Macleod returned to Scotland to become chairman of the physiology department at the University of Aberdeen. He continued his research into carbohydrate metabolism there and at the Rowett Institute, publishing numerous papers on insulin, experimental glycosuria—the presence of sugar in the urine—respiration and lactic acid metabolism. Arthritis forced him to discontinue his laboratory work, but he continued supervising the work of the physiology department.

Macleod was named fellow of the Royal Society in 1923 and president of the Royal Canadian Institute in 1925. He received the Cameron Prize of Edinburgh University in 1923, and honorary degrees from the University of Toronto, Western Reserve University, Aberdeen University and the University of Pennsylvania. He was a member of numerous professional societies in Canada, the United States and Europe. Macleod married Mary Watson McWalter in 1903. The prize-winning physiologist's favorite recreation was golf. He died on March 16, 1935.

SELECTED WRITINGS BY MACLEOD:

Books

Practical Physiology, [London], 1903.
Diabetes: Its Physiological Pathology, Longmans, Green, 1913.
(With Roy G. Pearce and others) *Physiology and Biochemistry in Modern Medicine,* C. Volume Mosby, 1918.
Insulin: Its Use in the Treatment of Diabetes, Williams & Wilkins, 1925.
Carbohydrate Metabolism and Insulin, Longmans, Green, 1926.

SOURCES:

Books

Parkinson, Claire, *Breakthroughs: A Chronology of Great Achievements in Science,* G. K. Hall, 1985.
Williams, Trevor, *Science: A History of Discovery in the Twentieth Century,* Oxford University Press, 1990.

Periodicals

Best, Charles, "The Late John James Rickard Macleod, M.B., Ch.B. LL.D., F.R.C.P.," *Canadian Medical Association Journal,* Volume 32, 1935, p. 556.
Collip, J. B., "John James Rickard Macleod (1876–1935)," *Biochemical Journal,* Volume 29, number 1, 1935, pp. 1253–156.

—*Sketch by Margo Nash*

Robert Maillart
1872-1940
Swiss structural engineer

Robert Maillart worked almost exclusively with reinforced concrete, defining the possibilities of the then-relatively new medium. For buildings, he developed the beamless floor slab technique known as mushroom slab construction. However, he is most famous for designing strikingly beautiful and highly efficient bridges. In 1947, New York City's Museum of Modern Art held the first art museum exhibition devoted purely to engineering; its subject was Maillart's Salginatobel Bridge in the Swiss Alps.

Maillart was born in Berne, Switzerland, on February 6, 1872. His father, Edmond Maillart, came from a Belgian family of professionals, businesspeople, and artists who had immigrated twenty years earlier. His mother, Bertha Kupfer Maillart, came from a prominent family in Berne. The future engineer was the fifth of six children; he was two years old when his father died. As a teenager, Maillart was a good student at the Berne Gymnasium, excelling in mathematics and drawing. At the age of seventeen, he qualified for admission to the Swiss Federal Technical University (ETH) in Zurich; however, since its minimum age for students was eighteen, he studied watchmaking for a year in Geneva until he could matriculate.

After graduating from the ETH as a structural engineer in 1894, Maillart took a job with a Berne engineering firm; within two years, he was assigned to supervise the construction of a small bridge, the first he had designed himself, at Pampigny. Following the completion of that project, he began employment with the Zurich department of public works' heavy construction division in early 1899. His design for the Stauffacher Bridge over the Sihl River in Zurich was lauded as being the most economical alternative, and it was built within the year. Maillart's first major work, the bridge was a single-span concrete arch with three hinges (one at the center of the arch and one at each end) to minimize cracking from foundation settlements and temperature changes.

In October of 1899, Maillart went to work for the engineering firm of Froté and Westermann, where he was able to develop further some of his new structural ideas. His first task involved performing design calculations on the Solis Bridge, which was the first in Switzerland to be analyzed according to the theory of elasticity—that a body of matter tends to resist deformation, reverting to its former configuration. Its masonry arch was constructed in three stages; wood scaffolding was required only for the first stage, a thin arch that subsequently supported the next two layers of masonry. Significant savings were achieved by reducing the necessary strength of the scaffolding by two-thirds; such economic considerations would become characteristic of Maillart's own designs.

In 1900, Maillart's proposed design was chosen for the Zuoz Bridge across the Inn River, eleven miles downstream from St. Moritz. It was a major innovation in that, for the first time, a bridge's arched slab, roadway slab, and connecting longitudinal walls functioned as a unified arch. In traditional bridges, the roadway slab and longitudinal walls simply added to the loading on the supporting solid arch; in this new design, all three elements formed a "hollow box" that transmitted loads as a unit. Since the deck slab

effectively helped support the arch slab below, the arch slab could be built much thinner than normal. By way of comparison, the deck and arch of Maillart's more traditional Stauffacher Bridge weighed three metric tons per square meter of roadway, while the corresponding weight for the deck, walls, and arch of the Zuoz Bridge was only 1.3 metric tons. This much more efficient design required a less massive structure, thus saving money on materials and labor; its thin, graceful lines were also more aesthetically pleasing.

The hollow box design exceeded the limits of the analytical techniques of the time. As David P. Billington wrote in *Robert Maillart's Bridges,* "Maillart traded analytical rigor for efficiency of design.... Maillart could not convince his doubters with mathematical arguments, because such research was way behind his design practice." Instead, he relied on full-scale load tests on his completed structures; these tests not only established the stability of the structure and generated empirical data for designers, but they also gave the local community an opportunity to celebrate a project's completion.

While supervising the construction of the Zuoz Bridge, Maillart met Maria Ronconi, a resident of Bologna, Italy; her parents had died recently, and she was traveling with a Swiss family. After a brief courtship, they were married on November 11, 1901, in Berne. A Zurich newspaper notice of the engagement attested to Maillart's growing prominence. The couple eventually had two sons and one daughter.

In 1902, Maillart established his own engineering firm in Zurich, and during the next eleven years he built seventy-four works. One of the most important was a bridge over the Rhine in the little town of Tavanasa. It was another application of his hollow-box system, but in a visually dramatic departure from the past, he omitted the vertical wall sections connecting the arch and the roadway deck near both ends of the bridge. The result was a thin, graceful structure that appeared much lighter than a typical bridge.

Since there was a limited market for bridges, Maillart constructed many reinforced concrete buildings during this period as well. His major contribution to the design of multi-story structures was a "mushroom" slab system that integrated beamless floor slabs with supporting columns. He also introduced the notion that structural safety factors should be split, and that the dead load (the weight of the structure itself) could reasonably be multiplied by a smaller safety factor than the live load (the building's contents), which could vary significantly.

Maillart also found time to educate others, lecturing at Zurich Technical College in 1911. A year later, already successful in Switzerland, Maillart took his family to Russia to expand his business. They were unable to return home during World War I, and his wife died in Russia of a gallbladder infection in 1916. Penniless, he returned to Switzerland in 1919 after the Russian Revolution and subsequently founded a new engineering office in Geneva.

His last ten years were his most creative. The period began with construction of the Salginatobel Bridge, which was completed in 1930. It was noted for spanning a spectacular gorge with exquisite gracefulness. His most significant accomplishment was construction of the Schwandbach Bridge, which was finished in 1933. Its astonishingly thin arch is connected by a series of equally thin trapezoidal columns to a roadway deck that curves horizontally in an ellipse.

Maillart suffered from ill health during the 1930s. His children had all left Switzerland, and he moved into an apartment in his office. He died in Geneva on April 5, 1940.

Maillart was an honorary member of the Royal Institute of British Architects, and in 1940 he was chosen as the sole honorary member of the Special Department for Bridge-builders of the Schweizerischer Ingenieur-und-Architekten-Verein. On the hundredth anniversary of Maillart's birth, Princeton University honored him as the subject of the Second National Conference on Civil Engineering: History, Heritage, and the Humanities.

SOURCES:

Books

Background Papers for the Second National Conference on Civil Engineering: History, Heritage, and the Humanities, edited by John F. Abel, Princeton University, 1972.

Bill, Max, *Robert Maillart: Bridges and Constructions,* translated into English by W. P. M. Keatinge Clay, Praeger, 1969.

Billington, David P., *Robert Maillart and the Art of Reinforced Concrete,* MIT Press, 1990.

Billington, David. P., *Robert Maillart's Bridges: The Art of Engineering,* Princeton University Press, 1979.

Periodicals

Schlaich, Jörg, "The Bridges of Robert Maillart: A Legacy of Ingenuity and Art," *Concrete International,* June, 1993, pp. 30–36.

—*Sketch by Sandra Katzman*

Theodore Maiman
1927-
American physicist

Theodore Maiman has spent all of his professional career in industry. His first job was at the Hughes Research Laboratory; he later founded three companies of his own: Korad Corporation, 1961, Maiman Associates, 1968, and Laser Video Corporation, 1972. The role of the Korad Corporation is especially significant in Maiman's career, largely because the company was set up to further develop the product its founder discovered in 1960—the ruby laser. Capable of producing an intense, monochromatic beam of visible light which can be directed with great precision, Maiman's lasers have demonstrated their usefulness in a variety of fields, from business to medicine.

Maiman was born in Los Angeles, California, on July 11, 1927. His father was an electrical engineer whose experiments yielded inventions such as a vibrating power supply for automobiles. Young Maiman inherited an interest in electronics from his father, earning the money he needed for his college education by repairing electrical appliances and radios. Maiman entered the University of Colorado in 1945 and received his bachelor of science in engineering physics in 1949. He then transferred to Stanford University, where he earned his master of science degree in 1951 and his doctorate in physics in 1955. Maiman's doctoral advisor at Stanford was Willis E. Lamb, winner of the 1955 Nobel Prize winner in physics.

After graduating from Stanford, Maiman accepted a job at Hughes Research Laboratories, a division of Hughes Aircraft Company. It was at Hughes that Maiman became interested in the development of a coherent, high-intensity, monochromatic light source. In the course of his research, Maiman looked at work done on the maser by Charles H. Townes in the United States and Nikolai Basov and Aleksandr Prokhorov in the Soviet Union. In 1953, Townes had invented a device for generating coherent, monochromatic beams of microwaves, a device that became known as the maser (*m*icrowave *a*mplification by *s*timulated *e*mission of *r*adiation). Townes and his colleague A. L. Schawlow suggested the possibility of making a similar device that would generate beams of visible light rather than microwaves. This development of this concept was the task to which Maiman turned his attention at Hughes.

Townes and Schawlow originally suggested using an alkali vapor as the medium for generating the monochromatic light source. Maiman took a different tack, one that had been proposed and studied by **Nicolas Bloembergen**, Satoru Sugano, Yukito Tanabe and I. Wieder. In this latter approach, a solid, rather than a gas, was used as the active medium. Maiman decided to investigate the use of a ruby-based device in his experiments. Others, including Schawlow, had also studied using rubies—minerals composed of corundum with chromium as an impurity—with mixed results. One of the most serious problems appeared to be that the amount of amplification obtained with the ruby was insufficient to produce the desired beam.

Maiman continued to work with rubies, eventually making a critical discovery: earlier calculations on the expected amplification required for beam generation had been incorrect. Using this new information, Maiman constructed his own ruby-based device, which consisted of a ruby rod with a silver coating at both ends. When an intense beam of light from a xenon lamp was fed into the rod, the rod emitted a coherent, monochromatic beam of visible light (a successful modification of the maser process in the visible region). Maiman's device was named the laser, (*l*ight *a*mplification by *s*timulated *e*mission of *r*adiation).

Light produced by Maiman's first laser consisted of a very narrow beam of electromagnetic radiation with a wavelength of precisely 6943 angstroms. The beam had the ability to travel great distances without dispersing, a property that made it ideal, for example, in measuring the distance from the Earth to the moon. Because the energy of the beam was so highly concentrated, it also produced very high temperatures at the point where it came into contact with a material, making it useful in welding and cutting and in surgical procedures.

Laser research and development have continued to be the focus of Maiman's professional interests. After Korad Corporation was acquired by Union Carbide in 1968, Maiman established Maiman Associates to specialize in optical and laser problems. Four years later, Maiman co-founded another company, Laser Video, for the development of large-screen, laser-driven color video display systems. In 1976, Maiman accepted a position at TRW Electronics as vice president for advanced technology. Maiman has been honored for his work with a variety of awards, including the Ballantine Medal from the Franklin Institute, 1962, the Buckley Solid State Physics Prize from the American Physical Society, and the Fanny and John Hertz Foundation Award for Applied Physical Science, both 1966, the Wood Prize from the American Optical Society, 1976, the Wolf Prize in Physics from Israel's Wolf Foundation, 1984, and the Japan Prize, 1987. Maiman has also been a member of numerous professional organizations, including the National Academy of Engineering and the Optical Society of America.

SELECTED WRITINGS BY MAIMAN:

Periodicals

"Stimulated Optical Radiation in Ruby," *Nature,* August 6, 1960, pp. 493–494.

SOURCES:

Books

McGraw-Hill Modern Scientists and Engineers, Volume 2, McGraw-Hill, 1980, pp. 271–272.

Periodicals

Swinbanks, David, "International Winners for Japan's Version of Nobel Prize," *Nature,* February 26, 1987, p. 749.
"Wolf Prizes in Physics for Hahn, Hirsch, and Maiman," *Physics Today,* April 1984, pp. 93–94.

—Sketch by David E. Newton

Arnold Hamilton Maloney
1888-1955
Trinidadian-born American physician and pharmacologist

Arnold Hamilton Maloney began his career planning to be a druggist in his native Trinidad, but his ultimate influence in the field of pharmacology was to be far greater than the local level. Maloney immigrated to the United States in 1909 where he completed his education and eventually became the first black professor of pharmacology in the nation. He had a varied career as ordained minister in the Episcopal Church, professor, researcher, consultant, and author. Through his research, he is perhaps most known for discovering an antidote for barbiturate poisoning (or an overdose of sedatives). He was also the second person of African descent to obtain both a medical degree and a doctorate of philosophy in the United States.

Maloney, the oldest male of ten children, was born July 4, 1888, in Cocoye Village, Trinidad, British West Indies. His father, Lewis Albert Maloney, was a building contractor and grocery chain operator, and his mother, Estelle Evetta (Bonas) Maloney, taught needlework to young women and later operated a general store. As a student, Maloney excelled and won numerous awards. He had a love of learning that led him to pursue many different interests as an adult. He studied at Naparima College in Trinidad, which is affiliated with Cambridge University, England, earning his bachelor's degree in 1909. That same year, he immigrated to the United States where he attended Lincoln University in Pennsylvania. In 1910, he received his master's degree from Columbia University. Maloney then received a bachelor of science degree in theology from the General Theological Seminary, New York, in 1912. He began his ministry at age 23 with the distinction of being the youngest minister in the Protestant Episcopal Church.

After practicing for several years, Maloney felt that the Episcopal Church was neglecting young black men. A suggestion he made prompted the church to establish St. Augustine in Raleigh, North Carolina, as a college for black youth. Although there were aspects of the ministry that Maloney enjoyed, he became disillusioned and left the church in 1922. He published a book outlining his views, *The Essentials of Race Leadership,* in 1924. On leaving the ministry, Maloney turned to teaching, accepting a professorship of psychology at Wilberforce University in Ohio. While he was very enthusiastic about teaching and found it rewarding, he decided to continue his own education.

Enters Medical Field and Discovers Cure for Sedative Overdose

Maloney entered Indiana University School of Medicine in 1925, graduating with a medical degree in 1929. He then attended the University of Wisconsin, where he engaged in research in pharmacology, earning a doctorate in this field in 1931. Maloney has the distinction of being the second man of African descent to earn both the M.D. and the Ph.D. degrees. Upon accepting a position at Howard University in the same year, he also became the first black professor of pharmacology in the United States.

From 1931 until 1953, Maloney worked in the department of pharmacology at Howard University School of Medicine in Washington, D.C. He began as an associate professor of pharmacology, becoming a full professor, and then head of the department. During these years, he also worked as a consultant in pharmacology for Freedmen's Hospital. Maloney's research involved several areas of pharmacology, but his most important work was the discovery of an antidote for barbiturate overdose. High levels of barbiturates (drugs used as sedatives) cause potentially deadly symptoms such as shallow respiration, central nervous system depression, and deep anesthesia. Maloney determined that administering picrotoxin (a potentially lethal poison) quickly reversed these

symptoms. His first paper on this subject was published in 1931.

Maloney was hugely affected by the written word. He devoted two chapters of his autobiography, *Amber Gold: An Adventure in Autobiography,* to books he had been influenced by or enjoyed. He also wrote more than 50 articles during his career before retiring in 1953. Maloney was a member of many learned societies and several medical associations, including the American Negro Academy, American Academy of Political Sciences and the National Medical Association. In 1916, he married Beatrice Pocahontas Johnston; they had two children: Arnold Maloney, Jr. and Louise Beatrice. Maloney died in Washington, D.C., on August 8, 1955.

SELECTED WRITINGS BY MALONEY:

Books

The Essentials of Race Leadership, Aldine Company, 1924.
Amber Gold: An Adventure in Autobiography, Meador, 1946.

Periodicals

(With R. H. Fitch and A. L. Tatum) "Picrotoxin as an Antidote in Acute Poisoning by the Shorter Acting Barbiturates," *Journal of Pharmacology and Experimental Therapeutics,* April, 1931, pp. 465–482.
(With A. L. Tatum) "Picrotoxin as an Antidote in Acute Poisoning by the Longer Acting Barbiturates," *Journal of Pharmacology and Experimental Therapeutics,* March, 1932, pp. 337–352.

SOURCES:

Periodicals

Journal of the National Medical Association, November, 1955, pp. 424–426.

—*Sketch by Barbara Proujan*

Benoit B. Mandelbrot
1924-
Polish-born American mathematician

Benoit B. Mandelbrot is a mathematician who conceived, developed, and named the field of fractal geometry. This field describes the everyday forms of nature—such as mountains, clouds, and the path traveled by lightning—that do not fit into the world of straight lines, circles, and smooth curves known as Euclidean geometry. Mandelbrot was also the first to recognize fractal geometry's value as a tool for analyzing a variety of physical, social, and biological phenomena.

Mandelbrot was born November 20, 1924, to a Lithuanian Jewish family in Warsaw, Poland. His father, the descendant of a long line of scholars, was a manufacturer and wholesaler of children's clothing. His mother, trained as a doctor and dentist, feared exposing her children to epidemics, so instead of sending her son to school, she arranged for him to be tutored at home by his Uncle Loterman. Mandelbrot and his uncle played chess and read maps; he learned to read, but he claims that he never did learn the whole alphabet. He first attended elementary school in Warsaw. When he was eleven years old, his family moved to France, first to Paris and then to Tulle, in south central France. When Mandelbrot entered secondary school, he was thirteen years old instead of the usual eleven, but he gradually caught up with his age group. His uncle Szolem Mandelbrojt, a mathematician, was a university professor, and Mandelbrot became acquainted with his uncle's mathematician colleagues. Mandelbrot's teenage years were disrupted by World War II, which rendered his school attendance irregular. From 1942 to 1944, he and his younger brother wandered from place to place. He found work as an apprentice toolmaker for the railroad, and for a time he took care of horses at a château near Lyon. He carried books with him and tried to study on his own.

After the war, at the age of twenty, Mandelbrot took the month-long entrance exams for the leading science schools. Although he had not had the usual two years of preparation, he did very well. He had not had much formal training in algebra or complicated integrals, but he remembered the geometric shapes corresponding to different integrals. Faced with an analytic problem, he would make a drawing, and this would often lead him to the solution. He enrolled in Ecole Polytechnique. Graduating two years later, he was recommended for a scholarship to study at the California Institute of Technology. In 1948, after two years there, he returned to France with a master's degree in aeronautics and spent a year in the Air Force.

Mandelbrot next found himself in Paris, looking for a topic for his Ph.D. thesis. One day his uncle, rummaging through his wastebasket for something for Mandelbrot to read on the subway, pulled out a book review of *Human Behavior and the Principle of Least Effort,* by George Zipf. The author discussed examples of frequency distributions in the social sciences that did not follow the Gaussian "bell-shaped curve," the so-called normal distribution according to which statistical data tend to cluster around the average, scattering in a regular fashion. Mandelbrot wrote part of his 1952 University of Paris Ph.D. thesis on Zipf's claims about word frequencies; the second half was on statistical thermodynamics. Much later, Mandelbrot commented that the book review greatly influenced his early thinking; he saw in Zipf's work flashes of genius, projected in many directions yet nearly overwhelmed by wild notions and extravagance, and he cited Zipf's career as an example of the extraordinary difficulties of doing scientific work that is not limited to one field. At the time, Mandelbrot had read Norbert Weiner on cybernetics and **John von Neumann** on game theory, and he was inspired to follow their example in using mathematical approaches to solve long-standing problems in other fields.

Mandelbrot was invited to the Institute for Advanced Studies at Princeton University for the academic year 1953–54. On returning to Paris, he became an associate at the Institut Henri Poincaré. In 1955, he married Aliette Kagan, who later became a biologist; they had two children, Laurent and Didier. From 1955 to 1957 Mandelbrot taught at the University of Geneva. In 1957 and 1958 he was junior professor of applied mathematics at Lille University and taught mathematical analysis at Ecole Polytechnique. In 1958 he became a member of the research staff at the IBM Thomas J. Watson Research Center in Yorktown Heights, New York.

Studies Statistical Irregularity

In the 1960s Mandelbrot studied stock market and commodity price variations and the mathematical models used to predict prices. A Harvard professor had studied the changes in the price of cotton over many years and had found that the changes in price did not follow the bell-shaped distribution. The variations appeared to be chaotic. Existing statistical models for stock-market prices assumed that the rise and fall was continuous, but Mandelbrot noted that prices may jump or drop suddenly. He showed that a model that assumes continuity in prices will turn out to be wrong. He used IBM computers to analyze the data, and he found that the pattern for daily price changes matched the pattern for monthly price changes. Statistically, the choice of time scale made no difference; the patterns were self-similar. Using this concept, he was able to account for a great part of the observed price variations, where earlier statistical techniques had not succeeded.

Shortly thereafter, IBM scientists asked for Mandelbrot's help on a practical problem. In using electric current to send computer signals along wires, they found occasional random mistakes, or "noise." They suspected that some of the noise was being caused by other technicians tinkering with the equipment. Mandelbrot studied the times when the noise occurred. He found long periods of error-free transmission separated by chunks of noise. When he looked at a noisy chunk in detail, he saw that it, in turn, consisted of smaller error-free periods interspersed with smaller noisy chunks. As he continued to examine chunks at smaller and smaller scales, he found that the chance of the noise occurring was the same, regardless of the level of detail he was looking at. He described the probability distribution of the noise pattern as self-similar, or scaling—that is, at every time scale the ratio of noisy to clean transmission remained the same. The noise was not due to technicians tinkering with screwdrivers; it was spontaneous. In understanding the noise phenomenon, Mandelbrot used as a model the Cantor set, an abstract geometric construction of **Georg Cantor**, a nineteenth-century German mathematician. The model changed the way engineers viewed and addressed the noise problem.

For centuries humankind has tried to predict the water level of rivers like Egypt's Nile in order to prevent floods and crop damage. Engineers have relied on such predictions in building dams and hydroelectric projects. In the 1960s, Mandelbrot studied the records of the Nile River level and found that existing statistical models did not fit the facts. He found long periods of drought along with smaller fluctuations, and he found that the longer a drought period, the more likely the drought was to continue. The resulting picture looked like random noise superimposed on a background of random noise. Mandelbrot made graphs of the river's actual fluctuations. He showed the unlabeled graphs to a noted hydrologist, along with graphs drawn from the existing statistical models and other graphs based on Mandelbrot's statistical theories. The hydrologist dismissed the graphs from the old models as unrealistic, but he could not distinguish Mandelbrot's graphs from the real ones. For Mandelbrot, this experience illustrated the value of using visual representations to gain insight into natural and social phenomena. Other researchers found similar support for Mandelbrot's statistical model when they showed fake stock charts to a stockbroker; the stockbroker rejected some of the fakes as unrealistic, but not Mandelbrot's.

Early in this century, mathematicians and geometers created curves that were infinitely wrinkled and solids that were full of holes. Much later, Mandelbrot found their abstract mathematics useful in models for shapes and phenomena found in nature. He had read an article about the length of coastlines in which **Lewis Fry Richardson** reported that encyclopedias in Spain and Portugal differed on the length of the border between the two countries; Richardson found similar discrepancies—up to twenty percent—for the border between Belgium and the Netherlands. Mandelbrot took up the question in a paper he called "How Long Is the Coast of Britain?" The answer to the question, according to Mandelbrot, depended on the length of the ruler you used. Measuring a rocky shoreline with a foot ruler would produce a longer answer than measuring it with a yardstick. As the scale of measurement becomes smaller, the measured length becomes infinitely large. Mandelbrot also investigated ways of measuring the degree of wiggliness of a curve. He worked with programmers to develop computer programs to draw fake coastlines. By changing a number in the program, he could produce relatively smooth or rough coastlines that resembled New Zealand or those of the Aegean Sea. The number determined the degree of wiggliness and came to be known as the curve's fractal dimension.

Fascinated with this approach, Mandelbrot looked at patterns in nature, such as the shapes of clouds and mountains, the meanderings of rivers, the patterns of moon craters, the frequency of heartbeats, the structure of human lungs, and the patterns of blood vessels. He found that many shapes in nature—even those of ferns and broccoli and the holes in Swiss cheese—could be described and replicated on the computer screen using fractal formulas.

Formulates Fractal Geometry

In Mandelbrot's reports and research papers during this period, he made clear that his methods were part of a more general approach to irregularity and chaos that was applicable to physics as well. Editors, however, usually preferred a more narrowly technical discussion. But then he was invited to give a talk at the Collège de France in 1973. Rather than selecting one of his many areas of research, he decided to explain how his many different interests fit together. Mandelbrot wanted a name for this new family of geometric shapes, which typically involved statistical irregularities and scaling. Looking through his son's Latin dictionary, he found the adjective *fractus,* meaning "fragmented, irregular," and the verb *frangere,* "to break," and he came up with *fractal.* His lecture aroused considerable interest and was published in expanded form in 1975 in French as *Les Objets Fractals: Forme, Hasard et Dimension.* Revised and expanded versions were published later in English in the United States as *The Fractal Geometry of Nature.*

The publication of his book, which Mandelbrot called a manifesto and a casebook, attracted interest from researchers in fields from mathematics and engineering to economics and physiology. Mandelbrot remained at IBM as an IBM fellow but with various concurrent positions and visiting professorships at universities, including Harvard University, Massachusetts Institute of Technology, Yale University, Albert Einstein College of Medicine, and the University of California.

Using fractal formulas, computer programmers could produce artificial landscapes that were remarkably realistic. This technology could be used in movies and computer games. Among the first movies to use fractal landscapes were George Lucas's *Return of the Jedi,* for the surface of the Moons of Endor, *Star Trek II: The Wrath of Khan,* and *The Last Starfighter.* Some fractal formulas produced fantastic abstract designs and strange dragon-like shapes. Mathematicians of the early twentieth century had done research in this area, but they did not have the advantage of seeing visual representations on a computer screen. The formulas were studied as abstract mathematical objects and, because of their strange properties, were called "pathological."

Discovers "Mandelbrot Set"

In the 1970s, Mandelbrot became interested in investigations carried out during World War I by French mathematicians Pierre Fatou and Gaston Julia, the latter having been one of his teachers years before at Polytechnique. Julia had worked with mathematical expressions involving complex numbers (those which have as a component the square root of negative one). Instead of graphing the solutions of equations in the familiar method of Descartes, Julia used a different approach; he fed a number into an equation, calculated the answer, and then fed the answer back into the equation, recycling again and again, noting what was happening to the answer. Mandelbrot used the computer to explore the patterns generated by this approach. For one set, he used a relatively simple calculation in which he took a complex number, squared it, added the original number, squared the result, continuing again and again; he plotted the original number on the graph only if its answers did not run away to infinity. The figure generated by this procedure turned out to contain a strange cardioid shape with circles and filaments attached. As Mandelbrot made more detailed calculations, he discovered that the outline of the figure contained tiny copies of the larger elements, as well as strange new shapes resembling fantastic seahorses, flames, and spirals. The figure represented what came to be known as the Mandelbrot set. Representations of the Mandelbrot set and the related sets studied by Julia, some in psychedelic colors, soon appeared in books and magazines—some even in exhibits of computer art.

Through his work with fractals and computer projections of various equations, Mandelbrot had discovered tools that could be used by scientists and engineers for strengthening steel, creating polymers, locating underground oil deposits, building dams, and understanding protein structure, corrosion, acid rain, earthquakes, and hurricanes. Physicists studying dynamical systems and fractal basin boundaries could use Mandelbrot's model to better understand phenomena such as the breaking of materials or the making of decisions. If images could be reduced to fractal codes, the amount of data necessary to transmit or store images could be greatly reduced.

Fractal geometry showed that highly complex shapes could be generated by repeating rather simple instructions, and small changes in the instructions could produce very different shapes. For Mandelbrot, the striking resemblance of some fractal shapes to living organisms raised the possibility that only a limited inventory of genetic coding is needed to obtain the diversity and richness of shapes in plants and animals.

In 1982 Mandelbrot was elected a fellow of the American Academy of Arts and Sciences. In 1985 he received the Barnard Medal for Meritorious Service to Science, awarded every five years by the National Academy of Sciences for a notable discovery or novel application of science beneficial to the human race. In 1986 he received the Franklin Medal for his development of fractal geometry. In 1987 he became a foreign associate of the U. S. Academy of Sciences. In 1988 he received the Harvey Prize and in 1993 the Wolf Prize for physics for having changed our view of nature. He officially retired from IBM in 1993, but he continued to work at Yale and at IBM as a fellow emeritus, preparing a collection of his papers and doing further research in fractals.

SELECTED WRITINGS BY MANDELBROT:

Books

The Fractal Geometry of Nature, W. H. Freeman, 1982.

SOURCES:

Books

Albers, Donald J., and G. L. Anderson, editors, *Mathematical People: Profiles and Interviews,* Birkhauser, 1985.

Briggs, John, *Fractals, the Patterns of Chaos: A New Aesthetic of Art, Science, and Nature,* Simon & Schuster, 1992.

Gardner, Martin, *Penrose Tiles to Trapdoor Ciphers,* W. H. Freeman, 1989.

Gleick, James, *Chaos: Making a New Science,* Viking Penguin, 1987.

Peitgen, Heinz-Otto, and Dietmar Saupe, editors, *The Science of Fractal Images,* Springer-Verlag, 1988.

Peitgen, Heinz-Otto, and P. H. Richter, *The Beauty of Fractals,* Springer-Verlag, 1986.

Periodicals

"Franklin Institute Honors Eight Physicists," *Physics Today,* April, 1987, pp. 101–102.

Gleick, James, "The Man Who Reshaped Geometry," *New York Times Magazine,* December 8, 1985, p. 64 ff.

"Interview: Benoit B. Mandelbrot," *Omni,* February, 1984, pp. 65–66, 102–107.

Jürgens, Hartmut, Heinz-Otto Peitgen, and Dietmar Saupe, "The Language of Fractals," *Scientific American,* August, 1990, pp. 60–67.

"Tomorrow's Shapes: The Practical Fractal," *The Economist,* December 26, 1987, pp. 99–103.

Other

Mandelbrot, Benoit B., interview with C. D. Lord conducted August 17, 1993.

—*Sketch by C. D. Lord*

Leonid Isaakovich Mandel'shtam
1879-1944
Russian physicist

Although best known for his work in optics and radiophysics, Leonid Isaakovich Mandel'shtam was engaged in a much wider variety of fields. His approach to physics began with his early studies of electromagnetic oscillations and waves in radio measurements. His work with light scattering proved the fluctuations in motion were due to density and not molecular motion, and he proposed the theory that oscillations can be nonlinear, leading to the discovery of other nonlinear phenomena. He was also an educator, and many of his students became prominent in their fields. Mandel'shtam's influence on Russian science was so great that he was later credited as a "founder [with **Abram F. Ioffe**] of 'big' Soviet physics" by his former student S. M. Rytov in an article for the journal *Soviet Physics Uspekhi.*

Mandel'shtam was born in Mogilev, Russia, on May 5, 1879. His father, Isaak Grigorievich Mandel'shtam, was a well-known physician, and his mother, Minna Lvovna Kahn, was an accomplished pianist and linguist. Two of his uncles were also scientists—the biologist Alexander Gavrilovich Gurvich, and the petroleum chemist L. G. Gurvich. The Mandel'shtam family moved to Odessa when Leonid was still very young, and his early education took place at home. At the age of twelve, he enrolled at the local high school, graduating in 1897.

Mandel'shtam enrolled at Novorossysk University in Odessa, where he intended to major in mathematics. Two years later, however, he was expelled for taking part in anti-government riots. On the advice of his parents, he traveled to Strasbourg (then a part of Germany) and became a student in the university's faculty of physics and mathematics. There, he fell under the influence of Ferdinand Braun, whose own field of interest was electromagnetic radiation and radiotelegraphy.

Mandel'shtam received his doctorate in natural philosophy from Strasbourg University in 1902. He then stayed on as Braun's assistant and was appointed professor in 1913 (a position seldom offered to foreigners). Mandel'shtam's work at Strasbourg, according to Rytov, brought him recognition "not only as a radio specialist, but also as a broad-profile physicist." His Strasbourg years were notable for two other reasons as well. First, he met and married Lidya Solomonovna Isakovich, the first female Russian architect, in 1907. Second, he became especially interested in art, music, and literature, interests that remained with him throughout his life.

With the first World War looming on the horizon, Mandel'shtam returned to Russia, arriving in Odessa on the day war was declared. He then began a phase of his life in which he traveled from job to job for more than a decade. During this period, he was an instructor in physics at Novorossysk University (1914–15), a scientific consultant at the Siemens and Halske radiotelegraph factory in Petrograd (1915–17), professor of physics at the Polytechnical Institute in Tiflis (1917–18), and scientific consultant at the Central Radio Laboratory, first in Moscow (1918–21) and then in Petrograd (1922–25). He finally settled in for a much longer stay as professor of theoretical physics at Moscow State University in 1925.

Mandel'shtam's teaching influenced many important Soviet physicists, including the theoretical physicists **Igor Tamm** and M. A. Leontovich, oscillation theorist A. A. Andronov, and G. S. Landsberg in ultraacoustics and physical optics (with whom Mandel'shtam collaborated on some of his most important research). In 1934, Mandel'shtam accepted a joint appointment at the P. N. Lebedev Institute of Physics of the Academy of Sciences of the U.S.S.R. He was evacuated from Moscow at the beginning of World War II because of ill health, but he returned toward the end of the war and continued his work in Moscow and at the Lebedev Institute until his death on November 27, 1944.

Mandel'shtam published on a wide variety of topics. His first notable discovery was made in 1907 when he showed that the scattering of light at the interface between two liquids is caused by irregularities in the liquid (not by the motion of liquid molecules, as **John William Strutt**, Lord Rayleigh, had suggested). In 1928, Mandel'shtam and his long-time collaborator, Landsberg, discovered the change in wavelength that occurs when light is scattered in crystals, a phenomenon now named the Raman effect for its simultaneous discoverer, Sir **C. V. Raman**. In one of his major achievements, Mandel'shtam (with another long-time collaborator, Nikolay Papaleksi) devised a method for making precise long-distance measurements using radio interference techniques. In recognition of Mandel'shtam's achievements, he was awarded the V. I. Lenin Award in 1931, the State Prize of the U.S.S.R. in 1942, and was the recipient of the Order of Lenin and the Order of the Red Banner of Labor.

SELECTED WRITINGS BY MANDEL'SHTAM:

Books

Polnoe sobranie trudov (collection of Mandel'shtam's complete works), edited by S. M. Rytov and M. A. Leontovich, five volumes, [Leningrad], 1947–55.

SOURCES:

Books

Dictionary of Scientific Biography, Scribner, 1970–90, pp. 76–77.

Periodicals

Soviet Physics Uspekhi, October, 1979, pp. 826–32.

—*Sketch by David E. Newton*

Sidnie Milana Manton
1902-1979
English zoologist

Sidnie Milana Manton was fascinated with animals. The focus of her professional life as a zoologist in England was the comparative anatomy and embryology of invertebrates, especially arthropods, a phylum that includes such creatures as insects, spiders, and crustaceans and makes up about seventy-five percent of all known animals. Away from work, Manton bred new varieties of house cats and published a book about domestic felines.

Manton was born in London on May 4, 1902, to George S. F. Manton and Milana Manton. After attending a girls' school, she earned an M.A., a Ph.D., and a Sc. D. from Cambridge University in the 1920s. From there, Manton went on to teach at Cambridge, serving as a demonstrator in comparative anatomy from 1927 to 1935 and as director of natural science studies at Cambridge's Girton College from 1935 to 1942. Manton moved on to the University of London in 1943, serving as a visiting lecturer in zoology until 1946, an assistant lecturer from 1946 to 1949, and a reader in zoology from 1949 to 1960.

Manton began a long research career while at Cambridge, initially examining the form and structure and the embryology of crustaceans and Onychophora, another class of invertebrate animals. Manton's work, particularly on crustaceans, became the basis of many later studies of crustacean development by scientists around the world. As a member of an expedition to Australia's Great Barrier Reef in 1928 and 1929 she studied crustaceans in Tasmania and explored the growth of a coral species. Another important achievement for Manton was her demonstration, in an extensive seventeen-year study beginning in 1950, that form and structure must have evolved concurrently with habits in Onychophora, and that these elements were central to the development of different classes and orders of arthropods. As a result of her work, Manton was one of the first women to be elected to the Royal Society of London in 1948 and was awarded a gold medal in 1963 by the Linnean Society of London. The University of Lund in Sweden awarded Manton an honorary doctorate in 1968. Manton married J. P. Harding in 1937 and they had one son and one daughter. She died January 1, 1979.

SELECTED WRITINGS BY MANTON:

Books

(With J. T. Saunders) *A Manual of Practical Vertebrate Morphology,* Oxford University Press, 1959.

Colourpoint, Longhair, and Himalayan Cats,
   Crown Publishers, 1971.
*The Arthropoda: Habits, Functional Morphology
   and Evolution,* Clarendon Press, 1977.

                              —*Sketch by Joel Schwarz*

Vance H. Marchbanks, Jr.
1905-1988
American flight surgeon

Vance H. Marchbanks, Jr. was a much-decorated Air Force flight surgeon who served in the military for 23 years. His combat mission work and bravery earned him several medals, including the Bronze Star and Air Force Commendation Medals. Marchbanks was one of the project physicians for Project Mercury, the United States' first manned space craft mission. He and ten other physicians monitored the health of the astronauts by collecting medical flight data from them as they orbited the Earth. This data enabled Marchbanks and others to determine the impact that space flight has on humans.

Marchbanks, the second of two children, was born on January 12, 1905, at Fort Washikie, Wyoming, to Vance H. Marchbanks, Sr. (a cavalry sergeant) and Callie Hatton. He received his baccalaureate degree from the University of Arizona in 1931, and his medical degree from Howard University, Washington, D.C., in 1937. After graduation, Marchbanks worked for the Veterans Administration Hospital in Tuskegee, Alabama, until April 1941, when he entered the Army Air Corps as a First Lieutenant. (At the time, medical officers who were in the Army Air Corps were considered part of the Army.) Marchbanks was awarded the Bronze Star for his heroism while fighting in Italy in World War II. He advanced in the Air Force ranks and was assigned to the Air Force Hospital in Nagoya, Japan, as the deputy commander and chief of the professional service; a year later, in 1955, his work there earned him a promotion to full Colonel in the Medical Corps.

Marchbanks wrote several papers about stress related to flying and combat fatigue, published in research journals and military manuals. While participating in a marathon 10,600-mile, 22.5-hour non-stop flight from Florida to Argentina to New York, he discovered a marker for identifying fatigue in flight crew members. During the flight, Marchbanks measured the amount of adrenal hormone in blood and tissue samples taken from the crew members. He determined that a certain level indicated physical fatigue, a condition which often presages a fatal crash. Marchbanks received an Air Force Commendation Medal in November 1957 for this research. He also received a medal for developing an oxygen mask tester, a device that reminds Air Force flight crew members to clean their oxygen masks frequently. His military record earned him two Commendation Medals, one in 1950 and another in 1958.

Selected as Project Physician for Project Mercury

By 1960, Marchbanks' work, his rating of Chief Flight Surgeon (with its prerequisite 1,500 flying hours and 15 years of flying status), and his research in aviation medicine qualified him as one of the eleven Air Force surgeons assigned to Project Mercury, the first manned space craft launched by the United States. Assigned a position as a project physician, Marchbanks was stationed in Kano, Nigeria, at one of the eighteen tracking stations utilized on February 20, 1962, when Colonel **John Glenn** and the other astronauts circled the Earth three times. Marchbanks' role in the mission was to monitor the astronauts' physical well-being by looking at readings of respiration rate, temperature, and heart reaction for the few minutes that they passed overhead. To determine whether they were having heart problems or not, Marchbanks compared their electrocardiograms (ECG) during spaceflight to a set of similar tests taken earlier at the Johnson Space Center while the astronauts were under both normal and stressed conditions. Prior to leaving for Nigeria, Marchbanks had spent more than a year studying Colonel Glenn's various ECG readings. Each time the Mercury passed, Marchbanks recorded normal ECG readings for the astronaut, indicating that the flight was not causing any physiological problems. After this assignment, Marchbanks helped to design the space suits and the monitoring systems the astronauts used for the Apollo moon shot. As Chief of Environmental Health Services at Hamilton Standard, a division of United Aircraft Corporation in Connecticut, Marchbanks was responsible for the human safety aspects of the simulated training for the backpack being built for the Apollo astronauts.

Marchbanks spent much of his career studying the sickle-cell trait, which differs from the disease sickle cell anemia. In 1983 he was recognized by Howard University in Washington, D.C., for pioneering the initiative that resulted in the Department of Defense rescinding restrictions on the admission of persons with this trait to the Air Force Academy and to the Department of Defense.

Marchbanks married Lois Gilkey and they had two daughters. He was a member of the AeroMedical Association and the Society of Flight Surgeons. He died in 1988 of complications from Alzheimer's disease.

SELECTED WRITINGS BY MARCHBANKS:

Periodicals

"The Black Physician and the USAF," *Journal of the National Medical Association,* January, 1972, pp. 73–74.
"The Sickle Trait and the Black Airman," *Aviation, Space, and Environmental Medicine,* March, 1980, pp. 299–300.

SOURCES:

Periodicals

Ebony, April 1962, pp. 36–40.

—*Sketch by Barbara Proujan*

Guglielmo Marconi

Guglielmo Marconi
1874-1937
Italian physicist and engineer

Before he was thirty, Guglielmo Marconi entered the limited ranks of scientists whose reputations have spread beyond the confines of their community. An amateur, Marconi accomplished the first transatlantic transmission of radio waves without ever having received any academic degrees in physics. Although unquestionably gifted in that field, Marconi expressed his true genius in assembling the backing, the information, and the engineers he needed to pursue his vision of linking the globe in a network of radio waves. With the advantages of ready money, social access, and entrepreneurial drive, Marconi realized his dream. He received many honors and awards from governments, academic institutions, and scientific associations, but undoubtedly the principal one was the 1909 Nobel Prize in physics, which he shared with **Karl Ferdinand Braun** for their advancement of radio technology. It would not be accurate to the scientific record to call Marconi the father of radio. However, he greatly accelerated the establishment of radio in all its current applications—military, industrial, and commercial.

Marconi's father, Giuseppe, was a successful landowner who split his time between Bologna, Italy,

and his estate, the Villa Grifone, eleven miles outside of Bologna in a town called Pontecchio. When already a widower with one son, Luigi, Giuseppe met and fell in love with Annie Jameson, a young Irishwoman who had come to Italy to study operatic singing. Her father, a whiskey distiller from Dublin, and her mother did not approve of the relationship. Against the wishes of her parents, they were married in 1864. Marconi was born in Bologna on April 25th, 1874. He had a brother nine years his senior called Alfonso. Life was very strict in his father's household, where he was educated in his early years. At age twelve, he went to the Istituto Cavallero in Florence. The following year Marconi enrolled in the Technical Institute in Leghorn. His schooling there was augmented with private tutoring from Professor Vincenzo Rosa of the Liceo Niccolini. Professor Rosa was an important early influence on the future scientist.

Accomplishes the First Successful Radio Transmission

In 1894 Marconi became acquainted with the work of Heinrich Hertz, who had died that year. He was so fascinated with Hertz's radio waves that he sought as much information as he could by auditing the courses of physicist and professor Augusto Righi, the expert on radio waves at the University of Bologna. At Villa Grifone, in 1895, Marconi built his first crude transmitter and receiver. The transmitter consisted of Hertz's oscillator, in which an electrical circuit generated radio waves as a spark jumped back and forth across a gap between two metal balls. In order to work up the voltage to power such a spark, Marconi used induction coils, two sets of wires wrapped around a soft iron core, to increase the current from a low-voltage battery. In the receiver, Marconi used a device introduced by French physicist Édouard-Eugéne Branly and English physicist Oliver Joseph Lodge called a coherer—a glass tube full of metal filings connected to a battery—to pick up the radio signals. Through painstaking trial and error, he introduced improvements of his own, such as insulated wire antennae and grounding of both the transmitter and the receiver. In the fall of 1895, Marconi succeeded in sending radio signals across his father's estate, a distance of about a mile.

Giuseppe Marconi, who until that point had been skeptical of the practicality of his son's experiments, realized that Marconi's discoveries should become public domain. The family petitioned the Italian Minister of Post and Telegraph to underwrite the development of Marconi's invention. The minister showed no interest. Marconi's Irish mother suggested asking the English government, because surely England, as the greatest naval power at the time, would realize the value of wireless ship-to-shore communication. In February of 1986, Marconi and his mother traveled to England. Once they arrived in London, his cousin Henry Jameson-Davis, as promised in correspondence prior to the trip, helped to guide Marconi through the English bureaucracy.

In 1896, after a successful radio transmission on England's Salisbury plain across a distance of nine miles, Marconi gained some notoriety, getting mail from all over the world and an offer to buy the rights to his system. On July 2, 1897, Patent Number 12,039 was granted for Marconi's invention of the "wireless," as radio was called then. Instead of selling his rights, however, Marconi formed the Wireless Telegraph and Signal Company, which was renamed Marconi's Wireless Telegraph Company in 1900. The English government, very impressed with the wireless, invited Marconi to become an English citizen in order to evade his three years of required service in the Italian military.

Marconi, a lifelong patriot of Italy, declined and through the auspices of Italy's ambassador in England became a cadet in training in the Italian navy with the understanding that he could pursue his work without interruption. Returning to Italy, Marconi performed a ship-to-shore demonstration of his system for the Italian navy at Spezia, where he reached a limit of twelve miles for good reception. In 1898 he returned to England for another demonstration, increasing the range to eighteen miles. English physicist and mathematician William Thomson (Lord Kelvin), who had earlier disparaged radio communication, made the first paid wireless transmission in 1899 and thereafter

became an ally. The same year, at Queen Victoria's invitation, Marconi set up a system so that the royal family could get news of the Kingstown regatta in Ireland. Although this feat had no scientific value, he shrewdly calculated that it would give him enormous publicity.

Permanent radio stations were beginning to be put into place. In March of 1899, with the cooperation of the respective governments, radio communications began between Chelmsford in England and Wimereux in France, a new record of eighty-five miles. Marconi believed, unlike many other scientists of his day, that radio waves would follow the earth's curve rather than shoot straight into space. Therefore he decided to prove his point by transmitting across the Atlantic Ocean.

Demonstrates Radio's Potential for Transatlantic Communication

With the company he had created to finance him, he began to build stations at Poldhu, in Cornwall, England, and at Cape Cod, Massachusetts. Unfortunately, before Marconi was ready to test his theory, the antennas at both sites were destroyed in storms. The mast at Poldhu's antenna was repaired. On the other side of the Atlantic, Marconi, impatient to get on with his tests, improvised an antenna in St. John's, Newfoundland, Canada, by lofting a kite four hundred feet into the air with a wire attached to it. The first signal coming out of Poldhu, the Morse code for the letter *s,* was heard in St. John's on December 12, 1901, at a distance this time of eighteen hundred miles. Marconi had proved to his own satisfaction that the earth's curvature was no obstacle.

The Anglo-American telegraph company, sensing, as did other telegraph companies, that its time was passing, fought back by bringing a suit against Marconi for trespassing on a monopoly it had been granted in Newfoundland. If the business community was convinced of Marconi's success, the scientific community was not. Many scientists expressed the opinion that the transatlantic transmission had been a hoax, or perhaps a fluke. No one knew then, as scientists later determined, that the type of radio waves Marconi generated are reflected by certain layers in the earth's atmosphere and thus can travel great distances despite the earth's curvature. Skepticism faded when in February of 1902 Marconi, on the boat *Philadelphia* in front of technically reliable witnesses, received clear signals from Poldhu at 1550 miles and intermittent signals at 2100 miles. The Canadian government decided that Marconi could be licensed to operate in Newfoundland but that he could charge no more than ten cents a word, a rate far lower than the cable companies charged.

In 1902, not yet thirty years old, Marconi had reached the pinnacle of his career. His company was operating on two continents. The transmission across the Atlantic had won him the awe and admiration of his fellow scientists. He had overcome the limitations of the coherer in his receiver by designing and patenting a superior radio wave detector that operated with magnets and wires. The helpers that he had assembled were of the highest caliber: George S. Kemp, his assistant; Andrew Gray, chief engineer; and R. N. Vyvyan, engineer and expert finagler of bureaucracies.

Marconi returned to Italy in 1902, and the Italian navy offered him a ship, the *Carlo Alberto,* as his first floating laboratory. Although he successfully transmitted messages between U.S. President Theodore Roosevelt and England's King Edward VII on January 19, 1903, Marconi was having a hard time convincing anyone that transatlantic communication could become more reliable and profitable. The Marconi Company began making money that year, but not much. Most of the income came from ship-to-shore communications, although negotiations were underway with the London *Times* and the British Post Office. Unhappy with the English domination of radio technology, Germany was looking for ways to get around the Marconi patents. The Marconi Company's monopoly on radio broadcasting was beginning to slip.

The next year, 1904, was a year of mixed blessings. Marconi's father died and he met his future first wife, Beatrice O'Brien, the daughter of the thirteenth Baron Inchiquin. On March 16, 1905, they were married. They had three daughters—Lucia, who died as an infant, Degna, who later wrote a biography of her father, and Gioia Jolanda—and one son, Giulio. Marconi proved a difficult husband. Beatrice tried to weather his long absences and frequent philandering but, after falling in love with another man, asked Marconi for a divorce in 1923. Their marriage was annulled in 1927.

Shares the 1909 Nobel Prize in Physics with Braun

In December of 1909 Marconi went to Stockholm to accept his Nobel Prize in physics. He was puzzled, as were many others, as to why he was splitting his award for radio with K. F. Braun. In fact, Braun's modifications on Marconi's designs had increased radio's range fivefold. Something very close to Braun's improvements had allowed Marconi to transmit across the Atlantic. In spite of the awkward circumstances, when the two men met they became friends. Marconi was the first Italian in his field to receive the Nobel Prize.

With the onset of World War I, Marconi became a technical consultant to the Italian military, which was badly in need of modernization. He was also attached to the Italian War Mission to the United States. During his service in Italy, a new benchmark for radio range was reached in 1918 when England made its first transmission to Australia. In 1919 the king of Italy sent Marconi to the Peace Conference in Paris as a delegate. He signed the treaties with Austria and Bulgaria for the Italian government. After the war Marconi bought a yacht he christened the *Elettra,* which became his laboratory and home.

Establishes Worldwide Short-Wave Radio Network

In 1923 Marconi's experiments with short-wave radio began to pay off. Marconi had been plagued by the greatly reduced performance of long-wave radio during daylight but did not understand the reasons for it—physics had not advanced to that stage. Yet in October of that year he found that waves thirty meters long—a tiny fraction of his original waves' length—could be transmitted across vast distances without interference from the sun's radiation. In July of 1924 the Marconi Company contracted with the British government to supply short-wave radio relay stations throughout the Empire. By 1927 the world was completely encircled with a short-wave radio network.

After the annulment of his first marriage in the spring, Marconi married Cristina Bezzi-Scali, a daughter of the papal nobility, on June 12, 1927. They had a daughter, Elettra. After complex negotiations beginning in 1925, the Marconi Company merged with the telegraph companies in 1928, making Marconi a wealthy man. By then, he had received the hereditary title of *Marchese* or Marquis from the Italian king. His last ten years, however, were marred by a decline in his health and estrangement from his ex-wife and the children of his first marriage. Marconi's involvement in politics also ended on a sour note. His public embrace of fascist dictator Benito Mussolini alienated much of the European and American public after Italy invaded Abyssinia in 1935. When Marconi sought to explain Italy's conduct to his adopted country, England, the British Broadcasting Corporation would not cooperate.

Yet Marconi persevered. In 1932 he proved with tests from aboard the *Elettra* that microwaves, waves less than one centimeter in length, could be received well beyond the horizon-line limit that the theory of the day mandated. It was not until after the technological advances spawned by World War II that this discovery received commercial application. He even, in 1934, demonstrated a radio beacon, a primitive form of radar, with which he piloted the *Elettra* blind into a difficult harbor. After 1936 Marconi's heart condition confined him to his native Italy, where he died on July 20, 1937.

Musically gifted, involved in Italian and international politics, always in the society pages, Marconi was anything but one-sided. A man of enormous energy, he managed not only to invent long-wave and short-wave radio transmission but to run a company besides. With his business skill, scientific creativity, technical know-how, and determination, Marconi resembled another famous scientist-engineer, America's **Thomas Alva Edison**. Edison, in fact, greatly admired Marconi for his successful transatlantic radio transmission. In 1903, the old inventor invited the young one to his home in Orange, New Jersey, where they spent a pleasant afternoon.

SOURCES:

Books

Heathcote, Niels H. de V., *Nobel Prize Winners in Physics, 1901–1950,* Schuman, 1953, pp. 70–81.
Marconi, Degna, *My Father, Marconi,* McGraw, 1962.

Periodicals

Fitch, Richard D., "Inventors and Inventions," *Radio-Electronics,* March, 1987, p. 86.
Reese, K. M., "Marconi's Floating Lab Being Re-created in Italy," *Chemical and Engineering News,* December 5, 1988, p. 78.
Schueler, Donald G., "Inventor Marconi: Brilliant, Dapper, Tough to Live With," *Smithsonian,* March, 1982, p. 126.

—*Sketch by Hovey Brock*

Rudolph A. Marcus
1923-
Canadian-born American physical chemist

In recognition for his contributions to the theory of electron-transfer reactions in chemical systems, Rudolph A. Marcus was awarded the 1992 Nobel Prize in chemistry. Marcus received the news of his award while attending a meeting of the Electrochemical Society in Toronto, Canada; the award recognized work he had done in the 1950s and 1960s, but some controversy had surrounded his discoveries until they were validated in the 1980s. Marcus was able to understand the way a basic chemical reaction occurs, where electron transfers take place, how fast the electrons travel, and how they affect the results. His work was a breakthrough for chemists because it enabled them to make selections on the basis of

bringing about specific outcomes. His work has been applied in a variety of areas, such as photosynthesis, electrically conducting polymers, chemiluminescence (cold light), and corrosion.

Rudolph Arthur Marcus, the only son of Myer and Esther Cohen Marcus, was born on July 21, 1923, in Montreal, Canada. He has described his parents as loving and noted that he admired his father's athletic abilities and his mother's musical talents. Marcus traced his interest in science to his high school years, when he explored mathematics and later chemistry. After graduating from high school, he attended McGill University, receiving his Bachelor of Science degree in 1943 and his doctorate in 1946. At McGill, he was supervised by Carl A. Winkler, who specialized in the rates of chemical reactions. Marcus's first work after McGill was in two research positions, one with the National Research Council (NRC) of Canada in Ottawa and the other at the University of North Carolina. At the NRC, he did experimental work under E. W. R. Steacie on free-radical reactions, which concern atoms or groups of atoms with unpaired valence electrons.

Move to the United States Leads to Research Shift

Marcus credited his move to the United States as the beginning of his theoretical work. For the first three months at North Carolina he read everything he could find on reaction rate theory. After concentrating on a particular problem, he was able within several months to consolidate several theories from early statistical ideas developed in the 1920s and 1930s. What had been called the Rice-Ramsperger-Kassel (RRK) theory became the Rice-Ramsperger-Kassel-Marcus (RRKM) theory, published in the early 1950s. Attempting to explain observed differences in reaction rates, Marcus identified simple mathematical expressions to explain how the energy of a molecular system is affected by structural changes. Counterintuitive and highly controversial, his contribution to the RRKM theory of unimolecular reactions—which related molecular properties and the lifespan of transition states to reaction rates—was validated by experimental findings announced in 1985 by Gerhard L. Closs of the University of Chicago and John R. Miller of Argonne National Laboratory.

After his postdoctoral grants, Marcus began the search for a faculty position; he received an offer from the Polytechnic Institute of Brooklyn, New York, and joined the staff as an assistant professor in 1951. Ten years later, he was the acting head of the division of physical chemistry. It was here that Marcus became an independent researcher. He experimented on gas phase and solution reaction rates at first, but a student brought his attention to a problem in polyelectrolytes. By 1960, Marcus felt he needed to commit his time completely to theoretical work.

While he was a faculty member at the University of Illinois at Champaign-Urbana from 1964 until 1978, Marcus concentrated his interest in electron transfer and reaction dynamics. During these years, he extended his knowledge into astronomy, including classical mechanics, celestial mechanics, quasiperiodic motion, and chaos. In a year spent as a visiting professor at Oxford and Munich from 1975 to 1976, Marcus explored electron transfer in photosynthesis. In 1978, he accepted an offer from the California Institute of Technology in Pasadena to become the Arthur Amos Noyes Professor of Chemistry. At Caltech, Marcus was influenced by the work that his colleagues were doing and he returned to the RRKM theory to treat more complicated problems. This was a fertile association for Marcus, and more than half of his articles were published after he went to Caltech.

Theories Become Highly Influential

The theories of electron-transfer reactions in chemical systems for which Marcus was recognized by the Nobel Committee have been applied extensively by other scientists in numerous areas. Several groups have used computer simulations in the study of electron transfer, employing Marcus's theory for the framework of their studies. One research group has been able to apply Marcus's theory to effects present in photosynthetic proteins. It was Marcus's ability to formulate a simple mathematical method for calculating the energy change that takes place in electron-transfer reactions that has made his work so valuable to other researchers. He was also able to find the driving force of the electron-transfer exchange.

It was while he was at North Carolina that Marcus met and married Laura Hearne, a graduate student in sociology, on August 27, 1949. They have three sons: Alan Rudolph, Kenneth Hearne, and Raymond Arthur. In 1958, Marcus became a naturalized U.S. citizen. He continues his father's interest in sports by skiing and playing tennis; his other leisure interests include music and history.

Marcus has received many awards and honors other than the Nobel Prize, notably the Irving Langmuir Award in Chemical Physics in 1978, the Wolf Prize in 1985, and the Linus Pauling Award in 1991. Marcus has been an active member of important scientific societies in his field and serves on the editorial boards of several scientific journals. He has lectured widely in the United States, Canada, Europe, the Middle East, and the Far East. He is highly respected and warmly regarded among his colleagues, who generally praise him for the warmth of his personality and his enthusiasm for his work.

SELECTED WRITINGS BY MARCUS:

Periodicals

"Unimolecular Dissociations and Free Radical Recombination Reactions," *Journal of Chemical Physics,* Volume 20, 1952, pp. 359–364.
"Calculation of Thermodynamic Properties of Polyelectrolytes," *Journal of Chemical Physics,* Volume 23, 1955, pp. 1057–1068.
(With D. M. Wardlaw) "RRKM Reaction Rate Theory for Transition States of Any Looseness," *Chemical Physics Letters,* Volume 110, 1984, pp. 230–234.
(With N. Sutin) "Electron Transfers in Chemistry and Biology," *Biochimica Biophysica Acta,* Volume 811, 1985, pp. 265–322.

SOURCES:

Books

Biographical Dictionary of Nobel Laureates, American Chemical Society, 1993.
McGraw-Hill Modern Scientists and Engineers, McGraw-Hill, 1980, pp. 275–277.

Periodicals

Levi, Barbara Goss, "Marcus Wins Nobel Prize in Chemistry for Electron Transfer Theory," *Physics Today,* January, 1993, pp. 20–22.
Robert A. Marcus Commemorative Issue, *Journal of Physical Chemistry,* July 31, 1986, pp. 3453–3466.

Other

Rudolph A. Marcus Autobiographical Sketch, courtesy of Office of Public Relations, California Institute of Technology.

—*Sketch by Vita Richman*

Gregori Aleksandrovitch Margulis
1946-
Russian mathematician

The study of Lie groups has proved to be extremely useful both within mathematics and in various other fields; by describing the relationships between algebraic, geometric and analytic structures, it has impacted on the fields of astrophysics, chemistry, unified field theory, and high-energy particle physics. Perhaps no one has done more to unlock their secrets than the Russian mathematician Gregori Aleksandrovitch Margulis. Through his exploration of the Lie group's basic substructure known as a lattice, Margulis uncovered the various interrelationships between the lattice and the Lie group, allowing for a clearer definition of both. These results had such far-reaching effects that in 1978 the International Mathematics Union awarded him the highest honor in mathematics, the Fields Medal.

Margulis was born in Moscow in 1946, the son of Aleksander and Tsilya Osharenko Margulis. His father was a mathematician, and Margulis showed an early interest in both mathematics and chess. However, he largely lost interest in chess playing when he began his mathematical studies at Moscow University. He studied there until 1970, when he received his Ph.D. under the direction of Yakov G. Sinai. By the time he received his degree, Margulis had already made his first major contribution to mathematics, a partial proof of the Selberg conjecture.

Atle Selberg, a Norwegian, had conjectured that lattices, which are discrete subgroups of continuous topological groups known as Lie groups, were all arithmetic in nature. In other words, Selberg said that they behaved in predictable ways, not unlike integers. Proof of his conjecture would have phenomenal effects on the applications of Lie groups in general, because it would provide a link between the lattices and the larger Lie groups. Selberg, however, only succeeded in proving that lattices fall into two different cases, cocompact and noncocompact. Still, by doing this he paved the way for the work Margulis would undertake.

In 1968, while working with D. A. Kazhdan, Margulis managed to prove Selberg's conjecture for noncocompact lattices, which formed a major part of the Lie group. Margulis and Kazhdan proved that these lattices contained nontrivial unipotent elements—points which, through repeated multiplication, would result in a return to the original element. By using the orbits, or repeated multiplication paths, to describe the lattice of these noncocompact groups, Margulis proved their arithmeticity. This result, while important, was only the first step toward a complete proof of the Selberg conjecture.

Proof of Conjecture Leads to Medal

Next, Margulis undertook the study of the more difficult cocompact lattices. Cocompact lattices have a smaller structure with fewer elements, and thus the idea of the nontrivial unipotent element does not apply. Margulis therefore had to develop a whole new approach for these lattices. Using results obtained earlier by G. D. Mostow, who showed that lattices are

rigid or unchangeable, Margulis considered a certain lattice in an alternative setting. By combining elements of algebra, analysis and number theory, and then applying them to the lattice, Margulis was able to define the structure of not only this but all cocompact lattices. These included the most complex form, lattices based on the p-adic Lie groups, whose structure is related to prime numbers.

He obtained these results while at Moscow's Institute for Transmission of Information, where he had worked since completing his education. Unlike many mathematicians, he did not have the opportunity to travel and lecture, due to restrictions imposed upon scientists by the Soviet government. This did not prevent Western mathematicians from recognizing the importance of what he was doing, though, and it came as no surprise to anyone familiar with Margulis's work when his name was announced as a recipient of the 1978 Fields Medal.

The International Congress of Mathematicians convened in Helsinki that year to award Fields Medals to Margulis and three others. Most of the mathematicians in attendance had heard of Margulis only through his work and were eagerly anticipating the opportunity to hear him speak. Margulis, however, was denied permission from the Soviet government to attend the conference. Jacques Tits, who spoke about Margulis's work at the conference, did not hide his dismay at the Soviet government's position and led the crowd in a standing ovation in honor of his achievements.

Back in the Soviet Union, Margulis continued his research into Lie groups. He explored various aspects of the groups and their subgroups and attempted to find applications for the work he had done. The many papers he wrote on this subject over the next ten years would form the basis for a 1989 textbook explaining group theory. He received a great deal of encouragement to write the book from Tits, who had praised him so highly in Helsinki.

With the breakup of the Soviet Union, Margulis was free to travel, and in 1990 he gave one of the plenary addresses at the International Congress of Mathematicians in Kyoto. He came to Harvard as a visiting professor that same year with his wife Raisa, a computer programmer, and their teenaged son. He decided to stay in the United States and gained permanent residency in 1991; after a brief appointment at Princeton's Institute for Advanced Study, he settled at Yale University.

SELECTED WRITINGS BY MARGULIS:

Books

Discrete Subgroups of Semisimple Lie Groups, Springer-Verlag, 1989.

Periodicals

"Discrete groups of motions of manifolds with nonpositive curvature," *Proceedings of the International Congress of Mathematics,* Volume 2, 1975, pp.

SOURCES:

Periodicals

"Four Mathematicians Receive Fields Medals," *Notices of the American Mathematical Society,* August, 1978, p. 432.

Mostow, G. D., "The Fields Medals (I): Relating the Continuous and the Discrete," *Science,* October 20, 1978, pp. 297–298.

Tits, Jacques, "The Work of Gregori Aleksandrovitch Margulis," *Proceedings of the International Congress of Mathematicians,* 1979, pp. 56–63.

Other

Margulis, Gregori, interview with Paul Becker conducted March 12, 1994.

　　　　　　　　　　　　—Sketch by Karen Sands

Lynn Margulis
1938-
American biologist

Lynn Margulis is a renowned theoretical biologist and professor of botany at the University of Massachusetts at Amherst. Her research on the evolutionary links between cells containing nuclei (eukaryotes) and cells without nuclei (prokaryotes) led her to formulate a symbiotic theory of evolution that was initially spurned in the scientific community but has become more widely accepted.

Margulis, the eldest of four daughters, was born in Chicago on March 5, 1938. Her father, Morris Alexander, was a lawyer who owned a company that developed and marketed a long-lasting thermoplastic material used to mark streets and highways. He also served as an assistant state's attorney for the state of Illinois. Her mother, Leone, operated a travel agency. When Margulis was fifteen, she completed her second year at Hyde Park High School and was accepted into an early entrant program at the University of Chicago.

Education and Early Career

Margulis was particularly inspired by her science courses, in large part because reading assignments consisted not of textbooks but of the original works of the world's great scientists. A course in natural science made an immediate impression and would influence her life, raising questions that she has pursued throughout her career: What is heredity? How do genetic components influence the development of offspring? What are the common bonds between generations? While at the University of Chicago she met **Carl Sagan**, then a graduate student in physics. At the age of nineteen, she married Sagan, received a B.A. in liberal arts, and moved to Madison, Wisconsin, to pursue a joint master's degree in zoology and genetics at the University of Wisconsin under the guidance of noted cell biologist Hans Ris. In 1960 she and Sagan moved to the University of California at Berkeley, where she conducted genetic research for her doctoral dissertation.

The marriage to Sagan ended before she received her doctorate. She moved to Waltham, Massachusetts, with her two sons, Dorion and Jeremy, to accept a position as lecturer in the department of biology at Brandeis University. She was awarded her Ph.D. in 1965. The following year, she became an adjunct assistant of biology at Boston University, leaving twenty-two years later as full professor. During her tenure at Boston University she taught two or three courses per semester and directed a $100,000-a-year research lab. In 1967 she married crystallographer Thomas N. Margulis. The couple had two children before they divorced in 1980. Since 1988, Margulis has been a distinguished university professor with the Department of Botany at the University of Massachusetts at Amherst.

Her interest in genetics and the development of cells can be traced to her earliest days as a University of Chicago undergraduate. She always questioned the commonly accepted theories of genetics, however, challenging the traditionalists by presenting hypotheses that contradicted current beliefs. She has been called the most gifted theoretical biologist of her generation by numerous colleagues. A profile of Margulis by Jeanne McDermott in the *Smithsonian* quotes Peter Raven, director of the Missouri Botanical Garden and a MacArthur fellow: "Her mind keeps shooting off sparks. Some critics say she's off in left field. To me she's one of the most exciting, original thinkers in the whole field of biology." Although few know more about cellular biology, Margulis considers herself a "microbial evolutionist," mapping out a field of study that doesn't in fact exist.

Evolutionary Theory

As a graduate student, Margulis became interested in cases of non-Mendelian inheritance, occurring when the genetic make-up of a cell's descendants cannot be traced solely to the genes in a cell's nucleus. For several years, she concentrated her research on a search for genes in the cytoplasm of cells, the area outside of the cell's nucleus. In the early 1960s, Margulis presented evidence for the existence of extranuclear genes. She and other researchers had found DNA in the cytoplasm of plant cells, indicating that heredity in higher organisms is not solely determined by genetic information carried in the cell nucleus. Her continued work in this field led her to formulate the serial endosymbiotic theory, or SET, which offered a new approach to evolution as well as an account of the origin of cells with nuclei.

Prokaryotes—bacteria and blue-green algae, now commonly referred to as cyanobacteria—are single-celled organisms that carry genetic material in the cytoplasm. Margulis proposes that eukaryotes (cells with nuclei) evolved when different kinds of prokaryotes formed symbiotic systems to enhance their chances for survival. The first such symbiotic fusion would have taken place between fermenting bacteria and oxygen-using bacteria. All cells with nuclei, Margulis contends, are derived from bacteria that formed symbiotic relationships with other primordial bacteria some two billion years ago. It has now become widely accepted that mitochondria—those components of eukaryotic cells that process oxygen—are remnants of oxygen-using bacteria. Margulis' hypothesis that cell hairs, found in a vast array of eukaryotic cells, descend from another group of primordial bacteria much like the modern spirochaete still encounters resistance, however.

The resistance to Margulis' work in microbiology may perhaps be explained by its implications for the more theoretical aspects of evolutionary theory. Evolutionary theorists, particularly in the English-speaking countries, have always put a particular emphasis on the notion that competition for scarce resources leads to the survival of the most well-adapted representatives of a species by natural selection, favoring adaptive genetic mutations. According to Margulis, natural selection as traditionally defined cannot account for the "creative novelty" to be found in evolutionary history. She argues instead that the primary mechanism driving biological change is symbiosis, while competition plays a secondary role.

Gaia Hypothesis

Margulis doesn't limit her concept of symbiosis to the origin of plant and animal cells. She subscribes to the "Gaia" hypothesis first formulated by **James E. Lovelock**, British inventor and chemist. The "Gaia theory" (named for the Greek goddess of the earth) essentially states that all life, as well as the oceans, the atmosphere, and the earth itself are parts of a single, all-encompassing symbiosis and may fruitfully be considered as elements of a single organism.

Margulis has authored more than one hundred and thirty scientific articles and ten books, several of which are written with her son Dorion. She has also served on more than two dozen committees, including the American Association for the Advancement of Science, the MacArthur Foundation Fellowship Nominating Committee, and the editorial boards of several scientific journals. Margulis is co-director of NASA's Planetary Biology Internship Program and, in 1983, was elected to the National Academy of Sciences.

SELECTED WRITINGS BY MARGULIS:

Books

Origins of Life, 2 volumes, Gordon & Breach, 1970 and 1971.

(With Dorion Sagan) *Microcosmos: Four Billion Years of Microbial Evolution,* Summit Books, 1986.

(With Karlene Volume Schwartz) *Five Kingdoms: An Illustrated Guide to the Phyla of Life on Earth,* W. H. Freeman, 1987.

(With Dorion Sagan) *Garden of Microbial Delights,* Harcourt, 1988.

SOURCES:

Periodicals

"The Creativity of Symbiosis," *Scientific American,* Volume 266, Number 1, 1992, p. 131.

McCoy, Dan, "The Wizard of Ooze," *Omni,* Volume 7, Number 49, 1985, pp. 49–78.

McDermott, Jeanne, "A Biologist Whose Heresy Redraws Earth's Tree of Life," *Smithsonian,* Volume 20, Number 72, 1989, pp. 72–80.

"The Microbes' Mardi Gras," *Economist,* Volume 314, Number 7643, 1990, pp. 85–86.

—Sketch by Benedict A. Leerburger

Frère Marie-Victorin
1885-1944
Canadian botanist

Frère Marie-Victorin achieved international acclaim for his botanical work on the plants of the Laurentian Mountains of Quebec, Canada. A member of many Canadian and international learned societies, Marie-Victorin wrote a number of works that are considered important to the field of botany and have often received awards. He taught at the University of Montreal for more than two decades and advocated the popularization of science, often working with children's groups. "He can truly be said to have been one of the founding fathers of modern intellectual enterprise in French Canada," *Dictionary of Literary Biography* contributor Michel Gaulin wrote of the botanist.

Marie-Victorin was born Conrad Kirouac on April 3, 1885, in Kingsey Falls, Quebec, Canada, to Cyrille, the owner of a prosperous grain business, and Philomène (Luneau) Kirouac. He attended primary school in St-Sauveur and secondary school at Quebec's Académie Commerciale, which was run by the Christian Brothers religious order. In 1900, he left the school and joined the Christian Brothers at the Mont-de-la-Salle de Maisonneuve seminary a year later.

Marie-Victorin, the religious name Kirouac assumed, began teaching in the Christian Brothers' schools despite his lack of a *licence,* the diploma that was awarded in French Canada by diverse religious *collèges* (until the second half of the twentieth century, education in French-speaking Canada was the privileged domain of Catholic religious orders). After teaching at several secondary schools, Marie-Victorin took up permanent residence in Longueuil, a city located across the St. Lawrence River from Montreal.

In 1903, Marie-Victorin fell ill with tuberculosis. After his physician prescribed outdoor exercise, Marie-Victorin became fascinated by the vegetation of the Lower St. Lawrence River. He studied botany with members of his order and he took his pupils on field excursions. In 1908, he began publishing studies on his findings, which included the discovery of new species and the determination of their ranges. He corresponded avidly with Merrit Lyndon Fernald, an assistant professor of botany at Harvard University and the leading authority on Northeast vegetation. At the same time, Marie-Victorin emerged as a prominent essayist and novelist, focusing on French-Canadian themes. In 1916, three of his works received literary prizes from the Société St-Jean Baptiste, a conservative, religiously-inspired association.

In 1920, as a result of his work in botany and his popularity in the pedagogical world of Catholic French Canada, Marie-Victorin became an associate professor of botany at the University of Montreal. Because he did not have a university diploma, Marie-Victorin wrote a study of the ferns of the province of Quebec and submitted the text as a doctoral thesis to his prospective employer. The University of Montreal awarded him its first doctorate in 1922 though no staff member could claim competence in botany or attest to the quality of the work. Marie-Victorin became director the University's Botanical Institute and held a chair in botany at the University until his death.

During the last twenty years of his life, Marie-Victorin was the most visible scientist in French Canada. He built the Botanical Institute on the grounds that became the Botanical Gardens of Montreal, a municipal fiefdom that Marie-Victorin also directed. He created a respected botanical monograph series. In the 1920s, Marie-Victorin helped found the Association Canadienne pour l'Avancement des Sciences (ACFAS), an organization focused on popularizing science. An ardent advocate of the scouting movement, Marie-Victorin was involved with a number of naturalist groups, especially those appealing to children. In 1935, he published his authoritative account of botany, *Flore laurentienne* ("Laurentian Flora"), which identifies roughly two thousand flora species of the St. Lawrence Valley. The book was widely appreciated and received the Prix Coincy of the Paris Academy of Sciences, among other awards. Gaulin wrote that *Flore laurentienne* made "French Canadians . . . conscious of a large part of their natural heritage that had been largely unknown and thus widely ignored." Marie-Victorin died in an automobile accident on July 15, 1944.

SELECTED WRITINGS BY MARIE-VICTORIN:

Books

Récits laurentiens, Frères des Ecoles Chrétiennes (Montreal), 1919, translation by James Ferres published as *The Chopping Bee and Other Laurentian Stories,* Musson (Toronto), 1935.

Croquis laurentiens (title means "Laurentian Sketches"), Frères des Ecoles Chrétiennes, 1920.

Flore laurentienne (title means "Laurentian Flora"), Imprimerie de La Salle (Montreal), 1935.

SOURCES:

Books

Dictionary of Literary Biography, Volume 92: *Canadian Writers, 1890–1920,* Gale, 1989.

Lavallée, Madeleine, *Marie-Victorin: Un itinéraire exceptionnel,* Saint-Lambert, Editions Héritage (Quebec), 1983.

Lefebvre, André, *Marie-Victorin: Le poète èducateur,* Guérin (Montreal), 1987.

Rumilly, Robert, *Le Frère Marie-Victorin et son temps,* Frères des Ecoles Chrétiennes, 1949.

—Sketch by Lewis Pyenson

Andrei Andreevich Markov
1856-1922
Russian mathematician

Andrei Andreevich Markov's research covered a number of fields in mathematics, including number theory, differential equations, and quadrature formulas. He is best known, however, for his work in probability theory and his derivation of a powerful predictive tool now known as Markov chains. Although Markov himself saw few applications for this tool, Markov chains are now widely used in many fields of modern science.

Markov was born in Ryazan, Russia, on June 14, 1856. His mother was Nadezhda Petrovna, daughter of a government worker, and his father was Andrei Grigorievich Markov, an employee of the state forestry department who also managed a private estate. Markov suffered from poor health as a child, walking with crutches until the age of ten. He was not a particularly good student, although he demonstrated an interest and skill in mathematics at an early age. While still in high school he wrote a paper on the integration of linear differential equations that drew the attention of members of the mathematics faculty at the University of St. Petersburg. Markov entered that university in 1874, where he studied with the renowned Pafnuty L. Chebyshev. Markov formed a long-term working relationship with Chebyshev, with whom he wrote a number of papers. In one of his earliest papers, Markov reworked one of Chebyshev's theorems, called the central limit theorem, and corrected certain errors his teacher had made.

Markov received his bachelor's degree in 1878 for a thesis on differential equations and continuing fractions, for which he was also awarded a gold medal. Markov then stayed on at St. Petersburg to work for his master's degree, which was granted in 1880, then for his doctorate, which he received in 1884. His doctoral thesis was also on continuing fractions, and this was a subject that would remain central to much of his career.

Markov began teaching at the University of St. Petersburg in 1880 while still a graduate student. By 1886 he was named extraordinary professor of mathematics and in 1893 full professor, a post he would hold until his retirement in 1905. Markov also held parallel appointments in the St. Petersburg Academy of Sciences during this period. He was elected an adjunct member of the academy in 1886, extraordinary academician in 1890, and an ordinary academician in 1896. During his years at St. Petersburg Markov pursued a rather wide variety of topics in mathematics, including the search for minima in indefinite quadratic functions; the evaluation of limits for functions, integrals, and derivatives; and the method of moments. It was not until 1907, however, after his retirement from St. Petersburg, that he completed the work in probability theory for which he is now best known.

Markov Chains

His most important contribution to probability theory began when he was writing a textbook on probability calculus, originally published in 1900. During preparation of the book, Markov encountered a particular type of probabilistic event, in which it is sometimes possible to predict the future status of some collection of random events if certain information is available about the present status of the sequence of events. As an example, the movement of gas molecules in a container is random. It can never be predicted exactly what any one molecule will do at any given moment. But, Markov showed, there are certain circumstances under which a later state of molecules in the container can be predicted if certain conditions exist among the molecules now. The sequence of events under which this situation can occur is called a Markov chain.

Markov apparently saw few practical applications for his theorem, mostly because of the state of science at that time, when it was believed that natural laws determined most events. Within a decade, however, the nature of science had undergone a dramatic revolution. Phenomena were seen to be the result of the *probable* behavior of fundamental particles and waves, though these actions often could not be proved. Markovian analysis became useful for predicting this type of probable behavior, and today Markov's work finds applications in a countless number of ways in the biological and physical sciences and in technology.

Beyond his academic work, Markov was also involved with Russian politics in the years leading up to the Russian revolution. He vigorously supported the liberal movement that swept through the country in the early twentieth century. In 1902, for example, he protested the action of Czar Nicholas II in withholding membership in the St. Petersburg Academy from dissident writer Maxim Gorky. Markov refused government honors later offered to him and in 1907 resigned from the academy in protest of the czar's opposition to government reform. During the revolution of 1917 Markov volunteered to teach mathematics without pay at the remote village of Zaraisk. He became ill shortly after his return to St. Petersburg and died there in 1922.

SELECTED WRITINGS BY MARKOV:

Books

Differential Calculus, 2 volumes, [St. Petersburg], 1889–1891.
Probability Calculus, [St. Petersburg], 1900.

Periodicals

"Functions Generated by Developing Power Series in Continuing Fractions," *Duke Mathematical Journal,* Volume 7, 1940, pp. 85–96.

SOURCES:

Books

Dictionary of Scientific Biography, Volume 9, Charles Scribner's Sons, 1975, pp. 124–130.
World of Scientific Discovery, Gale Research, 1994, pp. 421–422.

—*Sketch by David E. Newton*

A. J. P. Martin
1910-
English biochemist

One of Great Britain's most noted biochemists, A.J.P. Martin developed techniques of paper chromatography in addition to pioneering the separation of gases by chromatography, which revolutionized basic research in organic chemistry. For the development of paper partition chemistry, Martin and his colleague **Richard Synge** were awarded the Nobel Prize in chemistry in 1952.

Archer John Porter Martin, the only son of four children, was born on March 1, 1910, in London, England, to William Archer Porter Martin, a physician, and Lilian Kate Brown, a nurse. Martin attended high school in Bedford and graduated in 1929. Intent on becoming a chemical engineer, he entered Peterhouse, Cambridge, on a merit scholarship and studied chemistry, physics, mathematics, and mineralogy. While at Cambridge, he met Professor **John Burdon Sanderson Haldane**, became interested in biochemistry, and changed his major to that subject. He received a B.S. degree in 1932 and became a researcher in the physical chemistry laboratory of the university. With a colleague, Nora Wooster, he published an article in *Nature* in 1932, describing the preparation and mounting of deliquescent materials, solid substances that become liquid as they absorb moisture from the air.

Begins Research into Chromatography

In their laboratories at Cambridge, Martin and Synge became interested in chromatography in the early 1930s. Chromatography is a technique that separates parts of a mixture as it moves over a porous solid. **Richard Willstätter**, a German scientist, had developed a technique for separating plant pigments but had not been able to separate more complex substances. Martin and Synge had been searching for a method that would isolate the constituents of carotene, a ruby-red pigment that is present in various plants and animals and is the precursor of vitamin A. They found the compounds would move in columns or zones in a tube packed with porous materials like starch, cellulose, or silicagel.

While continuing his work at Cambridge, Martin held the Grocers' Scholarship for original medical research from 1934 to 1936. He worked under Sir Charles Martin, and he later credited this distinguished scientist as the greatest influence on his work in biochemistry. He received his M.A. degree in 1935 and a Ph.D. in 1936 from the University of Cambridge. In 1938 Martin became a biochemist at the Wool Industries Research Association Laboratory in Leeds. He stayed there through 1946. His studies involved the composition of wool felting and amino acid analysis. While working at this laboratory, he conceived the idea of separating amino acids using porous paper.

Work in Chromatography Leads to Nobel Prize

Several previous researchers had been frustrated in their efforts to break down proteins into amino acids. Building on their earlier studies at Cambridge, Martin and Synge devised paper partition chromatography in 1944. In this new technique, substances move in columns on sheets of paper instead of in an absorbent in a glass tube. The technique proved an instant success in separating proteins into their base amino acids. Martin and Synge worked the paper chromatography technique in the following manner. A drop of amino acid mixture is put near the bottom of a strip of porous paper and allowed to dry. The edge of the paper is dipped in a solvent which spreads through the strip by capillary action. As the solvent goes through the dried amino acid mixture, different amino acids move with the solvent at varying rates. Hence, the amino acids are separated and can be studied. The news of this new technique spread rapidly throughout the scientific community. Because of chromatography, other scientists made great strides. For example, **Frederick Sanger** was able to identify the order of amino acids in the insulin molecule, and **Melvin Calvin** was able to work out the mechanism of photosynthesis. Paper chromatography also contributed to advances in the biochemical knowledge of the sterols, an enormous array of substances that play a role in the life processes. Martin's work in chromatography received the highest recognition in 1952, when he and Synge were awarded the Nobel Prize in chemistry.

Martin worked at Boots Pure Drug Research Company, Nottingham, from 1946 to 1948. During this time, he and colleagues R. Consden and A. H. Gordon identified lower peptides in complex mixtures using paper chromatography. He joined the Medical Research Council at Lister Institute, Chelsea, London, in 1948 and accepted a post as head of the physical chemistry division of the National Institute of Medical Research in Mars Hill, London, in 1952. Continuing to apply paper chromatography, Martin studied sugars in a variety of substances and the partition of fatty acids. In 1953 his studies led him to gas-liquid chromatography, a method of separating volatile substances by blowing them down a long tube filled with inert gas. Gas-liquid chromatography is an adaptation of the paper chromatography technique.

Martin has written many articles on chromatography for journals and worked at major international universities. From 1956 to 1959 he was a chemical consultant, and he acted as a director to Abbotsbury Laboratories from 1959 to 1970. He was consultant to the Wellcome Foundation from 1970 to 1973. He has held professorships at Eindoven Technological University, Holland; at the University of Sussex; at the University of Houston, Texas; and at the Ecole Polytechnique Fédérale de Lausanne in France. He was elected a fellow of the Royal Society in 1950 and in 1951 received the Berzelius Gold Medal from the Swedish Medical Society. He is also the recipient of honorary doctorates from the universities of Leeds, Glasgow, and Urbino.

Martin married Judith Bagenal, a teacher, on January 9, 1943. They have two sons and three daughters. While in college he developed a love for the self-defense art of Jiu-Jitsu and in the past has enjoyed gliding and mountaineering. The Martins reside in Cambridge, England.

SELECTED WRITINGS BY MARTIN:

Periodicals

(With Nora Wooster) "Preparation and Mounting of Deliquescent Substances," *Nature,* April 16, 1932.

SOURCES:

Periodicals

New York Times, November 5, 1952, p. 29.
New York Tribune, November 7, 1952, p. 36.

—*Sketch by Evelvn B. Kelly*

Alla G. Massevitch
1918-
Russian astronomer

Alla G. Massevitch (also spelled Masevich) was a force behind the Russian space program for over three decades. In addition to establishing an academic career as an astrophysicist, she planned, put into operation, and administered the network of stations charting the motion of Soviet sputniks. A product of the system that enabled **Valentina Tereshkova** to become the first woman in history to orbit the earth in 1963, Massevitch enjoyed a reputation for effectiveness matched by personal charisma. She was committed to the popularization of technology, and traveled widely as an ambassador for Russian science.

Alla Genrikhovna Massevitch was born October 9, 1918, in Tbilisi, the capital of the Georgian Republic of the former Soviet Union. She was the eldest child of Genrikh Massevitch, a lawyer, and Natalie Zhgenty, a nurse. At age thirteen, Massevitch discovered the popular scientific works of Professor Y. Perelman of the Polytechnical Institute in Leningrad, and began a correspondence with him that would guide her education in astronomy, physics, and mathematics. After graduating from secondary school in 1936 Massevitch hoped to be able to study with Perelman, but her parents thought her too young to go so far away and proposed Moscow instead.

In 1937 Massevitch entered the Moscow Industrial Pedagogical Institute at Moscow University, majoring in physics, and earned her degree in 1940. She remained at Moscow University for postgraduate studies, which were cut short in the summer of 1941 by Hitler's advance into Russia. In November, Massevitch married Joseph Friedlander, a metallurgical engineer she met only days before in an air-raid shelter while taking cover from German bombs. The Institute of Physics and Metals, where Friedlander worked, and the University of Moscow were being evacuated to different parts of the country, and Massevitch chose to follow Friedlander to Kuibyshev on the Volga. At Kuibyshev, Massevitch worked with her husband at the Institute of Physics and taught astronomy at Kuibyshev Teacher's College, attending classes there in the evening to learn English. In the summer of 1943, with Hitler in retreat, the institute returned to Moscow. Massevitch enrolled in the Sternberg State Astronomy Institute to work on her doctorate. Massevitch specialized in the internal structure of stars and stellar evolution, and her thesis concerned the structure and internal energy sources of red giant stars. (Red giant stars are cool red stars, ten to one hundred times the radius of the Sun, but of similar mass.) At the time Soviet scientists had little experience in building stellar models, and automatic computers were practically nonexistent. Massevitch spent weeks painstakingly performing calculations on a model of the star Betelgeuse, a variable red giant near the shoulder of the constellation Orion. She took her candidate's degree (similar to a Ph.D.) in 1946, and accepted a position as assistant professor of astrophysics at the University of Moscow. In 1948, at the age of thirty, she was made full professor. She continued her work on the structure of red giants and began a study of the evolution of the sun.

Supervises Tracking of Soviet Space Vehicles

In 1952 Massevitch accepted a concomitant appointment as vice president of the Astronomical Council of the USSR (now Russian) Academy of Sciences that would involve her closely with space research programs for the next thirty years. Six months before the launching of *Sputnik I* in 1957, the Astronomical Council was given the task of tracking space vehicles. Massevitch came up with a clever system of specially adapted telescopes and simulated space vehicles to train operating personnel for the large network of tracking stations scattered across the country; on launch date the seventy-station network functioned without incident. In addition to organizing and administering the network, she was responsible for publishing data collected by the tracking stations. Since 1988 Massevitch has been chief scientific researcher for the council in charge of visual, photographic, and laser-ranging tracking of space vehicles, and maintains her own experimental station near Moscow. She divides her time between her professorial duties at the university and her work for the council.

Massevitch was awarded the USSR State Prize in 1975. She is a strong believer in international cooperation, as evidenced by the range of her activities. From 1961 to 1966 she chaired a working group for the Committee on Space Research (COSPAR) of the International Council of Scientific Unions. She was president of the section on satellite tracking for Geodesy from 1968 to 1989, and in 1982 served as deputy secretary general of the United Nations Conference on the Exploration and Peaceful Uses of Outer Space (UNISPACE). She was elected a foreign member of the Royal Astronomical Society in 1963, and holds membership in the Austrian and Indian academies of science and (since 1964) the International Academy of Astronautics.

Fluent in four languages, Massevitch is a much sought after speaker the world over. She enjoys ballet, music, theater, and cooking, and has been an avid skier and swimmer. She has written three books on stellar evolution and over 140 papers on the internal structure of stars, stellar evolution, and the optical tracking of satellites, mainly in the *Astronomical Journal of the USSR* and other Russian journals.

—Sketch by Sebastian Thaler

Walter E. Massey
1938-
American physicist

A respected physicist, Walter E. Massey has had a respected career as an educator, administrator, and researcher. He was also nominated by President George Bush to be director of the National Science Foundation and became the second African American to hold this post. In the early 1990s, after his tenure as the director of the National Science Foundation, he accepted an appointment as senior vice president for academic affairs and provost at the University of California. Massey also distinguished himself during his directorship of Argonne National Laboratory.

Walter Eugene Massey was born in Hattiesburg, Mississippi, on April 5, 1938. His parents were Almar and Essie Nelson Massey. He became interested in mathematics early in his childhood, and in an interview for *Scientific American* he explained that "there was just something about sitting down and working through problems" that intrigued him. Massey attended the Royal Street High School in Hattiesburg but left at the end of the tenth grade to accept a scholarship at Morehouse College in Atlanta, one of the premier black colleges in the nation. His early departure from high school meant that he entered Morehouse with no background in advanced mathematics, physics, or chemistry. As a result, he became discouraged during his first few weeks at Morehouse and wanted to return home. Massey's mother insisted that he remain, however, and four years later he graduated with a bachelor's degree in physics. Massey credits physicist Sabinus H. Christensen for his survival at Morehouse. Since he was the only physics major in his class at Morehouse, Massey received one-on-one tutorials from Christensen in many of his courses.

Establishes Himself in the Academic and Research Fields

Massey stayed on at Morehouse as an instructor for one year after graduation and then enrolled as a graduate student in physics at Washington University in St. Louis. Again, he was fortunate enough to encounter a concerned and inspiring teacher, the theoretical physicist Eugene Feenberg. "If he [Feenberg] had not taken extraordinary care," Massey told *Scientific American,* "I would have quit." Instead, he remained at Washington to complete his doctoral degree in physics in 1966.

Massey's research interests have included solid-state theory (study of properties of solid material) and theories of quantum liquids and solids. While still a graduate student, he studied the behavior of both solid and liquid helium–3 and helium–4, publishing a series of papers on this work in the early 1970s. Massey began his professional career as a research fellow at the Argonne National Laboratory in Batavia, Illinois, in 1966. Over the next two years he became a staff physicist and soon thereafter, he was appointed assistant professor of physics at the University of Illinois. But he stayed at this post only a year before moving to Brown University as associate professor of physics. He was promoted to full professor in 1975 and named dean of the college in the same year. Massey's best-known accomplishment at Brown was his development of the Inner City Teachers of Science (ICTOS) program, a program for the improvement of science instruction in inner city schools. He was awarded the American Association for the Advancement of Science's Distinguished Service Citation for his development of ICTOS.

In 1979 the University of Chicago invited Massey to become professor of physics and director of the Argonne National Laboratory, which the university operates for the U.S. Department of Energy. The latter appointment was a particular challenge, since the concept of national laboratories financed by federal tax funds was very much in question at the time. Massey made a concerted effort to see that Argonne research was made more readily available to

private industry, and because of this, Charles E. Till, head of engineering research at Argonne, has credited Massey for the survival of the research facility.

Accepts Post at National Science Foundation

During his tenure at Brown, Massey's administrative adeptness led him to become involved in activities such as the Physics Review Committee of the National Academy of Sciences-National Research Council (1972–1975), the Advisory Panel of the Division of Physics for the National Science Foundation (1975–1977), and the Advisory Committee on Eastern Europe and the U.S.S.R. of the National Science Foundation (1973–1976). He also served on the National Science Board, the policy-making arm of the National Science Foundation, from 1978 to 1984.

In the fall of 1990, Massey was chosen by President George Bush to head the National Science Foundation (NSF), a position he held until 1993 when he was offered the post of provost and senior vice president for academic affairs at the University of California. The *New York Times* reported that Massey had hoped to complete his six-year term at NSF, but he said that the California offer was "an opportunity that I cannot pass up."

Massey has received honorary degrees from a number of institutions, including Lake Forest College, Williams College, Elmhurst College, Atlanta University, Rutgers University, Marquette University, Boston College, and his alma mater, Morehouse College. He also served on the board of directors of the American Association for the Advancement of Science from 1981 to 1985 and was elected the organization's president in 1988. Massey has also been appointed to the board of directors of various corporations, including Motorola and the (Chicago) Tribune Company. He married Shirley Streeter in 1969. The Masseys have two sons, Keith Anthony and Eric Eugene. Massey lists his hobbies as sailing, skiing, tennis, and jogging.

SELECTED WRITINGS BY MASSEY:

Periodicals

(With C. Woo) "Variational Calculations on Liquid Helium 4 and Helium 3," *Physical Review,* December 5, 1967, p. 256.

(With H. Eschenbacher) "Training Science Teachers for the Inner City," *The Physics Teacher,* February 1976.

SOURCES:

Periodicals

Beardsley, Tim, "Scientist, Administrator, Role Model," *Scientific American,* June 1992, pp. 40–41.

Bradburn, Norman M., and David Rosen, "Walter E. Massey: President-Elect of AAAS," *Science,* December 18, 1987, pp. 1657–1658.

Leary, Warren E., "Head of Science Education Will Take a University Post," *New York Times,* January 28, 1993, p. A14.

Lepkowski, Wil, "Walter Massey Takes Over Helm of National Science Foundation," *Chemical & Engineering News,* April 22, 1991, pp. 22–24.

—*Sketch by David E. Newton*

Samuel P. Massie
1919-
American chemist

Samuel P. Massie's outstanding educational career as a chemistry professor has led him to be recognized as a leader in the field of chemical education. For his contributions to both the scientific and academic community, Massie received the 1961 Chemical Manufacturers Association award for "excellence in chemistry teaching" and "in recognition of service to the scientific community in instructing and inspiring students." Massie was nominated for this award by his colleagues and students at Fisk University.

Samuel Proctor Massie was born in North Little Rock, Arkansas, on July 3, 1919. An excellent student, Massie graduated from high school at the age of thirteen. He then attended Dunbar Junior College. When Massie graduated from Dunbar he went to the Agricultural Mechanical and Normal College of Arkansas, where he received a bachelor of science degree in 1938. In 1939 he began working as a laboratory assistant in chemistry at Fisk University, where he also obtained his master of arts degree in 1940. Between 1940 and 1941 Massie was an associate professor of mathematics at the Agricultural Mechanical and Normal College of Arkansas. He was a research associate in chemistry at Iowa State University beginning in 1943 and received a doctorate in organic chemistry from that university in 1946. That same year he returned to Fisk University as an instructor. The year following, Massie married Gloria Tompkins. They have three sons.

Begins a Distinguished Teaching Career

During his long teaching career, Massie held several positions, including professor and chair of the chemistry department at Langston University from 1947 to 1953. From 1953 to 1960 he held a similar post at Fisk University. In addition to his regular teaching position at Fisk, Massie also served as Sigma Xi Lecturer at Swarthmore College. In 1960 Massie became associate program director at the National Science Foundation (NSF), an agency that works to support a national science policy by sponsoring research, science curriculum development, teacher training, and various other programs. In 1961 Massie went on to become chair of pharmaceutical chemistry at Howard University, a post he gave up in 1963 to become president of North Carolina College at Durham. In 1966 he joined the faculty at the United States Naval Academy as a professor of chemistry, also serving as chair of the chemistry department from 1977 to 1981.

In addition to the award from the Chemical Manufacturers Association in 1961, Massie received an honorary doctorate from the University of Arkansas in 1970. In 1980 he was named Outstanding Professor by the National Organization of Black Chemists, and in 1981 he received a Distinguished Achievement Citation from Iowa State University. He is a member of the American Chemical Society. Massie has been active outside academia as chair of the Maryland State Board for Community Colleges, and he has also served on the Governor's Science Advisory Council. He has contributed to his community in many capacities, including membership on the Board of Directors of the Red Cross, and distinguished service with United Fund.

SOURCES:

Books

Sammons, Vivian Ovelton, *Blacks in Science and Medicine,* Hemisphere, 1990, p. 164.

—*Sketch by M. C. Nagel*

William Howell Masters
1915-
American obstetrician and gynecologist

William Howell Masters was the first to study the anatomy and physiology of human sexuality in the laboratory, and the publication of the reports on his findings created much interest and criticism. Since then, Masters and his colleague, **Virginia E. Johnson**, have become well-known as researchers and therapists in the field of human sexuality, and together they have established the Reproduction Biology Center and later the Masters and Johnson Institute in St. Louis, Missouri.

Masters was born on December 27, 1915, in Cleveland, Ohio, to Francis Wynne and Estabrooks (Taylor) Masters. He attended public school in Kansas City through the eighth grade and then went to the Lawrenceville School in Lawrenceville, New Jersey. In 1938 he received a B.S. degree from Hamilton College, where he divided his time between science courses and sports such as baseball, football, and basketball. He was also active in campus debate. He entered the University of Rochester School of Medicine and started working in the laboratory of Dr. George Corner, who was comparing and studying the reproductive tracts of animals and humans.

During his junior year in medical school, Masters became interested in sexuality because it was the last scientifically unexplored physiological function. After briefly serving in the navy, he received his M.D. degree in 1943. Masters became interested in the work of Dr. **Alfred Kinsey**, a University of Indiana zoology professor who had interviewed thousands of men and women about their sexual experiences. Choosing a field that would help him prepare himself for human sexuality research, Masters became an intern and later a resident in obstetrics and gynecology at St. Louis Hospital and Barnes Hospital in St. Louis. He also did an internship in pathology at the Washington University School of Medicine. In 1947 he joined the faculty at Washington and advanced from instructor to associate professor of clinical obstetrics and gynecology. Masters conducted research in the field and contributed dozens of papers to scientific journals. One of his areas of interest was hormone treatment and replacement in post-menopausal women.

By 1954 Masters decided that he was ready to undertake research on the physiology of sex. He was concerned that the medical profession had too little information on sexuality to understand clients' problems. Kinsey had depended on case histories, interviews, and secondhand data. Masters took the next step, which was to study human sexual stimulation using measuring technology in a laboratory situation.

Pioneers Studies of Human Sexuality in the Laboratory

Masters launched his project at Washington University, assisted by a grant from the United States Institute of Health. At first he recruited prostitutes for study, but found them unsuitable for his studies of "normal" sexuality. In 1956 he hired Virginia Eshelman Johnson, a sociology student, to help in the

interviewing and screening of volunteers. The study was conducted over an eleven-year period with 382 women and 312 men participating. Subjects ranged in age from eighteen to eighty-nine and were paid for their time. Masters found a four-phased cycle relating to male and female sexual responses. To measure physiological changes, he used electroencephalographs, electrocardiographs, color cinematography, and biochemical studies.

Masters was very cautious and meticulous about protecting the identity of his volunteers. In 1959 he sent some results to medical journals, but continued to work in relative secrecy. After the content of the studies leaked out, the team had difficulty procuring grant money, so in 1964 Masters became director of the Reproductive Biology Foundation, a nonprofit group, to obtain private funds. In November of that same year, Dr. Leslie H. Farber, a respected Washington D.C. psychiatrist, wrote an article in *Commentary* entitled "I'm sorry, Dear," in which he attacked the "scientizing" of sex. This attack was only the beginning of the criticism the research would receive.

In 1966 Masters and Johnson published *Human Sexual Response.* In this book, the researchers used highly technical terminology and had their publisher, Little, Brown and Co., promote the book only to medical professionals and journals. Nevertheless, the book became a popular sensation and the team embarked on a speaking and lecture tour, winning immediate fame. As early as 1959 Masters and Johnson had begun counseling couples as a dual-sex team. Believing that partners would be more comfortable talking with a same-sex therapist, the team began working with couples' sexual problems. In their second book, *Human Sexual Inadequacy* (1970), they discuss problems such as impotence.

Establishes Masters and Johnson Institute

Masters divorced his first wife, Elisabeth Ellis, not long after the publication of *Human Sexual Inadequacy* and married Johnson on January 1, 1971, in Fayetteville, Arkansas. In 1973 they became codirectors of the Masters and Johnson Institute. In 1979 Masters and Johnson studied and described the sexual responses of homosexuals and lesbians in *Homosexuality in Perspective.* They also claimed to be able to change the sexual preferences of homosexuals who wanted it. Masters also maintained a biochemistry lab and continued to receive fees from a gynecology practice. He retired from practice in 1975 at the age of sixty. In 1981 Masters and Johnson sold their lab and moved to another location in St. Louis. At this time they had a staff of twenty-five and a long list of therapy clients.

Further controversy over their work developed when in 1988 Masters and Johnson coauthored a book with an associate, Dr. Robert Kolodny. The book, *Crisis: Heterosexual Behavior in the Age of AIDS* predicted an epidemic of AIDS among the heterosexual population. Some members of the medical community severely condemned the study, and C. Everett Koop, then surgeon general of the United States, called Masters and Johnson irresponsible. Perhaps as a result of the negative publicity, the number of clients seeking sex therapy at the institute decreased. In early 1992, Bill Walters, acting director of the institute, announced that Masters and Johnson were divorcing after twenty-one years of marriage—conflict in their ideas about retirement was cited as the reason for the breakup. Masters vowed he would never retire and continued speaking and lecturing at the institute, in addition to working on another book. The divorce ended their work together at the clinic.

For his pioneering efforts in making human sexuality a subject of scientific study, Masters received the Paul H. Hoch Award from the American Psychopathic Association in 1971, the Sex Information and Education Council of the United States (SIECUS) award in 1972, and three other prestigious awards. He belongs to the American Association for the Advancement of Science (AAAS), the American Fertility Society, and several other medical associations.

SELECTED WRITINGS BY MASTERS:

Books

(With Virginia E. Johnson) *Human Sexual Response,* Little, Brown, 1966.
(With Johnson) *Human Sexual Inadequacy,* Little, Brown, 1970.
(With Johnson) *The Pleasure Bond: A New Look at Sexuality and Commitment,* Little, Brown, 1975.
(With Johnson) *Homosexuality in Perspective,* Little, Brown, 1979.
(With Johnson and Robert Kolodny) *On Sex and Human Loving,* Little, Brown, 1986.
(With Kolodny) *Crisis: Heterosexual Behavior in the Age of AIDS,* Grove, 1988.

SOURCES:

Books

Robinson, Paul A., *The Modernization of Sex: Havelock Ellis, Albert Kinsey, William Masters, and Virginia Johnson,* Harper, 1976.

Periodicals

Fried, Stephen, "The New Sexperts," *Vanity Fair,* December 1992, p. 132.

"Repairing the Conjugal Bed," *Time,* March 25, 1970.

—*Sketch by Evelyn B. Kelly*

Alva T. Matthews
19(?)-
American engineer

A consultant in engineering mechanics, Alva T. Matthews has conducted research in varied fields, including the effect of nuclear weapons blasts on soils and structures, the dynamic analysis of helicopter blades and blade design, and improvements in automobile crash safety. She also has developed and adapted large computer codes for scientific calculations, and developed software for the design and development of Telstar tracking antennae. Since the birth of her child in 1977, Matthews has been retired from full-time work, choosing instead to consult for Xerox and other firms on a part-time basis.

Matthews decided to become an engineer at age fifteen; her parents had always encouraged her to achieve without limitations, and accompanying her father, an industrial builder, to construction sites opened her eyes to the possibilities in engineering. As she told Sam Merrill in *Cosmopolitan,* "It never occurred to me I *couldn't* be an engineer." When Matthews enrolled in an engineering program at Middlebury College in Vermont, however, an advisor told her that the field was too difficult for a girl and that she would never be hired. "I was hurt and surprised," Matthews said in an address to the Society of Women Engineers. "After the hurt wore off I decided to ignore him." Later, while a student working in a contractor's field office, she was prohibited from entering the tunnels because of a superstition about women causing tunnel collapses. Matthews persevered, and eventually transferred to Barnard College and later Columbia University, where she became the first woman to attend the Engineering School's surveying camp; there she met her future husband, A. R. Solomon. Matthews received a B.S from Columbia in 1955, an M.S. in 1957, and a Ph.D. of Engineering Science in 1965. Matthews joined the staff of Paul Weidlinger, a New York construction engineering firm, as Design Engineer in 1957; upon completion of her degree, she was named Senior Research Engineer. Although she had confronted barriers during her education, Matthews noted in her address that once her career began, she experienced "no problems which can be related to being a female."

During this period, Matthews conducted research into the mechanical behavior of materials under great pressures, research which influenced models of how waves move through materials such as rock and soil. Applications of this research included study of how nuclear weapons blasts might affect buildings. Concurrently, Matthews was a senior research engineer with Rochester Applied Science Associates in Rochester, New York, where she conducted research on the dynamics of helicopter blades and worked on the reconstruction and analysis of automobile accidents. At the same time, she became an instructor of civil engineering at Columbia University School of Engineering. She lectured in the evenings at the University of Rochester, where she was an adjunct associate professor with the department of mechanical and aerospace sciences, and also taught one year at Swarthmore College's Engineering School.

Speaking in her 1973 address of her dual love of education and the private sector, Matthews noted, "I hope always to be able to go back to teaching once in a while for the rejuvenation it brings to your thinking." She received the Society of Women Engineers 1971 Achievement Award for her work in "shock analysis, elasticity and structural design." In 1976, she was given the Engineering Award of the Federation of Engineering and Scientific Societies of Drexel University.

In addition to her continued consulting, Matthews has pursued her love of dressage, producing horse shows and riding with her daughter. "One has to define life—because it's a longer life now—in different rooms. You go from room to room," she said in an interview with contributor Karen Withem. Even though her aspirations have shifted from engineering to other activities, she noted, "I have no regrets. The engineering training is a precious thing to have for any endeavor."

SELECTED WRITINGS BY MATTHEWS:

Periodicals

(With H. Bleich) "Effects of a Step Wave Moving Superseismically over the Surface of a Half-Space of Non-Mises Material," *International Journal of Solids and Structures,* November, 1967.

SOURCES:

Periodicals

"Award Winner," *Society of Women Engineers Newsletter,* August, 1971, p. 1.

Merrill, Sam, "Women in Engineering," *Cosmopolitan,* April, 1976, pp. 162–164.
"Who's Doing What Where," *Society of Women Engineers,* Spring, 1976, p. 13.

Other

Matthews, Alva, "Engineering as an Ideal Woman's Career," address, Society of Women Engineers and Engineering Foundation Conference, August 19–24, 1973.
Matthews, Alva, interview with Karen Withem conducted March 31, 1994.

—Sketch by Karen Withem

Motonori Matuyama
1884-1958
Japanese geophysicist

Motonori Matuyama, who discovered that the direction of the earth's magnetic field has actually changed its polarity since the Pleistocene era (which ended approximately 10,000 years ago), began life in a very different context from the world of science. In fact Matuyama, who was born in Uyeda, Japan, on October 25, 1884, was the son of a Zen abbot, Tengai Sumiye. In 1910 Matuyama was adopted as an adult into the Matsuyama family, taking that name as his own (the difference in spelling is explained by the convention of the time towards transliteration). Matuyama also became a part of the family through marriage when he wed the Matsuyamas' daughter, Matsuye.

Matuyama earned degrees in physics and mathematics from Hiroshima Normal College (later the University of Hiroshima) in 1907. He taught at a junior high school in Tomioka for a year before beginning his graduate studies in physics at the Imperial University in Kyoto. After receiving his degree in 1911, Matuyama decided to concentrate his postgraduate studies in the field of geophysics under the tutelage of Toshi Shida.

It was during this time that Matuyama began to focus on what would become one of his major research topics, the determination of gravity by pendulum. In fact, his research was incorporated into Shida's "On the Elasticity of the Earth and the Earth's Crust," which was published in 1912. That work won Matuyama a lectureship at the Imperial University beginning in 1913. Three years later he began an assistant professorship at the Geophysical Institute, where he continued his probing of gravitational theory.

For his doctoral dissertation, Matuyama examined the results of experiments to determine the depth of a coral reef called Jaluit atoll, on which he had spent a month in 1915. His paper daringly suggested that by determining the minute features of the earth's field of gravity at a certain location, one could make assumptions about the geological substructure of the spot. This assertion became the basis of the torsion-balance method used in Japan to prospect for underground mineral deposits.

Matuyama spent two years in the United States, where he studied under **T. C. Chamberlin** at the University of Chicago and published his paper "On Some Physical Properties of Ice," which was based on experiments that explained the movement of glaciers. Upon returning to Japan, Matuyama was named professor of theoretical geology at the Imperial University, where he began teaching in January of 1922. In 1927 Matuyama resumed the work of the gravity survey, begun by the Imperial Japanese Geodetic Commission, to further include Korea and Manchuria.

Lends Name to an Epoch

Matuyama's most influential work was his discovery of the reversal of the earth's magnetic field. Subjecting specimens of basalt from sites in Japan, Korea, and Manchuria to remnant magnetization tests, Matuyama determined that the magnetic field of the earth had not only changed over relatively short periods of time, but had almost reversed. His findings were published in 1929 in a paper entitled "On the Direction of Magnetization of Basalt in Japan, Tyosen [Korea] and Manchuria," and the term "Matuyama reversed epoch" has come to describe the time from the late Pliocene to the middle Pleistocene eras (0.7 million to 2.4 million years ago), when the direction of the earth's magnetic field is thought to have been opposite what it is today. Later research based on Matuyama's findings revealed that the magnetic field has reversed more than 20 times during the past five million years, apparently at random.

Matuyama began a project in the mid–1930s that would be of great importance to his homeland. Having been witness to one of the tremendous earthquakes that plague Japan, Matuyama undertook a survey of marine gravity in the area of the Japan Trench, using an elaborate pendulum mounted in a naval submarine. Based on his findings, a relationship was established between the great irregularities in the equilibrium of the earth's crust and earthquakes that occurred in the region.

From 1936 to 1937, Matuyama served as the dean of the Faculty of Science at the Imperial University, where he continued to teach until 1944. In 1949 he became president of the University of Yamaguchi. Matuyama died in Yamaguchi, Japan, on January 27, 1958.

SELECTED WRITINGS BY MATUYAMA:

Periodicals

"Gravity Measurements in Tyosen and Manchuria," *Proceedings of the Fourth Pacific Science Congress* (Djakarta), 1929, pp. 745–747.
"On the Direction of Magnetization of Basalt in Japan, Tyosen and Manchuria," *Proceedings of the Fourth Pacific Science Congress* (Djakarta), 1929, pp. 567–569. (Also appeared in *Proceedings of the Imperial Academy of Japan* 5, 1929, pp. 203–205.)
"Gravity Survey by the Japanese Geodetic Commission Since 1932," *Travaux* (Association internationale de geodesie), Japan Report no. 2, 12, 1936, pp. 1–8.

SOURCES:

Books

Dictionary of Scientific Biography Volume IX, Charles Scribner's Sons, 1974, pp. 180–182.

—*Sketch by Joan Oleck*

John William Mauchly
1907-1980
American computer engineer

John William Mauchly, a physicist and computer engineer, is widely credited with co-inventing two of the most important early computers. With **J. Presper Eckert**, Mauchly invented the first general-purpose digital electronic computer, the Electronic Numerical Integrator and Computer (ENIAC). Also with Eckert, Mauchly developed the first commercial digital electronic computer, the Universal Automatic Computer (UNIVAC). Their work together effectively began the commercial computer revolution in America and throughout the world.

Mauchly was born on August 30, 1907, in Cincinnati, Ohio, to Sebastian J. Mauchly and Rachel Scheidemantel Mauchly. His father was an electrical engineer who, in 1915, moved the family east to accept a position as head of the Section of Terrestrial Electricity and Magnetism at the Carnegie Institute in Washington, D.C. Mauchly attended the Johns Hopkins University from 1925 to 1927, when he was admitted to the graduate school there without an undergraduate degree. He received a Ph.D. in physics from Johns Hopkins in 1932. He spent another year there as a research assistant, and then in 1933 he was appointed head of the physics department at Ursinus College, near Philadelphia.

Mauchly had a strong early interest in meteorology, but he found studying the weather to be particularly difficult because it took so much time to coordinate all the data. Computations could only be done by hand or with the primitive calculating machines then available. Interested in using statistics to prove the effect of sun flares on the weather, he began trying to develop a better machine for calculating. During the late 1930s, Mauchly began to experiment with vacuum tubes in place of the slower gears and wheels used in mechanical computing devices.

Inventing the First Computer

Mauchly did not publish anything on his experiments until December of 1940, when he gave a paper to the American Association for the Advancement of Science on using computing machines to solve meteorology problems. After presenting his paper, he was approached by **John Atanasoff**, a professor at Iowa State University, who told him he was building an electronic computer. In June of 1941, Mauchly went to Iowa State to see Atanasoff's computer—a visit which was later used against his patent claim that he and Eckert had invented the first computer. Atanasoff said later that Mauchly had been fascinated by it; Mauchly said that seeing the computer had been of little value. It had run slowly and had only done simple arithmetic functions.

When the United States entered World War II, Mauchly agreed to study electrical engineering at the Moore School of Engineering at the University of Pennsylvania in order to further the war effort. It was there he met Eckert and they began their famous collaboration. The Moore School had already developed one of the most advanced electro-mechanical computational devices in the world, the differential analyzer. At the beginning of the war, the United States Army had awarded the school a contract to compute the tables of trajectories for artillery shells. Both Mauchly and Eckert became deeply involved in this project.

Mauchly and Eckert were both fascinated with the idea of using vacuum tubes to create an electronic digital computer. They used vacuum tubes, photoelectric cells, and other devices to make the existing mechanical computer at the Moore School work ten times faster. In August of 1942, Mauchly wrote a five-page memo to an administrator at the school, John Grist Brainerd. The memo, "The Use of High-Speed Vacuum Tube Devices for Calculating," outlined how vacuum tubes could be used to add, subtract, multiply, and divide much more rapidly than mechanical calculators. Brainerd, Herman H. Goldstine, and Oswald Veblen saw the potential for an electronic computer, and in April of 1943 the Moore School got permission from the army to go ahead with what is now called the ENIAC.

Eckert and Mauchly designed and built the ENIAC with a team of fifty other people at the Moore School, overcoming a number of technical and logistical obstacles. Unfortunately for the war effort, the ENIAC did not run its first full-scale test until December of 1945, several months after World War II had ended. After the war, ENIAC was used to solve trajectory problems and compute ballistics tables at the army's Aberdeen Proving Ground. Later, it performed calculations for the development of the hydrogen bomb.

Faces Legal Battles over Computer Patent

Mauchly and Eckert applied for a patent on the ENIAC in 1947. By then, they had resigned from the Moore Engineering School and had begun their own corporation, the Eckert and Mauchly Computer Corporation. They assigned their patent to their corporation, where they developed the first commercial computer, the UNIVAC. Eckert took care of the engineering functions, and Mauchly ran the business. Neither Mauchly nor Eckert, however, was a good businessman. Mauchly was very easy going and jovial, but he was also unconventional. When he and Eckert visited IBM and its famous president, Thomas Watson, Sr., Mauchly flopped down on the couch and put his feet up on the coffee table. Eckert and Mauchly eventually ran into financial troubles, and in 1950 they sold their company along with their computer patents to Remington Rand. Sperry Rand later bought out Remington. Mauchly worked for Remington and Sperry until 1959, when he left to form his own consulting corporation, Mauchly Associates. In 1968, he founded a second computer consulting corporation, which he called Dynatrend.

In February 1964, after seventeen years, the ENIAC patent was finally issued to one of Sperry Rand's subsidiaries, Illinois Scientific Developments. The patent, however, was very broad and vaguely written. When Sperry Rand sued the Honeywell Corporation in 1967 for infringing the ENIAC patent, Honeywell countersued. Honeywell claimed, among other things, that the patent was a fraud and that

Eckert and Mauchly did not invent the first general-purpose digital electronic computer. Honeywell's suit claimed that Atanasoff was the real inventor. There was a lengthy trial, and each side presented thousands of pages of documents to support its arguments. In October, 1973, Judge Earl Larson of Minneapolis issued his judgment, which made Honeywell the winner. Judge Larson's decision to invalidate the patent was based primarily on the facts that the patent on the ENIAC was filed after the computer had been in use for over a year and that information about the ENIAC had already been published, making the technology "prior art" and thus unpatentable.

In his decision, the judge also held that Atanasoff was the real inventor of the electronic digital computer. This last reason especially bothered Mauchly. Atanasoff had never considered himself the originator of the electronic digital computer until an IBM lawyer mentioned the idea to him in 1954. Atanasoff never even built a working electronic computer; he attempted a prototype but he could not get all the parts to work together before he abandoned it. His computer was also highly specialized and could only compute linear equations, whereas the ENIAC could add, subtract, multiply, divide, extract square roots, compare quantities, and perform other functions. Many people who have studied the case believe that Mauchly and Eckert were wronged by Judge Larson's decision. Mauchly himself believed he had been wronged, and the patent decision left him bitter. Even though he won many awards for his accomplishments, including the Howard N. Potts Medal in 1949, the John Scott Award in 1961, and the Harry Goode Award in 1966, Mauchly never ceased to feel he had been denied full credit for his role in the development of the computer.

Mauchly had married Mary Augusta Walzl in 1930. They had two sons. But in September of 1946, while they were swimming in the Atlantic, his wife was swept out to sea and drowned. On February 7, 1948, Mauchly married Kathleen R. McNulty, who had been one of the programmers on the ENIAC. He had five more children with her, four daughters and a son. Mauchly suffered all his life from a hereditary genetic disease called hemorrhagic telangiectasia, which caused bloody noses and internal bleeding, among other symptoms. In his later life he had to carry around oxygen to breathe properly. He died on January 8, 1980, of complications from an infection.

SELECTED WRITINGS BY MAUCHLY:

Books

"The ENIAC," N. Metropolis and others, editors, *A History of Computing in the Twentieth Century,* Academic Press, 1980, pp. 541–550.

Periodicals

"Mauchly on the Trials of Building the ENIAC," *IEEE Spectrum,* April, 1975, pp. 70–76.
"Mauchly: Unpublished Remarks," *Annals of the History of Computing,* July, 1982, pp. 245–256.

SOURCES:

Books

Shurkin, Joel, *Engines of the Mind,* W. W. Norton, 1984.
Slater, Robert, *Portraits in Silicon,* MIT Press, 1987.
Stern, Nancy, *From ENIAC to UNIVAC: An Appraisal of the Eckert-Mauchly Computers,* Digital Press, 1981.

—Sketch by Patrick Moore

Annie Russell Maunder
1868-1947
Irish astronomer

Annie Russell Maunder specialized in sunspot research with her husband, Edward Walter Maunder, detecting dark spots appearing on the sun's surface. In 1898, she obtained a photograph of a solar prominence (a cloud of gas arising from the atmosphere of the sun) six solar radii in length—the largest captured on film up to that time. Maunder was also active in the British Astronomical Association, serving as vice-president of the association several times up to 1942, and planning the general form of their official journal (*Journal of the British Astronomical Association*) and serving as editor from 1894 to 1896 and from 1917 to 1930. She also held a paid position at the Greenwich Observatory, at the time a distinction most unusual for a woman.

Annie Russell was born on April 14, 1868, in County Tyrone, Ireland. The daughter of Rev. W. A. Russell, she was educated at Victoria College in Belfast and Girton College in Cambridge. In 1889 she received the highest mathematical honor available to women at Girton, a Senior Optime in the Mathematical Tripos. In 1891 Russell was hired as a "computer" to assist Edward Maunder, head of the solar photography department at the Royal Observatory in Greenwich and founder of the British Astronomical Association. Her job was to examine and measure daily sunspot photographs. Russell and Maunder became friends and were married in 1895. In 1897 and 1898 Annie Russell Maunder was a Pfeiffer student for research at Girton College. Throughout her career she worked in close collaboration with her husband on a variety of astronomical subjects, though her own favorite was the sun; among her contributions were eclipse observations and photographs made during expeditions to Lapland in 1896, India in 1898, Algiers in 1900, Mauritius in 1901, and Labrador in 1905. The Maunders were prolific writers, and contributed frequently as coauthors to *Monthly Notices of the Royal Astronomical Society* and the *Journal of the British Astronomical Association.*

Obtains Longest Coronal Streamer on Film

While in India for the 1898 eclipse, Maunder obtained on film the longest coronal extension (or solar prominence) then known. She equipped a camera to photograph the greatest possible extension of coronal streamers (or solar extensions), and she did in fact photograph one with a length of six solar radii. In related work Maunder proposed that the Earth influenced the number and areas of sunspots, and that sunspots frequency decreased from the eastern to the western edge of the Sun's disk as viewed from the Earth. She also proposed that changes in the Sun caused changes in the Earth's climate, and contributed (with support from a research grant from Girton College) to a photographic survey of the Milky Way.

In 1892 she failed to obtain membership in the Royal Astronomical Society, but she did become a member of the British Astronomical Association, which welcomed female members. On several occasions, she was asked to be president of the association, but refused on account of her soft-spokenness. She was a representative at the Womens' International Congress in London in 1899.

Maunder was interested in the history of astronomy, especially in the origin of the forty-eight ancient constellations, noting that the southern limit of those constellations gave clues to the latitude of their observers. She shared with her husband a fascination for the astronomy of the early Hindus and Persians, and wrote many articles on the subject. Maunder survived Edward, who died in 1928, by nineteen years; she died on September 15, 1947.

SELECTED WRITINGS BY MAUNDER:

Books

(With Edward Maunder) *The Heavens and Their Story,* R. Culley, 1908.
Catalogue of Recurrent Groups of Sun Spots for the Year 1874 to 1906, Neill, 1909.

SOURCES:

Books

Women in Science, MIT Press, 1986, pp. 129–230.

Periodicals

Journal of the British Astronomical Association, December, 1947, p. 238.

—*Sketch by Sebastian Thaler*

Antonia Maury
1866-1952
American astronomer

Antonia Maury's long career included twenty-five years at the Harvard College Observatory. While there, she used her expertise in spectroscopy (the study of light wavelengths) to create a classification system of spectral lines that later proved to correspond to the appearance of particular stars. Maury's system in fact improved on the system developed by **Annie Jump Cannon**, the famed "census taker of the skies" who also worked out of Harvard. The Maury classification system is considered an integral element of the development of theoretical astrophysics.

Antonia Caetana de Paiva Pereira Maury was born in Cold Spring, New York, on March 21, 1866. Her family had long been involved in science. Her mother, Virginia Draper Maury, was a sister of the astronomer Henry Draper and daughter of the chemist John Draper. Her father, Mytton Maury, was a cousin of the oceanographer Matthew Fontaine Maury; although a minister himself, he was an amateur naturalist and editor of a geography magazine. Maury's younger sister, **Carlotta Joaquina Maury**, was a noted paleontologist.

Maury was educated at home and attended Vassar College, from which she obtained a bachelor of arts degree in 1887. Because of her interest in astronomy, her father wrote to the Harvard astronomer Edward Pickering asking him to hire the young Antonia. Pickering had doubts about hiring a Vassar graduate for a mere assistant's position (for which he could pay no more than 25 cents an hour), but he decided to give her a chance.

Devises Stellar Classification System

Her first task at Harvard was the classification of northern stars according to spectra. She assisted Pickering in identifying binary stars, groups of two stars that revolve around each other under mutual gravitation. She quickly mastered spectroscopy and set to work on revising the classification system then in place, which she found inadequate. Light which passes through chemical elements is absorbed at specific wavelengths characteristic to the elements. These chemical signatures show up as absorption lines in light spectra, making it possible to study both the chemical constitution of stars and the light they emit by means of spectroscopy. Maury realized that classifications could be made on the basis of the lines themselves—their intensity, width, and distance from one another. By 1891, she had mapped out her classification scheme.

During this time, however, Pickering's fear had become reality; Maury had grown bored with the Harvard routine. Moreover, she felt stifled by Pickering's supervision. Maury was an innovator—something Pickering did not admire, although he recognized her talents. Maury left the Observatory in 1891 to become a teacher, but returned periodically to continue her work on the classification system. She published her system in 1897, and left the Harvard Observatory, to which she would not return for more than twenty years.

Maury served as a visiting teacher and lecturer; she also tutored students privately. In 1918, she returned to Harvard as a research associate and continued her work on binary stars, in particular spectroscopic binaries. In 1920, **Harlow Shapley** became director of the Observatory, and Maury's working relationship with him was far more amiable than her experience with Pickering had been.

She retired from Harvard in 1935 and moved to Westchester County, New York, where she became curator of the Draper Observatory and Museum in Hastings-on-Hudson; the museum had formerly been part of the Draper family estate. She retired from that position in 1938 and spent the rest of her life pursuing, in addition to astronomy, such other interests as ornithology and conservation. In 1943, Maury was awarded the Annie J. Cannon Prize by the American Astronomical Society. She died in Dobbs Ferry, New York, on January 8, 1952.

SELECTED WRITINGS BY MAURY:

Periodicals

"Spectra of Bright Stars Photographed with the 11-inch Draper Telescope as a Part of the Henry Draper Memorial and Discussed by An-

tonia C. Maury under the direction of Edward C. Pickering," *Annals of the Astronomical Observatory of Harvard College,* Volume 28, part 1, 1897.

"The Spectral Changes of Beta Lyrae," *Annals of the Astronomical Observatory of Harvard College,* Volume 84, number 8, 1933.

SOURCES:

Books

Abbott, D., editor, *Biographical Dictionary of Scientists: Astronomers,* Bedrick Books, 1984, pp. 590–591.

Ogilvie, Marilyn Bailey, *Women In Science: Antiquity through the Nineteenth Century,* MIT Press, 1986.

—*Sketch by George A. Milite*

Carlotta Joaquina Maury
1874-1938
American paleontologist

Carlotta Joaquina Maury was a specialist in the stratigraphy and fossil fauna of Brazil, Venezuela, and the West Indies, contributing a number of scientific reports on these regions and describing several new fossil genera and species. In 1916, she headed up her own paleontological expedition to the Dominican Republic. Maury taught, traveled and consulted widely, acting for many years as an advisor to the Venezuelan division of the Royal Dutch Shell Petroleum Company, and as the official paleontologist to the government of Brazil.

Maury was born January 6, 1874, at Hastings-on-Hudson, New York, one of three children of Mytton Maury, who was an Episcopal minister, and Virginia (Draper) Maury. The Maury family line dated back to Matthew Maury, who left England and arrived in Virginia in 1718. Maury's great-grandfather, James Maury, was appointed by George Washington to be the first U.S. consul to Liverpool, a post he held for forty years. Many of the other Maury family members had scientific backgrounds. The hydrographer and meteorologist Commodore Matthew Fontaine Maury was a cousin, and Carlotta's father edited many revisions of his treatises. Maury's elder sister, **Antonia Maury**, had a distinguished career as a research astronomer at the Harvard Observatory, classifying the spectra of stars. Carlotta's grandfather on her mother's side was the physicist John William Draper.

Maury displayed an early interest in zoology and geology. She attended Radcliffe College for a year, then spent three years at Cornell University, graduating in 1896 with a bachelor of philosophy degree. She received the Schuyler Fellowship for graduate research from Cornell, studied at the University of Paris for two years, then received a Ph.D. degree from Cornell in 1902, with a thesis titled "A Comparison of the Oligocene of Western Europe and the Southern United States."

Maury also studied at Columbia University and from 1904 through 1906 was an assistant in the department of paleontology there. From 1907 through 1909 she was a geologist for the Louisiana state geological survey, preparing reports on the region's petroleum and rock salt deposits. From 1909 through 1912 she lectured in geology at Barnard College, accepting only a token salary for her services. From 1912 through 1915 she was professor of geology and zoology at Huguenot College of the University of the Cape of Good Hope, South Africa.

Maury was a paleontologist for the Venezuelan geological expedition headed by Arthur Clifford Veatch conducted from 1910 to 1911. In 1916, as a Sarah Berliner Fellow, she organized and conducted the Maury expedition to the Dominican Republic. In addition to her paleontological work for the Royal Dutch Petroleum Company and the Brazilian government, Maury provided reports to New York City's American Museum of Natural History. Her specialty was the study of South American and West Indian stratigraphy and fossil fauna. Maury was known to have a sparkling personality, to enjoy philosophical discussions, and to sprinkle her prolific writings with humor and poetic charm.

Maury was a fellow of the American Association for the Advancement of Science, the Geological Society of America, and the American Geographical Society, and a corresponding member of the Brazilian Academy of Sciences. She never married. In 1936 she moved from Hastings-on-Hudson to Yonkers, New York, and she died January 3, 1938, at her home in Yonkers.

SELECTED WRITINGS BY MAURY:

Periodicals

"The Soldado Rock Section," *Science,* Volume 82, 1935, pp. 192–193.

SOURCES:

Books

The National Cyclopedia of American Biography, Volume 28, White, 1940, pp. 25–26.

Periodicals

"Miss C. J. Maury, Paleontologist," *New York Times,* January 4, 1938, p. 23.

—*Sketch by Jill Carpenter*

John Maynard Smith
1920-
English biologist

John Maynard Smith has utilized his expertise in various disciplines, including mathematics, biology, engineering, and ecology, to study the mechanics of evolution from a behavioral standpoint. His research in the 1980s concentrated on adapting game theory (the study of the dynamics of the outcome of conflict) to what he called evolutionary stable strategy (ESS). Later research sought to explain evolution as a process of an "adaptive landscape" in which organisms with the most desirable genotypes survive and contribute to evolutionary change. Maynard Smith began his professional career as a lecturer at University College, London, and later became a professor of biology and dean of the school of biological sciences at the University of Sussex in England.

Born in London on June 1, 1920, to Sidney Maynard and Isobel Mary (Pitman) Smith, John Maynard Smith developed a passionate interest in animals and birdwatching as a young child. His father, a surgeon, died when Maynard Smith was eight, and he moved with his family to the south of England to be with his mother's family until he was sent to boarding school.

As a teenager Maynard Smith attended Eton, though he never cared much for the school. His early education lacked sufficient training in science but allowed him to develop extensive mathematical abilities that he later applied to biology. Ironically, the gaps in Maynard Smith's early training helped shape his later career as a scientist. In a short autobiography in D. A. Dewsbury's *Leaders in the Study of Animal Behavior,* Maynard Smith commented, "My knowledge of science at the age of eighteen, and, indeed, until I was almost thirty, consisted in an excellent training in solving problems—including problems in applied mathematics, which in those days meant Newtonian mechanics—and a fair understanding of some of the more fundamental theoretical ideas in physics. It included no practical or experimental work, and no chemistry or geology."

At age sixteen, miserable and lonely at Eton, Maynard Smith began to channel his energy into studying biology, particularly the work of Charles Darwin and British biologist **John Burdon Sanderson Haldane**, a former Eton student himself who was not highly regarded by the teachers at the school. Fascinated by the work of Haldane, Maynard Smith sought out every one of his books in Eton's library. Haldane, whose thinking blended the abstract and the specific, became a major influence in Maynard Smith's work. Faced with a problem, be it the action of enzymes, the progress of evolution, or protection against air raids, Haldane made mathematical models to provide concrete illustrations of his conclusions. Unaware at the age of eighteen that one could earn a living in biology and unwilling to enter his grandfather's stock brokerage firm, Maynard Smith entered Cambridge to study engineering. Around that time he also became active in politics and joined the Communist party, an affiliation he did not sever until 1956. Thus, he spent more time at Cambridge engaged in political activity than he did studying.

In 1941, the same year he got married, he obtained a bachelor of arts degree in engineering from Cambridge University. Until 1947 he worked in aircraft design, a pursuit that increased his problem-solving skills and allowed him to perform massive numerical calculations with nothing more than a slide rule, an ability rare among biologists.

In 1947 he entered the University College of London, where his earliest influence, John Haldane, was a professor, and within several years Maynard Smith received a bachelor of science degree in zoology. It was during these years that he developed the interest in evolution that has dominated his career. Following his graduation, Maynard Smith became a lecturer, and later a reader, at the college. Many of his publications from this era are rooted in the teaching he received from Haldane and his wife, Helen Spurway, on genetics, ecology, and systematics (the classification of animals and plants into categories by characteristics).

Research Explores the Theory of Natural Selection

Most of Maynard Smith's research has focused on three problems: the evolution and physiology of aging, the evolution of sex and breeding systems, and the evolution of behavior. He was attracted to these areas because they seemed to contradict the theory of natural selection. Natural selection refers to Darwin's theory of evolution, the process by which members of

a species become best-fitted for their environments. According to the theory, organisms with genetic variations that are favorable to their environments should survive in order to pass the desirable traits on to subsequent generations. Accumulated variations over generations can result in descendants different from their ancestors.

From 1951 to about 1965, Maynard Smith spent most of his time on experimental work with *Drosophila subobscura*, a fly ideal for heredity experiments because of its short life cycle and high rate of reproduction. He left theoretical work to his colleague Haldane, who solved those types of problems faster. Focusing on a central issue in ecology in the 1960s— the regulation of the number of individuals in a population—Maynard Smith set out to learn why most eggs produced by inbred lines of *D. subobscura* failed to hatch. One possible explanation for the failure was that the female had not mated.

Based on his observations, Maynard Smith asserted that a side-to-side dance of the females enabled them to distinguish between males. Untrained in the mind set of ethologists, who usually explained differences among animals observed in natural contexts as differences in motivation, Maynard Smith concluded that the males did not mate because, despite their best efforts, they were unable to keep up with the females. In other words, he offered a functional (work- or performance-related) explanation for the selective processes responsible for evolution by assuming that the males were unable to mate, not that they did not want to mate.

In 1965 Haldane left for India, and Maynard Smith left London to become the first dean of biological sciences at the new University of Sussex in Brighton. Since the administrative work of a dean was incompatible with the daily routines of experiments and since he was confident that he could contribute to evolutionary theory, Maynard Smith switched from experimental to mathematical and theoretical work.

Maynard Smith developed a new interest in 1970 when he spent three months at the University of Chicago studying mathematical biology. Influenced by a paper written by George Price, Maynard Smith became intrigued by the recently derived concept of game theory. Game theory is the mathematical study of games or abstract models of conflict situations with a goal of arriving at an optimal policy or strategy.

Price's paper contradicted the accepted notion that fighting behavior benefits a species. Instead, he suggested that animals often refrained from escalating a fight because their opponents might retaliate. Maynard Smith incorporated this idea into his ESS theory and applied it to conflict situations. Since 1970 Maynard Smith has sought to clarify the concept of evolutionary game theory in order to apply it to specific problems and thus extend the range of the ESS concept.

A January 13, 1990, *Science News* article entitled "Taking Proteins for a Walk" described Maynard Smith's other main research interest. In 1970 he contributed to a concept formulated by evolutionary theorist **Sewall Wright** in the 1930s, which suggested that evolution occurs in an "adaptive landscape."

An adaptive landscape in an environment in which organisms survive to the extent that they have acquired adaptive traits. These traits are based on specific collections of genes or genotypes. (Genotype refers to an organism's genetic constitution with respect to one gene or a few genes relevant in a particular context.)

Wright proposed making a map of the range of possible genotypes in which neighboring genotypes differed by a single mutation (an abrupt change not due to a routine recombination of genetic material). Fitness values associated with the differences produced a detailed landscape that charted the organism's evolutionary changes. Such a map might show what happens over time when an animal such as the giraffe develops a progressively longer neck in a struggle with other species for ground-level food.

Maynard Smith extended the idea of adaptive landscapes to what he called "protein space," a mathematical model whose points represent particular sequences of proteins built by the twenty amino acids that serve as the proteins' building blocks. Arrangements that differ by a single amino acid are represented by adjacent points in space. Each point is given a fitness value in accordance with the work it does. The points and their fitness values create a landscape that demonstrates the relationship between a protein's structure and its function.

Maynard Smith has received many awards. In 1977 he was elected a fellow of the Royal Society and a foreign member of the American Academy of Arts and Sciences. In 1982 he became a foreign member of the American Philosophical Society, and in 1982 a foreign associate of the U.S. National Academy of Sciences. He has been awarded honorary degrees by the University of Kent, Oxford University, the University of Chicago, and the University of Sussex. In 1986 he was given the Darwin Medal; in 1990, the Frink Medal of the Zoological Society of London; and in 1991 the Balzan Prize.

Married for more than fifty years, Maynard Smith and his wife have two sons, a daughter, and grandchildren. He collects flowers, is an enthusiastic gardener, and remains an avid birdwatcher.

SELECTED WRITINGS BY MAYNARD SMITH:

Books

The Theory of Evolution, Penguin, 1958.

Mathematical Ideas in Biology, Cambridge University Press, 1968.
The Evolution of Sex, Cambridge University Press, 1978.
Evolution and the Theory of Games, Cambridge University Press, 1983.
"In Haldane's Footsteps," in *Leaders in the Study of Animal Behavior*, edited by D. A. Dewsbury, Bucknell University Press, 1985, pp. 347–354.
Evolutionary Genetics, Oxford University Press, 1989.

SOURCES:

Periodicals

Amato, Ivan, "Taking Proteins for a Walk: Mathematical Mountains Offer Sweeping Views of Evolution," *Science News*, January 13, 1990, pp. 26–27.

—*Sketch by Margaret DiCanio*

Ernst Mayr
1904-
German-born American biologist

Considered one of the century's most important evolutionary biologists, Ernst Mayr has made major contributions to ornithology, evolutionary theory, and the history and philosophy of biology. He is best known for his work on speciation—how one species arises from another. In his more than sixty years in the United States, however, he has published hundreds of articles and more than a dozen books. Through these writings, he has not only clarified certain aspects of earlier scientific theories but proposed new theories which have changed the course of biological research.

Mayr was born on July 5, 1904, in Kempten, Germany, near the borders of Austria and Switzerland. He was one of three sons of Helene Pusinelli Mayr and Otto Mayr, who was a judge. As a boy, Mayr enjoyed bird watching. He received a broad education, including Latin and Greek. In 1923, he followed in the footsteps of several physicians in his family and began studying for a medical degree at the University of Greifswald. Within two years, however, he had become so enthralled with the evolutionary

Ernst Mayr

theories and the exploratory voyages of nineteenth-century British naturalist Charles Darwin that he switched from medicine to zoology. He moved to the University of Berlin, where he had once worked at the zoological museum during his summer vacations. In 1926, he received his Ph.D. in zoology, *summa cum laude* from the university. Soon afterward, he became the zoological museum's assistant curator.

Leads Expeditions to New Guinea and the Solomon Islands

While still working at the museum, Mayr went to Budapest in 1928 to attend a zoological conference. There he met Lionel Walter Rothschild, a British baron and well-known zoologist. Impressed by the young man, Lord Rothschild asked him to lead an ornithological expedition to Dutch New Guinea, in the southwest Pacific. Mayr jumped at the chance. New Guinea at that time was extremely inaccessible, but Mayr was eager to investigate the birds of several remote mountain ranges. The trip was not easy, and Mayr's party suffered a variety of illnesses and injuries. But Mayr was undaunted and he decided to remain in the region, making a second expedition sponsored by the University of Berlin to mountain ranges in the Mandated Territory of New Guinea. Then in 1929 and 1930, Mayr participated in a third expedition, the American Museum of Natural History's Whitney South Sea Expedition to the Solomon Islands. The experiences and insights crowded into

these few years in the south Pacific were to stimulate Mayr's thinking about biology and the development of species for decades to come.

When the expedition to the Solomons was over, Mayr was invited to be a Whitney research associate in ornithology at the American Museum of Natural History in New York City. In 1932, he was named associate curator of the museum's bird collection and he decided to stay in the United States, eventually becoming an American citizen. Over the next decade, Mayr worked at identifying and classifying bird species, studying their geographical distribution and relationships. These years resulted in two of his most influential books.

He published the first of these books in 1941, the *List of New Guinea Birds.* This book is much more complex than its title might imply; it explores the ways closely related species can be distinguished from one another and how variations can arise within a species. In a short article in *Science,* Stephen Jay Gould calls each species Mayr discusses in this book "a separate puzzle, a little exemplar of scientific methodology." In writing the *List of New Guinea Birds,* Gould observes, Mayr "sharpened his notion of species as fundamental units in nature and deepened his understanding of evolution."

Proposes Theory of Geographic Speciation

While most biologists in the 1930s and 1940s accepted the broad premise of Darwin's theory about evolution—that species change and evolve through a process called natural selection, sometimes loosely called "the survival of the fittest"—there was little understanding of how the process worked. If the fittest members of an animal population were the ones that survived, where did those especially well adapted creatures come from in the first place? These questions were complicated during this period by the fact that there was no clear understanding of exactly what constituted a plant or animal species. Instead, there were two conflicting approaches: one school of thought tried to classify species by their shape and appearance, and another tried to identify species through their genes.

In December 1939, Mayr attended a lecture series at Yale University given by a well-known geneticist named **Richard Goldschmidt**, who argued that new species can arise through sudden genetic mutation. Goldschmidt believed that these changes could take place within a single generation, and Mayr was appalled by what he heard. As Fred Hapgood explained in *Science 84,* "What Mayr heard in those lectures seemed so wrong that he decided, in his own words, to 'eliminate' those ideas 'from the panorama of evolutionary controversies.'" Mayr was convinced that extremely long periods of time were required for the development of a new species, and he set out to demolish Goldschmidt's argument.

The result was *Systematics and the Origin of Species,* which he published in 1942. Based partly on what he had learned in the South Pacific, Mayr argued that geographic speciation is the basic process behind the formation of new species. This theory had been advanced more than a hundred years earlier—even before Darwin—but it had never taken hold. Mayr showed how the process works: when a few animals become separated from their original population and breed among themselves over a great many generations, they eventually change so much that they can no longer breed with their original group. For example, birds from the mainland who once settled on an island may look like their ancestors and will have many similar genetic traits, yet the two groups will not be able to interbreed. The island birds have then become a new species. This concept, which Mayr gradually elaborated, was to form the core of his thinking.

Mayr's ideas about speciation not only found general acceptance but won him great respect. *Systematics and the Origin of Species* has been called the "bible" of a generation of biologists. E. O. Wilson remembers how in this book Mayr offered him the "theoretical framework on which to hang facts and plan enterprises" as reported in *Science 84.* Wilson continued, "He gave taxonomy an evolutionary perspective. He got the show on the road."

Accepts Professorship at Harvard

Over the next several years, Mayr continued to expand and refine his ideas about speciation. In 1946, he founded the Society for the Study of Evolution, becoming its first secretary and later its president. In 1947, he founded the Society's journal, *Evolution,* and served as its first editor. In 1953, at the age of forty-nine, he was named Alexander Agassiz Professor of Zoology at Harvard. From 1961 to 1970, he was director of Harvard's Museum of Comparative Zoology, and during those years he brought about an important expansion of the museum, which is now a major center of biological research. By this time, Mayr was recognized as a leader of what has been called "the modern synthetic theory of evolution." In this context, he is often mentioned with three other eminent researchers in the field: **George Gaylord Simpson**, **Theodosius Dobzhansky**, and **Julian Huxley**. In 1963, Mayr published *Animal Species and Evolution,* in which he wrote of man's place in the ecosystem.

In a 1983 interview with Carol A. Johmann in *Omni,* Mayr discussed many of the concerns he has expressed throughout his career: "Man must realize that he is part of the ecosystem and that his own survival depends on not destroying that ecosystem."

But Mayr remained pessimistic about the future of the human race. Implicit in his work is the firm belief that animal species, including the human one, do not improve toward some higher state as they evolve; they merely adapt to changing conditions. And though it might someday be possible to alter the human race by manipulating its genetic structure, Mayr found this idea not only morally offensive but futile, since even with scientific advances there can never be any agreement about which genes are worth manipulating.

Still, Mayr has said, all this does not mean that humankind cannot improve, but improvement must be through education and cultural advances. Writing in *Scientific American* in 1978, Mayr pointed out that it is cultural evolution, not genetic changes, which has permitted the human species to fly more powerfully than birds, bats, or insects. He explained that cultural evolution "is a uniquely human process by which man to some extent shapes and adapts to his environment. . . . Cultural evolution is a much more rapid process than biological evolution."

Life's Work Culminates in Balzan Prize

In 1975, Mayr retired from Harvard as emeritus professor of zoology. But he continued to work intensely and his interests continued to expand. He changed careers, as Stephen Jay Gould has observed; from a scientist he became a historian of science. He undertook to write not only about evolution, but also about the entire history of biology. In 1982, he published *The Growth of Biological Thought,* intended to be the first of two volumes. Then in 1991, at the age of eighty-seven, he published yet another carefully wrought discussion of evolution, *One Long Argument.* In that book, he wrote, "The basic theory of evolution has been confirmed so completely that modern biologists consider evolution simply a fact. . . . Where evolutionists today differ from Darwin is almost entirely on matters of emphasis. While Darwin was fully aware of the probabilistic nature of selection, the modern evolutionist emphasizes this even more. The modern evolutionist realizes how great a role chance plays in evolution."

Mayr married Margarete Simon on May 4, 1935, and they had two daughters. For many years, Mayr was a familiar figure around Harvard, a lean man with brown eyes and white hair. Many people noted that Mayr's natural assertiveness and strong writing style added to the weight of his arguments, helping to win over others. During an exceptionally long career, Mayr was awarded ten honorary degrees, including Doctor of Science degrees from both Oxford and Cambridge Universities and a Doctor of Philosophy degree from the University of Paris. In 1954, he was elected to the National Academy of Sciences. His numerous prizes include the Darwin-Wallace Medal in 1958, the Linnean Medal in 1977, the Gregor

Mendel medal in 1980, and the Darwin Medal of the Royal Society in 1987. In 1983, he received the Balzan Prize, which has been called the equivalent of the Nobel Prize in the biological sciences. Commenting on Mayr's winning the Balzan Prize in the article in *Science,* Stephen Jay Gould called Mayr "our greatest living evolutionary biologist."

SELECTED WRITINGS BY MAYR:

Books

List of New Guinea Birds, American Museum of Natural History, 1941.
Systematics and the Origin of Species, Columbia University Press, 1942.
Animal Species and Evolution, Belknap Press- Harvard University Press, 1963.
Evolution and the Diversity of Life, Belknap Press- Harvard University Press, 1976.
The Growth of Biological Thought, Belknap Press- Harvard University Press, 1982.
One Long Argument, Harvard University Press, 1991.

Periodicals

"Evolution," *Scientific American,* September, 1978, pp. 47–55.

SOURCES:

Periodicals

Gould, Stephen Jay, "Balzan Prize to Ernst Mayr," *Science,* January 20, 1984, pp. 255–257.
Hapgood, Fred, "The Importance of Being Ernst," *Science 84,* June, 1984, pp. 40–46.
"Interview: Ernst Mayr," *Omni,* February, 1983, pp. 73–78, 118–119.

—*Sketch by Wallace Mack White*

Walter S. McAfee
1914-

American astrophysicist

Walter S. McAfee is best known as the mathematician for the U.S. Army's Project Diana. As mathematician for the project, he was responsible for making the essential calculations that led to the first human contact with the moon: a radar signal sent in January 1946.

Walter Samuel McAfee was born in Ore City, Texas, on September 2, 1914. He was the second of nine children born to Luther F. McAfee, a carpenter, and Susie A. Johnson McAfee. He received a bachelor's degree from Wiley College in 1934 and earned an M.S. from Ohio State in 1937. Unable to afford further graduate work, McAfee turned to teaching, and from 1939 to 1942 he taught physics at Champion Junior High School in Columbus, Ohio. There he met Viola Winston, a French teacher, whom he married in 1941; they have two daughters. In 1946 McAfee was awarded a Rosenwald fellowship and enrolled in the doctoral program at Cornell University. There he studied with theoretical physicist **Hans Bethe**, receiving a doctorate in physics from Cornell in 1949.

In May 1942, McAfee joined the theoretical studies unit of the Electronics Research Command, part of the U.S. Army's Signal Corps at Fort Monmouth, New Jersey. A civilian physicist, he remained with the group in various capacities for more than forty years, studying and experimenting in theoretical nuclear physics and electromagnetic theory, quantum optics, and laser holography. From 1958 to 1975 he also taught graduate and undergraduate courses at nearby Monmouth College as a lecturer in nuclear physics and electronics. He retired in 1985.

Project Diana Pioneers Space Communications

Project Diana was an effort to bounce a radar signal off the moon's surface. It was not known at the time if a high-frequency radio signal could penetrate the Earth's ionosphere or stratosphere. Early experiments with low- and medium-frequency radio waves had failed. In sending a signal, Project Diana scientists needed to account accurately for the moon's speed, which varies from 750 miles per hour slower than the earth's rotation to 750 miles per hour faster. As mathematician for the project, McAfee made the necessary calculations. On January 10, 1946, a radar pulse was sent through a special forty-foot square antenna toward the moon. Two and a half seconds later, a faint radar echo was heard, and Project Diana was recorded a success. Made public two weeks later by the Signal Corps, the experiment provided an important breakthrough in space exploration, establishing that communication was possible across the enormous distances of outer space.

The official news report of the accomplishment did not include McAfee's name, nor give any hint of the role he had played. Public recognition did not come until twenty-five years later, at the anniversary of Project Diana in 1971. Since then, however, he has been honored by the Stevens Institute of Technology and by Wiley College, which in 1982 inducted

McAfee into its Science Hall of Fame, founded to inspire students to excel in the sciences. In an interview at the time, quoted in *ERADCOM Currents,* he said, "If the [Hall of Fame] program bears fruit, and if my presence helped in some small way, then that shall have been reward enough." McAfee subsequently established a math and physical science fellowship at Wiley College to encourage minority students in math and science. He is a member of the American Association for the Advancement of Science, the American Astronomy Society, the American Physical Society, the American Association of Physics Teachers, and is a senior member of the Institute of Electrical and Electronics Engineers. He and his wife live in South Belmar, New Jersey.

SELECTED WRITINGS BY MCAFEE:

Periodicals

"Determination of Energy Spectra of Backscattered Electrons by Use of Everhart's Theory," *Journal of Applied Physics,* Volume 47, number 3, 1976, pp. 1179–1184.

(With others) "Electron Backscattering from Solids and Double Layers," *Journal of Vacuum Science Technology,* Volume 13, number 4, 1976, pp. 843–847.

SOURCES:

Periodicals

Gould, Jack, "Contact with Moon Achieved by Radar in Test by the Army," *New York Times,* January 25, 1946, pp. 1, 19.

"McAfee Named to Wiley's Science Hall of Fame," *ERADCOM Currents,* May, 1982.

"Original Participants Mark Diana's 25th Anniversary," *Army Research and Development Newsmagazine,* January/February, 1971.

Other

McAfee, Walter S., interview with F. C. Nicholson conducted on February 9, 1994.

—*Sketch by F. C. Nicholson*

John McCarthy
1927-
American computer scientist

John McCarthy coined the term artificial intelligence (AI) and is recognized as the father of AI research. He founded two of the most important AI laboratories in the world and wrote the primary computer programming language for AI research, List Processing Language (LISP). While his quest for an intelligent machine has yet to be fulfilled, his work in computers has produced a number of other important advances, including interactive time-sharing, computer semantics, and one of the first proposals to link home computers to a public network.

A Red Diaper Baby

The oldest of two brothers, McCarthy was born in Boston, Massachusetts, on September 4, 1927. His father, John Patrick McCarthy, was an Irish immigrant and working-class militant. His mother, Ida Glatt, was a Jewish Lithuanian active in the suffrage movement. Both were members of the Communist party in the 1930s, so McCarthy is what is known among political activists as a "red diaper" baby. John Patrick McCarthy worked as a carpenter, a fisherman, a union organizer, and also as an inventor. He held two patents, one for a ship caulking machine and the other for a hydraulic orange juice squeezer. Young John McCarthy and his brother Patrick were raised to think politically and logically, and although McCarthy eventually decided that Marxism was hardly scientific, he never renounced science, logic, or politics.

McCarthy was a bookish lad whose health problems eventually spurred his family's move to Los Angeles. He attended public school and skipped three grades before entering the California Institute of Technology (Cal Tech) in 1944 with plans to become a mathematician. After several interruptions, including a stint as an army clerk, he graduated in 1948. From Cal Tech, McCarthy went to Princeton University, where he earned his doctorate in mathematics and took his first academic job as an instructor in mathematics in 1951. Two years later he became an acting assistant professor of mathematics at Stanford University before moving to Dartmouth College in 1955. While at Dartmouth in the summer of 1956, he was the principle organizer of the first conference on modeling intelligence in computers and coined the term artificial intelligence for the conference proposal. McCarthy was working on a chess-playing computer program at the time. In order to limit the moves the computer had to consider, McCarthy invented a search strategy and mathematical method that is now called the alpha-beta heuristic, which allowed the computer to eliminate any moves that permit the computer's opponent to quickly gain an advantage.

Invents a Language Used Around the World

In 1958 McCarthy moved to the Massachusetts Institute of Technology (MIT), where he became an associate professor and founded the first AI laboratory. It was here that McCarthy constructed the computer programming language called List Processing Language, or LISP, which is still the most common computer language used in AI research. He also began work on the idea of giving a computer "common sense"—a difficult problem that became the focus of many AI researchers in the late 1980s—and developed the first means of interactive time-sharing on computers which allows hundreds, or even thousands of people, to use one large computer at the same time. During his tenure at MIT, McCarthy married for the first time and had the first of his two daughters, Susan Joanne. In 1962 he moved his family to Stanford to take up a professorship in computer science and start a second AI laboratory. He has two other children, Sarah Kathleen and Timothy Talcott.

While at Stanford McCarthy continued to contribute to AI research in a number of ways, from mentoring many of the best young scientists in the field, to clarifying the different roles played by mathematical logic and common sense (called non-monotonic reasoning by McCarthy) in AI. But his greatest contribution has been in the area of artificial languages, especially semantics. Philip J. Hilts, in his book *Scientific Temperaments,* quotes one mathematician on LISP: "The new expansion of man's view of the nature of mathematical objects, made possible by LISP, is exciting. There appears to be no limit to the diversity of problems to which LISP will be applied. It seems to be a truly general language, with commensurate computing power." In addition, McCarthy has speculated on machines that could make copies of themselves (automata) as well as artificial intelligence smarter than its creator.

McCarthy's adventurous impulses have not been confined to academic speculations. He has been a rock climber, a pilot, and he has even made a dozen parachute jumps. After McCarthy's first marriage ended in divorce in the 1960s, he married Vera Watson, a computer programmer and a world-class mountain climber. She was the first woman to solo the 22,800-foot Aconcagua peak in the Andes, and for a number of years she and McCarthy climbed lesser peaks together. Tragically, Watson died while a member of the women's expedition attempting to scale Annapurna peak in the Himalayas.

Calls for an Electronic Bill of Rights

Politics have always been important to McCarthy, as they were to his parents. While he has called himself a reactionary because of his rejection of Marxism, in many ways his views defy simple categories. In the 1960s he was involved in many political campaigns and projects, such as the Free University in Palo Alto, California, but he eventually became disillusioned by the methods of some of the leftist groups with which he worked. Still, he felt that his own work on computer technology could benefit democracy by allowing people easy access to information. The danger of authoritarian control over computer technology led him to propose an extension of the Bill of Rights to cover electronic data and communications, an idea that became part of the national debate on computer networks in the 1990s. Specifically, McCarthy called for limiting control of public data files and allowing each person the right to read, correct, and limit access to his or her own files.

In 1971 McCarthy won the prestigious Alan Mathison Turing Award from the Association for Computing Machinery, of which he is a member. In addition, he is a former president of the American Association for Artificial Intelligence. He also received the Kyoto Prize in 1988 and the National Medal of Science in 1990. In 1987 he assumed the Charles M. Pigott chair of the Stanford University School of Engineering and became a professor in Stanford's Computer Science Department and director of the Stanford Artificial Intelligence Laboratory.

McCarthy has argued that making artificially intelligent robots that are more intelligent than human beings is quite possible, since (according to McCarthy) intelligence is made up of logic and common sense that can be mathematically represented. Despite his optimism in the goal of constructing intelligent machines, McCarthy has been one of the most rigorous critics of AI research. In a survey conducted in the 1970s and reprinted in his collection of essays, *Formalizing Common Sense,* McCarthy concluded that "artificial intelligence research has so far been only moderately successful; its rate of solid progress is perhaps greater than most social sciences and less than many physical sciences. This is perhaps to be expected, considering the difficulty of the problem."

SELECTED WRITINGS BY MCCARTHY:

Books

Information: A Scientific American Book, W. H. Freeman, 1966.
Formalizing Common Sense: Papers by John McCarthy, edited by Vladimir Lifschitz, Ablex Publishing Corporation, 1990.

SOURCES:

Books

Graubard, Stephen R., editor, *The Artificial Intelligence Debate: False Starts, Real Foundations,* MIT Press, 1988.

Hilts, Philip J., *Scientific Temperaments: Three Lives in Contemporary Science,* Simon & Schuster, 1982.

—*Sketch by Chris Hables Gray*

Maclyn McCarty
1911-
American bacteriologist

Maclyn McCarty is a distinguished bacteriologist who has done important work on the biology of streptococci and the origins of rheumatic fever, but he is best known for his involvement in early experiments which established the function of DNA. In collaboration with **Oswald Avery** and **Colin Munro MacLeod**, McCarty identified DNA as the substance which controls heredity in living cells. The three men published an article describing their experiment in 1944, and their work opened the way for further studies in bacteriological physiology, the most important of which was the demonstration of the chemical structure of DNA by **James Watson** and **Francis Crick** in 1953.

McCarty was born on June 9, 1911, in South Bend, Indiana. His father worked for the Studebaker Corporation and the family moved often, with McCarty attending five schools in three different cities by the time he reached the sixth grade. In his autobiographical book, *The Transforming Principle,* McCarty recalled the experience as positive, believing that moving so often made him an inquisitive and alert child. He spent a year at Culver Academy in Indiana from 1925 to 1926, and he finished high school in Kenosha, Wisconsin. His family moved to Portland, Oregon, and McCarty attended Stanford University in California. He majored in biochemistry under James Murray Luck, who was then launching the *Annual Review of Biochemistry.* McCarty presented public seminars on topics derived from articles submitted to this publication, and he graduated with a B.A. in 1933.

Although Luck asked him to remain at Stanford, McCarty entered medical school at Johns Hopkins in Baltimore in 1933. Although McCarty had lived all over the country, he was initially uncomfortable on the East Coast, suffering from what he later described as "culture shock." He was married during medical school days, and he spent a summer of research at the Mayo Clinic in Minnesota. After graduation, McCarty spent three years working in pediatric medicine at the Johns Hopkins Hospital. Even in the decade before penicillin, new chemotherapeutic agents had begun to change infectious disease therapy. He treated children suffering from pneumococcal pneumonia, and he was able to save a child suffering from a streptococcal infection, then almost uniformly fatal, by the use of the newly available sulfonamide antibacterials. Both of these groups of bacteria, the streptococci and the pneumococci, would play important roles throughout the remainder of McCarty's career.

McCarty spent his first full year of medical research at New York University in 1940, in the laboratory of W. S. Tillett. In 1941, McCarty was awarded a National Research Council grant, and Tillett recommended him for a position with Oswald Avery at the Rockefeller Institute, which was one of the most important centers of biomedical research in the United States. For many years, Avery had been working with Colin Munro MacLeod on pneumococci. In 1928, the British microbiologist **Frederick Griffith** had discovered what he called a "transforming principle" in pneumococci. In a series of experiments now considered a turning point in the history of genetics, Griffith had established that living individuals of one strain or variety of pneumococci could be changed into another, with different characteristics, by the application of material taken from dead individuals of a second strain. When McCarty joined Avery and MacLeod, the chemical nature of this transforming material was not known, and this was what their experiments were designed to discover.

Identifying the "Transforming Principle" as DNA

In an effort to determine the chemical nature of Griffith's transforming principle, McCarty began as more of a lab assistant than an equal partner. Avery and MacLeod had decided that the material belonged to one of two classes of organic compounds: it was either a protein or a nucleic acid. They were predisposed to think it was a protein, or possibly RNA, and their experimental work was based on efforts to selectively disable the ability of this material to transform strains of pneumococci. Evidence that came to light during 1942 indicated that the material was not a protein but a nucleic acid, and it began to seem increasingly possible that DNA was the molecule for which they were searching. McCarty's most important contribution was the preparation of a deoxyribonuclease which disabled the transforming power of the material and established that it was DNA. They achieved these results by May of 1943, but Avery remained cautious, and their work was not published until 1944.

In 1946, McCarty was named head of a laboratory at the Rockefeller Institute which was dedicated to the study of the streptococci. A relative of pneumococci, streptococci is a cause of rheumatic fever. McCarty's research established the important role played by the outer cellular covering of this bacteria. Using some of the same techniques he had used in his work on DNA, McCarty was able to isolate the cell wall of the streptococcus and analyze its structure.

McCarty became a member of the Rockefeller Institute in 1950; he served as vice president of the institution from 1965 to 1978, and as physician in chief from 1965 to 1974. For his work as co-discoverer of the nature of the transforming principle, he won the Eli Lilly Award in Microbiology and Immunology in 1946 and was elected to the National Academy of Sciences in 1963. He won the first Waterford Biomedical Science Award of the Scripps Clinic and Research Foundation in 1977 and received honorary doctorates from Columbia University in 1976 and the University of Florida in 1977.

SELECTED WRITINGS BY MCCARTY:

Books

The Transforming Principle: Discovering That Genes Are Made of DNA, Norton, 1985.

Periodicals

(With Oswald Theodore Avery and Colin M. MacLeod) "Studies on the Chemical Nature of the Substance Inducing Transformation of Pneumococcal Types," *Journal of Experimental Medicine,* Volume 79, 1944, pp. 137–158.
(With S.D. Elliott and R.C Lancefield) "Teichoic Acids of Group D Streptococci with Special Reference to Strains from Pig Meningitis," *Journal of Experimental Medicine,* Volume 145, 1977, pp. 490–499.

SOURCES:

Books

McGraw-Hill Modern Scientists and Engineers, McGraw-Hill, 1980, pp. 259–260.

—*Sketch by Donald J. McGraw*

Barbara McClintock
1902-1992
American geneticist

Barbara McClintock was a pioneering American geneticist whose discovery of transposable or "jumping genes" in the 1940s baffled most of her contemporaries for nearly three decades. A recluse by nature, McClintock spent nearly fifty years working apart from the mainstream of the scientific community. Yet her colleagues had such a high regard for her as an adherent to rigid scientific principles that they accepted her discovery of transposable genes decades before others could confirm her observations. McClintock was eventually awarded the Nobel Prize in medicine or physiology in 1983 for this prescient discovery.

McClintock's childhood years shaped her to be a woman who lived outside of the conventional expectations of both the scientific and secular worlds. The third of four children, she was born on June 16, 1902, in Hartford, Connecticut. Her parents, Thomas Henry McClintock and Sara Handy, were married in 1898. Her father graduated with a medical degree from Boston University shortly after their marriage, but it took him several years to establish a solid and profitable practice. After the birth of the fourth child, her mother began to show emotional strain. McClintock had an adversarial relationship with her mother, and so to relieve some of the tension she was sent off to live with an aunt and uncle in rural Massachusetts. This was an arrangement that continued off and on throughout the early years of her life, and McClintock, characteristically, insisted that she was never homesick while away from her parents. She was happy to roam the outdoors, where she developed a love of nature that was to last a lifetime.

McClintock's differences with her mother continued when she returned home, and she grew to be solitary and independent. Her family moved to Brooklyn, New York in 1908, where her father had obtained a position as a company physician with Standard Oil. Interestingly, this future scientist's father forbade any of his children's teachers to give them homework, regarding six hours a day in school as ample education, and as a result McClintock had plenty of time to pursue outside interests, such as playing the piano and ice skating. An inveterate tomboy, she asked to wear boys' clothes at a young age, a wish her parents granted. Once, a neighbor who saw her playing sports with boys chided McClintock to do girl things; despite her own conventional views of a woman's role in society, Sara quickly called the neighbor and told her never to reprimand her daughter again.

Barbara McClintock

Begins Investigations in Cytology

After graduating from Erasmus High School in Brooklyn, McClintock enrolled at Cornell University in 1919. During her freshman and sophomore years she had a normal college social life, including dating and even playing tenor banjo in a jazz band. Elected president of the freshman class, she was popular among her fellow students and was asked to join a sorority. But when McClintock learned that the sorority would not accept Jewish students, she refused the invitation. This kind of reaction was to be characteristic of McClintock throughout her life. She never hesitated to snub the social conventions of her time, especially those concerning women's role in society. She decided early on to remain an independent, single woman devoted to her work; she had little inclination to marry or start a family.

McClintock became interested in the study of the cells, known as cytology, under the tutelage of Lester Sharp, a professor who gave her private lessons on Saturdays. She exhibited a keen intellect as an undergraduate and was invited to take graduate-level genetics courses while still in her junior year. She received her B.S. in 1923 and entered graduate school, where she majored in cytology and minored in genetics and zoology. At that time, geneticists favored studies of the fruit fly *Drosophila*, which produces a new offspring every ten days. This rapid production of successive generations offered geneticists the opportunity to see quickly the results of genetic traits passed on through crossbreeding. It was studies of

Drosophila that produced much of the early evidence of the relationship between genes and chromosomes. Chromosomes are the strands of biological material seen at the time of cell division, and studies confirmed that they carried the genes that passed hereditary traits from one generation to the next. At Cornell, the main focus of genetic research was corn, or maize, whose varicolored kernels, relatively long life spans, and larger chromosomes (which could be more easily viewed under the microscope) offered geneticists the opportunity to identify specific genetic processes.

While still in graduate school, McClintock had refined and simplified a technique originally developed by John Belling to prepare slides for the study of chromosome structures under a microscope. McClintock made modifications to this technique that enabled her to apply it to detailed chromosomal studies of maize. She obtained her M.A. degree in 1925 and her Ph.D. two years later and then was appointed an instructor in Cornell's botany department. McClintock's research at that time focused on linkage groups, the inherited sets or groups of genes that appear on a chromosome. Geneticists had already discovered these linkage groups in *Drosophila,* and McClintock set out to relate specific linkage groups to specific chromosomes in maize.

Robert A. Emerson, a pioneer in the genetics of maize, was a professor at Cornell at this time, and he was drawing promising young geneticists to the university. Marcus Rhoades, who would become a renowned geneticist in his own right, came to do his graduate work at Cornell and formed an immediate friendship with McClintock that was to last throughout their lives. Years later, in an interview with McClintock's biographer, Evelyn Fox Keller, Rhoades said: "I've known a lot of famous scientists. But the only one I thought was really a genius was McClintock." Other young graduate students migrating to Cornell included **George Beadle**, who went on to win a Nobel Prize for his work in molecular genetics, and Harriet Creighton, who was a student of McClintock's. Together, these young scientists formed the core of a supportive and enthusiastic group of geneticists at Cornell studying the sequences of genes on chromosomes.

In 1931, McClintock and Creighton published a landmark study proving a theory geneticists had previously believed without proof: that a correlation existed between genetic and chromosomal crossover. Their study revealed that genetic information was exchanged during the early stages of meiosis, the process of cell division. They found that this exchange occurred when parts of homologous chromosomes (chromosomes on which particular genes are identically located) were exchanged in the same division that produced sex cells. These experiments were to become recognized as the cornerstone of modern genetic research; Horace Freeland Judson has called them "one of the truly great experiments of modern biology." This groundbreaking work and McClintock's successive studies further establishing this relationship eventually led to her election to the National Academy of Sciences in 1944 and presidency of the Genetics Society of America in 1945.

Works for Many Years without a Permanent Appointment

Despite having achieved worldwide recognition among her colleagues, the 1930s were difficult years for McClintock. The Great Depression had impacted university funding and she found herself in the precarious position of having no stipend from Cornell University and no large grants to support her research. She received a Guggenheim Fellowship in 1933 that enabled her to go to the Kaiser Wilhelm Institute in Berlin, but she left after only a short stay because of her concerns over Hitler's rise to power and his anti-Semitic beliefs. Fortunately, by this time funding had been garnered from the Rockefeller Foundation to help support her efforts. In 1936, she received an appointment to the University of Missouri as an assistant professor of botany, her first faculty appointment. During this time, she performed further experiments delineating the cellular processes of chromosomal interactions, especially their effects on large-scale mutations. Although this appointment provided a secure base for McClintock to continue her work, her relationship with the University of Missouri did not develop. After five years, the university decided that McClintock did not fit into its future plans.

Embarks on Nobel Prize-winning Research

In the following decade, as war dominated much of the world, McClintock had perhaps her most productive years as a geneticist. In the summer before the bombing of Pearl Harbor, Marcus Rhoades obtained an invitation for his out-of-work friend and colleague to spend the summer at the Cold Springs Harbor Laboratory in New York. Run by the Carnegie Institute of Washington, the laboratory was a self-contained facility that had its own summer houses for researchers. On the first of December, 1941, McClintock was offered a one-year position at Cold Springs, where she would spend the remainder of her career. By the summer of 1944, McClintock had initiated the studies that would lead to her discovery of genetic transposition. She had noticed different-colored spots that did not belong on the green or yellow leaves of a particular plant. She surmised that the larger the discoloration patch, the earlier the mutation had occurred, believing that many large patches on the leaves meant the mutation had occurred early in the plant's development. From this observation, McClintock determined that mutations occurred at a con-

stant rate that did not change within a plant's life cycle, which led her to the concept of regulation and control in the passing on of genetic information. Investigating how this passing on of genetic information could be regulated, McClintock next noticed that in addition to these regular mutations there also occurred exceptions, in which there were different types of mutations not normally associated with the plant. Convinced that something must occur at the early stages of meiosis to cause these irregular mutations, McClintock put the full forces of her intellect into identifying what it might be, again working with maize.

McClintock discovered kernels on a self-pollinated ear of corn that had distinctive pigmentation but should have been clear, suggesting a loss of some genetic information that normally would have been passed on to inhibit color. Finally, after two years, she found what she called a controlled breakage in the chromosome, and in 1948 she coined the term "transposition" to describe how an element is released from its original position on the chromosome and inserted into a new position. As a result of this "jumping gene," plant offspring could have an unexpected pattern of heredity due to a specific genetic code that other offspring did not have. In fact, two transposable genes were involved in the process: one, which she called a "dissociator" gene, allowed the release of the "activator" gene, which could then be transposed to a different site.

In 1950, McClintock published her research on transposition, but her work was not well received. Her discovery went against the genetic theory then current that genes were stable components of chromosomes; also, very few of her contemporaries could actually understand her work. It wasn't until the 1970s—when technology had been developed that enabled geneticists to study genes on the molecular, rather than cellular, level—that McClintock's ideas were truly understood by the scientific community. Her discovery presaged many later discoveries, such as genetic imprinting or the "presetting" of genetic activity. Her work also would eventually be used to explain inheritance patterns that seemed to lie outside the strict Mendelian law based on simple ratios of dominant and recessive genes. In 1983, McClintock was awarded the Nobel Prize for physiology or medicine for her discovery of mobile genetic systems.

One of the most intriguing aspects of McClintock's discovery is how she deduced the theory of transposition and proved it while other pioneering geneticists remained in the dark. Some have called her a "prophet" of genetics, and her discovery may have owed much to her ability to have "a feeling for the organism," as she told Evelyn Fox Keller. Forming an intense identification with the plants she studied, McClintock was able to notice the slightest differences, even on a cellular level. Although

McClintock adhered strictly to the scientific method in proving her theories, she told Keller that as scientists she and her colleagues were also "limiting ourselves" by using this method. Interested in Eastern thought and religion, she practiced methods to control her own body temperature and blood flow, and she seemed to some to have the ability to see what was going on in her own mind long before she could prove it.

McClintock spent the remainder of her life at Cold Spring Harbor, studying transposition. Although very private, McClintock could be sociable and she loved to talk about science, philosophy, and art. She was known, at times, to accompany the local children home from the school bus, describing to them the intricacies of nature as they walked. She often complained in her later years that scientists no longer stayed over the summer at Cold Spring Harbor, and she rarely became well acquainted with them. She died on September 2, 1992, shortly after friends had celebrated her ninetieth birthday. She was acknowledged as a true pioneer in every sense of the word, and many of her fellow scientists believe that her accomplishments came from an intense desire for knowledge and the commitment to keep working on a problem. In an obituary in *Nature*, Gerald R. Fink aptly notes that her "burning curiosity, enthusiasm, and uncompromising honesty serve as a constant reminder of what drew us all to science in the first place."

SELECTED WRITINGS BY MCCLINTOCK:

Books

The Control of Gene Action in Maize, Brookhaven Symposia in Biology, 1965.

SOURCES:

Books

Batstein, David, and Nina Federoff, editors, *The Dynamic Genome: Barbara McClintock's Ideas in the Century of Genetics,* Cold Spring Harbor Laboratory Press, 1991.
Judson, Horace Freeland, *The Eighth Day of Creation: Makers of the Revolution in Biology,* Simon and Schuster, 1979, p. 216.
Keller, Evelyn Fox, *A Feeling for the Organism: The Life and Work of Barbara McClintock,* W. H. Freeman, 1983.

Periodicals

Fincham, J. R. S., "Moving with the Times," *Nature,* August 20, 1992, p. 631–632.

Fink, Gerald R., "Barbara McClintock (1902–1992)," *Nature,* September 24, 1992, p. 272.

—*Sketch by David Petechuk*

Elmer Verner McCollum
1879-1967
American biochemist, organic chemist, and nutritionist

Elmer Verner McCollum was a distinguished biochemist, organic chemist, and nutritionist who studied nutrition and its effects on health and metabolism. The discoverer of vitamins A, B and D, McCollum also found the nutritional cause of rickets, a bone disease. His twenty-six years of research at the School of Hygiene and Public Health at the Johns Hopkins Medical School in Baltimore continued his earlier research and made him an authority on how diets lacking certain vitamins or trace minerals can cause diseases. He developed a biological method to analyze foods and popularized the use of rats as an extremely valuable experimental model. By modifying the rats' diets, McCollum produced animals with rickets. Because of these studies, rickets, a disease in which bones become deformed, is virtually nonexistent in developed countries. In a field of research that had few findings of importance for decades, he was instrumental in ushering in a new era.

McCollum, the fourth of five children and the first son, was born on March 3, 1879, near Fort Scott, Kansas, to Cornelius Armstrong McCollum, a farmer believed to be of Scottish descent, and Martha Catherine Kidwell McCollum, the daughter of mountain people also originally from Scotland. McCollum grew up on a farm, and as a child he was very inquisitive, a trait he had all of his life. Oddly enough for a man who would devote his life to researching nutrition and the role vitamins play in having good health, as an infant he suffered from scurvy, a nutritional disease later determined to be caused by the lack of vitamin C. He was cured when his mother fed him apple peels, which contain this vitamin. His parents understood the value of advanced education, and his mother in particular was determined that her children should receive higher education. He attended the University of Kansas in Lawrence, where as a sophomore he became interested in organic chemistry. At the end of his junior year, he was elected to membership in Sigma Xi, the honorary scientific society. He graduated with a baccalaureate degree in 1903 and a master's of arts degree a year later. McCollum continued his education at Yale University in New Haven, Connecticut, and graduated in 1906 with a doctorate in organic chemistry.

Develops Animal Model and Discovers Vitamin A

After an unsuccessful search for a position in the field of organic chemistry, McCollum began to study biochemistry. In 1907 he became an instructor in agricultural chemistry at the Wisconsin Agricultural Experimental Station and quickly rose through the academic ranks, becoming a full professor in 1913. In his early work he performed chemical analyses on the diets of dairy cattle and studied how different diets affected the cows' health and reproductive capacities. However, he thought the procedures were long and tedious in such large animals. Fortuitously, references in scientific journals about using mice in other experiments led him to develop a rat colony for his nutritional research. This was the first rat colony used in the study of nutritional aspects of disease. The rats were fed various diets, each one lacking certain substances. Their short life span quickly enabled McCollum to determine what effect the diets had. This work helped to popularize the use of rats in other experimental situations.

In 1912 McCollum noticed that rats fed a diet deficient in certain fats grew normally again when the fats were added back in. This discovery was the first of a fat-soluble nutrient, which McCollum named vitamin A. Subsequent studies have shown that vitamin A helps makes teeth and bones strong and is necessary for normal vision and healthy skin. McCollum later demonstrated that a water-soluble substance, which he called vitamin B, was also necessary for normal health. He had created the alphabetical nomenclature for vitamins.

Although pleased with his rapid rise at the Wisconsin Agricultural Experimental Station, McCollum felt somewhat restricted in his research. At this time, funds from the Rockefeller Foundation established a School of Hygiene and Public Health at Johns Hopkins Medical School in Baltimore. Highly respected among his peers, McCollum was offered a position as the first faculty member—professor of biochemistry—which he assumed in 1917. He was made emeritus professor in 1945.

Coincidence Leads to Discovery of Rickets

A coincidence led to the discovery for which McCollum is best known: producing rickets in rats. The rats had bending, fractures, and swellings of the ends of the long bones in their legs. But McCollum did not know recognize it as rickets until John Howland, professor of pediatrics at Johns Hopkins

Medical School, stopped by McCollum's office to inquire whether anyone had ever produced rickets in rats. After McCollum described his rats, he and Howland concluded the rats had rickets. The discovery threw new light on the disease. McCollum identified the missing factor in the rats' diets that resulted in rickets, which he named vitamin D. (Another researcher had discovered a different vitamin, so *C* was taken.) Vitamin D aids in the absorption of calcium, which is used in bones and teeth, and is found in fortified milk, fish such as tuna and sardines, dairy products, and egg yolks. It also is formed in the body when a person is exposed to sunlight. Because of this discovery, people changed their diets to include vitamin D, and now rickets is rare in most developed countries. Some of McCollum's research efforts focused on trace elements, simple substances essential to life in very small quantities. Through his research he started to isolate these substances. McCollum showed that a deficiency of calcium eventually would produce muscular spasms. Other trace elements he focused on include fluorine, zinc, and manganese.

In addition to his laboratory research, McCollum lectured widely about progress and problems in nutritional studies. In 1923 he started writing articles for the popular press in *McCall's* magazine. In honor of his outstanding contributions in the field of nutrition, he received many awards. He was a member of numerous national and international organizations devoted to public health, including the international committee on vitamin standards of the League of Nations in 1931, the food and nutrition board of the National Research Council starting in 1942, and the World Health Organization. In 1948 the McCollum-Pratt Institute was created at Johns Hopkins for the study of trace elements. Years after his retirement in 1946, he remained actively interested in nutrition and related health fields and published the comprehensive book *A History of Nutrition* in 1957. He died in Baltimore, Maryland, November 15, 1967.

SELECTED WRITINGS BY MCCOLLUM:

Books

(With Elsa Orent-Keiles and Harry G. Day) *The Newer Knowledge of Nutrition,* 5th edition, Macmillan, 1939.
A History of Nutrition, Houghton, 1957.
From Kansas Farm Boy to Scientist: The Autobiography of Elmer Verner McCollum, University of Kansas Press, 1964.

Periodicals

"Fifty Years of Progress in Nutritional Research," *Scientific Monthly,* 1950, pp. 376–379.

SOURCES:

Books

Biographical Memoirs of Fellows of the Royal Society, Volume 15, Royal Society, 1969, pp. 159–171.

Day, Harry G., *Biographical Memoirs,* National Academy of Science, 1974, pp. 263–335.

—*Sketch by Barbara J. Prouian*

Harden McConnell

Harden McConnell
1927-
American chemist

Harden McConnell is known for his innovative work dealing with nuclear magnetic resonance (NMR). He created his namesake equation, the McConnell Relation, in the late–1950s; the equation has proved beneficial in studying atomic and molecular structure. He also introduced the technique of spin labeling that has aided scientists in identifying the motion and location of molecules, and he has used the procedure to research several subjects including the relationship of antibodies and antigens in immune systems. His more recent work has used silicone technology to detect changes within human cells.

Harden Marsden McConnell was born to George and Frances (Coffee) McConnell in Richmond, Virginia, on July 18, 1927. He attended George Washington University, where he majored in chemistry and minored in mathematics. After receiving his B.S. degree in 1947, McConnell enrolled at the California Institute of Technology where he earned a Ph.D. in chemistry, with a minor in physics, in 1951. After completing a two-year National Research Council fellowship at the University of Chicago in 1952 with **Robert S. Mulliken** and John Platt, McConnell began his career at Shell Development Company in Emeryville, California, where he worked as a research chemist for the next four years.

In 1956, McConnell married Sofia Glogovac, with whom he would eventually have two sons and a daughter. The same year McConnell was married, Caltech delegated a team of faculty members including **Linus Pauling**, who had won the Nobel Prize in chemistry two years earlier, to recruit him as an assistant professor of chemistry. McConnell accepted the position and was subsequently promoted to associate professor in 1958, professor in 1959, and professor of chemistry and physics in 1963.

First at Shell and then at Caltech, McConnell spent a great deal of time developing theoretical models for the purpose of explaining nuclear magnetic resonance (NMR) spectra in organic systems. NMR deals with the magnetic forces that exist in various atoms and result from the spin of the atom's nucleus. By subjecting atoms to both an alternating magnetic field and a radio signal of specific frequency, the nucleus of the atoms can be made to reverse their spin. The radio frequency at which this reverse occurs reveals much information about the atoms, and the spectra produced by the process is also important to scientists. During the 1950s, McConnell published a highly influential series of 12 papers on the subject. This work validated chemical shielding and the use of NMR in determining molecular electronic structure and chemical kinetics. Using his background in mathematics, McConnell applied group theory to the analysis of NMR spectra of complex molecules with several spin-spin couplings between different nuclei.

The McConnell Relation

One of McConnell's papers, written with D. B. Chesnut in 1958, introduced what has become known as the McConnell Relation, an equation that deals with the relationship between spin density the proton bonding of a carbon atom. The March 25, 1993, issue of *The Journal of Physical Chemistry,* dedicated to McConnell's achievements, notes that "This relationship has made possible a means of testing theoretical predictions of molecular orbital theory and valence bond theory." The *Journal of Physical Chemistry* also points out that the McConnell Relation has been important in allowing scientists to fully understand the organization of free radicals—atoms or molecules that contain an electron that is not paired with another electron in the same orbital.

As a result of his research, McConnell was often able to theorize scientific occurrences that, years later, turned out to be correct. His 1963 theoretical analysis of ferromagnetics (iron substances that possess magnetic attraction in the absence of magnetic fields) preceded experimental validation by twenty years. It also took research chemists a decade to empirically verify his 1961 conclusions (with Himan Sternlicht) about the existence and properties of paramagnetic excitons in organic crystals. In the words of the *Journal of Physical Chemistry*'s tribute, "Not only has McConnell been at the forefront of major theoretical developments in interpreting magnetic resonance spectra, but his theoretical contributions have always been balanced by significant experimental innovations and systematic verification in his laboratory."

Spin Labeling

In 1964 McConnell accepted a professorship at Stanford University and was elected the following year to the National Academy of Sciences. In 1979 he was named Robert Eckles Swain Professor of Chemistry at Stanford; he served as head of the Department of Chemistry from 1989 to 1992. Shortly after joining the Stanford faculty, he introduced a fruitful technique called spin labeling. In a free radical, the spin of the unpaired electron creates a magnetic moment that can be detected by electron spin resonance (ESR) spectroscopy. When a free radical is chemically bonded to another molecule, it acts as a "tag" or "marker" to make the molecule recognizable to scientists, so that its motion or orientation with respect to surrounding molecules can be studied. The technique has been used in many applications, including the dynamics of nonmembrane proteins (notably hemoglobin), biological membranes, and investigation of the antibody-antigen combining site—a subject of importance in studying immune systems and resistance to disease.

His invention of spin labeling brought McConnell the Irving Langmuir Award in Chemical Physics in 1971. McConnell used spin labeling to solve several biochemical problems that had defied previous techniques. He was the first to demonstrate the existence of conformational intermediates during oxygenation of hemoglobin, and he helped Syva Associates develop a fast, convenient, and sensitive test for the presence in the human body of hard drugs such as morphine. During the mid–1970s, McConnell applied spin labeling to several topics related to biological membranes, including membrane fusion and the interactions of hormones on cell membranes. He also used spin labels to investigate immune responses, developing new information about the interactions of antibodies and antigens.

In 1983, McConnell founded the Molecular Devices Corporation to develop hybrid instruments applying silicon technology to biology and biochemistry. An instrument called Threshold was produced in 1988 to perform rapid and very sensitive immunoassays (determinations of the amounts of an antigen or antibody present in a sample). Four years later, the company introduced a microphysiometer to detect substances (including toxins, drugs, and hormones) that affect biological cells. This instrument can be used to detect changes that might occur within the cell. For example, cellular metabolic changes caused by virus infection can be continuously monitored with the microphysiometer.

McConnell's productivity can be found not only in research journals and in the instruments and techniques used in laboratories but also in the activities of the students and colleagues he has inspired. During his teaching career, he has mentored over 75 graduate students and over 60 postdoctoral fellows, as well as collaborating with numerous colleagues. In summarizing his career up to the age of 65, *The Journal of Physical Chemistry* concludes "McConnell is without question one of the most imaginative, stimulating, and productive chemists of this generation. His profound insights and his incisive theories and experiments have provided fertile ground for literally thousands of subsequent investigators." In addition to the Langmuir Award in 1971, McConnell has received the 1961 California Section Award of the American Chemical Society, the 1962 National American Chemical Society Award in Pure Chemistry, and the National Medal of Science in 1989.

SELECTED WRITINGS BY MCCONNELL:

Periodicals

"The Cytosensor Microphysiometer: Biological Applications of Silicon Technology," *Science*, September 25, 1992, pp. 1906–1912.
"Elementary Theory of Brownian Motion of Trapped Domains in Lipid Monolayers," *Biophysical Journal*, March, 1993, pp. 577–80.

SOURCES:

Books

Modern Scientists and Engineers, Volume 2, McGraw-Hill, 1980, pp. 260–261.

Periodicals

"California Award to McConnell," *Chemical and Engineering News,* October 23, 1961, p. 103.

"Harden M. McConnell: A Celebration of His Scientific Achievements," *The Journal of Physical Chemistry,* March 25, 1993, pp. 2805–2810.

"Harden M. McConnell: ACS Award in Pure Chemistry," *Chemical and Engineering News,* April 2, 1962, p. 99.

"Harden McConnell Wins Pauling Award," *Chemical and Engineering News,* December 21, 1987, p.45.

Other

McConnell, Harden M., curriculum vitae, December, 1993.

—Sketch by Amy M. Punke

Edwin M. McMillan
1907-1991
American physicist

Edwin M. McMillan's first important discovery was made in 1940 when he, **Philip Abelson**, and **Glenn T. Seaborg** produced and identified samples of transuranium elements, later named neptunium and plutonium. After World War II McMillan became involved in the development of particle accelerators. Simultaneously with but independent of the Russian physicist **V. I. Veksler**, McMillan found a way to compensate for the relativistic mass increase that occurs in high energy accelerators. He won a share of the 1951 Nobel Prize for chemistry (with Seaborg) for his discovery of neptunium and a share of the 1963 Atoms for Peace Award (with Veksler) for his work on accelerators.

McMillan was born in Redondo Beach, California, on September 18, 1907. His father was Edwin Harbaugh McMillan, a physician, and his mother was Anna Marie Mattison. The McMillan family moved to Pasadena when Edwin was a year old. He attended local primary and secondary schools, graduating from Pasadena High School in 1924.

After completing his B.S. and M.S. degrees at the California Institute of Technology in 1928 and 1929, McMillan enrolled at Princeton University for his graduate study. In 1932, he was awarded a Ph.D. degree for his thesis, entitled "Electric Field Giving Uniform Deflecting Force on a Molecular Beam."

McMillan then received a National Research fellowship that allowed him to begin his postdoctoral studies at the University of California at Berkeley.

In 1934, **Ernest Orlando Lawrence**, inventor of the cyclotron, established the Berkeley Radiation Laboratory on the University of California campus and invited McMillan to join its staff. McMillan maintained his relationship with the laboratory (later renamed the Lawrence Radiation Laboratory) for the next forty years. He was made associate director of the laboratory in 1954 and director in 1958, a post he held until his retirement in 1973.

In the late 1930s, McMillan turned his attention to one of the most exciting topics in scientific research at the time: the bombardment of atomic nuclei by neutrons. This type of research had been inspired by a series of experiments conducted by **Enrico Fermi** in the mid–1930s. Fermi had found that nuclei will often capture a neutron and undergo a nuclear transformation in which they are converted to a new element one place higher in the atomic table than the original element. Over a period of time, Fermi used this technique to transform more than sixty different elements.

The one element in which Fermi was most interested, however, was uranium. It was obvious that neutron capture by a uranium nucleus would result in the formation of the next heavier element, an element that does not exist naturally on the earth. When Fermi actually conducted this experiment, however, he obtained confusing results that could not be interpreted as the formation of a new element. A few years later, **Otto Hahn**, **Fritz Strassmann**, and **Lise Meitner** correctly interpreted Fermi's experiments, showing that the bombardment of uranium with neutrons had resulted in nuclear fission.

Working first with Abelson and later with Seaborg, McMillan repeated Fermi's original experiments. They bombarded uranium with neutrons and found that, while fission did occur, a small fraction of the uranium nuclei did undergo the kind of transformation to a heavier element that Fermi had anticipated. Later studies found that the uranium 235 isotope undergoes fission, while the uranium 238 isotope, under the proper conditions, is transformed to a heavier element. McMillan and Abelson suggested the name neptunium for the element after the planet Neptune, located one planet beyond Uranus, the namesake of uranium. A year later, McMillan and Seaborg found that the radioactive decay of neptunium produces yet another element, heavier than itself, an element they called plutonium. Again, the element's name was taken from that of a planet, Pluto, the furthest from the sun. The two researchers were later to share the 1951 Nobel Prize in chemistry for their research on the transuranium elements.

Contributes to Accelerator Development

With the onset of World War II, McMillan left Berkeley to conduct military research at the Massachusetts Institute of Technology, at the United States Navy Radio and Sound Laboratory in San Diego, and finally at the Manhattan Project laboratories at Los Alamos. At the war's conclusion, McMillan returned to Berkeley and the radiation laboratory, and immediately became immersed in problems of accelerator design. The cyclotron, invented by Lawrence in the early 1930s, had served the research community well for more than a decade, but the limits of the machine's usefulness were now becoming apparent. The most serious problem with traditional cyclotrons was relativistic mass increase.

Relativistic mass increase refers to the fact that as particles gain velocity in an accelerator, they also gain mass; the mass gain subsequently causes them to lose velocity. Before long, high energy particles begin to fall out of phase with the electrical fields that are used to accelerate them, and they become lost inside the machine. McMillan's solution for this problem was simple and elegant. He modified the electrical field in the accelerator so that, as particles speed up and gain mass, the rate at which the electrical field changes direction slows down. In that way, the electrical field can be kept in phase with the particles even while they gain energy and mass.

For many years thereafter, this concept was employed in the development of more advanced circular accelerators, such as the synchrotron and synchrocyclotron. In 1963, McMillan was awarded a share of the Atoms for Peace award with Veksler, who had developed the same concept at about the same time.

McMillan married Elsie Walford Blumer on June 7, 1941. She was the daughter of the former dean of the Yale University school of medicine and the sister of Mrs. Ernest Lawrence. The McMillans had three children, Ann, David, and Stephen. McMillan died of complications from diabetes on September 7, 1991, in El Cerrito, California.

SELECTED WRITINGS BY MCMILLAN:

Books

(With J. Peterson and R. White) *Lecture Series in Nuclear Physics,* U.S. Government Printing Office, 1947.

Periodicals

"The Synchrotron—A Proposed High-Energy Particle Accelerator," *Physical Review,* Volume 68, September, 1945, pp. 143–144.

"Production of Mesons by X-Rays," *Science,* Volume 110, 1949, pp. 579–583.

SOURCES:

Books

Annual Obituary, 1991, St. Martin's Press, 1991, pp. 570–572.

—*Sketch by David E. Newton*

Peter Brian Medawar
1915-1987
Brazilian-born English biologist

Peter Brian Medawar was a renowned biologist who made major contributions to the study of immunology. Working extensively with skin grafts, he and his collaborators proved that one's immune system "learns" to distinguish between "self" and "non-self"—that is, such distinctions are not inherent. During his career, Medawar also became a prolific author, penning books such as *The Uniqueness of the Individual* and *Advice to a Young Scientist.* Winner of the Nobel Prize in physiology or medicine in 1960, he was also knighted in 1965.

Medawar was born on February 28, 1915, in Rio de Janeiro, Brazil, to businessperson Nicholas Medawar and the former Edith Muriel Dowling. When he was a young boy, his family moved to England, which he thereafter called home. Medawar attended secondary school at Marlborough College, where he first became interested in biology. He once described his biology master at Marlborough as a rough individual whose selection for the position was meant to discourage the students from taking up science. However, Medawar acknowledged his teacher's devotion to biology, while the educator, in turn, recognized the pupil's interest. The biology master encouraged Medawar to pursue the science under the tutelage of one of his former students, **John Young**, at Magdalen College. Medawar followed this advice and enrolled at Magdalen in 1932 as a zoology student. He found Young to be an excellent teacher.

Medawar earned his bachelor's degree from Magdalen in 1935, the same year he accepted an appointment as Christopher Welch Scholar and Senior Demonstrator at Magdalen College. He followed Young's recommendation that he work with patholo-

Peter Brian Medawar

gist **Howard Florey**, who was undertaking a study of penicillin, work for which he would later become well-known. Medawar leaned toward experimental embryology and tissue cultures. While at Magdalen, he met zoology student Jean Shinglewood Taylor, who also joined Florey's lab. They married in 1937. In a 1984 interview with *New Scientist,* she recalled her impressions of Medawar at Magdalen: "Nobody could forget him, because he was very tall, very untidy, obviously extremely clever, and very dominant." She spent less than a year in Florey's lab. The couple had their first child in 1938. In all they had four children, sons Charles and Alexander, and daughters Caroline and Louise.

Begins to Study Tissue Transplants

In 1938, Medawar, by examination, became a fellow of Magdalen College and received the Edward Chapman Research Prize. A year later, he received his master's from Oxford. When World War II broke out in Europe, the Medical Research Council asked Medawar to concentrate his research on tissue transplants, primarily skin grafts. While this took him away from his initial research studies into embryology, his work with the military would come to drive his future research and eventually lead to a Nobel Prize. During the war, Medawar developed a concentrated form of fibrinogen, a component of the blood. This substance acted as a glue to reattach severed nerves, and found a place in the treatment of skin grafts and

in other operations. More importantly to Medawar's future research, however, were his studies at the Burns Unit of the Glasgow Royal Infirmary in Scotland. His task was to determine why patients rejected donor skin grafts. He observed that the rejection time for donor grafts was noticeably longer for initial grafts, compared to those grafts that were transplanted for a second time. Medawar noted the similarity between this reaction and the body's reaction to an invading virus or bacteria. He formed the opinion that the body's rejection of skin grafts was immunological in nature; the body built up an immunity to the first graft and then called on that already-built-up immunity to quickly reject a second graft.

Upon his return from the Burns Unit to Oxford, he began his studies of immunology in the laboratory. In 1944 he became a senior research fellow of St. John's College, Oxford, and university demonstrator in zoology and comparative anatomy. Although he qualified for and passed his examinations for a doctorate in philosophy while at Oxford, Medawar opted against accepting it because it would cost more than he could afford. In his autobiography, *Memoir of a Thinking Radish,* he wrote, "The degree served no useful purpose and cost, I learned, as much as it cost in those days to have an appendectomy. Having just had the latter as a matter of urgency, I thought that to have both would border on self-indulgence, so I remained a plain mister until I became a prof." He continued as researcher at Oxford University through 1947.

During that year Medawar accepted an appointment as Mason professor of zoology at the University of Birmingham. He brought with him one of his best graduate students at Oxford, Rupert Everett "Bill" Billingham. Another graduate student, Leslie Brent, soon joined them and the three began what was to become a very productive collaboration that spanned several years. Their research progressed through Medawar's appointment as dean of science, through his several-month-long trip to the Rockefeller Institute in New York in 1949—the same year he received the prestigious title of fellow from the Royal Society—and even a relocation to another college. In 1951 Medawar accepted a position as Jodrell Professor of Zoology and Comparative Anatomy at University College, London. Billingham and Brent followed him.

Their most important discovery had its experimental root in a promise Medawar made at the International Congress of Genetics at Stockholm in 1948. He told another investigator, Hugh Donald, that he could formulate a foolproof method for distinguishing identical from fraternal twin calves. He and Billingham felt they could easily tell the twins apart by transplanting a skin graft from one twin to the other. They reasoned that a calf of an identical pair would accept a skin graft from its twin because the two originated from the same egg, whereas a calf would reject a graft from its fraternal twin because they came from two separate eggs. The results did not bear this out, however. The calves accepted skin grafts from their twins regardless of their status as identical or fraternal. Puzzled, they repeated the experiment, but received the same results.

They found their error when they became aware of work done by Dr. **Frank Macfarlane Burnet** of the University of Melbourne, and Ray D. Owen of the California Institute of Technology. Owen found that blood transfuses between twin calves, both fraternal and identical. Burnet believed that an individual's immunological framework developed before birth, and felt Owen's finding demonstrated this by showing that the immune system tolerates those tissues that are made known to it before a certain age. In other words, the body does not recognize donated tissue as alien if it has had some exposure to it at an early age. Burnet predicted that this immunological tolerance for non-native tissue could be reproduced in a lab. Medawar, Billingham, and Brent set out to test Burnet's hypothesis.

Research Proves Acquired Immunological Tolerance

The three-scientist team worked closely together, inoculating embryos from mice of one strain with tissue cells from donor mice of another strain. When the mice had matured, the trio grafted skin from the donor mice to the inoculated mice. Normally, mice reject skin grafts from other mice, but the inoculated mice in their experiment accepted the donor skin grafts. They did not develop an immunological reaction. The prenatal encounter had given the inoculated mice an acquired immunological tolerance. They had proven Burnet's hypothesis. They published their findings in a 1953 article in *Nature*. Although their research had no applications to transplants among humans, it showed that transplants were possible. The scientific world previously held no hope for successful transplants. In *Memoir of a Thinking Radish*, Medawar explained: "Thus the ultimate importance of the discovery of tolerance turned out to be not practical, but moral. It put new heart into the many biologists and surgeons who were working to make it possible to graft, for example, kidneys from one person to another."

In the years following publication of the research, Medawar accepted several honors, including the Royal Medal from the Royal Society in 1959. A year later he and Burnet accepted the Nobel Prize for Physiology or Medicine for their discovery of acquired immunological tolerance: Burnet developed the theory and Medawar proved it. Medawar shared the prize money with Billingham and Brent.

Medawar's scientific concerns extended beyond immunology, even during the years of his work toward acquired immunological tolerance. While at Birmingham, he and Billingham also investigated pigment spread, a phenomenon seen in some guinea pigs and cattle where the dark spots spread into the light areas of the skin. "Thus if a dark skin graft were transplanted into the middle of a pale area of skin it would soon come to be surrounded by a progressively widening ring of dark skin," Medawar asserted in his autobiography. The team conducted a variety of experiments, hoping to show that the dark pigment cells were somehow "infecting" the pale pigment cells. The tests never panned out. "It was a weary and disheartening business representing a loss of about two years' work, at the end of which I had to admit that the hypothesis on which I had been working was mistaken."

Medawar also delved into animal behavior at Birmingham. He edited a book on the subject by noted scientist **Nikolaas Tinbergen**, who ultimately netted a Nobel Prize in 1973. Medawar felt Tinbergen's work was important enough that he went beyond his literary assistance, and wrote to a granting agency to assure that Tinbergen's work was funded. In 1957, Medawar also became a book author with his first offering, *The Uniqueness of the Individual,* which was actually a collection of essays. In 1959, his second book, *The Future of Man,* was issued, containing a compilation of a series of broadcasts he read for British Broadcasting Corporation (BBC) radio. The series examined the impacts of evolution on man.

Medawar remained at University College until 1962 when he took the post of director of the National Institute for Medical Research in London, where he continued his study of transplants and immunology. While there, he continued writing with mainly philosophical themes. *The Art of the Soluble,* published in 1967, is an assembly of essays, while his 1969 book, *Induction and Intuition in Scientific Thought,* is a sequence of lectures examining the thought processes of scientists. In 1969 Medawar, then president of the British Association for the Advancement of Science, experienced the first of a series of strokes while speaking at the group's annual meeting. As soon as possible, he returned to work, sometimes relying on research assistants to conduct the laboratory bench work. He finally retired from his position as director of the National Institute for Medical Research in 1971. In spite of his physical limitations, he went ahead with scientific research in his lab at the clinical research center of the Medical Research Council. There he began studying cancer. In the 1984 interview with *New Scientist,* he said, "I believe that vaccination is possible against a wide range of cancers, in principle. This is now our principal line of research."

Through the 1970s and 1980s, Medawar produced several other books—some with his wife as co-author—in addition to his many essays on growth, aging, immunity, and cellular transformations. In one of his most well-known books, *Advice to a Young Scientist,* he states that scientists are not geniuses, but people who have the combined characters of common sense and curiosity. He writes, "Like any other human being, a young scientist growing up will probably say to himself at the end of each decade, 'Ah well, that's it then. It has all been great fun, but nothing now remains except to play out time with dignity and composure and hope that some of my work will last a bit longer than I do.'" Medawar died on October 2, 1987, at the age of seventy-two.

SELECTED WRITINGS BY MEDAWAR:

Books

The Uniqueness of the Individual, Basic Books, 1957.
The Future of Man, Mentor, 1959.
The Art of the Soluble, Methuen, 1967.
Induction and Intuition in Scientific Thought, American Philosophical Society, 1969.
The Life Science, Harper, 1977.
Advice to a Young Scientist, Harper, 1979.
The Limits of Science, Harper, 1984.
Memoir of a Thinking Radish, Oxford University Press, 1986.
"Immunological Tolerance," *Nobel Lectures,* Nobel Foundation, 1964, pp. 704–715.

SOURCES:

Books

A Very Decided Preference, W. W. Norton, 1990.

Periodicals

"The Art of the Soluble," *Nature,* October 8, 1987, p. 472.
Mitchison, N. A., "Sir Peter Medawar (1915–1987)," *Nature,* November 12, 1987, p. 112.
"Sir Peter Medawar," *New Scientist,* April 12, 1984, pp. 14–20.

—*Sketch by Leslie Mertz*

Lise Meitner
1878-1968
Austrian physicist

The prototypical female scientist of the early twentieth century was a woman devoted to her work, sacrificing family and personal relationships in favor of science; modestly brilliant; generous; and underrecognized. In many ways Austrian-born physicist Lise Meitner embodies that image. In 1938, along with her nephew **Otto Robert Frisch**, Meitner developed the theory behind nuclear fission that would eventually make possible the creation of the atomic bomb. She and lifelong collaborator **Otto Hahn** made several other key contributions to the field of nuclear physics. Although Hahn received the Nobel in 1944, Meitner did not share the honor—one of the more frequently cited examples of the sexism rife in the scientific community in the first half of this century.

Elise Meitner was born November 7, 1878 to an affluent Vienna family. Her father Philipp was a lawyer and her mother Hedwig travelled in the same Vienna intellectual circles as Sigmund Freud. From the early years of her life, Meitner gained experience that would later be invaluable in combatting—or overlooking—the slights she received as a woman in a field dominated by men. The third of eight children, she expressed interest in pursuing a scientific career, but her practical father made her attend the Elevated High School for Girls in Vienna to earn a diploma that would enable her to teach French—a much more sensible career for a woman. After completing this program, Meitner's desire to become a scientist was greater than ever. In 1899, she began studying with a local tutor who prepped students for the difficult university entrance exam. She worked so hard that she successfully prepared for the test in two years rather than the average four. Shortly before she turned twenty three, Meitner became one of the few women students at the University of Vienna.

At the beginning of her university career in 1901, Meitner could not decide between physics or mathematics; later, inspired by her physics teacher Ludwig Boltzmann, she opted for the latter. In 1906, after becoming the second woman ever to earn a Ph.D. in physics from the University of Vienna, she decided to stay on in Boltzmann's laboratory as an assistant to his assistant. This was hardly a typical career path for a recent doctorate, but Meitner had no other offers, as universities at the time did not hire women faculty. Less than a year after Meitner entered the professor's lab, Boltzmann committed suicide, leaving the future of the research team uncertain. In an effort to recruit the noted physicist **Max Planck** to take Boltzmann's

Lise Meitner

place, the university invited him to come visit the lab. Although Planck refused the offer, he met Meitner during the visit and talked with her about quantum physics and radiation research. Inspired by this conversation, Meitner left Vienna in the winter of 1907 to go to the Institute for Experimental Physics in Berlin to study with Planck.

Soon after her arrival in Berlin, Meitner met a young chemist named Otto Hahn at one of the weekly symposia. Hahn worked at Berlin's Chemical Institute under the supervision of **Emil Fischer**, surrounded by organic chemists—none of whom shared his research interests in radiochemistry. Four months older than Hahn, Meitner was not only intrigued by the same research problems but had the training in physics that Hahn lacked. Unfortunately, Hahn's supervisor balked at the idea of allowing a woman researcher to enter the all-male Chemical Institute. Finally, Fischer allowed Meitner and Hahn to set up a laboratory in a converted woodworking shop in the Institute's basement, as long as Meitner agreed never to enter the higher floors of the building.

This incident was neither the first nor the last experience of sexism that Meitner encountered in her career. According to one famous anecdote, she was solicited to write an article by an encyclopedia editor who had read an article she wrote on the physical aspects of radioactivity. When she answered the letter addressed to Herr Meitner and explained she was a woman, the editor wrote back to retract his request, saying he would never publish the work of a woman.

Even in her collaboration with Hahn, Meitner at times conformed to gender roles. When British physicist Sir **Ernest Rutherford** visited their Berlin laboratory on his way back from the Nobel ceremonies in 1908, Meitner spent the day shopping with his wife Mary while the two men talked about their work.

Becomes First Woman Professor in Germany

Within her first year at the Institute, the school opened its classes to women, and Meitner was allowed to roam the building. For the most part, however, the early days of the collaboration between Hahn and Meitner were filled with their investigations into the behavior of beta rays as they passed through aluminum. By today's standards, the laboratory in which they worked would be appalling. Hahn and Meitner frequently suffered from headaches brought on by their adverse working conditions. In 1912 when the Kaiser-Wilhelm Institute was built in the nearby suburb of Dahlem, Hahn received an appointment in the small radioactivity department there and invited Meitner to join him in his laboratory. Soon thereafter, Planck asked Meitner to lecture as an assistant professor at the Institute for Theoretical Physics. The first woman in Germany to hold such a position, Meitner drew several members of the news media to her opening lecture.

When World War I started in 1914, Meitner interrupted her laboratory work to volunteer as an X-ray technician in the Austrian army. Hahn entered the German military. The two scientists arranged their leaves to coincide and throughout the war returned periodically to Dahlem where they continued trying to discover the precursor of the element actinium. By the end of the war, they announced that they had found this elusive element and named it protactinium, the missing link on the periodic table between thorium (previously number 90) and uranium (number 91). A few years later Meitner received the Leibniz Medal from the Berlin Academic of Science and the Leibniz Prize from the Austrian Academy of Science for this work. Shortly after she helped discover protactinium in 1917, Meitner accepted the job of establishing a radioactive physics department at the Kaiser Wilhelm Institute. Hahn remained in the chemistry department, and the two ceased working together to concentrate on research more suited to their individual training. For Meitner, this constituted a return to beta radiation studies.

Throughout the 1920s, Meitner continued her work in beta radiation, winning several prizes. In 1928, the Association to Aid Women in Science upgraded its Ellen Richards Prize—billing it as a Nobel Prize for women—and named Meitner and chemist **Pauline Ramart-Lucas** of the University of Paris its first recipients. In addition to the awards she received, Meitner acquired a reputation in physics circles for some of her personal quirks as well. Years later, her nephew Otto Frisch, also a physicist, would recall that she drank large quantities of strong coffee, embarked on ten mile walks whenever she had free time, and would sometimes indulge in piano duets with him. By middle age, Meitner had also adopted some of the mannerisms stereotypically associated with her male colleagues. Not the least of these, Hahn later recalled, was absent-mindedness. On one occasion, a student approached her at a lecture, saying they had met earlier. Knowing she had never met the student, Meitner responded earnestly, "You probably mistake me for Professor Hahn."

Begins Work on Uranium

Meitner and Hahn resumed their collaboration in 1934, after **Enrico Fermi** published his seminal article on "transuranic" uranium. The Italian physicist announced that when he bombarded uranium with neutrons, he produced two new elements—number 93 and 94, in a mixture of lighter elements. Meitner and Hahn joined with a young German chemist named **Fritz Strassmann** to draw up a list of all the substances the heaviest natural elements produced when bombarded with neutrons. In three years, the three confirmed Fermi's result and expanded the list to include about ten additional substances that resulted from bombarding these elements with neutrons. Meanwhile, physicists **Irène Joliot-Curie** and Pavle Savitch announced that they had created a new radioactive substance by bombarding uranium by neutrons. The French team speculated that this new mysterious substance might be thorium, but Meitner, Hahn, and Strassmann could not confirm this finding. No matter how many times they bombarded uranium with neutrons, no thorium resulted. Hahn and Meitner sent a private letter to the French physicists suggesting that perhaps they had erred. Although Joliet-Curie did not reply directly, a few months later she published a paper retracting her earlier assertions and said the substance she had noted was not thorium.

Current events soon took Meitner's mind off these professional squabbles. Although her father, a proponent of cultural assimilation, had all his children baptized, Meitner was Jewish by birth. Because she continued to maintain her Austrian citizenship, she was at first relatively impervious to the political turmoil in Weimar Germany. In the mid–1930s she had been asked to stop lecturing at the university but she continued her research. When Germany annexed Austria in 1938, Meitner became a German citizen and began to look for a research position in an environment hospitable to Jews. Her tentative plans grew urgent in the spring of 1938, when Germany announced that academics could no longer leave the country. Colleagues devised an elaborate scheme to smuggle her out of Germany to Stockholm where she

had made temporary arrangements to work at the Institute of the Academy of Sciences under the sponsorship of a Nobel grant. By late fall, however, Meitner's position in Sweden looked dubious: her grant provided no money for equipment and assistance, and the administration at the Stockholm Institute would offer her no help. Christmas found her depressed and vacationing in a town in the west of Sweden.

Posits Theory of Nuclear Fission

Back in Germany, Hahn and Strassmann had not let their colleague's departure slow their research efforts. The two read and reread the paper Joliet-Curie had published detailing her research techniques. Looking it over, they thought they had found an explanation for Joliet-Curie's confusion: perhaps instead of finding one new substance after bombarding uranium, as she had thought, she had actually found two new substances! They repeated her experiments and indeed found two substances in the final mixture, one of which was barium. This result seemed to suggest that bombarding uranium with neutrons led it to split up into a number of smaller elements. Hahn immediately wrote to Meitner to share this perplexing development with her. Meitner received his letter on her vacation in the village of Kungalv, as she awaited the arrival of her nephew, Frisch, who was currently working in Copenhagen under the direction of physicist **Niels Bohr**. Frisch hoped to discuss a problem in his own work with Meitner, but it was clear soon after they met that the only thing on her mind was Hahn and Strassmann's observation. Meitner and Frisch set off for a walk in the snowy woods—Frisch on skis, with his aunt trotting along—continuing to puzzle out how uranium could possibly yield barium. When they paused for a rest on a log, Meitner began to posit a theory, sketching diagrams in the snow.

If, as Bohr had previously suggested, the nucleus behaved like a liquid drop, Meitner reasoned that when this drop of a nucleus was bombarded by neutrons, it might elongate and divide itself into two smaller droplets. The forces of electrical repulsion would act to prevent it from maintaining its circular shape by forming the nucleus into a dumbbell shape that would—as the bombarding forces grew stronger—sever at the middle to yield two droplets—two completely different nuclei. But one problem still remained. When Meitner added together the weights of the resultant products, she found that the sum did not equal the weight of the original uranium. The only place the missing mass could be lost was in energy expended during the reaction.

Frisch rushed back to Copenhagen, eager to test the revelations from their walk in the woods on his mentor and boss, Bohr. He caught Bohr just as the scientist was leaving for an American tour, but as Bohr listened to what Frisch was urgently telling him, he responded: "Oh, what idiots we have been. We could have foreseen it all! This is just as it must be!" Buoyed by Bohr's obvious admiration, Frisch and Meitner spent hours on a long-distance telephone writing the paper that would publicize their theory. At the suggestion of a biologist friend, Frisch coined the word "fission" to describe the splitting of the nucleus in a process that seemed to him analogous to cell division.

Theory Makes Possible Atom Bomb

The paper "On the Products of the Fission of Uranium and Thorium" appeared in *Nature* on February 11, 1939. Although it would be another five and a half years before the American military would successfully explode an atom bomb over Hiroshima, many physicists consider Meitner and Frisch's paper akin to opening a Pandora's box of atomic weapons. Physicists were not the only ones to view Meitner as an important participant in the harnessing of nuclear energy. After the bomb was dropped in 1944, a radio station asked First Lady Eleanor Roosevelt to conduct a transatlantic interview with Meitner. In this interview, the two women talked extensively about the implications and future of nuclear energy. After the war, Hahn found himself in one of the more enviable positions for a scientist—the winner of the 1944 Nobel prize in chemistry—although, because of the war, Hahn did not accept his prize until two years later. Although she attended the ceremony, Meitner did not share in the honor.

But Meitner's life after the war was not without its plaudits and pleasures. In the early part of 1946, she travelled to America to visit her sister—working in the U.S. as a chemist—for the first time in decades. While there, Meitner delivered a lecture series at Catholic University in Washington, D.C. In the following years, she won the Max Planck Medal and was awarded numerous honorary degrees from both American and European universities. In 1966 she, Hahn, and Strassmann split the $50,000 Enrico Fermi Award given by the Atomic Energy Commission. Unfortunately, by this time Meitner had become too ill to travel, so the chairman of the A. E. C. delivered it to her in Cambridge, England, where she had retired a few years earlier. Meitner died just a few weeks before her 90th birthday on October 27, 1968.

SELECTED WRITINGS BY MEITNER:

Periodicals

(With Otto R. Frisch), "On the Products of the Fission of Uranium and Thorium," *Nature,* Volume 143, March, 1939, p. 239.

"Looking Back," *Bulletin of the Atomic Scientists,* November, 1964.

SOURCES:

Books

Crawford, Deborah, *Lise Meitner, Atomic Pioneer,* Crown, 1969.
Irving, David, *The German Atomic Bomb: The History of Nuclear Research in Nazi Germany,* Simon & Schuster, 1967.
Rhodes, Richard, *The Making of the Atom Bomb,* Simon & Schuster, 1988.

Periodicals

Watkins, Sallie, "Lise Meitner and the Beta-ray Energy Controversy: An Historical Perspective," *American Journal of Physics,* Volume 51, 1983, pp. 551–553.
Watkins, Sallie, "Lise Meitner: The Making of a Physicist," *Physics Teacher,* January, 1984, pp. 12–15.

—*Sketch by Shari Rudavsky*

Dorothy Reed Mendenhall
1874-1964
American obstetrician and medical researcher

Dorothy Reed Mendenhall was a well-respected researcher, obstetrician, and pioneer in methods of childbirth. She was the first to discover that Hodgkin's disease was not a form of tuberculosis, as had been thought. This finding received international acclaim. As a result of her work, the cell type characteristic of Hodgkin's disease bears her name. The loss of her first child due to poor obstetrics changed her research career to a lifelong effort to reduce infant mortality rates. Mendenhall's efforts paid off with standards being set for weight and height for children ages birth to six, and also in programs that stressed the health of both the mother and child in the birthing process.

Dorothy Reed Mendenhall, the last of three children, was born September 22, 1874, in Columbus, Ohio, to William Pratt Reed, a shoe manufacturer, and Grace Kimball Reed, both of whom had descended from English settlers who came to America in the seventeenth century. Mendenhall attended Smith

College and obtained a baccalaureate degree. Although she initially contemplated a career in journalism, Mendenhall's interest in medicine was inspired by a biology course she attended.

When they opened the school up to women, Mendenhall applied to Johns Hopkins Medical School in Baltimore, Maryland. In 1900, she was one of the first women to graduate from this school with a doctorate of medicine degree. The next year she received a fellowship in pathology at Johns Hopkins. While there, she taught bacteriology and performed research on Hodgkin's disease, which physicians then believed was a form of tuberculosis. She disproved this theory when she discovered a common link between diagnosed patients. She found that the blood of these patients carried a specific type of cell. The presence of these giant cells, now known as the Reed cell, distinctly identifies the disease. Mendenhall's work produced the first thorough descriptions, both verbal and illustrated, of the tissue changes that occur with Hodgkin's. She was the first to describe the disease's growth through several progressive states. Mendenhall determined that a patient's prognosis worsened with each successive stage. She incorrectly speculated, however, that the disease was a chronic inflammatory process. Her finding of the distinctive cell had world-wide importance and was a significant step forward in the understanding and treatment of Hodgkin's disease. Today, researchers know that Hodgkin's is a type of cancer characterized by a progressive enlargement of the lymph nodes.

Pioneering Efforts Lower Infant Mortality Rates

Because she felt that there were few opportunities for advancement at Johns Hopkins, Mendenhall transferred her work to Babies Hospital of New York, becoming the first resident physician there. In 1906, she married Charles Elwood Mendenhall and began to raise a family. She had four children, one who died a few hours after birth. This loss was to shape the rest of her career. Mendenhall undertook a study of infant mortality, that, when released, brought government attention to the problems of maternal and child health. To determine the extent of infant mortality in the United States, she obtained epidemiological data for the Wisconsin State Board of Health. A major problem she identified was the prevalence of malnutrition among children. In her efforts to remedy the problems of childbearing and childrearing, Mendenhall developed correspondence courses for new and prospective mothers. She also lectured to groups across Wisconsin and wrote bulletins on nutrition for the United States Department of Agriculture. Mendenhall's efforts helped create some of Wisconsin's first infant welfare clinics, particularly in Madison. In 1937, she was gratified when Madison had the lowest infant mortality rate in the United States.

While employed as a field lecturer for the Department of Home Economics at the University of Wisconsin, in 1918, Mendenhall initiated a nationwide effort in which all children under six years of age were weighed and measured. This project helped establish standards for that normal, healthy children of these ages should weigh and how tall they should be. In 1926, Mendenhall undertook a study of birthing methods in Denmark, which had one of the lowest rates of childbirth complications. She later travelled to the country to gain firsthand information on their techniques, which included the utilization of specialized midwives and a reduced role of medical procedures. Through this, Mendenhall determined that there was too much medical intervention in normal childbirth, and that this intervention is often the source of health problems for the mother and child. She helped institute natural childbirth in the U.S. and also suggested that obstetrics become a specialty profession. From 1917 to 1936, Mendenhall also worked intermittently as a medical officer for the United States Children's Bureau. After her husband's death, she withdrew from public life. In her spare time she loved to read Marcus Aurelius. As a tribute to her dedication as a researcher, teacher, and physician, Smith College dedicated Sabin-Reed Hall in 1965. The hall honors Mendenhall and Florence Sabin, a fellow student at both Smith and Johns Hopkins. Mendenhall died July 31, 1964, in Chester, Connecticut, from heart disease.

SELECTED WRITINGS BY MENDENHALL:

Periodicals

"On the Pathological Changes in Hodgkin's Disease with Especial Reference to Its Relation to Tuberculosis," *Johns Hopkins Hospital Reports,* Volume 10, 1902, pp. 133–96.
"Prenatal and Natal Conditions in Wisconsin," *Wisconsin Medical Journal,* March, 1917, pp. 353–69.

SOURCES:

Books

Sicherman, Barbara, Carol Hurd Green, Ilene Kantrov, and Harriette Walker, editors, *Notable American Women: The Modern Period,* Belknap Press of Harvard University Press, 1980, pp. 468–70.

—*Sketch by Barbara Proujan*

R. Bruce Merrifield
1921-
American biochemist

American biochemist R. Bruce Merrifield is recognized as a leading figure in peptide research. He was awarded the 1984 Nobel Prize in chemistry for his development of an automated laboratory technique for rapidly synthesizing peptide chains in large quantities. His research into peptide-protein and nucleic acid chemistry has significantly advanced the fields of biochemistry, molecular biology, and pharmacology.

Merrifield was born July 15, 1921, in Fort Worth, Texas, the only son of George E. and Lorene Lucas Merrifield. Two years after his birth the family moved to California, moving frequently during the Great Depression as his father sought work as a furniture salesman. By Merrifield's count he attended more than forty schools before the family finally settled in Montebello, California. It was at a high school there that he became interested in science, especially chemistry and astronomy. He joined the astronomy club, eventually building his own telescope, grinding its mirror himself, and won runner-up honors in the annual science contest. When he graduated high school in 1939, Merrifield initially entered Pasadena Junior College, but at the end of two years transferred to the University of California at Los Angeles (UCLA) to continue his studies in the field of chemistry. Working in the laboratory of Max S. Dunn, he assisted in the synthesis of a complex amino acid called dihydroxyphenylalanine (DOPA), essential in nerve transmission and used in the treatment of certain illnesses such as Parkinson's disease.

After receiving a Bachelor of Arts degree with a major in chemistry from UCLA in 1943, Merrifield went to work at the Philip R. Park Research Foundation as a chemist. During his stay at the lab, Merrifield assisted in growth experiments feeding test animals a synthetic amino acid diet. The experience lasted only a year, but it was enough to convince Merrifield that to pursue his goals he would need to return to school. An Anheuser-Busch Inc. fellowship allowed him to continue his studies at UCLA's graduate school in the chemistry department. He served as a chemistry instructor from 1944 until 1947, then returned to Professor Dunn's laboratory as a research assistant from 1948 through 1949. His work with Dunn included the development of microbiological methods for the study of yeast purines and the pyrimidines, organic bases that make up such compounds as the nucleotides and nucleic acids. In 1949, he received his Ph.D. in biochemistry. Upon graduating, Merrifield was offered an appointment as assistant chemist at the Rockefeller University, then known as the Rockefeller Institute for Medical Research, in New York City. He remained at the institute, becoming a John D. Rockefeller Jr. Professor—the institution's highest academic rank—in 1984.

Improves Peptide Synthesis

At the Institute, Merrifield first worked as an assistant to Dr. Dilworth W. Woolley, whom he considered a profound influence on his later career. At this time, having recognized that proteins are the key components of all living organisms, he chose to focus on this aspect of their research. Their studies centered on peptide growth factors that Dr. Woolley had discovered and on the dinucleotide growth factors Merrifield had discovered during his graduate study. Merrifield's research required him to isolate biologically active peptides. For his experiments, he had to synthesize analogues of the materials. However, the research pointed up the need to improve the techniques of peptide synthesis. The methods pioneered by **Emil Fischer** at the turn of the century for peptide synthesis were laborious and time consuming. Preparing a single experiment's sample could take months of work. Fischer's process involved activating the link in a chain of peptides to which one would attach the next peptide. Before the bond could be activated, however, all the other bonds in the chain would have to be protected. Then, after the required bond had formed, all other protected bonds needed to be cleared of their chemical caps. The process would then be repeated however many times necessary to gradually build the desired molecule.

In May of 1959, a note in his laboratory book records the moment Merrifield conceived the idea of a new approach to the synthesis. Understating the urgency, his note read: "There is a need for a rapid, quantitative, automatic method for synthesis of long chain peptides." Realizing that the critical step involved activating the peptide bond while protecting all others in a long chain, Merrifield hit on the notion of anchoring the chain to a solid base. The first amino acid in the sequence would be tightly bonded to a polymeric support, an insoluble foundation that would not react during the peptide bond additions but, following the reactions, could easily be removed by the proper solvents. This solid-phase method acted like the frame of a loom, holding the ends of the chain taut while link after link was sewn in. Not only did this save one of the most cumbersome steps in the Fischer process, the need to purify the intermediate product prior to the addition of another bond, it also allowed much more reagent to be flushed in due to the secure hold at the polymeric end. The reactions could be driven longer and harder, producing a purer product. Purities of 99.5 percent were achieved, as Merrifield announced at a 1962 meeting of the

Federation of American Societies of Experimental Biology.

Develops Automated Technique

Despite being simplified, however, the steps were still so repetitive Merrifield felt they could be automated. Working in the basement of his house, he devised the first prototype of an automated peptide synthesizer by 1965. The machine was a technological success. In 1969, Merrifield used his box of computer switches filled with jars and tubes to carry out the complete synthesis of one of the first enzymes he had begun his work on years earlier. It took 369 separate chemical reactions in 11,391 steps to make the ribonuclease molecule, but it took far less time than before. However, the practical advantage had a price. Because the step of isolating—and thereby purifying—the intermediates had been circumvented, trace side reactions were no longer washed out of the product during a protein's synthesis. While Merrifield could boast that each stage's yield had a high degree of purity, the overall synthesis after so many steps may have had an appreciable number of undesirable side products. Advances since then, such as in liquid chromatography, a method of identifying substances using light, and the use of stronger reagents, have dramatically improved product purity. But the key advance was in the speed and simplification of a once unimaginably complex task. The process—which has never been patented, either by Merrifield or Rockefeller University—has been used widely and is seen as one of the fundamental techniques of genetic and biochemical research.

Merrifield was invited to be a Nobel Guest Professor and traveled to Uppsala University in 1968. Since 1969 he has edited the *International Journal of Peptide and Protein Research*. In addition to his Nobel Prize, he has received many academic and professional awards, including: the Lasker Award for Basic Medical Research (1969); the Gairdner Award (1970); the Intra-Science Award (1970); American Chemical Society Award for Creative Work in Synthetic Organic Chemistry (1972); the Nichols Medal (1973); the Instrument Specialties Company Award of the University of Nebraska (1977); the Second Alan E. Pierce Award of the American Peptide Symposium (1979); the Ralph F. Hirschmann Award in Peptide Chemistry, American Chemical Society (1990); and the Josef Rudinger Award (1990). Merrifield and his wife, Elizabeth, live in Cresskill, New Jersey. They have six children: daughters Nancy, Betsy, Cathy, Laurie, and Sally, and their son James. In the 1980's, Elizabeth, a trained biologist, joined Dr. Merrifield in his lab at Rockefeller University.

SELECTED WRITINGS BY MERRIFIELD:

Periodicals

"Solid-Phase Peptide Synthesis I: The Synthesis of a Tetrapeptide," *Journal of the American Chemical Society,* Volume 85, 1963, pp. 2149–54.

(With John Morrow Stewart) "Automated Peptide Synthesis," *Nature,* July 31, 1965, pp. 522–523.

(With John Morrow Stewart and N. Jernberg) "Instrument for Automated Synthesis of Peptides," *Anal. Chem.,* Volume 38, 1966, pp. 1905–1914.

(With B.F. Gisin and D.C. Tosteson) "Solid-Phase Synthesis of the Cyclododecadepsipeptide Valinomycin," *Journal of the American Chemical Society,* Volume 91, 1969, pp. 2691–95.

"An Assessment of Solid Phase Peptide Synthesis," *Peptides: Structural Function, Proceedings of the American Peptide Symposium, 8th,* 1983, pp. 33–44.

(With D. Andreu and H.G. Boman) "Solid-Phase Synthesis of Cecropin A and Related Peptides," *Proceedings of the National Academy of Sciences USA,* Volume 80, 1983, pp. 6475–79.

(With James P. Tam and William F. Heath) "SN2 Deprotection of Synthetic Peptides with a Low Concentration of Hydrogen Fluoride in Dimethyl Sulfide: Evidence and Application in Peptide Synthesis," *Journal of the American Chemical Society,* Volume 105, 1983, pp. 6442–55.

"Solid Phase Synthesis," *Science,* Volume 232, 1986, pp. 341–347.

SOURCES:

Books

Stewart, John Morrow, and Janis Dillaha Young, *Solid Phase Peptide Synthesis,* foreword by Merrifield, W.H. Freeman, 1969.

Synthetic Peptides: A User's Guide, edited by Gregory A. Grant, W.H. Freeman, 1992.

Periodicals

New Scientist, October 25, 1984.

"R. Bruce Merrifield: Designer of Protein-Making Machine," *Chemical and Engineering News,* August 2, 1971, pp. 22–26.

"The 1984 Nobel Prize in Chemistry," *Science,* December 7, 1984, pp. 1151–53.

—*Sketch by Nicholas Williamson*

Matthew Meselson
1930-
American molecular biologist

Matthew Meselson, in collaboration with biologist Franklin W. Stahl, showed experimentally that the replication of deoxyribonucleic acid (DNA) in bacteria is semiconservative. Semiconservative replication occurs in a double stranded DNA molecule when the two strands are separated and a new strand is copied from the "parental" strand to produce two new double stranded DNA molecules. The new double stranded DNA molecule is semiconservative because only one strand is conserved from the "parent"; the other strand is a new copy. (Conservative replication occurs when one offspring of a molecule contains both parent strands and the other molecule offspring contains new copies of the strands) The classical experiment revealing semiconservative replication in bacteria was central to the understanding of the living cell and to modern molecular biology.

Matthew Stanley Meselson was born May 24, 1930, in Denver, Colorado, to Hymen Avram, a businessman, and Ann (Swedlow) Meselson, a homemaker. Matthew, an only child, spent most of his childhood in Denver, until he left home to attend college at the University of Chicago. After graduating in 1951 with a Ph.B. in liberal arts he continued his education with graduate studies at the California Institute of Technology in the field of chemistry. Meselson graduated with a Ph.D. in 1957, and remained at Cal Tech as a research fellow. He acquired the position of assistant professor of chemistry at Cal Tech in 1958. In 1960, Meselson moved to Cambridge, Massachusetts to fill the position of associate professor of natural sciences at Harvard University. In 1964, he was awarded professor of biology, which he held until 1976. He was appointed the title of Thomas Dudley Cabot professor of natural sciences in 1976. From that time on, Meselson held a concurrent appointment on the council of the Smithsonian Institute in Washington, DC.

An Early Call to Science

From an early age, Matthew Meselson was interested in the sciences. As a child he had his own chemistry laboratory in the basement of his home. His fascination with science continued to grow throughout his youth. When it came time to decide on a field of study at the University of Chicago, Meselson showed no hesitation. After graduating from the University of Chicago, Meselson continued his education in chemistry at the California Institute of Technology. It was during his final year at Cal Tech that

Meselson collaborated with Franklin Stahl on the classical experiment of semiconservative replication of DNA. Meselson and Stahl wanted to design and perform an experiment that would show the nature of DNA replication from parent to offspring using the bacteriophage T4 (a virus that destroys other cells, also called a phage). The idea was to use an isotope to mark the cells and centrifuge to separate particles that could be identified by their DNA and measure changes in the new generations of DNA. This technique of isolating phage samples was originally designed by Meselson, Stahl and Jerome Vinograd. The phage samples isolated would contain various amounts of the isotope based on the rate of DNA replication. The amount of isotope incorporated in the new DNA strands, they hoped, would be large enough to determine quantitatively. The experiments, however, were not successful. After further contemplation, Meselson and Stahl decided to abandon the use of bacteriophage T4 and the isotope and use instead the bacteria *Echerichia coli* (*E. coli*) and the heavy nitrogen isotope 15N as the labeling substance. This time when the same experimental steps were repeated, the analysis showed three distinct types of bacterial DNA, two from the original parent strands and one from the new offspring. Analysis of this offspring showed each strand of DNA came from a different parent. Thus the theory of semiconservative replication of DNA had been proven. With this notable start to his scientific career Meselson embarked on another collaboration, this time with biologists **Sydney Brenner**, from the Medical Research Council's Division of Molecular Biology in Cambridge, England, and **François Jacob** from the Pasteur Institute Laboratories in Paris, France. Together, Meselson, Brenner and Jacob performed a series of experiments in which they showed that when the bacteriophage T4 enters a bacterial cell, the phage DNA incorporates into the cellular DNA and causes the release of a substance called "messenger RNA" which instructs the cell to manufacture phage proteins instead of the bacterial cell proteins that are normally produced. These experiments led to the discovery of the role of messenger RNA as the instructions which the bacterial cell reads to produce the desired protein products. These experiments also showed that the bacterial cell can produce proteins from messenger RNA that are not native to the cell in which it occurs. These findings laid considerable ground work in the field of molecular biology.

Restriction, Replication, Recombination

In his own laboratory at Harvard University, Meselson and a postdoctoral fellow, Robert Yuan, were developing and purifying one of the first of many known restriction enzymes commonly used in molecular biological analyses. Restrictions enzymes are developed by cultivating bacterial strains with phages. Bacterial strains that have the ability to restrict foreign DNAs produce a protein called an "enzyme," that actually chews up or degrades the foreign DNA. This enzyme is able to break up the foreign DNA sequences into a number of small segments by breaking the double stranded DNA at particular locations. Purification of these enzymes allowed mapping of various DNA sequences to be accomplished. The use of purified restriction enzymes became a common practice in the field of molecular biology to map and determine contents of many DNA sequence.

After many years working with the bacteria *E. coli,* Meselson decided to investigate the fundamentals of DNA replication and repair in other organisms. He chose to work on the fruit fly called *Drosophila melanogaster.* Meselson discovered that the fruit fly contained particular DNA sequences that would be transcribed only when induced by heat shock or stress conditions. These particular "heat shock genes" required a specific setup of DNA bases upstream of the initiation site in order for transcription to occur. If the number of bases was increased or reduced from what was required, the gene would not be transcribed. Meselson also found that there were particular DNA sequences that could be recombined or moved around within the entire chromosome of DNA. These moveable segments are termed transposons. These transposons, when inserted into particular sites within the sequence, can either turn on or turn off expression of the gene that is near it, causing mutations within the fly. These studies contributed to the identity of particular regulatory and structural features of the fruit fly as well as to the overall understanding of the properties of DNA.

Throughout his scientific career, Meselson has been awarded for his contributions to the field of molecular biology. In 1963, Meselson received the National Academy of Science Prize for Molecular Biology, followed by the Eli Lilly Award for Microbiology and Immunology in 1964. He was awarded the Lehman Award in 1975 and the Presidential award in 1983, both from the New York Academy of Sciences. In 1990, Meselson received the Science Freedom and Responsibility Award from the American Association for the Advancement of Science.

During a personal interview, when asked what was a leading factor in his choosing scientific research as a career, Dr. Meselson responded, "research gives you the freedom to think about problems, and science gives you the ability to solve the problems." According to Meselson, his greatest contribution to the scientific world has been "the invention of particular methods of analysis that have contributed to the understanding of how nature works." He attributes his successful career as a scientist to the many people with whom he has interacted in the field of science. With each person he has encountered, ideas and knowledge are exchanged, contributing to the advancement of the understanding of basic biology.

Throughout his career as a scientist, Meselson has written over 50 papers published in major scientific journals and received many honors and awards. Matthew Meselson married Jeanne Guillemin in 1986 and has two children, Zoe and Amy Valor. In his spare time, Meselson has delved into political issues, particularly on government proposals for worldwide chemical and biological weapon disarmament. He has also enjoyed traveling throughout the world.

SELECTED WRITINGS BY MESELSON:

Periodicals

"The Replication of DNA in *Escherichia coli,*" *Proceedings of the National Academy of Sciences,* Volume 44, 1958, pp. 671–682.
"DNA Restriction Enzyme from *E. coli,*" *Nature,* Volume 217, 1968, pp. 1110–1114.
"Interspecific Nucleotide Sequence Comparisons Used to Identify Regulatory and Structural Features of the *Drosophila* hsp82 gene." *Journal of Molecular Biology,* Volume 188, pp. 499–515, 1986.

SOURCES:

Books

Daintith, John, Sarah Mitchell, and Elizabeth Tootill, *A Biographical Encyclopedia of Scientists,* Facts on File, 1981.
Modern Scientists and Engineers, Volume 3, McGraw-Hill, 1980.

Other

Meselson, Matthew S., interview with Karen S. Kelly conducted December 2, 1993.

—*Sketch by Karen S. Kelly*

Élie Metchnikoff
1845-1916
Russian immunologist

Élie Metchnikoff was a pioneer in the field of immunology and won the 1908 Nobel Prize in physiology or medicine for his discoveries of how the body protects itself from disease-causing organisms.

Later in life he became interested in the effects of nutrition on aging and health, which led him to advocate some controversial diet practices.

Metchnikoff, the youngest of five children, was born in the Ukrainian village of Ivanovka on May 16, 1845, to Emilia Nevahovna, daughter of a wealthy writer, and Ilya Ivanovich, an officer of the Imperial Guard in St. Petersburg. He enrolled at the Kharkov *lycee* in 1856, where he developed an especially strong interest in biology. At age 16 he published a paper in a Moscow journal criticizing a geology textbook. After graduating from secondary school in 1862, he entered the University of Kharkov, where he completed a four year program in two years. He also became an advocate of the theory of evolution by natural selection after reading Charles Darwin's *On the Origin of Species by Means of Natural Selection.*

In 1864 he traveled to Germany to study, where his work with nematodes (a species of worm) led to the surprising conclusion that the organism alternates between sexual and asexual generations. His studies at Kharkov, coupled with his interest in Darwin's theory, convinced him that highly evolved animals should show structural similarities to more primitive animals. He pursued his studies of invertebrates in Naples, Italy, where he collaborated with Russian zoologist Alexander Kovalevsky. They demonstrated the homology (similarity of structure) between the germ layers—embryonic sheets of cells that give rise to specific tissue—in different multicellular animals. For this work the scientists were awarded the Karl Ernst von Baer Prize.

Metchnikoff was only twenty-two when he received the prize and had a promising career ahead of himself. However, he soon developed severe eye strain, a condition that hampered his work and prevented him from using the microscope for the next fifteen years. Nevertheless, in 1867 he completed his doctorate at the University of St. Petersburg with a thesis on the embryonic development of fish and crustaceans. He taught at the university for the next six years before moving to the University of Odessa on the Black Sea where he studied marine animals.

During the summer of 1880 he spent a vacation on a farm where a beetle infection was destroying crops. In an attempt to curtail the devastation, Metchnikoff injected a fungus from a dead fly into a beetle to see if he could kill the pest. Metchnikoff carried this interest in infection with him when he left Odessa for Italy, following the assassination of Czar Alexander II in 1884. A zoologist up to that point, Metchnikoff began to focus more on pathology, or the study of diseases.

This transformation was due primarily to his study of the larva of the Bipinniara starfish. While studying this larva, which is transparent and can be easily observed under the microscope, Metchnikoff saw special cells surrounding and engulfing foreign bodies, similar to the actions of white blood cells in humans that were present in areas of inflammation. During a similar study of the water flea *Daphniae,* he observed white blood cells attacking needle-shaped spores that had invaded the insect's body. He called these cells "phagocytes," from the Greek word *phagein,* meaning, "to eat."

While scientists thought that human phagocytes merely transported foreign material throughout the body, and therefore spread disease, Metchnikoff realized they performed a protective function. He recognized that the human white blood cells and the starfish phagocytes were embryologically homologous, both being derived from the mesoderm layer of cells. He concluded that the human cells cleared the body of disease-causing organisms. In 1884 he injected infected blood under the skin of a frog and demonstrated that white blood cells in higher animals served a similar function as those in starfish larvae. The scientific community, however, still did not accept his idea that phagocytic cells fought off infections.

Metchnikoff married Ludmilla Federovna in 1869. When she died from complications of tuberculosis four years later, Metchnikoff overdosed on morphine in an unsuccessful suicide attempt. In 1875 he married fifteen-year-old Olga Belokopitova, who shortly thereafter contracted typhoid fever. Distraught, Metchnikoff once again attempted suicide by infecting himself with a dangerous bacteria. Neither of Metchnikoff's wives bore him children, but he and his second wife became the guardians of her two brothers and three sisters upon the death of her parents.

Metchnikoff returned to Odessa in 1886 and became the director of the Bacteriological Institute. He continued his research on phagocytes in animals and pursued vaccines for chicken cholera and sheep anthrax. Hounded by scientists and the press because of his lack of medical training, Metchnikoff fled Russia a year later. A chance meeting with French scientist Louis Pasteur led to a position as the director of a new laboratory at the Pasteur Institute in Paris. There, he continued his study of phagocytosis for the next twenty-eight years.

But conflict with his fellow scientists continued to follow him. Many scientists asserted that antibodies triggered the body's immune response to infection. Metchnikoff accepted the existence of antibodies but insisted that phagocytic cells represented another important arm of the immune system. His work at the Pasteur Institute led to many fundamental discoveries about the immune response, and one of his students, **Jules Bordet**, contributed important insights into the nature of complement, a system of antimicrobial enzymes triggered by antibodies. Metchnikoff received the Nobel Prize for physiology and medicine in

1908 jointly with **Paul Ehrlich** for their work in initiating the study of immunology and greatly influencing its development.

Metchnikoff's interest in immunity led to writings on aging and death. His book *The Nature of Man,* published in 1903, extolled the health virtues of "right living," which for him included consuming large amounts of fermented milk or yogurt made with a Bulgarian bacillus. In fact, his own name became associated with a popular commercial preparation of yogurt, although he received no royalties. By 1913 Metchnikoff publicly supported the erroneous theory that cancer is caused by microbes and warned people not to eat uncooked food. Metchnikoff claimed he even plunged bananas into boiling water after unpeeling them and passed his silverware through flames before using it. "Water is filtered and then boiled. I never eat uncooked fruit," the *New York Times* quoted him as saying.

On July 15, 1916, after a series of heart attacks, Metchnikoff died in Paris at the age of 71. He was a member of the French Academy of Medicine, the Swedish Medical Society, and the Royal Society of London, from which he received the Copley Medal. He also received an honorary doctorate from Cambridge University.

SELECTED WRITINGS BY METCHNIKOFF:

Books

The Nature of Man: Studies in Optimistic Philosophy, [New York], 1903.
Lectures on the Comparative Pathology of Inflamation, Dover, 1905.
Immunity in Infectious Diseases, Cambridge University Press, 1905.

SOURCES:

Books

Lépine, Pierre, *Élie Metchnikoff et l'immunologie,* [Vichy], 1966.
Metchnikoff, Olga, *Life of Élie Metchnikoff, 1845–1916,* translated by E. Ray Lankester, [Boston], 1921.

Periodicals

"Prof. Metchnikoff, Scientist, Is Dead," *New York Times,* July 16, 1916.
Vaughn, R. B., "The Romantic Rationalist, a Study of Élie Metchnikoff," *Medical History,* Volume 10, 1965, pp. 201–215.

—*Sketch by Marc Kusinitz*

Otto Meyerhof
1884-1951
German American biochemist

In the course of a long and distinguished career both in Germany and the United States, Otto Meyerhof helped lay the foundations for modern bioenergetics, the application of the principles of thermodynamics (the science of physics in relation to heat and mechanical action) to the analysis of chemical processes going on within the living cell. Meyerhof's was the first attempt at explaining the function of a cell in terms of physics and chemistry; his research into the chemical processes of the muscle cell paved the way for the full understanding of the breakdown of glucose to provide body energy. For his discovery of the fixed relationship between the consumption of oxygen and the metabolism of lactic acid in the muscle, Meyerhof shared the 1922 Nobel Prize for Physiology or Medicine.

Born Otto Fritz Meyerhof on April 12, 1884, in Hannover, he was the second child and first son of Felix Meyerhof, a Jewish merchant, and Bettina May Meyerhof. Brought up in a comfortable middle class home, Meyerhof attended secondary school at the Wilhelms Gymnasium in Berlin where the family had moved. As a 16-year-old, he developed kidney trouble, necessitating a long period of bed rest. It was during this time that Meyerhof began reading extensively, especially the works of Goethe, which were to influence him deeply in his later life. A trip to Egypt in 1900 also provided him with a lasting love of archaeology. Once his health had improved, Meyerhof began studying medicine, receiving his medical degree from the University of Heidelberg in 1909. As a doctoral dissertation, Meyerhof wrote on the psychological theory of mental disturbances. His interests in psychology and psychiatry were ongoing, though he soon changed the direction of his professional passions.

From 1909 to 1912 Meyerhof was an assistant in internal medicine at the Heidelberg Clinic, and it was there he came under the influence of physiologist **Otto Warburg** who was researching the causes of cancer. Meyerhof soon joined this young man in a study of cell respiration, for Warburg was examining the changes that occur when a normal living cell becomes cancerous. It was this early work that set Meyerhof on a course of biochemical research. He also spent some time at the Stazione Zoologica in Naples, and by 1913 had joined the physiology department at the University of Kiel where, as a young lecturer, he first introduced his theory of applying the principles of thermodynamics to the analysis of cell processes. It was one thing to lecture about such an application; quite another to apply such principles to his own research.

Muscle Contraction as Focus

Meyerhof decided to focus on the chemical changes occurring during voluntary muscle contraction, applying thermodynamics to the study of cellular function. The chemical and mechanical changes occurring during muscle contraction were on a large enough scale that he could measure them with the primitive instruments he had at Kiel, and there had been some earlier research on which to build. Specifically, physiologist **Archibald Vivian Hill** in England had observed the heat production of muscles, and others, including physiologist Claude Bernard of France and English biochemist **Frederick Gowland Hopkins**, had shown both that glycogen, a carbohydrate made up of chains of glucose molecules, is stored in liver and muscle cells, and that working muscles accumulated lactic acid. But Meyerhof's research had to be put on hold during the First World War.

In 1914, as Europe was becoming increasingly unsettled, Meyerhof married Hedwig Schallenberg, a painter. The couple had three children in the course of their marriage: George Geoffrey, Bettina Ida, and Walter Ernst. There was still time for some research during this period. In 1917 he was able to show that the carbohydrate enzyme systems in animal cells and yeast are similar, thus bolstering his philosophical conviction in the biochemical unity of all life. During the war, Meyerhof served briefly as a German medical officer on the French front, after the war resuming his research into the physicochemical mechanics of cell function and being appointed assistant professor at the University of Kiel. It was while examining the contraction of frog muscle in 1919 that Meyerhof proved in a series of careful experiments that there was a quantitative relationship between depletion of glycogen in the muscle cell and the amount of lactic acid that was produced. He also demonstrated that this process could occur without oxygen, in what is termed anaerobic glycolysis. Meyerhof went on to demonstrate further that when the muscle relaxed after work, then molecular oxygen would be consumed, oxidizing part of the lactic acid—actually only about one-fifth of it. He concluded that the energy created by this oxidative process was used to convert the remaining lactic acid back to glycogen, and thus the cycle could begin again in the muscle cell. Such an understanding, though not completely explaining all the steps in such a metabolic pathway, did pave the way for other research into the glucose cycle and energy production in the body. Meyerhof won the 1922 Nobel Prize for this pioneering work, sharing it with Hill whose work on heat in muscle contraction had inspired much of Meyerhof's own research. The prize could not have come at a better time. Just prior

to the announcement, Meyerhof had been passed over for the position of chair of the physiology department at the University of Kiel, largely because of anti-Semitism. The Nobel Prize secured for him laboratory space at the Kaiser Wilhelm Institute for Biology in Berlin, where he was appointed a professor in 1924. During his stay there, from 1924 to 1929, he trained many notable biochemists, **Hans Adolf Krebs**, **Fritz Lipmann**, and **Severo Ochoa** among them. He brought his colleague Karl Lohmann into the group, and Meyerhof and his team continued with further research at Berlin-Dahlem where the institute was located. In 1925 Meyerhof managed to extract the glycolytic enzymes of muscle, thereby making it possible to isolate these enzymes and study the individual steps involved in the complex pathway in the muscle cell from glycogen to lactic acid. It took another two decades to fully delineate the pathway, and many other brilliant scientists worked on it, but it is today called the Embden-Meyerhof pathway in recognition of Meyerhof's groundbreaking work.

Discovers Role of Energy-Rich Phosphate Derivatives

In 1926 researchers in the U.S. and in England discovered a new phosphorylated compound in muscle, phosphocreatine. Searching for another possible source of chemical energy in addition to lactic acid, Meyerhof tested this compound and found that its breakdown did produce heat. But more importantly, in 1929, Meyerhof's assistant, Lohmann, discovered adenosine triphosphate (ATP). Meyerhof and Lohmann went on to show that ATP is the most important molecule that powers the biochemical reactions of the cell, and to demonstrate its role in muscle contraction as well as in other energy-requiring processes of biological systems. That same year Meyerhof was appointed director of the new Kaiser Wilhelm Institute for Medical Research in Heidelberg, and for the first time had expansive and modern work space at his disposal.

Meyerhof remained at Heidelberg until 1938, continuing his work with ATP and providing striking evidence of the unity of biochemical processes amid the amazing diversity of life forms. But such philosophical proofs would not help him in the new Germany. Starting with Hitler's rise to power in 1933, Jewish scientists like Meyerhof had been steadily emigrating. Finally in 1938 he realized that he could no longer stay. His daughter and oldest son were already out of the country. Together with his wife and youngest child, Meyerhof, on the pretext of taking a few weeks vacation, escaped to Paris where he continued his research at the Institute of Physico-chemical Biology. In 1940, when the Germans invaded France, Meyerhof and his family were forced to flee once again, this time to Spain and eventually, via an arduous trip over the Pyrenees, to neutral Portugal where they caught a ship to the United States. There he joined his friend Hill—with whom he had shared the 1922 Nobel Prize—at the University of Pennsylvania where the Rockefeller Foundation had created a professorship in physiological chemistry for him. He continued research into the bioenergetics of cell function, summering at Woods Hole Marine Laboratory on Cape Cod and meeting with other refugees from the European conflagration. He suffered a severe heart attack in 1944, but recovered and became a United States citizen in 1946. In 1949 he was elected to the National Academy of Sciences in recognition of his life's work that included not only original research, but also the publication of over 400 scientific articles. He died of a second heart attack on October 6, 1951.

SELECTED WRITINGS BY MEYERHOF:

Books

Chemical Dynamics of Life Phenomena, Lippincott, 1924.

Die Chemischen Vorgänge im Muskel und ihr Zusammenhang mit Arbeitsleistung und Wärmebildung, Springer, 1930.

Chimie de la contraction musculaire, Delmas, 1932.

Nobel Lectures in Physiology or Medicine, Volume 2, Elsevier, 1965, pp. 27–41.

SOURCES:

Books

Dictionary of Scientific Biography, Scribner, 1974, p. 359.

Nachmansohn, David, *German-Jewish Pioneers in Science, 1900–1933,* Springer-Verlag, 1979, pp. 268–311.

Nobel Laureates in Medicine or Physiology, Garland Publishing, pp. 392–395.

Nobel Prize Winners, H. W. Wilson, 1987, pp. 696–698.

Periodicals

Gemmill, C. L., *Medical College of Virginia Quarterly,* Volume 2, 1966, pp. 141–142.

Nachmansohn, David, Severo Ochoa, and Fritz Lipmann, *Science,* Volume 115, 1952, pp. 365–369.

—*Sketch by J. Sydney Jones*

Hartmut Michel
1948-
German biochemist

A biochemist known for his wide range of technical skills in the laboratory, Hartmut Michel has spent his career studying the complex proteins involved in photosynthesis. He shared the 1988 Nobel Prize in chemistry with **Johann Deisenhofer** and **Robert Huber** for a project he initiated: a detailed analysis of the atomic structure of a cluster of proteins called the photosynthetic reaction center.

Hartmut Michel was born July 18, 1948, in Ludwigsburg, Germany, to Karl and Freda Kachler Michel. His father was a joiner and his mother was a dressmaker, though in previous generations, Michel's family on both sides had been farmers. Michel graduated in 1967 from the Friedrich Schiller Gymnasium, with a strong interest in molecular biology and biochemistry, but before pursuing his education, served for two years in the military.

In 1969, Michel enrolled in the University of Tubingen. During 1972, he did laboratory work at the University of Munich and at the Max Planck Institute for Biochemistry at Martinsred, and by the end of that year he had decided to pursue a career in academic research. Michel passed his exams in 1974, and began work in the Friedrich Miescher Laboratory of the Max Planck Society in Tubingen under Dieter Oesterhelt, a biochemist. Oesterhelt moved to the University of Wurzburg in 1975, and Michel went with him. It was here he completed work for his Ph.D. in 1977.

Begins Work on Photosynthesis

A good portion of Michel's work under Oesterhelt was devoted to the study of photosynthesis. This is considered the most important chemical reaction in the biosphere. At its most basic level, photosynthesis is the conversion of water and carbon dioxide with the use of sunlight into oxygen and nutrients, but the process is actually extremely complicated and not well understood. At the time Michel began his work, it was surmised that an area of protein, known as the photosynthetic reaction center, was a major actor in the process of photosynthesis; scientists believed that the electrons somehow picked up the charge that drove the reaction here, but little else was known about it.

Scientists usually study proteins, as they study many substances, by crystallizing them. The crystallized form of a substance is a good subject because crystals are characterized by a very organized internal atomic structure—they are predictable solids. X-ray crystallography is a tool commonly used in analysis of crystals. This process uses radiation of known wavelength, X rays; the radiation is aimed at crystals, and crystallographers study the reaction of the rays after they come in contact with the crystal. Electron clouds present in the crystal cause interference with the X rays, so knowing how the direction of the rays is changed tells the scientist where the electrons are located and thus determines atomic structure.

X-ray crystallography was first used in 1912 by **Max von Laue**, so it was not a new procedure. The difficulty for Michel was not in finding the technology to examine the crystal, but in finding a method to create a crystal out of the protein. It was considered almost impossible to crystallize membrane proteins, the type present in the photosynthetic reaction center. Water is generally used in crystallization, but membrane proteins interact with water as part of their function, so they are not water soluble. Michel decided that this did not mean membrane proteins could not be crystallized, but that they must be crystallized with a different solution. He originally worked on this problem with bacteriorhodopsin, one of the halobacteria, which means salt-loving. By using different detergents instead of water, he was able to form a two-dimensional crystal and a very small three-dimensional crystal, neither suitable for study with X-ray crystallography.

At this point in his research, Michel had planned to pursue a postdoctoral position. His limited success, however, excited him enough to move once again with Oesterhelt, this time to the Max Planck Institute for Biochemistry in Martinsred in 1979. Once settled, Michel decided to try a different membrane protein, choosing that of *rhodopseudomonas viridis,* a purple bacterium containing the simplest known photosynthetic reaction center. Success came two years later; in 1981 he formed a crystal that could be studied.

Joins Team that Wins Nobel Prize

With a crystal well-formed enough to study, Michel turned to Robert Huber, a department head at the Max Planck Institute, to help find a suitable expert in X-ray crystallography to run the tests. Huber directed Michel to Johann Deisenhofer, and a four-year collaboration was begun. By the end of this period, they had identified and placed more than 10,000 atoms in the membrane protein. This work led to the award of the 1988 Nobel Prize in chemistry to Michel, Huber, and Deisenhofer. In receiving this award, the scientists were credited for work which had implications far beyond photosynthesis, including the understanding of respiration, nerve impulses, hormone action, and the process of nutrient introduction to the cells. The understanding of photosynthesis alone, however, is an important advance in scientific knowledge; their research may even make it possible

to create artificial reaction centers, which would have implications for many aspects of technology.

Before the award of the Nobel Prize, Michel won two other awards jointly with Deisenhofer—the Biophysics Prize of the American Physical Society in 1986, and the Otto-Bayer Prize in 1988. Michel was also the recipient of the 1986 Otto Klung Prize for Chemistry and the Leibniz Prize of the German Research Association in 1986. Michel is a member of the European Molecular Biology Organization, the Max Planck Society, the Society for Biological Chemistry, the German Chemists' Society, and the Society for Physical Biology. In 1987, he was named department head and director at the Max Planck Institute for Biophysics in Frankfurt/Main. His work continues in the area of photosynthesis and crystallization, and he was the editor of *Crystallization of Membrane Proteins* in 1989.

Michel has been married to Ilona Leger-Michel since 1979. They have a son and a daughter together, and a daughter from his wife's previous marriage. In his spare time, Michel enjoys reading history, traveling, and growing orchids.

SELECTED WRITINGS BY MICHEL:

Books

(Editor) *Crystallization of Membrane Proteins,* CRC Press, 1991.

Periodicals

(With Johann Deisenhofer) "Nobel Lecture: The Photosynthetic Reaction Center from the Purple Bacterium Rhodopseudomonas Viridis," *Embo J,* August 1989, pp. 2149–2170.

SOURCES:

Books

McGuire, Paula, editor, *Nobel Prize Winners Supplement, 1987–1991,* H. W. Wilson, 1992.

Periodicals

Dagani, Ron, and Stinson, Stephen, "Nobel Prizes: Photosynthesis, Drug Studies Honored," *Chemical and Engineering News,* October 24, 1988, pp. 4–5.
Levi, Barbara Goss, "Nobel Chemists Shed Light on Key Structure in Photosynthesis," *Physics Today,* February, 1989, pp. 17–18.
Lewin, Roger, "Membrane Protein Holds Photosynthetic Secrets," *Science,* November 4, 1988, pp. 672–673.

"Stories of Patience and Triumph," *Time,* October 31, 1988 p. 65.

"Winners of Nobel Prizes," *The New York Times,* October 20, 1988, p. B13.

—*Sketch by Kimberlyn McGrail*

Evangelia Micheli-Tzanakou

Evangelia Micheli-Tzanakou
19(?)-
Greek-born American physicist

A native of Greece, physicist Evangelia Micheli-Tzanakou has been based for most of her career at Rutgers University, where she has done extensive theoretical and practical research on brain function. In 1992, she received the Society of Women Engineers (SWE) Achievement Award for "outstanding contributions to the understanding and modeling of visual systems with neural networks."

Born in Athens, Micheli-Tzanakou received a B.S. degree in physics from Athens University in 1968. She taught high school in Athens before coming to the United States to resume her education. She studied physics at Syracuse University, earning her M.S. degree in 1974 and her Ph.D. in 1977. Micheli-Tzanakou then joined the staff of Rutgers University, where she was named assistant professor in 1981 and associate professor in 1985. In 1990, she was appointed professor and chair of the biomedical engineering department. She was named codirector of the graduate program in biomedical engineering in 1992. She also serves as a full member of the faculty in the computer science and electrical engineering departments.

Devises Models for Brain and Nervous System

In her research, Micheli-Tzanakou uses optimization techniques to gain understanding of brain functions and dysfunctions. She has compared those who age normally with patients who have Alzheimer's and Parkinson's diseases. Some of the methods she developed are now used in cardiology to predict the prognosis of heart-attack patients. Micheli-Tzanakou also developed a set of algorithms for modeling the visual system, and she has applied this technique to other functions of the nervous system and to research other brain functions, such as pattern recognition. Micheli-Tzanakou has also studied the effect of education on the functioning of the brain through the aging process, establishing that educated people do in fact maintain their brain functions better, on average, than those with less education.

Micheli-Tzanakou advises aspiring scientists to pursue the field that inspires their passion, telling contributor Karen Withem, "Go for whatever education pleases you the most, because that is where you will be successful." She also spoke of being surprised by the lack of ethics among some scientists: "A lot of people sacrifice their ethics for their science because they're under pressure, but without ethics, I don't believe the science," she said. Micheli-Tzanakou encourages young women to seek role models from among scientists of integrity whether they are men or women. "Many women think they need a woman as a role model; gender doesn't matter."

In addition to receiving the SWE Achievement Award, Micheli-Tzanakou is a fellow of the Institute for Electrical and Electronics Engineers (IEEE), a fellow of the Academy of Medicine of New Jersey, and a member of the scientific society Sigma Xi. She was the recipient in 1985 of the IEEE Outstanding Advisor Award. She is a Founding Fellow of the American Institute for Medical and Biomedical Engineering, an honorary member of the British Brain Research Association, and an honorary member of the European Brain and Behavior Society. Micheli-Tzanakou has served as a member of the editorial board and associate editor of IEEE Transactions on Neural Networks, as well as numerous committees and offices for IEEE. She has served in the Science

Advisory Group on the Douglass Project for Rutgers Women in Math, Science and Engineering. She has also received numerous honorary university degrees.

SOURCES:

Books

Society of Women Engineers Achievement Awards, 1993 edition.

Other

Micheli-Tzanakou, Evangelia, interview with Karen Withem conducted February 14, 1994.

—*Sketch by Karen Withem*

Albert Michelson
1852-1931
Prussian-born American physicist

Albert Michelson devoted his life almost exclusively to the study of one subject: light. For his accomplishments in the study of optics, he was awarded the Nobel Prize for physics in 1907, the first American ever to receive that prestigious award. In experiments carried out over nearly half a century, Michelson repeatedly refined his attempts to determine the speed of light, a topic on which he became the world's foremost authority, and attained an accuracy of about three parts in a million for the value of this constant. In addition to his work on the speed of light, Michelson became an expert on the use of optical techniques to make a wide variety of physical measurements.

Albert Abraham Michelson was born on December 19, 1852, in Strelno, Prussia, not far from the Polish border. At the age of two, he came to the United States with his parents, Samuel and Rosalie Przlubska Michelson. The Michelsons landed in New York City, but shortly thereafter left for San Francisco. Samuel planned to take his family to the gold fields of California and Nevada where he could open a general store.

After a short stay in San Francisco, young Albert traveled with his parents to their new home in Murphys Camp, in California's Calaveras County. He was soon sent back to San Francisco, however, to complete his education. There he fell under the influence of Theodore Bradley, headmaster of the Boys' High School, where Michelson was enrolled. Bradley apparently recognized Michelson's talents and placed him in charge of the school's scientific equipment. At the age of 16, Michelson returned to live with his parents, whose home was now in Virginia City, Nevada. A brother, Charles, was born the following year and a sister, Miriam, two years later.

Perseverance Wins an Appointment to the Naval Academy

In 1869, Michelson decided to take the entrance examination for the U.S. Naval Academy in Annapolis. He passed the exam, but lost the appointment to another boy who had tied with him on the test. Undeterred, Michelson decided to travel to Washington and ask President Ulysses S. Grant personally for an appointment to the Academy. The Academy traditionally saved ten "open" appointments for special cases such as Michelson's, and he hoped to earn one of them. He got his appointment with Grant, but the President explained that all ten open appointments had already been made. He encouraged Michelson, however, to take his case directly to the Commandant in Annapolis. When Michelson did so, he was surprised to hear that the Commandant was willing to offer him a "special eleventh appointment." In later years, Michelson was to look back on this stroke of good fortune and explain that he owed his career in science to that early "illegal act."

Michelson graduated from the Naval Academy in 1873 and then served his required two years as an ensign on a series of cruises. At the end of this period, he accepted an appointment as an instructor of chemistry and physics at the Academy, a position he held until 1879. On April 10, 1877, Michelson married Margaret McLean Heminway, daughter of New York City banker and lawyer, Albert Gallatin Heminway. The Michelsons' marriage lasted for twenty years and resulted in three children, Albert Heminway, Truman, and Elsa.

Michelson carried out his earliest scientific research during his years of teaching at the Naval Academy. The topic that captured his attention, and was to hold it during the rest of his life, was the speed of light. Prior to his own work, several other scientists, including physicist Jean Bernard Leon Foucault, had done significant research on finding the speed of light, all with varying degrees of success. Working on the problem at the same time was a colleague of Michelson's at the Academy, Simon Newcomb. Michelson and Newcomb both adopted the approach used by Foucault, and the extensive correspondence between the two Annapolis instructors about their respective experiments is now a classic part of the literature of American science.

By 1879, Michelson had devised a modification of Foucault's technique that gave a value for the speed of light of 186,500 miles per second, a result that was accurate to one part in 10,000. His research results were published in the April, 1879, issue of the *American Journal of Science.* In the same year, Michelson accepted a job at the Nautical Almanac office in Washington. He stayed only briefly, however, as he wanted to learn more about current research on the speed of light in particular and on optics in general, and that research was taking place largely in Europe. Michelson left for Europe in 1880 with his wife and two young children, Elsa and Truman. For the next two years, he visited a number of universities, including those in Berlin and Heidelberg, as well as the College de France and the Ecole Polytechnique in Paris.

His Research Fails to Detect the Luminiferous Ether

Michelson's first stop in Europe was at the laboratories of Hermann Helmholtz in Berlin. It was here that Michelson began his first studies of a question that was to earn him international fame: the movement of light through the "luminiferous ether." At the time, scientists believed that light travels as a wave, somewhat similar to water waves. But the existence of waves implies the presence of some material through which the waves can move. In the case of water waves, that "something" is water. In order to account for the existence of light waves, scientists had invented the concept of a "luminiferous ether." They envisioned this ether as a very thin substance that flowed much like water and permeated the whole universe. Light waves could then be explained as undulations within this ether. Efforts to detect the presence of this ether had been entirely unsuccessful, however. It was to this question that Michelson addressed himself during his stay at Helmholtz's laboratory in 1880–1881.

Michelson's investigation led him to create an experiment in which a beam of light was split into two parts and then projected at right angles to each other. The experiment was meant to create one beam of light that traveled parallel to the flow of the ether and a second beam that traveled perpendicular to it. As a simple analogy, think of a pair of boats traveling on a river, one moving downstream with the river's motion, and the other moving across the stream, at right angles to the river's flow. If both boats are traveling at the same speed, their actual motions will be somewhat different because of the additional velocity imparted by the motion of the river.

Michelson expected that in his experiment, one beam of light would be slowed down as it moved across the ether, while the other beam would be speeded up as it traveled with the ether. When the two beams were brought together by mirrors, then, they would no longer coincide, but would be slightly out of phase with each other. The device that Michelson developed to look for this change was an interferometer, a device that he was to use over and over again in many other applications in later years.

When Michelson actually carried out this experiment, however, he was able to detect no effect caused by an invisible ether. After being split, sent in two directions at right angles to each other, and then recombined, the light beams were exactly in phase with each other. There was no evidence that their travel had been at all affected by the ether. The result was especially troubling in Michelson's opinion because his equipment had been designed to detect very small changes in the speed of the two beams of light. Within a short time, flaws in the experiment's design were pointed out by Dutch physicist **Hendrik Lorentz**. These flaws, together with his inability to find a difference in speed between the two light beams, led Michelson to conclude that his effort was a failure. He began to think of modifications that would correct the problems in his experiment.

Meets Morley at Case

In the midst of his European tour, Michelson decided to resign his commission in the Navy. When he returned to the United States in 1882, he accepted an appointment in the physics department of the newly created Case School of Applied Science in Cleveland. While there, he continued his research on the speed of light. He also made the acquaintance of **Edward W. Morley** of Western Reserve College, also in Cleveland. Beginning in 1886, Michelson and Morley returned to the nagging problem of the ether, looking for ways to improve on Michelson's earlier "failed" experiment.

Over a five-day period in July of 1887, Michelson and Morley once more conducted a test for the differential velocity of light in the ether, this time using an interferometer sensitive to about one part in four billion. Again, the experiment produced no observable effect due to the ether. Somewhat disappointed about their results, Michelson and Morley abandoned their plans to repeat the experiment and went on to other fields of research. In particular, they were eager to explore other ways of using the very precise instruments they had built for the ether experiment.

The null results obtained by Michelson and Morley were not ignored by others, however. Indeed, a number of theorists began to ask what it meant that the speed of light appeared always to be the same. Several physicists devised equations to explain how this could happen in an ether. Irish physicist George Francis FitzGerald even argued that the lengths of objects shrink as their velocity increases, thus material measuring devices themselves are never completely accurate since they are affected by such things as the velocity of the Earth moving through space. (This theory became known as the Lorentz-FitzGerald contraction.) The Michelson-Morley results also had profound effects on **Albert Einstein**, then working on his theory of general relativity. One key assumption of Einstein's theory, that the speed of light is always a constant, can be traced directly to Michelson's "failed" experiment.

Honors and Awards Mark His Years at Clark and Chicago

In 1889, Michelson accepted an invitation to join the faculty at the newly created Clark University in Worcester, Massachusetts. While at Clark, he continued to collaborate with Morley on applications of their interferometer. Among the new uses to which the instrument was put during this period was a more precise measurement of the length of the meter. This was accomplished by measuring the Paris meter bar then used as an international standard and rendering that measurement in terms of red cadmium lightwaves (these lightwaves being unaffected by conditions that might render a material measuring device inaccurate). This experiment allowed the length of an object to be determined through spectroscopic study.

After four years at Clark, Michelson changed institutions once more, this time accepting an offer to become chairman of the department of physics at the University of Chicago. He remained at Chicago for the rest of his academic career, eventually assuming the chair of Distinguished Service Professor of Physics in 1925. During his first decade at Chicago, Michelson's international fame reached its zenith. He served for two years as president of the American Physical Society (1901–1903) and later as president of the American Association for the Advancement of Science (1910–1911). He also received a number of national and international awards, including the Copley Medal of the Royal Society (1907), the Elliott Cresson Medal of the Franklin Institute (1912), the Draper Medal of the National Academy of Sciences (1916), and the Nobel Prize for Physics in 1907.

Academic honors also came his way. Although he never earned a graduate degree himself, he was awarded honorary doctorates by a number of institutions including Cambridge (1889), Yale (1901), Pennsylvania (1906), Leipzig (1909), Clark (1909), and Gottingen (1911). While at Chicago, his personal life also underwent some major changes as he divorced his first wife of 20 years and married Edna Stanton of Lake Forest, Illinois, on December 23, 1899. With his new wife, Michelson had three more daughters, Madelaine, Beatrice, and Dorothy. Michelson's tenure at Chicago was interrupted by World War I, during which he served as a naval officer. In the

Navy, he used his expertise to develop an optical range finder and to improve optical glasses used by the military.

In the years following the war, Michelson turned his attention to a problem that had long interested him: measurements of astronomical objects and phenomena. He adapted his interferometer to determine the size of objects such as the moons of Jupiter and the star Betelgeuse. The latter accomplishment was recorded in daily newspapers across the nation.

Late in life, Michelson turned once more to the subject that never lost its fascination for him: the speed of light. At the invitation of astronomer **George Ellery Hale**, Michelson designed an experiment to measure the speed of a light beam transmitted over the 22-mile distance between Mount Wilson and Mount San Antonio near Pasadena, California. Work actually began on the project in 1930 and continued through the next year. Michelson had become so ill, however, that he could not carry out the actual measurements himself, but left that task to assistants Fred Pearson and Francis Pease. In the midst of the experiment that was ultimately to conclude in 1933, Michelson died of a cerebral hemorrhage on May 9, 1931.

Michelson was interested in a number of leisure time activities including billiards, sailing, and tennis. He also had some talent as a musician (he played the violin) and as an artist. At one point, in fact, he was persuaded to give an exhibition of his water colors at the University of Chicago. Michelson has been described as a quiet, withdrawn man with a "simplicity of character." In *Popular Astronomy,* F. R. Moulton described Michelson as "unhurried and unfretful. . . . He pursued his modest serene way along the frontiers of science, entering new pathways, and ascending to unattained heights as leisurely and as easily as though he were taking an evening stroll."

SELECTED WRITINGS BY MICHELSON:

Books

Light Waves and Their Uses, University of Chicago Press, 1903.
Studies in Optics, University of Chicago Press, 1927.

SOURCES:

Books

Gillispie, Charles Coulson, editor, *Dictionary of Scientific Biography,* Volume 9, Scribner, 1975, pp. 371–374.

Livingston, Dorothy Michelson, *The Master of Light,* [New York], 1973.

Periodicals

Lemon, Harvey B., "Albert Abraham Michelson: The Man and the Man of Science," *American Physics Teacher,* February, 1936, pp. 1–11.
Popular Astronomy, June/July, 1931.

—*Sketch by David E. Newton*

Thomas Midgley, Jr.
1889-1944
American engineer and chemist

Though trained as an engineer, Thomas Midgley, Jr. is best known as an industrial chemist. He was primarily responsible for four important advances in the field of chemistry: discovering effective antiknock additives for gasoline; developing a practical process for the extraction of bromine from seawater; advancing knowledge of the vulcanization of rubber and the composition of both natural and synthetic rubbers; and developing nontoxic and nonflammable gases for use in refrigeration and air-conditioning. As a result of his endeavors, he was awarded all four of the major American medals for achievements in chemistry.

Midgley was born on May 18, 1889, in Beaver Falls, Pennsylvania, the son of Thomas Midgley and Hattie Lena Emerson Midgley. His father was a prolific inventor, especially of improvements in automobile tires; he was also an entrepreneur, whose business ventures usually proved unprofitable. When he was about six years old, Midgley moved with his family to Columbus, Ohio, where he attended elementary school and the early years of high school. In 1905 he went to Betts Academy, a preparatory school in Stamford, Connecticut. Midgley entered Cornell University in 1907 to study mechanical engineering, and he graduated in 1911.

On August 3, 1911, Midgely married Carrie M. Reynolds. They would eventually have two children. He went to work that same year as a draftsman and designer for the National Cash Register Company in Dayton, Ohio. He left after a year to work with his father in a small company the older man had established to manufacture his improved auto tires. This venture failed, and in 1916 Midgley joined the Dayton Engineering Laboratories Company, known as Delco. The company was headed by **Charles Franklin Kettering**, a noted engineer and inventor who became Midgley's boss, mentor, and friend; their close relationship was to last until the end of Midgley's life.

Discovers Antiknock Additives

Kettering soon put him to work investigating the problem of knock in internal-combustion engines, ignoring Midgley's protest that he was an engineer, not a chemist. Midgley was to spend the next five years on this project, becoming in the process a largely self-taught chemist. "Knock" was an audible pinging sound that developed in internal-combustion engines when they were driven near their maximum load capacity. The knock became worse at high engine-compression ratios, and it could destroy an engine if it continued long enough. Since higher compression ratios were essential to improve engine power and fuel efficiency, the problem had to be solved. Midgley soon determined that knock occurred after ignition of the fuel and that it was the result of a sudden increase in pressure and temperature within the engine cylinders. He also determined that it was caused by the fuel rather than by the engine itself. The problem then became one of finding a substance to add to gasoline that would lower the temperature, and hence the pressure, within the cylinder and thus end the knock.

Searching for a gasoline additive, Midgley and his coworkers at first simply tested a large number of chemical compounds in a process of trial and error. Some substances were found which effectively ended the knock, but they all had some serious drawback. Some were expensive to produce and some had a foul exhaust odor. As time passed and the research grew more sophisticated, Midgley and his colleagues discovered that all of the substances that reduced knock contained chemical elements that occupied a certain part of the periodic table. It then became possible to try compounds of other elements in the same area of the table. On December 9, 1921, they tested tetraethyl lead in an engine and found that a minute amount of it completely suppressed knock.

There were some problems even with tetraethyl lead. In the first place, it tended to foul engine valves and spark plugs. It was eventually discovered that adding bromine to the additive would solve this problem, but bromine was a scarce chemical. Midgely solved this by inventing a method for extracting bromine from seawater, where it is present in very small quantities. A more serious problem was the fact that lead compounds are poisonous and are especially dangerous to workers producing them. At the time tests done by the United States Bureau of Mines concluded that tetraethyl lead could be manufactured safely if proper precautions were followed. It was not until the 1970s that growing concern about lead pollution led to a ban on lead compounds in gasoline and the substitution of less toxic substances as antiknock additives.

Delco was absorbed by General Motors in 1920, and in 1924 General Motors and Standard Oil of New Jersey jointly formed a new concern, the Ethyl Corporation, whose purpose was to manufacture tetraethyl lead. Midgley became a vice president of the new organization but continued his chemical research for General Motors. In 1926 he became interested in natural and synthetic rubber and persuaded Alfred Sloan, the president of General Motors, to fund a research project on these materials. His research resulted in a series of scientific papers which greatly advanced the knowledge of the exact composition of natural rubber; he also improved the understanding of the process of vulcanization of rubber, and he was able to outline possible methods for the production of synthetic rubber. In 1928 Sloan ended financial support of this work because it seemed unlikely to produce any practical commercial results, but Midgley continued the work on his own time and with his own money for many years. He considered his rubber research to be the most truly scientific work he had done, precisely because it produced no immediate practical results.

Develops Nontoxic and Nonflammable Refrigerants

In 1928, Kettering asked Midgley to do research on a new refrigerant suited for home use. The Frigidaire division of General Motors was then in serious financial difficulties, due primarily to the deficiencies of the refrigeration equipment it produced. One of the most basic problems with all the refrigerators then being made was the refrigerants that were being used, such as sulfur dioxide, methyl chloride, ammonia, and butane. All were either toxic or inflammable. Kettering and Midgley agreed that a suitable refrigerant must be stable, noncorrosive, nontoxic, nonflammable; they also wanted a substance which had a boiling point between –0 and –40° centigrade, and they wanted it to be at least relatively cheap.

When Midgley examined his periodic table, he found that all elements of sufficient volatility for this purpose were clustered on the right-hand side. After rejecting all the elements which were either too unstable or too toxic, he was left with carbon, nitrogen, oxygen, hydrogen, fluorine, sulfur, chlorine, and bromine. Midgley and his assistants examined the physical properties of these elements for flammability and toxicity, and they decided that some compound of fluorine would be ideal. After experimentation, they synthesized dichlorodifluoromethane (soon called "freon"). Subsequent testing that the compound was stable and that it met the other criteria. Midgley revealed his discovery in April 1930 at the annual meeting of the American Chemical Society in

Atlanta. He breathed in some freon and then exhaled to extinguish a candle flame, thus dramatically demonstrating that the gas was both nontoxic and nonflammable. General Motors and the Du Pont Company joined together in August 1930 to form Kinetic Chemicals Inc. for the production of freon. Midgley became vice president of the new company. Freon soon became the standard refrigerant for home use.

Midgley devoted most of the remainder of his life to research at the laboratories of Ohio State University in Columbus. He had been awarded the Nichols Medal of the American Chemical Society in 1922; he subsequently received the Perkin Medal of the Society of Chemical Industry in 1937, the Priestley Medal of the American Chemical Society in 1941, and the Willard Gibbs Medal of the American Chemical Society in 1942. He was granted honorary degrees by the College of Wooster in 1936 and Ohio State University in 1944. He published fifty-seven scientific papers and was awarded 117 patents in the course of his career. He was president of the American Chemical Society at the time of his death in 1944.

Midgely was stricken with polio in 1940. In the *National Academy of Sciences, Biographical Memoirs,* Kettering remembers Midgely computing the odds of a man his age catching polio as "substantially equal to the chances of drawing a certain individual card from a stack of playing cards as high as the Empire State building." Although severely crippled, Midgely remained active, making the best he could of his infirmities. He rigged up a system of ropes and pulleys to assist him in rising from bed. On November 2, 1944, he somehow entangled himself in the apparatus and strangled to death at his home in Worthington, Ohio. He was fifty-five.

SELECTED WRITINGS BY MIDGLEY:

Periodicals

(With Thomas A. Boyd) "The Chemical Control of Gaseous Detonation with Particular Reference to the Internal-Combustion Engine," *Journal of Industrial and Engineering Chemistry,* Volume 14, October, 1922, pp. 894–898.

"From the Periodic Table to Production," *Industrial and Engineering Chemistry,* Volume 29, February, 1937, pp. 241–244.

SOURCES:

Books

Farber, Eduard, editor, *Great Chemists,* Interscience Publishers, 1961, pp. 1589–1597.

Gillispie, Charles Coulson, editor, *Dictionary of Scientific Biography,* Volume 9, Scribner, 1970, pp. 375–376.

Leslie, Stuart W., *Boss Kettering,* Columbia University Press, 1983.

Periodicals

Boyd, Thomas A., "Thomas Midgley, Jr., May 18, 1889-November 2, 1944," *Journal of the American Chemical Society,* Volume 75, June, 1953, pp. 2791–2795.

Kettering, Charles F., "Thomas Midgley, Jr., 1889–1944," *National Academy of Sciences, Biographical Memoirs,* Volume 24, 1947, pp. 361–380.

Leslie, Stuart W., "Thomas Midgley and the Politics of Industrial Research," *Business History Review,* Winter, 1980, pp. 480–503.

—*Sketch by John E. Little*

Elizabeth C. and James A. Miller

Elizabeth C. Miller
1920-1987
James A. Miller
1915-
American biochemists

Elizabeth C. Miller and James A. Miller are known for their ground-breaking research into the mechanism of chemical carcinogenesis. The Millers' discoveries laid the foundations for understanding the metabolic interactions with carcinogenic chemicals that produce cancer in experimental animals. Their work sparked intensive research into carcinogenesis and public interest in carcinogens.

James A. Miller was born in 1915 in Dormont, Pennsylvania, a small town just south of Pittsburgh. His father, John, was the manager of circulation for the *Pittsburgh Press,* and his mother, Emma Stenger, was a homemaker. Two brothers died in their youth. In 1929, his mother died and his father became seriously ill. "All the children had been taught to earn their keep," Miller told Laura Newman in an interview. "It fell to the four boys to stick together, absent mother and father." Despite the economic pressures, Miller completed high school in 1933, gaining high grades in science.

Miller credits the National Youth Administration, a New Deal youth employment program, with giving him his first job in chemistry—filling reagent

bottles at the chemistry department at the University of Pittsburgh. Within two years, Miller began the day program and an honors chemistry course. At the University of Pittsburgh, Miller got a job in an animal room lab with Charles Glen King, a well-known biochemist who had crystallized the first vitamin, vitamin C, and Max Schultze, who had trained at the University of Wisconsin. "I finally found myself," Miller told Newman. He graduated with a B.S. in chemistry in 1939. Schultze urged Miller to apply for a Wisconsin Alumni Research Foundation (WARF) scholarship in biochemistry at the University of Wisconsin, which he was awarded in 1939. He began laboratory research on the metabolism of recently identified chemicals that could induce cancer in animals. Miller received an M.S. and Ph.D. degrees in biochemistry from the University of Wisconsin in 1941 and 1943 respectively. Miller met Elizabeth Cavert in his second year at Wisconsin when he became her teaching assistant in a biochemistry lab. Miller soon found her to be an outstanding student and the two shared research interests. In August of 1942, the couple married.

Elizabeth Cavert Miller was born on May 2, 1920 in Minneapolis, the second daughter of Mary Elizabeth Mead and William Lane Cavert. Her father was the Director of Research in Agricultural Economics at the Federal Land Bank in Minneapolis, Minnesota. Her mother was a graduate of Vassar College. In 1941, Elizabeth Cavert received a bachelor's degree in biochemistry from the University of Minnesota and was elected to Phi Beta Kappa. She also received a Wisconsin Alumni Research Foundation (WARF) scholarship and began graduate work in a joint biochemistry and home economics program. Initially, she was denied entry to the biochemistry program, which Miller attributed to a sex bias and the lack of jobs for graduating male Ph.D.'s.

Before Cavert met James A. Miller, her goal of pursuing biochemistry research seemed unattainable. Miller became an important advocate, however, and succeeded in convincing Dr. Carl Baumann to take her on as a biochemistry graduate student. Cavert obtained an M.S. degree in biochemistry in 1943 and a Ph.D. in 1945. She began to study the metabolism of the vitamin pyridoxine in mice in Baumann's lab.

McArdle Laboratory Forges Coequal Working Relationship

In 1944, Miller joined the new McArdle Laboratory for Cancer Research at the University of Wisconsin and continued to study experimental chemical carcinogenesis. Elizabeth A. Miller joined McArdle as a postdoctoral fellow in 1945. There, the Millers began their productive partnership in research into the mechanisms of chemical carcinogenesis. "When we started our work, little was known about chemical carcinogenesis," said Miller.

In 1947, the Millers became the first researchers to demonstrate that a foreign chemical, an aminoazo dye caused cancer in rats, by binding with proteins in the liver in a process referred to as covalent binding. In tissues that were not sensitive to the carcinogenic effect of the azo dye, there was no binding. The Millers' subsequent research described the molecular events leading to metabolic activation of a large number of carcinogens. In 1949, Miller further demonstrated that one chemical may alter the carcinogenicity of a second chemical by influencing its enzymatic metabolism. Allan Conney, chairman of cancer research, Rutgers University said in a commemorative interview published in the *Journal of NIH Research* in 1992: "This study set the stage for many aspects of modern toxicology and led to an enhanced understanding of mechanisms of toxicity of drugs, environmental toxins, and carcinogens."

Carcinogenic Binding with DNA Initiates Carcinogenic Process

After the structure of DNA was discovered in 1953, the Millers realized that DNA played a major role in the binding of chemical carcinogens. The Millers and their associates were the first to recognize that initiation of carcinogenesis is dependent on metabolic reactions of carcinogenic chemicals with DNA. They also demonstrated that mutagenicity depends upon alteration of genetic material. The

Millers' work stimulated intensive research on the binding of carcinogens to DNA, the mechanisms of mutagenesis, the activation of proto-oncogenes, and the inactivation of tumor suppressor genes.

In 1960, the Millers reported that a metabolite proved to be much more carcinogenic than its parent compound and produced tumors in tissues including the site of administration. This research demonstrated that the initiation of carcinogenesis depended on metabolic activation to electrophiles, a major unifying concept of their research. These findings not only were significant for cancer research, they also opened up a new field of study of drug interactions in metabolic studies in toxicology and pharmacology.

Between 1968 and 1971, the Millers and their associates were the first to demonstrate that chemical carcinogens are potential mutagens, with mutagenicity dependent on metabolic conversion and access to the genetic material. This work set the stage for more rapid testing of potential mutagens and risk assessments of chemicals in humans. Subsequently, the Millers evaluated the carcinogenecity of food additives, contaminants, drugs, environmental pollutants and industrial chemicals, stimulating a growing public awareness and concern about potential carcinogens.

The Millers' commitment to cancer research and public health policy spanned more than forty-five years. Elizabeth C. Miller was editor of *Cancer Research,* the journal of the American Association for Cancer Research (AACR), between 1954–64; James A. Miller was associate editor between 1978–81. Elizabeth served as president of the American Association for Cancer Research between 1976 and 1978 and was twice elected to its board of directors. She was appointed to President Carter's Cancer Panel of the National Cancer Institute from 1978 to 1980. The Millers were concurrently admitted to the National Academy of Sciences in 1978. They participated in grant review and policy committees for numerous groups including the National Cancer Institute, the American Cancer Society, and the National Academy of Science. In 1973, Elizabeth became associate director of the McArdle Laboratory and served in this capacity until her retirement in 1987. Both were appointed WARF Senior Distinguished Research Professor of Oncology and Emeritus Professor of Oncology. By the time they retired in the 1980s, the Millers had written more than 300 papers on chemical carcinogenesis and mentored 42 McArdle researchers.

Lifetime Achievements Culminate in Numerous Honors

The Millers' preeminent contributions to the study of carcinogenesis have been recognized with over 25 awards, including the Papanicolaou, 1975, First Founder's Award from Chemical Industry Institute of Toxicology, 1978, and Mott Award from General Motors Cancer Research Foundation, 1980.

The Millers had two children, Linda Ann, a fiber artist, and Helen Louise, an associate professor of botany. When her children were young, Elizabeth held a half-time appointment, but worked full-time in research and administration. The family enjoyed hiking, camping and travel. Elizabeth died on October 14, 1987, of kidney cancer. In 1988, Miller remarried Barbara Butler, a teacher of religious studies. In 1992, the *Journal of NIH Research* commemorated the Millers' 45-year contributions to cancer research by reprinting the 1947 landmark study and interviewing Miller.

SELECTED WRITINGS BY THE MILLERS:

Periodicals

Miller, James A. and Elizabeth C., "The Presence and Significance of Bound Aminoazo Dyes in the Livers of Rats Fed p-Dimethylaminoazobenzene" *Cancer Research* 7, 1947, pp. 468–480.

Miller, James A., "Carcinogenesis by Chemicals: An Overview," *Cancer Research* 30, 1970, pp. 559–576.

Miller, Elizabeth C., "Some Current Perspectives on Chemical Carcinogenesis in Humans and Experimental Animals," (Presidential Address), *Cancer Research,* Volume 38, 1978, pp. 1479–1496.

Miller, E. C. and J. A., "Milestones in Chemical Carcinogenesis," *Seminars in Oncology* 6, 1979, pp. 445–460.

Books

Miller, E. C. and J. A., "Some Historical Perspectives on the Metabolism of Xenobiotic Chemicals to Reactive Electrophiles." In: *Bioactivation of Foreign Compounds,* M. W. Anders, editor, Academic Press, 1985.

Miller, J. A., "Elizabeth Cavert Miller." In: *Women in Chemistry and Physics. A Biobibliographic Sourcebook,* Grinstein, L. S. and others, editors, Greenwood Press, 1993.

SOURCES:

Periodicals

Fogel, S., "The Landmark Interviews: In Search of the Ultimate Carcinogen," *Journal of NIH Research,* February, 1992, p. 66.

Kadlubar, F. F., "Obituary: Elizabeth Cavert Miller," *Carcinogenesis* 9, 1988, pp. 517–18.

Books

Conney, A. H., "Introduction of Elizabeth C. Miller and James A. Miller," in Fortner, J. G. and Rhoads, J. E., editors, *Accomplishments in Cancer Research,* Lippincott, 1980.

McMahon, B., "Presentation of 1980 Charles S. Mott Prize," in Fortner and Rhoads, editors, *Accomplishments in Cancer Research,* Lippincott, 1980.

Other:

James A. Miller interview with Laura Newman conducted on March 7, 1994.

—*Sketch by Laura Newman*

Stanley Lloyd Miller
1930-
American chemist

Stanley Lloyd Miller is most noted for his experiments that attempted to replicate the chemical conditions that may have first given rise to life on earth. In the early 1950s he demonstrated that amino acids could have been created under primordial conditions. Amino acids are the fundamental units of life; they join together to form proteins, and as they grow more complex they eventually become nucleic acids, which are capable of replicating. Miller has hypothesized that the oceans of primitive earth were a mass of molecules, a prebiological "soup," which over the course of a billion years became a living system.

Miller was born in Oakland, California, on March 7, 1930, the youngest of two children. His father, Nathan Harry Miller, was an attorney and his mother, Edith Levy Miller, was a homemaker. Miller attended the University of California at Berkeley and received his B.S. degree in 1951. He began his graduate studies at the University of Chicago in 1951.

Conducts Pathbreaking Experiment as a Graduate Student

In an autobiographical sketch entitled "The First Laboratory Synthesis of Organic Compounds under Primitive Earth Conditions," Miller recalled the events that led to his famous experiment. Soon after arriving at the University of Chicago, he attended a seminar given by **Harold Urey** on the origin of the solar system. Urey postulated that the earth was reducing when it was first formed—in other words,

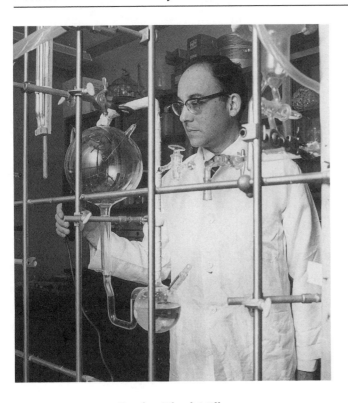

Stanley Lloyd Miller

there was an excess of molecular hydrogen. Strong mixtures of methane and ammonia were also present, and the conditions in the atmosphere favored the synthesis of organic compounds. Miller wrote that when he heard Urey's explanation, he knew it made sense: "For the nonchemist the justification for this might be explained as follows: it is easier to synthesize an organic compound of biological interest from the reducing atmosphere constituents because less chemical bonds need to be broken and put together than is the case with the constituents of an oxidizing atmosphere."

After abandoning a different project for his doctoral thesis, Miller told Urey that he was willing to design an experiment to test his hypothesis. However, Urey expressed reluctance at the idea because he considered it too time consuming and risky for a doctoral candidate. But Miller persisted, and Urey gave him a year to get results; if he failed he would have to choose another thesis topic. With this strict deadline Miller set to work on his attempt to synthesize organic compounds under conditions simulating those of primitive earth.

Miller and Urey decided that ultraviolet light and electrical discharges would have been the most available sources of energy on earth billions of years ago. Having done some reading into amino acids, Miller hypothesized that if he applied an electrical discharge to his primordial environment, he would probably get a deposit of hydrocarbons, an organic compound

containing carbon and hydrogen. As he remembered in "The First Laboratory Synthesis of Organic Compounds": "We decided that amino acids were the best group of compounds to look for first, since they were the building blocks of proteins and since the analytical methods were at that time relatively well developed." Miller designed an apparatus in which he could simulate the conditions of prebiotic earth and then measure what happened. A glass unit was made to represent a model ocean, atmosphere, and rain. For the first experiment, he filled the unit with the requisite "primitive atmosphere"—methane, hydrogen, water, and ammonia—and then submitted the mixture to a low-voltage spark over night. There was a layer of hydrocarbons the next morning, but no amino acids.

Miller then repeated the experiment with a spark at a higher voltage for a period of two days. This time he found no visible hydrocarbons, but his examination indicated that glycine, an amino acid, was present. Next, he let the spark run for a week and found what looked to him like seven spots. Three of these spots were easily identified as glycine, alpha-alanine, and beta-alanine. Two more corresponded to a-amino-n-butyric acid and aspartic acid, and the remaining pair he labelled A and B.

At Urey's suggestion, Miller published "A Production of Amino Acids under Possible Primitive Earth Conditions" in May of 1953 after only three-and-a-half months of research. Reactions to Miller's work were quick and startling. Articles evaluating his experiment appeared in major newspapers, and a Gallup poll even asked people whether they thought it was possible to create life in a test tube; seventy-nine percent of the respondants said no.

After Miller finished his experiments at the University of Chicago, he continued his research as an F. B. Jewett Fellow at the California Institute of Technology from 1954 to 1955. Miller established the accuracy of his findings by performing further tests to identify specific amino acids. He also ruled out the possibility that bacteria might have produced the spots by heating the apparatus in an autoclave for eighteen hours (fifteen minutes is usually long enough to kill any bacteria). Subsequent tests conclusively identified four spots that had previously puzzled him. Although he correctly identified the a-amino-n-butyric acid, what he had thought was aspartic acid (commonly found in plants) was really iminodiacetic acid. Furthermore, the compound he had called A turned out to be sarcosine (N-methyl glycine), and compound B was N-methyl alanine. Other amino acids were present but not in quantities large enough to be evaluated.

Results Support by Evidence from Fallen Meteorite

Although other scientists repeated Miller's experiment, one major question remained: was Miller's apparatus a true representation of the primitive atmosphere? This question was finally answered by a study conducted on a meteorite which landed in Murchison, Australia, in September of 1969. The amino acids found in the meteorite were analyzed and the data compared to Miller's findings. Most of the amino acids Miller had found were also found in the meteorite. On the state of scientific knowledge about the origins of human life, Miller wrote in "The First Laboratory Synthesis of Organic Compounds" that "the synthesis of organic compounds under primitive earth conditions is not, of course, the synthesis of a living organism. We are just beginning to understand how the simple organic compounds were converted to polymers on the primitive earth. . . . Nevertheless we are confident that the basic process is correct."

Miller's later research has continued to build on his famous experiment. He is looking for precursors to ribonucleic acid (RNA). "It is a problem not much discussed because there is nothing to get your hands on," he told Marianne P. Fedunkiw in an interview. He is also examining the natural occurrence of clathrate hydrates, compounds of ice and gases that form under high pressures, on the earth and other parts of the solar system.

Miller has spent most of his career in California. After finishing his doctoral work in Chicago, he spent five years in the department of biochemistry at the College of Physicians and Surgeons at Columbia University. He then returned to California as an assistant professor in 1960 at the University of California, San Diego. He became an associate professor in 1962 and eventually full professor in the department of chemistry.

Miller served as president of the International Society for the Study of the Origin of Life (ISSOL) from 1986 to 1989. The organization awarded him the Oparin Medal in 1983 for his work in the field. Outside of the United States, he was recognized as an Honorary Councillor of the Higher Council for Scientific Research of Spain in 1973. In addition, Miller was elected to the National Academy of Sciences and he belongs to Sigma Xi and Phi Beta Kappa. His other memberships include the American Chemical Society, the American Association for the Advancement of Science, and the American Society of Biological Chemists. Miller is unmarried.

SELECTED WRITINGS BY MILLER:

Books

(With Leslie E. Orgel) *The Origins of Life on the Earth,* Prentice-Hall, 1974.
"The First Laboratory Synthesis of Organic Compounds under Primitive Earth Conditions," *The Heritage of Copernicus: Theories "Pleasing to the Mind,"* edited by J. Neyman, MIT Press, 1974, pp. 228–242.

Periodicals

"A Production of Amino Acids under Possible Primitive Earth Conditions," *Science,* Volume 117, 1953, pp. 528–529.
"The Formation of Organic Compounds on the Primitive Earth," *New York Academy of Sciences,* Volume 69, 1957, pp. 260–274.
(With H. C. Urey) "Organic Compound Synthesis on the Primitive Earth," *Science,* Volume 130, 1959, pp. 245–251.
(With D. Ring, Y. Wolman, and N. Friedmann) "Prebiotic Synthesis of Hydrophobic and Protein Amino Acids," *Proceedings of the National Academy of Sciences USA,* Volume 69, 1972, pp. 765–768.
(With Y. Wolman and W. J. Haverland) "Nonprotein Amino Acids from Spark Discharges and Their Comparison with the Murchison Meteorite Amino Acids," *Proceedings of the National Academy of Sciences USA,* Volume 69, 1972, pp. 809–811.

SOURCES:

Miller, Stanley Lloyd, interview with Marianne P. Fedunkiw conducted December 23, 1993.

—Sketch by Marianne P. Fedunkiw

Robert A. Millikan
1868-1953
American physicist

Robert A. Millikan vaulted from obscurity to international fame on the strength of his classic experiment designed to measure the charge on the electron. His "oil-drop" method for determining the electron charge earned him the 1923 Nobel Prize for physics. He solidified his role as a leader in American science by presiding over the rise of the California Institute of Technology into a world-famous center of scientific research.

Millikan was born March 22, 1868, the second of six children, to Silas Franklin Millikan and Mary Jane Andrews Millikan in Morrison, Illinois. His mother, a graduate of Oberlin College in Ohio, served as dean of women at Olivet College in Michigan before moving to Illinois, and his father later earned a degree at the Oberlin Theological Seminary and became a Congregational preacher. The family moved to Maquoketa, Iowa in 1875.

Millikan graduated with high marks from Maquoketa High School in 1886. Following in his parents' footsteps, he then entered the Oberlin college preparatory program, and then the college itself the next year. He followed their classical course of study, taking classes in higher mathematics and basic physics, along with Latin and Greek. In 1889, he was asked to teach an introductory course in physics; the physics program at that time contained a large number of Greek terms, and he seemed to have been asked simply because he had done so well in Greek. His interest in physics began with his efforts to prepare himself for teaching this course. Millikan earned a B.A. in 1891, but stayed two more years as a physics tutor, taking additional science courses. He earned an M.A. in 1893 for his analysis of Silvanus P. Thomson's 1884 book, *Dynamic Electric Machinery.* On the strength of this achievement, Millikan earned a fellowship to Columbia University in New York as its sole graduate student in physics.

Receives Direction from Illustrious Scientists

At Columbia, Millikan gravitated to Michael I. Pupin of the electrical engineering department. Pupin schooled Millikan in mathematical precision in experimentation. In the summer of 1894, Millikan, with the aid of Columbia professor of physics Ogden Rood, enrolled at the Ryerson Laboratory at the University of Chicago. There, Millikan first met **Albert Michelson**, the noted scientist who had measured the speed of light in 1879–80. Michelson's emphasis on precise measurement and rigorous attention to detail, as well as his faith in the evolutionary pace of scientific progress, appealed strongly to Millikan.

Millikan received his Ph.D. in 1895 for his research on the polarization of incandescent light. With financial assistance from Pupin, Millikan went to Europe for postgraduate study. This was a common practice for American scientists at the time, and he studied under such luminaries as **Jules Henri Poincaré**, **Max Planck**, and **Walther Nernst**. He was in Europe when the revolutionary discoveries of X rays and radioactivity were made. Millikan returned to the United States in 1896 to take a position as a physics instructor at the University of Chicago, where Michelson was still head of the department of physics and director of the Ryerson Laboratory. Millikan had a heavy teaching load at first; he was responsible for establishing the physics curriculum and preparing textbooks. In 1906, he published his *First Course in Physics,* which was widely used.

Despite his teaching success, Millikan remained anxious to pursue original research in physics. He was aware of the rapid progress in Europe on atomic theory, and he understood that advancement in his profession depended upon research results. Initial work in thermodynamics met with little success. In April of 1902 he took time off from research to marry Greta Irvin Blanchard, the daughter of a wealthy local businessman, and to travel in Europe. The couple later had three sons. After his honeymoon, Millikan focused his attention on radioactivity, and then on the behavior of electrons in metals. In particular, he studied the photoelectric effect, the ability of certain electromagnetic waves to detach electrons from metal surfaces.

Measures Electron Charge with Oil Drops

In 1908, Millikan, now an assistant professor, began to focus on a problem involving precise measurement: the charge on the electron. The electron was playing an increasingly important role in the atomic theories then being assembled, and the precise measurement of its charge had become a pressing problem. The standard technique for measuring the charge had been developed by British physicist H. A. Wilson. First, water droplets would be given an electric charge, and the rate at which they fell would be measured. Next, an electric field would be introduced to attract the charged droplets upward and oppose the force of gravity. By determining the strength of the electric field and the mass of the water droplets, one could calculate the charge on the droplets and on the electrons.

Millikan tried Wilson's technique but found that the rapid evaporation of the water droplets made measurement difficult and the results erratic. He decided to measure the charge on a single drop of water by balancing it between the electric field and gravity. He observed in 1909 that the charge on any drop was an integral multiple of a fundamental value. His findings, however, were still complicated by evaporation of the droplets. In 1909 Millikan hit upon the idea of using slow-evaporating oil drops instead of water. He could now observe charged drops for several hours, instead of only seconds. By balancing charged oil drops between an electric field and gravity, Millikan proved that the electron was a fundamental particle with a fundamental charge. In 1913, he published his value for the charge, which remained the accepted value for decades. The determination of this value, and the ingenuity of the experiment, earned Millikan international recognition and the 1923 Nobel Prize in physics.

After determining the charge on the electron, Millikan returned to his research on the photoelectric effect. In 1905, Albert Einstein had explained the phenomenon by suggesting that small packages or quanta of light—photons—were responsible for knocking the electrons off the metal surfaces. Millikan, like many other physicists of the day, resisted this particle view of light, preferring instead to consider light as waves. He set out to test the validity of **Albert Einstein**'s hypothesis by observing the liberation of electrons from metals by ultraviolet light. By careful observation and elimination of the errors of previous methods, in 1916 Millikan was able to verify the validity of Einstein's calculations, although Millikan himself refused to abandon the wave theory of light.

Europe was engulfed in World War I by this time. As it became more likely that the United States would enter the war, **George Ellery Hale**, the astronomer and observatory builder, successfully lobbied for the National Academy of Sciences to establish a National Research Council, dedicated to research for the war effort. Millikan assisted Hale in his plans and in 1917 took a leave of absence from the University of Chicago to serve as head of a committee on submarine detection. Soon after the United States entered the war, Millikan joined the U.S. Army Signal Corps and became director of the Corps Division of Science and Research, rising to the rank of lieutenant colonel. His work for the National Research Council in antisubmarine warfare helped to establish the council as a permanent body.

Develops Institute into a World-Class Research Institution

Millikan returned to the University of Chicago after the war. But in 1921, Hale and chemist Arthur A. Noyes persuaded him to chair the Executive Council of the California Institute of Technology in Pasadena. Millikan was also named director of its Norman Bridge Laboratory. Despite his initial misgivings, Millikan quickly turned the Institute into an internationally respected center of research. He lured talented students to the school by inviting such prominent scientists as Einstein, Michelson, **Arnold Sommerfeld**, **Paul Ehrenfest**, and **C. V. Raman** to take faculty assignments. By the end of the 1920s, the California Institute of Technology was the leading research institution in the United States, boasting of such faculty giants as **Thomas Hunt Morgan**, **Theodore von Kármán**, and **Linus Pauling**.

Many Americans of the 1920s considered Millikan to be the foremost American scientist of the day. He continued to be active in the National Research Council, and from 1922 to 1932 he was the American representative to the Committee on International Cooperation of the League of Nations. He served as president of the American Association for the Advancement of Science in 1929. It was also during this period that he earned the Hughes Medal of the Royal Society of London and the Faraday Medal of the British Chemical Society. He would eventually hold honorary doctorates from twenty-five universities and belong to twenty-one foreign scientific academies.

Millikan still found time outside his administrative duties to conduct original research. With graduate student Carl F. Eyring, Millikan studied the ability of strong electric fields to draw electrons out of cold metals. His classical explanation for the phenomenon was eventually replaced by a quantum mechanical approach. He also studied the ultraviolet spectra of light elements with graduate student Ira S. Bowen. Their research supported Sommerfeld's relativistic explanation of spectra, rather than the atomic model of **Niels Bohr**; the conflict was resolved in 1925 by the hypothesis of electron spin.

Studies the Source of Cosmic Rays

Most of Millikan's research at the Institute, however, focused on cosmic rays, the penetrating rays that had been discovered by Austrian physicist **Victor Hess** in 1912. Millikan's initial objective was to determine whether the rays came from space or from radioactive elements in the earth. He launched a large number of sounding balloons, even mounting an expedition to the top of Pike's Peak in 1923, to detect and measure ionization of atmospheric gases by the rays. These experiments failed to settle the issue, and in 1925 Millikan decided to approach the problem by measuring the variation in ionization from Lake Arrowhead (5,000 feet above sea level) to Muir Lake (12,000 feet above sea level) in California. The atmosphere between the two lakes had the absorbing power of six feet of water, and a cosmic source for the rays could be assumed if the intensity of ionization at Lake Arrowhead matched the intensity of ionization six feet lower at Muir Lake. Millikan discovered this to be the case. Moreover, he observed that the ionization effects continued day and night, and that the rays were about eighteen times more energetic than the most energetic gamma rays then known. It was Millikan who dubbed these ionizing rays "cosmic."

Millikan became embroiled in controversy, however, when he attempted to build upon his cosmic ray work. He failed to convince other scientists that the cosmic rays were photons emitted by the spontaneous fusing of hydrogen atoms into heavier elements; he abandoned the theory himself by 1935. In 1932, **Arthur Holly Compton** detected that the intensity of the rays varied with latitude, suggesting that the rays were charged particles deflected by the earth's magnetic field. Millikan fiercely denied Compton's assertion, and he supported his argument by conducting his own experiments that failed to detect this latitude effect. In 1933, however, after determining that a local irregularity in cosmic ray intensity had interfered with his observations, Millikan ceded that some cosmic rays were charged particles.

Millikan remained a determined conservative throughout his career, both in politics and in science.

True to his scientific training under Michelson and Pupin, he preferred to think of scientific progress as evolutionary and not revolutionary. Though he encouraged original research, he never quite accepted the revolutionary ideas of the new quantum mechanics. In his later years, he even fought back attempts to reexamine his determination of the charge on the electron. In politics he was a staunch Republican; he was strongly opposed to the New Deal and, after the war, to the formation of the National Science Foundation. Despite his conservative inclinations, however, he was a religious modernist, promoting the compatibility of science and religion even as the 1925 Scopes trial pitted science against fundamentalist Christianity.

Millikan retired from his professorship and presidency of the California Institute in 1946. He then wrote his autobiography, which was published in 1950. He died in Pasadena on December 19, 1953.

SELECTED WRITINGS BY MILLIKAN:

Books

(With Henry Gordon Gale) *A First Course in Physics,* Ginn, 1906.
The Electron: Its Isolation and Measurement and the Determination of Some of Its Properties, University of Chicago Press, 1917.
Electrons (+ and -), Protons, Photons, Neutrons, and Cosmic Rays, University of Chicago Press, 1935.
The Autobiography of Robert A. Millikan, Prentice-Hall, 1950.

SOURCES:

Books

Kargon, Robert H., *The Rise of Robert Millikan: Portrait of a Life in American Science,* Cornell University Press, 1982.
Kevles, Daniel J., *The Physicists,* Vintage Books, 1979.

Periodicals

DuBridge, Lee A., and Paul S. Epstein, "Robert A. Millikan," *Biographical Memoirs, National Academy of Sciences* 33, 1959, pp. 241–282.
Epstein, Paul S., "Robert Andrews Millikan as Physicist and Teacher," *Review of Modern Physics* 20, January, 1948, pp. 10–25.
Kevles, Daniel J., "Millikan: Spokesman for Science in the Twenties," *Engineering and Science* 32, April, 1969, pp. 17–22.

—*Sketch by Michael Boersma*

Edward Arthur Milne
1896-1950
English mathematician and astrophysicist

Edward Arthur Milne was known for his important theoretical analyses of the conditions on the surface and of the atmospheres of stars. He also developed his own competing theory to **Albert Einstein**'s general theory of relativity called "kinematic relativity." Milne was born in Hull, Yorkshire, on February 14, 1896, the son of the chief administrator of a private Church of England school. The young Milne won a scholarship to Hymer's College, located in his hometown of Hull, and displayed an exceptional aptitude for mathematics. He entered Trinity College, Cambridge, in 1914, just as war was breaking out in Europe. His poor eyesight prevented him from assuming active duty, but in 1916 his mathematical skills were employed by the Munitions Inventions Department in the Anti-Aircraft Experimental Section. There, Milne performed significant military research, which gave him the opportunity to meet some of Britain's most prominent scientists.

Milne's successful work for the military in ballistics and atmospherics earned him the respect of the scientific community. When he returned to Trinity College in 1919 he published three papers related to his work during the war, which culminated in his being elected Prize Fellow of Trinity College. Extending his atmospheric research to the theoretical study of the sun, Milne became the Director of the Solar Physics Laboratory at Cambridge and taught courses in mathematics and astrophysics. In the mid–1920s, he accepted the Chair of Applied Mathematics at Manchester University, where he stayed for several years. During this time, he was also accepted as a Fellow of the Royal Society. The inevitable job-hopping that characterizes the careers of many successful scientists came to an end for Milne in 1929 when he assumed the newly created post of Rouse Ball Chair of Mathematics at Oxford. He remained at Oxford for the rest of his life.

Embarks on Studies of Stars

Milne's early work involved developing mathematical studies of the surfaces and atmospheres of stars. The composition of a star's gaseous atmosphere is revealed when the light from the star is spread into a rainbow, or spectrum. Each star's spectrum has a characteristic pattern of lines and other features which astronomers use to classify the star according to its spectral type. A star's spectral type is dependent upon the temperature of the star's surface. Collaborating with Cambridge colleague and fellow astrophysicist Ralph H. Fowler, Milne was able to mathematically derive specific surface temperatures for stars of any spectral type, thus greatly strengthening astronomers' understanding of stellar structure.

Milne's investigation into the equilibrium between gravity and radiation pressure in the atmosphere of stars also led to his prediction of the occurrence of periodic, explosive outbursts of electrically charged particles from near a star's surface. Years after Milne's prediction, the existence of a "solar wind," consisting of charged particles emanating from the sun, was confirmed. The challenge of understanding the complex behavior of stellar atmospheres continued to occupy Milne's attention after his appointment at Oxford, where he revised and amended the work of English physicist and astronomer **Arthur Stanley Eddington** on stellar structure. Milne's adjustments to Eddington's theories were not generally accepted, however, and it was at this moment in his career that Milne embarked on a new direction of research.

Creates His Own Cosmology

By the early 1930s, Einstein's theory of relativity had firmly gripped the minds and imaginations of scientists. Many members of the scientific community accepted the logic and consequences of Einstein's special theory of relativity, with its specific formulation of the effects of linear, non-accelerated motion upon the measurement of time and space. Einstein's general theory of relativity was a different matter, however. The consequences of the general theory's space-time geometry were, and still are, difficult to interpret and confirm experimentally. But a more subtle problem was the implication of the theory that a phenomenon such as gravity was an illusion, of sorts, generated by underlying geometric principles. Many scientists were disturbed by this—not so much by the specific idea of geometric "illusions," but by the possibility that all of nature could consist of unknown structures disguised by a scrim of subjective "forces" that did not lend themselves to the scrutiny of experimental confirmation. There was also a strong feeling that Einstein's general theory, though immensely profound, was too broadly conceived to be a really useful physical theory. Almost as soon as it was introduced, and for years afterward, mathematicians and scientists worked to improve the theory. Milne was among them.

From 1932 until the time of his death, Milne developed a parallel cosmological theory of his own. He accepted Einstein's special theory of relativity and the geometry of Greek philosopher Euclid, but Milne rejected the general theory of relativity. From this, Milne developed his "kinematic relativity" which enabled him to derive a gravitational theory and to formulate a system of electrodynamics. A conse-

quence of his theory was the formulation of the "cosmological principle," which asserts that the universe appears the same from wherever it is observed. Milne also derived a more acceptable measurement for the age of the universe using his kinematic theory than others were able to produce using the general theory of relativity of Einstein. Unfortunately, Milne's theory was not well received because of its Cartesian-style philosophical foundation based upon supposedly self-evident "first principles." In the mind boggling era of relativity and Quantum Mechanics, which were founded upon complex empirical phenomena, most scientists had developed the habit of distrusting philosophical cosmologies based on intuitive "truths." The fact that Milne's kinematic relativity was regarded with skepticism, though, did not deter him from tinkering with it throughout his life, reminiscent of the manner in which German astronomer Johannes Kepler, centuries earlier, persistently clung to his own discredited theory of planetary motion based on Perfect Solids.

Milne's work was interrupted from 1939 to 1944 when, in response to wartime necessities, he served the Ministry of Supply on the Ordnance Board. After World War II, Milne's health began to deteriorate. On September 21, 1950, he died suddenly while attending a conference in Dublin. He is remembered and respected for having contributed substantially to the understanding of stellar structure. Milne received numerous awards during his relatively short life, including the Gold Medal of the Royal Astronomical Society in 1935, the Royal Medal of the Royal Society in 1941, and the Bruce Medal of the Astronomical Society of the Pacific in 1945.

SELECTED WRITINGS BY MILNE:

Books

The White Dwarf Stars: Being the Halley Lecture, Delivered on 19 May 1932, Clarendon Press, 1932.
Relativity, Gravitation and World Structure, Clarendon Press, 1935.
Kinematic Relativity: A Sequel to Relativity, Gravitation and World Structure, Clarendon Press, 1948.
Vectorial Mechanics, Interscience Publishers, 1948.

—*Sketch by Jeffery Bass*

John Milnor
1931-
American mathematician

John "Jack" Milnor, one of the leading topologists in the second half of the twentieth century, has studied the generalized spaces known as manifolds and has had a particular interest in working out the relations among the various ways to view these spaces. In 1956 he astounded the mathematical world with the first example of manifolds that are distinct when considered in the context of calculus, but are equivalent when viewed geometrically. For this discovery he received the Fields Medal in 1962, an award in mathematics comparable to the Nobel Prize.

John Willard Milnor was born in Orange, New Jersey, on February 20, 1931, to John Willard and Emily (Cox) Milnor. He published his first paper, "On the Total Curvature of Knots," in 1950 while he was an undergraduate at Princeton. It has been said that Milnor mistook an unsolved conjecture written on the board for the homework assignment, and his simple yet ingenious solution was the catalyst for this paper. He received his A.B. degree in 1951 and continued his doctoral work at Princeton. He and Brigitte Weber were married on January 5, 1954. They had three children, Stefan, Daniel, and Gabrielle.

In 1954, Milnor received his Ph.D. under the direction of Ralph Fox, a mathematician known as the dean of American knot theorists. Knot theory was a branch of topology developed in the twentieth century. The following year Milnor was the Higgins Lecturer at Princeton and he quickly moved through the ranks of assistant, associate, and full professor. In 1962 Princeton appointed him the Henry Putnam University Professor of mathematics.

Explores Manifolds and Spheres

Milnor's primary work concerned the study of manifolds. These spaces arise in topology—a branch of mathematics related to geometry—and are the analogs of curves and surfaces. Near any point, a coordinate system can be introduced so that the immediate neighborhood of the point looks like ordinary Euclidean space (although it may be of any finite dimension). The coordinate systems for various points can be different but must fit together in a continuous fashion. A smooth manifold results if corners and other sharp folds are prohibited, which can be related to conditions from calculus. In 1956 Milnor published the paper "On Manifolds Homeomorphic to the 7-Sphere," which presented the first example of a pair of manifolds that are equivalent from the continuous point of view (homeomorphic), but distinct as smooth manifolds when calculus considerations are introduced. The 7-sphere is a sphere in seven dimensions. Over the next ten years, he studied these "exotic" spheres and found a way to combine them. Milnor has always been recognized as a master of using current algebraic techniques to analyze complex geometrical objects.

In addition to his mathematical innovations, Milnor was known for the clarity of his lectures. As Lisa Goldberg and Anthony Phillips mention in *Topological Methods in Modern Mathematics,* "When Milnor speaks, you understand." Graduate students would frequently volunteer to write up their notes from Milnor's courses. They would work with him through countless revisions, each time making further improvements over the previous draft. By means of the resulting mimeographed documents, Milnor's ability to organize new and complicated fields of mathematics was influential far beyond his immediate students.

Milnor was a visiting professor at the University of California at Berkeley during the academic year 1959–60, and at the University of California at Los Angeles in 1967–68. He spent two years as professor of mathematics at the Massachusetts Institute of Technology, and then returned to Princeton in 1970 as professor at the Institute for Advanced Study. At around that time, Milnor became interested in the use of computer graphics to experiment with the new field of dynamical systems. Although he did not begin to publish his work in this area until 1985, he was nevertheless influential through preprints of his work in progress and his collaboration with other mathematicians.

In addition to receiving the 1962 Fields Medal, Milnor was elected to the National Academy of Science in 1963, and has been awarded the National Medal of Science in 1967, the Steele Prize of the American Mathematical Society in 1982, and the Wolf Prize in 1989.

In 1989 Milnor accepted the position of director at the newly formed Institute for Mathematical Sciences at the State University of New York at Stony Brook. In June of 1991, the Institute and the Mathematics Department at Stony Brook organized a conference in honor of Milnor's sixtieth birthday. The proceedings of the conference contain summaries of Milnor's work and its influence on geometry, topology, mathematical physics, algebraic geometry, dynamical systems, and others. The participation by 220 mathematicians (including one hundred graduate students) from around the world testifies to Milnor's lasting influence on these many branches of mathematics.

SELECTED WRITINGS BY MILNOR:

Books

Topology from the Differential Viewpoint, University Press of Virginia, 1965.
(With William Thurston) "On Iterated Maps of the Interval," in *Dynamical Systems,* edited by J. C. Alexander, Springer-Verlag, 1988, pp. 465–563.
Collected Papers, Publish or Perish, 1994-.

Periodicals

"On the Total Curvature of Knots," *Annals of Mathematics,* Volume 52, number 2, 1950, pp. 248–257.
"On Manifolds Homeomorphic to the 7-Sphere," *Annals of Mathematics,* Volume 64, number 2, 1956, pp. 399–405.

SOURCES:

Books

Goldberg, Lisa, and Anthony Phillips, editors, *Topological Methods in Modern Mathematics: Proceedings of a Symposium in Honor of John Milnor's Sixtieth Birthday,* Publish or Perish, 1993.

Periodicals

"John W. Milnor," *Notices of the American Mathematical Society,* October, 1982, p. 507.

—*Sketch by Robert Messer*

César Milstein
1927-
Argentine-born English biochemist

César Milstein

César Milstein conducted one of the most important late-twentieth-century studies on antibodies. In 1984 he was granted the Nobel Prize for physiology or medicine, shared with **Niels K. Jerne** and **Georges Kohler**, for his outstanding contributions to this field. Milstein's research on the structure of antibodies and their genes, through the investigation of deoxyribonucleic acid (DNA) and ribonucleic acid (RNA), has been fundamental for a better understanding of how the human immune system works.

Milstein was born on October 8, 1927, in the eastern Argentine city of Bahía Blanca, one of three sons of Lázaro and Máxima Milstein. He studied biochemistry at the National University of Buenos Aires from 1945 to 1952, graduating with a degree in chemistry. Heavily involved in opposing the policies of President Juan Peron and working part-time as a chemical analyst for a laboratory, Milstein barely managed to pass with poor grades. Nonetheless, he pursued graduate studies at the Instituto de Biología Química of the University of Buenos Aires and completed his doctoral dissertation on the chemistry of aldehyde dehydrogenase, an alcohol enzyme used as a catalyst, in 1957.

With a British Council scholarship, he continued his studies at Cambridge University from 1958 to 1961 under the guidance of **Frederick Sanger**, a distinguished researcher in the field of enzymes. Sanger had determined that an enzyme's functions depend on the arrangement of amino acids inside it. In 1960 Milstein obtained a Ph.D. and joined the Department of Biochemistry at Cambridge, but in 1961, he decided to return to his native country to continue his investigations as head of a newly-created Department of Molecular Biology at the National Institute of Microbiology in Buenos Aires.

Collaborates in Development of Monoclonal Antibodies

A military coup in 1962 had a profound impact on the state of research and on academic life in Argentina. Milstein resigned his position in protest of the government's dismissal of the Institute's director, Ignacio Pirosky. In 1963 he returned to work with Sanger in Great Britain. During the 1960s and much of the 1970s, Milstein concentrated on the study of antibodies, the protein organisms generated by the immune system to combat and deactivate antigens. Milstein's efforts were aimed at analyzing myeloma proteins, and then DNA and RNA. Myeloma, which are tumors in cells that produce antibodies, had been the subject of previous studies by Rodney R. Porter, MacFarlane Burnet, and Gerald M. Edelman, among others.

Milstein's investigations in this field were fundamental for understanding how antibodies work. He searched for mutations in laboratory cells of myeloma but faced innumerable difficulties trying to find antigens to combine with their antibodies. He and Köhler produced a hybrid myeloma called hybridoma in 1974. This cell had the capacity to produce antibodies but kept growing like the cancerous cell from which it had originated. The production of monoclonal antibodies from these cells was one of the most relevant conclusions from Milstein and his colleague's research. The Milstein-Köhler paper was first published in 1975 and indicated the possibility of using monoclonal antibodies for testing antigens. The two scientists predicted that since it was possible to hybridize antibody-producing cells from different origins, such cells could be produced in massive cultures. They were, and the technique consisted of a fusion of antibodies with cells of the myeloma to produce cells that could perpetuate themselves, generating uniform and pure antibodies.

In 1983 Milstein assumed leadership of the Protein and Nucleic Acid Chemistry Division at the Medical Research Council's laboratory. In 1984 he shared the Nobel Prize with Köhler and Jerne for developing the technique that had revolutionized many diagnostic procedures by producing exceptionally pure antibodies. Upon receiving the prize, Milstein heralded the beginning of what he called "a new era of immunobiochemistry," which included production of molecules based on antibodies. He stated that his method was a by-product of basic research and a clear example of how an investment in research that was not initially considered commercially viable had "an enormous practical impact." By 1984 a thriving business was being done with monoclonal antibodies for diagnosis, and works on vaccines and cancer based on Milstein's breakthrough research were being rapidly developed.

In the early 1980s Milstein received a number of other scientific awards, including the Wolf Prize in Medicine from the Karl Wolf Foundation of Israel in 1980, the Royal Medal from the Royal Society of London in 1982, and the Dale Medal from the Society for Endocrinology in London in 1984. He is a member of numerous international scientific organizations, among them the U.S. National Academy of Sciences and the Royal College of Physicians in London. His hobbies include walking, outdoor cooking, and attending the theater. Milstein is married to biochemist Celia Prilleltensky; they have no children.

SELECTED WRITINGS BY MILSTEIN:

Periodicals

(With G. Winter) "Man-Made Antibodies," *Nature,* 349, 1991.
(With Georges Köhler) "Continuous Cultures of Fused Cells Secreting Antibody of Predefined Specificity," *Biotechnology,* 24, 1992, pp. 524–26.
"From the Structure of Antibodies to the Diversification of the Immune Response," The Nobel Lectures in Immunology, Lecture for the Nobel Prize for Physiology or Medicine, 1984, *Scandinavian Journal of Immunology,* April, 1993.
"Affinity Maturation Leads to Differential Expression of Multiple Copies of a Kappa Light-Chain Transgene," *Nature,* May 20, 1993, pp. 271–3.

SOURCES:

Books

Ahmad, Fazal, *From Gene to Protein,* Academic Press, 1982.
Nobel Prize Winners, H. W. Wilson, 1987, pp. 705–07.

—*Sketch by Rodolfo A. Windhausen*

Hermann Minkowski
1864-1909
Russian-born German physicist and mathematician

In spite of a relatively short career, Hermann Minkowski played an important role in the development of modern mathematics. His work formed the basis for modern functional analysis, and he did much to expand the knowledge of quadratic forms. He also developed the mathematical theory known as the geometry of numbers and laid the mathematical foundation for **Albert Einstein**'s theory of relativity.

Minkowski was born in Alexotas, Russia on June 22, 1864, of German parents. The family returned to their native Germany in 1872, to the city of Königsberg, where Minkowski spent the rest of his childhood and also attended university.

Awarded Grand Prix des Sciences Mathématiques

Even as a student at the University of Königsberg, Minkowski demonstrated a rare mathematical talent. In 1881, the Paris Academy of Sciences offered a prize, the Grand Prix des Sciences Mathématiques, for a proof describing the number of representations of an integer as a sum of five squares of integers—a proof that, unbeknownst to the Paris Academy, the British mathematician J. H. Smith had in fact already outlined at the time. Minkowski produced the proof independently while Smith sent in his own work. In 1883 both Smith and Minkowski received the prize. At that time, the nineteen-year-old Minkowski was two years away from receiving his doctorate from the University of Königsberg. The work contained in the 140-page manuscript he submitted to the Academy was, in fact, considered a better formulation than Smith's because the young Minkowski used more natural and more general definitions in arriving at his proof.

After receiving his doctorate from the University of Königsberg, Minkowski taught at the University of Bonn until 1894. Returning to teach at the University of Königsberg for two years, he then taught until 1902 at the University of Zurich. One of his closest colleagues at Zurich was a former teacher, A. Hurwitz, who is best known for his theorem on the composition of quadratic forms.

Develops Geometry of Numbers

After working on the arithmetic of quadratic forms for several years and making contributions particularly to work in *n* variables, Minkowski extended his work to what is most commonly known as the geometry of numbers. In 1889, he introduced what has been characterized as his most original achievement, when he included volume in his work with ternary quadratic forms. With this extension it became possible to give mathematical descriptions of the properties of, for example, convex bodies in both two and three dimensions. Common examples of convex regions are those bounded by circles, ellipses, and parallelograms. Using the two- and three-dimensional versions of Minkowski's convex body theorem, mathematicians are able to prove some fundamental facts about algebraic number theory and can derive new proofs of some theorems from elementary number theory. Minkowski extended these ideas to investigations of the geometrical properties of convex sets in *n*-dimensional space, and his observations ultimately formed the basis for modern functional analysis.

Builds Foundation for the Theory of Relativity

At the urging of a former classmate, the great mathematician **David Hilbert**, the University of Göttingen created a new professorship for Minkowski in 1902. It was during his tenure at Göttingen that Minkowski turned his attention to relativity theory. Albert Einstein had been one of Minkowski's pupils, and Minkowski was very interested in the special theory of relativity formulated by Einstein, which at the time competed with the more widely accepted electron theory of the Dutch physicist **Hendrik Lorentz** as an explanation of subatomic phenomena. Minkowski was the first to recognize the consequences of the relativity theory in consideration of time and space. "From now on," he said, "space by itself and time by itself are mere shadows and only a blend of the two exists in its own right." By 1907, Minkowski had placed a formal geometric interpretation upon relativity. He believed that in the universe, time and space exist as a fused "time-space." In his book *Raum und Zeit* (translated into English as *Time and Space*), he demonstrated that relativity made it necessary mathematically to take time into account as a fourth dimension besides the spatial dimensions of length, width, and depth. Einstein used Minkowski's ideas to develop his general theory of relativity, published nine years later, several years after Minkowski's death in Göttingen, Germany, on January 12, 1909.

SELECTED WRITINGS BY MINKOWSKI:

Books

Geometrie der Zahlen, [Leipzig], 1896, 2nd edition, 1910.

Raum und Zeit (title means "Time and Space"), 1907.
Diophantische Approximationen, [Leipzig], 1907.
Zwei Abhandlungen uber die Grundgleichungen der Elektrodynamik, 1909.
Minkowski's writings were collected in *Gesammelte Abhandlungen,* two volumes, edited by David Hilbert, [Leipzig-Berlin], 1911.

SOURCES:

Books

Hancock, Harris, *Development of the Minkowski Geometry of Numbers,* [New York], 1939.
Lanchester, Frederick W., *Relativity: An Elementary Explanation of the Space-Time Relations as Established by Minkowski,* [London], 1935.

—*Sketch by Maureen L. Tan*

Rudolph Minkowski
1895-1976

German-born American astronomer

Rudolph Minkowski was an astronomer who, along with his long-time collaborator **Walter Baade**, did important research into radio astronomy and planetary nebulae. He was also in charge of the 1950 Sky Survey conducted under the auspices of the National Geographic Society and the Palomar Observatory. This survey, consisting of 935 high-quality overlapping photographs covering the entire Northern sky, is still an important research tool used today. In 1951, Minkowski discovered an asteroid, which he named Geographos in honor of the National Geographic Society.

Rudolph Leo Minkowski was born on May 28, 1895, in Strassburg, which was then part of Germany. Rudolph's grandfather had moved the family to Strassburg from Russia in the 1870s to escape the pogroms of the Czarist government. His mother was Marie Siegel Minkowski, and his father, Oscar Minkowski, was a renowned physician and pathologist who had demonstrated the role of the pancreas in diabetes in 1889 and the role of the pituitary gland in acromegaly in 1887. He is sometimes referred to as the "grandfather of insulin." One of Rudolph's uncles was Hermann Minkowski, famed as the developer of

a mathematical system used in Einstein's special theory of relativity.

As Rudolph's father moved from city to city, the boy's education was completed in a series of gymnasia, first at Cologne, then at Greifswald, and finally at Breslau. During World War I, he served in the German army. In 1921, Minkowski was granted his Ph.D. in physics from the University of Breslau. He stayed on briefly at Breslau, continuing his research on spectroscopy and optics before moving on to Göttingen and then, in 1922, to the University of Hamburg. There he became an assistant in the Physikalishces Staatsinstitut and, in 1931, a full professor.

At Hamburg, Minkowski made the acquaintance of Walter Baade, another young research assistant. As Minkowski began to collaborate with Baade, he took on more problems in astronomy, a field in which he had been interested since his childhood. In 1933, he an Baade (along with Fritz Goos and Peter Paul Koch) published their first joint paper on research they had done on the Orion nebula.

The paper appeared the same year in which Nazi Party leader Adolf Hitler became chancellor of the German Reich. One of Hitler's first acts was to expel Jews from positions of authority within the government and universities. Minkowski's father-in-law, German Supreme Court justice Alfons David, was one of the first to be expelled from his post. Although the Minkowskis had themselves converted to Christianity, they realized how dangerous the situation in Germany had become for anyone with Jewish associations. So, in 1935, they left Germany to join Baade, who was then working at the Mt. Wilson Observatory in Pasadena, California.

Minkowski became a naturalized citizen in 1940. During World War II, he worked in the government's Office of Scientific Research and Development at the California Institute of Technology. His wife, Luise, took a course in drafting at night school and then took a job at a Lockheed plant. Minkowski returned to Mt. Wilson after the war and continued his association with the institution for the next two decades. In 1961 he accepted an appointment as research astronomer at the University of California's Berkeley Radio Astronomy Laboratory. During the year between his departure from Mt. Wilson and his joining the University of California, he served as visiting professor at the University of Wisconsin.

Minkowski's arrival at Mt. Wilson was significant for the research program there. Astronomers already on the staff tended to be pure astronomers with relatively modest backgrounds in physics. Minkowski was able to provide, therefore, a new perspective on much of the research then being carried out, applying his own background in physics—especially optics and spectroscopy—to the analysis of astronomical questions. In 1951, for example, he was able to confirm an earlier discovery of a remnant of a supernova (a star explosion) in the Crab nebula. With Baade, he discovered that there were two types of supernovae and developed a system for classifying them. Minkowski also became especially interested in planetary nebulae—ring-shaped galaxies—and organized a program at Mt. Wilson for a systematic search and study of these objects in the sky. That program eventually resulted in the doubling of the number of planetary nebulae known to science.

The early 1950s saw the development of a revolutionary new form of astronomy, radio astronomy. During World War II, scientists working on radar had discovered that unknown radio sources existed in the deep reaches of outer space. Following the war, many of these same scientists returned to their universities and observatories determined to find out just what these mysterious radio sources were. Minkowski made many contributions to this effort. Working in conjunction with radio astronomers, Minkowski and Baade trained the Palomar telescope on locations where radio sources had been found to see if there were any stars or other astronomical objects to be seen there. In 1951, Minkowski and Baade identified for the first time a radio source, called Cygnus A, with a specific object in the sky, an object they believed was two colliding galaxies. (Later research rejected this idea.) In 1960, Minkowski showed that a radio source first recorded by astronomer John Bolton was associated with a galaxy with the largest velocity observed to that time, 0.46 that of the speed of light.

As his biographer Donald E. Osterbrock has pointed out, Minkowski "made important contributions to nearly every branch of nebular and extragalactic astronomy, but his most important contribution was to the identification and interpretation of cosmic radio sources." In addition to his research findings, Minkowski also "guided, encouraged and counseled a generation of radio and optical astronomers."

SELECTED WRITINGS BY MINKOWSKI:

Books

"Optical Investigations of Radio Sources," in H. C. Van der Hulst, editor, *Radio Astronomy,* Cambridge University Press, 1957, pp. 107–122.
"Planetary Nebulae," in Adriaan Blaauw and Maarten Schmidt, editors, *Galactic Structure,* University of Chicago Press, 1965, pp. 321–343.
"Twenty Years Astronomy with the 48-inch Schmidt Telescope on Palomar Mountain," in U. Haug, editor, *The Role of Schmidt Telescopes in Astronomy,* Hamburg Observatory, 1972, pp. 5–8.

SOURCES:

Books

Osterbrock, Donald E., "Rudolph Leo Bernhard Minkowski," in *Biographical Memoirs,* Volume 54, National Academy Press, 1983, pp. 270–298.

Periodicals

Osterbrock, Donald E., "Rudolph Minkowski: Observational Astrophysicist," *Physics Today,* April, 1985, pp. 50–57.

—*Sketch by David E. Newton*

George Richards Minot
1885-1950
American hematologist and physician

George Richards Minot was a pioneer in the medical field of hematology, the study of blood and blood-forming organs. His most important contribution was the discovery that pernicious anemia could be effectively treated by feeding patients large doses of liver or liver extract. For this discovery, he shared the 1934 Nobel Prize in medicine with his Boston colleague **William P. Murphy** and with **George Hoyt Whipple** of the University of Rochester medical school.

Minot was born on December 2, 1885, in Boston, Massachusetts, the eldest of three sons of James Jackson Minot and Elizabeth Whitney Minot. The Minots were an old and well-to-do family of Boston. James Jackson Minot was a physician, and several other men on both sides of the family had been distinguished medical practitioners as well. Minot was a sickly child who spent a good deal of his early life in bed, but he grew stronger as he got older, partly by spending much time out of doors. He became a keen observer of nature and developed a love of the sea and sailing. He entered Harvard College in 1904, did well in his studies, and graduated in 1908.

Like many upper-class young men of his time, Minot was casual about choosing a vocation and finally decided to enter Harvard medical school only five days before the opening of the fall term on October 1, 1908. Nevertheless, he performed well in his class work and gradually grew more serious about his career. It was in medical school that he became interested in the study of human blood, and after he received his M.D. in 1912 he immediately began his internship at the Massachusetts General Hospital in Boston. In 1914 he became an assistant at the Johns Hopkins University medical school in Baltimore. There he continued his studies of blood in the laboratory and did some of the research that led to Dr. William H. Howell's discovery of the anticoagulant drug heparin. Minot returned to Boston to join the staff of the Massachusetts General Hospital in January 1915, and on June 29 of that year, he married Marian Linzee Weld. The couple eventually had two daughters and a son.

Early Research on Anemia

It was in 1915 at the Massachusetts General Hospital that Minot began to focus his attention on various forms of anemia, but especially on pernicious anemia, a disease for which there was then no known cure and which was almost always fatal to the patient. In his prolonged study of blood smears under the microscope, Minot made the important discovery that the number of reticulocytes (young red blood cells) found in a sample provided a good index of the activity of the bone marrow, the part of the body which produces all red blood cells. He also began to suspect that the cause of pernicious anemia was some malfunction in the bone marrow, and that this in turn was somehow related to the diet of the patient. However, his study of this problem, while never entirely abandoned, was put partially aside for a number of years while he worked in several other areas of hematology.

Around 1917 he began to spend an increasing amount of time at the recently opened Collis P. Huntington Memorial Hospital, also in Boston, which specialized in cancer research and treatment. There he did significant research on several forms of leukemia, a cancerous disease of the blood. In 1918 he became an assistant professor at the Harvard Medical School.

In October 1921 Minot found himself in a serious medical crisis of his own. Always a man of delicate health, he now discovered that he was suffering from diabetes. His doctors placed him on a strict, semi-starvation diet. At the time, this was the only known way of alleviating the effects of the disease. Minot continued his work but he grew terribly weak. Then, in January 1922, the discovery of insulin was announced, and by January 1923 the hormone was available in sufficient quantity that Minot could begin taking it. His condition improved rapidly, and although required to remain on a strict diet (weighed out in grams at each meal) for the rest of his life, Minot was able to maintain a heavy schedule of activity until 1947. His return to relatively good health was signaled by his acceptance of the positions of chief of medical services at Huntington Hospital and associate in medicine at Peter Bent Brigham Hospital, both in 1923.

Liver as a Cure for Pernicious Anemia

In 1925 Minot returned to the problem of the treatment of pernicious anemia. He was partly inspired by reading reports of experiments by Dr. George Hoyt Whipple of Rochester, who had bled dogs to make them anemic and then restored their health by feeding them a diet rich in red meat, especially liver. Minot speculated that feeding liver to human patients with pernicious anemia might have a beneficial effect. Minot enlisted a young colleague, Dr. William P. Murphy, to assist him in the experiment, and together they began feeding up to half a pound of liver per day to as many patients with pernicious anemia as they could persuade to eat it. This simple treatment produced dramatic results: nearly all the patients showed striking improvement, many within only two weeks or so. More important, they continued to improve with further liver feeding rather than suffering relapses following temporary remission of symptoms, as victims of pernicious anemia often did.

On May 4, 1926, at a meeting of the American Medical Association in Atlantic City, New Jersey, Minot and Murphy presented a report on the successful treatment of forty-five patients suffering from pernicious anemia. A year later, at a meeting in Washington, D.C., they reported favorable results in the treatment of 105 patients. The next step was to develop an extract of pure liver which would be less bulky and more palatable to the patient. Minot persuaded Dr. Edward J. Cohn, a professor of physical chemistry at the Harvard medical school, to work on this problem, and Cohn soon isolated what was called Fraction G from pure liver. The Eli Lilly Company then began to manufacture the substance as a commercial product. In 1929 Minot and others discovered that much smaller dosages of the extract, given intravenously, had the same effect as large doses taken by mouth.

The discovery of a cure for pernicious anemia marked the culmination of Minot's career as a scientific researcher. He was appointed professor of medicine at the Harvard medical school and director of the Thorndike Memorial Laboratory at Boston City Hospital in 1928. Subsequently, he was primarily an administrator rather than an active participant in research. He remained very active until April 16, 1947, when he suffered a severe stroke. He died on February 25, 1950, in Brookline, Massachusetts.

SELECTED WRITINGS BY MINOT:

Periodicals

(With William P. Murphy) "Treatment of Pernicious Anemia by a Special Diet," *Journal of the American Medical Association,* August 14, 1926, p. 470.

(With Murphy) "A Diet Rich in Liver in the Treatment of Pernicious Anemia," *Journal of the American Medical Association,* September 3, 1927, pp. 759–66.

"The Development of Liver Therapy in Pernicious Anemia: A Nobel Lecture," *The Lancet,* February 16, 1935, pp. 361–64.

SOURCES:

Books

De Kruif, Paul, *Men Against Death,* Harcourt, Brace, 1932.

Dictionary of Scientific Biography, Scribner, 1970–90.

Fox, Daniel M., Marcia Meldrum, and Ira Rezak, editors, *Nobel Laureates in Medicine or Physiology: A Biographical Dictionary,* Garland Publishing, 1990, pp. 401–04.

Magill, Frank N., editor, *The Nobel Prize Winners: Physiology or Medicine,* Volume 1, Salem Press, 1991, pp. 381–89.

Rackemann, Francis M., *The Inquisitive Physician: The Life and Times of George Richards Minot,* Harvard University Press, 1956.

Wintrobe, Maxwell M., *Hematology, the Blossoming of a Science,* Lea & Febiger, 1985.

—*Sketch by John E. Little*

Marvin Minsky

Marvin Minsky
1927-
American computer scientist

Marvin Lee Minsky is an educator and computer scholar at Massachusetts Institute of Technology and a pioneer in the field of artificial intelligence. Since the early 1950s, he has attempted to define and explain the thinking process and design a machine that can duplicate it. His 1987 book, *The Society of Mind,* put forward a detailed and mechanistic theory of how the mind works, and how it might be artificially duplicated. For his original and outstanding achievements in science and technology, Minsky was awarded the Japan Prize in 1990. Marvin Lee Minsky was born in New York City on August 9, 1927, to Dr. Henry Minsky and Fannie Reiser. His father was an eye surgeon and an artist. His mother was active in the Zionist movement. For the most part, Minsky attended private schools during his childhood, where his intelligence and later his interest in electronics and chemistry were nurtured. He learned early that he was most comfortable in the intellectually stimulating world of academia. This perception was enhanced in 1945, when, following his high school graduation, he enlisted in the United States Navy. He took his basic training at the Great Lakes Naval Training Center north of Chicago, with about one hundred and twenty other recruits. He later told Jeremy Bernstein, an interviewer for the *New Yorker,* that "they provided my first, and essentially my last, contact with nonacademic people."

Minsky enrolled at Harvard University in 1946, majoring in physics, but his eclectic interests kept him attending classes in a wide variety of subjects, including genetics, mathematics, and the nature of intelligence. He associated briefly with the researchers in the psychology department, but questioned the prevailing theories of what happens deep inside the mind. He confided to Bernstein in a *New Yorker* interview that he found B. F. Skinner's theories unacceptable "because they were an attempt to fit curves to behavior without any internal ideas."

Skinner had enjoyed considerable success in conditioning animal behavior using these hypotheses, but Minsky felt there must be a better explanation. Minsky switched his major to mathematics in his senior year, and graduated in 1950.

From Harvard, Minsky moved to Princeton to begin his doctoral studies. In the same environment in which mathematician **Alan Turing** had constructed the first electrical multiplier just prior to World War II, Minsky applied his budding theories of mentation to the construction of a learning machine which he called the Snarc, whose purpose was to learn how to traverse a maze using forty "agent" components and a system to reward success. However, Minsky's accomplishments with the Snarc were limited; although he felt himself on the right track with the "reward" principle, it was not versatile enough for Minsky's purposes.

Minsky began to explore how a machine might use memory to use past experience. This thought is elaborated on in his doctoral dissertation, in which he tries to show ways that a learning machine can predict the results of its behavior, based on its knowledge of past actions. There was some question at the time whether this line of inquiry properly belonged in a program that was ostensibly about mathematics. This is a recurring problem for Minsky, whose interests typically draw from so many disciplines that it becomes difficult to determine exactly what to label them. After receiving his Ph.D., Minsky accepted a three-year junior fellowship at Harvard, where, as he later said, he had no obligations except to pursue his theories about intelligence.

Co-founder of MIT Artificial Intelligence Laboratory

In 1958 Minsky joined the staff at the Massachusetts Institute of Technology's Lincoln Laboratory. He became an assistant professor of mathematics, and, in 1959, he and a colleague, **John McCarthy**, founded the MIT Artificial Intelligence Project. This project eventually became the Artificial Intelligence Laboratory, of which Minsky was the director from 1964 until 1973. In 1974, he was promoted to Donner professor of science in the department of electrical engineering and computer science. In 1989, he moved to MIT's media laboratory, where he became Toshiba Professor of Media Arts and Sciences.

Minsky has made it his life's work to finalize an overall theory of how minds work. He has disturbed, and perhaps alienated, many of his co-researchers by insisting that what we think of as "consciousness" or "self-awareness" is actually a myth—a convenient fallacy which allows us to function as a society. According to Minsky's theory (which he has outlined in *The Society of Mind* as well as in numerous articles in popular magazines), there is no difference between humans and machines, because, he believes, humans are machines whose brains are made up of many semi-autonomous but unintelligent "agents," but who mistakenly consider themselves intelligent individuals. According to Eugene F. Mallove in a *Tech Talk* article, "it is Minsky's view that hundreds of specialized 'computers' make up the human brain—or any other large brain for that matter. Many of these are at work cooperatively and unconsciously." Some have expressed concern that Minsky's mechanistic view of how minds work flies in the face of much established knowledge in the fields of biology and psychology, and contradicts what we seem to perceive about ourselves. But Minsky dismisses such objections, maintaining that most research on how the mind works has been crippled by researchers who simply ask the wrong questions.

Although Minsky still holds a professorship at the Artificial Intelligence Laboratory, most of the recent activity there has gone in directions that do not fully support his theories. For the past few years, Minsky has devoted himself to private research, fleshing out his Society of Mind theory. His professional writings are not prolific, but he writes often in such publications as *Omni* and *Discover,* and has co-authored a science fiction novel (not surprisingly based on his theory) with Harry Harrison titled *The Turing Option.* Artificial intelligence itself is a field in stasis; no major steps toward developing—or even defining—a truly intelligent machine have been made in decades. Minsky believes this could change if more researchers would pay attention to his theory. Whether or not that turns out to be true, it is very likely that when the field of artificial intelligence does move forward, Minsky will be somewhere nearby, giving it a push.

Minsky married Gloria Rudisch, a doctor, in 1953. The couple has three children: Margaret, Henry, and Juliana. Minsky has won many honors for his pioneering work: the Donner professorship, the Turing award in 1970, and the prestigious Japan award in 1990.

SELECTED WRITINGS BY MINSKY:

Books

(Editor) *Robotics,* Doubleday, 1985.
The Society of Mind, Simon & Schuster, 1987.
(With Harry Harrison) *The Turing Option* (a novel), Warner Books, 1992.

Periodicals

Omni, October, 1986, p. 38.
Discover, October, 1989, p. 52; June, 1992, p. 84; July, 1993, p. 24.
Byte, January, 1989, p. 343.

Ad Astra, June, 1990, p. 34.

SOURCES:

Periodicals

Boston Globe, February 9, 1990.
Business Week, March 2, 1992, p. 104.
Current Biography, September, 1988, p. 398–402.
New Yorker, December 14, 1981.
New York Times, April 18, 1990.
Tech Talk, April 25, 1990.

—*Sketch by Joel Simon*

Beatrice Mintz

Beatrice Mintz
1921-
American embryologist

Beatrice Mintz is an embryologist who has been responsible for a number of advances in the understanding of cancer while working in the laboratories at the Institute for Cancer Research in Philadelphia. She has published over 150 papers on a wide range of experimental approaches in the field of developmental biology, helping to establish the role of genes in differentiation and disease. She developed new strains of mice with a genetic predisposition to melanoma, thus offering the first experimental opportunity to analyze the progression of this disease, which is the fastest growing cancer among young people in the United States. In one experiment, she successfully accomplished the hereditary transmission of human skin melanoma cells to transgenic mice. In another experimental approach, she injected the human betaglobulin gene into fertilized mouse eggs, and this gene was then transmitted by that generation of mice to their offspring in a Mendelian ratio.

Mintz was born in New York City on January 24, 1921 to Samuel and Janie Stein Mintz. She attended Hunter College and received her A.B. in 1941; she graduated *magna cum laude,* and a member of Phi Beta Kappa. In the following year she did graduate work at New York University and then transferred to the University of Iowa where she received an M.S. in 1944 and a Ph.D in 1946. She served as a professor of biological science at the University of Chicago from 1946 to 1960. Since then, she has devoted her efforts to investigations at the Institute for Cancer Research.

Of Mice and Men

Mintz has made her most important contributions to cancer research with her experiments on the embryos of mice. The techniques she has developed to manipulate the embryos have made it possible to establish the genetic transmission of certain kinds of cancer, such as melanoma, a dangerous skin cancer. She has utilized a number of delicate laboratory techniques, such as injecting a few individual cells into the blastocysts—or early embryos—of mice in vitro, and then surgically transferring these early embryos into surrogate mothers, who then gave birth to mice whose traits were traceable. She has managed to inject the liver cells of fetal mice into the placental circulation of other mouse fetuses, thus ultimately developing a new pool of donor-strain stem cells for red and white blood cells. She has also developed techniques for in-vitro freezing of cells in liquid nitrogen before culturing them. She concluded from her investigations that human DNA could be assimilated into the germ line of mice for in-vivo research into the regulation of genetic diseases.

In the early 1960s, Mintz pioneered techniques for producing mammalian chimeras using mouse embryos. Chimera is a word from Greek mythology which describes an animal with a goat's head, a lion's body, and a serpent's tail. The mammalian chimeras Mintz produced were also composites, though they were merely the composites of genetic strains from different mice. She invented methods to develop them from more than one fertilized egg; she would take as many as fifteen embryos of different strains of mice and push them together until the cells aggregated into a single large blastocyst, which was then implanted into a foster mother. The offspring of these mice often reveal differing patterns of pigmentation and skin graft reactions.

In another experiment, Mintz succeeded in producing individuals with four, rather than two, parents. Early embryos consisting of only a few cells were removed from pregnant mice and placed in close contact with similar cells of genetically unrelated embryos to form a composite, unified embryo; this was then surgically implanted in the uterus of a mouse, which gave birth to a mouse that was a cellular mosaic—its tissues comprising genetically different kinds of cells. This technique is particularly valuable for tracing the tissue site of specific genetic diseases. In addition, Mintz established that when mouse embryo cells from a malignant tumor known as tetracarcinoma were combined with normal mouse embryo cells, the cancer cells developed into normal cells.

Named Outstanding Woman in Science

Mintz was awarded a Fulbright research fellowship at the universities of Paris and Strasbourg in 1951, and she has continued to receive many honors and awards, including the Papanicolaou Award for Scientific Achievement in 1979, and an Outstanding Woman in Science citation from the New York Academy of Sciences in 1993. She was also the recipient of two other honors, the Genetics Society of America Medal in 1981, and the Ernst Jung Gold Medal for Medicine in 1990. Five colleges, including her alma mater, have awarded her honorary doctorate degrees. She has been invited to deliver over twenty-five special lectureships, including the Ninetieth Anniversary Lecture at the Woods Hole Marine Biological Laboratory in 1978, and the first Frontiers in Biomedical Sciences Lecture at the New York Academy of Sciences in 1980. She is a member of the National Academy of Sciences and serves on the editorial boards of various scientific journals.

SELECTED WRITINGS BY MINTZ:

Books

"Experimental embryology," *McGraw-Hill Yearbook of Science and Technology,* McGraw-Hill, 1978, pp. 160–162.
"Gene Therapy: Production of Four-Parent Individuals," *Encyclopedia of Bioethics,* edited by W. T. Reich, Macmillan, 1978, pp. 519–520.

Periodicals

"Changing the Mammalian Genome," *Proceedings of the Pontifical Academy of Science,* Volume 73, 1980, pp. 216–223.
(With T. A. Stewart and E. F. Wagner) "Human Betaglobulin Gene Sequences Injected into Mouse Eggs, Retained in Adults and Transmitted to Progeny," *Science,* Volume 217, 1982, pp. 1046–1048.
(With W. K. Silvers) "Transgenic Mouse Models of Malignant Skin Melanoma," *Proceedings of the National Academy of Sciences,* Volume 90, 1993, pp. 8817–8821.

SOURCES:

Books

McGraw-Hill Encyclopedia of Science and Technology, Volume 3, McGraw-Hill, 1992, p. 5593.

Periodicals

Hawkes, Nigel, "A Weapon to Change the World," *Times* (London), March 2, 1993, p. 16.
Runkle, Guy, and Arlene J. Zaloznik, "Malignant Melanoma," *American Family Physician,* Volume 49, January, 1994, p. 91.

—Sketch by Maurice Bleifeld

Peter D. Mitchell
1920-
English biochemist

Peter D. Mitchell was awarded the 1978 Nobel Prize in Chemistry for his chemiosmotic theory, which explained how organisms use and synthesize energy. In his Nobel Prize address, Mitchell honored his long association with Professor David Keilin of Cambridge University, whose work provided the takeoff point for Mitchell's discoveries. Keilin had discovered cytochromes—electron-carrier proteins that assist in energy transfer via a respiratory chain. Mitchell's revolutionary chemiosmotic hypothesis changed the way scientists view energy transformation, and though it was initially viewed as controversial, it eventually won almost universal acceptance.

In 1961, when Mitchell's idea was first introduced, it was greeted by some in the scientific community with skepticism: what he was proposing was radically different than the prevailing thought on energy conversion at that time, and those opposing his conclusions questioned the validity of his research. Also, although Mitchell viewed his small research staff and unconventional laboratory at Glynn House mansion in Cornwall as positive elements conducive to productive research, others viewed his unorthodox working environment with suspicion. Mitchell's chemiosmotic theory generated intense debate, but the positive result for science as a whole was the creation of much additional scientific experimentation and productivity attempting to prove or disprove his theory, and advancing the discipline of bioenergetics—the study of energy exchanges and transformations between living things and their environments—in the process. Peter Dennis Mitchell was born in Mitcham, Surrey, England, on September 29, 1920, the son of Christopher Gibbs Mitchell, a civil servant, and Kate Beatrice Dorothy Taplin Mitchell. He received his secondary education at Queens College in Taunton, England, and was admitted to Jesus College at Cambridge University in 1939. A graduate student of James F. Danielli in the department of biochemistry at Cambridge, Mitchell earned his doctorate degree in 1951. He taught biochemistry at Cambridge from 1951 until 1955, when he left to develop a chemical biology unit at Edinburgh University. He was to remain there until 1963, when poor health caused him to look for a calmer working atmosphere.

Mitchell found a peaceful environment in an eighteenth-century manor house in Cornwall. The manor house, called Glynn House, was in disrepair and was restored by Mitchell and converted to family living quarters and a research laboratory. Glynn Research Laboratories was organized and directed in 1964 by Mitchell and his colleague, Jennifer Moyle, whose background work was instrumental to Mitchell's development of the chemiosmotic hypothesis. By the time Mitchell received the Nobel Prize, the laboratory had grown to require a staff of six.

Development of the Chemiosmotic Theory

The intriguing question of how organisms take energy from their surroundings and transform it for use in specialized functions, such as movement and respiration, was thought to have been answered by a theory called chemical coupling. This theory postulated that energy was carried down the respiratory chain by an unknown high-energy intermediate compound formed during oxidation. The energy derived from the intermediate compound was thought to form a "universal energy currency" known as adenosine triphosphate (ATP).

The search was on to identify the energy-rich intermediary when Mitchell upset prevailing thought by proposing that the process was an electrical, not a chemical, one. He coined the term "proticity" to explain the process by which protons flow across cell membranes to synthesize ATP. Mitchell likened this process to the way electricity moves from a high concentration to a concentration low enough to power an electric appliance. Laboratory experiments crucial for the support of his chemiosmotic theory were successfully carried out during the 1960s by Mitchell and Moyle at Glynn Research Laboratories, as well as in other research labs throughout the world. These experiments included identifying the membrane protons that provide a link to the movement of other molecules across the cell membrane and showing that the membrane also serves to halt the movement of other molecules.

Recognition for his work on cell energy transfer culminated in Mitchell's receipt of the Nobel Prize in 1978. Later, Mitchell and his staff at the Glynn laboratory studied the biochemical actions involved in energy transfer within cells, seeking precise details of this complex process. Those contributions advanced scientific knowledge of how cells use, transform, and generate energy. Mitchell had a strong philosophical sense that he was just one more link in science's intellectual and historical chain. He believed that the practice of science was a continuing process, whereby one scientist builds on the discoveries and knowledge of another, and was quick to give credit to those whose past work had advanced and made possible his own. In the December 15, 1978, issue of *Science,* Frank Harold quoted Mitchell as saying, "Science is not a game like golf, played in solitude, but a game like tennis in which one sends the ball into the opposing court and expects its return."

Many awards other than the Nobel Prize have been presented to Mitchell. Among them were the CIBA Medal and Prize, Biochemical Society, England; the Warren Triennial Prize, Massachusetts General Hospital; the Louis and Bert Freedman Award of the New York Academy of Sciences; the Lewis S. Rosenstiel Award for Distinguished Work in Basic Medical Research of Brandeis University; and the Copley Medal of the Royal Society. He has held membership in various professional societies and has been awarded honorary degrees from universities in Berlin and Chicago, as well as from numerous British institutions. Although immersed in his work, Mitchell found time to participate in local affairs, respond to environmental issues, and restore medieval farmhouses. He and his wife, Mary Helen French, were married in 1958; they had six children: Jeremy, Daniel, Jason, Gideon, Julia, and Vanessa.

SELECTED WRITINGS BY MITCHELL:

Periodicals

"Coupling of Phosphorylation to Electron and Hydrogen Transfer by a Chemi-Osmotic Type of Mechanism," *Nature,* Volume 191, 1961.

"Chemiosmotic Coupling in Oxidative and Photosynthetic Phosphorylation," *Biological Reviews,* Volume 41, 1966.

"Vectorial Chemistry and the Molecular Mechanics of Chemiosmotic Coupling: Power Transmission by Proticity," *Transactions of the Biochemical Society,* Volume 4, 1976.

"Vectorial Chemiosmotic Processes," *Annual Review of Biochemistry,* Volume 46, 1977.

"David Keilin's Respiratory Chain Concept and Its Chemiosmotic Consequences," *Science,* Volume 206, 1979.

"Compartmentation and Communication in Living Systems. Ligand Conduction: A General Catalytic Principle in Chemical, Osmotic, and Chemiosmotic Reaction Systems," *European Journal of Biochemistry,* Volume 95, 1979.

SOURCES:

Periodicals

Gwynne, Peter, "Nobel Quartet," *Newsweek,* October 30, 1978, pp. 105–106.

Harold, Franklin M., "The 1978 Nobel Prize in Chemistry," *Science,* December 15, 1978, pp. 1174 and 1176.

—*Sketch by Jane Stewart Cook*

Russell Mittermeier

Russell Mittermeier
1949-

American rain forest ecologist

Russell Mittermeier's exploration of rain forest ecology in places such as Costa Rica and Guatemala has provided much insight into the diversity and importance of preserving ecosystems. Through his field studies and writing, Mittermeier has sought to raise awareness among the general public on issues pertaining to biodiversity. His high-profile positions have included tenures as vice-president of science for the World Wildlife Fund and chairperson of the World Bank Task Force of Biological Diversity.

Mittermeier's observation of South American monkeys landed him a position with the New York Zoological Society in 1976, where he began his efforts to understand the cultural factors that affect the environment. In 1989 he became president of Conservation International, a Washington, DC-based nonprofit organization concerned with maintaining biodiversity and conserving rain forest ecosystems.

Russell Alan Mittermeier, born November 8, 1949, was the only child of Francis Xavier and Bertha Mittermeier, German immigrants who settled in New York City. While her husband tended to his stamp business, Bertha entertained her young son with stories of the jungle and frequent trips to the Bronx Zoo and the American Museum of Natural History. By the time Mittermeier was six, he had announced his intention to someday become an explorer.

An ambitious child, Mittermeier had read all the works of adventure writer Edgar Rice Burroughs while he was still in grade school. Growing up on Long Island, the budding anthropologist entertained himself with pet turtles, snakes, and frogs. By the time he was 16, he had helped form a local conservation group and began writing articles for their journal.

Though Mittermeier had wanted to attend Harvard as an undergraduate, he landed at Dartmouth in Hanover, New Hampshire, instead. The decision proved fortuitous, since Dartmouth had the best foreign language and overseas studies program in the country at the time. He spent considerable time engaged in field studies, which helped him develop the research and language skills he would need to eventually attend Harvard. A trimester each was devoted to studying in Costa Rica, France, and the University of Mainz in Germany. During these travels, Mittermeier studied with European herpetologists—scientists who study reptiles and amphibians—and South American primatologists, who study primates.

Dartmouth's senior fellow program awarded grants that enabled the recipients to spend an entire year on a project of their choice. When Mittermeier was granted this award, he proposed a trip to Central America, but the review board was initially skeptical. They could not imagine the young student "camping out" in the wild by himself. However, his proposal was eventually accepted on the condition that he show some proof that he would not be putting himself in too much danger.

Studies in Costa Rica Lead to Work in Conservation

On his way to Costa Rica, Mittermeier stopped at the Smithsonian Tropical Research Institute at Barro Colorado Island near the Panama Canal. "They were worried I was going to get lost down in the jungle," Mittermeier told Jennifer Kramer in an interview. "So I just went down to Panama, wrote them from the field station down there and said, 'I'm already in the field, so why don't you give me the senior fellowship?' And they did!" His subsequent research on New World monkeys along with his summa cum laude and Phi Beta Kappa honors from Dartmouth gained him entry into graduate school at Harvard. In 1973 he was awarded an M.A. in biological anthropology from the Massachusetts university, and in 1977 he completed his dissertation on the distribution, synecology, and conservation of Surinam monkeys.

The New York Zoological Society recruited Mittermeier for the position of conservation associate in 1976. A series of high-profile positions followed in the next several years with such organizations as the World Wildlife Fund, the International Union for the Conservation of Nature and Natural Resources in Switzerland, the World Health Organization, and the World Bank. In these positions Mittermeier helped focus the attention of government officials and citizens alike to the problems of the environment. Regarding various governmental policies that seek to protect vanishing and damaged ecosystems, Mittermeier told Kramer: "I don't believe in protectionist barriers; I think they're very artificial. The greatest enemy of the environment is poverty." Mittermeier further explained that poor economic conditions often coerce people in Third World countries to

engage in environmentally dangerous practices in order to sustain themselves financially.

Beginning in 1987, Mittermeier initiated the process of "debt swap" to combat these damaging practices. Debt swap was a policy in which countries with struggling economies were forgiven some overseas debts in exchange for protecting land which they might have otherwise been forced to clear for farming or other developments with negative environmental impact. Although the idea is credited to Thomas Lovejoy of the Smithsonian Institution, it was Mittermeier and his colleagues at Conservation International who implemented the first deals with Mexico, Madagascar, and Guatemala.

Mittermeier took this idea further in his concept of the "megadiversity country," described in detail in the first Conservation International Policy Paper in 1993. In this type of initiative, areas of the world containing a wealth of genetic material, which other countries have either lost or never had at all, would become protected areas. This would enable scientists to fill in the glaring gaps in their knowledge of primates and other species—simple facts regarding survival status and geographic distribution which Mittermeier has tried to gather during his travels. An example of science's incomplete knowledge is Mittermeier's 1992 discovery, along with Marco Schwarz and Jose Marcio Ayres, of a species of marmoset (a small variety of monkey) previously unknown in the scientific community.

Mittermeier's popularity has not been confined to scientific circles. In 1989 he posed for a Gap jeans ad along with an "organ-grinder's" monkey, a member of an endangered species. He has also given numerous interviews and speeches worldwide with mass-media organizations such as the BBC-TV network in England and *People* magazine. Through such means he has sought to broaden support for his mission, and in the process he has been awarded numerous accolades, ranging from important research grants to a citation in *Esquire* magazine as one of the most influential people under forty who is changing the United States.

Mittermeier's first marriage in 1985 to fellow biologist Isabel Constable produced a son, John. Following their divorce, Mittermeier married Christina Goettsch, who was affiliated with Conservation International, in 1991. The couple's son, Michael, was born in April of 1992.

In addition to his work with policy and advocacy organizations, Mittermeier has served as an advisor to zoological societies around the world and has been an adjunct professor for the State University of New York at Stony Brook since 1977. The information Mittermeier has collected has been published in the various newsletters he has edited since 1981, including *Neotropical Primates, Asian Primates, Primate*

Conservation and *Lemur News.* After successfully touring with two conservationist films, *Monkey of the Clouds* and *Cry of the Muriqui,* he began planning a series of tropical field guides in book and CD-ROM formats, patterned after the long-popular Peterson Guides.

SELECTED WRITINGS BY MITTERMEIER:

Books

(With Federico Medem and Anders G.J. Rhodin) *Vernacular Names of South American Turtles,* Society for the Study of Amphibians and Reptiles, 1980.

(Editor with Clive W. Marsh) *Primate Conservation in the Tropical Rain Forest,* Alan R. Liss, Inc., 1987.

(Editor with others) *Ecology and Behavior of Neotropical Primates Volume 2,* World Wildlife Fund/Littera Maciel Ltda, 1988.

Periodicals

"Monkey In Peril," *National Geographic,* March 1987, pp. 386–395.

"Strange and Wonderful Madagascar," *International Wildlife,* July 1988, pp. 4–13.

SOURCES:

Periodicals

Jackson, Donald Dale, "Making the World a Safer Place for Primates in Peril," *Smithsonian,* December 1985, pp. 100–110.

Klinkenborg, Verlyn, "The Making of a Biopolitician," *Audubon,* January/February 1992, pp. 90–93.

Shapiro, Harriet, "Destruction of Rain Forests, Warns a Conservationist, Is Endangering Many Species—Including Our Own," *People,* November, 28, 1988, pp. 165–167.

Other

Mittermeier, R.A., interview with Jennifer Kramer conducted September 17, 1993.

—Sketch by Jennifer Kramer

Andrija Mohorovičić
1857-1936
Croatian meteorologist and seismologist

The boundary between the earth's mantle and its crust is known as the Mohorovičić discontinuity in honor of Croatian seismologist Andrija Mohorovičić, who discovered it in 1909. He recognized that when seismic waves generated by an earthquake reach a certain depth, their speed increases. These deeper-moving waves travel much faster than waves nearer the surface. Mohorovičić correctly reasoned that a boundary, or discontinuity, existed since the velocity of seismic waves depends on the density and elasticity of the materials through which they move. Waves move slowly through the rocky, segmented crust and faster through the smooth mantle. Therefore, he concluded, a crust and a mantle of different physical and chemical composition must exist along with a relatively narrow boundary region. This discovery had important implications for seismological research concerning the cause and exact location of earthquakes.

Mohorovičić was born in Volosko, Istria, Croatia, on January 23, 1857. Little is known about his parents or his early life. His mother died shortly after his birth, and his father worked as a shipbuilder. Mohorovičić was a precocious youth who excelled at the grammar school he attended in Rijeka. In 1875 he entered the University of Prague where he attended lectures by the controversial Austrian physicist Ernst Mach. After graduating with a degree in math and physics, he taught in a secondary school for a short period.

In 1882 Mohorovičić received an appointment at the Royal Nautical School in Bakar to teach meteorology and oceanography. Meteorology soon became his scientific passion, and in 1887 he helped establish the Meteorological Station of Bakar. Mohorovičić accepted a professorship at the Main Technical School in Zagreb in 1891 and later became director of the school's meteorological observatory. After earning a doctorate from the University of Zagreb in 1897, he received an appointment as an unsalaried lecturer and was promoted to reader in 1910. In 1898 he was elected to the Yugoslav Academy of Sciences and served as secretary of its mathematics and science section from 1918 to 1922.

On October 8, 1909, a minor earthquake struck the Kulpa valley of Croatia. Mohorovičić began a systematic study of this event, examining seismographs and other physical evidence obtained from the earthquake. His work focused on the behavior of seismic waves, which were first postulated by English geologist **Richard Dixon Oldham**. When an earthquake occurs, tiny vibrating rock particles distribute the energy in wave form. These waves, known as "body" waves, radiate in all directions. Primary, or "P" waves, are compressed and cause a bumping, rebound motion. Secondary, or "S" waves, have an up-and-down motion. Mohorovičić noted that two distinct sets of both P and S waves were recorded from earthquakes originating less than five hundred miles away. He examined records of other earthquakes at various distances within this range and concluded that one set of waves moved more slowly but directly through the outer part of the earth. The faster waves, he reasoned, must have taken a path below this outer layer, moving down from the earthquake's focus point and later travelling back to the surface.

Mohorovičić identified the boundary between the two layers, and his initial calculations suggested that this boundary layer was between thirty to thirty-five miles thick. Later calculations by other researchers verified the existence of the discontinuity but reduced his estimate of the thickness to approximately twenty miles in depth. The Mohorovičić discontinuity is now known as the boundary that separates the crust and the mantle. This discontinuity is found throughout the world, though it is somewhat deeper under major mountain ranges.

Much of Mohorovičić's success can be attributed both to his rigorous attention to detail and his ability to sidestep bureaucracy. He was considered a good-humored man who made friends easily, in part because he spoke fluent Croatian, English, French, and Italian. Using his social skills, he was able to procure state-of-the-art seismographic and meteorologic equipment, which enabled him to make precise scientific measurements and to verify new theories.

His seismological research included the development of a method for accurately determining the epicenter (origin) of earthquakes and a model for estimating the travel time of seismic waves over distances of up to 10,000 miles. In his later years, he attempted to develop earthquake-proof buildings and he studied ways to improve the mechanics of seismographs. Although he is remembered for his contributions to geology, his meteorological research was equally meticulous. He authored a number of important papers on meteorology, including articles on cloud movement, tornadoes, atmospheric temperatures, and precipitation patterns.

Mohorovičić died in Zagreb on December 18, 1936, at the age of 79. His name was known primarily in scientific circles until 1957 when the "Mohole" project was launched—an attempt by scientists to drill beneath the Mohorovičić discontinuity and reach the earth's mantle. The project was underwritten by

the International Association of Seismology and Physics of the Earth's Interior.

SELECTED WRITINGS BY MOHOROVIČIĆ:

Books

"Sur la propagation des ondes sismiques au voisinage de l'épicentre. Préliminaires continues et tragets à réfraction," *Publications du Bureau central sèismologique international,* edited by E. Roth, Travaux scientifiques, 1924.

Periodicals

"Das Beben vom 8.X.1909," *Jahrbuch des meteorologischen Observatoriums in Zagreb,* 1909.

SOURCES:

Books

Dictionary of Scientific Biography, Volume 9, Scribner, 1970, pp. 443–445.
Great Events from History II, edited by Frank Magill, Salem Press, 1991, pp. 340–344, 1065–1068.

—*Sketch by Tom Crawford*

Henri Moissan
1852-1907
French chemist

Henri Moissan, who occupied the chair of Inorganic Chemistry at the Sorbonne from 1900 until his death, was the first person to isolate and characterize the element fluorine. He also invented the high-temperature electric arc furnace and prepared many new fluorine compounds, elemental transition metals, and carbides, borides, and silicides. For his work on fluorine and the electric furnace he was awarded the Nobel Prize in chemistry in 1906.

Ferdinand Frédéric Henri Moissan was born in Paris on September 28, 1852, the son of Francois Ferdinand and Josephine Mitel Moissan. The family lived modestly; his father was a clerk and his mother a seamstress. In 1864 they moved to Meaux, about twenty-five miles east of Paris. He was educated at the municipal school and was influenced by a mathematics and science teacher who gave him private lessons. His family, however, could not afford to pay for him to complete the courses in physics and classical languages that would have given him his baccalaureate, a necessity for university admission. In 1870 he was apprenticed briefly to a watchmaker before joining the army to defend Paris from the Prussians. He was finally apprenticed to a pharmacist in 1871. He planned to enroll in the three-year course at the École Supérieure de Pharmacie to earn the only qualification open to him, pharmacist second-class. Instead he was attracted into the laboratories of Edmond Fremy's School of Experimental Chemistry at the Paris Museum of Natural History. There he engaged in research, supported himself by tutoring, and finished the courses needed for his degree. He received the baccalaureate in 1874, and thereafter a series of higher degrees: *license* (B.S.) in 1877, pharmacist first-class in 1879, and a doctorate in 1880.

Although his earlier research had been in the chemistry of plant respiration, his doctoral dissertation dealt with pyrophoric iron and various oxides of that metal. He was interested only in inorganic chemistry, and this was the direction he would take for the rest of his career. In the course of this research he also concerned himself with chromium salts, and he developed a process for the preparation of pure chromium by reduction in a stream of hydrogen. Moissan began teaching at the École Supérieure de Pharmacie, and in 1880 he was named associate professor. In 1882 he married Marie Leonie Lugan, the daughter of a Meaux pharmacist who took an interest in Moissan's scientific progress and provided financial support. In 1885 they had their only child, Louis Ferdinand Henri, who was killed in 1915 in one of the early battles of World War I.

Isolates the Element Fluorine

In 1884 Moissan attempted to isolate the element fluorine. This was a long-standing problem that had eluded many notable scientists of the day. It was also a dangerous problem because of the high toxicity of fluoride compounds. Moissan's mentor Fremy had claimed production of fluorine by electrolysis (passing an electric current through it) of molten potassium fluoride, but at the temperature necessary for fusion the gas immediately attacked the platinum electrodes and thus could not be isolated. Fremy had also produced anhydrous hydrogen fluoride, but it could not be electrolyzed because it did not conduct electricity.

Moissan found that potassium acid fluoride which had been dissolved in hydrogen fluoride did conduct electricity. With an apparatus consisting of a platinum U-tube capped with plugs of fluorite (calcium fluoride) and fitted with iridium-platinum electrodes that resisted attack by fluorine, he produced

the gaseous element at –50 degrees Celsius to keep its reactivity to a minimum. This was in 1886, and over the next several years he devoted his major research efforts to reactions and compounds of fluorine, producing thionyl fluoride and sulfuryl fluoride and the unreactive carbon tetrafluoride and sulfur hexafluoride, as well as a number of organic alkyl fluorides. Later, with James Dewar, he produced liquid fluorine and, in 1903, solid fluorine. The element proved reactive down to its liquefaction temperature of –188 degrees Celsius. It is in fact the most reactive of all the elements, forming compounds even with the "inert" gases krypton, xenon, and radon; water itself "burns" in a fluorine atmosphere with a visible flame.

Invents High-Temperature Furnace in Effort to Synthesize Diamonds

After an excursion into the chemistry of boron, during which time he produced the pure element and studied a number of its compounds, Moissan became interested in the laboratory production of diamonds. To force carbon from its graphite form into the density of a diamond, great heat and pressure was required. Moissan reasoned that this might be accomplished by dissolving carbon into molten iron at very high temperature, then quickly cooling the solution in such a way that the mass formed a solid "skin" that would generate pressure on the still-liquid interior. However, the crystals he produced in this way were considered by later researchers not to be true diamonds because the pressure required to create diamonds is about five times greater than Moissan's method produced. The most important result of these experiments proved to be an instrument he had developed to conduct them. Moissan devised an electric arc furnace capable of producing temperatures as great as 3500 degrees Celsius.

The design of the furnace was simple. Two blocks of lime were laid on top of one another; the lower block was grooved to admit the electrodes and their leads, and the center had room for a crucible. A smaller hollow in the upper block formed a lid for the chamber. The electric furnace opened a new world of high-temperature chemistry. Within a few years of its development, Moissan prepared pure samples of metallic vanadium, chromium, manganese, zirconium, niobium, molybdenum, tantalum, tungsten, thorium, and uranium. He also synthesized previously unknown metallic borides, carbides, and silicides, including the extremely hard and refractory silicon carbide, which was later produced by a more practical method under American patent as the abrasive Carborundum.

Moissan was professor of toxicology at the Ecole Surérieure de Pharmacie from 1886 to 1899, when he became professor of inorganic chemistry. The following year, he accepted the chair of Inorganic Chemistry in the Faculty of Sciences of the University of Paris (Sorbonne), which he held until his death. In addition to receiving the Nobel Prize in 1906, Moissan's other awards and honors include the Prix Lacaze of the French Academy of Sciences in 1887, and he was elected to that body in 1891. He received the Davy Medal of the Royal Society of London in 1896 and was made a foreign member of that society in 1905. Moissan's health was adversely affected by his work with fluorine and its compounds. He was stricken with appendicitis and died on February 20, 1907, after an operation.

SELECTED WRITINGS BY MOISSAN:

Books

Le Four électrique, G. Steinheil, 1897, published as *The Electric Furnace,* Edward Arnold, 1904.
Le Fluor et ses composés, G. Steinheil, 1900.
Traite de chimie Minerale, [Paris], 1906.

SOURCES:

Books

Dictionary of Scientific Biography, Volume 11, Scribner, 1974, pp. 450–452.
Farber, Eduard, *Great Chemists,* Interscience, 1961, pp. 960–979.
Harrow, Benjamin, *Eminent Chemists of Our Time,* Van Nostrand, 1920, pp. 134–154.

Periodicals

Bundy, F.P. et al., "Man-made diamonds," *Nature,* Volume 176, 1955, pp. 51–55.
Huntress, Ernest H., "Moissan, (Ferdinand Frederic) Henri," *Proceedings of the American Academy of Arts and Sciences,* Volume 81, 1952, pp. 75–78.
Lonsdale, Kathleen, "Further Comments on Attempts by H. Moissan, J.B. Hannay and Sir Charles Parsons to Make Diamonds in the Laboratory," *Nature,* Volume 196, 1962, pp. 104–106.

—*Sketch by Robert M. Hawthorne Jr.*

Mario Molina
1943-
Mexican-born American chemist

Mario Molina is an important figure in the development of a scientific understanding of our atmosphere. Molina earned national prominence by theorizing, with fellow chemist **F. Sherwood Rowland**, that chlorofluorocarbons (CFCs) deplete the Earth's ozone layer. In his years as a researcher at the Jet Propulsion Lab at CalTech and a professor at the Massachusetts Institute of Technology (MIT), Molina has continued his investigations into the effects of chemicals on the atmosphere.

Mario José Molina was born in Mexico City on March 19, 1943. His father was Roberto Molina-Pasquel; his mother, Leonor Henriquez. Following his early schooling in Mexico, he graduated from the Universidad Nacional Autónoma de México in 1965 with a degree in chemical engineering. Immediately upon graduation, Molina went to West Germany to continue his studies at the University of Freiburg, acquiring the equivalent of his master's degree in polymerization kinetics in 1967. Molina then returned to Mexico to accept a position as assistant professor in the chemical engineering department at his alma mater, the Universidad Nacional Autónoma de México.

In 1968, Molina left Mexico to further his studies in physical chemistry at the University of California at Berkeley. He received his Ph.D. in 1972 and became a postdoctoral associate that same year. His primary area of postdoctoral work was the chemical laser measurements of vibrational energy distributions during certain chemical reactions. The following year, 1973, was a turning point in Molina's life. In addition to marrying a fellow chemist, the former Luisa Y. Tan (the couple have one son, Felipe), Molina left Berkeley to continue his postdoctoral work with physical chemist, Professor F. Sherwood Rowland, at the University of California at Irvine.

Conducts Landmark Investigation into the Dangers of Chlorofluorocarbons

Both Molina and Rowland shared a common interest in the effects of chemicals on the atmosphere. And both were well aware that every year millions of tons of industrial pollutants were bilged into the atmosphere. Also, there were questions about emissions of nitrogen compounds from supersonic aircraft. What impact did these various chemical discharges have on the envelope of air that surrounds the Earth? Molina and Rowland decided to conduct experiments to determine what happens to chemical pollutants that reach both the atmosphere directly above us but also at stratospheric levels, some ten to twenty-five miles above the Earth. Both men knew that within the stratosphere, a thin, diffuse layer of ozone gas encircles the planet which acts as a filter screening out much of the sun's most damaging ultraviolet radiation. Without this ozone shield, life could not survive in its present incarnation.

The two scientists concentrated their research on the impact of a specific group of chemicals called chlorofluorocarbons, which are widely used in such industrial and consumer products as aerosol spray cans, pressurized containers, etc. They found that when CFCs are subjected to massive ultraviolet radiation they break down into their constituent chemicals: chlorine, fluorine, and carbon. It was the impact of chlorine on ozone that alarmed them. They found that each chlorine atom could destroy as many as 100,000 ozone molecules before becoming inactive. With the rapid production of CFCs for commercial and industrial use—millions of tons annually—Molina and Rowland were alarmed that the impact of CFCs on the delicate ozone layer within the stratosphere could be life-threatening.

Mario Molina published the results of his and Rowland's research in *Nature* magazine in 1974. Their findings had startling results. Molina was invited to testify before the House of Representatives's Subcommittee on Public Health and Environment. Suddenly CFCs were a popular topic of conversation. Manufacturers began searching for alternative propellant gases for their products.

Over the next several years, Molina refined his work and, with Rowland, published additional data on CFCs and the destruction of the ozone layer in such publications as *Journal of Physical Chemistry, Geophysical Research Letter* and in a detailed piece entitled "The Ozone Question" in *Science*. In 1976, Mario Molina was named to the National Science Foundation's Oversight Committee on Fluorocarbon Technology Assessment.

In 1982, Molina became a member of the technical staff at the Jet Propulsion Laboratory at CalTech; two years later he was named senior research scientist, a position he held for an additional five years. In 1989, Mario Molina left the West coast to accept the dual position of professor of atmospheric chemistry at the MIT's department of Earth, atmosphere and planetary sciences, and professor in the department of chemistry. In 1990, he was one of ten environmental scientists awarded grants of $150,000 from the Pew Charitable Trusts Scholars Program in Conservation and the Environment. In 1993, he was selected to be the first holder of a chair at MIT established by the Martin Foundation, Inc., "to support research and education activities related to the studies of the environment."

Molina has published more than fifty scientific papers, the majority dealing with his work on the ozone layer and the chemistry of the atmosphere. In 1992 Molina and his wife, Luisa, wrote a monograph entitled "Stratospheric Ozone" published in the book *The Science of Global Change: The Impact of Human Activities on the Environment* published by the American Chemical Society.

His later work has also focused on the atmosphere-biosphere interface which Molina believes is "critical to understanding global climate change processes." He is the recipient of more than a dozen awards including the 1987 American Chemical Society Esselen Award, the 1988 American Association for the Advancement of Science Newcomb-Cleveland Prize, the 1989 NASA Medal for Exceptional Scientific Advancement, and the 1989 United Nations Environmental Programme Global 500 Award.

SELECTED WRITINGS BY MOLINA:

Periodicals

(With F. Sherwood Rowland) "Stratospheric Sink for Chlorofluormethanes-Chlorine Atom Catalyzed Destruction of Ozone," *Nature*, Volume 249, number 810, 1974.
(With Rowland) "The Ozone Question," *Science*, Volume 190, number 1038, 1974.
"The Antarctic Ozone Hole," *Oceanus*, Volume 31, number 47, 1990.

—Sketch by Benedict A. Leerburger

Egas Moniz
1874-1955
Portuguese neurologist

Egas Moniz was the professional name of Antonio Caetano de Abreu Freire, a scientist who made extensive contributions to the study of the human brain. A neurologist at the University of Lisbon, Moniz developed cerebral angiography in the 1920s, an important breakthrough in brain study that is still used today to diagnose tumors and strokes. Moniz also pioneered surgical procedures to address psychiatric disorders; with the help of Almeida Lima, he developed the psychosurgical technique called frontal leucotomy, which severed the frontal lobes from the rest of the brain and reduced the patient's anxiety and other symptoms of neurosis. For his work on the frontal leucotomy, Moniz shared the 1949 Nobel Prize in Physiology or Medicine with **Walter Rudolf Hess**.

Moniz was born Antonio Caetano de Abreu Freire in Avança, Portugal, on November 29, 1874. A member of an aristocratic family, his father was Fernando de Pina Rezende Abreu and his mother was Maria do Rosario de Almeida e Sousa. Moniz received his early education from an uncle who was an abbot, and in 1891 he entered the University of Coimbra where he studied medicine. Graduating as an M.D. in 1899 with a thesis on diphtheria, Moniz chose neurology as his field of specialization. He went on to study in France at the University of Paris and the University of Bordeaux, although he began to suffer from gout, a disease that impaired the use of his hands. After writing a paper on the physiological pathology of sexual activity, he became a professor at the University of Coimbra in 1902, the same year he married Elvira de Macedo Dias. In 1911 he was appointed professor of neurology at the University of Lisbon, where he would remain until his retirement in 1945.

Along with his medical career, Egas became immersed in Portuguese politics. In his years as a student at Coimbra, he had authored political literature promoting the cause of the liberal republicans that opposed Portugal's monarchical government. He first used the name Egas Moniz in writing these pamphlets, eventually adopting this moniker for all of his professional and political activities. Beginning in 1899, he served as a deputy in the Portuguese parliament. After the monarchy was overthrown in Portugal in 1910, Moniz became involved in rebuilding and reshaping his country's political system. In 1917, he was named Ambassador to Spain and Minister of Foreign Affairs, and he signed the Versailles Treaty as Portugal's delegate to the peace conference at the end of World War I. A political quarrel got him entangled in a duel in 1919, however, and he finally abandoned his political activities as a liberal republican when a conservative government took power in 1922.

Mapping the Brain

Moniz studied head injuries during World War I, and in 1917 he published *A Neurología na Guerra,* in which he described some of his findings. One of the early obstacles for neurology was the absence of a reliable and safe technology for examining the brain when it was still alive. Attempting to find an improved method of locating intracranial brain tumors, Moniz to begin experimenting on corpses by injecting radioactive solutions into the arteries and taking X rays of them. By 1927 he had developed this technique, known as cerebral angiography, to the point where the radioactive solution coursing through the

brain's vessels and arteries made it possible to x-ray live brain tissues. Moniz mapped out the distribution of blood vessels in the head, and he was therefore able to detect and measure tumors that displaced the normal location of the arteries. To this day, angiography continues to be the most widely used method for diagnosing tumors, strokes, and other injuries. The contribution Moniz made to psychosurgery was the result of his determination to find physical cures for mental illness. Attending the 1935 International Neurological Conference in London, Moniz was particularly impressed by the work of John F. Fulton and Carlyle G. Jacobsen, American scientists who had removed the frontal lobes from the brains of chimpanzees and observed certain behavioral changes. Known as frontal leucotomy, the procedure consists of severing the nerves connecting the frontal lobes to the rest of the brain. Moniz and his colleague Almeida Lima developed the technique so it could be applied to humans to alleviate certain psychiatric problems such as anxiety and neurosis. The procedure was considered successful; there were no fatalities in the original twenty patients, and the mental condition of most of them was declared improved or cured by the operation. Widely hailed as the most important psychiatric procedure yet discovered, Moniz shared the Nobel Prize in 1949 for his frontal leucotomy research. This method was abandoned after World War II, however, when psychopharmacology made considerable inroads in treating nervous and mental disorders with drugs. Nonetheless, frontal leucotomy played an important role in educating neurologists about the human brain and the surgical procedures that can be applied to it.

SELECTED WRITINGS BY MONIZ:

Books

A Neurología na Guerra, (published in Lisbon), 1917.

SOURCES:

Periodicals

Perino, F.R., "Egas Moniz," *Journal of the International College of Surgeons,* Volume 36, 1961, p. 261.

—Sketch by Rodolfo A. Windhausen

Jacques Lucien Monod
1910-1976
French biologist

Jacques Lucien Monod

The structure of all living matter is determined by the composition of its deoxyribonucleic acid, or DNA, molecule; the discovery in the early 1950s that the genetic code carried by DNA is responsible for the shape of all the proteins that make up skin, eyes, hair—all the tissues of life—astounded the scientific community at the time. But how this master plan is carried out, and how its instructions are read and followed by the body, were facts discovered much later by French biologist Jacques Lucien Monod and a small cadre of scientists working with him. Monod and his colleagues postulated, and later demonstrated, the process by which messenger ribonucleic acid (mRNA) carries instructions for protein synthesis from the DNA in a cell's nucleus to its cytoplasm, where the instructions are carried out. Monod and two fellow researchers, **Francois Jacob** and **André Lwoff**, won the 1965 Nobel Prize for physiology or medicine.

Early Interest in Biology

Monod was born in Paris, on February 9, 1910, to Lucien Hector Monod, a painter and intellectual of Swiss Huguenot descent, and Charlotte Todd (MacGregor) Monod, a Scottish-American from Milwaukee, Wisconsin. At the age of seven, Monod moved with his family to Cannes in the South of France. His parents were very influential in his education, and Monod later credited his father for his own passionate interest in music, and, later, biology. The young Monod learned to play the cello at an early age, and even during the years he was doing research in molecular biology, he played in and directed a string quartet and a Bach choir. Although Monod later confessed a serious inclination towards a career in conducting, he also showed an early interest in biology, collecting beetles and tadpoles in the woods around his southern France home. His interest developed further, and he entered the College de Cannes from where he graduated in the summer of 1928. Monod went on to receive a B.S. from the Faculte des Sciences at the University of Paris, Sorbonne, in 1931. Although he stayed on at the university for further studies, Monod felt that the academic curriculum at the Sorbonne was deficient and did not reflect contemporary biological research. Therefore, it was through the personal contacts he developed during excursions to the nearby Roscoff marine biology station that Monod received his true scientific grounding.

While working at the Roscoff station, Monod met Andre Lwoff, with whom he would establish a life-long collaboration. Lwoff introduced Monod to the potentials of microbiology and microbial nutrition, and these became the focus of Monod's early research. Boris Ephrussi, another scientist working at Roscoff, opened Monod to the importance of physiological and biochemical genetics. And Louis Rapkine, also a Roscoff contemporary, impressed upon Monod the importance of learning the chemical and molecular aspects of living organisms.

Embarks on His Career

During the autumn of 1931 Monod took up a fellowship at the University of Strasbourg in the laboratory of Edouard Chatton, France's leading protistologist. Then, in October, 1932, he won a Commercy Scholarship that called him back to Paris to work at the Sorbonne once again. This time he was an assistant in the Laboratory of the Evolution of Organic Life, which was directed by the French biologist Maurice Caullery at the time. Moving to the zoology department in 1934, Monod became an assistant professor of zoology in less than a year. That summer, Monod also embarked on a natural history expedition to Greenland aboard the *Pourquoi pas?* This expedition was a great success and developed in Monod a life-long love for sailing. In 1936 Monod left for the United States with Ephrussi, where he spent time at the California Institute of Technology on a

Rockefeller grant. His research centered on studying the fruit fly (*Drosophila melanogaster*) under the direction of **Thomas Hunt Morgan**, an American geneticist. Here Monod not only met with refreshingly new opinions, but he also got his first look at a new way of studying science—a research style based on collective effort and a free passage of critical discussion. This was in contrast to the rigid, sometimes sterile, attitude among the faculty at the Sorbonne. Returning to France, Monod completed his studies at the Institute of Physiochemical Biology. In this time he also worked with Georges Teissier, a scientist at the Roscoff station, who influenced Monod's interest in the study of bacterial growth. This later became the subject of Monod's doctoral thesis at the Sorbonne.

This was a time of war in Europe, and despite a medical exemption from military service which allowed him to retain his academic position, Monod joined the French resistance movement. His Sorbonne laboratory became an underground meeting place and propaganda print shop. Thereafter Monod also joined the Franc-Tireurs Partisans and was captured by the Gestapo. He managed to escape and continued his underground resistance efforts. Monod is also credited with helping to organize the general strike that led to Paris' ultimate liberation, and he was honored with several military commendations for his efforts.

During this period Monod also continued his pursuit of music, forming a Bach choir, La Cantate, which he would direct until 1948. In 1938, he met his future wife, Odette Bruhl, an archeologist and orientalist, through the choir. In the post-war period Monod served as the laboratory director of Lwoff's Department, and he also became an officer in the Free France Forces. As a member of General de Lattre de Tassigny's staff, he met a number of American scientists. They provided Monod with several scientific journals in which he read articles about the spontaneous mutations of bacteria. Monod later recalled the influence these articles had on the course of his career. He noted that these journals in particular, lead him to the study of genetics and later, his research into the structure of DNA.

Studies Enzyme Induction

Monod's work comprised four separate but interrelated phases beginning with his practical education at the Sorbonne. In the early years of his education, he concentrated on the kinetic aspects of biological systems, discovering that the growth rate of bacteria could be described in a simple, quantitative way. The size of the colony was solely dependent on the food supply; the more sugar Monod gave the bacteria to feed on, the more they grew. Although there was a direct correlation between the amount of food Monod fed the bacteria and their rate of growth,

he also observed that in some colonies of bacteria, growth spread over two phases, sometimes with a period of slow or no growth in between. Monod termed this phenomenon "diauxy" (double growth), and guessed that the bacteria had to employ different enzymes to metabolize different kinds of sugars.

When Monod brought the finding to Lwoff's attention in the winter of 1940, Lwoff suggested that Monod investigate the possibility that he had discovered a form of "enzyme adaptation," in which the latency period represents a hiatus during which the colony is switching between enzymes. In the previous decade, a similar phenomenon had been recorded by the Finnish scientist, Henning Karstroem while working with protein synthesis. Although the outbreak of war and a conflict with his director took Monod away from his lab at the Sorbonne, Lwoff offered him a position in his laboratory at the Pasteur Institute where Monod would remain until 1976. Here he began working with Alice Audureau to investigate the genetic consequences of his kinetic findings, thus beginning the second phase of his work.

To explain his findings with bacteria, Monod shifted his focus to the study of enzyme induction. He theorized that certain colonies of bacteria spent time adapting and producing enzymes capable of processing new kinds of sugars. Although this slowed down the growth of the colony, Monod realized that it was a necessary process as the bacteria needed to adapt to varying environments and foods to survive. Therefore, in devising a mechanism that could be used to sense a change in the environment, and thereby enable the colony to take advantage of the new food, a valuable evolutionary step was taking place. In Darwinian terms, this colony of bacteria would now have a very good chance of surviving, by passing these changes on to future generations. Monod would summarize his research and views on relationship between the roles of random chance and adaptation in evolution in his 1970 book *Chance and Necessity*.

Between 1943 and 1945, working with Melvin Cohn, a specialist in immunology, Monod hit upon the theory that an "inducer" acted as an internal signal of the need to produce the required digestive enzyme. This hypothesis challenged the German biochemist Rudolf Schoenheimer's theory of the "dynamic state" of protein production, which stated that it was the mix of proteins that resulted in a large number of random combinations. Monod's theory, in contrast, projected a fairly stable and efficient process of protein production which seemed to be controlled by a master plan. In 1953, Monod and Cohn published their findings on the generalized theory of induction.

Discovers Role of Messenger Ribonucleic Acid (mRNA)

That year Monod also became the director of the department of cellular biology at the Pasteur Institute and began his collaboration with Francois Jacob and Jacob's team. In 1955, working with Jacob, he began the third phase of his work by investigating the relationship between the roles of heredity and environment in enzyme synthesis, that is, how the organism creates these vital elements in its metabolic pathway and how it knows when to create them.

It was this research that led Monod and Jacob to formulate their model of protein synthesis. They identified a gene cluster they called the operon, at the beginning of a strand of bacterial DNA. These genes, they postulated, send out messages signalling the beginning and end of the production of a specific protein in the cell, depending on what proteins are needed by the cell in its current environment. Within the operons, Monod and Jacob discovered two key genes, which they named the "operator" and "structural" genes. The scientists discovered that during protein synthesis, the operator gene sends the signal to begin building the protein. A large molecule then attaches itself to the structural gene to form a strand of messenger RNA (mRNA). In addition to the operon is the regulator gene, which codes for a repressor protein. The repressor protein either attaches to the operator gene and inactivates it, in turn, halting structural gene activity and protein synthesis; or the repressor protein binds to the regulator gene instead of the operator gene, thereby freeing the operator and permitting protein synthesis to occur. As a result of this process, the mRNA, when complete, acts as a template for the creation of a specific protein encoded by the DNA, carrying instructions for protein synthesis from the DNA in the cell's nucleus, to the ribosomes outside the nucleus, where proteins are manufactured. With such a system, a cell can adapt to changing environmental conditions, and produce the proteins it needs when it needs them.

Word of the importance of Monod's work began to spread, and in 1958 he was invited to become professor of biochemistry at the Sorbonne, a position he accepted conditional to his retaining his post at the Pasteur Institute. At the Sorbonne, Monod was the chair of chemistry of metabolism, but in April, 1966, his position was renamed the chair of molecular biology in recognition of his research in creating the new science. His Nobel prize in 1965 both increased his responsibilities and thrust him to the center of a growing limelight in the field of biochemistry.

Monod's life following the Nobel prize reveals a dramatic shift to the administrative side of scientific research. Elected to the College de France and named chair of molecular biology in 1967, Monod used his influence and fame to bolster the cause of the organized student movement against the academic establishment in France. In 1971 he was offered the directorship of the Pasteur Institute and, on April 15, 1971, he was named director general of the institute. At this time the institute was on the verge of financial collapse, and Monod set aside his research to devote all his efforts to modernize and revitalize the organization. As his administrative duties grew, his research activities rapidly slowed and finally stopped in 1972 after the death of his wife. Not long thereafter, Monod himself fell ill with aplastic anemia. Four years later, with his own death imminent, and having completed only the first phase of his intended sweeping changes at the institute, Monod returned to his home in Cannes. He died there on May 31, 1976.

His twin sons, Olivier and Philippe, followed him into scientific research, Olivier as a geologist and Philippe as physicist. Monod's list of awards and honors was impressive, and it included the Montyon Physiology Prize, the Louis Rapkine Medal, and the Charles Leopold Mayer Prize. He was made a Chevalier de l'Ordre des Palmes Academiques and later an officer in the Legion of Honor. He also received both the Croix de Guerre and the Bronze Star Medal.

SELECTED WRITINGS BY MONOD:

Books

Chance and Necessity, translation from the original French manuscript, *Le hasard et la necessite. Essai sur la philosophie naturelle de la biologie moderne,* by Austryn Wainhouse, Random House, 1971.

Periodicals

(With Francois Jacob) "Genetic Regulatory Mechanisms in the Synthesis of Proteins," *Journal of Molecular Biology,* March, 1961, pp. 318–56.

SOURCES:

Books

Dictionary of Scientific Biography, Scribner, 1980, pp. 636–49.
Nobel Lectures: Physiology or Medicine, 1963–1970, Elsevier, 1972, pp. 143–47, 188–211.

Periodicals

"Jacques Monod, 1910–1976," *Nature,* Volume 262, 1976, pp. 429–30.
Science, October 22, 1965, pp. 462–63.

—Sketch by Nicholas Williamson

Luc Montagnier
1932-
French virologist

Luc Montagnier of the Institut Pasteur in Paris has devoted his career to the study of viruses. He is perhaps best known for his 1983 discovery of the human immunodeficiency virus (HIV), which has been identified as the cause of acquired immunodeficiency syndrome (AIDS). However, in the twenty years before the onset of the AIDS epidemic, Montagnier made many significant discoveries concerning the nature of viruses. He made major contributions to the understanding of how viruses can alter the genetic information of host organisms, and significantly advanced cancer research. His investigation of interferon, one of the body's defenses against viruses, also opened avenues for medical cures for viral diseases. Montagnier's ongoing research focuses on the search for an AIDS vaccine or cure.

Montagnier was born in Chabris (near Tours), France, the only child of Antoine Montagnier and Marianne Rousselet. He became interested in science in his early childhood through his father, an accountant by profession, who carried out experiments on Sundays in a makeshift laboratory in the basement of the family home. At age fourteen, Montagnier himself conducted nitroglycerine experiments in the basement laboratory. His desire to contribute to medical knowledge was also kindled by his grandfather's long illness and death from colon cancer.

Montagnier attended the Collège de Châtellerault, and then the University of Poitiers, where he received the equivalent of a bachelor's degree in the natural sciences in 1953. Continuing his studies at Poitiers and then at the University of Paris, he received his *licence ès sciences* in 1955. As an assistant to the science faculty at Paris, he taught physiology at the Sorbonne and in 1960 qualified there for his doctorate in medicine. He was appointed a researcher at the Centre National de la Recherche Scientifique (C.N.R.S.) in 1960, but then went to London for three and a half years to do research at the Medical Research Council at Carshalton.

Investigates the Nature of Viruses

Viruses are agents which consist of genetic material surrounded by a protective protein shell. They are completely dependent on the cells of a host animal or plant to multiply, a process which begins with the shedding of their own protein shell. The virus research group at Carshalton was investigating ribonucleic acid (RNA), a form of nucleic acid that normally is involved in taking genetic information from deoxyribonucleic acid (DNA) (the main carrier of genetic information) and translating it into proteins. Montagnier and F. K. Sanders, investigating viral RNA (a virus that carries its genetic material in RNA rather than DNA), discovered a double-stranded RNA virus that had been made by the replication of a single-stranded RNA. The double-stranded RNA could transfer its genetic information to DNA, allowing the virus to encode itself in the genetic make-up of the host organism. This discovery represented a significant advance in knowledge concerning viruses.

From 1963 to 1965, Montagnier did research at the Institute of Virology in Glasgow, Scotland. Working with Ian MacPherson, he discovered in 1964 that agar, a gelatinous extractive of a red alga, was an excellent substance for culturing cancer cells. Their technique became standard in laboratories investigating oncogenes (genes that have the potential to make normal cells turn cancerous) and cell transformations. Montagnier himself used the new technique to look for cancer-causing viruses in humans after his return to France in 1965.

From 1965 to 1972, Montagnier worked as laboratory director of the Institut de Radium (later called Institut Curie) at Orsay. In 1972, he founded and became director of the viral oncology unit of the Institut Pasteur. Motivated by his findings at Carshalton and the belief that some cancers are caused by viruses, Montagnier's basic research interest during those years was in retroviruses as a potential cause of cancer. Retroviruses possess an enzyme called reverse transcriptase. Montagnier established that reverse transcriptase translates the genetic instructions of the virus from the viral (RNA) form to DNA, allowing the genes of the virus to become permanently established in the cells of the host organism. Once established, the virus can begin to multiply, but it can do so only by multiplying cells of the host organism, forming malignant tumors. In addition, collaborating with Edward De Mayer and Jacqueline De Mayer, Montagnier isolated the messenger RNA of interferon, the cell's first defense against a virus. Ultimately, this research allowed the cloning of interferon genes in a quantity sufficient for research. However, despite widespread hopes for interferon as a broadly effective anti-cancer drug, it was initially found to be effective in only a few rare kinds of malignancies.

Discovers the AIDS Virus

AIDS (acquired immunodeficiency syndrome), a tragic epidemic that emerged in the early 1980s, was first adequately characterized around 1982. Its chief feature is that it disables the immune system by which the body defends itself against numerous diseases. It is eventually fatal. By 1993, more than three million people had developed full-blown AIDS. Montagnier believed that a retrovirus might be responsible for

AIDS. Researchers had noted that one pre-AIDS condition involved a persistent enlargement of the lymph nodes, called lymphadenopathy. Obtaining some tissue culture from the lymph nodes of an infected patient in 1983, Montagnier and two colleagues, Françoise Barré-Sinoussi and Jean-Claude Chermann, searched for and found reverse transcriptase, which constitutes evidence of a retrovirus. They isolated a virus they called LAV (lymphadenopathy-associated virus). Later, by international agreement, it was renamed HIV, human immunodeficiency virus. After the virus had been isolated, it was possible to develop a test for antibodies that had developed against it—the HIV test. Montagnier and his group also discovered that HIV attacks T4 cells which are crucial in the immune system. A second similar but not identical HIV virus called HIV–2 was discovered by Montagnier and colleagues in April 1986.

HIV Patent Dispute Sparks Controversy with Robert Gallo

A controversy developed over the patent on the HIV test in the mid–1980s. **Robert C. Gallo** of the National Cancer Institute in Bethesda, Maryland, announced his own discovery of the HIV virus in April 1984 and received the patent on the test. The Institut Pasteur claimed the patent (and the profits) on the basis of Montagnier's earlier discovery of HIV. Despite the controversy, Montagnier continued research and attended numerous scientific meetings with Gallo to share information. Intense mediation efforts by **Jonas Salk** (the scientist who developed the first polio vaccine) led to an international agreement signed by the scientists and their respective countries in 1987. Montagnier and Gallo agreed to be recognized as codiscoverers of the virus, and the two governments agreed that the profits of the HIV test be shared (most going to a foundation for AIDS research).

The scientific dispute continued to resurface, however. Most HIV viruses from different patients differ by six to twenty percent because of the remarkable ability of the virus to mutate. However, Gallo's virus was less than two percent different from Montagnier's, leading to the suspicion that both viruses were from the same source. The laboratories had exchanged samples in the early 1980s, which strengthened the suspicion. Charges of scientific misconduct on Gallo's part led to an investigation by the National Institutes of Health in 1991, which initially cleared Gallo. In 1992 the investigation was reviewed by the newly created Office of Research Integrity. The ORI report, issued in March of 1993, confirmed that Gallo had in fact "discovered" the virus sent to him by Montagnier. Whether or not Gallo had been aware of this fact in 1983 could not be established, but it was found that he had been guilty of misrepresentations in reporting his research and that his supervision of his

research lab had been desultory. The Institut Pasteur immediately revived its claim to the exclusive right to the patent on the HIV test. Gallo objected to the decision by the ORI, however, and took his case before an appeals board at the Department of Health and Human Services. The board in December of 1993 cleared Gallo of all charges, and the ORI subsequently withdrew their charges for lack of proof.

Montagnier's continuing work includes investigation of the envelope proteins of the virus that link it to the T-cell. He is also extensively involved in research of possible drugs to combat AIDS. In 1990 Montagnier hypothesized that a second organism, called a mycoplasma, must be present with the HIV virus for the latter to become deadly. This suggestion, which has proved controversial among most AIDS researchers, is the subject of ongoing research.

Montagnier married Dorothea Ackerman in 1961. They have three children, Jean-Luc, Anne-Marie, and Francine. He has described himself as an aggressive researcher who spends much time either in the laboratory or traveling to scientific meetings. He enjoys swimming and classical music, and loves to play the piano, especially Mozart sonatas.

SELECTED WRITINGS BY MONTAGNIER:

Books

"Europe Against AIDS," in *Scientific Europe: Research and Technology in 20 Countries,* edited by Nigel Calder, Foundation Scientific Europe, 1990.

Periodicals

(With others) "LAV Revisited: Origins of the Early HIV–1 Isolates from Institut Pasteur," *Science,* Volume 252, May 17, 1991, pp. 961–965.

SOURCES:

Periodicals

Altman, Lawrence K., "Accomplice in AIDS Deaths? Clues Are Sifted," *New York Times,* Volume 139, May 11, 1990, p. A12.
Bass, Thomas, "Interview: Luc Montagnier," *Omni,* Volume 11, December 1988.
Cohen, Jon, "HHS: Gallo Guilty of Misconduct," *Science,* Volume 259, January 8, 1993, pp. 169–170.
Gladwell, Malcolm, "1984 AIDS Strain Was French, Gallo Concedes," *Washington Post,* Volume 114, May 31, 1991, p. A3.

Hilts, Philip J., "Evidence Is Said to Increase on Microbe's Role in AIDS," *New York Times,* Volume 139, June 22, 1990, p. A18.

Hilts, Philip J., "Scientist in AIDS Rift Offers 2d Look at Virus," *New York Times,* Volume 140, March 1, 1991, p. A18.

Hilts, Philip J., "U.S. and France Finally Agree in Long Feud on AIDS Virus," *New York Times,* Volume 140, May 7, 1991, p. A1.

—Sketch by Pamela O. Long

Charlotte E. Moore

Charlotte E. Moore
1898-1990
American astrophysicist

Charlotte E. Moore, a physicist who gained international acclaim for her analysis of solar and atomic spectra, worked in the atomic physics division of the National Bureau of Standards for over twenty years. In this capacity, she supervised the compilation of numerous solar spectroscopic tables containing analytic information about the chemical and physical properties of the elemental gases comprising the sun and the solar atmosphere. She received worldwide recognition for her analytic interpretations and compilations of solar and stellar spectra, including the honor of being among six women to receive the first Federal Woman's Award from the United States Government in 1961 for her outstanding contributions in a federal career. She was also the first woman scientist elected as a foreign associate, in 1949, into the Royal Astronomical Society of London.

Moore was born on September 24, 1898, in Ercildoun, Pennsylvania, to George Winfield Moore, superintendent of the Chester County Schools, and Elizabeth Palmer (Walton) Moore, a school teacher. Her parents, through their occupations and Quaker following, instilled a disciplined appreciation for learning that Moore maintained throughout her life. Upon graduating from high school in 1916, she entered Swarthmore College, graduating in 1920 with a bachelor's degree in mathematics and membership in Phi Beta Kappa. John A. Miller, Moore's physics professor at Swarthmore, was influential in her decision to pursue a career in physics.

Develops Astrophysics Interests at Princeton

Moore's mathematical inclinations landed her a position in mathematical computation at the Princeton University Observatory in 1920. There, she worked with the astrophysicist **Henry Norris Russell**, whose research had resulted in a theory of stellar evolution. Typical of most astrophysicists, Moore and Russell used spectroscopy to measure certain cosmological objects' spectra or distribution of radiation at particular wavelengths of light. By determining the wavelength at which certain spectral lines appeared, they identified the elements making up the object under investigation. Russell guided Moore's initial research into atomic spectra, and in 1928 they collaborated on the publication of a monograph on the solar spectrum of elemental iron.

Although Moore's academic astrophysics career began and would later end at Princeton, she spent eight years researching in California. For five years she worked with Dr. Charles E. St. John at the renowned Mt. Wilson Observatory in Pasadena. Their spectroscopical researches resulted in a 1928 revision of Henry Rowland's classic *Preliminary Table of Solar Spectrum Wavelengths* published between 1893 and 1896. This work, together with her previous research, earned Moore the Lick fellowship as she pursued doctoral studies at the University of California at Berkeley. She wrote her dissertation on the atomic lines in the sunspot spectrum and received her degree in 1931.

Upon completing her doctorate, Moore returned to the Princeton University Observatory as a researcher and remained until 1945. While at Princeton, she met astronomer and physicist Bancroft

Walker Sitterly; they were married on May 30, 1937. Moore had established her scientific career and received recognition under her maiden name, so she continued publishing many journal articles under that name throughout her life, although a few publications appear under the name Sitterly or Moore-Sitterly.

Appointed Physicist and Astronomer at the National Bureau of Standards

Moore left the academic surrounds of Princeton and joined the National Bureau of Standards (now the National Institute of Standards and Technology) in Washington, D.C., in 1945. Joining William F. Meggers's section on spectroscopy, Moore was soon placed in charge of a project involving the compilation of data on atomic energy levels. According to her colleague William C. Martin, who authored her obituary for *Physics Today,* Moore regarded her position as much more than the gatherer of previously published data. She scrutinized the data and sought to correct any shortcomings by persuading spectroscopists to provide new analyses. The voluminous amount of unpublished data Moore received attested, Martin claimed, to the spectroscopists' great confidence in Moore's competence. The chief result of her stringent and persistent efforts in collecting data was the publication in 1949, 1952, and 1958 of the three-volume reference source *Atomic Energy Levels as Derived from the Analyses of Optical Spectra* containing an organized representation of the atomic energy information for 485 atomic species and described by Martin as "one of the most highly respected and frequently cited sources of basic atomic data ever published." While at the Bureau of Standards, Moore published other valuable reference sources including *The Masses of the Stars* in 1940 with Russell, her previous Princeton colleague, and *The Solar Spectrum* in 1947 with Harold D. Babcock. In the following decade, Moore began collaborations with Richard Tousey at the Naval Research Laboratory which were to continue until her death, using data gathered from V–2 rockets to analyze ultraviolet solar spectra. Also among Moore's accomplishments was her discovery of the existence of technetium in the sun; technetium is a highly unstable element which naturally occurs only at trace levels on earth.

In 1968, Moore officially retired from the Bureau of Standards. Her career, however, was hardly finished. She spent the next three years working at the Office of Standard Reference Data, then joined Tousey's group working at the Space Science Division of the Naval Research Laboratory from 1971 to 1978. Throughout this time, Moore retained strong working relationships with her previous colleagues at the National Bureau of Standards. She also increased her involvement in professional astronomical societies. Among those in which she held leadership positions were the American Association for the Advancement of Science, American Astronomical Society, and International Astronomical Union. Moore was the recipient of the Annie Jump Cannon prize of the American Astronomical Society in 1937 and the William F. Meggers award of the Optical Society of America in 1972; her alma mater, Swarthmore College, recognized Moore with an honorary doctorate degree in 1962, as did Germany's University of Kiel in 1968 and the University of Michigan in 1971. Moore died of heart failure in her Washington, D.C., home on March 3, 1990.

SELECTED WRITINGS BY MOORE:

Books

(With Henry Norris Russell) *Presence of Predicted Iron Lines in the Solar Spectrum of Iron,* Carnegie Institute, 1928.

(With Charles E. St. John, Louise M. Ware, Edward F. Adams, and Harold D. Babcock) *Revision of Rowland's Preliminary Table of Solar Spectrum Wavelengths, With an Extension to the Present Limit of Infrared,* Carnegie Institute, 1928.

Some Results from the Study of the Atomic Lines in the Sun-Spot Spectrum (monograph), Carnegie Institution of Washington, 1932.

A Multiplet Table of Astrophysical Interest, Observatory at Princeton, 1933, revised edition, 1945.

(With Russell) *The Masses of the Stars* (monograph), University of Chicago Press, 1940.

(With Babcock) *The Solar Spectrum,* Carnegie Institute, 1947.

Atomic Energy Levels as Derived from the Analyses of Optical Spectra, U.S. Government Printing Office, Volume 1, 1949, Volume 2, 1952, Volume 3, 1958.

"Collaboration with Henry Norris Russell over the Years," *In Memory of Henry Norris Russell,* edited by A. G. Davis Philip and David H. DeVorkin, Dudley Observatory, 1977, pp. 27–41.

SOURCES:

Books

Minnaert, M. "Forty Years of Solar Spectroscopy," *The Solar Spectrum,* edited by C. de Jager, D. Reidel, 1966, pp. 3–25.

Periodicals

Martin, William C., "Charlotte Moore Sitterly," *Physics Today,* April, 1991, pp. 128, 130.

—Sketch by Philip K. Wilson

Raymond Cecil Moore
1892-1974
American stratigraphist and paleontologist

An exemplary teacher and administrator, and a tireless contributor of scientific prose, Raymond Cecil Moore was a formidable figure in the field of geology during the first half of the twentieth century. As director of the Kansas Geological Survey for thirty-eight years, he reshaped the Survey's mission to create an important agency for scientific research and helped define the stratigraphy of the midcontinent of North America. His interest in invertebrate paleontology, particularly his intensive study of the fossil crinoids and corals, evolved into the massive *Treatise on Invertebrate Paleontology.* Moore received several scientific awards and honors, including the first Paleontological Society Medal in 1963, the Wollaston Medal from the Geological Society of London in 1968, and the Prix Paul Fourmarier, the highest geological award in Europe, from the Royal Academy of Belgium.

Moore was born in Roslyn, Washington, on February 20, 1892, to the Reverend Bernard Harding Moore and Winnifred Denney Moore. His father, a Baptist minister, moved the family around the Midwest, where Moore attended high schools in Milwaukee, Wisconsin, and Chicago, Illinois. In 1909, he entered Denison University in Granville, Ohio, as a classical languages major, but he later transferred into geology. His interest in the former may have been the basis for his fluency in nine languages. While at Denison, Moore ran track in 1912 and 1913, and he also began his teaching career as a substitute in general geology. He graduated Phi Beta Kappa, with honors, in 1913.

Begins Work with the Kansas Geological Survey

Moore then returned to Chicago, where he earned his Ph.D. in geology, *summa cum laude,* from the University of Chicago in 1916. There he served as an assistant instructor during his second year, and came under the direct influence of such notable geologists as **Thomas C. Chamberlin** and Samuel Wendell Williston. He continued to teach at Chicago after graduation, first as an instructor in the summer session, and later as an assistant professor. In this time he also joined the geology department at the University of Kansas as an assistant professor, where he became a full professor in 1919. In 1916 Moore was appointed state geologist and director of the Kansas Geological Survey. He immediately steered the Survey out of the safe confines of its role as collector and disseminator of statistical information into the broader waters of scientific investigation. By the following year, 1917, he had coauthored *Oil and Gas Resources of Kansas,* which described and named the Nemaha Ridge in east-central Kansas, one of the state's most significant subsurface geological features. The publication was considered a excellent source of petroleum-related information for years to come. In 1920 Moore became chairman of the geology department at the University of Kansas, where he remained until 1939. Moore returned to serve two more terms, first in 1940–41, and again from 1952–54. In 1921 and 1922, Moore also had occasion to work as a field geologist for the United States Geological Survey, including a survey of the Colorado River and dam sites between Lees Ferry and Black Canyon. This was the first such undertaking since the John Wesley Powell expeditions of 1869 and 1871.

Tireless Researcher and Publisher

In 1929, Moore published an article in the *Bulletin of the American Association of Petroleum Geologists* in which he refers to his early study concerning cycles of deposition in Pennsylvanian period strata, laid some 300 million years ago. Moore addressed the issue in more detail two years later, attributing the alternate layers of limestone and shale and their respective marine and nonmarine inhabitants to the periodic advance and retreat of the midcontinental sea present during that period. Moore concluded that these changes in sea-level were caused by the geologic movement of the continents, but he would later concede to the theory that mechanisms for sea-level change included displacement by glaciers and polar ice caps. Moore's interests in the Pennsylvanian and Permian environments led him to hypothesize on various types of cyclothems, or different types of rock units deposited by the encroachment and regression of seas. Moore continued his publishing activities in the 1930s, adding to his own output, while also increasing greatly, the amount and diversity of work produced by the Survey. Editor of the Survey's bulletins from 1917 to 1942, he also served as editor to the *Journal of Paleontology* and the *Journal of Sedimentary Petrology,* which he helped establish. In 1933 Moore published his first major text, *Historical Geology.* In 1943 Moore was placed on active duty as a captain in the U.S. Army Reserves Corp of Engineers. He worked as Assistant Chief of Planning in the Fuels and Lubricants Division, Office of the Quartermaster General until 1945. Moore left the University of Kansas to go to Japan in 1949, where he served as a consultant to General Douglas MacArthur, in a study of Japan's coal resources.

In 1936 Moore married his second wife, Lillian Boggs. His daughter, Marjorie Ann, had been born in 1929 through a previous marriage. In his spare time, Moore played the piano and was an artist. He retired from the University of Kansas as professor emeritus in 1962, and he was distinguished as the University of Kansas' first appointment as Solon E. Summerfield Distinguished Professor. Moore received many other scientific awards and honors during his career, and one of his most prized possessions was a small doll presented to him by a group of Soviet women scientists during a 1967 fossil expedition to Russia.

Moore's major scientific contribution was in the area of invertebrate paleontology, a subject to which he contributed some 350 works. While his early research focused on bryozoans, most of his major published works in this field detail corals and crinoids. His intense interest in the entire expanse of invertebrate paleontology lead him to the concept, in 1948, of an encyclopedia of fossil invertebrates, the voluminous *Treatise on Invertebrate Paleontology,* to which he served as editor-in-chief and chief architect. Originally intended as a twenty-four-volume treatise, Moore secured the cooperation of more than 200 scientists from around the world, as well as funding from the National Science Foundation and the Geological Society of America. After his retirement from the Kansas Geological Survey in 1954, Moore devoted the better part of the next twenty years writing, editing, and creating his own artwork for this monumental project. Scientific lore suggests that he was editing a volume on echinoderms only several days before his death on April 16, 1974, at the age of 82.

SELECTED WRITINGS BY MOORE:

Books

Historical Geology, McGraw-Hill, 1933.
Introduction to Historical Geology, McGraw-Hill, 1958, second edition, 1949.
Editor-in-chief, *Treatise on Invertebrate Paleontology,* thirty-five volumes, Geological Society of America, 1970–74.

SOURCES:

Books

Dott, Robert H., Jr., editor, *Eustasy: The Historical Ups and Downs of a Major Geological Concept,* Geological Society of America, 1992, pp. 73–81.
Maples, Christopher G., and Rex Buchanan, *Raymond Cecil Moore (1892–1974): Memorial and Bibliography,* Paleontological Society, 1989, pp. 1–29.
Teichert, Curt, and Ellis L. Yochelson, editors, *R.C. Moore Commemorative Volume,* University of Kansas Press, 1967, pp. 5–7.

Other

Buchanan, Rex, conversation with John Spizzirri on October 20, 1993.
Denison University Archives, Granville, OH.

—Sketch by John Spizzirri

Ruth Moore
1903-
American bacteriologist

Ruth Moore achieved distinction when she became the first African American woman to earn a Ph.D. in bacteriology from Ohio State in 1933. Her entire teaching career was spent at Howard University in Washington, D.C., where she remained an associate professor emeritus of microbiology until 1990.

Ruth Ella Moore was born in Columbus, Ohio, on May 19, 1903. After receiving her B.S. from Ohio State in 1926, she continued at that university and received her M.A. the following year. In 1933 she earned her Ph.D. in bacteriology from Ohio State, becoming the first African American woman to do so. Her achievement was doubly significant considering that her minority status was combined with that era's prejudices against women in professional fields. During her graduate school years (1927–1930), Moore was an instructor of both hygiene and English at Tennessee State College. Upon completing her dissertation at Ohio State—where she focused on the bacteriological aspects of tuberculosis (a major national health problem in the 1930's)—she received her Ph.D. in 1933.

That same year she took a position at the Howard University College of Medicine as an instructor of bacteriology. In 1939 she became an assistant professor of bacteriology, and in 1948 she was named acting head of the university's department of bacteriology, preventive medicine, and public health. In 1955 she became head of the department of bacteriology and remained in that position until 1960 when she became an associate professor of microbiology at Howard. She remained in that department until her retirement in 1973, whereupon she became an associate professor emeritus of microbiology. Throughout her career, Moore has been concerned with public health issues, and as such is a member of the American Public Health Association and the American Society of Microbiologists.

SOURCES:

Books

Sammons, Vivian O., *Blacks in Science and Medicine,* Hemisphere, 1990, p. 176.

—*Sketch by Leonard C. Bruno*

Stanford Moore
1913-1982
American biochemist

Stanford Moore

Stanford Moore's work in protein chemistry greatly advanced understanding of the composition of enzymes, the complex proteins that serve as catalysts for countless biochemical processes. Moore's research focused on the relationship between the chemical structure of proteins, which are made up of strings of amino acids, and their biological action. In 1972 he was awarded the Nobel Prize in chemistry with longtime collaborator **William Howard Stein** for providing the first complete decoding of the chemical composition of an enzyme, ribonuclease (RNase). This discovery provided scientists with insight into cell activity and function, which has had important implications for medical research.

Moore was born on September 4, 1913, in Chicago, Illinois, but spent most of his childhood in Nashville, Tennessee, where his father, John Howard Moore, was a professor at Vanderbilt University's School of Law. His mother was the former Ruth Fowler. In 1935 Moore earned a B.A. in chemistry from Vanderbilt. Moore continued his education in organic chemistry at the graduate school of the University of Wisconsin and completed the Ph.D in 1938. Though Moore considered attending medical school, he accepted a position in 1939 as a research assistant in the laboratory of German chemist Max Bergmann at the Rockefeller Institute for Medical Research (RIMR), later renamed the Rockefeller University.

Bergmann's research group focused on the structural chemistry of proteins. During his early years at RIMR, Moore questioned whether proteins actually had specific structures. The direction of research in Bergmann's laboratory was greatly influenced by the arrival of William Howard Stein. At Bergmann's suggestion, Moore and Stein began a long-lived and successful collaboration. With the exception of his wartime service, the years abroad, and a year at Vanderbilt University, Moore remained at RIMR all of his professional life. In 1952 he became a member of the institute, and his association with RIMR/Rockefeller University continued until his death in 1982.

From 1942 to 1945, Moore worked as a technical aide in the National Defense Research Committee of the Office of Scientific Research and Development (OSRD). As an administrative officer for university and industrial projects, Moore studied the action and effects of mustard gas and other chemical warfare agents. As a technical aide, Moore also coordinated academic and industrial studies on the actions of chemical agents. In 1944 he was appointed to the project coordination staff of the Chemical Warfare Service and continued to contribute to this research until the end of the war in 1945.

Though his initial investigation of chromatography—the process of separating the components of a solution—began in the late 1930s, the war interrupted this work. After the war and following the death of Max Bergmann in 1944, Moore returned to RIMR to resume work with William Howard Stein. This marked a productive period for the two men, leading to their work on chromatographic methods for separating amino acids, peptides (compounds of two or more amino acids), and proteins. Moore's work in chromatography was influenced by the methods of paper chromatography developed by **A. J. P. Martin** and **Richard L. M. Synge** of England. However, limitations in these earlier methods prohibited the study of protein chemistry; new techniques in chromatography had to be developed so that amino acids could be separated. Moore and Stein utilized column chromatography, in which a column or tube is filled with material that separates the components of a solution. In 1948 they successfully separated amino acids by passing the solution through a column filled with potato starch. The process was time consuming, however, and presented inadequate separations for amino acid analysis. To facilitate the procedure, Moore and Stein replaced the filler material with a synthetic ion exchange resin, which separated components of a solution by electrical charge and size. In 1949 they successfully separated amino acids from blood and urine.

Study and Work Abroad

Further interruptions in the work at RIMR occurred in 1950, when Moore held the Francqui Chair at the University of Brussels (where he established a laboratory for amino acid analysis), and in 1951, when he was a visiting professor at the University of Cambridge (England) working with **Frederick Sanger** on the amino acid sequence of insulin.

In 1958 Moore and Stein contributed to the development of the automated amino acid analyzer. This instrument facilitated the complete amino acid analysis of a protein in twenty-four hours; previously employed procedures, such as chromatography, had required up to one week. The automated technique afforded researchers a tool with which to separate and study the large chemical sequences in protein molecules. This instrument is used worldwide for the study of proteins, enzymes, and hormones as well as the analysis of food. While Moore and Stein endeavored to determine the chemical composition of proteins, scientists concurrently worked to determine their three-dimensional structure.

Discovery of the Chemical Nature of Enzymes

By 1959 Moore and Stein had determined the amino acid sequence of pancreatic ribonuclease (RNase), a digestive enzyme that breaks down ribonucleic acid (RNA) so that its components can be reused. They discovered that ribonuclease is made up of a chain of 124 amino acids, which they identified and sequenced. This marked the first complete description of the chemical structure of an enzyme, a discovery that earned Moore and Stein the 1972 Nobel Prize in chemistry (an award shared with **Christian Boehmer Anfinsen** of the National Institutes of Health). Understanding protein structure is essential to understanding biological function, which opens the door to the treatment of disease. Moore's findings influenced research in neurochemistry and the study of such diseases as sickle-cell anemia. Scientists later discovered that related ribonucleases

are present in nearly all human cells, which prompted studies in the fields of cancer and malaria research.

In 1969, Moore returned to Rockefeller University following one year spent at Vanderbilt University School of Medicine as a visiting professor of health sciences. Upon his return, the team of Moore and Stein resumed their studies of protein chemistry with an investigation of deoxyribonuclease, the enzyme that breaks down deoxyribonucleic acid (DNA).

In addition to scientific work, Moore also served as an editor of *The Journal of Biological Chemistry*, treasurer and president of the American Society of Biological Chemistry, and president of the Federation of American Societies for Experimental Biology. Moore received many honors, including membership in the National Academy of Sciences and receipt of the Richards Medal of the American Chemical Society and the Linderstrøm-Lang Medal. He was also awarded honorary degrees by the University of Brussels, the University of Paris, and the University of Wisconsin.

Moore was diagnosed with amyotrophic lateral sclerosis (Lou Gehrig's disease) some time in the early 1980s. On August 23, 1982, he committed suicide in his home in New York City. Upon his death Moore, who never married, left his estate to Rockefeller University.

SELECTED WRITINGS BY MOORE:

Periodicals

(With William Howard Stein) "The Chemical Structure of Proteins," *Scientific American,* February, 1961, pp. 81–92.
(With William Howard Stein) "Chemical Structures of Pancreatic Ribonuclease and Deoxyribonuclease," *Science,* May, 1973, pp. 458–464.

SOURCES:

Books

Corner, George W., *A History of the Rockefeller Institute: 1901–1953, Origins and Growth,* The Rockefeller Institute Press, 1964.

Periodicals

Manning, James M., "Recollections: The Contributions of Stein and Moore to Protein Science," *Protein Science,* 1993, pp. 1188–1191.
Smith, Emil L., and C. H. W. Hirs, "Stanford Moore, Biographical Memoirs," *National Acad-*

emy of Sciences, Volume 56, 1987, pp. 355–385.

—*Sketch by Renee D. Mastrocco*

Cathleen Synge Morawetz
1923-

American mathematician

In 1984 Cathleen Synge Morawetz became the first woman in the United States to head a mathematical institute, the Courant Institute of Mathematical Sciences at New York University. Since receiving her Ph.D. from the university in 1951, her research on fluid dynamics and transonic flow has been influential in the fields of aerodynamics, acoustics, and optics. In 1993 she was elected president of the American Mathematical Society.

Born on May 5, 1923, to mathematician John Synge and Eleanor Mabel Allen Synge, Morawetz grew up in Toronto, Canada, and won a scholarship in mathematics to the University of Toronto. She served in a wartime post in 1943–44 before earning her B.A. in 1945. That same year she married chemist Herbert Morawetz (with whom she eventually had four children) and began graduate studies at the Massachusetts Institute of Technology (MIT), from which she received her master's degree in 1946. At a time when few scientific fields were open to women, Morawetz briefly considered working for Bell Laboratories in New Jersey but decided to pursue a Ph.D. instead.

While editing the book *Supersonic Flow and Shock Waves,* written by New York University mathematicians **Richard Courant** and Kurt Friedrichs, she became interested in the phenomenon of transonic flow, or the behavior of air at speeds approximating that of sound. Spurred by the urgency of this research (in the late years of World War II, the new jet engine enabled aircraft to approach supersonic flight) she decided to pursue a Ph.D. in the subject. Working under Friedrichs at New York University (NYU), she wrote her doctoral thesis on imploding shock waves and received her degree in 1951. After a brief stint as a research associate at MIT, she joined NYU's mathematics faculty as a research assistant in 1952, publishing scores of scientific articles during her upward climb to full professor in 1965. Morawetz also rose within NYU's Courant Institute of Mathematical Sciences, where she received the ultimate honor of being named the institute's director in 1984—the first woman ever to head a mathematical institution of

that stature in the United States. She has also served as the editor of several scientific journals, including the *Journal of Mathematical Analysis and Applications* and *Communication in Pure and Applied Mathematics.*

Morawetz continued research in the field of fluid dynamics, the study of forces exerted upon liquids and gases and the effects of those forces on motion. She conclusively demonstrated that all airplane wings produce shock waves if they are moving fast enough. Her findings have contributed to important advances in aerodynamics, acoustics, and optics. Similarly, her work on transonic flow has been applied in two widely different areas: the use of seismic waves (movement caused by vibrations within the earth) in prospecting for oil and the development of medical imaging techniques.

A member of the American Academy of Arts and Sciences, Morawetz has received several major awards, including two Guggenheim Fellowships, the Gibbs Lectureship of the American Mathematical Society, and the Lester R. Ford Award from the Mathematical Association of America. She also holds honorary degrees from Smith College, Brown University, Princeton University, and Duke University. In 1994, in addition to being the only woman member of the Applied Mathematics Section of the National Academy of Sciences, Morawetz was elected the second woman president to head the American Mathematical Society. In a university press release, NYU President L. Jay Oliva summarized the esteem in which she is held by her peers: "Morawetz is an outstanding mathematician, and has long been one of the leading lights at our prestigious Courant Institute. I know that the American Mathematical Society will benefit greatly by her considerable acumen and compelling leadership."

SELECTED WRITINGS BY MORAWETZ:

Periodicals

(With I. Kolodner), "On the Non-existence of Limiting Lines in Transonic Flows," *Communication in Pure and Applied Mathematics,* February, 1953, pp. 97–102.

"Energy Flow: Wave Motion and Geometrical Optics," *Bulletin of the American Mathematical Society,* July, 1970, pp. 661–74.

"The Mathematical Approach to the Sonic Barrier," *Bulletin of the American Mathematical Society,* March, 1982, pp. 127–45.

"Giants," *American Mathematical Monthly,* November, 1992, pp. 819–28.

SOURCES:

Books

Grinstein, Louise S., and Paul J. Campbell, editors, *Women of Mathematics,* Greenwood Press, 1987, pp. 152–55.

Periodicals

"Cathleen Morawetz, First Woman to Head a Mathematics Institute," *Series in Applied Mathematics News,* Volume 17, number 4, 1984, p. 5.
Kolata, Gina Bari, "Cathleen Morawetz: The Mathematics of Waves," *Science,* Volume 206, 1979, pp. 206–07.

Other

"NYU Mathematician Cathleen Morawetz Elected Next President of 30,000-Member American Mathematical Society," New York University press release, December 20, 1993.

—*Sketch by Nicholas Pease*

Arthur E. Morgan
1878-1975
American civil engineer

Arthur E. Morgan directed seventy-five water control projects, constructing two thousand miles of drainage canals and reclaiming more than two million acres of land. He was the first chairperson of the Tennessee Valley Authority (TVA), a government-sponsored administrative agency charged with developing the area's river network to improve transportation and flood control as well as generate electricity. His post-secondary training was informal, but he became a college president and instituted the innovative "Antioch Plan" of cooperative education. As a philosopher, he was intrigued with the literature on utopian societies and implemented some of his ideas through his business practices.

Arthur Ernest Morgan was born on June 20, 1878, in Cincinnati, Ohio. A year later, the family moved to St. Cloud, Minnesota. His father, John D. Morgan, was a surveyor, and his mother, Anna Frances Wiley Morgan, was a former high school teacher. Encouraged by his mother, Morgan began a prolific writing career when he sold his first articles to *Popular Science News* in 1896, the year he finished high school. Following his father's example, he was an active Quaker throughout his life.

During the next four years, Morgan searched for his vocation. After teaching briefly in a country school, he headed westward to Boulder, Colorado, working variously as a farm hand, miner, logger, book vendor, and typesetter. He began attending the University of Colorado, Boulder, but quit after a few weeks because of eyestrain. Upon his return to Minnesota in 1900, he persuaded his father to train him as a surveyor. Young Morgan studied other engineering topics as well and became interested in the newly developing area of drainage and flood control. Recognizing the inadequacy of current drainage laws, he submitted a new code that was adopted by the Minnesota legislature in 1905.

In 1907, Morgan passed a civil service exam in hydraulic engineering and was appointed supervising engineer in the Department of Agriculture's Office of Experiment Stations. In this position, he designed reclamation works in the southern United States. Two years later, he left government service to found the Morgan Engineering Company in Memphis, Tennessee.

Meanwhile, Morgan's first marriage ended tragically when his wife of a year, Urania T. Jones, died in 1905. She was survived by their infant son, Ernest. Six years later, Morgan married again; he and Lucy Middleton Griscom had a son, Griscom, and a daughter, Frances.

Following major flooding in Dayton in 1913, Morgan moved to Ohio as chief engineer for the Miami River Conservancy District. Under Morgan's direction, the thirty-million-dollar flood control project was planned and constructed without letting any outside contracts. He later conducted a similar project for the Pueblo (Colorado) Conservancy District.

While living in Dayton, Morgan implemented some of his social theories. His Dayton Morgan Engineering Company built model villages for its employees. With the help of local business people, he founded the progressive Moraine Park School in 1917. He became a trustee of Antioch College in Yellow Springs, Ohio, a school founded by Horace Mann in 1853 but struggling to survive by 1920. Morgan assumed the institution's presidency and initiated a major reorganization. Under the "Antioch Plan," students alternated five weeks of classroom work with five weeks of full-time job experience, a strategy he hoped would produce men and women who could make a living on their own. By the end of his sixteen-year presidency, the school's enrollment had grown from 35 to 560, and 150 businesses around the country were participating in its cooperative education program.

Upon Congress' enactment of the Tennessee Valley Authority (TVA) in 1933, President Franklin D. Roosevelt asked Morgan to chair the new organization's three-person board. Their job was to administer the building of eleven dams and associated locks and power plants on the Tennessee and lower Mississippi rivers, and to oversee the distribution of the resulting electricity. Morgan implemented his Miami Conservancy District strategy, and the TVA built its own projects. Again, the workers' housing was provided; additionally, they were supplied with schools, clubs, traveling libraries, and adult education programs. Morgan's labor policy was based on cooperation, not antagonism, between unions and management. Interpreting the TVA's authorizing act broadly in its provision to delve into various aspects of social and economic planning, the board implemented programs to educate local residents in the use of electricity and in new agricultural methods, to relocate families from land needed for the dams, and to support research and development in such diverse areas as forestry and agricultural fertilizers.

The TVA board was philosophically divided, however. Morgan favored cooperation with private utility companies, while the other two members (Harcourt A. Morgan and David E. Lilienthal) espoused a "yardstick" approach for establishing electric rates independently in competition with power companies that were not government subsidized. Tensions mounted, with the chairperson charging fellow board members with conspiracy and bureaucratic manipulation involving the determination of costs for electric power. In 1938, following a personal meeting, President Roosevelt dismissed Morgan from the board, citing "contumacy" (a stubborn refusal to submit to authority). Morgan responded that only Congress had the authority to remove him from office; the dispute was settled by a Supreme Court decision in favor of Roosevelt.

Morgan returned to Yellow Springs, Ohio, where he founded Community Service, Inc., which promotes the concept of the community as the basis of a wholesome society. In the preface to his 1944 biography of social reformer Edward Bellamy, Morgan asserted his own philosophical bent: "It was the genius of Edward Bellamy that he took Utopia out of the region of hazy dreamland and made it a concrete program for the actual modern world." He was a charter member of the American Eugenics Society, and belonged to the Rural Sociology Society as well as the more technical American Association for the Advancement of Science and American Society of Civil Engineers.

In 1947 the American Friends Service Committee sent Morgan to Finland as a consultant in the development of small industries. The following year, he served on a national commission in India organizing a series of rural universities. Returning to the United States, he served as temporary chairperson of a conciliation and arbitration board involving the U.S. Steel Corporation and the Congress of Industrial Organizations. In 1954, he visited Africa to advise the Gold Coast government on a major hydroelectric project.

In addition to several honorary degrees that he eventually garnered in engineering and science, he was also awarded an honorary LL.D. from Antioch College in 1943. In his forty books and numerous published articles, Morgan wrote about engineering projects, technical organizations (including the TVA and the Corps of Engineers), and frequently about philosophy and social planning (especially utopian ideas). He died on November 16, 1975, in a nursing home in Xenia, Ohio, at the age of 97.

SELECTED WRITINGS BY MORGAN:

Books

The Small Community, Harper, 1942.
The Philosophy of Edward Bellamy, Greenwood, 1945.
Nowhere Was Somewhere: How History Makes Utopias and How Utopias Make History, University of North Carolina press, 1946.
Search for Purpose, Antioch, 1955.
Dams and Other Disasters: A Century of the Army Corps of Engineers in Civil Works, P. Sargent, 1971.
The Making of the TVA, Prometheus Books, 1974.

SOURCES:

Periodicals

Fowle, Farnsworth, "Arthur Morgan of Antioch, First T.V.A. Head, Dies," *New York Times,* November 17, 1975.
"Induction of Four Honorary Members Will Be Annual Convention Feature," *Civil Engineering,* September 1953, pp. 622–623.

—Sketch by Sandra Katzman

Garrett A. Morgan
1877-1963
American inventor

Apioneer inventor, Garrett A. Morgan was responsible for the creation of such life-saving inventions as the gas mask and traffic lights. In a long and productive career that spanned over forty years, Morgan worked diligently to create new products and services to enhance safety in modern-day living. His creations, for many of whom he held patents, brought him much fame and prosperity in his lifetime, and he was nationally honored by many organizations, including the Emancipation Centennial in 1963.

Garrett Augustus Morgan was born in Paris, Kentucky, on March 4, 1877. He was the seventh of eleven children born to Sydney Morgan, a former slave who was freed in 1863, and Elizabeth (Reed) Morgan. Leaving home at age fourteen with only an elementary school education, Morgan eventually settled in Cleveland. He taught himself to repair sewing machines, working with a number of companies before opening his own business specializing in sewing machine sales and repair in 1907. The venture was successful, enabling Morgan to set up house in Cleveland, and in 1908, he married Mary Anne Hassek. Together they had three sons.

Eventually, Morgan opened his own tailoring shop, and it was here that he developed his first unique product. Like other people in the clothing industry, Morgan was trying to solve a prevalent problem inherent in sewing woolen material: the sewing machine needle operated at such high speed that it often scorched the material. Morgan, who was working with a chemical solution to reduce this friction, noticed that the solution he was developing caused hairs on a pony-fur cloth to straighten instead. Intrigued, he tried it on a neighbor's dog, and when it straightened the hair on the dog's coat, Morgan finally tried the new solution on his own hair. The success of the solution led Morgan to form G. A. Morgan Refining Company, the first producers of hair refining cream.

Invents Two Life-Saving Devices

During his lifetime, Morgan continued to experiment with new products, inventing such things as hat and belt fasteners and a friction drive clutch. His most significant invention, however, came in 1912, when he developed the "safety hood," the precursor to the modern-day gas mask. Morgan's patent application for the contraption referred to it as a "Breathing Device." Granted a patent in 1914, the device, which consisted of a hood with an inlet for fresh air and an outlet for exhaled air, drew a number of awards, including the First Grand Prize from the Second International Exposition of Safety and Sanitation in New York City. Although Morgan tested and demonstrated the use of the safety hood over the next few years, its most critical test occurred on July 24, 1916, during a tunnel explosion at the Cleveland Waterworks. The whole area was filled with noxious fumes and smoke, trapping workers in a tunnel under Lake Erie. Aided by his Breathing Device, Morgan went into the tunnel and carried workers out on his back, saving a number of men from an underground death. For this act of heroism, Morgan received the Carnegie Medal and a Medal of Bravery from the city, and the International Association of Fire Engineers made Morgan an honorary member. Not much later, Morgan established a company to manufacture and sell the Breathing Device in response to numerous orders from fire and police departments and mining industries. Fire fighters came to rely upon the gas mask in rescue attempts, and the invention helped save thousands from chlorine gas and other noxious fumes during World War I.

Next Morgan created the three-way traffic signal, a device responsible for saving thousands of lives over the years. The idea to build the warning and regulatory signal system came to him after he witnessed a carriage accident at a four-way street crossing. Once again, Morgan made sure to acquire a patent for his product, this time in Britain as well as the United States and Canada. Eventually, Morgan sold the rights to his invention to the General Electric Company for $40,000.

In addition to inventing new and unique products Morgan was actively involved in promoting the welfare of African Americans. In 1920, therefore, he began publishing the *Cleveland Call,* a newspaper devoted to publishing local and national black news. Additionally, Morgan served as an officer of the Cleveland Association of Colored Men, remaining an active member after it merged with the National Association for the Advancement of Colored People (NAACP). He developed glaucoma in 1943, losing most of his sight, and died in 1963.

SOURCES:

Books

Haber, Louis, *Black Pioneers of Science and Invention,* Harcourt, 1970, pp. 61–72.
Sammons, Vivian Ovelton, *Blacks in Science and Medicine,* Hemisphere Publishing, 1990, p. 176.

—*Sketch by Sharon F. Suer*

Thomas Hunt Morgan
1866-1945
American geneticist and embryologist

Thomas Hunt Morgan, working alongside his associates in the "fly room," a small laboratory at Columbia University, bred not only fruit flies for genetics research but new ideas that helped to establish the infant science of genetics as one of the most important scientific fields of the twentieth century. Morgan also pioneered genetic research and published extensively in genetics, morphology, embryology and evolution, drawing together concepts and ideas to relate these varied disciplines.

Thomas Hunt Morgan was born in Lexington, Kentucky, on September 25, 1866, the newest in an already illustrious family: his father, Charlton Hunt Morgan, had been the American consul at Messina, Sicily during the early 1860s when Giuseppe Garibaldi was seeking to unify Italy; his uncle, John Hunt Morgan, was a general in the Confederate Army and led a group of guerrillas known as "Morgan's Raiders"; his maternal great grandfather was Francis Scott Key, composer of the "Star Spangled Banner." As a boy, Morgan spent his childhood in the countryside of Kentucky with occasional visits to his mother's family in Maryland, where he enjoyed exploring and looking for fossils. For two summers during his youth he worked with the United States Geological Survey in the Kentucky mountains. These experiences gave him an appreciation and fondness for natural history that stayed with him into adulthood.

Early Work in Embryology and Evolution

After attending prep school at the State College of Kentucky (which later became the University of Kentucky), Morgan stayed on as an undergraduate, receiving his B.S. in zoology in 1886; during his stay, his interest in science was especially influenced by his geology professor, A. R. Crandall. After graduation Morgan spent a summer at the marine biological station on the Massachusetts coast—an experience that further kindled what would become a life-long interest in diverse species.

In 1886 Morgan entered Johns Hopkins University in Baltimore, Maryland to begin his graduate work. His choice for grad school was probably influenced by Joseph Kastle, an undergraduate friend who had preceeded him to Johns Hopkins. Though he studied biology, anatomy, embryology and physiology, he preferred morphology (the study of form) and its attempts to discover the evolutionary relationships among organisms.

Thomas Hunt Morgan

Morgan's mentor at Hopkins was W. K. Brooks; a former student of Louis Agassiz, Brooks, like many of his contemporaries, stressed comparative anatomy and embryology as a method for determining the nature of life. Under Brooks, Morgan studied the embryology of sea spiders in an attempt to classify these organisms as either arachnids (like spiders) or crustaceans (like crayfish). In 1890 he finished his doctoral work on sea spiders and received his Ph.D. However, Morgan felt hemmed in by the rigors and structure of classical morphology—a very descriptive discipline that did not easily allow for the type of experimentation Morgan sought.

After staying at Hopkins an extra year on a Bruce fellowship, Morgan went to Bryn Mawr College in 1891; he remained there until 1904, when he was offered a position as head of experimental zoology at Columbia University in New York. In that same year he married Lilian Vaughan Sampson, a classmate of his from Bryn Mawr; a student of cell biology, Lilian would make important contributions to her husband's fruit fly research.

While at Bryn Mawr, Morgan had become friends with **Jacques Loeb** and was influenced by Loeb's mechanistic view of living things, which proposes that living things are governed by certain laws and principles, rather than by some vitalistic force. Morgan had also spent ten months at a zoological station in Naples, Italy, where he met Hans Driesch, a European who was also of the mechanistic school of thought. His contact with these two scientists convinced Morgan that the questions raised in embryology would be best answered experimentally, and spent the years from 1895 to 1902 applying experimental methods to embryology.

In Europe, there was a controversy raging among scientists over the factors governing the development of the embryo; some scientists believed this development was dictated by heredity, while others felt that environmental factors held sway. Morgan's observations of sea urchin eggs led him to believe that the environment may indeed help shape an embryo's development, but that inheritance was the more influential factor. His findings made him even more curious as to the hereditary information carried by each cell, and what chemical and physical processes controlled the inheritance of that information.

In 1903 Morgan published *Evolution and Adaptation,* an attack on Charles Darwin's theory of natural selection as it was interpreted at the turn of the century. Morgan believed that these proponents were relying too heavily on natural selection as the mechanism for evolution, feeling that no single theory could encompass so many natural phenomena. The concept of mutation, as introduced by Dutch botanist **Hugo de Vries**, made more sense to Morgan; De Vries' theory proposed that chance variations, called mutations, can be introduced into a population, providing the variation necessary for evolutionary changes to occur. It was this theory that Morgan offered as an alternative to Darwinism.

From 1903 to 1910 Morgan concentrated on the determination of sex in living things—a topic about which there were many varying views at the time. Was the sex of an organism determined by environmental factors, such as temperature or food, or was it a matter of inheritance? Those scientists who explained sex in terms of inheritance cited the work of Gregor Mendel, the Austrian monk whose work on the inheritance of pea plants had just been "rediscovered"—forty years after Mendel had submitted his papers to scientific societies. Mendel had postulated that all of an organism's traits were caused by inherited "factors," though he was unable to determine the nature of those factors. Some scientists speculated that Mendel's factors could be found within the chromosomes of cells, and they had named those factors "genes".

Morgan agreed that chromosomes probably did have something to do with inheritance; he was skeptical of Mendel's laws of inheritance, however, thinking that they were too simplistic to explain sex determination. In these early days of research, Morgan did not believe that an organism's sex was determined at the moment of fertilization, but rather was a developmental process guided by natural law. After Morgan observed sex inheritance in some insects, though, he came to realize that the presence of chromosomes must have something to do with inheriting sex. Around 1910 his colleagues at Columbia and Bryn Mawr gathered evidence to show that the large X chromosome had the most to do with sex inheritance.

Fruit Fly Research Leads to the Nobel Prize

Sometime around 1908 or 1909 Morgan began breeding *Drosophila melanogaster,* commonly known as the vinegar fly or fruit fly, for use in the laboratory. Morgan originally wanted to use the flies to test de Vrie's theory of mutations in animals by exposing the insects to radium, but he was not as successful in producing mutations as de Vries had been with his experimental plants. In 1910, though, Morgan discovered a natural variation in a male fruit fly—white eyes instead of the wild type red eyes. After Morgan mated the white-eyed male with his red-eyed sisters, he found all the offspring to have red eyes. However, the mating of those red-eyed flies brought about a generation in which there were some white-eyed offspring—all of which where male. Whereas before Morgan was skeptical of such attributes being inherited so precisely, he now found himself explaining this phenomenon in terms of Mendel's factors, or genes. He hypothesized that the genes for eye color were carried on (and therefore linked to) the X chromosome; this type of gene became known as a sex-limited or sex-linked gene. Morgan further hypothesized that the gene for white eyes was recessive to the dominant red—the fly would possess white eyes only if *all* of its X chromosomes possessed the white-eye gene. Since male flies have just one X chromosome, they were more likely to display the recessive trait than the females, whcih have two X chromosomes. With this experiment, Morgan showed clearly that hereditary characteristics were associated with specific chromosomes.

After this breakthrough, Morgan began in earnest a *Drosophila* breeding project with help from several others, including undergraduates **A. H. Sturtevant** and Calvin B. Bridges and a grad student named **Hermann Joseph Muller**. The project soon brought gratifying results, as new mutations appeared and were carefully tracked. The flies proved to be ideal test subjects, having a breeding cycle of just three weeks and only four chromosomes on which all the genes for their traits were carried. Morgan's team maintained two small laboratories—a winter lab at Columbia University and a summer lab at the Marine Biological Laboratory in Woods Hole, Massachusetts—that were collectively known as the "fly room". Although Morgan acted as the team's leader, the work was done in an informal give-and-take atmosphere; the "fly room" became something of a proving ground for many future geneticists.

Because the actual genes could not be seen, the team inferred that a particular part of each chromosome carried a particular trait. This inference was made based on a phenomenon called "crossing over," which had been discovered by the Belgian scientist F. A. Janssens in 1909. Janssens had noticed that during the duplication and separation of like chromosomes, part of one chromosome occasionally broke off and reattached to a comparable place on the other chromosome; the further apart two genes were on a single chromosome, the more likely it would be that a break could occur between them. A high frequency of crossing over observed between any two traits would indicate a long distance between the genes, whereas a low frequency of crossing over between two traits would mean the genes were close together. Sturtevant figured out a way to use this information to "map" each chromosome, and the team used this mapping technique to show how various genes for each trait might be arranged along each chromosome. Although the work had its drawbacks, the findings of the group were published in *The Mechanism of Mendelian Heredity,* written by the four in 1915. This gave the new experimental science of genetics a place in the world of biology. In 1916 Morgan published *A Critique of the Theory of Evolution.* Rather than discounting natural selection as he had before, Morgan now used his new understanding of chromosome mutation to offer a genetic explanation for Darwin's discoveries. For his works on this subject Morgan was awarded the Darwin Medal in 1924.

By the mid 1920s Morgan's focus was no longer on *Drosophila;* rather, he sought to explain larger questions of development and evolution using what he had learned about genetics. In 1927, he left Columbia for Cal Tech in Pasadena, California, where he had been invited to establish a biology department. Aided by a substantial budget, Morgan was able to set up a first-rate department and assemble an excellent staff. It would be this Cal Tech research group—which later included **George Beadle** and Max Delbruck—who would help pioneer the next wave of genetics research, exploring the gene at the molecular level.

Morgan was known for his sense of humor and quick wit, and for his generosity towards those with whom he worked. When he won the Nobel Prize for Physiology or Medicine in 1933, for example, he shared his prize money with his assistants to help their children to go to college. During his career Morgan served as the president of the Association for the Advancement of Science and of the National Academy of Sciences, and in 1939 he was awarded the Copley Medal of the Royal Society. Morgan continued doing administrative work at Cal Tech until his death in 1945.

SELECTED WRITINGS BY MORGAN:

Books

(With A. H. Sturtevant, J. J. Muller and C. B. Bridges), *The Mechanism of Mendelian Heredity,* [New York], 1915.
A Critique of the Theory of Evolution, [Princeton], 1916.
The Scientific Basis of Evolution, [New York], 1932.

Periodicals

"Sex-Limited Inheritance in *Drosophila*", *Science,* Volume 32, 1910, pp. 120–122.
(With E. B. Wilson) "The Theory of the Gene," *American Naturalist,* Volume 51, 1920, pp. 193–219.

SOURCES:

Books

Carlson, E. A., *The Gene, A Critical History,* [Philadelphia], 1966.
Gillispie, Charles Coulston, editor, *Dictionary of Scientific Biography,* Scribner, 1985, pp. 515–526.
World of Scientific Discovery, Gale, 1994.

Periodicals

Biographical Memoirs, National Academy of Sciences, Volume 33, 1959, pp. 283–325.

—*Sketch by Barbara A. Branca*

Shigefumi Mori
1951-
Japanese mathematician

Shigefumi Mori has made important contributions to the field of algebraic geometry. His major work, the creation of a minimal model theory for certain algebraic varieties, has been dubbed Mori's Program. Writing in the *Proceedings of the ICM–90,* Heisuke Hironaka called Mori's Program "the most profound and exciting development in algebraic geometry during the last decade." For research on his program, Mori has received numerous awards, including the 1990 Fields Medal.

Mori was born in Nagoya, Japan, on February 23, 1951. His father, Fumio Mori, and mother, Fusa Mori, were business people who ran a trading company. Mori attended Kyoto University where he received his B.A. in 1973, his M.A. in 1975, and his Ph.D. in 1978. While working on his dissertation, Mori was appointed an assistant instructor at the university. He would teach there until 1980, also spending part of the time as a visiting professor at Harvard University in the United States.

In 1979, Mori published his first major results, a proof of the Hartshorne conjecture, which stated that a certain class of algebraic varieties are projective in nature. In other words, these varieties or sets of solutions to given polynomial equations could be described using projective geometry. Although Hartshorne, the mathematician who first put forth the theory, had felt certain that he was correct, he had not been able to prove his conjecture. Mori proved the conjecture true, and his approach was only his first step in classifying three-dimensional varieties. Previous to Mori's research, one- and two-dimensional algebraic varieties had been classified, or grouped, according to the way they behaved under certain conditions. However, it was generally believed that three-dimensional varieties, which involved four variables, were impossible to categorize because they could not be easily represented or described. With the success of his work on the Hartshorne conjecture, Mori had enough evidence to proceed in his attempts to completely classify all three-dimensional algebraic varieties, the project that would eventually become know as Mori's Program.

Work in Third Dimension Leads to International Fame

In 1980, Mori returned to his hometown of Nagoya in order to accept a position as lecturer there. However, he soon found he was much in demand, especially after the publication of his paper entitled "Threefolds Whose Canonical Bundles Are Not Nef" that same year. "Nef" was Mori's abbreviation for "numerically effective." Essentially, this paper split the three-dimensional algebraic varieties into two groups, those that are nef and those that are "not nef." Using an extended version of his proof of Hartshorne's conjecture, Mori was able to classify all the not-nef cases into a small number of possibilities, which meant that all the not-nef cases had been reduced to their minimal model, making them easy to describe. Because of the recognition this paper brought him, over the course of the next few years, Mori lectured in Italy and Poland, and he did research at Princeton's Institute for Advanced Studies (IAS) as well as the Max Planck Institute in Germany.

During this period, Mori continued his efforts to finish his program. The nef cases turned out to be far more difficult than the not-nef cases, and he had to invent a entirely new terminology to describe these varieties. In some cases he had to "blow up", or expand, a piece of the surface of the variety; in other cases, he had to perform divisorial contraction, the opposite operation. He "flipped" varieties into simpler ones and "flopped" to avoid problems. In every case, he was trying to reach the ultimate goal of achieving the minimal model, or simplest description, of each variety.

Throughout the 1980s, Mori worked on classifying the nef cases of three-dimensional algebraic varieties. He received several awards, including the 1983 Japan Mathematical Society's Iyanaga Prize, the 1984 Chunichi Culture Prize, and the 1989 Inoue Science Prize. In the United States, C. Herbert Clemens and János Kollár, both of the University of Utah, arranged for Mori to spend one-quarter of each academic year there beginning in 1987.

Finally, in January of 1988, Mori published a paper which proved the existence of minimal models for all three-dimensional algebraic varieties. In just ten years, Mori had completed what many said could never be done. In recognition of this outstanding feat, Mori received both the American Mathematical Society's Cole Prize and the Japan Academy Prize, as well as the highest honor in mathematics, the Fields Medal. He accepted the Fields Medal at the 1990 International Congress of Mathematicians, held that year in his native Japan.

Taking the Fields Medal as a challenge to achieve even further success, Mori began work the following year on a project with Kollár and Y. Miyaoka to further define the varieties he had studied. While continuing to spend part of the academic year in Utah, Mori moved with his wife and four children to Kyoto University's Research Institute for Mathematics and Science. Here he would continue his study of algebraic varieties, a study which had already marked him as a leader in the field of algebraic geometry.

SELECTED WRITINGS BY MORI:

Periodicals

"Threefolds Whose Canonical Bundles Are Not Numerically Effective," *Annals of Mathematics,* Volume 116, 1982, pp. 133–176.
"Flip Theorem and the Existence of Minimal Models for 3-Folds," *Journal of the American Mathematical Society,* Volume 1, 1988, pp. 117–253.
"Birational Classification of Algebraic Threefolds," *Proceedings of ICM–90, Kyoto,* Springer-Verlag, 1991, pp. 235–248.

SOURCES:

Periodicals

Clemens, H. C., and J. Kollár, "Shigefumi Mori," *Notices of the American Mathematical Society,* Volume 37, November 1990, pp. 1213–14.

Hironaka, Heisuke, "On the Work of Shigefumi Mori," *Proceedings of ICM–90, Kyoto,* Springer-Verlag, 1991, pp. 19–25.

"Shigefumi Mori Awarded 1990 Cole Prize in Algebra," *Notices of the American Mathematical Society,* Volume 37, February 1990, pp. 118–19.

—*Sketch by Karen Sands*

Edward Williams Morley
1838-1923
American chemist and physicist

Originally trained for the ministry, Edward Williams Morley decided instead in 1868 to pursue a career in science, the other great love of his life. At first he devoted himself primarily to teaching, but gradually became engaged in more original research. His work can be divided into three major categories: the first two involved the determination of the oxygen content of the atmosphere and efforts to evaluate Prout's hypothesis; his third field of research involving experiments on the velocity of light with **Albert Michelson**, are those for which his name will always be most famous.

Morley was born in Newark, New Jersey, on January 29, 1838. His mother was the former Anna Clarissa Treat, a schoolteacher, and his father was Sardis Brewster Morley, a Congregational minister. According to a biographical sketch of Morley in the December 1987 issue of the *Physics Teacher,* the Morley family had come to the United States in early Colonial days and "was noted for its deep patriotism and religious devotion."

Morley's early education took place entirely at home, and he first entered a formal classroom at the age of nineteen when he was admitted to Williams College in Williamston, Massachusetts, as a sophomore. His plans were to study for the ministry and to follow his father in a religious vocation. But he also took a variety of courses in science and mathematics, including astronomy, chemistry, calculus, and optics. His courses at Williams were a continuation of an interest in science that he had developed at home as a young boy.

Morley graduated from Williams as valedictorian of his class with a bachelor of arts degree in 1860. He then stayed on for a year to do astronomical research with Albert Hopkins. Morley's biographers allude to the "careful" and "precise" calculations required in this work as typical of the kind of research Morley most enjoyed doing. Certainly the later research for which he is best known was also characterized by this high level of precision and accuracy.

After completing his work with Hopkins, Morley entered the Andover Theological Seminary to complete his preparation for the ministry, while concurrently earning his master's degree from Williams. Morley graduated from Andover in 1864 but rather than finding a church he took a job at the Sanitary Commission at Fortress Monroe in Virginia. There he worked with Union soldiers wounded in the Civil War.

His work completed at Fortress Monroe, Morley returned to Andover for a year and then, failing to find a ministerial position, took a job teaching science at the South Berkshire Academy in Marlboro, Massachusetts. It was at Marlboro that Morley met his future wife, Isabella Ashley Birdsall. The couple was married on December 24, 1868. They had no children.

Leaves the Ministry and Commits His Life to Science

Morley had finally received an offer in September, 1868, to become minister at the Congregational church in Twinsburg, Ohio. He accepted the offer but, according to biographers David D. Skwire and Laurence J. Badar in the *Physics Teacher,* became disenchanted with "the low salary and rustic atmosphere" at Twinsburg and quickly made a crucial decision: he would leave the ministry and devote his life to science.

The opportunity to make such a change had presented itself shortly after Morley arrived in Twinsburg when he was offered a job teaching chemistry, botany, geology, and mineralogy at Western Reserve College in Hudson, Ohio. Morley accepted the job and when Western Reserve was moved to Cleveland in 1882, Morley went also. While still in Hudson, Morley was assigned to a full teaching load, but still managed to carry out his first major research project. That project involved a test of the so-called Loomis hypothesis that during periods of high atmospheric pressure air is carried from upper parts of the atmosphere to the Earth's surface. Morley made precise measurements of the oxygen content in air for 110 consecutive days, and his results appeared to confirm the theory.

In Cleveland, Morley became involved in two important research studies almost simultaneously. The first was an effort at obtaining a precise value for the atomic weight of oxygen, in order to evaluate a well-known hypothesis proposed by the English chemist William Prout in 1815. Prout had suggested that all atoms are constructed of various combinations of hydrogen atoms.

Morley (as well as many other scientists) reasoned that should this hypothesis by true, the atomic weight of oxygen (and other elements) must be some integral multiple of that of hydrogen. For more than a decade, Morley carried out very precise measurement of the ratios in which oxygen and hydrogen combine and of the densities of the two gases. He reported in 1895 that the atomic weight of oxygen was 15.897, a result that he believed invalidated Prout's hypothesis.

Begins Research with Michelson on Ether Drift

Even better known than his oxygen research, however, was a line of study carried out by Morley in collaboration with Albert A. Michelson, professor of physics at the Case School of Applied Science, adjacent to Western Reserve's new campus in Cleveland. Morley and Michelson designed and carried out a series of experiments on the velocity of light. The most famous of those experiments were designed to test the hypothesis that light travels with different velocities depending on the direction in which it moves, a hypothesis required by current theories regarding the way light is transmitted through space. A positive result for that experiment was expected and would have confirmed existing beliefs that the transmission of light is made possible by an invisible "ether" that permeates all of space.

In 1886 Michelson and Morley published their report of what has become known as the most famous of all negative experiments. They found no difference in the velocity with which light travels, no matter what direction the observation is made. That result caused a dramatic and fundamental rethinking of many basic concepts in physics and provided a critical piece of data for **Albert Einstein**'s theory of relativity.

The research on oxygen and the velocity of light were the high points of Morley's scientific career. After many years of intense research, Morley's health began to deteriorate. To recover, he took a leave of absence from Western Reserve for a year in 1895 and traveled to Europe with his wife. When he returned to Cleveland, he found that his laboratory had been dismantled and some of his equipment had been destroyed. Although he remained at Western Reserve for another decade, he never again regained the enthusiasm for research that he had had before his vacation.

Morley died on February 24, 1923, in West Hartford, Connecticut, where he and Isabella had moved after his retirement in 1906; she predeceased him by only three weeks. Morley had been nominated for the Nobel Prize in chemistry in 1902 and received a number of other honors including the Davy Medal of the Royal Society in 1907, the Elliot Cresson Medal of the Franklin Institute in 1912, and the Willard Gibbs Medal of the Chicago section of the American Chemical Society in 1917. He served as president of the American Association for the Advancement of Science in 1895 and of the American Chemical Society in 1899.

SOURCES:

Books

Clark, F. W., "Edward Williams Morley, *Biographical Memoirs,* Volume 21, National Academy of Sciences, 1927, pp. 1–8.
Dictionary of American Biography, Volume 13, Scribner, 1934, pp. 192–193.
Dictionary of Scientific Biography, Volume 9, Scribner, 1975, pp. 530–531.
Williams, Howard R., *Edward Williams Morley,* [Easton, PA], 1957.

Periodicals

Skwire, Daniel D., and Lawrence J. Badar, "The Life and Legacy of Edward Williams Morley," *Physics Teacher,* December, 1987, pp. 548–555.

—*Sketch by David E. Newton*

Philip Morrison
1915-
American physicist

Philip Morrison has led a distinguished career highlighted by research into a great variety of applications of physics to the study of astronomical phenomena. He has written on topics such as the origin of cosmic rays; the production of helium in radioactive rocks and minerals; the structure of atomic nuclei; and astronomical phenomena such as quasars, neutrinos, supernovas, and black holes. Although the vast majority of his work has involved theoretical research in physics and astrophysics, he is almost certainly best known for other accomplishments: his work on the atomic bomb during World War II; his efforts on behalf of international nuclear controls after the war; his promotion of programs searching for intelligent life in the universe; and his campaign to improve science education in the United States.

Morrison was born in Somerville, New Jersey, on November 7, 1915. His father was in business, and his mother was a homemaker, a "rather conventional family pattern in the twenties and thirties," as he was later to describe his home in a 1981 interview with David Swift in *SETI Pioneers*. His early schooling took place in a suburb of Pittsburgh, but was delayed until about second grade because of an attack of polio. When he was able to begin his education, he entered a small private school where he remained until sixth grade. He then transferred to the public school system, where he completed his pre-college education.

Morrison became interested in science at an early age, even before entering grade school. He told Swift that he "was always fooling around with electrical, chemical, and mechanical things." He seemed especially interested in radios and was given a simple crystal set by his father in 1920. Later, at the Carnegie Institute of Technology, he helped establish the institution's radio station W8NKI.

In 1932, Morrison enrolled at Carnegie in Pittsburgh, where he earned his bachelor's degree in physics four years later. He then went on to the University of California at Berkeley, where he studied theoretical physics under **J. Robert Oppenheimer**. He graduated with a Ph. D. from Berkeley in 1940 and then taught briefly at San Francisco State College (now San Francisco State University) and the University of Illinois.

By 1942, the Manhattan Project to build the first atomic bomb was well under way and many scientists in the United States were leaving their personal work to join that effort. Morrison was assigned at first to work at the Metallurgical Laboratory at the University of Chicago (1943–1944). He was then transferred to the Los Alamos Scientific Laboratory in New Mexico where he became intimately involved in the testing of the first nuclear device. The story is told that Morrison was assigned the task of delivering the plutonium core for the first device from Los Alamos to the test site, which he did by carrying the core in the back seat of his car.

After the first successful test of the plutonium device in July 1945, Morrison traveled to the Pacific, where he assisted in the assembling of the second atomic bomb that was dropped on Japan. A few weeks after the bomb was dropped, he was asked to fly over regions damaged by the atomic bombs. He was startled to see the devastation caused by the bombs and became convinced that a rapid and massive effort was needed to bring the awesome power of nuclear energy under international civilian control. He began to write and speak on this topic, arguing in an article for *New Republic* in 1946 that "the atomic bomb is not merely a new weapon; it is a revolution in war." The silver lining to this terrible cloud, he went on, was the opportunity it gave the world "to build a working peace on the novelty and terror of the atomic bomb."

In the decade following the end of the war, Morrison continued to work for the control of nuclear weapons and the development of peaceful applications of nuclear energy. At times, his activities brought him into conflict with politicians who were caught up in the hysteria of the McCarthy era and, on one occasion, resulted in his being called to testify before the Senate Internal Security Subcommittee.

Morrison was appointed associate professor of physics at Cornell University in 1946. He was later promoted to full professor and remained at Cornell until 1965. During the academic year 1964–1965, he served as Francis L. Friedman Lecturer and Visiting Professor at the Massachusetts Institute of Technology (MIT). At the completion of that year, he was offered a permanent position at MIT, an offer that he accepted. Over the next two decades, he was promoted from professor to Institute Professor (1976) and finally, at his retirement in 1986, to Emeritus Professor of Physics. Throughout this period, in spite of his public visibility on other topics, Morrison continued to spend the vast majority of his time on theoretical research.

One of those topics for which he had become so well known among the general public was the search for extraterrestrial intelligence (SETI). Like many other scientists and nonscientists, Morrison claims to have long had a interest in the possibility that intelligent life exists elsewhere in the universe. But it was not until 1959 that interest matured. In that year, he wrote a paper for the journal *Nature* with a colleague at Cornell, Giuseppe Cocconi. In that paper, Morrison and Cocconi outlined the arguments for the existence of intelligent life outside our solar system and described a program for using radio signals to search for such life forms. The Morrison-Cocconi agenda was eventually adopted by the U.S. National Space and Aeronautics Administration and put into operation on October 12, 1992.

Morrison and his second wife Phyllis have long been active in efforts to improve the quality of science education in the United States, In 1991, for example, they were both chosen as Bernard Osher Fellows at San Francisco's Exploratorium, a famous "hands-on" science museum. Morrison has also been a prodigious writer, producing more than a dozen books and over 1000 book reviews. He has also written and narrated a short film about cosmic tand subatomic time and distance measurements, "Powers of Ten," and a PBS television series about scientific research, "The Ring of Truth." Among his many honors are the Pregel Prize (1955), the Babson Prize of the Gravity Foundation (1957), the Oersted Medal of the American Association of Physics Teachers (1965), and the Klumpke-Roberts Award of the Astronomical Society of the Pacific (1992).

SELECTED WRITINGS BY MORRISON:

Books

(With Hans Bethe) *Elementary Nuclear Theory,* Wiley, 1956. *Charles Babbage and His Calculating Machine,* Dover, 1961.
My Father's Watch: Aspects of the Physical World, Prentice-Hall, 1969.
The Price of Defense: A New Strategy for Military Spending, Times Books, 1979.
The Search for Extraterrestrial Intelligence, Dover, 1979.

Periodicals

New Republic, Februrary 11, 1946.
(With Giuseppe Cocconi) "Searching for Interstellar Communication," *Nature,* September 19, 1959.

SOURCES:

Books

Current Biography 1981, H. W. Wilson, 1981, pp. 308–311.
Swift, David, *SETI Pioneers,* University of Arizona Press, 1990, pp. 19–48.

Other

Ferris, Timothy, "The Klumpke-Roberts Award to Philip Morrison," *Mercury,* November-December, 1992, pp. 198–199.
Morrison, Philip, letter to David E. Newton, May 28, 1993.

—*Sketch by David E. Newton*

Henry Gwyn Jeffreys Moseley
1887-1915
English physicist

Henry Gwyn Jeffreys Moseley's great contribution to science was his ordering of the elements by examining their X-ray spectra, thus creating the periodic table. His work, which ranks among the most profound discoveries of the twentieth century, was cut short when the scientist was killed during World War I. Although he never received a major award for his research, Moseley's accomplishments laid the groundwork for a number of later scientific developments.

Henry Gwyn Jeffreys Moseley (widely known as "Harry") was born on November 23, 1887, at Weymouth, England. He was the only son of Henry Nottidge Moseley, a professor of human and comparative anatomy at the University of Oxford. He had also served as a naturalist on the famous voyages of the *Challenger* in that vessel's studies of the world's oceans. Both sides of the family included a number of eminent scientists, including a paternal grandfather who was the first professor of natural philosophy at King's College, London, and a great grandfather who was an expert on tropical diseases.

Moseley's father died when Harry was four years old. The family then moved to the small town of Chilworth, in Surrey, where Harry and his two sisters began their education. Moseley's interest in science surfaced at a young age. He was fortunate in having the constant encouragement of his mother and friends in this interest which was to lead not only to a professional career in science, but also to a lifelong fascination with natural history.

In 1896, at the age of nine, Moseley was enrolled at the Summer Fields school, an institution that specialized in preparing boys for Eton. Five years later, he won a King's Scholarship that allowed him to enroll at Eton. At Eton, Moseley studied with T. C. Porter, one of the first scientists in England to work with X rays. Although Moseley studied a number of other subjects, X rays became the topic in which he was interested during his career in science.

After leaving Eton in 1906, Moseley was awarded a scholarship to continue his education at Trinity College, Oxford. Though he earned only second class honors in science, Moseley was able to get letters of recommendation that allowed him to take a position at the University of Manchester, where he worked with **Ernest Rutherford**. His assignment at Manchester involved a full teaching load, but he still found time to carry out an ambitious program of original research.

Moseley Discovers Atomic Number

At the conclusion of his first year at Manchester, Moseley was relieved of his teaching responsibilities and allowed to devote all his time to research. The topic he selected for that research was the diffraction of X rays, a phenomenon that had just been discovered by the German physicist **Max von Laue**. For a period of some months, Moseley collaborated with C. G. Darwin, a mathematical physicist, on a study of the general characteristics of diffracted X rays. In the fall of 1913, however, the two men went their separate ways, and Moseley began to focus on the nature of the spectra produced by scattered X rays.

Moseley saw that when X rays are beamed at certain crystalline materials, they are diffracted by atoms within the crystals, forming a continuous spectrum on which is superimposed a series of bright lines. The number and location of these lines are characteristic of the element or elements being studied. Much of the basic research on X-ray spectroscopy had been done in England by **William Lawrence Bragg**, with whom Moseley studied for a short period of time at the University of Leeds.

In his own research, Moseley devised a system that allowed him to study the X-ray diffraction pattern produced by one element after another in an orderly and efficient arrangement. Very quickly, he found that the frequencies of one set of spectral lines, the "K" lines, differed from element to element in a very consistent and orderly way. That is, when the elements were arranged in ascending order according to their atomic masses, the frequency of their K spectral lines differed from each other by a factor of one. To Moseley, the meaning of these results was clear. Some property inherent in the structure of atoms was responsible for the regular, integral change he observed. That property, he decided, was the charge on the nucleus. When the elements are arranged in ascending order to their atomic masses, he pointed out, they are also arranged in ascending order according to their nuclear charge. The main difference is that the variation in atomic masses between adjacent elements is never consistent, whereas the variation in nuclear charge is always precisely one. This property is such a clear defining characteristic of atoms and elements that it was given the special name of atomic number. Of all the properties of an atom, atomic number has come to be the single most important characteristic by which an atom can be recognized.

The implications of Moseley's discovery were manifold and profound. In the first place, the concept of a unique, identifying and characteristic number of an element—its nuclear charge—provided a new basis for the periodic table. The Russian chemist Dmitri Ivanovich Mendeleev's original proposal for arranging the elements on the basis of their atomic masses had worked extraordinarily well, but it did have its flaws. Moseley found, however, that the discrepancies found in Mendeleev's proposal disappeared when the elements were arranged according to their atomic numbers. It was obvious, therefore, that atomic number was an even more fundamental property of atoms and elements than was atomic mass.

Moseley's research also allowed him to predict the number and location of elements still missing from the periodic table. Since each element could be assigned its own unique atomic number (hydrogen=1, helium=2, lithium=3, beryllium=4, and so on), any missing numbers must mean that an element remains to be discovered for this particular position in the periodic table. Based on that logic, Moseley was able to predict with confidence the existence of an as-yet-undiscovered element #43, between molybdenum (#42) and ruthenium (#44) and another between neodymium (#60) and samarium (#62). Furthermore, he was able to predict the spectral pattern to be expected for each missing element and thereby provide a valuable tool in the search for those elements.

As his initial work on X-ray spectra was being concluded, Moseley decided to resign his position at Manchester and return to Oxford in the hope of securing a position as professor of experimental physics. At Oxford, Moseley continued to work on X-ray spectra, concentrating on the study of the relatively unknown group of elements known as the lanthanides.

In June of 1914, Moseley left for a meeting of the British Association for the Advancement of Science scheduled to be held in Australia. He received word while still aboard ship of the outbreak of World War I and decided to return to England immediately. He enlisted in the Royal Engineers and, after completing an eight-month training period, was sent to the Turkish battlefront at Gallipoli. There, during the battle of Sulva Bay on June 15, 1915, he was killed by a sniper's bullet. Moseley was never married and, in his short lifetime, received no great honors. His contributions to science, however, were enormous, in that many later advances in physics and chemistry were based on his work.

SELECTED WRITINGS BY MOSELEY:

Periodicals

"The High Frequency Spectra of the Elements," *Philosophical Magazine,* Volume 26, 1913, pp. 1025–1034, and Volume 27, 1914, pp. 703–713.

(With C. G. Darwin) "The Reflexion of X Rays," *Philosophical Magazine,*Volume 26, 1913, pp. 210–232.

SOURCES:

Books

Gillispie, Charles Coulson, editor, *Dictionary of Scientific Biography,* Volume 9, Scribner's, 1975, pp. 542–545.

Heilbron, J. L., *H. G. J. Moseley: The Life and Letters of an English Physicist, 1878–1915,* University of California Press, 1970.

Jaffe, Bernard, *Moseley and the Numbering of the Elements,* Doubleday, 1971.

Williams, Trevor, editor, *A Biographical Dictionary of Scientists,* Wiley, 1974, pp. 379–380.

—*Sketch by David E. Newton*

Rudolf Mössbauer
1929-
German physicist

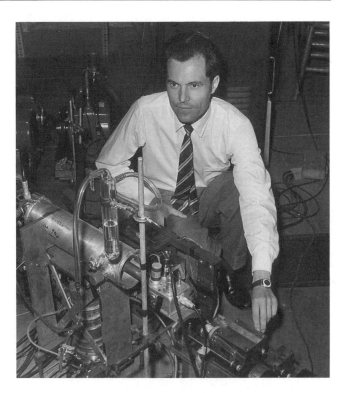

Rudolf Mössbauer

Rudolf Mössbauer's study of the recoilless emission of gamma rays and nuclear resonance florescence led to the discovery of methods for making exact measurements in solid-state physics, archeology, biological sciences, and other fields. His measurement method was used to verify **Albert Einstein's** theory of relativity and is known as the Mössbauer effect. He was honored with a 1961 Nobel Prize in physics for his work.

Rudolf Ludwig Mössbauer was born on January 31, 1929, in Münich, Germany. He was the only son of Ludwig and Erna (Ernst) Mössbauer. Ludwig Mössbauer was a phototechnician who printed color post cards and reproduced photographic materials. Mössbauer grew up during a difficult time in Germany, during the disruptions accompanying the rise of Adolf Hitler's National Socialism (Nazi party) and the onset of World War II. Still, he was able to complete a relatively normal primary and secondary education, graduating from the Münich-Pasing Oberschule in 1948. His plans to attend a university were thwarted because, due to Germany's loss in the war, the number of new enrollments was greatly reduced.

Through the efforts of his father, Mössbauer was able to find a job working as an optical assistant first at the Rodenstock optical firm in Münich and later for the U.S. Army of Occupation. Eventually Mössbauer saved enough money from these jobs to enroll at the Münich Institute for Technical Physics. In 1952 he received his preliminary diploma (the equivalent of a B.S. degree) from the institute, and

three years later he was awarded his diploma (the equivalent of an M.S. degree). For one year during this period, 1953–54, he was also an instructor of mathematics at the institute.

Begins Doctoral Research at Münich

After receiving his diploma in 1955, Mössbauer began his doctoral studies at the Münich Institute for Technical Physics. His advisor there was Heinz Maier-Leibnitz, a physicist with a special interest in the field of nuclear resonance fluorescence. As a result of Maier-Leibnitz's influence, Mössbauer undertook his thesis research in that field. His research was not carried out primarily in Münich, however, but at the Max Planck Institute for Medical Research in Heidelberg, where Mössbauer received an appointment as a research assistant.

Nuclear resonance fluorescence is similar to widely-known phenomena such as, for example, the resonance in tuning forks. When one tuning fork is struck, it begins to vibrate with a certain frequency. When a second tuning fork is struck close to the first, it begins vibrating with the same frequency, and is said to be "resonating" with the first tuning fork. Fluorescence is a form of resonance involving visible light. When light is shined on certain materials, the atoms that make up those materials may absorb electromagnetic energy and then re-emit it. The emitted energy has the same frequency as the original light as a result of the resonance within atoms of the material. This principle explains the ability of some materials to glow in the dark after having been exposed to light.

The discovery of fluorescence by R. W. Wood in 1904 suggested some obvious extensions. If light, a form of electromagnetic radiation, can cause fluorescence, scientists asked, can other forms of electromagnetic radiation do the same? In 1929, W. Kuhn predicted that gamma rays, among the most penetrating of all forms of electromagnetic radiation, would also display resonance. Since gamma rays have very short wavelengths, however, that resonance would involve changes in the atomic nucleus. Hence came the term nuclear resonance fluorescence.

For two decades following Kuhn's prediction, relatively little progress was made in the search for nuclear resonance fluorescence. One reason for this delay was that such research requires the use of radioactive materials, which are difficult and dangerous to work with. A second and more important factor was the problem of atomic recoil that typically accompanies the emission of gamma radiation. Gamma rays are emitted by an atomic nucleus when changes take place among the protons and neutrons that make up the nucleus. When a gamma ray is ejected from the nucleus, it carries with it a large amount of energy resulting in a "kick" or recoil, not unlike the recoil experienced when firing a gun. Measurements of gamma ray energy and of nuclear properties become complicated by this recoil energy.

Discovers Recoilless Gamma Ray Release

Researchers looked for ways of compensating for the recoil energy that complicated gamma ray emission from radioactive nuclei. Various methods that were developed in the early 1950s had been partially successful but were relatively cumbersome to use. Mössbauer found a solution to this problem. He discovered that a gamma emitter could be fixed within the crystal lattice of a material in such a way that it produced no recoil when it released a gamma ray. Instead, the recoil energy was absorbed by and distributed throughout the total crystal lattice in which the emitter was imbedded. The huge size of the crystal compared to the minute size of the emitter atom essentially "washed out" any recoil effect.

The material used by Mössbauer in these experiments was iridium–191, a radioactive isotope of a platinum-like metal. His original experiments were carried out at very low temperatures, close to those of liquid air, in order to reduce as much as possible the kinetic and thermal effects of the gamma emitter. Mössbauer's first report of these experiments appeared in issues of the German scientific journals *Naturwissenschaften* and *Zeitschrift fur Physic* in early 1958. He described the recoilless release of gamma rays whose wavelength varied by no more than one

part in a billion. Later work raised the precision of this effect to one part in 100 trillion.

In the midst of his research on gamma ray emission, Mössbauer was married to Elizabeth Pritz, a fashion designer. The couple later had three children, two daughters and a son. In 1958, Mössbauer was also awarded his Ph.D. in physics by the Technical University in Münich for his study of gamma ray emission.

The initial reactions to the Mössbauer papers on gamma ray emission ranged from disinterest to doubt. According to one widely-repeated story, two physicists at the Los Alamos Scientific Laboratory made a five-cent bet on whether or not the Mössbauer Effect really existed. When one scientist was in fact able to demonstrate the effect, the scientific community gained interest.

Physicists found a number of applications for the Mössbauer Effect using a system in which a gamma ray emitter fixed in a crystal lattice is used to send out a signal, a train of gamma rays. A second crystal containing the same gamma ray emitter set up as an absorber so that the gamma rays travelling from emitter to absorber would cause resonance in the absorber. Therefore, the emission of gamma rays stays resonating and constant until a change, or force such as gravity, electricity, or magnetism enters the field. By noting the changes in the gamma ray field, unprecedented measurements of these forces became available.

Mössbauer Effect Used to Test Theory of Relativity

One of the first major applications of the Mössbauer Effect was to test Einstein's theory of relativity. In his 1905 theory, Einstein had predicted that photons are affected by a gravitational field, and therefore an electromagnetic wave should experience a change in frequency as it passes near a massive body. Astronomical tests had been previously devised to check this prediction, but these tests tended to be difficult in procedure and imprecise in their results.

In 1959, two Harvard physicists, **Robert Pound** and Glen A. Rebka, Jr., designed an experiment in which the Mössbauer Effect was used to test the Einstein theory. A gamma ray emitter was placed at the top of a sixty-five-foot tower, and an absorber was placed at the bottom of the tower. When gamma rays were sent from source to absorber, Pound and Rebka were able to detect a variation in wavelength that clearly confirmed Einstein's prediction. Today, similar experimental designs are used for dozens of applications in fields ranging from theoretical physics to the production of synthetic plastics.

Mössbauer's Nobel Prize citation in 1961 mentioned in particular his "researches concerning the resonance absorption of gamma-radiation and his discovery in this connection of the effect which bears his name." The Nobel citation went on to say how Mössbauer's work has made it possible "to examine precisely numerous important phenomena formerly beyond or at the limit of attainable accuracy of measurement." The physics community acknowledged the enormous scientific and technical impact the discovery would eventually make.

After receiving his Ph.D. in 1958, Mössbauer took a position as research fellow at the Institute for Technical Physics in Münich. Two years later he was offered the post of full professor at the Institute, but, according to his entry in *Nobel Prize Winners,* declined the offer because he was "frustrated by what he regarded as the bureaucratic and authoritarian organization of German universities." Instead, he accepted a job as research fellow at the California Institute of Technology and was promoted to full professor a year later, shortly after the announcement of his Nobel award.

In 1964, Mössbauer once more returned to Münich, this time as full professor and with authority to reorganize the physics department there. In 1972, he took an extended leave of absence from his post at Münich to become director of the Institute Max von Laue in Grenoble, France. After five years in France, he returned to his former appointment in Münich. In addition to the Nobel Prize, Mössbauer has received the Science Award of the Research Corporation of America (1960), the Elliott Cresson Medal of the Franklin Institute (1961), the Roentgen Prize of the University of Giessen (1961), the Bavarian Order of Merit (1962), the Guthrie Medal of London's Institute of Physics (1974), the Lomonosov Gold Medal of the Soviet Academy of Sciences (1984), and the Einstein Medal (1986).

SOURCES:

Books

Abbott, David, *The Biographical Dictionary of Scientists—Physicists,* P. Bedrich, 1984, p. 118.
Current Biography 1962, H. W. Wilson, 1962, pp. 306–08.
Frauenfelder, Hans, *The Mössbauer Effect* (collection of Mössbauer's papers with a critical review of his work), W. A. Benjamin, 1962.
Halacy, D. S., Jr., *They Gave Their Names to Science,* Putnam, 1967, pp. 118–29.
McGraw-Hill Modern Scientists and Engineers, Volume 2, McGraw-Hill, 1980, pp. 331–32.
Nobel Prize Winners, H. W. Wilson, 1987, pp. 733–35.
Weber, Robert L., *Pioneers of Science: Nobel Prize Winners in Physics,* American Institute of Physics, 1980, pp. 184–85.

—Sketch by David E. Newton

Nevill Francis Mott
1905-
English physicist

Sir Nevill Francis Mott began his career applying the then-recently discovered laws of quantum mechanics and ultimately became a leading figure in solid state physics. He shared the 1977 Nobel Prize with **Philip Warren Anderson** and **John Van Vleck** for work on semiconductors, the materials that drove the modern revolution in electronics and led to improved electronic circuits and increases in the memory of computers. Mott also worked on theories explaining the physical underpinnings of the properties of many materials, and with R. W. Gurney, developed a theory explaining how a photographic image is formed when the film is exposed to light.

Mott was born September 30, 1905, in Leeds, England, the first of two children of Charles Francis and Lilian Mary (Reynolds) Mott, both of whom worked for a time in the Cavendish Laboratory at Cambridge University under **J. J. Thomson**, who had just discovered the electron. His parents moved to Stafford when Mott was six years old, but Mott studied at home with his mother until he was ten because of concerns about his health. He wrote in his autobiography that he wanted to be a physicist from the time he understood what physics was. At age thirteen, he began five years of secondary study at Clifton College. In 1927, he received a baccalaureate degree in mathematics from Cambridge, where he did his first work in theoretical physics studying the scattering of electrons by nuclei. He continued those studies during a 1928 term in Copenhagen with **Niels Bohr**, who in 1913 had put forth the theoretical model of the atom. Mott went on to teach at Manchester University during the 1929–1930 school year and received an introduction to solid state physics from **William Lawrence Bragg**, who with his father, **William Henry Bragg**, won a Nobel Prize for his work in X-ray crystallography. In 1930, Mott returned to Cambridge, received a master's degree, became a lecturer at Cambridge's Gonville and Caius College and made his first big discovery in the scattering of particles by atoms and nuclei. These collisions between charged particles are now known as

Mott scattering. Mott became Melville Wills Professor of Theoretical Physics at Bristol in 1933 and held this position until he became chair of the physics department there in 1948. Mott's group of researchers at Bristol led the world in the development of solid state physics. Mott's approach focused on using physics to explain the properties of materials, particularly metals and alloys. As he wrote in *Scientific American* in 1967, "In solid state perhaps more than anywhere else quantum mechanics has ceased to be restricted to pure science and has become a working tool of technology."

Mott's studies of electrons in metals and dislocations and defects in crystals resulted in the 1936 publication of the seminal work, "Theory of the Properties of Metals and Alloys," which he wrote with Harry Jones. Mott, with Gurney, also became the first to formulate a theory explaining how photographic plates work, an explanation that led to improvements in the field. They theorized that free electrons produced when light strikes the plates became trapped at dislocations or other imperfections and attract silver ions, which become silver atoms and form a latent image.

Work in Semiconductors Leads to Nobel Prize

Mott then became interested in semiconductors, which are materials that can act as insulators or conductors and are used in many electronic devices. In 1940, Mott wrote *Electronic Processes in Ionic Crystals* with Gurney, and did important work on transition metals, becoming the first to theorize that all electrons in such materials are involved in electrical conductivity. He also postulated that certain non-metals can act like metals when placed under pressure and that all electrons become free to move at once; these processes are called Mott transitions.

In 1954, Mott became Cavendish Professor of Physics at Cambridge, a post he held until his retirement in 1971. He also served as the master of Gonville and Caius College from 1959 to 1966. Mott was involved in confirming by observations with the electron microscope the existence of moving dislocations, or tiny defects, responsible for hardening in alloys. During the mid–1960s, Mott became interested in non-crystalline, or amorphous, semiconductors, a research shift that stemmed in part from his work on metal-insulator transitions and eventually brought him the Nobel Prize. Mott added considerably to science's knowledge of the electronic properties of amorphous (disordered) materials such as glasses, alloys and impure semiconductors, where atoms are not arranged in regular arrays. Adding impurities to semiconductors, for example, can improve conductivity.

Mott married Ruth Horder in 1930 and had two daughters, Elizabeth and Alice. During his career, he was involved in scientific publishing and a number of social and philosophical issues, including the control of nuclear armaments. A popular public speaker who organized and participated in many scientific conferences, Mott was elected a fellow of the Royal Society of London in 1936 and knighted in 1962. In addition, he has been a member of several foreign societies, including the U.S. National Academy of Sciences. Mott received the Royal Society's Hughes Medal in 1941, the Royal Medal in 1953, and the Copley Medal in 1972, in addition to many other awards and honorary degrees.

SELECTED WRITINGS BY MOTT:

Books

(With H. S. W. Massey) *The Theory of Atomic Collisions,* Clarendon Press, 1933, third edition 1965, Oxford University Press, 1987.
(With Harry Jones) *The Theory of the Properties of Metals and Alloys,* Clarendon Press, 1936.
(With R. W. Gurney) *Electronic Processes in Ionic Crystals,* Clarendon Press, 1940, 2nd edition, 1957, Dover, 1964.
(With E. A. Davis) *Electronic Processes in Non-Crystalline Materials,* Clarendon Press, 1971, 2nd edition, Oxford University Press, 1979.

Periodicals

"The Solid State," *Scientific American,* September, 1967, pp. 80–89.
"Metal-Insulator Transitions," *Physics Today,* November, 1978, pp. 42–47.

SOURCES:

Books

Contemporary Authors, Volume 129, Gale, 1990.
Modern Scientists and Engineers, McGraw-Hill, 1980, pp. 332–333.
Mott, Sir Nevill, *A Life in Science,* Taylor and Francis, 1986.

Periodicals

Cohen, Marvin L., and L. M. Falicov, "The 1977 Nobel Prize in Physics," *Science,* November 18, 1977, pp. 713–715.

—*Sketch by Julie Anderson*

Ben R. Mottelson
1926-
American-born Danish physicist

In 1953, Ben R. Mottelson and his colleague **Aage Bohr** published a theory combining the two previously popular but inconsistent models of the nucleus, the shell and liquid-drop models. Mottelson and Bohr shared the 1975 Nobel Prize in physics with **James Rainwater** for this accomplishment. Mottelson was born in Chicago on July 9, 1926. His parents were Goodman Mottelson, an engineer, and Georgia Blum. He graduated from La Grange High School in 1943 and immediately enlisted in the United States Navy. Mottelson was sent to Purdue University for officer training and then, at the war's conclusion, returned to Purdue to complete his B.S. degree. Upon graduation from Purdue in 1947, Mottelson began his doctoral program in physics at Harvard University. He was granted his Ph.D. in 1950 for a dissertation on nuclear physics written under the direction of Nobel Laureate **Julian Schwinger**.

In the same year, Mottelson was awarded a Sheldon traveling fellowship by Harvard, allowing him to do postdoctoral studies at the Institute for Theoretical Physics (later renamed the Niels Bohr Institute) in Copenhagen. At the end of his first year there Mottelson was given a second fellowship, this time from the U.S. Atomic Energy Commission, permitting him to remain in Denmark for two more years. From 1953 to 1957, his ongoing research in Copenhagen was sponsored by the European Organization for Nuclear Research (CERN). At the conclusion of this period, Mottelson was appointed to the staff at the newly-created Nordic Institute for Theoretical Atomic Physics (NORDITA), whose buildings are adjacent to the Institute for Theoretical Physics (now called the Niels Bohr Institute). Mottelson has continued his association with NORDITA ever since and, in 1981, was named director of the institute.

Proposes Model of the Atomic Nucleus

During his early years in Copenhagen, Mottelson's primary research interest was the structure of the atomic nucleus. In that research he collaborated with Aage Bohr, one of six sons of the great Danish physicist **Niels Bohr**. The problem with which Mottelson and Bohr dealt was that two quite different theories of nuclear structure had been proposed in the preceding fifteen years. One, the liquid-drop model, had been suggested by Aage's father, Niels Bohr, in 1936. According to that model, the nucleus acts as if it were made from an incompressible fluid that oscillates back and forth around a basically spherical shape. The liquid-drop model successfully described a number of known nuclear properties, especially the phenomenon of nuclear fission.

Over time, however a number of deficiencies in the Bohr model became apparent. Finally, in 1949, **Maria Goeppert-Mayer** and a team led by **J. H. D. Jensen** independently suggested an alternative theory, the shell model. According to this theory, nucleons (protons and neutrons) travel in specific orbitals within the nucleus, roughly similar to the way electrons orbit the nucleus in specific energy levels. The shell model explained a number of phenomena for which the liquid-drop model had been inadequate, but it failed when applied to many properties observed for the nucleus as a whole.

Mottelson and Aage Bohr were able to find a way of combining the liquid-drop and shell models into a single collective theory of nuclear structure. Their work was aided by the work of James Rainwater, with whom Aage Bohr had worked while at Columbia University from 1949 to 1950. Rainwater had suggested in a 1950 paper that the outermost nucleons in a nucleus might undergo dislocations that would change the shape of the nucleus from spherical to oblate. That idea provided one of the first links between the liquid-drop and shell models of the nucleus.

Between 1950 and 1953, Mottelson and Bohr expanded upon and revised Rainwater's theory. They suggested a mechanism by which nucleons can still be assigned energy levels within the nucleus, but in such a way that their motions can produce overall liquid-drop-type effects. For their contributions to the development of this model, Mottelson, Bohr, and Rainwater shared the 1975 Nobel Prize in physics.

Mottelson married Nancy Jane Reno on May 31, 1948; they have two sons and a daughter. Mottelson and his wife became citizens of Denmark in 1971. Four years later, a few days before word of her husband's Nobel Prize, Nancy Mottelson died of cancer.

SELECTED WRITINGS BY MOTTELSON:

Books

(With Aage Bohr) *Collective and Individual Particle Aspects of Nuclear Structure,* Munksgaard, 1957.

(With Bohr) *Nuclear Structure,* 2 volumes, Addison-Wesley, 1969.

Periodicals

"Elementary Modes of Excitation in the Nucleus," *Review of Modern Physics,* July, 1976, pp. 375–83.

SOURCES:

Books

A Biographical Encyclopedia of Scientists, Facts on File, 1981, pp. 575–76.

McGraw-Hill Modern Scientists and Engineers, McGraw, 1980, pp. 333–34.

Wasson, Tyler, editor, *Nobel Prize Winners,* H. W. Wilson, 1987, pp. 739–40.

Weber, Robert L., *Pioneers of Science: Nobel Prize Winners in Physics,* American Institute of Physics, 1980, pp. 241–42.

Periodicals

"Bohr, Mottelson and Rainwater Win Nobel Physics Prize," *Physics Today,* December, 1975, p. 69.

Feshbach, H., "The 1975 Nobel Prize for Physics," *Science,* November 28, 1975, pp. 868–70.

—*Sketch by David E. Newton*

Forest Ray Moulton
1872-1952
American astronomer

Forest Ray Moulton is best remembered for his hypothesis, conceived with **Thomas Chrowder Chamberlin,** that the planets formed when gas emitted by our sun was compressed under gravitational influence from a passing star. In this so-called Chamberlin-Moulton hypothesis, the gas solidified and condensed into "planetesimals," which later accumulated into the existing planets. While this model was superseded by later ideas, it brought to light certain theories about spiral motion in gas clouds which preceded important measurements of spiral galaxies. Moulton also served as chair of the University of Chicago's astronomy department; and, as secretary of the American Association for the Advancement of Science in Washington, D.C., saw the organization double its membership and find permanent housing. Moulton's interests also led to pioneering work in radio broadcasting and motion picture technology as well as contributions to the field of ballistics.

Moulton was born on April 29, 1872, to Belah G. Moulton, a farmer, and Mary G. (Smith) Moulton, a schoolteacher in a small school. Moulton was raised on a farm in southern Michigan's forest-rich Osceola County, near the town of Reed City (which later became Le Roy, Michigan). As noted in *Dictionary of American Biography Supplement 5 (1951–1955),* his mother named him Forest Ray because he was, in her words, "a perfect ray of light and happiness in that dense forest." The oldest child in his family, Moulton had five brothers and a sister: Mary, Charles, Vern, E. L., Elton J. (later a professor of astronomy at Northwestern University), and Harold G. (later a president of the Brookings Institution in Washington, D.C.). Moulton was sixteen when he began his teaching career, in a rural school near home, from 1888 to 1889. Moulton didn't begin secondary school until he was 17. He attended Albion College in 1892, where he played on the football team and taught astronomy, receiving his B.A. in 1894. He earned a Ph.D. in astronomy, summa cum laude, from the University of Chicago in 1899. Three years earlier he started working as an assistant instructor in the University of Chicago's astronomy department. In 1898, he was promoted to associate instructor and to instructor in 1900. In 1903, he became assistant professor, then served as associate professor from 1908 to 1912. From then on he was a professor and department chair, until his resignation in 1926.

Proposes Planetesimal Theory of Solar System Formation

In 1898, Moulton first met with Thomas Chrowder Chamberlin, chair of the geology department at the University of Chicago. Under the sponsorship of the University of Chicago and the Carnegie Institution of Washington, the two scientists studied photographs of the total eclipse of the sun occurring on May 28, 1900. They were impressed by the flares of gas flying off the sun's surface. In 1904, they published the first complete statement of their theory of planetesimals to account for the solar system's formation. Chamberlin had been critical of Pierre-Simon Laplace's nebular hypothesis, which said a gas cloud contracted to form the sun, with rings of matter being left out at their present-day distances and later condensing into the planets. This scenario presupposed a warmer past for the Earth, but Chamberlin's study of ice ages on Earth contradicted this. Moulton and Chamberlin thought a star had passed close to the sun, which had caused the sun to throw off material. Over time, the smaller pebbles that solidified became rocks, then boulders, etc., with gravity speeding up the process. (Today, it is believed that gas thrown off of the sun will *not* condense into solid matter.) Moulton prepared tables showing that if the Earth had really been much hotter in the past, as Laplace had implied, all its water vapor would have escaped into space. Chamberlin and Moulton theorized that our own solar system, in its primitive gaseous state, might have exhibited spiral structure. This part of the Chamberlin-Moulton hypothesis may have influenced later observations of the rotation in spiral galaxies, as well as specific observations of the Andromeda Galaxy's rotation.

During World War I, Moulton worked at Fort Sill as a Major in the Ordnance Department of the U.S. Army. He was in charge of ballistics in the American Artillery from 1918 to 1919, and carried out mathematical and test research on high velocity guns (and on improving the accuracy of firing data). He helped increase the range of guns by streamlining shells, and after the war, became a Lieutenant Colonel in the U.S. Army Reserve.

Moulton took on a variety of academic responsibilities, serving as associate editor of the *Transactions of the American Mathematical Society* from 1907 until 1912, and more significantly, as a research associate at the Carnegie Institution from 1908 to 1923. After leaving the University of Chicago in 1926, Moulton became director of the Utilities Power and Light Corporation until 1938. In perhaps his most influential administrative role, Moulton was elected permanent secretary of the American Association for the Advancement of Science (AAAS) in 1937, a duty he carried out until 1946 (staying on as administrative secretary for two more years). During Moulton's tenure as secretary, the AAAS took over the publication of *Science* magazine, found permanent housing for the association in Washington, D.C., and saw its membership rise from less than 20,000 in 1937 to 43,000 in 1946. Moulton also edited twenty-five science symposium volumes for the AAAS.

For several years Moulton gave weekly broadcasts on astronomy, mathematics, and physics over the Columbia Broadcasting Company's radio network. From 1919 until 1923, Moulton was a trustee and president of the board of Albion College, and he received a Sc.D. in astronomy and mathematics there in 1923. From 1933 to 1934, Moulton served as trustee and director to Concessions of the Chicago World's Fair, also known as the Century of Progress Exposition. Trying to make ends meet during the Depression proved stressful, and Moulton suffered (but recovered from) heart problems during this time. In 1939, Moulton received an LL.D. from Drake University, and an honorary Sc.D. from the Case School of Applied Science the following year.

Moulton founded the Society for Visual Education, gave the first radio address broadcast from the University of Chicago, and invented a way to prevent the flickering of motion pictures. He gave hundreds of public lectures across America, and enjoyed membership in the AAAS, the National Academy of Sciences, the American Mathematical Society, and the American Astronomical Society. Moulton played tennis and handball, occasionally played billiards, and enjoyed opera. He was also fond of farming, poetry, classical literature, and painting. Moulton died at age eighty on December 7, 1952, at the home of a friend in Wilmette, Illinois.

Moulton married twice and divorced twice. He married Estella Laura Gillette in Owosso, Michigan, on March 25, 1897, and with her had four children: Gail Francis, Vieva Gillette, Mary Elizabeth, and Merle Gordon. This first marriage ended in 1938, and Moulton remarried on July 28, 1939, to Alicia Pratt, in Norristown, Pennsylvania. This marriage ended in a 1951 divorce.

SELECTED WRITINGS BY MOULTON:

Books

(With T. C. Chamberlin) *The Tidal and Other Problems,* Carnegie Institution of Washington, 1909.
New Methods in Exterior Ballistics, University of Chicago Press, 1926.
The World and Man as Science Sees Them, University of Chicago Press, 1937.
(Editor with J. J. Schifferes) *The Autobiography of Science,* second edition, J. Murray, 1963.

Periodicals

"The Planetesimal Hypothesis," *Science,* December 7, 1929, pp. 549–559.

SOURCES:

Books

Current Biography: Who's News and Why 1946, The H. W. Wilson, 1946, p. 421.
Garraty, John A., *Dictionary of American Biography Supplement 5 (1951–1955),* Scribner, 1977, pp. 508–509.
Hetherington, Norris H., "Chamberlin-Moulton Hypothesis," *Encyclopedia of Cosmology,* Garland, 1993, p. 56.
National Cyclopedia of American Biography, Volume 43, James T. White, 1961, p. 314.

Periodicals

New York Times, December 9, 1952, p. 33.

—*Sketch by Sebastian Thaler*

Hermann Joseph Muller
1890-1967
American geneticist

Hermann Joseph Muller

Hermann Joseph Muller was the first to show that genetic mutations can be induced by exposing chromosomes to X rays. For this demonstration he was awarded the 1946 Nobel Prize in physiology or medicine. He also took up a crusade to improve the condition of the human gene pool by calling for a cessation of the unnecessary use of X rays in medicine and a halt to nuclear bomb testing in order to prevent further damage to the genetic makeup of the human population.

Hermann Joseph Muller was born on December 21, 1890, in New York City. His father was also named Hermann Joseph Muller; his mother was the former Frances Lyons. Muller's paternal grandfather had come to the United States from Germany after the revolution that had swept Europe in 1848. Muller's father had wanted to be a lawyer, but instead had taken up the family business of producing bronze art work. The elder Muller died when young Hermann was only nine.

Hermann attended Morris High School in the borough of the Bronx in New York City. When he founded its science club, perhaps the first of its kind in the country, it seemed obvious that science would be his calling. On a scholarship, Muller enrolled at Columbia University in 1907 and by his sophomore year decided that he would major in genetics. He received his bachelors degree in 1910 and then continued at both Cornell Medical School and Columbia for his master's degree, studying the transmission of nerve impulses.

An Early Interest in Fruit Fly Mutations

Two of Muller's classmates, **A. H. Sturtevant** and Calvin B. Bridges, were working at Columbia with **Thomas Hunt Morgan**, a zoologist who was performing ground-breaking work in genetics. In 1912, Muller joined this group. Together the four became something of a legend at Columbia, where the "fly room" buzzed with talk of chromosomes, genes, crossing over, and mutations. The flies in this case were *Drosophila melanogaster*, fruit flies with a brief three-week breeding cycle making them ideal for genetic study. These fruit flies also have just four pairs of chromosomes, the dark-staining microscopic structures within the nucleus of each cell. Experiments were done to study mutations, abnormal traits that seem to arise spontaneously in the fruit fly population. The mutations were tracked in order to infer which part of each chromosome contained the

gene responsible for a particular trait, such as eye color or wing shape.

Muller's doctoral thesis in 1916 was on "crossing over," a phenomenon discovered in 1909 by a Belgian scientist, F. A. Janssens, when he noticed that during the duplication and separation of like chromosomes, sometimes part of a chromosome would break off and reattach at a comparable place on the other chromosome. If two genes were far apart on a chromosome, then it would be more likely that a break could occur between them. Thus, a high frequency of crossing over observed between any two traits would mean a long distance between the genes, while a low frequency of crossing over between two traits would mean the genes were close together. The team used this information to "map" each chromosome in order to show how genes for each trait might be arranged along its length. The findings of the group were published in *The Mechanism of Mendelian Heredity,* written by the four in 1915.

In 1916, Muller took a teaching position at Rice Institute in Texas, where he did further research in genetics, especially mapping "modifier" genes, which seem to control the expression of other genes. Upon his return to Columbia two years later, Muller did some of his most important theoretical work. Realizing that genes on the chromosomes are self-replicating and are responsible for synthesizing the other components of cells, he theorized that all life must have started out with molecules that were able to self-replicate, which he likened to "naked genes." These molecules, he suggested, must have been something like viruses, a very astute hypothesis given the little that was known about viruses at the time.

In 1921, Muller returned to Texas, this time to the University of Texas in Austin, where he remained until 1932. Muller had grown impatient with waiting for mutations to happen on their own, so he began seeking methods of hastening rates of mutation. In 1919, he had discovered that higher temperatures increase the number of mutations, but not always in both chromosomes in a chromosome pair. He deduced that mutations must involve changes at the molecular or sub-molecular level. He struck on the idea of using X rays instead of heat to induce mutations, and by 1926 he was able to confirm that X rays greatly increased the mutation rate in *Drosophila.* He also concluded that most mutations are harmful to the organism, but are not passed on to future generations since the individual affected is unlikely to reproduce; nonetheless, he suggested, if the rate of harmful mutations were too become too high, a species might die out.

Muller reported his success in inducing mutations in a 1927 article in *Science* entitled "Artificial Transmutation of the Gene." The article gained him international status as an innovator and introduced other scientists to a technique for studying a large number of mutations at once. This led to the realization that mutations are actually chemical changes that can be artificially induced with any number of other chemicals. It also help spawn the infant study of radiation genetics.

Genetics and Politics Prove a Volatile Mix

In the early 1930s, personal problems led Muller to leave the United States. In 1923 he had married Jessie Mary Jacob, a mathematician. But the pressure of his work and a divorce from his wife led to a nervous breakdown. Muller left Texas in 1932 and moved to Berlin to work at the Kaiser Wilhelm Institute. There he spent a year as a Guggenheim fellow doing research on mutations and exploring the structure of the gene. However, Hitler was rising to power and Muller, being a strong supporter of socialism, left Germany.

Muller's next stop was the Soviet Union, where he stayed from 1933 to 1937. At the Academy of Sciences in both Leningrad and Moscow he studied radiation genetics, cytogenetics and gene structure. However, he soon became openly critical of Trofim Denisovich Lysenko's theories of genetics, which were dominant in the Soviet Union in the mid 1930s. Lysenko held a number of erroneous beliefs about how genetic traits are passed on to future generations. As Lysenko's hypotheses were compatible with certain aspects of Marxist theory, he was a favorite among those in political power. Disputing Lysenko proved dangerous, so in 1937 Muller was forced to leave the Soviet Union. Still following his socialist beliefs, Muller volunteered to fight in the Spanish Civil War.

The next year Muller got a job at the Institute of Animal Genetics in Edinburgh, Scotland, again working on radiation genetics. There he met Dorothy Kantorowitz, a German refugee. In 1939 they married and, as both of them were of part Jewish heritage, left for the safety of the United States in 1940. He continued his research at Amherst College and, starting in 1945, at Indiana University, where he was appointed professor of zoology and where he stayed until his death in 1967.

In 1946 Muller was awarded the Nobel Prize for medicine or physiology for his important work on mutations. Muller was also a member of the National Academy of Sciences and a fellow of the Royal Society. He used the opportunity of his world fame to campaign for many social concerns sparked by his interest in the genetic health of the human population. He spoke out against needless X rays in medicine and for safety in protecting people regularly exposed to X rays. In the 1950s he campaigned to outlaw nuclear bomb tests because he believed that nuclear fallout would cause mutations in future generations. Toward the end of his life, Muller believed that the human race should take action in order to keep healthy genes in the population. His idea came out of the belief that modern culture and technology suspend the process of natural selection and thus increase the number of mutations in human genes. He believed that there should be programs to promote eugenics, literally "good genes." He supported the idea of establishing sperm banks in which the sperm of exceptionally healthy and gifted men would be frozen as an "endowment" to be used for future generations. The concept of such massive intervention in the human gene pool and in the private lives of individuals was and remains highly controversial.

SELECTED WRITINGS BY MULLER:

Books

(With Thomas Hunt Morgan, Alfred H. Sturtevant and Calvin B. Bridges) *The Mechanism of Mendelian Heredity,* Holt, 1915.

Periodicals

"Artificial Transmutation of the Gene," *Science,* Volume 66, 1927, pp. 84–87.

SOURCES:

Books

Abbott, David, editor, *The Biographical Dictionary of Scientists: Biologists,* Peter Bedrick, New York, 1984.

Biographical Memoirs of Fellows of the Royal Society, Volume 14, Royal Society (London), 1968, pp. 349–389.

Gillispie, Charles Coulston, editor, *Dictionary of Scientific Biography,* Scribner's, York, 1985, pp. 564–565.

Periodicals

Carlson, E. A., "The Legacy of Hermann Joseph Muller: 1890–1967," *Canadian Journal of Genetics and Cytology,* Volume 9, number 3, 1967, pp. 437–448.

—Sketch by Barbara A. Branca

K. Alex Müller
1927-

Swiss physicist

P hysicist K. Alex Müller's Nobel Prize-winning work focused on his discovery of using metal-based ceramics to enable superconductivity at high temperatures, a feat previously unattainable by scientists using metals and other materials for the same purpose. This discovery later resulted in the development of materials that become superconductive at even higher temperatures.

Karl Alexander Müller was born in Basel, Switzerland, on April 20, 1927. His father was Paul Rudolf Müller, a music student at the time of his son's birth, and his mother was the former Irma Feigenbaum. Müller's childhood was spent in Basel, Salzburg, Austria, and Donach and Lugano, Switzerland. After his mother died in 1938, Müller moved to eastern Switzerland where he completed his secondary education at Evangelical College. Müller's interest in science developed during his years at Evangelical, eventually deciding to major in physics.

After graduating from Evangelical in 1945, Müller completed his required tour of duty with the Swiss army and then enrolled at the Swiss Federal Institute of Technology in Zürich. Tempted by a possible career in engineering, he decided to remain a physics major, at least partly because of his contact with **Wolfgang Pauli**, 1945 Nobel Laureate in physics, at the Federal Institute of Technology. Müller was awarded his diplomate (comparable to a master's degree) in 1952.

Müller Begins Studies of Ceramics

By this time, Müller's interests had begun to focus on problems of solid-state physics, especially on a class of compounds known as ceramics. Ceramics are glass-like compound of oxygen and at least one metallic element. Brick, tile, and terra cotta are examples of ceramics. Although ceramics have been used for a myriad of practical applications over the centuries, they have long been regarded as somewhat uninteresting subjects of scientific research. That attitude has changed rather dramatically over the last few decades, however, at least partly as a result of Müller's research. Müller's own doctoral thesis dealt with a new ceramic he had synthesized, an oxide of strontium and titanium. For this work, he was awarded his Ph.D. from the Federal Institute of Technology in 1958.

Müller's first work experience, at the Battelle Memorial Institute in Geneva, involved him in a very different line of research from the one of his graduate days. He was made manager of a group studying magnetic resonance, a subject on which he was also asked to lecture at the University of Zürich in 1962. In 1963, Müller accepted an appointment as researcher at the IBM Zürich Research Laboratory, where he was able to return to his study of ceramics.

Müller and Bednorz Work on Superconducting Ceramics

In 1972, the direction of Müller's career took an unexpected turn from the area of research in solid state physics. **J. Georg Bednorz**, a student from the Federal Institute of Technology, spent a summer working in Müller's laboratory at IBM. Bednorz then returned for two more summers and then joined Müller's staff at the IBM laboratory, working in the area of superconducting materials. Superconductivity, the tendency of a material to lose all resistance to the flow of an electrical current, had been discovered by the Dutch physicist **Heike Kamerlingh Onnes** in 1911. Physicists quickly realized the practical significance of Onnes's discovery, the possibility of having materials that can carry an electrical current essentially forever with no loss of energy due to resistance. The problem with Kamerlingh Onnes's discovery was that it was based on superconductivity observed only in metals cooled nearly to absolute zero (0 K, or –273°C). In the seven-decade period following his discovery, researchers have been able to raise this temperature to 23 K (–250°C), still far below the range at which practical devices would be able to operate economically.

During the mid–1980s, Müller and Bednorz explored another approach to the study of superconducting materials: the use of ceramics instead of metals. A key turning point in their research came in January 1986 when Bednorz read about a newly-invented ceramic that had certain metallic properties. It seemed to be a likely compound in which to look for superconductivity.

This research went forward with unexpectedly quick results. By April 1986, Müller and Bednorz had observed superconductivity in the new ceramic at 35 K, 12 K higher than the previous upper limit for the phenomenon. News of the accomplishment spread rapidly, and physicists around the world quickly began experiments to confirm the Müller-Bednorz discovery and, if possible, to extend the limit at which superconductivity was observable. Less than a year later, University of Houston researcher **Paul Ching-Wu Chu** had done so, not only repeating Müller-Bednorz's success, but also raising the critical temperature to 90 K (–183°C). In one of the most immediate decisions in the history of the award, the Nobel Prize committee awarded the 1987 prize to Müller and Bednorz for their achievement.

Müller has continued to work on superconducting ceramics at the IBM Laboratory since receiving his Nobel Prize. He was made manager of the Physics Department in 1972 and IBM Fellow in 1982. Since 1985, he has been relieved of all duties except to work solely on his own research. In addition to the Nobel Prize, Müller has been awarded the 1986 Marcel-Benoist Foundation Prize, the 1987 Fritz London Memorial Award, the 1987 Dannie Heineman Prize, the 1987 Robert Wichard Pohl Prize of the German Physical Society, and the 1988 Hewlett-Packard Europhysics Prize. Müller was married to Ingeborg Winkler in 1956. They have two children, Eric and Sylvia.

SELECTED WRITINGS BY MÜLLER:

Periodicals

"Possible High Tc Superconductivity in the Ba-La-Cu-O System," with J. G. Bednorz, *Zeitschrift für Physik B*, 64, 1986, pp. 189–193.
"The Discovery of a Class of High Temperature Superconductors," with J. G. Bednorz, *Science*, 237, 1987, pp. 1133–1139.

SOURCES:

Books

Weber, Robert L., *Pioneers of Science: Nobel Prize Winners in Physics,* American Institute of Physics, 1980, pp. 300–301.

Periodicals

Gleick, James, "In the Trenches of Science," *New York Times Magazine,* August 16, 1987, p. 29.
Khurana, Anil, "Bednorz and Müller Win Nobel Prize for New Superconducting Materials," *Physics Today,* December 1987, pp. 17–19.
Waldrop, M. Mitchell, "The 1987 Nobel Prize for Physics," *Science,* October 25, 1987, pp. 481–482.

—*Sketch by David E. Newton*

Paul Müller
1899-1965
Swiss chemist

Paul Müller was an industrial chemist who discovered that dichlorodiphenyltrichloroethane (DDT) could be used as an insecticide. This was the first insecticide that could actually target insects; in small doses it was not toxic to humans and yet it was stable enough to remain effective over a period of months. When DDT was introduced in 1942, the effects it would have on the environment were not well understood. It was widely hailed, in particular for its ability to reduce the incidence of tropical diseases by reducing insect populations. For his work with DDT and the role his discovery played in the fight against diseases such as typhus and malaria, Müller was awarded the 1948 Nobel Prize in medicine or physiology.

Paul Hermann Müller was born in Olten, Switzerland on January 12, 1899, to Gottlieb and Fanny Leypoldt Müller. His father was an official on the Swiss Federal Railway, and the family moved to Lenzburg and then to Basel, where Müller was educated until the age of seventeen. After finishing his secondary education, Müller worked for several years in a succession of jobs with local chemical companies. In 1919, he entered the University of Basel to study chemistry. He did his doctoral work under F. Fichter and H. Rupe, and his dissertation examined the chemical and electrochemical reactions of m-xylidine and some related compounds. Xylidines are used in the manufacture of dyes, and when Müller received his Ph.D. in 1925 he went to work in the dye division of the J. R. Geigy Corporation, a very large Swiss chemical company. Müller married Friedel Rügsegger in 1927; they had two sons and a daughter. Müller initially conducted research on the natural products that could be derived from green plants, and the compounds he synthesized were used as pigments and tanning agents for leather. In 1935, he was assigned to develop an insecticide. At that time the only available insecticides were either expensive natural products or synthetics ineffective against insects; the only compounds that were both effective and inexpensive were the arsenic compounds, which were just as poisonous to human beings and other mammals. Müller noticed that insects absorbed and processed chemicals much differently than the higher animals, and he postulated that for this reason there must be some material that was toxic to insects alone. After testing the biological effects of hundreds of different chemicals, in 1939 he discovered that the compound DDT met most of his design criteria. First synthesized in 1873 by German chemist Othmar Zeidler, who had not known of its insecticide potential, DDT could be sprayed as an emulsion with water or could be mixed with talcum or chalk powder and dusted on target areas. It was first used against the Colorado potato beetle in Switzerland in 1939; it was patented in 1940 and went on the market in 1942.

Müller had set out to find a specific compound that would be cheap, odorless, long-lasting, fast in killing insects, and safe for plants and animals. He almost managed it. DDT in short term application is so non-toxic to human beings that it can be applied directly on the skin without ill effect. It is cheap and easy to make, and it usually needs to be applied only once during a growing season, unlike biodegradable pesticides which must often be applied several times, in larger amounts and at much higher cost. Typhus and malaria are very severe, often fatal illnesses, which are carried by body lice and mosquitoes respectively; in the 1940s several potentially severe epidemics of these diseases were averted by dusting the area and the human population with DDT. The insecticide saved many lives during World War II and increased the effectiveness of Allied forces. Soldiers fighting in both the Mediterranean and the tropics were dusted with DDT to kill lice, and entire islands were sprayed by air before invasions.

Despite these successes, environmentalists were concerned from the time DDT was introduced about the dangers of its indiscriminate use. DDT was so effective that all the insects in a dusted area were killed, even beneficial ones, eradicating the food source from many birds and other small creatures. Müller and other scientists were actually aware of these concerns, and as early as 1945 they had attempted to find some way to reduce DDT's toxicity to beneficial insects, but they were unsuccessful. Müller also believed that insecticides must be biodegradable.

Hailed as a miracle compound, DDT came into wide use, and the impact on beneficial insects was not the only problem. Because it was such a stable compound, DDT built up in the environment; this was a particular problem once it began to be used for agricultural purposes and applied over wide areas year after year. Higher animals, unharmed by individual small doses, began to accumulate large amounts of DDT in their tissues (called bio-accumulation). This had serious effects and several bird species, most notably the bald eagle, were almost wiped out because frequent exposure to the chemical caused the shells of their eggs to be thin and fragile. Many insects also developed resistances to DDT, and so larger and larger amounts of the compound needed to be applied yearly, increasing the rate of bio-accumulation. The substance was eventually banned in many countries; in 1972 it was banned in the United States.

In addition to the 1948 Nobel Prize in physiology or medicine, Müller received an honorary doctorate from the University of Thessalonica in Greece in recognition of DDT's impact on the Mediterranean region. He retired from Geigy in 1961, continuing his research in a home laboratory. He died on October 13, 1965.

SELECTED WRITINGS BY MÜLLER:

Periodicals

(With P. Läuger and H. Martin) "Über Konstitution und toxische Wirkung von natürlichen und neuen synthetischen insektentötenden Stoffen," *Helvetica Chimica Acta,* Volume 27, 1944.
"Dichlorodiphenyltrichloroäthan und neuere Inzekticide," *Les Prix Nobel en 1948,* Stockholm, 1949.

SOURCES:

Books

Dictionary of Scientific Biography, Scribner, 1980.
Nobel Prize Winners, H.W. Wilson, 1987.

—*Sketch by Gail B. C. Marsella*

Robert S. Mulliken
1896-1986
American chemical physicist

Robert S. Mulliken's early interests and education were in the field of chemistry, especially in the structure of molecules. He eventually discovered that quantum mechanical theory offered an effective tool for the study of the topic and switched his allegiance to the field of physics, a subject that he taught for more than three decades at various institutions. His work ultimately contributed to the establishment of a new interdisciplinary subject, combining these two great fields of science in what is known as chemical physics. Mulliken's research has led to a new understanding of the way in which atoms are held together in molecules and the ways in which molecules interact with each other. In recognition of these accomplishments, he was awarded the 1966 Nobel Prize in chemistry.

Robert Sanderson Mulliken was born in Newburyport, Massachusetts, on June 7, 1896. His father was Samuel Parsons Mulliken, a professor of organic chemistry at the Massachusetts Institute of Technology (MIT). His mother was Katherine W. Mulliken, which was her maiden name as well as her married name. Robert's father was the first Mulliken in many generations not to choose a seafaring career. In fact, his grandfather (Samuel Parson's father) had chosen to become a ship's captain rather than attend college, as his parents had wanted.

Mulliken's interest in chemistry developed early, largely as a result of his father's work. Through his father, Robert Mulliken made an important professional contact early in his life. Arthur A. Noyes, later to become one of the nation's and world's leading physical chemists, was also a resident of Newburyport and faculty member at MIT. While still in high school, the young Robert proofread galleys of his father's textbooks, books that were later to become standards in the field and make the elder Mulliken famous. Robert Mulliken wrote in "Molecular Scientists and Molecular Science: Some Reminisces" that the proofreading experience helped him to become "well acquainted with the rather formidable names of organic compounds."

Career Influenced by Early Training

In a 1975 interview with the *Journal of Chemical Education,* Mulliken praised the education he had at Newburyport High School. While there, he studied a full academic program, including Latin, French, German, physics, biology, and mathematics. The salutatory address he gave at his high school graduation made it clear that his scientific interests were fixed even at that early age. The topic of his address was "The Electron: What It Is and What It Does."

There seemed little doubt that Mulliken would follow his father to MIT and major in chemistry. In 1913, he was awarded a Wheelwright Scholarship, given to young men from Newburyport that allowed him to enroll at MIT. Once settled into MIT, Mulliken began to consider the possibility of concentrating in chemical engineering rather than chemistry. During one summer, he took part in a Chemical

Engineering Practice School that required him to spend a week at each of a half dozen chemical plants in Massachusetts and Maine. He found the experience highly rewarding.

Mulliken eventually returned to chemistry, however, and graduated with a bachelor of science in that field in 1917, just as the United States was entering World War I. Instead of going on to graduate school, therefore, he took a job in war-related research at American University in Washington, D.C. His job was to work on the development of poison gases, but he was not very good at the work. On one occasion, he spilled mustard gas on the floor, much to the horror of his superior, James B. Conant. He later came down with a severe case of the flu and was still recovering in the hospital when the war ended. After the war, Mulliken briefly held a job at the New Jersey Zinc Company, where he studied the effects of zinc oxide and carbon black on the compounding of rubber. He apparently realized rather quickly that this was not the kind of work he wanted to do, and he enrolled in a doctoral program in chemistry at the University of Chicago.

Research Focuses on Isotopes at Chicago and Harvard

He chose Chicago because he wanted especially to work with Professor W. D. Harkins on the study of atomic nuclei. The work to which he was assigned involved finding ways to separate the isotopes of mercury from each other. Mulliken experienced extraordinary success in this line of research and, in 1921, he received his Ph.D. for this work. He went on to improve the system by which mercury isotopes can be separated from each other and later called the construction of this "isotope factory" one of his proudest accomplishments.

One reason for his sense of pride was that it confirmed that he had finally become a "proper experimentalist." In his earlier years, he had not been very proficient in the laboratory (witness the mustard gas event), leading Noyes to express some doubt that he could become a successful researcher. Although Mulliken's practical skills obviously had improved at Chicago, it was ultimately as a theorist, and not an experimentalist, that he was to gain his greatest fame.

In 1923, Mulliken applied to have his National Research Council Fellowship extended for two more years. He was told, however, that he would have to go to a different institution and study a different field of chemistry. His request to work with British physicist **Ernest Rutherford** on radioactivity was denied by the board, so he chose instead to go to Harvard. At Harvard, he became interested in studying the spectral lines of diatomic molecules, a subject he began with the compound boron nitride (BN). His hypothesis was that when analyzed scientists would find isotopes (such as boron–10 and boron–11) present in the molecule. When he actually carried out this research, his hypothesis was confirmed. Faint bands reflecting the presence of less abundant isotopes— bands that no one had noticed to that point—were apparent.

European Visits Motivate the Study of Quantum Theory in Chemistry

A turning point in Mulliken's career was marked by two visits to Europe in 1925 and 1927. During these visits, he made an effort to visit all of the major researchers who were working on molecular spectra. But, inevitably, he also came into contact with physicists who were developing the quantum theory.

The 1920s were a decade of revolution in physics as researchers were developing, elaborating, and refining the new view of physics arising out of the work of **Max Planck**, **Louis Victor de Broglie**, **Albert Einstein**, **Erwin Schrödinger**, and others. A very few chemists—**Linus Pauling**, perhaps most obviously— were also looking for ways in which quantum theory could be used to explain chemical phenomena.

Mulliken had already been introduced to quantum theory at MIT and Chicago. But it was his trips to Europe that really focused his attention on the problem that had now become foremost in his mind: how quantum theory could be used to explain the structure of molecules. He explained later in "Molecular Scientists and Molecular Science: Some Reminisces" that his earlier studies of spectra had "led naturally to attempts also to understand molecular electronic states as more or less like those of atoms."

Perhaps the most important single event on his visits to Europe was his meeting with the German chemist, Friedrich Hund. Hund had been working on many of the same problems as had Mulliken with one important exception. While Mulliken was using a deterministic form of quantum mechanics, stressing a more narrow range of likely outcomes for experiments in the field, Hund had employed the uncertainty principle developed by **Werner Karl Heisenberg** in his study of molecular electronic structure. The uncertainty principle states that it is impossible to specify precisely both the position and momentum of a particle at the same time. Applying such a concept to the study of quantum mechanics opened up possibilities for Hund's work. Mulliken began to adopt Hund's approach and soon achieved success. In 1928, he published a classic paper that was crucial in his being awarded the Nobel Prize in 1966. In that paper, Mulliken proposed an entirely new model for molecular structure. Previously, chemists had assumed that when two or more atoms combine to form a molecule, the atoms tend to retain their independent characteristics. The molecule was thought to be an assemblage of essentially independent, recognizable atoms "tied together" in some fashion.

Mulliken argued that individual atoms lose their identify when they combine to form a molecule. Electrons that once "belonged" to one or another atom in the molecule now became part of an overall molecular structure. The bonding electrons involved in the molecular structure now had energy levels whose quantum mechanical descriptions were determined by *molecular* characteristics, not *atomic* characteristics.

In succeeding decades, Mulliken derived a number of specific applications from this general theory. For example, he found ways to measure the relative ionic character of a chemical bond and the properties of conjugated double bonds using this model.

Serves on Faculties at New York University and Chicago

Mulliken's first academic appointment was as assistant professor of physics at the Washington Square College of New York University in 1926. The appointment was significant in that Mulliken, trained as a chemist, was now recognized as a physicist also. He held the New York position until 1928 when he was invited to join the faculty at the University of Chicago. Again, this appointment was in the department of physics, as associate professor. In 1931, he was promoted to full professor.

Mulliken continued to hold an appointment at Chicago for the rest of his academic career, a period of more than five decades. From 1956 to 1961, he was Ernest de Witt Burton Distinguished Service Professor of Physics and Chemistry and, at the end of that period, he was given a joint appointment as professor of physics and chemistry. Beginning in 1965, Mulliken also spent part of each year at Florida State University in Tallahassee, where he was a distinguished research professor of chemical physics at the Institute of Molecular Biophysics.

Mulliken was married on December 24, 1929, to the former Mary Helen von Noé, daughter of a colleague in the geology department at the University of Chicago. The Mullikens had two daughters, Lucia Maria and Valerie Noé. Mrs. Mulliken accompanied her husband on many of his overseas trips, one of which was particularly noteworthy. During their 1932 trip to Europe, Mrs. Mulliken came down with an infection of the appendix, a condition that grew increasingly more severe as they moved from city to city on the continent. Eventually an operation in Berlin solved the problem. Their stay in Berlin was further troubled, however, by the growing aggressiveness of Nazi supporters. In "Molecular Scientists and Molecular Science: Some Reminisces" Mulliken described how upset his German colleagues had become about "coming events" and how he himself could "see and hear the Nazi storm troopers marching up and down in the street" below his hotel room early every morning.

During World War II, Mulliken served as director of editorial work and information at the University of Chicago's Plutonium Project, a division of the Manhattan Project, set up to develop the atomic bomb. He also served briefly as Scientific Attaché at the American Embassy in London in 1955. As Mulliken approached formal retirement age in 1961, he was offered a number of prestigious teaching and lecturing assignments. He was the Baker Lecturer at Cornell University in 1960 and the Silliman Lecturer at Yale in 1965. In the latter year, he also served as John van Geuns Visiting Professor at the University of Amsterdam.

Mulliken continued working on problems of molecular structure, molecular spectra, and molecular interactions throughout his life. In 1952, for example, he applied quantum mechanical theory to an analysis of the interaction between Lewis acid and base molecules. In the 1960s, his studies of molecular structure and spectra ranged from the simplest of cases (hydrogen and diatomic helium, for example) to complex molecular aggregates. During this decade, Mulliken also received most of the major awards available to chemists in the United States, including the Gilbert Newton Lewis, Theodore William Richards, John G. Kirkwood, and Willard Gibbs Medals and the Peter Debye Award. Mulliken died in Arlington, Virginia, on October 31, 1986.

SELECTED WRITINGS BY MULLIKEN:

Books

Selected Papers of Robert S. Mulliken, edited by D. A. Ramsay and Jurgen Hinze, University of Chicago Press, 1975.

Periodicals

"Molecular Scientists and Molecular Science: Some Reminiscences," *The Journal of Chemical Physics,* November 15, 1965, pp. S2-S11.

SOURCES:

Books

Current Biography 1967, H. W. Wilson, 1967, pp. 307–309.
McGraw-Hill Modern Men of Science, Volume 1, McGraw-Hill, 1984, pp. 342–343.

Nobel Lectures in Chemistry, 1963–1970, Amsterdam, 1972, pp. 161–162.

Periodicals

Nachtrieb, Norman H., "Interview with Robert S. Mulliken," *Journal of Chemical Education,* September, 1975, pp. 560–564.

—*Sketch by David E. Newton*

Kary Mullis
1944-
American biochemist

Kary Mullis is a biochemist who designed polymerase chain reaction (PCR), a fast and effective technique for reproducing specific genes or DNA fragments that is able to create billions of copies in a few hours. Mullis invented the technique in 1983 while working for Cetus, a California biotechnology firm. After convincing his colleagues of the importance of his idea, they eventually joined him in creating a method to apply it. They developed a machine which automated the process, controlling the chain reaction by varying the temperature. Widely available because it is now relatively inexpensive, PCR has revolutionized not only the biotechnology industry, but many other scientific fields, and it has important applications in law enforcement, as well as history. Mullis shared the 1993 Nobel Prize in chemistry with **Michael Smith** of the University of British Columbia, who also developed a method for manipulating genetic material.

Kary Banks Mullis was born in Lenoir, North Carolina, on December 28, 1944, the son of Cecil Banks Mullis and Bernice Alberta (Barker) Fredericks. He grew up in Columbia, North Carolina, a small city in the foothills of the Blue Ridge Mountains, where his temperament and his curiosity about the world set him apart from others. As a high school student, for example, Mullis designed a rocket that carried a frog some 7,000 feet in the air before splitting open and allowing the live cargo to parachute safely back to earth. Even at a young age, Mullis was considered a maverick and nonconformist. He entered Georgia Institute of Technology in 1962 and studied chemistry. As an undergraduate, he created a laboratory for manufacturing poisons and explosives. He also invented an electronic device stimulated by brain waves that could control a light switch.

Kary Mullis

Upon graduation from Georgia Tech in 1966 with a B.S. degree in chemistry, Mullis entered the doctoral program in biochemistry at the University of California, Berkeley. In Berkeley at that time there was growing interest in hallucinogenic drugs; Mullis taught a controversial neurochemistry class on the subject. His thesis adviser, Joe Nielands, told *Omni* that as a graduate student Mullis was "very undisciplined and unruly; a free spirit." Yet at the age of twenty-four, he wrote a paper on the structure of the universe that was published by *Nature* magazine. He was awarded his Ph.D. in 1973, and he accepted a teaching position at the University of Kansas Medical School in Kansas City, where he stayed for four years. In 1977, he assumed a postdoctoral fellowship at the University of California, San Francisco. After two years there, discouraged by universities and uncertain what to do with his life, he left and took a job in a restaurant. One day his graduate advisor encountered him there and convinced him that he was wasting both his mind and his education waiting tables. In 1979, he accepted a position as a research scientist with a growing biotech firm, Cetus Corporation, in Emeryville, California, which was in the business of synthesizing chemicals used by other scientists in genetic cloning.

Invents PCR to Reproduce Small Sections of DNA

At Cetus, Mullis was bored by the routine demands of corporate life. He spent much of his time sunbathing on the roof and writing computer programs that would automatically respond to certain kinds of administrative requests. "I'd no real responsibilities for about two years," he told *Omni* magazine. "I was playing," he told *Parade Magazine.* "I think really good science doesn't come from hard work. The striking advances come from people on the fringes, being playful." He conceived of polymerase chain reaction (PCR) while driving out to his ranch in Mendocino county and thinking, as he describes it, somewhat "randomly" about ways to look at individual sections of the genetic code.

Reproducing deoxyribonucleic acid or DNA had long been an obstacle to anyone working in molecular biology. The most effective way to reproduce DNA was by cloning, but however much of a scientific advance this process represented, it was still cumbersome in certain respects. DNA strands are long and complicated, composed of many different chromosomes; the problem was that most genetic engineering projects were tasks that involved tiny fragments of the DNA molecule, almost infinitesimal sections of a single strand. Cloning works by inserting the DNA into bacteria and waiting while the reproducing bacteria creates copies of it. The cloning process is not only time-consuming, it replicates the whole strand, increasing the complexity. The revolutionary advantage of PCR is its selectivity: It is a process that reproduces specific genes on the DNA strand millions or billions of times, effectively allowing scientists to amplify or enlarge parts of the DNA molecule for further study.

Mullis remembers that it took a long time to convince his colleagues at Cetus of the importance of this discovery. "No one could see any reason why it wouldn't work," he told *Popular Science.* "But no one seemed particularly enthusiastic about it either." Once they had become convinced of its importance, however, PCR became the focus of intensive research at Cetus. Scientists there developed a commercial version of the process and a machine called the Thermal Cycler; with the addition of the chemical building blocks of DNA, called nucleotides, and a biochemical catalyst called polymerase, the machine would perform the process automatically on a target piece of DNA. The machine is so economical that even a small laboratory can afford it, and the technique, as one microbiologist told *Time,* "can reproduce genetic material even more efficiently than nature."

The selectivity of the PCR process, as well as the fact that it is simple and economical, have profoundly changed the course of research in many fields. In an interview with *Omni,* Mullis remarked of PCR: "It's so widely used by molecular biologists that its future direction is the future of molecular biology itself." In the field of genetics, the process has been particularly important to the Human Genome Project—the massive effort to map human DNA. Nucleotide sequences that have already been mapped can now be filed in a computer, and PCR enables scientists to use these codes to rebuild the sequences, reproducing them in a Thermal Cycler. The ability of this process to reproduce specific genes, thus effectively enlarging them for easier study, has made it possible for virologists to develop extremely sensitive tests for acquired immunodeficiency syndrome (AIDS), capable of detecting the virus at early stages of infection. There are many other medical applications for PCR, and it has been particularly useful for diagnosing genetic predispositions to diseases such as sickle cell anemia and cystic fibrosis.

PCR has also revolutionized evolutionary biology, making it possible to examine the DNA of woolly mammoths and the remains of ancient humans found in bogs. PCR can also answer questions about more recent history; it has been used to identify the bones of Czar Nicholas II of Russia who was executed during the Bolshevik revolution, and scientists at the National Museum of Health and Medicine in Washington, DC, are preparing to use PCR to amplify DNA from the hair of Abraham Lincoln, as well blood stains and bone fragments, in an effort to determine whether he suffered from a disease called Marfan's syndrome. In law enforcement, PCR has made genetic "fingerprinting" more accurate and effective; it has been used to identify murder victims, and to overturn the sentences of men wrongly convicted of rape. Some have suggested the PCR can be used to create tags or markers for industrial and biotechnological products, including oil and other hazardous chemicals, to insure that they are used and disposed of in a safe manner.

Cetus awarded Mullis only ten-thousand dollars for developing the PCR patent. Frustrated both by the size of this award and the restrictions the company continued to place on his scientific research, Mullis left Cetus in 1986. He became director of molecular biology at Xytronyx, a San Diego research firm, but two years later, again frustrated with the routine of corporate research, he left to become a private biochemical research consultant. The Du Pont Corporation challenged Cetus for Mullis's patent for PCR, filing suit in the late 1980s; they argued that while working for them in the early 1970s, Nobel laureate **Har Gobind Khorana** had written a paper which anticipated the process. Although he had already left Cetus, Mullis agreed to testify on their behalf, and in February 1991 a federal jury decided against Du Pont. That same year, Cetus sold the process to Hoffman-LaRouche, Inc., for 300 million dollars, the most money ever paid for a patent. When he invents something again, Mullis told *Omni*, "I'm not going to hand it over to some company like Cetus without something saying it's mine. If anyone makes $300 million off it, I'm going to be part of that."

In 1990, Mullis received both the Preis Biochemische Analytik Award from the German Society of Clinical Chemistry and the Allen Award from the American Society of Human Genetics; in 1991, he received the Gairdner Foundation Award and the National Biotech Award. In 1993, he was presented with the Japan Prize, in addition to the Nobel Prize. He is a member of the American Chemical Society. He has been married and divorced three times and is the father of three children. He works and lives in an apartment overlooking the Pacific Ocean in La Jolla, California.

SOURCES:

Periodicals

Dwyer, Jim, "The Quirky Genius Who Is Changing Our World," *Parade Magazine,* October 10, 1993, p.8.
Liversidge, Anthony, "Interview: Kary Mullis," *Omni,* April 1992, p. 69.
Marini, Richard A., "Polymerase Chain Reaction," *Popular Science,* May, 1992, pp. 99–100, 115–16.
Nash, J. Madeleine, "Ultimate Gene Machine: A Method of Multiplying DNA is Revolutionizing Medical Diagnosis, Speeding Forensic Work and Solving Old Mysteries," *Time,* August 12, 1991, p. 54.
New York Times, October 12, 1993, p. 89.

—*Sketch by Benedict A. Leerburger*

Walter Munk
1917-
Austrian-born American geophysicist and oceanographer

For more than four decades Walter Munk has been a leading oceanographer and geophysicist whose research at the University of California at San Diego's Scripps Institution of Oceanography has contributed to an understanding of ocean currents and circulation, tides, wave propagation, and irregularities in the rotation of the earth. Munk's work has ranged from helping to predict the tides prior to the D-Day invasion of Normandy during World War II to a long-range international project to detect global warming by measuring ocean temperatures with sound waves. During his career Munk has been a pioneer in adapting new technology to oceanographic and geophysical research. He was an early user of scuba diving equipment and was among the first scientists who employed computers to analyze geophysical data.

Walter Heinrich Munk was born on October 19, 1917, in Vienna, Austria, the son of Hans and Rega Brunner Munk; the family moved to the United States in 1932 where Munk worked in a bank owned by his grandfather. He began his study of physics at Columbia University but transferred to the California Institute of Technology in Pasadena where he earned a bachelor's degree in physics in 1939, the same year he became a U.S. citizen. Munk received a master's degree in geophysics from Cal Tech in 1941. He then attended the Scripps Institution and in 1947 earned his doctorate in oceanography from the University of California.

Observes A-Bomb Test from Raft

Munk enlisted in the Army during World War II and with Harald Sverdrup, then the director of the Scripps Institution, developed a method for forecasting the height of breaking waves and the condition of surf on beaches. This system was vital in planning for the successful Normandy invasion and a number of other amphibious landings in the South Pacific. During the war, Munk also served in the U.S. Army's Ski Battalion, as a meteorologist for the Army Air Force, and as an oceanographer with the University of California Division of War Research. Following the war, Munk participated in studies of ocean currents and waves created by nuclear explosions during weapons testing at the Bikini Atoll in the South Pacific Ocean in 1946, where he observed one test from a raft anchored just ten miles from ground zero. Munk described the blast to Associated Press correspondent Connie Cass in an interview published in the *Orange County Register:* "It's stunning; it's horrible. It's not dark, it's quite white. You see the boiling and the water vapor above you, like a curtain coming down all around you."

After earning his Ph.D., Munk joined the faculty at the University of California's Scripps Institution as an assistant professor of geophysics in 1947. Two years he later became an associate professor. Munk was named a professor of geophysics in 1954 and was appointed a member of the university's Institute of Geophysics, which was headquartered in Los Angeles. In 1960 Munk went on to establish a branch of the institute in La Jolla, near San Diego, at what later became the University of California at San Diego. The new branch was created to study the atmosphere, oceans, and interior of the earth using experimental and mathematical physics. Munk served as its director and as associate director of the system-wide

University of California Institute, which was renamed the Institute of Geophysics and Planetary Physics, until 1982.

In the early 1960s, Munk began studying the attenuation or loss of intensity in ocean waves. By using pressure sensing devices that were lowered to the ocean floor at six different locations, Munk and colleague Frank Snodgrass were able to track very long ocean swells over a distance of 12,000 kilometers across the Pacific Ocean from Australia to Alaska. In 1969 Munk began exploring ways of improving tide prediction. Munk developed sophisticated pressure-sensing instruments that were dropped to the ocean floor and then retrieved after an acoustical signal returned instrument-filled capsules back to the sea surface. The instruments allowed Munk to measure tides in the deep sea with precision off the coast of California, in the Antarctic Ocean, and in the Atlantic Ocean in the Bay of Biscay and south of Bermuda. This led Munk to further research in using sound waves as a tool to monitor the seas.

Munk's work has won him international recognition. He was elected to the National Academy of Sciences in 1956 and to the Royal Society of London in 1976. In 1993 he was awarded the Vetlesen Prize, considered to be the premier honor in the earth sciences. In addition, he is a member or fellow of more than a dozen professional societies, has been a Guggenheim Fellow three times and has published more than two hundred scientific papers. Munk and his wife, Judith, an architect, have two children, Edith and Kendall.

Attempts to Confirm Global Warming

Munk continues to be fascinated by the ocean and is involved in what he described to Cass as the most exciting experiment of his life, the effort to detect global warming by measuring ocean temperatures with sound waves. The $35-million project involving scientists from seven nations is called Acoustic Thermometry of Ocean Climate (ATOC) and resulted in part from a successful experiment headed by Munk in 1991 off Heard Island in the southern Indian Ocean. That test proved that low-frequency sounds emitted by underwater speakers could be transmitted and picked up by listening devices up to 18,000 kilometers away. The Heard Island experiment showed that sound waves cross the earth's oceans in sound channels, 3,000-foot-deep bands of water that are unaffected by surface climate fluctuations. These channels act as a kind of superhighway, restricting and focusing sound waves to particular paths so they do not dissipate quickly and can be heard over long distances. Though ATOC has been put on hold due to environmental concerns, the project was designed to duplicate the Heard Island work on a much larger scale. Transmitting stations off

California and Kauai, Hawaii, would send pulses of sound to listening stations throughout the Pacific basin. Scientists would then use the transoceanic channels to take water-temperature measurements over the entire Pacific, hoping to gain enough data to detect whether the earth's surface, seventy percent of which is ocean, has become measurably warmer over a period as short as one to two decades.

SELECTED WRITINGS BY MUNK:

Books

(With G. J. F. Macdonald) *The Rotation of the Earth: A Geophysical Discussion,* Cambridge University Press, 1960.

SOURCES:

Books

Modern Men of Science, McGraw-Hill, 1968.
Modern Scientists and Engineers, McGraw-Hill, 1980, pp. 339–340.

Periodicals

Cass, Connie, "Life at Sea," *Orange County Register,* April 21, 1993.

—*Sketch by Joel Schwarz*

William P. Murphy
1892-1987
American physician and pathologist

William P. Murphy won the 1934 Nobel Prize for physiology or medicine for his role in the discovery of liver as the successful dietary treatment for pernicious anemia, a deadly disorder in which bone marrow ceases to produce the fully mature red blood cells needed to carry oxygen to all parts of the body. Murphy's professional persistence following the discovery led to the simple, effective, and inexpensive treatment of the disease by intramuscular injection of a highly-concentrated liver extract. Murphy shared the Nobel Prize with **George Hoyt Whipple**, who had observed that a diet of liver, kidney, meat, and vegetables had a regenerative effect on the blood of dogs in which he had induced anemia; and **George**

Richards Minot, who, building on Whipple's research, isolated liver as the effective dietary factor. Murphy and Minot collaborated on the highly successful study in which pernicious anemia patients were fed one-quarter to one-half pound of liver daily. Reputed for his diligence and dedication, Murphy assumed the painstaking, time-consuming responsibility of counting the microscopic reticulocytes (red blood cells) in the blood samples of pernicious anemia patients before and during the liver diet. The dramatic increase in reticulocytes in the samples following the patient's consumption of liver clearly identified the critical connection between liver ingestion and the production of mature red blood cells.

William Parry Murphy was born on February 6, 1892, in Stoughton, Wisconsin, to Congregational minister Thomas Francis Murphy and his wife, Rose Anna Parry. He attended public schools in Wisconsin and Oregon and received his B.A. in 1914 from the University of Oregon. Murphy taught high school math and physics for two years in Oregon before entering the University of Oregon Medical School in Portland, where he also worked in the anatomy department as a laboratory assistant. In 1918, he took a summer course at Rush Medical School in Chicago. He later received the William Stanislaus Murphy Fellowship award and entered Harvard Medical School in Boston, from which he graduated in 1922. He interned at Rhode Island Hospital, Providence, then returned to Boston to become an assistant resident physician at Peter Bent Brigham Hospital.

Two Men Battle Pernicious Anemia

In 1925, Minot had put pernicious anemia patients at Boston's Huntington Memorial Hospital on a liver-rich diet and observed their improvement. Wanting more evidence, he told no one of his experiment, not even the resident from Boston's Peter Bent Brigham Hospital whose collaboration he recruited. Minot was an attending physician at Brigham where Murphy, a hard-working resident with a keen interest in blood disorders, attracted his attention. Without saying why, Minot asked Murphy to feed liver to pernicious anemia patients at Brigham. Murphy followed Minot's instructions, and two independent surveys were underway at two different institutions.

Murphy encountered difficulties, however. Not only did he have to convince the hospital to obtain and prepare tender, palatable liver on a daily basis, he also had to convince patients to eat it every day. Murphy himself was a lover of liver—he ate it because he liked it. He virtually became a liver salesman to his patients and observed results identical to Minot's: he watched with excitement as life returned to patients who had been dying and, in fact, should have been dead.

Overcomes Obstacles to Therapy

The liver diet therapy for pernicious anemia presented certain problems. Patients found it difficult to eat half a pound of liver every day of their lives. Particularly troublesome was the question of how to feed it to patients so ill they could no longer eat. This problem was partially overcome by a suggestion from one of Murphy's female patients: Couldn't uncooked liver be pulverized and fed to patients in orange juice? Not too proud to listen to a suggestion from a nonprofessional, Murphy tried it. He and Minot literally force-fed their dying patients, pouring liquid liver into stomach tubes as long as the patient showed any sign of life. Within a week, patients who had been too ill to eat were sitting up asking for food.

Murphy, however, was not satisfied. The two doctors enlisted the expertise of Edwin J. Cohn, a physical chemistry professor at Harvard Medical School. Cohn chemically reduced large amounts of liver to a concentrated extract fifty to one hundred times more potent than the liver itself. Ingestion of three vials a day of this extract, which cost $17.00 a month, proved just as effective as the cheaper but less palatable liver diet, which cost approximately $5.50 a month. Still not satisfied, Murphy felt the cost of the extract was prohibitive for many people and continued to search for a less expensive method of administering it. He sought the help of Guy W. Clark of the Lederle Laboratories; soon they developed an extremely concentrated extract. Injected into the muscle only once a month, the extract provided the same therapeutic effect as the liver diet or the oral extract. The monthly cost of this injection was $1.20.

Medical professionals, however, virtually refused to believe the results of the carefully documented study, which Murphy and Minot presented at a medical meeting in Atlantic City in 1926. The treatment was entirely too simple. Pernicious anemia had been thought to be caused by some type of poison, and patients were treated with arsenic, blood transfusions, or removal of the spleen, the organ which breaks down red blood cells, all to no avail. But worldwide treatment by the liver diet soon convinced the skeptics. Murphy's lifesaving contribution to society was further advanced by Harvard physician William Castle, who, in 1948, isolated the active ingredient in liver which promoted the development of fully mature red blood cells in patients suffering from pernicious anemia. That factor, named cyanocobalamin for its high concentration of cobalt, is commonly called Vitamin B_{12}, which is now used universally via intramuscular injection for the lifesaving treatment of pernicious anemia.

In addition to working with Minot on the liver diet study, Murphy became Minot's partner in private practice in Boston. In 1924, he was appointed assistant in medicine at Harvard Medical School, promoted to associate in medicine at the Brigham Hospital in 1935, and became a senior associate in medicine and consultant in hematology there. Harvard and Brigham both granted him emeritus status in 1958, when he retired to a suburb of Boston. He married Pearl Harriet Adams in 1919; they had a son, William Murphy, Jr., and a daughter, Priscilla Adams. Murphy's honors include the Cameron Prize and Lectureship of the University of Edinburgh, the Bronze Medal of the American Medical Association, and the Gold Medal of the Massachusetts Humane Society. He died on October 9, 1987, in Brookline, Massachusetts.

SELECTED WRITINGS BY MURPHY:

Periodicals

"Treatment of Pernicious Anemia by a Special Diet," *Journal of the American Medical Association,* Volume 87, 1926, pp. 470–476.
"The Nature of the Material in Liver Effective in Pernicious Anemia I," *Journal of Biological Chemistry,* Volume 74, 1927, pp. 69–74.

SOURCES:

Books

De Kruif, Paul, *Men against Death,* Harcourt, 1932, pp. 108–114.
Nobel Prize Winners, H. W. Wilson, 1987, pp. 746–747.
The Nobel Prize Winners—Physiology or Medicine, Salem Press, 1991, pp. 393–398.

Periodicals

Science News Letter, November, 1934, pp. 276–277.

—*Sketch by David Petechuk*

Joseph E. Murray
1919-

American surgeon

Joseph E. Murray has combined the traits of bench and bedside, of the basic scientific researcher along with the clinical physician, to pioneer renal (kidney) transplantation. Since his first successful kidney transplant in 1954, over a quarter of a million have taken place worldwide. Organ transplants, once a medical dream—some would even say fantasy—have become a commonplace reality, with the list of donor organs ever expanding: liver, heart, lung, and pancreas. In 1990 the Nobel committee in Stockholm honored Murray for his work that has brought prolonged life to millions by awarding him the Nobel Prize for physiology or medicine.

Joseph Edward Murray was born on April 1, 1919, in Milford, Massachusetts. The son of William Andrew Murray and Mary DePasquale Murray, he grew up and went to high school in Milford, excelling in baseball as well as science. He entered Holy Cross College upon graduation from high school and earned an A.B. in 1940, and then went on to Harvard University to earn his medical degree in 1943. At Peter Bent Brigham Hospital, a Harvard-affiliated hospital, Murray interned in surgery for one year before the U. S. Army gave him a commission in the Medical Corps and assigned him to Valley Forge General Hospital. For the next three years Murray worked in plastic surgery, his specialties being reconstructive surgery of the eye and hand. He performed over 1,800 operations in this period, working under and learning from Drs. J. Barrett Brown and Bradford Cannon. It was a training that would stand Murray in good stead with his later research, for one of the major problems plastic surgeons had to deal with was the rejection of skin grafts by the immune system. Murray and other plastic surgeons soon learned that grafts would take between identical twins.

Joins Renal Transplant Team at Harvard

Returning from the military in 1947, Murray assumed a residency at the Peter Bent Brigham Hospital (now Brigham and Women's Hospital). His first love continued to be plastic surgery, but this was a fledgling discipline in the late 1940s and Murray was encouraged to go into general surgery, keeping plastic surgery as a sideline. This he did, soon winning a reputation for his head and neck surgical reconstructions on cancer patients and gaining recognition for the discipline of plastic surgery in the process. Murray was also drawn to the work of a team of doctors at Brigham Hospital who were studying end-stage renal disease, and one of the directions their researches was taking was transplantation. Research had been progressing over the past half century on kidney transplants in dogs, but there had never been a successful human transplant. These Harvard researchers, led by John Merrill and David Hume, had been doing experiments transplanting kidneys from cadavers onto the thigh of patients with kidney failure, grafting the third kidney to the femoral vessel of the recipient. One such thigh transplant functioned for about six months, enough time to allow the patient's own kidneys to heal and resume functioning. Kidney

dialysis was also being perfected at this time, but Murray felt that it was only a temporary solution. He developed a surgical technique to connect the blood vessels of the donor kidney with those in the abdomen of the recipient, implanting the ureter directly into the urinary bladder.

All was in readiness to test the new procedure, except for the right patient: he or she would have to be one of a pair of identical twins with the other twin willing and able to donate a kidney, thus avoiding rejection by the immune system of the recipient. Such an opportunity came in December, 1954, when the Herrick brothers turned up at Brigham Hospital. Richard Herrick had end-stage renal failure and his twin, Ronald, was prepared to donate a kidney. Murray reasoned there should be no problem with rejection as the introduced kidney would be genetically identical to the one being replaced. The subsequent operation, performed on December 23, lasted five and one-half hours and was an immediate success. Herrick lived another seven years on the transplanted kidney before dying of heart failure.

Searches for Immunosuppressant

Murray continued to perform more successful operations on identical twins, including Edith Helm, who went on to have children and grandchildren, but the real problem now became how to suppress the immune reaction so that the operation would be more generally available. At first Murray and other researchers tried total body X rays and infusions of bone marrow from the donor to adapt the recipient's immune system. In most cases the transplants functioned for several weeks, but there were many failures. Finally in 1959, after a course of total body X rays, a non-identical twin survived a kidney transplant from his brother and went on to lead a normal life. Later in 1959 two Boston hematologists, William Dameshek and Robert Schwartz, demonstrated that the compound 6-mercaptopurine would prevent a host animal from rejecting a foreign protein. This was the opening Murray was looking for, and working with chemists and other researchers, Murray developed a drug regimen to suppress the immune system and thus allow an organ from a non-related donor to be accepted by the recipient's body. In 1962 Murray successfully completed the first organ transplant from a cadaver.

Murray's successes became known worldwide and inspired other surgeons to experiment with a variety of organ transplants. With the development of less toxic immune suppressants such as azathioprine, transplants became a growth industry with registries for organs documented worldwide. In the first three decades after the development of the surgical technique, there had been 8,890 kidney transplants, 2,160 liver, 1673 heart, 413 pancreas, and 67 heart-lung transplants in the U.S. alone. The success rate for kidney transplants is high: the new kidney thrives for at least ten years in 70 percent of the patients. A related medical benefit was the increase in research into the rejection phenomenon, and thus into the functioning of the human immune system, research that has proved invaluable with the onset of Acquired Immunodeficiency Syndrome (AIDS).

After this work on renal transplants, Murray went back to his first love, plastic surgery, developing ways to repair inborn facial defects in children. He headed the plastic surgery divisions of Peter Bent Brigham Hospital from 1951–1986 and Children's Hospital Medical Center from 1972–1985, and he has also been a professor of surgery at Harvard Medical School since 1970. Murray was the recipient of the Gold Medal from the International Society of Surgeons in 1963. Four years after retiring from surgery, but not from administrative duties at Brigham Hospital, Murray was awarded the Nobel Prize for physiology or medicine along with **E. Donnall Thomas,** whose work in bone marrow transplants was closely related to Murray's research. The two split the $703,000 award.

Murray's private life is as full as his professional life. Married in 1945 to Virginia Link, he has six children: Virginia, Margaret, Joseph, Katherine, Thomas, and Richard. An avid mountaineer, he was 52 when he climbed the Matterhorn, and he has trekked in high mountain areas in India, China, and Nepal. Joseph Murray is a man for whom—as a sign in his office says—difficulties are opportunities. By tackling the difficult problem of organ transplants, he provided a definitive solution to end-stage renal disease as well as stimulating worldwide research into immunology. His work in craniofacial reconstruction as a plastic surgeon has not only mended and saved lives, but also enlarged the scope and diversity of plastic surgery.

SELECTED WRITINGS BY MURRAY:

Periodicals

"Organ Transplantation: Status and a Look into the Future," *New York Journal of Medicine,* October 1, 1961, pp. 3245–3248.

"Organ Transplantation—The Kidney and the Skin," *Southern Medical Journal 55,* September, 1962, pp. 890–893.
"Prolonged Survival of Human-Kidney Homografts by Immunosuppressive Drug Therapy," *New England Journal of Medicine,* June 13, 1963, pp. 1315–1323.
"Human Organ Transplantation: Background and Consequences," *Science,* June 5, 1992, pp. 1411–1416.

SOURCES:

Periodicals

Goldwyn, Robert M., "Joseph E. Murray, M. D., Nobelist," *Plastic and Reconstructive Surgery,* June, 1991, pp. 1110–1112.
Jurkiewicz, Maurice J., "Nobel Laureate: Joseph E. Murray, Clinical Surgeon, Scientist, Teacher," *Archives of Surgery,* November, 1990, pp. 1423–1424.
Los Angeles Times, October 9, 1990, pp. A1, A23.
Moore, F.D., "A Nobel Award to Joseph E. Murray, M. D.," *Archives of Surgery,* May, 1992, pp. 627–632.
New York Times, October 9, 1990, p. C3.
Noe, Joel, "An Interview with Joseph E. Murray, M. D.," *Annals of Plastic Surgery,* January, 1984, pp. 84–89.
Palca, Joseph, "Overcoming Rejection to Win a Nobel Prize," *Science,* April 26, 1990, p. 378.
Sweeney, Francis, "Joseph E. Murray on the Mountaintop," *America,* March 2, 1991, p. 230.
Time, October 22, 1990, p. 62.
Washington Post, October 9, 1990, pp, A1, A5.

—*Sketch by J. Sydney Jones*

Samuel Milton Nabrit
1905-
American biologist

Samuel Milton Nabrit is known for his research into animal regeneration, the ability of body parts to regrow or repair themselves after injury, and for his academic career as a promoter of science instruction among young African Americans. The first black Ph.D. from Brown University, Nabrit served as chairman of the biology department and as dean of the graduate school of arts and sciences at Atlanta University, and as president of Texas Southern University.

Born in Macon, Georgia, February 21, 1905 to James M. Nabrit, a Baptist minister and teacher, and Augusta Gertrude West Nabrit, Nabrit studied at Morehouse College, where he received his bachelor's degree in 1925. Taking to heart the desire to teach inherited from his father, Nabrit returned to Morehouse College as a professor of biology from 1925–31, while he attended Brown University, working towards his advanced degrees. He obtained his M.S. in 1928 and his Ph.D. in biology in 1932.

While teaching during the school year at Morehouse, Nabrit conducted research at the Marine Biological Laboratory in Woods Hole, Massachusetts, every summer from 1927 to 1932. His specialty was the regenerative abilities of fish, particularly studying their ability to regrow tail fins. He found that the size of the fin rays on fishes' fins determined the rate of regeneration. The results of his research were published in the *Biological Bulletin*. A citation presented to Nabrit on April 30, 1982, by the Beta Kappa Chi Scientific Honor Society to which Nabrit belonged, noted that a study published by Nabrit in 1928 was still being quoted in studies of animal regeneration as late as the 1980s.

After earning his doctorate in 1932, Nabrit was appointed chairman of Atlanta University's biology department, a position he held until 1947. He continued his regenerative research at Atlanta University, focusing on fish embryo regeneration in particular. His work was described in articles appearing in such scientific publications as the *Anatomical Record, Journal of Parasitology,* and the *Journal of Experimental Zoology.* In 1947, Nabrit became dean of Atlanta University's graduate school of arts and sciences. In 1955 he was appointed president of Texas Southern University, where he served until 1966. During his tenure as president, Nabrit also served as president of the Association of Colleges and Secondary Schools and as a member of the board of directors of the American Council on Education. He also joined several committees for the Departments of State and Health and Human Services, and was appointed by President Eisenhower to a six-year term on the National Science Board in 1956. In 1966 President Johnson selected Nabrit for a term on the Atomic Energy Commission. The following year Nabrit became director of the Southern Fellowships Fund, an operating agency of the Council of Southern Universities, where he stayed until his retirement in 1981.

Nabrit was one of the founders of Upward Bound, a program designed to increase the numbers of qualified youth staying in college beyond one year. While a guest speaker at Kashmere Gardens High School, Nabrit was told that most of the scholarship winners would drop out during their first year in college. Nabrit decided to do something about this problem. In 1957, scholarship winners and other high potential students were invited to Texas Southern for the summer, essentially enrolling in the college for 11 weeks. Three nationally established specialists in reading, logical thinking and mathematics were recruited to hold classes daily, and the students were paired with volunteers who stayed with them in the dormitories and tutored them every night. The number of students remaining in college was greatly increased by the program.

Speaking to Sharon F. Suer in a phone interview, Nabrit recalled that when he began his academic career the "leading scientist in our field . . . produced only one or two biology students. All of his students he steered into medicine. My notion was that we needed to increase the number of young people who would be able to get the Ph.D. in biology and all the other sciences. At Brown, where I was the first Negro to graduate with a Ph.D. in Biology, I made sure that the next four black Ph.D.s were all out of my lab."

Throughout his college career, Nabrit played baseball and football. The game he loved playing the most, though, and continued playing into the 1940's was bridge; he and his foursome became expert enough to advance to a national bridge championship. Nabrit married Constance T. Crocker in 1927; she passed away in 1984. They had no children. Dr. Nabrit still lives in Georgia.

SELECTED WRITINGS BY NABRIT:

Periodicals

"The Role of the Fin Rays in Tailfins of Fishes Fundulus and Goldfish," *Biological Bulletin,* April, 1929.
"The Role of the Basal Plate of the Tail in Regeneration of Fishes Fundulus," *Biological Bulletin,* February, 1931.
"Human Ecology in Georgia," *Science Education,* October, 1944.
"The Negro in Science," *Negro History Bulletin,* January, 1957.

SOURCES:

Books

Sammons, Vivian O., *Blacks in Science and Technology,* Hemisphere Publishing Corp. p. 179, 1990.

Other

Beta Kappa Chi, text of citation, April 30, 1982.
Nabrit, Samuel Milton, interview with Sharon F. Suer conducted January 18, 1994.

—Sketch by Sharon F. Suer

Takesi Nagata
1913-1991
Japanese geophysicist

Takesi Nagata was one of the first scientists to investigate the magnetic properties of volcanic rocks. Additional studies into what he termed thermoremanent magnetization (TRM) led to a renewal in the 1950s of the theory of continental drift and ocean floor spreading. Nagata was also an active field scientist, leading Japan's Antarctic expeditions in the mid- to late–1950s, and establishing a Japanese base there for the study of polar magnetism. His interests in space physics led to his becoming the primary geophysical investigator of lunar matter from the Apollo space missions. Additionally, Nagata was a

science administrator of international stature, organizing and chairing conferences and committees worldwide for the advancement of geophysical observation.

Born in Okazaki City, in the prefecture of Aichi, on June 24, 1913, Nagata graduated from Tokyo Imperial University (later the University of Tokyo) in 1936. He then became a research associate at the Earthquake Research Institute of the university, studying the electric and magnetic properties of seismic and volcanic occurrences and focusing particularly on volcanic rocks. It was in the late 1930s that he discovered the strong magnetism of such rocks, classifying both natural remanent (NRM) and thermoremanent magnetism of lavas as they cooled. In May, 1941, Nagata accepted a position as associate professor at the Geophysical Institute of Tokyo Imperial University, his research interests broadening to include rock magnetism in general and the measurement of the NRM of sedimentary rocks in hopes of uncovering the course of early development of the Earth. He continued his research during World War II in addition to working for the Japanese navy on the military applications of magnetism.

Takes on an International Research Agenda

After the war, Nagata became more involved in organizational work, heading various geophysical and geomagnetic research groups in Japan, founding the Society of Terrestrial Magnetism and Electricity of Japan among others. In 1951 he was a research fellow at the Department of Terrestrial Magnetism at the Carnegie Institute in Washington, D.C., a turning point in his career that pointed him in new research directions, particularly toward geomagnetism as it relates to the ionosphere and outer space. That same year he was awarded the prestigious Japan Academy prize in recognition for his work in rock magnetism, and the following year he became a full professor at the University of Tokyo.

With the advent of the International Geophysical Year from 1957 to 1958, Nagata pushed for Japan to mount an Antarctic expedition, which he led in 1956, establishing a Japanese observation base at Syowa Station. Nagata also led subsequent expeditions to the base, and later, after retirement from the University of Tokyo in 1973, he became the director general of Japan's newly created National Institute of Polar Research, responsible for overseeing the functions of Syowa Station, particularly the space launches from Antarctica to study the upper atmosphere. He also set up an additional two Japanese stations in Antarctica. Nagata's interest in space physics grew over the years: a full one-third of his four hundred professional articles deal with that subject. In the 1960s and 1970s much of his time was spent in studying lunar samples from the various Apollo missions, measuring and discovering surprisingly strong magnetism in various rocks, as well as high electrical conductivity of crystalline rock samples containing metallic iron.

From 1961, Nagata held an adjunct professorship at the University of Pittsburgh, where he continued to do research in between international meetings. But much of his time in later years was taken up with administration. He was the president of the International Association of Geomagnetism and Aeronomy (IAGA) from 1967 to 1971, as well as vice-president of the Scientific Committee on Antarctic Research (SCAR) from 1972 to 1976. Later honors included Japan's Order of Culture in 1974 and the Gold Medal from the Royal Astronomical Society of Great Britain in 1987. He was also elected a member of the National Academy of Sciences in the United States in 1959. Nagata remained active in scientific affairs until his death on June 3, 1991, at the age of seventy-seven. Two mountains were named after the renowned geophysicist: One is in the Pacific Ocean and the other in Victoria Land of Antarctica.

SELECTED WRITINGS BY NAGATA:

Books

Rock Magnetism, Maruzen, 1953.
*National Report of Japanese Antarctic Research Expeditions, 1958–1960,*Ministry of Education, 1960.
(With others) "Magnetic Properties of Apollo 11–17 Lunar Materials with Special Reference to Effects of Meteorite Impact," *Physical Properties,*Volume 3, Pergamon, 1974, pp. 2827–2839.

Periodicals

"Magnetism of the Earth's Crust and the Earth's Interior," *American Association of Petroleum Geologists' Bulletin,* Volume 49, number 3, 1965, p. 354.
"Effects of Uniaxal Compression on Remanent Magnetizations of Igneous Rocks," *Pure and Applied Geophysics,* Volume 78, 1970, pp. 100–109.
"Geomagnetic Secular Variation in the Antarctic Region during 1960–1975," *Nankyoku Shiryo,* Volume 74, 1982, pp. 27–44.
"Geophysical Studies on Mount Erebus," *Antarctic Journal of the United States,* Volume 19, number 5, 1985, pp. 22–24.

SOURCES:

Periodicals

Fukushima, N., "Nagata, Takesi (1913–1991)," *Journal of Geomagnetism and Geoelectricity,* Volume 43, number 11, 1991, pp. 883–884.
Fukushima, N., "Nagata, Takesi (1913–1991)," *Planetary and Space Science,*October, 1991, pp. 1323–1324.
"Japan Will Send Antarctic Party," *New York Times,* September 23, 1956, p. 30.
Rikitake, Tsuneji, "Takesi Nagata: Portrait of a Scientist," *Earth Science Review,* Volume 9, number 1, 1973, pp. 81–86.
Yukutake, Takesi, "To the Memory of Dr. Takesi Nagata," (Japanese language), *Kasan—Bulletin of the Volcanological Society of Japan,* October, 1991, pp. 389–390.

—*Sketch by J. Sydney Jones*

Yoichiro Nambu
1921-
Japanese-born American physicist

Yoichiro Nambu is a theoretical physicist whose research has contributed to the understanding of elementary atomic particles. In 1982, he was awarded the National Medal of Science by President Ronald Reagan "for seminal contributions to the understanding of elementary particles and their interactions." Since 1991 he has been Professor Emeritus of Physics at the University of Chicago.

Nambu was born in Tokyo, Japan, on January 18, 1921. Despite the tumult of World War II, he completed his studies in physics at the University of Tokyo, receiving his B.S. in 1942 and his Ph.D. in 1952. He was appointed professor of physics at Osaka City University before his doctorate was granted; his six-year appointment there began in 1950, although the latter years of this period were spent largely in the United States. In 1952 Nambu became a member of the Institute for Advanced Study in Princeton, New Jersey, and in 1954 he joined the physics department at the University of Chicago as a research associate. Nambu has remained affiliated with the University of Chicago for most of his career. In 1956 he was promoted to associate professor and in 1958, professor. From 1974 until 1977 he was the chair of the department of physics, and in 1977 he became a Henry Pratt Judson Distinguished Service Professor.

In the 1950s, when Nambu entered the field of particle physics, only a few subnuclear particles were known to exist. The existence of these particles can only be demonstrated by using powerful nuclear accelerators, and during that period it was only possible to push particles through an accelerator with

500 million electron volts of energy. By the mid–1980s, accelerators could attain energies a thousand times higher and several hundred subnuclear particles had been identified. Throughout his career, Nambu's research has been aimed not only at predicting the existence of various subnuclear particles, but at making sense of their behavior. He has advanced ideas and explanations that have helped to create a body of intellectual work known as the grand unification theories. Known also as "GUTs," these theories are an attempt to explain the fundamental forces of nature in a single framework.

Nambu's best known contribution to the GUTs is his concept of "spontaneous symmetry breaking" in particle physics. The laws of physics predict that subatomic particles should behave symmetrically, but experimental results show that they do not. Nambu proposed that while the laws of nature may predict symmetry in subatomic interactions, the stage or space-time continuum in which the interactions occur causes symmetry to break down. In the mid–1980s physicists built on Nambu's work to advance a GUT explanation that describes at least two of nature's forces, weak force and electromagnetism. This theory, now widely embraced by physicists, is known as the electroweak theory.

Nambu has been highly decorated for his contributions to the understanding of elementary particles and their interactions. He was awarded the Dannie Heineman Prize for Mathematical Physics from the American Institute of Physics in 1970. He was elected to the National Academy of Sciences in 1971. In 1976 he was awarded the J. Robert Oppenheimer Prize. In 1978 he received the Order of Culture Award of the Japanese government. The Max Planck Medal was awarded to him in 1985, and the P. A. M. Dirac Medal in 1986. Nambu holds honorary degrees from universities in the United States and Japan. He has published numerous professional articles as well as a popular book on particle physics, entitled *Quarks.* Nambu became a citizen of the United States in 1970. He is married to Chieko Hida, with whom he has had two sons.

SELECTED WRITINGS BY NAMBU:

Books

Quarks, World Scientific, 1985.

SOURCES:

Periodicals

"Nambu Looks at Past and Future of Particle Physics," *University of Chicago News,* March 29, 1984, p. 7.

—Sketch by Leslie Reinherz

Daniel Nathans
1928-
American molecular biologist

Daniel Nathans is best known for his work with restriction enzymes, which are used to cut or break DNA (deoxyribonucleic acid) molecules. This technique, first applied to gene study by Nathans, led the way in studying the structure of viruses and opened the door for recombinant DNA research and genetic mapping. His work was recognized in 1978, when he shared the Nobel Prize in physiology or medicine with **Werner Arber** and **Hamilton O. Smith**.

Nathans was born on October 30, 1928, in Wilmington, Delaware. He was the last of nine children born to Samuel and Sarah Nathans, Russian Jewish immigrants. Nathans received his B.A. from the University of Delaware in 1950 and his M.D. from Washington University in St. Louis in 1954. It was during the summer after his first year of medical school that Nathans had his initial exposure to laboratory work.

After medical school, Nathans completed a one-year internship at Columbia-Presbyterian Medical Center. After this, he spent two years (1955–57) at the National Cancer Institute as a clinical associate studying protein synthesis. In 1956, Nathans married Joanne Gomberg, with whom he had three sons. Returning to Columbia-Presbyterian, Nathans completed his residency in 1959. That same year Nathans won a United States Public Health Service grant to do biochemical research at Rockefeller University in New York with **Fritz Lipmann** and **Norton Zinder**. It was at this point that Nathans fully committed to work in the laboratory rather than in a clinical practice. In New York, Nathans continued his work on protein synthesis and began viral research, mostly related to host-controlled variations in viruses.

In 1962, Nathans began his long relationship with Johns Hopkins University as assistant professor of microbiology and director of genetics. He was elevated to associate professor in 1965 and full professor in 1967. He was named director of the molecular biology and genetics department in 1972 and Boury Professor of Molecular Biology and Genetics in 1976, positions he retained for many years.

Pioneers Research in DNA

In 1962, when Nathans first arrived at Johns Hopkins, Werner Arber, at Basel University in Switzerland, predicted the existence of an enzyme capable of cutting DNA at specific sites. Deoxyribonucleic

Daniel Nathans

acid (DNA) is assumed to be the source of autoreproduction in many viruses. An ability to cut or cleave the DNA into specific and predictable fragments was important to greatly improving our capabilities for researching and understanding viruses. The necessity of "specific" and "predictable" fragments relates to the need of the scientist to know the fragment he or she is studying is identical to the fragment any other scientist would get following the same laboratory procedure.

In 1968, Arber got halfway to his goal, finding an enzyme (type I) capable of cleaving DNA, but in seemingly random patterns. In 1969, Hamilton O. Smith, a colleague of Nathans at Johns Hopkins, wrote to Nathans (who was in Israel at the time) to tell him he had developed a type II enzyme. This enzyme, named Hind II, was capable of cleaving DNA into specific and predictable fragments.

At this time, Nathans was working on a simian virus (SV40) which causes tumors in monkeys. SV40 was particularly impervious to then-current methods of study, so Nathans immediately saw an application of Smith's tool. Nathans, with Kathleen Danna, used Hind II to cut SV40 into eleven pieces and show its method of replication. One technique they employed in this process was radioactive labeling. The combined efforts of Arber, Smith, and Nathans over a period of more than a decade led to their receipt of the Nobel Prize in physiology or medicine in 1978. Their inter-laboratory cooperation greatly advanced the potential for consistent DNA and gene research.

Nathans continued his work with Hind II and cleared the path for much of the work that has been done since in research on DNA function and structure (such as restrictions maps, used to define DNA structure). This early work has also led to the area of recombinant DNA research, which involves the process of joining two DNA fragments from separate sources into one molecule. Since this field of research was uncharted territory and carried some risks, including the creation of new pathogens, Nathans was among an early group of scientists who, in 1974, encouraged the publication of research guidelines and some self-imposed limits on DNA research. Despite the risks, recombinant DNA research has been put to good use in creating supplies of heretofore scarce enzymes and hormones, including human-produced insulin.

In the 1980s, Nathans's research continued to be linked closely to DNA and genetics. A good portion of his scientific work during this time related to the effect of growth factors on genes and gene regulation. Nathans is a member of the American Academy of Arts and Sciences. He is a senior investigator at the Howard Hughes Medical Institute and a member of the National Academy of Sciences. He has served on the editorial board of *Proceedings of the National Academy of Sciences* and has been a regular contributor. He has maintained his association with the National Cancer Institute and authored dozens of articles for several scientific journals. He has been a major player in scientific research and education in the mid to late part of the twentieth century.

SELECTED WRITINGS BY NATHANS:

Periodicals

(With H.O. Smith) "Restriction Endonucleases in the Analysis and Restructuring of DNA Molecules," *Annual Review of Biochemistry,* 1975, pp. 273–93.

(With K. Ryder) "Induction of Protooncogene c-jun by Serum Growth Factors," *Proceedings of the National Academy of Sciences,* November 1, 1988, pp. 8464–66.

(With B. Christy) "DNA Binding Site of the Growth Factor-inducible Protein Zif268," *Proceedings of the National Academy of Sciences,* November 1, 1989, pp. 8737–39.

SOURCES:

Books

Daintith, J., S. Mitchell, and E. Tootill, editors, *A Biographical Encyclopedia of Scientists,* Volume 2, Facts on File, 1981, pp. 584–85.

Fox, D., M. Meldrum, and I. Rezak, editors, *Nobel Laureates in Medicine or Physiology: A Biographical Dictionary,* Garland, 1990, pp. 427–29.

McGraw-Hill Modern Scientists and Engineers, Volume 2, McGraw-Hill, 1980, pp. 348–49.

Periodicals

New York Times, October 13, 1978, p. 60.
Science, December 8, 1978, pp. 1069–71.

—*Sketch by Kim McGrail*

Giulio Natta
1903-1979
Italian chemist

Giulio Natta was a highly regarded Italian chemist who, during an active career spanning almost fifty years, worked closely with the Italian chemical industry to create many new processes and products. His studies of high polymers and his discovery of the hard plastic substance polypropylene ushered in the age of plastics with immense worldwide impact. For his work in this field he shared the 1963 Nobel Prize in chemistry with the German chemist **Karl Ziegler**.

Natta was born on February 26, 1903, in Imperia, Italy, a resort town located about sixty miles southwest of Genoa on the Ligurian Sea. His parents were Francesco Natta, a lawyer and judge, and Elena Crespi Natta. He received his primary and secondary education in Genoa. Having read his first chemistry book at age twelve, he quickly became fascinated by the topic. At age sixteen, Natta graduated from high school and entered the University of Genoa, intending to study mathematics. Finding this subject too abstract, he then transferred to the Milan Polytechnic Institute in 1921 and earned his doctorate in chemical engineering in 1924, at the early age of twenty-one.

Following graduation, Natta remained at the Polytechnic Institute as an instructor. He was promoted to assistant professor of general chemistry in 1925, and to full professor in 1927. Moving to the University of Pavia in 1933, Natta served as professor and director of the school's chemical institute. Next, in 1935, he became professor and chairman of the department of physical chemistry at the University of Rome, then professor and director of the institute of industrial chemistry at the Turin Polytechnic Institute in 1937. He returned to the Milan Polytechnic

Institute as professor and director of the Industrial Chemical Research Center in 1938 and remained there for the rest of his career. He married Rosita Beati, a professor of literature at the University of Milan, in 1935. The couple had a daughter, Franca, and a son, Giuseppe. In his younger days, Natta was an enthusiastic skier, mountain climber, and hiker.

Natta's decision to seek a degree in chemical engineering rather than in chemistry, or some other pure science, was the earliest manifestation of the basic attitude which characterized his entire career. He was always concerned with the practical results of scientific research and believed that science should serve chiefly to meet the needs of business and industry. His research in the 1920s and early 1930s was largely devoted to X-ray and electron diffraction analyses to determine the structure of various inorganic substances. One of his early practical breakthroughs was the discovery of an effective catalyst for the synthetic production of the important chemical, methanol.

In the early 1930s Natta became interested in the chemistry of polymers, or large molecules, thus shifting his focus from inorganic to organic chemistry, the study of carbon compounds. In the late 1930s the Italian government headed by Benito Mussolini actively promoted scientific research in order to increase Italy's self-sufficiency in the production of vital materials. Natta, using his recently acquired expertise in polymer chemistry, contributed to the national effort especially in the development of new methods to produce synthetic rubber. Following the conclusion of World War II, Natta continued his research in polymer chemistry, his work being subsidized by the large Milan chemical firm, the Montecatini Company.

Discovery of High Polymers

In 1952 Natta attended a lecture at Frankfurt, Germany, given by the chemist, Karl Ziegler, then the director of the Max Planck Institute for Coal Research in Mulheim. Ziegler spoke about his recently discovered Aufbau ("growth") reaction, which could be used to create large molecules from ethylene molecules, a gaseous product of the refining of petroleum. Though Ziegler had lectured frequently on his discovery, Natta was one of the first scientists other than Ziegler to grasp its potential importance for the production of high polymers (very large molecules), a venture which might have significant practical applications. Natta and representatives of the Montecatini Company soon invited Ziegler to Milan where they reached an agreement under which Montecatini would have commercial rights to exploit Ziegler's discoveries in Italy and Ziegler and Natta would exchange information on their respective research projects.

In the autumn of 1953 Ziegler and his research staff developed a catalytic process which allowed them to synthesize from ethylene a true high polymer, linear polyethylene, a plastic substance much harder and stronger than any plastic then known. Ziegler promptly patented the new substance but not the process which had produced it. Natta learned of the new discovery through representatives of the Montecatini Company who had been stationed in Ziegler's laboratory in Mulheim. Natta and his research group decided to try Ziegler's catalytic process on propylene, another gaseous product of petroleum which was much cheaper than ethylene. On March 11, 1954, they synthesized linear polypropylene, another high polymer with even more desirable chemical properties than polyethylene. The new plastic proved capable of being molded into objects stronger and more heat resistant than polyethylene. It could be spun into fiber stronger and lighter than nylon, spread into clear film, or molded into pipes as sturdy as metal ones.

Natta and his associates followed up on their discovery with a careful series of X-ray and electron diffraction experiments which demonstrated conclusively the exact nature of the polymer they had created. It was a molecular chain structure in which all of the subgroups were arranged on the same side of the chain. The substance had a high degree of crystallinity which was the cause of its strength. Natta and his colleagues soon discovered other high polymer plastics, including polystyrene. Natta did not inform Ziegler of his discovery of polypropylene until after he had filed for a patent on the new substance. Ziegler was greatly disturbed by what he considered to be Natta's failure to live up to their earlier agreement to share their research and the incident disrupted their previously close friendship to the extent that they were not on speaking terms for many years. The two scientists patched up their quarrel sufficiently to appear together at the 1963 ceremony in Stockholm at which they jointly received the Nobel Prize in chemistry.

In 1959 Natta contracted Parkinson's disease and was already seriously crippled by it at the time of the Nobel Prize award ceremony. He retired from active work in the early 1970s and died at Bergamo, Italy, on May 2, 1979, from complications following surgery for a broken femur bone. In the course of his career, Natta authored or coauthored over five hundred scientific papers and received nearly five hundred patents. He was the recipient of numerous gold medals and at least five honorary degrees for his scientific contributions.

SELECTED WRITINGS BY NATTA:

Books

(Editor with Ferdinando Danusso) *Stereoregular Polymers and Stereospecific Polymerizations,* 2 volumes, translated by Luisa M. Vaccaroni, Pergamon Press, 1967.

(With Mario Farina) *Stereochemistry,* translated by Andrew Dempster, Longmans, 1972.

Periodicals

(With Piero Pino) "Crystalline High Polymers of c-Olefins," *Journal of the American Chemical Society,* March 20, 1955, pp. 1708–1710.

"How Giant Molecules Are Made," *Scientific American,* September, 1957, pp. 98–104.

"Precisely Constructed Polymers," *Scientific American,* August, 1961, pp. 33–41.

"Macromolecular Chemistry," *Science,* January 15, 1965, pp. 261–272.

SOURCES:

Books

Carra, Sergio, and others, editors, *Giulio Natta: Present Significance of His Scientific Contribution,* Editrice di Chimica, 1982.

Magill, Frank N., editor, *The Nobel Prize Winners: Chemistry,* 3 volumes, Salem Press, 1990, pp. 757–764.

McMillan, Frank M., *The Chain Straighteners,* Macmillan, 1979.

Periodicals

New York Times, June 7, 1956, p. 43; November 6, 1963, p. 46.

—*Sketch by John E. Little*

Homer Alfred Neal
1942-
American physicist

A physicist, physics educator, and university administrator, Homer Alfred Neal has devoted much of his career to researching high-energy physics. He has carried out extensive studies of elementary particle interactions and has also made some of the first experimental studies of spin effects in proton-proton collisions at high energies. In addition, he is concerned with methods of particle detection (including spark chamber and scintillation counter techniques), digital and analog electronics, and computer analysis.

Neal was born in Franklin, Kentucky, on June 13, 1942. The son of Homer Neal and Margaret Elizabeth Holl, he was educated at Indiana University, receiving his B.Sc. in physics with honors in 1961. On June 16, 1962, Neal married Donna Jean Daniels; the couple has two children, Homer Alfred, Jr. and Sharon Denise. Neal's son is also a scientist, studying laser physics and computer programming, and helping his father prepare work for publication.

Neal earned his M.Sc. at the University of Michigan as a John Hay Whitney fellow in 1963, and received his Ph.D. in 1966. Neal's dissertation was titled "Polarization Parameter in Elastic Proton-Proton Scattering from .75 to 2.84 GeV," a topic he has returned to in several subsequent papers for such journals as the *American Physical Review* and the Italian *Nuovo Cimento*.

After graduation, Neal became a National Science Foundation (NSF) fellow at the European Organization of Nuclear Research until 1967, and a Sloan Foundation Fellow in 1968. During 1967, he returned to Indiana University at Bloomington, as an assistant professor of physics between 1967 and 1970. He became an associate professor in 1970, professor in 1972, and dean of research and graduate development in the late 1970s. His research at Indiana consisted of extending his previous work on elastic proton-proton scattering, studying pion-proton interactions, and other phenomena of high-energy physics.

Between 1970 and 1972, Neal was chairperson of the Argonne Zero Gradient Synchrotron (ZGS) Accelerator Users Group. The ZGS was a proton acceleratordeveloped by the Argonne National Laboratory, a physics research center founded in 1946 and operated by the University of Chicago. Neal used the ZGS to measure large-angle elastic proton-proton polarization and recoil-proton polarization. An Argonne University Association trustee from 1971 to 1974 and 1977 to 1980, Neal continued his ZGS work until its closure in 1979, studying hadron-induced reactions and elastic scattering, spin-flip amplitudes, asymmetry, and other effects of elementary particle physics. Neal then took on a substantial role as administrator and advisor to various science organizations and corporate boards. During 1976 to 1979 he served on a physics advisory panel for the NSF; he chaired a similar panel in the late 1980s. In 1977, Neal joined a U.S. Department of Energy advisory panel on high-energy physics, a position he held for four years. He was also a National Science Board member between 1980 and 1986.

In addition, Neal served on the Ogden Corporation's Board of Directors and the New York Sea Grant Institute. His Ogden Corporation work dealt with the increasing problem of urban garbage disposal. This led to his 1987 book, *Solid Waste Management and the Environment: The Mounting Garbage and Trash Crisis,* written with J. R. Schubel. Neal surveyed the many technical, economic, environmental, and societal issues surrounding solid waste disposal, and suggested novel methods of disposal. These included the notion of making artificial ocean reefs from stable ash blocks.

Despite Neal's increasing administrative work in the 1980s, he continued his elementary particle physics research, becoming a Guggenheim Fellow at Stanford University in 1980. In 1981, after an unsuccessful bid for the presidency of City College in New York, Neal moved on to the State University of New York (SUNY) in Stony Brook as its provost. His continued studies of high-energy interactions resulted in his 1983 election as a fellow of the American Association for the Advancement of Science. In 1984 he received an honorary doctorate from Indiana University.

In 1986, Neal became department chair and professor of physics at the University of Michigan in Ann Arbor. His research during the late 1980s and early 1990s involved meson and lepton decays, studies of quarks, and experimental tests of quantum electrodynamics (QED), a theory explaining the electromagnetic forces of charged particles. Many of Neal's experiments were carried out at the Stanford Linear Accelerator Center (SLAC) in California.

During the 1990s, Neal has taken on additional administrative positions, including membership in the Superconducting Super Collider's board of overseers in 1989. In the same year he joined the Smithsonian Institution's Board of Regents. He also become a Center for Strategic and International Studies trustee in 1990.

SELECTED WRITINGS BY NEAL:

Books

(With J. R. Schubel) *Solid Waste Management and the Environment: The Mounting Garbage and Trash Crisis,* Prentice-Hall, 1987.

Periodicals

"The Universities and the ZGS in the Seventies," *American Institute of Physics Conference Proceedings,* Volume 60, 1980, pp. 269–289.

Other

"Polarization Parameter in Elastic Proton-Proton Scattering from .75 to 2.84 GeV" (dissertation), University of Michigan, 1966.

SOURCES:

Books

Sammons, Vivian Ovelton, *Blacks in Science and Medicine,* Hemisphere Publishing, 1990, p. 180.

Periodicals

"Search for New President of City College Is Narrowed to 3 Candidates," *New York Times,* February 9, 1981, p. B2.

—*Sketch by Julian A. Smith*

Louis Néel
1904-
French physicist

Louis Néel is a French physicist who explored the magnetic properties of solids. He is famous for discovering antiferromagnetism—a property possessed by some metals, alloys, and salts by which their magnetic fields line up in a way that negates their magnetism. He also explained some of the magnetic properties of ferrites (iron salt compounds), making it possible to prepare synthetic ferrites with properties that could be used in computer memories. For his fundamental work and discoveries, Néel received the 1970 Nobel Prize in physics along with the Swedish physicist **Hannes Olof Gösta Alfvén**.

Louis Eugène Félix Néel was born in Lyons, France, to Antoinette Hartmayer and Louis Néel, a director in the civil service. Néel received his secondary education at the Lycée du Parc in Lyons and the Lycée St.-Louis in Paris. He studied at the distinguished Ecole Normale Supérieure in Paris, was graduated in 1928, and continued there as a lecturer. Néel received his doctorate in 1932 from the University of Strasbourg. He studied under Pierre Weiss, a leading investigator of magnetization (a solid's capability of being magnetized). After receiving his doctorate, Néel joined the faculty of the University of Strasbourg and remained there until 1945.

Advances Heisenberg's Work

When Néel was beginning his doctoral work, German physicist **Werner Karl Heisenberg** announced his finding that large scale magnetic attraction is produced by neighboring atoms of ferromag-netic substances orienting in the same direction. Heisenberg also showed that the alignment of magnetic moments—the small amount of magnetism around each atom—became parallel at low temperatures.

In 1930, Néel, building on Heisenberg's work, suggested that there are also "antiferromagnetic" substances, with interactions that cause the magnetic moments of neighboring atoms to realign in opposing directions, resulting in zero magnetization. The realignment only occurs at a very low temperature, a temperature that has come to be known as the Néel Point or Néel temperature. During World War II, Néel used his expertise to protect French warships against magnetic mines by "neutralizing" them. He gave them a magnetization opposite the normal terrestrial magnetic field.

In 1945, Néel joined the faculty of the University of Grenoble and established the Laboratory of Electrostatics and the Physics of Metals. In 1947, he also developed the concept of ferrimagnetic substances. When the temperature of antiferromagnetic substances is raised, the spontaneous magnetization slightly deforms the antiparallel arrangement of the two sets of atoms, leaving one set slightly stronger than the other, previously equal, set. The result is paramagnetism, in which the substances are slightly attracted to an external field but are essentially independent of one another. Ferrites, which are not electrical conductors, are ferrimagnetic substances. Ferrimagnetic substances share some of the properties of ferromagnetic elements (such as iron, nickel, and cobalt) and some of the properties of antiferromagnetics. They have been used to coat magnetic tape in computer memory cores and in other types of communication technology.

Néel developed a theory of magnetization that described the subdivision of ferromagnetic substances into elementary domains, regions of ferromagnetic material, with spikes and walls. He also analyzed the process of magnetic creep, the effect of time on magnetization of ferromagnetic substances. There are two classes of creep, one due to temperature changes and the other due to the redistribution of atoms in the crystal that accompanies spontaneous magnetization.

Work in Magnetics Leads to Nobel Prize

In 1956 Néel was asked to found the Center for Nuclear Studies at Grenoble. Through his involvement, Grenoble became an important center for physics research. Néel was also president of the Institut National Polytechnique de Grenoble. Between 1963 to 1983 he was French delegate to the NATO Scientific Council. In 1970 Louis Néel received the Nobel Prize in physics for his fundamental work and discoveries concerning antiferromagnetism and ferrimagnetism. That year the prize for physics was also given to Hannes Alfvén for his research into magnetohydrodynamics.

Néel received many honors besides the Nobel Prize. He was named to the French Legion of Honor and received the Gold Medal of the National Center for Scientific Research and the Holweck Medal of the Institute of Physics, London. He was also elected to the Academy of Sciences of Paris, the scientific academies of Moscow, Warsaw, Romania, and Amsterdam and to the Royal Society of London and the American Academy of Arts and Sciences.

Néel married Hélène Hourticq in 1931. The couple had a son and two daughters. Néel's pastimes include carpentry, strolling in the country, and reading mystery stories and eighteenth-century French literature.

SOURCES:

Books

McGraw-Hill Modern Scientists and Engineers, McGraw-Hill, 1980.
Wasson, Tyler, editor, *Nobel Prize Winners,* H. W. Wilson, 1987.

—Sketch by Margo Nash

Erwin Neher
1944-
German biophysicist

Erwin Neher, along with **Bert Sakmann**, was awarded the 1991 Nobel Prize in physiology or medicine for the development of the patch clamp technique. The use of this technique enabled Neher and Sakmann to forge new paths in the study of membrane physiology and to understand the structure and functions of ion channels found in the plasma membranes of most body cells. The patch clamp technique has given physiologists a precise understanding of cellular microelectrical activity and has contributed significantly to the research and treatment of cystic fibrosis, diabetes, epilepsy, and other disorders of the cardiovascular and neuromuscular systems.

Neher was born in Landsberg, Germany, on March 20, 1944, the son of Franz Xavier Neher and Elisabeth Pfeiffer Neher. In 1965 he completed his undergraduate studies at the Institute of Technology in Munich with a major in physics. Two years later he earned his master's degree from the University of Wisconsin under a Fulbright scholarship. He then went on to complete his doctorate at the Institute of Technology in Munich, Germany, in 1970.

While the existence of ion channels that transmit electrical charges was hypothesized as early as the 1950s, no one had been able to see these channels. As a doctoral student, Neher was drawn to the question of how electrically charged ions control such biological functions as the transmission of nerve impulses, the contraction of muscles, vision, and the process of conception. He realized that in order to get answers to these questions he would have to look for the ion channels.

Collaboration with Sakmann Begins

It was in his doctoral thesis that Neher first developed the concept of the patch clamp technique as a way of discovering the ion channels. In 1974 he shared a laboratory space with Bert Sakmann at the Max Planck Institute in Göttingen. They both agreed that understanding the nature of ion channels was the most important problem in the biophysics of the cell membrane, and they set out to develop the techniques of patch clamping.

Neher briefly worked with Charles F. Stevens at the University of Washington. When Stevens moved to Yale, Neher followed him while maintaining his collaboration with Sakmann. From 1975 to 1976, Neher was a research associate in the department of physiology at Yale University, and much of the data for the paper on patch clamps came from the Yale studies.

In 1976 Neher and Sakmann published their landmark paper on the use of glass recording electrodes with microscopic tips, called micropipettes, pressed against a cell membrane. With these devices, which they called patch clamp electrodes, they were able to electrically isolate a tiny patch of the cell membrane and to study the proteins in that area. They could then see how the individual proteins acted as channels or gates for specific ions, allowing certain ions to pass through the cell membrane one at a time, while preventing others from entering. Their work with patch clamps allowed them to remove a patch of the membrane and to enter the interior of the cell. They then were able to conduct various experiments to observe the intricate mechanism of ion channels.

Refinement to Reduce Noise Improves Technique

Several years passed after they presented their findings to an audience at the Biophysical Society meeting in 1976 in which Neher and Sakmann, along with their co-workers, refined the technique of patch clamping. Creating a better seal between the micropipette and the patch of cell membrane it pressed against was one of the refinements they sought. Without a tight seal there was interference by "noise" that overshadowed the smaller electrical currents.

The problem of outside noise interference was solved by Neher in 1980 when he was able to observe on his oscilloscope a marked drop in the noise level to almost zero. From this drop he was able to infer that he had produced a seal that was one hundred times better than previously attained. While other researchers had noticed an abatement of noise at times, Neher was the first to realize the significance of the drop in noise level.

Neher found that by using a light suction with a super clean pipette, he could create a high-resistance seal of 10–100 gigohms (a gigohm is a measure of electrical resistance equal to one billion ohms). He called this seal a "gigaseal." With the gigaseal, background noise could be decreased, and a number of new ways could be used to control cells for patch clamp experimentation. Patches from the cell could now be torn away from the membrane to act as a membrane coating over the mouth of the pipette, thus allowing for more exact measurement of electrical ion movement. A strong suction could force the pipette into the cell while still maintaining a tight seal for the cell as a whole.

In 1976 Neher returned to the Max Planck Institute in Göttingen. On December 26, 1978, he married Eva-Maria Ruhr, a microbiologist. They have five children: Richard, Benjamin, Carola, Sigmund, and Margret. He became director of the membrane biophysics department at the Max Planck Institute in 1983, and in 1987 he was made an honorary professor. In 1991 Neher and Sakmann won the 1991 Nobel Prize in physiology or medicine for proving the existence of ion channels.

Researchers using the patch clamp technique were able to discover a defective ion channel that was responsible for cystic fibrosis. Because of the use of patch clamps in research, there is now a better understanding of hormone regulation and the production of insulin as it relates to diabetes. The Nobel Committee also praised the work of Neher and Sakmann for helping in research on heart disease, epilepsy, and disorders affecting the nervous and muscle systems. Patch clamp research has helped in the development of new drugs for these conditions.

SELECTED WRITINGS BY NEHER:

Books

Single Channel Recording, Plenum, 1983.

(Contributor) *Molecular Mechanisms in Secretion,* edited by N. A. Thron, [Copenhagen], 1988, pp. 262–270.

Periodicals

(With Bert Sakmann) "The Patch Clamp Technique," *Scientific American,* March, 1992, pp. 44–51.
"Ion Channels for Communication between and within Cells," *Science,* April 24, 1992, pp. 498–502.

SOURCES:

Periodicals

Aldous, Peter, "Patch Clamp Brings Honour," *Nature,* October 10, 1991, p. 487.
Altman, Lawrence K., "Cell Channel Finding Earns Nobel Prize," *New York Times,* October 13, 1992, pp. C1, C3.
Brown, Phyllida, "Ion Channels Bring Nobel Prize to Germany," *New Scientist,* October 12, 1991, p. 14.
"Ion Channels: Discoverers Win Physiology Nobel," *Chemical and Engineering News,* October 14, 1991, p. 4.
Zeman, Ellen J., "Neher and Sakmann Win Physiology Nobel for Cell Membrane Studies," *Physics Today,* January, 1992, pp. 17–18.

—*Sketch by Jordan Richman*

Walther Nernst
1864-1941
German chemist

Walther Nernst made a significant breakthrough with his statement of the Third Law of Thermodynamics, which holds that it should be impossible to attain the temperature of absolute zero in any real experiment. For this accomplishment, he was awarded the 1920 Nobel Prize for chemistry. He also made contributions to the field of physical chemistry. While still in his twenties, he devised a mathematical expression showing how electromotive force is dependent upon temperature and concentration in a galvanic, or electricity-producing, cell. He later developed a theory to explain how ionic, or charged, compounds break down in water, a problem

Walther Nernst

that had troubled chemists since the theory of ionization was proposed by **Svante A. Arrhenius**.

Born Hermann Walther Nernst in Briesen, West Prussia (now Wąbrzeżno, Poland), on June 25, 1864, he was the third child of Gustav Nernst, a judge, and Ottilie (Nerger) Nernst. He attended the gymnasium at Graudenz (now Grudziadz), Poland, where he developed an interest in poetry, literature, and drama. For a brief time, he considered becoming a poet. After graduation in 1883, Nernst attended the universities of Zurich, Berlin, Graz, and Würzburg, majoring in physics at each institution. He was awarded his Ph.D. summa cum laude in 1887 by Würzburg. His doctoral thesis dealt with the effects of magnetism and heat on electrical conductivity.

Nernst's first academic appointment came in 1887 when he was chosen as an assistant to professor **Friedrich Wilhelm Ostwald** at the University of Leipzig. Ostwald had been introduced to Nernst earlier in Graz by Svante Arrhenius. These three, Ostwald, Arrhenius, and Nernst, were to become among the most influential men involved in the founding of the new discipline of physical chemistry, the application of physical laws to chemical phenomena.

The first problem Nernst addressed at Leipzig was the diffusion of two kinds of ions across a semipermeable membrane. He wrote a mathematical equation describing the process, now known as the Nernst equation, which relates the electric potential of the ions to various properties of the cell.

In the early 1890s, Nernst accepted a teaching position appointment at the University of Göttingen in Leipzig, and soon after married Emma Lohmeyer, the daughter of a surgeon. The Nernsts had five children, three daughters and two sons. In 1894, Nernst was promoted to full professor at Göttingen. At the same time, he also received approval for the creation of a new Institute for Physical Chemistry and Electrochemistry at the university.

At Göttingen, Nernst wrote a textbook on physical chemistry, *Theoretische Chemie vom Standpunkte der Avogadroschen Regel und der Thermodynamik* (*Theoretical Chemistry from the Standpoint of Avogadro's Rule and Thermodynamics*). Published in 1893, it had an almost missionary objective: to lay out the principles and procedures of a new approach to the study of chemistry. The book became widely popular, going through a total of fifteen editions over the next thirty-three years.

Pursues Questions of Solution Chemistry

During his tenure at Göttingen, Nernst investigated a wide variety of topics in the field of solution chemistry. In 1893, for example, he developed a theory for the breakdown of ionic compounds in water, a fundamental issue in the Arrhenius theory of ionization. According to Nernst, dissociation, or the dissolving of a compound into its elements, occurs because the presence of nonconducting water molecules causes positive and negative ions in a crystal to lose contact with each other. The ions become hydrated by water molecules, making it possible for them to move about freely and to conduct an electric current through the solution. In later work, Nernst developed techniques for measuring the degree of hydration of ions in solutions. By 1903, Nernst had also devised methods for determining the pH value of a solution, an expression relating the solution's hydrogen-ion concentration (acidity or alkalinity).

In 1889, Nernst addressed another fundamental problem in solution chemistry: precipitation. He constructed a mathematical expression showing how the concentration of ions in a slightly soluble compound could result in the formation of an insoluble product. That mathematical expression is now known as the solubility product, a special case of the ionization constant for slightly soluble substances. Four years later, Nernst also developed the concept of buffer solutions—solutions made of bases, rather than acids—and showed how they could be used in various theoretical and practical situations.

Around 1905, Nernst was offered a position as professor of physical chemistry at the University of Berlin. This move was significant for both the institution and the man. Chemists at Berlin had been resistant to many of the changes going on in their field, and theoretical physicist and eventual Nobel Prize winner **Max Planck** had recommended the selection of Nernst to revitalize the Berlin chemists. The move also proved to be a stimulus to Nernst's own work. Until he left Göttingen, he had concentrated on the reworking of older, existing problems developed by his predecessors in physical chemistry. At Berlin, he began to search out, define, and explore new questions. Certainly the most important of these questions involved the thermodynamics of chemical reactions at very low temperatures.

Research Leads to the Third Law of Thermodynamics

Attempting to extend the Gibbs-Helmholtz equation and the Thomsen-Berthelot principle of maximum work to temperatures close to absolute zero—the temperature at which there is no heat—Nernst eventually concluded that it would be possible to reach absolute zero only by a series of infinite steps. In the real world, that conclusion means that an experimenter can get closer and closer to absolute zero, but can never actually reach that point. Nernst first presented his "Heat Theorem," as he called it, to the Göttingen Academy of Sciences in December of 1905. It was published a year later in the *Nachrichten von der Gesellschaft der Wissenschaften zu Göttingen.* The theory is now more widely known as the Third Law of Thermodynamics. In 1920, Nernst was awarded the Nobel Prize in chemistry in recognition of his work on this law.

The statement of the Heat Theorem proved to be an enormous stimulus for Nernst's colleagues in Berlin's chemistry department. For at least a decade, the focus of nearly all research among physical chemists there was experimental confirmation of Nernst's hypothesis. In order to accomplish this objective, new equipment and new techniques had to be developed. Nernst's Heat Theorem was eventually integrated into the revolution taking place in physics, the development of quantum theory. At the time he first proposed the theory, Nernst had ignored any possible role of quantum mechanics. A few years later, however, that had all changed. In working on his own theory of specific heats, for example, **Albert Einstein** had quite independently come to the same conclusions as had Nernst. He later wrote that Nernst's experiments at Berlin had confirmed his own theory of specific heats. In turn, Nernst eventually realized that his Heat Theorem was consistent with the dramatic changes being brought about in physics by quantum theory. Even as his work on the Heat Theorem went forward, Nernst turned to new topics. One of these involved the formation of hydrogen chloride by photolysis, or chemical breakdown by light energy. Chemists had long known that a mixture of hydrogen and chlorine gases will explode when exposed to light. In 1918, Nernst developed an explanation for that reaction. When exposed to light, Nernst hypothesized, a molecule of chlorine (Cl_2) will absorb light energy and break down into two chlorine atoms ($2Cl$). A single chlorine atom will then react with a molecule of hydrogen (H_2), forming a molecule of hydrogen chloride and an atom of hydrogen ($HCl + H$). The atom of hydrogen will then react with a molecule of chlorine, forming a second molecule of hydrogen chloride and another atom of chlorine. The process is a chain reaction because the remaining atom of chlorine allows it to repeat.

In 1922, Nernst resigned his post at Berlin in order to become president of the Physikalisch-technische Reichsanstalt. He hoped to reorganize the institute and make it a leader in German science, but since the nation was suffering from severe inflation at the time, there were not enough funds to achieve this goal. As a result, Nernst returned to Berlin in 1924 to teach physics and direct the Institute of Experimental Physics there until he retired in 1934.

Makes a Fortune with Invention

In addition to his scientific research, Nernst was an avid inventor. Around the turn of the century, for example, he developed an incandescent lamp that used rare-earth oxide rather than a metal as the filament. Although he sold the lamp patent outright for a million marks, the device was never able to compete commercially with the conventional model invented by **Thomas Alva Edison**. Nernst also invented an electric piano that was never successfully marketed.

The rise of the Nazi party in 1933 brought an end to Nernst's professional career. He was personally opposed to the political and scientific policies promoted by Adolf Hitler and his followers and was not reluctant to express his views publicly. In addition, two of his daughters had married Jews, which contributed to his becoming an outcast in the severely anti-Semitic climate of Germany at that time.

Walther Nernst was one of the geniuses of early twentieth-century German chemistry, a man with a prodigious curiosity about every new development in the physical sciences. He was a close colleague of Einstein, and was a great contributor to the organization of German science—he was largely responsible for the first Solvay Conference in 1911, for example. In his free time, he was especially fond of travel, hunting, and fishing. Nernst also loved automobiles and owned one of the first to be seen in Göttingen. Little is known about his years after his retirement. Nernst died of a heart attack on November 18, 1941, at his home at Zibelle, Oberlausitz, near the German-Polish border.

SELECTED WRITINGS BY NERNST:

Books

Theoretische Chemie vom Standpunkte der Avogadroschen Regel und der Thermodynamik, [Göttingen], 1893.

(With A. Schönflies) *Einführung in die mathematische Behandlung der Naturwissenschaften-Kurzgefasstes Lehrbuch der Differential- und Integralrechnung mit besonderer Berücksichtigung der Chemie,* [Leipzig], 1895.

Die Ziele der physikalischen Chemie, [Göttingen], 1896.

Experimental and Theoretical Applications of Thermodynamics to Chemistry, [London], 1907.

Die Theoretischen und experimentellen Grundlagen des Neuen Wärmesatzes, [Halle-Salle], 1918.

Periodicals

"Ueber die Berechnung chemischer Gleichgewichte aus thermischen Messungen," *Nachrichten von der Gesellschaft der Wissenschaften zu Göttingen,* 1906, pp. 1–40.

SOURCES:

Books

Concise Dictionary of Scientific Biography, Macmillan, 1981, pp. 499–501.

Farber, Eduard, editor, *Great Chemists,* Interscience, 1961, pp. 1203–1208.

Gillispie, Charles Coulson, editor, *Dictionary of Scientific Biography,* Volume 15, Scribner, 1975, pp. 432–453.

Mendelsohn, Kurt, *The World of Walther Nernst: The Rise and Fall of German Science, 1864–1941,* Pittsburgh, 1973.

Periodicals

Einstein, Albert, "The Work and Personality of Walther Nernst," *Scientific Monthly,* February, 1942, pp. 195–196.

Partington, James R., "The Nernst Memorial Lecture," *Journal of the American Chemical Society,* 1953, pp. 2853–2872.

—*Sketch by David E. Newton*

Elizabeth F. Neufeld
1928-
French-born American biochemist

Elizabeth F. Neufeld is best known as an authority on human genetic diseases. Her research at the National Institutes of Health (NIH) and at University of California, Los Angeles (UCLA), provided new insights into mucopolysaccharide storage disorders (the absence of certain enzymes preventing the body from properly storing certain substances). Neufeld's research opened the way for prenatal diagnosis of such life-threatening fetal disorders as Hurler syndrome. Because of this research, she was awarded the Lasker Award in 1982 and the Wolf Prize in Medicine in 1988.

She was born Elizabeth Fondal in Paris, on September 27, 1928. Her parents, Jacques and Elvire Fondal, were Russian refugees who had settled in France after the Russian revolution. The impending occupation of France by the Germans brought the Fondal family to New York in June 1940. Her parents' experience led them to instill in Neufeld a strong commitment to the importance of education "They believed that education was the one thing no one could take from you," she told George Milite in a 1993 interview.

Neufeld first became interested in science while a high school student, her interest sparked by her biology teacher. She attended Queens College in New York, receiving her bachelor of science degree in 1948. She worked briefly as a research assistant to Elizabeth Russell at the Jackson Memorial Laboratory in Bar Harbor, Maine. From 1949 to 1950 she studied at the University of Rochester's department of physiology. In 1951 she moved to Maryland, where she served as a research assistant to Nathan Kaplan and Sidney Colowick at the McCollum-Pratt Institute at Johns Hopkins University. In 1952 Neufeld moved again, this time to the West Coast. From 1952 to 1956 she studied under W. Z. Hassid at the University of California, Berkeley. She received her Ph.D. in comparative biochemistry from Berkeley in 1956 and remained there for her postdoctoral training. She first studied cell division in sea urchins. Later, as a junior research biochemist (working again with Hassid) she studied the biosynthesis of plant cell wall polymers—which would prove significant when she began studying Hurler syndrome and related diseases.

Neufeld began her scientific studies at a time when few women chose science as a career. The historical bias against women in science, compounded with an influx of men coming back from the Second World War and going to college, made positions for

Elizabeth F. Neufeld

women rare; few women could be found in the science faculties of colleges and universities. Despite the "overt discrimination" Neufeld often witnessed, she decided nonetheless to pursue her interests. "Some people looked at women who wanted a career in science as a little eccentric," she told Milite, "but I enjoyed what I was doing and I decided I would persevere."

Begins Research on Hurler Syndrome

After spending several years at Berkeley, Neufeld moved on to NIH in 1963, where she began as research biochemist at the National Institute of Arthritis Metabolism and Digestive Diseases. It was during her time at NIH that Neufeld began her research on mucopolysaccharidoses (MPS), disorders in which a complex series of sugars known as mucopolysaccharides cannot be stored or metabolized properly. Hurler syndrome is a form of MPS. Other forms of MPS include Hunter's Syndrome, Scheie Syndrome, Sanfillipo, and Morquio. These are all inherited disorders. Defectively metabolized sugars accumulate in fetal cells of victims. The disorders can cause stunted physical and mental growth, vision and hearing problems, and a short life span.

Because some plant cell wall polymers contain uronic acids (a component of mucopolysaccharides), Neufeld, from her work with plants, could surmise how the complex sugars worked in humans. When she first began working on Hurler syndrome in 1967, she initially thought the problem might stem from faulty regulation of the sugars, but experiments showed the problem was in fact the abnormally slow rate at which the sugars were broken down.

Working with fellow scientist Joseph Fratantoni, Neufeld attempted to isolate the problem by tagging mucopolysaccharides with radioactive sulfate, as well as mixing normal cells with MPS patient cells. Fratantoni inadvertently mixed cells from a Hurler patient and a Hunter patient—and the result was a nearly normal cell culture. The two cultures had essentially "cured" each other. Additional work showed that the cells could cross-correct by transferring a corrective factor through the culture medium. The goal now was to determine the makeup of the corrective factor or factors.

Identifies Enzyme Deficiency

Through a combination of biological and molecular techniques, Neufeld was able to identify the corrective factors as a series of enzymes. Normally, the enzymes would serve as catalysts for the reactions needed for cells to metabolize the sugars. In Hurler and other MPS patients, enzyme deficiency makes this difficult. A further complication is that often the enzymes that do exist lack the proper chemical markers needed to enter cells and do their work. Neufeld's subsequent research with diseases similar to MPS, including I-Cell disease, showed how enzymes needed markers to match with cell receptors to team with the right cells.

This research paved the way for successful prenatal diagnosis of the MPS and related disorders, as well as genetic counseling. Although no cure has been found, researchers are experimenting with such techniques as gene replacement therapy and bone marrow transplants.

In 1973 Neufeld was named chief of NIH's Section of Human Biochemical Genetics, and in 1979 she was named chief of the Genetics and Biochemistry Branch of the National Institute of Arthritis, Diabetes, and Digestive and Kidney Diseases (NIADDK). She served as deputy director in NIADDK's Division of Intramural Research from 1981 to 1983.

In 1984 Neufeld went back to the University of California, this time the Los Angeles campus, as chair of the biological chemistry department, where she continues her research. In addition to MPS, she has done research on similar disorders such as Tay-Sachs disease. But her concerns go beyond research. She strongly believes that young scientists just starting out need support and encouragement from the scientific community, because these scientists can bring new and innovative perspectives to difficult questions and issues. At the same time, young scientists can learn much from the experience of established scientists. In her capacity as department chair, Neufeld encourages interaction among established scientists, young scientists, and students.

Neufeld has chaired the Scientific Advisory Board of the National MPS Society since 1988 and was president of the American Society for Biochemistry and Molecular Biology from 1992 to 1993. She was elected to both the National Academy of Sciences (USA) and the American Academy of Arts and Sciences in 1977 and named a fellow of the American Association for Advancement in Science in 1988. In 1990 she was named California Scientist of the Year.

Married to Benjamin Neufeld (a former official with the U.S. Public Health Service) since 1951, she is the mother of two children. Although her work takes up a great deal of her time, she enjoys hiking when she gets the chance, and travel "when it's for pleasure and not business."

SELECTED WRITINGS BY NEUFELD:

Books

(Editor with V. Ginsburg) *Methods in Enzymology,* Volume 8, Academic Press, 1966.
(Contributor) *NIH: An Account of Research in its Laboratories and Clinics,* edited by DeW. Stetten and W. T. Carrigan, Academic Press, 1984, pp. 330–336.

SOURCES:

Books

O'Neill, Lois Decker, editor, *The Women's Book of World Records and Achievements,* Anchor Press, 1979.

Other

Neufeld, Elizabeth F., interview with George Milite conducted December 17, 1993.

—*Sketch by George A. Milite*

Allen Newell
1927-1992
American computer scientist

Allen Newell, an expert on how people think and a developer of complex information processing programs, was a pioneer in the field of artificial intelligence. From his development in the 1950s of Logic Theorist, one of the initial forays into artificial intelligence, to his presentation of the sophisticated problem-solving software system know as "SOAR" in the 1980s, Newell worked to link computer science and advances in understanding human cognition.

Newell was born in San Francisco on March 19, 1927, the son of Robert R. and Jeannette (LeValley) Newell. Robert Newell, a professor of radiology at Stanford Medical School, had a strong influence on his son. "[My father] was in many respects a complete man," Newell told Pamela McCorduck in an interview reported in *Machines Who Think.* "We used to go up and spend our summers on the High Sierra. He'd built a log cabin up in the mountains in the 1920s. And my father knew all about how to do things out in the woods—he could fish, pan for gold, the whole bit. At the same time, he was the complete intellectual. . . . My father knew literature, all the classics, and he also knew a lot of physics." Newell told McCorduck, however, that his own desire for scientific achievement had led him to focus his interests much more narrowly than had his father.

Newell served for two years on active duty in the Naval Reserve during World War II. In 1947, he married Noel Marie McKenna; they would have one son, Paul Allen Newell. After obtaining his B.S. in physics from Stanford University in 1949, Newell spent a year at Princeton University doing postgraduate work in mathematics, then went to work in 1950 as a research scientist for the RAND (Research and Development) Corporation in Santa Monica, California.

A Pioneer in the Field of Artificial Intelligence

While at RAND, Newell worked with the Air Force to simulate an early warning monitoring station with radar screens and a crew. His need to simulate the crew's reactions led to his interest in determining how people think. Working together throughout the 1950s and into the 1960s, Newell and his colleagues **Herbert A. Simon** and Clifford Shaw were able to identify general reasoning techniques by observing the problem-solving behavior of human subjects. One of the best known of these techniques is means-ends analysis, a process that analyzes the gap between a current situation and a desired end and searches for the means to close that gap.

In order to make use of computers in studying problem-solving behavior, Newell, Simon, and Shaw observed individuals as they worked through well-structured problems of logic. Subjects verbalized their reasoning as they worked through the problems. The three scientists were then able to code this reasoning in the form of a computer program. To make the program work, the scientists used a language called Information Processing Language (IPL) that they had developed previously for a computerized chess game. Their program, known as Logic Theorist, was not subject-matter specific; rather, it focused on the problem-solving process. Newell, Simon, and Shaw followed Logic Theorist with the development of General Problem Solver, a program that used means-end analysis to solve problems. Like Logic Theorist, General Problem Solver used the IPL language they had developed earlier.

During the summer of 1956, Newell and Simon were among a group of about a dozen scientists that gathered at Dartmouth College. The scientists came from a wide variety of fields, including mathematics, psychology, neurology, and electrical engineering. Though their backgrounds differed, they all had one thing in common: all were using computers in their research in an effort to simulate some aspect of human intelligence. With their Logic Theorist program, however, Newell and Simon were the only participants who could offer a working program in what would come to be known as "artificial intelligence." The Dartmouth Conference is generally viewed as the formal beginning of the field of artificial intelligence.

In 1957, Newell earned his Ph.D. in industrial administration from Carnegie Institute of Technology in Pittsburgh, Pennsylvania. In 1961 he left his position at RAND to join the faculty of Carnegie-Mellon University (formerly the Carnegie Institute of Technology), where he helped develop the School of Computer Science.

Problem-solving Software That Thinks

During the 1980s, Newell, along with his former students John Laird and Paul Rosenbloom, developed a more sophisticated software system that solved problems in a manner similar to the human mind. This system, called SOAR (State, Operator, and Result), was a general problem-solving program that learned from experience in that it was able to remember how it solved problems and to make use of that knowledge in subsequent problem-solving. SOAR, like humans, used working memory and long-term memory to solve problems. If SOAR was working toward a desired goal, it used working memory to keep track of the current situation, or

"state," in the problem-solving process compared with the desired goal or "result." In order to make the decisions necessary to achieve a goal, people use information they have accumulated through experience. People use long-term memory to access information; SOAR also used long-term memory, programmed as a series of IF/THEN statements.

While the use of IF/THEN statements in a computer program wasn't a new idea, the way in which SOAR processed those statements was new. In the past, only one IF/THEN statement could control a computer program at any given time. If conflicting statements could apply to a problem, the problem-solving process would break down. SOAR, on the other hand, was designed to look at all of the programmed IF/THEN statements at once. After looking at all of the statements, SOAR would weigh them as suggestions, then decide which move, or "operator," would best advance it towards the desired result. If there were no IF/THEN statements stored in memory that applied specifically to the problem at hand, SOAR would use any available information that seemed potentially useful to try to resolve the problem. Whenever it solved one of these unexpected problems, SOAR would remember how it solved the problem, adding this information to its long-term memory. Like the human mind, SOAR was thus able both to generate original responses to new problems and to "learn" from its experiences.

In the late 1980s, Newell began an active campaign to promote the use of SOAR as the basis for a new effort to develop a unified theory of cognition. Whereas current research in artificial intelligence tended to focus on narrow and isolated aspects of cognition, Newell hoped SOAR would help cognitive psychologists devise broad theories of human cognition and advance towards an integrated understanding of all aspects of human thought.

Career Capped with National Medal of Science

Newell received the National Medal of Science from President George Bush just a month before his death from cancer on July 19, 1992. His work had already brought him a number of other honors, including the Harry Goode Memorial Award, which he received from the American Federation of Information Processing Societies in 1971, and the A. M. Turing Award, presented jointly to Newell and Simon by the Association for Computing Machinery in 1975. Newell was founding president of the American Association for Artificial Intelligence and also served as head of the Cognitive Science Society. Along with his colleague Herbert Simon and computer scientists **Marvin Minsky** and **John McCarthy**, he is considered one of the fathers of artificial intelligence.

SELECTED WRITINGS BY NEWELL:

Books

(With Herbert A. Simon) *The Logic Theory Machine: A Complex Information Processing System,* RAND Corp., revised edition, 1956.
(With George W. Ernst) *GPS, A Case Study in Generality and Problem Solving,* Academic Press, 1969.
(With Simon) *Human Problem Solving,* Prentice-Hall, 1972.
(With S. Card and T. Moran) *The Psychology of the Human Computer,* L. Erlbaum Associates, 1983.
Unified Theories of Cognition, Harvard University Press, 1990.

SOURCES:

Books

McCorduck, Pamela, *Machines Who Think,* W.H. Freeman, 1979, pp. 122–123.
Mishkoff, Henry C., *Understanding Artificial Intelligence,* Howard W. Sams, 1985, pp. 31–35, 152.

Periodicals

Fox, John, "Models of Mind," *Nature,* September 26, 1991, pp. 312–313.
New York Times, July 20, 1992, p. D8.
Waldrop, M. Mitchell, "SOAR: A Unified Theory of Cognition?," *Science,* July 15, 1988, pp. 296–298.
Waldrop, M. Mitchell, "Toward a Unified Theory of Cognition," *Science,* July 1, 1988, pp. 27–29.

—Sketch by Daniel Rooney

Norman Dennis Newell
1909-
American paleontologist and geologist

Paleontologists spend their lives investigating the events of millions of years ago through the fossil record and stratigraphy, or the examination of the layers of the earth's crust. It is a complex record, and since the nineteenth century when such studies bur-

geoned, a debate has raged between uniformitarians, who argue that life has evolved over the ages in a relatively smooth progression, and the catastrophists, who counter that life forms have undergone radical changes through the millennia as a result of climatic and geologic catastrophes. Norman Dennis Newell, through painstaking research of the fossil record around the world, has added greatly to this debate, and his findings suggest a much more radical and episodic process of evolution than was thought possible. Newell has done much to popularize the understanding of rapid extinctions and introductions of life forms on earth, and has explored the changes in sea level brought about by geographic or climatic changes as one cause of such rapid alterations. In his long career as a paleontologist and geologist, Newell has surveyed parts of the earth from Texas to the Bahamas to the Pacific atolls, and as an academic, curator, and writer, he has introduced paleontology to new generations of scholars and lay people alike. Born on January 7, 1909, in Chicago, Illinois, Newell is the son of Virgil Bingham and Nellie (Clark) Newell. His father was a dental surgeon and amateur geologist who instilled in the young Newell a lasting interest in rocks and in nature in general. Newell grew up in central Kansas, attended the University of Kansas, and earned his B.S. there in 1929 and his A.M. in 1931. He worked with the Kansas Geologic Survey during this time and performed in a jazz band to help put himself through school. While a graduate student he married his first wife, Valerie Zirkle, in 1928. After graduating from the University of Kansas, Newell attended Yale University, where he earned his Ph.D. in 1933.

Early Interest Focuses on Bivalves

Newell stayed on at Yale as a Sterling Fellow, and it was during this fellowship at the Yale Peabody Museum that he became intensely interested in bivalve mollusks (animals with two-part shells, such as clams) as indicators of evolutionary principles. He studied both living and fossil mollusks and developed a classification system that was adapted internationally. He was made an assistant professor of geology at the University of Kansas in 1934. In 1937 he was chosen as a delegate to the 17th International Geologic Congress in Moscow, and that same year accepted a position at the University of Wisconsin as an associate professor of geology, where he remained until 1945. From 1939 to 1942, he was the co-editor of the *Journal of Paleontology.* While at Wisconsin, Newell led a research team to Peru to survey for petroleum reserves. Once in Peru, he also surveyed the entire Lake Titicaca basin, the results of which led to a revised theory of the geological formation of the Andes mountains. After World War II, Newell moved on to Columbia University in New York, where he was made a full professor of geology, holding also a concurrent position as chairman and curator of invertebrate paleontology at the American Museum of Natural History.

Conducts Worldwide Geologic Surveys

The next decades were a period of intense research and rich field work for Newell, as he conducted field surveys from the South Pacific to the Bahamas. His work in the Guadalupe Mountains of western Texas from 1949 to 1952 uncovered such a rich and varied fossil record that the area was subsequently designated a national park. Working in the South Pacific at the Raroia coral atoll in 1952, Newell verified Darwin's theory of the development of coral atolls, and surveying in the Great Bahama Bank in 1950 and 1951, he demonstrated that such islands were indeed remnants of a huge barrier reef, one that was once far more extensive even than modern day Australia's Great Barrier Reef. In 1967 he was also a member of a Scripps Institute of Oceanography expedition to Micronesia. Other field work took him to North Africa for surveys in Tunisia and Morocco. Through all of these studies, Newell was able to put together a picture of the earth's geologic and fossil record that suggests a less than gradual evolution of life forms. Indeed, the differences in fossilized life forms that Newell found embedded in rock strata indicated what he termed episodic revolutions in life, or large and radical changes over relatively brief periods of geologic time.

The author of numerous books and articles on geology and paleontology, Newell has been internationally honored for his work in these fields. In 1960 he was awarded the Mary Clark Thompson Medal from the National Academy of Sciences (of which he is a member); a medal from the University of Hiroshima in 1964; the Hayden Memorial Award in paleontology and geology from the Academy of Natural Sciences in 1965; Yale University's Verrill Medal in 1966; the Gold Medal for Distinguished Achievement in Science from the National Museum of Natural History in 1978; and the Raymond C. Moore Medal in 1980. Newell's first wife died in the early 1970s and he married Gillian Wendy Wormall Schacht in 1973. Retiring from both Columbia University and the American Museum of Natural History in 1977, Newell continued on at both institutions in an emeritus capacity. The year after his retirement he was an exchange scholar to the Soviet Union under the sponsorship of the American Academy of Sciences. In his retirement, Newell spends several days a week at the American Museum of Natural History and enjoys field expeditions and collecting minerals.

SELECTED WRITINGS BY NEWELL:

Books

(With John M. Jewett) *The Geology of Johnson and Miami Counties, Kansas, and the Geology of Wyandotte County, Kansas,* University of Kansas, 1935.
Late Paleozoic Pelecypods: Pectinacea and Mytilacca, University of Kansas, 1937.
Geology of Lake Titicaca Region, Peru and Bolivia, Geological Society of America, 1949.
(With others) *The Permian Reef of the Guadalupe Mountains Region, Texas and New Mexico: A Study in Paleoecology,* W. H. Freeman, 1953.
(With others) *Upper Paleozoic of Peru,* Geological Society of America, 1953.
Organism Communities and Bottom Facies, Great Bahama Bank, American Museum of Natural History, 1959.
Creation and Evolution: Myth or Reality?, Columbia University Press, 1982.

SOURCES:

Books

Contemporary Authors, Volume 104, Gale, 1982, pp. 338–339.
McGraw-Hill Modern Scientists and Engineers, McGraw-Hill, 1980, pp. 358–359.

—*Sketch by J. Sydney Jones*

Margaret Morse Nice
1883-1974
American ornithologist

Margaret Morse Nice became one of America's leading ornithologists due to her insistence on the importance of studying the behavior of individual birds to better understand the nature of each species as a whole. Her detailed observations provided a major contribution to the study of birds and have had a lasting effect on the field of ornithology, despite the fact that she never held a faculty appointment or received university funding. Nice was also a wife and the mother of four children, with a traditional role in her family, and most of her contributions were made by investigating birds in her own backyard.

Nice was born Margaret Morse on December 6, 1883, in Amherst, Massachusetts, to Anson and Margaret (Ely) Morse. Her father was a professor of history at Amherst College; he was also a dedicated gardener and had a deep love of the wilderness. Her mother had studied botany at Mount Holyoke and helped inspire in her daughter a love of nature, teaching her the name of wild flowers as they walked in the woods. In her autobiography, *Research Is a Passion with Me,* Nice would later describe how in her family's two-acre orchard and garden, "we learned of nature at first hand, planting and weeding in our own small gardens." Her interest in ornithology began early: she was recording her observations of birds by the age of twelve.

Nice attended a private elementary school and the public high school in Amherst, and then in 1901 she enrolled in Mount Holyoke College, as had her mother. At first she concentrated on languages, but later switched to the natural sciences. She graduated in 1906 and the following year received a fellowship to study biology for two years at Clark University in Worcester, Massachusetts. In August of 1909, she married Leonard Blaine Nice, whom she had met there. That same year, the couple moved to Cambridge, where Leonard Nice entered Harvard Medical School. In 1913, he was appointed the head of the physiology department at the University of Oklahoma and Nice moved with him to Norman, Oklahoma.

Nice's first paper, which dealt with bobwhites, was published after more than two years of research. Mostly confined to the house during the following years as her four daughters were born and she tended to them, Nice would not publish any more ornithological research until 1920. Frustrated by her inability to pursue her studies in this field, Nice began studying how her daughters acquired language. This work later earned her a master's degree in psychology from Clark University in 1915, and she published eighteen articles on child psychology.

Researches Territorial Behavior of Birds

In the 1920s, Nice was influenced to return to the study of birds by an older friend, Althea Sherman, an amateur ornithologist. In 1920, Nice published a description of Oklahoma bird life. Thirty-five more articles about Oklahoma birds followed, and in 1924 she published a book on the subject, *The Birds of Oklahoma.* In 1927, her husband accepted a teaching position in Columbus, Ohio, and the family moved to a house on the bank of a river which attracted a number of nesting and migratory birds, including sparrows. There, Nice studied the territorial behavior of birds by placing colored bands on them and following them for years in a way no one had before. Her studies resulted in several publications, the most important of which was her two-part *Studies in the*

Life History of the Song Sparrow, published in 1937 and 1943. With the publication of these volumes, she became one of the world's leading ornithologists. *Notable American Women* quoted German evolutionary biologist **Ernst Mayr** as saying that Nice had "almost singlehandedly, initiated a new era in American ornithology."

Nice and her family moved to Chicago in 1936, where her husband had accepted an appointment at the University of Chicago Medical School. She was not able to do nearly as many field observations there, but she continued to write and study. Her knowledge of languages enabled her to expose Americans to European ornithology through translations and reviews of articles in German and other languages. During this period she became increasingly active as a conservationist, advocating the preservation of wildlife and restrictions on the use of pesticides.

Nice was president of the Wilson Ornithological Society in 1938 and 1939, the first woman to be elected president of a major American ornithological society. She was also associate editor of the journal *Bird-Banding* from 1935 to 1942 and 1946 to 1974. Mount Holyoke awarded her an honorary doctorate in 1955. In 1969, the Wilson Ornithological Society inaugurated a grant in her name to be given to self-trained amateur researchers. Nice died in Chicago on June 26, 1974, at the age of ninety.

SELECTED WRITINGS BY NICE:

Books

(With Leonard Blaine Nice) *The Birds of Oklahoma,* University of Oklahoma, 1924, revised edition, 1931.
Studies in the Life History of the Song Sparrow, two volumes, [New York], 1937 and 1943, Dover, 1964.
The Watcher at the Nest, Macmillan, 1939.
Research Is a Passion with Me, Consolidated Amethyst, 1979.

SOURCES:

Books

Conway, Jill K., editor, *Written by Herself,* Vintage Books, 1991.
Sicherman, Barbara, and Carol Hurd Green, editors, *Notable American Women: The Modern Period,* Belknap, 1980.

Periodicals

Trautman, Milton B., "In Memoriam: Margaret Morse Nice," *The Auk,* July, 1977.

—Sketch by Margo Nash

Roberta J. Nichols
1931-
American engineer

As a principal research engineer with Ford Motor Company since 1979, Roberta J. Nichols is an internationally recognized innovator in alternative fuel for transportation vehicles. She is the holder of three patents for the Flexible Fuel Vehicle (FFV), which can run on alcohol, gasoline, or any combination of these substances mixed in one fuel tank. Nichols has delivered lectures or seminars in Europe, Japan, Australia, China, and India. She has served as consultant for the Office of Technology Assessment (OTA) of the U.S. Congress, and has been a witness at numerous federal and state government hearings on the use of alcohol-fueled vehicles.

Nichols was born on November 29, 1931, in Los Angeles, California, and received her education there. She first began her career as a mathematician with Douglas Aircraft Company in 1957, working in the company's data analysis section in missiles engineering. She held a similar position at TRW's Space Technology Laboratory from 1958 to 1960 in the propulsion department.

In 1960 Nichols accepted a position as research associate of the Aerodynamics and Propulsion Laboratory with the Aerospace Corporation in El Segundo, California. During her employment with the firm, she was widowed and decided, with two children to raise, to return to school to better her career prospects. Her interest in boat and car racing propelled her to study engineering. Nichols thus completed work on her bachelor of science degree in physics at the University of California at Los Angeles in 1968. She earned a master of science degree in environmental engineering in 1975 and a Ph.D. in engineering in 1979, both at the University of Southern California. In addition to her schooling, she conducted research on Air Force-related projects, such as wind-tunnel testing of re-entry vehicles, from 1960 until 1969.

During 1969 Nichols was also named co-manager of the Chemical Kinetics Department at the Aerospace Corporation and subsequently established and operated the Air Pollution Laboratory. She conducted various studies, developing emission reductions through two-stage combustion and the use of lead-free, high-octane fuel.

In 1978, Nichols served as consultant to the State of California's Synthetic Fuels Program, where she developed engine and vehicle modifications used to create a station wagon which ran only on methanol fuel. Her work in the late 1970s also encompassed research on police vehicles and hydrogen-powered vehicles.

Earns Patents for Multi-Fuel Burning Engines

Nichols began her leadership role in Flexible Fuel Vehicles (FFV) soon after joining Ford in 1979. She has earned three patents for technologies used in engines which burn fuels of different octane, volatility, and volumetric energy content. In 1992, she was named as electric vehicle external strategy and planning manager in the Electric Vehicle Program Office of Car Product Development. While at Ford, Nichols developed ethanol-fueled engines for Ford of Brazil; designed and developed 630 methanol-fueled Escorts, which were used primarily for California government fleets; designed and developed the powertrain for the Alternate Fuel Vehicle (AFV), an auto which was displayed at the Knoxville, Tennessee, World's Fair in 1982; gave seminars in Europe, New Zealand, Australia, the Philippines, and Japan; consulted on alternative fuels in India and China; and served as Ford spokesperson to the media. Nichols also has participated on numerous advisory committees, and has been a guest lecturer at universities across the United States and Canada.

Among the honors received by Nichols are the Outstanding Engineer Merit Award, given by the Institute for the Advancement of Engineering; the Aerospace Corporation's Woman of the Year Award; and the South Coast Air Quality Management District's Clean Air Award for Advancing Air Pollution Technology. She was also the recipient of the Society of Women Engineers Achievement Award in 1988 and was nominated for the National Medal of Technology in 1989. An avid boat and auto racer, she held the women's world water speed record from 1966 to 1969. She has designed and built the boat and auto engines, including her first methanol engine, that she has driven in various competitions. Her husband, Lynn Yakal, shares her love of racing.

On being a woman pioneer in engineering, Nichols told *UCLA Magazine:* "I was the typical tomboy, and always went to welding shops and junkyards with my dad. I didn't know I wasn't supposed to like that stuff!"

SOURCES:

Periodicals

"A Woman's Driving Passions," *Michigan Woman,* September/October 1988, p. 30–31.
"Roberta Nichols, Designing Superwoman," *UCLA Magazine,* winter, 1990, p. 96.

—Sketch by Karen Withem

Charles J. H. Nicolle
1866-1936
French bacteriologist

Charles J. H. Nicolle, the recipient of the 1928 Nobel Prize for physiology or medicine, was recognized by the Swedish Academy for his research into the cause of typhus, a severe and widespread disease during the early twentieth century. Nicolle's discovery that typhus is transmitted by the human body louse—and therefore can be readily prevented—was of great benefit to both military and civilian medicine.

Born September 21, 1866, in Rouen, France, Charles Jules Henri Nicolle was the son of physician Eugène Nicolle. Charles's father was a medical doctor at the municipal hospital, as well as a professor of natural history at the École des Sciences et des Art. Encouraged by his brother, the noted bacteriologist Maurice Nicolle, Charles took a course in bacteriology at the Institute Pasteur in Paris, studying under the renowned bacteriologists, Émile Roux and **Élie Metchnikoff**. For his doctoral dissertation, Nicolle investigated the bacterium then called Ducrey's Bacillus (also known as *Hemophilus ducreyi*), the causative agent of soft chancre, a type of venereal disease.

Charles took his medical degree in 1893 in Paris, then returned to Rouen for a staff position in a hospital. Shortly thereafter, he married Alice Avice; their two sons, Marcelle and Pierre, would eventually become physicians. Unable to develop a major biomedical research center in Rouen as he desired, Nicolle agreed in 1902 to assume the directorship of the Institute Pasteur in Tunis, Tunisia. For the remainder of his life, Nicolle lived and worked primarily in Tunis with occasional lecturing in Paris.

Investigating the Source of Typhus

Affiliated with the original Institute Pasteur (which was founded in Paris in 1888), the institute in Tunis was basically an organization in name only. Over the years to come, however, Nicolle improved a run-down antirabies vaccination unit into a leading center for the study of North African and tropical diseases. It was in Tunis where Nicolle accomplished his groundbreaking work on typhus. He became intrigued by the observation that an outbreak of typhus did not seem to take hold in hospital wards as it did among the general populace of the city. Although the contagion infected workers who admitted patients into the hospital, it did not affect other patients or attendants in the actual wards. Those who collected or laundered the dirty clothes of newly admitted patients typically came down with the disease.

Realizing that the washing, shaving, and providing of clean clothes to the new patient was possibly the key to the pattern of infection, Nicolle initiated a series of experiments in 1909 to confirm his suspicion of the arthropod-borne nature of typhus. He theorized that lice, which attached themselves to the bodies and clothes of human beings, transmitted the disease, so he began his investigation by infusing a chimpanzee with human blood infected with typhus, then transferred the chimpanzee's blood to a healthy macaque monkey. When the fever and rash of typhus was seen on the monkey, Nicolle placed twenty-nine human body lice obtained from healthy humans on the skin of the macaque. These lice were later placed on the skin of a number of healthy monkeys, which all contracted the disease.

Once Nicolle isolated the relationship between typhus and the louse, preventative measures were established to counter unsanitary conditions. Nevertheless, the trenches of World War I remained major breeding places for the louse and typhus killed an enormous number of soldiers on all sides of the conflict. The development of the insecticide DDT by **Paul Müller** in 1939 was the most effective prophylactic against typhus, nearly eradicating the disease among soldiers during World War II.

Nicolle is also responsible for other important contributions to the science of bacteriology. Stemming from his research into typhus was his recognition of a phenomenon known as "inapparent infection," a state in which a carrier of a disease exhibits no symptoms. This theoretical discovery suggested how diseases survived from one epidemic to another.

Nicolle, along with a variety of other colleagues over time, also researched African infantile leishmaniasis, which affected humans, and a related disease in dogs. Another significant discovery concerned the role of flies in the transmission of the blinding disease trachoma. For these and other works, Nicolle received the French Commander of the Legion of Honor and was named to the French Academy of Medicine. In 1932 he became a professor in the College de France.

Besides his work in science, Nicolle was an accomplished literary figure, having published several novels. His scientific writings include five major books as well as numerous articles. Nicolle died on February 28, 1936 in Tunis.

SELECTED WRITINGS BY NICOLLE:

Books

La destinee humaine, par Charles Nicolle, Felix Alcan, 1936.

Destin des Maladies Infectieuses, Presses universitaires de France, 1939.

Periodicals

"Recherches expérimentales sur le typhus ex-
anthématique," *Annales de l'Institut Pasteur,*
Volume 24, pp. 243–275, 1910.

—*Sketch by Dr. Donald J. McGraw*

Alfred O. C. Nier
1911-
American physicist

Alfred O. C. Nier's research and discoveries in the
area of examining and defining isotopes through
mass spectroscopy have led to important findings,
particularly in the areas of uranium isotopes used in
nuclear fission, and the use of isotopes for geological
dating methods. Nier invented the double-focusing
mass spectrometer which was used in the Viking
Spacecraft's visit to Mars, bringing back the first on-
site data from that planet.

Alfred Otto Carl Nier was born on May 28, 1911,
in St. Paul, Minnesota. His parents were August C.
and Anna J. Stoll Nier, both immigrants to the United
States from Germany. Nier attended the University of
Minnesota, from which he received a bachelor of
science degree in 1931 and a master of science degree
in 1933, both in the field of electrical engineering. He
then changed his major to physics and earned his
Ph.D. in that subject in 1936.

Begins Studies in Mass Spectroscopy

From his days as a graduate student, Nier's
career has reflected his ability to look at problems
from two perspectives: that of the technologically-
oriented engineer, and that of the research-oriented
physicist. Much of his work has involved the use of
mass spectrometers to analyze the isotopic composition of elements.

The principle of mass spectroscopy was developed in the first decade of the twentieth century by
Francis W. Aston. In a mass spectrometer, atoms are
ionized and then accelerated through electrical and
magnetic fields. Since these fields act with different
force on ions of different mass, the spectrometer can
be used to separate particles according to their
masses. That separation is relatively clear-cut when

mass differences are large, but becomes less clear as
the masses of two particles become closer in size.

An important objective of Nier's work has been
to refine the mass spectrometric process so that it can
distinguish smaller and smaller mass differences. One
such refinement is the double-focusing mass spectrometer. In Nier's version of the double-focusing
mass spectrometer, a beam of ions is accelerated first
through an electrical field at an angle of ninety
degrees, and then through a magnetic field at an angle
of sixty degrees. Nier found that this arrangement
could be used to achieve a high degree of separation
of ions with similar masses at a cost much less than
that of conventional mass spectrometers.

Mass Spectrometer Used to Discover Important Isotopes

Nier's first major discovery, the radioactive
isotope potassium–40, was made while he was still a
graduate student in Minnesota. That discovery was of
considerable importance, since potassium is one of
the most abundant elements in the Earth's crust, and
potassium–40 is, therefore, an important source of
background radiation. In 1934, Nier and Lyman T.
Aldrich were able to show how the decay of potassium–40 to argon–40 can be used to measure the age of
very old objects. That technique has since become
extraordinarily useful in the dating of geological
objects and materials.

From 1936 to 1938, Nier worked at Harvard
University under a National Research Council fellowship. While there, he used the mass spectrometer to
determine the isotopic composition (the percentage of
each isotope of a given mass) for a number of
elements. During this work he discovered a number of
new isotopes whose abundance is so low that they had
never been identified previously. These included
sulfur–36, calcium–46, calcium–48, and osmium–186. He also carried out studies on the relative
abundance of two isotopes of carbon, carbon–12 and
carbon–13, and showed that the ratio of the two is a
function of the source from which the carbon is taken.
This research has been put to use in recent attempts to
estimate the temperature of past geological years.

Nier's most important research was his study of
the isotopes of uranium. His earliest research was
aimed at determining the relationship between the
radioactive isotopes of this element and the isotopes
of lead, some of which are formed during the decay of
uranium. This work eventually provided scientists
with a second method for estimating the age of rocks,
a method based on the ratio of radiogenic lead (from
uranium) to non-radiogenic lead.

The early uranium studies led to even more
significant research during World War II. In 1938,
Otto Hahn and **Fritz Strassmann** discovered that

fission occurs when uranium is bombarded by neutrons. Physicists immediately understood the enormous potential of this discovery as a source of energy for both peaceful applications and, more relevant at the time, for the development of weapons. One practical problem of the development of nuclear fission as a source of energy was the uncertainty as to which isotope of uranium actually undergoes fission. Nier answered this question in 1940, working with J. R. Dunning, E. T. Booth, and A. V. Grosse at Columbia University, as they were able to show that it is the relatively uncommon uranium–235, rather than the more common uranium–238, that undergoes fission. During and after the war, Nier was active in the development of methods for separating these two isotopes from each other.

In 1938, at the conclusion of this postdoctoral work at Harvard, Nier returned to Minnesota. He remained there for the rest of his academic career as assistant professor (1938–40), associate professor (1940–44), professor (1944–66), and finally, Regents' Professor of Physics (after 1966).

Nier's research using mass spectographs to measure isotopes and other atomic masses led to his invention of the first double-focusing mass spectrometer, miniature versions of which were later used on satellites observing the lower thermosphere. Nier was appointed by the National Aeronautics and Space Administration to lead the Entry Science team to study the composition and structure of the Martian atmosphere during the Viking spacecraft's descent to the planet's surface. On this mission, Nier's mass spectrometer provided the first on-site information known about the make-up of the atmosphere of Mars.

Nier has been married twice, first to Ruth E. Andersen in 1937, and then to Ardish L. Hovland in 1969. He has one son and one daughter. His work has been recognized by the American Geological Society's Arthur L. Day Medal (1956), the Goldschmidt Medal of the Geochemical Society (1984), the U.S. Atomic Energy Commission's Field and Franklin Award (1985), and the Thomson Medal of the International Mass Spectrometry Conference (1985).

SOURCES:

Books

McGraw-Hill Modern Scientists and Engineers, Volume 2, McGraw-Hill, 1980, pp. 361–363.

—*Sketch by David E. Newton*

Marshall Warren Nirenberg
1927-
American biochemist

Marshall Warren Nirenberg is best known for deciphering the portion of DNA (deoxyribonucleic acid) that is responsible for the synthesis of the numerous protein molecules which form the basis of living cells. His research has helped to unravel the DNA genetic code, aiding, for example, in the determination of which genes code for certain hereditary traits. For his contribution to the sciences of genetics and cell biochemistry, Nirenberg was awarded the 1968 Nobel Prize in physiology or medicine with **Robert W. Holley** and **Har Gobind Khorana**.

Nirenberg was born in New York City on April 10, 1927, and moved to Florida with his parents, Harry Edward and Minerva (Bykowsky) Nirenberg, when he was ten years old. He earned his B.S. in 1948 and his M.Sc. in biology in 1952 from the University of Florida. Nirenberg's interest in science extended beyond his formal studies. For two of his undergraduate years he worked as a teaching assistant in biology, and he also spent a brief period as a research assistant in the nutrition laboratory. In 1952, Nirenberg continued his graduate studies at the University of Michigan, this time in the field of biochemistry. Obtaining his Ph.D. in 1957, he wrote his dissertation on the uptake of hexose, a sugar molecule, by ascites tumor cells.

Shortly after earning his Ph.D., Nirenberg began his investigation into the inner workings of the genetic code as an American Cancer Society (ACS) fellow at the National Institutes of Health (NIH) in Bethesda, Maryland. Nirenberg continued his research at the NIH after the ACS fellowship ended in 1959, under another fellowship from the Public Health Service (PHS). In 1960, when the PHS fellowship ended, he joined the NIH staff permanently as a research scientist in biochemistry.

Nirenberg Cracks the Genetic Code

After only a brief time conducting research at the NIH, Nirenberg made his mark in genetic research with the most important scientific breakthrough since **James D. Watson** and **Francis Crick** discovered the structure of DNA in 1953. Specifically, he discovered the process for unraveling the code of DNA. This process allows scientists to determine the genetic basis of particular hereditary traits. In August of 1961, Nirenberg announced his discovery during a routine presentation of a research paper at a meeting of the International Congress of Biochemistry in Moscow.

Marshall Warren Nirenberg

Nirenberg's research involved the genetic code sequences for amino acids. Amino acids are the building blocks of protein. They link together to form the numerous protein molecules present in the human body. Nirenberg discovered how to determine which sequences patterns code for which amino acids (there are about 20 known amino acids).

Nirenberg Honored with Nobel Prize

Nirenberg's discovery has led to a better understanding of genetically determined diseases and, more controversially, to further research into the controlling of hereditary traits, or genetic engineering. For his research, Nirenberg was awarded the 1968 Nobel Prize for physiology or medicine. He shared the honor with scientists Har Gobind Khorana and Robert W. Holley. After receiving the Nobel Prize, Nirenberg switched his research focus to other areas of biochemistry, including cellular control mechanisms and the cell differentiation process.

Since first being hired by the NIH in 1960, Nirenberg has served in different capacities. From 1962 until 1966 he was Head of the Section for Biochemical Genetics, National Heart Institute. Since 1966 he has been serving as the Chief of the Laboratory of Biochemical Genetics, National Heart, Lung and Blood Institute. Other honors bestowed upon Nirenberg, in addition to the Nobel Prize, include honorary membership in the Harvey Society, the Molecular Biology Award from the National Academy of Sci-

ences (1962), National Medal of Science presented by President Lyndon B. Johnson (1965), and the Louisa Gross Horwitz Prize for Biochemistry (1968). Nirenberg also received numerous honorary degrees from distinguished universities, including the University of Michigan (1965), University of Chicago (1965), Yale University (1965), University of Windsor (1966), George Washington University (1972), and the Weizmann Institute in Israel (1978). Nirenberg is a member of several professional societies, including the National Academy of Sciences, the Pontifical Academy of Sciences, the American Chemical Society, the Biophysical Society, and the Society for Developmental Biology.

Nirenberg married biochemist Perola Zaltzman in 1961. While described as being a reserved man who engages in little else besides scientific research, Nirenberg has been a strong advocate of government support for scientific research, believing this to be an important factor for the advancement of science.

SELECTED WRITINGS BY NIRENBERG:

Periodicals

Scientific American, March, 1963, p. 33.

SOURCES:

Books

Wasson, Tyler, editor, *Nobel Prize Winners,* H. W. Wilson, 1987, pp. 767–768.

Periodicals

New York Times, October 12, 1982, p. C3.

—*Sketch by Carla Mecoli-Kamp*

Jun-ichi Nishizawa
1926-
Japanese electrical engineer

Inventor, educator, and engineer Jun-ichi Nishizawa has made significant contributions to the field of semiconductor devices, which are materials that can act as insulators or conductors; they are used in electronics and are a main component in computers. Nishizawa's inventions include the "pin" diode, which is a type of diode (a device which carries electrical current in one direction only) that is a building block in semiconductors and also used in motor drives and power supplies. He also developed the static induction transistor (SIT), which is a high-power, high-frequency device which operates as a kind of switch and is applied in AM/FM transmittors, ultrasonic generators, and high voltage power supplies. Nishizawa has twice received the Director's Award of the Japanese Science and Technology Agency for his work on semiconductors, and received the Medal of Honor with Purple Ribbon from the Japanese Government in 1976 for his invention of the SIT.

Jun-ichi Nishizawa was born in Sendai, Japan on September 12, 1926, the second of five children. His father, Kyosuke Nishizawa, was the director of the Faculty of Engineering of Tohoku University. Nishizawa attended elementary and high school in Sendai before attending Tohoku University where he studied electrical engineering, receiving his bachelor of science in 1948.

In 1950, while doing postgraduate work at Tohoku University, he invented the pin diode and the "pnip" transistor, a variation on a bipolar transistor, which is a semiconductor used in almost all types of electronic circuits. Nishizawa's transistor was an improvement because it has an additional layer of high resistivity semiconductor material between the usual positive and negative semiconductor layers. During this time he also invented the SIT and the avalanche photo diode, which is a type of semiconductor that converts optical signals to electrical signals; they are highly sensitive devices with quick response speed and low noise. Avalanche photo diodes have many uses, especially in fiber-optic communications. Nishizawa also proposed the use of ion implantation in semiconductors.

Nishizawa joined the staff of the Research Institute of Electrical Communication at Tohoku University in 1953 as a research assistant; he became an assistant professor the following year. Throughout this period he conducted research which led to his invention of semiconductor injection lasers, transit time effect negative resistance diodes, which are among the most powerful sources of solid-state microwave power, and the hyperabrupt variable capacitance diode, a type of diode used in resonant circuits.

Nishizawa also continued his education, earning his doctor of engineering degree in 1960. Two years later he was made a full professor. During his tenure, he was appointed to various directorships at Tohoku University including director of the Semiconductor Research Institute, a position he has held since 1968, and director of the Research Institute of Electrical Communication, which he held in 1983 and again from 1989 to 1990. He remained active as a full professor until 1990, when he was elected president of the university. Nishizawa has written numerous technical papers on semiconductor devices, and has been granted over two hundred Japanese and fifty U.S. patents. Besides the positions held at Tohoku, he was also head of the Perfect Crystal Technology Research Project. This was an Exploratory Research Project for Advanced Technology sponsored by the Japanese Science and Technology Agency.

Nishizawa's extensive honors include the 1966 Imperial Inventions Prize, the 1985 Asahir Prize, the 1986 Honda Prize, and the 1989 Order of Cultural Merits. In addition, he was made a fellow of the Institute of Electrical and Electronics Engineers in 1969 for his technical contributions to solid state electronics, and received the Jack A. Morton Award from this organization in 1983. He was made a foreign member of the USSR Academy of Sciences (later the Russian Academy of Sciences) in 1988. Nishizawa has also been active in other technical societies including the Institute of Physics, the Institution of Electrical Engineers, and the Electrochemical Society. In 1991 he served as president of the Institute of Electronics and Communication Engineers of Japan.

In 1956, Nishizawa married Takeko Hayakawa and the first of their three children was born a year later. Besides his technical interests, he enjoys China ceramics, classical music, and French Impressionist paintings.

SELECTED WRITINGS BY NISHIZAWA:

Books

(Editor) *Semiconductor Technologies 1982,* Ohmsha Ltd, Tokyo, 1981.

Periodicals

(With K. Yamamoto) "High-Frequency High-Power Static Induction Transistor," *IEEE Transactions on Electron Devices,* Volume 25, March, 1978, pp. 314–322.

(With T. Tamamushi, K. Nonaka, and S. Shimomura) "Current Amplification in Nonhomogeneous Base Structure and Static Induction Transistor Structure," *Journal of Applied Physics,* Volume 57, May, 1985, pp. 4783–4797.

(With K. Aoki and T. Akamine) "Simple Structured PMOSFET Fabricated Using Molecular Layer Doping," *IEEE Electron Device Letters,* March, 1990, pp. 105–106.

—Sketch by George A. Ferrance

Yasutomi Nishizuka
1932-
Japanese biochemist

Yasutomi Nishizuka is a celebrated biochemist who discovered protein kinase C, an enzyme which controls the biology of cells. In further studies, he and his group found that tumor-promoting agents could trigger unregulated cell growth by activating protein kinase C. In 1989, Nishizuka won the Lasker Basic Medical Research Award "for his profound contributions to the understanding of signal transduction in cells and for his discovery that carcinogens trigger cell growth by activating protein kinase C." In 1988, he received The Order of Culture from the Emperor of Japan. Nishizuka is professor and chairman of the department of biochemistry at Kobe University School of Medicine and director of the Biosignal Research Center in Kobe.

Nishizuka was born on July 12, 1932. He received his medical degree in 1957 and his Ph.D. in 1962, both from Kyoto University. For the next two years, Nishizuka was a research associate in the laboratory of Osamu Hayaishi in the department of medical chemistry at Kyoto University. While still a research associate, Nishizuka was named an NIH International Postdoctoral Research Fellow in 1964; he went to Rockefeller University in New York City, where he worked in the laboratory of **Fritz Lipmann** for two years. Nishizuka remained on the faculty of Kyoto University until 1969, when he was appointed professor and chairman of the department of biochemistry at Kobe University Medical School.

It was at Kobe University, in 1977, that Nishizuka and his group announced the discovery of protein kinase C, with characteristics which resemble an enzyme. An enzyme is an organic catalyst produced by living cells but capable of acting independently; they are proteins that can cause chemical changes in other substances without being changed themselves. At first, the role of protein kinase C in intracellular signalling was not recognized. But later Nishizuka and his colleagues showed that it could be activated by tumor-promoting agents known as phorbol esters. These substances can remain in a cell membrane, causing it to continually produce protein kinase C— which can lead to uncontrollable cell growth, the basis of many types of carcinogenesis, or cancer.

The work done by Nishizuka and his team initiated many new lines of research; scientists began looking for substances that activate protein kinase C. Nishizuka's work also revealed the overwhelming importance of protein kinase C in the maintenance of normal health in all living things above the level of unicellular microorganisms. Exploration of the enzyme continues. It is now understood that it is part of a large family of proteins with multiple sub-species exhibiting individual enzymological characteristics and distinct patterns of tissue distribution.

Among the many prizes Nishizuka has received for his work are the Award of the Japan Academy in 1986; the Cultural Merit Prize from the Japanese Government in 1987; the Alfred P. Sloan Jr. Prize in 1988 from the General Motors Cancer Research Foundation; the Gairdner Foundation International Award in 1988; the Order of Culture in 1988 from the Emperor of Japan; the Albert Lasker Basic Medical Research Award in 1989, and the Kyoto Prize in 1992. In 1994, he received the Dale Medal from the British Endocrine Society. He was elected a foreign associate of the National Academy of Sciences in the United States in 1988 and a foreign member of the Royal Society of the United Kingdom in 1990. In addition to being a member of the Japan Academy, he is also a foreign associate of l'Academie des Sciences in France and a foreign honorary member of the American Academy of Arts and Sciences. The magazine *Science* noted that of the ten most cited Japanese papers of the 1980s, five were written by Nishizuka.

In June of 1992, Nishizuka was appointed director of the Biosignal Research Center at Kobe University and continues in the position. Nishizuka is married and has two daughters. The family lives in Ashiya.

SELECTED WRITINGS BY NISHIZUKA:

Periodicals

"The Role of Protein Kinase C in Cell Surface Signal Transduction and Tumor Promotion," *Nature,* Volume 308, 1984, pp. 696–697.
"Studies and Perspectives of Protein Kinase C, *Science,* Volume 233, 1986, pp. 305–312.

SOURCES:

Periodicals

"Science News," *Science,* Volume 258, 1992, p. 574.

Other

Nishizuka, Yasutomi, written communication to Margo Nash sent February 17, 1994.

—Sketch by Margo Nash

G. K. Noble
1894-1940
American zoologist and naturalist

Zoologist and naturalist G. K. Noble was one of those rare individuals who was able to transform a childhood fascination into his life's work. As a young boy Noble was attracted to animals and nature and these early interests carried over to a career as a naturalist and zoologist with the American Museum of Natural History in New York. Noble's interest in the natural world ranged from reptiles, amphibians, birds, and fish to animal behavior based on psychological and biological factors.

Gladwyn Kingsley Noble was born in Yonkers, New York, on September 20, 1894, the son of Gilbert Clifford Noble and Elizabeth Adams. He spent his youth in Yonkers and fixed on a career as a naturalist even before graduating from Yonkers High School. His career choice led him to Harvard University, where he earned his bachelor's and master's degrees in zoology in 1916 and 1918, respectively. As a college student, Noble's initial interest was in birds, and he published his first scientific paper—on the predation of cats on nesting seagull colonies—at age 19. At Harvard he participated in two field trips, to the islands of Newfoundland and Guadeloupe, to collect bird specimens. An expedition as a general zoologist to Peru in 1916 prompted Noble's deep interest in reptiles and amphibians.

After serving in the Office of the Chief of Naval Operations during World War I, Noble began his long affiliation with American Museum of Natural History in 1919. He joined the institution as an assistant curator of herpetology, which is the study of reptiles and amphibians. Simultaneously, he began work on his doctorate in zoology at Columbia University, which he completed in 1922. Noble's thesis reclassified frogs and toads and almost immediately was hailed as a significant contribution to herpetology. Meanwhile, he became an associate curator in 1922 and then, in 1924, curator of herpetology at the museum.

Noble married Ruth Crosby, an assistant curator in the museum's education department, in 1921, and she and their two sons often accompanied him on field trips. During his relatively short career, Noble was a prolific writer and lecturer. He published nearly 200 scientific papers—many of them on amphibians—as well as the 1931 guide to amphibian animals, *The Biology of the Amphibia*. In the final decade of his life, Noble switched his zoological attention to behavioral and physiological pursuits and expanded his field of research to fish and birds. This work and his

lectures and notes resulted in the posthumous publication of the book *The Nature of the Beast,* a popular account of animal psychology, edited by his wife. Noble rejected a number of job offers from universities and remained at the American Museum of Natural History for his entire career. He did, however, dedicate time to the education of others, giving biology lectures at Columbia and serving as a visiting professor at the University of Chicago and New York University.

SELECTED WRITINGS BY NOBLE:

Books

The Biology of the Amphibia, McGraw-Hill, 1931.
The Nature of the Beast, edited by Ruth Crosby Noble, Doubleday, 1945.

—Sketch by Joel Schwarz

Ida Tacke Noddack
1896-1979
German chemist

Working with fellow chemist Walter Noddack (her future husband) and X-ray specialist Otto Berg, Ida Tacke discovered element 75, rhenium, in 1925, thus solving one of the mysteries of the periodic table of elements introduced by Russian chemist Dmitri Ivanovich Mendeleev in 1869. Ida Tacke Noddack's continuing study of the periodic table also led her to be the first to suggest in 1934 that physicist **Enrico Fermi** had not made a new element in an experiment with uranium as he thought, but instead had discovered nuclear fission. Her prediction was not verified until 1939.

Ida Tacke was born in Germany on February 25, 1896 and studied at the Technical University in Berlin, where she received the first prize for chemistry and metallurgy in 1919. In 1921, soon after receiving her doctorate, she set out to isolate two of the elements that Mendeleev had predicted when he proposed the Periodic System and displayed all known elements in a format now called the periodic table. Mendeleev had left blank spaces on his table for several elements that he expected to exist but that had not been identified. Two of these, elements 43 and 75, were located in Group VII under manganese.

Assuming that these elements would be similar in their properties to manganese, scientists had been searching for them in manganese ores. Tacke and Walter Noddack, who headed the chemical laboratory at the Physico-Technical Research Agency in Berlin, focused instead on the lateral neighbors of the missing elements, molybdenum, tungsten, osmium, and ruthenium. With the assistance of Otto Berg of the Werner-Siemens Laboratory, who provided expertise in analyzing the X-ray spectra of substances, Tacke and Noddack isolated element 75 in 1925 and named it rhenium, from *Rhenus,* Latin for the Rhine, an important river in their native Germany. It took them another year to isolate a single gram of the element from 660 kilograms of molybdenite ore. They also believed they had discovered traces of element 43, which they dubbed masurium. Later research, however, did not confirm their results. Now known as technetium, element 43 has never been found in nature, although it has been produced artificially.

In 1926, Ida Tacke married Walter Noddack. They would work together in their research until Walter Noddack's death in 1960, and together would publish some one hundred scientific papers. The Noddacks were awarded the Leibig Medal of the German Chemical Society in 1934 for their discovery of rhenium.

In 1934 Ida Noddack challenged the conclusions of Enrico Fermi and his group that they had produced transuranium elements, artificial elements heavier than uranium, when they bombarded uranium atoms with subatomic particles called neutrons. Although other scientists agreed with Fermi, Noddack suggested he had split uranium atoms into isotopes of known elements rather than added to uranium atoms to produce heavier, unknown elements. She had no research to support her theory, however, and for five years her hypothesis that atomic nuclei had been split was virtually ignored. "Her suggestion was so out of line with the then-accepted ideas about the atomic nucleus that it was never seriously discussed," fellow chemist **Otto Hahn** would later comment in his autobiography. In 1939, after much research had been done by many scientists, Hahn, **Fritz Strassmann** and **Lise Meitner** discovered that Noddack had been right. They named the process nuclear fission.

The Noddacks moved from Berlin to the University of Freiburg in 1935, to the University of Strasbourg in 1943, and to the State Research Institute for Geochemistry in Bamberg in 1956. In 1960, Walter Noddack died. Ida Noddack received the High Service Cross of the German Federal Republic in 1966. During her life she received honorary membership in the Spanish Society of Physics and Chemistry and the International Society of Nutrition Research, as well as an honorary doctorate of science from the University of Hamburg. Ida Noddack retired in 1968 and moved to Bad Neuenahr, a small town on the Rhine. She died in 1979.

SOURCES:

Books

Hahn, Otto, *A Scientific Autobiography,* Scribner, 1966.

Weeks, Mary E., *The Discovery of the Elements,* Mack, 1954, pp. 321–322.

Periodicals

Habashi, Fathi, "Ida Noddack, 75 & Element 75," reprint from *Chemistry,* February, 1971, in *Element Profiles,* American Chemical Society, 1972, pp. 81–82.

Starke, Kurt, "The Detours Leading to the Discovery of Nuclear Fission," *Journal of Chemical Education,* December, 1979, pp. 771–775.

—Sketch by M. C. Nagel

Emmy Noether
1882-1935
German-born American mathematician

Emmy Noether was a world-renowned mathematician whose innovative approach to modern abstract algebra inspired colleagues and students who emulated her technique. Dismissed from her university position at the beginning of the Nazi era in Germany—for she was both Jewish and female—Noether emigrated to the United States, where she taught in several universities and colleges. When she died, **Albert Einstein** eulogized her in a letter to *New York Times* as "the most significant creative mathematical genius thus far produced since the higher education of women began."

Noether was born on March 23, 1882, in the small university town of Erlangen in southern Germany. Her first name was Amalie, but she was known by her middle name of Emmy. Her mother, Ida Amalia Kaufmann Noether, came from a wealthy family in Cologne. Her father, Max Noether, a professor at the University of Erlangen, was an accomplished mathematician who worked on the theory of algebraic functions. Two of her three younger brothers became scientists—Fritz was a mathematician and Alfred earned a doctorate in chemistry.

Noether's childhood was unexceptional, going to school, learning domestic skills, and taking piano lessons. Since girls were not eligible to enroll in the gymnasium (college preparatory school), she attended

Emmy Noether

the Städtischen Höheren Töchterschule, where she studied arithmetic and languages. In 1900 she passed the Bavarian state examinations with evaluations of "very good" in French and English (she received only a "satisfactory" evaluation in practical classroom conduct); this certified her to teach foreign languages at female educational institutions.

Begins a Teaching Career

Instead of looking for a language teaching position, Noether decided to undertake university studies. However, since she had not graduated from a gymnasium, she first had to pass an entrance examination for which she obtained permission from her instructors. She audited courses at the University of Erlangen from 1900 to 1902. In 1903 she passed the matriculation exam, and entered the University of Göttingen for a semester, where she encountered such notable mathematicians as **Hermann Minkowski**, Felix Klein, and **David Hilbert**. She enrolled at the University of Erlangen where women were accepted in 1904. At Erlangen, Noether studied with Paul Gordan, a mathematics professor who was also a family friend. She completed her dissertation entitled "On Complete Systems of Invariants for Ternary Biquadratic Forms," receiving her Ph.D., summa cum laude, on July 2, 1908.

Noether worked without pay at the Mathematical Institute of Erlangen from 1908 until 1915, where her university duties included research, serving as a

dissertation adviser for two students, and occasionally delivering lectures for her ailing father. In addition, Noether began to work with **Ernst Otto Fischer**, an algebraist who directed her toward the broader theoretical style characteristic of Hilbert. Noether not only published her thesis on ternary biquadratics, but she was also elected to membership in the Circolo Matematico di Palermo in 1908. The following year, Noether was invited to join the German Mathematical Society (Deutsche Mathematiker Vereinigung); she addressed the Society's 1909 meeting in Salzburg and its 1913 meeting in Vienna.

Formulates the Mathematics of Relativity

In 1915, Klein and Hilbert invited Noether to join them at the Mathematical Institute in Göttingen. They were working on the mathematics of the newly announced general theory of relativity, and they believed Noether's expertise would be helpful. Einstein later wrote an article for the 1955 Grolier Encyclopedia, characterizing the theory of relativity by the basic question, "how must the laws of nature be constituted so that they are valid in the same form relative to arbitrary systems of co-ordinates (postulate of the invariance of the laws of nature relative to an arbitrary transformation of space and time)?" It was precisely this type of invariance under transformation on which Noether focused her mathematical research.

In 1918, Noether proved two theorems that formed a cornerstone for general relativity. These theorems validated certain relationships suspected by physicists of the time. One, now known as Noether's Theorem, established the equivalence between an invariance property and a conservation law. The other involved the relationship between an invariance and the existence of certain integrals of the equations of motion. The eminent German mathematician **Hermann Weyl** described Noether's contribution in the July 1935 *Scripta Mathematica* following her death: "For two of the most significant sides of the general theory of relativity theory she gave at that time the genuine and universal mathematical formulation."

While Noether was proving these profound and useful results, she was working without pay at Göttingen University, where women were not admitted to the faculty. Hilbert, in particular, tried to obtain a position for her but could not persuade the historians and philosophers on the faculty to vote in a woman's favor. He was able to arrange for her to teach, however, by announcing a class in mathematical physics under his name and letting her lecture in his place. By 1919, regulations were eased somewhat, and she was designated a Privatdozent (a licensed lecturer who could receive fees from students but not from the university). In 1922, Noether was given the unofficial title of associate professor, and was hired as an adjunct teacher and paid a modest salary without fringe benefits or tenure.

Noether's enthusiasm for mathematics made her an effective teacher, often conducting classroom discussions in which she and her students would jointly explore some topic. In *Emmy Noether at Byrn Mawr*, Noether's only doctoral student at Bryn Mawr, Ruth McKee, recalls, "Miss Noether urged us on, challenging us to get our nails dirty, to really dig into the underlying relationships, to consider the problems from all possible angles."

Lays the Foundations of Abstract Algebra

Brilliant mathematicians often make their greatest contributions early in their careers; Noether was one of the notable exceptions to that rule. She began producing her most powerful and creative work about the age of 40. Her change in style started with a 1920 paper on noncommutative fields (systems in which an operation such as multiplication yields a different answer for a x b than for b x a). During the years that followed, she developed a very abstract and generalized approach to the axiomatic development of algebra. As Weyl attested, "she originated above all a new and epoch-making style of thinking in algebra."

Noether's 1921 paper on the theory of ideals in rings is considered to contain her most important results. It extended the work of Dedekind on solutions of polynomials—algebraic expressions consisting of a constant multiplied by variables raised to a positive power—and laid the foundations for modern abstract algebra. Rather than working with specific operations on sets of numbers, this branch of mathematics looks at general properties of operations. Because of its generality, abstract algebra represents a unifying thread connecting such theoretical fields as logic and number theory with applied mathematics useful in chemistry and physics.

During the winter of 1928–29, Noether was a visiting professor at the University of Moscow and the Communist Academy, and in the summer of 1930, she taught at the University of Frankfurt. Recognized for her continuing contributions in the science of mathematics, the International Mathematical Congress of 1928 chose her to be its principle speaker at one of its section meetings in Bologna. In 1932 she was chosen to address the Congress's general session in Zurich.

Noether was a part of the mathematics faculty of Göttingen University in the 1920s when its reputation for mathematical research and teaching was considered the best in the world. Still, even with the help of the esteemed mathematician Hermann Weyl, Noether was unable to secure a proper teaching position there, which was equivalent to her male counterparts. Weyl once commented: "I was ashamed to occupy such a preferred position beside her whom I knew to be my superior as a mathematician in many respects." Nevertheless, in 1932, on Noether's fiftieth birthday, the university's algebraists held a celebration, and her colleague Helmut Hasse dedicated a paper in her honor, which validated one of her ideas on noncommutative algebra. In that same year, she again was honored by those outside her own university, when she was named cowinner of the Alfred Ackermann-Teubner Memorial Prize for the Advancement of Mathematical Knowledge.

Teaches in Exile

The successful and congenial environment of the University of Göttingen ended in 1933, with the advent of the Nazis in Germany. Within months, anti-Semitic policies spread through the country. On April 7, 1933, Noether was formally notified that she could no longer teach at the university. She was a dedicated pacifist, and Weyl later recalled, "her courage, her frankness, her unconcern about her own fate, her conciliatory spirit were, in the midst of all the hatred and meanness, despair and sorrow surrounding us, a moral solace."

For a while, Noether continued to meet informally with students and colleagues, inviting groups to her apartment. But by summer, the Emergency Committee to Aid Displaced German Scholars was entering into an agreement with Bryn Mawr, a women's college in Pennsylvania, which offered Noether a professorship. Her first year's salary was funded by the Emergency Committee and the Rockefeller Foundation.

In the fall of 1933, Noether was supervising four graduate students at Bryn Mawr. Starting in February 1934, she also delivered weekly lectures at the Institute for Advanced Study at Princeton. She bore no malice toward Germany, and maintained friendly ties with her former colleagues. With her characteristic curiosity and good nature, she settled into her new home in America, acquiring enough English to adequately converse and teach, although she occasionally lapsed into German when concentrating on technical material.

During the summer of 1934, Noether visited Göttingen to arrange shipment of her possessions to the United States. When she returned to Bryn Mawr in the early fall, she had received a two-year renewal on her teaching grant. In the spring of 1935, Noether underwent surgery to remove a uterine tumor. The operation was a success, but four days later, she suddenly developed a very high fever and lost consciousness. She died on April 14th, apparently from a post-operative infection. Her ashes were buried near the library on the Bryn Mawr campus.

Over the course of her career, Noether supervised a dozen graduate students, wrote forty-five technical publications, and inspired countless other research results through her habit of suggesting topics of investigation to students and colleagues. After World War II, the University of Erlangen attempted to show her the honor she had deserved during her lifetime. A conference in 1958 commemorated the fiftieth anniversary of her doctorate; in 1982 the university dedicated a memorial plaque to her in its Mathematics Institute. During the same year, the 100th anniversary year of Noether's birth, the Emmy Noether Gymnasium, a coeducational school emphasizing mathematics, the natural sciences, and modern languages, opened in Erlangen.

SELECTED WRITINGS BY NOETHER:

Books

Collected Papers, Springer-Verlag, 1983.

SOURCES:

Books

Brewer, James W., *Emmy Noether: A Tribute to Her Life and Work,* edited by Martha K. Smith, Marcel Dekker, 1981.
Kramer, Edna E., *The Nature and Growth of Modern Mathematics,* Princeton University, 1981, pp. 656–672.
Magill, Frank N., editor, *Great Events from History II,* Books International, 1991, pp. 650–654, 716–719.
Osen, Lynn M., *Women in Mathematics,* Massachusetts Institute of Technology, 1979, pp. 141–152.
Perl, Teri, *Math Equals: Biographies of Women Mathematicians,* Addison-Wesley, 1978, pp. 172–178.
Srinivasan, Bhama and Judith D. Sally, *Emmy Noether in Bryn Mawr: Proceedings of a Symposium,* Springer-Verlag, 1983.

Periodicals

Kimberling, Clark H., "Emmy Noether," *The American Mathematical Monthly,* February, 1972, pp. 136–149.

—*Sketch by Loretta Hall*

Hideyo Noguchi
1876-1928
Japanese microbiologist and pathologist

Hideyo Noguchi was a controversial microbiologist who overcame poverty, a physical handicap, and linguistic and cultural barriers to make some pioneering contributions to the field of bacteriology. Chosen by bacteriologist **Simon Flexner** to be a member of the original scientific staff at the Rockefeller Institute, Noguchi's most important achievements advanced the understanding of syphilis, trachoma, and Bartonellosis. He worked tirelessly, almost day and night, on a number of scientific problems, but the energy which made his accomplishments possible also made him hasty and occasionally careless. Some of the claims he made for his research have not been substantiated; his work on yellow fever, in particular, was discredited, and Noguchi succumbed to this disease while studying it in Africa.

Hideyo Seisaku Noguchi was born in Japan in the mountain village of Inawashiro, Fukushima, on November 24, 1876. Given the childhood name Seisaku, he was the second child and only son of Sayosuke, a peasant farmer who soon deserted the family; his mother, Shika, worked in the rice fields to support her household. When very young, Noguchi fell into an open hearth fire and was severely burned, losing the use of his left fingers. He nevertheless excelled in school, and he was noticed by the superintendent, Sokae Kobayashi, who became something of a foster father to him, coordinating financial support and overseeing the rest of his education.

Kobayashi arranged for a surgeon to restore some functioning to the child's crippled hand, and it was as a result of his experience that Noguchi decided to study medicine. The surgeon retained him as an apprentice; in his office Noguchi used a microscope and first encountered spirochetes—microbes that would become a major focus of his research. In 1894, Noguchi entered the Tokyo Medical College, and in 1897 he passed the government examinations for a medical degree. He served as a lecturer at a dental college and studied the bubonic plague briefly in China before accepting a position as an assistant under bacteriologist Shibasaburo Kitasato at his Institute for Infectious Diseases. About this time, Noguchi changed his first name to Hideyo, meaning "great man of the world."

In 1899, a medical commission was sent from the United States to study tropical diseases afflicting American soldiers stationed in the Philippines. Flexner, who was a leading bacteriologist from Johns Hopkins University, was a member of this commis-

Hideyo Noguchi

sion; he was with the group when it passed through Japan and visited Kitasato's Institute for Infectious Diseases. Noguchi met Flexner there and told him he wanted to study bacteriology in the United States. In a memorial piece originally published in *Science,* Flexner remembers that "no particular encouragement was given to this request." He only encouraged him to write; he told Noguchi he would be moving to the University of Pennsylvania and gave him his address there.

Later that same year, about six months after he had met Flexner, Noguchi simply arrived at the University of Pennsylvania. He travelled on borrowed money and, as Flexner remembers, "presented himself at the dormitories unexpectedly, and in accordance with eastern custom bearing several gifts, which the writer still possesses and cherishes." Flexner arranged for him to be appointed as a research assistant to Silas Weir Mitchell, with whom he studied the hemolysins and agglutinins of snake venoms and the protective sera against them. The work he did with Mitchell won Noguchi a year-long Carnegie fellowship at the Statens Seruminstitut in Copenhagen. Here, under Thorvald Madsen, he mastered certain quantitative and chemical methods that were related to his snake venom studies.

Works on Syphillis at the Rockefeller Institute

Flexner became the organizing director of the Rockefeller Institute in New York City when it

opened in 1904, and he immediately asked Noguchi to work in his laboratory on poliomyelitis. In 1905, the two men were the first scientists in the United States to confirm Fritz Schaudinn's identification of *Treponema pallidum* as the spirochete responsible for syphilis. Noguchi's research on syphilis continued for a number of years, and the energy he devoted to this resulted in a major breakthrough. Syphilis patients had long been observed to suffer from paresis, a kind of partial paralysis. The connection had long been assumed but never proven until 1913, when Noguchi found a spiral organism in the brains of patients who had died of paresis. His work proved that general paresis and tabes dorsalis are the late stages of tertiary syphilis in the brain and spinal cord. He made the discovery early one morning, after spending the entire night inspecting 200 slides from paretic brain specimens. Flexner remembers being woken in bed and brought to the laboratory to confirm the discovery.

Despite this success, Noguchi's research during this period also resulted in some notorious failures. In 1911, he claimed he had obtained *T. pallidum* in pure culture, but no other investigator has ever duplicated his results, and the organisms have never been successfully isolated. He also developed a single diagnostic test for syphilis, which involved the injection of *T. pallidum* into the skin of patients believed to be suffering from the disease. The skin test proved unreliable, and according to Paul Franklin Clark in the *Bulletin of the History of Medicine* even a researcher who worked with Noguchi on this project was unable to duplicate his results in a different laboratory. In another study, Noguchi and Flexner reported that they had cultivated the "globoid bodies" of the virus that produces polio in monkeys, but this finding was later discredited as well, though their mistake may have been the result of the generally imperfect understanding at the time of the difference between bacteria and viruses.

On April 10, 1912, Noguchi married Mary Dardis. She was the daughter of Irish immigrants from Scranton, Pennsylvania, where her three brothers worked as coal miners. Noguchi was initially very secretive about his wife, even with his closest colleagues, and this may have been because of the interracial nature of his marriage. They had no children.

Researches the Origins of Infectious Diseases

In 1918, Noguchi turned to experiments on the etiology of obscure infectious diseases. Each required a different method of approach, and he made field expeditions to the American West as well as Central and South America. In the Peruvian Andes, he worked on Carrion's disease, now called Bartonellosis, and he established the existence of two different manifestations of the disease which had the same etiology. In one disease, there is an acute febrile anemia (Oroya fever), and in the other a local cutaneous eruption (Verruga peruana). Noguchi also did invaluable work in trachoma, a disease of the eyes. He attributed its cause to a bacterium; his findings were later challenged and the cause identified as a virus, but today the causative organism of trachoma is considered a unique microbe which is more closely related to bacteria than to viruses. Despite this controversy, Noguchi's critical work on trachoma's secondary bacterial infection contributed to its cure. During this period, he also searched for the causes of rabies and Rocky Mountain spotted fever.

The most controversial work that Noguchi did was on yellow fever. Using evidence he had gathered during four expeditions to the southern hemisphere, Noguchi became convinced that yellow fever was caused by a spiral organism which he had isolated. He named it *Leptospira icteroides,* and he published several reports based on these field observations. He even prepared an experimental vaccine against the disease that was distributed by the Rockefeller Institute. Noguchi's research, however, was almost totally invalid. The evidence he had been examining had been taken from patients who had been misdiagnosed by local physicians; instead of suffering from yellow fever, they had hemorrhagic jaundice, also known as Weil's disease or leptospirosis. In addition, Noguchi had assumed without conducting sufficient research that the spirochete which caused leptospirosis differed from the one he believed caused yellow fever. By 1924, other researchers had showed that the two spirochetes were identical.

In 1927, Adrian Stokes determined that a filterable virus was the cause of yellow fever. Stokes made this discovery in African patients from whom no *Leptospira* could be recovered, but he died from yellow fever before his report was published. In October of that year, Noguchi sailed for Africa to compare yellow fever there with that of South America. He wanted to test Stokes' findings for himself, and he worked for six strenuous, hectic months in a crude field laboratory with William Young, the resident British director of the Medical Research Institute. Noguchi was stricken with yellow fever just as he was about to return to New York. He died on May 21, 1928, at the age of fifty-one. Young confirmed the diagnosis of yellow fever during an autopsy and then succumbed to the disease himself a week later.

For indefatigable research into infectious diseases, Noguchi received honorary degrees from many universities and was decorated by many foreign governments. In 1915, he returned to Japan to receive the Order of the Rising Sun and an Imperial Prize from the Emperor. He received the John Scott Medal in 1920 and was the first recipient of the Kober Medal in 1925. Noguchi and his wife are buried in Woodlawn Cemetery in New York City. He is remembered in Japan as well, where, among many memorials, his portrait was issued on a postage stamp in 1950. His family home is a museum where many of his papers and memorabilia are preserved.

SELECTED WRITINGS BY NOGUCHI:

Books

Snake Venoms, Carnegie Institution of Washington, 1909.
Serum Diagnosis of Syphilis and the Butyric Acid Test for Syphilis, [Chicago], 1910.

Periodicals

(With J. W. Moore) "A Demonstration of *Treponema Pallidum* in the Brain in Cases of General Paralysis," *Journal of Experimental Medicine,* Volume 17, 1913, pp. 232–238.
"The Etiology of Verruga Peruana," *Journal of Experimental Medicine,* Volume 45, 1927, pp. 175–189.
"The Etiology of Trachoma," *Journal of Experimental Medicine,* Volume 48, 1928, supplement 2, pp. 1–53.
"The Spirochetes," *The Newer Knowledge of Bacteriology and Immunology,* edited by E. O. Jordan and I. S. Falk, University of Chicago Press, 1928, pp. 452–497.

SOURCES:

Books

Eckstein, Gustav, *Noguchi,* Harper & Brothers, 1931.
Plesset, Isabel R., *Noguchi and His Patrons,* Associated University Presses, 1980.

Periodicals

Clark, Paul Franklin, "Hideyo Noguchi, 1876–1928," *Bulletin of the History of Medicine,* Volume 33, 1959, pp. 1–20.
Flexner, Simon, "Hideyo Noguchi. A Biographical Sketch," *Science,* Volume 69, 1929, pages 653–660.
"Pioneer Bacteriologist," *MD,* April 1976, pp. 143–150.
Williams, Greer, *The Plague Killers,* Scribner, 1969, pp. 215–249.

—*Sketch by Carol L. Moberg*

Masayasu Nomura
1927-
Japanese-born American molecular biologist

Masayasu Nomura is the American molecular biologist who demonstrated that those ribosomes present in bacteria can be reduced to their molecular components of ribonucleic acid (RNA) and proteins. Four years later he further demonstrated that they can then be reunited to regenerate themselves.

Nomura was born on April 27, 1927, in Hyogo-ken, Japan. He married Junko Hamashima on February 10, 1957; they had two children—Keiko and Toshiyasu. After receiving his Ph.D. in microbiology at the University of Tokyo in 1957, Nomura went to the United States to work as a postdoctoral fellow in Sol Spiegelman's laboratory. While at Spiegelman's lab, Nomura isolated a kind of RNA that receives information from a bacteriophage (a virus that infects bacteria) genome, then serves as a model for producing the proteins within the bacteriophage. This type of RNA later became known as messenger RNA (mRNA). He then briefly returned to Japan as an assistant professor at the Osaka University Institute of Protein Research before emigrating to the United States in 1963 to join the faculty of the University of Wisconsin's department of genetics, where he became a full professor in 1966.

Demonstrates the Reversibility of Protein Splitting in Ribosomes

By the early 1960s, the basic decoding of genetics had been clarified and the protein biosynthesis components identified, thanks to the efforts of such scientists as Paul Zamecnik and **Marshall Warren Nirenberg**. The term "ribosome" had been introduced in 1958 to describe the tiny organs that are present in all living cells, and that synthesize proteins; furthermore, it was known that ribosomes were the site where amino acids were assembled to form proteins, and that ribosomes were made up of two different subunits, one larger than the other, each with its own complicated structure consisting of RNA molecules and various protein molecules. But what was not known was how the molecular components were assembled into sophisticated ribosome structures, or how the assembled structures performed their functions.

Using the work of Zamecnik and Nirenberg as a springboard, Nomura discovered that by centrifuging bacterial ribosomes in heavy salt concentrations some ribosomal proteins would split off from the ribosomes, and it occurred to him that the situation might be reversible. Four years later, under very specific conditions, Nomura mixed those particles lacking protein with the split-off proteins; like magic, functionally active ribosomal particles were formed. The significance of this reconstitution proved that the necessary information for the proper construction of ribosomal particles was contained in their molecular components, rather than in some extraneous factor. It also opened the way for study of the molecular components of ribosomes. In 1968 Nomura and his colleagues actually reconstituted the small ribosome subunits from purified RNA and dissociated ribosomal proteins, and in 1970, as professor of genetics and biochemistry, he did the same with the larger ribosomal subunit. He and his team also did significant research into the ribosomal makeup of chromosomes, isolating a number of genes from *Escherichia coli* (also known as E coli) cells.

During the 1960s and 1970s, Nomura also showed how certain strains of enterobacteria, called colicins, have a tendency to kill other, related bacterial strains. Some colicins kill bacteria by splitting RNA in ribosomes, while others eliminate it by causing deoxyribonucleic acid (DNA) breakdown. This discovery initiated many modern studies of colicins.

Nomura shed much light on the processes of information transfer from genes to proteins. In 1970 he was appointed co-director of the Institute for Enzyme Research at the University of Wisconsin. He was elected to the National Academy of Sciences in 1978.

SELECTED WRITINGS BY NOMURA:

Books

(Editor) *Ribosomes,* Cold Spring Harbor Laboratory, 1974.
(Editor) *Ribosomes: Structure, Function and Genetics,* University Park Press, 1980.

Periodicals

(With Sol Spiegelman) "Characterization of RNA Synthesized in *Escherichia coli* After Bacteriophage T2 Infection," *Journal of Molecular Biology,* Volume 2, 1960, p. 306.
"Assembly of Bacterial Ribosomes," *Science,* March 2, 1973, p. 864.
(With Strycharz and Lake) "Ribosomal Proteins L7/L12 Localized at a Single Region of the Large Subunit by Immune Electron Microscopy," *Journal of Molecular Biology,* Volume 128, 1976, pp. 123–140.

SOURCES:

Books

McGraw-Hill Modern Scientists and Engineers,
    McGraw, 1980, pp. 365–366.

                    —*Sketch by Janet Kieffer Kelley*

Ronald G. W. Norrish
1897-1978
English physical chemist

The English chemist Ronald G. W. Norrish spent his academic life studying reaction kinetics, a discipline in chemistry concerned with rates of chemical reactions and factors influencing those rates. Norrish received the 1967 Nobel Prize for Chemistry—which he shared with a former student, **George Porter**, and German scientist **Manfred Eigen**—for his work in this realm. A pioneer researcher in flash photolysis (chemical reactions induced by intense bursts of light), Norrish developed a process which allowed minute intermediate stages of a chemical reaction to be measured and described. He also contributed to chemistry an understanding of chain reactions, combustion, and polymerization (the formation of large molecules from numerous smaller ones). Over his career, Norrish was awarded the Liversidge Medal of the Chemical Society and the Davy Medal of the Royal Society, both in 1958, and the Bernard Lewis Gold Medal from the Combustion Institute in 1964. In addition, he was a member of scientific academies in eight foreign countries.

Ronald George Wreyford Norrish was born on November 9, 1897, in Cambridge, England. The son of Amy and Herbert Norrish, he attended the Perse Grammar School and won a scholarship to study natural sciences at Emmanuel College in Cambridge University. Although Norrish entered Cambridge in 1915, World War I intervened and he served in France as a lieutenant in the Royal Field Artillery. Captured by the Germans in 1918, he spent a year in a prisoner of war camp before being repatriated. Norrish then returned to his academic career at Cambridge and finished his bachelor of science degree in chemistry by 1921.

Norrish studied for his doctorate under the renowned physical chemist E. K. Rideal, who directed him to investigations of chemical kinetics and photochemistry (the effect of light upon solutions of potassium permanganate). By 1924 he had earned his Ph.D. in chemistry, staying on at the university to become a fellow of Emmanuel College and then, in 1925, a demonstrator in chemistry. The following year Norrish married Anne Smith who was a lecturer at the University of Wales. They would eventually have twin daughters together.

Norrish served for the rest of his academic and research life at Cambridge University. He became the Humphrey Owen Jones Lecturer in Physical Chemistry in 1930, then seven years later, he was named professor of physical chemistry as well as the director of the department of physical chemistry. He retained this position until 1965, when he retired.

Researches Chemical Kinetics and Polymerization

Norrish's early work at Cambridge involved the photochemistry of rather simple compounds, such as ketones, aldehydes, and nitrogen peroxide. He discovered that light breaks down these compounds in one of two directions, creating either stable molecules or unstable "free radicals," which are molecules that have unpaired electrons. As a corollary to this work, Norrish and his laboratory also began studying chemical chain reactions. Working with M. Ritchie, Norrish was able to describe the process by which hydrogen and chlorine react when initiated by light. Studies of other chain reactions led Norrish and his fellow workers to a study of hydrocarbon combustion, building on **Nikolai N. Semenov**'s work in branching chain reactions to describe the means by which methane and ethylene are combusted. They discovered that formaldehyde formation is a necessary intermediate step in such a chain reaction.

Norrish also conducted an investigation into the mechanics of polymerization, primarily in vinyl compounds. It was Norrish who coined the term 'gel effect' to describe the final slowing-down stages of polymerization as a solution undergoing the process becomes increasingly semi-fluid or viscous. With the advent of World War II, Norrish's laboratory work increasingly involved military projects, such as research into gun-flash suppression. Norrish became chairman of the Incendiary Projectiles Committee during this period and also assisted in the development of incendiary devices.

Flash-Photolysis Techniques Win the Nobel

After the war, Norrish worked with Porter to pioneer the study of flash-photolysis. This involved the measurement of very fast chemical reactions while exposing the substance to extremely strong and short blasts of light. Unstable molecules turned into free radicals, thus resulting in a dissociative reaction. Intermediate stages and products of such fast chemical reactions were then gauged by use of spectrographic analysis—the illumination by weaker flashes of light following at millisecond intervals upon the initial flash. Such analysis went a long way toward proving intermediate stages of reactions which had been, until the Norrish-Porter work, only theoretical.

Norrish and Porter continued their research together from 1949 to 1965, perfecting their technique to allow analysis of short-lived intermediate compounds down to a thousandth of a millionth of a second. They published numerous articles and opened new vistas of research in fast reactions. For such work, Norrish and Porter shared the 1967 Nobel Prize for Chemistry with Eigen, who was doing similar work (although he employed a "relaxation technique," whereby small disturbances of equilibrium were induced rather than the intense ones elicited by flash-photolysis).

After his retirement in 1965, Norrish remained a senior fellow at his old college, Emmanuel. Having lived in Cambridge most of his life, Norrish felt an abiding affection for all things dealing with the university. Famous for his hospitality, Norrish held at-homes with an eclectic blend of cultural personalities in attendance. He died on June 7, 1978, in Cambridge.

SELECTED WRITINGS BY NORRISH:

Periodicals

(With G. Porter) "Chemical Reactions Produced by Very High Light Intensities," *Nature,* Volume 164, 1949, p. 658.
(With G. Porter) "The Application of Flash Techniques to the Study of Fast Reactions," *Discussions of the Faraday Society,* Volume 17, 1954, pp. 40–46.
"The Gas Phase Oxidation of n-Butenes," *Proceedings of the Royal Society,* Series A272, 1963, pp. 164–191.
"The Kinetics and Analysis of Very Fast Reactions," *Chemistry in Britain,* Volume 1, 1965, pp. 289–311.

SOURCES:

Books

Biographical Memoirs of Fellows of the Royal Society, Volume 27, Royal Society (London), 1981, pp. 289–311.

Periodicals

Bamford, C. H., "R. G. W. Norrish, 1897–1978," *Nature,* September 7, 1978, pp. 78–79.

Eyring, Henry and Edward M. Eyring, "Nobel Prize Winners: Chemistry," *Science,* November 10, 1967, pp. 746–748.

—Sketch by J. Sydney Jones

John Howard Northrop
1891-1987
American biochemist

John Howard Northrop, a Nobel laureate in chemistry, is best known for his work on the purification and crystallization of enzymes, which regulate important body functions like digestion and respiration. Northrop's studies on the chemical composition of enzymes enabled him to confirm the hypothesis that enzymes are proteins—a discovery that spurred much additional research on these critical catalysts of biochemical reactions. For this discovery, Northrop was awarded the Nobel Prize in chemistry in 1946. In addition to these studies, he also contributed to the development of techniques for isolating—and thus identifying—a variety of substances, including bacterial viruses and valuable antitoxins.

Northrop was born in Yonkers, New York, on July 5, 1891, to John Isaiah and Alice Belle (Rich) Northrop. The Northrops hailed from a long list of notable ancestors; well-known relations include the Reverend Jonathan Edwards, president of Princeton University in 1758. Prior to his son's birth, Isaiah Northrop was killed in a laboratory fire at Columbia University, where he taught zoology. Alice Northrop, a biology teacher at Normal (Hunter) College, influenced her son's interest in zoology and biology. John Northrop received a B.S. in 1912 from Columbia University, where he majored in biochemistry. He continued his studies in Columbia's chemistry department and was awarded an M.A. in 1913 and a Ph.D. in 1915.

Research at RIMR

In 1915 Northrop accepted a position in the laboratory of **Jacques Loeb** at the Rockefeller Institute for Medical Research (RIMR). Loeb, an experimental physiologist, headed RIMR's laboratory of general physiology. There Northrop studied the effect of environmental factors on heredity through experimentation with *Drosophila* (fruit flies). He developed a method for producing *Drosophila* free of microorganisms, which revolutionized studies that investigated factors affecting the flies' lifespan. Using these flies,

Northrop and Loeb demonstrated that heat affected the life and health of the flies—not light or expenditure of energy, as previously believed.

Northrop's work in Loeb's laboratory was interrupted by the advent of World War I. At that time he became involved with research geared toward wartime concerns. Northrop developed a fermentation process for acetone that was used in the production of explosives and airplane wing coverings. As a result of these efforts, he was commissioned a captain in the U.S. Army Chemical Warfare Service. He was subsequently sent to the Commercial Solvents Corporation in Terre Haute, Indiana, to oversee the plant development of acetone production.

Although Loeb and Northrop remained close associates, Northrop was ready for independent work upon his return to the institute in 1919. At this time he studied the digestive enzymes pepsin and trypsin; these studies continued throughout the 1920s and 1930s, but Northrop was also interested in a myriad of other scientific investigations. He studied vision in the *Limulus* crab; with RIMR colleague Moses Kunitz he analyzed the chemical composition of gelatin; and he worked with Paul De Kruif on bacterial suspensions.

Shortly after Loeb's death in 1924, Northrop transferred to the institute's Princeton, New Jersey, department of animal pathology; at this time he was made a full member of the institute. The animal pathology department was opened in 1917 to study basic research in animal diseases and later expanded in 1931 to include a department of plant pathology. Inspired by the work of **James B. Sumner**, who had isolated and crystallized an enzyme called urease, Northrop continued his studies of the protein-splitting enzymes pepsin, trypsin, and chymotrypsin; he eventually isolated and crystallized all three substances. In 1929, Northrop and M. L. Anson developed the diffusion cell, a relatively simple means for isolating materials. In 1931, with Kunitz, Northrop validated the usefulness of the phase rule solubility method of studying the purity of substances, which tests for the homogeneity of dissolved solids. By applying this testing method to crystalline pepsin, chymotrypsin, and trypsin, he corroborated Sumner's controversial belief that enzymes were proteins. The research of this period was presented in *Crystalline Enzymes* (1939), written by Northrop, Kunitz, and Roger Herriott.

Northrop's investigation of bacteriophages (viruses that attack bacteria) began in the 1920s, but did not flower until the 1930s. He and associate **Wendell Stanley** applied their techniques for isolating enzymes to crystallizing the tobacco mosaic virus—isolation being the first step in determining the chemical composition of any substance. From 1936 to 1938 Northrop examined the chemical nature of bacteriophages and successfully isolated purified nucleoprotein (protein plus DNA and RNA) from cultures of *Staphylococcus aureus,* the bacteria that causes boils; this finding was one of the earliest indications that nucleoproteins are an essential part of a virus. Using his ability to isolate and crystallize substances, in 1941 Northrop produced the first crystalline antibody, for diphtheria. He would later, with W. F. Goebel, produce an antibody for pneumococcus.

With the start of World War II, Northrop was once again called on to become involved with government research undertaken at RIMR. In 1941, RIMR and the U.S. Office of Scientific Research and Development (OSRD) initiated the investigation of lethal gases used in battle. One of Northrop's biggest wartime achievements was developing the Northrop Titrator and the portable, battery-operated Northrop Field Titrator. These devices measure the concentration of mustard gas in the air at some distance from the gassed zone. The Northrop Titrator is considered an important prototype for subsequent development of the more sophisticated defensive instruments used in chemical warfare today.

Accepts Position at Berkeley

In 1949, RIMR's Princeton facility closed, prompting Northrop's move to the University of California, Berkeley. During his tenure as visiting professor, Northrop maintained his association with RIMR and was named professor emeritus in 1961. While at Berkeley, Northrop continued his work with bacteriophages. He conducted research on the life cycle of *B. megatherium* cells from their normal stage to that of a phage. He also investigated the origin of bacterial viruses and found that they were mutations of normal cells.

In addition to the Nobel Prize, which he shared with Stanley and Sumner, Northrop was also awarded the W. B. Cutting Travelling Fellowship and the Stevens Prize of the College of Physicians and Surgeons of Columbia University, and he was elected to the National Academy of Sciences. Beginning in 1924, he also served on the editorial board of the *Journal of General Physiology,* an association that spanned a sixty-two year period.

Northrop retired from Berkeley in 1959 and moved to Wickenburge, Arizona, where he died on May 27, 1987. He left his wife, Louise Walker, whom he married in June, 1918, and two children, Alice Havemeyer and John.

SELECTED WRITINGS BY NORTHROP:

Books

(With Moses Kunitz and Roger Herriott) *Crystalline Enzymes,* Columbia University Press, 1939.

Periodicals

"The Chemistry of Pepsin and Trypsin," *Biological Review,* Volume 10, 1935, pp. 263.
"Factors Controlling the Production of Lysogenic Cultures of B. megatherium," *Journal of General Physiology,* March, 1961, pp. 859–867.

SOURCES:

Books

Corner, George W., *A History of the Rockefeller Institute: 1901–1953,* The Rockefeller Institute Press, 1964.

Periodicals

Herriott, Roger M., "A Biographical Sketch of John Howard Northrop," *Journal of General Physiology,* March, 1962 (Part 2), pp. 1–16.
Herriott, Roger M., "John Howard Northrop," *Journal of General Physiology,* June, 1981, pp. 597–599.

—*Sketch by Renee D. Mastrocco*

Sergei Novikov
1938-
Russian mathematician

Sergei Novikov, a mathematician interested in everything from topology to theoretical physics, made important contributions to several fields. He has worked on finding links between high-level mathematics and theoretical physics, but he is best known for his research on Pontryagin classes, which led to the classification of certain types of manifolds. For his work on Pontryagin classes, he was awarded both his own country's Lenin Prize and the international recognition of the Fields Medal.

Sergei Petrovich Novikov was born into a mathematical family on March 20, 1938, in Gorky, Russia. His father, Petr Sergeevich Novikov, had founded the Soviet Union's school of mathematical logic and made outstanding contributions to the field of set theory. His mother, Lyudmila Vsevolodovna Keldysh, was also a mathematician, whose research was concentrated on geometric topology, a field in which her son would later excel. (Topology is a branch of mathematics concerned with properties of geometric configurations that are not altered by changes in shape—sometimes described as the study of continuity.) Novikov entered Moscow University as an undergraduate in 1955, and very early on he showed signs of mathematical brilliance. His first paper, a short work on a part of topological theory, was published when he was only twenty-one; his second, published a year later, held the beginnings of his later research on manifolds. Novikov graduated from the faculty of mathematics and mechanics of Moscow University in 1960, and he entered the Steklov Institute of Mathematics as a doctoral student.

Breakthrough Research Leads to Top Award

Under the supervision of M. M. Postnikov, Novikov began his research at Steklov, where he would stay for five years. In 1962, he married Eleonora Tsoi (with whom he had three children); he received his Ph.D. in 1964 and his doctor of science degree in 1965. At Steklov, Novikov uncovered the crucial ideas of his manifold research. A manifold can be broadly described as a topological space containing a set of items—for example, a plane can be understood as a two-dimensional manifold of points. At the time of Novikov's research, three different categories of manifolds were discussed: differentiable, piecewise linear (also known as combinatorial), and topological. In differentiable manifolds, those on which calculus is performed, the items in the set are connected by curves or twists. Piece-wise linear manifolds, on the other hand, are connected by straight lines. This distinction was already recognized at the time of Novikov's work. However, very little was known about topological manifolds. Did they behave more like differentiable manifolds or piece-wise linear ones? This was the question Novikov set out to answer.

He began by looking at the Pontryagin classes. On a differentiable manifold, a Pontryagin class is a structure related to the manifold which is unchanged, or invariant, when the manifold is manipulated. They can be used to describe the amount of twisting or curvature present in the manifold. However, in 1957, French mathematician **René Thom** and others had proved that, when using real or rational numbers, the Pontryagin classes are piece-wise linear invariants; in other words, they are a characteristic feature of a piece-wise linear manifold, just as they are of a differentiable manifold. Finally, in 1965, Novikov was able to show that they were also topologically invariant. This dramatic result showed that topological manifolds are, in the last analysis, most similar to piece-wise linear ones, a result which had great impact on future work in topology. An impressive aspect of this research was that Novikov was relatively isolated from other mathematicians working in this field at the time, and yet he solved a problem which had puzzled the entire mathematical community.

Moscow University, where Novikov had been teaching since 1964, recognized the importance of his work by appointing him to a full professorship in 1966. Other recognitions soon followed. In 1967, he won the Soviet Union's Lenin Prize, and in 1970, the International Mathematical Union awarded him the Fields Medal, the most prestigious honor a mathematician can receive.

After receiving the Fields Medal, Novikov turned his attention to a new topic, theoretical physics. He wanted to help form connections between the two subjects, using the research being done in modern mathematics to inform the progress of theoretical physics. His extensive research after 1971 varied between articles strictly concerned with algebraic geometry and those on modern mathematical physics. In particular, Novikov concentrated on equations involving solitons, or non-linear waves; he also worked in spectral theory and other areas. This work, much of which he did in collaboration with his students, helped further not only the fields of physics and algebraic geometry, but related areas as well. In 1975, he accepted a position as head of the mathematics department at the L.D. Landau Institute.

In 1981 Novikov received belated recognition for work he had done over ten years earlier. As part of his research on manifolds, he had studied foliations, which are decompositions of manifolds into smaller ones (called leaves). Leaves could be either open or closed, but the closed type was most mathematically interesting because at the time its existence had not been proved. Novikov, using geometric proofs, solidified the existence of closed leaves in the case of a sphere, and became the first person ever to do so. The mathematical community began using this research immediately, but it was not until 1981 that Novikov was honored for the work with the Lobachevsky International Prize of the Academy of Sciences of the Soviet Union.

In 1983, in addition to his professorship at Moscow University and his directorship of the Landau Institute, Novikov accepted the position of head of the department at the Steklov Mathematical Institute. A year later, he was appointed chair of the department of geometry and topology at Moscow University. In spite of these prestigious appointments, Novikov did not limit himself to administrative duties. The mid–1980s also saw the publication of two important mathematical texts by Novikov and his colleagues, one in mathematical physics called *Theory of Solitons: The Inverse Scattering Methods* and one in geometry, *Modern Geometry: Methods and Applications*. Throughout his career, Novikov looked for ways to link the three major areas of modern-day pure mathematics: calculus, geometry, and topology. His 1990 work, *Basic Elements of Differential Geometry and Topology,* showed not only his ability to achieve the goal of finding connections within mathe-

matics but also his concern that future mathematicians might be capable of doing so as well.

SELECTED WRITINGS BY NOVIKOV:

Books

(With B. A. Dubrovin and A. T. Fomenko) *Modern Geometry: Methods and Applications,* 2 volumes, Springer-Verlag, 1984.
(With S. Volume Manakov, L. P. Pitaevskii, and Volume E. Zakharov) *Theory of Solitons: The Inverse Scattering Methods,* Consultants Bureau, 1984.
Basic Elements of Differential Geometry and Topology, Kluwer Academic Publishers, 1990.

Periodicals

"Homotopic and Topological Invariance of Certain Classes of Pontryagin," *Journal of the Academy of Science of the USSR,* Volume 162, 1965, pp. 854–57.

SOURCES:

Periodicals

Atiyah, M. F., "On the Work of Serge Novikov," in *Actes, Congrès International Mathématiques,* Volume 1, International Mathematics Union, pp. 11–13.
"Sergei Petrovich Novikov (on His Fiftieth Birthday)," *Russian Mathematical Surveys,* Volume 43, 1988, pp. 1–10.

—*Sketch by Karen Sands*

Robert Noyce
1927-1990
American physicist and inventor

Robert Noyce coinvented the integrated circuit, an electronic component which is considered to be among the twentieth century's most significant technological developments. The laptop computer, the ignition control in a modern automobile, the "brain" of a VCR that allows for its programming, and thousands of other computing devices all depend for their operation on the integrated circuit. Noyce

Robert Noyce

was not only a brilliant inventor, credited with more than a dozen patents for semiconductor devices and processes, but a forceful businessman who founded the Fairchild Semiconductor Corporation and the Intel Corporation and who, at the time of his death, was president and CEO of Sematech.

Robert Norton Noyce was born December 12, 1927, in Burlington, Iowa, the third of four boys in the family. His parents were Ralph Noyce, a minister who worked for the Iowa Conference of Congregational Churches, and Harriet Norton Noyce. Growing up in a two-story church-owned house in Grinnell, a small town in central Iowa, Noyce was gifted in many areas, excelling in sports, music, and acting as well as academic work. He exhibited a talent for math and science while in high school and took the Grinnell college freshman physics course in his senior year. Noyce went on to receive his baccalaureate degree in physics from Grinnell, graduating Phi Beta Kappa in 1949. It was at Grinnell that he was introduced to the transistor (an electronic device that allows a small current to control a larger one in another location) by his mentor Grant Gale, head of Grinnell's physics department. Noyce was excited by the invention, seeing it as freeing electronics from the constraints of the bulky and inefficient vacuum tube. After he received his Ph.D. in physics from the Massachusetts Institute of Technology in 1954, Noyce—who had no interest in pure research—started working for Philco in Philadelphia, Pennsylvania, where the company was making semiconductors (materials whose conduc-

tivity of an electrical current puts them midway between conductors and insulators).

After three years, Noyce became convinced Philco did not have as much interest in transistors as he did. By chance in 1956 he was asked by **William Shockley**, Nobel laureate and coinventor of the transistor, to come work for him in California. Excited by the opportunity to develop state-of-the-art transistor technology, Noyce moved to Palo Alto, which is located in an area that came to be known as Silicon Valley (named for the silicon compounds used in the manufacture of computer chips). But Noyce was no happier with Shockley than he had been with Philco; both Shockley's management style and the direction of his work—which ignored transistors—were disappointing. In 1957 Noyce left with seven other Shockley engineers to form a new company, financed by Fairchild Camera and Instrument, to be called Fairchild Semiconductor. At age twenty-nine, Noyce was chosen as the new corporation's leader.

Invents the Integrated Circuit

The first important development during the early years at Fairchild was the 1958 invention, by Jean Hoerni (an ex-Shockley scientist), of a process to protect the elements on a transistor from contaminants during manufacturing. This was called the planar process, and involved laying down a layer of silicon oxide over the transistor's elements. In 1959, after prodding from one of his patent attorneys to find more applications for the planar process, Noyce took the next step of putting several electronic components, such as resistors and transistors, on the same chip and layering them over with silicon oxide. Combining components in this fashion eliminated the need to wire individual transistors to each other and made possible tremendous reductions in the size of circuit components with a corresponding increase in the speed of their operation. The integrated circuit, or microchip as it became commonly known, had been born. More than one person, however, was working toward this invention at the same time. **Jack Kilby** of Texas Instruments had devised an integrated circuit the year before, but it had no commercial application. Nevertheless, both Kilby and Noyce are considered coinventors of the integrated circuit. In 1959 Noyce applied for a semiconductor integrated circuit patent using his process, which was awarded in 1961.

Both technological advances and competition in the new microchip industry increased rapidly. The number of transistors that could be put on a microchip grew from ten in 1964 to one thousand in 1969 to thirty-two thousand in 1975. (By 1993 up to 3.1 million transistors could be put on a 2.15-inch-square microprocessor chip.) The number of manufacturers eventually grew from two (Fairchild and Shockley) to dozens. During the 1960s Noyce's company was the leading producer of microchips, and by 1968 he was a millionaire. However, Noyce still felt constricted at Fairchild; he wanted more control and so—along with Gordon Moore (also a former Shockley employee)—he formed Intel in Santa Clara, California. Intel went to work making semiconductor memory, or data storage. Subsequently, Ted Hoff, an Intel scientist, invented the microprocessor and propelled Intel into the forefront of the industry. By 1982 Intel could claim to have pioneered three-quarters of the previous decade's advances in microtechnology.

Noyce's management style could be called "roll up your sleeves." He shunned fancy corporate cars, offices, and furnishings in favor of a less-structured, relaxed working environment in which everyone contributed and no one benefited from lavish perquisites. Becoming chairman of the board of Intel in 1974, he left the work of daily operations behind him, founding and later becoming chairman of the Semiconductor Industry Association. In 1980 Noyce was honored with the National Medal of Science and in 1983, the same year that Intel's sales reached one billion dollars, he was made a member of the National Inventor's Hall of Fame. He was dubbed the Mayor of Silicon Valley during the 1980s, not only for his scientific contributions but also for his role as a spokesperson for the industry. Noyce spent much of his later career working to improve the international competitiveness of American industry. Early on he recognized the strengths of foreign competitors in the electronics market and the corresponding weaknesses of domestic companies. In 1988 Noyce took charge of Sematech, a consortium of semiconductor manufacturers working together and with the United States government to increase U.S. competitiveness in the world marketplace.

Noyce was married twice. His first marriage to Elizabeth Bottomley ended in divorce (which he attributed to his intense involvement in his work); the couple had four children together. In 1975 he married Ann Bowers, who was then Intel's personnel director. Noyce enjoyed reading Hemingway, flying his own airplane, hang gliding, and scuba diving. He believed that microelectronics would continue to advance in complexity and sophistication well beyond its current state, and that the question would finally lead to what use society would make of the technology. Noyce died on June 3, 1990, of a sudden heart attack.

SOURCES:

Books

Bonner, M., W. L. Boyd, and J. A. Allen, *Robert N. Noyce, 1927–1990,* Sematech, 1990.
Encyclopedia of Computer Science, Van Nostrand, 1993, pp. 522–523.
Fifty Who Made the Difference, Villard Books, 1984, pp. 270–303.
Palfreman, Jon, and Doron Swade, *The Dream Machine,* BBC Books, 1991.
Slater, Robert, *Portraits in Silicon,* MIT Press, 1987.

—Sketch by Frank Hertle

Hermann Oberth
1894-1989
Austro-Hungarian-born German physicist

Hermann Oberth is one of three scientists considered to be the founders of space flight. The other two, Russian aerospace engineer **Konstantin Tsiolkovsky** and American physicist **Robert Goddard**, may have preceded him in many discoveries, but Oberth's writings enjoyed a much wider audience, inaugurating a movement which lead first to the development of the long-range military missile, the German V–2 guided missile, and then to human space flight. In recognition of his important contributions to space flight, Oberth was the first recipient of the international R. E. P. Hirsch Astronautics Prize in 1929; he also received the Diesel medal of the Association of German Inventors in 1954, the American Astronautical Society Award in 1955, and the Federal Service Cross First Class from the German Federal Republic in 1961.

Hermann Julius Oberth was born on June 25, 1894, in the German town of Hermannstadt, Transylvania; formerly a part of Austria-Hungary, the town is now known as Sibiu, Romania. His father was Dr. Julius Gotthold Oberth, and in 1896 he became the director and chief surgeon of the county hospital in Schässburg, Transylvania, where Oberth grew up. His mother was Valerie Emma (Krassner) Oberth, the daughter of a doctor who had prophesied accurately in July of 1869 that humans would land on the moon in a hundred years. In an autobiographical piece published in *Astronautics,* Oberth remembered that "at the age of eleven, I received from my mother as a gift the famous books, *From the Earth to the Moon* and *Travel to the Moon* by Jules Verne, which I . . . read at least five or six times and, finally, knew by heart." He was fascinated by space flight, and even as a child began to perform various calculations about how it could be done. Although Oberth learned infinitesimal calculus at the Schässburg secondary school, he taught himself differential calculus, and he successfully verified the magnitude of escape velocity.

In 1913, Oberth began studying medicine at the University of Münich, but he also attended lectures in physics and related subjects at the nearby technical institute. During World War I, he served in the Infantry Regiment on the eastern front. He was

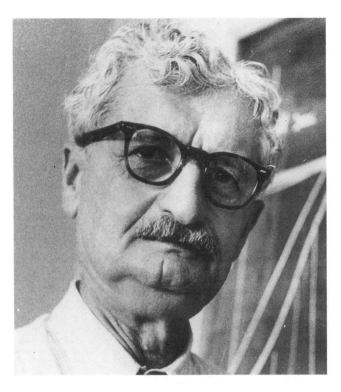

Hermann Oberth

wounded in February of 1916, and was detailed to a reserve hospital, where he had the opportunity to continue the experiments with weightlessness which he had begun as a teenager. He experimented on himself with drugs, including scopolamine, which is still used to treat motion sickness. Although Oberth's pioneering work in the field of space medicine has received some recognition, it does not appear to have had any direct influence on later developments.

Develops Space-Flight Theory

After leaving the army, Oberth began to work more seriously on developing solutions to the problems posed by space flight. In an autobiographical piece published in *First Steps Toward Space,* Oberth recalled that in 1918 the German Ministry of Armament rejected his proposal for "a long-range rocket powered by ethyl alcohol, water, and liquid air, somewhat similar to the V–2, only bigger and not so complicated." This was also the same year that he married Mathilde Hummel; the wedding was on June 6, and the couple would have four children, two of whom would die during World War II. In 1919 Oberth resumed his schooling, this time studying physics. He began at the University of Klausenburg in his native Transylvania, but subsequently transferred several times: first back to the University of Münich and the technical institute there, then to the University of Göttingen, and finally to the University of Heidelberg. He submitted his doctoral dissertation at Heidelberg; the thesis was on rockets and space-flight theory and it was not accepted. Denied his doctorate, Oberth taught physics and mathematics at a girls' school for teachers in Sighisoara (also known as Schassburg) from 1922 to 1923, when the University of Klausenburg granted him the title of professor. He taught for a year at his former secondary school before transferring in 1925 to the secondary school in nearby Mediasch, where he taught physics and mathematics periodically until 1938.

In 1928, Oberth published his doctoral dissertation under the title *Die Rakete zu den Planeträumen* (title means "The Rocket into Planetary Space"). Although filled with complicated equations, Oberth's book sold well. In it he set forth the basic principles of space flight and discussed possible solutions to a number of specific problems. He examined such matters as liquid-propellant rocket construction, the use of propellants for different stages of rockets, and the employment of successive stages that would disengage as their propellants were used up, thereby enabling the rocket to achieve the velocities necessary to escape from the earth's atmosphere. He also discussed the use of pumps to inject the propellants into a rocket's combustion chamber, reviewed procedures to prevent burnout of that chamber, speculated on the effects of space flight upon humans, and proposed the idea of a space station. In 1929, Oberth published a considerably expanded version of this book, now entitled *Wege zur Raumschiffahrt* (translated and published as *Ways to Spaceflight*); this volume was more popularly written and the highly technical material was highlighted. Both versions of the book were important for their new ideas and for the inspiration they provided to other spaceflight pioneers.

One of the most important consequences of this publication was the German Rocket Society (Verein für Raumschiffahrt), which was founded in 1927 to raise money for Oberth's rocket experiments. With Oberth as president from 1929 to 1930, the society provided considerable practical training in rocketry to several of its members, including **Wernher von Braun**, who later became part of the German Army's rocket center at Peenemünde and participated in developing the V–2 guided missile. As public interest in space flight increased, the German film director Fritz Lang decided to make a movie on the subject; it was called *Frau im Mond* (title means "Woman on the Moon"), and he employed Oberth as technical advisor. Lang and his film company also provided funds for Oberth to construct a liquid-propellant

rocket which would be launched at the movie's premier, but Oberth was unable to meet the deadline. He designed and built a rocket which never flew, but it did undergo a static test on July 23, 1930, that was certified by the Government Institute for Chemistry and Technology. Soon after this, Oberth returned to his teaching duties in Romania, but the German Rocket Society continued their work, and rocket development benefitted from the increased credibility that had been bestowed on it by government certification.

Participates Less in Later Development of Rocketry

Oberth's most important contributions to rocketry were his initial theoretical work and the publicity he was able to generate during the 1920s. After 1930, he resumed liquid-propellant rocket experiments while continuing to teach at Mediasch. He succeeded in launching one rocket in 1935, but during these years he remained outside the mainstream of rocket development. In 1938 he received an appointment to the Technical Institute in Vienna to work on liquid-propellant rockets under a contract with the German Air Force, but he was not given adequate facilities or sufficient staff to do anything significant. In 1940 he was transferred to the Technical Institute of Dresden to develop a fuel pump for what turned out to be the V–2 rocket. But the system for this rocket had already been designed when he started, and Oberth left Dresden once he discovered that his work had no purpose. He went to Peenemünde, where he worked under his former assistant, Wernher von Braun, but by the time he arrived the V–2 rocket was already essentially developed. Oberth, who became a German citizen in 1941, was put to work examining patents and other technical information for possible use on rockets. After doing some analytical work with the supersonic wind tunnel at Peenemünde in 1943, he began work on an antiaircraft rocket, using a solid propellant. He was transferred to a firm that dealt in solid fuels, Westfälisch-Anhaltische Sprengstoff A.G., where he worked until the end of the war.

After World War II, he moved to Feucht in what became West Germany. In 1948, Oberth obtained a position in Switzerland as an advisor and technical writer on matters related to rocketry, and in 1950 he was hired by the Italian Navy to develop a solid-propellant rocket. The project was discontinued in 1953, and he returned to Feucht, where in 1954 he published *Menschen im Weltraum* (translated and published as *Man into Space*), in which he discussed electric spaceships and a vehicle for moving about on the moon, as well as many of the topics covered in his previous books. In 1955 Oberth published another book, *Das Mondauto* (translated and published as *The Moon Car*), in which he elaborated on his conception for a vehicle to operate on the moon.

Also in 1955, von Braun obtained for Oberth a position with the U.S. Army Ballistic Missile Agency (ABMA) at Redstone Arsenal in Huntsville, Alabama. At ABMA, Oberth was involved in advanced planning for projects in space, including electrical and thermonuclear propulsion for rockets, guidance devices, and vehicles for the moon. Von Braun believed that Oberth had inspired the roving vehicle used on the Apollo 15 flight to the moon. The concept of inspiration is what best characterizes Oberth's other designs at Huntsville as well, for they seem to have contributed little directly to the space effort. In 1958 he returned to Feucht where he resided for the rest of his life, although he did return to the United States in July of 1969 to witness the launch of Apollo 11 that carried the first humans to the moon.

In *The Spaceflight Revolution,* William Sims Bainsbridge writes of Oberth that "his rocket work was conducted simultaneously with the development of a theosophical system that must be described, delicately, as variant, if not deviant." As early as 1930 but increasingly during the 1950s, Oberth was publishing and expressing a number of views that many of his admirers found disconcerting. These included claims that unidentified flying objects could be space vehicles carrying intelligent people from beyond our world, and that each human cell had its own immortal soul; he also supported such movements as parapsychology and the occult. Oberth's real importance lay in his two first books, which launched the space flight movement in Germany and laid the foundations for the exploration of space after 1957. Of the three preeminent founders of space flight, Oberth alone lived to witness the results of his early ideas. He died at age ninety-five in Nuremberg, West Germany, on December 29, 1989.

SELECTED WRITINGS BY OBERTH:

Books

Die Rakete zu den Planeträumen (title means "The Rocket into Planetary Space"), [Germany], 1923, reprinted, Uni-Verlag, 1960.

Wege zur Raumschiffahrt, [Germany], 1929, translation published as *Ways to Spaceflight,* The National Aeronautics and Space Administration, 1972.

Menschen im Weltraum, [Germany], 1954, translation by G. P. H. de Freville published as *Man into Space,* Harper, 1957.

Das Mondauto, [Germany], 1959, translation by Willy Ley published as *The Moon Car,* Harper, 1959.

"My Contributions to Astronautics," in *First Steps Toward Space,* edited by Frederick C. Durant and George S. James, Smithsonian Institution Press, 1974, pp. 129–140.

Periodicals

"Hermann Oberth: From My Life," *Astronautics,* June, 1959, pp. 38–39, 100–105.

SOURCES:

Books

Bainbridge, William Sims, *The Spaceflight Revolution,* Wiley, 1976.

Barth, Hans, *Hermann Oberth: "Vater der Raumfahrt,"* Bechtle, 1985.

Ley, Willy, *Rockets, Missiles, and Men in Space,* Viking, 1968.

Ordway, Fred, and Wernher von Braun, with Dave Dooling, *Space Travel: A History,* Harper, 1975.

Winter, Frank H., *Rockets into Space,* Harvard University Press, 1990.

Periodicals

Ad Astra, March, 1990, pp. 37–40.

Spaceflight, July-August, 1977, pp. 243–256.

Other

Harwit, Martin, and Frank Winter, oral interview with Hermann Oberth, National Air and Space Museum, Smithsonian Institution, November 14–15, 1987.

Von Braun, Wernher, letter to Dr. C. Stark Draper, 30 June 1971.

—Sketch by J. D. Hunley

Adriana C. Ocampo
1955-
Colombian-born American planetary geologist

Adriana C. Ocampo is a geologist whose duties at the National Aeronautics and Space Administration (NASA) have involved coordinating aspects of the flight of the unmanned spacecraft *Mars Observer* and the long-term Jupiter mission called Project Galileo. The ongoing Project Galileo mission is the most complex flown by NASA in nearly twenty years, and Ocampo is responsible for one of the spacecraft's four remote sensing instruments. She has served her profession as national secretary of the Society of

Hispanic Professional Engineers (SHPE) and later as its national vice president.

Adriana C. Ocampo was born on January 5, 1955, in Barranquilla, Colombia. When she was only a few months old, her family moved to Buenos Aires, Argentina. When she was fifteen they emigrated to the United States, settling in Pasadena, California. Although the results from aptitude tests she had taken in Argentina directed her toward a career in the fields of business or accounting, Ocampo was able to convince her school counselors in Pasadena that she was serious about taking physics and calculus. When she participated in a science program sponsored by NASA's Jet Propulsion Laboratory (JPL) during her junior year as an aerospace engineering major at Pasadena City College, her resolve and ability became apparent.

Located in Pasadena, the Jet Propulsion Laboratory (JPL) would play an important role in shaping Ocampo's education and career. She worked there part-time during her last two years of high school and continued to do so after entering Pasadena City College. It was during this time that Ocampo discovered her real scientific focus and decided to switch to geology. She also entered California State University at Los Angeles, where she received her B.S. in geology in 1983, accepting a full-time position at JPL.

The Jet Propulsion Laboratory put her skills as a planetary geologist to the test during their Viking mission to Mars when they assigned her the task of producing a photo atlas of one of the moons of Mars. Published by NASA in 1984, this volume is the only available atlas of the moon Phobos. Ocampo subsequently became science coordinator for separate sensing instruments on two major planetary missions. For the *Mars Observer* mission, NASA's first Mars venture in seventeen years, she was responsible for the thermal emission spectrometer—an instrument that would measure the heat produced by the planet, thus enabling cartographers to create more accurate maps. This mission failed, however, during 1993 when, after an eleven-month journey, the spacecraft inexplicably fell silent, spinning out of control due to a malfunction. Ocampo's instrument thus remained untested.

Ocampo, however, became involved with another assignment at JPL, overseeing the operation of the Near-Infrared Mapping Spectrometer (NIMS) mounted on NASA's Project Galileo spacecraft. As one of four remote sensing instruments mounted on the space probe, NIMS will measure reflected sunlight and heat from Jupiter's atmosphere and help scientists to determine the planet's composition, cloud structure. and temperature. Using the data gathered by Ocampo's instrument, scientists will begin to learn more about the surface chemistry and mineralogy of Jupiter's four moons. The Galileo mission was launched successfully in 1989 and is on track for a Jupiter encounter during December, 1995. During its voyage, it has successfully returned images of the Earth, the Moon, Venus, and the crater-pocked asteroid named Gaspra. Ocampo's NIMS instrument scanned that asteroid's surface as it flew past and revealed valuable new information—indicating that the asteroid is covered by a "soil" of pulverized rock and dust thinner than the Moon's, and that its peak temperature is about 230 degrees Kelvin.

Ocampo is fluent in Spanish and English and reads French and Italian, so it is not surprising that she originated the idea of an international sharing of space information. Called the Pan American Space Conference and sponsored by the United Nations, this symposium met in Costa Rica in 1990 and in Chili in 1993 and provided a forum for scientists and engineers of North and South America to discuss cooperative efforts in space research and technology. Ocampo is married to archeologist Kevin O. Pope who shares her interest in geology and whose company does remote-sensing geological and ecological research.

SELECTED WRITINGS BY OCAMPO:

Books

Phobos: Close Encounter Imaging from the Viking Orbiters, NASA, 1984.

SOURCES:

Periodicals

Mellado, Carmela, "Adriana Ocampo," *Hispanic Engineer,* fall, 1987, pp. 22–24.
Mellado, Carmela, "The Women Leaders of the SHPE National Board of Directors," *Hispanic Engineer,* fall, 1989, pp. 22–25.

—*Sketch by Leonard C. Bruno*

Ellen Ochoa
1958-
American electrical engineer and astronaut

A specialist in optics and optical recognition in robotics, Ellen Ochoa is noted both for her distinguished work in inventions and patents and for her role in American space exploration. Among her

Ellen Ochoa

optical systems innovations are a device that detects flaws and image recognition apparatus. In the late 1980s she began working with the National Aeronautics and Space Administration (NASA) as an optical specialist. After leading a project team, Ochoa was selected for NASA's space flight program. She made her first flight on the space shuttle Discovery in April 1993, becoming the first Hispanic woman astronaut.

The third of five children of Rosanne (Deardorff) and Joseph Ochoa, she was born May 10, 1958, in Los Angeles, California. She grew up in La Mesa, California; her father was a manager of a retail store and her mother a homemaker. Ochoa attended Grossmont High School in La Mesa and then studied physics at San Diego State University. She completed her bachelor's degree in 1980 and was named valedictorian of her graduating class; she then moved to the department of electrical engineering at Stanford University. She received her master's degree in 1981 and her doctorate in 1985, working with Joseph W. Goodman and Lambertus Hesselink. The topic of her dissertation was real-time intensity inversion using four-wave mixing in photorefractive crystals. While completing her doctoral research she developed and patented a real-time optical inspection technique for defect detection. In an interview with Marianne Fedunkiw, Ochoa said that she considers this her most important scientific achievement so far.

In 1985 she joined Sandia National Laboratories in Livermore, California, where she became a member of the technical staff in the Imaging Technology Division. Her research centered on developing optical filters for noise removal and optical methods for distortion-invariant object recognition. She was coauthor of two more patents based on her work at Sandia, one for an optical system for nonlinear median filtering of images and another for a distortion-invariant optical pattern recognition system.

Becomes an Astronaut for NASA

It was during her graduate studies that Ochoa began considering a career as an astronaut. She told Fedunkiw that friends were applying who encouraged her to join them; ironically, she was the only one from her group of friends to make it into space. Her career at NASA began in 1988 as a group leader in the Photonic Processing group of the Intelligent Systems Technology Branch, located at the NASA Ames Research Center in Moffett Field, California. She worked as the technical lead for a group of eight people researching optical-image and data-processing techniques for space-based robotics. Six months later she moved on to become chief of the Intelligent Systems Technology Branch. Then in January 1990 she was chosen for the astronaut class, becoming an astronaut in July of 1991.

Her first flight began April 8, 1993, on the orbiter Discovery. She was mission specialist on the STS–56 Atmospheric Research flight, which was carrying the Atmospheric Laboratory for Applications and Science, known as Atlas–2. She was responsible for their primary payload, the Spartan 201 Satellite, and she operated the robotic arm to deploy and retrieve it. This satellite made forty-eight hours of independent solar observations to measure solar output and determine how the solar wind is produced. Ochoa was the lone female member of the five-person team which made 148 orbits of the earth.

Ochoa's technical assignments have also included flight-software verification in the Shuttle Avionics Integration Laboratory (SAIL), where she was crew representative for robotics development, testing and training, as well as crew representative for flight-software and computer-hardware development. Ochoa's next flight will be on the STS–66 Atmospheric Laboratory for Applications and Science–3 (ATLAS–3) flight scheduled for October 1994. ATLAS–3 will continue the Spacelab flight series to study the Sun's energy during an eleven-year solar cycle; the primary purpose of this is to learn how changes in the irradiance of the Sun affect the Earth's environment and climate. On this mission Ochoa will be Payload Commander. She is currently based at the Lyndon B. Johnson Space Center in Houston, Texas.

Ochoa is a member of the Optical Society of America and the American Institute of Aeronautics and Astronautics. She has received a number of awards from NASA including the NASA Group Achievement Award for Photonics Technology in 1991 and the NASA Space Flight Medal in 1993. In 1994, she received the Women in Science and Engineering (WISE) Engineering Achievement Award. She has also been recognized many times by the Hispanic community. Ochoa was the 1990 recipient of the National Hispanic Quincentennial Commission Pride Award. She was also given *Hispanic* magazine's 1991 Hispanic Achievement Science Award, and in 1993 she won the Congressional Hispanic Caucus Medallion of Excellence Role Model Award.

Ochoa is married to Coe Fulmer Miles, a computer research engineer. They have no children. Outside of her space research, Ochoa counts music and sports as hobbies. She is an accomplished classical flautist—in 1983 she was the Student Soloist Award Winner in the Stanford Symphony Orchestra. She also has her private pilot's license and in training for space missions flies "back seat" in T–38 aircraft.

SELECTED WRITINGS BY OCHOA:

Periodicals

(With George F. Schils and Donald W. Sweeney) "Detection of Multiple Views of an Object in the Presence of Clutter," *Optical Engineering,* Volume 27, 1988, p. 266.

(With Joseph W. Goodman and Lambertus Hesselink) "Real-time Enhancement of Defects in a Periodic Mask Using Photorefractive BSO," *Optics Letters,* Volume 10, 1985, p. 430.

(With Goodman and Hesselink) "Real-time Intensity Inversion Using Two-Wave and Four-Wave Mixing in Photorefractive BGO," *Applied Optics,* Volume 24, 1985, p. 1826.

SOURCES:

NASA Johnson Space Center, "Missions Highlights STS–56," May 1993.

NASA Johnson Space Center, "Biographical Data—Ellen Ochoa," August 1993.

Ochoa, Ellen, interview with Marianne Fedunkiw conducted March 18, 1994.

—Sketch by Marianne Fedunkiw

Severo Ochoa
1905-
Spanish biochemist

Spanish-born biochemist Severo Ochoa has spent his life engaged in research into the workings of the human body. In the 1950s, he was one of the first scientists to synthesize the newly discovered ribonucleic acid (RNA) in the laboratory. This feat marked the first time that scientists managed to combine molecules together in a chain outside a living organism, knowledge that would later prove to be an essential step in enabling scientists to create life in a test tube. For this work, Ochoa received the Nobel Prize in 1959. In addition to his laboratory work, Ochoa, who was trained as a physician in Spain, taught biochemistry and pharmacology to many generations of New York University medical students.

Severo Ochoa was born on September 24, 1905, in Luarca, a small town in the north of Spain. Named after his father, a lawyer, Ochoa was the youngest son in the family. He lived in this mountain town until the age of seven, when his parents decided to move to Málaga, Spain. The move gave young Severo access to a private school education that prepared him for entrance into Málaga College, which is comparable to an American high school. By this time, Ochoa knew that he eventually would enter a career in the sciences; the only question in his mind was in which field he would specialize. Because Ochoa found mathematics at Málaga College very taxing, he decided against pursuing an engineering career, in which such skills would be essential. Instead, he planned to enter biology. After Ochoa received his B.A. from Málaga in 1921, he spent a year studying the prerequisite courses for medical school, at that time physics, chemistry, biology, and geology. In 1923 he matriculated at the University of Madrid's Medical School.

Acquires a Medical Education

At Madrid, Ochoa had dreams of studying under the Spanish neurohistologist Santiago Rámon y Cajal, but these were quickly dashed when he discovered that the 70-year-old histology professor had retired from teaching, although he still ran a laboratory in Madrid. Ochoa hesitated to approach Cajal even at the lab, however, because he thought the older man would be too busy to be bothered by an unimportant student. Nonetheless, by the end of his second year in medical school, Ochoa had confirmed his desire to do biological research and jumped at one of his professor's offers of a job in a nearby laboratory.

The Medical School itself housed no research facilities, but Ochoa's physiology teacher ran a small

Severo Ochoa

research laboratory under the aegis of the Council for Scientific Research a short distance away. Working with a classmate, Ochoa first mastered the relatively routine laboratory task of isolating creatinine—a white, crystalline compound—from urine. From there he moved to the more demanding task of studying the function and metabolism of creatine, a nitrogenous substance, in muscle. The summer after his fourth year of medical school he spent in a Glasgow laboratory, continuing work on this problem. Ochoa received his medical degree in 1929.

In an attempt to further his scientific education, Ochoa applied for a postdoctoral fellowship working under **Otto Meyerhof** at the Kaiser-Wilhelm Institute in a suburb of Berlin. Although the Council for Scientific Research had offered him a fellowship to pursue these studies, Ochoa turned down their offer of support because he could afford to pay his own way. He felt the money should be given to someone more needy to himself. Ochoa enjoyed his work under Meyerhof, remaining in Germany for a year.

On July 8, 1931, he married Carmen García Cobian, a daughter of a Spanish lawyer and businessman, and moved with his newlywed wife to England, where he had a fellowship from the University of Madrid to study at London's National Institute for Medical Research. In England Ochoa met Sir **Henry Hallett Dale**, who would later win the 1936 Nobel in medicine for his discovery of the chemical transmission of nerve impulses. During his first year at the

Institute, Ochoa studied the enzyme glyoxalase, and the following year he started working directly under Dale, investigating how the adrenal glands affected the chemistry of muscular contraction. In 1933 he returned to his alma mater, the University of Madrid, where he was appointed a lecturer in physiology and biochemistry.

Spanish Civil War Forces Him to Flee Native Country

Within two years, Ochoa accepted a new position. One of the heads of the Department of Medicine was planning to start an Institute for Medical Research with sections on biochemistry, physiology, microbiology, and experimental medicine. The institute would be partially supported by the University of Madrid, which offered it space in one its new medical school buildings, and partially supported by wealthy patrons, who planned to provide a substantial budget for equipment, salaries, and supplies. The director of the new institute offered the young Ochoa the directorship of the section on physiology, which he accepted, and provided him with a staff of three. However, a few months after Ochoa began work, civil war broke out in Spain. In order to continue his work, Ochoa decided to leave the country in September, 1936. He and his wife immigrated to Germany, hardly a stable country itself in late 1936.

When Ochoa arrived, he found that his mentor Meyerhof, who was Jewish, was under considerable political and personal pressure. The German scientist had not allowed this to interfere with his work, though Ochoa did find to his surprise that the type of research Meyerhof conducted had changed dramatically in the six years since he had seen him last. As he wrote of the laboratory in a retrospective piece for the *Annual Review of Biochemistry:* "When I left it in 1930 it was basically a physiology laboratory; one could see muscles twitching everywhere. In 1936 it was a biochemistry laboratory. Glycolysis and fermentation in muscle or yeast extracts or partial reactions of these processes catalyzed by purified enzymes, were the main subjects of study." Meyerhof's change in research emphasis influenced Ochoa's own work, even though he studied in the laboratory for less than a year before Meyerhof fled to France.

Before Meyerhof left, however, he ensured that his protege was not stranded, arranging for Ochoa to receive a six-month fellowship at the Marine Biological Laboratory in Plymouth, England. Although this fellowship lasted only half a year, Ochoa enjoyed his time there, not the least because his wife Carmen started working with him in the laboratory. Their collaboration later led to the publication of a joint paper in *Nature.* At the end of six months, though, Ochoa had to move on, and friends at the lab found him a post as a research assistant at Oxford University. Two years later, when England entered the war, Oxford's Biochemistry Department shifted all its efforts to war research in which Ochoa, an alien, could not take part. So in 1940 the Ochoas picked up stakes again, this time to cross the Atlantic to work in the laboratory of **Carl Ferdinand Cori** and **Gerty T. Cori** in St. Louis. Part of the Washington University School of Medicine, the Cori lab was renowned for its cutting edge research on enzymes and work with intermediary metabolism of carbohydrates. This work involved studying the biochemical reactions in which carbohydrates produce energy for cellular operations. Ochoa worked there for a year before New York University persuaded him to move east to take a job as a research associate in medicine at the Bellevue Psychiatric Hospital, where he would for the first time have graduate and postdoctoral students working beneath him.

Appointed Chair of NYU's Pharmacology Department

In 1945, Ochoa was promoted to assistant professor of biochemistry at the medical school. Two years later when the pharmacology chair retired, Ochoa was offered the opportunity to succeed him and, lured by the promise of new laboratory space, he accepted. He remained chairperson for nine years, taking a sabbatical in 1949 to serve as a visiting professor at the University of California. His administrative work did not deter him from pursuing his research interests in biochemistry, however. In the early 1950s, he isolated one of the chemical compounds necessary for photosynthesis to occur, triphosphopyridine nucleotide, known as TPN. Ochoa continued his interest in intermediary metabolism, expanding the work of **Hans Adolf Krebs**, who posited the idea of a cycle through which food is metabolized into adenosine triphosphate, or ATP, the molecule that provides energy to the cell. The Spanish scientist discovered that one molecule of glucose when burned with oxygen produced 36 ATP molecules. When the chairman of the biochemistry department resigned in 1954, Ochoa accepted this opportunity to return to the department full-time as chair and full professor.

Once more ensconced in biochemistry research, Ochoa turned his attentions to a new field: the rapidly growing area of deoxyribonucleic acid (DNA) research. Earlier in his career, enzymes had been the hot new molecules for biochemists to study; now, after the critical work of **James Watson** and **Francis Crick** in 1953, nucleic acids were fascinating scientists in the field. Ochoa was no exception. Drawing on his earlier work with enzymes, Ochoa began investigating which enzymes played roles in the creation of nucleic acids in the body. Although most enzymes assist in breaking down materials, Ochoa knew that he was looking for an enzyme that helped combine nucleotides into the long chains that were nucleic acids. Once he

isolated these molecules, he hoped, he would be able to synthesize RNA and DNA in the lab. In 1955, he found a bacterial enzyme in sewage that appeared to play just such a role. When he added this enzyme to a solution of nucleotides, he discovered that the solution became viscous, like jelly, indicating that RNA had indeed formed in the dish. The following year, **Arthur Kornberg**, who had studied with Ochoa in 1946, applied these methods to synthesize DNA.

Wins Nobel for Synthesis of RNA

In 1959, five years after he assumed the directorship of the biochemistry department, Ochoa shared the Nobel Prize for Physiology or Medicine with Kornberg, for their work in discovering the enzymes that help produce nucleic acids. While Ochoa was particularly delighted to share the prize with his old colleague, by this time he was no stranger to academic plaudits. The holder of several honorary degrees from both American and foreign universities, including Oxford, Ochoa had also been the recipient of the Carl Neuberg Medal in biochemistry in 1951 and the Charles Leopold Mayer Prize in 1955. Ochoa served as chairperson of NYU's biochemistry department for 20 years, until the summer of 1974, just before his seventieth birthday. When he retired from this post, he rejected the department's offer to make him an emeritus professor, preferring to remain on staff as a full professor. But even that could not keep Ochoa sufficiently occupied. In 1974, he joined the Roche Institute of Molecular Biology in New Jersey.

In 1985 he returned to his native Spain as a professor of biology at the University Autonoma in Madrid to continue his lifelong fascination with biochemical research. At the age of 75 Ochoa wrote a retrospective of his life, which he titled "Pursuit of a Hobby." In the introduction to this piece, he explained his choice of title: At a party given in the forties in honor of two Nobel laureate chemists Ochoa listed his hobby in the guest register as biochemistry, although he was at the time professor of pharmacology at New York University. Sir Henry Dale, one of the party's honorees, joked, "now that he is a pharmacologist, he has biochemistry as a hobby." Ochoa concluded this tale with the statement, "In my life biochemistry has been my only and real hobby."

SELECTED WRITINGS BY OCHOA:

Books

"Recollections from the NYU Department of Pharmacology (1946–1954)," *An Era in Biochemistry: A Festschrift for Sarah Ratner,* edited by Maynard Pullman, New York Academy of Sciences, 1983.

Periodicals

"The Pursuit of a Hobby," *Annual Review of Biochemistry,* Volume 48, 1980, pp. 1–30.

SOURCES:

Books

Moritz, Charles, editor, *Current Biography,* H. W. Wilson, 1962.
Nobel Prize Winners, H. W. Wilson, 1987.

—*Sketch by Shari Rudavsky*

Eugene Pleasants Odum
1913-
American ecologist and ornithologist

Ecologist and ornithologist Eugene Pleasants Odum is renowned for his views concerning the interrelationship between man and environment, having researched the ecology of birds, wetland ecology, landscape ecology, and vertebrate populations, as well as the general principles of ecology. The author of numerous works, including the widely used textbooks *Fundamentals of Ecology* and *Ecology,* Odum was the recipient of the 1987 Crafoord Prize from the Royal Swedish Academy of Science for his investigations into ecological issues (the Crafoord Prize is regularly awarded to scientists working in disciplines not addressed by the Nobel Prize). This honor was bestowed jointly upon Eugene P. Odum and his brother, **Howard T. Odum**, also an ecologist.

A native of Lake Sunapee, New Hampshire, Odum was born September 17, 1913. He received his undergraduate education at the University of North Carolina at Chapel Hill in 1934, then obtained his doctorate degree in ecology and ornithology from the University of Illinois in 1939. During his studies, Odum was assistant zoologist at the University of Georgia from 1934 to 1936. Upon completion of his doctoral studies, he was named resident biologist at the Edmund Niles Huyck Preserve in New York, a position he held from 1938 to 1940, and again during the summer of 1941.

Odum became an instructor at the University of Georgia in 1940 and was named assistant professor in 1942, then associate professor in 1945, receiving full professorship at the university in 1954. Odum also held two adjunct positions during his career: in the summers of 1942 and 1945, he carried out research at the Mountain Lake Biological Station at the University of Virginia, and from 1957 to 1961 he was an instructor of marine ecology during the summer training program of the Marine Biological Laboratory at Woods Hole, Massachusetts. Named Callaway Professor of Ecology at the University of Georgia in 1977, Odum also served as director of the university's Institute of Ecology from 1960 until 1984, when he became director emeritus.

Authors Primary Ecology Textbook

Odum wrote the influential textbook *Fundamentals of Ecology* in 1953, when ecological science was generally regarded as a subtopic within the field of biology. In the book, Odum describes the delicate balance of life among plants, herbivores, and carnivores, and their interaction with microorganisms. These complex relationships play a crucial role in the recycling of nutrients and the continuation of each species.

By 1989, when Odum authored *Ecology and Our Endangered Life-Support Systems,* ecology had not only emerged as its own field of study, but was evolving into an integrative discipline which encompasses human life and the environment in which we live. In this volume, which was written for general readers as well as students of science, Odum declares that we have reached a "turning point in history . . . when we cannot continue to postpone the environmental and human costs of development without incurring widespread damage to our global life-support systems." Reiterating basic ecological principles, Odum then demonstrates that each life form, rather than engaging in a merely competitive struggle, is connected with the others as part of a unified, dynamic process. Species of plants, herbivores, and carnivores maintain a beneficial interdependence upon one another. Odum also explains how human economic activities have disturbed both local and global ecosystems.

Discussing ecological and human systems, Odum notes that human communities are similar to organic communities, since each pass through phases from pioneering—when resources abound—to maturity, when resources are less plentiful and their consumption must be moderated. In *Ecology and Our Endangered Life-Support Systems* Odum describes biological organization within a hierarchical framework, applying the concept to such examples as endangered species, prescribed burning, population biology, and the Gaia hypothesis, which views the Earth as an organism able to regulate its own biosphere. Also included in the volume are sketches of prominent scientists in the field of ecology.

Odum has received numerous honors for his work in ecological science. In addition to the Crafoord Prize, he was awarded the prestigious Prix de l'Institute de la Vie by the French government in 1975. Odum was honored in 1956 with the Mercer Award of the Ecological Society of America and was presented with the Tyler Ecological Award by United States president Jimmy Carter in 1977. A member of the National Academy of Science, the American Academy of Arts and Sciences, and the American Society of Limnology and Oceanography, Odum also served as president of the Ecological Society of America from 1964 to 1965.

SELECTED WRITINGS BY ODUM:

Books

Fundamentals of Ecology, Saunders College, 1953.
Ecology, Holt, 1963.
Ecology: The Link Between the Natural and the Social Sciences, Saunders College, 1975.
Basic Ecology, Saunders College, 1983.
Ecology and Our Endangered Life-Support Systems, Sinauer Associates, 1989.

Periodicals

"Input Management of Production Systems," *Science,* January 13, 1989, pp. 177–81.
"Great Ideas in Ecology for the 1990s," *BioScience,* July/August, 1992, pp. 542–45.

—*Sketch by Karen Withem*

Howard T. Odum
1924-

American ecologist

Howard T. Odum is a systems ecologist whose research encompasses biological oceanography, ecological engineering, energy analysis, biogeochemistry, and tropical meteorology. He is most noted for his concept of the self-organizing system and its relation to energy production and consumption. He has done some of his most important work with his brother, **Eugene Pleasants Odum**, who is also an ecologist, and they have been the joint recipients of two prestigious international awards: the 1987 Crafoord Prize, which in the field of ecology is equivalent to the Nobel Prize, and the 1976 Prix de l'Institute de la Vie, a comparable award from the French government.

Howard Thomas Odum was born on September 1, 1924, in Durham, North Carolina. He served with the U.S. Air Force from 1944 to 1945 as a meteorologist in the Panama Canal Zone. He completed his undergraduate education at the University of North Carolina at Chapel Hill, graduating in 1947. He then entered the doctoral program in zoology at Yale University, receiving his Ph.D. in 1951.

From 1950 to 1954, Odum was assistant professor of biology at the University of Florida, followed by two years as assistant professor of zoology at Duke University, where he continued his research at Duke Marine Laboratory. In 1956, Odum accepted a post as director and resident scientist of the Institute of Marine Sciences, University of Texas at Port Arkansas, where he also served as editor of publications. Odum left this post in 1963 to study as chief scientist on the rain forest program at the Puerto Rico Nuclear Center at Rio Piedras, staying until 1966. In that year, he was named professor of ecology at the University of North Carolina, Chapel Hill, where he remained until he began his association with the University of Florida in 1970. He has served there as Graduate Research Professor of Environmental Engineering Sciences since 1970, and as director of the Center for Wetlands since 1972.

One of the primary fields of research for Odum is how what he calls self-organizing systems use energy. He has defined self-organizing systems to include an ecosystem in nature or an economy in human society, and in an article in *Science* he has observed that "ecosystem study has generated concepts that may apply to all complex systems when appropriately generalized." Odum has questioned the traditional model for these systems, the steady-state paradigm, which proposes that growth of production is followed by growth of consumption until both factors become level in a steady state. He has argued that the organization of these systems is more dynamic, and that the production and consumption of energy actually affects the development of the system itself. The systems tend toward the maximum utilization of energy as Odum has explained in *Science:* "During the trials and errors of self-organization, species and relations are being selectively reinforced as more energy becomes available to those designs that feed products back into increased production." Odum believes that the long-range performance of such systems are maximized by what he calls "pulsing": intense, short-term consumption that does not interfere with production, such as cattle being allowed to graze for a few weeks on grass that has been allowed to grow for months.

In his analysis of these self-organizing systems, including ecosystems, Odum has examined why energy is distributed in such a way that, as he claimed in *Science,* "hierarchies are universal in physical and biological systems." In examining the transformation of energy, he has distinguished between low-quality energy, which is generally present in large quantities, and high-quality energy, which is generally available in smaller amounts. Sunlight would be an example of a lower-quality energy; plant matter would be higher-quality energy. Odum has noted the difficulty of actually calculating the passage of energy through such a system, because it is constantly being transformed from one type to another. He has proposed the concept of "emergy" to clarify this problem, defining emergy in his *Science* article as "the energy of one type required in transformation to generate a flow or storage."

Odum's career in ecology has been recognized with the prestigious Crafoord Prize and Prix de l'Institute de la Vie. He also received the George Mercer Award from the Ecological Society of America in 1957. He was honored by the International Technical Writers Association, which gave him their Award of Distinction in 1971. In 1973, he received a million-dollar grant jointly awarded by the Rockefeller Foundation and the National Science Foundation to study the feasibility of putting treated sewage in wetlands. Odum is a member of the American Society of Limnology and Oceanography, the American Meteorological Society, the Ecological Society of America, and the Geochemical Society. He is a fellow of the American Association for the Advancement of Science, and in 1979 he was appointed Erskine Fellow by the University of Canterbury in New Zealand to help that nation use its natural and human resources to produce energy.

SELECTED WRITINGS BY ODUM:

Books

(With E. C. Odum) *Energy: Basis for Man and Nature,* McGraw-Hill, 1976.
Systems Ecology, Wiley, 1983.
(With Katherine Ewel Carter) *Cypress Swamps,* University Presses of Florida, 1984.

Periodicals

"Self-Organization, Transformity, and Information," *Science,* November 25, 1988, pp. 1132–1139.

—Sketch by Karen Withem

Ida H. Ogilvie
1874-1963
American geologist

Ida H. Ogilvie was instrumental in making careers in geology accessible to women. The founder and first chair of Barnard College's geology department, she was also a renowned field researcher, conducting explorations in Maine, New Mexico, Mexico, California, and her home state of New York. Her areas of specialization included glacial geography and petrology.

Born on February 12, 1874, in New York City, Ida Helen Ogilvie was the daughter of Clinton Ogilvie, who traced his ancestry to the Earl of Airlie in Scotland, and of Helen Slade Ogilvie, a Mayflower descendant who was related to many of the colonial founders of America. The wealthy family expected their daughter to follow the usual debutante-wife-matron progression of the Gilded Age. But Ogilvie had different plans. She received her early education at home, being taught to speak French before English and learning how to draw expertly, before going to the Brearley School. She also attended schools in Europe before entering Bryn Mawr, and it was at that women's college that she found an abiding interest in geology, studying under Florence Bascom who had just founded Bryn Mawr's program in geology. She earned an A.B. from Bryn Mawr in 1900 and then studied at the University of Chicago for two years, where she began to focus on both petrology, or the origin of rocks, and glacial geology. She published her first paper in petrology in 1902 and then went to Columbia University, where she earned her doctorate in 1903.

Founds the Geology Department at Barnard

That same year she became the first lecturer in geology at Columbia University's Barnard College. She did not want to give up teaching graduate courses at Columbia, however, so she focused on the one field in geology where a lecturer was needed, glacial geology, even though her real love was petrology. From 1903 until her retirement in 1941, Ogilvie was the chair of Barnard's geology department, responsible not only for administration, but also for instruction and research. She was honored for her work in geology by being the second woman elected to the Geological Society of America.

Additionally, she took on the responsibilities of a farm she purchased at Bedford, New York, where she raised registered Jersey cattle, as well as horses, dogs, and ponies. During World War I she turned this into a model farm, recruiting young women from across the

United States into agriculture during the manpower shortage created by the hostilities. After the war, some of her recruits stayed on, and Ogilvie bought a larger farm of 660 acres in Germantown, New York, the Hermitage, where she continued to breed her prize-winning herd.

With all of these responsibilities, Ogilvie was still able, until 1920, to do distinguished research, investigating glaciation in Canada, conducting field mapping in Maine and New York, and studying volcanic activities. Thereafter, she concentrated on instruction, becoming a noted lecturer who fretted over each presentation and who encouraged and nurtured her students. She also helped endow scholarships for young women in the sciences at Barnard, Columbia, and Bryn Mawr. After retiring from teaching in 1941, she devoted herself full time to her farm and to her hobby of knitting afghans in geologic designs. She died at the age of eighty-nine on October 13, 1963, at her farm in Germantown, having, as Elizabeth Wood reported in the *Bulletin of the Geological Society of America,* "lived a long and mostly happy life, doing the things she wanted to do."

SELECTED WRITINGS BY OGILVIE:

Periodicals

"Glacial Phenomena in the Adirondacks and Champlain Valley," *Journal of Geology,* Volume 10, 1902, pp. 397–412.

"An Analcite-Bearing Camptonite from New Mexico," *Journal of Geology,* Volume 10, 1902, pp. 500–507.

"Geological Notes on the Vicinity of Banff, Alberta," *Journal of Geology,* Volume 12, 1904, pp. 408–414.

"The Effect of Superglacial Debris on the Advance and Retreat of Some Canadian Glaciers," *Journal of Geology,* Volume 12, 1904, pp. 722–743.

"Geology of the Paradox Lake Quadrangle, N.Y.," *New York State Museum Bulletin,* number 96, 1905, pp. 461–509.

"The High-Altitude Conoplain; A Topographic Form Illustrated in the Ortiz Mountains," *American Geologist,* Volume 36, 1905, pp. 27–34.

"A Contribution to the Geology of Southern Maine," *New York Academy of Sciences Annals,* Volume 17, 1907, pp. 519–558.

"Some Igneous Rocks from the Ortiz Mountains, New Mexico," *Journal of Geology,* Volume 16, 1908, pp. 230–238.

"The Interrelation of the Sciences in College Courses," *Columbia University Quarterly,* Volume 17, number 3, 1915, pp. 241–252.

"Field Observations on the Iowan Problem," *New York Academy of Sciences Annals,* Volume 26, 1916, pp. 432–433.

SOURCES:

Books

Arnold, Lois Barber, *Four Lives in Science,* Schocken Books, 1984, pp. 117-119.

Periodicals

"Dr. Ida Ogilvie of Barnard Dies; First Geology Chairman Was 89," *New York Times,* October 15, 1963, p. 39.

"Geology Attracts Feminine Workers," *New York Times,* November 27, 1938, p. 4.

"38-Year Career at Barnard Ends," *New York Times,* May 26, 1941, p. 17.

Wood, Elizabeth A., "Memorial to Ida Helen Ogilvie," *Bulletin of the Geological Society of America,* February, 1964, pp. 35–39.

—*Sketch by J. Sydney Jones*

Kenneth Olden
1938-
American cellular biologist and biochemist

Kenneth Olden has been investigating the possible links between the properties of cell-surface molecules and cancer for more than two decades. In 1991 he was named director of the National Institute of Environmental Health Sciences and the National Toxicology Program, the first African American to become director of one of the National Institutes of Health.

Olden was born in Parrottsville, Tennessee, on July 22, 1938, the son of Mack and Augusta Christmas Olden. In 1960, he received a bachelor's degree in biology from Knoxville College. He was awarded a master of science in genetics from the University of Michigan in 1964 and a doctorate in biology and biochemistry from Temple University in 1970. During the summers of 1964 and 1965, Olden worked in New York City at two academic institutions at the same time, a pattern that he has followed throughout much of his career. He was a research assistant at Columbia University's Department of Biological Chemistry and a biology instructor at the Fashion

Institute of Technology, part of the State University of New York.

In September 1970, Olden went to Harvard University Medical School as a research fellow and a physiology instructor. In 1973, the fellowship ended and he continued as a physiology instructor through 1974. That year, Olden joined the Laboratory of Molecular Biology, Division of Cancer Biology and Diagnosis of the National Cancer Institute at the National Institutes of Health in Bethesda, Maryland, as a senior staff fellow. He was promoted to expert in biochemistry in 1977 and in 1978 became a research biologist in the same division. During this time Olden published two articles on cell biology which in 1980 were listed among the 100 most cited papers of 1978 and 1979: "The Role of Carbohydrates in Protein Secretion and Turnover," and "Fibronectin Adhesion Glycoprotein of Cell Surface and Blood."

Olden is now considered a leading authority on the structure and function of the extracellular matrix glycoprotein fibronectin, one of a family of proteins involved in interactions between cells and the supporting structure around cells. The interactions are important to the spread of cancer. Olden was first to demonstrate that sugar residues of glycoproteins are not required for the export or secretion of glycoproteins. He was also the first to show that metastasis of malignant cells in particular organs could be prevented by blocking the interaction between fibronectin and the glycoprotein receptor around the cell.

In 1979, Olden left NIH to become associate professor of oncology and associate director for research at the Howard University Cancer Center in Washington, D.C. In 1982 he became its deputy director and in 1984 director of research; in that year he was also named professor and in 1985 chairman of the oncology department. In 1991, Olden became director of the National Institute of Environmental Health Sciences and the National Toxicology Program. He was the first African American to become director of any of the seventeen National Institutes in the organization's 100 year history. During his tenure at NIH, Olden has devoted particular attention to the anticancer drug Swainsonine. In 1991, the drug was approved by the Treatment Division of the National Cancer Institute to be on its list of drugs for high-priority development for possible clinical trials on humans.

Olden was named by President George Bush to the National Cancer Advisory Board in January 1991 but resigned six months later due to his appointment to NIH causing a conflict of interest. He has participated widely as an invited speaker at scientific symposia and seminars and as a reviewer for programs in his field; he has authored and coauthored more than 108 publications. Olden is a member of the American Society of Cell Biology; the American Society of Biological Chemistry; the American Association of Cancer Research, for which he is on the board of directors; the Society for Biological Response Modifiers; the North Carolina Institute of Medicine; and the International Society for the Study of Comparative Oncology.

Olden lives in Durham, North Carolina, and is married to the former Sandra L. White. The couple has four children. Olden likes to play tennis, hike, bicycle, and cook.

SELECTED WRITINGS BY OLDEN:

Periodicals

(With K. M. Yamada) "Fibronectin Adhesive Glycoprotein of Cell Surface and Blood," *Nature,* Volume 275, 1978, pp. 179–184.

(With R. M. Pratt and K. M. Yamada) "Role of Carbohydrates in Protein Secretion and Turnover: Effects of Tunicamycin on the Major Cell Surface Glycoprotein of Chick Embryo Fibroblasts," *Cell,* Volume 13, 1978, pp. 461–473.

"Opportunities in Environmental Health Science Research," *Environmental Health Perspectives,* April 22, 1993, pp. 6–7.

"A Preliminary Pharmacokinetic Evaluation of the Antimetastatic Immunomodulator Swainsonine; Clinical Implications," *Anticancer Research,* July-August 1993, pp. 841–844.

SOURCES:

Periodicals

"Ken Olden Heals NIEHS's Split Brain," *Science,* March 5, 1993, pp. 1398–9.

Other

Roberts, John, interview with Margo Nash conducted March 11, 1994.

—*Sketch by Margo Nash*

Richard Dixon Oldham
1858-1936
Irish geologist and seismologist

Richard Dixon Oldham was a geologist whose most important contributions were to the field of seismology, in the era after useful seismographs had been developed and accurate records of earthquakes had begun to be kept. He became famous for his study of the great earthquake of June 12, 1897, in Assam in northeast India; approaching the evidence with unprecedented rigor, he made several discoveries which became the foundation of modern seismology, including the identification of three types of seismic waves. Later in his career, Oldham used his knowledge of these waves and some of their irregularities to establish that the earth has a central core.

Oldham was born in Dublin, Ireland, on July 31, 1858. He was the third son of noted geologist Thomas Oldham, a professor of geology at Trinity College, Dublin, and director of the geological surveys that were being done of Ireland and India. The younger Oldham was educated in England, first at Rugby School and then at the Royal School of Mines; he joined the staff at the Geological Survey of India in 1879. His father had died in 1878, leaving behind an exhaustive study he had begun of an 1869 earthquake in Cachar, India; one of Oldham's first contributions to the group was to finish this study.

Oldham eventually occupied his father's position as superintendent of the Geological Survey of India, and among his primary concerns were investigating the earthquakes and hot springs of India, and researching the structure of the Himalaya Mountains and the plain of the Ganges River. Members of the group made geodetic observations of these various conditions and locations—that is, by measurements and mathematical calculations they determined both their proportions and their exact location on the surface of the earth. Oldham's analyses of these observations provided the material for about forty publications he wrote while he held this position.

Conducts Landmark Earthquake Study

Oldham directed and carried out most of the investigation of the great Assam earthquake of June 12, 1897. This remains one of the largest earthquakes known; though the seismographic records are not entirely compatible with modern measurements, its force has been estimated at 8.7 on the Richter scale. It destroyed an area of more than 9,000 square miles. In his search for a greater understanding of the activity of the earthquake and the physical properties of the earth itself, Oldham reviewed a wide body of evidence. He spoke with people who had seen stones bouncing "like peas on a drumhead," and he photographed boulders that had been thrown from the ground without touching the edges of the dirt that had lain around them. He made careful examinations of cracks in buildings and a pair of damaged tombs, as well as a hill he had been told was "rent from top to bottom." As **Charles F. Richter** writes in *Elementary Seismology:* "His observations were minutely careful and his reasoning ingenious."

Oldham made a number of discoveries about the geology of India, including the location of two major faults. He also made a number of discoveries that contributed to the knowledge of geology in general. By citing evidence of fractures in the earth that were not accompanied by rock displacement, he was able to argue that the surface of the earth was more elastic than had previously been recognized. This theory was supported by other evidence; he was able to identify places where increases in the speed at which the ground was moving during the earthquake had not increased the height at which it was moving. A further consequence of his work on the elasticity of the earth was his discovery of three types of seismic waves. First predicted in theory by the mathematician Siméon Poisson, Oldham established the existence of primary or longitudinal waves, secondary or transverse waves, and surface waves. Oldham's conclusions set precedents for the field of seismology, establishing a new relationship between the changes in the earth's surface and the study of seismic waves.

Oldham left India in 1903 because of health problems. He returned to England, where he continued his research on the Isle of Wight with the distinguished seismologist John Milne. Through analysis of Milne's research on large earthquakes, Oldham was able to establish in 1906 that the earth has a central core. Earlier geologists and seismologists had suggested its existence, but Oldham's work provided the first indisputable confirmation, and his conclusions were based on his discovery of primary and secondary waves.

Oldham observed that when an earthquake occurred on one side of the earth, the primary waves it created could be recorded by a seismograph on the other side of the earth. But he also observed that the arrival of these waves was delayed. It had already been established that the earth had a crust and a mantle, but the mantle was not elastic enough to delay the primary waves in this fashion. Thus Oldham was able to hypothesize the existence of core matter within the earth which was less dense and rigid than the rocks of the mantle and so slowed the transmission of the waves. Later analyses, using Oldham's findings about the arrival and distortion of primary and secondary waves, provided significant insight for scientists into the structure of the earth. By 1914, geologists had prepared a comprehensive set of tables, including tables for a number of phases corresponding to waves that penetrate into the central core, and it was estimated that the depth of the boundary of this core was 2900 kilometers below the earth's outer surface.

In 1903, Oldham retired and became the director of the Indian Museum in Calcutta. He was awarded the Lyell Medal of the Geological Society of London in 1908 and was elected to the Royal Society in 1911. He continued to make contributions to the fields of geology and seismology through the late 1920s. He died in Llandrindod Wells, Wales, on July 15, 1936.

SELECTED WRITINGS BY OLDHAM:

Periodicals

"Report on the Great Earthquake of 12th June 1897," *Memoirs of the Geological Survey of India,* Volume 29, 1899, pp. i-xxx.
"On the Propagation of Earthquake Motion to Great Distances," *Philosophical Transactions of the Royal Society,* 1900, pp. 135–174.
"The Earthquake of 7th August, 1895, in Northern Italy," *Quarterly Journal,* Volume 79, 1923, pp. 231–236.
"The Depth of the Origin of Earthquakes," *Quarterly Journal,* Volume 82, 1926, pp. 67–92.

SOURCES:

Books

Bullen, K. E., *An Introduction to the Theory of Seismology,* Cambridge University Press, 1947, pp. 2, 168, 206.
Richter, Charles F., *Elementary Seismology,* W. H. Freeman, 1958, pp. 49–55.

—*Sketch by Kelly Otter Cooper*

Lars Onsager

Lars Onsager
1903-1976
Norwegian American chemist

Born in Norway, Lars Onsager received his early education there before coming to the United States in 1928 to do graduate work at Yale University. After receiving his Ph.D. in theoretical chemistry he stayed on at Yale and ultimately spent nearly all of his academic career at that institution. Onsager's first important contribution to chemical theory came in 1926 when he showed how improvements could be made in the Debye-Hückel theory of electrolytic dissociation. His later (and probably more significant) work involved non-reversible systems—systems in which differences in pressure, temperature, or some other factor are an important consideration. For his contributions in this field, Onsager received a number of important awards including the Rumford Medal of the American Academy of Arts and Sciences, the Lorentz Medal of the Royal Netherlands Academy of Sciences, and the 1968 Nobel Prize in Chemistry.

Lars Onsager was born in Oslo (then known as Christiania), Norway, on November 27, 1903. His parents were Erling Onsager, a barrister before the Norwegian Supreme Court, and Ingrid Kirkeby Onsager. Onsager's early education was somewhat unorthodox as he was taught by private tutors, by his own mother, and at a somewhat unsatisfactory rural private school. Eventually he entered the Frogner School in Oslo and did so well that he skipped a grade and graduated a year early. Overall, his early schooling provided him with a broad liberal education in philosophy, literature, and the arts. He is said to have become particularly fond of Norwegian epics and continued to read and recite them to friends and family throughout his life.

In 1920, Onsager entered the Norges Tekniski Høgskole in Trondheim where he planned to major in chemical engineering. The fact that he enrolled in a technical high school suggests that he was originally interested in practical rather than theoretical studies. Onsager had not pursued his schooling very long, however, before it became apparent that he wanted to go beyond the everyday applications of science to the theoretical background on which those applications are based. Even as a freshman in high school, he told of making a careful study of the chemical journals, in order to gain background knowledge of chemical theory.

Refines Arrhenius and Debye-Hückel Theories

One of the topics that caught his attention concerned the chemistry of solutions. In 1884, **Svante Arrhenius** had proposed a theory of ionic dissociation that explained a number of observations about the conductivity of solutions and, eventually, a number of other solution phenomena. Over the next half century, chemists worked on refining and extending the Arrhenius theory.

The next great step forward in that search occurred in 1923, when Onsager was still a student at the Tekniski Høgskole. The Dutch chemist **Peter Debye** and the German chemist Erich Hückel, working at Zurich's Eidgenössische Technische Hochschule, had proposed a revision of the Arrhenius theory that explained some problems not yet resolved—primarily, whether ionic compounds are or are not completely dissociated ("ionized") in solution. After much experimentation, Arrhenius had observed that dissociation was not complete in all instances.

Debye and Hückel realized that ionic compounds, by their very nature, already existed in the ionic state *before* they ever enter a solution. They explained the apparent incomplete level of dissociation on the basis of the interactions among ions of opposite charges and water molecules in a solution. The Debye-Hückel mathematical formulation almost perfectly explained all the anomalies that remained in the Arrhenius theory.

Almost perfectly, but not quite, as Onsager soon observed. The value of the molar conductivity predicted by the Debye-Hückel theory was significantly different from that obtained from experiments. By 1925, Onsager had discovered the reason for this discrepancy. Debye and Hückel had assumed that most—but not all—of the ions in a solution move about randomly in "Brownian" movement. Onsager simply extended that principle to *all* of the ions in the solution. With this correction, he was able to write a new mathematical expression that improved upon the Debye-Hückel formulation.

Onsager had the opportunity in 1925 to present his views to Debye in person. Having arrived in Zurich after traveling through Denmark and Germany with one of his professors, Onsager is reported to have marched into Debye's office in Zurich and declared, "Professor Debye, your theory of electrolytes is incorrect." Debye was sufficiently impressed with the young Norwegian to offer him a research post in Zurich, a position that Onsager accepted and held for the next two years.

In 1928, Onsager emigrated to the United States where he became an associate in chemistry at Johns Hopkins University. The appointment proved to be disastrous: he was assigned to teach the introductory chemistry classes, a task for which he was completely unsuited. One of his associates, Robert H. Cole, is quoted in the *Biographical Memoirs of Fellows of the Royal Society:* "I won't say he was the world's worst lecturer, but he was certainly in contention." As a consequence, Onsager was not asked to return to Johns Hopkins after he had completed his first semester there.

Fortunately, a position was open at Brown University, and Onsager was asked by chemistry department chairman Charles A. Krauss to fill that position. During his 5-year tenure at Brown, Onsager was given a more appropriate teaching assignment, statistical mechanics. His pedagogical techniques apparently did not improve to any great extent, however; he still presented a challenge to students by speaking to the blackboard on topics that were well beyond the comprehension of many in the room.

Law of Reciprocal Relations Developed while at Brown

A far more important feature of the Brown years was the theoretical research that Onsager carried out in the privacy of his own office. In this research, Onsager attempted to generalize his earlier research on the motion of ions in solution when exposed to an electrical field. In order to do so, he went back to some fundamental laws of thermodynamics, including Hermann Helmholtz's "principle of least dissipation." He was eventually able to derive a very general mathematical expression about the behavior of substances in solution, an expression now known as the Law of Reciprocal Relations.

Onsager first published the law in 1929, but continued to work on it for a number of years. In 1931, he announced a more general form of the law that applied to other non-equilibrium situations in which differences in electrical or magnetic force, temperature, pressure, or some other factor exists. The Onsager formulation was so elegant and so general that some scientists now refer to it as the Fourth Law of Thermodynamics.

The Law of Reciprocal Relations was eventually recognized as an enormous advance in theoretical chemistry, earning Onsager the Nobel Prize in 1968. However, its initial announcement provoked almost no response from his colleagues. It is not that they disputed his findings, Onsager said many years later, but just that they totally ignored them. Indeed, Onsager's research had almost no impact on chemists until after World War II had ended, more than a decade after the research was originally published.

The year 1933 was a momentous one for Onsager. It began badly when Brown ended his appointment because of financial pressures brought about by the Great Depression. His situation improved later in the year, however, when he was offered an appointment as Sterling and Gibbs Fellow at Yale. The appointment marked the beginning of an affiliation with Yale that was to continue until 1972.

Prior to assuming his new job at Yale, Onsager spent the summer in Europe. While there, he met the future Mrs. Onsager, Margarethe Arledter, the sister of the Austrian electrochemist H. Falkenhagen. The two apparently fell instantly in love, became engaged a week after meeting, and were married on September 7, 1933. The Onsagers later had three sons, Erling Frederick, Hans Tanberg, and Christian Carl, and one daughter, Inger Marie.

Onsager had no sooner assumed his post at Yale when a small problem arose: the fellowship he had been awarded was for postdoctoral studies, but Onsager had not as yet been granted a Ph.D. He had submitted an outline of his research on reciprocal relations to his alma mater, the Norges Tekniski Høgskole, but the faculty there had decided that, being incomplete, it was not worthy of a doctorate. As a result, Onsager's first task at Yale was to complete a doctoral thesis. For this thesis, he submitted to the chemistry faculty a research paper on an esoteric mathematical topic. Since the thesis was outside the experience of anyone in the chemistry or physics departments, Onsager's degree was nearly awarded by the mathematics department, whose chair understood Onsager's findings quite clearly. Only at the last moment did the chemistry department relent and agree to accept the judgment of its colleagues, awarding Onsager his Ph.D. in 1935.

Onsager continued to teach statistical mechanics at Yale, although with as little success as ever. (Instead of being called "Sadistical Mechanics," as it had been by Brown students, it was now referred to as "Advanced Norwegian" by their Yale counterparts.) As always, it was Onsager's theoretical—and usually independent—research that justified his Yale salary. In his nearly four decades there, he attacked one new problem after another, usually with astounding success. Though his output was by no means prodigious, the quality and thoroughness of his research was impeccable.

Continued Productivity with Increasing Age

During the late 1930s, Onsager worked on another of Debye's ideas, the dipole theory of dielectrics. That theory had, in general, been very successful, but could not explain the special case of liquids with high dielectric constants. By 1936, Onsager had developed a new model of dipoles that could be used to modify Debye's theory and provide accurate predictions for all cases. Onsager was apparently deeply hurt when Debye rejected his paper explaining this model for publication in the *Physikalische Zeitschrift,* which Debye edited. It would be more than a decade before

the great Dutch chemist, then an American citizen, could accept Onsager's modifications of his ideas.

In the 1940s, Onsager turned his attention to the very complex issue of phase transitions in solids. He wanted to find out if the mathematical techniques of statistical mechanics could be used to derive the thermodynamic properties of such events. Although some initial progress had been made in this area, resulting in a theory known as the Ising model, Onsager produced a spectacular breakthrough on the problem. He introduced a "trick or two" (to use his words) that had not yet occurred to (and were probably unknown to) his colleagues—the use of elegant mathematical techniques of elliptical functions and quaternion algebra. His solution to this problem was widely acclaimed.

Though his status as a non-U.S. citizen enabled him to devote his time and effort to his own research during World War II, Onsager was forbidden from contributing his significant talents to the top-secret Manhattan Project, the United State's research toward creating atomic weapons. Onsager and his wife finally did become citizens as the war drew to a close in 1945.

The postwar years saw no diminution of Onsager's energy. He continued his research on low-temperature physics and devised a theoretical explanation for the superfluidity of helium II (liquid helium). The idea, originally proposed in 1949, was arrived at independently two years later by Princeton University's Richard Feynman. Onsager also worked out original theories for the statistical properties of liquid crystals and for the electrical properties of ice. In 1951 he was given a Fulbright scholarship to work at the Cavendish Laboratory in Cambridge; there, he perfected his theory of diamagnetism in metals.

During his last years at Yale, Onsager continued to receive numerous accolades for his newly appreciated discoveries. He was awarded honorary doctorates by such noble universities as Harvard (1954), Brown (1962), Chicago (1968), Cambridge (1970), and Oxford (1971), among others. He was inducted to the National Academy of Sciences in 1947. In addition to his Nobel Prize, Onsager garnered the American Academy of Arts and Sciences' Rumford Medal in 1953 and the Lorentz Medal in 1958, as well as several medals from the American Chemical Society and the President's National Medal of Science. Upon reaching retirement age in 1972, Onsager was offered the title of emeritus professor, but without an office. Disappointed by this apparent slight, Onsager decided instead to accept an appointment as Distinguished University Professor at the University of Miami's Center for Theoretical Studies. At Miami, Onsager found two new subjects to interest him, biophysics and radiation chemistry. In neither field did he have an opportunity to make any significant contributions, however, as he died on October 5, 1976, apparently the victim of a heart attack.

Given his shortcomings as a teacher, Onsager still seems to have been universally admired and liked as a person. Though modest and self-effacing, he possessed a wry sense of humor. In *Biographical Memoirs*, he is quoted as saying of research, "There's a time to soar like an eagle, and a time to burrow like a worm. It takes a pretty sharp cookie to know when to shed the feathers and . . . to begin munching the humus." In a memorial some months after Onsager's death, Behram Kursunoglu, the director of the University of Miami's Center for Theoretical Studies, described him as a "very great man of science—with profound humanitarian and scientific qualities."

SELECTED WRITINGS BY ONSAGER:

Periodicals

"Report on a Revision of the Conductivity Theory," *Transactions of the Faraday Society,* Volume 23, 1927, pp. 341–49.
"Reciprocal relations in irreversible processes, pt. I," *Physical Review,* 1931, Volume 37, pp. 405–26.
"Reciprocal relations in irreversible processes, pt. II," *Physical Review,* 1931, Volume 38, pp. 2265–79.
"Crystal Statistics, pt. I," *Physical Review,* Volume 65, 1944, pp. 117–49.
"The Electrical Properties of Ice," *Vortex,* Volume 23, 1962, pp. 138–41.

SOURCES:

Books

Biographical Memoirs of Fellows of the Royal Society, Volume 24, Royal Society (London), 1978.
Current Biography 1958, H. W. Wilson, 1958.
Nobel Lectures in Chemistry, 1963–1970, [Amsterdam], 1972.

—Sketch by David E. Newton

Jan Hendrik Oort
1900-1992
Dutch astronomer

One of the fathers of modern astronomy, Jan Hendrik Oort altered commonly held perspectives of the universe as profoundly as the great classical astronomers changed ancient views of the Earth's relationship to the solar system. "Like a modern Copernicus, Oort showed that our position in nature's grand scheme was not so special," commented astronomer Seth Shostak in Oort's obituary in the *New York Times,* referring to Oort's repudiation of the belief that the Earth and Sun were near the center of the galaxy. Oort proved that the solar system is in the galactic hinterlands, thirty thousand light years away from the galaxy's center. Oort's accomplishments were many; he calculated the structure of the Milky Way, discovered the existence of dark matter, and pioneered radio astronomy. He is best known, however, for his theory on the source of comets and an astronomical phenomenon known as the Oort cloud.

Oort was born on April 28, 1900, in Franeker, a small farming town in Friesland, one of the northern provinces of the Netherlands. His parents were Abraham Hermanus Oort, a physician, and Ruth Hannah Faber Oort. He had two brothers and two sisters. Oort's grandfather, a professor of Hebrew at the University of Leiden, was one of the principal contributors to a translation of the bible into Dutch, known as the Leiden translation. When he was three years old, his family moved to Wassenaar, near Leiden.

In 1917 Oort graduated from the gymnasium in Leiden, but instead of staying at the university where his grandfather had taught, he decided to go back north and enroll at the University of Groningen. His express intention was to study under Jacobus Kapteyn, a prominent astronomer and the first scientist to quantitatively measure and compute the position of stars in the Milky Way. Prior to the efforts of Kapteyn and others at the turn of the century, astronomers had little concrete knowledge concerning the size and mass of the galaxy. Using photographic plates of the southern sky, Kapteyn correctly ascertained that the Milky Way was convex in shape, like an eyeglass lens or a discus, with a bulge in the middle. Throughout his life, Oort cherished his studies under Kapteyn and kept a portrait of his teacher, who died in 1922, on his office wall.

Gains International Recognition

Oort's gift for astronomy was evident by 1920 when he won the Bachiene Foundation Prize for a paper he cowrote on stars of the spectral types F, G, K, and M. After graduating from Groningen in 1922, he became a research assistant for two years at the Yale University Observatory in New Haven, Connecticut. During this time, Oort studied the work of **Harlow Shapley** at Harvard, whose study of the galaxy correctly postulated that its size was much larger than Kapteyn had estimated. Oort returned to the Netherlands in 1924 and received his Ph.D. from Groningen in 1926 for his dissertation on high-velocity stars. He then became an instructor at the University of Leiden, where he was to spend the remainder of his career.

Oort quickly gained worldwide recognition in 1927 when he built on the work of Swedish astronomer Bertil Lindblad and correctly ascertained the rotation of the Milky Way. With his knowledge of high-velocity stars, Oort was able to use complex mathematical calculations to measure the relative velocities of stars as they moved in the rotating galaxy; he showed that they did not rotate as an aligned unit like a wheel, but rather the stars nearer the Milky Way's center moved faster than those further away. These calculations allowed him to estimate the center's gravitational field, from which he deduced that the mass of the galaxy is one hundred billion times that of the Sun, that the galaxy contains some one hundred billion stars, and that it measures one hundred thousand light years across and twenty thousand light years deep at the center. When Oort received the Vetlesen Prize in 1966 from Columbia University, Bengt Stromgren noted that Oort's early paper analyzing the galaxy's mass and structure was responsible for changing the astronomical community's outlook, including the once-held belief that the solar system was near the center of the galaxy. According to Oort's calculations, the solar system was thirty thousand light years away from the galactic center, around which it took three hundred million light years to make a complete orbit.

In 1935 Oort was appointed professor of astronomy at Leiden, and he continued his work at the observatory there. His studies of galaxies NGC 3115 and NGC 4494 as well as his work on the velocity of stars in the solar system convinced him that galaxies contain much more mass than can be detected either visually or by current calculations. Far ahead of his time, Oort's early recognition of dark matter, or "missing mass," in the universe continues to baffle astronomers. According to some calculations, more than ninety percent of the universe could be made up of dark matter, which also might be responsible for gravitational clustering of stars into galaxies.

Oort's work was disrupted during World War II when the Germans, who had occupied The Netherlands, forced him from his position at the observatory in 1940 because he opposed the firing of fellow professors who were Jewish. Soon the observatory was closed, and Oort and his family went into hiding in a rural area east of Leiden. Oort and his colleagues still continued their work, however, although with great difficulty.

In 1942 Oort began collaborations with J. L. L. Duyvendak, an Asian language professor who had translated Chinese texts concerning the "guest star" of July 4, 1054, the sudden appearance of which had confounded contemporary Chinese and Japanese astronomers. The star was so bright that for several months it remained visible even during daylight. By studying the light curve of this star, Oort and Nicholas Mayall hypothesized that is was a supernova. (A supernova occurs when a hugely massive star implodes or bursts inward from extreme pressure and the resulting shock wave blows the stars apart, releasing energy equal to at least fifteen million Suns.) They also identified the Crab Nebula—named by the nineteenth-century Irish astronomer William Parsons Rosse because it appeared crablike in structure in his homemade telescope—as a supernova remnant of this 1054 event.

Begins Radio Astronomy Research

Following the war, Oort was appointed director of the Leiden Observatory. In collaboration with Hendrik van de Hulst, he discovered that clouds of gas and dust surround extremely bright, hot stars and provide the material for spontaneous formation of new stars. But the two also collaborated on a much more important project that was to thrust astronomy light years ahead of previous efforts. Working with a German radar antenna that had been made into a radio telescope, the two began their pioneering efforts in radio astronomy.

Although scientists in the United States were leading the way in radio astronomy in the 1930s, World War II had halted most efforts in this area. Oort knew that radio waves would be an unparalleled tool for the study of the galaxy's structure because they are not hampered by gas and dust as is visible light. As a result, astronomers could observe the galaxy in detail not possible with normal optical telescopes. The first task was to find a wavelength that radio telescopes could be tuned into. In 1944, at the request of Oort, van de Hulst had calculated that the hydrogen atom emits radio waves at a constant wavelength of twenty-one centimeters. After several years of research, in 1951 the pair detected the twenty-one-centimeter hydrogen line, a gaseous cloud of cold hydrogen that passes through the Milky Way. Oort and van de Hulst used the newfound knowledge of a moving mass of hydrogen gas to confirm the speed of the galaxy's rotation at 225 million years. They also completed a comprehensive map of the galaxy's spiral structure at the outer region. Their efforts not only placed the Netherlands at the forefront of modern astronomy but also firmly established radio astronomy as one of the most important technological advances in astronomy in that era.

Oort's work in the fifties continued to shed light on the structure of the Milky Way. Working with Australian astronomer Frank Kerr, he discovered that the galaxy's core consists of so-called turbulent hydrogen and hypothesized that this turbulence was caused by a massive explosion some ten million years ago. Oort eventually proved that the galaxy is a rapidly whirling disk with two spiral arms moving outward from the core. In 1964 he and G. W. Rougoor discovered a corona of hydrogen encircling the galaxy and rapidly moving outward, approximately at the same speed as the galaxy's rotational velocity. Oort went on to theorize that the location of the densest part of the corona above the galaxy was forcing the galaxy upward. He estimated that the galaxy would change in shape every three billion years due to some of the gases moving inward or being "absorbed."

Postulates the Source of Comets

Oort was most widely recognized by the public, however, for his postulation of the Oort cloud, a mass of icy objects that surround the Sun from one light year away and reach almost to the nearest stars. Oort theorized that when other stars pass in close proximity to the solar system, some of these "cometary nuclei" (numbering from one hundred-ninety billion to one hundred trillion) are perturbed from the orbit by a gravitational flurry and thrust into the solar system's inner orbit where they can be seen. Although no astronomer has ever observed the Oort cloud, few doubt its existence, a testament to Oort's scientific integrity. During the course of his career, Oort headed several international astronomical groups, including serving as president of the International Astronomical Union from 1958 to 1961. In 1962, he was one of the cofounders of the European Southern Observatory, one of the preeminent optical observatories in the world.

Although Oort retired in 1970, he continued his astronomical studies, much to the chagrin of his wife, Mieke, a poet whom he had married on May 24, 1927. According to Govert Schilling in an article in *Sky & Telescope,* she politely complained, "For me, nothing seemed to change." Oort relished the outdoors, especially hiking, rowing, and skating, which he often did in the company of fellow astronomers from the Leiden Observatory. He was also fond of reading poetry. The Oorts had two sons, Coenraad and Abraham, a daughter, Marijke, and several grandchildren and great grandchildren.

Oort published more articles in the 1970s than he did the previous decade and, for several years, shared an office with his grandson, Marc, at the Leiden Observatory. Many of these articles have become

landmarks in astronomical literature, especially those concerning the center of the Milky Way and on super clusters of galaxies. Oort's enthusiasm for the study of the sky was remembered by Gart Westerhout and noted in the *Sky & Telescope* article. On a visit to the Southern Hemisphere to pick a site for the Leiden Southern Station, Westerhout saw Oort "flat on his back in the wet grass, risking pneumonia" to ponder the southern sky. "His fascination, and the theories that must have formed in his mind at that time, almost physically radiated from him." Up until his death at the age of ninety-two on November 5, 1992, Oort continued to keep his family informed of the latest astronomical discoveries with cosmology lectures.

SELECTED WRITINGS BY OORT:

Books

The Stars of High Velocity, Gebroeders Hoitsema, 1926.

SOURCES:

Books

The Biographical Dictionary of Scientists: Astronomers, Peter Bedrick Books, 1989, pp. 119–120.
The Great Scientists, Volume 9, Grolier, 1989, pp. 110–115.
McGraw-Hill Modern Men of Science, McGraw, 1966, pp. 359–360.
Seargent, David A., *Comets: Vagabonds of Space,* Doubleday, 1982, pp. 100–102.

Periodicals

Schilling, Govert, "Jan Oort Remembered," *Sky & Telescope,* April, 1993, pp. 44–45.
Wilford, John Noble, "Jan H. Oort, Dutch Astronomer in Forefront of Field, Dies at 92," *New York Times,* November 12, 1993, p. 15.

—Sketch by David Petechuk

Aleksandr Ivanovich Oparin
1894-1980
Russian biochemist

Aleksandr Ivanovich Oparin was a prominent biochemist in the former Soviet Union whose achievements were recognized throughout the international scientific community. He is best known for his theory that life on earth originated from inorganic matter. Although a belief that life formed through spontaneous generation was prevalent up to the nineteenth century, that theory was disputed by the development of the microscope and the experiments of French scientist Louis Pasteur. Oparin's materialistic approach to the subject was responsible for a renewed interest in how life on earth originated. His book *The Origin of Life* outlined his basic theory, which was that life originated as a result of evolution acting on molecules created in the primordial atmosphere through energy discharges. In addition to his work on the origin of life, he played a major role in the development of technical botanical biochemistry in the Soviet Union.

Aleksandr Ivanovich Oparin

Oparin was born near Moscow on March 2, 1894. He was the youngest child of Ivan Dmitrievich Oparin and Aleksandra Aleksandrovna. He had a sister, Aleksandra, and a brother, Dmitrii. His secondary education was marked by his achievements in science. He studied plant physiology at Moscow State University, graduating in 1917. He was a graduate student and teaching assistant there from 1921 to 1925. He also studied at other institutes of higher learning in Germany, Austria, Italy, and France, but it is thought that he never earned a graduate degree (he was awarded a doctorate in biological sciences in 1934 by the U.S.S.R. Academy of Sciences).

Aleksei N. Bakh, Oparin's mentor during his years of graduate study, was to have great influence on Oparin's later role in the development of Soviet biochemistry. Bakh was well known internationally for his research in medical and industrial chemistry, and played an important role in the organization of the chemical industry in Russia. After the Russian Revolution in 1917, Bakh helped develop the chemical section of the National Economic Planning Council (VSNKh) and founded its Central Chemical Laboratory. Oparin studied plant chemistry with Bakh in 1918, and from 1919 through 1925, he worked under Bakh at the VSNKh and the Central Chemical Laboratory. Bakh and Oparin cofounded the Institute of Biochemistry at the Academy of Sciences of the Soviet Union in Moscow in 1935. Oparin was appointed deputy director of the institute and held that position until 1946. After Bakh's death that same year, Oparin assumed the director's position, which he held until his death.

The practical aspects of Oparin's work during his association with Bakh in the early thirties involved biochemical research for increasing production in the food industry, work that was of extreme importance to the Soviet economy. Through his study of enzymatic activity in plants, he found that it was necessary for molecules and enzymes to combine in order to create starches, sugars, and other carbohydrates and proteins. He was able to show that this biocatalysis was the basis for producing many food products in nature. He held a post from 1927 through 1934 as assistant director and head of the laboratory at the Central Institute of the Sugar Industry in Moscow, where he conducted research on tea, sugar, flour, and grains. During this same period, he also taught technical biochemistry at the D. I. Mendeleev Institute of Chemical Technology. As professor at the Moscow Technical Institute of Food Production from 1937 to 1949, he continued his research of plant processes and began the study of nutrition and vitamins.

Oparin's biochemical research on plant enzymes and their role in plant metabolism, so important for its practical application, would also be important for what was to be the focus of his career, the question of how life first appeared on earth. His first paper on this subject was presented to a meeting of the Moscow Botanical Society in 1922. This paper, which was never published, was revised and published in 1924 by the *Moscow Worker*. In it, Oparin discussed the problem of spontaneous generation, arguing that any differences between living and nonliving material could be attributed to physicochemical laws. This work went largely unnoticed, and Oparin did not seriously consider the topic again until the mid-thirties. In 1936, he published *The Origin of Life,* which modified and enlarged his earlier ideas. His ideas at this time were influenced not only by contemporary international thinking on astronomy, geochemistry, organic chemistry, and plant enzymology, but also by the dialectic philosophy espoused by Friedrich Engels, and the work of H. G. Bungenburg de Jong on colloidal coacervation. Translated into English in a 1938 edition, *The Origin of Life* was also revised and updated in 1941 and 1957. Although the later versions amended the original, the concept that life arose through a natural evolution of matter remained central, and he often described this concept metaphorically by comparing life to a constant flow of liquid in which elements within are constantly changed and renewed.

The Origin of Life Theory

Oparin's theory that the origin of life had a biochemical basis was based on his suppositions concerning the condition of the atmosphere surrounding the primeval earth and how those conditions interacted with primitive organisms. It was his idea that the primeval atmosphere (consisting of ammonia, hydrogen, methane and water) in conjunction with energy (probably in the form of sunlight, volcanic eruptions, and lightning) gave this primitive matter its metabolic ability to grow and increase. He speculated that the first organisms had appeared in ancient seas between 4.7 and 3.2 billion years ago. These living organisms would have evolved from a nonliving coagulate, or gel-like, solution. Oparin argued that a separation process called coacervation occurred within the gel, causing nonliving matter at the multimolecular level to be chemically transformed into living matter. He further theorized that this chemical transformation was dependent upon protoenzymatic catalysts and promoters contained in the coacervates. From there, a process of natural selection began, which resulted in the formation of increasingly complex organisms and, eventually, primitive systems of life. Although others, such as de Jong and T. H. Huxley, would postulate that life arose from a kind of "sea jelly," Oparin's theory that nonliving material was a catalyst for the formation of living organisms is considered by many to be his special contribution to the issue.

His suppositions on life's origins were not merely theoretical. In laboratory experiments, he showed how molecules might combine to produce the needed protein structure for transformation. Experiments of other scientists, such as **Stanley Lloyd Miller**, **Harold**

Urey, and **Cyril Ponnamperuma**, confirmed his initial experiments on the chemical structure necessary to produce life. Ponnamperuna took the work a step further when he altered Oparin's original experiments and was able to easily produce nucleotides, dinucleotides, and adenosine triphosphate, which also contribute to the formation of life. Building on Ponnamperuna's research, Oparin was able to produce droplets of gel that he called protobionts. He believed these protobionts were living organisms because of their ability to metabolize and reproduce. Although later research of scientists in both the Soviet Union and the West would develop independently of Oparin's biochemical experiments, he must be given credit for putting the question of the origin of life into the realm of modern science. It has been said that his work in this area opened the door, and scientists in the West walked through.

Biochemistry in the Service of Dialectical Materialism

Oparin was a man of his time, and his thinking was greatly influenced by Charles Darwin's theory of natural selection and the ideological climate of dialectical materialism which pervaded Soviet society during the 1930s. Although Oparin was never a Communist Party member, both his writings and his research methods reflect a bias toward dialectical materialism. However, it has been suggested that his denigration of the science of genetics and his support of Trofim Denisovich Lysenko and the Marxist-Leninist ideology which permeated and controlled Soviet genetics at that time may have resulted from political pressure and a desire to protect his career, as much as philosophical and scientific belief. Whatever the reasons, Oparin used his influence and prestige as chief administrator of the U.S.S.R. Academy of Sciences from 1948 through 1955 to implement policies that advanced Lysenko's views at the expense of the advancement of Soviet genetics. The influence of Lysenko and the Marxist-Leninist view of biology waned after Stalin's death in 1953. In 1956, as the result of a petition by 300 scientists calling for his resignation, Oparin was removed from his top position in the academy's biology division. He was replaced by Vladimir A. Engelhardt, a leading Soviet advocate of molecular biology. The 1950s saw an international explosion in the growth of molecular biology, but Oparin was severely critical of its principles. Although he considered the discoveries made by Watson and Crick concerning DNA to be important, he was skeptical of the idea of a genetic code, calling it "mechanistic reductionism." He did, however, support DNA research within his own Institute of Biochemistry during this time, and was a coauthor of papers discussing DNA and RNA in coacervate droplets.

Although Oparin's influence in Soviet science weakened in the early sixties, his international reputation, based on the origin of life theory, remained strong. This, coupled with his political reliability, led his government to send him abroad as a Soviet representative. Traveling by scientists in the Soviet Union was severely restricted in the 1950s, but Oparin was sent on official Soviet business not only to countries in the Eastern bloc and Asia, but to Europe and the United States as well. He also represented his country at international scientific and political conferences, such as the World Peace Council and the World Federation of Scientists.

His work brought him numerous honors. His awards from the Soviet Union include the A. N. Bakh Prize in 1950, the Elie Metchnikoff Gold Prize in 1960, the Lenin Prize in 1974, and the Lomonosov Gold Medal in 1979. The International Society for the Study of the Origin of Life elected him as its first president in 1970. He also was elected a member of scientific societies in Finland, Bulgaria, Czechoslovakia, East Germany, Cuba, Spain, and Italy.

Beginning in 1965 and continuing through 1980, the Soviet Union placed new emphasis on the science of genetics and molecular biology. However, Oparin's Institute of Biochemistry remained a stronghold of old-style biochemistry, and it eventually was bypassed by more progressive research institutions. Oparin died of heart disease in Moscow on April 21, 1980.

SELECTED WRITINGS BY OPARIN:

Books

The Origin of Life, translated by Sergius Morgulis, Macmillan, 1938.
The Chemical Origin of Life, translated by Ann Synge, Charles C. Thomas, Springfield, Illinois, 1964.

SOURCES:

Books

Graham, Loren R., *Science and Philosophy in the Soviet Union,* Knopf, 1972.

—*Sketch by Jane Stewart Cook*

J. Robert Oppenheimer
1904-1967
American physicist

Theoretical physicist J. Robert Oppenheimer was a pioneer in the field of quantum mechanics, the study of the energy of atomic particles. His research on protons and their relation to electrons led directly to the discovery of a new particle, the positron. His later work shed light on deuterons, the nuclei of heavy hydrogen atoms. He was a charismatic teacher and effective administrator who directed the laboratory at Los Alamos, New Mexico, where the atomic bomb was developed during World War II. In the postwar years, however, Oppenheimer staunchly opposed the proliferation of nuclear weapons. This stance brought him before Congress during the McCarthy era and cost him his security clearance as a government consultant.

Julius Robert Oppenheimer was born in New York City on April 22, 1904, to a wealthy and cultured family. His father, Julius Oppenheimer, who emigrated from Germany as a young man, had a successful business importing textiles. His mother, the former Ella Friedman, was a painter and a great lover of the arts. Oppenheimer, his parents, and his younger brother, Frank, divided their time between a spacious New York apartment overlooking the Hudson River and a summer house on Long Island.

It became apparent when he was quite young that Oppenheimer had a quick mind, a vast appetite for learning, and a wide range of interests. At age eleven, he was the youngest person ever admitted to the New York Mineralogical Society, and at the age of twelve he presented a paper there. He attended the Ethical Culture School in New York, and after graduating he spent the summer in Europe. Unfortunately, he contracted dysentery there, and needed the following year to recuperate. When he was well again he took his first trip to the West, where the expanse of the Pecos Valley of New Mexico captured his imagination. His family eventually bought a ranch there, returning year after year.

Oppenheimer entered Harvard College in 1922. He studied a broad curriculum, which included several languages as well as chemistry and physics. As an undergraduate he was especially close to physicist **Percy Bridgman**, also a man of many interests, who may have shaped the way Oppenheimer combined physics with philosophy in his later career. Despite his course load, Oppenheimer graduated from Harvard *summa cum laude* in just three years, and in 1925 he left the United States for Europe to study theoretical physics.

J. Robert Oppenheimer

It was in Europe during that period that the most important advances were being achieved in the study of the behavior and energy of particles that make up the atom—a discipline known as quantum mechanics. Such brilliant theoreticians as **Werner Heisenberg**, **Erwin Schrödinger** and **Paul Dirac** were formulating their theories about quantifying and predicting the movement and location of atomic particles. Oppenheimer initially went to the Cavendish Laboratory in Cambridge, England, and within just a few months he had submitted his first paper, which used some of the most recent theoretical advances in nuclear physics to explain aspects of molecular behavior.

Explains Molecular Activity

In 1926 Oppenheimer left the Cavendish for the University of Göttingen in Germany. He did independent research on radiation at Göttingen and also collaborated with the physicist **Max Born** in a further investigation of molecular activity. The two scientists tackled variations in the vibration, rotation, and electronic properties of molecules. Their results led to the so-called "Born-Oppenheimer method," which is in effect a quantum mechanics at the molecular rather than the atomic level. After receiving his doctorate in 1927, he left Göttingen for Leiden, Holland, and then went on to Zurich where he worked with another distinguished physicist, **Wolfgang Pauli**. Throughout this period, Oppenheimer consistently demonstrated his ability to synthesize ideas, draw connections

between theories, and detect their inherent contradictions.

Oppenheimer's work in Europe had been of such quality that he was able to arrange teaching positions both at the University of California at Berkeley and at the California Institute of Technology. For the next thirteen years he taught and did research at these schools during alternating semesters. During this period, Oppenheimer evolved into an extraordinary, charismatic teacher. Although many students complained that he set an impossible pace in the classroom, he attracted a number of students and even some colleagues to theoretical physics by his quick wit and probing questions. He inspired many of his students, and some even adopted his gestures and way of speaking. Oppenheimer's social life was very much involved with his teaching; he would often discuss subjects such as astrophysics and cosmic rays or nuclear physics and electrodynamics for hours on end.

Some of his best work in particle physics was also done during these years. In 1930 he was able to demonstrate that the proton is not the antimatter equivalent of the electron (or antielectron) as had until then been supposed. One of Oppenheimer's students, **Carl Anderson**, used this work in his search for the true antielectron and found the positron. Oppenheimer's earlier work on radiation led to his contribution to the discovery that cosmic ray particles could break down into another generation of particles, a phenomenon commonly called the "cascade process." In 1935, he discovered that it was possible to accelerate deuterons, made up of a proton and a neutron, to much higher energies than neutrons alone. Deuterons, as a consequence, could be used to bombard positively charged atomic nuclei at high energies, enabling further research into atomic particles.

Leads the Manhattan Project

For years physicists had been aware of the possibility of manipulating nuclear fission. Bombarding the nuclei of certain molecules, they suspected, could result in a chain reaction that would release an extremely large amount of energy. In the United States and Nazi Germany, scientists were rushing to work on a weapon that could harness this energy—the atomic bomb. At Berkeley's Radiation Laboratory under the direction of Oppenheimer's colleague, **Ernest Orlando Lawrence**, researchers selected uranium as the chemical element most likely to lend itself to nuclear fission for military purposes. However, no coordinated effort to design and fabricate an actual atomic weapon was made.

According to Oppenheimer's colleague Victor Weisskopf, "many physicists were drawn into this work by fate and destiny rather than enthusiasm," and Oppenheimer was one of them. Early in 1942 he brought together a group of theoretical physicists—many of whom had been working in separate laboratories under the umbrella of the Manhattan Project—and became director of the new research lab at Los Alamos to develop the first nuclear weapon.

The administration of the research at Los Alamos presented its challenges, which Oppenheimer handled effectively. The intense and sustained work that was done on the Manhattan Project was due in large part to his evident sense of purpose and his ability to provide a creative, cooperative environment for scientists forced to work in secret. A design for the bomb was ready and a fissionable form of plutonium produced to fuel it by mid–1945. On the fateful morning of July 16, 1945, Oppenheimer stood silently awaiting the detonation of the test bomb nicknamed "Fat Man" at nearby Alamogordo. He wrote in his *Letters and Recollections* that, upon seeing the power it unleashed, he thought the play of the light had the "radiance of a thousand suns," but he was also reminded of a dark, foreboding line from the Hindu *Bhagavad-Gita:* "I am become death, the Shatterer of Worlds."

Oppenheimer was one of a panel of four scientists including Ernest Orlando Lawrence, **Enrico Fermi**, and **Arthur Compton** that was asked to formulate an opinion regarding the use of the atomic bomb to end the war against Japan. They were told that there was a choice between a military invasion of Japan, which was certain to cost many American lives, and a nuclear attack on a military target that would also kill many civilians. Confronted with this choice, the panel voted to use the bomb. Oppenheimer later regretted his decision, saying that the intentional slaughter of civilians had been unnecessary and wrong.

Political Controversies

After the war, Oppenheimer became more and more concerned about the devastating potential of atomic weaponry. With this concern foremost in his mind, he cowrote the "Acheson-Lilienthal Report," which opposed the nuclear arms race at its very outset, instead proposing stringent international controls on the development of nuclear arsenals. The report was rewritten and presented to the United Nations as the Baruch Plan, but the Soviet Union vetoed its adoption. In 1946 Oppenheimer became chair of the general advisory committee of the Atomic Energy Commission and continued to advocate controls on the development of nuclear power.

In October of 1947, Oppenheimer became director of the Institute for Advanced Study at Princeton University, New Jersey. Under his directorship, the institute became one of the foremost centers of research in theoretical physics, even though Oppen-

heimer himself did little research from this time forward. He was keenly aware of what others were doing at the institute both inside and outside theoretical physics, but much of his energy was now spent on policy issues rather than science, and many considered his scientific judgment no longer as keen as it had been.

As the 1940s drew to a close, President Truman decided that it was in the country's best interest to develop the hydrogen bomb. Oppenheimer's position was clear; he did not believe in the proliferation of nuclear weapons, and he did not hesitate to express his opinion in public. His position disturbed many of those in power in Washington. In November of 1953 William Borden, former executive director of Congress' Joint Atomic Energy Committee, sent a registered letter to J. Edgar Hoover of the FBI, stating he had considerable evidence to show that Oppenheimer was a Soviet agent. In December Oppenheimer was informed that his security clearance, which he needed to have access to classified information, was revoked on suspicion of unpatriotic activities on his part.

A Congressional hearing giving Oppenheimer the opportunity to clear himself did little to dispel the myth of his lack of patriotism. It was the era of the Cold War and the anti-communist hysteria spearheaded by Senator Joseph McCarthy. Oppenheimer's association with Communists during the 1930s, never a secret nor an obstacle to his receiving clearance when he was director of Los Alamos, was now presented as a blot on his character and a challenge to his patriotic commitment. Both his position on nuclear weapons and his arrogance and ability to argue had made him unpopular in some quarters, and there were those who wanted to see him removed from his public position. After many grueling hours of testimony, the majority of a three-man panel found that Oppenheimer was "a loyal citizen," but still denied him clearance on the basis of "defects of character."

After this very public hearing was finally over, Oppenheimer emerged somewhat aged and wounded. Yet he continued to lecture on science and express his opinions on politics. In 1963 Oppenheimer received the prestigious Enrico Fermi Award, which was something of a public vindication but did not undo all the harm done earlier.

Almost every published photograph showed Oppenheimer with a cigarette or pipe in hand, and he knew for some time that he had throat cancer. He died at home in Princeton on February 18, 1967. After his cremation, his wife Kitty spread his ashes in the sea near their vacation retreat in the Virgin Islands.

SELECTED WRITINGS BY OPPENHEIMER:

Books

Letters and Recollections, edited by Alice Kimball Smith and Charles Weiner, Harvard University Press, 1980.

Periodicals

"On the Quantum Theory of Field Currents," *Physical Review,* May, 1928, p. 914.
"The Disintegration of Lithium by Protons of High Energy," *Physical Review,* March, 1933, p. 380.
(With R. Serber) "The Density of Nuclear Levels," *Physical Review,* August, 1936, p. 391.
"On the Applicability of Quantum Theory to Mesotron Collisions," *Physical Review,* February, 1940, p. 353.

SOURCES:

Books

Contemporary Authors, New Revisions Series, Volume 34, Gale, 1991.
Kunetka, James W., *Oppenheimer: The Years of Risk,* Prentice-Hall, 1982.
Rabi, I. I., et al., *Oppenheimer,* Scribner, 1969.
Stern, Philip M., *The Oppenheimer Case: Security on Trial,* Harper, 1969.

Periodicals

Biographical Memoirs of Fellows of the Royal Society, Volume 14, Royal Society (London), 1968, pp. 391–416.

—*Sketch by Barbara A. Branca*

Mary J. Osborn
1927-
American biochemist

Mary J. Osborn is the first person to demonstrate the mode of action of methotrexate, a major cancer chemotherapeutic agent and folic acid antagonist (in other words, it opposes the physiological effects of folic acid). Best known for her research into the biosynthesis of a complex polysaccharide known as lipopolysaccharide—a molecule that is essential to bacterial cells—Osborn helped to identify a potential target for the development of new antibiotics and chemotherapeutic agents.

Mary Jane Osborn was born in Colorado Springs, Colorado, on September 24, 1927, and raised in west Los Angeles and Beverly Hills, California. Her father, Arthur Merten, had an eighth-grade education and was a machinist; her mother, Vivian, went to secretarial classes and also taught school. "Both parents were high achievers and their ambitions for me were considerable," Osborn told Laura Newman in an interview. Osborn noted that her background was somewhat atypical for girls growing up in the 1930s. She recalled reading a book for young girls about being a nurse when she was ten years of age. "I got very interested in being a nurse, but when I told my parents, they asked me, 'Why don't you want to be a doctor?'" Osborn credited her parents for their early support of her interest in science; from her mother and father she gained "a very naive and blind assumption that I could do whatever I wanted to do." In describing her academic progress as a girl Osborn noted, "The thing that amazes me about my primary and secondary education is that I remained interested in biology. What I remember of the teaching was pretty awful."

Osborn entered the University of California at Berkeley as a pre-med student. "By senior year I realized that there was no way in the world that I wanted to treat patients." She then pursued biochemistry courses. Osborn recalled, "I realized that I liked bench research and could do it well. I was good at planning experiments and thinking about the results and going on to the next step." She was awarded a B.A. in physiology from the University of California at Berkeley in 1948, then went on to the University of Washington, attaining a Ph.D. in biochemistry in 1958. Osborn's thesis examined the functions of the vitamins and enzymes whose action depended on folic acid. In 1957, Osborn reported the mode of action of methotrexate, which became a major cancer chemotherapeutic agent, especially for leukemia.

In 1959, Osborn moved into a new area, the study of the structure and building blocks—or biosynthesis—of a molecule complex polysaccharide named lipopolysaccharide. Lipopolysaccharide is unique to a certain class of bacteria that includes pathogens such as salmonella, shigella, and the cholera bacillus. Abundant on the surface of these bacteria, lipopolysaccharide is responsible for major immunological reactions and for the bacteria's characteristic toxicity. Osborn's work led to a new understanding of a previously unknown mechanism of polysaccharide formation.

For her contributions to biochemistry, Osborn was accepted as a fellow of the American Academy of Arts and Sciences in 1977 and was elected to the

National Academy of Sciences in 1978. Other major distinctions include having served as president of the American Society of Biological Chemists from 1981 to 1982 and as president of the Federation of American Societies for Experimental Biology from 1982 to 1983. She has been appointed to numerous scientific advisory councils, including the National Institute for General Medical Sciences, National Institutes of Health Division of Research Grants, and the National Science Board. In addition, Osborn has served as editor of several journals, including *Biochemistry, Journal of Biological Chemistry,* and the *Annual Review of Biochemistry.*

Osborn became professor of microbiology at the University of Connecticut Health Center School of Medicine in 1968 and she has been head of the department since 1980. Her interest in the development of antibiotics and chemotherapeutic agents continues on into the 1990s. She is married to a painter, Ralph, and they have no children. In her leisure time, Osborn gardens.

SELECTED WRITINGS BY OSBORN:

Periodicals

(With I. M. Weiner, T. Higuchi, L. Rothfield, M. Saltmarsh-Andrew, and B. L. Horecker) "Biosynthesis of Bacterial Lipopolysaccharide V. Lipid-Linked Intermediates in the Biosynthesis of the O-Antigen Groups of *Salmonella typhimurium,*" *Proceedings of the National Academy of Science,* Volume 54, 1965, pp. 228–33.

(With P. D. Rick) "Isolation of a Mutant of *Salmonella typhimurium* Dependent on D-Arabinase–5-phosphate for Growth and Synthesis of 3-deoxy-D-mannoctulosonate (Ketodeooxyoctonate)," *Proceedings of the National Academy of Science,* Volume 69, 1972, pp. 3756–60.

"Biogenesis of the Outer Membrane of *Salmonella,*" *The Harvey Lectures,* Series 78, 1984, pp. 87–103.

Other

Osborn, Mary J., interview with Laura Newman conducted March 8, 1994.

—*Sketch by Laura Newman*

Donald E. Osterbrock
1924-
American astronomer

Donald E. Osterbrock, an admired astronomer and author of astronomy books, has been among the most significant players in the study of gas in space and the determination of its structure and composition. Because of him, twentieth-century astronomers gained a greater understanding of gas motions and the centers of galaxies. His work on radiation emitted from gas regions and the hearts of galaxies opened these fields to a wider audience of astronomers, while his textbooks and popular books allowed students and lay audiences to share in the excitement of astronomy.

Donald Edward Osterbrock was born in Cincinnati, Ohio, on July 13, 1924, to William Carl Osterbrock and Elsie Wettlin Osterbrock. After serving in the U.S. Air Force from 1943 to 1946, he received both a Ph.B. and a B.S. degree from the University of Chicago in 1948; his M.S. degree followed the next year, and in 1952, he received his Ph.D. in astronomy. He worked as an astronomy fellow at Princeton University for a year before joining the faculty of the California Institute of Technology in 1953. Until he left that position five years later, he also served on the staff of the Mount Wilson and Palomar observatories. While at Caltech, Osterbrock began training young astronomers, among them George O. Abell, future president of the Astronomical Society of the Pacific. He worked at the University of Wisconsin at Madison from 1958 to 1973, taking time off from 1960–61 to work at the Institute for Advanced Study at Princeton. At Madison, Osterbrock became an astronomy professor in 1961, serving as department chairman in 1966–7 and 1969–72. In the early 1970s, he took on other duties, including a stint as letters editor of the *Astrophysical Journal* (1971–73) and president of Commission 34 (on interstellar matter and planetary nebulae) of the International Astronomical Union (1967–70). In 1972, Osterbrock joined the faculty of the University of California at Santa Cruz, as professor of astronomy and astrophysics at Lick Observatory, where he also served as director until 1981. He was president of the American Astronomical Society for two years, succeeding Bernard F. Burke of MIT in 1988.

In the 1950s, Osterbrock's research on middle-aged stars gave astronomers a clue to the importance of motion in the stars' outer layers. The motion, called convection, occurred when chunks of matter physically percolated out from inner layers of the star towards the surface. Before Osterbrock's work on convection, such noted astronomers as Karl Schwarzschild, Arthur Eddington, and S. Chandrasekhar thought convection was *not* an important process in stars. Osterbrock opened the path to better models of stars.

Penetrated Mysteries of Interstellar Gas

Osterbrock explored diffuse clouds of gas in regions between stars. These clouds of gas shine because of the ultraviolet light given off by stars concealed in them. The gas, affected by this ultraviolet light, "ionizes"—that is, its electrons are ejected from its atoms. Once freed, these electrons combine with other atoms, and the processes of ionization and recombination balance each other. When electrons recombine, the gas emits a spectrum. Spectra may give clues to the temperature, density, and types of elements in the gas. Some parts of spectra appear brighter than others, and comparing brightness provides clues to the physical makeup of the gas. In the late 1950s, Osterbrock and Michael J. Seaton used brightness ratios to explore small, bright regions of gas with a single central star. Osterbrock also examined dimmer and more diffuse gas regions. He made a detailed model of the Orion Nebula, showing what physical phenomena would account for the observed spectrum. The Orion Nebula work was adopted by other astronomers in their studies of other gas regions. In the mid–1970s, Osterbrock and students at Santa Cruz took advantage of the capabilities of the Lick Observatory to study the nature of spiral galaxies with bright centers—the so-called "Seyfert" galaxies. They also looked at galaxies emitting strong radio waves. Osterbrock's student Alan T. Koski found that extreme amounts of radiation in galaxy centers were coming not from stars but from the cores of the galaxies themselves. Koski's finding added fuel to the argument that the tremendous energy in galactic centers is due to disks of matter surrounding giant black holes. Into the 1980s, Osterbrock strove to collect data of uniform quality from different galaxies so they could be compared and contrasted.

Osterbrock's studies of the relative strengths of spectra helped astronomers understand both the Milky Way's center and the center of other galaxies. By the late 1980s, Osterbrock had extended his research interests to the spectra of unusually bright galactic centers. As with clouds of gas, the components of spectra in galactic centers can be analyzed to estimate their temperature and density. While most of the atoms in gas clouds have two or three electrons stripped away, the atoms in galaxy centers can have as many as six missing. Osterbrock and student Ross D. Cohen compared galaxies that emitted in the radio part of the spectrum with those that did not. They found very few differences, but suggested that those few differences could hold the key to why some galaxies give off a lot of radio emission and others do not.

Osterbrock has written several books; his two most widely praised and popular ones are *James E. Keeler, Pioneer American Astrophysicist, and the Early Development of American Astrophysics* and *Eye on the Sky: Lick Observatory's First Century.* "Osterbrock is not content to give superficial descriptions of the work of others, but always integrates their results into his own thinking and writes about it with as much depth and clarity as if it were his own," said Nancy Morrison of the University of Toledo and chair of the Astronomical Society of the Pacific Awards Committee on the occasion of Osterbrock's winning the Bruce medal. A more recent book, *Pauper & Prince,* concerned the life of George Willis Ritchey, the guiding force behind Mount Wilson Observatory's 60- and 100-inch reflecting telescopes.

Osterbrock has been highly decorated for his contributions to the fields of astronomy and astrophysics. In January 1991, he won the Henry Norris Russell Lectureship, the highest honor of the American Astronomical Society, for "lifetime achievement." The award citation called him "a leader in the investigation of the properties of gaseous nebulae." Also in 1991, Osterbrock won the Catherine Bruce Wolfe medal of the Astronomical Society of the Pacific, for his research, writing, and educational efforts.

Having a keen interest in the history of astronomy, Osterbrock served as chairman of the history committee of the Astronomical Society of the Pacific from 1982 until 1986, and as vice chairman of the history of astronomy division of the American Astronomical Society from 1985 until 1987. A Congregationalist, he married Irene L. Hansen on September 19, 1952, and has three children: Carol Ann, William Carl, and Laura Jane. At the time of his professorship at the Lick Observatory, Osterbrock resided in Santa Cruz, California.

SELECTED WRITINGS BY OSTERBROCK:

Books

Astrophysics of Gaseous Nebulae, W. H. Freeman, 1974.
James E. Keeler, Pioneer American Astrophysicist, and the Early Development of American Astrophysics, Cambridge University Press, 1984.
Eye on the Sky: Lick Observatory's First Century, University of California Press, 1988.
Pauper & Prince: Ritchey, Hale, and Big American Telescopes, University of Arizona Press, 1993.

SOURCES:

Periodicals

Morrison, Nancy, "The 1991 A.S.P. Award Winners," *Mercury: The Journal of the Astronomi-*

cal Society of the Pacific, November/December, 1991, pp. 182–184.

—*Sketch by Sebastian Thaler*

Friedrich Wilhelm Ostwald
1853-1932
Latvian-born German physical chemist

Around the turn of the twentieth century, Friedrich Wilhelm Ostwald was responsible for organizing physical chemistry into a discipline distinct from organic chemistry. He wrote a basic textbook on the subject and co-founded a journal that provided physical chemists with a forum for their theories and experimental results. For his work in the measurement of chemical reactions, electrochemistry, and the acceleration of chemical reactions by the use of catalysts, Ostwald won the 1909 Nobel Prize for chemistry. He was also a prolific writer in both the philosophy and psychology of science, and he culminated a long academic career with valuable independent research into color theory.

Ostwald was born on September 2, 1853, in Riga, Latvia (now Estonia) into a family of master artisans. His parents, Gottfried and Elisabeth (Leuckel) Ostwald, were descendants of German immigrants; his father was a master cooper who had been a painter as a young man. The humanities were emphasized in the Ostwald home, and young Friedrich Wilhelm learned to paint and play the viola and piano; he was also an avid reader. These passions stayed with him throughout his life, but at an early age he also became enthralled with chemical experimentation, creating his own fireworks when he was eleven. He studied at the Riga Realgymnasium and in 1872 enrolled at the University of Dorpat (now the State University of Tartu in Estonia), where he studied both chemistry and physics. At this time, chemists were almost exclusively concerned with research on organic molecules, but Ostwald's natural inclinations led him to a study of physical chemistry. He received his bachelor's degree in 1875 from Dorpat and stayed on to lecture and complete his master's degree in 1876 and his Ph.D. in 1878.

Explores the Nature of Chemical Affinities

Ostwald's early interests in the measurement of chemical reactions were spurred by the work of Julius Thomsen, who had measured the heat accompanying chemical reactions. Ostwald had realized that other properties could serve equally well for such measurements; his master's thesis had concerned the density of substances by volume in a watery solution, and his doctoral thesis dealt with optical refraction. The result of the laboriously repetitive experiments he performed were affinity tables for twelve acids. During this period, he became increasingly interested in the subject of chemical affinities, or the combinational reactions between various chemicals. In 1881 Ostwald was appointed professor of chemistry at the Riga Polytechnic University, where he expanded his research into chemical affinities by measuring the rate at which chemical changes take place. He confirmed his earlier measurements of volume and density with measurements of the velocity at which acids will split esters into alcohol and organic acid, and he was able to assign precise numerical values to chemical reactions and affinities.

Ostwald's name was becoming known for such discoveries, and he was soon joined in his work establishing physical chemistry by two younger scientists: **Svante Arrhenius** from Sweden and Jacobus Van't Hoff from Holland. In 1884, Arrhenius sent Ostwald his doctoral dissertation; hotly contested by many of the scientists at his university, it concerned affinity and electrical conductivity. Ostwald immediately saw the importance of Arrhenius's work, and he recognized that it included the beginning of the idea of electrolytic dissociation and thus of ionization, or the conversion of a neutral atom into a positive ion and a free electron. He did all he could to sponsor Arrhenius. In 1886, Ostwald became interested in van't Hoff's work on the similarities between solutions and gases; he was no longer working alone in physical chemistry.

In 1885 Ostwald had begun work on the *Lehrbuch der allgemeinen Chemie,* a textbook of general chemistry which he finished in 1887, the year he received an appointment at the University of Leipzig as the first professor of physical chemistry in Germany. There van't Hoff joined him as an assistant and the two soon created a center for the study of physical chemistry and founded the influential journal for the new discipline, *Zeitschrift für physikalische Chemie.* In 1889, Ostwald published a book on analytical chemistry, *Grundriss der allgemeinen Chemie,* which further distinguished physical chemistry from organic chemistry. By this time, Ostwald had begun to understand the world in terms of energy; he believed that everything could be reduced to that single concept, and this was a theme that would dominate the rest of his life and work. By 1898 Leipzig University had created a physical chemistry institute, a training and research center where much of Ostwald's later work was done.

Work on Catalysis Leads to Nobel Prize

Ostwald's research into the dynamics of chemical reactions in solutions led to the dilution law of 1888, which established a relationship between elecrolytic dissociation and conductivity. Arrhenius's theory of electrolytic dissociation states that atoms will come apart (dissociate) in water, creating charged ions that have gained or lost electrons. Excited by this theory, Ostwald and his researchers turned their attention to electrochemistry, seeing it as a model for chemical reactions that are accelerated or catalyzed by weak bases or acids. This led to his most important research, which was in the area of catalysis, whereby a substance is used to speed up a chemical reaction but remains unaffected by that reaction. Though the process of catalysis had been described some sixty years earlier, Ostwald made such processes measurable and also connected them with his own work on chemical affinity. Although his theory that catalysis operates simply by having catalysts present and that catalysts do not take part in the reaction is now known to be incorrect, his work on catalysis was otherwise productive. In 1901, Ostwald's work led to the process for converting ammonia to nitric acid, which was accomplished by burning ammonia in the presence of platinum. This process was patented in 1902 and allowed mass manufacturing of the basic component of explosives. Renewed interest in catalysis also led to great strides in the chemical industry: oil, for example, is transformed into fuel and natural gas by the catalytic process. In 1909, Ostwald was awarded the Nobel Prize in chemistry for this work.

In 1905, Ostwald spent a year as an exchange professor at Harvard University in the United States, spreading the word of physical chemistry across the Atlantic. The following year he retired from his chair of physical chemistry at Leipzig, tired of administrative duties and political infighting. His working life was far from over, however. He bought an estate in a Leipzig suburb, which he dubbed 'Energie,' and there he continued a number of experimental and writing projects. Along with editing professional journals, he also worked on a history and classification of people who were considered geniuses, reprints of significant papers in chemistry and physics, and a three-volume autobiography. Some of his many interests included the philosophy and history of science, pacifism, internationalism, and the creation of a world language—he was very interested in Esperanto while he was a visiting professor at Harvard and later he wrote his own language, Ido. Ostwald also made important contributions to color theory—standardization of colors and a theory of color harmony. This was an outgrowth of his own interest in painting.

In 1880 Ostwald had married the daughter of a medical doctor in Riga, Helene von Reyher. They had three sons and two daughters. One of his sons, Wilhelm Wolfgang, would grow up to be a well-known chemist himself. Until his death from uremia in early April of 1932, Ostwald continued to work tirelessly for the causes he espoused.

SELECTED WRITINGS BY OSTWALD:

Books

Lehrbuch der allgemeinen Chemie, 2 volumes, Engleman, 1885–1887.
Grundriss der allgemeinen Chemie, Engleman, 1889.
Die wissenschaftlichen Grundlagen der analytischen Chemie, Engleman, 1894.
Grundlinien der anorganischen Chemie, Engleman, 1900.

Periodicals

"Über physico-chemische Messmethoden," *Zeitschrift für physikalische Chemie,* Volume 17, 1895, pp. 427–445.
"Über Katalyse," *Verhandlungen der Gesellschaft Deutsche Naturforscher und Ärtze,* Volume 73, 1901, pp. 184–201.

SOURCES:

Books

Concise Dictionary of Scientific Biography, Charles Scribner's Sons, 1981, pp. 522–523.
Gillespie, Charles Coulson, editor, *Dictionary of Scientific Biography,* Volume 15, Scribner, 1978, pp. 455–469.
Farber, Eduard, editor, *Great Chemists,* Interscience Publishers, 1961, pp. 1021–1030.

Periodicals

Donnan, F. G., "Ostwald Memorial Lecture," *Journal of the Chemical Society,* 1933, pp. 316–332.

—*Sketch by J. Sydney Jones*

David Packard
1912-
American electrical engineer

David Packard

David Packard is an electrical engineer and entrepreneur who has had a profound impact on politics and industry in the United States. With **William Hewlett**, he founded Hewlett-Packard in 1939, one of the nation's first high-technology companies. He served as Deputy Secretary of Defense under President Nixon and as vice chairman of the President's Commission on Defense Management, known as the Packard Commission, under President Reagan. He has also made large charitable contributions through the David and Lucile Packard Foundation.

Packard was born in Pueblo, Colorado, on September 7, 1912, the second child of Sperry and Ella (Graber) Packard. His mother was a high school teacher of German descent, and his father was a lawyer descended from New England colonialists. Packard was educated at Somerlid Grade School, where he first became interested in electrical engineering, and Centennial High School in Pueblo. He later attended Stanford University, where he first met Hewlett. Packard played football and received his B.A. in electrical engineering in 1934. In 1935, he was hired by the General Electric company to work in the vacuum-tube engineering division at Schenectady, New York. Offered a fellowship by an engineering professor, **Frederick Terman**, he returned to Stanford and in 1939 took a master's degree in electrical engineering with a focus on radio engineering.

Cofounds Hewlett-Packard Company

In 1939, Packard and Hewlett, two of the most successful partners in the history of industry, used $538 to start their firm in Packard's garage in Palo Alto. Many of their early inventions were related to work that Hewlett had done at Stanford. One of Packard and Hewlett's first projects was production of a new kind of audio oscillator, called a "resistance-capacitance oscillator," the design of which was the subject of Hewlett's master's thesis at Stanford. The oscillator, named the 200A, produced electrical signals in the range of human hearing, from 20 to 20,000 cycles per second. The device was used primarily to measure the intensity of recorded sound. Hewlett and Packard presented the oscillator, which sold at a quarter the cost of similar instruments of its day, at a 1938 meeting of the International Radio Engineers in Portland, Oregon. Here, they met Walt Disney; later, the chief sound engineer at Disney Studios ordered eight of these devices for use in making the landmark film *Fantasia*.

Hewlett-Packard was incorporated a year later, and the two men flipped a coin to see whose name would go first. Packard cofounded the West Coast Electronics Foundation in 1942 and was awarded the Medal of Honor of the Electronics Industry for his involvement. Packard, who was more the businessman than Hewlett, served as president of Hewlett-Packard from 1947 to 1964 and as chairman of the board and chief executive officer from 1964 to 1968. During World War II, the company grew rapidly as the result of defense contracts; forced to reorganize and redefine their objectives after the war, Hewlett and Packard decided to focus development and marketing efforts on the engineering industry. The company specialized in instruments for measuring and testing; they were also one of the first companies to make use of semiconductors and in 1966 they introduced their first computer.

Hewlett-Packard was a highly successful technology firm by the 1960s, but almost none of their market was outside of industry; their first successful product in the popular market was the hand-held calculator, introduced in 1968 as the HP 9100. Growth at Hewlett-Packard was the result of continuing technological innovation, but as *Fortune* magazine observed in a 1988 profile of Packard, "No single product ... has brought the company as much distinction as its management style." An informal management style, which often involved what Hewlett remembered as "wandering around," cultivated loyalty and commitment from their work force and encouraged creative participation.

Becomes Involved in National Politics

Packard was chairman of the board of trustees of Stanford University in 1958 and 1959. Packard was also a friend of Herbert Hoover, and in keeping with Hoover's wishes, he prevented a takeover by liberal faculty of the Hoover Institution, where he sat on the advisory board. He became acquainted with Richard Nixon during this period and supported him for president in the election of 1968. In 1969, Packard was asked by the Secretary of Defense, Melvin Laird, to serve under Nixon as Deputy Secretary of Defense, a post he held until 1971. During his tenure at the Pentagon, Packard prevented himself from benefitting from any changes in the value of Hewlett-Packard stock; during the three years he was in his office, the value of his stock rose over twenty million dollars, but he arranged his holdings so he never received this increase.

Another California politician to whom Packard developed strong ties was Ronald Reagan. In 1985, he was chosen by President Reagan to head the Packard Commission, which was charged with making recommendations to overhaul defense-procurement policies. This was during a period when government was spending a great deal of money on defense, and Packard was appointed in the midst of a scandal over the prices many defense contractors were charging the Pentagon. In the report his committee submitted to the president, Packard recommended strengthening the role of the chair of the Joint Chiefs of Staff and stimulating better long-term planning, as well as appointing what *U.S. News and World Report* called "a high-level civilian procurement czar to oversee the services' buying plans." After the report was released, Packard told *U.S. News and World Report:* "There's no question that, because of long-term structural problems, we've wasted tens of billions of dollars out of the more than a trillion that's been spent." The Reagan administration submitted to Congress most of the recommendations he included in his report.

Both Packard and Hewlett retired from active leadership of their company in 1978, but they returned to take the helm at Hewlett-Packard in 1990, guiding the company through difficulties caused by mismanagement and changing circumstances in the computer industry. They restructured the divisions of the company and reduced the power of the centralized bureaucracy, and Hewlett-Packard was posting a profit again within two years.

On April 8, 1938, Packard married Lucile Laura Salter, a Stanford classmate; the couple had four children. His wife has shared many of his interests, and they founded the David and Lucile Packard Foundation to support scientific and health research, as well as a broad range of social and educational programs. The foundation made a $70 million contribution to the children's hospital at Stanford University. The Packards were also the major contributors to the construction of the Monterey Bay Aquarium, where Packard designed a machine to simulate tidal movements. He once financed a project to salvage four U.S. Navy Sparrowhawk biplanes that had gone down in 1,500 feet of water off the Pacific coast in 1935 aboard the U.S.S. Macon. In 1988, Packard announced that he would give most of his fortune, which was estimated to amount to over two billion dollars, to the David and Lucile Packard Foundation. Their children supervise many of the foundation's programs, particularly those in archaeology and marine biology.

SELECTED WRITINGS BY PACKARD:

Periodicals

"The Real Scandal in Military Contracts," *Across the Board,* November, 1988, pp. 17–23.

SOURCES:

Books

Kanter, Rosabeth Moss, *The Change Masters,* Simon & Schuster, 1983.
Peters, Thomas J., and Robert H. Waterman, *In Search of Excellence,* Warner Books, 1982.
Schoenbaum, Elenora, editor, *Political Profiles: The Nixon/Ford Years,* Facts on File, 1979.

Periodicals

"Calling for a Pentagon Shake-Up," *U.S. News and World Report,* March 10, 1986, pp. 23–24.
Goff, T. J., "The Best in Business: 1986," *California Business Magazine,* December, 1986, pp. 40–45.

Guzzardi, Walter, Jr., "The U.S. Business Hall of Fame," *Fortune,* March 14, 1988, pp. 142–144.

"Packard's Big Giveaway," *Time,* May 9, 1988, p. 70.

"A Pentagon Manifesto," *Newsweek,* March 10, 1986.

"A Quartet of High-Tech Pioneers," *Fortune,* October 12, 1987, pp. 148–149.

"Silicon Valley's Troubled Olympus," *California,* February, 1991, pp. 12–13.

Other

Packard, David, interview with John Henry Dreyfuss conducted February 9, 1994.

—Sketch by John Henry Dreyfuss

George Palade

George Palade
1912-
Romanian-born American cell biologist

George Palade entered the science of cell biology at a time when techniques such as electron microscopy and sedimentation of discrete bits of cell structure were beginning to reveal the minute structure of the cell. He not only advanced these techniques, but also, by investigating the ultrastructure or fine structure of animal cells, identified and described the function of mitochondria as the powerhouse of the cell and of ribosomes as the site of protein manufacture. For his research in the function and structure of such cell components, he shared the 1974 Nobel Prize in physiology or medicine with two other cell researchers, **Albert Claude** and **Christian R. de Duvé**.

George Emil Palade was born on November 19, 1912, in Jassy (Iaşi), in northeastern Romania. One of three children, Palade came from a professional family—his father, Emil, was a philosophy professor at the University of Jassy, while his mother, Constanta Cantemir, taught elementary school. Palade's two sisters, Adriana and Constanta, would grow up to be a professor of history and a pediatrician, respectively.

Attending school in Buzau, Palade entered the University of Bucharest in 1930 as a medical student. Ten years later he received his degree, having completed his internship as well as a thesis on the microanatomy of the porpoise kidney. Having earned his medical degree, Palade chose to focus on research instead of practicing medicine. His particular interest was histology, or the microscopic structure of plant and animal tissue. With the advent of the World War II, Palade was drafted into the army and stationed at the University of Bucharest Medical School as an assistant professor of anatomy. In 1941, he married Irina Malaxa; they eventually had two children together, a daughter, Georgia Teodora, and a son, Philip Theodore.

Proceeds with Research in United States

In 1945, after being discharged from the army, Palade obtained a research position at New York University. While there he met the eminent cell biologist Albert Claude, who had pioneered both the use of the electron microscope in cell study and techniques of cell fractionation (the separation of the constituent parts of cells by centrifugal action). The older scientist invited Palade to join the staff at the Rockefeller Institute (now Rockefeller University), and in 1946 Palade accepted a two-year fellowship as visiting investigator. In 1947 the communist-led government in Romania declared the country a people's republic and forced the abdication of King Michael. Palade, who had always planned to return home to work, now opted to remain in the United States. He became a U.S. citizen in 1952 and a full professor of cytology at Rockefeller in 1958.

At the Rockefeller Institute, Palade's first achievements came in the preparation of cell tissue for both the fractionation process and electron microscopy. In the former, collaborating with W. C. Schneider and George Hogeboom, Palade introduced as a fixative the use of gradient sucrose, and in the latter, buffered osmium tetroxide. But his accomplishments soon went beyond improvements in methodology. Claude left the institute in 1949, and in the next decade Palade and his collaborators, building on Claude's work, reported groundbreaking descriptions of the fine appearance of the cell and of its biochemical function. Concentrating on the cytoplasm—the living material in the cell outside the nucleus—Palade was first attracted to larger organelles (bodies of definite structure and function in the cytoplasm) which Claude had earlier called "secretory granules." Palade showed that these tiny sausage-shaped structures, mitochondria, are the site where energy for the cell is generated. Animal cells typically contain a thousand such mitochondria, each creating adenosine triphosphate—ATP, a high-energy phosphate molecule—through enzymic (enzyme-catalyzed) oxidation or breakdown of fat and sugar. The ATP is then released into the cytoplasm where it powers energy-requiring mechanisms such as nerve impulse conduction, muscle contraction, or protein synthesis.

Using the high-power electron microscope (a device that utilizes electrons instead of light to form images of minute objects), Palade next revealed a delicate tracery, subsequently termed the endoplasmic reticulum by his collaborator, Keith R. Porter. The endoplasmic reticulum is a series of double-layered membranes present throughout all cells except mature erythrocytes, or red blood cells. Its function is the formation and transport of fats and proteins. By far Palade's most significant work was with so-called microsomes, small bodies in the cytoplasm that Claude had earlier identified and shown to have a relatively high ribonucleic acid (RNA) content. RNA is the genetic messenger in protein synthesis. Palade observed these microsomes both as free bodies within the cytoplasm, and attached to the endoplasmic reticulum. In 1956, using a high-speed centrifuge, Palade and his colleague Philip Siekevitz were able to isolate microsomes and observe them under the electron microscope. They discovered that these microsomes were made of equal parts of RNA and protein.

Traces the Pathway of Protein Synthesis

Palade assumed that these RNA-rich microsomes were in fact the factories producing protein to sustain not only the cell but the entire organism. The microsome was renamed the ribosome, and Palade and his team went to work to investigate the pathway of protein synthesis in the cell. Palade and Siekevitz began a series of experiments on ribosomes of the liver and pancreas, employing autoradiographic tracing, a sophisticated process similar to X-ray photography in which a picture is produced by radiation.

Investigating in particular exocrine cells (those that secrete externally) of the guinea pig pancreas, the team was able, by 1960, to show that ribosomes do in fact synthesize proteins that are then transported through the endoplasmic reticulum. Further research with Lucien Caro, J. D. Jamieson, C. Redman, David Sabatini, and Y. Tashiro elucidated the function of the larger ribosomes attached to the endoplasmic reticulum, establishing them as the site where amino acids assemble into polypeptides (chains of amino acids). Palade's team also traced the transportation network as well as the function of the Golgi complex, tubelike structures where proteins are sorted before final transport to the cell surface for export.

Having completed his work on protein synthesis, Palade turned his attention to cellular transport—the means by which substances move through cell membranes. Working with **Marilyn G. Farquhar**, Palade demonstrated by electron micrography (images formed using an electron microscope) that molecules and ions were engorged by sacs or vesicles that move to the surface from within the cell. These vesicles actually merge with the outer membrane for a time, and then swallow up and bring the substances inside the cell. This vesicular model was in distinct contrast to the then current pore model whereby it was thought that molecules simply entered the cell through pores in the membrane.

Following the death of his wife in 1969, Palade married Marilyn Gist Farquhar. In 1972 he left the Rockefeller Institute and became a full professor of cell biology at Yale University, continuing his research in cell morphology and function, but also turning to practical clinical uses of his discoveries. His later work is an attempt to establish links between defects in cellular protein production and various illnesses. In 1974 Palade shared the Nobel Prize in Physiology or Medicine with his former mentor, Albert Claude, and with Christian R. de Duvé, for their descriptions of the detailed microscopic structure and functions of the cell. He was also the recipient of the Passano Award in 1964, the Albert Lasker Basic Medical Research Award in 1966, the Gairdner Foundation Special Award in 1967, and the Horowitz Prize in 1970. In addition, Palade is the founding editor of the *Journal of Cell Biology*.

In 1990, Palade left Yale to become the dean for scientific affairs at the University of California, San Diego. He is also serving at the university as a professor-in-residence in cellular and molecular medicine.

SELECTED WRITINGS BY PALADE:

Periodicals

(With Albert Claude) "The Nature of the Golgi Apparatus, I and II," *Journal of Morphology,* Volume 85, 1949, pp. 35–111.

(With P. Siekevitz) "Liver Microsomes: An Integrated Morphological and Biochemical Study," *Journal of Biophysical and Biochemical Cytology,* Volume 2, 1956, pp. 171–200.

(With Siekevitz) "Pancreatic Microsomes: An Integrated Morphological and Biochemical Study," *Journal of Biophysical and Biochemical Cytology,* Volume 2, 1956, pp. 671–690.

"Functional Changes in the Structure of Cell Components," *Woods Hole Subcellular Particles Symposium,* 1958, pp. 64–80.

(With Siekevitz) "A Cytochemical Study on the Pancreas of the Guinea Pig, 1–4," *Journal of Biophysical and Biochemical Cytology,* Volume 4, 1958, pp. 203–218, 309–319, 557–566; Volume 5, 1959, pp. 1–10.

(With Marilyn Gist Farquhar) "Functional Evidence for the Existence of a Third Cell Type in the Renal Glomerulus: Phagocytosis of the Filtration Residues by a Distinctive 'Third Cell,'" *Journal of Cell Biology,* Volume 13, April, 1962, pp. 55–87.

SOURCES:

Books

McGraw-Hill Modern Scientists and Engineers, McGraw, 1980, pp. 388–389.
Nobel Laureates in Medicine or Physiology, Garland, 1990, pp. 442–445.
Nobel Prize Winners, H. W. Wilson, 1987, pp. 789–791.

Periodicals

New York Times, October 11, 1974, p. 22.
Science, November 8, 1974, pp. 516–520.

—*Sketch by J. Sydney Jones*

Angeliki Panajiotatou
1875-1954
Greek physician

Angeliki Panajiotatou and her sister were the first women to graduate from the University of Athens with medical degrees. Because of discrimination against her on the basis of her sex, however, it took Panajiotatou many years to be accepted as a physician in her native country. She had to leave Greece in order to practice medicine, moving to Egypt where she became an internationally recognized authority on tropical diseases.

Panajiotatou was born in Greece in 1875. She and her sister enrolled at the University of Athens in 1896, then Panajiotatou pursued her medical studies in Germany after graduation. She returned to the University of Athens in 1905, where she was appointed lecturer on the faculty of medicine and became the subject of bitter controversy. The sight of a woman teaching medicine proved too much for the medical students. According to the *Continuum Dictionary of Women's Biography,* the students shouted at her, "Back in the kitchen, back in the kitchen!" They refused to take her classes and she was eventually forced to resign.

Panajiotatou went to Alexandria, Egypt, where she practiced as a municipal doctor and was appointed professor at Cairo University. Later, she became chief of laboratories at the Greek Hospital in Alexandria, remaining in that position for twenty years. Upon passing a competitive examination, she also became a member of the Quarantine Service of Egypt, a post she held for more than thirty years.

Panajiotatou was interested in tropical diseases such as cholera and typhus, and she experimented to find ways of controlling them. Throughout her career, she journeyed to many international conferences to present the results of her work. The hygiene of ancient Greece was another of her interests, and her book on the subject has often been quoted by medical historians. A popular figure for many years in Alexandria's Greek community, she was often visited by artists and intellectuals who valued her interest in Greek culture.

Panajiotatou returned to Greece in 1938 and was appointed professor at the University of Athens. She died in Athens in 1954.

SELECTED WRITINGS BY PANAJIOTATOU:

Books

The Hygiene of the Ancient Greeks, Vigot Freres, 1923.

Periodicals

"Dysentery and Enteritis in Tropical Countries," *Grammata,* Volume 27, 1932, pp. 737–783.

SOURCES:

Books

Uglow, Jennifer, editor, *The Continuum Dictionary of Women's Biography,* Continuum, 1989.

Periodicals

Morton, Rosalie S., "Report of Work of Women Physicians in the Near East," *The Medical Woman's Journal,* August, 1936, p. 203.

Quarterly Bulletin of the Medical Women's National Association, Volume 42, 1932.

—*Sketch by Margo Nash*

Wolfgang K. H. Panofsky
1919-
German-born American physicist

Wolfgang K. H. Panofsky is known for his research in the area of atomic particles, especially in pi-mesons, and for his part in designing, building, and maintaining the Stanford Linear Accelerator, a two-mile-long atomic accelerator which has been the site of many important nuclear discoveries. He has also held prominent positions with governmental science, energy, and defense agencies.

Wolfgang Kurt Hermann Panofsky was born in Berlin, Germany, on April 24, 1919. His parents were Erwin Panofsky, an eminent art historian, and the former Dorothea Mosse. His older brother, Hans, later became professor of meteorology at Pennsylvania State University. Both Panofsky children showed signs of unusual intelligence at an early age, and Wolfgang was a strong chess player by the age of eight.

Panofsky received his early education at the Johanneum Gymnasium in Hamburg, where his father had taken a job at the local university. By the early 1930s, however, the Panofskys realized that they would have to leave their homeland. Adolf Hitler's anti-semitic laws and policies made it clear that those of the Jewish faith, such as the Panofskys, were certain to lose their jobs and, very likely, their lives as well. As a result, they left Germany for the United States, where the elder Panofsky accepted an appointment at the Institute for Advanced Studies in Princeton, New Jersey. Wolfgang enrolled at Princeton University in 1934, at the age of 15, and received his B.A. in physics four years later. He then continued his graduate studies at the California Institute of Technology, earning his Ph.D. there in 1942.

Becomes Involved in Government Research

Having graduated just as World War II was getting under way, Panofsky immediately became involved in military research. From 1942 to 1943 he served as director of the Office of Scientific Research and Development Projects at the California Institute of Technology. He then became a consultant to the Manhattan Project at the Los Alamos Scientific Laboratory in New Mexico. At the war's end, he was appointed a research physicist at the University of California's Radiation Laboratory and then, in 1946, joined the university's physics department as assistant professor. In 1951, Panofsky began his long-term affiliation with Stanford University when he accepted a position as professor of physics there.

Panofsky's most notable research during his years in Berkeley involved the study of pi mesons ("pions"), first discovered by English physicist **Cecil Frank Powell** in 1947. Pions are mesons, or fundamental particles, that consist of combinations of elementary particles known as quarks, and that are subject to the strong force. Panofsky's approach was to generate pions by bombarding a target with protons from the 184-inch synchrocyclotron on the Berkeley campus. Gamma rays released during this reaction were then analyzed to determine the characteristics of the pi mesons with which they were associated. Among the discoveries resulting from this series of experiments was a new and more precise value for the mass of the pion and surprising new data about the pion's parity.

Oversees the Construction of Stanford's Linear Accelerator

At Stanford, Panofsky became involved in the university's program of research on elementary particles and the machinery needed to carry out that research. In his capacity as director of the Stanford High Energy Physics Laboratory, he was responsible for the design of the projected two-mile-long linear accelerator (linac) planned for the campus. In 1961, he obtained a grant of $114 million from the U.S. government for the construction of the machine. It was designed to lie about 25 feet underground along a line directly under interstate highway 280 connecting San Francisco and San Jose. The linac was completed five years later and opened officially on September 10, 1967. By that time, initial tests had confirmed that the accelerator was capable of generating the 20 billion electron volt beams for which it had been designed. It took its place as one of the half dozen most powerful particle accelerators in the world.

In the meantime, Panofsky had been appointed director of the newly created Stanford Linear Accelerator Center (SLAC), the facility responsible for the linac's operation. In the twenty-three years that he held this position, Panofsky oversaw the expansion and re-design of the linac necessitated by new needs and changing technology. In 1984, he was named Director Emeritus of SLAC and, in 1989, added the title of Professor Emeritus of Physics.

Panofsky's wartime work marked the beginning of a long commitment to serving the government in a number of capacities. He served, for example, as a member of the President's Science Advisory Committee from 1960 to 1964, as consultant to the Office of Science and Technology from 1965 to 1973, as a member of the steering committee for JASON, a project of the Institute for Defense Analyses, from 1965 to 1973, as a consultant to the Arms Control and Disarmament Agency from 1959 to 1980, and as a member of the Department of Energy Panel on Nuclear Warhead Dismantlement and Special Nuclear Materials Controls beginning in 1991. Panofsky was also president of the American Physical Society from 1974 to 1975 and a member of the Commission on Particles and Fields of the International Union of Pure and Applied Physics.

Panofsky was married to Adele Irene DuMond on July 21, 1942. The couple has five children, Richard Jacob, Margaret Anne, Edward Frank, Carol Eleanor, and Steven Thomas. His awards include the Ernest Orlando Lawrence Memorial Award (1961), the National Medal of Science (1969), the Franklin Institute Award (1970), and the Leo Szilard Award (1982).

SELECTED WRITINGS BY PANOFSKY:

Books

(With M. Phillips) *Classical Electricity and Magnetism,* Addison-Wesley, 1955.
Particles and Policy, AIP Press, 1993.

SOURCES:

Books

McGraw-Hill Modern Scientists and Engineers, Volume 2, McGraw-Hill, 1980, pp. 390–391.

—*Sketch by David E. Newton*

George Papanicolaou
1883-1962
Greek-born American physician and anatomist

George Papanicolaou was a physician and researcher who was associated with the Cornell University school of medicine for forty-eight years. While studying microscopic slides of cells that had been cast off (exfoliated) in body fluids of laboratory animals and humans, he recognized the presence of abnormal cancer cells. The discovery led to the famous test that bears the first syllable of his last name, the Pap test. He is recognized by his colleagues as the father of modern cytology.

George Nicholas Papanicolaou was born on May 13, 1883, in Coumi, Greece, to Nicholas (a physician) and Mary Critsutas Papanicolaou. He received an M.D. degree from the University of Athens in 1904 and a Ph.D. from the University of Munich in 1910. He married Mary A. Mavroyeni on September 15, 1910. His first position was as a physiologist for an expedition of the Oceanographic Institute of Monaco for one year. In 1912, during the Balkan War, he became an officer in the Greek army medical corps. He came to the United States in 1913, working initially as a salesman, but soon securing work in his field as an anatomy assistant at Cornell University, where he eventually became a full professor in 1924. He also served on the pathology staff of New York Hospital from 1913. Papanicolaou became a United States citizen in 1927.

Finds Cancer Cells in Vaginal Fluid

In the pathology lab at Cornell, Papanicolaou began working with microscope slides of vaginal secretions of guinea pigs. He found that changes in forms of the epithelial cells (the outer layer of the skin or of an organ) correspond with the animal's estrus or menstrual cycle. Using the changes as a measuring device, he was able to study sex hormones and the menstrual cycles of other laboratory animals.

In 1923 Papanicolaou studied vaginal smears of women who had cervical cancer and found cancer cells present. Writing in the medical journal *Growth* in 1920, he outlined his theory that a microscopic smear of vaginal fluid could detect the presence of cancer cells in the uterus. At this time physicians relied on biopsy and curettage to diagnose and treat cancer and ignored the possibilities of a new test based on Papanicolaou's research.

Papanicolaou himself paid little attention to his research in this area for the next decade. At the encouragement of a colleague, Dr. Herbert F. Traut, and with the support of Dean Joseph C. Hinsey of Cornell medical college, he later continued his work in this field and was allowed to devote full time to his research. In 1943 he published conclusive findings that showed smears of vaginal fluid could indicate cervical and uterine cancer before symptoms appear. This time the medical community took notice, and the "new cancer diagnosis," the Pap smear test, won acceptance and became a routine screening technique.

During a Pap test, a scraping or smear is taken from the woman's cervix (the mouth of the uterus) or from the vagina, then is stained and examined under the microscope, where cells may appear normal, cancerous, or suspicious. It is a simple, painless, and effective means of early cancer detection.

Wins International Fame for the Pap Test

Papanicolaou soon won international acclaim for his discovery. The American Cancer Society (ACS) launched massive education campaigns for the test, and Dr. Charles Cameron, a Philadelphia surgeon (who was director of the ACS), said that this test was the most significant and practical discovery in our time. Papanicolaou spent much of his time promoting the test and trained thousands of students in the microscopic detection techniques. Once the test had been accepted, he began to apply the same principle of exfoliate cytology to cancers of the lung, stomach, and bladder.

At Cornell Papanicolaou founded the Papanicolaou Research Center and worked six and a half days a week peering at slides and looking for malignant cells. He seldom took a vacation. When associates advised him to rest, he stated that the work was so interesting and that there was so much to be done. His wife worked as his research assistant and driver.

Papanicolaou was a member of many societies and won twelve prestigious awards including the Borden award of the Association of Medical Colleges in 1940, the Lasker award of the Public Health Association in 1950, and the honor medal from the American Cancer Society in 1952. The king of Greece gave him the medal of the Cross of the Grand Commander award, and his native town of Coumi renamed their town square in his honor. He was the author of four books and over one hundred articles.

At the age of seventy-eight, Papanicolaou ended his forty-eight year association with Cornell and took over the Papanicolaou Cancer Institute in Miami. He maintained a busy schedule and was planning for the further expansion of the institute when he suffered a heart attack and died on February 19, 1962. He was buried in Clinton, New Jersey.

In 1983, the hundredth anniversary of Papanicolaou's birth, several articles appeared in scientific journals honoring him and his persistent spirit of scientific discovery. In December, 1992, the *Journal of the Florida Medical Association* issued a thirty year commemorative of his death, which states that because of his persistence, there has been a seventy-percent decrease in cervical and uterine cancer. His techniques are also being applied to other organs and systems in the use of fine needle aspiration.

SELECTED WRITINGS BY PAPANICOLAOU:

Books

The Sexual Cycle of Human Females as Revealed in Vaginal Smears, 1933.

(With Herbert Traut) *Diagnosis of Uterine Cancer by the Vaginal Smear,* 1943.
(With Traut and Andrew Marchetti) *Epithelia of Women's Reproductive Organs,* 1948.
Atlas of Exfoliate Cytology, 1954.

SOURCES:

Books

Carmichael, D. Erskine, *The Pap Smear: Life of George N. Pananicolaou,* 1973.

Periodicals

Cameron, Charles S., "Dedication of the Papanicolaou Cancer Research Institute," *Journal of the American Medical Association,* 1962, pp. 556–59.
Koprowski, I., "Remembering George N. Papanicolaou," *Journal of the American Medical Women's Association,* November-December, 1984, pp. 200–202.
Palatianos et al., "George N. Papanicolaou, M.D., Father of Modern Cytology," *Journal of the Florida Medical Association,* December, 1992, pp. 837–38.

—*Sketch by Evelyn B. Kelly*

Mary Lou Pardue
1933-
American biologist

Mary Lou Pardue is a biologist noted for her work in insect genetics. She was born in Lexington, Kentucky, on September 15, 1933, the daughter of Mary Allie Marshall and Louis Arthur Pardue, professor of physics and administrator at the University of Kentucky and Virginia Polytechnic Institute. She received a B.S. in biology from the College of William and Mary in 1955, an M.S. in radiation biology from the University of Tennessee in 1959, and a Ph.D. in biology from Yale University in 1970. At Yale, Pardue's mentor was Joseph G. Gall, with whom she conducted some of her most important research as well as coauthoring several significant articles. In 1972 she became an associate professor of biology at the Massachusetts Institute of Technology, where she has been a professor since 1980. She also participated in summer courses at the Cold Spring Harbor Laboratory between 1970 and 1980.

Pardue's area of specialization is the structure and function of chromosomes in eukaryotic organisms. Eukaryotic organisms are those whose deoxyribonucleic acid (DNA), which provides the information for reproduction, is contained in their cell's nuclei or centers. Pardue's work excludes lower organisms such as bacteria and viruses, which are prokaryotic organisms, having their genetic material located in the cytoplasm (the cell area surrounding the nucleus). Her studies primarily centered on the breed of fruit fly (*Drosophila*) known as *D. melanogaster;* the rapid succession of fruit fly generations—due to their short lifespans—facilitates a time-saving study of genetic developments. Also of importance to Pardue and her coworkers is the fact that the flies' gene activity is similar, and therefore applicable, to higher organisms.

In the late 1960s, Pardue and Gall developed a technique called in situ hybridization for localizing, with intact chromosomes, specific nucleotic sequences, which determine traits imparted during reproduction. These experiments were carried out using the chromosomes for *Drosophila*'s salivary glands. This method, designed to locate genes on the chromosomes, is used to identify the chromosomal regions of DNA that are complementary to specific nucleic acid molecules, or RNAs. The technique involves squashing chromosomes and fixing them on a slide; the DNAs are denatured (a process that diminishes their biological activity) by means of a mild alkaline solution to break hydrogen bonds without separating the DNA from the chromosome. Radioactive RNA is then introduced to the chromosomes under incubating heat which bonds the RNA with the DNA. Once hybridization occurs, the unbonded, single-stranded RNA is removed. Photographic emulsion is then placed on the chromosomes to detect DNA-RNA hybrids by autoradiography, which registers an image through a substance's radioactive properties.

During the mid–1970s Pardue concentrated on the heat-shock response. This refers to the effects of temperature on genetic activity. Studies of the fruit fly showed that increases in its normal environmental temperature exceeding ten degrees resulted in the suspension of some genetic activity; the studies attempted to determine what genes are affected by the heat increase. In a related area of research, insect muscle cell biology of stress response, Pardue found that stress also resulted in the suspension of some genetic activity and the associated synthesis of proteins. An understanding of this, the most basic cellular stress mechanism, is significant because of its potential application in cancer treatment; it points to a relationship between stress and the cellular processes associated with the development of that disease. An understanding of how to turn genetic activity on and off carries potential benefits in establishing new forms of cancer therapy as well as other scientific/medical treatments.

As a result of her work, Pardue received the Esther Langer Award for Cancer Research in 1977. In 1989 the Yale Graduate School awarded her its Lucius Wilbur Cross Medal. She has also received an honorary D.Sc. from Bard College (1985).

SELECTED WRITINGS BY PARDUE:

Books

(With N. C. Hogan, K. L. Traverse, and D. E. Sullivan) "The Nucleus-limited Hsr-omega–1 Transcript Is a Polyadenylated RNA with a Regulated Intranuclear Turnover," *Journal of Cellular Biology,* Volume 125, Number 1, April, 1994, pp. 21–30.

Periodicals

(With J. G. Gall) "Formation and Detection of RNA-DNA Hybrid Molecules in Cytological Preparations," *Proceedings of the National Academy of Science USA,* Volume 63, 1969, pp. 378–83.

(With Gall) "Chromosomal Localization of Mouse Satellite DNA," *Science,* Volume 168, 1970, pp. 1356–58.

(With A. Spradling and S. Penman) "Analysis of Drosophila mRNA by In Situ Hybridization: Sequences Transcribed in Normal and Heat-shocked Cultured Cells," *Cell,* Volume 4, 1975, pp. 395–404.

(With H. Biessmann, K. Valgeirsdottir, A. Lofsky, C. Chin, B. Ginther, and R. W. Levis) "HeT-A, a Transposable Element Specifically Involved in 'Healing' Broken Chromosome Ends in *Drosophila Melanogaster,*" *Molecular Cellular Biology,* Volume 12, 1992, pp. 3910–18.

SOURCES:

Pardue, Mary Lou, interview with Michael Sims conducted January, 1994.

—Sketch by Michael Sims

Charles Stewart Parker
1882-1950
American botanist

Charles Stewart Parker was a botanist whose research led to the control of stone-fruit blight, which, until the 1920s, had been responsible for hundreds of thousands of dollars in lost harvests each year. He also discovered dozens of new plants, and both a new species of sweet pea and a new subspecies rose have been named after him.

Parker was born in Corinne, Utah, on March 31, 1882. He attended Trinity College, receiving his bachelor of arts degree in 1905. Before continuing his education, he served as director of a field expedition to Mexico for a brief period, from 1908 to 1912. He then attended the State College of Washington (now Washington State University) where he earned his B.S. in 1922 and his M.S. in 1923. Parker then moved to Pennsylvania State College, where he worked toward his Ph.D. in botany. He titled his dissertation "A Taxonomic Study of the Genus *Hypholoma* in North America." He joined Howard University as an associate professor of botany in 1925 and was promoted the following year to professor. In 1936 he became head of the botany department, where he remained until his retirement in 1947.

For a year, beginning with the spring of 1922, Parker had conducted a field study of orchards in the state of Washington. In January 1925, he published an article titled "Coryneum Blight of Stone Fruits" in the *Howard Review,* where he described the life history of the blight that particularly attacked stone fruits such as cherries, plums, peaches, and apricots. He wrote: "Coryneum Blight is a fungus disease of stone fruits . . . which has been reported in many of the peach growing sections of the United States, east of the Rocky Mountains, since the first announcement of its presence on the Pacific Coast in 1900. . . . Coryneum blight attacks the twigs, leaves, blossoms and fruit of its host plants, causing a spotting, gumming and death of affected parts."

According to Parker's study, the disease attacked the twigs most often and most severely, developing small spots that could culminate in the formation a canker. He also found that infections near buds either killed the buds directly or killed the leaves and flowers afterward. The fruits that did mature often carried spots that enlarged with ripening. Parker also noted that weather patterns affected the disease. For example, he explained in his *Howard Review* article, a damp summer led to "continued spore production and new infections," while a dry summer resulted in scattered spores which "lie dormant or are protected within the stromatic tissue, gum, etc." Parker also put forth that in 1920, the blight had resulted in $250,000 of damage to the cherry crop in one region of Washington alone.

Over the course of his career, Parker discovered and described thirty-nine species of plants, wrote many papers, and described a new subgenus and section of the genus *Carex.* Additionally, Parker was a member of the Botanical Survey Party in Washington from 1921 to 1922, as well as the Mycology Society, the Botanical Society, the Phytopathological Society, and the Torrey Botanical Club. Perhaps the two greatest recognitions of his work, however, were the naming of a new species of sweet pea, *Lathyrus Parkeri,* and a new variety of rose, *Rosa Spaldingii, var. Parkeri,* after him. He died on January 10, 1950, in Seattle, at the age of sixty-eight.

SELECTED WRITINGS BY PARKER:

Periodicals

"Coryneum Blight of Stone Fruits," *The Howard Review,* Volume 2, January 1925, pp. 3–40.

SOURCES:

Periodicals

Downing, Lewis K., "Contributions of Negro Scientists," *Crisis,* June, 1939, pp. 167–68.
"Necessity Is Again Mother of Invention," *Washington D.C. News,* September 16, 1938.
Science, February 3, 1950, p. 122.

—*Sketch by Leslie Mertz*

John T. Parsons
1913-
American inventor

John T. Parsons is an industrialist whose inventions revolutionized machining and tooling, making American manufacturing much more precise and uniform. In addition, the changes he made in the tooling used for metalworking have greatly simplified that industry, while his work with composites and adhesively bonded structures have led directly to some of the most recent technologies used in aviation manufacturing.

John Thoren Parsons was born to Carl and Edith (Thoren) Parsons on October 11, 1913, in Detroit, Michigan. His mother was very involved in the work of the church, and his father ran his own company, the Parsons Corporation, which supplied Detroit automakers with various parts. From the age of five, Parsons liked to visit his father's company and observe the work that went on there; the experience awakened in him his lifelong fascination with machining and metalworking.

Parsons was working for his father's company by the time he was in high school, having been put on the payroll in August of 1928. In September of 1933, he entered Wayne University (now Wayne State University) in Detroit, but the financial pressures of the Great Depression forced his father to choose which of his two sons should finish college. He decided that Parsons' brother would be the one to get his degree, and part way through his second semester at Wayne University, Parsons withdrew. He never went back to college. In an interview with Susan E. Kolmer, Parsons said that not having a college degree initially hampered him in some ways, but that all in all it was a positive development for him. He believes that his mind was not forced into a predetermined way of approaching problems which might have prevented him from finding solutions no one had before. After leaving Wayne University, Parsons returned to his father's company, where he remained for the next nineteen years. During that time, he became a division manager.

The advent of World War II diversified the Parsons Corporation; by 1940 they were doing work for the U.S. Army and Air Force. Under the military contracts, the Parsons Corporation manufactured land mines, bomb fins, and bomb casings. Looking ahead to the end of the war and the specialized contracts that went with it, Parsons began searching for a product which was both useful to the military during the war but would also be in demand during peacetime as well. He settled on the idea of manufacturing helicopter and other rotor blades, initially manufacturing them out of wood, but later progressing to steel, aluminum, titanium, and finally composites, which most are still made of today.

Develops Numerical Control for Manufacturing

Under contract with the U.S. Air Force in the late 1940s, Parsons started work on the idea of manufacturing by numerical control. Since the early 1900s, machining was done mostly by hand, with the most experienced and skillful machinists able to turn out relatively uniform and precise products. However, there was always variation, sometimes quite slight and sometimes significant. In 1948, Parsons started working in earnest on a system that used a binary punched card system that was coded to tell a machine

tool exactly what lines to follow, how fast to operate, and at what depth to cut. This innovation in manufacturing proved to be far more precise than any person could be in turning out parts to exact specifications; the parts produced were also far more uniform than human hands could make them. In 1952, Parsons was awarded his patents for the numerical control process.

By 1952, Parsons' father no longer had control of the company, although he retained ownership. Parsons became embroiled in a dispute with a superior who fired him, despite his contributions. The Danville Division of F. L. Jacobs Company initially employed him as a salesperson, but he was made division manager there after only three months. Parsons stayed only eleven months before being re-hired at the Parsons Corporation by the same manager who had fired him. Determined not to let such a thing happen to him again, Parsons was able to buy control of the corporation in 1954. While a division still manufactured auto parts, Parsons Corporation continued its work on rotor blades. Some of the blades the corporation manufactured were for wind tunnels, most notably the tunnel at the Arnold Engineering Development Center in Tullahoma, Tennessee.

Blades were not the only aviation-related item the Parsons Corporation produced. The company also developed a process for metal-to-metal adhesive bonding, a very sophisticated process because of the great obstacle involved in bonding different metals having different specific heats. Adhesive bonding paved the way for the modern manufacture of aircraft. During 1954 and 1955, the Parsons Corporation developed composites for aircraft using fiberglass, an improvement over titanium. The process was so complicated that over fifty patents, both foreign and domestic, were issued for it. Under the Parsons Corporation, licensees in England and France turned out rotor blades. Later the company established an aircraft division in Stockton, California for manufacturing helicopter blades and other bonded structures.

Uses Polysterene Foam to Form Casts

In 1968, Parsons sold the Parsons Corporation, which is now owned by British Petroleum, and he founded the John T. Parsons Company. The focus of the new company was process development. Using the adhesive bonding technology which he had developed, Parsons engaged in research for jet fan blades and marine propellers, such as those that drive the largest ships. This research led Parsons to pioneer the development of polystyrene foam patterns. Used mainly to package goods and in the production of drinking cups, Parsons put polystyrene foam to an entirely different use. Working with only a small number of employees, he engineered the idea of using polystyrene foam to form the casts of body dies. This process proved to be much faster and more accurate than conventional methods, resulting in much less machining needed to get a part right. The use of polystyrene foam for castings also greatly reduced the weight of castings, thus saving industry much money. In fact, this process was such a boon to Detroit automakers that the lead time needed to get a car into production dropped from five to three years.

Parsons also worked extensively on metal machining. Because metals tend to warp as they are tooled, the conventional method of machining a piece was to do one surface, then turn it to do the other surfaces. As each surface is done to perfection, the others warp, albeit a little less each time, and a part is flipped over and over again until all of the surfaces are machined to within tolerable limits. Parsons developed a means of machining metal that minimized warping so greatly that each surface needed only be machined once. With the new process, even metal as thin as three-one-thousands of an inch could be machined with minimal warping.

In 1968, Parsons received the Jacquard Medal from the Numerical Control Society for his development of numerical control. Named for the inventor of the Jacquard loom, this award previously had never been presented. In 1975, the Society of Manufacturing Engineers presented Parsons with an engineering citation that claimed his " . . . brilliant concept of numerical control ushered in the second Industrial Revolution." In an interview with Kolmer, Parsons said one of the highlights of his life was receiving the National Medal for Technology from the United States Department of Commerce in 1985. He received the medal from the hand of President Ronald Reagan in a White House ceremony held in the East Room. Parsons was inducted in the National Inventor's Hall of Fame in 1993.

Parsons considers his home and family as his hobbies, although he gives the lion's share of credit for raising their six children to his wife. Born Elizabeth Mae Shaw, she married Parsons in 1940. While still busy with John T. Parsons Company, Parsons began working on an autobiography. He devoted much of his time to that effort as well as directing the Society of Manufacturing Engineers. He was first elected as one of its directors at the age of seventy-eight.

SOURCES:

Parsons, John T., interview with Susan E. Kolmer conducted November 29, 1993.

—Sketch by Susan E. Kolmer

Jennie R. Patrick
1949-
American chemical engineer

Jennie R. Patrick is the first African American woman to earn a doctorate degree in chemical engineering. A successful chemical engineer, manager, and educator who has applied her skills with a number of different companies and universities, she has also been honored with the Outstanding Women in Science and Engineering Award in 1980, and by CIBA-GEIGY Corp. in its Exceptional Black Scientist poster series in 1983.

Patrick was born January 1, 1949, in Gadsden, Alabama, one of five children of James and Elizabeth Patrick, working-class parents who emphasized knowledge as an escape from poverty. Patrick was both nurtured and challenged in a segregated elementary school and junior high, but in high school she was one of the first participants in a controversial and sometimes explosive program of racial integration, where she successfully overcame violence and unsupportive white teachers to graduate with an A-minus average in 1969.

Patrick was accepted at several prestigious universities, but chose to begin her pursuit of engineering at Tuskegee Institute, which she attended until 1970 when the chemical engineering program was eliminated. She then transferred to the University of California at Berkeley to finish her degree, receiving her B.S. in 1973 and meanwhile working as an assistant engineer for the Dow Chemical Company in 1972 and for the Stauffer Chemical Company in 1973. She continued her education at the Massachusetts Institute of Technology (MIT), receiving a Gilliland Fellowship in 1973, a DuPont Fellowship in 1974, and a Graduate Student Assistant Service award in 1977. She was also awarded a fellowship in 1975 from the American Association of University Women, and a National Fellowship Foundation Scholarship in 1976.

Conducts Research on Superheated Liquids

Her research at MIT involved the concept of superheating, where a liquid is raised above its boiling temperature but does not become a vapor. She investigated the temperature to which pure liquids and mixtures of two liquids could be superheated. Patrick finished her research and completed her doctorate in 1979. While pursuing her graduate studies, Patrick worked as an engineer with Chevron Research in 1974 and with Arthur D. Little in 1975.

Jennie R. Patrick

After completing her doctorate, Patrick joined the Research and Development Center at General Electric (GE) in Schenectady, New York, where she held the position of research engineer. Her work there involved research on energy-efficient processes for chemical separation and purification, particularly the use of supercritical extraction. In supercritical processes, the temperature and pressure are varied so that a substance is not a liquid or a gas, but a fluid. Unique properties make these fluids useful in both separations and purification processes. She has published several papers on this work, and has received patents for some of her advancements.

Patrick remained at GE until 1983, when she accepted a position at Philip Morris as a project manager in charge of the development of a program to improve several of the company's products. Patrick transferred to the Rhom and Haas Company in 1985, as manager of fundamental chemical engineering research. In this position she interacted with all aspects of the chemical business, from engineering to marketing to manufacturing. By being exposed to the overall business she was able to direct development of new research technology within her division and promote its implementation throughout the company. In 1990, Patrick became assistant to the executive vice president of Southern Company Services, a position that emphasized her management skills in both the business and technical aspects of the company. Having earlier held adjunct professorships at Rensselaer Polytechnic Institute from 1982 to 1985

and the Georgia Institute of Technology from 1983 to 1987, Patrick decided to make teaching a bigger part of the her life. In January 1993, she left Southern Company Services and returned to Tuskegee University, as the 3M Eminent Scholar and Professor of Chemical Engineering. In addition to her teaching duties, Patrick is developing research projects in material sciences, is actively involved in leadership roles at Tuskegee, and remains firmly committed to helping minority students find success, particularly in the fields of science and engineering.

SELECTED WRITINGS BY PATRICK:

Books

(With F. Palmer) "Supercritical Extraction of Dixylenol Sulfone," in *Supercritical Fluid Technology,* edited by J. M. L. Penninger and others, Elsevier, 1985, pp. 379–384.

Periodicals

(With R. C. Reid) "Superheat-Limit Temperature of Polar Liquids," *Industrial and Engineering Chemistry Fundamentals,* November, 1981, pp. 315–317.
(With R. D'Souza and A. S. Teja) "High Pressure Phase Equilibria in the Carbon Dioxide-n-Hexadecane and Carbon Dioxide-Water Systems," *Canadian Journal of Chemical Engineering,* February, 1988, pp. 319–325.
"Let Others' Experience Be Your Roadway to Success," *The Black Collegian,* September/October, 1992, p. 39.

SOURCES:

Books

Outstanding Young Women of America, Junior Chamber of Commerce, 1979, p. 981.
Sammons, V. O., editor, *Blacks in Science and Medicine,* Hemisphere Publishing Co., 1990, p. 185.

Periodicals

Bradby, Marie, "Professional Profile: Dr. Jennie R. Patrick," *US Black Engineer,* fall, 1988 pp. 30–33.
"Engineering Their Way to the Top," *Ebony,* December 1984, pp. 33–36.
Kazi-Ferrouillet, Kuumba, "Jennie R. Patrick: Engineer Extraordinaire," *NSBE Journal,* February, 1986, pp. 32–35.

—Sketch by Jerome P. Ferrance

Ruth Patrick
1907-
American limnologist

R uth Patrick has pioneered techniques for studying the biodiversity of freshwater ecosystems over a career that spans sixty years. Her studies of microscopic species of algae, called diatoms, in rivers around the world have provided methods for monitoring water pollution and understanding its effects. Federal programs to monitor the status of freshwater rely on Patrick's method of growing diatoms on glass slides. Her studies of the impact of trace elements and heavy metals on freshwater ecosystems have demonstrated how to maintain a desired balance of different forms of algae. For example, she showed that addition of small amounts of manganese prevents the overgrowth of blue-green algae and permits diatoms to proliferate.

Patrick received the prestigious Tyler Ecology Award in 1975, and serves on numerous governmental advisory committees. She advanced the field of limnology, the study of freshwater biology, and in the late 1940s established the Department of Limnology at the Academy of Natural Sciences in Philadelphia. She remained its director for more than four decades. Headquarters for her research are in Philadelphia, with a field site in West Chester, Pennsylvania. An estuary field site at Benedict, Maryland, on the Patuxent River near Chesapeake Bay, serves for studies of pollution caused by power plants.

Patrick was born in Topeka, Kansas, on November 26, 1907. Her undergraduate education was completed at Coker College, where she received a B.S. degree in 1929. She obtained both her M.S. degree in 1931 and her Ph.D. in botany in 1934 from the University of Virginia. The roots of Patrick's long and influential career in limnology can be traced to the encouragement of her father, Frank Patrick. He gave his daughter a microscope when she was seven years old and told her, "Don't cook, don't sew; you can hire people to do that. Read and improve your mind." Patrick's doctoral thesis, which she wrote at the University of Virginia in Charlottesville, was on diatoms, whose utility derives from their preference for different water chemistries. The species of diatoms found in a particular body of water says a lot about the character of the water.

Confronted with Bias against Women Scientists

When Patrick joined the Academy of Natural Sciences in 1933, it was as a volunteer in microscopy to work with one of the best collections of diatoms in the world; she was told at the time that women

Ruth Patrick

scientists were not paid. For income she taught at the Pennsylvania School of Horticulture and made chick embryo slides at Temple University. In 1937 persistence paid off, and she was appointed curator of the Leidy Microscopical Society with the Academy of Natural Sciences, a post she held until 1947. She also became associate curator of the academy's microscopy department in 1937, and continued in that capacity until 1947, when she accepted the position of curator and chairman of the limnology department at the academy. Continuing as curator, in 1973 she was offered the Francis Boyer Research Chair at the academy.

Conducts Pioneering Studies of Freshwater Ecosystems

In the late 1940s Patrick gave a paper at a scientific meeting on the diatoms of the Poconos. In the audience was William B. Hart, an oil company executive, who was so impressed with the possibilities of diatoms for monitoring pollution that he provided funds to support Patrick's research. Freed from financial constraints, Patrick undertook a comprehensive survey of the severely polluted Conestoga Creek, near Lancaster, Pennsylvania. It was the first study of its kind, and launched Patrick's career. She matched types and numbers of diatoms in the water to the type and extent of pollution, an extremely efficient procedure now used universally.

By her own account Patrick has waded into 850 different rivers around the globe in the course of her research. She participated in the American Philosophical Society's limnological expedition to Mexico in 1947 and led the Catherwood Foundation's expedition to Peru and Brazil in 1955. Patrick was an advisor to several presidential administrations and has given testimony at many hearings on environmental problems and before congressional committees on the subject of environmental legislation. She was an active participant in drafting the federal Clean Water Act.

Pens Book on Groundwater Concerns

In 1987 Patrick coauthored a book, *Groundwater Contamination in the United States,* which provides an overview of groundwater as a natural resource, and a state-by-state description of policies designed to manage growing problems of contamination and depletion. Another of her concerns is global warming, the rise in the earth's temperature attributed to the buildup of carbon dioxide and other pollutants in the atmosphere. In an interview reported in the *Philadelphia Inquirer* in 1989, Patrick said, "We're going to have to stop burning gasoline. And we're going to have to conserve more energy, develop ways to create electricity from the sun and plants, and make nuclear power both safe and acceptable."

Patrick has received many awards in addition to the Tyler prize, including the Gimbel Philadelphia Award for 1969, the Pennsylvania Award for Excellence in Science and Technology in 1970, the Eminent Ecologist Award of the Ecological Society of America in 1972, and the Governor's Medal for Excellence in Science and Technology in 1988. She holds many honorary degrees from United States colleges and universities. Patrick has authored over 130 papers, and continues to influence thinking on limnology and ecosystems. Her contributions to both science and public policy have been vast.

SELECTED WRITINGS BY PATRICK:

Books

(With E. Ford and J. Quarles) *Groundwater Contamination in the United States,* University of Pennsylvania Press, 1987.

Periodicals

"Managing the Risks of Hazardous Waste," *Environment,* April, 1991, pp. 13–35. :

SOURCES:

Periodicals

Detjen, Jim, "In Tiny Plants, She Discerns Nature's Warning on Pollution," *Philadelphia Inquirer,* February 19, 1989.

Other

"The Wonderful World of Dr. Ruth Patrick," unpublished paper by Geraldine J. Gates, Wharton School, University of Pennsylvania, February 16, 1987.

—*Sketch by Karen Withem*

Claire Patterson
1922—
American geochemist

Claire Patterson's contributions to science ranged from developing dating techniques using radioactive decay to alerting the public about the dangers of lead, although he began his career as an emission and mass spectroscopist with the Manhattan Project in 1944. Much of Patterson's professional career was spent as a research associate of environmental science at California Institute of Technology (Caltech) until his retirement in 1992. His early studies focused on using isotopes to date rocks—a process that enabled him to estimate the age of the earth. Later research on lead levels in the environment and their dangers to public health proved fundamental to the enactment of the Clean Air Act in 1970. He was elected to the National Academy of Sciences in 1987; his other honors include having a mountain and an asteroid named after him.

Claire Cameron Patterson was born in Des Moines, Iowa, on June 2, 1922, to Claire Cameron Patterson, a rural letter carrier, and his wife Vivian Ruth (Henny) Patterson. He obtained an A.B. in chemistry in 1943 from Grinnell College in Iowa, an M.S. in 1944 from the University of Iowa, and a Ph.D. in 1951 from the University of Chicago. Patterson met his wife Lorna (McCleary) Patterson while at Grinnell; the two married in 1944 and had two sons and two daughters. Lorna worked as a high school chemistry and physics teacher until her retirement.

Early in his career at Caltech, Patterson conducted studies to determine the age of various rocks. He did this by using the radioactive elements uranium and thorium to measure the rate of decay of an element's isotopes (forms of atoms) into lead. Decay is the process whereby rocks and minerals are transformed into new, more stable chemical combinations. While studying meteorites using his method, Patterson solved a problem that had mystified scientists for over 300 years—he calculated the age of the earth. Patterson determined the earth to be about 4.6 billion years old. Estimates prior to his 1953 calculations put the earth at approximately three billion years old. Subsequent research by others has not overturned Patterson's findings.

In 1973, twenty years after his historic finding, Patterson was elected to the National Academy of Science (NAS), one of the highest honors to be bestowed on a U.S. scientist or engineer. Caltech vice president and provost, geophysicist Barclay Kamb, as quoted in a California Institute of Technology press release, commented on the occasion by heralding Patterson's "thinking and imagination [as] so far ahead of the times that he has often gone misunderstood and unappreciated for years, until his colleagues finally caught up and realized he was right."

Patterson was often recognized as a scientist who did not follow the status quo. This reputation was gained in part by his inclination to challenge the findings of his peers and his disdain for what he calls "ivory-tower scientists." In a 1990 interview with the *Los Angeles Times,* Patterson asserted that science as it is practiced in United States has lost its imagination and creativity. It was this view of progress that prompted novelist Saul Bellow to pattern his disillusioned scientist in *The Dean's December* after Patterson.

Patterson's renegade stature may have originated during World War II when, as a member of the Manhattan Project, he contributed to the development of the atomic bomb by analyzing the uranium isotopes that went into the bombs. He told the *Los Angeles Times* that developing such a destructive force was "the greatest crime that science has committed yet," and that science, which "remains an abstract, beautiful refuge within the mind," is often misguided.

Discovers Dramatic Increase in Lead Levels

Continuing his work with isotopes, Patterson began studying the evolution of the earth's crust from the mantle (an area between the earth's outer crust and its inner core). During this research he discovered that millions of years ago the amount of lead stored in plankton (microscopic plant and animal life) and in ocean sediments was only 1/10th to 1/100th the amount of lead now being introduced into the ocean by rivers. Lead, the end product of the decay of

radioactive minerals, is normally one of the rarest elements in ocean water.

Interested in this dramatic increase in the ocean's lead levels, Patterson set out to measure the amount of lead present in the atmosphere, the polar ice caps, and other oceans to see if they showed similar shifts. In December of 1963, Patterson, Tsaihwa J. Chow of University of California's Scripps Institution of Oceanography, and M. Tatsumoto of the U.S. Geological Survey in Denver reported the results of a study in which they had sampled waters of the Pacific and Atlantic oceans and the Mediterranean sea. The scientists determined that nearly 500,000 tons of lead were annually entering the oceans in the Northern Hemisphere. But more startling than the amount was the fact that quantities of lead this high were apparently a new phenomenon; for centuries the rate had remained at 10,000 tons per year.

To arrive at these estimates, small amounts of a particular form of lead (an isotope called lead 208), called a tracer, were added to lead-free containers. When the container was submerged in the ocean, the water mixed with the tracer lead. Using chemicals, the scientists removed the tracer lead, and from the residue they were able to calculate the proportions of tracer lead to the lead already present in the sea water.

The three geochemists proposed that the increase in lead was the result of automobile exhaust emissions, which introduced small particles of lead oxide into the atmosphere. From the 1930s to the 1960s, the lead content of gasoline increased from near zero to about 175,000 tons a year in the United States alone. Winds carried vehicles' exhaust particles through the atmosphere to the world's rivers and oceans either as dry particles or in the form of rain. Once thought a natural, relatively benign part of the environment, lead was being consumed by humans in hundreds of times the quantities taken in by pre-industrial people, Patterson's studies revealed. These high levels of lead were contributing to damage to bones, kidneys, blood circulation, and brain cells, especially in children. Armed with Patterson's research, environmentalists and scientists successfully lobbied for passage of the Clean Air Act of 1970. Enactment of the legislation reduced lead emissions from cars and trucks by about 96 percent, but Patterson remained concerned about the quantity of lead remaining in the atmosphere, which may continue to affect public health for years to come.

Findings Lead to Changes in Laboratory Procedures

Patterson also determined that biological laboratories are highly contaminated with industrial lead. This finding had wide ramifications because it implied that previous biochemical knowledge was based on studies of biological systems that were grossly contaminated by lead. Patterson believed that knowledge of the biochemistries of natural systems unaffected by lead toxicity probably do not exist.

As a result, Patterson formulated strict and sterile laboratory procedures which since have become standard in the field. To protect his experiments from lead drifting through the air, Patterson pressurized and lined his lab with plastic. Before entering his lab, he washed his hands with distilled water and put on a lab coat and surgical cap.

Patterson, with the help of graduate students, post doctoral fellows, and research associates from all over the United States and the world, has focused on delineating the extent to which industrial lead during the past two centuries has altered natural biogeochemical cycles of lead. They have measured lead in the earth's atmosphere, hydrosphere (the water on earth and in the atmosphere), and ecosystems on both land and water. Patterson's research has demonstrated that the magnitude of global pollution can be determined only after pre-industrial chemical levels are established. To do this, Patterson analyzed lead concentrations in buried skeletal remains of pre-Colombian Southwest Native Americans. The natural level of lead in the remains was found to be about 1/1000th of the average amount of lead in twentieth-century adult Americans.

Patterson's most recent work has involved investigating the factors that encouraged humans to poison the earth's biosphere with lead. To do this, he studied the development of lead technologies and production over the past 10,000 years. In the process he utilized isotopes to determine methods of medieval metallurgy (the science of making and manipulating metals). Another alarming statistic he uncovered was that tuna packed in cans sealed with lead contains 10,000 times more lead than tuna from the pre-industrial era. This study from 1980 also found that lead pollution in United States and its effects on public health have been vastly underestimated.

Based on his study, Patterson proposed that there is a feed-back link (a self-perpetuating mechanism) between the development of engineering technologies and the emergence of social institutions that define a culture. He reports that the geometries of the brains of those who lived in cultures that used metals and alloys for utilitarian purposes appear to be different from those who used lead for artistic purposes.

Despite Patterson's criticism of some scientific institutions' methods and focus, he has received many honors. These include the J. Lawrence Smith medal given by the National Academy of Science in 1975, the V.M. Goldschmidt medal given by the Geochemical Society in 1980, and the Professional Achievement award given by the University of Chicago in 1980.

SELECTED WRITINGS BY PATTERSON:

Books

(Contributor with M. Tatsumoto) *Earth Science and Meteoritics,* edited by J. Geiss and E. D. Golding, Amsterdam: North Holland Publishing, 1963.

Periodicals

(With G. Tilton and M. Inghram) "Age of the Earth," *Science,* 1955, pp. 69–75.
(With M. Tatsumoto) "Concentrations of Common Lead in Some Atlantic and Mediterranean Waters and in Snow," *Nature,* 1963, pp. 350–352.
(With H. Shirahata and J. E. Erickson) "Lead in Ancient Human Bones and its Relevance to Historical Developments of Social Problems with Lead," *Science of the Total Environment,* 1987, pp. 167–200.

SOURCES:

Periodicals

"Earth's Age: 4.6 Billion Years," *Chemical and Engineering News,* November 1953, pp. 4874–4878.
"News Notes," *On Campus,* November 1992.
Newton, Edmund, "Lead Man," *Los Angeles Times,* October 14, 1990.

Other

"Clair Patterson of Caltech Elected to National Academy of Sciences," California Institute of Technology Press Release, May 11, 1987.

—*Sketch by Margaret DiCanio*

Frederick Douglass Patterson
1901-1988
American veterinarian

Founder of the United Negro College Fund (UNCF), Frederick Douglass Patterson was known for his visionary and pioneering efforts in promoting higher education for African American higher education. Under his guidance, the UNCF became the nation's largest independent source of monetary aid to educational institutions that were traditionally African American. Patterson also went on to establish the College Endowment Funding Plan, and he was the founder of the first African American school of veterinary medicine in the United States at Tuskegee Institute. All through his life, Patterson acted on his conviction that education was the best means to achieve African American mobility. For his lifelong efforts in promoting education, Patterson was awarded the Presidential Medal of Freedom, the nation's highest civilian honor, in 1987.

Born to William Ross Patterson and Mamie Lucille (Brooks) Patterson in Washington, D.C., on October 10, 1901, Patterson was named after the African American journalist and antislavery leader, Frederick Douglass. Patterson, who was orphaned at the age of two, was raised in Texas by his sister, Wilhelmina, who was a schoolteacher there. After attending Prairie View State College in Texas from 1915 to 1919, he attended Iowa State College in Ames, Iowa, and received his doctorate in veterinary medicine in 1923. In 1927 he earned his M.S. degree at that same school and later entered Cornell University at Ithaca, New York. He was awarded a Ph.D. in veterinary medicine from Cornell in 1932.

Begins a Teaching Career

Patterson also began teaching as an instructor in veterinary science at Virginia State College in Petersburg, Virginia, while he was still a student. Later, from 1927 to 1928, Patterson was appointed director of agriculture at Virginia State. In 1928 he was invited to join the Tuskegee Normal and Industrial Institute, an organization he remained affiliated with for the next twenty-five years. Patterson held various positions at Tuskegee, including serving as the first head of the school's new veterinary division and later as director of the School of Agriculture. From 1935 to 1953, he served as the Institute's third president, raising the school to new heights of achievement and national recognition. Tuskegee had been founded by Booker T. Washington, a black American educator, who believed that African Americans should receive vocational training. Patterson's ideas went beyond that, and he stressed the importance of both job training as well as the need to develop confident leadership skills. After he retired as president of the Tuskegee Institute in 1953, Patterson remained president emeritus until his death.

The Founding of the United Negro College Fund

In 1943, a few years after he had become president of Tuskegee, Patterson proposed that a group of African American colleges form a consortium to raise funds for their mutual benefit. Called the United Negro College Fund (UNCF), the organization had twenty-seven original members who amassed

an endowment of $765,000. Thirty-five years later, the Fund had grown to include forty-two members with a combined monetary legacy of $42 million. The UNCF provided money for scholarships, staff salaries, library resources, and laboratories, and their motto, "A mind is a terrible thing to waste," became a well-known slogan. In addition to establishing the UNCF, Patterson was also instrumental in creating the College Endowment Funding Plan, which would encourage private businesses to donate funds by matching their gifts with Federal funds.

Patterson also served as president and trustee of the Phelps-Stokes Fund, which worked for the improvement of the status of blacks in Africa and the United States, the welfare of the Native American, and the improvement of low-income housing in New York City. In 1987, Patterson was honored by the White House, along with actor Danny Kaye and composer Meredith Wilson, when former President Ronald Reagan named him a recipient of the Presidential Medal of Freedom for his life's work. When Patterson died of a heart attack on April 26, 1988, at his home in New Rochelle, New York, he was survived by his wife of fifty-three years, Catherine Elizabeth (Moton), and his son, Frederick Patterson.

SELECTED WRITINGS BY PATTERSON:

Books

College Endowment Funding Plan, American Council on Education, 1976.

SOURCES:

Periodicals

New York Times, April 27, 1988, Section D, p. 27.
Washington Post, April 28, 1988, Section D, p. 4.

—*Sketch by Leonard C. Bruno*

Wolfgang Paul
1913-
German physicist

Wolfgang Paul's Nobel Prize-winning research included the invention of an "ion trap" (also known as an "electrical bottle" or "Paul trap") which holds particles in place by means of two electrical plates and a ring-shaped electrode for the purpose of very precise measuring and observation. Paul has been celebrated for his research in the fields of molecular-beam physics, mass spectroscopy, high-energy physics, and radiobiology.

Paul was born in Lorenzkirch, Saxony, Germany, on August 10, 1913. He was the fourth of six children born to Theodor and Elizabeth (Ruppel) Paul. Theodor Paul was professor of pharmaceutical chemistry at the University of Münich and a colleague of the eminent theoretical physicist **Arnold Sommerfeld**. Wolfgang developed an interest in science at an early age and, after graduating from high school, entered the Technical University of Münich in 1932. Two years later he transferred to the Technical University of Berlin, from which he received his diplomate (comparable to a master's degree) in 1937.

Paul then stayed on in Berlin to work on his doctoral degree under Hans Kopfermann, a specialist in nuclear and atomic physics. He was nearly prevented from completing his degree by his induction into the German military at the onset of World War II. His service was cut short, however, when he was allowed to return to graduate school and excused from further military obligations. Paul was granted his Ph.D. in 1939 for a thesis on the properties of the beryllium nucleus.

After completing his doctoral studies, Paul joined his former advisor Kopfermann, who was then at the University of Kiel. The two worked together for sixteen years, moving to the University of Göttingen in 1942, where Paul was appointed assistant professor two years later. He remained at Göttingen until 1952.

Works on Mass Spectrometry and Radiobiology

Paul's earliest research interest at Kiel and Göttingen was mass spectrometry, a technique in which magnetic and electrical fields are used to separate ions of different masses from each other. The devastation caused by Germany's defeat in World War II eventually made a continuation of this line of research impossible, however. It was a difficult time for physicists, with an acute lack of equipment and severe governmental restrictions on the type of research allowed. As a consequence, Paul briefly refocused his studies to the field of radiobiology, where these limitations were not as serious.

Shortly after receiving his Ph.D., Paul had married Liselotte Hirsche. The couple later had four children, two sons and two daughters. Mrs. Paul died in 1977. Paul was later married to Doris Walch, a professor of medieval literature at the University of Bonn.

Paul moved to the University of Bonn in 1952 to become a professor of physics. He remained there for three decades until his retirement in 1983. It was at Bonn that Paul carried out the research for which he is best known and which won him the 1989 Nobel Prize for physics. That research involved the development of methods for focusing the path of ions, and was done with collaborating scientists **Norman Foster Ramsey** of Harvard University, and **Hans Dehmelt** of the University of Washington.

Develops Electric and Magnetic Lenses and Traps

The development of devices that can be used to divert the path of moving particles goes back to the invention of the mass spectrometer by the English physicists, **J. J. Thomson** and **Francis W. Aston** in the first decade of the twentieth century. In the mass spectrometer, a beam of charged particles is deflected as it is forced to travel through a strong magnetic field. The device is used to separate particles of differing masses from each other since those particles are deflected differentially by the magnetic field.

In the 1950s, Paul began to work on modifications of the mass spectrometric principle known as electrical and magnetic lenses. In a lens of this type, electrical and magnetic fields are arranged to focus a beam of particles in much the same way that glass and plastic lenses can focus a beam of light. Paul's electrical and magnetic lenses have become valuable tools in the use of atomic and molecular beams used for the study of the structure and properties of atoms and molecules.

An electrical or magnetic lens is a device for limiting the movement of a particle beam in two directions. The logical extension of this device is to find a way of restricting movement in three dimensions, that is, of stopping the motion of an individual particle and holding it in a suspended state for some period of time. A device of this type is of enormous value to scientists since it makes possible very precise studies of the changes that take place within an individual atom or ion and the changes that occur when energy interacts with that particle.

In the late 1950s, Paul invented such a device. It consists of a ring-shaped electrode placed between two electrical plates. A particle placed within the ring is prevented from moving in any direction by the electrical field that surrounds it. The device has been described as an "electrical bottle" or a "Paul trap." With it, scientists have been able to observe transitions within an atom with far greater precision than had ever been possible before.

In the 1970s, Paul turned his attention to an even more challenging task, the trapping of uncharged particles. Since traditional mass spectrometric and beam focusing methods do not work on uncharged particles, Paul and his associates (including his two sons, Lorenz and Stephan) found variations on the Paul trap to use with such particles.

Paul has become increasingly interested in the study of elementary particles. He was responsible for the construction at Bonn of Germany's first particle accelerator, a 500 million-electron-volt electron synchrotron, and later for the installation of a more powerful 2.5 billion-electron-volt accelerator.

Paul's non-academic affiliations have included serving both as director of the nuclear physics division at CERN, the European Center for Nuclear Research in Geneva, and as executive director of DESY, Germany's national particle accelerator laboratory. In addition to the Nobel Prize, Paul has been awarded the Robert W. Pohl Prize of the German Physical Society and the Gold Medal of the Czech Academy of Sciences.

SELECTED WRITINGS BY PAUL:

Periodicals

"A New Mass Spectrometer without Magnetic Field," *Zeitschrift fur Naturforsch,* 89, 1953, pp. 448–450.
"Production of Elementary Particles in the Laboratory," *Naturwissenschaften,* 46, 1959, pp. 277–283.

SOURCES:

Periodicals

Hall, Nina, "Perfect Timing Wins Belated Nobel Prize for Paul," *New Scientist,* October 21, 1989, p. 29.
Levi, Barbara Goss, "Ramsey, Dehmelt, Paul Win Nobel for Helping to Set High Standards," *Physics Today,* December, 1989, pp. 17–19.
Pool, Robert, "Basic Measurements Lead to Physics Nobel," *Science,* October 20, 1989, pp. 327–328.

—*Sketch by David E. Newton*

Wolfgang Pauli
1900-1958
Austro-Hungarian-born Swiss physicist

Wolfgang Pauli's exclusion, or "Pauli," principle asserted the later-proven existence of the neutrino, a chargeless, massless particle. This discovery led to the Nobel Prize-winning theory of a fourth

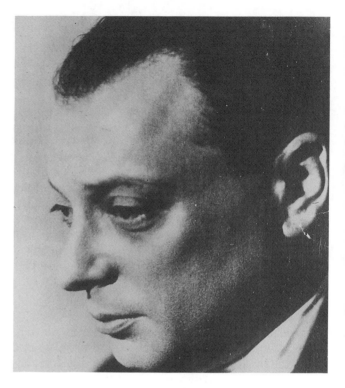

Wolfgang Pauli

quantum number with only two possible values (a quantum number expresses the distinct state of a quantum system). The exclusion principle limits the number of electrons possible in the first level of energy to two, a restriction not previously seen in quantum physics.

Wolfgang Ernst Pauli was born on April 25, 1900, in Vienna, in what was then Austria-Hungary. His father was Wolfgang Joseph Pauli, a medical doctor and biochemist who later became a professor at the University of Vienna. His mother was the former Bertha Schültz, an author. R. E. Peierls reports in *Biographical Memoirs of Fellows of the Royal Society* that Pauli's parents' "background and their acquaintance with the leading authorities in many fields had a profound effect in creating the high standards and the impatience with anything but the best of its kind, which became later an important characteristic of the young Pauli."

Masters Relativity Theory at an Early Age

Pauli was a very bright student who sometimes found Vienna's schools dull and boring. He took to reading advanced treatises on modern physics during his most tedious classes, gaining familiarity with such new and revolutionary concepts as American physicist **Albert Einstein**'s general theory of relativity. In 1918, Pauli graduated from high school in Vienna and entered the University of Münich. He chose Münich because it was the home of German theoretical physicist **Arnold Sommerfeld**, then one of the greatest teachers of theoretical physics alive. Two years into his course of study, Pauli was given a special assignment by Sommerfeld: he was asked to write an entry on the subject of relativity for the forthcoming *Encyclopedia of Mathematical Sciences*. The two-hundred-fifty-page article that Pauli produced was not only a summary of all that was known on the subject but also an analysis of the information. In a letter to Einstein, Sommerfeld described Pauli's work as "simply masterful." A year later, after the shortest time allowed by the university, Pauli was awarded his Ph.D. for a thesis on the hydrogen molecule ion.

When Pauli was a graduate student, the field of physics was in a state of disarray, stumbling towards new perspectives on the nature of matter and energy. The development of quantum mechanics and relativity theory was still encumbered by remnants of classical theory. Pauli made important contributions to the clarification of the nature of modern theory, especially with his enunciation of the exclusion principle. In addition, Pauli tackled a then-troublesome problem in which the emission of electrons during beta decay (a form of radiation) does not appear to obey the law of conservation of energy. To resolve this difficulty, Pauli hypothesized the existence of a chargeless, massless particle later given the name neutrino.

After receiving his degree, Pauli was offered a job as assistant in theoretical physics at the University of Göttingen. There he came into contact not only with English physicist **Max Born**, professor of theoretical physics, but also with Danish physicist **Niels Bohr**, who was guest lecturer at Göttingen in 1922. It was through Bohr's lectures that Pauli began to think about some of the fundamental difficulties that still remained in Bohr's quantum theory of the atom. One of these problems was the existence of various electron energy levels within an atom. Nothing in classical physics could explain the fact that electrons are distributed in various energy levels outside the nucleus, with each energy level having a maximum permitted number of electrons. Bohr had derived such a model from empirical data rather than any theoretical concept, and the fact that the model worked did not detract from questions as to *why* it worked.

Solving the Zeeman Effect Leads to the Exclusion Principle

Over the next three years, Pauli worked on this question. He continued to do so when he went to the University of Copenhagen as Bohr's assistant in 1922 and then to the University of Hamburg as assistant professor of theoretical physics in 1923. At Hamburg, he also began to think about another puzzle in atomic theory, the Zeeman effect. In 1896, the Dutch physicist **Pieter Zeeman** had found that the presence of a strong magnetic field causes the lines of an atomic spectrum to split. More than twenty years later, no one had yet devised an explanation for this phenomenon, but, early in 1925, Pauli found a possible explanation. He suggested that a fourth quantum number—in addition to the three already known—was needed to describe completely the energy state of an electron. In addition to its principle quantum number (n), its azimuthal quantum number (ℓ), and its magnetic quantum number (m), an electron must also have a fourth quantum number, Pauli said. This fourth number could have one of two (but only two) possible values.

At the time, Pauli had no idea as to how this fourth quantum number could be interpreted in physical terms. That problem was solved three years later when Dutch physicists **Samuel Goudsmit** and **George Uhlenbeck** discovered electron spin. Goudsmit and Uhlenbeck suggested that an electron could spin in one of two directions, clockwise or counterclockwise. Their designation of these spins as +½ or -½ corresponded precisely to the two-valuedness of the fourth quantum number that Pauli had predicted.

Proposes the Exclusion Principle

As significant as the discovery of the fourth quantum number was, it was perhaps even more important in terms of what it led to: the exclusion principle. Prompted by a 1924 paper by the English physicist E. D. Stoner, Pauli was able to develop an explanation for the fact that all electrons in an atom do not occupy the lowest energy level. The reason, he said, is that no two electrons can have exactly the same set of quantum numbers. An electron in the first energy level (n = 1) is restricted to an azimuthal quantum number of zero (because ℓ = n - 1) and a magnetic quantum number of 0 (because m = ±ℓ). It can have spin quantum numbers of +½ or -½. These restrictions mean that electrons in the first energy level can have quantum numbers of 1,0,0,+½ or 1,0,0,-½, but no others. Therefore, since the exclusion principle says that there can be no more than one electron of each of these two kinds, only two electrons can occupy that first energy level. By a similar argument, it is possible to show how the second energy level can hold no more than eight electrons, the third level no more than eighteen, and so on. In this way, a theoretical basis is provided for the electron orbital capacities originally devised empirically by Bohr more than a decade earlier.

In 1928, Dutch American chemical physicist **Peter Debye** retired as professor of theoretical physics at the Eidgennössische Technische Hochschule (ETR, or Federal Institute of Technology) in Zürich and Pauli was appointed as his successor. Pauli was to remain at this post until his death, with two brief interruptions. The first came in the academic year 1935–36 when he was visiting professor at the Institute for Advanced Studies in Princeton, New Jersey. The second came five years later when German leader Adolf Hitler's armies had begun to sweep through Europe. Even though he lived in a neutral country, Pauli decided that it would be safer to leave Europe. He traveled back to the Institute for Advanced Studies, where he again held an appointment. Although Pauli returned to Zürich in 1946, he continued to hold a permanent appointment at the Institute and went back for short visits several times.

Pauli Proposes the Existence of the Neutrino

During his first years in Zürich, Pauli turned to another problem troubling physicists: beta decay. According to quantum theory at the time, the loss of a beta particle by a radioactive particle should be accompanied by the loss of a discrete quantity of energy. The spectrum produced by beta decay should, therefore, be characterized by a series of lines. Instead, the spectra associated with beta decay were always continuous spectra. In 1930, Pauli proposed a solution for this dilemma. He suggested that the loss of a beta particle by a nucleus was accompanied by the loss of a second particle. The characteristics of beta decay required that this particle have no electrical charge and no—or almost no—mass. At first, Pauli referred to the particle as a "neutron," a name later given to the chargeless nuclear particle discovered by English physicist **James Chadwick** in 1932. After Chadwick's discovery, American physicist **Enrico Fermi** rechristened Pauli's particle as the "neutrino," or "little neutron." A year later, Fermi had also incorporated the neutrino into an elegant and totally satisfactory mathematical theory of beta decay. Because of the characteristics of this elusive particle, the neutrino itself was not actually discovered for more than two decades after the work of Fermi and Pauli. Shortly before his return to Switzerland in 1945, Pauli was informed of his selection as the winner of the Nobel Prize in physics. After resuming his post in Zürich, he became a Swiss citizen and continued his research on elementary particles.

Pauli was married twice, first to Kate Depner, then to Franciska Bertram on April 4, 1934. There were no children from either marriage. Pauli's work was acknowledged not only by the Nobel Prize but also by the Lorentz Medal of the Royal Dutch Academy of Sciences in 1930, the Franklin Medal of the Franklin Institute in 1952, and the Max Planck Medal of the German Physical Society in 1958. Pauli died unexpectedly in Zürich on December 14, 1958.

SELECTED WRITINGS BY PAULI:

Books

"Relativitätstheorie," *Encyklopädie Mathematische Wissenschaft*, [Leipzig], 1921.

(With C. C. Jung) *Natureklarung und Psyche*, Rasher, 1952.
Collected Scientific Papers, edited by R. Kronig and V. F. Weisskopf, Interscience, 1964.

Periodicals

"Über den Zusammenhang des Abschlusses der Elektron Engruppen im Atom mit der Komplex Struktur der Spektren," *Zeitschrift fur Physik*, Volume 31, 1925, pp. 765–783.
"Zür Älteren und Neuen Geschichte des Neutrinos," *Viert. Naturf. Ges. Zürich*, Volume 102, 1957, pp. 387–388.

SOURCES:

Books

Biographical Memoirs of Fellows of the Royal Society, Volume 5, Royal Society (London), 1959, pp. 175–192.
Current Biography 1946, H. W. Wilson, 1946, pp. 468–470.
Gillispie, Charles Coulson, editor, *Dictionary of Scientific Biography*, Volume 10, Scribner, 1975, pp. 422–425.
McGraw-Hill Modern Scientists and Engineers, Volume 2, McGraw, 1980, pp. 398–399.
Wasson, Tyler, editor, *Nobel Prize Winners*, H. W. Wilson, 1987, pp. 795–798.
Weber, Robert L., *Pioneers of Science: Nobel Prize Winners in Physics*, American Institute of Physics, 1980, pp. 125–126.

—Sketch by David E. Newton

Linus Pauling
1901-1994
American chemist

Linus Pauling is the only person ever to win two unshared Nobel Prizes. His 1954 prize for chemistry was given in recognition of his work on the nature of the chemical bond, while the 1963 Nobel Peace Prize was awarded for his efforts to bring about an end to the atmospheric testing of nuclear weapons. Pauling has made important contributions to a number of fields, including the structure of proteins and

Linus Pauling

Early Interest in Chemistry Leads to Oregon Agricultural College

During his high school years, Pauling continued to pursue his interest in chemistry. He was able to obtain much of the equipment and materials he needed for his experiments from the abandoned Oregon Iron and Steel Company in Oswego. Since his grandfather was a night watchman at a nearby plant, Linus was able to "borrow" the items he needed for his own chemical studies. Pauling would have graduated from Portland's Washington High School in 1917 except for an unexpected turn of events. He had failed to take the necessary courses in American history required for graduation and so did not receive his diploma. The school corrected this error 45 years later when it awarded Pauling his high school diploma—after he had been awarded two Nobel Prizes.

In the fall of 1917, Pauling entered Oregon Agricultural College (OAC), now Oregon State University, in Corvallis. He was eager to pursue his study of science and signed up for a full load of classes. Finances presented a serious problem, however. His mother was unable to send him any money for his expenses and, in fact, Pauling was soon forced to help her pay family bills at home. As a result, Pauling regularly had to work 40 hours or more in addition to studying and attending classes. By the end of his sophomore year, it became apparent that Pauling could not afford to stay in school. He decided to take a year off and help his mother by working in Portland. At the last minute, however, those plans charged. OAC offered him a job teaching quantitative analysis, a course he had completed as a student only a few months earlier. The $100-a-month assignment allowed him to return to OAC and continue his education.

During his last two years at OAC, Pauling learned about the work of **Gilbert Newton Lewis** and **Irving Langmuir** on the electronic structure of atoms and the way atoms combine with each other to form molecules. He became interested in the question of how the physical and chemical properties of substances are related to the structure of the atoms and molecules of which they are composed and decided to make this topic the focus of his own research. An important event during Pauling's senior year occurred when he met Ava Helen Miller, a student in one of his classes. Ava Helen and Linus were married on June 17, 1923, and later had four children: Linus, Jr., born in 1925, Peter Jeffress, born in 1931, Linda Helen, born in 1932, and Edward Crellin, born in 1937.

Pursues Studies at Cal Tech and in Europe

After graduation from OAC in 1922, Pauling entered the California Institute of Technology (Cal Tech) in Pasadena. At the time, Cal Tech was a vigorous, growing institution that served as home to

other biologically important molecules, mineralogy, the nature of mental disorders, nuclear structure, and nutrition.

Linus Carl Pauling was born in Portland, Oregon, on February 28, 1901. He was the first of three children born to Herman Henry William Pauling and Lucy Isabelle (Darling) Pauling, usually called Belle. Herman Pauling was a druggist who struggled continuously to make a decent living for his family. With his business in Portland failing, Herman moved his family to Oswego, seven miles south of Portland, in 1903. He was no more successful in Oswego, however, and moved on to Salem in 1904, to Condon (in northern Oregon) in 1905, and finally back to Portland in 1909. A year later, Herman died of a perforated ulcer, leaving Belle to care for the three young children.

Linus was a precocious child who read every book he could get his hands on. At one point, his father wrote the local paper asking for readers to suggest additional books that would keep his son occupied. Pauling's interest in science was apparently stimulated by his friend Lloyd Jeffress during grammar school. Jeffress kept a small chemistry laboratory in a corner of his bedroom where he performed simple experiments. Pauling was intrigued by these experiments and decided to become a chemical engineer.

some of the leading researchers in chemistry and physics in the nation. Pauling quickly became immersed in a heavy load of classes, seminars, lectures, and original research. He was assigned to work with Roscoe Gilley Dickinson on the X-ray analysis of crystal structure. As a result of this research, his first paper, "The Crystal Structure of Molybdenite," was published in the *Journal of the American Chemical Society* (*JACS*) in 1923. During his remaining years at Cal Tech, Pauling was to publish six more papers on the structure of other minerals.

Pauling was awarded his Ph.D in chemistry *summa cum laude* in 1925 and decided to continue his studies in Europe. He planned to spend time with three leading researchers of the time, **Arnold Sommerfeld** in Munich, **Niels Bohr** in Copenhagen, and **Erwin Schrödinger** in Zurich. Sommerfeld, Bohr, and Schrödinger were all working in the new field of quantum mechanics. The science of quantum mechanics, less than a decade old at the time, was based on the revolutionary concept that particles can sometimes have wave-like properties, and waves can sometimes best be described as if they consisted of massless particles. Pauling had been introduced to quantum mechanics at OAC and was eager to see how this new way of looking at matter and energy could be applied to his own area of interest, the electronic structure of atoms and molecules. After two years in Europe, Pauling was determined to make this subject the focus of his future research. He and Ava Helen left Zurich in the summer of 1927 and returned to Cal Tech, where Pauling took up his new post as Assistant Professor of Theoretical Chemistry.

Pauling's first few years as a professor at the college were a time of transition. He continued to work on the X-ray analysis of crystals, but also began to spend more time on the quantum mechanical study of atoms and molecules. He wrote prolifically, turning out an average of ten papers a year during his first five years at Cal Tech. His reputation grew apace, and he was promoted quickly to associate professor in 1929 and then to full professor a year later. By 1931, the American Chemical Society had awarded Pauling its Langmuir Prize for "the most noteworthy work in pure science done by a man 30 years of age or less."

In the meanwhile, Pauling had spent another summer traveling through Europe in 1930, visiting the laboratories of Laurence Bragg in Manchester, Herman Mark in Ludwigshafen, and Sommerfeld in Munich. In Ludwigshafen, Pauling learned about the use of electron diffraction techniques to analyze crystalline materials. Upon his return to Cal Tech, Pauling showed one of his students, L. O. Brockway, how the technique worked and had him build an electron diffraction instrument. Over the next 25 years, Pauling, Brockway, and their colleagues used the diffraction technique to determine the molecular structure of more than 225 substances.

Work on Chemical Bond Leads to First Nobel Prize

In some ways, the 1930s mark the pinnacle of Pauling's career as a chemist. During that decade he was able to apply the principles of quantum mechanics to solve a number of important problems in chemical theory. The first major paper on this topic, "The Nature of the Chemical Bond: Applications of Results Obtained from the Quantum Mechanics and from a Theory of Paramagnetic Susceptibility to the Structure of Molecules," appeared in the April 6, 1931 issue of *JACS*. That paper was to be followed over the next two years by six more on the same topic and, in 1939, by Pauling's magnum opus, *The Nature of the Chemical Bond, and the Structure of Molecules and Crystals*. The book has been considered one of most important works in the history of chemistry, and the ideas presented in the book and the related papers are the primary basis upon which Pauling was awarded the Nobel Prize for chemistry in 1954.

Pauling's work on the chemical bond proved crucial in understanding three important problems in chemical theory: bond hybridization, bond character, and resonance. Hybridization refers to the process by which electrons undergo a change in character when they form bonds with other atoms. For example, the carbon atom is known to have two distinct kinds of bonding electrons known as 2s and 2p electrons. Traditional theory had assumed, therefore, that carbon would form two types of bonds, one type using 2s electrons and a second type using 2p electrons. Studies had shown, however, that all four bonds formed by a carbon atom are identical to each other. Pauling explained this phenomenon by illustrating that carbon's electrons change their character during bonding. All four assume a new energy configuration that is a hybrid of 2s and 2p energy levels. Pauling called this hybrid an sp^3 energy level.

In a second area, Pauling examined the relationship between two kinds of chemical bonding: ionic bonding, in which electrons are totally gained and lost by atoms, and covalent bonding, in which pairs of electrons are shared equally between atoms. Pauling was able to show that ionic and covalent bonding are only extreme states that exist in relatively few instances. More commonly, atoms bond by sharing electrons in some way that is intermediate between ionic and covalent bonding.

Pauling's third accomplishment involved the problem of the benzene molecule. Until the 1930s, the molecular structures that were being written for benzene did not adequately correspond to the properties of the substance. The German chemist Friedrich Kekulé had proposed a somewhat satisfactory model in 1865 by assuming that benzene could exist in two states and that it shifted back and forth between the two continuously. In his work on the chemical bond,

Pauling suggested another answer. Quantum mechanics showed, he said, that the most stable form of the benzene molecule was neither one of Kekulé's structures, but some intermediate form. This intermediate form could be described as the superposition of the two Kekulé structures formed by the rapid interconversion of one to the other. This "rapid interconversion" was later given the name resonance.

Turns to Research on Biological Molecules

By the mid–1930s, Pauling was looking for new fields to explore. The questions he soon addressed concerned the structure of biological molecules. These molecules are complex substances that are found in living organisms and can contain thousands of atoms in each molecule rather than the relatively simple molecules that Pauling had studied previously that contained only twenty or thirty atoms. This was a surprising choice for Pauling, because earlier in his career he had mentioned that he wasn't interested in studying biological molecules. One reason for his change of heart may have been the changes taking place at Cal Tech itself. In an effort to expand the institution's mission beyond chemistry and physics, its administration had begun to build a new department of biology. Among those recruited for the department were such great names as **Thomas Hunt Morgan**, **Theodosius Dobzhansky**, Calvin Bridges, and Alfred Sterdevant. Pauling's almost daily interaction with these men opened his eyes to a potentially fascinating new field of research.

The first substance that attracted his attention was the hemoglobin molecule. Hemoglobin is the substance that transports oxygen through the bloodstream. Pauling's initial work with hemoglobin, carried out with a graduate student Charles Coryell, produced some fascinating results. Their research showed that the hemoglobin molecule undergoes significant structural change when it picks up or loses an oxygen atom. In order to continue his studies, Pauling decided he needed to know much more about the structure of hemoglobin, in particular, and proteins, in general.

Fortunately, he was already familiar with the primary technique by which this research could be done: X-ray diffraction analysis. The problem was that X-ray diffraction analysis of protein is far more difficult than it is for the crystalline minerals Pauling had earlier worked with. In fact, the only reasonably good X-ray pictures of protein available in the 1930s were those of the British crystallographer, **William Astbury**. Pauling decided, therefore, to see if the principles of quantum mechanics could be applied to Astbury's photographs to obtain the molecular structures of proteins.

The earliest efforts along these lines by Pauling and Coryell in 1937 were unsuccessful. None of the molecular structures they drew based on quantum mechanical principles could account for patterns like those in Astbury's photographs. It was not until eleven years later that Pauling finally realized what the problem was. The mathematical analysis and the models it produced were correct. What was wrong was Astbury's patterns. In the pictures he had taken, protein molecules were tilted slightly from the position they would be expected to have. By the time Pauling had recognized this problem, he had already developed a molecular model for hemoglobin with which he was satisfied. The model was that of a helix, or spiral-staircase-like structure in which a chain of atoms is wrapped around a central axis. Pauling had developed the model by using a research technique on which he frequently depended: model building. He constructed atoms and groups of atoms out of pieces of paper and cardboard and then tried to fit them together in ways that would conform to quantum mechanical principles. Not surprisingly, Pauling's technique was also adopted by two contemporaries, **Francis Crick** and **James Watson**, in their solution of the DNA molecule puzzle, a problem that Pauling himself very nearly solved.

Pauling also turned his attention to other problems of biological molecules. In 1939, for example, he developed the theory of complementarity and applied it the subject of enzyme reactions. He later used the same theory to explain how genes might act as templates for the formation of enzymes. In 1945, Pauling attacked and solved an important medical problem by using chemical theory. He demonstrated that the genetic disorder known as sickle-cell anemia is caused by the change of a single amino acid in the hemoglobin molecule.

Efforts on Behalf of Peace Movement Bring Second Nobel Prize

The 1940s were a decade of significant change in Pauling's life. He had never been especially political and, in fact, had voted in only one presidential election prior to World War II. But he rather quickly began to immerse himself in political issues. One important factor in this change was the influence of his wife, Ava Helen, who had long been active in a number of social and political causes. Another factor was probably the war itself. As a result of his own wartime research on explosions, Pauling became more concerned about the potential destructiveness of future wars. As a result, he decided while on a 1947 boat trip to Europe that he would raise the issue of world peace in every speech he made in the future, no matter what topic.

From that point on, Pauling's interests gradually shifted from scientific to political topics. He devoted more time to speaking out on political issues, and the majority of his published papers dealt with political rather than scientific topics. In 1958 he published his views on the military threat facing the world in his book *No More War!*. Pauling's views annoyed many of his scientific colleagues, fellow citizens, and many legislators. In 1952 he was denied a passport to attend an important scientific meeting in London, and in 1960 he was called before the Internal Security Committee of the United States Senate to explain his antiwar activities. Neither professional nor popular disapproval could sway Pauling's commitment to the peace movement, however, and he and Ava Helen continued to write, speak, circulate petitions, and organize conferences against the world's continuing militarism. In recognition of these efforts, Pauling was awarded the 1963 Nobel Prize for Peace.

Studies of Vitamin C Provoke Controversy

At the age of 65, when many men and women look forward to retirement, Linus Pauling had found a new field of interest: the possible therapeutic effects of vitamin C. Pauling was introduced to the potential value of vitamin C in preventing colds by biochemist Irwin Stone in 1966. He soon became intensely interested in the topic and summarized his views in a 1970 book, *Vitamin C and The Common Cold*. Before long, he became convinced that the vitamin was also helpful in preventing cancer.

Pauling's views on vitamin C have received relatively modest support in the scientific community. Many colleagues tend to feel that the evidence supporting the therapeutic effects of vitamin C is weak or nonexistent, though research on the topic continues. Other scientists are more convinced by Pauling's argument, and he is regarded by some as the founder of the science of orthomolecular medicine, a field based on the concept that substances normally present in the body (such as vitamin C) can be used to prevent disease and illness.

Pauling's long association with Cal Tech ended in 1964, at least partly because of his active work in the peace movement. He accepted an appointment at the Study of Democratic Institutions in Santa Barbara for four years and then moved on to the University of California at San Diego for two more. In 1969 he moved to Stanford University where he remained until his compulsory retirement in 1974. In that year, he and some colleagues and friends founded the Institute of Orthomolecular Medicine, later to be renamed the Linus Pauling Institute of Science and Medicine, in Palo Alto.

Pauling died of cancer at his ranch in the Big Sur area of California on August 19, 1994. He was 93 years old.

SELECTED WRITINGS BY PAULING:

Books

The Nature of the Chemical Bond, and the Structure of Molecules and Crystals, Cornell University Press, 1939.
General Chemistry, California Institute of Technology, 1941.
College Chemistry, W. H. Freeman, 1950.
No More War!, Dodd, Mead & Company, 1958.
Vitamin C and the Common Cold, W. H. Freeman, 1970.
Vitamin C, the Common Cold, and the Flu, W. H. Freeman, 1976.
(With Ewan Cameron) *Cancer and Vitamin C,* Linus Pauling Institute of Science and Medicine, 1979.
How to Live Longer and Feel Better, W. H. Freeman, 1986.

Periodicals

"The Social Responsibilities of Scientists and Science," *The Science Teacher,* May, 1966, pp. 14–18.
"Fifty Years of Progress in Structural Chemistry and Molecular Biology," *Daedalus,* fall, 1970, pp. 988–1014.
"Chemistry and the World of Tomorrow," *Chemical & Engineering News,* April 16, 1984, pp. 54–56.
"Why Modern Chemistry is Quantum Chemistry," *New Scientist,* November 7, 1985, pp. 54–55.

SOURCES:

Books

Goodell, Rae, *The Visible Scientists,* Little, Brown, 1977.
Gray, Tony, *Champions of Peace,* Paddington Press, 1976.
Judson, Horace Freeland, *The Eighth Day of Creation,* Simon and Schuster, 1979.
"Linus Pauling," *Current Biography 1949,* H. W. Wilson, 1949, pp. 473–475.
"Linus Pauling," *Current Biography 1964,* H. W. Wilson, 1964, pp. 339–342.
Newton, David E., *Linus Pauling,* Facts on File, 1994.
Olby, Robert, *The Path to the Double Helix,* University of Washington Press, 1974.
Serafini, Anthony, *Linus Pauling: A Man and His Science,* Paragon House, 1989.
White, Florence Meiman, *Linus Pauling: Scientist and Crusader,* Walker & Co., 1980.

Periodicals

Campbell, Neil A., "Crossing the Boundaries of Science," *BioScience,* December, 1986, pp. 737–739.

Fry, William F., Jr., "What's New with You, Linus Pauling?" *The Humanist,* November/December, 1974, pp. 16–19.

Goertzel, Ted G., Mildred George Goertzel, and Victor Goertzel, "Linus Pauling: The Scientist as Crusader," *Antioch Review,* summer, 1980, pp. 371–382.

Goodstein, Judith R., "Atoms, Molecules, and Linus Pauling," *Social Research,* autumn, 1984, pp. 691–708.

Grosser, Morton, "Linus Pauling: Molecular Artist," *Saturday Evening Post,* fall, 1971, pp. 147–149.

Hogan, John, "Profile: Linus C. Pauling," *Scientific American,* March, 1993, p. 36.

"Interview: Linus Pauling," *Omni,* December, 1986, pp. 102–110.

"The Plowboy Interview: Dr. Linus Pauling," *Mother Earth News,* January/February, 1978, pp. 17–22.

Pogash, Carol, "The Great Gadfly," *Science Digest,* June, 1981, pp. 88–91.

Ridgway, David, "Interview with Linus Pauling," *Journal of Chemical Education,* August, 1976, pp. 471–476.

—*Sketch by David E. Newton*

Ivan Petrovich Pavlov
1849-1936
Russian physiologist

Ivan Petrovich Pavlov was a Russian physiologist whose research on mammalian digestion earned him the Nobel Prize and whose research on conditioned reflexes brought him international recognition. The colloquial expression "Pavlov's dog" refers to Pavlov's famous experiments in which he taught a dog to salivate at the sound of a bell by associating the bell with feeding. This research helped spawn a physiologically-oriented school of psychology that focused on the influence of conditioned reflexes on learning and behavior. Because of his contribution to the fields of psychology and physiology, Pavlov became one of Russia's most revered scientists in his day and was even tolerated by the communist Soviet regime, of which he was openly critical.

Ivan Petrovich Pavlov

Pavlov was born in Ryazan, Central Russia, on September 26, 1849. His father, Pyotr Dmitrievich Pavlov, was a priest who rose through the ranks and eventually headed one of the most influential parishes in the area. A devoted reader and scholar, Pyotr taught his son at an early age to read all worthwhile books at least twice so that he would understand them better—a bit of fatherly advice that helped shape Pavlov's intense dedication to his work. Pavlov's mother, Varvara Ivanova, also came from a family of clergy and had ten children after Pavlov, six of whom died in childhood.

The family expected the young Pavlov to follow the family tradition of entering the clergy. Thus, Pavlov attended Ryazan Ecclesiastical High School and the Ryazan Ecclesiastical Seminary. During his studies at the seminary, Pavlov became seriously interested in science, physiology in particular, and was greatly influenced by a radical philosopher named Dmitri Pisarev who espoused many of evolutionist Charles Darwin's theories.

In 1870 when the government decreed that divinity students could attend nonsectarian universities, Pavlov decided to leave the seminary and attend St. Petersburg University to study the natural sciences. At St. Petersburg, Élie de Zion, a professor of physiology, made a formidable impression on Pavlov. By all accounts the two scientists had a mutual admiration for one another. According to Boris Babkin in his book *Pavlov: A Biography,* Pavlov said of his early mentor, "Never can such a teacher be forgotten," and in turn Zion called Pavlov a "skilled surgical operator."

Upon graduation from St. Petersburg University in 1875, Pavlov followed Zion to the Military Medical Academy in St. Petersburg, where Zion had been appointed chair of physiology. Pavlov became an assistant in Zion's laboratory and worked toward his medical degree. But Zion was soon dismissed because he was Jewish, and Pavlov, intolerant of his mentor's dismissal, left the Medical Academy in favor of the Veterinary Institute where he spent the next two years studying digestion and circulation. In 1877 Pavlov traveled to Breslau, Germany (later Poland), to study with Rudolf Heidenhain, a specialist in digestion. After receiving his medical degree from the Military Medical Academy in 1879, Pavlov went on to earn his postdoctoral degree and was honored with a Gold Medal for his doctoral dissertation in 1883.

Upon graduation, Pavlov was one of ten students awarded a government scholarship for postgraduate studies abroad. Thus, Pavlov returned to Germany to work with Carl Ludwig on cardiovascular physiology and blood circulation; he also collaborated with Heidenhain again on further digestion research. Another mentor, Sergei Botkin, eventually asked Pavlov to direct an experimental physiological laboratory. This lab, devoted to the school of "scientific medicine," focused on the physiological and pathological relations in an organism. Under Botkin's guidance, Pavlov first developed his interest in "nervism," the pathological influence of the central nervous system on reflexes.

Awarded Nobel Prize for Digestion Research

Pavlov returned to St. Petersburg University and began his exhaustive research on digestion which eventually gained him worldwide recognition in scientific circles. Focusing on the physiology of digestion and gland secretions, Pavlov devised an ingenious experiment in which he severed a dog's gullet, forcing the food to drop out before it reached the animal's stomach. Through this sham feeding, he was able to show that the sight, smell, and swallowing of food was enough to cause secretion of the digestive acidic "juices." He demonstrated that stimulation of the vagus nerve (one of the major cranial nerves of the brain) influences secretions of the gastric glands. In 1904 Pavlov received the Nobel Prize for Medicine or Physiology for these pioneering studies on the physiology of the digestive system.

Pavlov's work on blood circulation earned him a professorship at the Military Medical Academy. In 1895 Pavlov became the chairman of the physiology department at the St. Petersburg Institute for Experimental Medicine, where he spent the greater part of his remaining career. Ironically, by the time Pavlov received the Nobel Prize, his work delineating the central nervous system's effects on digestive physiology was soon to be overshadowed by subsequent investigations by **William Bayliss** and others, who demonstrated that chemical (hormone) stimulation induces digestive secretions from the pancreas. Ever curious, Pavlov himself conducted experiments that also confirmed this discovery.

Although Pavlov's "nervism" theory was relegated to secondary importance in the study of digestion, his experiments profoundly influenced biological research. Pavlov strongly believed that a healthy laboratory animal subject free from disease and the influence of pharmaceuticals was imperative to his work. "It has become abundantly clear that the usual simple cutting of an animal, the so-called acute test, is a source of many errors," Pavlov said, as noted by Alexander Vucinich in his book *Science in Russian Culture*. Among the laboratory techniques advanced by Pavlov were the use of aseptic surgical procedures on laboratory animals and the development of chronic, or long-lasting, experiments on the same animal. Pavlov believed in minimizing an animal's pain for both moral and scientific reasons and led the way for the humane treatment of laboratory animals.

Pavlov's Dog Becomes Conditioned

Ironically, Pavlov's most famous studies were conducted after he received the Nobel Prize. Concentrating on the neural influences of digestion, Pavlov set out to determine whether he could turn normally "unconditioned" reflexes or responses of the central nervous system into conditioned reflexes. Pavlov noticed that the laboratory dogs would sometimes salivate merely at the approach of lab assistants who often fed them. Through careful repeated experiments, Pavlov demonstrated that if a bell is rung each time a dog is given food, the dog eventually develops a "conditioned" reflex to salivate at the sound of the bell, even when food is not present. Thus, Pavlov showed that the unconditioned reflexes—gastric activity and salivation—could become conditioned responses triggered by a stimulus (the bell) not previously associated with the physiological event (eating).

Pavlov traced this phenomenon to the cerebral cortex and continued to study the brain's role in conditioned reflexes for the remainder of his life. Although this research led to a proliferation of studies of conditioned reflexes in physiology, the conditioned reflex theory became a popular subject in the fields of psychiatry, psychology, and education.

Pavlovian psychology contends that a person's behavioral development and learning are profoundly affected by conditioned nervous responses to life events, similar to the dog's learned response to the bell. This behavioral theory created a schism in the field of psychology, with Pavlovian psychologists opposing the views of Sigmund Freud, who theorized that an individual's thought processes—especially the unconscious—were the driving forces of human behavior. Eventually, Freudian psychology usurped Pavlovian psychology in popularity to become the primary approach to mental health treatment outside of Russia. But Pavlov maintained his devotion to the importance of conditioned reflexes in human behavior, believing that human language was probably the most intricate example of such conditioning. Pavlov also applied his theory to the treatment of psychiatric patients in which he placed patients in a quiet and isolated environment in order to remove any possible physiological or psychological stimuli that might negatively affect their mental health.

Pavlov Outspoken on Communist Regime

Pavlov's life spanned three distinct Russian political eras, which sometimes intruded upon his personal and professional life. He was born during the reign of Czar Nicholas I, an oppressive feudal monarch who sought to retain aristocratic rule at any price. Pavlov saw this oppressive regime give way to a new ideology of reform, known as post-Emancipation Russia, which heralded technological advancements but was mired in turmoil on both the social and political level. Shortly after the Bolshevik Revolution in 1917 which attempted to impose a socialist structure on society, Pavlov became a staunch and vocal opponent of the new and often hostile regime. Years earlier, Pavlov had shown a willingness to oppose authority when he resigned from the Medical Military Academy to protest the dismissal of his mentor, Zion, because he was Jewish.

By the time of the Bolshevik Revolution, Pavlov had achieved international recognition and was living a comfortable life. He had overcome the extreme economic hardships he faced early in his career when he had struggled to support his growing family on the meager salary of a lab assistant. In 1881 he married Seraphima Vasilievna Karchevskaya, a naval doctor's daughter and friend of Russian novelist Fyodor Dostoevsky. They eventually had four sons and a daughter.

Pavlov's legendary self-discipline and devotion to his work, however, often led him to disregard opportunities for advancement. His feud with the military academy over Zion's dismissal also hindered his career. So consumed was Pavlov with his scientific investigations that he once bought dogs for his experiments with money students had collected for him to give special lectures. Pavlov's wife had difficulty impressing upon her husband the severity of the family's needs. When she complained of his unwillingness to seek a higher position, he told her that their lack of money was nothing compared to the tragic deaths of his butterflies.

Despite these hardships, Pavlov was willing to risk his hard-earned success by opposing the new communist regime. His religious background caused him to become enraged when all clergymen's sons were expelled from the Medical Academy, and in 1924 he resigned from the Medical Academy as the chair of physiology in protest. The new Soviet government, however, was intent on accommodating a person they considered to be a shining example of Russian science, who, in addition to the Nobel Prize, had been awarded the Order of the Legion of Honor of France and the Copley Medal of the Royal Society of London. Vladimir Lenin, who emerged as the most powerful leader of the revolution, signed a decree guaranteeing Pavlov's personal freedom and his right to continue his research and even to attend church. These special privileges were in stark contrast to countless other scientists whose work was suppressed by the government. Pavlov, however, continued to speak out, once refusing extra rations of food unless all his laboratory assistants received the same privileges.

The rulers in the new Soviet republic believed that Pavlov's work with conditioned reflexes could be adapted for political purposes. For example, they hypothesized that the masses could be conditioned just as Pavlov had conditioned the dog. In a sense, they saw the opportunity to develop a type of mass mind control in which the Soviet system would appear to have complete power, even over those who were originally reluctant to follow the communist way. To appease their favorite scientist, in 1935 the government built Pavlov a spacious laboratory equipped with the latest scientific technology which the scientist called "the capitol of conditioned reflexes."

Although Pavlov was known in the last five years of his life to publicly praise the government for their efforts to foster education and science, he repeatedly denounced the Soviet "social experiment." He died of pneumonia on February 27, 1936, in Leningrad. While some of Pavlov's early research has not stood the test of time and further scientific inquiry, he remains one of the fathers of modern science whose observations provided a basis from which much scientific knowledge arose in the twentieth century.

SELECTED WRITINGS BY PAVLOV:

Books

Lectures on Conditioned Reflexes, International, 1928.
Conditioned Reflexes: An Investigation of the Physiological Activity of the Cerebral Cortex, Dover, 1960.

SOURCES:

Books

Babkin, Boris P., *Pavlov: A Biography,* University of Chicago Press, 1949.

The Great Scientists, Grolier Educational Corporation, 1989, pp. 186–191.

Vucinich, Alexander, *Science in Russian Culture,* Stanford University Press, 1963, pp. 301.

Wells, Harry K., *Ivan P. Pavlov: Toward a Psychology and Psychiatry,* International, 1956.

—Sketch by David Petechuk

Cecilia Payne-Gaposchkin
1900-1979

English-born American astronomer

Cecilia Payne-Gaposchkin was a pioneer in the field of astronomy and one of the most eminent female astronomers of the twentieth century. She was the first to apply the laws of atomic physics to the study of the temperature and density of stellar bodies and to conclude that hydrogen and helium, the two lightest elements, were also the two most common elements in the universe. Her revelation that hydrogen, the simplest of the known elements, was the most abundant substance in the universe has since become the basis for analysis of the cosmos. Yet she is not officially credited with the discovery, made when she was a 25-year-old doctoral candidate at Harvard, because her conservative male superiors convinced her to retract her findings on stellar hydrogen and publish a far less definitive statement. While she is perhaps best known for her later work in identifying and measuring variable stars with her husband, Sergei I. Gaposchkin, Payne-Gaposchkin helped forge a path for other women in the sciences through her staunch fight against sexual discrimination at Harvard College Observatory, where she eventually became the first woman appointed to full professor and the first woman named chairman of a department that was not specifically designated for a woman.

Cecilia Helena Payne was born on May 10, 1900, in Wendover, England, the eldest of three children born to Edward John and Emma Leonora Helena (Pertz) Payne of Coblenz, Prussia. Her father, a London barrister, died when she was four years old. Her mother, a painter and musician, introduced her to the classics, of which she remained fond throughout her life. Payne-Gaposchkin recalled that Homer's *Odyssey* was the first book her mother read to her as a child. She knew Latin by the time she was 12 years old, became fluent in French and German, and showed an early interest in botany and algebra. As a schoolgirl in London she was influenced by the works of Isaac Newton, Thomas Huxley, and Emmanuel Swedenborg.

In 1919 she won a scholarship to Newnham College at Cambridge University, where she studied botany, chemistry, and physics. During her studies there, she became fascinated with astronomy after attending a lecture on **Albert Einstein**'s theory of relativity given by Sir **Arthur Eddington**, the university's foremost astronomer. Upon completion of her studies in 1923 (at that time women were not granted degrees at Cambridge), Payne-Gaposchkin sought and obtained a Pickering Fellowship (an award for female students) from Harvard to study under **Harlow Shapley**, the newly appointed director of the Harvard Observatory. Thus, Payne-Gaposchkin embarked for the United States, hoping to find better opportunities as a woman in astronomy. Harvard Observatory in Boston, Massachusetts, became her home for the rest of her career—a "stony-hearted stepmother," she was said to have called it.

Harvard: A Stony-Hearted Stepmother

Payne-Gaposchkin's career at Harvard began in 1925, when she was given an ambiguous staff position at the Harvard Observatory. By that time she had already published six papers on her research in the field of stellar atmospheres. That same year, she was awarded the first-ever Ph.D. in astronomy at Radcliffe. Her doctoral dissertation, *Stellar Atmospheres,* was published as Monograph No. 1 of the Harvard Observatory. A pioneering work in the field, it was the first paper written on the subject and was the first research to apply Indian physicist Meghnad Saha's recent theory of ionization (the process by which particles become electrically charged by gaining or losing electrons) to the science of measuring the temperature and chemical density of stars. However, she was discouraged in her views and was convinced to alter them by **Henry Norris Russell**, a renowned astronomer at Princeton who several years later reached her same conclusions and published them, thereby receiving credit for their origin. Despite this, Payne-Gaposchkin's research remains highly regarded today; Otto Struve, a notable astronomer of the period, was quoted in *Mercury* magazine as saying that *Stellar Atmospheres* was "undoubtedly the most brilliant Ph.D. thesis ever written in astronomy."

In 1926 when she was 26 years old, she became the youngest scientist to be listed in *American Men of Science.* But her position at Harvard Observatory remained unacknowledged and unofficial. It was not until 1938 that her work as a lecturer and researcher was recognized and she was granted the title of astronomer, which she later requested to be changed to Phillips Astronomer. From 1925 until 1938 she was considered a technical assistant to Shapley, and none of the courses she taught were listed in the Harvard catalogue until 1945. Finally, in 1956 when her colleague Donald Menzel replaced Shapley as director of the Harvard Observatory, Payne-Gaposchkin was "promoted" to professor, given an appropriate salary, and named chairman of the Department of Astronomy—the first woman to hold a position at Harvard University that was not expressly designated for a woman.

Payne-Gaposchkin's years at Harvard remained productive despite her scant recognition. She was a tireless researcher with a prodigious memory and an encyclopedic knowledge of science. She devoted a large part of her research to the study of stellar magnitudes and distances. Following her 1934 marriage to Gaposchkin, a Russian emigre astronomer, the couple pioneered research into variable stars (stars whose luminosity fluctuates), including research on the structure of the Milky Way and the nearby galaxies known as the Magellanic Clouds. Through their studies they made over two million magnitude estimates of the variable stars in the Magellanic Clouds.

From the 1920s until Payne-Gaposchkin's death on December 7, 1979, she published over 150 papers and several monographs, including "The Stars of High Luminosity" (1930), a virtual encyclopedia of astrophysics, and *Variable Stars* (1938), a standard reference book of astronomy written with her husband. She also published four books in the 1950s on the subject of stars and stellar evolution. Moreover, though she retired from her academic post at Harvard in 1966, becoming Emeritus Professor of Harvard University the following year, she continued to write and conduct research until her death. Her autobiography, writings collected after her death by her daughter, Katherine Haramundanis, was entitled *Cecilia Payne-Gaposchkin: An Autobiography and Other Recollections* and was published in 1984.

Payne-Gaposchkin was elected to the Royal Astronomical Society while she was a student at Cambridge in 1923, and the following year she was granted membership in the American Astronomical Society. She became a citizen of the United States in 1931. She and her husband had three children: Edward, born in 1935, Katherine, born in 1937, and Peter, born in 1940—a noted programmer analyst and physicist in his own right. In 1934 Payne-Gaposchkin received the Annie J. Cannon Prize for significant contributions to astronomy from the American Astronomical Society. In 1936 she was elected to membership in the American Philosophical Society. Among her honorary degrees and medals, awarded in recognition of her contributions to sci-

ence, are honorary doctorates of science from Wilson College (1942), Smith College (1943), Western College (1951), Colby College (1958), and Women's Medical College of Philadelphia (1961), as well as an honorary master of arts and doctorate of science from Cambridge University, England (1952). She won the Award of Merit from Radcliffe College in 1952, the Rittenhouse Medal of the Franklin Institute in 1961, and was the first woman to receive the Henry Norris Russell Prize of the American Astronomical Society in 1976. In 1977 the minor planet 1974 CA was named Payne-Gaposchkin in her honor.

Payne-Gaposchkin is remembered as a woman of boundless enthusiasm who refused to give up her career at a time when married women with children were expected to do so; she once shocked her superiors by giving a lecture when she was five months pregnant. Jesse Greenstein, astronomer at the California Institute of Technology and friend of Payne-Gaposchkin, recalled in *The Sciences* magazine that "she was charming and humorous," a person given to quoting Shakespeare, T.S. Eliot, and Gilbert and Sullivan. Her daughter remembers her in the autobiography *Cecilia Payne-Gaposchkin* as a "world traveler,... an inspired seamstress, an inventive knitter and a voracious reader." Quoted in *Sky and Telescope,* Payne-Gaposchkin revealed that nothing compares to "the emotional thrill of being the first person in the history of the world to see something or to understand something."

SELECTED WRITINGS BY PAYNE-GAPOSCHKIN:

Books

Stellar Atmospheres, W. Heffer & Sons, 1925.
The Stars of High Luminosity, McGraw-Hill, 1930.
(With S. Gaposchkin) *Variable Stars,* Harvard Observatory Monograph No. 5, 1938.
Stars in the Making, Harvard University Press, 1952.
Introduction to Astronomy, Prentice-Hall, 1954; second edition, 1970.
The Galactic Novae, Interscience, 1957.
Stars and Clusters, Harvard University Press, 1979.
Cecilia Payne-Gaposchkin: An Autobiography and Other Recollections, edited by Katherine Haramundanis, Cambridge University Press, 1984.

Periodicals

"Stellar Evolution," *Science Monthly,* May 1926, p. 419.

(With H.N. Russell and D.H. Menzel) "The Classification of Stellar Spectra," *Astrophysical Journal,* 1935, pp. 107–108.

"New Stars," *Telescope,* no. 4, 1937, pp. 100–106.

"The Topography of the Universe," *Telescope,* no. 8, 1941, pp. 112–114.

"Interesting Variable Stars," *Popular Astronomy,* no. 49, 1941, pp. 311–319.

"Problems of Stellar Evolution," *Sky and Telescope,* Volume 2, no. 9, 1943, pp. 5–7.

"Variable Stars and Galactic Structure," *Nature,* no. 170, 1952, pp. 223–5.

"Myth and Science," *Journal for the History of Science,* Volume 3, 1972, pp. 206–211.

"Fifty Years of Novae," *Astronomical Journal,* no. 82, 1977, pp. 665–673.

"The Development of Our Knowledge of Variable Stars," *Annual Review of Astronomy and Astrophysics,* no. 16, 1978, pp. 1–13.

SOURCES:

Books

Abir-Am, P. and D. Outram, editors, *Uneasy Careers and Intimate Lives: Women in Science 1789–1979,* Rutgers University Press, 1987.

Kass-Simon, G. and Patricia Farnes, editors, *Women of Science: Righting the Record,* Indiana University Press, 1990.

Periodicals

Bartusiak, Marcia, "The Stuff of Stars," *The Sciences,* September/October, 1993, pp. 34–39.

Dobson, Andrea K. and Katherine Bracher, "A Historical Introduction to Women in Astronomy," *Mercury,* January/February 1992, pp. 4–15.

Lankford, John, "Explicating an Autobiography," *Isis,* March 1985, pp. 80–83.

Lankford, John and Ricky L. Slavings, "Gender and Science: Women in American Astronomy, 1859–1940," *Physics Today,* March 1990, pp. 58–65.

Smith, E., "Cecilia Payne-Gaposchkin," *Physics Today,* June 1980, pp. 64–66.

Whitney, C., "Cecilia Payne-Gaposchkin: An Astronomer's Astronomer," *Sky and Telescope,* March 1980, page 212–214.

—Sketch by Mindi Dickstein

Giuseppe Peano
1858-1932
Italian mathematician

Giuseppe Peano served most of his adult life as professor of mathematics at the University of Turin. His name is probably best known today for the contributions he made to the development of symbolic logic. Indeed, many of the symbols that he introduced in his research on logic are still used in the science today. In Peano's own judgment, his most important work was in infinitesimal calculus, which he modestly described as "not . . . entirely useless." Some of Peano's most intriguing work involved the development of cases that ran counter to existing theorems, axioms, and concepts in mathematics.

Peano was born in Spinetta, near the city of Cuneo, Italy, on August 27, 1858. He was the second of five children born to Bartolomeo Peano and the former Rosa Cavallo. At the time of Peano's birth, his family lived on a farm about three miles from Cuneo, a distance that he and his brother Michele walked each day to and from school. Sometime later, the family moved to Cuneo to reduce the boys' travel time.

At the age of twelve or thirteen, Peano moved to Turin, some fifty miles south of Cuneo, to study with his uncle, Michele Cavallo. Three years later he passed the entrance examination to the Cavour School in Turin, graduating in 1876. He then enrolled at the University of Turin and began an intensive study of mathematics. On July 16, 1880, he passed his final examinations with high honors and was offered a job as assistant to Enrico D'Ovidio, professor of mathematics at Turin. A year later he began an eight-year apprenticeship with another mathematics professor, Angelo Genocchi.

Writes "Genocchi's" Textbook on Calculus

Peano's relationship with Genocchi involved one somewhat unusual feature. In 1883 the publishing firm of Bocca Brothers expressed an interest in having a new calculus text written by the famous Genocchi. They expressed this wish to Peano, who passed it on to his master in a letter of June 7, 1883. Peano noted to Genocchi that he would understand if the great man were not interested in writing the book himself and, should that be the case, Peano would complete the work for him using Genocchi's own lecture notes and listing Genocchi as author.

In fact, that was just Genocchi's wish. A little more than a year later, the book was published, written by Peano but carrying Genocchi's name as author. Until the full story was known, however, many of Genocchi's colleagues were convinced that Peano had used his master's name to advance his own reputation. As others became aware of Peano's contribution to the book, his own fame began to rise.

Peano's first original publications in 1881 and 1882 included an important work on the integrability of functions. He showed that any first-order differential equation of the form $y' = f(x, y)$ can be solved provided only that f is continuous. Some of these early works also included examples of a type of problem of which Peano was to become particularly fond, examples that contradicted widely accepted and fundamental mathematical statements. The most famous of these, published in 1890, was his work on the space-filling curve.

Derives the Space-Filling Curve

At the time, it was commonly believed that a curve defined by a parametric function would always be limited to an arbitrarily small region. Peano showed, however, that the two continuous parametric functions $x = x(t)$ and $y = y(t)$ could be written in such a way that as t varies through a given interval, the graph of the curve covers every point within a given area. Peano's biographer Hubert Kennedy points out that Peano "was so proud of this discovery that he had one of the curves in the sequence put on the terrace of his home, in black tiles on white."

Peano's first paper on symbolic logic was an article published in 1888 in which he continued and extended the work of George Boole, the founder of the subject, and other pioneers such as Ernst Schröder, H. McColl, and C. S. Peirce. His magnum opus on logic was written about a year later. In it Peano suggested a number of new notations including the familiar symbol $\in$ to represent the members of a set. He wrote in the preface to this work that progress in mathematics was hampered by the "ambiguity of ordinary language." It would be his goal, he said, to indicate "by signs all the ideas which occur in the fundamentals of arithmetic, so that every proposition is stated with just these signs." In succeeding pages, then, we find the introduction of now familiar symbols such as $\cap$ for "and," $\cup$ for "or," $\supset$ for "one deduces that," $\exists$ for "such that," and Π for "is prime with." Also included in this book, *Arithmetices principia, nova methodo exposita* (*The Principles of Arithmetic, Presented by a New Method*), were Peano's postulates for the natural numbers, an accomplishment that Kennedy calls "perhaps the best known of all his creations."

In 1891 Peano founded the journal *Rivista di matematica* (*Review of Mathematics*) as an outlet for his own work and that of others; he edited the journal until its demise in 1906. He also announced in 1892 the publication of a journal called *Formulario* with the ambitious goal of bringing together all known theorems in all fields of mathematics. Five editions of *Formulario* listing a total of forty-two hundred theorems were published between 1895 and 1908.

By 1900 Peano had become interested in quite another topic, the development of an international language. He saw the need for the creation of an "interlingua" through which people of all nations—especially scientists—would be able to communicate. He conceived of the new language as being the successor of the classical Latin in which pre-Renaissance scholars had corresponded, a *latino sine flexione,* or "Latin without grammar." He wrote a number of books on the subject, including *Vocabulario commune ad latino-italiano-français-english-deutsch* in 1915, and served as president of the Akademi Internasional de Lingu Universal from 1908 until 1932.

While still working as Genocchi's assistant, Peano was appointed professor of mathematics at the Turin Military Academy in 1886. Four years later he was also chosen to be extraordinary professor of infinitesimal calculus at the University of Turin. In 1895 he was promoted to ordinary professor. In 1901 he resigned his post at the Military Academy, but continued to hold his chair at the university until his death of a heart attack on April 20, 1932.

Peano had been married to Carla Crosio on July 21, 1887. She was the daughter of the painter Luigi Crosio and was particularly fond of the opera. Kennedy points out that the Peanos were regular visitors to the Royal Theater of Turin where they saw the premier performances of Puccini's *Manon Lescaut* and *La Bohème.* The couple had no children. Included among Peano's honors were election to a number of scientific societies and selection as knight of the Crown of Italy and of the Orders of Saints Maurizio and Lazzaro.

SELECTED WRITINGS BY PEANO:

Books

(Ghostwriter) Angelo Genocchi, *Calcolo differenziale e principii di calcolo integrale, pubblicato con aggiante dal Dr. Giuseppe Peano,* Bocca, 1884.

Calcolo geometrico secondo l'Ausdehnungslehre di H. Grassmann, preceduto dalle operazioni della logica deduttiva, Bocca, 1888.

Arithmetices principia, nova methodo exposita, Bocca, 1889.

Gli elementi di calcolo geometrico, Candeletti, 1891.

Lezioni di analisi infinitesimale, Candeletti, 1893.

Notations de logique mathématique, Guadagnini, 1894.

Vocabulario commune ad linguas de Europa, Bocca, 1909.

Fundamento de Esperanto, Cavoretto, 1914.

Vocabulario commune ad latino-italiano-français-english-deutsch, Academia pro Interlingua, 1915.

SOURCES:

Books

Dictionary of Scientific Biography, Volume 10, Scribner, 1975, pp. 441–444.

Selected Works of Giuseppe Peano, translated and edited with a biographical sketch and bibliography by Hubert C. Kennedy, University of Toronto Press, 1973.

—Sketch by David E. Newton

Karl Pearson
1857-1936
English statistician

Karl Pearson is considered the founder of the science of statistics. He believed that a true understanding of human evolution and heredity required mathematical methods for analysis of the data. In developing ways to analyze and represent scientific observations, he laid the groundwork for the development of the field of statistics in the twentieth century and its use in medicine, engineering, anthropology, and psychology.

Pearson was born in London, England, on March 27, 1857, to William Pearson, a lawyer, and Fanny Smith. At the age of nine, Karl attended the University College School, but was forced to withdraw at sixteen because of poor health. After a year of private tutoring, he went to Cambridge, where the distinguished King's College mathematician E. J. Routh met with him each day at 7 A.M. to study papers on advanced topics in applied mathematics. In 1875, he was awarded a scholarship to King's College, where he studied mathematics, philosophy, religion, and literature. At that time, students at King's College were required to attend divinity lectures. Pearson announced that he would not attend the lectures and threatened to leave the college; the requirement was dropped. Attendance at chapel services was also required, but Pearson sought and was granted an exception to the requirement. He later attended chapel services, explaining that it was not the services themselves, but the compulsory attendance to which he objected. He graduated with honors in mathematics in 1879.

After graduation, Pearson traveled in Germany and became interested in German history, religion and folklore. A fellowship from King's College gave him financial independence for several years. He studied law in London, but returned to Germany several times during the 1880s. He lectured and published articles on Martin Luther, Baruch Spinoza, and the Reformation in Germany, and wrote essays and poetry on philosophy, art, science, and religion. Becoming interested in socialism, he lectured on Karl Marx on Sundays in the Soho district clubs of London, and wrote hymns for the Socialist Song Book. Pearson was given the name Carl at birth, but he began spelling it with a "K," possibly out of respect for Karl Marx.

During this period, Pearson maintained his interest in mathematics. He edited a book on elasticity as it applies to physical theories and taught mathematics, filling in for professors at Cambridge. In 1884, at age twenty-seven, Pearson became the Goldsmid Professor of Applied Mathematics and Mechanics at University College in London. In addition to his lectures in mathematics, he taught engineering students, and showed them how to solve mathematical problems using graphs.

In 1885, Pearson became interested in the role of women in society. He gave lectures on what was then called "the woman question," advocating the scientific study of questions such as whether males and females inherit equal intellectual capacity, and whether, in the future, the "best" women would choose not to bear children, leaving it to "coarser and less intellectual" women. He joined a small club which met to discuss questions of morality and sex. There he met Maria Sharpe, whom he married in 1890. They had three children, Egon, Sigrid, and Helga. Maria died in 1928, and Pearson married Margaret V. Child, a colleague at University College, the following year.

Develops Statistical Methods to Study Heredity

Pearson was greatly influenced by Francis Galton and his 1889 work on heredity, *Natural Inheritance.* Pearson saw that there often may be a connection, or correlation, between two events or situations, but in only some of these cases is the correlation due not to chance but to some significant factor. By making use of the broader concept of correlation, Pearson believed that mathematicians could discover new knowledge in biology and heredity, and also in psychology, anthropology, medicine, and sociology.

An enthusiastic young professor of zoology, W. F. R. Weldon came to University College in 1891, further influencing Pearson's direction. Weldon was interested in Darwin's theory of natural selection and, seeing the need for more sophisticated statistical methods in his research, asked Pearson for help. The two became lunch partners. From their association came many years of productive research devoted to the development and application of statistical methods for the study of problems of heredity and evolution. Pearson's goal during this period was not the development of statistical theory for its own sake. The result of his efforts, however, was the development of the new science of statistics.

Remaining at the University College, Pearson became the Gresham College Professor of Geometry in 1891. His lectures for two courses there became the basis for a book, *The Grammar of Science,* in which he presented his view of the nature, function, and methods of science. He dealt with the investigation and representation of statistical problems by means of graphs and diagrams, and illustrated the concepts with examples from nature and the social sciences. In later lectures, he discussed probability and chance, using games such as coin tossing, roulette, and lotteries as examples. He described frequency distributions such as the normal distribution (sometimes called the bell curve because its graph resembles the shape of a bell), skewed distributions (for which the graphed design is not symmetrical), and compound distributions (which might result from a mixture of the two). Such distributions represent the occurrence of variables such as traits, events, behaviors, or other incidents in a given population, or in a sample (subgroup) of a population. They can be graphed to illustrate where each subject falls within the continuum of the variable in question.

Pearson introduced the concept of the "standard deviation" as a measure of the variance within a population or sample. The standard deviation statistic refers to the average distance from the mean score for any score within the data set, and therefore suggests the average amount of variance to be found within the group for that variable. Pearson also formulated a method, known as the chi-square statistic, of measuring the likelihood that an observed relation is in fact due to chance, and used this method to determine the significance of the statistical difference between groups. He also developed the theory of correlation and the concept of regression analysis, used to predict the research results. His correlation coefficient, also known as the Pearson r, is a measure of the strength of the relationship between variables and is his best-known contribution to the field of statistics.

Between 1893 and 1901 Pearson published thirty-five papers in the *Proceedings* and the *Philosophical Transactions* of the Royal Society, developing new statistical methods to deal with data from a wide range of sources. This work formed the basis for much of the later development of the field of statistics. He was elected to the Royal Society in 1896, was awarded the Darwin Medal in 1898, and, in 1903, was elected an Honorary Fellow of King's College and received the Huxley Medal of the Royal Anthropological Institute.

Establishes Journal and Compiles Statistical Tables

In 1901, Pearson helped found the journal *Biometrika* for the publication of papers in statistical theory and practice. He edited the journal until his death. His research often required extensive mathematical calculation, which was carried out under his direction by students and staff mathematicians in his biometric laboratory. Since high-speed electronic computers had not yet been invented, performing the calculations by hand was tedious and time-consuming. The laboratory staff produced tables of calculations which Pearson made available to other statisticians through *Biometrika,* and later as separate volumes. Access to these tables made it possible for others to carry out statistical research without the support of a large staff, and, again, proved to be a valuable contribution to the early development of the field of statistics.

Pearson became the Galton Professor of Eugenics in 1911, and headed a new department of applied statistics as well as the biometric laboratory and a eugenics laboratory, established to study the genetic factors affecting the physical and mental improvement or impairment of future generations. During World War I, Pearson's staff served Britain's interest by preparing charts showing employment and shipping statistics, investigating stresses in airplane propellers, and calculating gun trajectories. From 1911 to 1930, Pearson produced a four-volume biography of Francis Galton. In 1925, he founded the journal *Annals of Eugenics,* which he edited until 1933. In 1932, Pearson was the first foreigner to be awarded the Rudolf Virchow Medal by the Anthropological Society of Berlin. He retired in 1933 at age seventy-seven, and received an honorary degree from the University of London in 1934. Pearson died on April 27, 1936, in Coldharbour, Surrey.

Pearson produced more than three hundred published works in his lifetime. His research focused on statistical methods in the study of heredity and evolution but dealt with a range of topics, including albinism in people and animals, alcoholism, mental deficiency, tuberculosis, mental illness, and anatomical comparisons in humans and other primates, as well as astronomy, meteorology, stresses in dam construction, inherited traits in poppies, and variance in sparrows' eggs. Pearson was described by G. U. Yule as a poet, essayist, historian, philosopher, and statistician, whose interests seemed limited only by the chance encounters of life. Colleagues remarked on his boundless energy and enthusiasm. Although some saw him as domineering and slow to admit errors, others praised him as an inspiring lecturer and noted his care in acknowledging the contributions of the members of his lab group. For Pearson, scientists were heroes. The walls of his laboratory contained quotations from Plato, Pascal, Huxley and others, including these words from Roger Bacon: "He who knows not Mathematics cannot know any other Science, and what is more cannot discover his own Ignorance or find its proper Remedies."

SELECTED WRITINGS BY PEARSON:

Books

The Ethic of Freethought, Fisher Unwin, 1888.
The Grammar of Science, Walter Scott, 1892.
The Chances of Death and Other Studies in Evolution, Edward Arnold, 1897.
Tables for Statisticians and Biometricians, Cambridge University Press, 1914.
The Life, Letters, and Labours of Francis Galton, four volumes, Cambridge University Press, 1914, 1924, 1930.

SOURCES:

Books

Froggatt, P., *Modern Epidemiology: The Pearsonian Legacy,* New Lecture Series No. 54, The Queen's University, Belfast, 1970.
Haldane, J. B. S., *Karl Pearson, 1857–1957, The Centenary Celebration at University College, London, 13 May 1957,* [privately issued by Biometrika Trustees], 1958.
Pearson, E. S., *Karl Pearson, An Appreciation of Some Aspects of His Life and Work,* Cambridge University Press, 1938.

Periodicals

Camp, Burton H., "Karl Pearson and Mathematical Statistics," *Journal of the American Statistical Association,* December, 1933, pp. 395–401.
"Karl Pearson," *Obituary Notices of Fellows of the Royal Society,* Volume 2, number 5, December, 1936, pp. 72–110.
Pearl, Raymond, "Karl Pearson, 1857–1936," *Journal of the American Statistical Association,* December, 1936, pp. 653–664.

—*Sketch by C. D. Lord*

Irene Carswell Peden
1925-
American electrical engineer

Irene Carswell Peden is a specialist in radio science and electromagnetic wave propagation and scattering. She built her niche as a scientist conducting geophysical studies of radio wave propagation in Antarctica, where she became the first American woman engineer/scientist to live and work in the interior of that continent. She was born September 25, 1925, in Topeka, Kansas, to Mr. and Mrs. J. H. Carswell. Her mother was a country school teacher specializing in mathematics and music education, and her father was in the automobile business.

Peden's interest in science was sparked in high school, when she enrolled in a required chemistry course. Eventually, her scientific interests were diverted to electrical engineering, the field in which she received her bachelor's degree from the University of Colorado in 1947. After graduating, she began work for the Delaware Power and Light Company and, in 1949, she joined the Stanford Research Institute's Aircraft Radio Systems Lab.

Peden earned her master's degree from Stanford University in 1958 and worked at the university's Hansen Lab. While studying for her doctorate at Stanford, Peden became an acting instructor of electrical engineering and physics. In 1962, she became the first woman to earn a Ph.D. in any engineering field at the university.

Achievements in the Antarctic

Peden achieved early recognition in her study of radio wave propagation through the Antarctic ice pack. Through her research in the 1970s at the Byrd Antarctic Research Station, she developed new methods to characterize the deep glacial ice by studying the effect it has on radio waves directed through it. She continued this line of research by studying certain properties in the lower ionosphere over Antarctica. Not only was she responsible for developing the methodology for her experiments, she also invented mathematical models to study and interpret the data collected. In so doing, Peden and her students were the first researchers to measure many of the electrical properties of Antarctic ice and to describe important aspects of very low frequency (VLF) propagation over long paths in the polar region. Peden later turned her attention to subsurface exploration technologies, using very high frequency (VHF) radio waves to detect and locate subsurface structures and other targets. Again, she found that she was paving new scientific

Irene Carswell Peden

ground and therefore had to design methodology and models to collect and interpret her data.

For her research, Peden has received a number of awards, including the Society of Women Engineers' Achievement Award in 1973, and the U.S. Army's Outstanding Civilian Service Medal in 1987. She has also been awarded Centennial Medals from the Institute of Electrical and Electronics Engineers, the University of Colorado and the American Society for Engineering Education, which named her to its 100-member Hall of Fame. A member of the national Academy of Engineering, Peden served a two-and-a-half-year term as director of the Division of Electrical and Communications Systems at the National Science Foundation. Peden was married in 1962 to attorney Leo J. Peden and has two step-daughters, Jefri, a high school athletic director, and Jennifer, a vocational and rehabilitational counselor. Peden continues her career at the University of Washington as a researcher in the Electromagnetics and Remote Sensing Laboratory, where she is a professor of electrical engineering.

SELECTED WRITINGS BY PEDEN:

Periodicals

"A Scale-model Study of Down-hole VHF Dipole Arrays with Application to Subsurface Exploration," *IEEE Transactions on Geoscience and Remote Sensing,* Volume 30, number 5, September, 1992, p. 845.

"Detection of Tunnels in Low Loss Media Illuminated by a Transient Pulse," *IEEE Transactions on Geoscience and Remote Sensing,* Volume 31, number 2, March, 1993, p. 503.

—*Sketch by Roger Jaffe*

Charles John Pedersen
1904-1989
Korean-born American organic chemist

Charles John Pedersen was a chemist and researcher credited with discovering how to make simple molecules that mimic the more complex molecules produced by living cells. These molecules, called macrocyclic crown polyethers or "crown ethers," shed light on the shape and size of organic molecules in general. For this work, Pedersen shared the Nobel Prize in chemistry in 1987 with the chemists **Donald J. Cram** and **Jean-Marie Lehn**.

Pedersen was born in Pusan, Korea, on October 3, 1904. His father was a Norwegian sailor who later became a mechanical engineer. His Japanese mother came from a family of silkworm traders. At the age of eight Pedersen started school in Nagasaki, Japan, and was educated in Roman Catholic schools. He emigrated to the United States in 1922 and later received his Bachelor of Science degree from the University of Dayton. His Master of Science degree was awarded by the Massachusetts Institute of Technology in 1927.

Pedersen worked for Du Pont in Wilmington, Delaware, as a researcher from 1927 to 1946. The company recognized his value and appointed him research associate in its Elastomers Chemicals Department in 1947. Pedersen remained in that position until his retirement in 1969. As a research associate, he was authorized to pursue whatever experiment he chose, free from the normal constraints of commercial or academic researchers. His work at Du Pont led to more than sixty patents, most of them in the field of petrochemicals.

Failure Leads to Fame

In the early 1960s Pedersen was trying to find a catalyst for polymerization processes. Polymerization is the combination of molecules into a more complex structure. Although he was unsuccessful in finding the catalyst, the end result of one of his failed experiments caught his attention and he began to study it more carefully. Pedersen found that his "mistake" was itself a small polymer that had some special properties. It later was determined to be the first recognized crown ether, named after its three-dimensional crown-like structure consisting of pairs of carbon and hydrogen atoms arranged in a ring. Pedersen found that the crown ethers he was able to synthesize formed complexes with a range of salts by trapping molecules within its ring structure. Complexes formed from a crown ether have distinctive electrical properties which have been the object of many subsequent studies by scientists. Pedersen's research helped to explain the relationship between a molecule's size and shape and its reactivity. The crown ether's ability to trap molecules within its structure has also led to the design of drugs with specific actions in pharmacology, and to an understanding of the transport of ions through biological membranes in biophysics.

In 1969, two years after publication of his work on crown ethers, Pedersen retired from Du Pont. He worked briefly at the Agricultural Research Council Unit of Structural Chemistry in London before retiring altogether. Over the course of his career he published some twenty-five papers in such periodicals as the *Journal of the American Chemical Society*. His work on crown ethers was continued by many researchers, including Donald J. Cram of the University of California at Los Angeles and Jean-Marie Lehn of the Collège de France in Paris and the Louis Pasteur Institute in Strasbourg. The three scientists were named co-winners of the 1987 Nobel Prize in chemistry.

Although Pedersen did collaborate with an occasional academic, the vast majority of his work was conducted on his own in the Du Pont laboratories. He never pursued a doctorate or an academic career. Pedersen married Susan J. Ault in 1947; the couple had two daughters, Shirley and Barbara. Susan Pedersen died in 1983. Pedersen became a United States citizen in 1953. After a long struggle with blood cancer and Parkinson's disease, Pedersen himself died on October 26, 1989, at the age of eighty-five, and was buried in Salem, New Jersey.

SOURCES:

Books

The Annual Obituary, St. James Press, 1990.

—*Sketch by Evelyn B. Kelly*

Laurence Delisle Pellier
19(?)-
French-born American metallurgist

Laurence Delisle Pellier is the owner of Pellier-Delisle Metallurgical Laboratory, a consulting firm in Westport, Connecticut. A metallurgist of great experience, Pellier has studies powder metallurgy, corrosion, and physical metallurgy. Additionally, Pellier holds two patents, including one granted in 1956 for gold plating surgical needles. Her other research interests include the study of construction metals for chemical plants and she is one of the pioneering researchers in applying electron microscopy to metallurgy. For her work and achievements in the field of metallurgy, Pellier received the Society of Women Engineers (SWE) Annual Achievement Award in 1962.

Born Laurence Delisle in Paris, France, Pellier came to the United States at a young age. After receiving her B.S. in chemical engineering from the College of the City of New York, from where she graduated *cum laude* in 1939, Pellier went on to obtain an M.S. in metallurgy from Stevens Institute of Technology in 1942. Following this she began doctoral work in physical metallurgy at Columbia University.

From 1940 to 1946 Pellier was a research associate and research fellow for the International Nickel Company and General Bronze Company; in this position she studied and designed alloys using powder metallurgy. She then accepted a position as senior metallurgical engineer with Sylvania Electric Products, where she developed techniques for the application of electron microscopy to problems in physical metallurgy. She remained at Sylvania until 1951, when she joined the American Cyanamid Company as a metallurgist. It was here that she studied corrosion, metals for construction of chemical plants, electron metallography, and electro-plating and electroless plating. It was also during this period that she received a patent for a process of preparing corrosion-resistant gold-plated needles for use in surgery.

In 1956 Pellier accepted a position as research metallurgist with the Sigmund Cohn Corporation, where she studied the design and processing of metal alloys for use in fine instruments. In 1958, she joined International Nickel Company as senior scientist. There she explored electron metallography of high temperature alloys, traveling to Europe in 1960 to attend meetings on metallurgy at various places, including Cambridge, England, Delft, Holland, and in

Paris. She returned to the United States in 1962 and formed her private consulting firm.

In addition to receiving the SWE Achievement Award, Pellier was awarded the Micrography Prize by the American Society for Metals in 1949 and the Micrography Prize by the American Society for Testing and Materials. Her affiliations include membership in the American Institute of Mining and Metallurgical Engineers, the French Society of Metallurgy, the Electron Microscope Society of America, French Engineers in the U.S.A., New York Electron Microscopists, and the New York Microscopical Society.

SELECTED WRITINGS BY PELLIER:

Periodicals

"Direct Examination by Electron Transfer of Inconel-X," *Fifth International Congress for Electron Microscopy,* Academic Press, 1962.

—*Sketch by Karen Withem*

Mary Engle Pennington
1872-1952
American chemist

Mary Engle Pennington was a bacteriological chemist who revolutionized methods of storing and transporting perishable foods. Denied a B.S. degree in 1895 because she was a woman, Pennington went on to head the U.S. Department of Agriculture's food research lab. As persuasive as she was resourceful, Pennington was able to convince farmers, manufacturers, and vendors to adopt her techniques. She developed methods of slaughtering poultry that kept them fresh longer, discovered ways to keep milk products from spoiling, and determined how best to freeze fruits and vegetables. Pennington was the first female member of the American Society of Refrigerating Engineers. She eventually went into business for herself as a consultant and investigator in the area of perishable foods.

Pennington was born October 8, 1872, in Nashville, Tennessee. She was the first of two daughters born to Henry and Sarah B. Molony Pennington. Pennington spent most of her early life in Philadelphia, where her family moved to be closer to their Quaker relatives. With her father, a successful label manufacturer, she shared a love of gardening.

Pennington found her way to the field of chemistry through a library book on that subject. Her interest prompted her to enter the Towne Scientific School of the University of Pennsylvania, an uncommon occurrence for a woman at that time. In 1895 she received a certificate of proficiency, having been denied a B.S. because of her gender. Not to be deterred, Pennington continued academic work, earning her Ph.D. at age twenty-two from the University of Pennsylvania with a major in chemistry and minors in zoology and botany. This degree was conferred under an old statute that made exceptions for female students in "extraordinary cases." Pennington then accepted a two-year fellowship at the university in chemical botany, followed by a one-year fellowship in physical chemistry at Yale.

From 1898 to 1906 Pennington served as instructor in physiological chemistry at Women's Medical College. During this same period, she started and operated a clinical laboratory performing analyses for physicians, and was a consultant to Philadelphia regarding the storage of perishable foods during the marketing process. Her reputation for quality work led to an appointment as head of the Philadelphia Department of Health and Charities Bacteriological Laboratory. One of her first goals here was the improvement of the quality of milk and milk products. Her natural gift of persuasion aided her in convincing ice-cream manufacturers and vendors to adopt simple steps to help avoid bacterial contamination of their foods.

The Pure Food and Drug Act was passed in 1906, and the U.S. Department of Agriculture planned to establish a research laboratory to help provide scientific information for prosecutions under the act. Specifically, this lab would be concerned with the quality of eggs, dressed poultry, and fish. With the encouragement of Harvey W. Wiley, chief of the chemistry section of the USDA and a longtime family friend, Pennington took and passed the civil service exam in 1907 under the name M. E. Pennington. Unaware that Pennington was a woman, the government gave her a post as bacteriological chemist. Wiley promoted her to head the food research lab in 1908. That same year she delivered an address for Wiley to a startled all-male audience at the First International Congress of Refrigeration.

During Pennington's tenure the laboratory effected alterations in the warehousing of food, its packaging, and use of refrigeration in transport. Pennington eventually developed techniques that were commonly used for the slaughter of poultry, ensuring safe transport and high quality long after the butchering occurred. In the area of eggs, a highly perishable item especially in warm weather, she again used her powers of persuasion. She worked to convince farmers to collect and transport eggs more frequently during warmer weather. She is also credited with developing the egg cartons that prevent excessive breakage during transport.

During World War I, Pennington consulted with the War Shipping Administration. The United States had forty thousand refrigerated cars available for food transport at the start of the war. Pennington determined only three thousand of these were truly fit for use, with proper air circulation. Following the war she was recognized for her efforts with a Notable Service Award given by Herbert Hoover.

Pennington made another career change in 1919 when she accepted a position as manager of research and development for New York's American Balsa Company, a manufacturer of insulating material. In 1922 she made her final career move, starting her own business in New York as a consultant and investigator in the area of perishable foods. She was particularly interested in frozen foods, helping to determine the best strains of fruits and vegetables for freezing, and the best method for freezing them.

Pennington was the author of books, articles, pamphlets, and several government bulletins. She gave many addresses and was the recipient of several awards, including the American Chemical Society's 1940 Garvan Medal to honor a woman chemist of distinction. Pennington, in fact, was one of the first dozen female members of the society. She was the first female member of the American Society of Refrigerating Engineers, and the first woman elected to the Poultry Historical Society's Hall of Fame. She served as director of the Household Refrigeration Bureau of the National Association of Ice Industries from 1923 to 1931.

Pennington earned herself the reputation for always producing quality work. She was accepted in industry even while she was working for the government in enforcing the Pure Food and Drug Act. She maintained her interest in gardening and botany, growing flowers in her apartment. She was a lifelong member of the Quaker Society of Friends. Pennington, who never married, was still working as a consultant and as vice president of the American Institute of Refrigeration when she died on December 27, 1952, in New York City.

SELECTED WRITINGS BY PENNINGTON:

Books

(With H. M. P. Betts) *How to Kill and Bleed Market Poultry,* Government Printing Office, 1915.
(With Paul Mandeville) *Eggs,* Progress Publications, 1933.

SOURCES:

Books

American Chemists and Chemical Engineers, edited by Wyndham Miles, American Chemical Society, 1976.
Notable American Women: The Modern Period, edited by Barbara Sicherman and Carol Green, Belknap Press, 1980.

Periodicals

"Mary E. Pennington," *Chemical and Engineering News,* January 5, 1953.

　　　　　　　　　—Sketch by Kimberlyn McGrail

Roger Penrose
1931-
English mathematical physicist

Roger Penrose explored a range of topics in mathematical theory and physics, including relativity theory, quantum mechanics, astrophysics, cosmology, possible and impossible geometric shapes, and how the human brain works. With theoretical physicist and professor **Stephen Hawking**, he extended our understanding of black holes and the "big bang" theory of the origin of the universe, and his work with geometric puzzles shed light on the nature of quasi-crystals.

Penrose was born August 8, 1931, in Colchester, England. His father, Lionel S. Penrose, was a geneticist, and his mother, Margaret Newman, a doctor; his uncle, Sir Roland Penrose, was a surrealist painter and a biographer of Picasso. Penrose's older brother Oliver became a mathematics professor, while his younger brother Jonathan, a professor of psychology, was British chess champion ten times. As a boy, Penrose shared his father's interest in nature and geometrical puzzles. In school, he showed an aptitude for mathematics, devising geometry problems that challenged his teachers.

As a mathematics student at University College, London, Penrose discovered a theorem concerning eight conics in a plane, for which three well-known theorems turned out to be special cases. He received a Bachelor of Science degree in 1952 and a Ph.D. from Cambridge in 1957, writing his dissertation on algebraic geometry. As a student, Penrose rediscovered and developed mathematician E. H. Moore's generalized inverse matrix, a method of solving equations that involves rectangular arrays of numbers. At St. John's College, Cambridge, Penrose heard lectures by Paul Dirac on quantum mechanics and by Hermann Bondi on the theory of relativity, and became interested in relating quantum mechanics and space-time structure.

Beginning as a research fellow at St. John's College from 1957 to 1960, Penrose pursued a career of research and teaching at major universities in England and the United States. He was a North Atlantic Treaty Organization (NATO) research fellow at Princeton, Syracuse, and Cornell universities from 1959 to 1961. In the 1960s he had visiting appointments at the University of Chicago, Yeshiva University in New York, the University of Texas in Austin, the University of California at Berkeley, and King's College and Bedford College in London. In 1973 Penrose was named the Rouse Ball professor at Oxford University, and in the 1980s he was the Edgar Odell Lovett Professor of Mathematics at Rice University. Penrose's early honors include the 1966 Adams Prize from Cambridge University and the Dannie Heineman Prize for Physics from the American Physical Society and the American Institute of Physics in 1971. He was elected to the Royal Society in 1972.

Developed Mathematics for Study of Black Holes

In 1965 Penrose showed that, as a consequence of Einstein's theory of general relativity, there must inevitably be points in space that are infinitely dense and hot. At such points—called singularities—the laws of classical physics do not apply; the gravitational field becomes infinite, or other pathological behavior occurs. Penrose's theorem proved that if a star of sufficient mass collapsed, a singularity—the core of what later became known as a black hole—would result. Penrose's work first convinced many physicists of the existence of black holes, and inspired the search for them.

A year later, Stephen Hawking of Cambridge University applied Penrose's theorem to cosmology, proving that the universe started in a singularity. In 1970, Penrose and Hawking, working together, succeeded in proving a singularity theorem much more powerful than their earlier efforts. Previous work by others had indicated that our universe did not begin with a "big bang" singularity; Penrose and Hawking's theorem challenged this view, asserting that in any universe with certain fundamental properties, a big bang singularity must occur. The two scientists proved their theorem using mathematical techniques from the theory of differential topology; using the same techniques, Penrose contributed to Hawking's work on black holes, which showed that the surface area of a black hole must increase as mass is added. In

1975, Penrose and Hawking shared the Royal Astronomical Society's Eddington Medal, and in 1988 they were awarded the Wolf Foundation Prize in Physics.

Penrose's efforts were aided by his invention of the "twistor," a mathematical tool for describing physical objects and space, incorporating energy, momentum, and spin—the three properties possessed by all objects moving through space-time. A twistor has either six or eight dimensions, each of which involves either movement or change in size.

Another of Penrose's primary areas of study is tiling, which involves completely covering a flat surface with a regular pattern of tiles. He shares this interest with numerous other mathematicians, including Johannes Kepler in the seventeenth century. Penrose has said that he inherited his love of puzzles from his father, who used models to understand or explain concepts in genetics. Speaking of his father in an interview for *Omni*, Penrose explained, "With him there was no clear line between making puzzles for his children and his serious work in genetics." While a graduate student in 1954, Penrose saw the drawings of Dutch artist M. C. Escher at a mathematics conference in Amsterdam. Escher's work incorporates geometry and perspective to produce drawings of "impossible" objects. Penrose was fascinated with the illustrations of objects which violate the rules of three-dimensional reality. He proceeded to draw his own such construct—a "tribar" of three beams—which he sent to Escher. The artist later used the tribar figure as the basis for a continuous flow of water in his lithograph, *Waterfall*.

The simplest tiling pattern utilizes identical tiles in the shape of squares, equilateral triangles, or regular hexagons. However, regular pentagons—five-sided tiles—will not tile a surface without leaving gaps. Penrose found that a floor, or any plane surface, can be covered with pentagons plus two other shapes—stars and hat-shaped pieces. The resulting pattern has regularities but does not repeat itself exactly. Some tiling patterns repeat themselves in a certain way: if you placed a sheet of thin paper over the design and traced it, and then moved the paper sideways without rotating it, the tracing would match. Such designs are called "periodic." Penrose's pattern was non-periodic. With some tile designs, such as hexagons, you know from the neighboring tiles where to put down the next one; such patterns are called "local." Penrose's pattern appeared to be non-local; it was necessary to look at the position of pieces some distance away in order to position the next tile correctly.

Penrose worked with pieces of various shapes, trying to find the smallest number of shapes that would force a non-periodic tiling. He discovered several combinations, and finally, in 1974, lowered the number of shapes to two. One of Penrose's most interesting designs used two shapes derived from a rhombus: one piece looked like a kite, and the other resembled a dart or a "stealth" airplane. Following rules about which edges could be fitted together, the two shapes forced a non-periodic tiling. In his book, *Penrose Tiles to Trapdoor Ciphers,* Martin Gardner displays some tiling patterns and explains how to make a set of "Penrose tiles."

Similar Pattern Found in Quasi-Crystals

Following Penrose's work, others extended the tiling concept to three dimensions, devising solid polyhedrons to fill space without any gaps; these tilings were also non-periodic. In the 1980s, crystallographers became interested in Penrose's findings. For a century, scientists had thought that the atoms in crystals were arranged periodically, and that crystals with five-fold symmetry were impossible. It was generally assumed that the atoms in solid matter took one of two forms: either a periodic crystal arrangement or a disordered arrangement in materials such as glass. But in studying an alloy of aluminum and manganese, Dan Schechtman at the National Bureau of Standards saw what appeared to be non-periodic crystals with five-fold symmetry. The complicated sequences in the pattern were only "quasi-periodic." Halfway between crystals and glass-like structures, this new form of matter, quasi-crystals, caused considerable excitement among chemists, physicists, and crystallographers. The similarity between the alloy pattern and the Penrose patterns was recognized by University of Pennsylvania physicist Paul Steinhardt and by crystallographer Alan MacKay of London. Soon scientists found similar non-periodic structures in other alloys. Alloys with five-fold symmetry, as well as seven-fold, nine-fold, and eleven-fold symmetry, proved to be possible.

The apparent non-locality of the structures puzzled scientists, because it was not clear how a growing quasi-crystal would attach new atoms, one at a time, in the right location and sequence. Then in 1988 Steinhardt and George Onoda, an IBM ceramics expert, devised rules for building a Penrose tiling, specifying which vacancy to fill first, which piece to use, and which way the tile should be turned. It was not necessary to pay attention to any distant part of the pattern. These results provided possible clues to the growth of three-dimensional quasi-crystals. Researchers proceeded to study the properties of the new alloys. Because of their intricate structure, it was thought that they might turn out to be harder than crystals and usable as substitutes for industrial diamonds, or as materials in electronic devices.

Possible Link Between the Human Mind and Quantum Gravity

Much of Penrose's work, including topics such as theoretical mathematics, cosmological singularities,

and quasi-crystals, came together in his 1989 book, *The Emperor's New Mind: Concerning Computers, Minds, and the Laws of Physics.* The book was on the *New York Times* best-seller list for nine weeks, attracting interest from people in a wide range of fields, and was the topic of more than twenty book reviews in periodicals in fields ranging from science and artificial intelligence to philosophy, as well as popular newspapers.

In the book Penrose disagrees with the view, held by some researchers in the field of artificial intelligence, that computers are capable of mimicking the function of human brains. A computer program, Penrose argues, uses an algorithm, a step-by-step mechanical procedure for working toward an answer from the input data. Certain kinds of human thinking are nonalgorithmic—not formalizable—so, Penrose concludes, the human brain must be making use of nonalgorithmic processes.

Penrose considers the nature of the physics that might underlie conscious thought processes. He sees a significant gap between our physical understanding at the small-scale quantum level (which includes the behavior of molecules, atoms and subatomic particles) and at the larger classical level (which includes the behavior of larger objects such as baseballs). Penrose suspects that a greater understanding of the functioning of the human brain may depend on a fundamentally new understanding of physics, to be sought in a radical new theory of quantum gravity. He believes that until we understand the borderline between quantum mechanics and classical mechanics, computers will not be able to work as human brains do.

SELECTED WRITINGS BY PENROSE:

Books

(With Wolfgang Rindler) *Spinors and Space-time,* Volume 1: *Two-Spinor Calculus and Relativistic Fields,* Volume 2: *Spinor and Twistor Methods in Space-Time Geometry,* Cambridge University Press, 1986.

(Editor with H. S. M. Coxeter, M. Emmer, and M. L. Teuber) *M. C. Escher, Art and Science,* North Holland, 1986.

The Emperor's New Mind: Concerning Computers, Minds, and the Laws of Physics, Oxford University Press, 1989.

SOURCES:

Books

Gardner, Martin, *Penrose Tiles to Trapdoor Ciphers,* W. H. Freeman and Co., 1989.

McGraw-Hill Modern Scientists and Engineers,
    Volume 2, McGraw-Hill, 1980, pp. 407–408.

Periodicals

Horgan, John, "The Artist, the Physicist and the
    Waterfall," *Scientific American,* February,
    1993, p. 30.
Horgan, "Quantum Consciousness: Polymath Rog-
    er Penrose Takes on the Ultimate Mystery,"
    Scientific American, November, 1989, pp.
    31–33.
"Interview: Roger Penrose," *Omni,* June, 1986,
    pp. 67–68, 70, 73, 106–107.
Landauer, Rolf, "Is the Mind More Than an Ana-
    lytic Engine?," *Physics Today,* June, 1990, pp.
    73–75.
"Many-sided Penrose," *The Economist,* September
    17, 1988, p. 100.
"Precis of The Emperor's New Mind: Concerning
    Computers, Minds, and the Laws of Physics,"
    "Open Peer Commentary," and "Author's Re-
    sponse," *Behavioral and Brain Sciences,* 1990,
    no. 13, pp. 643–705.
Siegel, Matthew, "Wolf Foundation Honors Hawk-
    ing and Penrose for Work on Relativity,"
    Physics Today, January, 1989, pp. 97–98.
von Baeyer, Hans C., "Impossible Crystals," *Dis-
    cover,* February, 1990, pp. 69–78.

—*Sketch by C. D. Lord*

Arno Penzias

1933-

German-born American astrophysicist

Arno Penzias shared the Nobel Prize for physics
in 1978 with **Robert Wilson** for a discovery
that supported the big bang theory of the universe.
The two radio astronomers at what was then American Telephone & Telegraph's (AT&T) Bell Telephone
Laboratories were using a 20-foot horn reflector
antenna that year to measure the intensity of radio
waves emitted by the halo of gas surrounding our
galaxy. And they were bothered by a persistent noise
which they could not explain. At first they pinned it
on two pigeons that were nesting in the antenna
throat. But even after they evicted the birds, the noise
continued. Eventually the scientists were able to
conclude that the noise came from cosmic background, or microwave, radiation. This came to be
widely considered as remnant microwave radiation
from the "big bang" in which the universe was created

billions of years ago. And the Penzias-Wilson discovery came to be considered a major finding in astrophysics.

Arno Allan Penzias was born in Munich, Germany, April 26, 1933, to Jewish parents Karl and Justine
(Eisenreich) Penzias. Hitler's campaign to wipe out
the Jews of Europe was well underway when the
family escaped in 1940. Arriving in New York,
Penzias had to acclimate to a new culture and
language and suffer through hard times for his family.
Naturalized in 1946, he demonstrated scientific acumen at Brooklyn Technical High School and went on
to obtain his B.S. at City College in New York in
1954. He married Anne Pearl Barras that same year;
the union produced three children. After a two-year
stint in the U.S. Army Signal Corps, Penzias obtained
both his master's and Ph.D. degrees at Columbia
University. He has said he chose to study physics
because he asked a professor if he could make a living
in the field and was told, "Well, you can do the same
things engineers can do and do them better."

Begins Research Career

In 1961 Penzias was hired at Bell Labs in
Holmdel, New Jersey. AT&T was a telecommunications monopoly at that time and Bell Labs was its
research center, attracting the best and brightest
scientific minds. In this context Penzias demonstrated
his capabilities early on. Asked to join a committee of
older scientists who were trying to devise how to
calculate the precise positions of communication
satellites by triangulation, young Penzias suggested
they use radio stars, which emit characteristic frequencies from fixed positions, as reference points.
The distinguished scientists nodded their heads in
agreement—and the committee immediately disband-
ed. For his abilities, Penzias rose through the Bell
ranks to become director of the facility's Radio
Research Laboratory in 1976, and executive director
of the Communications Sciences Research Division
in 1979. He also took part in the pioneering Echo and
Telstar communications satellite experiments of the
1970s.

Penzias's Cosmic Finding

It was astronomer **George Gamow** who in 1942
first calculated the conditions of temperature and
density that would have been required for a fireball
explosion or "big bang" origin of the universe 15
billion years ago. Astronomers Ralph Alpher and
Robert Herman later concluded that cosmic radiation
would have resulted from this event. This theory was
confirmed by Penzias and Wilson. According to the
theory, the background radiation resulting from the
big bang would have lost energy; it would have
essentially "cooled." Gamow and Alpher calculated in
1948 that the radiation should now be characteristic

of a perfectly emitting body—or black body—with a temperature of about 5 kelvin, or –268 degrees C. The scientists said this radiation should lie in the microwave region of the spectrum; their calculations were verified by physicists Robert Dicke and P. J. E. Peebles.

Penzias's and Wilson's contribution to the issue began with a 20-foot directional radio antenna, the same kind of radio antenna designed for satellite communication. Investigating an irritating noise emitted by the antenna, the two men realized in May of 1964 that what they heard was not instrumental noise but microwave radiation coming from all directions uniformly. Penzias and Wilson calculated the radiation's temperature as about 3.5 kelvin. Dicke and Peebles, who had made the earlier calculations, got reinvolved from nearby Princeton University with a scientific explanation of the Penzias-Wilson discovery. More experiments followed, confirming that the radiation was unchanging when measured from any direction. Even after the duo received the Nobel Prize in 1978 (also awarded that year to **Pyotr Kapitsa** for unrelated work in physics) they continued to collaborate on research into intergalactic hydrogen, galactic radiation and interstellar abundances of the isotopes.

Bringing Bell Labs into a New Era

At the time of the federal lawsuit which led to the breakup of AT&T in 1984, Penzias, who had become vice president of research in 1981, predicted that without the operating companies as a base, Bell Labs would become "a sinking ship." That did not happen. Instead, Penzias in September of 1990 presided over the realignment of Bell Labs into a facility whose research is streamlined and oriented towards the activities of its business units. "We adjusted the food chain," Penzias told *Science* magazine in 1991. "If we'd done everything in the old way we probably would have sunk." Picking up on his former marine metaphor, Penzias added: "But we've fixed the hull; we're back to a healthy operation."

While rearranging Bell Labs, Penzias has kept an eye on the outside world, writing *Ideas and Information: Managing in a High-Tech World* in 1989 and staying involved in the national dialogue regarding the growth of computer technology and competition with the Japanese. "You've got to understand the Japanese are not superhuman," he told *Forbes* magazine in March of 1989. "You go into Sears, the best cordless telephone you can buy is an AT&T phone. It works better. You try it."

In his personal life, Penzias, who is the proud grandfather of three, is also an avid skier, swimmer, and runner with an interest in kinetic sculpture and writing limericks. Penzias is a member of the National Academy of Sciences and the National Academy of Engineering, as well as the vice chairman of the

Committee of Concerned Scientists, devoted to political freedom for scientists internationally. He has written over 100 articles and collected 19 honorary degrees. In all this Penzias argues that technology can be liberating. As he wrote in *Fortune* magazine in March of 1990: "Everybody is overstressed.... We've got to stop going to meetings and have them electronically instead.... How far away are we from realizing this dream? My guess is that by the time *Fortune* marks its 100th anniversary, a lot of this will have happened. In fact, long before I retire in 1998, I hope to have at least a multimedia terminal in my office so that I can integrate voice, data, high-definition video, conference video, document access, and shared software ... who's going to do all this? I hope it's AT&T. But it could be IBM, Apple—it could be anybody."

SELECTED WRITINGS BY PENZIAS:

Books

Ideas and Information: Managing in a High-Tech World, Norton, 1989.

Periodicals

"The World Beyond Digital Switching: An Integrated Transport and Switching System Will Be Required In Order To Provide the Services of the Future," *Telephone Engineer and Management,* May 1, 1986.

"The World According To Penzias," *Discover,* Nov. 1988, p. 88.

"Present Shock: How Information Technology Transforms Organizations, Management and the Way Things Are Done," *Computerworld,* Oct. 23, 1989, p. 89.

"Networking in the Nineties: A Preview of Telecommunications in the 21st Century," *Telephone Engineer & Management,* Jan. 15, 1990, p. 511.

SOURCES:

Books

Weber, Robert L., *Pioneers of Science: Nobel Prize Winners in Physics,* Institute of Physics, 1980, p. 257.

Periodicals

"Bell Labs: Shakeout Follows Breakup," *Science,* June 14, 1991, p. 1480.

"The Japanese Are Not Superhuman," *Forbes,* March 20, 1989, p. 122.

"The New Look at America's Top Lab: How Has Bell Labs Weathered the Breakup of AT&T?" *Fortune,* Feb. 1, 1988, p. 60.

"We Simply Can't Afford Telephone Tag," *Science,* March 26, 1990, p. 72.

Other

Biographical Information Supplied by Bell Labs' Media Relations.

—Sketch by Joan Oleck

Marguerite Perey
1909-1975
French physicist

M arguerite Perey is best known for her discovery of francium, the 87th element in the Periodic Table. Francium, a rare, highly unstable, radioactive element, is the heaviest chemical of the alkali metal group. Perey's work on francium and on such scientific occurrences as the actinium radioactive decay series led to her admission to the French Academy of Sciences. Perey was the first woman to be admitted to the two-hundred-year-old Academy—even **Marie Curie** had been unable to break the sex barrier.

Marguerite Catherine Perey was born in Villemomble, France, in 1909. As a child, she showed an interest in science and wanted to become a doctor. Her father's early death, however, left her family without the resources for such an education. Nonetheless, Perey was able to study physics and showed a talent for scientific endeavors. Because of her technical prowess, she was able to secure a position as a lab assistant (initially for a three-month stint) in Marie Curie's laboratory at the Radium Institute in Paris. Curie, for all her influence, made an unpretentious first impression, so much so that Perey, upon first meeting her at the Institute, thought she was the lab's secretary. This incident, combined with Curie's tendency to be aloof with strangers, might have portended a short career at the Curie lab for Perey. In fact, after the initial meeting, Perey thought she would only stay at the Radium Institute for her three months and leave. But Curie saw that Perey was both talented and dedicated, and she encouraged the younger woman, thus building a working relationship that extended beyond Perey's initial intentions.

Discovers Francium

Perey worked with Curie until the latter's death in 1934; thereafter she continued her mentor's research. Perey discovered the sequence of events that lead to the process known as the actinium radioactive decay series. This research inadvertently led to her most important discovery. She was aware of the existence of actinouranium, actinium-B, actinium-C, and actinium-D as part of the decay series she was trying to interpret. During this time, scientists were still trying to discover what they then believed to be the only three elements missing in the Periodic Table (which at the time contained 92 elements). One of these was Element 87. As Perey attempted to confirm her results of actinium radioactive decay, she found that other elements kept cropping up, disrupting the procedure. One of the elements was Element 87, with an atomic weight of 223. The element was highly charged—in fact, the most electropositive of all the elements. Because of this property, she considered naming it catium (from cation, which is a term for positively charged ions). But the word sounded too much like "cat" to her colleagues. As a result, she decided on francium, in honor of her homeland (and the place where the element had been discovered).

The following year, Perey took a position at France's National Center for Scientific Research. She remained there until 1949, when she became a professor of nuclear physics at the University of Strassbourg. She later became director of Strassbourg's Nuclear Research Center, holding that post for the rest of her life. By the time of her admission into the French Academy, Perey had already been diagnosed with the cancer that would slowly kill her. (She was undergoing treatment at the time of her appointment and was unable to attend the ceremonies.) She remained at the Nuclear Research Center and continued to conduct research. Eventually, the battle against the cancer grew more fierce, and, after a fifteen-year struggle, she succumbed in Louveciennes, France, on May 14, 1975.

SOURCES:

Books

Brock, William H., *The Norton History of Chemistry,* Norton, 1992.

Heiserman, David L., *Exploring Chemical Elements and Their Compounds,* TAB Books, 1992.

Reid, Robert, *Marie Curie,* Saturday Review Press/Dutton, 1974.

Vare, Ethlie Ann and Greg Ptacek, *Mothers of Invention,* Morrow, 1988.

Periodicals

Times (London), May 15, 1975, p. 20.

—Sketch by George A. Milite

Jean Baptiste Perrin
1870-1942
French physicist

The contribution made by French physicist Jean Baptiste Perrin to the study of atomic physics was of the most fundamental kind: he helped to prove that atoms and molecules exist. This achievement, which quantitatively extended the original observations of botanist Robert Brown on the movement of pollen grains in water, and put scientific substance into **Albert Einstein**'s exquisite mathematical equations describing the distribution of those particles in solution, won for Perrin the 1926 Nobel Prize in chemistry.

Perrin was born in Lille, France, on September 30, 1870, and raised, along with two sisters, by his widowed mother. His father, an army officer, died of wounds he received during the Franco-Prussian War. The young Perrin attended local schools and graduated from the Lycée Janson-de-Sailly in Paris. After serving a year of compulsory military service, he entered the Ecole Normale Supérieure in 1891, where his interest in physics flowered and he made his first major discovery.

Between 1894 and 1897 Perrin was an assistant in physics at the Ecole Normale, during which time he studied cathode rays and X rays, the basis of his doctoral dissertation. At this time, scientists disagreed over the nature of cathode rays emitted by the negative electrode (cathode) in a vacuum tube during an electric discharge. Physicists disagreed among themselves over whether cathode rays were particles—a logical assumption, since they carried a charge—or whether they took the form of waves.

Confirms Nature of Cathode Rays

In 1895 Perrin settled the debate simply and decisively using a cathode-ray discharge tube attached to a larger, empty vessel. When the discharge tube generated cathode rays, the rays passed through a narrow opening into the vessel, and produced fluorescence on the opposite wall. Nearby, an electrometer, which measures voltage, detected a small negative charge. But when Perrin deflected the cathode rays with a magnetic field so they fell on the nearby electrometer, the electrometer recorded a much larger negative charge. This demonstration was enough to prove conclusively that cathode rays carried negative charges and were particles, rather than waves. This work laid the basis of later work by physicist **J. J. Thomson**, who used Perrin's apparatus to characterize the negatively charged particles, called electrons, which were later theorized to be parts of atoms.

Jean Baptiste Perrin

In 1897 Perrin married Henriette Duportal, with whom he had a son and a daughter. He received his doctorate the same year, and began teaching a new course in physical chemistry at the University of Paris (the Sorbonne). He was given a chair in physical chemistry in 1910 and remained at the school until 1940. During his early years at the University of Paris, Perrin continued his study of the atomic theory, which held that elements are made up of particles called atoms, and that chemical compounds are made up of molecules, larger particles consisting of two or more atoms. Although the atomic theory was widely accepted by scientists by the end of the nineteenth century, some physicists insisted that atoms and molecules did not actually exist as physical entities, but rather represented mathematical concepts useful for calculating the results of chemical reactions. To them, matter was continuous, not made up of discrete particles. Thus, at the dawn of the twentieth century, proving that matter was discontinuous (atomic in nature) was one of the great challenges left in physics. Perrin stood on the side of the "atomists," who believed that these tiny entities existed. In 1901 he even ventured (with no proof) that atoms resembled miniature solar systems. His interest in atomic theory led him to study a variety of related topics, such as osmosis, ion transport, and crystallization. However, it was colloids that led him to study Brownian motion, the basis of his Nobel Prize-winning discovery of the atomic nature of matter.

Verifies Einstein's Calculations of Brownian Motion

In 1827 the English botanist Robert Brown reported that pollen grains suspended in water were in violent and irregular motion, a phenomenon at first ascribed to differences in temperature within the fluid. Before the end of the century, however, scientists generally accepted the notion that the motion might be caused by bombardment of the pollen grains by molecules of the liquid—an apparent triumph for atomic theory. Yet some scientists remained skeptical.

In 1905 Albert Einstein calculated the mathematical basis of Brownian motion, basing his work on the assumption that the motion was due to the action of water molecules bombarding the grains. But Einstein's work, though elegant, lacked laboratory experiments needed to demonstrate the reality of his conclusions. It fell to Perrin to bolster Einstein's calculations with observations. From 1908 to 1913, Perrin, at first unaware of Einstein's published paper on the subject, devoted himself to the extremely tedious but necessary experiments—experiments now considered classics of their kind. He hypothesized that if Brownian movement did result from molecular collisions, the average movements of particles in suspension were related to their size, density, and the conditions of the fluid (e.g., pressure and density), in accordance with the gas laws. Perrin began by assuming that both pollen grains and the molecules of the liquid in which they were suspended behave like gas molecules, despite the much greater size of the grains.

According to Einstein's equations governing Brownian motion, the way the particles maintained their position in suspension against the force of gravity depended partly on the size of the water molecules. In 1908 Perrin began his painstaking observations of suspensions to determine the approximate size of the water molecules by observing suspensions of particles. He spent several months isolating nearly uniform, 0.1-gram pieces of gamboge—tiny, dense extracts of gum resin, which he suspended in liquid. According to Einstein's molecular theory, not all particles will sink to the bottom of a suspension. The upward momentum that some particles achieve by being bombarded by molecules of the fluid will oppose the downward force of gravity. At equilibrium, the point at which the reactions balance each other out, the concentrations of particles at different heights will remain unchanged.

Perrin devised an ingenious system to make thousands of observations of just such a system. He counted gamboge particles at various depths in a single drop of liquid only one twelve-hundredth of a millimeter deep. The particle concentration decreased exponentially with height in such close agreement with the mathematical predictions of Einstein's theory that his observations helped to prove that molecules existed.

In essence, his system behaved like the Earth's atmosphere, which becomes increasingly rarified with height, until, at the top of a very tall mountain, people may find it difficult to breathe. Furthermore, it was already known that a change in altitude of five kilometers is required to halve the concentration of oxygen molecules in the atmosphere, and that the oxygen atom has a mass of sixteen. Based on his knowledge of the gas laws, Perrin realized that if, in his tiny system, the height required to halve the concentration of particles was a billion times less than the height it took to halve the concentration of oxygen in the atmosphere, he could, by simple proportion, calculate the mass of a gamboge particle relative to the oxygen molecule.

Einstein had linked to Brownian motion the concept of Avogadro's number, the number of molecules in any gas at normal temperature and pressure, now known to be 6.023×10^{23}. According to Avogadro's hypothesis, equal volumes of all gases at the same temperature and pressure contain equal numbers of molecules. Furthermore, the total mass of a specific volume of gas is equal to the mass of all the individual molecules multiplied by the total number of these individual molecules. So a gram-molecule of all gases at the same temperature and pressure should contain the same number of molecules. (A gram-molecule, or mole, is a quantity whose mass in grams equals the molecular weight of the substance; for example, one gram-molecule of oxygen equals sixteen grams of oxygen.) Only if this were true would the concept that each individual molecule contributes a minute bit of pressure to the overall pressure hold true, and individual entities called molecules could be said to exist.

Perrin calculated the gram-molecular weight of the 0.1-gram particles in the equilibrium system and therefore knew the number of grams in a gram-molecule of the particles. Then he divided the gram-molecular weight by the mass in grams of a single particle. The result, 6.8×10^{23}, was extremely close to Avogadro's number. Thus, Perrin had demonstrated that uniform particles in suspension behave like gas molecules, and calculations based on their mass can even be used to calculate Avogadro's number. This demonstrated that Brownian motion is indeed due to bombardment of particles by molecules, and came as close as was possible at the time to detecting atoms without actually seeing them. "In brief," Perrin said during his Nobel Prize acceptance speech, "if molecules and atoms do exist, their relative weights are known to us, and their absolute weights would be known as soon as Avogadro's number is known."

Perrin's work ranged farther afield than equilibrium distribution of particles and Avogadro's number, however. As an officer in the engineering corps of the French army during World War I, he contributed his expertise to the development of acoustic detection of submarines. His commitment to science, however, did not inhibit his social graces. He was a popular figure who took a genuine interest in young people, and held weekly parties for discussion groups in his laboratory. Following the war, Perrin's reputation continued to grow. In 1925, he became one of the first scientists to use an electric generator capable of producing a continuous current of 500,000 volts. At the time, he predicted that someday much larger machines of this type would let physicists bombard atoms, and thus make important discoveries about the structure of these particles.

In 1929 after being appointed director of the newly founded Rothschild Institute for Research in Biophysics, he was invited to the United States as a distinguished guest at the opening of Princeton University's new chemical laboratory. In 1936 Perrin replaced Nobel laureate Irene Joliot-Curie as French undersecretary of state for scientific research in the government of Premier Léon Blum. The following year, as president of the French Academy of Science, he assumed the chair of the scientific section of an exhibit in the Grand Palais at the 1937 Paris exposition. The project enabled him to help the average person, including children, to appreciate the wonders of science, from astronomy to zoology.

His flourishing reputation was further enhanced in 1938 when he informed the French Academy of Science, of which he had been a member since 1923, and was then president, that his collaborators had discovered the ninety-third chemical element, neptunium, a substance heavier than uranium. Four years earlier, **Enrico Fermi** (who was awarded the 1938 Nobel Prize in physics and directed the first controlled nuclear chain reaction) had artificially created Neptunium, a so-called transuranium element, by bombarding uranium (element 92) with neutrons. Perrin's announcement that Neptunium existed in nature excited speculation among physicists that there also might exist even more undiscovered elements, which turned out to be the case.

Condemns Totalitarianism and Warns of Impending War

His blossoming career did not shield the French physicist from concerns over what he considered to be a steady encroachment by totalitarian governments around the world on the freedom of science to express itself. A socialist and outspoken opponent of fascism, Perrin expressed his concerns during a speech delivered at the Royal Opera House in London before the International Peace Conference, reported in the *New York Times*. He asserted that world science stands or falls with democracy, and decried the fact that

scientists seemed unable to understand "how financiers and capitalists as a whole cannot see that it is to their interest not to support those powers which, if they are successful, will ruin them." Perrin also criticized what he called "an irrational world that made it difficult to extend higher education or grant more aid to science but relatively easy to raise money for costly armaments." He voiced concern over what he believed was the coming war—World War II—which he feared would cost millions of lives, as well as threaten "the democracy that is the spirit of science." Perrin also warned that the victory of totalitarianism would mean "perhaps a thousand years of ruthless subjugation and standardization of thought, which will destroy the freedom of scientific research and theorizing."

Perrin's fears were realized in September of 1939, when France joined Great Britain in entering World War II against Germany following that country's invasion of Poland. By the end of September, the French government appointed Perrin president of a committee for scientific research to help the war effort. The situation became particularly grim in the summer of 1940, when German troops swept into Paris. Perrin fled the city and took up residence in Lyon as a refugee. In December 1941 he moved to the United States, where he lived with his son, Francis Perrin, a visiting professor of physics and mathematics at Columbia University. While in the United States, Perrin sought American support for the French war effort and helped to establish the French University of New York.

Perrin spoke out against the German occupation and French collaboration with the enemy. He was particularly disturbed when the Germans began operating an armaments industry in the suburbs of Paris using forced labor. Following Allied aerial bombardment of the factories, the *New York Times* reported that Perrin defended the action as "one of the sad necessities" of the war. Speaking before five hundred guests at the first dinner of the French American Club in New York City, in March 1942, Perrin asked, "Who does not understand that it was imperative to put an end to this?" A few weeks later, Perrin took ill, and ten days later he died at the age of seventy-one at Mount Sinai Hospital in New York.

Three years after the defeat of Germany and the end of the war, diplomats and scientists in New York paid homage to Jean Perrin at ceremonies held at the Universal Funeral Chapel. Afterwards, Perrin's ashes were placed aboard the training cruiser Jean d'Arc at Montreal, on which they were transported to France for burial at the Pantheon, a magnificent former eighteenth-century church converted to civic use. Among his many honors in addition to the Nobel Prize, Perrin received the Joule Prize of the Royal Society of London in 1896 and the La Caze Prize of the French Academy of Sciences in 1914. In addition, he held honorary degrees from the universities of Brussels, Liège, Ghent, Calcutta, and Manchester and from New York, Princeton, and Oxford universities. Perrin was also a member of the Royal Society of London and scientific academies in Italy, Czechoslovakia, Belgium, Sweden, Romania, and China.

SELECTED WRITINGS BY PERRIN:

Books

Brownian Movement and Molecular Reality, translated from the *Annales de chimie et de physique,* 8th series, September, 1909, by F. Soddy, Taylor and Francis, 1910.
Les éléments de la physique, A. Michel, 1929.
Oeuvres scientifiques, Centre National de la Recherche Scientifique, 1950.

SOURCES:

Periodicals

New York Times, March 27, 1938, p. 7; August 3, 1938, p. 21; March 10, 1942, p. 7; April 18, 1942, p. 15.

—*Sketch by Marc Kusinitz*

Candace B. Pert
1946-
American neuroscientist and biochemist

Candace B. Pert is a leading researcher in the field of chemical receptors, places in the body where molecules of a drug or natural chemical fit like a key into a lock, thus stimulating or inhibiting various physiological or emotional effects. As a graduate student, Pert codiscovered the brain's opiate receptors, areas that fit painkilling substances such as morphine. Her work led to the discovery of endorphins, the naturally occurring substances manufactured in the brain that relieve pain and produce sensations of pleasure.

Candace Dorinda Bebe Pert was born in New York City on June 26, 1946, to Mildred and Robert Pert. She went to General Douglas MacArthur High School in Levittown, New York. She attended Hofstra University but dropped out in 1966. That year she married Agu Pert and the couple moved to Philadel-

phia so that her husband could get a doctorate at Bryn Mawr College. In 1966, Candace Pert gave birth to the first of the couple's three children.

In 1967, to help support the family, Pert took a job as a cocktail waitress. On one occasion she chatted with a customer who turned out be an assistant dean at Bryn Mawr. The dean encouraged Pert to finish her B.A. at Bryn Mawr, and helped her through the admissions process. In 1970, Pert got her B.A. in biology and that year entered the doctoral pharmacology program at Johns Hopkins University in Baltimore.

Her first research assignment, working under Dr. Solomon Snyder, was to explore the mechanisms that regulate the production of acetylcholine, the body's most important neurotransmitter. Neurotransmitters are chemicals that stimulate or inhibit other neurons throughout the body, which in turn regulate the heart and other organs. Then in the summer of 1972, again working with Dr. Snyder, she embarked on her next project, the search for an opiate receptor. Opiate receptors were believed to exist, but finding them was another matter. Although techniques for locating receptors of hormones had been put into practice, many scientists thought it would be difficult, if not impossible, to transfer the technique to an opiate receptor.

Makes Surprising Discovery of Opiate Receptors

Receptors evolve from a chain of amino-acid molecules; these molecules are shaped by electrical forces into a three-dimensional shape with an electrically active indentation which recognizes correspondingly shaped molecules. These indentations are the points at which a receptor binds with a chemical substance or neurotransmitter. Using technology borrowed from identifying insulin receptors, Pert used radioactive drugs to identify receptor molecules that bonded with morphine and other opiate drugs in animal brain cells. The first report on her finding was published in *Science* in March 1973. Pert went on to investigate whether opiate receptors developed before birth. She used pregnant rats to evaluate the brains of the fetuses and found that during fetal development opiate receptors were present.

Pert and her colleagues mulled over why opiate receptors existed. It was certainly not that animals had evolved opiate receptors to interact with poppy plants, the natural source of opium. The scientist speculated that there might be an unknown neurotransmitter, naturally produced in the body, that fulfilled a similar function. Other experiments had already shown that stimulating the brainstem of rats caused pain relief, and that the best pain relief was obtained when a specific part of the brain was stimulated. After initial investigations proved inconclusive Pert turned to other areas of research. Eventually two Scottish scientists, John Hughes and Hans Kosterlitz, found the transmitters, which they called endorphins.

The discovery of endorphins led to the discovery of other types of receptors and corresponding chemicals in the brain. Uncovering the intricate system of chemicals changed the scientific conception of the brain as an organ that signals the rest of the body using just a few chemicals. Now it is understood that the nervous system uses many substances to signal pain, pleasure and emotions as well as sensory data. Many had mistakenly hoped that the discoveries would immediately result in a cure for drug addictions or a non-addicting pain killer for cancer patients, especially since the media had sensationalized these possibilities. Although these hopes proved overoptimistic, in 1978 Snyder, Hughes and Kosterlitz received the prestigious Lasker Award for their discoveries; Pert did not. The fact that the biochemist, who had received her Ph.D. in 1974, had not been recognized for her part in the discovery caused a controversy that even erupted on the editorial pages of the prominent journal *Science.*

Pert refused to become involved in any controversy, however, and continued on at Hopkins as a National Institutes of Health fellow from 1974 to 1975, as a staff fellow from 1975 to 1977, a senior staff fellow from 1977 to 1978, and then as research pharmacologist from 1978 to 1982. In 1982, she became chief of the section on brain chemistry at the National Institutes of Mental Health (NIMH). There, the neuroscientist turned her attention to Valium receptors in the brain and the receptors where the street drug PCP, or "angel dust," takes hold. In 1986, Pert led the NIMH team that discovered peptide T. Peptides are substances that are synthesized from amino acids and are intermediate in molecular weight and chemical properties between amino acids and proteins, and have been linked to the manifestation of emotions.

Pert left NIMH in 1987 and worked for laboratories in the private sector. She also started her own company, Peptide Design, to encourage research on peptides. The company was in existence from 1987 to 1990. Since then, Pert has become an adjunct professor in the department of physiology at Georgetown University. Among her other areas of research have been investigations into the immune system and the nature of the human immunodeficiency virus (HIV) that causes AIDS. Pert won the Arthur S. Fleming Award in 1979. She is a member of the American Society of Pharmacologists and Experimental Therapeutics; the American Society of Biological Chemists; the Society of Neuroscientists; and the International Narcotics Research Conference.

Since her first discovery of an opiate receptor, Pert has located endorphin receptors throughout the body, even in the pituitary gland. She suspects that the location of receptors in sites where there is no clear connection with conscious pain serves the function of signalling the central nervous system when there is a problem with an organ. She believes, as she told an *Omni* interviewer, that scientists will eventually be able to chart the various receptors of the brain and the reactions they produce. "There's no doubt in my mind that one day—and I don't think that day is all that far away—we'll be able to make a color-coded map of the brain. A color-coded wiring diagram, with blue for one neurochemical, red for another, and so on—that's the neuroscientist's ambition."

SELECTED WRITINGS BY PERT:

Periodicals

(With Solomon Snyder) "The Opiate Receptor: Demonstration in Nervous Tissue," *Science,* March 2, 1973.
(With others) "Octapeptides Deduced From the Neuropeptide Receptor-like Pattern of Antigen T4 in Brain Potently Inhibit Human Immunodeficiency Virus Receptor Binding and T-Cell Infectivity," *Academy of Science USA,* Volume 83, 1986, pp. 9254–9258.

SOURCES:

Books

Snyder, Solomon, *Brainstorming: The Science and Politics of Opiate Research,* Harvard University Press, 1989.
Weintraub, Pamela, editor, *The Omni Interviews,* Omni Press, 1984, pp. 118–131.

Periodicals

"The Body Telling the Mind," *Fortune,* Sept. 8, 1980, p. 97.

—*Sketch by Margo Nash*

Max Perutz
1914-
Austrian-born English crystallographer and biochemist

Max Perutz pioneered the use of X-ray crystallography to determine the atomic structure of proteins by combining two lines of scientific investigation—the physiology of hemoglobin and the physics

Max Perutz

of X-ray crystallography. His efforts resulted in his sharing the 1962 Nobel Prize in chemistry with his colleague, biochemist **John Kendrew**. Perutz's work in deciphering the diffraction patterns of protein crystals opened the door for molecular biologists to study the structure and function of enzymes—specific proteins that are the catalysts for biochemical reactions in cells. Known for his impeccable laboratory skills, Perutz produced the best early pictures of protein crystals and used this ability to determine the structure of hemoglobin and the molecular mechanism by which it transports oxygen from the lungs to tissue. A passionate mountaineer and skier, Perutz also applied his expertise in X-ray crystallography to the study of glacier structure and flow.

Perutz was born in Vienna, Austria, on May 19, 1914. His parents were Hugo Perutz, a textile manufacturer, and Adele Goldschmidt Perutz. In 1932, Perutz entered the University of Vienna, where he studied organic chemistry. However, he found the university's adherence to classical organic chemistry outdated and backward. By 1926 scientists had determined that enzymes were proteins and had begun to focus on the catalytic effects of enzymes on the chemistry of cells, but Perutz's professors paid scant attention to this new realm of research. In 1934, while searching for a subject for his dissertation, Perutz attended a lecture on organic compounds, including vitamins, under investigation at Cambridge University in England. Anxious to continue his

studies in an environment more attuned to recent advances in biochemical research, Perutz decided he wanted to study at Cambridge. His wish to leave Austria and study elsewhere was relatively unique in that day and age, when graduate students seldom had the financial means to study abroad. But Hugo Perutz's textile business provided his son with the initial funds he would need to survive in England on a meager student stipend.

In 1936, Perutz landed a position as research student in the Cambridge laboratory of Desmond Bernal, who was pioneering the use of X-ray crystallography in the field of biology. Perutz, however, was disappointed again when he was assigned to research minerals while Bernal closely guarded his crystallography work, discussing it only with a few colleagues and never with students. Despite Perutz's disenchantment with his research assignments and the old, ill-lit, and dingy laboratories he worked in, he received excellent training in the promising field of X-ray crystallography, albeit in the classical mode of mineral crystallography. "Within a few weeks of arriving," Perutz states in Horace Freeland Judson's *Eighth Day of Creation: Makers of the Revolution in Biology,* "I realized that Cambridge was where I wanted to spend the rest of my life."

Begins Work with Hemoglobin

During his summer vacation in Vienna in 1937, Perutz met with Felix Haurowitz, a protein specialist married to Perutz's cousin, to seek advice on the future direction of his studies. Haurowitz, who had been studying hemoglobin since the 1920s, convinced Perutz that this was an important protein whose structure needed to be solved because of the integral role it played in physiology. In addition to making blood red, hemoglobin red corpuscles greatly increase the amount of oxygen that blood can transport through the body. Hemoglobin also transports carbon dioxide back to the lungs for disposal.

Although new to the physical chemistry and crystallography of hemoglobin, Perutz returned to Cambridge and soon obtained crystals of horse hemoglobin from Gilbert Adair, a leading authority on hemoglobin. Since the main goal of X-ray crystallography at that time was to determine the structure of any protein, regardless of its relative importance in biological activity, Perutz also began to study crystals of the digestive enzyme chymotrypsin. But chymotrypsin crystals proved to be unsuitable for study by X ray, and Perutz turned his full attention to hemoglobin, which has large crystal structures uniquely suited to X-ray crystallography. At that time, microscopic protein crystal structures were "grown" primarily through placing the proteins in a solution which was then evaporated or cooled below the saturation point. The crystal structures, in effect, are repetitive groups of cells that fit together to fill each space, with the cells representing characteristic groups of the molecules and atoms of the compound crystallized.

In the early 1930s, crystallography had been successfully used only in determining the structures of simple crystals of metals, minerals, and salts. However, proteins such as hemoglobin are thousands of times more complex in atomic structure. Physicists **William Bragg** and **Lawrence Bragg**, the only father and son to share a Nobel Prize, were pioneers of X-ray crystallography. Focusing on minerals, the Braggs found that as X rays pass through crystals, they are buffeted by atoms and emerge as groups of weaker beams which, when photographed, produce a discernible pattern of spots. The Braggs discovered that these spots were a manifestation of Fourier synthesis, a method developed in the nineteenth century by French physicist Jean Baptiste Fourier to represent regular signals as a series of sine waves. These waves reflect the distribution of atoms in the crystal.

The Braggs successfully determined the amplitude of the waves but were unable to determine their phases, which would provide more detailed information about crystal structure. Although amplitude was sufficient to guide scientists through a series of trial and error experiments for studying simple crystals, proteins were much too complex to be studied with such a haphazard and time consuming approach.

Initial attempts at applying X-ray crystallography to the study of proteins failed, and scientists soon began to wonder whether proteins in fact produce X-ray diffraction patterns. However, in 1934, Desmond Bernal and chemist **Dorothy Crowfoot Hodgkin** at the Cavendish laboratory in Cambridge discovered that by keeping protein crystals wet, specifically with the liquid from which they precipitated, they could be made to give sharply defined X-ray diffraction patterns. Still, it would take twenty-three years before scientists could construct the first model of a protein molecule.

Research Interrupted by War and Internment

Perutz and his family, like many other Europeans in the 1930s, tended to underestimate the seriousness of the growing Nazi regime in Germany. While Perutz himself was safe in England as Germany began to invade its neighboring countries, his parents fled from Vienna to Prague in 1938. That same summer, they again fled to Switzerland from Czechoslovakia, which would soon face the onslaught of the approaching German army. Perutz was shaken by his new classification as a refugee and the clear indication by some people that he might not be welcome in England any longer. He also realized that his father's financial support would certainly dwindle and die out.

As a result, in order to vacation in Switzerland in the summer of 1938, Perutz sought a travel grant to apply his expertise in crystallography to the study of glacier structures and flow. His research on glaciers involved crystallographic studies of snow transforming into ice, and he eventually became the first to measure the velocity distributions of a glacier, proving that glaciers flow faster at the surface and slower at the glacier's bed.

Finally, in 1940, the same year Perutz received his Ph.D., his work was put to an abrupt halt by the German invasions of Holland and Belgium. Growing increasingly wary of foreigners, the British government arrested all "enemy" aliens, including Perutz. "It was a very nice, very sunny day—a nasty day to be arrested," Perutz recalls in *The Eighth Day of Creation*. Transported from camp to camp, Perutz ended up near Quebec, Canada, where many other scientists and intellectuals were imprisoned, including physicists Herman Bondi and Tom Gold. Always active, Perutz began a camp university, employing the resident academicians to teach courses in their specialties. It didn't take the British government long, however, to realize that they were wasting valuable intellectual resources and, by 1941, Perutz followed many of his colleagues back to his home in England and resumed his work with crystals.

Perutz, however, wanted to contribute to the war effort. After repeated requests, he was assigned to work on the mysterious and improbable task of developing an aircraft carrier made of ice. The goal of this project was to tow the carrier to the middle of the Atlantic Ocean, where it would serve as a stopping post for aircrafts flying from the United States to Great Britain. Although supported both by then British Prime Minister Winston Churchill and the chief of the British Royal Navy, Lord Louis Mountbatten, the ill-fated project was terminated upon the discovery that the amount of steel needed to construct and support the ice carrier would cost more than constructing it entirely of steel.

Embarks on Nobel Prize-Winning Research

Perutz married Gisela Clara Peiser on March 28, 1942; the couple later had a son, Robin, and a daughter, Vivian. After the war, in 1945, Perutz was finally able to devote himself entirely to pondering the smeared spots that appeared on the X-ray film of hemoglobin crystals. He returned to Cambridge, and was soon joined by John Kendrew, then a doctoral student, who began to study myoglobin, an enzyme which stores oxygen in muscles. In 1946 Perutz and Kendrew founded the Medical Research Council Unit for Molecular Biology, and Perutz became its director. Many advances in molecular biology would take place there, including the discovery of the structure of deoxyribonucleic acid (DNA).

Over the next years, Perutz refined the X-ray crystallography technology and, in 1953, finally solved the difficult phase dilemma with a method known as isomorphous replacement. By adding atoms of mercury—which, like any heavy metal, is an excellent X-ray reflector—to each individual protein molecule, Perutz was able to change the light diffraction pattern. By comparing hemoglobin proteins with mercury attached at different places to hemoglobin without mercury, he found that he had reference points to measure phases of other hemoglobin spots. Although this discovery still required long and assiduous mathematical calculations, the development of computers hastened the process tremendously.

By 1957, Kendrew had delineated the first protein structure through crystallography, again working with myoglobin. Perutz followed two years later with a model of hemoglobin. Continuing to work on the model, Perutz and Hilary Muirhead showed that hemoglobin's reaction with oxygen involves a structural change among four subunits of the hemoglobin molecule. Specifically, the four polypeptide chains that form a tetrahedral structure of hemoglobin are rearranged in oxygenated hemoglobin. In addition to its importance to later research on the molecular mechanisms of respiratory transport by hemoglobin, this discovery led scientists to begin research on the structural changes enzymes may undergo in their interactions with various biological processes. In 1962, Perutz and Kendrew were awarded the Nobel Prize in chemistry for their codiscoveries in X-ray crystallography and the structures of hemoglobin and myoglobin, respectively. The same year, Perutz left his post as director of the Unit for Molecular Biology and became chair of its laboratory.

The work of Perutz and Kendrew was the basis for growing understanding over the following decades of the mechanism of action of enzymes and other proteins. Specifically, Perutz's discovery of hemoglobin's structure led to a better understanding of hemoglobin's vital attribute of absorbing oxygen where it is plentiful and releasing it where it is scarce. Perutz also conducted research on hemoglobin from the blood of people with sickle-cell anemia and found that a change in the molecule's shape initiates the distortion of venous red cells into a sickle shape that reduces the cells' oxygen-carrying capacity.

In *The Eighth Day of Creation,* Judson remarks that Perutz was known to have a "glass thumb" for the difficult task of growing good crystals, and it was widely acknowledged that for many years Perutz produced the best images of crystal structures. In the book, published in 1979, Perutz's long-time colleague Kendrew remarks that little changed over the years, explaining, "If I had come into the lab thirty years ago, on a Saturday evening, Max would have been in a white coat mounting a crystal—just the same." Perutz retired in 1979.

SELECTED WRITINGS BY PERUTZ:

Books

Proteins and Nucleic Acids: Structure and Function, Elsevier Publishing Company, 1962.

SOURCES:

Books

Judson, Horace Freeland, *The Eighth Day of Creation: Makers of the Revolution in Biology,* Simon & Schuster, 1979.

Periodicals

"X-rays Mark the Spots," *The Economist,* November 21, 1992, pp. 100–101.

—*Sketch by David Petechuk*

Rózsa Péter
1905-1977
Hungarian mathematician

Rózsa Péter was one of the early investigators in the field of recursive functions, a branch of mathematical logic. Recursive functions are those mathematical functions whose values can be established at every point, for whole numbers one and above. These functions are used to study the structure of number classes or functions in terms of the complexity of the calculations required to determine them, and have useful applications to computers and other automatic systems. Péter wrote two books and numerous papers on recursive functions, which are related to **Alan Turing**'s theory of algorithms and machines and to **Kurt Gödel**'s undecidability theorem of self-referential equations. Péter also wrote a popular treatment of mathematics, *Playing with Infinity,* which was translated into fourteen languages. A teacher and teacher-training instructor before her appointment to a university post, Péter won national awards for her contributions to mathematics education and to mathematics.

Péter was born in Budapest on February 17, 1905. She received her high school diploma from Mária Terézia Girls' School in 1922, then entered the university in Budapest to study chemistry. Although her father, an attorney, wanted her to stay in that field, Péter changed to the study of mathematics. One of her classmates was László Kalmár, her future teacher and colleague. Péter graduated from the university in 1927, and for two years after graduation she had no permanent job, but tutored privately and took temporary teaching assignments.

In 1932, Péter attended the International Mathematics Conference in Zurich, where she presented a lecture on mathematical logic. She published papers on recursive functions in the period 1934 to 1936, and received her Ph.D. summa cum laude in 1935. In 1937, Péter became a contributing editor of the *Journal of Symbolic Logic.* Péter lost her teaching position in 1939 due to the Fascist laws of that year; Hungary was an ally of Nazi Germany and held similar purges of academics. Nevertheless, she published papers in Hungarian journals in 1940 and 1941.

In 1943, Péter published her book, *Playing with Infinity,* which described ideas in number theory, geometry, calculus and logic, including Gödel's undecidability theory, for the layman. The book, many copies of which were destroyed by bombing during World War II, could not be distributed until 1945. The war claimed the life of Péter's brother, Dr. Nicholas Politzer, in 1945, as well as the lives of her friend and fellow mathematician, Pál Csillag, and her young pupil, Káto Fuchs, who had assisted Péter with *Playing with Infinity.*

In the late 1940s, Péter taught high school and then became Head of the Mathematics Department of the Pedological College in Budapest. She also wrote textbooks for high school mathematics. In the fifties, Péter published further studies of recursive functions; her 1951 book, *Recursive Functions,* was the first treatment of the subject in book form and reinforced her status as "the leading contributor to the special theory of recursive functions," as S. C. Kleene observed in the *Bulletin of the American Mathematical Society.*

Péter was appointed Professor of Mathematics at Eötvös Loránd University in Budapest in 1955, where she taught mathematical logic and set theory. The official publication of *Playing with Infinity* occurred in 1957. In this book, she wrote in the preface, she tried "to present concepts with complete clarity and purity so that some new light may have been thrown on the subject even for mathematicians and certainly for teachers."

In the sixties and seventies, Péter studied the relationship between recursive functions and computer programming, in particular, the relationship of recursive functions to the programming languages Algol and Lisp. Péter retired in 1975. She continued her research, however, publishing *Recursive Functions in Computer Theory* in 1976.

Péter's awards included the Kossuth Prize in 1951 for her scientific and pedological work, and the State Award, Silver Degree in 1970 and Gold Degree in 1973. Péter was a member of the Hungarian Academy of Sciences and was made honorary President of the János Bolyai Mathematical Association in 1975. Interested in literature, film and art as well as mathematics, Péter translated poetry from German and corresponded with the literary critic Marcel Benedek. She noted in *Playing with Infinity* that her mathematical studies were not so different from the arts: "I love mathematics not only for its technical applications, but principally because it is beautiful; because man has breathed his spirit of play into it, and because it has given him his greatest game—the encompassing of the infinite." Péter died on February 17, 1977.

SELECTED WRITINGS BY PÉTER:

Books

Playing with Infinity: Mathematics for Everyman, translated by Z. P. Dienes, Simon & Schuster, 1962.
Recursive Functions, 3rd revised edition, translated by István Földes, Academic Press, 1967.
Recursive Functions in Computer Theory, translated by I. Juhász, Wiley, 1981.

SOURCES:

Books

"Algorithms and Recursive Functions," *Mathematics at a Glance,* 2nd edition, Van Nostrand Reinhold, 1989, pp. 340–342.

Periodicals

Császár, Akos, "Rózsa Péter: February 17, 1905-February 16, 1977," *Matematikai Lapok* (Hungarian), Volume 25, 1974, pp. 257–258.
Dömölki, Bálint, et al, "The Scientific Work of Rózsa Péter," *Matematikai Lapok* (Hungarian), Volume 16, 1965, pp. 171–184.
Kleene, S.C., "Rekursive Funktionen," *Bulletin of the American Mathematical Society,* March, 1952, pp. 270–272.
Nelson, D., "Rózsa Péter, Rekursive Funktionen," *Mathematical Reviews,* 1952, pp. 421–422.
"Playing with Infinity," Telegraphic Reviews, *American Mathematical Monthly,* Volume 84, February, 1977, p. 147.
Robinson, Raphael M., "Rózsa Péter. Rekursive Funktionen," *Journal of Symbolic Logic,* Volume 16, 1951, pp. 280–282.

Ruzsa, Imre Z. and János Urbán, "In Memoriam Rózsa Péter," *Matematikai Lapok* (Hungarian), Volume 26, 1975, pp. 125–137.

Sudborough, I. Hal, "Rózsa Péter, Rekursive Funktionen in der Komputer-Theorie," *Mathematical Reviews,* Volume 55, #6926.

Turán, Pál, "To the Memory of Mathematician Victims of Fascism," *Matematikai Lapok* (Hungarian), Volume 26, 1975, pp. 259–263.

Other

Kocsor, Klára, notes on articles in Hungarian, January, 1994.

—*Sketch by Sally M. Moite*

Mary Locke Petermann
1908-1975
American biochemist

Mary Locke Petermann isolated and worked out the structure of animal ribosomes, organelles that are now known as the sites of protein synthesis in cells. She began her original investigation of the particles (for a time they were known as "Petermann's particles") because they were interfering with her studies of DNA and RNA. Her work was fundamental and pioneering; her continued work established the importance of ions in stabilizing ribosomes and elucidated ribosomal transformations.

Peterman was born in Laurium, Michigan, on February 25, 1908, one of three children and the only daughter of Albert Edward and Anna Mae Grierson Petermann. Her mother was a graduate of Ypsilanti State Teachers' College. Her father, a graduate of Cornell University, became a lawyer for Calumet and Hecla Consolidated Copper Company in Calumet, Michigan, after World War I; he later was president and general manager. The Petermann family lived in a large company house and enjoyed high status in the community.

After graduating from Calumet High School in 1924, Petermann spent a year at a Massachusetts preparatory school before entering Smith College. In 1929, she graduated from Smith with high honors in chemistry and membership in Phi Beta Kappa. After a year at Yale University as a technician, she spent four years working at the Boston Psychopathic Hospital, investigating the acid-base balance of mental patients. In 1936 she entered the University of Wisconsin; she received a Ph.D. degree in physiological chemistry in 1939, with a thesis project on the role of the adrenal cortex in ion regulation.

In 1939 Petermann became the first woman chemist on the staff of the Department of Physical Chemistry at the University of Wisconsin. She remained at Wisconsin as a postdoctoral researcher until 1945. During these six years she and Alwin M. Pappenheimer began to investigate the physical chemisty of proteins. Petermann discovered what were at first called "Petermann's particles" but were named ribosomes at a meeting of the Biophysical Society in 1958. (It was at this meeting that **George Palade**, a research scientist who had independently played a pivotal role in discovering ribosomes, called Petermann "the mother of the particles.") Ribosomes are where protein synthesis occurs in a cell. Petermann's research isolated several types of ribosomes and clarified their properties. She also pioneered the study of antibodies. This research later led to **Rodney Porter** winning a Nobel Prize in 1972 for his work on the structure of immunoglobulins.

After leaving the University of Wisconsin in 1945, Petermann accepted the position of research chemist at Memorial Hospital in New York City to explore the role of plasma proteins in cancer. (According to Mary L. Moller, Petermann had been recommended to the director, Cornelius Rhoads, as "the girl out in Wisconsin.") In 1946 she was appointed Finney-Howell Foundation fellow at the newly founded Sloan-Kettering Institute, where she explored the role of nucleoproteins in cancer. She became an associate member of the institute in 1960, the first woman member in 1963, and member emeritus in 1973 when she retired. Concurrent with her work at Sloan-Kettering, she also taught biochemistry in the Sloan-Kettering Division, Graduate School of Medical Sciences, Cornell University. In 1966, she became the first woman appointed a full professor at Cornell. She authored or co-authored almost 100 scientific papers.

As the Sloan Award recipient in 1963, Petermann was honored for what the accompanying citation explained was her "many basic and distinguished contributions to the knowledge of the relevance of proteins and nucleoproteins in abnormal growth. An even greater contribution has been her fundamental work on the nature of the cell ribosome." Petermann used her award money to work for a year in the Swedish laboratory of Nobel laureate **Arne Tiselius**. She also lectured in several European countries, including England and France. In 1966 she received the Garvan Medal of the American Chemical Society, which honors contributions made by women scientists, an honorary doctorate from Smith College, and the Distinguished Service Award from the American Academy of Achievement.

Petermann never married. In 1974, the year before her death, she organized the Memorial Sloan-Kettering Cancer Center Association for Professional Women and served as its first president. She died in Philadelphia on December 13, 1975, of intestinal cancer, which had been misdiagnosed as a "nervous stomach" earlier that year. In 1976 the Educational Foundation of the Association for Women in Science named one of its graduate scholarships in her honor.

SELECTED WRITINGS BY PETERMANN:

Books

The Physical and Chemical Properties of Ribosomes, Elsevier Publishing Company, 1964.

SOURCES:

Books

Moller, Mary L., "Mary Locke Petermann (1908–1975)" in Grinstein, Louise S., Rose K. Rose, and Miriam H. Rafailovich, editors, *Women in Chemistry and Physics,* Greenwood Press, 1993, pp. 476–487.
O'Neill, Lois Decker, editor, *The Women's Book of World Records and Achievements,* Doubleday, 1979, p. 168.

—*Sketch by Jill Carpenter*

Edith R. Peterson
1914-1992
American medical researcher

A medical researcher specializing in cell cultures, Edith R. Peterson was the first scientist to grow myelin, the outer covering of nerve cells, in a test tube. Her discovery aided research into multiple sclerosis, muscular dystrophy, and other diseases of the nervous system.

Peterson was born Edith Elizabeth Runne on June 24, 1914, in Brooklyn, New York, to Hermann and Else Helmke Runne. Peterson's father, co-owner of a restaurant and catering establishment, died suddenly in 1920, shortly before he was to take a trip to Germany to join his wife and two daughters, who were visiting relatives. After staying in Germany for the next six years, the family returned to the United

Edith R. Peterson

States, where Peterson's mother obtained employment designing custom dresses. In 1937 Peterson received a B.S. degree from Barnard College; two years later she earned a master's degree in zoology from Columbia University. In September of 1941 she married Charles Peterson, a commercial artist. The couple had a son, Wesley, in 1952 and a daughter, Rhonda Lea, in 1954.

In the early 1940s Peterson went to work in the laboratory of Margaret Murray at Columbia University. While working there, she was able to grow functional nerve cells using cultures containing chicken embryos. She utilized organotype culture which, unlike other methods of growing cells, involves having cells simulate the actual structure and functions of the organs from which they have been taken. Peterson succeeded in growing the actual nerve cells, brain, and spinal cord of chickens. In doing so she was also able to grow myelin, the insulating sheath surrounding nerve cells—the first time this had been done. This discovery aided research on multiple sclerosis, a disease that involves the degeneration of the myelin in the brain and spinal cord.

In 1966 Peterson left Columbia to work with Dr. Murray Bornstein at the Albert Einstein College of Medicine of Yeshiva University in the Bronx, New York. There she concentrated her studies on muscular dystrophy, a wasting disease affecting skeletal muscles. In addition to her research, she taught her techniques for organotype culture to students from the United States, Asia, and Europe.

Peterson retired in 1990 following a stroke that hindered her ability to use her right hand. Shortly afterward, she and her husband moved to Middletown, New York. Peterson died of a stroke on August 15, 1992.

SOURCES:

Books

Edelson, Edward, *The Nervous System,* Chelsea House, 1991.
Rosner, Louis, and Shelley Ross, *Multiple Sclerosis,* Prentice-Hall, 1987.

Periodicals

"Edith Peterson, 78; Studied Cell Cultures" (obituary), *New York Times,* p. D14.

Other

Peterson, Wesley, personal communication with Francis Rogers, January 14, 1994.

—Sketch by Francis Rogers

Frank Piasecki
1919-
American helicopter engineer

Frank Piasecki, an aviation pioneer who helped develop the concept of vertical take-off/landing (VTOL), introduced many innovations to the design of helicopters. Among his accomplishments was the engineering of helicopters which could achieve heavier load-carrying capacities, an improvement that rendered them more efficient, thus more economical. Piasecki also engineered improvements in the helicopter's handling and stability.

Frank Nicholas Piasecki was born in Philadelphia, Pennsylvania, on October 24, 1919, to Nikodem (a tailor who had emigrated from Poland) and Emilia Piasecki. While growing up in Philadelphia, he worked as a teenager for the Kellet Autogyro Company and the Aero Service Corporation. Piasecki's early exposure to autogyros laid the foundation for his later work, since the autogyro, while not a true helicopter, was a fixed wing craft with a rotor.

Piasecki received his degree in mechanical engineering from the University of Pennsylvania's Towne School, then soon afterwards earned a bachelor's of science degree in aeronautical engineering from the Guggenheim School of Aeronautics of New York University in 1940. After college, Piasecki became a designer for Platte-LePage Aircraft Company, then worked for the Edward G. Budd Manufacturing Company as an aerodynamicist in its aircraft division.

Piasecki also founded a research group, the PV-Engineering Forum, which was composed of University of Pennsylvania engineering students. Their first helicopter was the PV–2, a single-seat, single-rotor helicopter built for the purpose of proving what were at the time advanced concepts of VTOL. The PV–2, which had the first dynamically balanced rotor blades, a tension-torsion pitch-change system, and overhead stick and a rigid, anti-torque tail rotor, was the second helicopter to fly successfully in the United States. Its maiden flight took place on April 11, 1943, with Piasecki at the controls. Up to that point, Piasecki had only fourteen hours of flying time, all of it in fixed-wing aircraft; nevertheless, he successfully taught himself to fly the PV–2. The following October, Piasecki demonstrated the PV–2 to military commanders and commercial operators in Washington, D.C., and impressed those present with the PV–2's precision finger-tip control.

Develops Choppers for Military Use

Due to his critical skills as an aeronautical engineer, Piasecki was exempted from military service during World War II, although he contributed in other ways to the war effort. In January, 1944, the U.S. Coast Guard signed a contract with Piasecki, who would produce for them a large helicopter capable of rescuing people from torpedoed ships along the coast; this aircraft would be known as the HRP–1. First flown by Piasecki in March, 1945, the HRP–1 was revolutionary as it featured—for the first time—tandem rotors mounted on a helicopter. Far from interfering with each other, the rotors allowed the machine to carry heavy loads without great concern for load balance. The U.S. Navy bought twenty of this model, soon to be dubbed the "Flying Banana," so-called because the ends of the elongated craft were bent up slightly so that the rotors did not interfere with each other.

The Flying Banana proved most useful for a number of military applications such as mine-sweeping, amphibious assault, search and rescue tasks, and heavy load transport. Another model, the HRP–2, was built for the Marine Corps' assault mission and was notable for its vertical landing capability; the craft also featured a thinner shell and stiffer sections which enhanced its strength while keeping its weight to a minimum (to produce the metal Piasecki developed a stretch-milling process now found throughout helicopter manufacturing).

In 1946, the PV Forum was transformed into the Piasecki Helicopter Corporation; Piasecki served as both president and chairman of the board of the new company. The next significant improvement to arrive in helicopter design was the development of the HUP models. Conceived for the U.S. Navy, the HUP–1 featured over-lapping rotors, a necessity when it came to swiftly storing the craft on a lower deck of a ship. The HUP–2 model was the first helicopter to have an autopilot. This permitted IFR (instrument flight rules) flying, as well as hands-off flying, even when the helicopter was hovering. So useful was the HUP–2 that it was not only flown by the military services of the United States, but by those of Canada and France.

While the HUP was the naval version of these helicopters, the army version was designated the H-series. Among them, the H–21 attained an altitude over 22,000 feet and featured a fixed tricycle-type landing gear. Doughnut-shaped floaters around the wheels allowed for landings on any type of terrains. Ideal for rescue operations—especially those where injuries were present, since it could carry up to twelve stretchers—the H–21 also had the distinction of being the first helicopter to make a non-stop transcontinental flight across the United States (the journey lasted thirty-seven hours and involved in-flight refueling). Other countries, such as West Germany, Sweden, Japan, and Canada, employed the H–21 for many years.

The U.S. Air Force commissioned the development of a long range rescue helicopter for picking up stranded bomber crews in 1946. The ensuing helicopter, the YH–16, was the largest in the world, with a length of 134 feet, and was also the first helicopter with twin engines. An improved version, the H–16, was produced for the U.S. Army; it could hold three jeeps and carried various pods for specialized functions, such as an electronics center, a field operating room, and a mobile repair center.

Forms New Company for Further VTOL Advancement

In the mid–1950s, the Piasecki Helicopter Corporation was purchased by Boeing Airplane Company, and Piasecki formed a new company called Piasecki Aircraft Corporation. He became committed to further research and development of VTOL, especially where higher speed and heavier lift capability were concerned. However, Piasecki still maintained his role in developing helicopters for the military. For instance, the deployment of nuclear submarines prompted the navy to seek a good weapons delivery system that could be ship-based; Piasecki not only developed the PA–4 for this need, but made it a drone and installed a system for maintaining a constant

azimuth heading no matter which direction the helicopter flew. Known as the "Sea-Bat," this model was followed by the "Mud-Bat" and the "Ice-Bat."

Piasecki's next innovation, the PA–59 "Air-Geep," was a terrain- following craft invisible to radar. Its maiden flight was in September, 1958. Unlike conventional helicopters, the AirGeep was unique because its rotors did not stir up clouds of sand, dust or snow as it skimmed the surface of the earth. This aircraft was followed by the PA–59N "SeaGeep" which could land on the water or easily land aboard ship; it first flew in November, 1961.

The army desired the capability to carry its biggest tank, weighing at sixty-two tons, by helicopter (a feat no helicopter could accomplish). One of the solutions Piasecki engineered was that of developing configurations wherein multiple helicopters were joined to provide the needed lift and fly as one unit. This system was known as the PA–39 and led later to a hybrid system where blimps were used connected to helicopters for maximum lift.

The PA–97, developed in the early 1980s, continued the hybrid lift concept, eventually being able to lift from sixty to two hundred tons. Piasecki believed that higher speeds and greater load capacity were the concerns of future helicopter development, along with such considerations as reduced noise and vibrations.

Piasecki, the recipient of twenty-three patents on helicopter development, was the first person the Civil Aeronautics Administration recognized as a helicopter pilot before being a fixed-wing pilot. The United States Coast Guard made him an honorary helicopter pilot on April 23, 1945, at Fort Bennett Field, and in 1955, he was awarded an honorary doctorate in aeronautical engineering from New York University. In addition, Piasecki received a doctor of science degree in 1970 from Alliance College in Cambridge Springs, Pennsylvania. In 1974, he was inducted into the Army Aviation Hall of Fame and also received the Leonardo da Vinci Award from the Navy Helicopter Association.

In December, 1958, Piasecki married the former Vivian O'Gara Weyerhaeuser with whom he had five sons and two daughters. The annual donator of the Dr. Alexander Klemin Award—presented by the American Helicopter Society—Piasecki has also served as both president and fellow of that organization. In addition, he is a founding member and fellow of what is now known as the American Institute of Aeronautics and Astronautics. A frequent lecturer to technological associations in the United States and abroad, Piasecki has testified before Congress on the concept of heavy vertical air lift.

SELECTED WRITINGS BY PIASECKI:

Periodicals

"Helicopter Air Travel," *Flight Magazine,* October 10, 1952.

"International Cooperation," *Aero Digest,* September 4, 1955.

SOURCES:

Books

Boyne, Walter J., and Donald S. Lopez, editors, *Vertical Flight,* Smithsonian Institution Press, 1984.
Carey, Keith, *The Helicopter,* Tab Books, 1986.
Lightbody, Andy, and Joe Poyer, *The Illustrated History of Helicopters,* Publications International, 1990.
Young, Warren R., *The Helicopters,* Time-Life, 1982.

Periodicals

Anderton, D. A., "Piasecki Tests Ring-Wing VTOL Design Concept," *Aviation Week,* September 26, 1960, p. 54.
Deigan, E., "Flying Bananas and How They Grew," *Flying,* July, 1949, p. 24.
Holt, W. J., Jr., "He Likes to Fly Straight Up," *Saturday Evening Post,* August 11, 1951, p. 32.
"Piasecki: Getting Set for Mass Transportation," *Business Week,* September 26, 1953, p. 144.

Other

Biography provided by Frank Piasecki, 1992.
The Piasecki Story of Vertical Lift, Piasecki Aircraft Corporation, Essington, PA.

—*Sketch by Susan E. Kolmer*

Auguste Piccard
1884-1962
Swiss physicist

Auguste Piccard earned his fame by exploring higher into the Earth's atmosphere and deeper into its oceans than had any person before him. Son of the chair of the department of chemistry at the University of Basel, he and his twin brother both earned doctorates in engineering, became professors themselves, and collaborated in a variety of research projects. In 1931, Piccard and a colleague traveled in a balloon to an altitude of about ten miles, more than three miles higher than any human had ever gone before. Shortly after this feat, Piccard became interested in the exploration of the ocean depths and designed a new vehicle—the bathyscaphe—by which they could be explored.

Auguste Piccard and his twin brother Jean Félix were born in Basel, Switzerland, on January 28, 1884. The Piccard family had a long and notable history in the area. Auguste and Jean Félix's grandfather had been chief commissioner of the region in which the family lived, and their uncle owned the Piccard-Pictet Company in Geneva, manufacturers of hydroelectric turbines. The twins' mother was Hélène Haltenhoff Piccard, and their father Jules Piccard was chairman of the department of chemistry at the University of Basel.

After graduation from the local high school, the twins entered the Federal Institute of Technology in Zürich where Auguste majored in mechanical engineering and Jean Félix majored in chemical engineering. They both received their bachelor of science degrees and then went on to complete doctorates in their respective fields. Between 1907 and 1920, Auguste taught in Zürich. He then accepted an appointment as professor of physics at the Brussels Polytechnic Institute, a post he held until his retirement in 1954.

Uses New Technology to Explore Upper Atmosphere

One of Piccard's earliest interests was the Earth's upper atmosphere and the cosmic rays to be detected there. He was not alone, of course, in this interest. As early as 1783, scientists had been using lighter-than-air balloons to carry themselves and their instruments into the atmosphere to study its properties. In 1804, for example, the French physicist Joseph Louis Gay-Lussac had ridden a balloon 23,000 feet into the atmosphere where he collected samples of air for later analysis. Auguste and Jean Félix made their own first balloon ascension from Zürich in 1913, after which, in 1915, they both joined the balloon section of the Swiss army for a period of service.

The use of balloons to study the atmosphere involved an inherent risk and limitation, however. At a certain altitude, the air becomes so thin that humans can no longer function. In 1862, the English meteorologist James Glashier lost consciousness as his balloon reached an altitude of 29,000 feet. He survived only because his companion was able to maneuver the balloon back to earth. Such occurrences made it clear to scientists that open-air balloons could be used only below certain altitudes.

One solution to this limitation was developed by the French meteorologist Léon Philippe Teisserenc de Bort. Teisserenc de Bort decided that unmanned balloons carrying instruments could more safely record the data that humans had been collecting previously. Between 1899 and 1902, he launched dozens of automated balloons that brought back information about the atmosphere. One discovery he made was the existence of layers in the atmosphere, the first evidence for the presence of the stratosphere. Piccard's view was that unmanned ascents could never provide the quality of data that could be obtained from balloons in which humans could travel. He resolved, therefore, to design a pressurized gondola in which observers could travel well beyond the 29,000 foot level that had marked the previous barrier to manned flight.

By 1930, his first design was ready for testing. The gondola was made of an air-tight aluminum shell that could be pressurized to sea-level pressures and was then suspended from a hydrogen-filled balloon. On May 27, 1931, Piccard and a colleague, Paul Kipfer, took off in their airship from Augsburg, Germany. They eventually reached an altitude of 51,775 feet, by far the highest altitude so far attained by human researchers. About 15 months later, on August 18, 1932, Piccard made another record-breaking ascent, this time to a height of 53,139 feet after departing from Zürich. His companion on this flight was Max Cosyns.

Piccard made more than two dozen more balloon ascensions before he retired from the activity in 1937. During that time, he collected valuable new information on atmospheric electricity and radioactivity , as well as cosmic radiation. Probably more important, he continued to improve on the design of his aircraft, making the kinds of improvements that would eventually allow other scientists to reach altitudes of more than 100,000 feet. In recognition of his many accomplishments in balloon flight, Piccard was awarded the Gold Medal of the Belgian Aero Club.

Descends to Record Depths

In the late 1930s, Piccard shifted his attention to a new challenge: the ocean depths. He became convinced that the same techniques used to study the thin upper atmosphere could be used in the high-pressure depths of the oceans. He began work on the design of a *bathyscaphe,* or "ship of the deep." The bathyscaphe consisted of two parts. The lower portion of the vessel was an air-tight steel sphere, built to withstand pressures of 12,000 pounds per square inch, where researchers rode. The upper part of the bathyscaphe consisted of a 5,200 cubic foot metal tank containing heptane that provided the vessel with buoyancy. The bathyscaphe operated under its own power and could rise or sink by having seawater pumped into the flotation chamber or iron pellets dumped from the same chamber.

The first test of the bathyscaphe took place in 1948, but the vessel was able to dive no deeper than about a mile below sea level, far less than Piccard had hoped. He continued to modify the design of his vessel, however, and a second test five years later was more successful. In 1953, he and his son Jacques traveled to a depth of 10,335 feet off the coast of Capri, a depth three times as great as the previous record set by William Beebe in his bathysphere in 1934. The Piccards also built another bathyscaphe, the *Trieste,* which was sold to the U.S. Navy for research use. The *Trieste* was used in a 1960 expedition that took Jacques Piccard and U.S. Navy lieutenant Don Walsh to a depth of 35,802 feet in the Mariana Trench off the coast of Guam. Piccard and his son Jacques were working on yet another modification of the bathyscaphe design—to be called a mesoscaphe—when Piccard died on March 25, 1962, in Lausanne, Switzerland.

SELECTED WRITINGS BY PICCARD:

Books

Audessus des nuages, B. Grasset (Paris), 1933.
Entre terre et ciel, Editions d'Ouchy (Lausanne), 1946, translation by Claude Apcher published as *Between Earth and Sky,* Falcon Press, 1950.
Au fond des mers en bathyscaphe, Arthaud (Paris), 1954, translation by Christina Stead published as *In Balloon and Bathyscaphe,* Cassell, 1956, and as *Earth, Sky, and Sea,* Oxford University Press, 1956.

SOURCES:

Books

Field, Adelaide, *Auguste Piccard, Captain of Space, Admiral of the Abyss,* Houghton Mifflin, 1969.
Honour, Alan, *Ten Miles High, Two Miles Deep: The Adventures of the Piccards,* Whitlesey House, 1957.
Malkus, Alida, *Exploring the Sky and Sea: Auguste and Jacques Piccard,* Kingston, 1961.
Stehling, Kurt R., and William Beller, "The First Space-Gondola Flight," in *Skyhooks,* Doubleday, 1962.

—*Sketch by David E. Newton*

David Pimentel
1925-
American entomologist and ecologist

David Pimentel is professor of insect ecology and agricultural sciences at Cornell University in Ithaca, New York. A widely recognized authority on ecologically sound methods of pest control, sustainable agriculture, and the relationship between human populations and environmental impacts, Pimentel has played a central role in national and international environmental policies.

Pimentel was born on May 24, 1925, in Fresno, California. His parents, Frank Freitas and Marion Silva Pimentel, were farmers raising vegetables and grapes. At age six, Pimentel moved with his family to a farm in Middleborough, Massachusetts. After completing high school, Pimentel left Massachusetts for Saint John's University in Collegeville, Minnesota, where in 1943 he received pilot and officer training as a member of the U.S. Air Force. Pimentel remained in the Air Force for two years before returning to the East Coast to attend the University of Massachusetts at Amherst beginning in 1945. He received his bachelor of science degree in 1948. Also during this period, he spent the summer semester of 1946 at Clark University in Worcester, Massachusetts. Pimentel's scientific career gained an auspicious start when his undergraduate research was published in 1949.

Pimentel earned his Ph.D. from Cornell University in 1951 following just three years of graduate school. Still a member of the Air Force Reserve, Pimentel was called back into active duty after receiving his Ph.D. Pimentel no longer desired a flying career and obtained a transfer into the U.S. Public Health Service (USPHS). He served as chief of the Tropical Research Laboratory in San Juan, Puerto Rico, from 1951 to 1955. Research there primarily focused on mongooses—important in the transmission of rabies—and snails, which contributed to the spread of other major diseases. From 1954 to 1955 Pimentel spent spring and summer in Savannah, Georgia, as project leader at the USPHS Technical Development Laboratory. During winters, Pimentel engaged in postdoctoral insect ecology research at the University of Chicago, Illinois.

Pimentel joined the faculty of Cornell University in 1955 as assistant professor of insect ecology. He has remained there for the duration of his career, becoming a full professor and chairman of the department of entomology and limnology in 1963. Pimentel's research broadened over the course of his career. He explained in an interview with Peter H.

David Pimentel

Taylor, "I began in entomology and pest control, and then became interested in environmental implications of pesticides. Studying this made me more broadly interested in issues surrounding water resources, soil resources, deforestation, and energy. Ultimately, I became interested in the whole question of human populations and their impact on the environment."

Pimentel has authored over four hundred publications, including seventeen books. One of the most important is a 1973 paper that reported the first-ever measurements of energy use in food production. It appeared at the height of the energy crisis in the 1970s. Other landmark publications include several articles related to reduction of pesticide use and a 1963 paper that led to new methods of selecting pest control agents.

Pimentel's expertise in environmental research led to his participation in numerous national and international committees. Among the most notable was the President's Science Advisory Council of 1964–66. The council assembled basic research information on a wide range of environmental pollution issues into a major report used in policy development. Also significant was a 1969 commission on pesticides that recommended the banning of DDT and that led to the formation of the Environmental Protection Agency. Serving more than sixteen years as an elected member of the Ithaca, New York, mayor's council, Pimentel has been active in the administration of local affairs, such as road repairs and the town budget.

He lives in Ithaca with his wife Maria Hutchins, a nutritionist also on the Cornell faculty, whom he married in 1949. They have two daughters and a son.

Pimentel's former students have become major players in research and environmental policy making throughout the world. His accomplishments have attracted many honors, including the 1992 Award for Distinguished Service to Rural Life. Anne H. Ehrlich, a researcher at Stanford University recognized for her expertise in related research areas, said of Pimentel in an interview with Peter H. Taylor, "He has had a substantial impact ... on the recognition of how agricultural systems fit into the larger ecological picture, and how people altering those systems end up damaging them. Beyond this, David Pimentel has played an important role in influencing public policy related to environmental issues."

SELECTED WRITINGS BY PIMENTEL:

Books

(With M. Pimental) *Food, Energy, and Society,* Edward Arnold, 1979.
(Editor with H. Lehman) *The Pesticide Question: Environment, Economics, and Ethics,* Chapman & Hall, 1993.
(Editor) *World Soil Erosion and Conservation,* Cambridge University Press, 1993.

Periodicals

(With L. E. Hurd, A. C. Bellotti, M. J. Forster, and others) "Food Production and the Energy Crisis," *Science,* Volume 182, 1979, pp. 443–449.

Other

Ehrlich, Anne H., interview with Peter H. Taylor conducted on January 28, 1994.
Pimentel, David, interview with Peter H. Taylor conducted on January 25, 1994.

—Sketch by Peter H. Taylor

Gifford Pinchot
1865-1946
American forester and conservationist

Gifford Pinchot was a pioneer of the forestry movement in the United States. He was the first American to receive formal training in forestry and practice systematic forest management, beginning with his work in the Biltmore Forest of North Carolina in 1892. Eventually serving under Presidents William McKinley, Theodore Roosevelt, and William Howard Taft as the chief of the Forest Service, Pinchot was a major force on the national scene. He was also an early conservationist in the United States and a two-term governor of Pennsylvania.

Born August 11, 1865, in Simsbury, Connecticut, Pinchot was the first of four children by James Wallace Pinchot, a wealthy New York merchant, and Mary Jane (Eno) Pinchot. The children were raised in an atmosphere rich with French culture and—because of their parents' place in society—were exposed to important personalities in the arts and politics. As a boy, Pinchot attended private schools in New York and Paris, as well as the Phillips Exeter Academy.

Upon entering Yale University in 1885, Pinchot had accepted the advice of his father and made up his mind to become a professional forester. Yale, like other American universities, did not offer courses in forestry at the time, so Pinchot took courses in botany, meteorology, and other sciences. After graduating in 1889 with a B.A. degree, he traveled to London to study the British government's forestry program in India. He also attended the National Forestry School in Nancy, France, where he studied silviculture (tree-growing) and forest economics. His examination of forest management in countries like France, Germany, and Switzerland convinced him that the right approach would be to treat forests as a public resource. When Pinchot returned home in 1890, he was determined to introduce the concept of public forestry in the United States.

In 1892 Pinchot was hired to manage the much-neglected Biltmore Forest, located in the North Carolina estate of the railroad magnate, George Vanderbilt. This was Pinchot's opportunity to apply the principles of scientific forestry as employed in Europe, and in a year, he was able to show a profit. Pinchot left North Carolina in 1894 to set up his own consultancy service in New York City. His work took him all over the United States and acquainted him with the nation's forest reserves. An advocate of regulating commercial use of public and private forests, he nevertheless favored selective harvesting and other measures to promote the well-being and regrowth of forests.

Pinchot was appointed in 1896 to the newly created National Forest Commission of the National Academy of Sciences. The commission's study of the national forest reserves in the western states culminated in the passage of the Forest Management Act of 1897, which was the legal framework for the commercial use of these reserves.

Enters Government Service

Offered a post in the United States Division of Forestry in 1897, Pinchot was chosen the following year to succeed Dr. Bernhard E. Fernow as the chief of the small agency, which was part of the federal Department of Agriculture. Pinchot then began a campaign for the transfer of all the United States forest reserves—which were then being controlled by the Interior Department—to the Department of Agriculture. He succeeded in 1905 and the division was renamed the Forest Service; in 1907, the transferred reserves became known as national forests. The success of Pinchot's mission largely depended on the support he received from President Theodore Roosevelt, with whom Pinchot developed a close association and friendship. Pinchot's administration of the nation's forests resulted in their increase from fifty-one million acres in area in 1901 to 175 million by 1910.

Pinchot also joined with Roosevelt in bringing conservation ideas to the forefront and helped formulate the conservation policies of the president's administration. He worked to ensure a systematic classification of the nation's natural resources by the United States Geographical Survey and, in 1908, influenced the Inland Waterways Commission (of which he was a member) to set forth proposals aimed at regional development of the nation's river systems. Also in 1908, Pinchot organized the White House Conference on the Conservation of Natural Resources, then served as chairman of the subsequent National Conservation Commission, which inventoried the country's natural resources.

Pinchot's fortunes, however, began to reverse when Taft succeeded Roosevelt at the White House. Losing his favored position as a close presidential advisor, Pinchot faced hostility from Richard A. Ballinger, the Secretary of the Interior and a close associate of Taft, who opposed many of Pinchot's conservation policies and attempted to undermine the smooth functioning of the Forest Service. In the power struggle that ensued between the two, Pinchot was dismissed from government service for publicly criticizing the president.

Begins a Career in Politics

Pinchot increasingly turned his attention to politics, prompted by the belief that public service should include a political career. He campaigned against Taft's reelection, helped found the National Progressive Republican League in 1911, and worked for Roosevelt's renomination in 1912 by the new Progressive Party. On August, 14, 1914, Pinchot married Cornelia Elizabeth Bryce, with whom he would have one son, Gifford Bryce. A suffragist and champion of women's rights, Cornelia took on an important role as Pinchot's closest political advisor, helping to guide her husband's career.

Pinchot was known for his strong views. During his unsuccessful run for the Senate against Pennsylvania's Boies Penrose in 1914, he favored some extreme views such as government ownership of railroads, public utilities, and the coal, copper, and lumber industries (later he softened his stand on these issues). He made an unsuccessful attempt at a senate nomination in 1920, then—the same year—became forestry commissioner of Pennsylvania under Governor William C. Sproul. Still determined to secure a political office, Pinchot was finally elected governor of Pennsylvania in 1922.

The high point of Pinchot's first term was the reform of government operations and state finances. In 1930, he was elected to a second term, but his conflicts with the public utilities prevented him from enacting any major accomplishments. He did succeed, however, in creating jobs during an era hard hit by the Great Depression. Pinchot's ambitions of a presidential or vice presidential nomination were never realized. He ran again—in vain—for a senate seat in 1932 and sought the nomination for governor in the state primary in 1938. Pinchot died of leukemia on October 4, 1946, at Columbia Presbyterian Medical Center in New York and was buried in Milford, Pennsylvania.

Through the years, Pinchot's interest in conservation did not wane. He played a key role in the passage of laws favoring conservation, such as the Weeks Act in 1911 and the Water Power Act of 1920. He became a nonresident lecturer and professor at the Yale School of Forestry, which had been established in 1900 by a grant from his family. He also founded and became president of the Society of American Foresters. His memo on forests for president Franklin D. Roosevelt resulted in the creation of the Civilian Conservation Corps, which recruited young men for reforestation projects.

In his belief that forests should be used, not just preserved, Pinchot ran into opposition from many conservationists of his day. His autobiography *Breaking New Ground* (which was published posthumously in 1947) is "one of the central documents of the American conservation movement," according to T. H. Watkins in *American Heritage*.

SELECTED WRITINGS BY PINCHOT:

Books

A Primer of Forestry, Government Printing Office, 1899.
The Fight for Conservation, Doubleday, 1910.
The Training of a Forester, Lippincott, 1914.
Breaking New Ground, Harcourt, 1947.

SOURCES:

Books

Faber, Doris and Harold Faber, *Great Lives ... Nature and the Environment,* Charles Scribner's Sons, 1991.

Fausold, Martin, L., *Gifford Pinchot: Bull Moose Progressive,* Syracuse University Press, 1961.

McGeary, M. Nelson, *Gifford Pinchot: Forester-Politician,* Princeton University Press, 1960.

Pinkett, Harold, T., *Gifford Pinchot: Private and Public Forester,* University of Illinois Press, 1970.

Squire, C. B., *Heroes of Conservation,* Fleet Press, 1974.

Wister, Owen, *Roosevelt: The Story of a Friendship, 1880–1919,* Macmillan, 1930.

Periodicals

Journal of Forestry 9 (Gifford Pinchot Commemorative Issue), Volume 63, No. 8, August, 1965.

Watkins, T. H., "Father of the Forests," *American Heritage,* February/March 1991, pp. 86–98.

—*Sketch by Kala Dwarakanath*

Gregory Goodwin Pincus
1903-1967
American biologist

Gregory Goodwin Pincus' research in endocrinology resulted in pathbreaking work on hormones and animal physiology. However, he is best known for developing the oral contraceptive pill. As his friend and colleague Hudson Hoagland remarked in *Perspectives in Biology and Medicine:* "[Pincus'] highly important development of a pill ... to control human fertility in a world rushing on to pathological overpopulation is an example of practical humanism at its very best." In addition, Pincus also participated in the founding of the Worcester Foundation for Experimental Biology and the annual Laurentian Hormone Conference.

Pincus was born in Woodbine, New Jersey, on April 9, 1903, the eldest son of Joseph and Elizabeth Lipman Pincus. His father, a graduate of Storrs Agricultural College in Connecticut, was a teacher and the editor of a farm journal. His mother's family came from Latvia and settled in New Jersey. Pincus' uncle on his mother's side, Jacob Goodale Lipman,

was dean of the New Jersey State College of Agriculture at Rutgers University, director of the New Jersey State Agricultural Experiment Station, and the founding editor of *Soil Science* magazine.

After attending a public grade school in New York City, Pincus became an honor student at Morris High School where he was president of the debating and literary societies. As an undergraduate at Cornell University, he founded and edited the *Cornell Literary Review.* After receiving his B.S. degree in 1924, he was accepted into graduate school at Harvard. He concentrated on genetics under W. E. Castle but also did work on physiology with animal physiologist W. J. Crozier. Pincus credited the two scientists with influencing him to eventually study reproductive physiology. He received both his Master of Science and Doctor of Science degrees in 1927 at the age of twenty-four. Pincus married Elizabeth Notkin on December 2, 1924, the same year he completed his undergraduate degree. They had three children—Alexis, John, and Laura Jane.

Pursues Research in Reproductive Biology

In 1927 Pincus won a three-year fellowship from the National Research Council. During this time, he travelled to Cambridge University in England where he worked with F. H. A. Marshall and John Hammond, who were pioneers in reproductive biology. He also studied at the Kaiser Wilhelm Institute with the geneticist **Richard Goldschmidt**. He returned to Harvard in 1930, first as an instructor in biology and then as assistant professor.

Much of the research Pincus did during the early part of his career concentrated on the inheritance of physiological traits. Later research focused on reproductive physiology, particularly sex hormones and gonadotrophic hormones (those which stimulate the reproductive glands). Other research interests included geotropism, the inheritance of diabetes, relationships between hormones and stress, and endocrine function in patients with mental disorders. He also contributed to the development of the first successful extensive partial pancreatectomy in rats.

The development of the oral contraceptive pill began in the early 1930s with Pincus' work on ovarian hormones. He published many studies of living ova (eggs) and their fertilization. While still at Harvard he perfected some of the earliest methods of transplanting animal eggs from one female to another who would carry them to term. He also developed techniques to produce multiple ovulation in laboratory animals. As a consequence of this work, he learned that some phases of development of an animal's ovum were regulated by particular ovarian hormones. Next, he analyzed the effects of ovarian hormones on the function of the uterus, the travel of the egg, and the maintenance of the blastocyst (the first embryonic stage) and later the embryo itself. By 1939 he had published the results of his research on breeding rabbits without males by artificially activating the eggs in the females. This manipulation was called "Pincogenesis," and it was widely reported in the press, but it was not able to be widely replicated by other researchers.

After returning from a year at Cambridge University in 1938, Pincus became a visiting professor of experimental zoology at Clark University in Worcester, Massachusetts, where he stayed until 1945. It was at Clark that Pincus began to work with Hoagland, though they had known each other as graduate students. Together they began to research the relationship between stress and hormones for the United States Navy and Air Force. Specifically, they examined the relationship between steroid excretion, adrenal cortex function, and the stress of flying. While at Clark University, Pincus was named a Guggenheim fellow and elected to the American Academy of Arts and Sciences.

Participates in the Founding of Scientific Organizations

In the spring of 1943, the first conference on hormones sponsored by the American Association for the Advancement of Science was held near Baltimore. Since the conference was held at a private club, African American scientist **Percy Julian** was excluded. Pincus protested to the management, and Julian was eventually allowed to join the conference. Although not an organizer the first year, Pincus was involved in reshaping the conference the following year, along with biochemist Samuel Gurin and physiological chemist Robert W. Bates. They held the conference in the Laurentian mountains of Quebec, Canada, and from then on the conference was known as the Laurentian Conference, and Pincus was its permanent chairperson. In addition to his administrative duties, he edited the twenty-three volumes of *Recent Progress in Hormone Research,* a compendium of papers presented at the annual conferences.

With Hoagland, Pincus also co-founded the Worcester Foundation for Experimental Biology (WFEB) in 1944. Hoagland served as executive director of the WFEB; Pincus served as director of laboratories for twelve years and then as research director. The WFEB served as a research center on steroidhormones and provided training for young biochemists in the methods of steroid biochemistry. From 1946 to 1950 Pincus was on the faculty of Tufts Medical School in Medford, Massachusetts, and then from 1950 until his death he was research professor in biology at Boston University Graduate School. Many of his doctoral students at these universities completed research at the WFEB.

Uses Hormone Research to Develop Oral Contraceptive

Pincus had been conducting research on sterility and hormones since the 1930s, but it was not until the 1950s that he applied his theoretical knowledge to the idea of creating a solution to the problem of overpopulation. In 1951 he was exposed to the work of Margaret Sanger, who had described the inadequacy of existing birth control methods and the looming problem of overpopulation, particularly in underdeveloped areas. By 1953, Pincus was working with Min-Chueh Chang at the WFEB, studying the effects of steroids on the fertility of laboratory animals.

Science had made it possible to produce steroid hormones in bulk, and Chang discovered a group of compounds called progestins which worked as ovulation inhibitors. Pincus took these findings to the G. D. Searle Company, where he had been a consultant, and shifted his emphasis to human beings instead of laboratory animals. Pincus also brought human reproduction specialists John Rock and Celso Garcia into the project. They conducted clinical tests of the contraceptive pill in Brookline, Massachusetts, to confirm the laboratory data. Pincus then travelled to Haiti and Puerto Rico, where he oversaw large-scale clinical field trials.

Oscar Hechter, who met Pincus in 1944 while at the WFEB, wrote in *Perspectives in Biology and Medicine* that "Gregory Pincus belongs to history because he was a man of action who showed the world that the population crisis is not an 'impossible' problem. He and his associates demonstrated that there is *a* way to control birth rates on a large scale, suitable alike for developed and underdeveloped societies. The antifertility steroids which came to be known as the 'Pill' were shown to be effective, simple, contraceptive agents, relatively safe, and eminently practical to employ on a large scale." Pincus spent much of the last fifteen years of his life travelling to explain the results of research. This is reflected in his membership in biological and endocrinological societies in Portugal, France, Great Britain, Chile, Haiti, and Mexico. His work on oral contraceptives was also recognized by awards such as the Albert D. Lasker Award in Planned Parenthood in 1960 and the Cameron Prize in Practical Therapeutics from the University of Edinburgh in 1966. He was elected to the National Academy of Sciences in 1965.

Pincus died before the issue of *Perspectives in Biology and Medicine* commemorating his sixty-fifth birthday was published. Although ill for the last three years of his life, he had continued to work and travel. He died in Boston on August 22, 1967, of myeloid metaplasia, a bone-marrow disease which some speculate was caused by his work with organic solvents.

SELECTED WRITINGS BY PINCUS:

Books

The Eggs of Mammals, Macmillan, 1936.
The Control of Fertility, New York Academic
Press, 1965.

Periodicals

(With O. S. Baum) "On the Interaction of Oestrin
and the Ovary-Stimulating Principles of Extracts of the Urine of Pregnancy," *American
Journal of Physiology,* Volume 102, 1932, pp.
241–248.
(With Priscilla White and Elliott P. Joslin) "The
Inheritance of Diabetes," *Journal of the American Medical Association,* Volume 103, 1934,
pp. 105–106.
(With Hudson Hoagland) "Steroid Excretion and
the Stress of Flying," *Journal of Aviation Medicine,* Volume 14, 1943, pp. 173–193.
"Chemical Control of Fertility," *Advances in
Chemistry Series,* Volume 44, 1964, pp.
177–189.

SOURCES:

Books

Dictionary of Scientific Biography, Volume 10,
Scribner, 1970, pp. 610–611.
Ingle, Dwight J., "Gregory Goodwin Pincus," *Biographical Memoirs,* Volume 42, Columbia University Press, 1971, pp. 228–270.

Periodicals

Hechter, Oscar, "Homage to Gregory Pincus,"
Perspectives in Biology and Medicine, spring,
1968, pp. 358–370.
Hoagland, Hudson, "Creativity—Genetic and Psy-
chosocial," *Perspectives in Biology and Medicine,* spring, 1968, pp. 339–349.

—*Sketch by Marianne P. Fedunkiw*

Max Planck
1858-1947
German physicist

Max Planck

Max Planck is best known as one of the founders
of the quantum theory of physics. As a result
of his research on heat radiation he was led to
conclude that energy can sometimes be described as
consisting of discrete units, later given the name
quanta. This discovery was important because it
made possible, for the first time, the use of matter-
related concepts in an analysis of phenomena involving energy. Planck also made important contributions
in the fields of thermodynamics, relativity, and the
philosophy of science. He was awarded the 1918
Nobel Prize in physics for his discovery of the
quantum effect.

Max Karl Ernst Ludwig Planck was born on April
23, 1858, in Kiel, Germany. His parents were Johann
Julius Wilhelm von Planck, originally of Göttingen,
and Emma Patzig, of Griefswald. Johann had previously been married to Mathilde Voigt, of Jena, with
whom he had two children. Max was the fourth child
of his father's marriage to Emma.

Johann von Planck was descended from a long
line of lawyers, clergyman, and public servants and
was himself Professor of Civil Law at the University
of Kiel. Young Max began school in Kiel, but moved
at the age of nine with his family to Münich. There he
attended the Königliche Maximillian Gymnasium
until his graduation in 1874.

As a child, Planck demonstrated both talent in
and enthusiasm for a variety of fields, ranging from
mathematics and science to music. He was accomplished at both piano and organ and gave some
thought to a career in music. He apparently abandoned that idea, however, when a professional musician told him that he did not seem to have the

commitment needed for that field. Planck did, however, maintain a life-long interest in music and its mathematical foundations. Later in life, he held private concerts in his home which featured eminent musicians, such as Joseph Joachim and Maria Scherer, as well as fellow scientists, including **Albert Einstein**, often with Planck at the piano.

Begins His Career at Münich and Berlin

Planck entered the University of Münich in 1874 with plans to major in mathematics. He soon changed his mind, however, when he realized that he was more interested in practical problems of the natural world than in the abstract concepts of pure mathematics. Although his course work at Münich emphasized the practical and experimental aspects of physics, Planck eventually found himself drawn to the investigation of theoretical problems. It was, biographer Hans Kango points out in *Dictionary of Scientific Biography,* "the only time in [his] life when he carried out experiments."

Planck's tenure at Münich was interrupted by illness in 1875. After a long period of recovery, he transferred to the University of Berlin for two semesters in 1877 and 1878. At Berlin, he studied under a number of notable physicists, including Hermann Helmholtz and Gustav Kirchhoff. By the fall of 1878, Planck was healthy enough to return to Münich and his studies. In October of that year, he passed the state examination for higher level teaching in math and physics. He taught briefly at his alma mater, the Maximillian Gymnasium, before devoting his efforts full time to preparing for his doctoral dissertation. He presented that dissertation on the second law of thermodynamics in early 1879 and was granted a Ph.D. by the University of Münich in July of that year.

Planck's earliest field of research involved thermodynamics, an area of physics dealing with heat energy. He was very much influenced by the work of Rudolf Clausius, whose work he studied by himself while in Berlin. He discussed and analyzed some of Clausius's concepts in his own doctoral dissertation. Between 1880 and 1892, Planck carried out a systematic study of thermodynamic principles, especially as they related to chemical phenomena such as osmotic pressure, boiling and freezing points of solutions, and the dissociation of gases. He brought together the papers published during this period in his first major book, *Vorlesungen über Thermodynamik,* published in 1897.

During the early part of this period, Planck held the position of Privat-Dozent at the University of Münich. In 1885, he received his first university appointment as extraordinary professor at the University of Kiel. His annual salary of 2,000 marks was enough to allow him to live comfortably and to marry a childhood sweetheart from Münich, Marie Merck. Marie was eventually to bear Planck three children.

Planck's personal life was beset with tragedy. Both of his twin daughters died while giving birth: Margarete in 1917, and Emma in 1919. His son, Karl, also met an untimely death when he was killed during World War I. Marie had predeceased all her children when she died on October 17, 1909. Planck later married Marga von Hoessli, with whom he had one son.

Nobel Prize Awarded for Discovery of the Quantum

Planck's research on thermodynamics at Kiel soon earned him recognition within the scientific field. Thus, when Kirchhoff died in 1887, Planck was considered a worthy successor to his former teacher at the University of Berlin. Planck was appointed to the position of assistant professor at Berlin in 1888 and assumed his new post the following spring. In addition to his regular appointment at the university, Planck was also chosen to head the Institute for Theoretical Physics, a facility that had been created especially for him. In 1892, Planck was promoted to the highest professorial rank, ordinary professor, a post he held until 1926.

Once installed at Berlin, Planck turned his attention to an issue that had long interested his predecessor, the problem of black body radiation. A black body is defined as any object that absorbs all frequencies of radiation when heated and then gives off all frequencies as it cools. For more than a decade, physicists had been trying to find a mathematical law that would describe the way in which a black body radiates heat.

The problem was unusually challenging because black bodies do not give off heat in the way that scientists had predicted that they would. Among the many theories that had been proposed to explain this inconsistency was one by the German physicist **Wilhelm Wien** and one by the English physicist John Rayleigh. Wien's explanation worked reasonably well for high frequency black body radiation, and Rayleigh's appeared to be satisfactory for low frequency radiation. But no one theory was able to describe black body radiation across the whole spectrum of frequencies. Planck began working on the problem of black body radiation in 1896 and by 1900 had found a solution to the problem. That solution depended on a revolutionary assumption, namely that the energy radiated by a black body is carried away in discrete "packages" that were later given the name *quanta* (from the Latin, *quantum,* for "how much"). The concept was revolutionary because physicists had long believed that energy is always transmitted in some continuous form, such as a wave. The wave, like a line in geometry, was thought to be infinitely divisible.

Planck's suggestion was that the heat energy radiated by a black body be thought of as a stream of "energy bundles," the magnitude of which is a function of the wavelength of the radiation. His mathematical expression of that concept is relatively simple: $E = \hbar v$, where E is the energy of the quantum, v is the wavelength of the radiation, and $\hbar$ is a constant of proportionality, now known as *Planck's constant.* Planck found that by making this assumption about the nature of radiated energy, he could accurately describe the experimentally observed relationship between wavelength and energy radiated from a black body. The problem had been solved.

The numerical value of Planck's constant, $\hbar$ can be expressed as 6.62×10^{-27} erg second, an expression that is engraved on Planck's headstone in his final resting place at the Stadtfriedhof Cemetery in Göttingen. Today, Planck's constant is considered to be a fundamental constant of nature, much like the speed of light and the gravitational constant. Although Planck was himself a modest man, he recognized the significance of his discovery. Robert L. Weber in *Pioneers of Science: Nobel Prize Winners in Physics* writes that Planck remarked to his son Erwin during a walk shortly after the discovery of the quantum concept, "Today I have made a discovery which is as important as Newton's discovery." That boast has surely been confirmed. The science of physics today can be subdivided into two great eras, classical physics, involving concepts worked out before Planck's discovery of the quantum, and modern physics, ideas that have been developed since 1900, often as a result of that discovery. In recognition of this accomplishment, Planck was awarded the 1918 Nobel Prize in physics.

Research on Relativity and Philosophical Speculations

After completing his study of black body radiation, Planck turned his attention to another new and important field of physics: relativity. Albert Einstein's famous paper on the theory of general relativity, published in 1905, stimulated Planck to look for ways on incorporating his quantum concept into the new concepts proposed by Einstein. He was somewhat successful, especially in extending Einstein's arguments from the field of electromagnetism to that of mechanics. Planck's work in this respect is somewhat ironic in that it had been Einstein who, in another 1905 paper, had made the first productive use of the quantum concept in his solution of the photoelectric problem.

Throughout his life, Planck was interested in general philosophical issues that extended beyond specific research questions. As early as 1891, he had written about the importance of finding large, general themes in physics that could be used to integrate specific phenomena. His book *Philosophy of Physics,* published in 1959, addressed some of these issues. He also looked beyond science itself to ask how his own discipline might relate to philosophy, religion, and society as a whole. Some of his thoughts on the correlation of science, art, and religion are presented in his 1935 book, *Die Physik im Kampf um die Weltanschauung.*

Planck remained a devout Christian throughout his life, often attempting to integrate his scientific and religious views. Like Einstein, he was never able to accept some of the fundamental concepts of the modern physics that he had helped to create. For example, he clung to the notion of causality in physical phenomena, rejecting the principles of uncertainty proposed by Heisenberg and others. He maintained his belief in God, although his descriptions of the Deity were not anthropomorphic but more akin to natural law itself.

Tragedy Fills Final Days

By the time Planck retired from his position at Berlin in 1926, he had become probably the most highly respected scientific figure in Europe, if not the world, except for Einstein. Four years after retirement, he was invited to become president of the Kaiser Wilhelm Society in Berlin, an institution that was then renamed the Max Planck Society in his honor. Planck's own prestige allowed him to speak out against the rise of Nazism in Germany in the 1930s, but his enemies eventually managed to have him removed from his position at the Max Planck Society in 1937. The last years of his life were filled with additional personal tragedies. His son by his second marriage, Erwin, was found guilty of plotting against Hitler and executed in 1944. During an air raid on Berlin in 1945, Planck's home was destroyed with all of his books and papers. During the last two and a half years of his life, Planck lived with his grandniece in Göttingen, where he died on October 4, 1947.

SELECTED WRITINGS BY PLANCK:

Books

Vorlesungen über Thermodynamik, Leipzig, 1897.
Vorlesungen über die Theorie der Wärmestrahlung, Leipzig, 1906.
Acht Vorlesungen über Theoretische Physik, Leipzig, 1910.
Einführung in die Theoretische Physic, 5 volumes, Leipzing, 1916–30.
Die Physik im Kampf um die Weltanschauung, Leipzig, 1935.
Abhandlungen and Vorträge, 3 volumes, Brunswick, 1958.

The New Science (Contains the works *Where Is Science Going?, The Universe in the Light of Modern Physics,* and *The Philosophy of Physics*), Meridian Books, 1959.
Scientific Autobiography and Other Papers, New York, 1968.

SOURCES:

Books

Hermann, A., *Max Planck,* Hamburg, 1973.
Weber, Robert L., *Pioneers of Science: Nobel Prize Winners in Physics,* American Institute of Physics, 1980, pp. 58–59.

Periodicals

Klein, M. J., "Thermodynamics and Quanta in Planck's Work," *Physics Today,* November 1966, pp. 23–27.

—*Sketch by David E. Newton*

William Reid Pogue

William Reid Pogue
1930-

American pilot and astronaut

William Reid Pogue achieved prominence as the pilot of the third and final Skylab mission, launched November 16, 1973. By the time they had returned to Earth on February 8, 1974, Pogue and his crew had set a record of eighty-four days in space, the longest spaceflight ever. This record stood until 1978, when it was broken by Soviet cosmonauts Yuri Romanenko and Georgi Grechko on space station Salyut 6.

Pogue was born in Okemah, Oklahoma, on January 23, 1930 to Alex W. and Margaret McDow Pogue. His early education took place at Oklahoma Baptist University, where he earned a Bachelor of Science degree in education in 1951. That same year he enlisted in the Air Force, finishing his B.S. and receiving a commission as a second lieutenant in 1952. In 1953 Pogue logged forty-three combat missions while serving with the Fifth Air Force in Korea. The next year, after returning to the United States, Pogue served as a gunnery instructor at Luke Air Force Base near Phoenix, Arizona. His experience as a combat fighter pilot and his exemplary service won him a place on the Air Force's air acrobatic team, the Thunderbirds.

Pogue returned to school in 1960 to earn his master's degree in mathematics at Oklahoma State University, after which he taught as an assistant professor of math at the Air Force Academy until 1963. Pogue then became an exchange test pilot with the British Royal Aircraft Establishment in Farnborough, England, graduating from the Empire Test Pilots' School in 1966. He also served for a year as an instructor at the USAF Aerospace Research Pilots School at Edwards Air Force Base, California.

Joins NASA

Probably the most interesting part of Pogue's career came with his assignment in 1966 as one of nineteen astronauts with NASA's Manned Spacecraft Center in Houston, Texas, for it was there that Pogue became the pilot for the final Skylab mission. This mission was in some respects unique: Pogue related how he and his crew felt the need for more time to reflect and contemplate on the human aspects of their mission than had previous Skylab crews. While still in space, Pogue explained to a *Science News* interviewer: "I think [the flight has] had a really great impact on me. I feel much more inclined toward humanistic feeling toward other people, other crewmen.... I think that I see myself in a much more realistic fashion, and when I see other people, I try to see them as operating human entities and to put myself into the human situation, instead of trying to operate like a machine."

While in space, Pogue was called upon to make a number of repairs to Skylab's equipment, including a potentially mission-ending coolant line leak, a malfunctioning radar antenna, and a misaligned X-ray telescope. Most of these repairs were made from the outside of the spacecraft, forcing Pogue to don a spacesuit and "spacewalk" for a then-record seven straight hours. For successfully enacting these repairs, Pogue was awarded 1974's General Thomas D. White USAF Space Trophy.

According to Henry S. F. Cooper, Jr., who wrote about the third Skylab mission in his *House in Space,* Pogue was "the earthiest of all the astronauts." When asked back on Earth why the final crew of Skylab complained so much more than previous crews, Pogue replied: "The purpose of these debriefings was to be hypercritical!" "If you try to be nice," he continued, "it's a crummy debriefing." For all their complaining, however, the third and longest Skylab mission was regarded by many as having revealed more data about living in prolonged periods of weightlessness than had any prior mission.

After taking an extended leave from NASA and the Air Force, Pogue toured the lecture circuit; this tour resulted in the book *How Do You Go to the Bathroom in Space?,* which sought to answer the types of questions most asked by audiences at his lectures. He retired from the Air Force as a full colonel in 1975, and now serves as a private consultant to aerospace and energy firms. He and his wife, Jean Ann Pogue, have three children: William Richard, Layna Sue, and Thomas Reid. In his leisure hours, Pogue enjoys running and playing handball, gardening, and biblical history. Pogue's many awards include an honorary Doctor of Science degree from Oklahoma Baptist University in 1974, the Air Medal with an oak leaf cluster, and the Robert H. Goddard Medal from the National Space Club. In view of Pogue's accomplishments and his Choctaw descent, he also won a place in the Five Civilized Tribes Hall of Fame.

SELECTED WRITINGS BY POGUE:

Books

How Do You Go to the Bathroom in Space?, Tom Doherty Associates, 1985.

SOURCES:

Books

Cooper, Henry S. F., Jr., *A House in Space,* Holt, 1976.

Periodicals

"What It's Really Like up There," *Science Digest,* March, 1985, p. 20.

Other

Grolier's Academic American Encyclopedia (online service), Grolier Electronic Publishing, 1993.
Interview with Alumni Office, Oklahoma Baptist University, February 28, 1994.
NASA Historical Archives, Biographical Data on William Reid Pogue.
NASA News Release, September 12, 1975.

—*Sketch by Karl Preuss*

Jules Henri Poincaré
1854-1912
French mathematician

Jules Henri Poincaré has been described as the last great universalist—"the last man," E. T. Bell wrote in *Men of Mathematics,* "to take practically all mathematics, pure and applied, as his province." He made contributions to number theory, theory of functions, differential equations, topology, and the foundations of mathematics. In addition, Poincaré was very much interested in astronomy, and some of his best known research is his work on the three-body problem, which concerns the way planets act on each other in space. He worked in the area of mathematical physics and anticipated some fundamental ideas in the theory of relativity. He also participated in the debate about the nature of mathematical thought, and he wrote popular books on the general principles of his field.

Poincaré was born in Nancy, France, on April 29, 1854. The Poincaré family had made Nancy their home for many generations, and they included a number of illustrious scholars. His father was Léon Poincaré, a physician and professor of medicine at the University of Nancy. Poincaré's cousin Raymond Poincaré was later to serve as prime minister of France and as president of the republic during World War I. Poincaré was a frail child with poor coordination; his larynx was temporarily paralyzed when he was five, as a result of a bout of diphtheria. He was also very bright as a child, not necessarily an advantage in dealing with one's peers. All in all he was, according to James Newman in the *World of Mathematics,* "a suitable victim of the brutalities of children his own age."

Poincaré received his early education at home from his mother and then entered the lycée in Nancy. There he began to demonstrate his remarkable mathematical talent and earned a first prize in a national student competition. In 1873, he was admitted to the École Polytechnique, although he scored a zero on the drawing section of the entrance examination. His work was so clearly superior in every other respect that examiners were willing to forgive his perennial inability to produce legible diagrams. He continued to impress his teachers at the École, and he is reputed to have passed all his math courses without reading the textbooks or taking notes in his classes.

After completing his work at the École, Poincaré went on to the École des Mines with the intention of becoming an engineer. He continued his theoretical work in mathematics, however, and three years later he submitted a doctoral thesis. He was awarded his doctorate in 1879 and was then appointed to the faculty at the University of Caen. Two years later, he was offered a post as lecturer in mathematical analysis at the University of Paris, and in 1886 he was promoted to full professor, a post he would hold until his death in 1912.

Discovers Automorphic Functions

One of Poincaré's earliest works dealt with a set of functions to which he gave the name Fuchsian functions, in honor of the German mathematician Lazarus Fuchs. The functions are more commonly known today as automorphic functions, or functions involving sets that correspond to themselves. In this work Poincaré demonstrated that the phenomenon of periodicity, or recurrence, is only a special case of a more general property; in this property, a particular function is restored when its variable is replaced by a number of transformations of itself. As a result of this work in automorphic functions, Poincaré was elected to the French Academy of Sciences in 1887 at the age of thirty-two.

For all his natural brilliance and formal training, Poincaré was apparently ignorant of much of the literature on mathematics. One consequence of this fact was that each new subject Poincaré heard about drove his interests in yet another new direction. When he learned about the work of Georg Bernhard Riemann and Karl Weierstrass on Abelian functions, for example, he threw himself into that work and stayed with the subject until his death.

Two other fields of mathematics to which Poincaré contributed were topology and probability. With topology, or the geometry of functions, he was working with a subject which had only been treated in bare outlines, and from this he constructed the foundations of modern algebraic topology. In the case of probability, Poincaré not only contributed to the mathematical development of the subject, but he also wrote popular essays about probability which were widely read by the general public. Indeed, he was elected to membership in the literary section of the French Institut in 1908 for the literary quality of these essays.

Contributes to Three-Body Problem

In the field of celestial mechanics, Poincaré was especially concerned with two problems, the shape of rotating bodies (such as stars) and the three-body problem. In the first of these, Poincaré was able to show that a rotating fluid goes through a series of stages, first taking a spheroidal and then an ellipsoidal shape, before assuming a pear-like form that eventually develops a bulge in it and finally breaks apart into two pieces. The three-body problem involves an analysis of the way in which three bodies, such as three planets, act on each other. The problem is very difficult, but Poincaré made some useful inroads into its solution and also developed methods for the later resolution of the problem. In 1889, his work on this problem won a competition sponsored by King Oscar II of Sweden.

The work Poincaré did in celestial mechanics was part of his interest in the application of mathematics to physical phenomena; his title at the University of Paris was actually professor of mathematical physics. Of the roughly 500 papers Poincaré wrote, about seventy deal with topics such as light, electricity, capillarity, thermodynamics, heat, elasticity, and telegraphy. He also made contributions to the development of relativity theory. As early as 1899 he suggested that absolute motion did not exist. A year later he also proposed the concept that nothing could travel faster than the speed of light. These two propositions are, of course, important parts of **Albert Einstein**'s theory of special relativity, first announced in 1905.

As he grew older, Poincaré devoted more attention to fundamental questions about the nature of mathematics. He wrote a number of papers criticizing the logical and rational philosophies of **Bertrand Russell**, **David Hilbert**, and **Giuseppe Peano**, and to some extent his work presaged some of the intuitionist arguments of **L. E. J. Brouwer**. As E. T. Bell wrote: "Poincaré was a vigorous opponent of the theory that all mathematics can be rewritten in terms of the most elementary notions of classical logic; something more than logic, he believed, makes mathematics what it is."

Poincaré died on July 17, 1912, of complications arising from prostate surgery. He was fifty-eight years old. During his lifetime he had received many of the honors then available to a scientist, including election to the Royal Society as a foreign member in 1894. Poincaré was married to Jeanne Louise Marie Poulain

D'Andecy, with whom he had four children, one son and three daughters.

SELECTED WRITINGS BY POINCARÉ:

Books

Electricité et Optique, G. Carré (Paris), second edition, 1901.
La science et l'hypothèse, [Paris], 1906.
The Value of Science, Science Press (New York), 1907.
Science et méthode; E. Flammarion (Paris), 1908.

SOURCES:

Books

Bell, E. T., *Men of Mathematics,* Simon & Schuster, 1937, pp. 526–554.
Gillispie, C. C., editor, *Dictionary of Scientific Biography,* Volume 1, Scribner, 1975, pp. 51–61.
Jones, Bessie Zaban, editor, *The Golden Age of Science,* Simon & Schuster, 1966, pp. 615–637.
Newman, James R., *The World of Mathematics,* Volume 2, Simon & Schuster, 1956, pp. 1374–1379.
Williams, Trevor, editor, *A Biographical Dictionary of Scientists,* Wiley, 1974, pp. 422–423.

—*Sketch by David E. Newton*

Hildrus A. Poindexter
1901-1987
American physician and bacteriologist

Hildrus A. Poindexter had a distinguished career as a medical school professor and a physician in the United States Army and Public Health Service. His careful scientific observations in many countries, including Africa, Asia, Europe, and South America, provided the basis for much medical research and discovery by others. In the preface to his autobiography *My World of Reality,* Poindexter wrote: "My major interest in life is the physical world, the physical aspects of man and the effects of environment on a human life."

Hildrus Augustus Poindexter, the sixth of eleven children, was born on May 10, 1901, on a farm near Memphis, Tennessee, the son of Fred Poindexter, a tenant farmer, and Luvenia Gilberta Clarke. Poindexter worked on the farm at a very early age and later recalled that he had announced his intention of becoming a physician at about the age of five. He attended the local segregated elementary school from age seven to fifteen, which was considered normal at the time. Poindexter furthered his own education, however, by learning Latin, Greek, and algebra. In 1916, he sold the horse and chickens his parents had given him to start in farm life and went off to Swift Memorial Academy, a secondary school located in eastern Tennessee. He worked his way through school, graduated in 1920, and then enrolled at Lincoln University. He graduated with honors in 1924, the same year he married Ruth Viola Grier, with whom he had one daughter, Patchechole Barbara.

After teaching for a year in a private secondary school in Oxford, North Carolina, and working as a Pullman porter to earn additional money, Poindexter entered the two-year program of the Dartmouth College Medical School in Hanover, New Hampshire. He did well enough there to be accepted for the third-year class at Harvard University Medical School in 1927, from which he received his M.D. in 1929. It was while at Dartmouth and Harvard that he decided to specialize in tropical medicine, the study and treatment of diseases and public health problems found in tropical lands. In late 1929, he entered Columbia University to do graduate work in bacteriology and parasitology; he received his Ph.D. in microbiology and immunology in 1932. Poindexter taught bacteriology, preventive medicine, and public health at the Howard University College of Medicine in Washington, D.C., from 1931 to 1943.

It was during this period that he did much of his scientific research, though he soon found himself preoccupied with administrative duties. From 1943 to 1946 he served as a physician in the U.S. Army in the South Pacific, New Guinea, the Philippines, and later in occupied Japan. In 1947, he became a physician in the U.S. Public Health Service. He served tours of duty in Liberia, Vietnam, Surinam, Iraq, Libya, Somali, Jamaica, and Sierra Leone. In all of these assignments, he used his knowledge of tropical medicine in efforts to improve the poor health situation of the citizens of these countries. In 1977, Poindexter retired from the Public Health Service as medical director and returned to the Howard University College of Medicine as a professor of community health practice.

Poindexter's importance as a medical researcher lies in his careful scientific observations of the many tropical diseases he encountered in his foreign duty posts and the very extensive reports he wrote concerning his findings. He often suggested possible medications to eliminate or alleviate the diseases, which were sometimes based upon his own field experiments. These reports served as valuable raw data upon which other scientists and public health physicians could base their own research. Poindexter received honorary doctorates from Lincoln University, Dartmouth College, and Howard University, and also was awarded the National Civil Service League Career Award in 1963 and the U.S. Public Health Service Meritorious Award in 1965. After a heart attack, Poindexter died in a Maryland suburb of Washington, D.C., on April 21, 1987.

SELECTED WRITINGS BY POINDEXTER:

Books

My World of Reality: An Autobiography, Balamp Publishing, 1973.

—*Sketch by John E. Little*

John C. Polanyi
1929-
German-born Canadian chemist

John C. Polanyi, a pioneer in the field of reaction dynamics, made major contributions toward scientists' knowledge of the molecular mechanisms of chemical reactions. His work on the use of infrared chemiluminescence paved the way for the development of powerful chemical lasers. In recognition of his achievement, he was awarded the Nobel Prize in chemistry in 1986.

Polanyi was born on January 23, 1929, in Berlin, Germany to Michael Polanyi, a chemistry professor, and Magda Elizabeth Kemeny Polanyi, both of Hungarian descent. Polanyi's family moved to Manchester, England, when he was four years old. There, his father took a position as professor of chemistry at Manchester University. Polanyi attended Manchester Grammar School as a child, and enrolled at Manchester University in 1946. That same year, his father stopped teaching chemistry and joined the university's philosophy department.

Polanyi's father had focused his research on the molecular basis of chemical reactions. Polanyi, who had taken his father's last chemistry classes, began to conduct his own chemistry research under the supervision of Ernest Warhurst, one of his father's former students. Where Warhurst, the senior Polanyi and their colleagues investigated the probability that a chemical reaction would result from a collision between molecules, the young Polanyi began to investigate the motions of the newly created reaction products.

Initially, Polanyi had been only marginally interested in science. As a student, he was more enthusiastic about politics, writing poetry, and newspaper editing. Eventually, however, he developed an interest in chemistry, especially "reaction dynamics," as the study of molecular motions in chemical reactions would eventually be called. He went on to earn a Ph.D. in chemistry in 1952, and then moved to Ottawa to conduct his postdoctoral work at Canada's National Research Council. There he attempted to determine whether the transition state theory of reaction rates, which his father had helped to develop, could predict the rates at which reactions would occur. He concluded that scientists had insufficient understanding of the forces in the transition state to accomplish this.

After two years in Ottawa, Polanyi worked for several months in the laboratory of **Gerhard Herzberg** studying vibrational and rotational motions in molecular iodine. In 1954, he was invited by the chemist Hugh Stott Taylor to a postdoctoral fellowship at Princeton University. There, the research of Taylor's colleagues, Michael Boudart and David Garvin, impressed Polanyi. In their study of the vibrations produced when atomic hydrogen chemically reacted with ozone, the reaction emitted a visible glow. From this, Polanyi concluded that it should be possible to determine the vibrational and rotational excitation in newly-formed reaction products from the wavelengths of the infrared radiation arising from chemical reactions.

In 1956, Polanyi returned to Canada to take a position as lecturer in the chemistry department at the University of Toronto. He advanced to assistant professor in 1957, and to full professor in 1974. At the University of Toronto, Polanyi and graduate student Kenneth Cashion conducted experiments on the reaction of atomic hydrogen and molecular chlorine. The reaction emitted a faint infrared light "chemiluminescence." The study was significant because it suggested a way to obtain quantitative information, for the first time, concerning the vibrational and rotational energy released in chemical reactions. Polanyi's subsequent report, "An Infrared Maser Dependent on Vibrational Excitation," followed up on **Arthur L. Schawlow**'s and **Charles Townes**' 1958 proposal that light could be amplified by passing it through a medium containing highly excited atoms and molecules, a proposal that led to the development of the laser (*l*ight *a*mplification by *s*timulated *e*mission of *r*adiation). Polanyi realized that products of the hydrogen-chlorine reaction—and similar chemical reactions—would provide a medium suitable for a laser—a chemical laser. His report, published in the

Journal of Chemical Physics in September 1960, after its initial rejection by *Physical Review Letters,* paved the way for the University of California, Berkeley's George Pimentel to develop the chemical laser, one of the most powerful lasers that exist.

Awarded Nobel Prize for Chemistry

In 1986, Polanyi and two other scientists, **Dudley R. Herschbach** and **Yuan T. Lee**, shared the Nobel Prize in chemistry for their contributions to "the development of a new field of research in chemistry—reaction dynamics." Polanyi was cited for his work on "the method of infrared chemiluminescence, in which the extremely weak infrared emission from a newly formed molecule is measured and analyzed." He was also recognized for his use of "this method to elucidate the detailed energy disposal during chemical reactions."

Speaks Out on Arms Control Issues

Polanyi's interests extended far beyond the laboratory. Beginning in the late 1950s, he became active in the arms control debate. In an article he'd written for the *Bulletin of the Atomic Scientists* after attending an arms control meeting in Moscow, he was struck by the "symmetry of fears" between the Soviets and Western powers that prompted the arms buildup as a precaution against surprise attacks. His concern as a scientist over "the mounting spiral of precaution, fear, increased precaution, increasing fear" led him to become the founding chairman of the Canadian Pugwash Group. He was also an active member of the American National Academy of Sciences' Committee on International Security Studies and the Canadian Center for Arms Control and Disarmament. In addition, he has given many lectures on the subject of arms control and has written approximately sixty articles on this topic.

Polanyi's contributions have been officially recognized by various quarters. His many honors and awards, in addition to the Nobel Prize, include the Marlow Medal of the Faraday Society, the Steacie Prize for the Natural Sciences, the Centennial Medal of the Chemical Society, the Remsen Award, and the Royal Medal of the Royal Society of London. He has been awarded more than two dozen honorary degrees from universities in Canada and the United States, including Harvard University and Rensselaer Polytechnic Institute. In recognition of his accomplishments, the Canadian government appointed him an officer and, later, a companion of the Order of Canada and a member of the Privy Council. A fellow of the Royal Society of Canada and the Royal Society of London, he is a foreign member of the American Academy of Arts and Sciences, the American National Academy of Sciences, and belongs to the Pontifical Academy of Rome.

Polanyi married musician Anne Ferrar Davidson in 1958. The couple has two children. Although Polanyi is more knowledgeable about art, literature and poetry than music, he and his wife have collaborated in writing professionally performed skits, for which she wrote the music and he wrote the words. For relaxation, he enjoys skiing and walking; he no longer engages in the white water canoeing and aerobatics he enjoyed when he was younger.

SELECTED WRITINGS BY POLANYI:

Periodicals

"An Infrared Maser Dependent on Vibrational Excitation," *Journal of Chemical Physics,* September, 1960.
"Armaments Policies for the Sixties," *Bulletin of the Atomic Scientists,* December, 1961, p. 403.

SOURCES:

Books

Wasson, Tyler, editor, *Nobel Prize Winners,* H.W. Wilson Company, 1987, pp. 824–26.

Periodicals

"The 1986 Nobel Prize in Chemistry," *Science,* November 7, 1986, p. 673.
Time, October 27, 1986, p. 67.

—Sketch by Donna Olshansky

Pelageya Yakovlevna Polubarinova-Kochina
1899-
Russian mathematician and hydrologist

In a remarkable career that spanned over seventy years, Pelageya Yakovlevna Polubarinova-Kochina played a major role in the worldwide development of the theory of hydrodynamics. "Kochina's research activity is characterized by a deep and well-organized link with practice, a subtle attention to the physical essence of the phenomena being considered, an exact mathematical formulation of the relevant physical problems, and by a brilliant mastery of the mathematical apparatus," once wrote the respected mathematician **P. S. Aleksandrov**, in an article later printed in the *Association for Women in Mathematics Newsletter.*

Kochina was born in the Russian city of Astrakhan on May 13, 1899. Her mother was Anisiya Panteleimonovna, and her father, an accountant named Yakov Stepanovich Polubarinov. Kochina had an older brother and a younger sister and brother. During her school years, Polubarinov moved the family to St. Petersburg to get the best possible education for his children. After Kochina graduated from the Pokrovskii Women's Gymnasium in 1916, she began taking courses in the Bestudzevskii women's program, which was incorporated into the University of Petrograd following the October Revolution of 1917.

After her father died in 1918, Kochina began working at the main physics laboratory to support her mother and younger siblings while also pursuing her education. Her sister, however, contracted tuberculosis and died; and though Kochina also developed the disease, she managed to graduate in 1921 with a degree in pure mathematics from Petrograd University. She continued to work in the main physics laboratory (now known as the geophysics laboratory) in the division of theoretical meteorology under the direction of A. A. Fridman, whose interest in hydrodynamics greatly influenced Kochina's later work.

Russia's experience in World War I had exposed the country's deficiencies in industrial capacity, and the new Soviet government expanded research efforts in order to apply mathematics to technological and industrial problems. Kochina excelled in this endeavor, as did Nikolai Evgrafovich Kochin, a colleague who attended night classes at Petrograd University. The two young people shared more than a professional interest; after three years of working together, they married in 1925. The couple embraced their country's post-revolutionary attitudes completely, and their wedding was a simple affair at a Leningrad office, followed by tea at a restaurant for their witnesses.

Begins Research on Filteration and Hydrodynamics

Although Kochina remained professionally active, she quit her job at the laboratory to raise her daughters, Ira and Nina. During these years, she taught at a worker's high school and at the Institute of Transportation and the Institute of Civil Aviation. She also served as a deputy in the Leningrad city soviet (legislature). In 1934 Kochina was appointed a professor at Leningrad University. However, the following year, her husband became head of the mechanics division of the Steklov Mathematics Institute, and the family moved to Moscow. Kochina now turned her attention from teaching to research, becoming a senior researcher in Kochin's division; she also served in the Moscow soviet, eventually becom-

ing a deputy in the Supreme Soviet of the Russian Republic. While working at the institute, Kochina began to concentrate on problems in filtration, and in 1940, after completing her dissertation on theoretical aspects of filtration, she was awarded a Ph.D. in physical and mathematical sciences. When her husband died in 1944, Kochina finished delivering his course of lectures on the theory of interrupted currents.

In addition to working at the Academy of Sciences, Kochina lectured on her research activities, teaching at the Hydrometeorological and Aircraft Building Institute and at the University of Moscow's Aviation Industry Academy. In 1946 she was named a corresponding member of the Academy of Sciences and awarded the State Prize of the Soviet Union. Two years later, she became director of the Institute of Mechanics' division of hydromechanics, which focused on filtration problems. In 1958, Kochina was named an academician of the Academy of Sciences, the highest ranking in that organization, and was asked to help create a Siberian branch of that institution. The following year, at age sixty, she left Moscow for a decade of work in Siberia. During this time she was a department director at the Hydrodynamics Institute as well as head of the department of theoretical mechanics at the University of Novosibirsk. She returned to Moscow in 1970 to direct the section for mathematical methods of mechanics at the Academy of Sciences' Institute for Problems in Mechanics.

Although Kochina's training was in pure mathematics, her professional life was dedicated to finding solutions for practical problems in hydrodynamics. In 1952, relatively early in her career, she wrote *Theory of Ground Water Movement;* J. M. Roger De Wiest's English translation of that work notes that "In this book, reference is made to over thirty of her original and significant contributions on the hydromechanics of porous media (groundwater and oil flow)." One of Kochina's major accomplishments was the development of a general method for solving two-dimensional problems of the steady seepage of subsurface water in homogeneous subsoils. This process has important applications in the design of dam foundations. She obtained significant results in the theory of tides and free-flowing currents, and she resolved problems relating to soil drainage and salt accumulation during her work on irrigation and hydroelectric projects. Her solution to the problem of describing the location of the boundary between an oil-bearing domain and surrounding water as the oil is removed by wells was a well-received innovation. Since Kochina's pioneering work, the topic has been widely researched by others.

In addition to technical topics in mathematics and hydrology, Kochina was also fascinated with the history of mathematics and mechanics. She wrote the first extensive studies of mathematician Sofia Kovalevskaia's life and work, published descriptions of the scientific legacy of Karl Weierstrass and A. A. Fridman, and wrote two biographies of her husband, one during the Stalin era and one in the post-Stalinist period beginning in 1970. On her seventieth birthday, Kochina was named a Hero of Socialist Labor. She has actively participated in women's movements for peace, and on her eightieth birthday she was awarded the order of the Friendship of Nations.

SELECTED WRITINGS BY KOCHINA:

Books

Theory of Ground Water Movement, translated by J. M. De Wiest, Princeton University Press, 1962.

SOURCES:

Books

Grinstein, Louise S., and Paul J. Campbell, editors, *Women of Mathematics,* Greenwood Press, 1987, pp. 95–102.

Periodicals

Aleksandrov, P. S., G. I. Barenblum, A. I. Ishlinskii, and O. A. Oleinik, "Pelageya Yakovlevna Kochina: On Her 80th Birthday," *Association for Women in Mathematics Newsletter,* January-February, 1982, pp. 9–12.

—*Sketch by Loretta Hall*

George Pólya
1887-1985
Hungarian-born American mathematician

The career of George Pólya was distinguished by the discovery of mathematical solutions to a number of problems originating in the physical sciences. He made contributions to probability theory, number theory, the theory of functions, and the calculus of variations. He also cared about the art of teaching mathematics; he worked with educators, advocating the importance of problem solving, for which the United States gave him a distinguished service award. Pólya continued to do innovative research well into his nineties, but he is probably best known for his book on methods of problem solving, called *How to Solve It,* which has been translated into many languages and has sold more than one million copies.

Pólya was born in Budapest, Austria-Hungary (now Hungary), on December 13, 1887, the son of Jakob and Anna Deutsch Pólya. As a boy, he preferred geography, Latin, and Hungarian to mathematics. He liked the verse of German poet Heinrich Heine and translated some into Hungarian. His mother urged him to become a lawyer like his father, and he began to study law at the University of Budapest, but soon turned to languages and literature. He earned teaching certificates in Latin, Hungarian, mathematics, physics, and philosophy, and for a year he was a practice teacher in a high school. Though physics and philosophy interested Pólya, he decided to study mathematics on the advice of a philosophy professor. In an interview published in *Mathematical People: Profiles and Interviews,* Pólya explained how he chose a career in mathematics: "I came to mathematics indirectly.... It is a little shortened but not quite wrong to say: I thought I am not good enough for physics and I am too good for philosophy. Mathematics is in between."

Pólya received his doctorate in mathematics from the University of Budapest in 1912 at the age of twenty-four with a dissertation on the calculus of probability. Traveling to Germany and France, he was influenced by the work of eminent mathematicians at the University of Göttingen and the University of Paris. In 1914, he took his first teaching position, at the Eidgenössische Technische Hochschule in Zurich, Switzerland; he taught there for twenty-six years, becoming a full professor in 1928.

During World War I, Pólya was initially rejected by the Hungarian Army because of an old soccer injury. When the need for soldiers increased later in the war, however, he was asked to report for military service, but by this time he had been influenced by the pacifist views of British mathematician and philosopher **Bertrand Russell** and refused to serve. As a result, Pólya was unable to return to Hungary for several years, and he became a Swiss citizen. He married Stella Vera Weber, the daughter of a physics professor, in 1918.

Pólya proved an important theorem in probability theory in a paper published in 1921, using the term "random walk" for the first time. Many years later, a display demonstrating the concept of a random walk was featured in the IBM pavilion at the 1964 World's Fair in New York; it recognized the work of Pólya and other distinguished scholars. Pólya's work with Gabor Szegö, also a Hungarian, resulted in *Problems and Theorems in Analysis,* published in 1925. The problems in the book were grouped not according to the topic but according to the methods that could be used to solve them. Pólya and Szegö continued to work together and they published another book, *Isoperimetric Inequalities in Mathematical Physics,* in 1951.

Pólya was awarded the first international Rockefeller Grant in 1924 and spent a year in England at Oxford and Cambridge, where he worked with English mathematician **Godfrey Harold Hardy** on *Inequalities,* which was published in 1934. During the 1930s, Pólya frequently visited Paris to collaborate on papers with Gaston Julia. He received another Rockefeller Grant in 1933, this time to visit the United States, where he worked at both Princeton and Stanford universities. In 1940, after World War II had begun in Europe, Pólya left Switzerland with his wife and emigrated to the United States. He taught for two years at Brown University and for a short time at Smith College before joining Szegö at Stanford University in 1942, where he would remain until his retirement in 1953 at age sixty-six. Pólya became a U.S. citizen in 1947.

Before leaving Europe, Pólya had begun writing a book on problem solving. Observing that Americans liked "how-to" books, Hardy suggested the title *How to Solve It.* The book, Pólya's most popular, was published in 1945; it examined discovery and invention and discussed the processes of creation and analysis. Although he officially retired in 1953, Pólya continued to write and teach. Another book on heuristic principles for problem solving, at a more advanced level of mathematics, was published in 1954, entitled *Mathematics and Plausible Reasoning.* A third book on problem solving, *Mathematical Discovery,* was published in 1962. In 1963, Pólya was the recipient of the distinguished service award from the Mathematical Association of America. The citation, as quoted in the *Los Angeles Times,* read: "He has given a new dimension to problem-solving by emphasizing the organic building up of elementary steps into a complex proof, and conversely, the decomposition of mathematical invention into smaller steps. Problem solving *a la Pólya* serves not only to develop mathematical skill but also teaches constructive reasoning in general."

Pólya also became interested in the teaching of mathematics teachers, and he taught in a series of teacher institutes at Stanford University supported by the National Science Foundation, General Electric, and Shell. His film, "Let Us Teach Guessing," won the Blue Ribbon from the Educational Film Library Association in 1968. In 1978, the National Council of Teachers of Mathematics held problem-solving competitions in *The Mathematics Student;* they named the awards the Pólya Prizes.

Pólya made significant contributions in many areas, including probability, geometry, real and complex analysis, combinatorics, number theory, and mathematical physics. Perhaps one indication of the breadth of his accomplishments is the range of fields that now contain concepts bearing his name. For example, the "Pólya criterion" and the "Pólya distribution" in probability theory; and "Pólya peaks," the "Pólya representation," and the "Pólya gap theorem" in complex function theory. Pólya's writings have been praised for their clarity and elegance; his papers were called a joy to read. The Mathematical Association of America established the Pólya Prize for Expository Writing in the *College Mathematics Journal.* Pólya's papers were collected and published by MIT Press in 1984.

Pólya received honorary degrees from the University of Wisconsin at Milwaukee, the University of Alberta, the University of Waterloo, and the Swiss Federal Institute of Technology. He was a member of the American Academy of Arts and Sciences, the National Academy of Sciences of the United States, the Hungarian Academy of Sciences, the Academie Internationale de Philosophie des Sciences in Brussels, and a corresponding member of the Academie des Sciences in Paris. The Society for Industrial and Applied Mathematics named an honorary award after him, the Pólya Prize in Combinatorial Theory and Its Applications.

Among his colleagues, Pólya was known as a kind and gentle man, full of curiosity and enthusiasm. In honoring him, Frank Harary praised his depth, his versatility, and his speed and power as a mathematician. The mathematician N. G. de Bruijn wrote of Pólya in *The Pólya Picture Album: Encounters of a Mathematician:* "All his work radiates the cheerfulness of his personality. Wonderful taste, crystal clear methodology, simple means, powerful results. If I would be asked whether I could name just one mathematician who I would have liked to be myself, I have my answer ready at once: Pólya." Pólya suffered a stroke at age ninety-seven and died in Palo Alto, California, on September 7, 1985.

SELECTED WRITINGS BY PÓLYA:

Books

(With Gabor Szegö) *Problems and Theorems in Analysis,* Springer-Verlag, 1925.
(With Godfrey Harold Hardy and J. E. Littlewood) *Inequalities,* Cambridge University Press, 1934.
How to Solve It, Princeton University Press, 1945.
(With Szegö) *Isoperimetric Inequalities in Mathematical Physics,* Princeton University Press, 1951.

SOURCES:

Books

Albers, Donald J., and G. L. Alexanderson, editors, *Mathematical People: Profiles and Interviews,* Birkhauser Boston, 1985.

Alexanderson, editor, *The Pólya Picture Album: Encounters of a Mathematician,* Birkhauser Boston, 1987.

Szegö, Gabor, editor, *Studies in Mathematical Analysis and Related Topics: Essays in Honor of George Pólya,* Stanford University Press, 1962.

Periodicals

Dembart, Lee, "George Pólya, 97, Dean of Mathematicians, Dies," *Los Angeles Times,* September 8, 1985, pp. 3, 29.

—*Sketch by C. D. Lord*

Cyril Ponnamperuma

Cyril Ponnamperuma
1923-

Sri Lankan-born American chemist

Cyril Ponnamperuma, an eminent researcher in the field of chemical evolution, rose through several National Aeronautics and Space Administration (NASA) divisions as a research chemist to head the Laboratory of Chemical Evolution at the University of Maryland, College Park. His career has focused on explorations into the origin of life and the "primordial soup" that contained the precursors of life. In this search, Ponnamperuma has taken advantage of recent discoveries in such diverse fields as molecular biology and astrophysics.

Born in Galle, Ceylon (now Sri Lanka) on October 16, 1923, Cyril Andres Ponnamperuma was educated at the University of Madras (where he received a B.A. in Philosophy, 1948), the University of London (B.Sc., 1959), and the University of California at Berkeley (Ph.D., 1962). His interest in the origin of life began to take clear shape at the Birkbeck College of the University of London, where he studied with J. D. Bernal, a well-known crystallographer. In addition to his studies, Ponnamperuma also worked in London as a research chemist and radiochemist. He became a research associate at the Lawrence Radiation Laboratory at Berkeley, where he studied with **Melvin Calvin,** a Nobel laureate and experimenter in chemical evolution.

Chemical Evolution—Searching for Life from Primordial Soup

After receiving his Ph.D. in 1962, Ponnamperuma was awarded a fellowship from the National Academy of Sciences, and he spent one year in residence at NASA's Ames Research Center in Moffet Field, California. After the end of his associate year, he was hired as a research scientist at the center and became head of the chemical evolution branch in 1965.

During these years, Ponnamperuma began to develop his ideas about chemical evolution, which he explained in an article published in *Nature.* Chemical evolution, he explained, is a logical outgrowth of centuries of studies both in chemistry and biology, culminating in the groundbreaking 1953 discovery of the structure of DNA by **James Watson** and **Francis Crick.** Evolutionist Charles Darwin's studies affirming the idea of the "unity of all life" for biology could be extended, logically, to a similar notion for chemistry: protein and nucleic acid, the essential elements of biological life, were, after all, chemical.

In the same year that Watson and Crick discovered DNA, two researchers from the University of Chicago, **Stanley Lloyd Miller** and **Harold Urey,** experimented with a primordial soup concocted of the elements thought to have made up earth's early atmosphere—methane, ammonia, hydrogen, and water. They sent electrical sparks through the mixture, simulating a lightening storm, and discovered trace amounts of amino acids.

During the early 1960s, Ponnamperuma began to delve into this primordial soup and set up variations of Miller and Urey's original experiment. Having changed the proportions of the elements from the original Miller-Urey specifications slightly, Ponnamperuma and his team sent first high-energy electrons, then ultraviolet light through the mixture, attempting to recreate the original conditions of the earth before life. They succeeded in creating large amounts of adenosine triphosphate (ATP), an amino acid that fuels cells. In later experiments with the same concoction of primordial soup, the team was able to create the nucleotides that make up nucleic acid—the building blocks of DNA and RNA.

Search for Life's Origins Extends to Space

In addition to his work in prebiotic chemistry, Ponnamperuma became active in another growing field: exobiology, or the study of extraterrestrial life. Supported in this effort by NASA's interest in all matters related to outer space, he was able to conduct research on the possiblity of the evolution of life on other planets. Theorizing that life evolved from the interactions of chemicals present elsewhere in the universe, he saw the research possibilities of spaceflight. He experimented with lunar soil taken by the Apollo 12 space mission in 1969. As a NASA investigator, he also studied information sent back from Mars by the unmanned Viking, Pioneer, and Voyager probes in the 1970s. These studies suggested to Ponnamperuma, as he stated in an 1985 interview with *Spaceworld,* that "earth is the only place in the solar system where there is life."

In 1969, a meteorite fell to earth in Muchison, Australia. It was retrieved still warm, providing scientists with fresh, uncontaminated material from space for study. Ponnamperuma and other scientists examined pieces of the meteorite for its chemical make-up, discovering numerous amino acids. Most important, among those discovered were the five chemical bases that make up the nucleic acid found in living organisms. Further interesting findings provided tantalizing but puzzling clues about chemical evolution, including the observation that light reflects both to the left and to the right when beamed through a solution of the meteorite's amino acids, whereas light reflects only to the left when beamed through the amino acids of living matter on earth. "Who knows? God may be left-handed," Ponnamperuma speculated in a 1982 *New York Times* interview.

Ponnamperuma's association with NASA continued as he entered academia. In 1979, he became a professor of chemistry at the University of Maryland and director of the Laboratory of Chemical Evolution—established and supported in part by the National Science Foundation and by NASA. He continued active research and experimentation on meteorite material. In 1983, an article in the science section of the *New York Times* explained Ponnamperuma's chemical evolution theory and his findings from the Muchison meteorite experiments. He reported the creation of all five chemical bases of living matter in a single experiment that consisted of bombarding a primordial soup mixture with electricity.

Ponnamperuma's contributions to scholarship have included hundreds of articles. He has written or edited numerous books, some in collaboration with other chemists or exobiologists, including annual collections of papers delivered at the College Park Colloquium on Chemical Evolution. He edited two journals, *Molecular Evolution* (from 1970 to 1972) and *Origins of Life* (from 1973 to 1983). In addition to traditional texts in the field of chemical evolution, he also coauthored a software program entitled "Origin of Life," a simulation model intended to introduce biology students to basic concepts of chemical evolution.

Although Ponnamperuma became an American citizen in 1967, he maintained close ties to his native Sri Lanka, even becoming an official governmental science advisor. His professional life has included several international appointments. He was a visiting professor of the Indian Atomic Energy Commission (1967); a member of the science faculty at the Sorbonne (1969); and director of the UNESCO Institute for Early Evolution in Ceylon (1970). His international work has included the directorship of the Arthur C. Clarke center, founded by the science fiction writer, a Sri Lankan resident. The center has as one of its goals a Manhattan Project for food synthesis.

Ponnamperuma is a member of the Indian National Science Academy, the American Association for the Advancement of Science, the American Chemical Society, the Royal Society of Chemists, and the International Society for the Study of the Origin of Life, which awarded him the A. I. Oparin Gold Medal in 1980. He married Valli Pal in 1955. They have one child and live in Washington D.C.

SELECTED WRITINGS BY PONNAMPERUMA:

Books

The Origins of Life, Dutton, 1972.
(With G. Field and G. Verschuur) *Cosmic Evolution,* Houghton, 1978.

(With Lynn Margulis) *Limits of Life,* Kluwer, 1980.
Comets and the Origin of Life, Kluwer, 1981.

Periodicals

Nature, January 25, 1964.

SOURCES:

Periodicals

Boffey, Philip, "Precursors of Life Found in Meteorite," *New York Times,* August 30, 1993.
"E.T. May Look Like Us," *USA Today Magazine,* June, 1987.
"Interview: Cyril Ponnamperuma," *Space World,* February, 1985.
"Is There a Cosmic Chemistry of Life?," *Science News,* September 20, 1986.

—*Sketch by Katherine Williams*

George Porter
1920-
English chemist

Sir George Porter shared the Nobel Prize in chemistry in 1967 with his former teacher, **Ronald G. W. Norrish**, and **Manfred Eigen** for their contributions to the study of rapid chemical reactions. Porter's efforts included research on flash photolysis, which has been used widely in the fields of organic chemistry, biochemistry, and photobiology. Porter, who is praised for having an outgoing personality and being a great promotor of science education, has also contributed to the scientific education of non-specialists and children, especially through his role in helping prepare television programs in Great Britain.

Porter was born on December 6, 1920, to John Smith Porter and Alice Ann (Roebuck) Porter in Stainforth, West Yorkshire, where he received his early education at Thorne Grammar School. With the award of an Ackroyd Scholarship, he entered Leeds University in 1938 to study chemistry and received his bachelor of science degree in 1941. While at Leeds he also studied radio physics and electronics, and he drew upon this background while serving in the Royal Navy Volunteer Reserve as a radar specialist during World War II. At the end of the war, Porter entered Emmanuel College at Cambridge University to do graduate work. There he met and studied under Norrish, who had pioneered research in the area of photochemical reactions in molecules. Porter received his doctorate degree from Cambridge in 1949.

Flash Photolysis Successfully Implemented

Using very short pulses of energy that disturbed the equilibrium of molecules, Porter and Norrish developed a method to study extremely fast chemical reactions lasting for only one-billionth of a second. The technique is known as flash photolysis. First, a flash of short-wavelength light breaks a chemical that is photosensitive into reactive parts. Next, a weaker light flash illuminates the reaction zone, making it possible to measure short-lived free radicals, which are especially reactive atoms that have at least one unpaired electron. Flash photolysis made it possible to observe and measure free radicals for the first time and also to study the sequence of the processes of reactants as they are converted into products. When Porter won the Nobel Prize in 1967, he was praised, along with Norrish and Eigen, for making it possible for scientists around the world to use their techniques in a wide range of applications, opening many passageways to scientific investigation in physical chemistry. In his own work, Porter was able to apply his methods from his early work with gases to later work with solutions. He also developed a method to stabilize free radicals, which is called matrix isolation. It can trap free radicals in a structure of a supercooled liquid (a glass). Porter also made important contributions in the application of laser beams to photochemical studies for the purpose of investigating biochemical problems. Some practical applications of photochemical techniques include the production of fuel and chemical feedstocks.

In 1949, Porter became a demonstrator in chemistry at Cambridge University and an assistant director of research in the Department of Physical Chemistry in 1952. While he was at the British Rayon Research Association as assistant director of research in 1954, Porter used his method of flash photolysis to record organic free radicals with a lifetime as short as one millisecond. Also at the Rayon Association, he worked on problems of light and the fading of dye on fabric.

Porter was appointed professor of physical chemistry at Sheffield University in 1955, and in 1963 he became the head of the chemistry department and was honored as Firth Professor. During his years at Sheffield, Porter used his flash photolysis techniques to study the complex chemical interactions of oxygen with hemoglobin in animals. He also investigated the properties of chlorophyll in plants with the use of his high-speed flash techniques. He was able to improve his techniques to the degree that he could examine chemical reactions that were more than a thousand times faster than with the use of flash tubes. Porter also studied chloroplasts and the primary processes of photosynthesis.

In 1966, Porter also became Fullerian Professor of Chemistry at the Royal Institution in London and the Director of the Davy Faraday Research Laboratory. He left there to take the position of chair for the Center for Photomolecular Sciences at Imperial College in London in 1990. During his career, Porter received many other honors and awards in addition to the Nobel Prize. He was knighted in 1972, and he has been granted numerous honorary doctorate degrees and awarded prizes from British and American scientific societies, including the Robertson Prize of the American National Academy of Sciences and the Rumford Medal of the Royal Society, both in 1978.

Promotes Science among Young People

Porter has been active outside scientific circles in the promotion of science to the general public. His concern about communication between scientists and the rest of society induced him to participate as an adviser on film and television productions. He has been praised for his activities in educating young people and people in non-scientific fields about the value of science. He was an active participant during his service with the Royal Institution in a science program series for British Broadcasting Company television (BBC-TV) called *Young Scientist of the Year.* Another BBC-TV program in which he participated was called *The Laws of Disorder* and *Time Machines.* Porter has also served on many policy and institutional committees that are involved in promoting science and education in Europe, England, and America.

Porter married Stella Brooke in 1949 and they have two sons, John Brooke Porter and Christopher Porter. His outgoing personality is considered an asset in promoting scientific knowledge. He has been an active contributor to scientific journals and has also played the role of advisor to industry. Besides sailing, Porter spends some leisure time vacationing on the coast of Kent with his family.

SELECTED WRITINGS BY PORTER:

Books

(Editor with K. R. Jennings and B. Stevens) *Progress in Reaction Kinetics,* Pergamon Press, 1961.
Chemistry for the Modern World, Barnes and Noble, 1962.

Periodicals

(With R. Norrish) "Chemical Reactions Produced by Very High Light Intensities," *Nature,* Volume 164, 1949, p. 658.

(With R. Norrish) "The Application of Flash Techniques to the Study of Fast Reactions," *Discussions of the Faraday Society,* Volume 17, 1954, pp. 40–46.

SOURCES:

Periodicals

New York Times, October 31, 1967.
Science, November 1967, p. 748.

—*Sketch by Vita Richman*

Rodney Porter
1917-1985
English biochemist

Rodney Porter was a biochemist who spent most of his professional life investigating the chemical structure and functioning of antibodies, a class of proteins which are also called immunoglobulins. Since 1890 scientists had known that antibodies are found in the blood serum and provide immunity to certain illnesses. However, when Porter began his research in the 1940s, little was known about their chemical structure, or how antigens (substances that cause the body to produce antibodies) interacted with them. Using the results of his own research as well as that of **Gerald M. Edelman**, Porter proposed the first satisfactory model of the immunoglobulin molecule in 1962. The model allowed the development of more detailed biochemical studies by Porter and others that led to a better understanding of the way in which antibodies worked chemically. Such understanding was key to research on the prevention and cure of a number of diseases and the solution to problems related to organ transplant rejection. For his work, Porter shared the 1972 Nobel Prize in physiology or medicine with Edelman.

Rodney Robert Porter was born October 8, 1917, in Newton-le-Willows, near Liverpool in Lancashire, England. His mother was Isobel Reese Porter and his father, Joseph L. Porter, was a railroad clerk. "I don't know why I became interested in [science]," Porter once told the *New York Times.* "It didn't run in my family." He attended Liverpool University, where he earned a B.S. in biochemistry in 1939. During World War II he served in the Royal Artillery, the Royal Engineers, and the Royal Army Service Corps, and participated in the invasions of Algeria, Sicily, and Italy. After his discharge in 1946, he resumed his biochemistry studies at Cambridge University under the direction of **Frederick Sanger.**

Investigates the Nature of Antibodies

Porter's doctoral research at Cambridge was influenced by Nobel laureate **Karl Landsteiner**'s book, *The Specificity of Serological Reactions,* which described the nature of antibodies and techniques for preparing some of them. Antibodies, at the time, were thought to be proteins that belonged to a class of blood-serum proteins called gamma globulins. From Sanger, who had succeeded in determining the chemical structure of insulin (a protein that metabolizes carbohydrates), Porter learned the techniques of protein chemistry. Sanger had also demonstrated tenacity in studying problems in protein chemistry involving amino acid sequencing that most believed impossible to solve, and he was a model for the persistence Porter would show in his later work on antibodies.

Fortunately, Porter chose rabbits to experiment on for his research. Although this was not known at the time, the antibody system is not as complex in this animal as it is in some. The most important antibody, or immunoglobulin, in the blood is called IgG, which contains more than 1,300 amino acids. The problem of discovering the active site of the antibody—the part that combines with the antigen—could be solved only by working with smaller pieces of the molecule. Porter discovered that an enzyme from papaya juice, called papain, could break up IgG into fragments that still contained the active sites but were small enough to work with. He received his Ph.D. for this work in 1948.

Porter remained at Cambridge for another year, then in 1949 he moved to the National Institute for Medical Research at Mill Hill, London. There, he improved methods for purifying protein mixtures and used some of these methods to show that there are variations in IgG molecules. He obtained a purer form of papaya enzyme than had been available at Cambridge and repeated his earlier experiments. This time the IgG molecules broke into thirds, and one of these thirds was obtained in a crystalline form which Porter called fragment crystallizable (Fc).

Obtaining the Fc crystal was a breakthrough; Porter now was able to show that this part of the antibody was the same in all IgG molecules, since a mixture of the different molecules would not have formed a crystal. He also discovered that the active site of the molecule (the part that binds the antigen) was in the other two-thirds of the antibody. These he called fragment antigen-binding (or FAB) pieces. After Porter's research was published in 1959, another research group, led by Gerald M. Edelman at

Rockefeller University in New York, split the IgG in another way—by separating amino acid chains rather than breaking the proteins at right angles between the amino acids as Porter's papain had done.

In 1960 Porter was appointed professor of immunology at St. Mary's Hospital Medical School in London. There he repeated Edelman's experiments under different conditions. After two years, having combined his own results with those of Edelman, he proposed the first satisfactory structure of the IgG molecule. The model, which predicted that the FAB fragment consisted of two different amino acid chains, provided the basis for far-ranging biochemical research. Porter's continuing work contributed numerous studies of the structures of individual IgG molecules. In 1967 Porter was appointed Whitley Professor of Biochemistry and chairman of the biochemistry department at Oxford University. In his new position, Porter continued his work on the immune response, but his interest shifted from the structure of antibodies to their role as receptors on the surface of cells. To further this research, he developed ways of tagging and tracing receptors. He also became an authority on the structure and genetics of a group of blood proteins called the complement system, which binds the Fc region of the immunoglobulin and is involved in many important immunological reactions.

Porter married Julia Frances New in 1948. They had five children and lived in a farmhouse in a small town just outside of Oxford. Porter was killed in an automobile accident a few weeks before he was to retire from the Whitley Chair of Biochemistry. He had been planning to continue as director of the Medical Research Council's Immunochemistry Unit for another four years; he had also intended to continue his laboratory work, attempting to crystallize one of the proteins of the complement system. Porter's awards in addition to the Nobel Prize include the Gairdner Foundation Award of Merit in 1966 and the Ciba Medal of the Biochemical Society in 1967.

SELECTED WRITINGS BY PORTER:

Books

Chemical Aspects of Immunology, Carolina Biological Supply Co., 1976.
"Complement," *Defense and Recognition IIB: Structural Aspects,* edited by E. S. Lennox, University Park Press, 1979, pp. 177–212.

SOURCES:

Periodicals

Cebra, John J., "The 1972 Nobel Prize for Physiology or Medicine," *Science,* October 27, 1972, pp. 384–386.

Chedd, Graham, "Nobel Prizes for Antibody Structure," *New Scientist,* October 19, 1972, pp. 142–143.

Steiner, L. A., "Rodney Robert Porter (1917–1985)," *Nature,* October 3, 1985, p. 383.

Weinraub, Bernard, "Pioneers in Immunology Research: Rodney Robert Porter," *New York Times,* October 13, 1972, p. A24.

—*Sketch by Pamela O. Long*

Valdemar Poulsen
1869-1942
Danish inventor

Valdemar Poulsen is known for his work in the development of magnetic recording and radio broadcasting, both of which involved converting sound waves into electrical energy. He invented the first recording device that was entirely electrical, called the telegraphone, as well as a device known as the Poulsen arc transmitter, which greatly extended the range of wireless communication.

Poulsen was born in Copenhagen, Denmark, on November 23, 1869, the son of a high-ranking judge. He studied natural sciences at the University of Copenhagen, but he left the university before graduating to take a position as assistant engineer with the Copenhagen Telephone Company. In 1898, while working for the telephone company, Poulsen developed a method for recording telephone conversations electromagnetically.

Patents the Telegraphone

Poulsen was the first to demonstrate that a generated electromagnetic field could be used to record sound. To do this, he connected a carbon telephone transmitter to an electromagnet. The telephone transmitter, when activated by sound waves, converted the sound waves into an electric current that varied in accordance with the amplitude and frequency of the waves. This current activated an electromagnet that contacted a moving steel wire or ribbon. As the wire moved past the electromagnet it became magnetized in a way that corresponded to the fluctuations in the electric impulses applied to it. These impulses reflected the fluctuations of the original sound waves. The original sound was then reproduced by reversing the process—that is, by moving the magnetized steel wire across the electro-

magnet connected to the telephone transmitter and earphones. Listening was accomplished by means of earphones. This invention, which Poulsen called the telegraphone, and for which he applied for a patent on December 1, 1898, was demonstrated at the Paris exposition of 1900 and was awarded a Grand Prix. The principle was identical to that of the modern tape recorder, which uses a ribbon of acetate covered with a coating of iron oxide or other magnetizable metal particles.

Poulsen's initial apparatus employed a steel wire moving at a rate of eighty-four inches per second; it could record continuously for thirty minutes. In 1900 Poulsen's telegraphone was used to record the voice of Emperor Franz-Joseph of Austria-Hungary. Over the following decade, Poulsen experimented with recording on four-and-a-half inch steel discs. These had a raised spiral that could be traced by the magnetic recording and playback head. He also designed a brass cylinder with an embedded steel wire to be used as the recording surface.

Poulsen's telegraphone had several advantages over the mechanical recording process used at that time, which employed wax cylinders and rubber discs. Because the playback apparatus was sensitive only to the magnetic energy in the wire and not to the wire's surface imperfections, the background noise of the recording was relatively low; in contrast, the mechanical playback method then in use by the phonograph could not differentiate between the vibrations incised or etched into the playing surface and the irregular surface of the playback medium. Nor was Poulsen's system limited to four minutes, the length of contemporary mechanical recordings. The wire also had another advantage: it could be erased and recorded over.

There were, however, some factors that kept the telegraphone from commercial success. The wire often became entangled, and rewinding took as much time as playback. But it was the lack of sufficient electrical amplification provided by the telephone transmitters through earphones that prevented the telegraphone from supplanting the phonograph. Electrical amplifiers and loudspeakers had not yet been developed, and this fact severely limited playback volume as compared to the phonograph, where large horns and weighted playback styli gave adequate volume despite the fact that the device depended solely on the unamplified mechanical energy of the original sound.

Probably because of the inadequate volume on the telegraphone and the perception that the practical uses of the apparatus were limited, Poulsen was not able to secure financial backing for the development of his invention in Europe. He travelled to the United States and founded the American Telegraphone Company in 1903 with the intention of manufacturing and selling an improved model of the device. With the exception of ten machines purchased by the DuPont Company, however, the machine was never successfully marketed. The telegraphone was relegated to being used as a dictating instrument in offices, and even this use lasted only a short time. It was not until the late 1920s and 1930s, with the development of electrical amplification and magnetic loudspeakers, that a practical magnetic recording instrument became feasible. The same developments, however, also had raised the quality of the phonograph and solidified the position of the 78 rpm record as the primary medium for recording and playback of sound.

Develops the Poulsen Arc

In 1903 Poulsen was awarded a patent for a device that generated continuous radio waves. Previous wireless stations employed spark transmitters based on a device developed by Reginald Fessenden, a chemist for Westinghouse. Poulsen's generator was an adaptation of W. Duddell's "singing arc," developed in 1900, which generated waves within the audio spectrum. Poulsen was able to increase the frequency limit of Duddell's arc from ten kHz to one-hundred kHz—that is, from an audible frequency to a radio frequency. Connecting the output of this arc to a transmitting antenna allowed the transmission of a continuous wave over a distance of 150 miles.

Poulsen's apparatus was manufactured by the Federal Telegraph Company, a chief rival of the American Marconi Company, and the company installed a Poulsen arc transmitter in the Arlington Radio Station, which had begun operations in February 1913. Since a Fessenden spark transmitter had already been in use in the station, it was possible to run comparisons between the two systems. Poulsen's apparatus proved to have a greater transmission range and a greater freedom from static interference. Poulsen's experiments led eventually to the development of a practical system for long-wave radio broadcasts. By the early 1920s Poulsen arc transmitters as powerful as 1,000 kilowatts, with ranges of up to 25,000 miles, had been constructed.

Among the awards bestowed on Poulsen were the gold medal of the Royal Danish Society for Science in 1907, an honorary doctorate of philosophy from the University of Leipzig in 1909, and the Danish Government's Medal of Merit. He was a fellow of the Danish Academy of Technical Science and the Swedish Institute for Engineering Research. He died in Denmark in 1942.

SELECTED WRITINGS BY POULSEN:

Periodicals

"Telegraphone," *Scientific American,* August 25, 1900, p. 20616; January 19, 1901, p. 29044.

"Telegraphone, Description," *Popular Science,* August, 1901, p. 413.

SOURCES:

Books

Archer, Gleason L., *History of Radio to 1926,* Arno Press, 1938.
Gelatt, Roland, *The Fabulous Phonograph, 1877–1977,* Collier Books, 1977, pp. 284–286.
Koenigsberg, Allen, *Patent History of the Phonograph, 1877–1912,* revised edition, A.P.M. Press, 1991.
Lewis, Tom, *Empire of the Air: The Men Who Made Radio,* Harper Perennial, 1993.
Read, Oliver, and Walter L. Welch, *From Tin Foil to Stereo: Evolution of the Phonograph,* Howard Sams, 1976.

Periodicals

"Poulsen's Telegraphone," *Scientific American,* September 22, 1900.

—*Sketch by Michael Sims*

Robert Pound
1919-
Canadian-born American physicist

During his early career as a Harvard professor, Robert Pound worked closely with Nobel Prize-winning physicist **Edward Mills Purcell** on the study of nuclear magnetic resonance (NMR) and established it as one of physics' most valuable analytical techniques. In the late 1950s, Pound became interested in the use of high-precision gamma rays produced by the Mössbauer process to study a variety of phenomena. In 1960, Pound and a colleague used the Mössbauer effect to measure the gravitational effects of electromagnetic radiation, and in the process they were able to confirm certain predictions of **Albert Einstein**'s theory of relativity.

Robert Vivian Pound was born in Ridgeway, Ontario, May 16, 1919, the son of Vivian Ellsworth and Gertrude C. (Prout) Pound. The Pounds moved to the United States when Robert was four years old and he became a naturalized citizen in 1932 at the age of thirteen. He attended the University of Buffalo where he earned his bachelor's degree in physics in

1941. On June 20, 1941, Pound married Betty Yde Andersen with whom he later had a son, John Andrew.

During the first year of World War II, Pound worked as a research physicist at the Submarine Signal Company before joining the staff of Massachusetts Institute of Technology's (MIT's) radiation laboratory, where he stayed until 1946. Pound's wartime research was related to the development of radar and microwave technology. A year before leaving MIT, Pound was appointed a junior fellow of Harvard University's Society of Fellows. He was a professor at Harvard from 1948 until his retirement in 1989. He also served as chair of the physics department (1968–1972), and as director of the physics laboratory (1975–1983).

While he was a junior fellow at Harvard, Pound worked with Purcell on the development of nuclear magnetic resonance techniques. These techniques make use of the fact that atomic nuclei can be identified on the basis of their behavior in the presence of a magnetic field. Nuclear magnetic resonance (NMR) has become a widely used analytical technique in chemical research, medical diagnosis, and a number of other fields. For his contribution to the development of these techniques, Purcell shared the 1952 Nobel Prize in physics.

Mössbauer Effect Leads to Red Shift Discovery

Pound began the research for which he is best known in 1959. The previous year, German physicist **Rudolf Mössbauer** had made an interesting discovery regarding the emission of gamma rays, the high-energy photons which are emitted by radioactive nuclei. Gamma rays often occur during radioactive decay where they carry away energy released in the nuclear transformation. However, the decay of any specific nucleus typically results in gamma rays with varying energies. The variability of gamma ray energies is the result of other changes taking place within the nucleus besides decay, most notably the recoil of the emitting nucleus.

Mössbauer found, however, that these gamma ray energy variations could be eliminated by binding decaying nuclei tightly within a crystal lattice. Within the lattice, the nuclei undergo little or no recoil and the gamma rays emitted are uniform in frequency. This discovery, called the Mössbauer effect, provided a powerful tool for detecting minute changes in electromagnetic waves, including gamma rays.

Pound realized that the Mössbauer effect would be useful in testing the assumptions of relativity theory. According to Einstein, an electromagnetic wave should be deflected from its path by a strong gravitational field. Scientists had attempted to test this hypothesis by measuring the apparent position of stars at various times. The assumption was that light from a distant star passing close to a massive astronomical body would be displaced and would, therefore, seem to be located in slightly different positions at various times.

These experimental efforts failed, however, because of the number of intervening factors, and the differences that were observed could not be specifically ascribed to the effect predicted by Einstein. Pound saw that monochromatic gamma rays produced by the Mössbauer effect (with their uniform frequencies) might be used to test the theory. The apparatus required was conceptually simple: a gamma ray emitter that produced a precise wave and a detector tuned to absorb the wave of that emitter's frequency. Any signal sent by the emitter and distorted by gravity would be detected by a drop of signal in the receiver. In actuality, the effect of gravity changed the frequency of the transmitted wave, resulting in a shift of the wavelength to the receiver—a change known as the "red shift." Pound carried out the necessary experiments with his associate Glen A. Rebka, Jr. between November 1959 and March 1960, and continued for four more years with the assistance of J. L. Snider. The final results confirmed with little uncertainty the existence and magnitude of the predicted red shift phenomenon.

In addition to his Harvard affiliation, Pound held a number of other appointments as visiting professor, including terms at the Clarendon Laboratory at Oxford in 1951, the College of France in 1973, the Joint Institute Laboratory of Astrophysics at the University of Colorado in 1979 and 1980, the University of Groningen in 1982, the Brookhaven National Laboratory in 1986 and 1987, and the University of Florida in 1987. Among his many honors and awards have been the Thompson Memorial Award of the Institute of Radio Engineers in 1948, the Eddington Medal of the Royal Astronomical Society in 1965, and the National Medal of Science in 1990. Pound became a professor emeritus of physics at Harvard in 1989 and retired from academic life.

SELECTED WRITINGS BY POUND:

Books

(Editor and contributor) *Microwave Mixers,* 1948.

—*Sketch by David E. Newton*

Cecil Frank Powell
1903-1969
English physicist

Cecil Frank Powell's research into cloud chambers and the detection of subatomic particles led to his development of photographic emulsion systems to detect and identify fast-moving particles, especially those found in cosmic rays. This enabled him to discover the pi-meson, a particle formed from nuclear reactions within cosmic rays. Powell was awarded the 1950 Nobel Prize in physics for his work in this area. He also was a member of the British Atomic Energy Project during World War II, though in his later years he became an advocate for nuclear disarmament.

Powell was born on November 5, 1903, at Tonbridge, Kent, England. His father, Frank Powell, was a gunsmith, and his mother, Elizabeth Caroline Bisacre, came from a family of skilled technicians. Powell developed an interest in science at an early age after becoming captivated by a chemistry book he saw in a store. Inspired by the book to conduct his own chemistry experiments, he eventually convinced his family to let him purchase the makings of a home chemistry set.

Studies at Cambridge under Rutherford and Wilson

In 1914 Powell won a scholarship to the Judd School in Tonbridge. Upon graduation from Judd, he earned two more scholarships that allowed him to attend Sidney Sussex College at Cambridge University. He graduated in 1925 with a degree in physics but turned down a teaching job to continue his graduate work at Cambridge.

At the time **Ernest Rutherford**, the Nobel-Prize winning physicist who had determined the structure of the atom, was the director of the Cavendish Laboratories at Cambridge. It was under **C. T. R. Wilson**, the inventor of the cloud chamber, that Powell conducted his doctoral research, a study of condensation phenomena in cloud chambers, for which he was awarded his Ph.D. in 1927. Cloud chambers are devices that reveal ionized particles by producing a trail of water droplets from air saturated with water. Powell accepted an appointment as research assistant to A. M. Tyndall at Bristol College. In succession he became lecturer in physics, a reader in physics, the Melville Wills Professor of Physics (1948), the Henry Overton Wills Professor of Physics and director of the H. H. Wills Physics Laboratory (1964), and vice-chancellor of the University at Bristol (1964).

Develops Photographic Detection Devices

Powell's initial work at Bristol involved the study of ion mobility in gases—the way electrically charged atoms behave in gases. By 1938, however, Powell became interested in particle detection devices. That interest, which first developed while he was studying cloud chambers, was rekindled when he learned that photographic emulsions could be used to detect particles in the atmosphere. For a number of years, Wilson's cloud chamber had been the instrument of choice for detecting subatomic particles, such as those produced in radioactive reactions and cosmic rays. However, the cloud chamber possessed one serious disadvantage—it required a brief resting phase each time it was used. In contrast, photographic emulsions were ready at all times to record events.

Like other scientists, Powell had been aware of the potential of photographic emulsions for this purpose, but no one had yet used them successfully. The main problem was that emulsions were not sensitive enough to be used for detection purposes, so Powell decided to find a way to overcome this limitation. His first year of research proved disappointing; he found that neither the emulsions nor the microscopes available were of sufficient quality to obtain the results he wanted. His research was interrupted by World War II, and he became involved with the British Atomic Energy Project for its duration. After the war, he again tackled the technical challenges of using photographic emulsions for detection purposes, this time with much greater success.

In 1946 at Powell's request, Ilford Ltd., a photographic company, developed a new emulsion that could more clearly record particle tracks. Powell and his colleagues used this new detection system to study cosmic radiation at altitudes of up to 9,000 feet. These studies resulted in the discovery of a new particle, the pion (or pi-meson), that had been predicted by the Japanese physicist **Hideki Yukawa** in 1935. The pion proved to be a cohesive force within the atomic nucleus, as was the K-meson, another particle discovered by Powell shortly thereafter. It was partly for these discoveries that Powell was awarded the 1950 Nobel Prize in physics. Over the next decade Powell continued his studies of cosmic radiation. As balloon technology improved, he launched his detectors higher into the atmosphere, in some cases reaching and maintaining altitudes of 90,000 feet for many hours. A key element in the success of this research program was the collaborative effort among scientists, technicians, and laypersons throughout Europe who collected and monitored his equipment. That experience proved to be especially helpful in the early 1960s, when Powell became involved in organizing the European Center for Nuclear Research (CERN) in Geneva, Switzerland. Powell served as chairman of CERN's Science Policy Committee from 1961 to 1963.

During the 1950s Powell became increasingly concerned about social problems related to scientific and technological development. He served as president of the Association of Scientific Workers from 1952 to 1954, and as president of the World Federation of Scientific Workers from 1956 until his death. A founding member of the Pugwash Movement for Science and World Affairs, he lent his signature to Bertrand Russell's 1955 petition calling for nuclear disarmament.

Powell was married in 1932 to Isobel Therese Artner, with whom he had two daughters. He died on August 9, 1969, at Bellano, Lake Como, Italy, while on vacation to celebrate his retirement from Bristol a few months earlier. Powell's awards in addition to the Nobel Prize included the Hughes Medal in 1949 and the Royal Medal of the Royal Society in 1961, the Rutherford Medal and Prize in 1961, the Lomonosov Gold Medal of the Soviet Academy of Sciences in 1967, and the Guthrie Prize and Medal of the Institute of Physics and Physical Society in 1969.

SELECTED WRITINGS BY POWELL:

Books

(With G. P. S. Occhialini), *Nuclear Physics in Photographs,* Oxford University Press, 1947.
(With P. H. Fowler and D. H. Perkins), *The Study of Elementary Particles by the Photographic Method,* Pergamon, 1959.
Selected Papers of Cecil Frank Powell, edited by E. H. S. Burhop, W. O. Lock, and M. G. K. Menon, North-Holland, 1972.

SOURCES:

Books

Biographical Memoirs of Fellows of the Royal Society, Volume 17, Royal Society (London), 1971, pp. 541–63.
McGraw-Hill Modern Scientists and Engineers, Volume 2, McGraw-Hill, 1980, pp. 436–37.

—*Sketch by David E. Newton*

David Powless
1943-
American environmental scientist

David Powless received the first National Science Foundation grant awarded to an individual Native American in 1977. This research funding allowed Powless to develop a successful method of recycling hazardous iron oxide wastes from steel mills. A member of the Oneida tribe, an Iroquoian-speaking group, Powless was named 1980 American Indian Business Owner of the Year by the United Indian Development Association. The following year, he was presented with the Small Business Administration's National Innovation Advocate of the Year Award by then Vice President George Bush at a ceremony in the White House Rose Garden.

David Allen Powless was born on May 29, 1943, in Ottawa, Illinois, the fifth of six children born to Merville and Adeline (Tucktenhagen) Powless. His father was a government employee who worked at various times for the Bureau of Indian Affairs, the Department of Navy, and the Department of Army. He was also a staunch believer in the value of education. As Powless recalled in an interview with Linda Wasmer Smith, "My father motivated us all. . . . When I was being raised, we were told that as Oneidas, we had a special obligation to our tribe to act well, because whatever we did, that was the way people would think all Oneida Indians acted. But we were also told that we had been given special skills and abilities with which to fulfill that duty. . . . We were Indian people, first. We were Indian people who were going to get a good education, second."

Powless lived up to his father's high expectations by winning a football scholarship to the University of Oklahoma. He stayed for one year before transferring to the University of Illinois, where he continued to pursue football while studying marketing and economics. After playing on a team that won the 1963 Rose Bowl, Powless graduated with a B.S. in 1966. He was drafted to play professional football for the New York Giants in 1965. He spent a season with them before being traded to the Washington Redskins, but a back injury brought an early end to his sports career.

Recycles Hazardous Wastes from Steel Mills

In 1967, Powless began nine years as a marketing representative for the Foseco company. His job, which involved selling chemical additives and insulation materials to steel mills, gave him a close-up view of how that industry worked. In 1976, he started his own company, convinced that the hazardous wastes generated by the steel mills represented a problem for which he could supply a practical solution. As he told Linda Wasmer Smith, "This is when I started seeking my identity as a Native person. All of our traditions are focused on care and concern for the Earth." Powless developed his recycling method with the aid of scientists at the Colorado School of Mines in Golden. They helped him write an unsolicited proposal to the National Science Foundation, and after almost half a year of negotiations he was awarded the grant. He then established a pilot plant at Kaiser Steel in California.

In Powless' recycling method, various contaminants are first removed from iron oxide wastes using an indirect fired rotary kiln—a constantly set furnace with an external flame hitting the shell. As materials enter the kiln, they become hot enough to ignite. But as the materials move farther into the furnace, there is less oxygen available to support the fire. In this high-temperature, low-oxygen environment, contaminants such as oil, zinc, lead, and cadmium wholly or partly come off the wastes. Then the cleaned-up materials are agglomerated, or collected, into briquettes, which can later be reintroduced into the steel-making process. According to Powless: "This was a spiritual experience for me, because it involved the use of fire and flame for purification."

Powless' company marketed this technology until 1986, when the search for his roots took Powless to the Oneida reservation in Wisconsin. There he soon became involved in the start-up of a tribally owned and managed environmental analytical testing laboratory called ORTEK. This profitable enterprise included an operating group that conducted organic and inorganic testing of soil, water, and air for contaminants. In 1992, Powless left his position as president of ORTEK and accepted a new one as vice president of marketing for the Arctic Slope Regional Corporation. There, Powless has assumed a key role in the Eskimo-owned firm's expansion outside Alaska.

Powless has served on the board of directors of the American Indian Science and Engineering Society. He is also a popular speaker on the relationship between traditional teachings, spiritual growth, and science. Powless was married in 1968 to Carol Monson, with whom he has a son. That marriage ended in divorce, and on November 6, 1983, Powless wed Anna Kormos in Los Angeles. The couple and their daughter make their home in Corrales, New Mexico.

SELECTED WRITINGS BY POWLESS:

Periodicals

"A Successful Economic Development Venture of the Oneida Tribe," *Winds of Change,* spring, 1989, pp. 27–28.

SOURCES:

Periodicals

Vogel, Mike, "Native American Parley Fuses Culture, Technology. 900 Expected at Conference," *Buffalo News,* November 9, 1990, p. B15.
Weidlein, Jim, "People of the Whale," *Winds of Change,* summer, 1993, pp. 10–15.
Weidlein, Jim, "Sharing a Piece of the Whale," *Winds of Change,* autumn, 1993, pp. 140–147.

Other

Powless, David Allen, interviews with Linda Wasmer Smith conducted February 14 and 22, 1994.

—Sketch by Linda Wasmer Smith

Ludwig Prandtl
1875-1953
German physicist and aerodynamicist

Generally considered the father of aerodynamics, Ludwig Prandtl taught for many years at Germany's Göttingen University and made important contributions to the fields of fluid mechanics, hydraulics, hydrodynamics, and aerodynamics. Prandtl also conducted original research in solid mechanics, heat transfer, elasticity, and even meteorology. He and his many students at Göttingen fundamentally shaped the new field of aerodynamics and its application in airplane design, permitting "aeronautical engineers to move from hit-and-miss methods into scientific design," as Hungarian-American aerodynamicist **Theodore von Kármán** wrote in *The Wind and Beyond.* "In my opinion," von Kármán noted, "Prandtl unraveled the puzzle of some natural phenomena of tremendous basic importance and was deserving of a Nobel Prize."

Prandtl was born in Freising, Bavaria, Germany, on February 4, 1875, to Alexander and Magdalene Ostermann Prandtl. Because his mother suffered from a long illness, Prandtl was especially close to his father, who taught surveying and engineering at the Weihenstephen agricultural college near Freising and inspired in his son an early interest in natural phenomenon. Following a humanistic secondary education in Freising and Munich, Germany, Prandtl earned an engineering degree from the Technical

Institute at Munich in 1898 and a Ph.D. in solid mechanics from the University of Munich in 1900. His major professor, August Föppl, was a noted authority in engineering mechanics and helped Prandtl obtain a job as an engineer in the Augsburg-Nürnberg Machine Factory. At the factory, Prandtl was assigned to improve a vacuum device that removed wood shavings. He was so successful that the firm rebuilt the piece of equipment according to his design and began to market a new line of shavings conveyors. This work led Prandtl to recognize some basic gaps in the knowledge of fluid mechanics.

Develops Boundary Layer Concept

In 1901, Prandtl became a professor of mechanics at the Technical Institute of Hannover, Germany, where he continued to investigate fluid motion. Existing fluid motion theories failed to explain why the flow of thin (inviscid) liquids in a pipe did not fill the pipe but separated from its wall. Prandtl observed that a thin layer of the fluid always formed between the pipe and the rest of the flowing liquid. In the next three years, he developed an explanation of this phenomenon, set forth in what became a famous paper delivered at the Third International Congress of Mathematics at Heidelberg, Germany, in 1904. Only eight pages long, the paper delineated the concept of a boundary layer in fluid flow that subsequently proved to be of critical importance in understanding such central aviation concepts as lift, the force that causes aircraft to fly, and drag, or air resistance. Subsequent innovations, such as streamlined aircraft designs, resulted from these findings.

Even before Prandtl presented this groundbreaking paper, the famous mathematician Felix Klein had brought him to Göttingen University in 1904 as an extraordinary (junior) professor of applied physics. Although this was a step down from his full professorship in Hannover, at Göttingen Prandtl received a higher salary and the promise of a research laboratory. Klein was attempting to bring together the disciplines of science and engineering that tended to be taught in separate institutions of higher learning throughout Germany; he was also interested in promoting the study of aerodynamics at Göttingen. Both goals fit well with Prandtl's own concerns and he had both a laboratory and a full professorship by 1907. He also played a key role in bringing about the construction of a thirty-five-horsepower wind tunnel, built in 1908 and 1909, which was later joined by several other wind tunnels at Göttingen. In 1909, Prandtl married Gertrude Föppl, the eldest daughter of his former professor, who gave birth to the couple's two daughters in 1914 and 1917.

Prandtl's studies led him to advocate the initially controversial single-winged aircraft at a time when designers favored bi- and tri-wings. His theoretical discoveries also led to improvements in the design of dirigibles, lighter-than-air carriers used by both civilians and the military. In the 1910s, Prandtl was also at work on one of his most important discoveries, induced drag. Induced drag is caused when air races over wing surfaces; though this motion produces lift, the air flowing over the wing from leading to trailing edge also results in two trailing vortices that extend back from the airplane and impede its flight. After struggling to comprehend this little understood phenomenon, Prandtl developed a mathematical explanation and went on to show how to reduce drag through wing design and streamlining, techniques that dramatically influenced the aircraft industry.

Studies Turbulent Air Flow

A problem remaining to be solved in the years between World Wars I and II was turbulent (irregular) air flow. Prandtl worked in friendly competition with von Kármán, who was teaching at the Technical Institute of Aachen. Following some preliminary findings by von Kármán in 1924, Prandtl presented his "mixing length concept" in 1926, which analyzed turbulent air flow in terms of elements colliding and producing molecular friction. Prandtl mathematically demonstrated the distances each fluid element has to travel before collision with other elements reduces its momentum. Thereafter, experimental work by Prandtl and his students, together with important experimental and theoretical findings by von Kármán and his collaborators, led to a summary paper delivered by Prandtl in 1933 that laid the foundation for subsequent knowledge about chaotic motion. The method and concepts von Kármán and Prandtl developed had important applications for avoiding drag in aircraft, describing liquid flow through pipes, and designing rockets.

These discoveries represented only some of the more important contributions Prandtl and his students made to aerodynamics—not to mention hydrodynamics and solid mechanics. Prandtl was instrumental in setting up aerodynamics and hydrodynamics institutes at Göttingen, including the famous Kaiser Wilhelm Institute for Fluid Mechanics, which was founded in 1925 and renamed the Max Planck Institute after World War II.

Prandtl's usual methodology in achieving his discoveries involved a painstaking comparison of theory with experimental data. He also abstracted the basic components from complex processes and described them in a simplified, mathematical way that allowed him to understand the fundamental principles involved. Beyond applying this methodology himself, he was also highly effective in teaching it to his students. Many of them then went on to make their own contributions to fluid and solid mechanics. Described by von Kármán as a "tedious lecturer" whose classroom presentations suffered from excessive precision, Prandtl impressed Adolf Busemann by displaying "amazing clarity in dissecting and composing mechanical phenomena and finding ways to reduce their complexity," as Busemann wrote in *Biographical Memoirs of the Fellows of the Royal Society.* According to Busemann, Prandtl "never [tried] to circumvent difficulties by omitting them," resulting in lectures that were "a rich source of information for all his pupils."

Besides being an accomplished scientist, Prandtl played piano, enjoyed hiking in the hills and mountains, gave annual parties for his laboratory staff, and took a childlike delight in toys and magic tricks. He resisted the Nazis on several occasions after 1933 and even signed a petition opposing the dismissal of Jewish professors from Göttingen. Prandtl's son-in-law was killed during World War II, and he lost his wife immediately afterwards, perhaps occasioning a physical decline that was arrested for a while but resumed in the year before his death in Göttingen on August 15, 1953.

SELECTED WRITINGS BY PRANDTL:

Books

Essentials of Fluid Dynamics, Hafner, 1952.
Gesammelte Adhandlungen zur angewandten Mechanik, Hydro- und Aerodynamik (title means "Collected Essays on Applied Mechanics, Hydro- and Aerodynamics"), three volumes, Springer-Verlag, 1961.

SOURCES:

Books

Biographical Memoirs of Fellows of the Royal Society, Volume 5, Royal Society (London), 1960, pp. 193–205.
The Daniel Guggenheim Medal for Achievement in Aeronautics, [New York], 1936, pp. 11–17.
Dictionary of Scientific Biography, Volume XI, Scribner, 1975, pp. 123–125.
The Great Scientists, edited Frank M. Magill, Volume 10, Grolier Educational Corporation, 1989, pp. 20–25.
von Kármán, Theodore with Lee Edson, *The Wind and Beyond,* Little, Brown, 1967.

—*Sketch by J. D. Hunley*

Fritz Pregl
1869-1930
Austrian analytical chemist

The work of Fritz Pregl is an example of the maxim that every difficulty is an opportunity. It was the problems inherent in analyzing organic matter that motivated Pregl to take microanalysis into new realms of exactitude, developing new instrumentation for the precise measurement of such substances. Such microanalytic tools paved the way for later biochemical research on pigments, hormones, and vitamins. Pregl's innovations in the field earned him the 1923 Nobel Prize in chemistry.

Pregl was born on September 3, 1869, in Laibach, Austria (now Ljubljana, Republic of Slovenia), the only son of Friderike Schlacker and Raimund Pregl, the treasurer of a bank in nearby Krain (now Kranj). Though his father died when he was quite young, Pregl finished Gymnasium or high school in Laibach before he and his mother moved in 1887 to Graz, where he studied medicine at the University of Graz. Early in his academic career, Pregl demonstrated the intelligence and skill that would become more evident in his subsequent work as an analytical chemist. While still a student, his physiology professor, Alexander Rollett, made him an assistant in his laboratory. Upon gaining his medical degree in 1893, Pregl began to practice medicine with a specialty in ophthalmology but also stayed on part-time at Rollett's laboratory.

Turns Attention to Chemistry

Becoming an assistant lecturer in physiology and histology at the University of Graz, and working in Rollett's laboratory, Pregl increasingly turned his attention to biological and physiological chemistry, focusing on organic matter. His early research centered on human physiology and, in particular, the properties of bile and urine. His research on the reaction of cholic acid, which is found in bile, and the causality of the high ratio of carbon to nitrogen in human urine, won him a university lectureship at Graz in 1899. In 1904, Pregl went to Germany to study chemistry with **Friedrich Wilhelm Ostwald** in Leipzig and **Emil Fischer** in Berlin. Fischer was a 1902 Nobel laureate in organic chemistry for his sugar and purine research, and Ostwald, a physical chemist, would win the Nobel in 1909 for his work in catalysis.

Returning to Graz in 1905, Pregl renewed his bile research and began protein investigations, having been intrigued by Fischer's recent work on the structure of proteins. He also became an assistant at the medical and chemical laboratory of the University of Graz, a position which provided him with valuable research space. In 1907 he was appointed as the forensic chemist for central Styria, the province of which Graz is the capital. In the course of his chemical investigations, Pregl continually came up against one problem: the methods of analysis employed by organic chemistry were much too cumbersome, lengthy, and overly complex for the new discipline of biochemistry in which he was becoming increasingly involved. In particular, Pregl found that he would have to prepare large amounts of test samples if he used traditional analytical methods in his studies on bile acids. Because these acids are complicated proteins, only small quantities can be isolated from liver bile, a process that is both time-consuming and costly: Pregl's research in bile acid alone would require processing several tons of raw bile in order to refine enough of the acid for traditional analysis. It was to overcome such difficulties that he set to improve the methods of microanalysis, thereby altering the direction of his research from biochemistry to analytical chemistry.

By the time Pregl entered the field, microanalysis was already over seventy years old, pioneered by Justus von Liebig, who had developed the combustion method. In Liebig's technique, proportionate amounts of elements in an organic substance could be determined by burning the substance in a glass tube under conditions that would convert the carbon to carbon dioxide (CO_2) and all the hydrogen into water. The water and CO_2 would in turn be absorbed by other materials such as potassium hydroxide or a lime and soda mixture, and the change of weight in the respective absorbing materials would thus give the relative amounts of carbon and hydrogen in the combusted substance. Additionally, a contemporary of Pregl's, Friedrich Emich, at the Technical University of Graz had shown the reliability of working with small quantities of substances in an inorganic framework. Pregl set out to achieve Emich's measurement techniques with organic material.

Microanalysis Improvements Lead to Nobel Prize

It was Pregl's achievement to build upon Liebig and Emich's developments, and to refine and improve them to the point where substantially less of the organic substances were required for analysis. In 1910 he left Graz for Innsbruck, where he took the position of professor of medical chemistry at the University of Innsbruck. With this position, Pregl could devote more time to his research. His first priority was to find or create a balance that would accurately weigh much smaller amounts of substances than those currently available. He turned to W. H. Kuhlman, a German chemist who had recently developed a microbalance accurate to between 0.01 and 0.02 milligrams; Pregl found that with careful adjustments he could

accurately utilize Kuhlman's balance to within 0.001 milligrams.

Pregl also took on the combustion analysis of carbon and hydrogen, improving that process by scaling down the size of the analytic equipment and adding a universal filling for the combustion tube that consisted of a mixture of lead chromate and copper oxide set in between two pieces of silver. This adaptation improved the absorption of the carbon dioxide and water. With such refinements, Pregl was able to obtain accurate analyses with between 2–4 milligrams of an organic substance—and fairly accurate readings with only 1 milligram—a significant reduction compared to the .2 to 1 grams needed for Liebig's method. With the new materials employed, Pregl was also able to reduce the time needed for such analysis from three hours to an hour. Pregl and his team also went on to devise new microanalytic techniques for boiling substances to determine their molecular weight by creating apparatus that impeded the substances' contamination with air. This allowed determinations to be made with greatly reduced amounts of such substances. Pregl made these advances known in two public presentations: in 1911 at the German Chemical Society in Berlin, and in 1913 at a scientific congress in Vienna.

Although improved techniques since Pregl's time now allow scientists to work with organic samples of only a few tenths of a milligram, his microanalytic improvements were revolutionary in their day and opened the way to new vistas of biochemical research in both science and industry. World renowned, Pregl returned to the University of Graz in 1913 as a full professor at the Medicochemical Institute, and here he perfected the methods he had pioneered, remaining in Graz—despite other tantalizing offers—until his death. In 1916, in the midst of the First World War, he was made dean of the medical school, and in 1920 became vice chancellor of the university. His major publication on his findings, *Die quantitative organische Mikroanalyse,* was published in 1917 and has since gone through numerous editions and translations. He subsequently won the Lieben Prize and membership in the Vienna Academy of Sciences. Pregl continued his research into a wide range of organic substances, employing his own methods of microanalysis on bile acids, enzymes, and sera. He also employed microanalysis in forensics, determining poisonous alkaloids from minute amounts of substance.

In 1923 Pregl was awarded the Nobel Prize in chemistry for his advances in microanalysis of organic substances. Though his work was an improvement rather than an invention, it was a well deserved honor for a man who tirelessly devoted his life to the cause of science. A life-long bachelor, Pregl's only pleasures aside from his research were mountain climbing and bicycling. He was also devoted to his students, lending both money and support when needed. In 1929 he endowed an award for chemistry through the Vienna Academy of Sciences, the Fritz Pregl Prize, which continues to provide yearly stipends to promising students. Pregl died following an illness in 1930 at the age of sixty-one.

SELECTED WRITINGS BY PREGL:

Books

Die quantitative organische Mikroanalyse, J. Springer, 1917.

SOURCES:

Books

A Biographical Dictionary of Scientists, Adam & Charles, 1982, pp. 425–26.
Dictionary of Scientific Biography, Volume 11, Scribner's, 1978, pp. 128–29.
Farber, Eduard, editor, *Great Chemists,* Interscience, 1961, pp. 1327–31.
Hinduja Foundation Encyclopedia of Nobel Laureates 1901–1987, Konark, 1988, pp. 145–46.
Nobel Prize Winners, H. W. Wilson, 1987, pp. 834–35.

Periodicals

"Fritz Pregl (1869–1930)," *Journal of Chemical Education,* December, 1958, p. 609.
Lieb, H., "Fritz Pregl," *Berichte der Deutschen chemischen Gesellschaft,* Volume 64A, 1931, p. 113.

—*Sketch by J. Sydney Jones*

Vladimir Prelog
1906-
Bosnian-born Swiss organic chemist

Vladimir Prelog spent most of his working life investigating the chemistry of natural products. He made major contributions to the synthesis and structure determination of hundreds of natural organic compounds. Additionally, he and his colleagues Robert Cahn and Sir Christopher Ingold formulated a set of rules (abbreviated CIP) for communicating the specific shape and configuration of highly complex organic compounds. Much of Prelog's work was characterized by an unusual cooperative spirit. Almost all of his major discoveries were made in conjunction with accomplished chemists in other laboratories. He shared the 1975 Nobel Prize in chemistry with Sir **John Cornforth**, who said about their work in his acceptance speech, as quoted in Prelog's autobiography (*My 132 Semesters of Chemistry Studies*): "Our backgrounds, and the experience that has shaped us as scientists, are very different. . . . What we have in common is a lifelong curiosity about the shapes, and changes in shape, of entities that we shall never see; and a lifelong conviction that this curiosity will lead us closer to the truth of chemical processes, including the processes of life."

Prelog was born on July 23, 1906, to Milan and Mara (Cettolo) Prelog in Sarajevo, in what was then the Austro-Hungarian monarchy. His father was a historian and teacher at both the high school and university level. Prelog's early life in general was surrounded by the political upheaval and war endemic to that part of the world—as a small child giving out flowers at a procession, he was within 200 yards of the assassination of Archduke Ferdinand, which touched off World War I. He wrote in his autobiography " . . . since then, I have been allergic to all violent mass demonstrations, even when held for just causes." Prelog's parents separated when he was nine, and he was raised for the next four years in Zagreb by an unmarried aunt who encouraged his interest in chemical experiments. At a science high school in Osijek he met a chemistry teacher, Ivan Kuria, who strongly encouraged his interests and helped him, at age 15, to publish his first chemistry paper in the journal *Chemiker Zeitung.* He completed high school in Zagreb in 1924 and moved to Prague to study chemistry at the Czech Institute of Technology.

Initially, Prelog was disillusioned with his university experience; chemistry seemed to consist entirely of disconnected facts, with nothing to hold them together. He eventually apprenticed himself to Rudolf Lukes, an older student in the laboratories of the sugar chemist Emil Votoček. Lukes introduced him to the organizing principles of organic chemistry and rekindled Prelog's interest in the subject. He had to work and learn very quickly because he was short of money, and in 1929 he received his doctorate under the supervision of Votocek. The topic of his dissertation was the structure determination of a natural product called rhamnoconvolvulinoic acid, a sugar derivative.

In the severely depressed economy of the time, and particularly since he was not a citizen of Czechoslovakia, it was impossible to obtain a job with any research organization. Thus, between 1929 and 1934, Prelog worked unofficially with Gothard J. Driza, an entrepreneur who set up a home laboratory to supply specialty chemicals to business, government, and the military. Among these chemicals were chloroacetophenone, which the police used for tear gas ammunition, and ammonium sulfite, which hairdressers used in their work. At the same time, he began trying to synthesize quinine (a principle anti-malarial drug), then available only from the bark of the *Cinchona* tree. He became even more interested in quinine and similar drugs when he himself contracted malaria serving in the Royal Yugoslav Navy in 1932, and that interest continued for many years.

A teaching position at the University of Zagreb materialized in 1935, but it proved to be a disappointment because the salary was so low and research funding so minimal. Prelog accepted the position anyway, and to make ends meet took a second job with a local pharmaceutical company, Kastel, Ltd. Among other chemicals, they made the sulfa drug called sulfanilamide.

Sanctuary and Research at the Swiss Federal Institute of Technology

The company and university connections proved fruitful, and Prelog finally made sufficient money to support himself for a few months in 1937 working with the chemist **Leopold Ružička** at the Swiss Federal Institute of Technology (Eidgenossische Technische Hochschule, or ETH) in Zurich, Switzerland. His friendship with Ruzicka may have saved his life; later, with World War II raging, Ruzicka obtained Swiss entry visas for Prelog and his wife. Officials who thought Prelog was going to Germany to give a scientific talk permitted him to leave the city, and the Prelogs were thus able to legally escape German-occupied Zagreb and settle in Zurich in late 1941. Prelog became a Swiss citizen in 1959 and spent the rest of his career at the ETH, financially supported for much of that time by the giant Swiss pharmaceutical company CIBA.

At ETH, Prelog initially worked on several natural products from various animal glands, but eventually he switched to research on alkaloids (natural nitrogen-containing compounds), his principle interest. In 1942, he received a promotion, and in 1945 received the title of Professor. During the war, there was no possibility of travel to other countries, or even contact with other scientists by mail, so Prelog and his colleagues caught up on their literature-reading and worked with readily available materials. During this time, he made important contributions to the structure determination and synthesis of both solanine (a chemical extractable from potatoes) and strychnine, among many others.

After the war, Prelog began traveling, meeting other chemists, and conducting joint projects with them. He traveled and lectured extensively in the United States in 1950 and 1951. He seriously considered moving to America when Harvard University and later the Hoffmann-LaRoche Company offered him attractive positions, but ETH created a special chaired professorship for him, so he retained his residence in Switzerland. For a few more years, he worked with naturally-occurring alkaloid compounds, collaborating with fellow chemists Sir **Derek Barton** and **Robert B. Woodward**, among others. He then switched his interest to elaborate ring structures, enzymes, and antibiotics, particularly the metabolic products of bacteria and other microbes. Most of these discoveries fall under the title of "basic" research, which develops the science of organic chemistry itself; the most commercially successful outcome was the eventual development of rifampicin, used to treat tuberculosis and leprosy.

In 1957, Prelog was named Ruzicka's successor at ETH and eventually found that he did not care for administrative work. He instituted a policy of rotating the administrative duties among a group of professors, which worked well and allowed him more time for research. In 1960, he joined the board of directors of CIBA (later CIBA-Geigy) and served until 1978. While a member, he helped set up the Woodward Institute in Basel, a research facility where the Nobel Laureate Woodward, also an organic chemist, could conduct research as he liked. The two became lifelong friends. Prelog also continued his world travels, lecturing and accepting guest professorships in many countries, including India, Israel, Australia, England, and South Africa.

Stereochemical Studies Lead to the 1975 Nobel Prize in Chemistry

Beginning in the 1950s, the electronic instrumentation applicable to chemical structure determination improved markedly. A process that once required slow, highly skilled, creative observation and analysis became routine, as various types of spectrometers and other analytical instruments gave almost instantaneous information on the layout of atoms in large molecules. In this environment, the identification and synthesis of new organic compounds grew exponentially.

It became apparent to Prelog, beginning with his work on alkaloids, that the naming of these new millions of organic compounds could be greatly improved. Natural products are not only extremely complex, they are also extremely specific in their three dimensional shapes. Small differences in the way atoms are oriented in space may change the biochemistry of a compound completely. Thus, new synthetic techniques are required to obtain exactly the desired configuration of a molecule. The entire branch of organic chemistry devoted to the shapes and configurations of molecules is called stereochemistry, and the individual configurations of a molecule are called its stereoisomers. Prelog spoke about the requirements in an oral history for the Chemical Heritage Foundation: "If, for example, you have sixty-four stereoisomers [of the same molecule] and only one is a natural compound that is biologically active, you have to be able first to assign to this molecule a model or a stereo formula. Secondly, you have to have a certain language, symbols, descriptors, to speak about it. Finally, you need to be able to [synthesize] this specific stereoisomer [uncontaminated with the others]. . . . We needed symbols to talk about our results."

Together with Robert Cahn and Sir Christopher Ingold, Prelog developed the CIP system of stereochemical nomenclature, which includes single letter symbols to designate specific characteristics of large molecules. The CIP system is now widely used as a standard in reference books and journals. Later, he developed new methods of synthesizing specific stereoisomers. For his body of work, specifically that related to stereochemical nomenclature and stereosynthesis, Prelog won the 1975 Nobel Prize (shared with Sir John Cornforth). He thus became the fifth director of ETH to win a Nobel. Additionally, he was the recipient of numerous honorary degrees throughout his life, as well as the Werner medal in 1945, and the Marcel Benoist award in 1965.

Prelog married Kamila Vitek in 1933, and their only child, a son named Jan, was born in 1949. Jan followed in his grandfather's rather than his father's footsteps and became an historian. Over the course of his life, Prelog learned to speak or read at least four languages fluently—among them English, Czech, Croatian, and German—although he was characteristically modest about the achievement and said that he spoke none of them, including his mother tongue, without an accent. During his career he supervised more than 100 doctoral students and published approximately 400 papers. He also wrote biographical material on the scientists he had worked with, particularly Ruzicka. After his official retirement in 1976, he maintained his attachment to ETH by signing on as a postdoctoral student and working on the separation of complex chemical mixtures by the technique of chromatography. Becoming a student again (at least in name) inspired the title of his autobiography, *My 132 Semesters of Chemistry Studies,* published in 1991 by the American Chemical Society.

SELECTED WRITINGS BY PRELOG:

Books

My 132 Semesters of Chemistry Studies, translated by Otto Theodor Benfey and David Ginsburg,

in the series *Profiles, Pathways, and Dreams: Autobiographies of Eminent Chemists,* series edited by Jeffrey I. Seeman, American Chemical Society, 1991.

SOURCES:

Prelog, Vladimir, interview with Tonja Koeppel, Zurich, 1984, tapes and transcript archived at the Chemical Heritage Foundation, Philadelphia, PA.

—Sketch by Gail B.C. Marsella

Ada I. Pressman
1927-
American control systems engineer

Ada I. Pressman is a recognized authority in power plant controls and process instrumentation. She specialized in the area of shutdown systems for nuclear power plants, working to find ways to ensure that a nuclear power plant's turbine, steam engine, and reactor work together properly and safely to generate electrical power. Pressman's contributions to the technology of emergency systems for nuclear power plants include the development of a secondary cooling system that operates from a diesel generator in the event of a primary power source loss. These measures safeguard people working on site against the danger of radiation as well as protect plant machinery against physical damage if malfunctions occur. She received the Society of Women Engineers (SWE) Annual Achievement Award in 1976 "in recognition of her significant contributions in the field of power control systems engineering."

Ada Irene Pressman was born on March 3, 1927, in Shelby County, Ohio. She graduated from Ohio State University with a bachelor of science degree in mechanical engineering in 1950 and then began her professional career as a project engineer with Bailey Meter Company in Cleveland. Five years later, she accepted a post as project engineer with Bechtel Corporation in Los Angeles. During the next two decades, she was promoted to instrument group leader, control systems engineering group supervisor, and assistant chief control systems engineer. In these capacities, Pressman managed eighteen design teams for more than twenty power generating plants throughout the world. Pressman returned to college to earn her master's degree in business administration, which she obtained from Golden Gate University in 1974, the same year she was named chief control systems engineer at Bechtel. In 1979, she became engineering manager; she retired in 1987.

In addition to her career at Bechtel, Pressman was noted for her involvement in science and women's organizations. She was president of the Society of Women Engineers in 1979–80, vice president of the Instrument Society of America from 1973 to 1978, and a member of the American Nuclear Society. She is a member of the Institute for Advancement of Engineering's College of Fellows. In the 1970s Pressman successfully campaigned to have control systems engineering classified as a separate field with the state engineering board of California and became the first person to be registered in the new discipline.

Honors awarded to Pressman include the Distinguished Alumna Award from Ohio State University, the E. G. Bailey Award from the Instrument Society of America, the Outstanding Engineer Merit Award, and the YWCA TWIN award. In an interview with contributor Karen Withem, Pressman said that her career in engineering was "a challenge and an opportunity to do a good job, to gain the feeling of accomplishment when something is done well." She believes that being one of a very few women in leadership in engineering caused her to develop resourcefulness. "I was never given the easiest jobs," she said. 'Some of those jobs that no one else wanted were opportunities in disguise. They gave me the chance to do things I wouldn't otherwise have had the opportunity to do." Her hobbies include traveling, bowling, and photography.

SOURCES:

Pressman, Ada I., interview with Karen Withem conducted March 28, 1994.

—*Sketch by Karen Withem*

Diana García Prichard
1949-
American chemical physicist

Diana García Prichard is a research scientist who conducts fundamental photographic materials research for the Eastman Kodak company. Her graduate work on the behavior of gas phases that she completed at the University of Rochester was lauded for its inventiveness and received unusual attention and recognition by the scientific community. She is also an active leader in the Hispanic community and has garnered numerous awards for her work.

Prichard was born in San Francisco, California, on October 27, 1949. Her mother, Matilde (Robleto) Dominguez García, was originally from Granada, Nicaragua. Her father, Juan García, was from Aransas Pass, Texas, and was of Mexican and Native American descent. He worked as a warehouse foreman at Ray-O-Vac. Although both of her parents received little education, they knew well the value of schooling and saw that Prichard appreciated the worth and the joys of learning. After graduating from El Camino High School in South San Francisco, Prichard entered the College of San Mateo and received her LVN degree (nursing) in 1969.

After taking some years to care for her two children, Erik and Andrea, Prichard chose a dramatic career shift and reentered academia in 1979. Interested in things scientific ever since she was young, and always intrigued and attracted by the thinking process and creativity required to do real scientific research, she enrolled at California State University at Hayward and earned her B.S. degree in chemistry/physics in 1983. She then continued her post graduate education at the University of Rochester in New York, obtaining her M.S. degree in physical chemistry in 1985. Continuing at Rochester, she entered the doctoral program and earned her Ph.D. in chemical physics in 1988.

Her graduate studies at Rochester emphasized optics, electronics, automation, vacuum technology, and signal processing with data acquisition and analysis. During this graduate work on the high resolution infrared absorption spectrum (which basically involves telling how much or what type of atoms or molecules are present), she was able to construct the first instrument ever to be able to measure van der Waals clusters. Named after Dutch Nobel prize-winning physicist, **Johannes Diderick van der Waals**, the van der Waals equation accounts for the non-ideal behavior of gases at the molecular level. An ideal or perfect gas is one which always obeys the known gas laws. The van der Waals equation allows scientists to predict the behavior of gases that do not strictly follow these laws by factoring in specific corrections. Van der Waals clusters are weakly bound complexes that exist in a natural state but are low in number. Prichard's work allowed other scientists to produce these rare clusters by experimental methods and thus be able to study them. Her graduate publications on this subject were themselves cited in more than one hundred subsequent publications.

Upon graduation, Prichard accepted a position with Eastman Kodak of Rochester, New York. A research scientist in the firm's PhotoScience Research Division, she conducts basic studies in silver halide materials for photographic systems. A member of Sigma Xi and Sigma Pi Sigma honor societies as well as a national board member of the Society for Hispanic Professional Engineers (SHPE) and a charter member of the Hispanic Democratic Women's Network of Washington, D.C., she also served on the Clinton/Gore Transition Cluster for Space, Science and Technology in 1992.

Prichard founded a program in Rochester called "Partnership in Education" that provides Hispanic role models in the classroom to teach science and math to limited English proficient students. She has also co-founded, within Eastman Kodak, the Hispanic Organization for Leadership and Advancement (HOLA). She is married to Mark S. Prichard, also a research scientist at Eastman Kodak. As to what she is most proud of in her career, she says that it is the fact that although her parents had little schooling, she was nevertheless able to come to love learning, obtain an advanced degree, and work in a professional field that she truly loves.

SELECTED WRITINGS BY PRICHARD:

Periodicals

Prichard, Diana G., R. N. Nandi, and J. S. Muenter, "Microwave and Infrared Studies of Acetylene Dimer in a T-Shaped Configuration," *Journal of Chemical Physics,* July 1, 1988, pp. 115–123.

Prichard, Diana G., R. N. Nandi, and J. S. Muenter, "Vibration-Rotation Spectrum of the Carbon Dioxide-Acetylene van der Waals Complex in the 3 u Region," *Journal of Chemical Physics,* August 1, 1988, pp. 1245–1250.

—*Sketch by Leonard C. Bruno*

Ilya Prigogine
1917-
Russian-born Belgian chemist

Ilya Prigogine was awarded the 1977 Nobel Prize in chemistry for his pioneering work on nonequilibrium thermodynamics. He revolutionized chemistry by introducing the concepts of irreversible time and probability in his approach to unstable chemical

Ilya Prigogine

states and providing mathematical models of dissipative structures and their self-organization, the processes by which disorder progresses to order. Taking a highly philosophical approach to science, Prigogine has redefined the framework of the laws of nature, insisting on a less deterministic understanding of the natural world.

Prigogine was born in Moscow, Russia, on January 25, 1917, two months before the collapse of the czarist regime and nine months before the Bolshevik revolution. His father, Roman, was a chemical engineer and a factory owner, and his mother, Julia (Wichman) Prigogine, had studied music at the Moscow conservatory of music. Prigogine's brother, Alexandre, who was four years older, also became a chemist.

Four years after he was born, Prigogine's father decided to leave Russia because of the restrictions placed on private ownership and enterprise by the new Soviet government. After a year in Lithuania, the family moved to Berlin where they remained until 1929. Their stay in Berlin coincided with the terrible inflation of the early twenties and the beginnings of Nazism in the latter half of the decade. After two of his business attempts failed, and with growing Nazi strength boding ill for Jewish émigrés, Prigogine's father took the family to Brussels, Belgium, where Prigogine, then twelve, was enrolled in the Latin-Greek section of the Athénée d'Ixelles, a secondary school with a strict classical curriculum.

Early Education

At this stage in his life, Prigogine was interested not in science but in history, archeology, art, and music; his mother claimed he could understand musical notes before he could understand words. Taught to play the piano by his mother, he even considered a career as a concert pianist, later regretting that he did not have as much time to devote to his music as he would have liked. He also read widely in the classics and philosophy during his teen years, and was particularly impressed by Henri Bergson's *L'évolution créatrice* and the Bergsonian view of the nature of time. He became a chemist as the result of a chance occurrence after his family had decided, and Prigogine concurred, that he should become a lawyer. Feeling that a first step to that end would be to learn about the criminal mind, he sought information about criminal psychology. In so doing, he came across a book dealing with the chemical composition of the brain, and he was so intrigued that he abandoned the law and took up chemistry.

Prigogine enrolled in the Free University of Brussels in 1935 to study chemistry, as had his brother before him. In 1939 he received his master's degree; he also won a prize for his performance of some Schumann pieces in a piano competition. Under the direction of Théophile De Donder, Prigogine received his Ph.D. in 1941 with the thesis, "The Thermodynamic Study of Irreversible Phenomena." De Donder was the founder of the Brussels school of thermodynamics (the branch of physics that deals with the behavior of heat and related phenomena) and one of the first scientists to attempt to deal with the thermodynamics of systems not at equilibrium, that is, not in balance. Prigogine has credited De Donder with developing the mathematical apparatus needed for studying nonequilibrium states, and these tools would prove important to Prigogine's own work. Another professor who had an influence on the course of Prigogine's career was Jean Timmermans, a chemist and experimentalist interested in applying classical thermodynamics to the study of solutions and other complex systems. In 1957, Prigogine co-wrote *The Molecular Theory of Solutions,* which explained that at a low temperature, liquid helium would spontaneously separate into two phases, one of helium–3 and the other of helium–4. This was later confirmed experimentally. The book also develops methods for dealing with polymer solutions, some of which are still in use.

Incorporates Time and Entropy into Chemistry

With his early interest in the nature of time, it was natural that Prigogine should be attracted to a study of the second law of thermodynamics that states that any spontaneous change in a closed system (one where neither matter nor energy flows into or out of the system) occurs in the direction that increases entropy, the measure of unavailable energy in a system or the measure of its disorder. This law indicates that as time passes in a closed system, disorder always increases, leading Sir **Arthur Stanley Eddington** to refer to the second law as supplying "the arrow of time." The move toward entropy described in the second law is irreversible, which contrasts with all other physical laws in which processes are reversible in time. This contrast begged the question of how the reversible, random workings of molecular and atomic motions could lead to processes that have a preferred direction in time. Furthermore, the second law, when extended to the largest known systems, suggests that the universe is moving toward eventual decay, a point when all energy and matter will reach a uniform state of equilibrium known as heat death.

Intrigued by these issues, Prigogine moved his focus away from the ideal "closed" system described in the second law and instead studied open systems that exchange matter and energy with an outside environment. Prigogine's first success in dealing with irreversible processes and open systems not at equilibrium came in 1945. In his doctoral research, he showed that for systems not too far from equilibrium, changes take place so as to achieve a steady state in which the production of entropy is at a minimum. This is true near equilibrium where the flux (or flow) of energy or matter through the system is directly proportional to the force creating that flux; that is, the flux and the force are linearly related. But such a steady state, once established, is stable and continues unchanged; it cannot evolve into a new state. Prigogine's work in this area led to his book *Thermodynamics of Irreversible Processes.*

In 1947 Prigogine succeeded De Donder to become full professor at the Free University of Brussels, where he assembled an interdisciplinary group to study irreversible processes. He went on to show that far from equilibrium, where fluxes and forces are no longer linearly related, a system can become unstable and evolve new, organized structures spontaneously. Prigogine called these organizations dissipative structures and developed the mathematical means of describing them. Prigogine theorized that such structures can be maintained as long as the energy and material fluxes are kept up. The process by which a new order evolves is labeled self-organization. In a nonlinear system there exist points—Prigogine referred to these as moments of choice or bifurcation points—at which the system is unstable, and small fluctuations can grow to a macroscopic or large size, creating a new structure. Randomness enters at the bifurcation points, so that predictions with respect to outcomes can only be expressed as probabilities. Common examples, although complicated and difficult to analyze, include the development of conduction cells in liquids heated from below (known as the Bénard instability), or the abrupt change from smooth flow to turbulent flow as the velocity of a liquid passing through a pipe is increased.

Empirical Confirmation

Prigogine's findings, while important, remained largely theoretical into the 1960s. Attempting to confirm his ideas, Prigogine worked with G. Nicolis and Réné Lefever to devise a simple mathematical model now called the Brusselator to better test his theories. Then in 1965 the Belousov-Zhabotinskii reaction, discovered in 1951 in the Soviet Union, became widely known abroad. One version of the reaction, in which the dissipative structures can be seen and do not have to be revealed by elaborate measurements, is a solution of malonic acid and bromate ion in sulfuric acid and ferrous phenanthroline (ferroin). Depending on the temperature and concentrations of the various species, the color of the solution may change back and forth from red to blue, or a pattern of red and blue may be formed that is either stationary or moves through the solution in a regular manner. These patterns gave striking visual proof of the existence of Prigogine's dissipative structures. In 1968 Richard Noyes at the University of Oregon was able to establish the mechanism of the reaction and, using Prigogine's work, to describe the phenomenon exactly.

The various processes that take place in cells involve complicated cycles of reactions catalyzed by special proteins called enzymes. Many of these enzymatic cycles meet the requirements for the formation of dissipative structures. For example, the breakdown of sugar in a cell has been shown to occur on a regular, periodic basis. Consequently, Prigogine's work is of great interest to biologists and biochemists. In fact, it was suggested by **Alan Mathison Turing** in 1952 that instabilities in chemical reaction systems could explain the patterns of stripes on a zebra or spots on a leopard. On a still larger scale, the thermodynamics of irreversible systems may explain how evolution, a process that gives rise to ever more specialized forms, is compatible with a physical picture of the world in which systems inevitably move from an ordered to a disordered state.

Prigogine and others have also applied the principles of irreversible thermodynamics to such disparate systems as the development of traffic patterns on a highway in response to driving conditions, the aggregation of slime molds in response to the depletion of nutrients in their environment, and the buildup of giant termite mounds in which a large number of independent termites behave in an orderly, seemingly purposeful, and intelligent fashion. On a larger scale, Prigogine's research allows a somewhat different and brighter view of the universe's ultimate fate. As explained in *Omni,* the theory of dissipative structures "offers a guardedly optimistic alternative to the pessimistic view of mankind's future—that winding down of nature toward a kind of heat death."

In 1949 Prigogine became a Belgian citizen, so that his Nobel Prize in 1977 was the first given to a Belgian. He was named director of the Instituts Internationaux de Physique et de Chimie (the Solvay Institute) in 1959, a post in which he continued after his retirement from the Free University in 1985. From 1961 to 1966 he spent time at the University of Chicago, and since 1967 spends three months of each year as director of the Ilya Prigogine Center for Statistical Mechanics and Thermodynamics at the University of Texas. He and his wife Marina Prokopowicz, an engineer whom he married in 1961, live in Brussels.

Prigogine has attempted to explain the implications of his work for the general public in two books: *From Being to Becoming: Time and Complexity in the Physical Sciences* in 1980 and, with Isabelle Stengers, *Order out of Chaos: Man's New Dialog with Nature* in 1984. For the latter work, Prigogine was made *commandeur* of the Ordre des Arts et des Lettres by the French government, an honor he especially prized because it is usually given to recognize achievement in the arts. Among the many honors conferred on him are the honorary foreign memberships in the U.S. National Academy of Sciences and the Academy of Sciences of the U.S.S.R. (now Russia).

SELECTED WRITINGS BY PRIGOGINE:

Books

(With A. Bellemans and Volume Mathout) *The Molecular Theory of Solutions,* North-Holland, 1957.

Thermodynamics of Irreversible Processes, 3rd edition, Interscience, 1967.

(With P. Glansdorff) *Thermodynamic Theory of Structure, Stability and Fluctuations,* Interscience, 1971.

(With G. Nicolis) *Self-Organization in Non-Equilibrium Systems: From Dissipative Structures to Order through Fluctuations,* Wiley, 1977.

From Being to Becoming: Time and Complexity in the Physical Sciences (first appeared in French as *La nouvelle alliance*), Freeman, 1980.

(With Isabelle Stengers) *Order out of Chaos,* Bantam, 1984.

Periodicals

(With G. Nicolis and A. Babloyantz) "Thermodynamics of Evolution," *Physics Today,* Volume 25, Number 11, 1972, pp. 23–28; Volume 25, Number 12, 1972, pp. 38–44.

"Time, Structure, and Fluctuations," *Science,* Volume 201, September 1, 1978, pp. 777–785.

SOURCES:

Books

Current Biography Yearbook, H. W. Wilson, 1987, pp. 447–450.
McGraw-Hill Modern Scientists and Engineers, Volume 2, McGraw-Hill, 1980, pp. 440–441.

Periodicals

Lepkowski, Will, "The Social Thermodynamics of Ilya Prigogine," *Chemical and Engineering News,* April 16, 1979, pp. 30–33.
Procaccia, I., and J. Ross, "The 1977 Nobel Prize in Chemistry," *Science,* Volume 198, November 18, 1977, pp. 716–717.
Snell, M. B., "Beyond Being and Becoming," *New Perspectives Quarterly,* Volume 9, spring, 1992, pp. 22–28.
Tucker, R. B., "Ilya Prigogine," *Omni,* Volume 5, Number 8, 1983, pp. 84–92, 120–121.

—Sketch by R. F. Trimble

Aleksandr Prokhorov
1916-
Australian-born Russian physicist

Aleksandr Prokhorov, a pioneer in the field of quantum electronics, began his scientific career by studying radio wave propagation. His application of these studies to the theoretical design of a molecular generator and amplifier in 1952 formed the basis for the invention of both masers and lasers. For his work in quantum electronics Prokhorov shared the 1964 Nobel Prize in physics with his colleague, **Nikolai G. Basov**, and the American physicist **Charles H. Townes**.

Aleksandr Mikhailovich Prokhorov was born on July 11, 1916, in Atherton, Australia. His parents, Mikhail Ivanovich and Mariya Ivanovna Prokhorov, had fled from Siberia to Australia in 1911 because of Mikhail's involvement in revolutionary activities. The family returned to the Soviet Union in 1923, and Prokhorov received his undergraduate education at the Leningrad State University, receiving his baccalaureate degree in 1939.

Prokhorov embarked on his graduate studies at the P. N. Lebedev Institute of Physics of the Soviet Academy of Sciences in Moscow. His research dealt with the propagation of radio waves and their use in studying the upper atmosphere of earth. In June 1941 the German invasion of Russia interrupted his studies and he was called to military service. Prokhorov was wounded in battle twice before being discharged in 1944. He then completed his research for the candidate's degree (comparable to a master's degree) with a thesis on nonlinear oscillators. In 1951 he was awarded a Ph.D. in physical and mathematical sciences for his research on the radiation produced by electrons in the high-energy orbits of the synchrotron, a circular particle accelerator that uses electrical and magnetic fields to propel the components of atoms to extremely high speeds. Prior to receiving his degree, Prokhorov had been appointed assistant director of the Oscillation Laboratory at the Lebedev Institute. He continued his research on the uses of radar and radio waves and applied them to the study of molecular structure and properties. In connection with this work, he came into contact with Nikolai G. Basov, with whom he was to collaborate on some of his most important work.

Prokhorov and Basov Develop the Molecular Generator

Prokhorov and Basov soon became involved in the stimulated emission of radiation from gas molecules. Three decades earlier in 1917, **Albert Einstein** had studied the effects of radiation on atoms. Using quantum mechanics, Einstein confirmed earlier hypotheses that electrons in an atom tend to absorb small amounts of energy and jump to higher energy levels in the atom. They then re-emit the absorbed radiation and return to lower, less energetic orbitals. But Einstein also discovered that in some instances an electron in a higher energy level can, simply by virtue of being exposed to radiation, jump to a lower energy level and emit a photon of a wavelength identical to that of the external radiation. This process became known as stimulated emission.

Prokhorov and Basov saw in Einstein's analysis a way of using molecules to amplify the energy of a given beam of radiation. Radiation could be used to stimulate the emission of more photons of the same wavelength within an atom, creating a domino effect among other atoms, thus stimulating the emission of more photons. This cascade of energy emission could result in a mechanism for generating more and more intense beams of radiation with a very narrow range of wavelengths. Later researchers used these findings to develop masers (microwave amplification by stimulated emission of radiation) and lasers (light amplification by stimulated emissions of radiation).

Prokhorov and Basov announced the discovery of their molecular generator in a paper read before the All-Union Conference on Radio Spectroscopy in May 1952. However, they did not publish their results for more than two years, by which time the American physicist Charles H. Townes had built a working maser and published his conclusions in *Physical Review.* In awarding the 1964 Nobel Prize in physics, the Nobel committee recognized the contributions of all three physicists. The discovery of the molecular generator provided the theoretical basis for the development of both masers and lasers, on which Prokhorov has concentrated his research efforts since the mid–1950s.

In 1941 Prokhorov married the former Galina Alekseyevna Shelepina, with whom he had one son, Kiril. He was appointed professor at Moscow State University in 1959 and eventually returned to the Lebedev Institute, where he was appointed deputy director in 1972. He has also been editor-in-chief of the *Great Soviet Encyclopedia* since 1969 and was made a corresponding (associate) member of the Soviet Academy of Sciences in 1960 and an academician (full member) in 1966. Prokhorov was awarded the Lenin Prize in 1959 and the Lomonosov Gold Medal of the Soviet Academy of Sciences in 1988.

SELECTED WRITINGS BY PROKHOROV:

Books

(With A. S. Prokhorov) *Problems in Solid-State Physics,* 1984.

Periodicals

(With N. G. Basov) "Application of Molecular Beams to Radio Spectroscopic Study of the Rotation Spectra of Molecules," *Zhur. Eksptl'. i Teoret. Fiz.,* Volume 27, 1954, pp. 431–438.
(With N. G. Basov) "Theory of the Molecular Generator and the Molecular Power Amplifier," *Zhur. Eksptl'. i Teoret. Fiz.,* Volume 30, 1956, pp. 560–563.

SOURCES:

Books

Nobel Prize Winners, H. W. Wilson, 1987, pp. 839–841.
Weber, Robert L., *Pioneers of Science: Nobel Prize Winners in Physics,* American Institute of Physics, 1980, pp. 199–200.

Periodicals

Gordon, J. P., "Research on Maser-Laser Principle Wins Nobel Prize in Physics," *Science,* November 13, 1964, pp. 897–899.
"Nobel Prize Winners," *Science News,* November 7, 1964, p. 295.

—*Sketch by David E. Newton*

R. C. Punnett
1875-1967
English morphologist and geneticist

Noted morphologist and geneticist R. C. Punnett was instrumental in introducing the field of genetics to lay audiences, especially to commercial breeders of livestock. His contributions significantly advanced knowledge of the genetics of fowl, ducks, rabbits, sweet pea plants, and humans; his research served as the foundation for poultry genetics for decades. Punnett was among the pioneering investigators who helped revolutionize scientific thought in the field of genetics after the rediscovery of Gregor Mendel's work with genetics and heredity.

Reginald Crundall Punnett, the eldest of three children, was born on June 20, 1875, at Tonbridge in Kent, England, to George Punnett, the head of a Tonbridge building firm, and Emily Crundall. He suffered from appendicitis as a child. During the treatment, which consisted of applying leeches to the lower stomach, and the daily bedrest required afterwards, he spent his time reading Jardine's *Naturalist's Library* and discovered a strong liking for natural history. He recovered and later was accepted to Cambridge University, where he developed an interest in human anatomy, human physiology, and zoology, and decided to pursue a career in zoology, not medicine as he originally had intended. As part of his zoological studies, Punnett observed sharks at the Zoological Station in Naples, Italy, for six months before graduating with first class honors from Cambridge's Caius College in 1898. He received his master's degree in 1902.

Studies Zoology of Worms

In 1899, Punnett was offered the position of demonstrator and part-time lecturer in the Natural History Department of St. Andrews University, where he stayed for three years. In 1901, he was elected a fellow of Caius College. During this time, his appendix had been troubling him sporadically and he decided to have it removed. As the scientific thought at the time was that worms caused appendicitis, he dissected the organ after the surgery, but found no worms. After he recovered from the operation, Punnett became unhappy with his teaching accommodations at St. Andrews and began a search for a new job. In 1902, he returned to Cambridge as a demonstrator in morphology in the Department of Zoology and remained in this position until 1904. While a demonstrator, Punnett had plenty of time to perform research and publish a number of papers on nemertines, a type of worm.

Discovers Several Mendelian Genetic Principles

Punnett then turned from the study of nemertines to genetics, working with **William Bateson**, an investigator also researching Mendelian principles, during a six-year period in which the pair produced noteworthy and lasting advances in Mendelian genetics. Gregor Mendel, an Augustinian monk, had used pea plants to demonstrate how genetic traits are inherited. Using the sweet-pea plant or fowl for their studies, Punnett and Bateson determined several basic classical Mendelian genetic principles, including the Mendelian explanations of sex-determination, sex-linkage, complementary factors and factor interaction, and the first example of autosomal linkage. It was early in his relationship with Bateson that Punnett was awarded the Balfour Studentship in the Department of Zoology, and he resigned as demonstrator. He held the Balfour Studentship position until 1908. Also, during this year he was awarded the Thurston medal of Gonville and Caius College. Punnett wrote *Mendelism,* the first published textbook on the subject of genetics, in 1905. As a reflection on his research, he was appointed superintendent of the Museum of Zoology in 1909. A year later, Punnett became professor of biology at the University of Cambridge. Punnett and Bateson started the *Journal of Genetics* in 1911 and edited it jointly until Bateson died in 1926. Punnett continued to edit the journal, credited with drawing numerous new students to the field of genetics, for twenty more years.

In 1912, the University of Cambridge changed the name of the chair of biology to the chair of zoology, and offered the position to Punnett, making him the first Arthur Balfour Professor of Genetics, a position that was the first of its kind in Great Britain. He held this prestigious position until his retirement at the age of sixty-five. Also in 1912, Punnett was elected a fellow of the Royal Society, and in 1922 he was awarded its Darwin Medal. Punnett's interests in genetics led him to a founding membership in the British Genetical Society; he served as one of the group's secretaries from 1919 to 1930, when he then became president.

During World War I, Punnett bought his expertise in poultry breeding to a position with the Food Production Department of the Board of Agriculture. He suggested that hens' plumage color could be used to determine the sex of the birds much earlier than previously was possible. This enabled the breeders to destroy most of the unwanted males, which were not used for food, and save precious resources for raising females for consumption. After the war ended, Punnett produced the first breed of poultry in which a trait is demonstrated uniquely in one sex or the other. This first auto-sexing breed, the Cambar, was followed a decade later by a second breed, the Legbar. Punnett's work laid the foundation for poultry breeding research for several more decades.

Punnett was married to Eveline Maude Froude, widow of Sidney Nutcombe-Quicke, at age forty-one; they had no children. In his leisure time, he enjoyed playing bridge, participated in many sports including cricket and tennis, and collected Japanese color prints, Chinese porcelain and old and rare biological and medical texts. Upon his death, his collection of Japanese prints was acquired by the Bristol Corporation for the city art gallery. Punnett died suddenly during a game of bridge in Bilbrook, Somerset, England, on January 3, 1967.

SELECTED WRITINGS BY PUNNETT:

Books

Mendelism, Macmillan & Bowes, 1905, sixth edition, 1922.
Embryogeny: An Account of Laws Governing the Development of the Animal Egg as Ascertained through Experiment (revision of *Embryogeny* by Hans Przibram, translated by R. Sollas), Cambridge University Press, 1908.
Mimicry in Butterflies, Cambridge University Press, 1915.
Heredity in Poultry, Macmillan, 1923.

Periodicals

(With W. Bateson) "The Heredity of Sex," *Science,* Volume 27, 1908, pp. 785–787.
"Applied Heredity," *Harper's,* December, 1908, pp. 115–122.

SOURCES:

Books

Biographical Memoirs of Fellows of the Royal Society, Volume 13, Royal Society (London), 1967, pp. 309–326.

—*Sketch by Barbara J. Proujan*

Edward Mills Purcell
1912-
American physicist

Edward Mills Purcell spent much of his lifetime studying the basic particles of matter. Ultimately focusing on the frequencies of atomic particles spinning in magnetic fields, he developed a method of measuring their magnetic moments and investigating their atomic structures. For his simultaneous but independent development of this method, known as nuclear resonance absorption, he shared the 1952 Nobel Prize in physics with physicist **Felix Bloch**. The principle of nuclear magnetic resonance itself has been applied to a wide range of applications, from studying space through radio astronomy to measuring magnetic fields with magnetometers.

Purcell was born August 30, 1912, in Taylorville, Illinois, to Edward A. and Mary (Mills) Purcell. His mother was a high school teacher, and his father was a former country school teacher, who, during Purcell's boyhood, was the general manager of an independent telephone company. Purcell read the Bell System technical magazine that his father received and decided to become an electrical engineer. Eventually, he also developed his parents' interest in teaching.

Purcell received a bachelor's degree in electrical engineering from Purdue University in 1933. During his undergraduate days, Purcell's interest in physics was encouraged and strengthened by Karl Lark-Horowitz, a professor from Vienna, who was building Purdue's physics department. After graduation, Purcell spent a year at the Technische Hochschule in Karlsruhe, Germany, as an international exchange student. He received a master's degree from Harvard in 1935 and a Ph.D. in physics in 1938. He remained at Harvard as a physics instructor until 1941, when he became leader of the Fundamental Developments Group at the Massachusetts Institute of Technology's Radiation Laboratory, contributing to the World War II effort by working on advanced radar for night fighting. At MIT, he worked with **I. I. Rabi** and some of Rabi's Columbia University colleagues, who were developing the field of nuclear moments and resonance. The work Purcell and his group did with higher frequencies and shorter wavelengths also played a role in Purcell's later research. He returned to Harvard as an associate professor in 1946, advancing to professor of physics in 1949. He served as Donner professor of science from 1958 to 1960, and Gerhard Gade University professor from 1960 until his retirement in 1980.

Shares Nobel Prize for Nuclear Measurement Method

During the 1930s, Rabi had experimented with a method of determining nuclear magnetic moments,

the rotating force exerted on nuclei when placed in a magnetic field. Purcell pursued a similar methodology by placing atoms in the field of a strong electromagnet and a second magnet activated by radio waves. He aligned the atoms in the magnetic field and then introduced varying frequencies of radio waves to change their orientation, allowing him to determine the one signature frequency at which the atoms absorbed energy, showing nuclear magnetic resonance. As Purcell wrote in his Nobel lecture, "Commonplace as such experiments have become in our laboratories, I have not yet lost a feeling of wonder, and of delight, that this delicate motion should reside in all the ordinary things around us, revealing itself only to him who looks for it. . . . To see the world for a moment as something rich and strange is the private reward of many a discovery."

Discovery Leads to Invention

Purcell put his discovery to work, when, with Harold Ewen, he built a radio telescope. In 1951, they detected for the first time radiation emitted by hydrogen clouds in space, noting a signature wavelength of twenty-one centimeters. Thus, they were able to exact a frequency by which radio astronomers could use to track hydrogen clouds. Purcell also found that the nuclear magnetic resonance signatures could change in substances like crystals or liquids because of the influence of their surroundings, a change known as a chemical shift. This phenomenon provided a means of studying molecular structures. Later in his career, Purcell ventured into biophysics to study bacterial behavior and locomotion, particularly the physics of swimming microscopic organisms.

In 1937, Purcell married Beth C. Busser, with whom he had two sons, Frank and Dennis. In addition to his work at Harvard, Purcell served on the scientific advisory board to the U.S. Air Force in 1947 and 1948, and from 1953 to 1957. A member of the President's Science Advisory Committee from 1957 to 1960 and 1962 to 1966, he was elected to the National Academy of Science in 1951 and received an honorary doctorate in engineering from Purdue in 1953. Purcell was a member of a number of scientific organizations and received the National Medal of Science from the National Science Foundation in 1978.

SELECTED WRITINGS BY PURCELL:

Books

Electricity and Magnetism, McGraw-Hill, 1965.

Periodicals

"Nuclear Magnetism in Relation to Problems of the Liquid and Solid States," *Science,* April 30, 1948, pp. 433–40.
"Research in Nuclear Magnetism," *Science,* October 16, 1953, pp. 431–36.

SOURCES:

Books

McGraw-Hill Encyclopedia of Science and Technology, McGraw-Hill, 1993, pp. 157–66.

Modern Scientists and Engineers, McGraw-Hill Book Company, 1980, pp. 445–46.
Pioneers of Science: Nobel Prize Winners in Physics, The Institute of Physics, 1980, pp. 145–46.

Periodicals

Science News Letter, November 15, 1952, p. 307.
Torrey, Volta, "Changing Partners in the Atom Dance," *Saturday Review,* May 6, 1961, pp. 68–69.

—*Sketch by Julie Anderson*

Alfred H. Qöyawayma
1938-
American engineer

Alfred H. Qöyawayma (ko-YAH-wy-ma), a Hopi Indian, co-founded and served as the first chairman of the American Indian Science and Engineering Society (AISES). He is a registered professional engineer in Arizona and California, and holds patents for his early work on aircraft guidance systems. In 1990, after a twenty-year career in environmental management, Qöyawayma turned his full attention to the art work he had begun to pursue in 1976. As a potter, he is known for his exceptionally thin-walled and perfectly symmetrical "flying saucer" vessels, fashioned with wooden tools and without the aid of a potter's wheel. His pieces appear in the permanent collections of several museums; they reflect years of research into the Hopi ceramic tradition. His work has been the subject of several videos and documentaries. Qöyawayma is also an investigator for a Smithsonian Institute project to identify clay sources for ancient Hopi ceramics.

Alfred H. Qöyawayma

Qöyawayma was born February 26, 1938, in Los Angeles, California, the only child of Alfred and Mamie (Colton) Cooyama. About 1980, Qöyawayma adopted his father's original Hopi name, which means "Grey Fox Walking at Dawn." His father worked in watercolors and oils, and at one time painted for Walt Disney. Of notable influence was Qöyawayma's aunt, Polingaysi Qöyawayma (Elizabeth White), who died in 1990. A noted Hopi potter, educator and writer, she taught him to work in clay.

Qöyawayma received a B.S. degree in mechanical engineering from California State Polytechnic University in 1961, and an M.S. in mechanical/control systems engineering from the University of Southern California in 1966. From 1961 through 1971, he worked as a project engineer for Litton Guidance and Control Systems in Woodland Hills, California, where his work in the development of inertial guidance systems and star trackers impelled Litton to open a new corporate division. He left Litton in 1971 to join the Salt River Project in Phoenix, Arizona, serving as a manager and planner in the power and water utility's environmental division. In 1977, he co-founded the American Indian Science and Engineering Society (AISES) to develop leaders and increase Native American participation in science and engineering. From its original seven members, it has expanded into an organization with more than 100 student chapters in the United States, Canada and Puerto Rico. Qöyawayma continues to work with AISES and its expansion into Mexico and Central America. In 1986, he received the society's Ely S. Parker Award for Engineering Achievement and Service to the American Indian Community.

Qöyawayma joined a Smithsonian Institute research team in 1982 as one of four principal investigators involved in the use of neutron activation and factor analysis techniques to identify the original clay sources used in making ancient Hopi pottery. In 1990, he started the Electric Power Research Institute's study on the removal of carbon dioxide from the atmosphere through halophytes, plants grown in sodium-rich soil that, like trees, can absorb and store carbon dioxide.

Qöyawayma's pottery has been exhibited at the Kennedy Center and the Smithsonian and appears in the permanent collections of several museums. Qöyawayma, who has served on the board of directors of the National Action Committee on Minorities and on the Arizona Commission on the Arts, is a consultant to the Hopi Tribe on environmental and economic issues. In 1986, he received an honorary doctorate of humane letters from the University of Colorado, Boulder. He was named 1989 Alumnus of the Year by California State Polytechnic Institute, and received a Fulbright Fellowship in 1991 to work with Maori Indians in New Zealand, helping to re-establish an ancient tradition in ceramics. Qöyawayma and his wife, Leslie (Thompson), live in Phoenix. They have two children, Kathleen and John.

SELECTED WRITINGS BY QÖYAWAYMA:

Books

Qöyawayma, the Potter, Santa Fe East Gallery, 1984.

Periodicals

(With Ronald Bishop, Veletta Canouts, Suzanne de Atley and C. W. Aikins) "The Formation of Ceramic Analytical Groups: Hopi Pottery Production and Exchange, A. D. 1300–1600," *Journal of Field Archaeology,* Volume 15, 1988, pp. 317–37.
"Between Two Worlds," *Santa Fe, Going Places with the Arts,* summer, 1991, pp. 8–13.
"Diversity at Work," *IEEE Spectrum,* June, 1992, pp. 28–29.

SOURCES:

Periodicals

Americana, March/April, 1984, pp. 52–55.
Native Peoples, winter, 1994, pp. 34–43, 48.
Southwest Profile, August, 1993, pp. 22–25.

—*Sketch by Jill Carpenter*

Lloyd Albert Quarterman
1918-1982
American chemist

Lloyd Albert Quarterman was one of only a handful of African Americans to work on the "Manhattan Project," the team that developed the first atom bomb in the 1940s. He was also noted as a research chemist who specialized in fluoride chemistry, producing some of the first compounds using inert gases and developing the "diamond window" for the study of compounds using corrosive hydrogen fluoride gas. In addition, later in his career, Quarterman initiated work on synthetic blood.

Quarterman was born May 31, 1918, in Philadelphia. He attended St. Augustine's College in Raleigh, North Carolina, where he continued the interest in chemistry he had demonstrated from an early age. Just after he completed his bachelor's degree in 1943 he was hired by the U.S. War Department to work on the production of the atomic bomb, an assignment code-named the Manhattan Project. Originally hired as a junior chemist, he worked at both the secret underground facility at the University of Chicago and at the Columbia University laboratory in New York City; the project was spread across the country in various locations. It was the team of scientists at Columbia which first split the atom. To do this, scientists participated in trying to isolate an isotope of uranium necessary for nuclear fission; this was Quarterman's main task during his time in New York.

Quarterman was one of only six African American scientists who worked on the development of atomic bomb. At the secret Chicago facility, where the unused football stadium had been converted into an enormous, hidden laboratory for the "plutonium program," Quarterman studied quantum mechanics under renowned Italian physicist **Enrico Fermi**. When the Manhattan Project ended in 1946, the Chicago facilities were converted to become Argonne National Laboratories, and Quarterman was one of the scientists who stayed on. Although his contributions included work on the first nuclear power plant, he was predominantly a fluoride and nuclear chemist, creating new chemical compounds and new molecules from fluoride solutions. Dr. Larry Stein, who worked at Argonne at the same time as Quarterman, told interviewer Marianne Fedunkiw that Quarterman was very good at purifying hydrogen fluoride. "He helped build a still to purify it, which he ran." This was part of the research which led to the production of the compound xenon tetrafluoride at Argonne. Xenon is one of the "inert" gases and was thought to be unable to react with other molecules, so Quarterman's work in producing a xenon compound was a pioneering effort.

After a number of years at Argonne National Laboratories, Quarterman returned to school and received his master's of science from Northwestern University in 1952. In addition to his fluoride chemistry work, Quarterman was a spectroscopist researching interactions between radiation and matter. He developed a corrosion resistant "window" of diamonds with which to view hydrogen fluoride. He described this to Ivan Van Sertima, who interviewed him in 1979: "It was a very small window—one-eighth of an inch. The reason why they were one-eighth of an inch was because I couldn't get the money to buy bigger windows. These small diamonds cost one thousand dollars apiece and I needed two for a window." Diamonds were necessary because hydrogen fluoride was so corrosive it would eat up glass or any other known container material. Quarterman was able to study the X-ray, ultraviolet, and Raman spectra of a given compound by dissolving it in hydrogen fluoride, making a cell, and shining an electromagnetic beam through the solution to see the vibrations of the molecules. His first successful trial was run in 1967.

Quarterman also began research into "synthetic blood" late in his career but he was thwarted by what he described as "socio-political problems" and later fell ill and died before he could complete it. Besides holding memberships in the American Chemical Society, American Association for the Advancement of Science, and Scientific Research Society of America, Quarterman was an officer of the Society of Applied Spectroscopy. He also encouraged African American students interested in science by visiting public schools in Chicago, and was a member of the National Association for the Advancement of Colored People. In recognition for his contributions to science, Quarterman's alma mater, St. Augustine's College, departed from 102 years of tradition to award him an honorary Ph.D. in chemistry in 1971 for a lifetime of achievement. He was also cited for his research on the Manhattan project in a certificate, dated August 6, 1945, by the Secretary of War for "work essential to the production of the Atomic Bomb thereby contributing to the successful conclusion of World War II."

Quarterman was also a renowned athlete. During his university days at St. Augustine's College he was an avid football player. Van Sertima, who interviewed Quarterman three years before his death, later wrote, "As he spoke, the shock of his voice and his occasional laughter seemed to contradict his illness and I began to see before me, not an aging scientist, but the champion footballer." Quarterman died at the Billings Hospital in Chicago in the late summer of 1982. He donated his body to science.

SOURCES:

Books

Le Blanc, Ondine E., "Lloyd Albert Quarterman," *Contemporary Black Biography,* Volume 4, Gale, 1993, pp. 199–201.
Sammons, Vivian O., editor, *Blacks in Science and Medicine,* Hemisphere Publishing, 1990, p. 196.
Van Sertima, Ivan, editor, *Blacks in Science: Ancient and Modern,* Transaction Books, 1983, pp. 266–272.

Periodicals

Ebony, September, 1949, p. 28.
Jet, August 9, 1982.

Other

Stein, Larry, interview with Marianne Fedunkiw conducted April 7, 1994.

—Sketch by Marianne Fedunkiw

Edith H. Quimby
1891-1982
American biophysicist

A pioneer in the field of radiology, Edith H. Quimby helped develop diagnostic and therapeutic applications for X rays, radium, and radioactive isotopes when the science of radiology was still in its infancy. Her research in measuring the penetration of radiation enabled physicians to determine the exact dose needed with the fewest side effects. Quimby also worked to protect those handling radioactive material from its harmful effects. While a radiology professor at Columbia University, she established a research laboratory to study the medical uses of radioactive isotopes, including their application in cancer diagnosis and treatments. In recognition of her contributions to the field, the Radiological Society of North America awarded her a gold medal for work which "placed every radiologist in her debt."

Quimby was born on July 10, 1891, in Rockford, Illinois, to Arthur S. Hinkley, an architect and farmer, and Harriet Hinkley (whose maiden name was also Hinkley). The family—Quimby was one of three children—moved to several different states during Quimby's childhood. She graduated from high school in Boise, Idaho, and went on a full tuition scholarship to Whitman College in Walla Walla, Washington, where she majored in physics and mathematics. Two of her teachers at Whitman, B. H. Brown and Walter Bratton, were major influences in directing her toward a career in scientific research. After graduating in 1912, Quimby taught high school science in Nyssa, Oregon, and then went to the University of California in 1914 to accept a fellowship in physics. While in the graduate program there, she married fellow physics student Shirley L. Quimby. She earned her M.A. in 1915 and returned to teaching high school science, this time in Antioch, California. In 1919, when her husband moved to New York to teach physics at Columbia University, she went with him. The move to New York was a pivotal point in Quimby's career, as she began working under Dr. Gioacchino Failla, chief physicist at the newly created New York City Memorial Hospital for Cancer and Allied Diseases. This began a scientific association that was to last forty years.

Quimby began studying the medical uses of X rays and radium, especially in treating tumors. At that time, physicians and researchers knew extremely little about this area; before Quimby's research, each doctor had to determine on a case-by-case basis how much radiation each patient needed for treatment. Quimby focused her attention on measuring the penetration of radiation so that radiotherapy doses could be more exact and side effects minimized. After several years of research, she successfully determined the number of roentgens (a now obsolete unit of radiation dosage) per minute emitted in the air, on the skin, and in the body. Her research on the effects of radiation on the skin was especially noteworthy to the scientific community, and her study was frequently quoted in the professional literature for many years.

From 1920 to 1940, Quimby conducted numerous experiments to examine various properties of radium and X rays. During this period she wrote dozens of articles for scientific journals, describing the results of her research and listing standards of measurement. In 1940 Quimby was the first woman to receive the Janeway Medal of the American Radium Society in recognition of her achievements in the field.

Becomes Professor and Establishes Isotope Laboratory

From 1941 to 1942, Quimby taught radiology courses at Cornell University Medical College. The following year she became associate professor of radiology at Columbia University College of Physicians and Surgeons, where she taught radiologic physics. While at Columbia, she and Failla founded the Radiological Research Laboratory. There they studied the medical uses of radioactive isotopes in cooperation with members of Columbia's medical departments. They focused their research on the application of radioactive isotopes (different forms of the same element whose unstable nuclei emit alpha, beta, or gamma rays) in treating thyroid disease, and for circulation studies and diagnosis of brain tumors. These inquiries made Quimby a pioneer in the field of nuclear medicine.

Quimby participated in other aspects of radiology research as well. She researched the use of synthetically produced radioactive sodium in medical research, and devoted considerable efforts to investigating ways to protect those handling radioactive substances from the harmful effects of exposure. Very early on, Quimby foresaw the potential for increased diagnostic and therapeutic use of atomic energy in medicine through radioactive isotopes.

In addition to her research and lecturing, Quimby worked on the Manhattan Project (which developed the atom bomb). She also worked for the Atomic Energy Commission, acted as a consultant on radiation therapy to the United States Veterans Administration, served as an examiner for the American Board of Radiology, and headed a scientific committee of the National Council on Radiation Protection and Measurements. A prolific writer, Quimby published a considerable amount of literature on various aspects of the medical uses of X rays, radium, and radioactive isotopes. She also coauthored a widely respected book entitled *Physical Foundations of Radiology*.

After her official retirement in 1960 as professor emeritus of radiology, Quimby continued to write, lecture, and consult well into the 1970s. She was a member of several radiology societies, including the American Radium Society, for which she served as vice president. In her nonprofessional life, Quimby was a member of the League of Women Voters.

On Quimby's death on October 11, 1962, at the age of ninety-one, Harald Rossi of Columbia University wrote in *Physics Today* that "all too often the creative achievements of scientific pioneers are overshadowed by further developments made by others or simply become anonymous components of accepted practice. Fortunately, Quimby's exceptional service to radiological physics was widely recognized."

SELECTED WRITINGS BY QUIMBY:

Books

(With Sergei Feitelberg and Solomon Silver) *Radioactive Isotopes in Clinical Practice*, Lea & Febiger, 1958.
Safe Handling of Radioactive Isotopes in Medical Practice, Macmillan, 1960.
(With Paul N. Goodwin) *Physical Foundations of Radiology*, Harper, 1970.

SOURCES:

Books

Current Biography, H. W. Wilson, 1949, pp. 492–493.

Periodicals

New York Times, October 13, 1982, p. 28.
Physics Today, December, 1982, pp. 71–72.

—*Sketch by Donna Olshansky*

William Samuel Quinland
1885-1953
West Indies-born American pathologist

William Samuel Quinland was a distinguished pathologist and educator who contributed twenty-eight studies to medical journals, including pioneering research on pathology in African Americans. His medical career spanned from Panama, to Brazil, to several regions of the United States, including Alaska. He was the first black member to be elected to the American Association of Pathologists and Bacteriologists, an appointment he received in 1920; the American Board of Pathology in 1937; and the College of American Pathologists in 1947.

Quinland was born on October 12, 1885 in All Saints, Antigua, in what was then the British West Indies, the son of William Thomas and Floretta Victoria (Williams) Quinland. After completing his secondary education in the West Indies, Quinland taught in public schools. He then embarked on his medical career, working for three years as a laboratory assistant in the Ancon Hospital in the Canal Zone, Panama, followed by four years as a laboratory worker at the Candelaria Hospital in Brazil.

After making his way to the United States, Quinland attended Howard University in Washington, D.C., from 1914 to 1915 and earned his B.S. degree from Oskaloosa College in Iowa in 1918. In 1919, he earned his medical degree, with an outstanding record, from Meharry Medical College in Nashville, Tennessee. Quinland was then awarded the first Rosenwald fellowship in pathology and bacteriology for study at Harvard Medical School, which he held from 1919 to 1922. In 1921, Quinland earned his certificate in pathology and bacteriology from Harvard, and also published his first professional article, a study of carcinoma, or malignant tumors. In 1922, Quinland's final year under the Rosenwald fellowship, he worked as an assistant in pathology at the Peter Bent Brigham Hospital in Boston.

Returns to Meharry Medical College

Although Harvard offered him a professorship in its Medical College, Quinland felt that Meharry, a ground-breaking institution for African-American medical practitioners, needed him more. In 1922, he accepted a post at Meharry as professor and head of the pathology department, a position he held until 1947. In 1923, he married Sadie Lee Watson; they had two children. In addition to his professorship at Meharry Medical College, Quinland worked as a pathologist at Meharry's George W. Hubbard Hospital, where he served as associate medical director from 1931 to 1937, and at the Millie E. Hale Hospital. In 1941 and 1942, he undertook post-graduate studies as a fellow of the University of Chicago.

During these years, Quinland published studies on tuberculosis, syphilis, heart disease, and carcinoma, among other subjects. Much of this research was particularly valuable for its focus on black patients; Quinland noted in his study on "Primary Carcinoma in the Negro," for example, that "while social differences in cancer have long been recognized," little research had been conducted on its occurrence among African Americans. That study looked at three hundred cases of carcinoma and documented which types of cancers were found in samples from African American men and women of various ages. In addition, Quinland served on the editorial board of the *Journal of the National Medical Association* and of the *Punjab Medical Journal,* held a post as a reserve surgeon for the United State Public Health Service, and directed public health clinics in Virginia, South Carolina, and Georgia.

In 1947, Quinland left Meharry Medical College for a post as pathologist and chief of laboratory service at the Veterans Administration Hospital in Tuskegee, Alaska. His publications in this final phase of his career included a study of tumors. Quinland served at the Veterans Administration Hospital until his death on April 6, 1953.

SELECTED WRITINGS BY QUINLAND:

Periodicals

"Tuberculosis from the Standpoint of Pathology," *Journal of the National Medical Association,* Volume 15, 1923, pp. 1–5.
"Primary Carcinoma of Prostrate," *Meharry News,* 1928.
"Syphilis in Combination with Certain Diseases," *Journal of the National Medical Association,* Volume 31, 1939, pp. 199–205.
"Primary Carcinoma in the Negro: Anatomic Distribution of Three Hundred Cases," *Archives*

of Pathology, Volume 30, 1940, pp. 393–402.

"Bronchogenic Carcinoma—Report of Three Cases in Negroes," *Southern Medical Journal,* Volume 35, 1942, pp. 729–732.

"Cancer of the Prostrate: A Clinico-pathologic Study of 34 Cases in Negroes," *Journal of Urology,* Volume 50, Number 2, 1943.

"Histologic and Clinical Response of Human Cancer to Irradiation," *Journal of the National Medical Association,* Volume 38, 1946, pp. 171–178.

SOURCES:

Books

Blacks in Science and Medicine, Hemisphere, 1990, pp. 196–197.
Dictionary of American Medical Biography, Greenwood, 1984, pp. 618–619.

Periodicals

The Crisis, December, 1919, pp. 64–65.
Journal of the American Medical Association, July, 1953, pp. 298–300.

—*Sketch by Miyoko Chu*

R

I. I. Rabi
1898-1988
Austrian-born American physicist

Born in Austria, I. I. Rabi came to the United States with his parents at an early age. He attended Cornell and Columbia Universities, receiving his Ph.D. in physics from the latter in 1927. During a post-doctoral year in Germany Rabi worked with **Otto Stern** and learned about Stern's experiments (conducted with Walther Gerlach) on the analysis of atomic and molecular structure by means of atomic and molecular beams. Upon his return to the United States in 1929, Rabi worked on methods for extending and refining the Stern-Gerlach techniques. He eventually made a number of important discoveries regarding the magnetic properties of the nucleus and of subatomic particles—discoveries that later found application in a number of fields, including nuclear magnetic resonance, masers and lasers, and time measurement by means of atomic clocks. During World War II, Rabi worked on the development of radar devices and nuclear weapons. At the war's conclusion, he devoted most of his time and energy to the political aspects of scientific and technological development, serving as chairman of the U.S. Atomic Energy Commission from 1952 to 1956. Rabi died in 1988 at the age of 91.

Isidor Isaac Rabi was born on July 29, 1898, in Rymanow (also given as Raymanou or Rymanov), Galicia, then a part of the Austro-Hungarian empire. Rabi's parents were David Rabi and the former Janet (also given as Jennie or Scheindel) Teig. The senior Rabi emigrated to the United States shortly after his son's birth and, in 1899, sent for his family to join him in New York City. David Rabi has been described by various biographers as an unskilled worker, a tailor, and an owner of a grocery store; Rabi himself said that his father started out by doing odd jobs, such as delivering ice, and then "graduated into work in the sweatshop, making women's blouses." Yiddish was the only language spoken in the Rabi household, and young Isidor learned his English on the streets. He was a quick learner, however, and did well in the public schools of New York City. After graduating from Brooklyn's Manual Training High School in 1916, he entered Cornell University with plans to major in electrical engineering. He eventually

changed his major to chemistry, though, graduating with a bachelor of science degree in 1919. He then spent three years working as a chemist before returning to Cornell for graduate work. Rabi soon discovered that his real interest was physics, and in 1923 enrolled in a doctoral program in this field at Columbia University. In order to support himself at Columbia, Rabi took a job teaching physics at the City College (now City University) of New York, a post he held until he received his Ph.D. in 1927.

Pursues Postgraduate Studies in Europe

For his postdoctoral studies, Rabi planned a two-year tour of the most important scientific institutions in Europe, including Münich, Copenhagen, Hamburg, Leipzig, and Zürich. While on tour he studied with such leading figures as **Arnold Sommerfeld**, **Niels Bohr**, **Wolfgang Pauli**, **Werner Heisenberg**, and Otto Stern. The visit with Stern may have been the most significant stop on the tour, because Stern's work at Hamburg closely corresponded to Rabi's own field of interest and the subject of his doctoral thesis, the effects of magnetic fields on matter. In 1922, Stern and Walther Gerlach had developed methods for creating beams of atoms or molecules that could be used to study the magnetic properties of the atomic nuclei in these beams. For his discoveries in this field, Stern would go on to win the 1943 Nobel Prize in physics.

In 1929, when Rabi returned to the United States, he began his own research on the use of atomic and molecular beams to study nuclear properties. This work took place at Columbia, where he had been appointed lecturer in physics; over the next decade, he worked his way up the professional ladder, being promoted to assistant professor in 1930, associate professor in 1932, and then full professor of physics in 1937. Throughout this period, Rabi refined his methods of atomic and molecular beam analysis, eventually making a number of important discoveries.

Discovers Atomic Spin Properties

The Stern-Gerlach experiment of 1922 had showed that a molecular beam passing through a magnetic field splits into two parts. The discovery of electron spin by **George Uhlenbeck** and **Samuel Goudsmit** in 1927 explained this phenomenon: they demonstrated that electrons in an atom can spin in only one of two directions; hence, electrons spinning in one direction split into one beam, while those spinning in the opposite direction split into another.

As Rabi studied this effect in more detail, he realized that the magnetic properties of an atom are more complex than first suggested by the Stern-Gerlach experiment. In the first place, the nucleus itself spins, creating its own magnetic field. Thus, there will be interactions among the magnetic field of the nucleus, the magnetic fields of the orbital electrons, and any external magnetic field that is applied to the atom.

In his research, Rabi was able to sort out and quantify many of these discrete properties. His most important accomplishment was to determine the magnetic moment of the nucleus, an important piece of information essential to the construction of an accurate model of the atom. By 1937, Rabi had made yet another discovery, namely that he could reverse the spin of a nucleus by imposing an external radiofrequency signal on an atomic or molecular beam. That discovery has been used in a number of important applications; one of these, nuclear magnetic resonance (NMR), is now among the most powerful analytical tools available to scientific investigators and medical diagnosticians. Rabi was awarded the 1944 Nobel Prize in physics for his work on "the resonance method for recording the magnetic properties of the atomic nucleus."

During World War II, Rabi took a leave of absence from Columbia to worked on the development of microwave radar devices at the Massachusetts Institute of Technology. Though most of his colleagues in the scientific community were devoting their wartime efforts to the development of atomic weapons, Rabi believed that, of the two projects, radar would be more immediately useful to the U.S. war effort—though he did consult on nuclear weapons projects as part of the Manhattan Project. At the war's conclusion, Rabi returned to Columbia as chairman of the physics department. He devoted his time primarily to administrative responsibilities and to the effort by scientists to restrict military control of nuclear technology. "Speaking for the group of men who created these weapons," Rabi once said in *Atlantic Monthly,* "I would say that we are frankly pleased, terrified, and to an even greater degree embarrassed when we contemplate the results of our wartime efforts." In order to monitor the use of atomic energy and weapons, Rabi became a member of the General Advisory Committee of the Atomic Energy Commission in 1945 and then served as chairman of the committee from 1952 to 1956 (after the retirement of J. Robert Oppenheimer). He was an advisor to NATO and the United Nations, and served as a member of the American delegation to UNESCO, overlooking the European Center for Nuclear Research (CERN) in Geneva.

Rabi was married to Helen Newmark in 1926. They had two daughters, Nancy Elizabeth and Margaret Joella. In addition to the Nobel Prize, Rabi won a host of other awards, including the Elliott Cresson Medal of the Franklin Institute in 1942, the U.S. Medal for Merit (the country's highest civilian service award) in 1948, the Niels Bohr International Gold Medal in 1967, the Atoms for Peace Award in 1967, the Franklin Delano Roosevelt Freedom Medal in 1985, and the Public Welfare Medal of the National Academy of Sciences in 1985. Rabi died in New York City on January 11, 1988.

SELECTED WRITINGS BY RABI:

Books

My Life and Times As a Physicist, Claremont College, 1960.
Science: The Center of Culture, World Publishing, 1970.

Periodicals

(With others) "A New Method of Measuring Nuclear Magnetic Moment," *Physical Review,* Volume 53, 1938, p. 318.
(With others) "The Magnetic Moments of 3-Li–6, 3-Li–7, and 9-F–19," *Physical Review,* Volume 55, 1939, pp. 526–535.

SOURCES:

Books

Current Biography Yearbook 1948, H. W. Wilson, 1949, pp. 509–510.
Heathcote, Niels H. de V., *Nobel Prize Winners in Physics, 1901–1950,* Henry Schuman, 1953, pp. 398–410.
McGraw-Hill Modern Scientists and Engineers, McGraw-Hill, 1980, pp. 1–2.
Nobel Prize Winners, H. W. Wilson, 1987, pp. 847–849.
Weber, Robert L., *Pioneers of Science: Nobel Prize Winners in Physics,* American Institute of Physics, 1980, pp. 122–124.

—*Sketch by David E. Newton*

James Rainwater
1917-1986
American physicist

James Rainwater, an American nuclear physicist who had a lifelong association with Columbia University, conducted some pioneering research in the study of the atomic nucleus, proving that its structure was not the symmetrical sphere many had believed it to be. For his role in formulating a new model of the nucleus, Rainwater, along with fellow physicists **Aage Bohr** and **Ben R. Mottelson**, was awarded the 1975 Nobel Prize in physics.

Leo James Rainwater was born in Council, Idaho, to Edna Eliza Teague and Leo Jasper Rainwater, a civil engineer and general store manager. The elder Rainwater died of influenza a year after his son was born, and the family moved to Hanford, California, where Rainwater's mother remarried. In high school, Rainwater entered a chemistry competition sponsored by the California Institute of Technology (Caltech). He got an outstanding score and after graduation enrolled at Caltech as a chemistry major. Later he switched to physics. After receiving a B.A. in physics from Caltech in 1939, Rainwater went to Columbia University and received a master's degree in physics in 1941. As a doctoral student at Columbia, Rainwater studied under such notable physicists as **Enrico Fermi** and **Edward Teller**.

In 1942 Rainwater was appointed a scientist in the Manhattan Project, thus delaying his thesis research in order to participate in the development of the atom bomb. Rainwater used the Columbia cyclotron particle accelerator to study the behavior of neutrons (uncharged elementary particles with a mass nearly equal to that of protons). In 1946 he received his Ph.D. and became a physics instructor at Columbia; in 1947 he was made assistant professor.

After the Second World War, Columbia University started building an improved particle accelerator, the so-called synchrocyclotron, at the Nevis Laboratory. Rainwater helped build this new accelerator at Nevis, marking the beginning of his own long-standing connection with this lab. His research at Nevis lasted for more than thirty years, during which Rainwater served as director from 1951 to 1953 and then again from 1956 to 1961. When the synchrocyclotron became operational in 1950, it enabled scientists to study other particles besides neutrons. Muons, rapidly decaying particles 200 times larger than electrons, and pi-mesons, other short-lived particles that carry a force binding nuclei together, were of particular interest to Rainwater.

Formulates New Model of Atomic Nucleus

During 1949 and 1950 Rainwater shared an office with Danish physicist Aage Bohr. Their conversations during this period led to the development of a new conception of the atomic nucleus. At the time, physicists were trying to construct a model of the nucleus that would account for the forces acting between the protons and neutrons. Bohr's father, the noted physicist **Niels Bohr**, had earlier suggested the analogy of a drop of liquid as one possible model. Bohr proposed that the nucleus vibrated and changed shape like a drop of liquid. Other possible explanations were suggested by scientists Maria Goeppert Mayer and **J. Hans D. Jensen**, who conceived of the nucleus as a series of onion-like layers or shells. According to this theory, the nucleons move independently in their own concentric orbits in shells. The forces are equal throughout the nucleus, creating a nucleus with a uniform spherical force field. The shell theory succeeded in describing the motion of the nucleons, but its assumption that the nucleus was a symmetrical sphere was proven wrong by later research showing that the electrical charge around the nuclei was not spherical. Rainwater would explain why. After attending a lecture by **Charles H. Townes** in 1949 on the inconsistencies of the two nuclear models, Rainwater came up with the idea that centrifugal forces within the nucleus might make the spherical shape around the nucleus more like an ellipsoid or football. In 1950, he published his hypothesis in a paper titled "Nuclear Energy Level Argument for a Spheroidal Nuclear Model."

Rainwater convinced Aage Bohr that his hypothesis was correct. After Bohr returned to Copenhagen, he and fellow Danish physicist Ben Mottelson developed a comprehensive theory of nuclear behavior, publishing their findings in 1952. The scientists used Rainwater's hypothesis to combine aspects of the liquid-drop model with the shell model, proposing that the collective action of the protons and neutrons made the surface of the nucleus act a like a drop of liquid, which could be deformed into a football-like shape if the outer shell of the nucleus was not filled with all the nucleons it could hold. It would then appear to oscillate and change its size. But if the outer shell of the nucleus had its complete number of nucleons, it appeared spherical.

While Bohr and Mottelson were publishing their theory, Rainwater was at work in the Nevis laboratory with a colleague, Val L. Fitch, observing X rays emanating from muons. His work revealed that the size of protons was being overestimated at the time. Other research by Rainwater focused on the properties of muons and their interactions with nuclei and advanced insight into the behavior of neutrons.

Receives International Recognition

In 1975, Bohr, Mottelson and Rainwater received the Nobel Prize for their discovery of the connection between collective motion and particle motion in atomic nuclei and for the development of the theory of the structure of the atomic nucleus based on this connection. The U.S. Atomic Energy Commission gave Rainwater the E. O. Lawrence Memorial Award in 1963, and the National Academy of Sciences elected him a member in 1968. He would also become a member of the Institute of Electrical and Electronic Engineers, the New York Academy of Sciences, the American Association for the Advancement of Science and the American Physical Society. In 1983, Rainwater was named Michael I. Pupin Professor of Physics.

In 1942, Rainwater married Emma Louise Smith. They had three sons and a daughter, who died in infancy. Rainwater's interests included geology, astronomy, and classical music. On May 31, 1986, shortly after retiring, Rainwater died in Yonkers, New York.

—Sketch by Margo Nash

Vulimiri Ramalingaswami
1921-
Indian medical scientist

A medical researcher for several decades, Vulimiri Ramalingaswami pioneered studies in nutritional disorders in India and other developing countries. His discovery of a syndrome known as protein-energy malnutrition in children has led to treatments that have greatly alleviated suffering around the world. His researches in liver pathology also led to the discovery of a syndrome that produces a fatal form of cirrhosis. A teacher of international repute, Ramalingaswami's later career has been devoted to the application of his and others' discoveries in nutrition and health care.

Vulimiri Ramalingaswami was born August 8, 1921, at Srikakulam, Andhra Pradesh, India. His father, V. Gumpaswami Ramalingaswami, was a government official, and his mother, V. Sundaramma, was a housewife. As a youth, Ramalingaswami attended a school funded by his grandfather, who was also its first headmaster. Ramalingaswami told contributor J. Sydney Jones that his grandfather, whose many interests ranged from English language studies to ancient Indian literature, classical Indian music, and

the science of human health, was an influential figure in Ramalingaswami's early life, especially in his choice to become a doctor. Ramalingaswami earned an M.B.B.S. in 1944 from Andhra Medical College, and his M.D. degree two years later from the same institution. In 1947 he married Surya Prabha, a training psychologist, and then attended Magdalen College at Oxford University, where he received his Ph.D. in 1951.

Research Accomplished at All India Institute

Returning to India, Ramalingaswami worked as a pathologist at the Indian Council of Medical Research until 1954 and then served as its deputy director until 1957, when he accepted a position at the All India Institute of Medical Sciences in New Delhi. For the next twenty-two years, he would help to develop an outstanding school of pathology at that institution, both in teaching and research. It was during his tenure at the All India Institute that he focused on some of the major health problems of developing countries, especially nutritional problems and liver disease. His work on protein-energy malnutrition; liver conditions such as non-cirrhotic portal hypertension; and goiter, a hormonal deficiency causing the enlargement of the thyroid gland that is prevalent in India, has done much to relieve suffering in his homeland and throughout the world. He has also worked to adapt European health care and medical education to the culture and structures of developing countries. In 1979, he left his position as director of the All India Institute of Medical Sciences to become director general of the Indian Council of Medical Research. Until his retirement seven years later, Ramalingaswami was responsible for coordinating and promoting biomedical research throughout India and for playing a principal role in establishing a government program called "Health for All by the Year 2000."

Honored worldwide for his research and organizational work, Ramalingaswami is one of the few scientists in the world to have been elected a foreign member of the major scientific academies of the United States, the United Kingdom, and the former Soviet Union. He was also chairman of the Global Advisory Committee on Medical Research for the World Health Organization (WHO) for several years, and was awarded an honorary doctorate from the Karolinska Institute in Sweden in 1974. An emeritus professor at the All India Institute of Medical Sciences since 1990, he is currently president of India's National Institute of Immunology in New Delhi. He has two children, Vulimiri Jagdish and Lakshmi V. Ramanathan. In his free time he enjoys music, literature, and sports.

SELECTED WRITINGS BY RAMALINGASWAMI:

Periodicals

"Perspectives in Protein Malnutrition," *Nature,* Volume 201, 1964, pp. 546–551.

"Experimental Protein Deficiency—Pathological Features in the Rhesus Monkey," *Archives of Pathology,* Volume 80, 1965, pp. 14–23.

(With M. G. Deo) "Reaction of the Small Intestine to Induced Protein Malnutrition in Rhesus Monkeys," *Gastroenterology,* Volume 49, 1965, pp. 150–157.

"Endemic Goiter in South-East Asia—New Clothes on an Old Body," *Annals of International Medicine,* Volume 78, 1973, pp. 277–283.

(With others) "Prevention of Endemic Goiter with Iodized Salt," *WHO Bulletin,* Volume 49, 1973, pp. 307–312.

(With others) "WHO Sponsored Collaboration Studies on Nutritional Anaemia in India," *Quarterly Journal of Medicine New Series,* Volume 44, 1975, 241–258.

(With others) "Under the Volcano—Biomedical Science and the Third World," *Annals of the New York Academy of Science,* Volume 569, 1989, pp. 25–35.

SOURCES:

Ramalingaswami, Vulimiri, interview with J. Sydney Jones conducted April 12, 1994.

—Sketch by J. Sydney Jones

C. V. Raman
1888-1970
Indian physicist

Physicist C. V. Raman helped to usher India into the world of twentieth-century science. Raman overcame obstacles of geographical isolation and political oppression to establish himself, and thus India, as a serious contributor to modern Western science. His primary research interests were acoustics, musical instruments, and wave optics. He was best known for his discovery of the Raman effect (first announced in 1928), a process by which a beam of light passing through a solid, liquid, or gas was diffracted and its frequencies (and so its colors) were

C. V. Raman

changed. In recognition of this discovery Raman was knighted in 1929 and awarded the Nobel Prize in physics in 1930.

Prior to Raman's time, India's development had proceeded along the lines of literature, art, and architecture. After the British colonized this land and set up trade, science was imported only to assist in furthering commerce. The British kept native Indians on the periphery of this activity and did not allow them training in modern scientific methods. It was only after the British introduced Western education that native Indians came in direct contact with twentieth-century European science. Raman, then, had to struggle against his country's delayed interest in science, its geographical isolation, and its oppression by the ruling British. By the end of the nineteenth century when European science had already become mature, science in India was a mere fledgling.

Childhood Education and Early Achievements

Chandrasekhara Venkata Raman, the second of eight children, was born on November 7, 1888, near Trichinopoly on the banks of the Kaveri. His father, Ramanathan Chandrasekaran Iyer, was a lecturer in physics, mathematics, and physical geography. Iyer read avidly, collected books, and played the violin. These pastimes came to have a great influence on his son. Raman's mother, S. Parvati Ammal, was the daughter of Saptarshi Sastri, a great Sanskrit scholar.

As a child, Raman was not strong or athletic, but he excelled at intellectual pursuits. He won many scholarships and prizes at school, and in 1903 at the age of 16 he won a scholarship and entered the prestigious Presidency College as one of its youngest undergraduates. At college Raman pursued his boyhood interest, physics, and also developed a fondness for English. Raman graduated first in his class and won gold medals in physics and English.

After Raman passed his B.A. examination, his teachers encouraged him to go to England to continue his studies. But because of his frail health he was counseled against subjecting himself to the unhealthy English climate. As a result, Raman decided to enroll in the Presidency College's M.A. program in physics. Raman's teacher at this time made few demands on him and let him explore on his own. Raman, guided by his own interests and goaded by his own motivation, conducted his own experiments in the diffraction of light passing through rectangular slits. When he had accumulated a number of findings, he wrote them up and sent a manuscript to the *Philosophical Magazine* in London, which published it as "Unsymmetrical Diffraction Bands Due to a Rectangular Aperture." This accomplishment was remarkable because Raman sent the manuscript on his own, his was the first paper to come out of the Presidency College, and he had done this at the age of eighteen.

After earning his M.A. in 1907, Raman found that there were no opportunities for a career in research open to Indians in India. So he secured through fierce competition a coveted position in the Indian Civil Service as an accountant. He pursued his scientific research in his spare time at home until 1917 when Calcutta University offered him the Palit Chair for Physics at about half the salary he was receiving from the government. Raman accepted the position without hesitation.

Promoting Indian Science

Because of India's great size and diversity, its centers of research often suffered from their isolation. Raman felt a need for some way of consolidating and promoting his country's interests in science. To that end he worked at inciting interest among Indian scientists in establishing an academy of science. His initial attempts were stymied in Bombay by intramural disputes among various scientific factions, so he independently founded his own academy in Bangalore.

The inaugural meeting of the Indian Academy of Sciences was held in August of 1934 in Bangalore. Raman became its first president, and he retained the office until his death. For this reason some called the organization Raman's Academy. Its stated objectives were to provide a forum for discussing the results of scientific research and to publish the achievements of

Indian science. G. Venkataraman, in his *Journey into Light: Life and Science of C. V. Raman,* called the Academy "one of Raman's gifts to India."

The Academy's journal, the *Proceedings of the Indian Academy of Sciences,* appeared in 1934 and featured as its opening paper Raman's work entitled "The Origin of the Colours of the Plumage of Birds." By 1935 the amount of publishable material had grown to such an extent that Raman divided the journal into two parts: physical and mathematical sciences, and biological sciences. Eventually the *Proceedings* was divided into six separate specialty journals in 1977.

Fascination with Light and Sound

Raman's fascination with the phenomenal world seemed to be behind most of his research interests. Raman once admitted to letting his attention wander from his English professor at the Presidency College because the glittering waves of the blue sea, which were visible from his lecture hall, caught his eye. Later, color was to become an ever-present aspect of his research on light and optics, which included studies on the color effects of shells, gems, minerals, flowers, and plumage.

Music also influenced Raman's research. His father inspired in his son a love for music, particularly the violin. Raman himself became a competent violinist, and later he approached musical instruments as a physicist. Raman was recognized as the first in this century to rekindle the research into the physics of the violin and other musical instruments. His research in this area included studies on the behavior of bowed strings, the influence of the violin's bridge, and the frequency response of the violin (known as the Raman curve). Raman also investigated the sound-producing mechanisms of the piano and of some traditional Indian instruments like the tabla and the tambura.

At one point, Raman was able to combine his interests in sound and light in the same research project. The fruit of this project was the Raman-Nath theory, perhaps his greatest achievement during his stay at the Indian Institute of Science. The Raman-Nath theory explained what happens to a beam of light as it passes through a liquid that is agitated by a sound wave. This theory became important later to the research on the propagation of starlight through the atmosphere and the propagation of laser emissions through plasma.

As a student, Raman had learned science in a setting where laboratory resources were modest. As a result he became adept at improvising the equipment he needed for his experiments. In a 1905 experiment on the surface tension of liquids, he devised a spark generator that illuminated a suspended drop so its shadow could be photographed. In 1927 while studying the scattering of light, Raman needed to keep the sensitivity of an observer's eye at a maximum, so he fashioned a light-tight wooden enclosure for the observer, which came to be called the "black hole of Calcutta." During his research on the physics of the violin, Raman needed a way to study and control the force of the bow, so he contrived his experimental apparatus from materials he had on hand including parts from an optical bench and the chain and hubs from a cycle. The result was a mechanical violin player where the violin moved while the bow remained stationary.

Soon after discovering the Raman effect (frequency and color changes with respect to light diffraction), Raman became interested in the diamond. Captivated by its beauty and physical properties, he referred to it as the "prince of solids." He began collecting them at his own expense, and by 1944 he had over 300. Raman even admitted that he had used part of his Nobel Prize money to buy diamonds. When he couldn't afford to buy them, he borrowed diamond rings from wealthy friends. Venkataraman reported that Raman once saw his brother sporting a diamond ring and said to him, "I say, why don't you put that thing on your finger to some use?" So strong was his scientific curiosity for diamonds that at one point every one of his students was studying some aspect of diamonds. Raman studied many optical phenomena in diamonds including light absorption, light scattering, and X-ray diffraction.

Later Interests

Raman did not want to become idle once he retired, so he began planning a new research institute two years before his retirement from the Indian Institute of Science. He conducted his own fund raising, and, by 1948, although he had not raised enough money, he had acquired a building. During the first year of its existence, the new Raman Research Institute had no electricity, but that did not prevent Raman from conducting some important optical experiments using sunlight. Eventually Raman had the financial support to complete his new facility, which included gardens for the trees and flowers that he loved and a museum for his collections of crystals, gems, minerals, shells, birds, and butterflies. Raman continued his work on optics at the Institute, which included, in conjunction with his nephew, the development of a theory to explain mirages.

Raman was known to be proud and at times even arrogant. Venkataraman reported that in 1924 at the age of 36, Raman was elected Fellow of the Royal Society. When he was congratulated and asked what was next, he replied, "the Nobel Prize, of course." When he actually did receive the prize six years later, it was discovered that he had booked passage to Stockholm, the site of the awards ceremony, four months before he received the official announcement of the award.

In the course of his 66 years as a physicist, Raman published over 450 research papers and inspired almost three times that number of papers among his students. In promoting Indian science, Raman was hailed as one of India's heroes along with Mohandas Gandhi and Motilal Nehru. Raman died at his research institute in Bangalore on November 20, 1970, and his ashes were scattered there among the trees.

SELECTED WRITINGS BY RAMAN:

Books

Ramaseshan, S., editor, *Scientific Papers of C. V. Raman,* 6 volumes, Indian Academy of Sciences, 1988.

SOURCES:

Books

Venkataraman, G., *Journey into Light: Life and Science of C. V. Raman,* Indian Academy of Sciences, 1988.

—Sketch by Lawrence Souder

S. I. Ramanujan
1887-1920
Indian mathematician

Mathematician S. I. Ramanujan was a self-taught prodigy from India. His introduction to the world of formal mathematics and subsequent fame arose from his correspondence and collaboration with the renowned British mathematician **Godfrey Harold Hardy**. In his short but prolific career Ramanujan made several important contributions to the field of number theory, an area of pure mathematics that deals with the properties of and patterns among ordinary numbers. Three quarters of a century after his death, mathematicians still work on his papers, attempting to provide logical proofs for results he apparently arrived at intuitively. Many of his theorems are now finding practical applications in areas as

S. I. Ramanujan

diverse as polymer chemistry and computer science, subjects virtually unknown during his own times.

Srinivasa Iyengar Ramanujan, born on December 22, 1887, was the eldest son of K. Srinivasa Iyengar and Komalatammal. He was born in his mother's parental home of Erode and raised in the city of Kumbakonam in southern India, where his father worked as a clerk in a clothing store. They were a poor family, and his mother often sang devotional songs with a group at a local temple to supplement the family income. Ramanujan received all his early education in Kumbakonam, where he studied English while still in primary school and then attended the town's English-language school. His mathematical talents became evident early on; at eleven he was already challenging his mathematics teachers with questions they could not always answer. Seeing his interest in the subject, some college students lent him books from their library. By the time he was thirteen, Ramanujan had mastered S. L. Loney's *Trigonometry,* a popular textbook used by students much older than him who were studying in Indian colleges and British preparatory schools. In 1904, at the age of 17, Ramanujan graduated from high school, winning a special prize in mathematics and a scholarship to attend college.

Pursues Mathematics Independently

Shortly before he completed high school, Ramanujan came across a book called *A Synopsis of*

Elementary Results in Pure and Applied Mathematics. This book, written by British tutor G. S. Carr in the 1880s, was a compilation of approximately five thousand mathematical results, formulae, and equations. The *Synopsis* did not explain these equations or provide proofs for all the results; it merely laid down various mathematical generalizations as fact. In Ramanujan, the book unleashed a passion for mathematics so great that he studied it to the exclusion of all other subjects. Because of this, although Ramanujan enrolled in the Fine Arts (F.A.) course at the local Government College, he never completed the course. He began to spend all his time on mathematics, manipulating the formulae and equations in Carr's book, and neglected all the other subjects that were part of his course work at the college. His scholarship was revoked when he failed his English composition examination. In all, he attempted the F.A. examinations four times from 1904 to 1907. Each time he failed, doing poorly in all subjects except mathematics.

During these four years, and for several more, Ramanujan pursued his passion with single-minded devotion. He continued to work independently of his teachers, filling up sheets of paper with his ideas and results which were later compiled in his famous *Notebooks.* Carr's book had merely been a springboard to launch Ramanujan's journey into mathematics. While it gave him a direction, the book did not provide him with the methods and tools to pursue his course. These he fashioned for himself, and using them he quickly meandered from established theorems into the realms of originality. He experimented with numbers to see how they behaved, and he drew generalizations and theorems based on these observations. Some of these results and conclusions had already been proved and published in the Western world, though Ramanujan, sequestered in India, could not know that. But most of his work was original.

Meanwhile, his circumstances changed. Without a degree, it was very difficult to find a job, and for many of these years Ramanujan was desperately poor, often relying on the good graces of friends and family for support. Occasionally he would tutor students in mathematics, but most of these attempts were unsuccessful because he did not stick to the rules or syllabus. He habitually compressed multiple steps of a solution, leaving his students baffled by his leaps of logic. In July 1909 he married Janaki, a girl some ten years his junior. Keeping with local customs and traditions, the marriage had been arranged by Ramanujan and Janaki's parents. Soon afterwards, he traveled to Madras, the largest city in South India, in search of a job. Because he did not have a degree, Ramanujan presented his notebooks as evidence of his work and the research he had been conducting in past years. Most people were bewildered after reading a few pages of his books, and the few who recognized them as the work of a genius did not know what to do with them. Finally, Ramachandra Rao, a professor of mathematics at the prestigious Presidency College in Madras, reviewed the books and supported him for a while. In 1912 Ramanujan secured a position as an accounts clerk at the Madras Port Trust, giving him a meager though independent salary.

During this time, Ramanujan's work caught the attention of other scholars who recognized his abilities and encouraged him to continue his research. His first contribution to mathematical literature was a paper titled "Some Properties of Bernoulli's Numbers," and it was published in the *Journal of the Indian Mathematical Society* c. 1910. However, Ramanujan realized that the caliber of his work was far beyond any research being conducted in India at the time, and he began writing to leading mathematicians in England asking for their help.

Sends Letter to Hardy

The first two mathematicians he approached were eminent professors at Cambridge University, and they turned him down. On January 16, 1913, Ramanujan wrote to **Godfrey Harold Hardy**, who agreed to help him. Hardy was a fellow of Trinity College, Cambridge, and he specialized in number theory and analysis. Although he was initially inclined to dismiss Ramanujan's letter, which seemed full of wild claims and strange theorems with no supporting proofs, the very bizarreness of the theorems nagged at Hardy, and he decided to take a closer look. Along with J. E. Littlewood, he examined the theorems more thoroughly, and three hours after they began reading, they both decided the work was that of a genius. "They must be true because, if they were not true, no one would have had the imagination to invent them," Hardy is quoted as saying in Robert Kanigel's book *The Man Who Knew Infinity.*

Hardy now set about the task of bringing Ramanujan to England. In the beginning, Ramanujan resisted the idea due to religious restrictions on traveling abroad, but he was eventually persuaded to go. Ramanujan spent five years in England, from 1914 to 1919, during which time he enjoyed a productive collaboration with Hardy, who personally trained him in modern analysis. Hardy described this as the most singular experience of his life, says Kanigel in *The Man Who Knew Infinity:* "What did modern mathematics look like to one who had the deepest insight, but who had literally never heard of most of it?" Ramanujan was to receive several laurels during this period, including a B.A. degree from Cambridge, and appointments as Fellow of the Royal Society (at 30 he was one of the youngest ever to be honored thus) and Trinity College. But the English weather affected Ramanujan's health, and he con-

tracted tuberculosis. In 1919 he returned to India, where he succumbed to the disease, dying on April 26, 1920.

Until the very end, Ramanujan remained passionately involved in mathematics, and he produced some original work even after his return to India. His great love for the subject and his genius are perhaps best exemplified in an incident described by Hardy in his book *A Mathematician's Apology.* He related that while visiting Ramanujan at a hospital outside London, where he lay ill with tuberculosis, Hardy mentioned the number of his taxicab, 1729. Hardy thought it a rather dull number. "No, Hardy! No, Hardy!" Ramanujan replied. "It is a very interesting number. It is the smallest number expressible as the sum of two cubes in two different ways." Kanigel reported another comment Hardy made later. He said that had Ramanujan been better educated, "he would have been less of a Ramanujan and more of a European professor and the loss might have been greater." Ramanujan himself attributed his mathematical gifts to his family deity, the goddess Namagiri. A deeply religious man, he combined his passion with his faith, and he once told a friend that "an equation for me has no meaning unless it expresses a thought of God."

SELECTED WRITINGS BY RAMANUJAN:

Books

Notebooks, 2 volumes, Tata Institute of Fundamental Research, 1957.
The Lost Notebook and Other Unpublished Papers, Narosa Publishing House, 1988.

SOURCES:

Books

Hardy, G. H., *A Mathematician's Apology,* Cambridge University Press, 1940.
Hardy, G. H., *Ramanujan: Twelve Lectures on Subjects Suggested by His Life and Work,* Cambridge University Press, 1940.
Kanigel, Robert, *The Man Who Knew Infinity: A Life of the Genius Ramanujan,* Macmillan, 1991.

Periodicals

Hardy, G. H., "Obituary, S. Ramanujan," *Nature,* June 17, 1920, pp 494–95.
Seshu Iyer, P. V., and Ramachandra Rao, R., "The Late Mr. S. Ramanujan, B.A., F.R.S." *Journal of the Indian Mathematical Society,* June, 1920, pp 81–86.

Other

Sykes, Christopher, *Letters from an Indian Clerk* (documentary), BBC.

—*Sketch by Neeraja Sankaran*

Pauline Ramart-Lucas
1880-1953
French organic chemist

Pauline Ramart-Lucas was the second woman (after French physicist **Marie Curie**) to become a full professor at the University of Paris. An organic chemist whose interests ranged widely, Ramart-Lucas studied the structure, chemical reactivity, and ultraviolet absorption spectrum of organic compounds. Through her efforts, she discovered a new type of isomerism that revised the electronic structure of carbon in a large class of organic molecules. In addition, she was a prominent educator and science administrator in the French university system. Born on November 22, 1880, Ramart-Lucas grew up in modest circumstances in Paris. Upon finishing elementary school, she worked as an arranger of artificial flowers in the shadow of the Sorbonne, France's premier university. She vowed then to attend the university, and with this goal in mind she took evening courses to obtain a secondary-school diploma. A pharmacist instructed her in English and kindled her passion for chemistry. At age 29 she completed the *licence* in physical sciences—corresponding roughly to an American bachelor of sciences degree—despite encountering prejudice because she was female.

Ramart-Lucas gravitated to the organic chemistry laboratory of Albin Haller, who himself had been apprenticed as a woodworker before finding an academic vocation. There she completed a doctorate in 1913. After a short time working in radiology during World War I, she returned to chemistry when Haller called her back to his laboratory. With the exception of the years between 1941 and 1944, when she was relieved of her post, she worked at the Sorbonne for the rest of her life, rising from laboratory manager to lecturer in 1925, and then to professor in 1930.

In the first part of her career, from 1908 to 1924, Ramart-Lucas concentrated on the molecular changes that occur when various alcohols—organic compounds that include the oxygen-hydrogen radical OH—are dehydrated. During the latter part of her career she studied the structure, chemical reactivity, and ultraviolet absorption spectrum of organic compounds. She cast her net wide, specializing in analyzing diverse dyes. Her research identified a new type of isomerism, or structural difference, that revised the electronic structure of carbon in a large class of organic molecules.

The recipient of many prizes before World War II—including the 1928 Ellen H. Richards Research Prize of the American Association of University Women—Ramart-Lucas emerged as one of France's senior science administrators after 1944, when she became vice-president of the educational section in the Consultative Assembly. She also sat on the councils of the Palais de la découverte, France's national science museum, and the École de physique et de chimie, Paris's famous municipal science school. Admitted as a Knight in the French Legion of Honor in 1928, she was promoted to Officer in 1938; she received the exceptional distinction of Commander in 1953.

Ramart-Lucas preferred original research over synthetic summary, although in 1936 she did contribute a long chapter on molecular structure and absorption spectra to **Victor Grignard**'s multi-volume handbook on organic chemistry. Over nearly half a century, she published more than two hundred scientific articles and directed fifty doctoral theses and graduate memoirs, a large number of these by women students. Her work was her life, and her students and colleagues became her family. She died on March 13, 1953.

SOURCES:

Periodicals

Denis, Paul, "Madame Pauline Ramart-Lucas," *Bulletin de la Société chimique de France: Mémoires et documentation,* Volume 21, 1954, pp. 269–271.

Martynoff, Modeste, "L'oeuvre scientifique de Pauline Ramart-Lucas" (bibliography), *Bulletin de la Société chimique de France: Mémoires et documentation,* Volume 21, 1954, pp. 272–280.

—*Sketch by Lewis Pyenson*

Estelle R. Ramey
1917-
American physiologist and educator

Estelle R. Ramey

Estelle Ramey is known for her research in the endocrine aspects of stress, including the relationship between sex hormones and longevity, as well as for her activism in the feminist movement. In 1989 she was named by *Newsweek* magazine as "one of twenty-five Americans who have made a difference."

Ramey was born in Detroit, Michigan, on August 23, 1917, to Henry, a businessman, and Sarah L. White. She graduated from Brooklyn College at the age of nineteen and took a job as a teaching fellow in the department of chemistry at Queens College, New York City. "Dr. Whittaker, my old teacher, was appointed chairman of the department at Queens College," Ramey recalled in correspondence with Jill Carpenter, "and he was a unique man for his times. He did not equate gender with ability."

Ramey completed her M.S. degree in chemistry at Columbia University in 1940 and was working toward a Ph.D. degree when she married law student James T. Ramey (they have two children, James and Drucilla). When her husband's career took them to Knoxville, Tennessee, Ramey applied for a job in the department of chemistry at the University of Tennessee. Ramey told Carpenter: "I was brusquely informed by the chairman that he had never hired a woman, would never hire a woman, and I ought to go home and take care of my husband. A few months later, Pearl Harbor was bombed and the war started. The chemistry department began to lose its male faculty and a chastened chairman called to offer me a job teaching thermodynamics to Air Cadets and biochemistry to Nurse Cadets." Ramey taught at the University of Tennessee from 1942 through 1947.

When her husband joined the newly created Atomic Energy Commission in Chicago, Ramey entered the University of Chicago. She was a Mergler Scholar in 1949, and earned a Ph.D. from the university's School of Medicine in 1950. Also in 1950, she received a U. S. Public Health Service postdoctoral fellowship in endocrinology and became an assistant professor of physiology at the medical school, the first woman faculty member in that department. In 1956 she joined the faculty of Georgetown University Medical School in Washington, D.C. Her tenure at Georgetown was punctuated by stints as visiting professor at Stanford University, Harvard University, and Yale University. In 1977 she was awarded an honorary doctorate by Georgetown, and in 1987 the university named her professor emerita of biophysics.

Advisory boards, boards of directors, and committees on which Ramey has served include Educational Telecommunications, Planned Parenthood, Big Sisters of Washington, the National Institutes of Health, the National Academy of Science, the Veteran's Administration for Women Veterans, the Chief of Naval Operations, the Admiral H. G. Rickover Foundation, the MacDonald Hospital for Women, and President Carter's Committee on the Status of Women. She is a member of the nominating committee of the MacArthur Foundation, and her honors include the Outstanding Alumna Award from the University of Chicago, 1973; the Public Broadcasting Company Woman of Achievement Award, 1984; and the National Women's Democratic Club Woman of Achievement Award, 1993. Ramey is a past president of the Association for Women in Science (AWIS) and founder of the AWIS Educational Foundation. She holds 17 honorary doctorates, has lectured at dozens of colleges and government agencies, and has published more than 150 articles in the scientific and popular press.

SELECTED WRITINGS BY RAMEY:

Periodicals

"Boredom: The Most Prevalent American Disease," *Harper's,* November, 1974, pp. 12–22.

SOURCES:

Ramey, Estelle R., correspondence with Jill Carpenter, January, 1994.

—*Sketch by Jill Carpenter*

Santiago Ramón y Cajal
1852-1934
Spanish neurohistologist

The anatomical research of the Spanish neurohistologist Santiago Ramón y Cajal is central to the modern understanding of the nervous system. By adopting and improving the nervous-tissue staining process developed by the Italian scientist **Camillo Golgi**, Ramón y Cajal established that individual nerve cells, or neurons, are the basic structural unit of the nervous system. He also made important discoveries relating to the transmission of nerve impulses and the cellular structures of the brain. For his work in histology, the branch of anatomy concerned with minute tissue structures and processes, Ramón y Cajal shared with Golgi the 1906 Nobel Prize for physiology or medicine.

Ramón y Cajal was born on May 1, 1852, in the remote country village of Petilla de Aragon, Spain. He was the son of Justo Ramón y Casasús, a poor and self-educated barber-surgeon, and Antonia Cajal. The family subsequently moved to the university city of Zaragoza, where against considerable odds Ramón y Cajal's father earned a medical degree and became a professor of anatomy. As a young man, Ramón y Cajal was rebellious and independent-minded. He preferred drawing to studying, and although this passion for drawing would ultimately serve him well, it was vigorously opposed by his iron-willed father, who had determined that his son should become a doctor. As a disciplinary measure, his father apprenticed him to a barber and later to a shoemaker. During these apprenticeships, Ramón y Cajal also studied anatomy with his father—investigations which partially relied on bone specimens taken from a local churchyard.

When he was sixteen years old, Ramón y Cajal began medical studies at the University of Zaragoza, earning a degree in medicine in 1873. He then joined the army medical service and served as an infantry surgeon in Cuba for one year. He contracted malaria, however, which led to his discharge, and he returned to Spain. In 1879, still convalescent, he passed his examinations at Zaragoza and Madrid for his doctorate in medicine.

Ramón y Cajal was almost exclusively interested in anatomical research, and he embarked on an academic career. Beginning in 1879, Ramón y Cajal turned himself into a skilled histologist, initially working with an old, abandoned microscope he had found at the University of Zaragoza. He studied various anatomical tissues and began to publish articles on cell biology—complete with beautifully rendered ink drawings. His work was not immediately recognized in other countries, but the increasing prestige of his posts attests to his success in Spain. From 1879 to 1883, he directed the anatomical museum at the University of Zaragoza. In 1883, he assumed a professorship of descriptive anatomy at the University of Valencia, and in 1887 he became professor of histology at the University of Barcelona. In 1892, Ramón y Cajal assumed the chair of histology and pathologic anatomy at the University of Madrid, a post he retained until 1922.

Research Provides Evidence for Neuron Theory

Ramón y Cajal eventually turned to the most complex tissues, those of the nervous system. His research method now drew on Camillo Golgi's method of staining tissue samples to reveal their minute components. Under Golgi's method, a potassium dichromate-silver nitrate solution stained the nerve cells and fibers black, while the neuroglia, or supporting tissues, remained much lighter. By refining this staining technique and applying it to embryonic tissue samples, Ramón y Cajal was able to isolate the neuron as the basic component of the nervous system; he also differentiated the neuron from the ordinary cells of the body. His work supported the neuron theory, which held that the nervous system consists of a network of discrete nerve fibers that end in terminal "buttons," which never actually touch the surrounding nerve cells. Up until that time, the majority of scientists were "reticularists," who held that the nervous system formed a continuous and interconnected system. Golgi was among these, and the rivalry between the two scientists was intense. Ramón y Cajal published fierce and relentless attacks both on this theory and on the scientists who held it.

Based on his studies, Ramón y Cajal became convinced that the conduction of nerve impulses occurs in one direction only—a postulate since formalized as the law of dynamic polarization. He also conducted important research on the tissues of the inner ear and the eye, as well as the tissues of the grey matter of the brain, establishing a cellular basis for the localization of different functions within the brain. This research has formed the physiological basis for the understanding of human psychology, intelligence, and memory.

Ramón y Cajal was a prolific writer and he published many articles, textbooks, and research monographs. In 1896, he established a journal of microbiology and published his *Manual de Anatomia Pathologica General* ("Manual of General Pathologic Anatomy"). His major neurohistological work, *Textura del Systema Nervioso del Hombre y de los Vertebrados* ("Texture of the Nervous System of Man and Vertebrates"), was published from 1899 to 1904. These publications were generally printed in Spanish, often at his own expense, and they were largely ignored by the international scientific community.

His struggle for due recognition of the importance of his work came to an end in 1906, when he shared the Nobel Prize in physiology or medicine with his rival Golgi for their work on the structure of the nervous system. In an apparent effort to emphasize what the two scientists had in common, rather than their area of disagreement, they were described by the prize committee as "the principal representatives and standard-bearers of the modern science of neurology." But the tension between them over the reticular doctrine was still evident on the awards platform.

Later Research and Writing

In the same year he received the prize, Ramón y Cajal turned to the problem of the degeneration of tissue in the nervous system and the regeneration of nerve fibers that had been severed. The result of these studies, the two-volume *Estudios Sobre la Degeneracion y Regeneracion del Sistema Nervioso* ("Studies on the Degeneration and Regeneration of the Nervous System"), was published in 1913 and 1914. In 1913, Ramón y Cajal also developed a gold-based method of staining neuroglia; he was able to use this to classify cell types in these tissues. This research provided the basis for the medical treatment of tumors and pathological tissues in the nervous system. A tireless researcher, Ramón y Cajal also studied the eyes and vision processes of insects.

Ramón y Cajal, a patriot, was always sensitive to the international and scientific reputation of Spain and the Spanish language—issues that had a significant impact on the dissemination of his research. It was thus fitting that in 1920 King Alfonso XIII commissioned the construction of the Instituto Cajal, which secured Madrid's position as an international histological research center. Ramón y Cajal worked at this institute named in his honor from 1922 until his death. In addition to sharing the Nobel Prize, Ramón y Cajal received numerous awards and honors, including the Fauvelle Prize of the Society of Biology in Paris in 1896; the Rubio Prize in 1897; the Moscow Prize in 1900; the Martinez y Molina Prize in 1902; the Helmholtz Gold Medal of the Royal Academy of Berlin in 1905; and the Echegaray Medial in 1922. He also received honorary degrees from various foreign universities and held memberships in scientific societies worldwide. The Spanish government bestowed an impressive series of posthumous honors on him, including the republication of his works.

Ramón y Cajal married Silveria Fananas Garcia in 1880. They had three daughters and three sons. In addition to drawing, his hobbies included chess and photography, which he pursued as single-mindedly as his research. In a merging of his work and recreational interests, Ramón y Cajal developed his own photographic process for the reproduction of his delicate histological drawings.

Between 1901 and 1917, Ramón y Cajal published the installments of his autobiographical *Recuerdos de mi Vida* ("Recollections of My Life"). His other published works include the anecdotal *Charlas de Cafe* ("Conversations at the Cafe") and *El Mundo Visto a los Ochenta Años* ("The World as Seen at Eighty"). Ramón y Cajal died in Madrid on October 18, 1934.

SELECTED WRITINGS BY RAMÓN Y CAJAL:

Books

Manual de Anatomia Pathologica General (title means "Manual of General Pathologic Anatomy"), Moya (Madrid), 1896.

Textura del Systema Nervioso del Hombre y de los Vertebrados (title means "Texture of the Nervous System of Man and Vertebrates"), Moya (Madrid), 1899–1904.

Estudios Sobre la Degeneracion y Regeneracion del Sistema Nervioso, 1913–14, translated by Raoul M. Day as *Degeneration and Regeneration of the Nervous System,* Oxford University Press (London), 1928.

Recollections of My Life, two volumes, 1937, Massachusetts Institute of Technology (Cambridge, MA), 1966.

SOURCES:

Books

Cannon, Dorothy F., *Explorer of the Human Brain: The Life of Santiago Ramón y Cajal,* H. Schuman, 1949.

Dictionary of Scientific Biography, Scribner's, 1975, pp. 273–76.

Shepherd, Gordon M., *Foundations of the Neuron Doctrine,* Oxford University Press, 1992.

Nobel Prize Winners, H. W. Wilson, 1987, pp. 852–55.

Periodicals

Knudtson, Peter, "Painter of Neurons," *Science,* September 1985, pp. 66–72.

—*Sketch by David Sprinkle*

William Ramsay
1852-1916
English chemist

The first two decades of William Ramsay's career were spent on a variety of comparatively insignificant studies, including work on the alkaloids, water loss in salts, the solubility of gases in solids, and a class of organic compounds known as the diketones. It was not until 1892 that he became engaged in the line of research for which he was eventually to win a Nobel Prize, the study of the inert gases. Those studies were to occupy Ramsay for most of the next decade and to win him worldwide fame for his participation in the discovery of five new chemical elements.

Ramsay was born on October 2, 1852, at Queen's Crescent, Glasgow, Scotland. He was the only child of William Ramsay, a civil engineer, and the former Catharine Robertson, who came from a family of physicians. In spite of this scientific background, young William showed no particular interest in the sciences and had a classical liberal education at Glasgow Academy.

When he entered the University of Glasgow at the age of fourteen in 1866, Ramsay chose to remain in a classical curriculum that included literature, logic, and mathematics, thinking that he might join the clergy. Over a period of time, however, his interests shifted toward the sciences and, from 1869 to 1870, he worked as an apprentice to a local chemist, Robert Tatlock. At the end of this period, Ramsay was ready to make a commitment to a career in chemistry, and in 1871 he enrolled in a doctoral program at the University of Tübingen under the noted organic chemist Rudolf Fittig. Ramsay received his Ph.D. from Tübingen only a year later at the early age of nineteen for a study of toluic and nitrotoluic acids.

After receiving his degree, Ramsay returned to Glasgow and became a research assistant at Anderson's College (later the Royal Technical College). At Anderson's, Ramsay's work dealt primarily with organic chemistry, especially with compounds related to quinine and cinchonine. Six years later, in 1880, he was appointed professor of chemistry at University College, Bristol (later, Bristol University). During his seven years at Bristol, Ramsay worked with an assistant, Sydney Young, on the relationships between the physical properties of a liquid and the liquid's molecular weight.

Resolves the Puzzle of Nitrogen's Atomic Weight

Ramsay's appointment in 1887 as professor of chemistry at University College, London, marked a turning point in his career. For a few years he continued to work on a variety of problems, such as surface tension, the metallic compounds of ethylene, and the atomic weight of boron. But then, in late 1892, Ramsay was confronted with a puzzle that was to captivate him. That puzzle went back to a discovery made by Henry Cavendish in 1785. Cavendish had found that the compete removal of oxygen and nitrogen from a sample of air still left a small bubble of some additional unknown gas. The puzzle was confounded by the work of **Robert Strutt** (Lord Rayleigh) in the late 1880s that showed the density of nitrogen to be slightly different depending on whether the gas came from air or from a compound of nitrogen.

Ramsay decided to resolve this dilemma. He began by removing all of the nitrogen and oxygen from a sample of air by burning magnesium metal (which reacts with both) in the air. He found a small bubble of gas, similar to that reported by Cavendish a century earlier. But then Ramsay took an additional step that Cavendish could not have taken: he did a spectroscopic analysis of the gas bubble. The result of that analysis was a set of spectral lines that had never been seen before—the gas bubble was clearly a new element. Because of the inertness of the element, Ramsay suggested the name argon for the element, from the Greek *argos,* for "lazy."

Begins the Search for Other Inert Gases

The discovery of argon immediately posed new research possibilities. Determination of the element's atomic weight placed it between chlorine and potassium in the periodic table. Clearly the element was located in a new column in the table, a column that Dmitri Ivanovich Mendeleev could never have imagined when he proposed the periodic law in 1869. The challenge that Ramsay recognized was to locate other members of this new chemical family, those that made up column "0" (or column 18) in the periodic table.

Shortly after announcing the discovery of argon, Ramsay heard about another inert gas that had been discovered by the American chemist William Hillebrand. To see if Hillebrand's gas might also be argon,

Ramsay heated a sample of the mineral clevite in sulfuric acid and had the gas produced tested by spectroscopic analysis. The results of that analysis showed that the gas was *not* argon, but it did have the same spectral lines as those of an element discovered in the sun in 1868 by Pierre Janssen and Joseph Lockyer, an element they had named helium. Ramsay's research showed that helium also existed on the Earth.

Over the next few years, Ramsay looked for the remaining missing inert gases in various minerals, always without success. Then in 1898 he decided on another approach. He and a colleague, Morris Travers, prepared fifteen liters of liquid argon, which they then allowed to evaporate very slowly. Eventually they identified three more new gases, krypton, neon, and xenon, which they announced to the world on June 6, June 16, and September 8, 1898, respectively.

Ramsay remained at London until his retirement in 1912. During the last decade of his tenure there, he became increasingly interested in radioactivity. Among his discoveries in this field was one made with **Frederick Soddy** in 1903, namely that helium is always a product of the radioactive decay of radium. This discovery was later explained when it was found that the alpha particles emitted by a radioactive substance are actually positively charged helium ions. In conjunction with Robert Whytlaw-Gray, Ramsay also determined the atomic weight of the one inert gas in whose discovery he was not involved, radon.

Ramsay was married to Margaret Buchanan in August, 1881; they had two children. After the outbreak of World War I, Ramsay attempted to carry on chemical research for military applications, but his health failed rapidly and he died on July 23, 1916, at his home in Hazlemere, Buckinghamshire, England. In addition to the 1904 Nobel Prize in chemistry for his discovery of the rare gases, Ramsay was awarded the 1895 Davy Medal of the Royal Society and the 1903 August Wilhelm von Hofmann Medal of the German Chemical Society. He was made a fellow of the Royal Society in 1888 and was knighted in 1902.

SELECTED WRITINGS BY RAMSAY:

Books

Modern Chemistry, J. M. Dent, 1900.
Modern Chemistry, Theoretical and Systematic, Macmillan, 1907.
The Electron as an Element, Rice Institute, 1915.
Elements and Electrons, Harper and Brothers, 1912.

Periodicals

(With J. W. Strutt) "Argon, a New Constituent of the Atmosphere," *Proceedings of the Royal Society,* Volume 57, 1895, pp. 265–287.

(With M. Travers) "On the Companions of Argon," *Proceedings of the Royal Society,* Volume 63, 1898, pp. 437–440.
(With F. Soddy) "Further Experiments on the Production of Helium from Radium," *Proceedings of the Royal Society,* Volume 73, 1904, pp. 346–358.

SOURCES:

Books

Davis, H. W. C., and J. R. H. Weaver, *Dictionary of National Biography, 1912–1921,* Oxford, 1923, pp. 444–446.
Dictionary of Scientific Biography, Volume 11, Scribner, 1975, pp. 277–284.
Hunter, Norman W., and Kimberly Zeigler, "William Ramsay," in Laylin K. James, editor, *Nobel Laureates in Chemistry: 1901–1992,* American Chemical Society and the Chemical Heritage Foundation, 1993, pp. 23–29.
Tilden, W. A., *Sir William Ramsay, K.C.B., F.R.S.,* Macmillan, 1918.
Travers, M. W., *A Life of Sir William Ramsay,* E. Arnold, 1956.
Wasson, Tyler, editor, *Nobel Prize Winners,* H. W. Wilson, 1987, pp. 855–856.
Williams, Trevor, editor, *A Biographical Dictionary of Scientists: Chemists,* Wiley, 1974, pp. 120–121.

—*Sketch by David E. Newton*

Frank Plumpton Ramsey
1903-1930
English mathematician

During his short life, Frank Plumpton Ramsey made important contributions to three fields: mathematics (in particular, mathematical logic), philosophy, and economics. He is perhaps best known for his efforts to deal with some fundamental issues in logic raised by **Alfred North Whitehead** and **Bertrand Russell** in their monumental work *Principia Mathematica.* Those issues involved Whitehead and Russell's theory of types and their axiom of reducibility. Ramsey's work in the field of economics was limited to two published papers on taxation and savings that drew high praise from the eminent economist John Maynard Keynes.

Ramsey was born in Cambridge, England, on February 22, 1903. He was the older son of A. S. Ramsey, a mathematician who later became president of Magdalene College at Cambridge University. Ramsey's mother is described by Nils-Eric Sahlin in *The Philosophy of F. P. Ramsey,* as "active in politics" and a person of "very profound social awareness." Ramsey's younger brother later became Archbishop of Canterbury and his two sisters both graduated from universities.

Ramsey showed an aptitude for mathematics at an early age. He demonstrated special skills in dealing with abstract problems, a promising beginning for one who was to make his mark in logic and philosophy. Ramsey was educated first at home by his mother and then at the Winchester Public School. At Winchester, Ramsey's intellectual prowess quickly became obvious to his teachers and colleagues. In a reminiscence reported by Sahlin, a friend named I. A. Richards recalled how Ramsey learned German; he announced he wanted to do so, went home with a German grammar and a dictionary, and a week or two later he was able to critique Austrian physicist and philosopher Ernst Mach's *Analysis of Sensations* in the author's native language.

After completing his studies at Winchester, Ramsey enrolled at Trinity College, Cambridge. He earned his bachelor's degree in mathematics with first class honors in 1923. He then traveled briefly to Vienna, and upon his return in 1924 he was appointed a fellow at King's College, Cambridge. Although he never earned a Ph.D., Ramsey was soon promoted to lecturer in mathematics at Cambridge (1926) and was then made director of studies in mathematics at King's College. He held these posts until his untimely death.

Contributes to Logic, Philosophy, and Economics

Ramsey's contributions in the field of mathematics rest largely on two papers that he published in 1925 and 1928. The first of these dealt with the efforts of Alfred North Whitehead and Bertrand Russell in *Principia Mathematica* to outline a comprehensive and logical foundation for all of mathematics. Ramsey reinterpreted some of the fundamental premises of the Whitehead-Russell work, and he was able do away with the axiom of reducibility, which Whitehead and Russell had been forced to use to deal with some basic contradictions arising out of their theory of types, which concludes that if classes belong to a particular type, and if they consist of homogenous members, then a class cannot be a member of itself. Contemporaries such as R. B. Braithwaite considered Ramsey's work in this area to be "almost the last word in the treatment of mathematics by this 'logical' school."

In 1928, Ramsey published a paper addressing what was then the most important question facing mathematical logicians, the so-called *Entscheidungs* problem. The focus of this problem was to find a method for determining the consistency of a logical formula. In his paper, Ramsey was able to solve this problem for a certain specified set of conditions: when the axioms, or generally accepted theories, consist of general laws.

John Maynard Keynes has illuminated Ramsey's early powers in economics. Keynes describes how economists at Cambridge were accustomed to bringing their ideas to Ramsey for testing while the young man was still only sixteen years old. Keynes wrote that Ramsey possessed the ability to handle "the technical apparatus of our science with the easy grasp of one accustomed to something far more difficult." Ramsey's actual contributions to economics were also limited to only two published papers, but they were of extraordinary quality. Keynes described the second of these two papers, "A Mathematical Theory of Saving," as "one of the most remarkable contributions to mathematical economics ever made, both in respect of the intrinsic importance and difficulty of the subject, the power and elegance of the technical methods employed, and the clear purity of illumination with which the writer's mind is felt by the reader to play about its subject."

Ramsey's published work on philosophy was even slimmer than that in logic and economics, consisting of a single important paper on universals in the journal *Mind*. But his unpublished works were significant enough to cause Braithwaite to claim that Ramsey's death had "deprived the world of one of its most promising philosophers."

Ramsey was an intriguing and complex individual. He weighed nearly 240 pounds at the time of his death and claimed to take no displeasure in his size. His lectures were popular among undergraduates not only because of his brilliance and clarity of presentation but also because of his subtle humor and booming laugh. He died of a chronic liver disorder on January 19, 1930, at the age of twenty-six. He left behind his wife, the former Lettice C. Baker, whom he had married in 1925, and two young daughters.

SELECTED WRITINGS BY RAMSEY:

Books

The Foundations of Mathematics, edited by R. B. Braithwaite, Routledge & Kegan Paul, 1931.

Periodicals

"The Foundations of Mathematics," *Proceedings of the London Mathematical Society,* Volume 25, 1926, pp. 338–384.

"Mathematical Logic," *Mathematical Gazette,* Volume 13, 1926, pp. 185–194.

"A Contribution to the Theory of Taxation," *Economic Journal,* March, 1927.

"A Mathematical Theory of Saving," *Economic Journal,* December, 1928.

"On the Problem of Formal Logic," *Proceedings of the London Mathematical Society,* Volume 30, 1930, pp. 264–286.

SOURCES:

Books

Gillispie, C. C., editor, *Dictionary of Scientific Biography,* Volume 11, Scribner, 1975, pp. 285–286.

Keynes, John Maynard, *Essays in Biography,* Harcourt, 1933, pp. 294–311.

Sahlin, Nils-Eric, *The Philosophy of F. P. Ramsey,* Cambridge University Press, 1990.

Periodicals

Braithwaite, R. B., "Frank Plumpton Ramsey," *Journal of the London Mathematical Society,* Volume 6, 1931, pp. 75–78.

—*Sketch by David E. Newton*

Norman Foster Ramsey
1915-
American physicist

Norman Foster Ramsey is a preeminent physicist whose research has focussed on the properties of molecules, atoms, nuclei, and elementary particles. The numerous awards and honors he won throughout his career culminated in the 1989 Nobel Prize in physics. Although the prize seemed to recognize a lifetime of achievements in the field, the Nobel committee specifically cited his work in developing a method of measuring the differences between atomic energy levels. His findings were key to the development of the cesium atomic clock, which measures time with an accuracy previously unknown.

Ramsey was born in Washington, D.C., on August 27, 1915. He was named after his father, a graduate of the United States Military Academy who was then a general serving as assistant to the Chief of Ordnance. His mother was Minnie Bauer Ramsey.

After several years in Washington, his father was transferred to the Command and General Staff School in Fort Leavenworth, Kansas. There, Norman Jr. attended high school, distinguishing himself as president of his class. He graduated in 1931. Ramsey studied physics at Columbia University in New York City, where he won the Van Aminge and Van Buren prizes in mathematics. He graduated Phi Beta Kappa from Columbia in 1935 and entered the doctoral program there.

As a graduate student, Ramsey studied at Cambridge University, receiving a B.A. in 1937 and an M.A. in 1941. From 1939 to 1940, he was also a Carnegie Fellow at the Carnegie Institution in Washington. In 1940 he received his Ph.D. from Columbia. His thesis, written on research he had performed with the Nobel laureate I. I. Rabi, focused on the rotational magnetic moments of hydrogen molecules. Ramsey and Rabi had found that magnetic moments were dependent on the weight of the nuclei, which led to the discovery of a new force, called the tensor force, between the neutron and the proton.

From 1940 to 1942 Ramsey continued his research as an associate at the University of Illinois. As the United States became involved in World War II, he also worked at the Massachusetts Institute of Technology Radiation Laboratory as the head of a group developing the magnetron transmitter for radar. The result of this work was the three-centimeter-wavelength radar system, the first of its kind, which was widely used during the war. From 1942 to 1945, Ramsey served as consultant to the Secretary of War, at first advising the Air Force on the use of radar and later consulting with the National Defense Research Committee. In this capacity, he was sent to Los Alamos to study the possibilities of building an atomic bomb, and from 1943 to 1945 he was group leader and associate division chief of the Laboratory of the Atomic Energy Project. In 1945 he went with his group to the Tinian Island bomber base to oversee the first atom bombing missions.

During the war, Ramsey remained active in academics. From 1942 to 1945 he was an assistant professor of physics at Columbia, and in 1945 he was promoted to associate professor. After the war he served as executive secretary of the group that founded the Brookhaven National Laboratory in Long Island, New York. He was named head of the physics department there in 1946. In 1947 he took a job as associate professor at Harvard University, becoming a full professor in 1950.

In 1948, Ramsey was named chair of the Harvard Nuclear Physics Committee and director of the Harvard Nuclear Laboratory. In this capacity he was involved with the development of Harvard's first postwar cyclotron, built in 1949. The 125,000,000-electron-volt cyclotron was designed to smash atoms in order to study the particles that constitute atomic nuclei and the forces that keep the particles together. By 1956, Harvard and MIT had joined forces to build another cyclotron, the world's best at the time, producing the fastest artificially accelerated particles. Ramsey chaired the committee that oversaw its construction.

Ramsey's research during these years led to several important discoveries. One was that some atoms which were thought to exist near a temperature of absolute zero, a value based on the Kelvin temperature scale, could actually have temperatures that were below absolute zero. It had previously been thought that temperatures of matter could never have negative values. Parts of the second law of thermodynamics had to be rephrased in order to accomodate this finding.

Discovers Separate Oscillating Fields

Ramsey also challenged the prevailing practice of measuring atomic energy spectra. Beams of atoms had been measured by passing them through an electromagnetic field tuned to the difference between the atom's two energy levels. The resulting pattern of interference was studied to deduce information regarding the structure and behavior of atoms. However, the accuracy of this technique was limited by the need to maintain a constant magnetic field throughout the process. Ramsey attempted to expose atoms to two separate electromagnetic fields—one as the atoms entered the field and another as they departed. The pattern of interference was much more accurate than the one previously produced by using a homogenous magnetic field. His experiments led to the development of the hydrogen maser (for Microwave Amplification by Stimulated Emission of Radiation).

Improving the techniques of studying atoms led Ramsey to the development of his Nobel-winning achievement: the cesium atomic clock. Announced by Ramsey in 1960, the atomic clock is believed to be a hundred-thousand times more accurate than previous atomic clocks, which used gaseous ammonia molecules. Ramsey's clock uses high-energy atomic hydrogen, which could be measured for the first time due to the method of using separate oscillating fields. It is now the time standard used throughout the world, in which the second is defined as the time in which it takes a cesium atom to make 9,192,631,770 oscillations.

Ramsey was awarded half the 1989 Nobel Prize in physics, the other half being divided between Wolfgang Paul and Hans Dehmelt. Ramsey was cited for his work on the hydrogen maser, as well as the atomic clock. Daniel Kleppner, with whom Ramsey often collaborated, told *Science* magazine: "His work was seminal in the theory of chemical shifts, which underlies the use of the magnetic resonance imaging units in hospitals."

Kleppner also called Ramsey a "statesman of science," and World War II was not the end of his government service. In 1958, Ramsey was named Scientific Advisor to the North Atlantic Treaty Organization. He took a leave from Harvard to head an advisory committee which oversaw all NATO activities in research and applied science. In the late 1970s he was again asked to be a government adviser, and he became the co-chairman of a federal committee to study the possible practical uses of cold nuclear fusion.

In addition to the Nobel Prize, Ramsey also received the Lawrence Award in 1960, and the Davisson-Germer Prize from the American Physical Society in 1974. He was awarded the Karl Compton Prize from the American Institute of Physics, the Rumford Prize, and the National Medal of Science, all in 1985. He was elected to the National Academy of Sciences in 1952.

Ramsey married Elinor Stedman Jameson in 1940; she died in 1983. They had four daughters. In 1985, Ramsey married again, this time to Ellie Welch. He is now Higgins Professor of Physics, Emeritus, at Harvard University.

SELECTED WRITINGS BY RAMSEY:

Books

Nuclear Moments, Wiley, 1953.
Molecular Beams, Oxford University Press, 1955.

Periodicals

"A New Molecular-Beam Resonance Method," *Physical Review,* Volume 76, 1949, p. 996.
"A Molecular-Beam Resonance Method with Separated Oscillating Fields," *Physical Review,* Volume 78, 1950, pp. 695–699.

SOURCES:

Books

Current Biography, H. W. Wilson, 1993, pp. 351–353.
McGraw-Hill Modern Men of Science, McGraw-Hill, 1966, pp. 387–388.

Periodicals

New York Times, February 6, 1958, pp. 1, 8.
New York Times, October 13, 1989, p. 10.

Science, Volume 246, October 20, 1989, pp. 327–328.

—Sketch by Dorothy Barnhouse

Lucie Randoin
1888-1960
French physiologist

Lucie Randoin is best known for work which demonstrates the role of vitamins in the human diet. She did much of her ground-breaking research on vitamins during the 1920s, when scientists were beginning to understand their relationship to nutrition. Randoin spent years examining both vitamins and blood sugars, and her findings paved the way for a better understanding of how different substances affect human physiology.

Lucie Fandard was born in 1888 in Boeurs-en-Othe, France. She attended schools in Paris and distinguished herself in science, particularly physiology, botany, and chemistry. Receiving a degree in physiology, she became the first woman to compete for a Natural Sciences fellowship, which was awarded to her in 1911 (another individual who received a fellowship was Arthur Randoin, Lucie's future husband). She went on to the University of Clermont-Ferrand, studying general physiology and the physiology of nutrition under Dr. A. Dastre. During World War I Randoin served as Dastre's assistant and, around 1917, began research on the still-vague substances known as vitamins. The work of such scientists as Dutch physician **Christian Eijkman**, British biochemist **Sir Frederick Gowland Hopkins**, and American biochemists **Elmer McCollum** and **Marguerite Davis** established the existence of vitamins, which are essential for adequate nutrition. Randoin was intrigued by how vitamins affect the human metabolism, and her curiosity sparked a lifelong interest in the topic.

Randoin received her doctorate in science in 1918. As World War I was drawing to a close, Dastre disappeared and the loss to Randoin was personal as well as professional—Dastre had enthusiastically encouraged and supported her work. She then went on to the laboratory of the Oceanographic Institute in Paris, where she continued her work on vitamins. In 1920 Randoin started working at the Physiology Laboratory of the Research Center of the Ministry of Agriculture, and became its director in 1924. During the 1920s she demonstrated how vitamins B and C affect the body's use of sugars and other chemicals. In addition, Randoin studied the composition of vitamins, producing research which further assisted scientists in understanding how the substances function.

Randoin remained at the Agricultural Research Center until 1953 (in 1942, however, she had also become director of the Institute of Nutritional Science, a position she held until her death). Over the four decades of Randoin's career, her work helped illustrate the roles of specific vitamins, the proper amount required for good health, the role of vitamins as a form of preventive medicine, and how such factors as age and illness affect the body's use of nutrients.

Besides helping to found a national school for dietary studies which trained students to become dieticians in hospitals and cafeterias, Randoin created a set of quality standards for vitamins used in foods and formed a nutritional information service. In 1931 and 1934 she was the official French representative to international conferences on vitamin standardization. She was a member of the French Biological Society and served as president of the French Society of Biological Chemistry as well as general secretary of the Institute of Nutritional Hygiene. She was also named a commander of the Legion d'Honneur (at a time when few women where so honored). Randoin died on September 13, 1960, after a lengthy illness.

SELECTED WRITINGS BY RANDOIN:

Books

(With Henri Simmonet) *Les Données et les Inconnus du Problème Alimentaire* (title means "Facts and Unknowns About Nutrition Problems"), Les Presses Universitaires, 1927.
(With Simmonet) *Les Vitamines,* A. Colin, 1932.

SOURCES:

Periodicals

Fabre, René, "Nécrologie: Lucie Randoin," *La Presse Medicale,*
Volume 68, Number 54, December 3, 1960, pp. 2109–2110.

—Sketch by George A. Milite

C. N. R. Rao
1934-
Indian chemist

An Indian professor of chemistry, C. N. R. Rao has been instrumental in the worldwide research into superconductivity. Superconductivity occurs when certain metals experience a total loss of electrical resistance, turning them into superconductors capable of carrying currents without any loss of energy. Electrical transmission through wires normally involves a substantial loss of energy; with superconductivity, this transmission could be vastly improved, saving costs. So far, superconductivity has occurred only at extremely cold temperatures, barring its use in commercial applications. Scientists have for years been working to create the phenomenon at normal temperatures.

Chintamani Nagesa Ramachandra Rao was born on June 30, 1934, in Bangalore, India, the son of Hanumantha Nagesa and Nagamma Nagesa Rao. In 1953 he earned a master's degree from Banares Hundu University; in 1958, a doctor of philosophy degree from Purdue University. In 1958 he became a research chemist at the University of California at Berkeley, returning to India in 1959 to work as a lecturer at the Indian Institute of Science in Bangalore. In 1960 he married Indumati. They have two children, Suchitra and Sanjay.

From 1963–76, Rao was a professor of chemistry at the Indian Institute of Technology in Kanpur. He served as head of the chemistry department from 1964 to 1968, and was dean of research for three years. He was chairman of the Solid State and Structural Chemistry Unit and Materials Research Laboratory at the Indian Institute of Science in Bangalore between 1976–84. Since 1984, Rao has been the director of the Institute of Science. Concurrent with his academic positions in India, Rao was a visiting professor at Purdue University in 1967–68, at Oxford University in 1974–75, and he held a fellowship at King's College of Cambridge University in 1983.

Conducts Superconductivity Research

Since its discovery in 1911 by **Heike Kamerlingh-Onnes**, scientists had considered superconductivity to be a laboratory curiosity, able to be produced only at temperatures approaching absolute zero. In 1986, however, physicists **J. George Bednorz** and **K. Alex Müller** discovered an alloy that was superconductive at 30°K, a much higher temperature than previously known. This discovery led a number of scientists to examine the question. In 1987, **Paul** **Ching-Wu Chu** found an alloy that was superconductive at an even higher temperature, 95°K.

In 1989 three researchers at Purdue University—Jurgen Honig, Zbigniew Kąkol and Józef Spałek—discovered a superconductive material that did not contain copper as part of the alloy. All previous materials were copper-oxide based; the Princeton researchers used nickel oxide, the first time such a compound had been successfully utilized as a superconductor. While initial results of the experiments were still being analyzed, and the crystalline structure of the compound was still a mystery, Rao conducted similar tests with nickel oxide compounds at the Indian Institute of Science and confirmed their superconductivity. His research on the chemical properties of superconductive materials resulted in the publication of three books, *Chemical and Structural Aspects of High Temperature Superconductors*, 1988, *Bismuth and Thalium Cuprate Superconductors*, 1989, and *Chemistry of High Temperature Superconductors*, 1991. During his career Rao has published more than 25 books and 700 research papers.

Contributions Are Well Rewarded

Rao has received numerous awards for his contributions to chemistry, including the Marlow Medal of the Faraday Society of London in 1967, the Jawaharlal Nehru fellowship in 1973, the American Chemical Society Centennial foreign fellow in 1976, the Indian Chamber of Commerce and Industry Award for Physical Sciences in 1977, the Royal Society of Chemistry (London) Medal in 1981, the Padma Vibhushan Award from the President of India in 1985, the General Motors Modi Award in 1989, and the Hevrosky gold medal from the Czechoslovak Academy of Sciences in 1989.

In addition, Rao has received honorary degrees from many universities, including Purdue University in 1982, the University of Bordeaux in 1983, and the University of Wroclaw (Poland) in 1989. For two years, 1985–87, he served as president of the International Union of Pure and Applied Chemistry (IUPAC), a board of chemists who decide such issues as rules for naming new chemical compounds. Rao is an elected foreign member of the Slovenian Academy of Sciences, the Serbian Academy of Sciences, the American Academy of Arts and Sciences, the Russian Academy of Sciences, the Czechoslovak Academy of Sciences, and the Polish Academy of Sciences. He was a founding member of the Third World Academy of Sciences.

SELECTED WRITINGS BY RAO:

Books

Chemical and Structural Aspects of High Temperature Superconductors, World Scientific Publishing, 1988.

(Editor) *Bismuth and Thalium Cuprate Superconductors,* Gordon & Breach, 1989.
(Editor) *Chemistry of High Temperature Superconductors,* World Scientific Publishing, 1991.

SOURCES:

Periodicals

Science, February 10, 1989, p. 741.

—*Sketch by M. C. Nagel*

Sarah Ratner
1903-
American biochemist

Sarah Ratner is a biochemist whose research has focused on amino acids, the subunits of protein molecules. Her use of nitrogen isotopes to study metabolism—the chemical processes by which energy is provided for the body—resulted in the discovery of argininosuccinic acid, a substance formed by a sequence of reactions that take place in the liver. Ratner's awards for her work include the Carl Neuberg Medal from the American Society of European Chemists in 1959.

Ratner was born in New York City on June 9, 1903, the daughter of Aaron and Hannah (Selzer) Ratner. She received her bachelor of arts degree from Cornell University before proceeding to Columbia University for graduate studies, where she received an M.A. in 1927. Ratner worked as an assistant in biochemistry in the College of Physicians and Surgeons of Columbia University until she received her Ph.D. in biochemistry from the university in 1937. Following her graduation she was appointed a resident fellow at the College of Physicians and Surgeons and rose to the position of assistant professor. In 1946 she became an assistant professor of pharmacology at the New York University College of Medicine in New York City. Later, she became associated with the New York City Public Health Research Institute as an associate member of the division of nutrition and physiology and became a member of the department of biochemistry in 1957.

In her research Ratner used an isotope of nitrogen to study chemical reactions involving amino acids, particularly arginine. Isotopes are atoms of an element that have a different atomic mass than other atoms of the same element. Through her studies she discovered an intermediate molecule, called argininosuccinic acid, which forms when the amino acid citrulline is converted to arginine. Ratner determined that argininosuccinic acid plays an important role in the series of chemical reactions that occurs in the liver and leads to the formation of urine. This sequence of reactions is known as the urea cycle. Urea, a product of protein metabolism, has a high nitrogen content and is excreted by mammals.

The American Chemical Society honored Ratner with the Garvan Medal in 1961, and in 1974 she was elected to the National Academy of Sciences. In addition, she received research grants from the National Institutes of Health (NIH) for over twenty years, and from 1978 to 1979 she was the institutes' Fogarty Scholar-in-Residence and served as a member of the advisory council. She has received honorary doctorates from the University of North Carolina-Chapel Hill, Northwestern University, and State University of New York at Stony Brook.

—*Sketch by M. C. Nagel*

Dixy Lee Ray
1914-1994
American marine biologist and government official

Through her career as a marine biologist, Dixy Lee Ray developed a concern about both threats to the environment and the need for greater public understanding of science. Her increasing scientific activities in the public sphere brought her to national attention with her appointment by President Richard Nixon to the Atomic Energy Commission (AEC) in 1972. Within a year she was designated to head the AEC as its first woman chair. Later, in 1977, putting into practice her conviction that scientists need to be more active in public affairs, she was elected governor of her home state of Washington.

Ray was born to Alvis Marion Ray, a commercial printer and Frances (Adams) Ray on September 3, 1914, and was one of five girls. Early on, she developed a love of the outdoors and a fascination with marine biology, when the Ray family spent their summers on Fox Island in Puget Sound. She went on to major in zoology at Mills College and graduated Phi Beta Kappa in 1937. One year later, she received her M.A. there and proceeded to teach science in the public schools of Oakland, California, until 1942. She

Dixy Lee Ray

then left to do graduate work on a John Switzer fellowship at Stanford University. Continuing there as a Van Sicklen fellow, she received her Ph.D. degree in biological science in 1945. That year, she started a twenty-seven-year career at the University of Washington, first as an instructor in zoology, then rising to the rank of assistant professor in 1947, and finally to associate professor in 1957. While affiliated with the university, from 1952 to 1953, she was awarded a Guggenheim fellowship.

Conducted Research in Marine Biology

Ray's particular field of marine biology research dealt largely with invertebrates, especially crustacea. She studied the effects of the isopod Limnoria and fungi in damaging submerged wood, and, as an executive committee member of the Friday Harbor Laboratories in Washington in 1957, she was director of a symposium on the damage caused by marine organisms to boats, drydocks, and wharf filings. She also found time to serve as a special consultant in biological oceanography to the National Science Foundation from 1960 to 1962. Ray sailed with the crew of the Stanford University research ship, *Te Vega,* in 1964, as chief scientist and visiting professor in the International Indian Ocean Expedition, which was a multinational exploration of the little-studied environment of the Indian Ocean.

A year earlier, she had accepted the position of director of the Pacific Science Center in Seattle and

converted a collection of six imposing buildings left over from the 1962 World's Fair in that city into an active science center. The complex featured a science museum and a meeting place for scientific symposia. The Pacific Science Center also began to sponsor the prestigious Arches of Science Award, which honors scientists for contributing to the understanding of the discipline by the general public.

When she was first appointed to the Atomic Energy Commission, she admitted that she had to learn a great deal more about the potential and problems of atomic energy. Because of the long-term limitations of the fossil fuel supply, she was convinced that atomic power plants could serve as an invaluable source of energy. She proposed a multibillion-dollar program to develop new sources of nuclear power and to generate new ways of converting coal to gaseous and liquid fuels. She also campaigned to eliminate defects in atomic power plants. Her own interest in protecting the environment often led her into disagreement with environmental groups, which she considered "too strident." She expressed outspoken views on the subject in two books, *Trashing the Planet* (1990), and *Environmental Overkill* (1993), as well as in magazine articles and television interviews.

Ray received honorary degrees from her alma mater, Mills College, as well as from a number of other colleges and universities. Among the many other honors she received was the Clapp Award in Marine Biology in 1958, the Seattle Maritime Award in 1967, the Frances K. Hutchinson Medal for Service in Conservation in 1973, the United Nations Peace Medal in 1973, the Francis Boyer Science Award in 1974, and the American Exemplar Medal of the Freedom Foundation at Valley Forge in 1978. She was a member of many scientific societies and was elected a foreign member of the Swedish Academy of Science and the Danish Royal Society for Natural History. Among her hobbies was the study of American Indians, which resulted in a collection of artifacts from the Kwikseutanik tribe. The tribe welcomed her as an honorary member with the name Oo'ma, signifying Great Lady. On the occasion of her death from bronchial complications at the age of seventy-nine, the *New York Times* obituary of January 3, 1994, which ran the day after her death, acknowledged that she showed her mettle early at the age of twelve, when she became the youngest girl to climb Washington's highest peak, Mount Rainier.

SELECTED WRITINGS BY RAY:

Books

(Editor) *Marine Boring and Fouling Organisms,* University of Washington Press, 1959.
(With Louis R. Guzzo) *Trashing the Planet,* Regnery Gateway (Washington, D.C.), 1990.

(With Guzzo) *Environmental Overkill,* Regnery Gateway (Washington, D.C.), 1993.

Periodicals

(With Daniel E. Stunts) "Possible Relation between Marine Fungi and Limnoria Attack on Submerged Wood," *Science,* January 9, 1959.

"An Integrated Approach to Some Problems of Marine Biological Deterioration and Destruction of Wood in Sea Water," *Marine Biology,* Oregon State College Biology Colloquium, 1959.

SOURCES:

Books

Current Biography, H. W. Wilson (New York), 1973, pp. 345–348.

Periodicals

Gillette, Robert, "Ray Nominated to AEC," *Science,* July 21, 1972, p. 246.

—*Sketch by Maurice Bleifeld*

Grote Reber
1911-
American radio astronomer, engineer, and inventor

Grote Reber is an American engineer and pioneer radio astronomer who built the world's first radio telescope and so spawned the twentieth-century science of radio astronomy. Radio telescopes are antennas that pick up cosmic radio waves—invisible signals from stars, galaxies, nebulae, and other bodies in outer space. Scientists study cosmic radio waves to better understand the nature and origins of the universe and its energy. Reber built his radio telescope in his back yard, at a time when he was only an amateur in the emerging science. Inspired by the work of **Karl Jansky**, who identified the presence of radio waves in outer space, Reber became one of the first scientists to devote his career to the study of radio astronomy and was responsible for much of its early development.

Reber was born on December 22, 1911, in Wheaton, Illinois. As a boy, he exhibited a keen interest in amateur (ham) radio. He attended the Illinois Institute of Technology, graduating as a radio engineer. He went to work as an electronics engineer for a Chicago radio manufacturer, all the while pursing his hobby during the evenings. His hobby became a passion, however, after the discovery in 1932 of short wave radio emissions from outer space by Jansky, a young American engineer working in the Bell Laboratories assigned to determine the cause of static interference with long-distance communications. Jansky observed that the strong steady hissing noise interfering with communication—unattributable to any source on earth—seemed to be coming from the direction of the constellation Sagittarius. He proposed that stars and other bodies in the universe emit energy not only in the form of light, but also in the form of radio waves. When Jansky's findings were published in the *Proceedings of the Institute of Radio Engineers* journal, Reber immediately recognized their significance. In this he was almost alone. Jansky's paper marked the beginning of radio astronomy, and for many years, Reber was the only person working in the field.

Builds Radio Telescope in Back Yard

Determined to investigate Jansky's findings further, Reber built his own paraboloidal radio telescope in his back garden at a cost of $1,300. It was a dish-shaped structure, constructed of two-by-fours and sheet metal and rotated using power generated by a Model-T engine. (The original telescope is now exhibited at the gate of the National Radio Astronomy Observatory in Greenback, West Virginia.) At first, Reber's efforts were confounded, as the dish was designed to receive radio waves of a shorter wavelength than those studied by Jansky. In 1938, he tried receiving waves of a longer length (up to six feet) and at last met with some success. He was able to confirm the presence of what Jansky had termed the "cosmic static" emanating from the Milky Way. While Reber carried out this early work, he continued to work full time at the radio factory. After the Second World War, Reber's work began to receive fairly widespread recognition as more scientists entered the field, and he was able to devote himself completely to radio astronomy.

After confirming Jansky's findings, Reber began to draw up a chart that mapped the source of the radio waves he was receiving. The pattern of radio wave sources on the chart seemed to coincide with the general positions of stars in the sky. He detected strong signals, for instance, from the areas of the constellations Cygnus, Taurus, and Cassiopeia. From bright individual stars, which he expected would send out strong signals, however, he could detect no activity. It became clear to him that luminosity bore no relation to the strength or location of radio waves. Reber concluded that some radio waves originated in the invisible gas clouds of neutral hydrogen between the stars. Others, of shorter wavelength, came from places near stars where ionized hydrogen atoms are found. Still others, of longer wavelength, emanated from the center of the Milky Way galaxy. In 1940, Reber decided to publish his findings. He sent his article "Cosmic Static" to the *Astrophysical Journal,* but the periodical's board of referees voted against publication. However, Otto Struve, the journal's editor, recognized the importance of Reber's findings and decided to accept the article, against the board's wishes.

In 1951, Reber moved to Hawaii, where his work was less affected by interference from man-made radio signals. He used a radio telescope operating at 5.5 –14 meters to locate new sources of radio waves. In 1954, he moved even further afield to Tasmania, where, on a remote 300-acre site, Reber continued to work with a larger version of his satellite dish that could pick up radio waves from distant galaxies. It consisted of eight-story poles, arranged in a giant circle linked by fifty-seven miles of remote controlled wire. With it he was able to design a radio map of the universe from the perspective of the Southern hemisphere. Reber has been described as a pioneer for his work in radio astronomy, particularly for his ingenuity and dogged persistence at a time when he lacked the support of the scientific community. George Seielstad, director of the National Observatory in West Virginia, said of Reber in the *Chicago Tribune,* "[Reber] didn't discover radio astronomy. But he was the only person in the world who pursued it. He did it on his own, with no support, in his own back yard. He did truly admirable work."

SOURCES:

Books

Knight, David C., *Eavesdropping on Space: The Quest for Radio Astronomy,* William Morrow, 1975.
Roger, Piper, *The Big Dish: The Fascinating Story of Radio Telescopes,* Harcourt, 1963.
Verschuur, Gerrit L., *The Invisible Universe Revealed: The Story of Radio Astronomy,* Springer-Verlag, 1987.
Wallace, Tucker, and Karen Wallace, *The Cosmic Inquirers: Modern Telescopes and Their Makers,* Harvard University Press, 1986.

Periodicals

Bagnato, Andrew, "Honoring a Hometown Star: Wheaton Hails Builder of First Radio Telescope," *Chicago Tribune,* October 23, 1985, p. C1.
Sullivan, Walter, "Radio Astronomy, 50 Years Old, Moves toward a New Frontier," *New York Times,* November 17, 1981, p. C1.

—*Sketch by Avril McDonald*

Raj Reddy
1937-
Indian-born American computer scientist

R aj Reddy is one of the world's leading experts on robotics and artificial intelligence. The director from 1979 to 1992 of the Robotics Institute at Carnegie Mellon University in Pittsburgh, Pennsylvania, Reddy was responsible for the operation of thirteen laboratories and three program centers, and oversaw the research performed at the institute on numerous topics related to computer-integrated manufacturing and robotics design. He is currently the dean of computer science at Carnegie Mellon University.

Dabblal Rajagopal Reddy was born on June 13, 1937, in Katoor, India, near Madras. His father, Srdenivasulu Reddy, was an agricultural landlord and his mother, Pitchamma, was a homemaker. His interest in civil engineering led him to study at the University of Madras College of Engineering, where he received his bachelor's degree in 1958. Soon after finishing his undergraduate work in India, Reddy moved to Australia, calling it home for a number of years. While in Australia, Reddy worked as an applied science representative for the International Business Machines Corporation (IBM) in Sydney. His primary job used computers for structural analysis. Although his formal education was in civil engineering, his first employment and early practical experience were with computers, which prepared him for future work in the computer field. Reddy studied for and received a master's degree in computer science from the University of New South Wales in 1961. During his post-baccalaureate education his interest and course of study changed from the civil to the computer engineering disciplines.

Reddy moved to the United States in 1966 and received his doctorate from Stanford in the same year. He became a naturalized citizen and joined the faculty of Stanford University as an assistant professor of computer science. His time at Stanford only lasted three years; in 1969 he moved to Pittsburgh and joined the faculty of Carnegie Mellon University as a professor. It was here that Reddy began his study of the rapidly expanding fields of robotics and artificial intelligence. He was named director of the Robotics Institute in 1979.

Reddy has focused on two areas within the field of robotics: automatons capable of performing manufacturing and assembly-line tasks, and fully functional robots that can perform, understand, and use more complex functions like speech, hearing, and sight. Although the later part of the twentieth century has seen a tremendous growth in the use of robots for assembly-line manufacturing chores, Reddy feels that researchers are still thirty to one hundred years away from creating machines capable of speech and sight. Aiming to make this goal a reality, Reddy developed an interdisciplinary program at the Institute that trains students in mechanical engineering, computer science, and management in order to give them the background they need to design the complex robotics manufacturing systems of the future.

Reddy remains at the forefront of studies in human-computer interaction. His research projects include building robots capable of speech recognition and comprehension systems, and the Automated Machine Shop, a full manufacturing facility using robotics technology. Reddy is also exploring an area he calls "white-collar robotics," that is, robots programmed to perform such white-collar tasks as production scheduling and other management functions. Reddy and his colleagues at Carnegie Mellon also investigate the possibilities for programming robots to make subjective decisions (artificial intelligence), for building robots that can learn from observation, and for designing robots that can work in environments that are hazardous for humans, such as waste disposal sites and nuclear reactors.

A lecturer in his field and contributor to scholarly journals, Reddy was presented the Legion of Honor by President Mitterrand of France in 1984 for his service at the World Center for Personal Computation and Human Resources in Paris. He was awarded the IBM Research Ralph Gomory Visiting Scholar Award in 1991. He is a member of the National Academy of Engineering, and a fellow of the Institute of Electrical and Electronics Engineers, the Acoustical Society of America, and the American Association for Artificial Intelligence, which he also served as president from 1987 to 1989. Reddy married his wife Anu in 1966 and has two children, Shyamala and Geetha. He looks forward to the day when advances in computer and communication technology will allow every person to use computers in their daily lives.

SOURCES:

Periodicals

Dworetzky, Tom, "Reddy's Machine Dreams," *Omni,* August, 1990, p. 80.

Goldstein, Gina, "Shaping the Next Generation of Robots," *Mechanical Engineering,* June, 1990, pp. 38–42.

Other

Reddy, Raj, interview with Roger Jaffe conducted March 25, 1994.

—*Sketch by Roger Jaffe*

Walter Reed
1851-1902
American physician and bacteriologist

Walter Reed, an Army surgeon and medical researcher, helped discover that mosquitoes transmitted yellow fever, an infectious, sometimes fatal, disease. During his career, Reed also made contributions toward the control of malaria and typhoid. Although some questioned his practice of using humans as test subjects for his yellow fever work, his findings saved thousands of lives. In honor of his efforts to control epidemics, the Army General Hospital in Washington D.C. was named after Reed.

The youngest of five children, Reed was born on September 13, 1851 in Belroi, Virginia, to Lemuel Sutton Reed, a Methodist minister, and Pharaba White. His father's ministry took the family to different parishes every few years and, as a result, Reed's early education was somewhat sporadic. In 1865, however, Reed began two years of study under William R. Abbot. He entered the University of Virginia at age fifteen and, a year later, took a medical course. Reed received a medical degree in 1869.

Reed subsequently traveled to New York to pursue additional medical studies at Bellevue Hospital. He earned a second medical degree in 1870, but it was not official until 1872, when he turned twenty-one. In the meantime, Reed secured the position of assistant physician at New York Infants' Hospital, undertook residency at Kings County Hospital of Brooklyn and at Brooklyn City Hospital, and acted as district physician for the New York Department of Public Charities. For a year beginning in June of 1873, he served as sanitary inspector for the Brooklyn Board of Health.

In June of 1874, Reed received a commission as assistant surgeon, first lieutenant, with the U.S. Army Medical Corps and moved to Arizona. Before he left, he married Emilie Lawrence, a woman he had met while visiting his father in Murfreesboro, North Carolina. For the next eleven years Reed worked variously at bases in Arizona, Nebraska, Minnesota, and Alabama. During this time, Reed and his wife had two children, Lawrence and Blossom.

In the 1890s, Reed wished to pursue his interest in pathology. Because army bases did not offer appropriate facilities, he applied for a leave of absence to conduct advanced work in the field. His request was not granted; instead he was transferred to Baltimore to act as attending surgeon. There he took a brief clinical course at Johns Hopkins Hospital and met William Henry Welch, a pathologist who opened the first pathology laboratory in the United States. Under Welch's tutelage, Reed delved into pathology, performing autopsies, conducting experiments, and refining medical techniques. Reed specifically worked on the bacteriology of erysipelas (an acute fibroid disease accompanied by severe skin inflammation) and diphtheria. This work halted when Reed was sent to an army outpost at Fort Snelling, Minnesota, where he was promoted to major and made a full surgeon.

However, when George Sternberg became the nation's surgeon general, Reed returned to Washington as curator of the Army Medical Museum and also taught bacteriology and clinical microscopy at the Army Medical College. At this time, Reed began to make an impact in his field. When a malaria epidemic broke out at Fort Myer, Virginia in 1896, Reed proved that contaminated drinking water—as commonly believed—was not the cause. He noted that many areas of Washington, including the infected section, drew water from the Potomac. Reed also realized that malaria was striking the base's enlisted men, not officers. He traced this to the fact that the enlisted men often traveled to the city via a swamp trail. Reed postulated that "bad air" caused the disease (although it was later determined that mosquitoes spread malaria).

When the Spanish-American War erupted in 1898, Reed volunteered to serve in Cuba. To take advantage of his qualifications, he was instead appointed to chair a board investigating typhoid outbreaks in army camps. Hundreds of new cases—many of which proved fatal—were reported each day. In fact, the epidemic that killed more than fifty times as many soldiers as did combat. The bacillus, or rod-shaped bacterium, was believed to be transmitted by contaminated water, but the typhoid board found that it was passed by flies and contact with infected feces. The board further discovered that the infectious organisms were harbored by carriers—people who showed no signs of the disease. The typhoid board's two-volume report on its investigation is considered a model for epidemiologists.

Confronts Yellow Fever Epidemic

In 1900 Reed was selected to head an army board trying to discover the cause of yellow fever. This disease had spread among army troops in Cuba. In addition, annual outbreaks occurred along the East Coast and in the southern United States, killing thousands of people. Referred to colloquially as yellow jack, the disease was most prevalent in urban areas and was characterized by jaundice, hemorrhaging, fever, bloodshot eyes, hiccups, and dark-colored vomit. Yellow fever regularly hit the same cities during warm weather. By late autumn it was gone.

Alabama physician Josiah Nott postulated that mosquitoes caused the disease, but his evidence was scanty. In 1881 Carlos Finlay, a Cuban physician and epidemiologist who worked with the U.S. yellow fever commission in Havana, suggested that yellow fever was transmitted by *Culex fasciatus* (a mosquito now classified as *Aëdes aegypti*), but he was not taken seriously. Despite these suggestions, Italian physician Giuseppe Sanarelli maintained that *Bacillus icteroides* was the cause. Reed and American army physician James Carroll were assigned to investigate Sanarelli's claim, and they disproved it. A rash of yellow fever subsequently broke out in Havana, killing thousands of soldiers. Reed traveled to Cuba to head a board including Carroll, Jesse W. Lazear and Aristides Agramonte—all physicians with the army medical corps. The board decided to test its theory that mosquitoes transmitted yellow fever.

Finlay secured mosquitoes and mosquito eggs to allow the group to raise the insects. Because animals were not affected by the disease, the board decided to use human test subjects. Participants in the study gave their consent and were paid $100, plus an additional $100 if they contracted the disease. Reed designed and conducted experiments that proved the *Aëdes aegypti* mosquito was a carrier, and not an originator, of the disease. The yellow fever board concluded that the female *Aëdes aegypti* mosquito could only become a carrier of yellow fever if it bit a victim during the first three days of the disease. The mosquito was unable to transmit the disease for two weeks, but could remain infectious for up to two months in a warm climate. The board also discovered that having had the disease provided immunity against further attacks.

During the course of the board's experiments, Lazear was accidentally bitten by an infected mosquito and died twelve days later. He left notes, however, to assist Reed and the others in their experiments. The board induced twenty-two other cases of yellow fever—none of which proved fatal. (Carroll became ill with the first experimental case but recovered.) Although a vaccination against the disease was not developed until the 1920s, yellow fever was virtually eradicated by 1902 in Cuba through mosquito control.

The board's accomplishment not only saved lives, but also paved the way for U.S. ventures in tropical regions of the world. (For instance, the U.S. government insisted that a way to control yellow fever was necessary before construction began on the Panama Canal.) Reed earned special recognition for heading the investigation. Harvard University awarded him an honorary masters degree for his work with the yellow fever board. Reed died November 23, 1902, in Washington following surgery for a ruptured appendix.

SELECTED WRITINGS BY REED:

Periodicals

(With James Carroll) "The Specific Cause of Yellow Fever: A Reply to Dr. G. Sanarelli," *Medical News,* Volume 75, 1899.
(With Carroll) "The Etiology of Yellow Fever," *Philadelphia Medical Journal,* Volume 6, 1900, pp. 790–96.

Other

Yellow Fever: A Compilation of Various Publications. Results of the Work of Major Walter Reed, Medical Corps., United States Army, and the Yellow Fever Commission (Senate document 822 from the Third Session of the 61st Congress), Washington, D.C., 1911.

SOURCES:

Books

De Kruif, Paul, *Microbe Hunters,* Harcourt, Brace & World, 1926, 1953, pp. 286–307.
Kelly, Howard A., *Walter Reed and Yellow Fever,* 3rd ed., The Norman Remington Company, 1923.
Truby, Albert E., *Memoir of Walter Reed, The Yellow Fever Episode,* P. B. Hoeber, 1943.
Wood, Laura N., *Walter Reed, Doctor in Uniform,* J. Messner, 1943.

Periodicals

"Walter Reed: 'He Gave Man Control of That Dreadful Scourge—Yellow Fever'," *Archives of Internal Medicine,* Volume 89, pp. 171–187.

—*Sketch by Janet Kieffer Kelley*

Mina S. Rees
1902-
American mathematician

Mina S. Rees is the founding president of the Graduate Center of the City University of New York, and was the first woman elected to the presidency of the American Association for the Advancement of Science. She has been recognized by both the United States and Great Britain for organizing mathematicians to work on problems of interest to the military during World War II. After the war she headed the mathematics branch of the Office of Naval Research, where she built a program of government support for mathematical research and for the development of computers.

Rees was born in Cleveland, Ohio, on August 2, 1902, to Moses and Alice Louise (Stackhouse) Rees. Educated in New York public schools, Rees received her A.B. summa cum laude from Hunter College in New York City in 1923, and taught at Hunter College High School from 1923 to 1926. She completed an M.A. at the Teacher's College of Columbia University in 1925, and became an instructor at the Mathematics Department of Hunter College the following year. She continued her training in mathematics at the University of Chicago, where she received a fellowship for 1931 to 1932, and earned a Ph.D. in mathematics in 1931 with a dissertation on abstract algebra. Returning to Hunter, Rees was promoted to assistant professor in 1932 and associate professor in 1940.

In 1943, in the midst of World War II, Rees joined the government as a civil servant, working as executive assistant and a technical aide to Warren Weaver, the chief of the Applied Mathematics Panel (AMP) of the National Research Committee in the Office of Scientific Research and Development. The AMP, located in New York City, established contracts with mathematics departments at New York University, Brown, Harvard, Columbia and other universities. Under these contracts, mathematicians and statisticians studied military applications such as shock waves, jet engine design, underwater ballistics, air-to-air gunnery, the probability of damage under anti-aircraft fire, supply and munitions inspection methods, and computers. In 1948, Rees was awarded the U.S. President's Certificate of Merit and the British King's Medal for Service in the Cause of Freedom for her work during the war.

Joins Office of Naval Research

From 1946 to 1953, Rees worked for the Office of Naval Research (ONR), first as head of the mathematics branch and then, from 1950, as director of the mathematics division. Under Rees, the ONR supported programs for research on hydrofoils, logistics, computers, and numerical methods. Rees emphasized the study and development of mathematical algorithms for computing. The ONR supported the development of linear programming and the establishment in 1947 of an Institute for Numerical Analysis at the University of California at Los Angeles, and also worked with other military and civilian government agencies on the acquisition of early computers. In addition, the ONR funded university research programs to build computers, such as Project Whirlwind at MIT, lead by **Jay Forrester**, and the Institute for Advanced Study project under **John von Neumann**. The ONR also awarded grants to support applied and basic mathematical research.

In 1953, Rees returned to Hunter College as Dean of Faculty and Professor of Mathematics. She was married in 1955, to Dr. Leopold Brahdy, a physician. In 1961, she was appointed dean of graduate studies for the City University of New York (CUNY), which established graduate programs by pooling distinguished faculty from the City Colleges, including Hunter. The following year, Rees became the first recipient of the Award for Distinguished Service to Mathematics established by the Mathematical Association of America. Rees was appointed provost of the Graduate Division in 1968 and the first president of the Graduate School and University Center in 1969. By the time Rees retired as emeritus president in 1972, CUNY's graduate school had created twenty-six doctoral programs and enrolled over two thousand students. During her post-war years at Hunter and CUNY, Rees served on government, scientific, and educational advisory boards and held offices in mathematical, scientific, and educational organizations. She became the first female president of the American Association for the Advancement of Science in 1971. In 1983 Rees received the Public Welfare Medal of the National Academy of Sciences, an award that confers honorary membership in that organization.

SELECTED WRITINGS BY REES:

Periodicals

"The Nature of Mathematics," *Science,* October 5, 1962, pp. 9–12.
"The Mathematical Sciences and World War II," *American Mathematical Monthly,* October, 1980, pp. 607–621.
"The Computing Program of the Office of Naval Research, 1946–1953," *Annals of the History of Computing,* Volume 4, number 2, April, 1982, pp. 102–120.

SOURCES:

Books

Dana, Rosamond, and Peter J. H. Hilton, "Mina Rees" (interview), in *Mathematical People,* edited by Donald J. Albers and G. L. Alexanderson, Birkhauser, 1985, pp. 256–265.

Periodicals

"Award for Distinguished Service to Mathematics," *American Mathematical Monthly,* February 1962, pp. 185–187.

—*Sketch by Sally M. Moite*

Elsa Reichmanis
1953-
Australian-born American chemist

Elsa Reichmanis is a chemist and engineer who has worked to develop sophisticated chemical processes and materials that are used in the manufacture of integrated circuits, or computer chips. She has served as supervisor of the Radiation Sensitive and Applications Group at AT&T Bell Laboratories in Murray Hill, New Jersey, since 1984. As of 1994 she holds eleven patents, and she received the R & D 100 Award for one of the one hundred most significant inventions of 1992. She received the 1993 Society of Women Engineers (SWE) Annual Achievement Award for her contributions in the field of integrated circuitry.

Several of Reichmanis's patents are for the design and development of organic polymers—known as resists—that are used in microlithography. Microlithography is the principal process by which circuits, or electrical pathways, are imprinted upon the tiny silicon chips that drive computers. During the multistage process of chip manufacture, layers of resist material are applied to a silicon base and exposed to patterns of ultraviolet light. Portions of the resists harden, becoming templates for the application of subsequent layers of positively and negatively charged semiconductors that serve as the channels through which electric current travels. Reichmanis received the 1992 award for the development of a resist material called Camp-6, which will be used in the late 1990s to make the next generation of integrated circuits smaller and more powerful than ever before.

Elsa Reichmanis

Reichmanis was born December 9, 1953, in Melbourne, Australia. She completed her undergraduate studies in chemistry at Syracuse University in 1972. She then performed her doctoral studies in organic chemistry, also at Syracuse, as a university research fellow. She earned her Ph.D. in 1975 at age twenty-two with a perfect grade point average. She was a postdoctoral fellow for scientific research at Syracuse from 1976 to 1978, when she left academia for the private sector. In 1978, Reichmanis accepted a position as a member of the technical staff of the organic chemistry research and development department at AT&T Bell Laboratories in New Jersey. In 1984, she was promoted to her current position as supervisor of the Radiation Sensitive and Applications Group at AT&T.

Reichmanis's awards and appointments are numerous. In 1986, she was a member of a National Science Foundation panel to survey Japanese technology in advanced materials. She also served as a member of a National Research Council committee to survey materials research opportunities and needs for the electronics industry. Reichmanis served on the American Chemical Society (ACS) advisory board from 1987 to 1990, and was chair-elect of the ACS Division of Polymeric Materials in 1994. She has authored nearly one hundred publications, and co-edited three books that were presented at American Chemical Society symposia. She was plenary lecturer at the 1989 International Symposium of Polymers for Microelectronics.

An American citizen, Reichmanis is a member of the American Association for the Advancement of Science, and the Society of Photographic Instrumentation Engineering. As the mother of four children, Reichmanis encourages women to embrace both career and family. "If something interests you and you like doing it, then go for it," she told contributor Karen Withem in an interview. "If you ask yourself, 'How can I manage having both a career and children?'—you'll never do it. If you just do it, things will fall into place."

SELECTED WRITINGS BY REICHMANIS:

Books

"Chemistry of Polymers for Microlithographic Applications," in *Polymers for Electronic and Photonic Application,* edited by C. P. Wong, Academic Press, 1992, pp. 67–117.

Periodicals

(With L. F. Thompson) "Polymer Materials for Microlithography," *Annual Review of Materials Science,* Volume 17, 1987, pp. 235–271.

SOURCES:

Reichmanis, Elsa, interview with Karen Withem conducted March 27, 1994.

—*Sketch by Karen Withem*

Tadeus Reichstein
1897-
Polish-born Swiss organic chemist

It is now known that the hormones of the adrenal gland are essential to controlling many challenges to the human body, from maintaining a proper balance between water and salt to responding to stress. Tadeus Reichstein is one of those responsible for this knowledge; **Edward Kendall** and **Philip Hench** also played an important role in these efforts, and the three men shared the 1950 Nobel Prize in physiology or medicine. Reichstein's work has had effects throughout medicine—in the treatments of Addison's disease and rheumatoid arthritis, for example, and in the understanding of the fundamental biochemical processes of steroid hormone metabolism.

The eldest son of engineer Gustava Reichstein and his wife, Isidor, Reichstein was born on July 20, 1897, near Warsaw in Poland. After moving first to Kiev in the Ukraine and then to Berlin, the family settled in Zürich and became Swiss citizens. Tadeus attended the Eidgenössiche Technische Hochshule and graduated in 1920 with a chemical engineering degree. He worked briefly in a factory, then returned to the Eidgenössiche Technische Hochshule where he earned his doctorate in organic chemistry in 1922.

For several years thereafter Reichstein continued to work with his doctoral advisor, **Hermann Staudinger**, who would later win the 1953 Nobel Prize in chemistry. Reichstein's early work focused on identifying and isolating the chemical species in coffee that give it its flavor and aroma. This interest in plant products was to remain with Reichstein throughout his career. He had an early success when he discovered how to synthesize the newly discovered compound ascorbic acid (vitamin C). He published this method in 1933, and later that year Reichstein developed a second method of synthesis which is still widely used in the commercial production of this dietary supplement.

Isolates and Identifies Adrenal Cortical Hormones

In 1934, Reichstein began work on what he originally believed to be a single hormone produced by the cortex or outer layers of the adrenal glands. He soon realized, however, that the adrenals were producing a milieu of active substances. His work began with 1,000 kilograms (more than a ton) of adrenal glands that had been surgically removed from cattle. His first stage of purification resulted in one kilogram (about 2.2 pounds) of biologically active extract. He established that the extract was biologically active by injecting it into animals whose adrenal cortices had been removed; if the compound was active it replaced what was missing as a result of the operation and allowed the animal to survive. The next stage of purification reduced the kilogram of extract to 25 grams (less than one ounce), only about one-third of which proved to be the critical hormone mixture. Instead of one hormone, this sample contained no fewer than twenty-nine distinct chemical species.

Reichstein isolated the twenty-nine species and then individually examined them. He identified the first four which were found to be biologically active, and later synthesized one of them. It was also Reichstein who demonstrated that these compounds were all steroids. Steroids are a group of chemicals which share a particular structure of four linked carbon-based rings; other important compounds having steroid structure include the sex hormones, cholesterol, and vitamin D.

Synthesizes Steroid Hormones

Reichstein built on his earlier work with plant extracts to synthesize the steroid hormones. He and his colleagues developed several different methods to this end, though a process that used an animal waste product (ox bile) proved to be the most economical. One of the most important syntheses that Reichstein accomplished was that of aldosterone, which controls both water balance and sodium-potassium balance in the body. Aldosterone has been widely used in medical practice. Reichstein's work was also critical to the eventual syntheses of desoxycorticosterone, which for many years was the preferred treatment for Addison's disease, and cortisone, which is used for treating rheumatoid arthritis. It was principally for this latter accomplishment that Reichstein shared the 1950 Nobel Prize in chemistry.

Reichstein moved to the University of Basel in 1938 where he was appointed director of the Pharmaceutical Institute; in 1946 he became head of the organic chemistry division. Here he turned his attention to plant glycosides, a group of compounds with wide-ranging biological effects. They are the basis for a number of widely used drugs, and one of these, digitalis, has proven useful in controlling the heart rate. Reichstein was able to identify both the plants and the parts of the plants that contained glycosides, and his contributions were critical for initiating many botanical studies. He was one of the first researchers to realize the value of the tropical rain forests to the pharmaceutical industry. His work has also been pivotal in the field of chemical taxonomy, where the identities of plants are determined through their chemical composition—a method which has a higher degree of certainty than identification through visible characteristics. This technique has had broad applications in the development of both natural insecticides and drugs.

Reichstein was presented with an honorary doctorate from the Sorbonne in 1947. He received the Marcel Benoist Award in 1947, the Cameron Award in 1951, and a medal from the Royal Society of London in 1968. He is a foreign member of both the Royal Society and the National Academy of Sciences.

Reichstein married Henriette Louise Quarles van Ufford in 1927, while still at the Eidgenössiche Technische Hochshule. They had one daughter. He retired from his academic posts in 1967, but continued to work in the laboratory until 1987.

SELECTED WRITINGS BY REICHSTEIN:

Books

(With C. W. Shoppee) "The Hormones of the Adrenal Cortex," *Vitamins and Hormones,* edited by R. S. Harris and K. Volume Thiman, 1943.

"Chemistry of the Adrenal Cortex Hormones," *Nobel Lectures: Physiology or Medicine, 1942–1962,* 1966.

Periodicals

(With A. Gruessner and R. Oppenhauer) "Synthesis of *d*- and *l*-Ascorbic Acid (Vitamin-C)," *Nature,* Volume 132, 1933, p. 280.

(With Volume Denole) "Synopsis of the Chemical and Biological Effect of the Ascorbic Acid Group," *Festschrift Emil C. Barell* (special issue of *Helvetica Chimica Acta*), 1936, pp. 107–138.

(With H. Staudinger) "The Aroma of Coffee," *Perfumery and Essential Oil Record,* Volume 46, 1955, pp. 86–88.

(With J. von Euw, L. Fischelson, J. A. Parsons, and M. Rothschild) "Cardenolides (Heart-Poisons) in a Grasshopper Feeding on Milkweeds," *Nature,* Volume 214, 1967, pp. 35–39.

SOURCES:

Books

Magill, F. N., editor, *The Nobel Prize Winners: Physiology or Medicine,* Volume 2, Salem Press, 1991, pp. 615–623.

—*Sketch by Ethan E. Allen*

Lonnie Reid
1935-
American engineer

Dr. Lonnie Reid became a nationally known expert in fluid dynamics through his work at the National Aeronautics and Space Administration's (NASA) Lewis Research Center in Cleveland, Ohio. For his pioneering work in integrating theoretical and experimental methods in fluid dynamics, Reid was inducted into the Ohio Science, Technology, and Industry (OSTI) Hall of Fame, becoming the first NASA researcher to attain this honor.

Reid was born September 5, 1935 in Gastonia, North Carolina, to Lonnie and Willie Reid. The youngest of seven children, Reid attended elementary and high school in Gastonia. After high school, Reid served in the U.S. Army and was stationed in Korea from February, 1955 until June, 1956. Following his honorable discharge in July, 1957, Reid attended Tennessee State University, where he studied engineering. During the spring of his freshmen year he married Christine Smith and the first of their four sons was born the following year. In June, 1961 Reid received his B.S. in Mechanical Engineering, and in July of that same year, he joined the Research Staff of NASA's Lewis Research Center.

Reid's early work at Lewis included research into improving efficiency and operating ranges for fans and compressors of "airbreathing" engines, and research on cryogenic fluid pumps for rocket engine applications. Reid did not concentrate solely on research, however; he also found time to continue his education, attaining his M.S. Degree in Mechanical Engineering from the University of Toledo, Ohio, in June, 1974. In 1978 Reid moved on to Lewis' Compressor Branch, serving first as Head of the Small Compressor Section and then as Head of the Multistage Compressor Section. He left the Compressor Branch to join the Altitude Wind Tunnel Research Office in 1984, where he spent two years as Head of the Aerodynamic Section.

Earns Rapid Promotions

The next few years were very active for Reid; in the span of three years he was promoted three times, with his responsibilities increasing with each change. In 1986 he became Chief of the Computational Applications Branch where he was responsible for coordinating and directing work on computational fluid dynamics (CFD) codes. CFD codes are a means of modeling or simulating fluid flow. These codes enable computer analyses of propulsion system components to be performed. The work conducted under Reid involved verifying the accuracy of the CFD codes, then applying these codes to the analysis and design of aeropropulsion system components.

Reid became Chief of the Turbomachinery Technology Branch in 1987, directing research focused on flow physics in turbomachinery for gas turbine engines. Results of this research were applied to a wide variety of aircraft, including supersonic cruise and general aviation aircraft. A year later Reid became Chief of the Internal Fluid Mechanics Division. In this position he was responsible for research designed to advance the state-of-technology concerning the fluid mechanics in advanced aerospace propulsion system components. The program's goal was to transfer the developed technologies to the civilian U.S. propulsion industry. Even with the rigors of adjusting to new responsibilities, Reid still found time to continue his education—in December, 1989, Reid received his Ph.D. in Engineering Science from the University of Toledo. Besides being honored by the OSTI Hall of Fame in February, 1993, Reid received the NASA Exceptional Service Medal in 1989, and was named Tennessee State University's Outstanding Mechanical Engineering Alumnus in 1985. He has authored more than twenty-five technical papers on transonic compressors for advanced gas turbine engines. In November, 1993, after thirty-two years of service, Reid left Lewis Research Center and joined NYMA Inc., where he continues to pursue research in fluid dynamics.

SELECTED WRITINGS BY REID:

Periodicals

"Experimental Evaluation of the Effects of a Blunt Leading Edge on the Performance of a Transonic Rotor," *Transactions of the ASME: Journal of Engineering for Power,* July, 1973, p. 199.

"Experimental Study of Low Aspect Ratio Compressor Blading," *Transactions of the ASME: Journal of Engineering for Power,* October, 1980, p. 875.

"Analytical and Physical Modeling Program for the NASA Lewis Research Center's Altitude Wind Tunnel," with J. M. Abbott, J. H. Diedrich, J. F. Groenewig, L. A. Povinelli, J. J. Reimnann, and J. R. Szuch; *NASA Technical Memorandum 86919,* 1985.

SOURCES:

Periodicals

Akron Reporter, February 20, 1993.
National Technical News, April 26, 1993, p. 1.

Other

NASA Biographical Data, Dr. Lonnie Reid, February 1993.
Reid, Lonnie, Resume, 1993.

—*Sketch by George A. Ferrance*

Frederick Reines
1918-
American physicist

Frederick Reines is best known for his discovery of the neutrino, a particle that is created during a nuclear reaction. Since that discovery, he has continued to concentrate on the search for neutrinos and

study their characteristics and behaviors. In later years, Reines studied the possibility of proton decay, an experiment whose negative results have had important significance for elementary particle theory.

Reines was born in Paterson, New Jersey, on March 16, 1918. His father was Israel Reines and his mother was Gussie Cohen Reines. After graduation from high school in 1935, Reines enrolled at the Stevens Institute of Technology, from which he earned a B.S. in mechanical engineering in 1939 and an M.A. in science in 1941. He then went to New York University, where he was awarded his Ph.D. in theoretical physics in 1944. His first job was at the Los Alamos Scientific Laboratory, where he was first a staff member and later a group leader responsible for studying the blast effects of nuclear weapons. In 1951, he was director of Operation Greenhouse, a group of experiments related to the testing of nuclear weapons at Eniwetok Atoll in the South Pacific.

Discovers the Neutrino

It was during his association with Los Alamos that Reines made the discovery for which he has become most famous, the detection of the neutrino. The neutrino had been predicted by **Wolfgang Pauli** in 1931 as a way of solving a puzzling nuclear phenomenon. When a beta particle is emitted from an unstable nucleus during beta decay (a radioactive nuclear interaction), the energy it carries away is insufficient to account for the energy lost within the nucleus itself. In order to account for this discrepancy, Pauli suggested that a second particle was formed that appropriated the energy discrepancy. **Enrico Fermi** later named this particle the neutrino. The name neutrino ("little neutron") arises from the properties postulated for the particle by Pauli. From the physics of beta decay, it was clear that the particle could have no charge, like the neutron, and no or very small mass; thus it was dubbed a "little neutron."

These properties guaranteed, however, that finding the neutrino would be very difficult. With no charge and perhaps no mass, it would be able to pass through matter (including detection instruments) without undergoing any type of interactions. In the early 1950s, Reines and a colleague, Clyde Cowan, undertook a search for the neutrino. The basis for their research was the assumption that although the chance of a neutrino's interacting with matter was very low, it was not zero. The key to success, they hypothesized, was to focus their detectors on a situation in which very large number of neutrinos would be expected to form, thus greatly increasing the chance of observing at least one reaction.

The best source for observing a flood of neutrinos, Reines and Cowan concluded, was a nuclear reactor. Their first experiments were carried out, therefore, at the Atomic Energy Commission's Hanford Nuclear Laboratory in Washington state. To search for the elusive neutrino, they decided to select one of the many reactions that physicists had hypothesized for it, one in which gamma rays of characteristic energy are generated. They then built a large eighty-gallon liquid scintillator with a bank of ninety photomultiplier tubes (a form of vacuum tube used for detecting very low levels of light) which they placed next to the Hanford reactor. The first evidence for neutrinos began to appear in 1953, but it was not entirely conclusive. Cowan and Reines decided to expand and improve their detection system and to move their experiment to the Savannah River National Laboratory in South Carolina. In 1956, they repeated their experiment there and obtained conclusive evidence for the existence of neutrinos.

In 1959, Reines left Los Alamos and accepted a position as professor of physics and head of the department at Case Institute of Technology (now Case Western Reserve University) in Cleveland. At the same time, he became chair of the Joint Case-Western Reserve High Energy Physics Program. Reines held these positions until 1966, during which time he continued to serve as a consultant at Los Alamos and was also a consultant to the Institute for Defense Analysis (1965–1969) and trustee of the Argonne National Laboratory.

Reines left Case-Western Reserve in 1966 to accept an appointment as professor of physics and the first dean of physical sciences at the University of California at Irvine. Four years later, he was also appointed professor of radiological sciences at Irvine's Medical School. He retired in 1988 and was named Distinguished Professor of Physics, Emeritus at Irvine.

Searches for Neutrinos in Varied Environments

Following his discovery of the neutrino, Reines continued his research on these elusive particles. He later built huge tanks containing the colorless liquid perchloroethylene in a search for atmospheric neutrinos, that is, neutrinos produced by solar cosmic rays in the Earth's atmosphere. That search achieved success, although the number of neutrinos detected was significantly less than the number predicted by current theories. The detectors constructed for the search for atmospheric neutrinos were also used to find neutrinos produced by the dramatic eruption of Supernova 1987A in 1987. (A supernova is an exploding star that, at the height of its luminosity, can be brighter than the sun.)

Reines's research has also involved a search for the possible decay of the proton in nuclear interactions. Although the proton has long been considered a stable particle, some current theories of elementary particles suggest that they may have a very long, but not infinite, half-life. Reines's research sought to

prove that these half-lives could be many billions of years long. Using detection devices that had been successful with neutrino research, Reines has shown that the minimum proton half-life predicted so far is not possible, although still longer half-lives may be.

Reines married Sylvia Samuels on August 30, 1940. They have two children, Robert and Alisa. Among his numerous honors and awards are the 1981 J. Robert Oppenheimer Memorial Prize, the 1985 National Medal of Science, the Bruno Rossi Prize of the American Astronomical Society in 1989, and the Michelson-Morley Award in 1990. Reines also received the W. K. H. Panofsky Prize and the Franklin Medal of the Benjamin Franklin Institute, both in 1992.

SOURCES:

Periodicals

Physics Today, July, 1992, p. 77.

—*Sketch by David E. Newton*

Roger Revelle
1909-1991
American geologist, oceanographer, and environmental scientist

Roger Revelle was a scientist who for more than fifty-five years was associated with the Scripps Institution of Oceanography. In association with the Institution, Revelle and his colleagues laid the foundations for the theory of plate tectonics, which maintains that the Earth's surface is composed of relatively thin plates bordered by earthquake and volcanic zones. He was also one of the first scientists to predict that continual accumulation of atmospheric carbon dioxide would lead to global warming. In addition, Revelle was a leading advocate of science's social responsibility and was influential in urging government leaders to utilize modern science and technology to assist poorer nations in improving their standards of living. Revelle was also highly instrumental in founding the University of California's San Diego campus (UCSD). An outspoken advocate of educational quality, Revelle told *Scientific American,* "We built from the roof first," appointing senior professors before establishing an undergraduate curriculum. "It is by far the most important thing I've

Roger Revelle

ever been involved with," he added. For Revelle's life-long work as a scientist of international repute, President George Bush presented him with the National Medal of Science in 1990.

Roger Randall Dougan Revelle was born in Seattle, Washington, on March 7, 1909, the son of William Roger and Ella Robena (Dougan) Revelle. He grew up in southern California, his family having left the Northwest for Claremont, California, when Roger was still a boy. He attended schools in Claremont, receiving his B.A. in geology from Pomona College (now Claremont College) in 1929. He remained at Pomona, doing graduate work in geology and serving as a teaching assistant. Then, in 1931, while pursuing a graduate program at the University of California, Berkeley, Revelle was recruited to study deep-sea mud at California's Scripps Institution of Oceanography, in La Jolla, near San Diego. At the time, Scripps was a remote research station, but the assignment appealed to Revelle. That same year Revelle married Ellen V. Clark, grandniece of Ellen Browning Scripps and Edward Willis Scripps, the major benefactors of the institution that bears their name.

Revelle served as a research assistant at Scripps until he received his Ph.D. in oceanography in 1936. He was then named to the faculty as an instructor. He was associated with the institution the remainder of his life. He was named an assistant professor in 1941, but before he could become immersed in university life, World War II intervened. Revelle was commissioned a commander in the U.S. Naval Reserves and,

in 1942, was attached to the Hydrographic Office in Washington and put in charge of the oceanographic section of the Bureau of Ships. Following the war he returned to Scripps as a full professor but remained active in Navy oceanographic work. As chief of the geophysics section of the U.S. Office of Naval Research from 1946 to 1947, he supervised scientific measurement of the government's atom bomb tests off Bikini Atoll in the Pacific.

In 1951 Revelle was named director of Scripps, a position he held for thirteen years. Under his leadership the Institution was involved in numerous oceanographic expeditions that laid the foundations for much of modern oceanography. Among his scientific achievements was his innovative work on the upward flow of heat through the ocean floor. Working with other scientists, he built a device to measure amounts of heat being radiated from the bottom of the ocean. His discovery that more heat was being radiated than originally expected led scientists to believe hot material was flowing under the oceans. This discovery was the prelude to the revolutionary theory of plate tectonics, which posits that the earth's crust is made of relatively thin plates that float atop a layer of lava. As new material erupts along ocean ridges, undersea mountain ranges and volcanoes can be created, causing large sections of the ocean floor to shift. This shifting moves the earth's plates, resulting in continental movement, a phenomenon known as continental drift. To further this line of investigation, Revelle became involved in the Deep Sea Drilling Project, which probed the ocean floors. According to the *New York Times,* "Some scientists regard this program as the most productive scientific enterprise ever conducted at sea."

Calls Attention to Global Warming

In 1957, Revelle became one of the first scientists to introduce the concept of global warming. He and a colleague, oceanographer Hans E. Suess, wrote a paper suggesting that the oceans could not absorb most of the carbon dioxide that is poured into the atmosphere when fossil fuels such as coal and gasoline are burned to supply power for industry and automobiles. Predicting a twenty to forty percent increase in atmospheric carbon dioxide levels in future decades, the scientists theorized that long-range climate changes, including a rise in average temperatures on Earth, would be the result—a phenomenon now known as the "greenhouse effect." Increased temperatures could in turn lead to the partial melting of glaciers and a consequent rise in sea levels, coastal flooding, and inland drought. They called the burning of fossil fuels "a large-scale geophysical experiment" and argued for worldwide cooperation in studying global changes in the environment.

Also in 1957, Revelle helped organize the International Geophysical Year of 1957–58, which inaugurated the Space Age and was one of the most ambitious programs of global research ever undertaken. As the result of some of this research, Revelle successfully advocated the institution of yearly global carbon dioxide level measurements from a station on the volcano of Mauna Loa in Hawaii. These measurements are still taken today and are viewed as an authoritative indication of global carbon dioxide levels in the atmosphere.

In 1956, Revelle had begun lobbying the regents of the University of California system for a new campus at San Diego, which would be closely affiliated with the Scripps Institution. Although there was much initial opposition by the regents, with the aid of great local support Revelle's efforts were successful. When the San Diego campus of the University of California was finally established in 1959, Revelle became dean of the School of Science and Engineering, while retaining his directorship of Scripps. As an educator, Revelle held strong views on the state of American education and was determined to make changes. As reported in *Scientific American,* he bemoaned "the god-awful public education too many of our students get in public schools." His educational goal was to separate the San Diego campus into individual colleges so that students and faculty could work more closely in smaller units. Unfortunately, the plan failed. "The faculty didn't give a damn," Revelle said. "Professors are journeyman-scholars with very little loyalty to their institutions. What you have now is a dozen little empires."

Revelle was science advisor to Interior Secretary Stewart L. Udall from 1961 to 1963, an experience that would alter his life. As head of a presidential panel to study the problems of water use in the Indus River basin of Pakistan, he was able to closely observe the problems of Third-World people. Seeing the desperation of millions firsthand left an indelible impression. In 1964 Revelle took leave from UCSD to found the Harvard University Center for Population Studies. His work in Pakistan revealed to him the importance of environmental resources in the study of population growth and improvement of life for those living in poverty in the Third World. "Much to everyone's disapproval," he recalled in *Scientific American,* Revelle and his colleagues concentrated on making resources "a real university subject." As it turned out, he noted, "we were right." Revelle had put into practice his belief that scientists must have a social conscience. He resumed his post at UCSD in 1975. When he led a scientific party to Africa in 1988 to study hunger, he returned with a sense of frustration. "Agriculture is going backward rather than forward," he stated. "It's very, very discouraging." Reversing the trend, he remarked, will require "a whole new green revolution."

Revelle died of complications following a cardiac arrest at the age of 82, on July 15, 1991, in San Diego. He was survived by his wife, Ellen, a son, William Roger, and three daughters, Anne Elizabeth Shumway, Mary Ellen Paci, and Carolyn Hufbauer. When asked how he managed to do so many things in his career, he responded, "Do them in sequence."

SELECTED WRITINGS BY REVELLE:

Books

(Editor with Hans Landsberg) *America's Changing Environment,* Houghton, 1970.
(Editor with Ashok Khosla and Maris Vinovskis) *The Survival Equation: Man, Resources, and His Environment,* Houghton, 1971.
(Editor) *Consequences of Rapid Population Growth,* 1972.
(Editor with David Glass) *Population and Social Change,* Crane, 1972.
Population and Environment, Harvard University Press, 1974.

SOURCES:

Periodicals

Beardsley, Tim, "Profile: Dr. Greenhouse," *Scientific American,* December, 1990, pp. 33–36.
Maranto, Gina, and Allen Chen, "Are We Close to the Road's End?," *Discover,* January, 1986, p. 28.
Sullivan, Walter, "Roger Revelle, 82, Early Theorist in Global Warming and Geology," *New York Times,* July 17, 1991.

—*Sketch by Benedict A. Leerburger*

Dickinson Woodruff Richards, Jr.
1895-1973
American physician

In refining the technique of cardiac catheterization, Dickinson Woodruff Richards made significant contributions to the study of cardiopulmonary function in human patients. In collaboration with his colleague **André F. Cournand,** Richards elaborated upon earlier research by German physician **Werner Forssmann**, leading ultimately to the discovery of how pulmonary efficiency could be measured. For their work, Richards, Cournand, and Forssmann shared the 1956 Nobel Prize.

Richards was born October 30, 1895 in Orange, New Jersey to Sally (Lambert) and Dickinson Woodruff Richards. The legacy of the medical profession was established by his maternal forebears, the Lamberts. Richards' grandfather practiced general medicine in New York City, as did three of Richards' uncles; all either received their training or were otherwise affiliated with Bellevue Hospital or Columbia University's College of Physicians and Surgeons, where Richards himself would eventually study.

Richards received his A.B. from Yale University in 1917, and three months later enlisted in the United States Army, serving in France with the American Expeditionary Force. Upon his return to the United States, he entered the College of Physicians and Surgeons at Columbia; there he completed his M.A. in physiology in 1922 and his M.D. in 1923. Richards immediately received his license to practice medicine and interned for two years at Presbyterian Hospital in New York, spending two additional years there as a resident physician once his internship had expired. In 1927, Columbia University granted him a research fellowship to train at London's National Institute for Medical Research. From 1927 to 1928 he studied experimental physiology, working closely with Dr. **Henry Hallett Dale**, who Richards would later refer to as one of his greatest influences. He then returned to Columbia University's Presbyterian Hospital to study pulmonary and circulatory physiology. In 1930 he became engaged to Constance Riley, a Wellesley College graduate who worked as a technician in his research lab at Presbyterian Hospital. They married in September 1931.

Teams with Cournand to Refine Catheterization Technique

Richards' collaboration with André Cournand began in 1931 at Bellevue Hospital. Basing their research on Richards' concept "that lungs, heart, and circulation should be thought of as one single apparatus for the transfer of respiratory gases between outside atmosphere and working tissues," these two physicians began a long and fruitful partnership. Their initial research involved the study of the physiological performance of the lungs and, in particular, a disorder known as chronic pulmonary insufficiency. Characterized by a malfunction in the heart's tricuspid and pulmonic valves, this defect causes blood to flow backward into the heart. Richards concluded, as had others before him, that it was necessary to be able to measure the amount of air in the lungs during different stages of pulmonary activi-

ty. Thus, he and Cournand unearthed studies done in 1929 by the German physician Werner Forssmann, wherein Forssmann had attempted to measure gases in the blood as it passed from the heart to the lungs.

Forssmann's technique was proven viable when he successfully inserted a narrow rubber catheter through a vein in his own arm and into the right atrium of his heart. This method gave access to blood as it entered the heart—blood that could then be examined in specific stages of pulmonary and cardiac activity and evaluated in terms of rate of flow, pressure relations, and gas contents. Catheterization would allow physicians to measure oxygen and carbon monoxide in blood returning from the right atrium, allowing for accurate measurement of blood flow through the lungs. Richards and Cournand sought to advance Forssmann's technique and to develop a safe procedure by first experimenting on animals. They began their research in 1936, and by 1941 they had successfully catheterized the right atrium of the human heart.

The measurements made possible through cardiac catheterization led Richards to other important assessments about functions of the heart and circulatory system. In 1941 he developed methods to measure the volume of blood pumped out of either ventricle (lower chamber) of the heart, and to measure blood pressure in the right atrium, the right ventricle, and the pulmonary artery, as well as total blood volume. More recent research has employed catheterization to diagnose abnormal exchange between the right and left sides of the heart, such as is present in some congenital cardiac defects. It has also contributed to the development of more sophisticated techniques such as angiocardiography (the X-ray examination of the heart after injection of dyes), which is used to determine whether normal circulation has resumed following a surgical procedure.

Richards and his colleagues also relied on their revolutionary research technique to study the effects of traumatic shock in heart failure and to identify congenital heart lesions. During World War II Richards and his colleagues were asked by the government to study the circulatory forces involved in shock, with Richards serving as chair of the National Research Council's subcommittee. The goal was to measure the effects of hemorrhage and trauma on the heart and cardiac circulation, and to evaluate various procedures for treatment. The most important result of this project was the discovery that whole blood, rather than just blood plasma, should be used in the treatment of shock to the cardiac system.

Richards was passionate about health issues in the social arena as well as in the laboratory: in 1957 he testified before the Joint Legislative Committee on Narcotics Study to suggest the construction of hospital clinics to legally distribute narcotics to recovering addicts; he lobbied for the building of a new hospital to replace the aging Bellevue; he spoke often about the need for constant reform within medical academia; and he supported the crusade to improve health care benefits for the elderly.

In 1945 Richards became the head of Columbia University's First Medical Division at Bellevue Hospital, and at the same time was promoted to the full-time Lambert Professorship of Medicine at the College of Physicians and Surgeons. He served as associate editor of *Medicine, Circulation, The Journal of the American Heart Association,* and of the *American Review of Tuberculosis.* His articles have appeared in many publications, including *Physiological Review, Journal of Clinical Investigation,* and *Journal of Chronic Diseases.*

Richards was elected to the National Academy of Sciences in 1958, and retired from practice in 1961, though he continued to lecture and publish frequent articles for several years. He died at his home in Lakeville, Connecticut on February 23, 1973, after suffering a heart attack.

Research Discoveries Rewarded with Nobel Prize and Other Honors

For their refinement of the catheterization procedure and the discoveries that followed, Richards, Cournand and Forssmann were awarded the Nobel Prize in physiology or medicine in 1956. In addition, Richards also received many individual honors and awards, including the John Phillips Memorial Award of the American College of Physicians (1960) and the Kober Medal of the Association of American Physicians (1970). He was made a chevalier of the Legion of Honor of France (1963), and was a fellow of the American College of Physicians, the American Medical Association, and the American Clinical and Climatological Association. He was offered numerous honorary degrees but accepted only two—Yale University, his alma mater, and Columbia University, where he did most of his work.

SELECTED WRITINGS BY RICHARDS:

Books

Editor, with Alfred P. Fishman, *Circulation of the Blood: Men and Ideas,* Oxford University Press, 1964.
Medical Priesthoods and Other Essays, Connecticut Printers, 1970.

SOURCES:

Books

Biographical Memoirs, Volume 58, National Academy Press, 1989, pp. 459–487.
Current Biography Yearbook, 1957, H.W. Wilson, 1957, pp. 457–459.
Nobel Prize Winners, H. W. Wilson, 1987, pp. 862–863.

—*Sketch by Kelly Otter Cooper*

Ellen Swallow Richards
1842-1911
American chemist

Ellen Swallow Richards was an applied scientist, sanitary chemist, and the founder of home economics. For twenty-seven years she was employed by the Massachusetts Institute of Technology (MIT), where she taught chemistry and developed methods for the analysis of air, water, and consumer products. Her work as a scientist and educator led to improvements in the home and opened the door to scientific professions for women.

Swallow was born on December 3, 1842, in Dunstable, Massachusetts. She was the only child of Peter Swallow, a teacher, farmer, and store keeper, and Fanny Gould Taylor, a teacher. She was educated at home by her parents until the family moved to Westford, Massachusetts, in 1859. There she attended Westford Massachusetts Academy, where she enrolled in mathematics, French, and Latin. In 1863 she graduated from the academy, and the family relocated to Littleton, Massachusetts.

Swallow worked at an assortment of jobs—storekeeping, tutoring, housecleaning, cooking, and nursing—to earn enough money to continue her education. Because of her mother's ill health, she struggled with exhaustion and mental depression for a period of several years.

By 1868 Swallow had saved enough money to attend Vassar college, where she excelled in astronomy and chemistry. Her chemistry professor, convinced that science should be applied to practical problems, contributed to Swallow's developing interest in consumer and environmental science. Receiving a bachelor of arts degree in 1870, Swallow decided to apply to MIT to further her study of chemistry and became one of the first women students at that institution. She received a bachelor of science degree from MIT in 1873. In that same year, after submitting a thesis on the estimation of vanadium in iron ore, she received her masters of arts degree from Vassar. Although she continued her studies at MIT an additional two years, she was never awarded a doctorate.

Swallow married Robert Hallowell Richards, a professor of mining engineering, on June 4, 1875. The couple had no children and were able to devote their full support to each other's professional career. In her leisure time Richards enjoyed gardening, entertaining, and traveling. She also took an active interest in improving her own home. At one time she boasted of having year-round hot water and a telephone.

A Successful Career at MIT

Richards helped establish a laboratory at MIT for women. While still an undergraduate, she had taught chemistry at the girls high school in Boston through a project funded by the Woman's Education Association. With the help of this association, Richards convinced MIT of the need for a women's lab, and in 1876, armed with the title of assistant, she began teaching chemical analysis, industrial chemistry, mineralogy, and biology to a handful of women students. In addition to their traditional studies, the students assisted in testing a variety of consumer products for composition and adulterations. After seven years, in which four students graduated and the rest were accepted as regular MIT students, the laboratory closed.

In 1884 MIT opened a new laboratory for the study of sanitation, and Richards was appointed assistant and instructor in sanitary chemistry. Her teaching duties included instruction in air, water, and sewage analysis. In addition, she was responsible for completing a two-year survey of Massachusetts inland waters (begun in 1887 for the state board of health). Her success in analyzing nearly forty thousand water samples was attributed to her knowledge of methodology, apparatus, and her excellent supervisory and record-keeping skills. The water survey work and her involvement with environmental chemistry were significant contributions to the new science of ecology.

Founder of Home Economics

Richards was a pioneer in the effort to increase educational opportunities for women. She was one of the founders of the Association of Collegiate Alumnae, which later changed its title to the American Association of University Women. She organized the science section for the Society to Encourage Studies at Home, a correspondence school founded in 1887 by Anna Tickenor. Her correspondence with students provided insight into the daily life and problems faced by women in the home. Richards learned that women were seeking help with a wide range of problems, not all of which were scientific in nature, including manners of dress, food preparation, and exercise.

In 1890 Richards opened the New England Kitchen in Boston as a means of demonstrating how wholesome foods could be selected and prepared. In 1899 she organized and chaired a summer conference at Lake Placid, New York, that established the profession of home economics. Conference participants explored new ways of applying sociology and economics to the home and developed courses of study for schools and colleges. Later she helped found the American Home Economics Association and provided financial support for its publication, the *Journal of Home Economics.*

In addition to her work at the sanitation laboratory, Richards consulted, lectured, authored ten books, and published numerous papers, including bulletins on nutrition for the United States Department of Agriculture. In 1910, in recognition of her commitment to education, she was appointed to supervise the teaching of home economics in public schools by the council of the National Education Association. In that same year she was awarded an honorary doctorate from Smith College. Richards died of heart disease in 1911 at the age of sixty-eight.

SELECTED WRITINGS BY RICHARDS:

Books

The Chemistry of Cooking and Cleaning: A Manual for House-keepers, Estes and Lauriat, 1882.

SOURCES:

Books

Ogilvie, Marilyn, *Women in Science,* Massachusetts Institute of Technology Press, 1986, pp. 149–52.

—*Sketch by Mike McClure*

Theodore William Richards
1868-1928
American chemist

Theodore William Richards, a professor of chemistry at Harvard University, was the first American chemist to receive a Nobel Prize. The prize was awarded to Richards in 1914 in chemistry for his accurate determination of the atomic weights of twenty-five chemical elements. He was renowned for his unsurpassed laboratory skill in chemical analysis. His work provided essential fundamental data for practical and theoretical chemists and physicists, and his graduate program at Harvard produced many eminent educators and research scientists.

Richards, the fifth of six children, was born on January 31, 1868, in Germantown, Pennsylvania, to William Trist Richards, a painter of seascapes, and Anna Matlack Richards, a writer and poet. Until he was fourteen, Richards received all his education from his mother, who had little regard for the public schools of Germantown. His interest in chemical experiments began when he was ten; when he was thirteen, he attended lectures in chemistry at the University of Pennsylvania. At the age of fourteen, Richards enrolled in Haverford College as a sophomore and graduated at the head of his class with a specialty in chemistry in 1885. Upon graduation, Richards enrolled at Harvard to study chemistry with Josiah Cooke, a professor whom he had met on summer vacation when he was six years old. Richards received his second baccalaureate, with *summa cum laude* distinction, at Harvard in 1886, and remained to study for the Ph.D. under Cooke's supervision. He received his doctorate in 1888, when he was twenty.

Richards's dissertation research marked the beginning of his study of atomic weights, which formed the major field of investigation in his long career. Richards published over 150 papers on atomic weights, beginning with his doctoral research on the atomic weight of hydrogen. At the time, chemists theorized that all elements were made from hydrogen and that there should be an integral ratio between the atomic weight of hydrogen and other elements. Although the theory called for the ratio of oxygen to hydrogen in water to be exactly 16, Richards's careful laboratory work, which involved difficult manipulations of gases, showed the ratio was actually 15.869 and strongly suggested that the theory was erroneous.

In the 1888–89 academic year, Richards received a fellowship and visited analytical laboratories in Europe. He returned to Harvard to become an assistant in the analytical chemistry course. He was promoted to instructor in 1891, assistant professor in 1894, and full professor in 1901 (after rejecting an offer from the University of Göttingen). He taught analytical chemistry until 1902 and physical chemistry from 1895, after the death of Josiah Cooke. He was chairman of the chemistry department from 1903 to 1911 and director of the Wolcott Gibbs Laboratory from 1912 until his death in 1928.

Measurement of Atomic Weights Recognized with Nobel Prize

The measurement of atomic weights coincides with the beginning of modern chemistry, with An-toine-Laurent Lavoisier's conception of chemical elements and with John Dalton's atomic theory, which established that atoms are the building blocks of matter. The chemists of the nineteenth century had determined the atomic weights of all the known elements, and Dmitry Mendeleyev based his periodic table of the elements on these values. However, all values of the atomic weights at the time were relative values, where ratios of atomic weights were actually determined in chemical compounds, and an error in a crucial ratio meant that the atomic weights of several elements would be inaccurate. For example, if the silver to chlorine ratio in silver chloride was inaccurate, then the atomic weight of sodium from sodium chloride or potassium from potassium chloride would consequently be erroneous.

Richards found that the long-accepted atomic weight values of the French chemist Jean-Servais Stas were incorrect because of several experimental errors which had been previously overlooked. The crucial part of the analysis of atomic weight involves the complete collection of a pure precipitate; Richards showed that Stas's compounds were impure and that Stas had not accounted for all of the chemical product. Richards and his students were able to redetermine accurately the atomic weights of twenty-five elements, and other chemists who had studied with Richards added thirty more elements. In his studies, Richards showed that the geographical origins of the elements does not affect their atomic weights (he determined that terrestrial and meteoric iron have identical values). Richards's determination of physical constants, which were used by all chemists, won the admiration of the chemistry community and led to his Nobel Prize.

Richards's work was also important to the dramatic new discoveries of early twentieth-century scientists in radioactivity and the structure of the atomic nucleus. Richards determined that the atomic weight of ordinary lead was different from that of lead which came from the radioactive decay of uranium. This critical evidence corroborated theories of radioactivity, and because of Richards's reputation for accuracy, the experimental result was readily accepted by many scientists.

In addition to his work on atomic weights, Richards also directed research in physical chemistry. Before he began to teach physical chemistry at Harvard, he was sent to Germany to study with two leaders in the field, Nobel Prize winners **Friedrich Wilhelm Ostwald** and **Walther Nernst**. Richards invented an improved calorimeter for measuring heat in chemical reactions and published sixty papers in thermochemistry. He also contributed to the field of electrochemistry. His sixty graduate students became distinguished professors at other universities and continued the research studies they began at Harvard.

Richards's influence on American chemical research in analytical and physical chemistry was exceptional.

In addition to the Nobel Prize, Richards won scientific awards from many nations. He also served as president of the American Chemical Society (1914), the American Association for the Advancement of Science (1917), and the American Academy of Arts and Sciences (1920–1921). Outside of his scientific interests, he enjoyed sketching, sailing, and golf.

In 1896, Richards married Miriam Stuart Thayer, daughter of Professor Joseph H. Thayer of the Harvard divinity school. Their son William studied chemistry with his father at Harvard and went on to teach at Princeton. Another son, Greenough, became an architect, and their daughter, Grace, married James B. Conant, one of Richards's graduate students. Conant became professor of organic chemistry and president of Harvard University. Richards died in Cambridge, Massachusetts, on April 2, 1928.

SELECTED WRITINGS BY RICHARDS:

Books

"Atomic Weights," in *Nobelstiftelsen: Nobel Lectures: Chemistry, 1901–1921,* Elsevier, 1966.

Periodicals

"Atomic Weights and Isotopes," *Chemical Reviews,* 1924, pp. 1–40.

SOURCES:

Books

Burke, Helen M., "Theodore William Richards," in *The Nobel Prize Winners: Chemistry,* edited by F. N. Magill, Salem, 1990, Volume 1, pp. 197–206.
Fleck, George, "Theodore William Richards," in *Nobel Laureates in Chemistry, 1901–1992,* edited by L. K. James, American Chemical Society, 1993, pp. 100–107.
Ihde, Aaron, "Richards—Corrector of Atomic Weights," in *Great Chemists,* edited by E. Farber, Interscience, 1961, pp. 822–829.
Kopperl, Sheldon J., "Theodore William Richards," in *American Chemists and Chemical Engineers,* edited by W. Miles, American Chemical Society, 1976, pp. 407–408.

—*Sketch by Martin R. Feldman*

Lewis Fry Richardson
1881-1953
English physicist and meteorologist

Lewis Fry Richardson was an English physicist with a penchant for trying to solve a wide range of scientific problems using mathematics. During his career as a scientist and educator, Richardson explored mathematical solutions to predict weather, to explain the flow of water through peat, and to identify the origins of war.

Richardson was the youngest of seven children born to David Richardson, a tanner, and his wife, Catherine Fry, who came from a family of corn merchants. Richardson was born on October 11, 1881, in Newcastle upon Tyne. After completing his high school education in 1898, Richardson studied science at Durham College in Newcastle for two years before entering King's College at Cambridge, where he ultimately earned a doctorate in physics and then later returned to study and receive a degree in psychology. After graduating from King's College, Richardson held a number of positions in the years leading up to World War I. These included working as a scientist for a tungsten lamp factory, the National Peat Industries, Ltd., and serving four years as superintendent of the Eskdalemuir Observatory operated by the National Meteorological Office.

Richardson, who was born into a Quaker family, served with the French army as a member of the Friends' Ambulance Unit during the war from 1916 to 1919. Following the end of hostilities, Richardson returned to England, where he combined his scientific inquiry with teaching. In 1920 he accepted a position as director of the physics department at Westminster Training College. This was followed by an appointment as principal of Paisley Technical College in 1929, a post that he held until his retirement in 1940. Retirement allowed Richardson continue his primary love, research.

Attempts to Predict Weather Mathematically

Richardson began his research looking at practical problems, such as examining the flow of water through peat while he worked for the National Peat Industries, Ltd. Using differential equations, Richardson came up with ways to determine water flow that were far more accurate than other methods. His work eventually led to attempts at developing a system of weather prediction based on newly understood knowledge of the upper atmosphere and the roles played by radiation and eddies, or atmospheric currents which move contrary to main air flow. Richardson's work led to the publication of his book, *Weather Prediction by Numerical Process,* in 1922. Richardson's experiences in France during the First World War also inspired him to probe the causes of human conflict using mathematics, and he published a paper in 1919 on the mathematical psychology of war. Eventually, he enlarged upon this early work in the book *Arms and Insecurity* and went on to complete a mathematical study of the world's wars. This work, which resulted in *Statistics of Deadly Quarrels,* examined the causes and magnitude of these conflicts. In his research, Richardson tried to define the relations between countries with mathematical equations.

Richardson's pioneering use of mathematics resulted in him being elected a fellow in the Royal Society in 1926. Richardson married Dorothy Garnett in 1909. The couple adopted a son and two daughters. He died on September 30, 1953.

SELECTED WRITINGS BY RICHARDSON:

Books

Weather Prediction by Numerical Process, Cambridge University Press, 1922.
Arms and Insecurity: A Mathematical Study of the Causes and Origins of War, edited by Nicolas Rashevsky and Ernesto Trucco, Boxwood Press, 1960.
Statistics of Deadly Quarrels, edited by Quincy Wright and C. C. Lienau, Boxwood Press, 1960.

SOURCES:

Books

Dictionary of National Biography, Oxford University Press, 1971.

—*Sketch by Joel Schwarz*

Owen W. Richardson
1879-1959
English physicist

Owen W. Richardson is best known for his work in thermionics, the emission of electrons from a heated surface, and specifically for the law that describes that phenomenon, now called Richardson's law. For his work on thermionics, Richardson was awarded the 1928 Nobel Prize in physics. In addition, Richardson's investigations into gyromagnetics led to his theory that a body's magnetism is caused by the movement of its electrons, a phenomenon known as the Richardson-Einstein-de Haas effect.

Owen Willans Richardson was born in Dewsbury, Yorkshire, England, on April 26, 1879. He was the eldest of three children born to Joshua Henry and Charlotte Maria Willans Richardson. Young Owen was a precocious boy and, according to William Wilson in *Biographical Memoirs of Fellows of the Royal Society,* "gained so many scholarships and exhibitions that his education cost his parents nothing at all." That education began at the St. John's Church Day School in Dewsbury, continued at Batley Grammar School in 1841, and then at Trinity College, Cambridge, in 1897. Richardson earned first-class honors in 1900 at Trinity in botany, chemistry, and physics, and was awarded his B.A. degree. He then stayed on at Trinity for his graduate studies in chemistry and physics and, in 1902, was appointed a fellow at the college. Two years later he was chosen for a Clerk Maxwell scholarship and was awarded his D.Sc. by University College, London.

Begins Thermionic Research at Cavendish

Richardson's earliest research dealt with the properties of the electron. As early as 1901 he began the studies for which he was to become most famous, thermionics, a term that Richardson himself coined. The term refers to the emission of electrons from a heated metal. In his first studies, Richardson used platinum metal since it had the highest melting point of any readily available metal, allowing him to heat the material to very high temperatures and observe the emission of electrons. When ductile tungsten (which can be drawn out or hammered down, and whose melting point is much higher than that of platinum) became available in 1913, Richardson was then able to extend his work to even higher temperatures.

The emission of electrons from heated metals was first described as early as 1603 by Sir William Gilbert, but was not studied systematically until the late nineteenth century. Then, a number of scientists, including Thomas Edison, described a number of phenomena associated with thermionics. In his own studies with platinum metal, Richardson found that the heating of the metal resulted in the loss of a certain number of electrons for each unit area of surface. In addition, the number of electrons lost from the metal increases exponentially with the temperature. He was able to devise a mathematical formula describing these results, a formula now known as Richardson's law. According to that formula, the current released by a metal is a function of certain characteristics of the metal and the temperature.

Richardson explained the thermionic phenomenon by assuming that heating a metal provides some electrons on the metal surface with enough energy to overcome the attraction of ions in the metal. These electrons then "evaporate" from the metal surface in much the way that liquid molecules escape from the surface of a liquid.

Becomes Professor of Physics at Princeton

In 1906 Richardson was offered an appointment as professor of physics at Princeton University. Before leaving England, however, he was married to Lilian Maude Wilson, daughter of a goods manager at the North Eastern Railway Company and sister of Richardson's fellow student at the Cavendish, H. A. Wilson. The couple's three children, two sons and a daughter, were all born during Richardson's tenure at Princeton.

Richardson continued his work on thermionic emission during his Princeton years, but also studied other phenomena, including the photoelectric effect, thermodynamics, X rays, and gyromagnetics. The latter term refers to attempts to explain various gravitational effects in terms of electromagnetic theory. Although this effort failed in its broadest goals, one phenomenon he did discover was eventually called the Richardson-Einstein-de Haas effect. This effect relates an object's magnetism to the movement of the object's electrons.

Richardson was just about to become a naturalized citizen of the United States when, in 1913, he was offered the Wheatstone Professorship of Physics at King's College at the University of London. He accepted the offer and returned to England just before the outbreak of World War I. During the war, Richardson worked on the development of more efficient vacuum tubes to be used in military communication systems. At the war's conclusion, Richardson returned to his teaching and research at King's College until 1924, when he was appointed Yarrow Research Professor of the Royal Society. This position relieved him of all teaching responsibilities, and he dedicated the next two decades of his life to research. One of the main foci of this research was an attempt to delineate the connections between chemistry and physics. Even after his retirement from the Royal Society post in 1944, Richardson continued his research activities, publishing his last paper in 1953.

Richardson was awarded the 1928 Nobel Prize in physics for his work on thermionics and was knighted in 1939. He served as president of the Physical Society from 1926 to 1928. After his first wife Lilian died in 1945, Richardson married Henrietta M. G. Rupp, a noted physicist who specialized in electron diffraction and luminescence in solids. Richardson died in Alton, Hampshire, on February 15, 1959.

SELECTED WRITINGS BY RICHARDSON:

Books

The Electron Theory of Matter, Cambridge University Press, 1914.
The Emission of Electricity from Hot Bodies, Longmans Green, 1916.
Molecular Hydrogen and Its Spectrum, Yale University Press, 1934.

Periodicals

"On the Negative Radiation from Hot Platinum," *Proceedings of the Cambridge Philosophical Society,* Volume 11, 1901, pp. 286–295.
"The Ionisation Produced by Hot Platinum in Different Gases," *Philosophical Transactions A,* Volume 207, 1906, pp. 1–64.
(With L. Simons) "Note on Gravitation; Experimental Test," *Philosophical Magazine,* Volume 43, 1922, pp. 138–145.

SOURCES:

Books

Biographical Memoirs of Fellows of the Royal Society, Volume 5, Royal Society (London), 1959, pp. 207–215.
Heathcote, Niels H. de V., *Nobel Prize Winners in Physics, 1901–1950,* Henry Schuman, 1953, pp. 278–286.
Wasson, Tyler, editor, *Nobel Prize Winners,* H. W. Wilson, 1987, pp. 865–867.
Weber, Robert L., *Pioneers of Science: Nobel Prize Winners in Physics,* American Institute of Physics, 1980, pp. 79–81.

—Sketch by David E. Newton

Charles Robert Richet
1850-1935
French physiologist

The French physiologist Charles Robert Richet won the 1913 Nobel Prize for his discovery of a nonprotective, toxic immune system process which he called anaphylaxis, a process related to the shock and allergic reactions which occur when foreign substances are injected into the body. Richet also tried to develop treatments for tuberculosis and to discover a serum to prevent tuberculosis. He was noted for his varied interests in scientific as well as non-scientific activities. He wrote poetry, novels, and plays, and for thirty years he studied and wrote about hypnotism, parapsychology, telepathy, and extrasensory perception. In 1890, he participated in an early attempt to design an airplane. He was a pacifist who was outspoken on social and political issues, and he wrote on the subject of vivisection.

Richet was born August 26, 1850, in Paris. His father, Alfred Richet, taught surgery at the University of Paris. His mother was Eugénie Rouard. After secondary school, Richet decided he wanted to practice medicine. He enrolled in the University of Paris medical school, but he soon found that he was more interested in research than in applied medicine. He also weighed the possibilities of a career in the humanities, and although he choose science instead, he maintained an active interest in literary, philosophical, and political subjects throughout his life.

In 1877 he received his medical degree. As a medical student he did research on hypnotism, digestive tract fluids, and the function of the nerves and muscles in the presence of pain. He quickly went on to obtain his degree as a doctor of science in 1878. In his doctoral thesis Richet showed that various forms of animal and marine life contain stomach hydrochloric acid. He also found the presence of a form of lactic acid in the human stomach. In that same year, he was appointed to the medical faculty of the University of Paris. With this appointment Richet focused his attention on the different ways the muscles contract.

After doing research in 1883 on heat maintenance in warm-blooded animals and the distribution of bacteria in the body fluids (an outgrowth of his work on the digestive system), in 1887 Richet began to work on the problem of creating a serum that could protect an animal against specific diseases. He followed the work of Louis Pasteur, who in 1880 found a way of protecting chickens from coming down with fowl cholera by injecting them with a weak form of the cholera microbe. The injection of the serum containing the weakened forms of the microbes created an antidote in the body that could then later fight off an invasion from a stronger force of the microbes. The injected serum contained the antigen, and the body receiving the injection produced the antibody.

Richet did extensive work in the development of techniques for immunization with his collaborator, Jules Hericourt. Over a ten year period, Richet and Hericourt tried to develop a serum for tuberculosis, without any success. They were frustrated by the fact that **Emil von Behring** had shown positive results for the development of an immunization serum for diphtheria during the same period of time.

Develops Concept of Anaphylaxis

In 1902 Richet was drawn to the problem of shock or allergic reactions in people after they received inoculations of disease-fighting serum. He noticed that some animals who had received a dosage of immunization serum would go into fatal shock when a second shot was administered. He found that the antibody produced by the first shot did not protect the animals against the second shot. The animal was now in a state of hypersensitivity caused by the production of too many antibodies against the foreign intruder. Richet called this condition anaphylaxis, a Greek word that means overprotection.

By 1906 the word allergy had been introduced to describe a wide range of adverse reactions to the use of antiserums and later antibiotics. The term also came into use to describe reactions to plants, animals, foods, chemicals, and many other substances. These substances fall into the category of antigens, meaning foreign substances that cause the immune system to produce antibodies, and they could therefore be understood in terms of Richet's concept of anaphylaxis. Richet was, therefore, a pioneer in the field of medicine dealing with the prevention and treatment of allergies.

For his development of the concept of anaphylaxis, Richet won the 1913 Nobel Prize. In his acceptance speech for the Nobel Prize, Richet acknowledged the difficulties anaphylaxis causes individuals, but he emphasized its biological significance in insuring the chemical integrity of the species. Such an argument was rooted in his philosophy of biological teleology, a view that maintains that there is a purpose in every biological process for the species concerned.

Richet married Amélie Aubry in 1877. The Richets had five sons and two daughters. In 1926 Richet received the Cross of the Legion of Honor from France for his work during World War I studying the problems of blood plasma transfusion. He died in Paris on December 3, 1935.

SELECTED WRITINGS BY RICHET:

Books

Des circonvolutions cérébrales, 1878, translation by E. Fowler, W. Wood, 1879.
Peace and War, 1906.
The Pros and Cons of Vivisection, 1908.
L'anaphylaxic, 1911.
Idiot Man, 1925
The Natural History of a Savant, G. H. Doran, 1927, translation by Oliver Lodge, Arno Press, 1975.
The Importance of Man, 1928.
Our Sixth Sense, 1929.

The Story of Civilization Through the Ages, 1930.

Periodicals

"Contribution à la physiologie des centres nerveux et des muscles de l'écrevisse," *Archives de physiologie normale et pathologique,* second series, Volume 6, 1879, pp. 262–84, 522–76.
"De l'anaphylaxie en général et de l'anaphylaxie par le mytilo-congestine en particulier," *Annales de l'Institut Pasteur,* Volume 21, 1907, pp. 497–534.

SOURCES:

Books

Berger, Arthur S., and Joyce Berger, *Encyclopedia of Parapsychology and Psychical Research,* Paragon, 1991.
Nobel Prize Winners, Wilson, 1987, pp. 867–69.
A Biographical Dictionary of Scientists, Wiley, 1982, p. 443.
Wolf, Stewart, *Brain, Mind, and Medicine: Charles Richet and the Origins of Physiological Psychology,* Transaction, 1993.

—*Sketch by Jordan P. Richman*

Burton Richter
1931-
American physicist

Burton Richter is a physicist at Stanford University who was largely responsible for the design of the eight-billion electron-volt accelerator called the Stanford Positron-Electron Accelerating Ring (SPEAR). Designed to cause collisions between electrons and positrons at almost unprecedented energy levels, SPEAR allowed scientists to perform experiments in 1974 that resulted in the discovery of an entirely new and unexpected particle, which Richter named psi (ψ). The discovery had revolutionary implications for particle physics; the lifetime of the psi-particle was many thousands of times longer than other particles, which indicated that it possessed a previously undiscovered property of matter. At almost the same time Richter made his discovery, **Samuel C. C. Ting**, working at the Massachusetts Institute of Technology (MIT), discovered the same particle using a different method. The two men were jointly awarded the Nobel Prize in physics in 1976.

Richter was born in Brooklyn, New York, on March 22, 1931. He was the oldest child and only son of Abraham Richter, a textile worker, and Fannie (Pollack) Richter. Burton attended Far Rockaway High School in Queens and Mercersburg Academy in Mercersburg, Pennsylvania. In 1948, he entered MIT, where he hesitated between studying chemistry or physics. His choice was determined by one of his professors, Francis Friedman, who "opened my eyes to the beauty of physics," as Richter is quoted as saying in *Current Biography.* At MIT, Richter worked with both Francis Bitter and Martin Deutsch, writing his senior thesis on the effect of external magnetic fields on the hydrogen spectrum.

After receiving his B.S. in 1952, Richter stayed on at Bitter's laboratory as a research assistant and doctoral student. His first assignment there was to find a way of producing a short-lived isotope of mercury, mercury–197, which he accomplished by bombarding gold foil with deuterons from the MIT cyclotron. The task accomplished, Richter found that he was interested in further work with particle accelerators. Physicist David Frisch provided him with the opportunity to work with one of the world's most powerful accelerators, the cosmotron at the Brookhaven National Laboratory. In 1953, Richter spent six months pursuing his interest in accelerators. After returning to MIT, Richter began his doctoral research on the production of pi-mesons in MIT's own synchrotron accelerator. He received his Ph.D. in 1956.

Richter accepted an appointment as a research assistant at Stanford University in 1956. This decision was based on his interest in pursuing research on quantum electrodynamics (QED), the modern version of electromagnetic theory. In particular, he wanted to find out if QED was valid at very small distances, such as those corresponding to the dimensions of the atomic nucleus. The 700-million-electron-volt linear accelerator at Stanford was, Richter later wrote in an edition of the University's *Stanford Linear Accelerator Beam Line,* "the perfect device with which to do an experiment on electron-electron scattering which I had been considering." He carried out these studies over the next decade, discovering that QED is indeed valid to distances of at least the diameter of an atomic nucleus, about 10^{-14} centimeter.

Uses Colliding Beams to Discovery the Psi-Particle

Even before the QED experiments had been completed, Richter began thinking about another approach to accelerator design. In all accelerators built at that time, particles were accelerated and caused to collide with a stationary target. There was, however, a major limitation to this approach: a large fraction of the energy of the incident beam was lost in the kinetic energy of particles produced in the collision. Richter realized that a more efficient way to study particle collisions would be to have two particle beams collide with each other while travelling in opposite directions. In 1970, Richter obtained funding for the machine he had in mind, the Stanford Positron-Electron Accelerating Ring (SPEAR). Three years later, SPEAR was in operation; with it, Richter was able to make what is considered one of the most important discoveries concerning elementary particles.

In this experiment, two concentric beams of particles, one of electrons and one of positrons, traveled around the circumference of the SPEAR accelerator. At a particular moment, the paths of the two beams were diverted and the particles allowed to collide. A fraction of the enormous energy released in this collision was converted into particles that do not exist at lower energy levels. One of these particles had never been observed before and had dramatically unexpected properties. It was about three times as massive as a proton with a lifetime about 5,000 times greater than would have been predicted for such a particle. Richter named the particle psi. Coincidentally, an identical discovery using a totally different approach was made at almost the same time on the other side of the continent. At the Brookhaven National Laboratory, a research team led by Ting discovered the same particle and gave it the name *J*. Richter and Ting made a joint announcement of their discoveries on November 11, 1974, at Stanford. Two years later, the two were awarded the Nobel Prize in physics for the discovery of the particle, now generally called the J/psi.

The primary significance of the J/psi discovery was the questions it raised. Traditional physical theory, which postulated the existence of three kinds of fundamental particles called quarks, was unable to explain the J/psi particle's peculiar properties. However, the discovery was consistent with a prediction made by American physicist **Sheldon Lee Glashow** in 1964; he had theorized that a previously unknown property, which he called charm, was needed to describe fully the properties of at least some elementary particles. The application of Glashow's theory to the J/psi particle was confirmed, and it is now widely accepted that the particle consists of a fourth quark.

Richter has remained at Stanford throughout his academic career. He was promoted to assistant professor in 1959, associate professor in 1963, and full professor in 1967. Since 1980, he has been Paul Pigott Professor of Physical Sciences. In 1975, he received the E. O. Lawrence Memorial Award from the U.S. Energy Research and Development Agency. In addition to his many awards and honors, Richter was Loeb Lecturer at Harvard University in 1974, De Sholit Lecturer at the Weizmann Institute in Israel in 1975, and visiting researcher at the European Center for Nuclear Research in Geneva from 1975 to 1976. Richter married Laurose Becker, an administrative

assistant at Stanford, on July 1, 1960; the Richters have a daughter and a son.

SELECTED WRITINGS BY RICHTER:

Books

(With M. Sands and A. M. Sessler) *Instabilities in Stored Particle Beams,* CFSTI, 1965.

Periodicals

"Two-body Photoproduction," *U.S. Atomic Energy Commission SLAC-PUB–501,* 1968, pp. 1–57.
"Plenary Report on e (+) e (-) Hadrons," *Proceedings of the 17th International Conference on High Energy Physics,* 1974, pp. 20–35.
"A Scientific Autobiography," *Stanford Linear Accelerator Beam Line,* November, 1976.

SOURCES:

Books

Current Biography 1977, H. W. Wilson, 1977, pp. 359–362.
Nobel Prize Winners, H. W. Wilson, 1987, pp. 869–871.
Weber, Robert L., *Pioneers of Science: Nobel Prize Winners in Physics,* American Institute of Physics, 1980, pp. 245–246.

Periodicals

Bjorken, J. D., "The 1976 Nobel Prize in Physics," *Science,* November 19, 1976, pp. 825–826, 865–866.
"Nobel Prize to Richter and Ting for Discovery of J/psi," *Physics Today,* December, 1976, p. 17.

—Sketch by David E. Newton

Charles F. Richter
1900-1985
American seismologist

Charles F. Richter is remembered every time an earthquake happens. With German-born seismologist **Beno Gutenberg**, Richter developed the scale that bears his name and measures the magnitude of earthquakes. Richter was a pioneer in seismological

Charles F. Richter

research at a time when data on the size and location of earthquakes were scarce. He authored two textbooks that are still used as references in the field and are regarded by many scientists as his greatest contribution, exceeding the more popular Richter scale. Devoted to his work all his life, Richter at one time had a seismograph installed in his living room, and he welcomed queries about earthquakes at all hours. Charles Francis Richter was born on April 26, 1900, on a farm near Hamilton, Ohio, north of Cincinnati. His parents were divorced when he was very young. He grew up with his maternal grandfather, who moved the family to Los Angeles in 1909. Richter went to a preparatory school associated with the University of Southern California, where he spent his freshman year in college. He then transferred to Stanford University, where he earned an A.B. degree in physics in 1920.

Richter received his Ph.D. in theoretical physics from the California Institute of Technology (Caltech) in 1928. That same year he married Lillian Brand of Los Angeles, a creative writing teacher. **Robert A. Millikan**, a Nobel Prize-winning physicist and president of Caltech, had already offered Richter a job at the newly established Seismological Laboratory in Pasadena, then managed by the Carnegie Institution of Washington. Thus Richter started applying his physics background to the study of the earth.

Develops the Richter-Gutenberg Scale

As a young research assistant, Richter made his name early when he began a decades-long collaboration with Beno Gutenberg, who was then the director of the laboratory. In the early 1930s the pair were one of several groups of scientists around the world who were trying to establish a standard way to measure and compare earthquakes. The seismological laboratory at Caltech was planning to issue regular reports on southern California earthquakes, so the Gutenberg-Richter study was especially important. They needed to be able to catalog several hundred quakes a year with an objective and reliable scale.

At the time, the only way to rate shocks was a scale developed in 1902 by the Italian priest and geologist Giuseppe Mercalli. The Mercalli scale classified earthquakes from 1 to 12, depending on how buildings and people responded to the tremor. A shock that set chandeliers swinging might rate as a 1 or 2 on this scale, while one that destroyed huge buildings and created panic in a crowded city might count as a 10. The obvious problem with the Mercalli scale was that it relied on subjective measures of how well a building had been constructed and how used to these sorts of crises the population was. The Mercalli scale also made it difficult to rate earthquakes that happened in remote, sparsely populated areas.

The scale developed by Richter and Gutenberg, which became known by Richter's name only, was instead an absolute measure of an earthquake's intensity. Richter used a seismograph—an instrument generally consisting of a constantly unwinding roll of paper, anchored to a fixed place, and a pendulum or magnet suspended with a marking device above the roll—to record actual earth motion during an earthquake. The scale takes into account the instrument's distance from the epicenter, or the point on the ground that is directly above the earthquake's origin. Richter chose to use the term "magnitude" to describe an earthquake's strength because of his early interest in astronomy; stargazers use the word to describe the brightness of stars. Gutenberg suggested that the scale be logarithmic, so that a quake of magnitude 7 would be ten times stronger than a 6, a hundred times stronger than a 5, and a thousand times stronger than a 4. (The 1989 Loma Prieta earthquake that shook San Francisco was magnitude 7.1.)

The Richter scale was published in 1935 and immediately became the standard measure of earthquake intensity. Richter did not seem concerned that Gutenberg's name was not included at first; but in later years, after Gutenberg was already dead, Richter began to insist that his colleague be recognized for expanding the scale to apply to earthquakes all over the globe, not just in southern California. Since 1935, several other magnitude scales have been developed. Depending on what data is available, different ones are used, but all are popularly known by Richter's name.

A Storehouse of Seismological Knowledge

For several decades Richter and Gutenberg worked together to monitor seismic activity around the world. In the late 1930s they applied their scale to deep earthquakes, ones that originate more than 185 miles below the ground, which rank particularly high on the Richter scale—8 or greater. In 1941 they published a textbook, *Seismicity of the Earth,* which in its revised edition became a standard reference book in the field. They worked on locating the epicenters of all the major earthquakes and classifying them into geographical groups. All his life, however, Richter warned that seismological records only reflect what people have measured in populated areas and are not a true representative sample of what shocks have actually occurred. He long remained skeptical of some scientists' claims that they could predict earthquakes.

Richter remained at Caltech for his entire career, except for a visit to the University of Tokyo from 1959 to 1960 as a Fulbright scholar. He became involved in promoting good earthquake building codes, while at the same time discouraging the overestimation of the dangers of an earthquake in a populated area like Los Angeles. He pointed out that statistics reveal freeway driving to be much more dangerous than living in an earthquake zone. He often lectured on how loss of life and property damage were largely avoidable during an earthquake, with proper training and building codes—he opposed building anything higher than thirty stories, for example. In the early 1960s, the city of Los Angeles listened to Richter and began to remove extraneous, but potentially dangerous, ornaments and cornices from its buildings. Los Angeles suffered a major quake in February of 1971, and city officials credited Richter with saving many lives. Richter was also instrumental in establishing the Southern California Seismic Array, a network of instruments that has helped scientists track the origin and intensity of earthquakes, as well as map their frequency much more accurately. His diligent study resulted in what has been called one of the most accurate and complete catalogs of earthquake activity, the Caltech catalog of California earthquakes.

Later in his career, Richter would recall several major earthquakes. The 1933 Long Beach earthquake was one, which he felt while working late at Caltech one night. That quake caused the death of 120 people in the then sparsely populated southern California town; it cost the Depression-era equivalent of $150 million in damages. Nobel Prize-winning physicist Albert Einstein was in town for a seminar when the earthquake struck, according to a March 8, 1981 story in the *San Francisco Chronicle.* Einstein and a colleague of Richter's were crossing the campus at the time of the quake, so engrossed in discussion that they were oblivious to the swaying trees. Richter also remembered the three great quakes that struck in 1906, when he was a six-year-old on the Ohio farm. That year, San Francisco suffered an 8.3 quake, Colombia and Ecuador had an 8.9, and Chile had an 8.6.

In 1958 Richter published his text *Elementary Seismology,* which was derived from the lectures he faithfully taught to Caltech undergraduates as well as decades of earthquake study. Many scientists consider this textbook to be Richter's greatest contribution, since he never published many scientific papers in professional journals. *Elementary Seismology* contained descriptions of major historical earthquakes, tables and charts, and subjects ranging from the nature of earthquake motion to earthquake insurance and building construction. Richter's colleagues maintained that he put everything he knew into it. The book was used in many countries.

Earthquakes in His Living Room

In the 1960s, Richter had a seismograph installed in his living room so that he could monitor quakes at any time. He draped the seismographic records—long rolls of paper covered with squiggly lines—over the backs of the living room chairs. (His wife, Richter maintained, considered the seismograph a conversation piece.) He would answer press queries at any hour of the night and never seemed tired of talking about his work. Sometimes he grew obsessive about speaking to the press; when a tremor happened during Caltech working hours, Richter made sure he would be the one answering calls—he put the lab's phone in his lap.

Richter devoted his entire life to seismology. He even learned Russian, Italian, French, Spanish, and German, as well as a little Japanese, in order to read scientific papers in their original languages. His dedication to his work was complete; in fact, he became enraged at any slight on it. For instance, at his retirement party from Caltech in 1970, some laboratory researchers sang a clever parody about the Richter scale. Richter was furious at the implication that his work could be considered a joke. During his lifetime he enjoyed a good deal of public and professional recognition, including membership in the American Academy of Arts and Sciences and a stint as president of the Seismological Society of America, but he was never elected to the National Academy of Sciences. After his retirement Richter helped start a seismic consulting firm that evaluated buildings for the government, for public utilities such as the Los Angeles Department of Water and Power, and for private businesses.

Richter enjoyed listening to classical music, reading science fiction, and watching the television series *Star Trek.* One of his great pleasures, ever since he grew up walking in the southern California mountains, was taking long solitary hikes. He preferred to camp by himself, far away from other people. But being alone had its drawbacks; once, he encountered a curious brown bear, which he chased away by loudly singing a raunchy song. After his marriage Richter continued his solo hikes, particularly at Christmas, when he and his wife would go their separate ways for a while. At these times Lillian indulged in her interest in foreign travel. The couple had no children. A little-known fact about them, according to Richter's obituary in the *Los Angeles Times,* is that they were nudists. Lillian died in 1972. Richter died in Pasadena on September 30, 1985, of congestive heart failure.

SELECTED WRITINGS BY RICHTER:

Books

(With Beno Gutenberg) *Seismicity of the Earth,* The Society, 1941, revised edition, Princeton University Press, 1954.
Elementary Seismology, Freeman, 1958.

SOURCES:

Books

Current Biography, H. W. Wilson, 1975, November, 1985.

Periodicals

Los Angeles Times, October 1, 1985.
Los Angeles Times Home Magazine, May 11, 1980.
Pasadena Star-News, May 13, 1991.
San Francisco Chronicle, March 8, 1981.

—*Sketch by Alexandra Witze*

Hyman G. Rickover

Hyman G. Rickover
1900-1986

Polish-born American nuclear engineer

Hyman G. Rickover was a charismatic and visionary United States naval officer who gained international fame as the principal architect of the nuclear navy. Although Rickover had an unusual early naval career—his ascension to senior service leadership did not follow the more conventional path from a sea command—he emerged during World War II as the head of the electrical section of the Bureau of Ships. This post allowed Navy Department leaders to view Rickover's effective maneuvering in the complex political environment of military bureaucracy. It also provided Rickover a jumping-off point for pursuing what became a lifelong ambition, the development of larger and more dominant naval vessels powered by nuclear reactors.

For more than thirty years Rickover headed the Navy's nuclear program. From this position he transformed the Navy from one propelled by coal and diesel to one in which nuclear reactors were used as power plants for most of the major warships, including the increasingly significant submarine fleet. At the same time, he worked to reorient the skills of naval officers along more technological lines. In the process, Rickover was largely responsible for creating one of the key weapons employed by the United States during its Cold War with the former Soviet Union.

Early Life, Entrance to Annapolis, and Early Naval Career

Hyman George Rickover was born on January 27, 1900, in Russian-occupied Poland, the son of Abraham and Rachel Unger Rickover. During the Russian anti-Jewish pogroms in the first decade of the century, the Rickovers traveled along with thousands of other immigrants to the United States. The family settled initially in New York City and set up a tailor shop. In 1910 they moved to Chicago, a city with a substantial Polish population, and it was there that young Rickover grew to maturity. As a boy in the public schools he was a good student—graduating with honors from John Marshall High School—but the family did not have the money to send him to college, and it appeared for a time that he would have to follow his father into the tailoring trade.

To help his son attend college, Abraham Rickover obtained the sponsorship of the local congressman for his son's appointment to the U.S. Naval Academy at Annapolis. Although he was once again a good student, Rickover was not well liked by his fellow midshipmen. He believed in later years that his Jewish, immigrant, and impoverished background aroused the prejudices of his classmates, and that nothing he could have done would have brought acceptance. Rickover's classmates, on the other hand, thought him too introverted and bookish and a difficult person to like. Rickover soon gave up trying to fit in and concentrated on mastering technical disciplines at Annapolis. His unpopularity among the midshipmen awakened a strong compensation impulse, and Rickover commented in later years on how committed he was to success in the Navy because of his treatment. On the strength of his academic abilities he graduated 107th out of a class of 540 in 1922.

After accepting his commission, Rickover was assigned to the destroyer *La Vallette,* but within a short time he transferred to the battleship *Nevada.* In both assignments he refrained from social activities, kept to himself, and rigorously studied engineering and mathematics; on the *Nevada,* Rickover earned honors for excelling at his work.

In the late 1920s, Rickover applied for shore duty so he could continue formal studies. Having persuaded the Navy to send him to Columbia University to complete a master of science degree in electrical engineering, he graduated in 1929 and immediately went to submarine school at New London, Connecticut, where he became a convert to the merits of the "silent service." For three years after completing this school Rickover served aboard the submarines S–9 and S–48. This experience reinforced his impression that submarines represented an important change in naval combat and deserved a greater role in the overall order of battle.

In 1933 Rickover returned to shore duty, where he was assigned to the Office of the Inspector of Naval Material in Philadelphia, Pennsylvania. Two years later he was sent as an engineering officer to the USS *New Mexico,* then, in 1937, he was reassigned as commander of the *Finch,* an old minesweeper used to tow gunnery targets. Rickover was so dissatisfied with

this assignment that he requested shore duty as an electrical engineer. As punishment for this request, in the fall of 1937 the Navy sent him as an "EDO" (engineering duty only) to the Cavite Navy Yard in the Philippine Islands. At the same time that most of his Annapolis classmates were entering command positions, Rickover seemed to be mired in staff and technical positions with little hope of receiving a major command.

Events began to change in 1939, however, when Rickover returned to the United States for assignment to the Bureau of Ships at the Navy Department in Washington, D.C. This proved to be a significant move for Rickover, as—throughout most of World War II—he headed the bureau's electrical section, directing improvements in the design and implementation of electrical systems. In this capacity he led efforts to maintain "shock-proof" electrical equipment on ships, reduce noise on submarines, and develop underwater detectors and infrared signaling devices. After a three month stint on temporary duty with the staff of the Commander Service Force of the U.S. Pacific Fleet, Rickover was assigned in 1945 as industrial manager and commanding officer of the Naval Repair Base at Okinawa. He held these positions until the end of the year, when he was assigned as inspector general of the Nineteenth Fleet headquartered at San Francisco, California.

Builds First Nuclear Submarine

Rickover's work with the Bureau of Ships during World War II led directly to his assignment in 1946 to a team which explored the use of nuclear energy for use on ships (work done as part of the Manhattan Project at its Oak Ridge, Tennessee, facility). The team's report recommended the construction of a nuclear submarine, and although this report was tabled by the Navy Department, the effort set the stage for the rest of Rickover's career. On his return to Washington, D.C., in 1947 Rickover resumed his campaign, and by the end of the year he had convinced the chief of naval operations, Admiral Chester A. Nimitz, of the viability of the atomic submarine. Support from the Atomic Energy Commission (AEC) and subsequent appointments as head of the Naval Reactors Branch at the AEC and the Nuclear Power Branch at the Bureau of Ships enabled him to bring his plans to fruition. Throughout the rest of the 1940s the AEC worked on the design and construction of a suitable reactor while Rickover and his staff evolved a scheme for the rest of the vessel.

A breakthrough for Rickover's efforts came in 1950 when he persuaded President Harry S. Truman to formally approve the construction of the first nuclear-powered submarine, the *Nautilus;* thereafter, Rickover presided over an impressive crash program to build the vessel. Pulling together some of the best personnel from the military, the government, industry, and academia, he worked toward the delivery of the new submarine by 1954 on a modest budget of forty million dollars. In 1952 the Navy laid the keel for the *Nautilus,* with Truman giving the keynote address. When the *Nautilus* was launched on January 21, 1954, it confirmed Truman's expectations. Much larger than ordinary submarines, the *Nautilus* was 319 feet long and displaced 3,180 tons. It could also remain underwater for prolonged periods and travel at a speed in excess of twenty knots or nautical miles. This craft set a baseline for the performance of all future submarines built by the U.S. Navy with its impressive submerged mission of August 1–5, 1958, under the polar cap between Alaska and Greenland.

While work on the *Nautilus* was underway, Rickover established an atomic submarine school at the Massachusetts Institute of Technology. Recruiting officers from the regular submarine fleet, he trained them over a three-year course for their new duties aboard nuclear submarines. This training effort reinforced for Rickover a long-held perception that naval officers were inadequately prepared by the academy for service in highly technical fields like nuclear energy. He began a crusade to revamp the Naval Academy's curriculum, expanding it essentially on his own to emphasize the skills necessary to serve in the nuclear navy. He followed this with a similar effort at other service schools and with the overall educational system. Three books he wrote in the late 1950s and early 1960s—*Education and Freedom, Swiss Schools and Ours: Why Theirs Are Better,* and *American Education: A National Failure*—each dealt with the necessity of expanding the educational base in the United States and emphasizing science and technology in the curriculum.

In the following years Rickover continued to expand his base of power within the Navy from his position as head of the Navy's nuclear program. He designed a nuclear aircraft carrier and other seagoing vessels that could be powered by reactors, and also championed and built land-based nuclear power stations. As time progressed Rickover—who had never served in combat or commanded any ship more important than a target towing barge—assumed power within the Navy to the extent that he personally chose commanders of nuclear vessels. Reaching mandatory retirement age in the early 1960s, Rickover was retained on active duty and remained in uniform for another twenty years as the director of the Division of Nuclear Reactors. In 1982, Secretary of the Navy John Lehman forced Rickover into retirement after a career which almost single-handedly brought the Navy into the nuclear age. Rickover died on July 8, 1986, in Washington, D.C., leaving a wife, Ruth Dorothy Masters, and a son.

SELECTED WRITINGS BY RICKOVER:

Books

Education and Freedom, E. P. Dutton, 1959.
Swiss Schools and Ours: Why Theirs Are Better, Little, Brown, 1962.
American Education: A National Failure, E. P. Dutton, 1963.
Liberty, Science, and Law, Newcomen Society in North America, 1969.
Eminent Americans: Namesakes of the Polaris Submarine Fleet, Government Printing Office, 1972.
How the Battleship Maine Was Destroyed, Government Printing Office, 1976.
No Holds Barred: The Final Congressional Testimony of Admiral Hyman Rickover, Center for the Study of Responsive Law, 1982.

SOURCES:

Books

Blair, Clay, *The Atomic Submarine and Admiral Rickover,* Holt, 1954.
David, Heather M., *Admiral Rickover and the Nuclear Navy,* Putnam, 1970.
Duncan, Francis, *Rickover and the Nuclear Navy: The Discipline of Technology,* Naval Institute Press, 1990.
Lewis, Eugene, "Hyman G. Rickover," *Leadership and Innovation: A Biographical Perspective on Entrepreneurs in Government,* edited by Jameson W. Doig and Erwin C. Hargrove, Johns Hopkins University Press, 1987.
Lewis, Eugene, *Public Entrepreneurship: Toward a Theory of Bureaucratic Political Power: The Organizational Lives of Hyman Rickover, J. Edgar Hoover, and Robert Moses,* Indiana University Press, 1980.
Polmar, Norman, and Thomas B. Allen, *Rickover,* Simon & Schuster, 1982.
Tyler, Patrick, *Running Critical: The Silent War: Rickover and General Dynamics,* Harper, 1986.

—Sketch by Roger D. Launius

Sally Ride
1951-
American astronaut and physicist

Sally Ride is best known as the first American woman sent into outer space. She also served the National Aeronautics and Space Administration (NASA) in an advisory capacity, being the only astronaut chosen for President Ronald Reagan's Rogers Commission investigating the mid-launch explosion of the space shuttle *Challenger* in January, 1986, writing official recommendation reports, and creating NASA's Office of Exploration. Both scientist and professor, she has served as a fellow at the Stanford University Center for International Security and Arms Control, a member of the board of directors at Apple Computer Inc., and a space institute director and physics professor at the University of California at San Diego. Ride has chosen to write primarily for children about space travel and exploration. Her commitment to educating the young earned her the Jefferson Award for Public Service from the American Institute for Public Service in 1984, in addition to her National Spaceflight Medals recognizing her two groundbreaking shuttle missions in 1983 and 1984. Newly elected president Bill Clinton chose her as a member of his transition team during the fall of 1992.

Sally Kristen Ride is the older daughter of Dale Burdell and Carol Joyce (Anderson) Ride of Encino, California, and was born May 26, 1951. As author Karen O'Connor describes tomboy Ride in her young reader's book, *Sally Ride and the New Astronauts,* Sally would race her dad for the sports section of the newspaper when she was only five years old. An active, adventurous, yet also scholarly family, the Rides traveled throughout Europe for a year when Sally was nine and her sister Karen was seven, after Dale took a sabbatical from his political science professorship at Santa Monica Community College. While Karen was inspired to become a minister, in the spirit of her parents, who were elders in their Presbyterian church, Ride's own developing taste for exploration would eventually lead her to apply to the space program almost on a whim. "I don't know why I wanted to do it," she confessed to *Newsweek* prior to embarking on her first spaceflight.

The opportunity was serendipitous, since the year she began job-hunting marked the first time NASA had opened its space program to applicants since the late 1960s, and the very first time women would not be excluded from consideration. NASA needed to cast a wider net than ever before, as *Current Biography* disclosed in 1983. The program paid less than private sector counterparts and offered no particular research specialties, unlike most job oppor-

Sally Ride

tunities in academia. All it took was a return reply postcard, and Ride was in the mood to take those risks. This was, after all, a young lady who could patch up a disabled Toyota with Scotch tape without breaking stride, as one of her friends once discovered. Besides, she had always forged her own way before with the full support of her open-minded family.

Student Sets Own Agenda

From her earliest years in school, Ride was so proficient and efficient at once, she proved to be an outright annoyance to some of her teachers. Though she was a straight-A student, she was easily bored, and her brilliance only came to the fore in high school, when she was introduced to the world of science by her physiology teacher. The impact of this mentor, Dr. Elizabeth Mommaerts, was so profound that Ride would later dedicate her first book primarily to her, as well as the fallen crew of the *Challenger*. While she was adaptable to all forms of sport, playing tennis was Ride's most outstanding talent, which she had developed since the age of ten. Under the tutelage of a four-time U.S. Open champion, Ride eventually ranked eighteenth nationally on the junior circuit. Her ability won her a partial scholarship to Westlake School for Girls, a prep school in Los Angeles. After graduating from there in 1968, Ride preferred to work on her game full time instead of the physics program at Swarthmore College, Pennsylvania, where she had originally enrolled. It was only after Ride had fully tested her dedication to the game that she decided against a professional career, even though tennis pro Billie Jean King had once told her it was within her grasp. Back in California as an undergraduate student at Stanford University, Ride followed her burgeoning love for Shakespeare to a double major, receiving B.S. and B.A. degrees in tandem by 1973. She narrowed her focus to physics for her masters, also from Stanford, awarded in 1975. Work toward her dissertation continued at Stanford; she submitted "The Interaction of X-Rays with the Interstellar Medium" in 1978.

Ride was just finishing her Ph.D. candidacy in physics, astronomy, and astrophysics at Stanford, working as a research assistant, when she got the call from NASA. She became one of thirty-five chosen from an original field of applicants numbering eight thousand for the spaceflight training of 1978. "Why I was selected remains a complete mystery," she later admitted to John Grossmann in a 1985 interview in *Health.* "None of us has ever been told." Even after three years of studying X-ray astrophysics, Ride had to go back to the classroom to gain skills to be part of a team of astronauts. The program included basic science and math, meteorology, guidance, navigation, and computers as well as flight training on a T–38 jet trainer and other operational simulations. Ride was selected as part of the ground-support crew for the second (November, 1981) and third (March, 1982) shuttle flights, her duties including the role of "capcom," or capsule communicator, relaying commands from the ground to the shuttle crew. These experiences prepared her to be an astronaut.

A Series of NASA Firsts

Ride would subsequently become, at thirty-one, the youngest person sent into orbit as well as the first American woman in space, the first American woman to make two spaceflights, and, coincidentally, the first astronaut to marry another astronaut in active duty. She and Steven Alan Hawley were married at the groom's family home in Kansas on July 26, 1982. Hawley, a Ph.D. from the University of California, had joined NASA with a background in astronomy and astrophysics. When asked during a hearing by Congressman Larry Winn, Jr., of the House Committee on Science and Technology, how she would feel when Hawley was in space while she remained earthbound, Ride replied, "I am going to be a very interested observer." The pair were eventually divorced.

Ride points to her fellow female astronauts Anna Fisher, Shannon Lucid, Judith Resnik, Margaret Seddon, and Kathryn Sullivan with pride. Since these women were chosen for training, Ride's own experience could not be dismissed as tokenism, which had been the unfortunate fate of the first woman in orbit,

the Soviet Union's **Valentina Tereshkova**, a textile worker. Ride expressed her concern to *Newsweek* reporter Pamela Abramson in the week before her initial shuttle trip. "It's important to me that people don't think I was picked for the flight because I am a woman and it's time for NASA to send one."

From June 18 to June 24, 1983, flight STS–7 of the space shuttle *Challenger* launched from Kennedy Space Center in Florida, orbited the Earth for six days, returned to Earth, and landed at Edwards Air Force Base in California. Among the shuttle team's missions were the deployment of international satellites and numerous research experiments supplied by a range of groups, from a naval research lab to various high school students. With Ride operating the shuttle's robot arm in cooperation with Colonel John M. Fabian of the U.S. Air Force, the first satellite deployment and retrieval using such an arm was successfully performed in space during the flight.

Ride was also chosen for *Challenger* flight STS–41G, which transpired between October 5 and October 13, 1984. This time, the robot arm was put to some unusual applications, including "ice-busting" on the shuttle's exterior and readjusting a radar antenna. According to Henry S. F. Cooper, Jr., in his book *Before Lift-off,* fellow team member Ted Browder felt that because Ride was so resourceful and willing to take the initiative, less experienced astronauts on the flight might come to depend upon her rather than develop their own skills, but this mission also met with great success. Objectives during this longer period in orbit covered scientific observations of the Earth, demonstrations of potential satellite refueling techniques, and deployment of a satellite. As STS–7 had been, STS–41G was led by Captain Robert L. Crippen of the U.S. Navy to a smooth landing, this time in Florida.

Ride had been chosen for a third scheduled flight, but training was cut short in January, 1986, when the space shuttle *Challenger* exploded in midair shortly after takeoff. The twelve-foot rubber O-rings that serve as washers between steel segments of the rocket boosters, already considered problematic, failed under stress, killing the entire crew. Judy Resnik, one of the victims, had flown as a rookie astronaut on STS–41G. Ride remembered her in *Ms.* magazine as empathetic, sharing "the same feelings that there was good news and bad news in being accepted to be the first one." As revealed a few months later in the *Chicago Tribune,* program members at NASA began to feel that their safety had been willfully compromised without their knowledge. "I think that we may have been misleading people into thinking that this is a routine operation," Ride was quoted as saying.

Responds to *Challenger* Tragedy

Ride herself tried to remedy that misconception with her subsequent work on the Rogers Commission and as special assistant for long-range and strategic planning to NASA Administrator James C. Fletcher in Washington, D.C., during 1986 and 1987. In keeping with the Rogers Commission recommendations, which Ride helped to shape, especially regarding the inclusion of astronauts at management levels, Robert Crippen was eventually made Deputy Director for Space Shuttle Operations in Washington, D.C., as well.

As leader of a task force on the future of the space program, Ride wrote *Leadership and America's Future in Space.* According to *Aviation Week and Space Technology,* this status report initiated a proposal to redefine NASA goals as a means to prevent the "space race" mentality that might pressure management and personnel into taking untoward risks. "A single goal is not a panacea," the work stated in its preface. "The problems facing the space program must be met head-on, not oversimplified." The overall thrust of NASA's agenda, Ride suggested, should take environmental and international research goals into consideration. A pledge to inform the public and capture the interest of youngsters should be taken as a given. Ride cited a 1986 work decrying the lack of math and science proficiency among American high school graduates, a mere six percent of whom are fluent in these fields, compared to up to ninety percent in other nations.

Top Priority: Educating Children

While with NASA, Ride traveled with fellow corps members to speak to high school and college students on a monthly basis. As former English tutor Joyce Ride once told a *Boston Globe* reporter, her daughter had developed scientific interests she herself harbored in younger days, before encountering a wall of silence in a college physics class as a coed at the University of California in Los Angeles. As Joyce remarked, she and the only other young woman in the class were "nonpersons." Speaking at Smith College in 1985, Sally Ride announced that encouraging women to enter math and science disciplines was her "personal crusade." Ride noted in *Publishers Weekly* the next year that her ambition to write children's books had been met with some dismay by publishing houses more in the mood to read an autobiography targeted for an adult audience. Her youth-oriented books were both written with childhood friends. Susan Okie, coauthor of *To Space and Back,* eventually became a journalist with the *Washington Post. Voyager* coauthor Tam O'Shaughnessy, once a fellow competition tennis player, grew up to develop workshops on scientific teaching skills.

Ride left NASA in 1987 for Stanford's Center for International Security and Arms Control, and two years later she became director of the California Space Institute and physics professor at the Universi-

ty of California at San Diego. She has flown Grumman Tiger aircraft in her spare time since getting her pilot's license. The former astronaut keeps in shape, when not teaching or fulfilling the duties of her various professional posts, by running and engaging in other sports, although she once told *Health* magazine she winds up eating junk food a lot. Ride admitted not liking to run but added, "I like being in shape."

SELECTED WRITINGS BY RIDE:

Books

(With Susan Okie) *To Space and Back,* Lothrop, 1986.
Leadership and America's Future in Space: A Report to the Administrator by Dr. Sally K. Ride, August 1987, NASA, August, 1987.
(With Tam O'Shaughnessy) *Voyager: An Adventure to the Edge of the Solar System,* Crown, 1992.

SOURCES:

Books

Astronauts and Cosmonauts Biographical and Statistical Data, U.S. Government Printing Office, 1989.
Cooper, Henry S. F., Jr., *Before Lift-off,* Johns Hopkins University Press, 1987.
Current Biography, H. W. Wilson, 1983, pp. 318–21.
Hearing before the Committee on Science and Technology, U.S. House of Representatives, Ninety-eighth Congress, First Session, July 19, 1983, U.S. Government Printing Office, 1983.
O'Connor, Karen, *Sally Ride and the New Astronauts: Scientists in Space,* F. Watts, 1983.

Periodicals

Adler, Jerry, and Pamela Abramson, "Sally Ride: Ready for Liftoff," *Newsweek,* June 13, 1983, pp. 36–40, 45, 49, 51.
Caldwell, Jean, "Astronaut Ride Urges Women to Study Math," *Boston Globe,* June 30, 1985, pp. B90, B92.
Covault, Craig, "Ride Panel Calls for Aggressive Action to Assert U.S. Leadership in Space," *Aviation Week and Space Technology,* August 24, 1987, pp. 26–27.
Goodwin, Irwin, "Sally Ride to Leave NASA Orbit; Exodus at NSF," *Physics Today,* July, 1987, p. 45.
Grossmann, John, "Sally Ride, Ph.D.," *Health,* August, 1985, pp. 73–74, 76.

Ingwerson, Marshall, "Clinton Transition Team Takes on Pragmatic Cast," *Christian Science Monitor,* November 30, 1992, p. 3.

Lowther, William, "A High Ride through the Sex Barrier," *Maclean's,* June 27, 1983, pp. 40–41.

Peterson, Sarah, "Just Another Astronaut," *U.S. News and World Report,* November 29, 1982, pp. 50–51.

Roback, Diane, "Sally Ride: Astronaut and Now Author," *Publishers Weekly,* November 28, 1986, pp. 42, 44.

Rowley, Storer, and Michael Tackett, "Internal Memo Charges NASA Compromised Safety," *Chicago Tribune,* March 9, 1986, section 1, p. 8.

Sherr, Lynn, "Remembering Judy: The Five Women Astronauts Who Trained with Judy Resnik Remember Her . . . and That Day," *Ms.,* June, 1986, p. 57.

Sherr, "A Mission to Planet Earth: Astronaut Sally Ride Talks to Lynn Sherr about Peaceful Uses of Space," *Ms.,* July/August, 1987, pp. 180–81.

—*Sketch by Jennifer Kramer*

and a Ph.D. in electrical engineering in 1963. She launched her professional career as an engineer at the Mayo Clinic, a post she held from 1956 to 1957. She then accepted a position as an instructor of physics, math, and engineering at Ventura College, remaining there for one year before becoming senior research engineer for Lockheed Missile and Space Company in 1963.

In 1965, Rigas began an association with Washington State University that would last nineteen years. In 1968, she was named manager of the Hybrid Facility, a post she held until 1980. Rigas was appointed professor of electrical engineering in 1976. At Washington University she created the university's computer engineering program, taking the responsibility for developing the curriculum and raising necessary funding. Rigas also held concurrent posts at the Naval Postgraduate School, where she was named chair of the electrical engineering department in 1980. In 1987, Rigas joined Michigan State University as professor and chair of the department of electrical engineering. She served as board member of the Institute for Electrical and Electronic Engineers (IEEE), and as the IEEE representative on the Accreditation Board for Engineering and Technology. Rigas was married in 1959; she died on July 26, 1989.

—*Sketch by Karen Withem*

Harriett B. Rigas
1934-1989
Canadian-born American electrical engineer

Harriett B. Rigas was an electrical engineer who specialized in computer technology, automatic patching, control system stability, and logic design. Prior to serving as professor and the chair of the department of electrical engineering at Michigan State University, she established the computer engineering program at Washington State University. Rigas made advances in computer coding theory; her research focused on improving methods for creating the digital (binary) code that allows computers to store and manipulate data. Application of her theories would reduce computer memory requirements and facilitate the discovery of software errors. She received the 1982 Annual Achievement Award from the Society of Women Engineers for her "significant contributions in the fields of electrical engineering and computer technology."

Rigas was born on April 30, 1934, in Winnipeg, Manitoba. She earned her undergraduate degree at Queen's University in Ontario in 1956. She pursued her graduate studies at the University of Kansas in Missouri, earning a master of science degree in 1959

Joseph Risi
1899-1993
Swiss Canadian chemist

Joseph Risi, the principal force behind the rise of university research laboratories in French Canada, was born March 13, 1899, in Ennetbürgen, near Lucerne, Switzerland, to Alois and Marie Rothenfluh Risi. His father was a cabinetmaker. The exacting and slow nature of his father's trade persuaded Joseph Risi to find another path in life. He decided on teaching. After completing his secondary education at the Collège St.-Michel in Zug in 1918, he enrolled in the Catholic University of Fribourg, which had received university status only in 1909. He first finished the four diplomas (*licences*) then required of Swiss science teachers—in mathematics, physics, chemistry, and biology. He stayed on for a doctorate in organic chemistry, which he completed in 1925 under the direction of A. Bistrzycki.

For the preceding five years, the ecclesiastical hierarchy of Laval University, in Quebec City, had been trying to establish an advanced school of chemistry. They had called in chemists (Paul Cardinaux, Julian J. Gutensperger, and Carl Faessler) and a physicist (Alphonse Cristen) from the University of Fribourg. But in 1925 Cardinaux and Cristen were fired, the former for financial improprieties and the latter for a sexual escapade. Other chemists came and went from both Switzerland and France. Offered a position as lecturer in organic chemistry, Risi immigrated to Canada in 1925. He became a full professor at the university in 1931.

Risi plunged immediately into organizing Laval's chemistry program. He supervised the installation of new laboratories, the funding for which had taken five years to obtain. In addition to teaching organic chemistry, he taught mineralogy and botany, served as librarian of his school, and from 1931 to 1936 was the scientific overseer of the first marine biological station on the St. Lawrence River, at Trois-Pistoles. Most importantly, he began original research with local students.

Research on the Chemistry of Aromatics

The research was inspired by the environment of French Canada. From the time of his arrival at Laval, Risi had tirelessly promoted the economic development of the region through industrial chemistry. By 1930, he was focusing on the aromatics of maple sugar. His interest was stimulated by the discovery of a vegetable product in South Africa that could mimic the distinctive taste of maple sugar—a development that threatened an important local industry. Beginning with the results of an experiment reported in a German publication, Risi and a student discovered that the aromatic could be produced artificially from oak resin, and in the process they identified a way to distinguish the true maple-syrup taste. This work was followed by a study of the chemical properties of Canadian rhubarb. At the same time, Risi explored the new domain of polymer chemistry (polymers are natural or synthetic materials, like rubber and plastics, that have a high molecular weight and are composed of repeating units). He and a student presented an early description of the polymerization of styrene. In all, Risi would publish more than fifty scientific papers during his career. The chemistry of aromatics from the natural world captured the attention of a number of chemists in the 1920s. Musk was the starting point for the Croatian-Swiss chemist **Leopold Ružička**, for example, who then moved on to explore the composition of hormones and who garnered a Nobel prize in 1939 for his work in this field. A measure of Risi's eminence is found in his being invited, in 1937, to propose a candidate for the Nobel Prize in chemistry. Although he was not the first to do so, Risi recommended Ruzicka to the Nobel authorities. By this act, Risi established Laval as the premier research university of French Canada.

Beginning about 1940, Risi became interested in the chemistry of wood products; in 1948 he joined the faculty of Forestry Engineering at Laval, and in 1950 he became director of the Canadian Institute of Forestry Products. Elected a fellow of the Royal Society of Canada in 1954, he directed Laval's graduate school from 1960 until his retirement in 1971.

Risi had married Alice Neuhaus in 1926; they had four children. A Roman Catholic, Risi enjoyed playing chess and fishing in his spare time. He died on July 21, 1993.

SOURCES:

Ouellet, Danielle, *L'Emergence de deux disciplines scientifiques à l'Université Laval entre 1920 et 1950: La chimie et la physique,* Ph.D. dissertation, Laval University, 1991.

—*Sketch by Lewis Pyenson*

Dennis Ritchie
1941-
American computer scientist

Dennis Ritchie is a computer scientist most well-known for his work with **Kenneth Thompson** in creating UNIX, a computer operating system. Ritchie also went on to develop the high-level and enormously popular computer programming language *C.* For their work on the UNIX operating system, Ritchie and Thompson were awarded the prestigious Turing Award by the Association for Computer Machinery (ACM) in 1983.

Dennis MacAlistair Ritchie was born in Bronxville, New York, on September 9, 1941, and grew up in New Jersey, where his father, Alistair Ritchie, worked as a switching systems engineer for Bell Laboratories. His mother, Jean McGee Ritchie, was a homemaker. Ritchie went to Harvard University, where he received his B.S. in Physics in 1963. However, a lecture he attended on the operation of Harvard's computer system, a Univac I, led him to develop an interest in computing in the early 1960s. Thereafter, Ritchie spent a considerable amount of time at the nearby Massachusetts Institute of Technology (MIT), where many scientists were developing computer systems and software. In 1967 Ritchie began working for Bell Laboratories. Ritchie's job increased his association with the programming world, and in the late 1960s he began working with the Computer Science Research Department at Bell. It was here that he met Kenneth Thompson. Ritchie's lifestyle at Bell was that of a typical computer guru: he was devoted to his work. He showed up to his cluttered office in Murray Hill, New Jersey, around noon every day, worked until seven in the evening, and then went home to work some more. His computer system at home was connected on a dedicated private line to a system at Bell Labs, and he often worked at home until three in the morning. Even in the early 1990s, after he became a manager at Bell Labs, his work habits did not change substantially. "It still tends to be sort of late, but not quite that late," Ritchie told Patrick Moore in an interview. "It depends on what meetings and so forth I have."

UNIX: The Operating System that Changed Everything

When Ritchie and Thompson began working for Bell Labs, the company was involved in a major initiative with General Electric and MIT to develop a multi-user, time-sharing operating system called Multics. This system would replace the old one, which was based on batch programming. In a system based on batch programming, the programmers had no opportunity to interact with the computer system directly. Instead, they would write the program on a deck or batch of cards, which were then input into a mainframe computer by an operator. In other words, since the system was centered around a mainframe, and cards were manually fed into machines to relate instructions or generate responses, the programmers had no contact with the program once it had been activated. Multics, or the multiplexed information and computing service, would enable several programmers to work on a system simultaneously while the computer itself would be capable of processing multiple sets of information. Although programmers from three institutions were working on Multics, Bell Labs decided that the development costs were too high and the possibility of launching a usable system in the near future too low. Therefore, the company pulled out of the project. Ritchie and Thompson, who had been working on the Multics project, were suddenly thrown back into the batch programming environment. In light of the advanced techniques and expertise they had acquired while working on the Multics project, this was a major setback for them and they found it extremely difficult to adapt.

Thus it was in 1969 that Thompson began working on what would become the UNIX operating system. Ritchie soon joined the project and together they set out to find a useful alternate to Multics. However, working with a more advanced system was not the only motivation in developing UNIX. A major factor in their efforts to develop a multi-user, multi-tasking system was the communication and information-sharing it facilitated between programmers. As Ritchie said in his article titled "The Evolution of the UNIX Time-sharing System," "What we wanted to preserve was not just a good environment in which to do programming, but a system around which a fellowship could form. We knew from experience that the essence of communal computing, as supplied by remote-access, time-shared machines, is not just to type programs into a terminal instead of a keypunch, but to encourage close communication."

In 1969 Thompson found a little-used PDP–7, an old computer manufactured by the Digital Equipment Corporation (DEC). To make the PDP–7 efficiently run the computer programs that they created, Ritchie, Thompson, and others began to develop an operating system. Among other things, an operating system enables a user to copy, delete, edit, and print data files; to move data from a disk to the screen or to a printer; to manage the movement of data from disk storage to memory storage; and so on. Without operating systems, computers are very difficult and time-consuming for experts to run.

It was clear, however, that the PDP–7 was too primitive for what Ritchie and Thompson wanted to do, so they persuaded Bell Labs to purchase a PDP–11, a far more advanced computer at the time. To justify their acquisition of the PDP–11 to the management of Bell Labs, Ritchie and Thompson said that they would use the PDP–11 to develop a word-processing system for the secretaries in the patent department. With the new PDP–11, Ritchie and Thompson could refine their operating system even more. Soon, other departments in Bell Labs began to find UNIX useful. The system was used and refined within the company for some time before it was announced to the outside world in 1973 during a symposium on Operating Systems Principles hosted by International Business Machines (IBM).

One of the most important characteristics of UNIX was its portability. Making UNIX portable meant that it could be run with relatively few modifications on different computer systems. Most operating systems are developed around specific hardware configurations, that is, specific microprocessor chips, memory sizes, and input and output devices (e.g., printers, keyboards, screens, etc.). To transfer an operating system from one hardware environment to another—for example, from a microcomputer to a mainframe computer—required so many internal changes to the programming that, in effect, the whole operating system had to be rewritten. Ritchie circumvented this problem by rewriting UNIX in such a way that it was largely machine independent. The resulting portability made UNIX easier to use in a variety of computer and organizational environments, saving time, money, and energy for its users.

Inventing a New Computer Language

To help make UNIX portable, Ritchie created a new programming language, called *C*, in 1972. C used features of low-level languages or machine languages (i.e., languages that allow programmers to move bits of data between the components inside microprocessor chips) and features of high-level languages (i.e., languages that have more complex data manipulating functions such as looping, branching, and subroutines). High-level languages are easier to learn than low-level languages because they are closer to everyday English. However, because C combined functions of both high- and low-level languages and was very flexible, it was not for beginners. C was very portable because, while it used a relatively small syntax and instruction set, it was also highly structured and modular. Therefore, it was easy to adapt it to different computers, and programmers could copy preexisting blocks of C functions into their programs. These blocks, which were stored on disks in various libraries and could be accessed by using C programs, allowed programmers to create their own programs without having to reinvent the wheel. Because C had features of low-level programming languages, it ran very quickly and efficiently compared to other high-level languages, and it took up relatively little computer time.

Interestingly, because of federal antitrust regulations, Bell Labs, which is owned by American Telephone & Telegraph (AT&T), could not copyright C or UNIX after AT&T was broken up into smaller corporations. Thus, C was used at many college and university computing centers, and each year thousands of new college graduates arrived in the marketplace with a lot of experience with C. In the mid and late 1980s, C became one of the most popular programming languages in the world. The speed at which C worked made it a valuable tool for companies that developed software commercially. C was also popular because it was written for UNIX, which, by the early 1990s, was shipped out on over $20 billion of new computer systems a year, making it one of the most commonly used operating systems in the world.

At the end of 1990, Ritchie became the head of the Computing Techniques Research Department at Bell Labs, contributing applications and managing the development of distributed operating systems. He has received several awards for his contributions to computer programming, including the ACM Turing award in 1983, which he shared with Thompson.

SELECTED WRITINGS BY RITCHIE:

Books

(Brian W. Kernighan) *The C Programming Language,* Prentice Hall, 1988.

Periodicals

(With Kenneth Thompson) "The UNIX Time-Sharing System," *Communications of the ACM,* Volume 17.7, July, 1974, pp. 365–375.

"The Evolution of the UNIX Time-Sharing System," *Language Design and Programming Methodology,* edited by Jeffrey M. Tobias, Springer-Verlag, 1980, pp. 25–35.

"Reflections on Software Research," *Communications of the ACM,* Volume 27.8, August, 1984, pp. 758–760.

SOURCES:

Books

Slater, Robert, *Portraits in Silicon,* MIT Press, 1987.

Periodicals

Hafner, Katherine, "Newsmaker: Dennis Ritchie," *Data Communications,* November, 1985, pp. 106–107.

Rosenblatt, Alfred, "1982 Award for Achievement: Dennis M. Ritchie and Ken Thompson," *Electronics,* October 20, 1982, pp. 108–111.

Other

Ritchie, Dennis M., telephone interviews with Patrick Moore conducted February 9 and February 14, 1994.

—Sketch by Patrick Moore

Frederick Robbins
1916-
American microbiologist

Frederick Robbins was co-winner of the Nobel Prize in physiology or medicine in 1954 with **John F. Enders** and **Thomas Weller** for his work on the poliomyelitis virus. They were the first to successfully grow poliomyelitis in non-neural tissue culture. This development provided the technology needed to produce a vaccination for polio, which was done in 1953 by virologist **Jonas Salk**.

Frederick Chapman Robbins was born June 21, 1916, in Auburn, Alabama. He was the eldest of three boys born to Dr. William Jacob Robbins and Christine F. (Chapman) Robbins. His father was a noted plant physiologist and was director of the New York Botanical Garden for a time and later a professor of botany at the University of Missouri. Robbins's mother was a Phi Beta Kappa graduate of Wellesley College who was also a researcher in botany before her marriage.

Robbins received his B.A. in 1936 and his B.S. in pre-medicine in 1938, both from the University of Missouri. He then went on to Harvard Medical School, where he met and roomed with Weller and studied virology under Enders. After graduating with his M.D. in 1940, Robbins began an internship and residency at Children's Hospital in Boston, as he had decided to specialize in pediatrics.

World War II interrupted his residency program, and Robbins ended up serving from 1942 to 1946 in North Africa and Italy. He worked as chief of the section of the 15th Medical General Laboratory devoted to viruses and certain kinds of bacterial diseases, and his research mainly concerned infectious hepatitis, Q fever, and typhus fever. He won the Bronze Star for his work during the war.

After the war, Robbins returned to Children's Hospital, where he was assistant resident from 1946 to 1947 and chief resident in 1948 when he finished his residency. Also in 1948, Robbins married Alice Havemeyer Northrop, who had been Weller's assistant in the Enders laboratory. She was the daughter of **John Howard Northrop**, co-winner of the 1946 Nobel Prize for chemistry. The Robbins had two daughters, Alice and Louise.

Cracks the Polio Puzzle

At this point, Robbins received a two-year senior fellowship from the National Research Council to study viral diseases and went to work in Enders's lab. Still concentrating on pediatrics, Robbins began work on infant epidemic diarrhea, which he had seen much of as a resident. He was also working with the mumps virus and because of this had a strain of mouse intestine cells in culture. Meanwhile, Weller was also working with the mumps virus, and at the end of one experiment he had a few tubes of human embryonic tissue left over. Weller decided to try to grow poliomyelitis in this. The results were positive enough to spark some interest, and next Weller grew the virus in foreskin cells, followed by some of Robbins's supply of mouse intestine. These experiments did not

work as well but did spur the two to try polio in human intestine.

Prior to this time, polio had only been shown to grow in neural and brain tissue of men or monkeys. Vaccinations from this type of growth were potentially deadly because of something present in this tissue which could not be refined out, so there was no vaccine for polio. Growth of viruses in tissue culture, or in vitro, had historically been difficult because of the threat of bacterial invasion into the cell cultures. By the 1950s, however, antibiotics had been developed and introduced into the laboratory, such as penicillin and streptomycin, which enabled scientists to begin to grow tissue cultures of viruses without the threat of a bacterial invasion.

Robbins and Weller, in their polio experiments, were taking advantage of the new antibiotics. The human intestine cultures grew, which proved for the first time that polio could grow outside neural tissue. This made the feasibility of a polio vaccine far greater, both because it provided a non-deadly vaccine source and because the supply could be grown more cheaply in vitro than in a live animal. This work was a major breakthrough for scientific research and led to the awarding of the Nobel Prize to Enders, Weller, and Robbins in 1954. Weller and Robbins had already been given the Mead Johnson Prize in 1953 for their contribution to pediatric research.

While working in Enders's laboratory, Robbins also served as associate professor of pediatrics at Harvard. In 1950 he took on the additional position of associate director of Isolation Service at Children's Hospital. Then in 1952 he moved to Cleveland to become director of the pediatrics and contagious diseases department at Cleveland City Hospital as well as a member of the medical faculty at Case Western Reserve Medical School.

Robbins's career then took a turn from laboratory work to the health policy arena. He served as president of the Society for Pediatric Research in 1961 and 1962 and in 1965 became dean of the school of medicine at Case Western Reserve. Robbins also began an intense involvement in national committees on a wide range of topics including human experimentation, Third World health policies, and public food and safety policy. From 1973 to 1974 he served as president of the American Pediatric Society.

In 1979 Robbins was appointed chairman of the advisory council for the congressional Office of Technology Assessment. He retired from his position at Case in 1980, but only to go on with other projects. Elected president of the Institute of Medicine (IOM) for a five-year term beginning in 1980, he also held a concurrent appointment as distinguished professor of pediatrics at Georgetown University from 1981 to 1985. Robbins's work for the Institute of Medicine began long before 1980 with his participation on many of their studies and reports. He chaired a study on the health effects of legalizing abortion and participated in another on the use of saccharin in food. For all his research work, Robbins's peers considered him more a consultant or negotiator than an innovator. When chosen as IOM president he was credited by Joyce McCann, a member of the minority view on the saccharin report, as having an "ability to deal with groups of people who are at opposite ends of the spectrum," according to a March, 1980, article in *Science.*

Robbins's career covered a great deal of territory, from the laboratory to the classroom to the meeting room. His contribution to science in terms of laboratory research has been memorialized by the receipt of the Nobel Prize. In the end, however, it is possible his greater legacy will be in the area of health policy. Regardless, his importance in the field of science is assured.

SELECTED WRITINGS BY ROBBINS:

Periodicals

Enders, J. F., Weller, T. H., and Robbins, F. C., "Cultivation of the Lansing Strain of Poliomyelitis Virus in Cultures of Various Human Embryonic Tissues," *Science,* January 28, 1949, pp. 85–87.

SOURCES:

Books

Current Biography, H. W. Wilson, 1955, p. 183.
Fox, D., Meldrum, M., and Rezak, I., editors, *Nobel Laureates in Medicine or Physiology: A Biographical Dictionary,* Garland Publishing, 1990, pp. 471–74.

Periodicals

"Institute of Medicine Names Robbins President," *Science,* March 14, 1980, pp. 1184–85.
Sun, Marjorie, "Institute of Medicine Gets New President," *Science,* November 7, 1980, pp. 616–17.

—*Sketch by Kimberlyn McGrail*

Lawrence Roberts
1937-
American computer scientist

Lawrence Roberts is best known for implementing ARPANET, the first computer network that moved information using what is called "packet switching," transmitting bursts of information via a shared network connection. The success of ARPANET in the late 1960s, while Roberts was director of the Information Processing Techniques Office of the Advanced Research Projects Agency (ARPA), proved that networks could move information economically and quickly, a crucial step toward the development of such computer networks as the vast Internet system of the late twentieth century and most other distributed computer networks. For his role in establishing the viability of networking, Roberts has been dubbed "the father of computer networks."

Lawrence G. Roberts was born in Norwalk, Connecticut, on December 21, 1937. He received a B.S. degree in 1959 from the Massachusetts Institute of Technology (MIT) and went on to receive an M.S. in 1960 and a doctorate in electrical engineering in 1963 from the same institution. His doctoral dissertation treated machine perception of three dimensional solids.

Establishes the First Computer Network

Until the late–1960s data was transmitted over interactive communication networks by circuit switching, where a particular bandwidth was preallocated for a particular transmission. This system, requiring a dedicated link between points, left more than 90 percent of the possible communication potential of the network unused. With packet switching, computers dynamically allocate unused portions of the communication network to transmission bursts, or "packets," allowing many users to share the same transmission line previously required for one user. Because of its greater efficiency in utilizing network potential, packet switching offers significant economic savings over circuit switching. Dynamic allocation was actually an idea that had been successfully used by early communications technologies, but what worked with postal service and telegraph traffic—which were controlled manually—was at first not considered possible with the complex communications systems of the mid-twentieth century. Computer professionals trying to improve networking capabilities applied dynamic allocation principles in the 1960s with favorable results, however. The application of packet switching to twentieth-century technologies was the work of a number of people, including

Paul Baran of the Rand Corporation, J. C. R. Licklider, then at the Advanced Research Projects Agency, Donald Davies of the National Physical Laboratory in the United Kingdom, and Roberts, then at MIT working on computers. In 1966 Roberts staged an early experiment in computer networking, when he created a network at MIT's Lincoln Labs linking a TX–2 with an SDC Q32.

In October 1967 Roberts proposed the ARPANET at a computer conference in Gatlinburg, Tennessee. His plan to link some of the main academic, commercial, and military computer sites originally encompassed four nodes, or database sites, comprising the network in 1969; that number grew to 111 by 1977. By the 1990s the descendants of ARPANET, including the National Science Foundation's Internet, had literally millions of subscribers and, in effect, all the larger networks had become linked into one vast network, where people from all over the world interact electronically.

Roberts has continued to develop networks through his role as a leader of key institutions involved in the fundamental technologies and processes. He remained with ARPA from 1967 to 1973. He then became the president of Telenet Communications Corporation, where, under Robert's leadership, the first public network utilizing packet switching was introduced in August 1975. It quickly grew from seven nodes to 187. Roberts served as president of GTE Telenet Corporation from 1980 to 1982 and of GTE's Subscriber Network during the same period. In 1982 he became president of DHL Corporation and Chair of the Board of NETEXPRESS Inc. The companies that Roberts has led have continued to introduce innovations in networking technologies, including integrating satellites into networks and in developing the technologies to transmit voices, images, and other forms of data.

Roberts is a member of the National Academy of Engineers, the Institute of Electrical and Electronics Engineers, and the Association of Computing Machinery. He has received several significant awards for his research, including the L. M. Erickson award in 1981 and the 1990 W. Wallace McDowell award from the IEEE Computer Society for bringing packet switching into practical use.

SELECTED WRITINGS BY ROBERTS:

Periodicals

"Multiple Computer Networks and Intercomputer Communication," *ACM Symposium on Operating System Principles,* October, 1967.
"The Evolution of Packet Switching," *Proceedings of the IEEE,* November, 1978, pp. 1307–13.

SOURCES:

Books

A History of ARPANET: The First Decade, Bolt Beranek & Newman, Inc. (BBN), 1981.

—*Sketch by Chris Hables Gray*

Richard J. Roberts
1943-
English biochemist

For decades scientists assumed that genes are continuous segments within deoxyribonucleic acid (DNA), the chemical template of heredity. In 1977, however, Richard. J. Roberts, a thirty-four year old British scientist working with adenovirus, the same virus that causes the common cold and pink eye, discovered that genes (the functional units of heredity) can be composed of several separate segments rather than of a single chain along the DNA strand. For his discovery of "split genes," Roberts was awarded the Nobel Prize in 1993.

Richard John Roberts was born on September 6, 1943, in Derby, England, a mid-sized industrial city about forty miles northeast of Birmingham. His father, John Roberts, was a motor mechanic, while his mother, Edna (Allsop) Roberts, took care of the family and served as Richard's first tutor. In 1947, the Roberts family moved to Bath, where Richard spent his formative years. At St. Stephen's junior school, Roberts encountered his first real mentor, the school's headmaster known only to the students as Mr. Broakes. Here he was exposed to a variety of mentally-stimulating games, ranging from crossword to logical puzzles. "Most importantly, I learned that logic and mathematics are fun!," Roberts wrote in a brief autobiography for the Nobel Foundation.

At the City of Bath Boys School (now Beechen Cliff School), Roberts became enamored with the life and literature of detectives, as they represented the ultimate puzzle solvers. His young career path changed abruptly, however, when he received a chemistry set from his parents. His ever supportive father had a large chemistry cabinet constructed and, with the aid of a local chemist who supplied the myriad chemicals he needed, Roberts soon discovered how to assemble fireworks and other concoctions not found in a beginner's chemistry manual. "Luckily I survived those years with no serious injuries or burns.

I knew I had to be a chemist," he wrote in the Nobel Foundation autobiography.

At the age of seventeen, Roberts entered Sheffield University, where he concentrated in chemistry. His initial introduction to biochemistry was totally negative, he recalled in his autobiography: "I loathed it. The lectures merely required rote learning and the laboratory consisted of the most dull experiments imaginable." After graduating with honors in 1965, Roberts remained at Sheffield to study for his doctoral degree under David Ollis, his undergraduate professor of organic chemistry. But the direction of Roberts' scientific interests were profoundly altered after reading a book by John Kendrewon crystallography and molecular biology. Roberts became hooked on molecular biology and was later invited to conduct his postdoctoral work as part of a research team assembled by his colleague, Jack Strominger, a professor of biochemistry and molecular biology at Harvard University.

In 1969, Roberts left the English countryside and moved to Cambridge, Massachusetts, where he spent the next four years deciphering the sequence of nucleotides in a form of ribonucleic acid known as tRNA. Using a new method devised by English biochemist **Frederick Sanger** at Cambridge, he was able to sequence the RNA molecule, while teaching other scientists Sanger's technique. His creative work with tRNA led to the publication of two papers in *Nature* and an invitation by genetic pioneer and Nobel laureate, **James Watson**, to join his laboratory in Cold Spring Harbor, Long Island, New York.

In 1972, Roberts moved to Long Island to research ways to sequence DNA. American microbiologists **Daniel Nathans** and **Hamilton Smith** had shown that a restriction enzyme, Endonuclease R, could split DNA into specific segments. Roberts thought that such small segments could be used for DNA sequencing and began looking for other new restriction enzymes to expand the repertoire. (Enzymes are complex proteins that catalyze specific biochemical reactions.) He noted in his autobiography that his laboratory was responsible for discovering or characterizing three-quarters of the world's first restriction enzymes. In 1977, he developed a series of biological experiments to "map" the location of various genes in adenovirus and found that one end of a messenger ribonucleic acid (mRNA) did not react as expected. With the use of an electron microscope, Roberts and his colleagues observed that genes could be present in several, well-separated DNA segments. As he told the *New York Times,* "Everybody thought that genes were laid out in exactly the same way, and so it came as a tremendous surprise that they were different in higher organisms, such as humans."

In 1986, Roberts married his second wife, Jean. He is the father of four children, Alison, Andrew, Christopher and Amanda. He moved back to Massachusetts in 1992 to join New England Biolabs, a small, private company in Beverly, Massachusetts, involved in making research reagents, particularly restriction enzymes. He serves as joint research director. In 1993, Roberts was awarded the Nobel Prize for his discovery of "split genes." The Nobel Committee stated that, "The discovery of split genes has been of fundamental importance for today's basic research in biology, as well as for more medically oriented research concerning the development of cancer and other diseases."

SELECTED WRITINGS BY ROBERTS:

Books

(With G. Akusjarvi and U. Pettersson) "Structure and Function of the Adenovirus–2 Genome," in *Adenovirus DNA, The Viral Genome and Its Expression,* edited by W. Doerfler, Martinus Nijhoff, 1986, pp. 53–95.

(With S. S. Halford) "Type II Restriction Endonucleases," in *Nucleases,* edited by S. M. Linn, R. S. Lloyd, and R. J. Roberts, Cold Spring Harbor Press, 1993, pp. 35–88.

Periodicals

"Restriction Endonucleases," *CRC Critical Reviews in Biochemistry,* Volume 4, 1976, pp. 123–64.

(With L. T. Chow, R. E. Gelinas, and T. R. Broker) "An Amazing Sequence Arrangement at the 5' Ends of Adenovirus–2 Messenger RNA," *Cells,* Volume 12, 1977, pp. 1–8.

(With T. R. Broker, L. T. Chow, A. R. Dunn, R. E. Gelinas, J. A. Hassell, D. F. Klessig, J. B. Lewis and B. S. Zain) "Adenovirus–2 Messenger—An Example of Baroque Molecular Structure," *Cold Spring Harbor Symposium on Quantitative Biology,* Volume 42, 1978, pp. 531–53.

SOURCES:

Periodicals

New York Times, October 12, 1993. p. B9.

Other

Richard J. Roberts, autobiographical sketch, provided by the Nobel Foundation to Benedict A. Leerburger.

—Sketch by Benedict A. Leerburger

Julia Robinson
1919-1985
American mathematician

Excelling in the field of mathematics, Julia Robinson was instrumental in solving Hilbert's tenth problem—to find an effective method for determining whether a given diophantine equation is solvable with integers. Over a period of two decades, she developed the framework on which the solution was constructed. In recognition of her accomplishments, she became the first woman mathematician elected to the National Academy of Sciences, the first female president of the American Mathematical Society, and the first woman mathematician to receive a MacArthur Foundation Fellowship.

Robinson was born Julia Bowman on December 8, 1919, in St. Louis, Missouri. Her mother, Helen Hall Bowman, died two years later; Robinson and her older sister went to live with their grandmother near Phoenix, Arizona. The following year their father, Ralph Bowman, retired and joined them in Arizona after becoming disinterested in his machine tool and equipment business. He expected to support his children and his new wife, Edenia Kridelbaugh Bowman, with his savings. In 1925, her family moved to San Diego; three years later a third daughter was born.

At the age of nine, Robinson contracted scarlet fever, and the family was quarantined for a month. They celebrated the end of isolation by viewing their first talking motion picture. The celebration was premature, however, as Robinson soon developed rheumatic fever and was bedridden for a year. When she was well enough, she worked with a tutor for a year, covering the required curriculum for the fifth through eighth grades. She was fascinated by the tutor's claim that it had been proven that the square root of two could not be calculated to a point where the decimal began to repeat. Her interest in mathematics continued at San Diego High School; when she graduated with honors in mathematics and science, her parents gave her a slide rule that she treasured and named "Slippy."

At the age of sixteen, Robinson entered San Diego State College. She majored in mathematics and prepared for a teaching career, being aware of no other mathematics career choices. At the beginning of Robinson's sophomore year, her father found his savings depleted by the Depression and committed suicide. With help from her older sister and an aunt, Robinson remained in school. She transferred to the University of California, Berkeley, for her senior year and graduated in 1940.

At Berkeley, she found teachers and fellow students who shared her excitement about mathematics. In December of 1941, she married an assistant professor named Raphael Robinson. At that time she was a teaching assistant at Berkeley, having completed her master's degree in 1941. The following year, however, the school's nepotism rule prevented her from teaching in the mathematics department. Instead, she worked in the Berkeley Statistical Laboratory on military projects. She became pregnant but lost her baby; because of damage to Robinson's heart caused by the rheumatic fever, her doctor warned against future pregnancies. Her hopes of motherhood crushed, Robinson endured a period of depression that lasted until her husband rekindled her interest in mathematics.

In 1947 she embarked on a doctoral program under the direction of **Alfred Tarski**. In her dissertation, she proved the algorithmic unsolvability of the theory of the rational number field. Her Ph.D. was conferred in 1948. That same year, Tarski discussed an idea about diophantine equations (polynomial equations of several variables, with integer coefficients, whose solutions are to be integers) with Raphael Robinson, who shared it with his wife. By the time she realized it was directly related to the tenth problem on Hilbert's list, she was too involved in the topic to be intimidated by its stature. For the next twenty-two years she attacked various aspects of the problem, building a foundation on which Yuri Matijasevic proved in 1970 that the desired general method for determining solvability does not exist. While working at the RAND Corporation in 1949 and 1950, Robinson developed an iterative solution for the value of a finite two-person zero-sum game. Her only contribution to game theory is still considered a fundamental theorem in the field.

Robinson's heart damage was surgically repaired in 1961, but her health remained impaired. Her fame from the Hilbert problem solution resulted in her appointment as a full professor at Berkeley in 1976, although she was expected to carry only one-fourth of the normal teaching load. Eight years later she developed leukemia and died on July 30, 1985.

SELECTED WRITINGS BY ROBINSON:

Books

(With Martin Davis and Yuri Matijasevic) "Hilbert's Tenth Problem. Diophantine Equations: Positive Aspects of a Negative Solution," in *Mathematical Developments Arising from Hilbert's Problems,* edited by F. E. Browder, American Mathematical Society, 1976.

Periodicals

"Definability and Decision Problems in Arithmetic," *Journal of Symbolic Logic,* Volume 14, 1949, pp. 98–114.

"Existential Definability in Arithmetic," *Transactions of the American Mathematical Society,* Volume 72, number 3, 1952, pp. 437–449.

(With Martin Davis and Hilary Putnam) "The Decision Problem for Exponential Diophantine Equations," *Annals of Mathematics,* Volume 74, number 3, 1961, pp. 425–436.

SOURCES:

Periodicals

"Julia Bowman Robinson, 1919–1985," *Notices of the American Mathematical Society,* November, 1985, pp. 738–742.

Reid, Constance, "The Autobiography of Julia Robinson," *The College Mathematics Journal,* January, 1986, pp. 2–21.

Smorynski, C., "Julia Robinson, In Memoriam," *The Mathematical Intelligencer,* spring 1986, pp. 77–79.

—*Sketch by Loretta Hall*

Robert Robinson
1886-1975
English chemist

Robert Robinson worked on many types of chemical problems, but he received the 1947 Nobel Prize for his work with the alkaloids, complex nitrogen-containing natural compounds that often exhibit high biological activity. His work in synthesis, identification, and reaction theory make him one of the founders of modern organic chemistry. Robinson summed up his philosophy about basic research when he said in his Nobel address, "In both [chemistry and physics] it is in the course of attack of the most difficult problems, without consideration of eventual applications, that new fundamental knowledge is most certainly garnered.... Such contributions as I have been able to make are to the science itself and do not derive their interest from the economic or biological importance of the substances studied."

Robinson was born to the inventor William Bradbury Robinson and Jane (Davenport) Robinson on September 13, 1886 near Chesterfield, England. His very large family included eight half-siblings from his father's first marriage, as well as four younger children. The family moved to New Brampton when Robinson was three years old. He received an excellent private education from the Fulneck School, run by the Moravian Church, and entered Manchester University in 1902. Robinson's family had manufactured bandages and other medical products for nearly a century and he was expected to enter the family business, so his father insisted that he study chemistry instead of mathematics. While at Manchester, Robinson studied under William H. Perkin, Jr., and after graduating with high honors in 1905, he worked in Perkin's private laboratory for five years before finishing his Ph.D. in 1910. In 1912, Robinson moved to Australia to take a teaching position at the University of Sydney. He returned to England in 1915 and held university appointments at Liverpool, St. Andrews, and Manchester, before finally landing at Oxford as Waynflete Professor of Chemistry, succeeding his mentor Perkin. Robinson remained at Oxford until his retirement in 1955. He also spent time as a consultant to the dye and petroleum industries.

Robinson's interests spanned all of organic chemistry (molecular structure elucidation, theoretical considerations, and synthesis), and most of them originated in Perkin's laboratory. He first studied such plant pigments as brazilin , a dyestuff obtainable from brazilwood, and the group of red/blue flower pigments called anthocyanins. He also worked on some of the steroid hormones, and synthesized several artificial estrogens. As did many scientists of the time, during World War II Robinson worked on war-related research efforts—from explosives to anti-malarial drugs to penicillin. Later in his life, Robinson became interested in geochemistry, particularly the origin and composition of petroleum. His work convinced him that plants must synthesize chemicals in certain ways, and he proposed a biosynthesis pathway (later confirmed by radioactive tracers) for some of the plant alkaloids. His contributions to chemical theory also include ideas on the electron distribution (and therefore the chemical reactivity) of aromatic compounds like benzene.

Alkaloid Research Leads to Nobel Prize

Alkaloids, although not the largest natural chemical compounds, are arguably the most complex, since they always contain nitrogen and usually some combination of carbon rings. Alkaloids as a group have profound biochemical effects on living things; cocaine, morphine and opium all belong to this class of natural products, as do many natural poisons. Robinson elucidated the structure of morphine and strychnine, and synthesized the alkaloids papaverine, hydrastine, narcotine, and tropinone.

In addition to receiving the 1947 Nobel Prize in chemistry for his work with the alkaloids, Robinson was knighted in 1939; he was also awarded the Order of Merit in 1949, and the Longstaff, Faraday, Davy, Royal, and Copley medals. In addition, he was an active member of numerous professional organizations around the world: at different times during his career, he served as president of the Royal Society, the British Association for the Advancement of Science, and the Society of the Chemical Industry. With the help of Nobel Laureate **Robert B. Woodward**, Robinson established the organic chemistry journal *Tetrahedron.*

Robinson married Gertrude Maude Walsh in 1912; they had a son and a daughter. Robinson's hobbies included music, literature, gardening, and photography, but his most enthusiastic pursuits outside of science were mountain-climbing (he and his wife explored ranges all over the world) and chess. He won several chess championships, served as president of the British Chess Federation, and collaborated on a book entitled *The Art and Science of Chess.* Three years after his wife's death in 1954, Robinson married Stearn Hillstrom. He retired from Oxford in 1955, and died on February 8, 1975.

SELECTED WRITINGS BY ROBINSON:

Periodicals

"A Theory of the Mechanisms of the Phytochemical Synthesis of Certain Alkaloids" *Journal of the Chemical Society,* Volume 111, 1917, p. 876; portions reprinted in *Source Book in Chemistry 1900–1950,* edited by H. M. Leicester, Harvard University Press, 1968, p. 279.

SOURCES:

Books

Nobel Prize Winners in Chemistry: 1901–1961, revised edition, Abelard Schuman, 1963, p. 198.
Wasson, Tyler, editor, *Nobel Prize Winners,* H. W. Wilson, 1987, p. 873.

—*Sketch by Gail B. C. Marsella*

John Rock
1890-1984
American gynecologist and obstetrician

John Rock was a gynecologist, obstetrician, and medical researcher who played a significant role in developing and promoting the use of oral contraceptives. As a leading authority on the reproductive system and embryology, he contributed to the understanding of infertility and reproductive problems and founded the Rock Reproductive Clinic in Brookline, Massachusetts. A devout Roman Catholic, he also challenged his church's opposition to the use of the birth control pill.

Rock, one of five children, was born March 24, 1890 in Marlborough, Massachusetts, to Frank Sylvester Rock and Ann Jane (Murphy) Rock. His father was an enterprising businessman who owned a liquor store, dealt in real estate, and promoted the local baseball team. The younger Rock graduated from Boston High School of Commerce and worked for a year and a half as an accountant for a fruit company in Guatemala and then with a construction firm in Rhode Island. Rock was fired from both jobs and decided to follow his father's advice to attend college.

Graduating with a baccalaureate degree from Harvard in 1915, he received the M.D. degree from Harvard Medical School in 1918. Rock interned at Massachusetts General Hospital, doing his residency in urology there and also at Boston Lying-in Hospital. After one year as a surgeon at Brookline Free Hospital for Women, he set up his own practice. His long professional relations with Harvard Medical School began in 1922 when he was appointed assistant professor of obstetrics.

Seeks Answers to Reproductive Problems

Rock opened one of the first fertility and endocrine clinics at the Free Hospital for Women in the mid-1920s. At that time his main concern was solving reproductive problems rather than birth control. In 1944, along with Harvard scientist Miriam F. Menkin, Rock fertilized the first human egg in a test tube. He is also credited with the first recorded recovery of human embryos 2 to 17 days after fertilization as well as establishing the fact that ovulation occurs 14 days before menstruation.

In the early 1950s Rock began experimenting with progesterone, the female hormone that suppresses ovulation. Progesterone is secreted by the body during pregnancy so that no eggs are discharged—nature's way of preventing overlapping pregnancies. He surmised that giving the reproductive system a "rest" by injecting childless women with progesterone might increase fertility when the injections were stopped. Though he was aware of the contraceptive possibilities of the hormone, he ignored those aspects for fear of the state's anti-birth control laws. At that time in Massachusetts, each instance of birth control advice would result in a fine of $1000 and a possible five-year prison sentence.

Rock corresponded with scientists **Gregory Pincus**, the world's foremost authority on the mammalian egg, and **M. C. Chang**, a specialist in the biology of sperm, about the possibility of developing a useful progestin, or synthetic progesterone, that could be given orally. With Pincus and Chang intent on investigating the hormones contraceptive properties, Rock's focus began to shift in that direction as well. Many pharmaceutical companies had developed progestins but none had been tried on humans. Chang and Pincus had methodically tested hundreds of variations of progestin and found two that could be safely tested on women. While Rock began the first tests for treatment of sterility on 50 females in 1954, simultaneous investigations into the effectiveness of progestin as a contraceptive were also undertaken. The researchers were amazed to discover that although 15 percent of the women on natural progesterone ovulated, none of those using the oral progestins did.

At this point Rock left the clinic at the Free Hospital for Women, having reached the mandatory retirement age of 65, and opened the Rock Reproductive Clinic. Realizing the need for more extensive tests, but aware of the legal and social complications involved, he chose to do field trials in Puerto Rico, Haiti, and Mexico, with a progestin manufactured by G. D. Searle Company. Of the women who followed directions, none became pregnant. The studies were now ready to present in the United States.

In 1959 Searle applied to license the "Pill"—as the oral progestin became known—as a contraceptive, choosing Rock to present the findings of the experiences of 897 women before the Food and Drug Administration (FDA). The requirement at the time was that a drug must be proven safe and not necessarily effective. However, the young reviewer, who was aware of the implications of the Pill, was thorough in his examination, requiring further lab tests before approval. On May 11, 1960 the FDA approved Searle's Enovid, the first drug approved in order to prevent a medical happening. By 1964 some four million women were on the pill.

Rock Takes on Goliath

Rock was a devout member of the Roman Catholic church, whose traditional position was that no unnatural form of birth control be used. Believing in the right of choice, Rock became an outspoken activist for the use of contraceptives to control population explosion, in direct opposition to the teachings of the church. In 1931 he worked for the repeal of a Massachusetts law against the sale of birth control devices, and in 1945 he began teaching students at Harvard Medical School how to prescribe them. Rock took on the hierarchy of the Catholic church, arguing that the pill was a variant of the rhythm method. Using a strategy of logic, he showed that the pill of natural hormones extended the time when a woman was naturally sterile, hence increasing the rhythm method.

In 1963 he took his case through the mass media in a book, *The Time Has Come: A Catholic Doctor's Proposal to End the Battle Over Birth Control*. The book defended the morality of the pill and urged science and religion to unite on a system of population control. He was strongly criticized by conservative Catholic theologians but was described in the press as David taking on Goliath. As a result Pope Paul IV appointed a papal commission to study the issue. Although the commission recommended the pill, the hierarchy said no. With a clear conscience that he was right and the church leaders had made a mistake, Rock remained a devout Catholic, attending mass daily until his death on December 4, 1984.

Rock was a member of many societies, including Planned Parenthood, and was a founding fellow of the American College of Obstetricians and Gynecologists. Among the awards he received were the Lasker award from Planned Parenthood in 1940 and the Ortho award from the American Gynecological Society in 1949. He is credited not only with being the "father" of the first birth control pill but also popularizing and selling it to a skeptical world.

SELECTED WRITINGS BY ROCK:

Books

(With David Loth) *Voluntary Parenthood,* Random House, 1949.
The Time Has Come: A Catholic Doctor's Proposal to End the Battle Over Birth Control, Knopf, 1963.

SOURCES:

Books

Henden, David, *The Life Givers,* William Morrow, 1976.
McLaughlin, Loretta, *The Pill, John Rock, and the Church: The Biography of a Revolution,* Little, Brown, 1983.

Periodicals

McLaughlin, Loretta, "Dr. Rock and the Birth of the Pill," *Yankee,* September, 1990, pp. 72–77, 152–155.

—*Sketch by Evelyn B. Kelly, Ph.D.*

Mabel M. Rockwell
19(?)-1979
American electrical and aeronautical engineer

Mabel M. Rockwell was an electrical and aeronautical engineer whose activities ranged from the development of aircraft manufacturing processes to the design of underwater propulsion systems and submarine guidance instrumentation. Believed to be the first woman aeronautical engineer in the United States, she was one of the designers of the control system for the Polaris missile and for the Atlas guided missile launcher. Rockwell also helped design and install electrical power systems for facilities on the Colorado River.

A native of Philadelphia, Pennsylvania, Mabel MacFerran Rockwell was the daughter of Edgar O. MacFerran and Mabel Alexander. She attended Bryn Mawr College before transferring to the Massachusetts Institute of Technology, where she received a bachelor's degree in science, teaching, and mathematics in 1925. Stanford University awarded her a degree in electrical engineering the next year. Rockwell began her career with the Southern California Edison Company as a technical assistant. In this capacity, she pioneered in the application of the method of symmetrical components to transmission relay problems in power systems. This was crucial to the tracing of system malfunctions and to making multiple-circuit lines more reliable. Rockwell was then named assistant engineer with the Metropolitan Water District in Southern California, where she continued to work in the area of power transmission. During this time Rockwell served on the team who designed the Colorado River Aqueduct's power system and was the only woman to participate in the creation of electrical installations at Boulder Dam.

Contributes to U.S. World War II Effort

Three years later Rockwell joined Lockheed Aircraft Corporation as plant electrical engineer. She was named production research engineer in 1940, overseeing twenty-five engineers and technicians in an effort to enhance the aircraft manufacturing process. Rockwell and her staff converted a small factory to a military aircraft plant during World War II. The innovations of Rockwell and many of her contemporaries were shared with other aerospace firms in order to optimize the design and speed the production of military craft during the war. While at Lockheed, Rockwell conducted research on refining the process of spotwelding and developed techniques for maintaining cleaner surfaces, which are necessary to ensure complete fusion of metals during the welding process. She also investigated electrical and mechanical problems in aircraft manufacture, such as the uniform application of heat pressure in welding, the production of aircraft parts from sheet metal, and methods for supplying the huge amounts of electrical power necessary to produce the high temperatures needed for welding metal pieces into sections of airplanes. One result of Rockwell's research was that riveting was replaced by the more sophisticated process of spotwelding, which reduced the cost and accelerated the rate of aircraft production.

Following her wartime endeavors with Lockheed, Rockwell joined the staff of Westinghouse, where she designed the electrical control system for the Polaris missile launcher. Later, while at Convair, she developed the launching and ground controls for the Atlas guided missile system. For her contributions to these programs, President Dwight D. Eisenhower named her Woman Engineer of the Year in 1958. Rockwell also served as an engineer at McClellan Air Force Base in California, the Mare Island Naval Installation, the U.S. Bureau of Reclamation, and the Naval Ordnance Test Station in Pasadena, California. Rockwell was appointed consulting technical editor at Stanford University's electrical engineering department, where her meticulous editing of scholarly papers became known as "Mabelizing." She continued to edit doctoral dissertations into her seventies, on such subjects as computer science, mathematics, and systems theory. In addition to Eisenhower's award, Rockwell was presented with the Society of Women Engineer's Achievement Award in 1958, for "her significant contributions to the field of electrical control systems." In 1935, she married engineer Edward W. Rockwell; the couple had one daughter. In her spare time she enjoyed tennis, horseback riding, and skiing. Rockwell died in June, 1979.

SOURCES:

Books

Goff, Alice C., *Women Can Be Engineers,* Edwards Brothers, 1946, pp. 94–112.

Periodicals

M.I.T. Technology Review, June/July 1980, p. B–7.

—*Sketch by Karen Withem*

Wendell L. Roelofs
1938-
American biochemist

Wendell L. Roelofs was instrumental in developing insect sex attractants—substances used to attract insects—for pest control in crops. An organic chemist by training, Roelofs has identified more than 100 attractants of different insect species, using a technique that was hailed as a major breakthrough. Roelofs conducted tests in fields to determine how to use the attractants to lure male insects to traps or to confuse them, thus preventing them from mating.

Wendell Lee Roelofs was born on July 26, 1938, in Orange City, Iowa, to Edward and Edith Beyers Roelofs. His father was a life insurance salesman and former superintendent of schools. Roelofs was the youngest of three boys; his two brothers also became scientists, one of them a chemist and the other an electrical engineer. As an undergraduate at Central College in Pella, Iowa, Roelofs majored in chemistry. He earned his bachelor's degree in 1960 and subsequently married Marilyn Joyce Kuiken. The couple raised four children: Brenda Jo, Caryn Jean, Jeffrey Lee, and Kevin Jon.

Roelofs attended graduate school at Indiana University in Bloomington and studied organic chemistry. He wrote his doctorate thesis on biologically active compounds with potential use in medicine. For his post-doctoral work, Roelofs moved on to the Massachusetts Institute of Technology (MIT). While looking for a job in 1965, Roelofs heard of an opening in the entomology department at Cornell University's New York State Agricultural Experiment Station. The department chair, Paul Chapman, was looking for an organic chemist to explore insect sex attractants called pheromones.

Rachel Carson's book, *Silent Spring,* published in 1962, had raised consciousness about the overuse of toxic pesticides to control insects and the need for alternatives. Female insects relied on pheromones to attract mates. Instead of poisons, pheromones could be used to prevent insects from mating and multiplying. Roelofs had never even taken a college course in biology, but the job piqued his interest in the subject. He was hired as an assistant professor, and his new research soon led him to the interface of the disciplines of chemistry and biology.

Every insect species used a unique blend of chemicals as a sex attractant; when Roelofs began his work in 1965, no more than a few had been identified. After nearly 30 years of research, one team of German researchers had discovered the composition of one sex attractant. The work required removing the glands from thousands of female insects, extracting the pheromone, and running it through tests to determine its chemical composition. The first task Roelofs faced at the agricultural station was to begin a mass breeding program to raise insects. He decided to study the voracious pest of apple crops, the redbanded leafroller moth. After extracting the pheromone from approximately 50,000 female moths, Roelofs used a new instrument called a gas chromatograph. He identified the pheromone's composition after about two years.

Roelofs then developed an even greater shortcut to identifying the pheromones. German researchers had been studying the response of silkworm antennae to pheromones by using an instrument called an electroantennogram. The antenna of a male moth was hooked up to a machine that recorded each time the moth responded to a pheromone. Roelofs realized that he could use the technique on male moths to identify sex attractants. Using the electroantennogram reduced identification time to a matter of days and, in some cases, hours. Roelofs isolated the sex attractants of more than 100 species, including the grape berry moth, the tobacco budworm moth, and the potato tuberworm.

As an anecdote about how the work became virtually routine, Roelofs recalled that he stopped identifying pheromones after those of the major pests of interest had been described. But upon retiring, a professor from the University of Michigan requested that Roelofs pinpoint one last pheromone. Roelofs offered to spend two days on it and pledged to quit if he could not get results. Within two days, he had found a blend that worked.

Once Roelofs knew the composition of the redbanded leafroller pheromone, he made an artificial blend in the lab. He tested it in the field, confirming that it did indeed attract male moths. From 1969 to 1972 Roelofs and his colleagues explored how to use the redbanded leafroller pheromones in pest control. They laced traps with pheromones to lure males. Moth populations could be suppressed, they found, using as few as one trap per tree. Since males detected pheromones in extremely minute amounts, the researchers also tried releasing enough pheromone to completely confuse and disorient them. In addition to using attractants to disrupt mating, Roelofs used them as a tool to lure insects to traps where their numbers could be monitored. Pesticide applications could then be reduced to times when they were strictly needed and most effective.

Throughout his career, Roelofs's work took him to many parts of the world. He joined delegations to the People's Republic of China in 1976, Japan in 1977, and the Soviet Union in 1978. Roelofs went to New Zealand in 1983 to help research the pheromones of pests attacking kiwifruit crops. Researchers there had successfully identified the pheromones, yet when the pheromones were used in the field, the insects failed to respond. Roelofs and his colleagues discovered the underlying reason: the populations were actually composed of different species that looked very similar but used different pheromones.

Continuing their work in the United States, Roelofs and his colleague Timothy J. Dennehy, an associate professor of entomology, found a way to use pheromones against grape berry moths, the most serious insect pest for grape crops in North America east of the Rocky Mountains. At the time, more than 100 tons of pesticides were required to control the insects each year in New York state alone. In 1984 Roelofs and Dennehy found a way to seal grape berry moth pheromones inside the hollow plastic and wire ties used to keep the grape plants on their trellises. The ties leaked the pheromones slowly over 100 days, distracting the males from finding the females. Experiments showed that vineyards that had been treated with the pheromone generally had less than one percent damage, compared to approximately twenty-three percent in untreated areas.

As Roelofs advanced in his career, he gained pleasure from exploring different facets of pheromone research, from chemical analysis to the design of traps. He investigated how insects made pheromones in their bodies. Once pheromones were in the air, he studied how males honed in on the source. In the basement of a campus building, Roelofs and his colleagues built a wind tunnel for flying insects. A pheromone was released into the tunnel, where they could watch an insect as it navigated toward the source.

Although Roelofs had not foreseen that his work would lead into insect biochemistry, he was pleased with the outcome and timing of his career. "I got in at the ground floor of pheromone research. The field was wide open," Roelofs told Miyoko Chu in an interview. One of the joys of his work, Roelofs said, was the privilege of being able to work in different subfields, including molecular biology, endocrinology, and behavior.

In his spare time, Roelofs coaches a youth league football team of kids aged eleven and twelve. Roelofs likened a cooperative effort in the laboratory to teamwork in football. With a coach's natural ability,

he fostered an atmosphere where people could contribute their academic strengths and interests. "With our wide range of interests, we can always follow the most interesting lead whether it's my area of expertise or not," he told Chu. "That's how we stay at the forefront. It's synergistic. There's more creativity among us all."

In 1978 Roelofs was named the Liberty Hyde Bailey Professor of Insect Biochemistry at the New York State Agricultural Experiment Station. He was awarded the 1982 Wolf Prize in Agriculture, considered the most prestigious international award in that field. The following year, former U.S. President Ronald Reagan awarded him the National Medal of Science.

SELECTED WRITINGS BY ROELOFS:

Books

Establishing Efficacy of Sex Attractants and Disruptants for Insect Control, Entomological Society of America, 1979.

SOURCES:

Roelofs, Wendell L., interview with Miyoko Chu conducted September 4, 1993.

—*Sketch by Miyoko Chu*

Marguerite M. Rogers
1916(?)-1989
American physicist

Marguerite M. Rogers was a physicist who played a significant role in the development of air-launched weapons systems for the United States Navy. For many years she led the Naval Air Warfare Center Weapons Division and was considered an authority on air-launched tactical weapons.

Rogers received her undergraduate degree, M.A. and Ph.D. in physics from Rice University. She served as assistant professor at the University of Houston from 1940 to 1943, before joining the Naval Avionics Facility in Indianapolis as manager of the Optics Section of the Research Department. In 1946, she returned to academia as a research associate at the University of North Carolina, a post she held for two years. In 1948, she joined Oak Ridge National Laboratory as senior physicist. Rogers joined the Naval Ordnance Test Station (NOTS) in 1949, but in 1953 accepted a post as professor of physics and chair of the science division at Columbia College in South Carolina.

In 1957, Rogers renewed her association with NOTS, which later became the Naval Air Warfare Center Weapons Division. She at first was appointed electronics scientist, working on the development of fire-control and navigational systems. She led the Heavy Attack Systems Analysis Branch in 1958, the Air-to-Surface Weapons Division in 1962, and the Weapons Systems Analysis Division in 1966.

During her years with the Naval Air Warfare Center, Rogers contributed to the development of early fire-control systems, weapons effectiveness analyses, aerial rocketry, the "eye" weapon series used in the Vietnam War, and computerized aircraft avionics systems. She rose from project leader to acting laboratory director, and during her career managed a staff of 150 and a $100 million budget.

For her work in Naval weapons development, Rogers received the Naval Weapons Center's highest honor, the L. T. E. Thompson Award, in 1966; the Naval Air Systems Command Superior Civilian Service Award, also in 1966; the Harvey C. Knowles Award of the American Ordnance Association in 1967; the Society of Women Engineers Achievement Award in 1967; the Federal Women's Award in 1976; and the Department of Defense Distinguished Civilian Service Award in 1981. In bestowing one of her many honors, Captain J. I. Hardy said of Rogers: "Her sustained individual performance has demonstrated a high degree of personal integrity, sound judgment, and quality of leadership."

Rogers was married to Dr. Fred Rogers, who passed away in 1956; the couple had five children. Her two sons also became physicists in the defense industry. Rogers organized a 4-H Club in China Lake, California, and served as an officer of her church.

SOURCES:

Books

Society of Women Engineers Achievement Awards, Society of Women Engineers, 1993.

Periodicals

"Rogers Led the Way for Women—Devoted Her Life to Science," *China Lake Rocketeer,* March 17, 1989, p. 3.

"'67 SWE Award Presented to Dr. Rogers," *Society of Women Engineers Newsletter,* September, 1967, pp. 1–3.

—Sketch by Karen Withem

Heinrich Rohrer
1933-
Swiss physicist

Heinrich Rohrer shared half of the 1986 Nobel Prize in physics with **Gerd Binnig** for their development of an entirely new type of microscope that revealed for the first time the atomic structure of the surface of solids. This scanning tunneling microscope (STM) has such a vast array of applications in such a wide range of fields that the Royal Swedish Academy of Sciences was prompted to award its prestigious prize even though the device had only been successfully tested for the first time in 1981.

Rohrer was born on June 6, 1933, in Buchs, St. Gallen, Switzerland, the son of Hans Heinrich Rohrer, a distributor of manufactured goods, and Katharina Ganpenbein Rohrer. When he was sixteen, Rohrer moved with his family from the country to the large city of Zurich. As a student, Rohrer was interested in both physics and chemistry and classical languages, finally settling on the study of physics when he entered the Federal Institute of Technology in Zurich in 1951. He received his diploma in 1955 and his Ph.D. in 1960, both in physics, from the Institute. His doctoral research involved superconductivity.

From 1960 to 1961 Rohrer was a research assistant at the Institute in Zurich and followed this with two years of postdoctoral research in superconducting at Rutgers University in the United States. On his return to Zurich in 1963, Rohrer joined the staff of the research laboratory of International Business Machines (IBM), eventually becoming manager of the physics department as well as an IBM Fellow. Rohrer has remained at the IBM lab throughout his career, except for an academic year as a visiting scholar at the University of California, Santa Barbara, in 1974–75, when he studied nuclear magnetic resonance. In 1961, Rohrer married Rose-Marie Eggar; the couple had two daughters.

After joining IBM, Rohrer expanded his research in physics beyond superconductivity, investigating magnetic fields and critical phenomena. He became interested in the little-understood and complex atomic structures of the surfaces of materials. While electron microscopes had been developed to probe the internal arrangements of atoms in materials, attempts to uncover the very different characteristics of surface atoms had been decidedly unsuccessful. In 1978 Gerd Binnig, a young German who had just received his Ph.D., joined Rohrer's research team in Zurich. Together, Rohrer and Binnig began to explore oxide layers on metal surfaces. They decided to develop a spectroscopic probe and in the process invented an entirely new type of microscope.

Rohrer and Binnig began with the phenomenon called tunneling. As revealed through quantum mechanics, electrons behave in a wavelike manner that causes them to produce a diffuse cloud as they leak out from the surface of a sample. When electron clouds from two adjacent surfaces overlap, electrons tunnel from one surface or cloud to the other. Tunneling through an insulating layer had been used often to reveal information about the materials on either side of the insulation. Rohrer and Binnig decided to tunnel through a vacuum and then use a sharp, needlelike probe within the vacuum to scan the sample's surface. As the scanning tip closely approached the sample, the electron clouds of each overlapped and a tunneling current began to flow. A feedback mechanism used the tunneling current to keep the tip at a constant height above the sample's surface. In this way, the tip followed the contours of the individual atoms of the scanned surface, and a computer processed the tip's motion to produce a three-dimensional, high-resolution image of that surface.

From the beginning, Rohrer told *Science* magazine, "We were quite confident. Even at the beginning, we knew it would be a significant development. The surprising thing is that it went so fast." One large problem was the sensitivity of the scanning tip to disturbances from vibration and noise. Here Rohrer's background in superconductors was helpful, because transducers too are extremely sensitive to vibration. Rohrer and Binnig solved the problem by shielding their scanner from disturbances with magnets and a heavy stone table set on inflated rubber tires. They successfully tested their new device in 1981 and then worked to refine it technologically. By the mid–1980s the STM could fit in the palm of the hand (except for the vacuum chamber) and could show some details as tiny as 0.1 angstrom (with 1 angstrom being about the diameter of a single atom, or 2.5 billionths of an inch). STMs were also developed that worked in water, air, and cryogenic fluids as well as vacuums. By 1987 Rohrer's group at IBM had developed an STM the size of a fingertip.

Rohrer may not have been surprised when he and Binnig shared half of the Nobel Prize in 1986 for their STM. After he received the honor, Rohrer told *Business Week* that when he explained to colleagues at the IBM lab what he and Binnig planned to try,

"They all said, 'You are completely crazy—but if it works, you'll get the Nobel Prize'." In awarding the prize, the Swedish Academy conceded that the STM was completely new and barely yet developed. Nevertheless, the Academy stated, because of the STM, "It is . . . clear that entirely new fields are opening up for the study of the structure of matter." This study has included living organisms such as viruses, catalysts used to produce chemical reactions in the pharmaceutical and petrochemical industries, and semiconductors and metals. (Interestingly, the other recipient of the 1986 Nobel Prize in physics was **Ernst Ruska**, for his design of the first electron microscope in 1931, fifty years before Rohrer and Binnig developed their scanning microscope.)

Rohrer shared other international awards with Binnig for his work on the STM. He is a member of many important scientific societies and has been awarded honorary doctorates by several universities.

SELECTED WRITINGS BY ROHRER:

Periodicals

(With Gerd Binnig) "The Scanning Tunneling Microscope," *Scientific American,* August, 1985, pp. 50–56.
(With Binnig) "Scanning Tunneling Microscopy: From Birth to Adolescence," *Review of Modern Physics,* Volume 59, No. 3, 1987.

SOURCES:

Books

Scanning Tunnelling Microscopy, Springer-Verlag, 1992.
Hansma, Paul K., *Tunneling Spectroscopy: Capabilities, Applications, and New Techniques,* Plenum Press, 1982.
Nobel Prize Winners, H. W. Wilson, 1987.
Nobel Prize Winners: Physics, Volume 3, Salem Press, 1989.

Periodicals

Business Week, November, 3, 1986, pp. 134–36.
The Lancet, September, 5, 1992, pp. 600–01.
New York Times, October 16, 1986, pp. A1 & B18.
Physics Today, January, 1987, pp. 17–21, S–70.
Science, November 14, 1986, pp. 821–22.
Science News, October 25, 1986, pp. 262–63.
Wickramasinghe, H. Kumar, "Scanned-Probe Microscopes," *Scientific American,* October, 1989, pp. 98–105.

—*Sketch by Kathy Sammis*

Nancy Grace Roman
1925-
American astronomer

Nancy Grace Roman is famous for developing satellite observatories to explore the universe from a vantage point that is free from atmospheric interference. She also pioneered using satellites for gamma, X ray, and radio observations. In addition, she has conducted observational astronomical research using traditional earth-based telescopes, studying topics such as stellar motions, photoelectric photometry and spectroscopy.

Roman was born in Nashville, Tennessee on May 16, 1925 to a U.S. Geological Survey geophysicist, Irwin Roman, and his wife, Georgia Frances (Smith) Roman. Educated at Western High School in Baltimore, Maryland, Roman graduated in 1943. She then earned a B.A. in astronomy at Pennsylvania's Swarthmore College, where she was named a Joshua Lippincott Memorial Fellow and worked in the Sproul Observatory. From 1946 to 1948 Roman attended graduate courses at the University of Chicago, assisting at the Yerkes Observatory in Williams Bay, Wisconsin. She earned her Ph.D. in astronomy in 1949; her doctoral research investigated the radial velocities, spectra, and convergent point of the Ursa Major group of stars. Her dissertation appeared in the September 1949 *Astrophysical Journal.*

Also in 1949, Roman worked as a summer research associate at the Case Institute of Technology's Warner and Swasey Observatory, cataloguing high luminosity objects and classifying objective spectra. That fall, she returned to Yerkes, where she served as a research associate between 1949 and 1952, and then as an astronomy instructor from 1952 to 1955. She also made a brief visit in 1953 to Toronto's David Dunlap Observatory to study the radial velocities of certain high-speed faint stars. At Yerkes she researched stellar astronomy and galactic structure, specializing in radial velocity measurements, photoelectric photometry, and spectral classification. She was particularly interested in stellar clusters.

In 1955, Roman moved to the United States Naval Research Observatory (NRO) in Washington, D.C., where she first worked in radio astronomy, soon becoming the head of the microwave spectroscopy lab. Using a 50-foot cast aluminum mirror, Roman researched radio star spectra and the galactic distribution of radio emitters. In addition, she used radar to find the distance between the earth and the moon. During this time she attended a 1957 Soviet Academy of Sciences Symposium to dedicate their new Bjuraken Astrophysical Observatory, and the following year she edited the fifth International Astronomical Union Symposium on large scale galactic structure. In 1958 and 1959 she worked as an NRO consulting astronomer, educating others about radio astronomy and planning the institution's research programs. Roman dramatically expanded her work when in March of 1959 she became the head of the observational astronomy program head at the National Aeronautics and Space Administration (NASA). At NASA Roman developed an ambitious plan to observe objects in space by using rockets and satellite observatories. Charged with developing these efforts, in February, 1960, she was named chief of astronomy and astrophysics at NASA's office of satellites and sounding rockets.

Throughout the 1960s Roman designed instrumentation and made substantial measurements from gamma ray, radio, and visible light satellites, such as the Orbiting Solar Observatories. Her programs gave astronomers the planetary surface knowledge that ultimately led to the successful 1976 *Viking* probes that were designed to collect data from Mars. She became the astronomy program head in 1964 and the chief of the astronomy and relativity program in 1972, remaining in this position until 1979. Her published work from this period generally deals with new satellite data, but she still did earth-based observation, such as her 1967 Kitt Peak Observatory radial velocity and spectral research. She received a NASA award for Exceptional Scientific Research in 1969, and a medal for Outstanding Leadership in 1978. Roman was also granted honorary doctorates from Russell Sage, Hood, Bates, and Swarthmore Colleges between 1966 and 1976.

Roman improved her orbiting observatories throughout the 1970s and 1980s. She measured X ray and ultraviolet readings from the enormously successful OAO–3 or *Copernicus* satellite, launched in 1972, and recorded stellar spectra from the U.S. space station *Skylab*, which circled the earth between 1973 and 1979. During 1979 and 1980 she was also NASA program scientist for a projected space telescope; unfortunately, a decade of cost overruns and delays postponed the launch of NASA's Hubble space telescope until April 25, 1990. Meanwhile, as a NASA consulting astronomer, beginning in 1980, and a senior scientist for the Astronomical Data Center from 1981 onwards, Roman worked to prepare computer-readable versions of astronomical catalogues, databases, and other bibliographic tools.

SELECTED WRITINGS BY ROMAN:

Books

(Editor) *Comparison of the Large Scale Structure of the Galactic System with That of Other Systems,* Cambridge University Press (Cambridge), 1958.

Periodicals

"The Ursa Major Group," *Astrophysical Journal,* Volume 110, 1949, pp. 205–241.

SOURCES:

Books

The Women's Book of World Records and Achievements, edited by Lois Decker O'Neill, Anchor Books, 1979, pp. 88, 153.

Periodicals

Blackburn, Harriet B., interview with Roman, *Christian Science Monitor,* June 13, 1957.
"Scientist Accepts Soviet Bid", *New York Times,* September 7, 1956, p. 21.
"6 Women Hailed for U.S. Service", *New York Times,* February 6, 1962, p. 39.

—*Sketch by Julian A. Smith*

Alfred Sherwood Romer
1894-1973

American vertebrate paleontologist and anatomist

Some scientists gain prominence through path-breaking research. Others write landmark publications, control key institutions, or train a generation of devoted and skilled disciples. Alfred Sherwood Romer did each of these and more, becoming one of the century's most important vertebrate paleontologists. His unique approach to vertebrate evolution through comparative anatomy led to his prominence in the field, and he also wrote a series of textbooks based on his work.

Born in White Plains, New York, to Harry Houston Romer and Evalyn (Sherwood) Romer on December 28, 1894, Romer claimed an ancestry of predominately New England Puritan, grounded in the 1628–1640 migration, and "a good dash of Scotch-Irish blood," as he wrote to Hugh L. Dryden. Romer's father was a newspaperman who frequently moved the family between New York State and Connecticut. His parents divorced when Alfred was ten; his father's second marriage also collapsed. During this period, Romer lived in a "somewhat miserable situation," often ill, poor, and on his own, as he noted in his letter to Dryden. The situation improved when he went to live with his paternal grandmother for his high school years. After graduating, Romer spent a year doing small jobs and saving money for college.

Romer entered Amherst University in 1914, majoring in German literature and history. He pledged Phi Kappa Psi fraternity, supported himself through small jobs and fraternity loans, and moved from sports reporter to editor-in-chief for *The Amherst Student.* Searching for an easy class to fulfill science requirements while a sophomore, Romer enrolled in a course on evolution, taught in part by vertebrate paleontologist Frederick Brewster Loomis. Captivated by Loomis' section of fossil vertebrates, Romer had, by year's end, chosen his career path, although completing his originally intended liberal arts degree.

Caught in the nation's patriotic fervor in 1917, Romer volunteered for the American Field Service shortly after graduation. He had hoped to drive ambulances in World War I, instead, he transported ammunition in the Soissons sector. Seeking a military commission after his unit was dissolved, Romer joined the U.S. Air Service, where he eventually commanded a repair facility and rose to the rank of second lieutenant. He returned to New York in 1919. With Loomis' recommendation, he entered Columbia University that fall, eager to study vertebrate paleontology at the graduate level. At the time, Columbia provided superb training from internationally renowned biologists and paleontologists. Romer studied under William King Gregory, well known for his understanding of the vertebrate skull, and became part of a close circle of students, including **G. Kinsely Noble**, Charles Camp, and James Chopin. His dissertation on the evolution of locomotory muscles in early reptile groups developed from a comparative myology course taught by Gregory.

After receiving his Ph.D. within a remarkably short period of time in 1921, Romer accepted an instructorship at Bellevue Medical College in New York. It was not uncommon for vertebrate paleontologists to support themselves by teaching anatomy in medical schools. For two years Romer taught histology, embryology, and gross anatomy. (He was a quick learner and often taught courses in specialties for which he had no formal training.) In 1923, Romer was scheduled to direct the human anatomy laboratory at Bellevue, but instead accepted an offer from the University of Chicago to succeed Samuel Williston as its vertebrate paleontologist.

A Foothold in the Profession

The Chicago associate professorship was an enormous opportunity for Romer. Williston had studied early reptiles and amphibians and, together with his chief preparator Paul Miller, had built a considerable collection along these lines. Also interested in the early evolution of tetrapods, Romer eagerly expanded both Williston's research and the Chicago collections. His first expedition to the Permian red-beds of Texas—from which the majority of the existing collection originated—came in 1926; over the years, he returned many times to that region. Furthermore in 1929, Romer and Miller spent six months in South Africa collecting in the Karroo formation, returning with an impressive set of discoveries. The result of this sustained campaign was one of the world's finest collections of early land vertebrates. Romer was promoted to full professor in 1931.

In Chicago, Romer was active in many social and academic circles, including the university's Quadrangle Club and the city-wide Chaos Club. At the university, Romer cooperated with innovators of the general biology curriculum, such as zoologist Horatio Hackett Newman. He even contributed a chapter on the history of vertebrates to Newman's coursebook, *The Nature of the World and of Man,* published in 1926. Stimulated in part by his participation in this effort, Romer decided to expand his chapter into books for two different markets. His *Man and the Vertebrates,* published in 1933, was a general-audience survey of comparative vertebrate anatomy and vertebrate evolution that hinted at Romer's political and social philosophy. As a textbook designed for training specialists, *Vertebrate Paleontology,* published in the same year, complimented his popular treatment by covering the same domain in considerable technical detail. Both books filled long-neglected markets, became standard reading, and were extensively reprinted and translated.

Vertebrate paleontology had marginal status at Chicago, largely because it operated within a geology department where most professors were uninterested in such "soft" geology. Romer's approach was biological, and he often found himself at odds with department colleagues on matters of financial and academic support. As the Depression grew and the University's administration lost its creativity, Romer found an increasing number of obstacles impeding his research and teaching interests.

Fed up with his departmental situation, Romer left Chicago in 1934 for Harvard University and the Museum of Comparative Zoology (MCZ). He had been offered the position of professor of zoology along with being named curator of vertebrate paleontology at the museum. The year before, the school's new president, James Conant, had begun a program to transform the antiquated college into a world-class, modern teaching and research institution. At Harvard, Romer pursued a diverse research program on early land vertebrates in an atmosphere extremely sympathetic to his biological approach. His annual courses on comparative vertebrate anatomy and

vertebrate paleontology were mainstays within the museum.

Romer became director of the MCZ in 1946, following the death of long-time patriarch Thomas Barbour. Knowing his appointment would mean the sacrifice of vital time for research, Romer still accepted the role. At the time, the museum's management was in a poor situation: its endowment was ridiculously small; staff labored under meager salaries and low budgets; and researchers demonstrated severely uneven talents. Romer immediately negotiated for improvements and increased support both from Conant's administration and from the family of Louis Agassiz, the influential nineteenth-century zoologist who had founded the MCZ. Slowly, the museum situation turned around. After nearly two decades as director, Romer believed he had succeeded in returning the MCZ to "first rate" status. Mandatory administration retirement brought his resignation from the post in 1961. Although he had managed to continue some of his research program while director, Romer returned to research and exploration in full force following retirement. Nearly half his bibliography was published following his sixty-fifth birthday. Romer continued at the MCZ until his unexpected death on November 5, 1973.

Central to Romer's life and career was his companionship with his wife, Ruth (Hibbard) Romer. They married in 1924, raised three children, and kept many close friends. Ruth Romer accompanied her husband on many of his travels. She also collected fossils with him and helped administer both his research and his social life. As Edwin H. Colbert pointed out in his article for the National Academy of Sciences, however, Ruth Romer was no mere assistant; rather she "complimented [Romer] in a marvelous fashion."

Building a Profession for Bone Hunters

Romer made many important contributions to vertebrate paleontology's professional development. Frustrated by a lack of recognition among geologists and invertebrate paleontologists regarding the biological interests of his "vertebrate" colleagues, Romer helped organize an independent Section of Vertebrate Paleontology within the Paleontological Society in 1934. By providing a meeting place for him and his colleagues, this Section provided a means for building the cadre of vertebrate workers into a cohesive group. In 1940, the Section transformed itself into the Society of Vertebrate Paleontology. Romer sought similar developments for comparative anatomy within the American Society of Zoologists in 1959. Throughout his life, Romer demanded informality and camaraderie within his profession. He firmly believed that everyone present at society meetings be given an opportunity to discuss any subject they wished during open forums.

Two themes unified Romer's research. Foremost was an interest in the functional implications of anatomical structures. Romer strove to reconstruct and understand extinct animals as once-living organisms. This emphasis found expression in his research on muscle evolution in amphibians and reptiles, the origin and evolution of limbs, the embryonic and evolutionary history of cartilage and bone, and the structure and function of the nervous system. Second, Romer focused on major evolutionary transitions, choosing research topics with implications for the transition from fish to amphibians, amphibians to reptiles, and reptiles to mammals.

Romer described himself as primarily a comparative anatomist. A comprehensive knowledge of vertebrate anatomy is clear from his classic descriptive monographs and from *Vertebrate Paleontology.* His skills as a technical anatomist and taxonomist were demonstrated in his many studies of vertebrate skull structures, Permian and Carboniferous reptiles, labyrinthodont amphibians, and mammal-like reptiles. Although a solid neo-Darwinian, Romer avoided theorizing about evolutionary mechanisms, preferring instead to emphasize empirical studies of evolutionary change. A non-geologist by preference, Romer occasionally ventured into stratigraphy. His last expedition to the Texas red-beds involved detailed mapping of the region's geological history. As Ronald Rainger notes in *Perspectives on Science,* Romer also was one of the first vertebrate paleontologists to suggest the plausibility of continental drift. Through his academic efforts, his writings, and devotion to his profession, Romer left a rich legacy. His effect on the direction of professional bodies and research institutions continues.

SELECTED WRITINGS BY ROMER:

Books

Man and the Vertebrates, University of Chicago Press, 1933.
Vertebrate Paleontology, University of Chicago Press, 1933.
The Vertebrate Body, W. B. Saunders, 1949.
Osteology of the Reptiles, University of Chicago Press, 1956.
(With N. E. Wright, T. Edinger, and R. Van Frank) *Bibliography of Fossil Vertebrates Exclusive of North America, 1509–1927,* two volumes, Geological Society of America, 1962.

Periodicals

(With L. I. Price) "Review of the Pelycosauria," *Geological Society of America Special Paper,* Volume 26, 1940, pp. i-x, 1–538.

"Review of the Labyrinthodontia," *Bulletin of the Museum of Comparative Zoology,* Volume 99, 1947, pp. 1–368.
(With D. M. S. Watson) "A Classification of Therapsid Reptiles," *Bulletin of the Museum of Comparative Zoology,* Volume 114, 1956, pp. 37–89.
"Early Reptilian Evolution Reviewed," *Evolution,* December, 1967, pp. 821–33.
"Cynodont Reptile with Incipient Mammalian Jaw Articulation," *Science,* November 14, 1969, pp. 881–82.

SOURCES:

Periodicals

Anatomical Record, Volume 189, 1977, pp. 314–24.
Biographical Memoirs of Fellows of the Royal Society, Volume 21, Royal Society (London), 1975, pp. 497–516.
Geological Society of America Memorials, Volume 5, 1977, p. 10.
National Academy of Sciences. Biographical Memoirs, 1982, pp. 265–94.
Perspectives on Science, Volume 1, 1993, pp. 478–519.

Other

Alfred Romer's letter to George Simpson, July 16, 1933, American Philosophical Society Library.
Alfred Romer's letter to Hugh L. Dryden, June 5, 1961, National Academy of Sciences Archives.

—*Sketch by Joseph Cain*

Juan Carlos Romero
1937-
Argentine-born American physiologist

Juan Carlos Romero is a renowned authority on the physiology of the kidney. As director of the Hypertension Research Laboratories at the Mayo Clinic since 1982, he has been a prolific investigator into the relationship of the kidney to the development of hypertension (high blood pressure) and has issued more than 175 research papers on kidney functioning during the past thirty years. Since 1984, he has been awarded grants from the National Institute of Health

Juan Carlos Romero

totaling over three million dollars for research and training programs dealing with kidney function and hypertension.

Romero was born on September 15, 1937, in Mendoza, Argentina, the son of Juan Romero and Graciela Vizcaya. He attended San Jose College in Mendoza and graduated with a B.S. in 1955. The next year, he was admitted to the University of Cuyo School of Medicine, Mendoza. While there, he was awarded a scholarship for being one of the two best qualified students. He left school for military service in the Argentine Army in 1958, and rose to the rank of sergeant. He then returned to medical education, married Silvia Divinetz in 1963, and received his M.D. in 1964. Romero began his career in scientific investigation when he became a research assistant in the Institute of Pathological Physiology in 1962 and then continued on as a Fellow at the Consejo Nacional de Investigaciones, also in Mendoza, in 1966.

After Romero was honored with the competitive award of Fellow in the Eli Lilly International Program for Development of Biological Sciences in 1967, he came to the United States to continue his research at the University of Michigan. There, he rose to the position of research associate in the hypertension section of the Department of Internal Medicine. In 1973, he transferred to the Mayo Foundation in Rochester, Minnesota, and has remained there ever since, becoming professor of physiology at the Mayo Medical School and director of the Hypertension Research Laboratories.

Romero has done considerable research on the renin-angiotensin system. It has been discovered that the kidney plays a key role in the incidence of hypertension. With its million or so microscopic nephrons filtering wastes out of the bloodstream, the kidney is a vital organ of excretion that cleanses the blood and also helps maintain the appropriate balance of water and mineral salts in the body. Under certain conditions, the kidney secretes the enzyme renin which reacts in the blood with a protein secreted by the liver to form angiotensin, a vasoconstrictor which causes the smooth muscles of small blood vessels to contract, resulting in elevated blood pressure. He has also explored the effects of the atrial natriuretic peptide, which is produced by the atria of the heart when the blood pressure and volume of blood entering the atria are too high, stimulating the kidneys to excrete more salt and water into the urine. This results in a lowering of blood volume and blood pressure.

Among other areas of his expertise are renal prostaglandin, renal synthesis of nitric oxide, responses of isolated glomeruli (the glomular filters help purify the blood), and evaluation of renal function with computerized tomography, a form of radiology, or X ray, used to examine an organ and the blood flow to an organ. In connection with the latter investigation, in 1991 he received the Cum Laude Research Award from the American Society of Computed Body Tomography for the best scientific work on cross-sectional imaging.

In addition to the Cum Laude Research award, Romero was elected to Sigma Xi and received a competitive award as Established Investigator of the American Heart Association from 1976–1981. He also won the Teacher of the Year Award of the Mayo School of Medicine in 1984. In 1991, he was elected by the Council for High Blood Pressure Research to give the Lewis K. Dahl Memorial Lecture in the American Heart Association's 464th Scientific Session. He has been a key member and chairman of numerous groups specializing in hypertension. Through the years, Romero has also been affiliated with twenty different scientific journals. He is now a U.S. citizen, and he and his wife have two children, Patricia and Gabriela.

SELECTED WRITINGS BY ROMERO:

Books

(With O. A. Carretero) "Production and Characteristics of Experimental Hypertension in Animals," *Hypertension Physiopathology and Treatment,* McGraw-Hill, 1977, pp. 485–507.

(With D. C. Munahan and C. C. Strong) "The Renin-Angiotensin System," *Renal Function Tests: Clinical Laboratory Procedures and Diagnosis,* Little, Brown, 1979, pp. 119–36.

Periodicals

"The Renin-Angiotensin System," *The Physiologist,* Volume 24, Number 5, 1981, p. 59.

"Renal Effects of ANP without Changes in Glomerular Filtration Rate and Blood Pressure," *American Journal of Physiology,* Volume 251, 1986, pp. F532–36.

"Are Renal Hemodynamics a Key Factor in the Development and Maintenance of Arterial Hypertension in Humans?" *Hypertension,* Volume 23, 1994, pp. 3–9.

—*Sketch by Maurice Bleifeld*

Wilhelm Conrad Röntgen

Wilhelm Conrad Röntgen
1845-1923
German physicist

For the first two decades of his scientific career, Wilhelm Conrad Röntgen studied a fairly diverse variety of topics, including the specific heats of gases, the Faraday effect in gases, magnetic effects associated with dielectric materials, and the compressibility of water. He is most famous, however, for his discovery in 1895 of X rays, which had a revolutionary effect not only on physics but also on a number of other areas, particularly medicine. For this discovery, Röntgen was awarded the first Nobel Prize in physics in 1901.

Röntgen was born in Lennep, Germany, on March 27, 1845. He was the only child of Friedrich Conrad Röntgen and the former Charlotte Frowein. His father was a textile merchant who came from a long line of metal workers and cloth merchants. His mother had been born in Lennep but then moved with her family to Amsterdam, where they had become wealthy as merchants and traders. When Röntgen was three years old, his family moved to Apeldorn, Holland. Otto Glasser speculates in *Dr. W. C. Röntgen* that the revolution of 1848 may have been a factor in this move because the family lost its German citizenship on May 23, 1848, and became Dutch citizens a few months later. In any case, Röntgen received his primary and secondary education in the public schools of Apeldorn and at a private boarding school in Middelann.

In December 1862, Röntgen enrolled at the Utrecht Technical School. His education at Utrecht was interrupted after about two years, however, when a childish prank went awry. He confessed to having drawn a caricature of an unpopular teacher for which another student had been responsible. As punishment, Röntgen was expelled from school, and his education was stalled until January 1865, when he was given permission to attend the University of Utrecht as an irregular student. There he attended classes on analysis, physics, chemistry, zoology, and botany. His future still seemed bleak, however, and, according to Glasser, "both Wilhelm and his parents had become resigned to his seeming inability to adjust to the requirements of the Dutch educational system and to obtain the credentials necessary to become a regular university student."

A friend of Röntgen's told him about the liberal admission policies at the Swiss Federal Institute of Technology in Zurich. Röntgen applied and was admitted at Zurich, and he arrived there to begin his studies in the mechanical technical branch of the institute on November 16, 1865. Over the next three years, Röntgen pursued a course of study that included classes in mathematics, technical drawing, mechanical technology, engineering, metallurgy, hydrology, and thermodynamics. On August 6, 1868, he was awarded his diploma in mechanical engineering. His degree had come in spite of his rather irregular attendance at classes. He later told Ludwig Zehnder that the lake and mountains surrounding Zurich were "too tempting." As a result, he became a devoted mountain climber and boater but an undistinguished student. Only when one of his professors told Röntgen that he would fail his examinations did he settle down to his studies.

Begins Scientific Career under the Influence of August Kundt

At Zurich, the most important influence on Röntgen was the German physicist August Kundt. Kundt suggested to him that he do his graduate studies in physics rather than engineering, and Röntgen took his advice. On June 22, 1869, he was granted his doctoral degree for a thesis entitled "Studies about Gases." Kundt then asked him to become his assistant, an offer he quickly accepted. A year later, when Kundt was offered the chair of physics at the University of Würzburg in Germany, he brought Röntgen with him as his assistant.

While still in Zurich, Röntgen had met his future wife, Anna Bertha Ludwig, the daughter of a German revolutionary who had emigrated to Switzerland. They were married on January 19, 1872, after his move to Würzburg. The couple never had children of their own, although in 1887 they did adopt his wife's six-year-old niece Josephine Bertha.

After two years at Würzburg, Kundt moved once more, this time to the newly established University of Strasbourg in France. Again, he asked Röntgen to accompany him as his assistant. At Strasbourg, in March 1874, Röntgen finally achieved a long-delayed ambition: He was appointed a privatdozent at the university, his first official academic appointment. The appointment was the result of more liberal policies at Strasbourg; his lack of the necessary credentials had prevented him from receiving a formal appointment in any German university.

In 1875, Röntgen accepted a position as professor of physics at the Hohenheim Agricultural Academy. Missing the superb research facilities to which he had become accustomed in Strasbourg, however, he returned there in 1876 as associate professor of physics. Three years later he was appointed professor of physics at the University of Giessen in Germany, where he remained until 1888. He then returned to the University of Würzburg to take a joint appointment as professor of physics and director of the university's Physical Institute. Röntgen would remain at Würzburg until 1900, serving as rector of the university during his last six years there.

Röntgen wrote forty-eight papers on a diverse range of phenomena including the specific heats of gases, the heat conductivity of crystals, the Faraday and Kerr effects, the compressibility of solids and liquids, and pyroelectricity and piezoelectricity. Probably his most significant contribution during this period was a continuation of research originally suggested by James Clerk Maxwell's theory of electromagnetism. That theory had predicted that the motion of a dielectric material within an electrostatic field would induce a magnetic current within the dielectric material. During his last year at Giessen, Röntgen completed studies that confirmed this effect, a phenomenon for which **Hendrik Lorentz** suggested the name "röntgen current."

Work on Cathode Rays Results in Discovery of X Rays

Yet there is no doubt that the discovery for which Röntgen will always be most famous is that of X rays. In 1894 Röntgen began research on cathode rays, which was then one of the most popular topics in physics. Much of the fundamental research on this topic had been carried out in the 1870s by the English physicist William Crookes. Crookes had found that the discharge of an electrical current within a vacuum tube produces a beam of negatively charged rays that causes a fluorescence on the glass walls of the tube. A number of scientists had followed up on this research, trying to discover more about the nature and characteristics of Crookes's cathode rays.

After repeating some of the earlier experiments on cathode rays, Röntgen's own research took an unexpected turn on November 8, 1895. In order to observe the luminescence caused by cathode rays more clearly, Röntgen darkened his laboratory and enclosed the vacuum tube he was using in black paper. When he turned on the apparatus, he happened to notice that a screen covered with barium platinocyanide crystals about a meter from the vacuum tube began to glow. This observation was startling, because Röntgen knew that cathode rays themselves travel no more than a few centimeters in air. It was not they, therefore, that caused the screen to glow.

Over the next seven weeks, Röntgen attempted to learn as much as he could about this form of energy. He discovered that its effect could be detected at great distances from the vacuum tube, suggesting that the radiation was very strong. He learned that the radiation passed easily through some materials, such as glass and wood, but was obstructed by other materials, such as metals. At one point, he even saw the bones in his hand as he held out a piece of lead before it. He also discovered that the radiation was capable of exposing a photographic plate. Because of the unknown and somewhat mysterious character of this radiation, Röntgen gave it the name *X strahlen*, or X rays.

On December 28, 1895, seven weeks after his first discovery of X rays, Röntgen communicated news of his work to the editors of a scientific journal published by the Physical and Medical Society of Würzburg. Six days earlier, he had made the world's first X-ray photograph, a picture of his wife's hand. Within weeks, news of Röntgen's discovery had reached the popular press, and the general public was captivated by the idea of seeing the skeletons of living people. On January 13, 1896, Röntgen was ordered to demonstrate his discovery before the Prussian court and was awarded the Prussian Order of the Crown, Second Class, by the Kaiser.

Röntgen actually devoted only a modest amount of attention to his momentous discovery. He wrote two more papers in 1896 and 1897, summarizing his findings on X rays, and then published no more on the subject. Instead, he went back to his work on the effects of pressures on solids. Röntgen chose not to ask for a patent on his work and refused the Kaiser's offer of an honorific "von" for his name. He did, however, accept the first Nobel Prize in physics, awarded to him in 1901. Even then, however, he declined to make an official speech and gave the prize money to the University of Würzburg for scientific research. His discovery had generated a surprising number of personal attacks, with many dismissing it as an accident or attributing it to other scientists. Glaser speculates that "Röntgen's reticence, bordering on bitterness with advancing years, was doubtless a defense against these attacks."

Röntgen had declined offers from other universities for many years, but in 1900, at the special request of the Bavarian government, he abandoned his chair at Würzburg in order to accept a similar position at the University of Munich. The decision was not an easy one for Röntgen because, as Zehnder later noted, "the nice quiet laboratory at Würzburg suited him so well." Röntgen remained at Munich until 1920 when he retired, a decision he made at least partly because of his grief over his wife's death a year earlier. She had suffered from a lingering disorder during which she became addicted to morphine. Zehnder was later to write that she was always "Röntgen's most understanding and truest friend."

Germany's defeat in World War I also had its effect on Röntgen: The inflationary period following the war resulted in his bankruptcy. He spent the last few years of his life at his country home at Weilheim, near Munich. He died there on February 10, 1923, after a short illness resulting from intestinal cancer. Among the many awards given to him were the Rumford Medal of the Royal Society (1896), the Royal Order of Merit, Bavarian (1896), the Baumgaertner Prize of the Vienna Academy (1896), the Elliott-Cresson Medal of the Franklin Institute (1897), the Barnard Medal of Columbia University (1900), and the Helmholtz Medal (1919).

SELECTED WRITINGS BY RÖNTGEN:

Periodicals

"Über eine neue Art von Strahlen," *Annalen der Physik und Chemie,* Volume 64, 1898.

"Eine Neue Art von Strahlen. 2. Mitteilung," *Annalen der Physik und Chemie,* Volume 64, 1898.

SOURCES:

Books

Daintith, John, et al., *A Biographical Encyclopedia of Scientists,* Facts on File, Volume XX, 1981, p. 686.

Gillispie, C. C., editor, *Dictionary of Scientific Biography,* Volume 1, Scribner, 1975, pp. 529–531.

Glasser, Otto, *W. C. Röntgen and the Early History of Röntgen Rays,* Charles C. Thomas, 1934.

Magill, Frank N., editor, *The Nobel Prize Winners—Physics,* Volume 1, *1901–1937,* Salem Press, 1989, pp. 23–32.

Nitske, Robert W., *The Life of W. C. Röntgen, Discoverer of the X-Ray,* University of Arizona Press, 1971.

Wasson, Tyler, editor, *Nobel Prize Winners,* Wilson, 1987, pp. 879–882.

Weber, Robert L., *Pioneers of Science: Nobel Prize Winners in Physics,* American Institute of Physics, 1980, pp. 7–9.

Zehnder, Ludwig, *Wilhelm Conrad Röntgen,* Basle University, 192?.

—*Sketch by David E. Newton*

Mary G. Ross
1908-
American aerospace engineer

Mary G. Ross's most notable contribution as an engineer has been her work in aerospace technology, particularly in areas related to space flight and ballistic missiles. She was part of the original engineering team at Lockheed's Missile Systems Division, where she worked on a number of defense systems. She also contributed to space exploration efforts with her work relating to the Apollo program, the Polaris reentry vehicle, and interplanetary space probes.

Born in Oklahoma in 1908, Ross took pride in her heritage as a Cherokee Indian. Her great-great-grandfather, John Ross, was the principal chief of the

Mary G. Ross

Cherokee Nation between 1828 and 1866. Mary Ross was later to remark that she had been brought up in the Cherokee tradition of equal education for both boys and girls. She was, however, the only girl in her math class, which did not seem to bother her. Indeed, her early interests were math, physics, and science.

Armed with these interests and a sense of purpose, Ross graduated from high school when she was sixteen. She attended Northeastern State Teacher's College and graduated from there in 1928, when she was twenty. After graduating from college, Ross taught mathematics and science for nine and one-half years in public schools. She also served as a girls' advisor at a Pueblo and Navajo school for boys and girls. Ross returned to school herself, this time to Colorado State Teachers College (now the University of Northern Colorado at Greeley), where she graduated with a master's degree in mathematics in 1938.

With the growth of the aviation industry in the early part of World War II, Ross found a position in 1942 as an assistant to a consulting mathematician with Lockheed Aircraft Corporation in Burbank, California. Her early work at Lockheed involved engineering problems having to do with transport and fighter aircraft. Meanwhile, with the support of Lockheed, Ross continued her education at the University of California, Los Angeles, where she took courses in aeronautical and mechanical engineering.

When Lockheed formed its Missiles Systems Division in 1954, it selected Mary Ross to be one of

the first forty employees, and she was the only female engineer among them. As the American missile program matured, Ross found herself researching and evaluating feasibility and performance of ballistic missile and other defense systems. She also studied the distribution of pressure caused by ocean waves and how it affected submarine-launched vehicles.

Her work in 1958 concentrated on satellite orbits and the Agena series of rockets that played so prominent a role in the Apollo moon program during the 1960s. As an advanced systems engineer, Ross worked on the Polaris reentry vehicle and engineering systems for manned space flights. Before her retirement from Lockheed in 1973, Ross undertook research on flyby space probes that would study Mars and Venus. After Ross retired she continued her interests in engineering by delivering lectures to high school and college groups to encourage young women and Native American youths to train for technical careers.

Mary Ross authored a number of classified publications relating to her work in national defense and received several awards during her career. A charter member of the Los Angeles chapter of the Society of Women Engineers since 1952, Ross has received a number of honors. In 1961 she garnered the *San Francisco Examiner*'s award for Woman of Distinction and the Woman of Achievement Award from the California State Federation of Business and Professional Clubs. Ross was elected a fellow and life member of the Society of Women Engineers, whose Santa Clara Valley Section established a scholarship in her name. She has also been the recipient of achievement awards from the American Indian Science and Engineering Society and from the Council of Energy Resource Tribes. In 1992 she was inducted into the Silicon Valley Engineering Hall of Fame.

SOURCES:

Ross, Mary G., interview with Karl Preuss conducted February 14, 1994.

—Sketch by Karl Preuss

Ronald Ross
1857-1932
Indian-born English physician and parasitologist

Ronald Ross is best known for his discovery of the method by which malaria is transmitted, research for which he was awarded the 1902 Nobel Prize in physiology or medicine. However, Ross's true passion was the arts, and he became a doctor only because of his father's insistence. Ross's interest in bacteriology led him to study the causes of malaria, a disease that was widespread in India where he lived. His determination that the affliction was transmitted through a parasite common to mosquitos led to more advanced treatments for the condition and more effective means of preventing it. In addition to his Nobel Prize and other honorary awards, Ross was knighted in 1911. Ross was born in Almora, Nepal, on May 13, 1857. He was the first of ten children to be born to General Sir Campbell Claye Grant Ross, a British officer stationed in India, and the former Matilde Charlotte Elderton. General Ross was described by Paul DeKruif in his book *Microbe Hunters* as "a ferocious looking border-fighting English general with belligerent side-whiskers, who was fond of battles but preferred to paint landscapes."

First Passion Is for the Arts

In 1865 at the age of eight, Ross was sent to England for his schooling. When he returned to his family in India, he declared to his father that he wanted to pursue a career in the arts. General Ross's view was that the arts were a legitimate vocation but not a sensible career for a young man. Instead, he insisted that his son plan for a medical career in the Indian Medical Service. Ross returned to England in 1874 and began his medical education at St. Bartholomew's Hospital in London. He did poorly in his classes because he spent most of his time writing novels and reading. His father became so upset with his grades that he threatened to withdraw his son's financial support. In response, Ross took a job as a ship's doctor on Anchor Line ships plying the London-New York City route. DeKruif reports that Ross spent much of his time aboard ship "observing the emotions and frailties of human nature," which gave him more material for his novels and poems.

In 1879 Ross completed his course at St. Bartholomew's and was awarded his medical degree. He returned to India and held a series of posts in Madras, Bangalore, Burma, and the Andaman Islands. He soon became more interested in research than in the day-to-day responsibilities of medical practice and spent long hours working out new algebraic formulas.

Attacks the Problem of Malaria

An important turning point in Ross's life came with his first leave of absence in 1888. He returned to England and became interested in research on tropical diseases, many of which he had seen during his years in India. Ross took a course in bacteriology offered by E. Emanuel Klein and earned a diploma in public health. During this furlough he also met Rosa Bessie Bloxam, whom he married on April 25, 1889, just prior to returning to India. The Rosses later had four children: Charles Claye, Dorothy, Sylvia, and Ronald.

With his new found knowledge of bacteriology, Ross turned his attention to what was then the most serious health problem in India: malaria. In 1880 the French physician **Alphonse Laveran** had discovered that malaria is caused by a one-celled organism called *Plasmodium*. Two decades of research had produced further data on the organism's characteristics, its means of reproduction, **and** its correlation with disease symptoms, but no **one** had determined how the disease was transmitted from one person to another.

Ross's original research led him to question Laveran's discovery, but for five years he made little progress in his studies. Then, on a second leave of absence in England during 1894, he met Patrick Manson, an English physician particularly interested in malaria. During Ross's year in England, he studied with Manson and became convinced that Laveran's theory was correct and that the causative agent for malaria was transmitted by mosquitoes.

When Ross returned to India in March of 1895, he was prepared to take up an aggressive research program on the mosquito-transmission theory. However, he was frustrated by working conditions in India—especially the lack of support from his superiors and the primitive equipment available to him—but with Manson's constant letters of support and encouragement, he eventually succeeded.

The key discovery came on August 20, 1897, when Ross first observed in the stomach of an *Anopheles* mosquito a cyst with black granules of the type described by Laveran. Ross worked out the life cycle of the disease-causing agent, including its reproduction within human blood, its transmission to a mosquito during the feeding process, its incubation within the mosquito, and then its transmission to a second human during a second feeding (a "bite") by the mosquito.

Ross's work, however, was complicated by several factors. For example, in the midst of his research he was transferred to Rajputana, a region in which human malaria did not exist. He spent his time there instead working on the transmission of another form of the disease that affects birds. In addition, Ross was continually distracted by his passion for writing, and he produced a number of poems when he could no longer work on his battle against malaria.

Adding to Ross's frustration was the news he received late in 1898 that an Italian research team led by Battista Grassi had published reports on malaria closely paralleling his own work. Although little doubt exists about the originality of the Italian studies, Ross called Grassi's team "cheats and pirates." The dispute was later described by DeKruif as similar to a spat between "two quarrelsome small boys."

To some extent, the dispute was resolved in 1902 when the Nobel Prize committee awarded Ross the year's prize in physiology or medicine. By that time, Ross had retired from the Indian Medical Service and returned to England as lecturer at the new School of Tropical Medicine in Liverpool. There he worked for the eradication of the conditions (such as poor sanitation) that were responsible for the spread of malaria. In 1917, after eighteen years at Liverpool, Ross was appointed physician of tropical diseases at King's College Hospital in London. In 1926 he became director of a new facility founded in his name, the Ross Institute and Hospital for Tropical Diseases near London. He remained in this post until his death on September 16, 1932. Among the honors granted to Ross were the 1895 Parke Gold Medal, the 1901 Cameron Prize, and the 1909 Royal Medal of the Royal Society. He was knighted in 1911.

SELECTED WRITINGS BY ROSS:

Books

Memoirs with a Full Account of the Great Malaria Problem, Keynes Press, 1888.
The Deformed Transformed, Chapman and Hall, 1892.
The Prevention of Malaria, J. Murray, 1910.
The Setting Sun, J. Murray, 1912.
The Revels of Orsera, J. Murray, 1920.
Poems, E. Matthews & Marrot, 1928.
Studies on Malaria, J. Murray, 1928.

Periodicals

"On Some Peculiar Pigmented Cells Found in Two Mosquitoes Fed on Malarial Blood," *British Medical Journal,* Volume 2, 1897, pp. 1786–1788.

SOURCES:

Books

DeKruif, Paul, *Microbe Hunters,* Harcourt, Brace, 1926.

Kamm, Jacqueline, *Malaria Ross,* Methuen, 1963.
Mégroz, Rodolphe L., *Ronald Ross: Discoverer and Creator,* Allen & Unwin, 1931.

Periodicals

Gorgas, William C., and Fielding H. Garrison, "Ronald Ross and the Prevention of Malaria Fever," *Scientific Monthly,* August, 1916, pp. 132–150.
Yoelli, Meir, "Sir Ronald Ross and the Evolution of Malaria Research," *Bulletin of the New York Academy of Medicine,* August, 1973, pp. 722–735.

—*Sketch by David E. Newton*

Carl-Gustaf Rossby
1898-1957
Swedish-born American meteorologist

Carl-Gustaf Rossby has been called one of the most brilliant theoretical meteorologists of this century—a scientist who helped transform meteorology into the modern science it is known as today. Among Rossby's scientific achievements are the discovery of planetary waves—also known as Rossby waves—that play a crucial role in weather patterns; the identification of the jet stream; and the development of equations for predicting the weather. Renowned as well for his organizational skills, Rossby revitalized the U.S. Weather Bureau by eliminating bureaucratic inefficiency and promoting innovative research. The United States became a leader in meteorology largely as a result of his efforts.

Carl-Gustaf Arvid Rossby was born on December 28, 1898, in Stockholm, Sweden, to Arvid Rossby, a construction engineer, and his wife Alma Charlotta Marelius. Rossby was the first of the four boys and one girl in the family. A good student, Rossby was described by his teachers as an excellent scholar. As a child he contracted rheumatic fever, which subsequently damaged his heart. Perhaps as a result, Rossby was not particularly athletic, preferring instead such interests as music, geology, and botany. According to one biographical account, Rossby enjoyed playing the piano and cultivating orchids.

In 1917 Rossby enrolled at the University of Stockholm. He initially chose to study medicine but quickly switched to mathematical sciences. Less than a year later he received his bachelor's degree ("filosofie kandidat") in mathematics, mechanics, and as-

Carl-Gustaf Rossby

tronomy. (Most students took at least three years to accomplish the same.) In 1919 Rossby abruptly embarked on his career in meteorology by joining the Geophysical Institute in Bergen, Norway. His career choice proved somewhat of a mystery, considering that he had no knowledge of the subject at the time. However, historians believe that Rossby's interest was piqued after attending a lecture on the atmosphere given by **Vilhem Bjerknes**, a pioneer in meteorology and a professor at the Bergen Institute. Evidence also suggests that Rossby's move was spurred by boredom with Stockholm. Meteorology may have also captivated Rossby because he happened to enter the field at a time when the effect of polar fronts on weather was just being discovered.

According to Tor Bergeron, a meteorologist who also worked at Bergen, the twenty-year-old Rossby had "amazing persuasive and organizing" abilities; though inexperienced, Rossby presented ideas that Bergeron reported "took our breath away." Rossby worked in Bergen until 1921, when he joined the Geophysical Institute of the University of Leipzig. In that institute Rossby began studying hydrodynamics and newly discovered features of the upper atmosphere. To help further these interests, he also worked during part of 1921 at the Prussian Aerological Observatory at Lindenberg, a center for research using kites and balloons.

In 1921 Rossby also returned to the University of Stockholm to study mathematical physics. While he worked toward his "filosofie licentiat" (the equivalent

of a PhD), Rossby earned a living as a junior meteorologist at the Swedish Meteorologic-Hydrologic Service. During his tenure there, he went on several scientific expeditions, including a meteorological and oceanographic expedition through pack-ice near Greenland and a meteorological expedition around the British Isles. In 1925, Rossby attained his licentiat degree in mathematical physics.

Initial Hostility at the U.S. Weather Bureau

After receiving a fellowship from the American-Scandinavian Foundation, Rossby came to the U.S. Weather Bureau in Washington, D.C., in 1926. Officially, his scholarship was for the purpose of studying "the application of the polar front theory to American weather." By all accounts, the enthusiastic 27-year-old Rossby did not fare well in the Weather Bureau, which the National Academy of Sciences biography describes as being headed by "unimaginative administrators." As a result, Rossby's attempts to introduce the polar front theory and other meteorological innovations of his day were regularly thwarted.

Despite these obstacles, Rossby published three papers in the *Monthly Weather Review* describing his investigations into atmospheric turbulence. He also received a temporary appointment as junior meteorologist in 1926. Simultaneously, the Daniel Guggenheim Fund for the Promotion of Aeronautics chose Rossby to work on the meteorological aspects of flight plans. Unfortunately, this project escalated tensions between Rossby and the Weather Bureau to the point that in 1927, when Rossby left the Bureau to work for the Guggenheim Fund full-time, the Weather Bureau officially declared him "persona non grata." Administrators also sent letters to all its stations warning them against Rossby.

In 1927 aeronautics had captured the country's attention following Charles Lindbergh's solo flight across the Atlantic. That year the Guggenheim, then at the forefront of aeronautics, proposed a model airway between San Francisco and Los Angeles. Rossby, in his capacity as chairman of the committee on aeronautical meteorology, was given the task of establishing an experimental weather service as part of the airway. Enlisting the help of the Weather Bureau in San Francisco (whose director ignored the letter warning against Rossby), he created a system that would later serve as the prototype for all of the Weather Bureau's airways weather services. Needless to say, this success redeemed Rossby in the eyes of the bureau's administrators.

Collaborations at MIT

Once the experimental service was operational, Rossby and the Guggenheim Fund turned it over to the Weather Bureau, and Rossby began a new era in his career: In 1928 he was appointed associate professor as part of the Daniel Guggenheim Aeronautical Laboratory at the Massachusetts Institute of Technology (MIT). Along with Hurd C. Willett, a colleague from the Weather Bureau whom he had persuaded to join him, Rossby taught a graduate-level class in meteorology, the first such course in the United States. Together, Rossby and Willett formed a team that forever changed American meteorology.

On a personal level, in 1929 Rossby married Harriet Alexander of Boston. Together they eventually had three children. According to friends, Rossby had difficulty mastering any mechanical devices, and except for a few brief experiences with a car, left driving to his wife. His favorite form of entertainment was getting together as many friends and colleagues as possible for dinner and conversation in an expensive restaurant.

Rossby quickly developed a following at MIT. An obituary written for the American Meteorological Society recalled the reverential attitude of his students toward him, and their belief that "they were participating in his great crusade—to bring modern meteorology to America where the science had been existing in a stifling atmosphere for many years." Rossby's research at MIT involved both the atmosphere and oceanography: he was a part-time associate at the Woods Hole Oceanographic Institute. Among the subjects he investigated: the application of the principles of thermodynamics to the analyses of air masses; turbulence and the air-ocean boundary; forces at work in the generation and maintenance of ocean currents; and the general circulation of the atmosphere.

Forecasting the Future

From a scientific standpoint, Rossby conducted some of his most significant work in 1938 and 1939: In two of his most important papers, he developed equations for what are now called Rossby waves. At the time, scientists knew that the circulation of the atmosphere controlled both weather and climate. They also knew that storms at the Earth's surface caused waves in the westerly winds above the Northern Hemisphere. According to Patrick Hughes in *A Century of Weather Service,* in 1937 meteorologist Jacob Bjerknes "showed that these waves were hemispheric in scale and circled the globe." Rossby added to this theory by determining that the waves extended vertically through the atmosphere and that they moved the warm and cold air masses that cause local weather. Rossby developed a mathematical equation to predict the motion of the waves.

Rossby waves exist in both the ocean and the atmosphere. They are the reason that weather in the tropics can affect weather in higher latitudes. Partly as a result of Rossby's work, scientists can now make

long-range weather forecasts, including the five-day forecast that has become a common part of our lives. In 1939 Rossby became an American citizen. That same year he left MIT to become Assistant Chief for Research and Development at the U.S. Weather Bureau. It was in this position that Rossby helped Weather Bureau chief F. W. Reichelderfer modernize the agency. Rossby established a training program for Weather Bureau personnel and even arranged for some staffers to enroll in the meteorological schools at MIT and New York University.

Rossby stayed only two years at the Weather Bureau, moving on in 1941 to become chairman of the meteorology department at the University of Chicago. He continued his studies of Rossby waves, but with the onset of World War II, he began commuting between Chicago and Washington to promote a training program for military meteorologists. As a result of his efforts, an intense, year-long training program in meteorology was established at the University of Chicago and other institutions. Rossby also assisted in solving the meteorological problems faced by Allied strategists, traveling to Africa, Italy and the South Pacific when necessary. To aid in the understanding of meteorological problems in the tropics, Rossby helped establish the Institute of Tropical Meteorology at the University of Puerto Rico. According to the National Academy of Sciences *Biographical Memoirs,* Rossby enjoyed making these decisions with "a Hollywoodian flair for dramatic executive action."

Throughout the war Rossby continued to work, publishing two other significant papers dealing with Rossby waves in 1942. In addition, after the war, Rossby and colleagues helped reorganize the American Meteorological Society and founded the *Journal of Meteorology.* During his ten years at the University of Chicago—a period known as the great days of the Chicago School in meteorology—Rossby gathered leading European meteorologists as well as talented graduate students. Under Rossby's leadership, this group identified the jet stream and explored theories to explain it.

In 1948 the Swedish government solicited Rossby's help in developing research and educational programs in meteorology. As part of a commitment that occupied him until his death, Rossby founded and directed the Institute of Meteorology at the University of Stockholm and established *Tellus,* a geophysical research journal. Despite these new administrative duties, Rossby continued his research and in 1950 formulated an equation for predicting the weather—the Rossby equation. In addition, Rossby's new interest in atmospheric chemistry helped motivate others to investigate this field. In a paper published after he died, Rossby described the atmosphere as a carrier of particles and chemicals that continually interacted with the earth and the oceans.

Rossby died in Stockholm on August 19, 1957. He received many awards during his lifetime, including the Symons Medal of the Royal Meteorological Society in 1953 and the American Meteorological Society Service Award in 1956.

SELECTED WRITINGS BY ROSSBY:

Periodicals

"Relation Between Variations in the Intensity of the Zonal Circulation of the Atmosphere and the Displacements of the Semi-Permanent Centers of Action," *Journal of Marine Research,* Volume 2, 1939, pp. 38–55.
"Planetary Flow Patterns in the Atmosphere," *Quarterly Journal of the Royal Meteorological Society,* Volume 66, 1940, pp. 68–87.

SOURCES:

Books

Bergeron, Tor, "The Young Carl-Gustaf Rossby," *The Atmosphere and the Sea in Motion,* The Rockefeller Institute, 1959, pp. 51–55.
Byers, Horace R., "Carl-Gustaf Arvid Rossby," *Biographical Memoirs, The National Academy of Sciences,* Columbia University Press, 1960, pp. 248–263.
Byars, Horace R., "Carl-Gustaf Rossby, the Organizer," *The Atmosphere and the Sea in Motion,* The Rockefeller Institute, 1959, pp. 56–59.
Dictionary of Scientific Biography, Charles Scribners' Sons, 1975, pp. 557–559.
Hughes, Patrick, *A Century of Weather Service,* Gordon and Breach, 1970, pp. 69–71, 131.

—*Sketch by Devera Pine*

Miriam Rothschild
1908-
English naturalist

Miriam Rothschild's best-known work has been in the fields of entomology and parasitology, and she is considered the world's foremost authority on fleas. Although she has made numerous scientific contributions in such fields as marine biology, chemistry, horticulture, and zoology, her scientific background is unorthodox. Rothschild, though widely respected for her work and extensive knowledge of fleas, was never formally educated in these fields. In fact, her scientific endeavors are wholly a result of a natural curiosity about the physical world and the encouraging atmosphere of learning she grew up in.

Miriam Louisa Rothschild was born into the famed Rothschild banking family on August 5, 1908, at Ashton Wold, her parents' estate near Peterborough, England. The oldest of four children of Nathaniel Charles and Rozsika von Wertheimstein Rothschild, her own grandfather was the first Baron Rothschild. Although Nathaniel Charles Rothschild, her father, was a banker by profession, he was a zoologist by avocation; he founded the Society for the Promotion of Nature Preserves, and he studied moths, butterflies, and fleas for years. Rozsika Rothschild, her mother, was Hungarian by birth, and in addition to being astute in business, a champion in women's lawn tennis.

As a child, Rothschild spent six months of every year with her grandparents and uncle Walter at their estate outside London. Although all the Rothschilds expressed an interest in nature, it was Walter Rothschild who most sparked Miriam's interest in science. Walter Rothschild was a prolific collector of natural specimens, and his collection included more than two million butterflies, 300,000 bird skins, 200,000 bird eggs, and numerous other animals. And so, even as a young child of four, Rothschild began her own collection of ladybugs and caterpillars.

Rothschild had no formal education while growing up; her father believed formal education stifled creativity and natural curiosity. She read avidly and was tutored by her governess. When her father committed suicide after several years of chronic illness and depression, she lost interest in natural history, but her enthusiasm eventually returned, and at seventeen years of age, Rothschild enrolled herself in several evening classes at a local polytechnic institute.

A naturalist at the British Natural History Museum recommended her to the University of London in the late 1920s, and Rothschild became a researcher at the University's Biological Station located in Naples, Italy, where she studied marine life. She continued her studies when she went to the Marine Biological Station in Plymouth in 1932. It was at this time that she became interested in the study of parasites after finding out that some of the mollusks were infested with flatworms. She worked tirelessly, studying parasites, hosts, and other related marine animals, and collected numerous specimens and cultures. In 1939, however, the Germans bombed the research station during the Second World War, destroying Rothschild's laboratory completely. Rothschild now returned to Ashton Wold, which had been converted to a military hospital and air field during the war. At this time she was actively involved in the resistance movement, and she worked with mathematician **Alan Turing** on the top-secret British *Enigma* project, trying to crack the German code. She and her family also opened their home to European refugees.

Rothschild continued her scientific pursuits even while helping relocate many refugees after the war. Like her father, she had become interested in fleas. She studied many specimens and worked to catalog her father's collection—her findings were eventually amalgamated into six volumes and took twenty years to compile. She showed through her extensive research how fleas reproduce, how and why they choose their hosts, and the mechanics of how fleas can leap enormous distances. She also showed through research with Nobel laureate **Tadeus Reichstein** how the monarch caterpillar's diet of milkweed plants protects it (the glycosides in the milkweed are distasteful and possibly harmful to birds and other animals, who bypass monarchs for safer, tastier fare).

Rothschild was married to George Lane, a British soldier who had emigrated from Hungary, in 1943. The couple had four children and adopted two more. They divorced in 1957. In addition to science, Rothschild's other interests include travel, reading, and philanthropy. She has written and contributed to numerous articles about nature, and continues her research at Ashton Wold. Her 1983 book, *Dear Lord Rothschild,* honors her family and in particular her uncle Walter, who eventually became the second Baron Rothschild. Her interest in science has a mechanical side as well; she claims to be the first person to put seat belts in an automobile, in 1940.

SELECTED WRITINGS BY ROTHSCHILD:

Books

Dear Lord Rothschild: Birds, Butterflies, and History, American Institute of Physics, 1983.

SOURCES:

Periodicals

Gibson, Helen, "Britain's Quirky Samaritans," *International Wildlife,* July-August 1993, pp. 38–43.
Scientific American, August 1990, p. 116.
Sullivan, Walter, "Miriam Rothschild Talks of Fleas," *New York Times,* February 10, 1984, p. C2.

—*Sketch by George A. Milite*

Peyton Rous
1879-1970
American physician and pathologist

Peyton Rous was a physician-scientist at the Rockefeller Institute for Medical Research (later the Rockefeller University) for over sixty years. In 1966, Rous won the Nobel Prize for his 1910 discovery that a virus can cause cancer tumors. His other contributions to scientific medicine include creating the first blood bank, determining major functions of the liver and gall bladder, and identifying factors that initiate and promote malignancy in normal cells.

Francis Peyton Rous was born on October 5, 1879, in Baltimore, Maryland, to Charles Rous, a grain exporter, and Frances Wood, the daughter of a Texas judge. His father died when Rous was eleven, and his mother chose to stay in Baltimore to ensure that her three children would have the best possible education. His sisters were professionally successful, one a musician, the other a painter.

Rous, whose interest in natural science was apparent at an early age, wrote a "flower of the month" column for the *Baltimore Sun* when he was twenty. He pursued his biological interests at Johns Hopkins University, receiving a B.A. in 1900 and an M.D. in 1905. After a medical internship at Johns Hopkins, however, he decided (as recorded in *Les Prix Nobel en 1966*) that he was "unfit to be a real doctor" and chose instead to concentrate on research and the natural history of disease. This led to a full year of studying lymphocytes with Aldred Warthin at the University of Michigan and a summer in Germany learning morbid anatomy at a Dresden hospital. After Rous returned to the United States, he developed pulmonary tuberculosis and spent a year recovering in an Adirondacks sanatorium. In 1909, **Simon Flexner**, director of the newly-founded Rockefeller Institute in New York City, asked Rous to take over cancer research in his laboratory. A few months later, a poultry breeder brought a Plymouth Rock chicken with a large breast tumor to the Institute and Rous, after conducting numerous experiments, determined that the tumor was a spindle-cell sarcoma. When he transferred a cell-free filtrate from the tumor into healthy chickens of the same flock, they developed identical tumors. Moreover, after injecting a filtrate from the new tumors into other chickens, a malignancy exactly like the original formed. Further studies revealed that this filterable agent was a virus, although Rous carefully avoided this word. Now called the Rous sarcoma virus (RSV) and classed as an RNA retrovirus, it remains a prototype of animal tumor viruses and a favorite laboratory model for studying the role of genes in cancer.

Rous's discovery was received with considerable disbelief, both in the United States and in the rest of the world. His viral theory of cancer challenged all assumptions, going back to Hippocrates, that cancer was not infectious but rather a spontaneous, uncontrolled growth of cells and many scientists dismissed his finding as a disease peculiar to chickens. Discouraged by his failed attempts to cultivate viruses from mammal cancers, Rous abandoned work on the sarcoma in 1915. Nearly two decades passed before he returned to cancer research.

Enters New Phase of Research on Urgent Medical Problems

After the onset of World War I, Rous, J. R. Turner, and O. H. Robertson began a search for emergency blood transfusion fluids. Nothing could be found that worked without red blood corpuscles so they developed a citrate-sugar solution that preserved blood for weeks as well as a method to transfuse the suspended cells. Later, behind the front lines in Belgium and France, they created the world's first blood bank from donations by army personnel. This solution was used again in World War II, when half a million Rous-Turner blood units were shipped by air to London during the Blitz.

During the 1920s, Rous made several contributions to physiology. With P. D. McMaster, he demonstrated the concentrating activity of bile in the gall bladder, the acid-alkaline balance in living tissues, the increasing permeability along capillaries in muscle and skin, and the nature of gallstone formation. In conducting these studies, Rous devised culture techniques that have become standard for studying living tissues in the laboratory. He originated the method for growing viruses on chicken embryos, now used on a mass scale for producing viral vaccines, and found a way to isolate single cells from solid tissues by using the enzyme trypsin. Moreover, Rous developed an ingenious method for obtaining pure cultures of Kupffer cells by taking advantage of their phagocytic ability; he injected iron particles in animals and then used a magnet to separate these iron-laden liver cells from suspensions.

Returns to Cancer Tumor Research

In 1933, a Rockefeller colleague's report stimulated Rous to renew his work on cancer. Richard Shope discovered a virus that caused warts on the skin of wild rabbits. Within a year, Rous established that this papilloma had characteristics of a true tumor. His work on mammalian cancer kept his viral theory of cancer alive. However, another twenty years passed before scientists identified viruses that cause

human cancers and learned that viruses act by invading genes of normal cells. These findings finally advanced Rous's 1910 discovery to a dominant place in cancer research.

Meanwhile, Rous and his colleagues spent three decades studying the Shope papilloma to understand the role of viruses in causing cancer in mammals. Careful observations, over long periods of time, of the changing shapes, colors, and sizes of cells revealed that normal cells become malignant in progressive steps. Cell changes in tumors were observed as always evolving in a single direction toward malignancy.

The researchers demonstrated how viruses collaborate with carcinogens such as tar, radiation, or chemicals to elicit and enhance tumors. In a report co-authored by W. F. Friedewald, Rous proposed a two-stage mechanism of carcinogenesis, or the causilng of cancer, called initiation and promotion. He further explained that a virus can be induced by carcinogens or it can hasten the growth and transform benign tumors into cancerous ones. For tumors having no apparent trace of virus, Rous cautiously postulated that these "spontaneous" growths might contain a virus that persists in a "masked" or latent state, causing no harm until its cellular environment is disturbed.

Rous eventually ceased his research on this project due to the technical complexities involved with pursuing the interaction of viral and environmental factors. He then analyzed different types of cells and their nature in an attempt to understand why tumors go from bad to worse.

In 1915, Rous married Marion de Kay, daughter of a scholarly commentator on the arts, and they had three daughters: Marion, Ellen, and Phoebe. He spent two months every summer in the country near New York City with his family, first on Long Island and later in Connecticut, savoring outdoor life, rambling in the countryside, collecting objects that caught his eye, growing flowers, and' fishing.

This carefree time greatly contrasts with Rous's rigorous workday schedule at Rockefeller. His meticulous editing and writing, both scientific and literary, took place during several hours of solitude at the beginning and end of each day. At midday, he spent two intense hours discussing science with colleagues in the Institute's dining room. Rous then returned to work in his laboratory on experiments that lasted into the early evening.

Rous was appointed a full member of the Rockefeller Institute in 1920 and member emeritus in 1945. Though officially retired, he remained active at his lab bench until the age of ninety, adding sixty papers to the nearly three hundred he published. He was elected to the National Academy of Sciences in 1927, the American Philosophical Society in 1939, and the Royal Society in 1940. In addition to the 1966 Nobel

Prize for medicine, Rous received many honorary degrees and awards for his work in viral oncology, including the 1956 Kovalenko Medal of the National Academy of Sciences, the 1958 Lasker Award of the American Public Health Association, and the 1966 National Medal of Science.

As editor of the *Journal of Experimental Medicine,* a periodical renowned for its precise language and scientific excellence, Rous dominated the recording of forty-eight years of American medical research. He died of abdominal cancer on February 16, 1970, in New York City, just six weeks after he retired as editor.

SELECTED WRITINGS BY ROUS:

Periodicals

"A Transmissible Avian Neoplasm (Sarcoma of the Common Fowl)," *Journal of Experimental Medicine,* Volume 12, 1910, pp. 696–705.

"A Sarcoma of the Fowl Transmissible by an Agent Separable from the Tumor Cells," *Journal of Experimental Medicine,* Volume 13, 1911, pp. 397–411.

(With J. R. Turner) "The Preservation of Living Red Blood Cells in vitro. I. Methods of Preservation. II. The Transfusion of Kept Cells," *Journal of Experimental Medicine,* Volume 23, 1916, pp. 219–248.

(With J. W. Beard) "A Virus-induced Mammalian Growth with the Characters of a Tumor (the Shope Rabbit Papilloma)," *Journal of Experimental Medicine,* Volume 60, 1934, pp. 701–766.

(With W. F. Friedewald) "The Initiating and Promoting Elements in Tumor Production. An Analysis of the Effects of Tar, Benzpyrene, and Methylcholanthrene on Rabbit Skin," *Journal of Experimental Medicine,* Volume 80, 1944, pp. 101–126.

"Francis Peyton Rous," *McGraw-Hill Modern Scientists and Engineers,* Volume 3, 1980, McGraw-Hill, pp. 48–49.

"The Challenge to Man of the Neoplastic Cell," *Les Prix Nobel en 1966,* 1967, P.A. Norstedt & Soner, pp. 162–171.

SOURCES:

Books

A Notable Career in Finding Out: Peyton Rous, 1879–1970, The Rockefeller University Press, 1971.

Periodicals

Biographical Memoirs of Fellows 'of the Royal Society, Volume 17, Royal Society (London), 1971, pp. 643–662.

Dulbecco, Renato, "Francis Peyton Rous," *Biographical Memoirs, National Academy of Sciences,* Volume 48, 1976, pp. 275–306.

Henderson, James Stuart, "Peyton Rous," *American Philosophical Society Yearbook,* 1971, pp. 168–179.

"The Long Road to Stockholm," *Roche Medical Image & Commentary,* Volume 12, May 1970, pp. 14–15; June 1970, pp. 18–21.

Moberg, Carol L., "Peyton Rous, Inquiring Naturalist: Cancer and the Sarcoma Virus," *Search,* Volume 1, 1991, p. 9.

Other

Letter from Peyton Rous to T. Mitchell Prudden, October 14, 1922, The Rockefeller University Archives.

—*Sketch by Carol L. Moberg*

F. Sherwood Rowland
1927-
American atmospheric chemist

In 1974 F. Sherwood Rowland and his research associate, **Mario Molina**, first sounded the alarm about the harmful effects of chlorofluorocarbons, or CFCs, on the earth's ozone layer. CFCs, which have been used in air conditioners, refrigerators, and aerosol sprays, release chlorine atoms into the upper atmosphere when the sun's ultraviolet light hits them; chlorine then breaks down atmospheric ozone molecules, destroying a shield that protects the earth from damaging ultraviolet rays. In the mid–1980s a National Aeronautics and Space Administration (NASA) satellite actually confirmed the existence of a continent-sized hole in the ozone layer over Antarctica. By the early 1990s NASA and National Oceanographic and Atmospheric Administration scientists were warning that yet another ozone hole, this one over the Arctic, could imperil Canada, Russia, Europe, and, in the United States, New England. This news might have been gratifying affirmation for Rowland, a professor of chemistry at the University of California at Irvine, but rather than rest on his laurels he continued to steadfastly—and soberly—warn the world of the ozone danger. His efforts have won him

F. Sherwood Rowland

worldwide renown and prestigious awards, including the Charles A. Dana Award for Pioneering Achievement in Health in 1987, the Peter Debye Award of the American Chemical Society in 1993, the Roger Revelle Medal from the American Geophysical Union for 1994, and the Japan Prize in Environmental Science and Technology, presented to Rowland by the Japanese emperor in 1989.

Frank Sherwood Rowland always seemed destined to do something in science. Born June 28, 1927, in Delaware, Ohio, the son of a math professor, Sidney A. Rowland, and his wife, Latin teacher Margaret (Drake), Rowland said in an interview with Joan Oleck that math always came easy for him. "I always liked solving puzzles and problems," he said. "I think the rule we had in our family that applied even to my own children was you had your choice in school as to *what order* you took biology, chemistry, and physics, but not *whether.*"

Sidetracked by World War II, Rowland was still in boot camp when peace arrived. In 1948 he received his bachelor of arts degree from Ohio Wesleyan University; after three years—the summers of which he spent playing semiprofessional baseball—he obtained his master's from the University of Chicago. His Ph.D. came a year later, in 1952. That same year he married the former Joan E. Lundberg; the couple would eventually have a son and daughter.

The year 1952 was a banner one in Rowland's life; along with marriage and his doctorate he got his

first academic job, an instructorship in chemistry at Princeton University, where he would remain four years. In 1956 Rowland moved his family west to the University of Kansas, where he was a professor for eight years, and then farther west still, to Irvine, California, where he took over as chemistry department chairman at the University of California in Irvine in 1964. He has stayed at Irvine ever since, enjoying stints as Daniel G. Aldrich, Jr., Professor of Chemistry from 1985 to 1989 and as Donald Bren Professor of Chemistry since 1989.

Discovers CFCs

At Chicago, Rowland's mentor had been **Willard F. Libby**, winner of the Nobel Prize for his invention of carbon–14 dating, a way to determine the age of an object by measuring how much of a radioactive form of carbon it contains. The radioactivity research Rowland conducted with Libby led the young scientist eventually to atmospheric chemistry. Realizing, as he told Oleck, that "if you're going to be a professional scientist one of the things you're going to do is stay out ahead of the pack," Rowland looked for new avenues to explore. In the 1970s Rowland was inspired by his daughter's dedication to the then-fledgling environmental movement and by the tenor of the times: 1970 was the year of the first Earth Day. In 1971 the chemist helped allay fears about high levels of mercury in swordfish and tuna by showing that preserved museum fish from a hundred years earlier contained about the same amount of the element as modern fish.

Later events pushed him further in the direction of environmental concerns. At a meeting in Salzburg, Austria, Rowland met an Atomic Energy Commission (AEC) staffer who was trying to get chemists and meteorologists into closer partnerships. Sharing a train compartment with the AEC man to Vienna, Rowland was invited to another professional meeting. And it was there, in 1972, that he first began to think about chlorofluorocarbons in the atmosphere.

In those days, production of CFCs for household and industrial propellants was doubling every five years. A million tons of CFCs were being produced each year alone, but scientists were not particularly alarmed; it was believed they were inert in the atmosphere. Rowland, however, wanted to know more about their ultimate fate. Ozone, a form of oxygen, helps make up the stratosphere, the atmospheric layer located between eight and thirty miles above the earth. Ozone screens out dangerous ultraviolet rays, which have been linked to skin cancer, malfunctions in the immune system, and eye problems such as cataracts. Performing lab experiments with Molina, Rowland reported in 1974 that the same chemical stability that makes CFCs useful also allows them to drift up to the stratosphere intact. Once they rise thorough the ozone shield, Rowland and Molina warned, they pose a significant threat to ozone: each chlorine atom released when CFCs meet ultraviolet light can destroy up to one hundred thousand ozone molecules.

Sounding the alarm in the journal *Nature* in June of 1974 and in a subsequent presentation to the American Chemical Society that September, Rowland attracted attention: A federal task force found reason for serious concern; the National Academy of Sciences (NAS) confirmed the scientists' findings; and by 1978 the Environmental Protection Agency (EPA) had banned nearly all uses of CFC propellants. There were setbacks: In the 1980s President Ronald Reagan's EPA administrator, Anne Gorsuch, dismissed ozone depletion as a scare tactic. And Rowland himself discovered that the whole matter was more complex than originally thought, that another chemical reaction in the air was affecting calculations of ozone loss. The NAS's assessment of the problem was similarly vague, generalizing future global ozone losses as somewhere between 2 and 20 percent.

The Hole in the Sky

Then came a startling revelation. In the mid–1980s a hole in the ozone shield over Antarctica the size of a continent was discovered; NASA satellite photos confirmed it in 1985. The fall in ozone levels in the area was drastic—as high as 67 percent. These events led to increased concern by the international community. In 1987 the United States and other CFC producers signed the Montreal Protocol, pledging to cut production by 50 percent by the end of the millennium. Later, in the United States, President George Bush announced a U.S. plan to speed up the timetable to 1995.

There were more accelerations to come: Du Pont, a major producer, announced plans to end its CFC production by late 1994, and the European Community set a 1996 deadline. And producers of automobile air conditioning and seat cushions—two industries still using CFCs—began looking for alternatives. These goals only became more urgent in the face of the 1992 discovery of another potential ozone hole, this one over the Arctic. Scientists have attributed the extreme depletion of ozone over the poles to weather patterns and seasonal sun that promote an unusually rapid cycle of chlorine-ozone chain reactions.

In addition to the development of holes in the ozone layer, the atmosphere is further threatened because of the time delay before CFCs reach the stratosphere. Even after a complete ban on CFC production is achieved, CFCs will continue to rise through the atmosphere, reaching peak concentrations in the late 1990s. Some remained skeptical of the dangers, however. In the early 1990s a kind of "ozone backlash" occurred, with a scientist as prominent as Nobel Prize-winning chemist **Derek Barton** joining those who called for a repeal of the CFC phaseout pact.

Meanwhile Rowland continued his examination of the atmosphere. Every three months, his assistants have fanned out around the Pacific Ocean to collect air samples from New Zealand to Alaska. The news from his research has been sobering, turning up airborne compounds that originated from the burning of rain forests in Brazil and the aerial pollution of oil fields in the Caucasus mountains. "The major atmospheric problems readily cross all national boundaries and therefore can affect everyone's security," Rowland said in his President's Lecture before the American Association for the Advancement of Science (AAAS) in 1993. "You can no longer depend upon the 12-mile offshore limit when the problem is being carried by the winds." An instructive reminder of the international nature of such insecurity was given by the arrival only 2 weeks later in Irvine, California, of trace amounts of the radioactive fission products released by the 1986 Chernobyl nuclear reactor accident in the former Soviet Union.

Rowland has said in interviews that he's pleased with the progress he's helped set in motion. "One of the messages is that it is possible for mankind to influence his environment negatively," Rowland told Oleck. "On the other side there's the recognition on an international basis that we can act in unison. We have the [Montreal] agreement, people are following it, and it's not only that they have said they will do these things but they *are* doing them because the measurements in the atmosphere show it. People have worked together to solve the problem."

SELECTED WRITINGS BY ROWLAND:

Periodicals

(With Mario J. Molina) "Stratospheric Sink for Chlorofluoromethanes: Chlorine Atom-Catalysed Destruction of Ozone," *Nature,* June 28, 1974, pp. 810–12.

(With Molina) "Chlorofluoromethanes in the Environment," *Reviews of Geophysics and Space Physics,* February, 1975.

(With Susan Solomon, Rolando R. Garcia, and Donald J. Wuebbles) "On the Depletion of Antarctic Ozone," *Nature,* June 19, 1986, pp. 755–58.

"Can We Close the Ozone Hole?" *Technology Review,* August-September, 1987, pp. 51–58.

"Chlorofluorocarbons and the Depletion of Stratospheric Ozone," *American Scientist,* January-February, 1989, pp. 36–45.

"President's Lecture: The Need for Scientific Communication with the Public," *Science,* June 11, 1993, pp. 1571–76.

SOURCES:

Books

Cagin, Seth, and Dray, Philip, *Between Earth and Sky: How CFCs Changed Our World and Endangered the Ozone Layer,* Pantheon, 1993.

Dotto, Lydia, and Schiff, Harold, *The Ozone War,* Doubleday, 1978.

Roan, Sharon, *Ozone Crisis: The 15-Year Evolution of a Sudden Global Emergency,* Wiley, 1989.

Periodicals

"Annals of Chemistry: Inert," *New Yorker,* April 7, 1975, pp. 47–51.

"Annals of Chemistry: In the Face of Doubt," *New Yorker,* June 9, 1986, pp. 70–83.

"Can We Repair the Sky?" *Consumer Reports,* May, 1989, pp. 322–26.

"Is the Ozone Hole in Our Heads?" *Newsweek,* October 11, 1993, p. 71.

"The Man Who Knew Too Much," *Popular Science,* January, 1989, pp. 60–65 and 102.

"Northern Exposure," *People,* April 20, 1992, p. 121.

"The Ozone Vanishes," *Time,* February 17, 1992, pp. 60–68.

"Pondering the Mysteries of a Growing Hole in the Ozone: Antarctic Expedition to Explore UCI Researchers' Theory that Man-Made Chemicals Are at Fault," *Register* (Santa Ana), August 27, 1986.

Other

Rowland, F. Sherwood, interview with Joan Oleck conducted on September 17, 1993.

—*Sketch by Joan Oleck*

Janet D. Rowley
1925-
American cytogeneticist

Janet D. Rowley's research on chromosome abnormalities in a form of leukemia have introduced new diagnostic tools for oncologists—those doctors specializing in cancer—and have also opened new avenues of inquiry in possible gene therapies for cancer. A specialist in cytogenetics (the investigation of the role of cells in evolution and heredity), Rowley has helped to pinpoint cancer gene locations and correlate them to chromosome aberrations.

Janet Davison Rowley was born on April 5, 1925, in New York City, the daughter of Hurford Henry and Ethel Mary (Ballantyne) Davison. She attended the University of Chicago where she earned a B.S. degree in 1946 and her M.D. in 1948. During the latter year she married Donald A. Rowley. The couple eventually had four sons: David, Donald, Robert, and Roger. Rowley's professional career took her from a research assistant job at the University of Chicago in 1949 and 1950 to an internship at Marine Hospital in Chicago, a residency at Cook County Hospital, and a clinical instructor position in neurology at the University of Illinois Medical School before returning to the University of Chicago Medical School in 1962. From 1962 to 1969 she was a research associate both in the department of medicine and at Argonne Cancer Research Hospital. Then from 1969 to 1977, she became an associate professor, and in 1977 was made a full professor at the medical school and at Franklin McLean Memorial Research Institute. In 1984 Rowley became the Blum-Riese Distinguished Service professor in the department of medicine and in the department of molecular genetics and cell biology at Franklin McLean Memorial Research Institute.

Pioneering Research in Oncogenes

During her work at the University of Chicago, Rowley has committed her research to understanding the cytogenetic causes of cancer. She developed the use of quinacrine and Giemsa staining to identify chromosomes in cloned cells. Once the chromosomes were easily identifiable, she could then study abnormalities that occur in some chromosomes in certain cancers. With the discovery of oncogenes, or cancer-inducing genes, Rowley focused on chromosome rearrangements which occur in a form of blood cancer known as chronic myeloid leukemia (CML). Studying the so-called Philadelphia chromosome, Rowley was able in 1972 to show a consistent chromosome translocation or shifting of genetic material in CML cells. This was the first recurring translocation to be discovered in any species. Since that time more than seventy such translocations have been detected in human malignant cells. In general, Rowley's research indicates that both translocations and deletions of genetic material occur in malignancy, and that cancer is caused by a complex series of events within a single cell, making some genes overactive (tumor producing) and eliminating other genes that would normally suppress growth. Any cell, according to Rowley's research, is therefore potentially cancerous. What is needed to activate malignant growth is this complex series of events, including translocation and deletion.

Co-founder and co-editor of the journal *Genes, Chromosomes and Cancer,* Rowley has received numerous honors and awards, including the Esther Langer Award in 1983; the Kuwait Cancer Prize in 1984; the A. Cressy Morrison Award from the New York Academy of Sciences in 1985; the Judd Memorial Award from the Sloan-Kettering Cancer Center, the Charles S. Mott Prize from the General Motors Research Foundation, and the G. H. A. Clowes Memorial Award from the American Association for Cancer Research, all in 1989; and the Robert de Villiers award from the Leukemia Society of America in 1993.

SELECTED WRITINGS BY ROWLEY:

Books

Chromosome Changes in Leukaemia, Leukaemia Research Fund, 1978.
(Editor, with John E. Ultmann) *Chromosomes and Cancer: From Molecules to Man,* Academic Press, 1983.
(Editor, with others) *Genes and Cancer,* Liss, 1984.
(Editor) *Consistent Chromosomal Aberrations and Oncogenes in Human Tumors,* Oxford University Press, 1984.
(Editor) *Advances in Understanding Genetic Changes in Cancer,* National Academy Press, 1992.

Periodicals

"Cytogenetics in Clinical Medicine," *Journal of the American Medical Association,* February 3, 1969, pp. 914–919.
"Identification of a Translocation with Quinacrine Fluorescence in a Patient with Acute Leukemia," *Annales de Genetique,* June, 1973, pp. 109–112.
"Acquired Trisomy 9," *Lancet,* August 18, 1973, p. 390.
(With others) "15/17 Translocation, a Consistent Chromosomal Change in Acute Promyelocytic Leukemia," *Lancet,* March 5, 1977, pp. 549–550.
(With V. Lindgren) "Comparable Complex Rearrangements Involving 8;21 and 9;22 Translocations in Leukemia," *Nature,* April 21, 1977, pp. 744–745.
"Mapping of Human Chromosomal Regions Related to Neoplasia: Evidence from Chromosomes 1 and 17," *Proceedings of the National Academy of Sciences of the United States of America,* December, 1977, pp. 5729–5733.
"Cytogenetic Patterns in Acute Nonlymphocytic Leukemia," with J. R. Testa, *Virchows Archive. B. Cell Pathology,* November 17, 1978, pp. 65–72.

"Human Oncogene Locations and Chromosome Aberrations," *Nature,* January 27, 1983, pp. 290–291.
"Heritable Fragile Sites in Cancer," with M. M. Le Beau, *Nature,* April 12, 1984, pp. 607–608.
"Chromosome Abnormalities in Leukemia," *Journal of Clinical Oncology,* February, 1988, pp. 194–202.
"The Philadelphia Chromosome Translocation," *Cancer,* May 15, 1990, pp. 2178–2184.
"Molecular Cytogenetics: Rosetta Stone for Understanding Cancer," *Cancer Research,* July 1, 1990.

—Sketch by J. Sydney Jones

Carlo Rubbia
1934-
Italian physicist

Carlo Rubbia was born in Italy and carried out his first serious scientific experiments as a young boy, using communication equipment abandoned at the end of World War II. Since his postdoctoral year at Columbia University in 1958 and 1959, Rubbia has been particularly interested in the study of elementary particles, and through his affiliations with the European Center for Nuclear Research (CERN) he has had some of the most powerful particle accelerators in the world available for his research. Since the late 1960s, Rubbia's primary research has involved the search for a trio of particles known as the W+, W-, and Z0 bosons, which were postulated in the 1960s as the force particles through which the electroweak force exerts its influence. By 1982, Rubbia and his colleagues at CERN had designed the equipment needed to carry out this search and had successfully located the first W particles. For this accomplishment, he and co-worker **Simon van der Meer** were awarded the 1984 Nobel Prize in physics.

Rubbia was born on March 31, 1934, in the small town of Gorizia, in northern Italy. His father was Silvio R. Rubbia, a telephone worker; his mother, Bice Liceni Rubbia, was a school teacher. When World War II ended in 1945, eleven-year-old Carlo "scaveng[ed] radio equipment that had been abandoned as various armies marched through on their various advances and retreats," according to Gary Taubes in his book *Nobel Dreams.* He used this equipment to learn everything about radios, becoming something of an "electronics freak," Taubes wrote.

Carlo Rubbia

Studies Elementary Particles in Italy and the United States

In 1945, Silvio Rubbia's job brought the family to Pisa, where Rubbia was enrolled at the prestigious Scuola Normale Superiore, a rigorous secondary school affiliated with the University of Pisa. After graduating from the Scuola, Rubbia went on to the university, earning a Ph.D. in physics in 1958 for his dissertation on cosmic radiation and particle detection devices. During the academic year 1958–59, Rubbia continued his studies at Columbia University in the United States, where he worked with some of the world's outstanding physicists, including **Tsung-Dao Lee**, **Chen Ning Yang**, **Chien-Shiung Wu**, **Charles H. Townes**, **Melvin Schwartz**, Leon Ledeberg, and **Steven Weinberg**, acquiring from them an interest in weak-interaction physics.

Rubbia returned to Italy in 1960 to continue his post-doctoral studies at the University of Rome. A year later, he accepted an appointment at CERN in Geneva. A consortium of more than a dozen European nations, CERN is one of the world's most important centers for the study of elementary particles. Rubbia quickly moved up the hierarchy at CERN and was appointed to the prestigious position of team leader before he was thirty years old.

Rubbia's goal during his first years at CERN was the discovery of three "intermediate vector bosons" known as the W+, W-, and Z0 particles. The existence of these particles had been predicted in the 1960s,

when **Sheldon Glashow**, **Abdus Salam** and Steven Weinberg had independently developed an electroweak theory proposing that two fundamental forces, the electromagnetic and weak forces, are manifestations of a more fundamental natural force, and predicting the existence of W and Z particles. In 1971, Salam and Weinberg suggested that the neutral Z particle could be detected in "neutral currents" that would be produced by the collision of neutrinos and matter. Rubbia's objective was to design and conduct the experiment that would, for the first time, produce this particle.

Improved Accelerator Design Leads to Discovery of W and Z Particles

In 1969, Rubbia joined a project at the Fermi National Accelerator Laboratory (Fermilab) near Chicago to search for the W particles. In 1971, however, the team switched their efforts to the attempt to prove the existence of neutral weak currents, thus putting them in direct competition with Rubbia's former colleagues at CERN. In 1973, the CERN team published nearly conclusive evidence that neutral weak currents existed. The Fermilab team immediately rushed to publish their own as yet incomplete results, which also supported the existence of the currents. At about the same time, Rubbia's visa expired and he returned to Europe. Soon thereafter, the Fermi team reconducted their experiments and announced that their original findings had been in error. They then realized, however, that this second set of experiments was flawed, and they retracted their earlier retraction. The confusion temporarily tarnished Rubbia's reputation.

Both teams now turned their attention to the search for the W and Z particles. However, no existing particle accelerator could generate the energy needed to produce them. Rubbia proposed a revolutionary new technique in which two particle beams, one composed of protons and one of antiprotons, would be set in motion in opposite directions and caused to collide with each other. The amount of energy released in such a collision, Rubbia said, should be sufficient to result in the formation of W and Z particles. Rubbia's idea was ridiculed by a number of physicists, including the director of Fermilab. Managers at CERN were more open-minded, however, and provided the $100 million needed to redesign the center's super proton synchrotron to Rubbia's specifications.

By 1982, that work had been completed and the search for the W+, W-, and Z bosons began. Within a month's time, the first W particles had been identified and, less than a year later, the first Z's were also discovered. For this accomplishment, Rubbia shared the 1984 Nobel Prize in physics with the Dutch scientist Simon van der Meer, who had devised a means of storing and regulating the erratic antiprotons.

Rubbia has been affiliated with Harvard University since 1970 (1972 according to some biographers), teaching one semester there each year. He has also continued an active program of research at CERN. Rubbia married Marissa Romé, a high school physics teacher, on June 27, 1960. They have two daughters, Laura and Andrea. Rubbia has been described as one of the most controversial figures in modern particle physics, a man driven by his love for science and, according to some, his own ego. His reputation at CERN, for example, has been described by Taubes as "very, very good and very, very bad," and an article in the October 25, 1984, issue of *New Scientist* called him "an ebullient yet irascible Italian whom fellow physicists love to hate."

SELECTED WRITINGS BY RUBBIA:

Periodicals

"The Physics of the Proton-Antiproton Collider," *Proceedings HEP83 of the International Europhysics Conference on High Energy Physics,* 1983, pp. 860–79.

SOURCES:

Books

Current Biography 1985, H. W. Wilson, 1985, pp. 347–51.
Taubes, Gary, *Nobel Dreams,* Random House, 1986, pp. 3–9 and *passim.*
Wasson, Tyler, editor, *Nobel Prize Winners,* H. W. Wilson, 1987, pp. 891–93.

Periodicals

Lederman, Leon M., and Roy F. Schwitters, "The 1984 Nobel Prize in Physics," *Science,* January 11, 1985, pp. 131–34.
Sutton, Christine, "CERN Scoops Up the Nobel Physics Prize," *New Scientist,* October 25, 1984, pp. 10–11.
Walgate, Robert, "CERN's First Nobel Prize," *Nature,* October 25, 1984, p. 701.

—*Sketch by David E. Newton*

Vera Cooper Rubin
1928-
American astronomer

Vera Cooper Rubin, one of America's foremost women astronomers, has spent her life observing galactic structure, rotation and dynamics. Her pioneering spectroscopic research of the 1970s demonstrated the possible existence of a large percentage of dark matter in the universe, matter that is invisible to the naked eye. Scientists now speculate that up to 90 percent of the universe may be composed of dark matter. Rubin was born on July 23, 1928, in Philadelphia, the daughter of electrical engineer Philip Cooper and Rose Applebaum, and was educated at Vassar College, receiving her B.A. in 1948. Rubin earned her M.A. at Cornell in 1951; her thesis studied the evidence for bulk rotation in the universe, and later influenced Gérard de Vaucouleurs' work on the "local supercluster" of galaxies. She received her Ph.D. in astronomy under Russian-American physicist **George Gamow** (1904–1968) three years later at Georgetown University. Rubin's pioneering dissertation studied galactic distribution, and demonstrated a "clumpiness" in the spread of galaxies; virtually ignored in 1954, this effect was not seriously studied until the 1970s.

Rubin spent a year as an instructor in math and physics at Montgomery County Junior College before moving back to Georgetown University as research associate (1955–65), lecturer (1959–62), and then assistant professor (1962–65). She also did observational work at Kitt Peak Observatory in Arizona, and became the first official female observer at Palomar Observatory in California in 1965 (Margaret Burbidge had previously observed there unofficially). Also in 1965, Rubin joined the Department of Terrestrial Magnetism (DTM) at Washington's Carnegie Institute. For the rest of the 1960s, Rubin studied spectroscopy and galactic rotations, structure and dynamics.

Dark Matter Discovered

In particular, Rubin studied the rotation of spiral galaxies. She and DTM physicist W. Kent Ford used a spectrograph to study the rate of rotation within galaxies. They found that the stars closest to the center of a galaxy and those farthest out were traveling at the same rate of speed. Mathematical research had suggested the stars farthest from a galaxy's center would travel at a slower pace. In addition, the amount of mass in both the darker and brighter parts of a galaxy was constant, suggesting that some form of unseen matter was present. Earlier astronomers, including Fritz Zwicky, had speculated that a previously unknown "dark matter" might exist. Rubin and Ford's observations of galactic rotation speed seemed to verify that hypothesis. Continuing investigation of dark matter has been a major research effort among astronomers since the 1980s.

Rubin has contributed numerous papers to *Astrophysical Journal, Astronomical Journal,* and *Bulletin of the American Astronomical Society*. She also served as associate editor of the *Astronomical Journal* from 1972 to 1977, of *Astrophysical Journal Letters* from 1977 to 1982, and joined the editorial board of *Science Magazine* from 1979 to 1987. Rubin has sat on numerous astronomical committees, including those of Harvard University, the National Academy of Sciences (to which she was elected in 1981), and the American Astronomical Society. She has also received honorary degrees from Creighton University in 1978, Harvard University in 1988, and Yale University in 1990.

To promote women in astronomy, Rubin joined the council of American Women in Science in 1984, and in 1987 became a president's distinguished visitor at Vassar College. In 1988 she became the Beatrice Tinsley visiting professor at the University of Texas. Meanwhile, to encourage young girls to study science, she wrote a children's book on astronomy. In recent years Rubin has sat on the board of directors of the Astronomical Society of the Pacific, and has been a member of several other scientific societies. She was also on the visiting committee of the Space Telescope Scientific Institute between 1990 and 1992. In 1948 Rubin married physicist Robert J. Rubin. The couple have four children: David, Allan, Judith, and Karl. All four have become scientists as well.

"Observing is spectacularly lovely," Rubin said in *Mercury*. "I enjoy analyzing the observations, trying to see what you have, trying to understand what you're learning. It's a challenge, but a great deal of fun. It's not only fun, but a lot of it is just plain curiosity—this incredible hope that somehow we can learn how the universe works. What keeps me going is this hope and curiosity."

SELECTED WRITINGS BY RUBIN:

Books

(Editor with George V. Coyne) *Large Scale Motions in the Universe,* Princeton University Press, 1988.

Periodicals

"Rotation of the Andromeda Nebula from a Spectroscopic Survey of Emission Regions," *Astrophysical Journal,* Number 159, 1970, p. 379.
(With W. K. Ford, Jr., N. Thonnard, M. S. Roberts, and J. A. Graham) "Motion of the Gal-

axy and the Local Group Determined from the Velocity Anisotropy of Distant Sc I Galaxies. I. The Data. II. The Analysis for the Motion," *Astrophysical Journal,* Number 81, 1976, pp. 681, 719.
"Women's Work," *Science '86,* July-August, 1986, pp. 58–65.

SOURCES:

Books

A Hand Up: Mentoring Women in Science, American Women in Science, 1993, pp. 75–78.
Lightman, Alan and Brawer, Roberta, "Vera Rubin," in *Origins: The Lives and Worlds of Modern Cosmologists,* Harvard University Press, 1990, pp. 285–305.
Tufty, Barbara, "First Woman Permitted to Observe the Universe at Palomar," in O'Neill, Lois Decker, editor, *The Women's Book of World Records and Achievements,* Anchor, 1979, p. 151.

Periodicals

Bartusiak, Marcia, "The Woman Who Spins the Stars," *Discover,* October, 1990, pp. 88–94.
Stephens, Sally, "Vera Rubin: An Unconventional Career," *Mercury: The Journal of the Astronomical Society of the Pacific,* January-February, 1992, pp. 38–45.

—*Sketch by Julian A. Smith*

S. K. Runcorn
1922-
English geophysicist

Geophysicist S. K. Runcorn has made significant contributions to the understanding of several areas within his field, including the Earth's magnetic field and the theory of continental drift. During the 1950s, he helped establish the discipline called paleomagnetism—the study of the intensity and direction of residual magnetization found in ancient rocks. More recently, his research has encompassed lunar magnetism. In a prolific career marked by the publication of more than one-hundred and eighty papers and the editing of over two dozen books, Runcorn has exerted a wide-ranging impact on his field.

S. K. Runcorn

Stanley Keith Runcorn was born on November 19, 1922, in Southport, England. He was the eldest of two children born to William Henry Runcorn, a businessman, and Lily Idina Roberts Runcorn. As Runcorn related to Linda Wasmer Smith in a letter, "My interest in science as a child was certainly stimulated . . . by excellent maths and physics teaching in my grammar school." In 1941 Runcorn began studies at Gonville and Caius College of Cambridge University. He passed the tripos, or final honors examination, in mechanical sciences two years later. Runcorn earned a B.A. degree from Cambridge in 1944 and an M.A. in 1948, before transferring to Manchester University to obtain a Ph.D. in 1949. Later, he returned to Cambridge, where he received an Sc.D. degree in 1963.

Advances the Theory of Continental Drift

Runcorn's early years at college coincided with World War II. From 1943 though 1946, he worked on radar research for the ministry of supply at Malvern. For three years afterward, he was a lecturer in physics at Manchester University. His department head there was **Patrick Maynard Stuart Blackett**, who won the 1948 Nobel Prize in physics. Under Blackett's leadership, Runcorn first began a long line of investigations into geomagnetism, which extended well past his move back to Cambridge as assistant director of geophysics research in 1950.

At the time, the idea was rapidly gaining currency in England that many rocks contain within them a fossilized record of the magnetic conditions under which they were formed. This is the basic assumption behind paleomagnetic research. Runcorn compared the results of tests done on rocks from Great Britain and the United States. His analyses seemed to support the hypothesis that over hundreds of millions of years the Earth's magnetic poles had undergone large-scale movement, or polar wandering. However, the polar migration routes were different depending on whether the tested rocks came from Europe or North America. This suggested that the continents themselves had actually moved. Thus Runcorn became a proponent of the theory called continental drift. Although this idea had first been put forth in 1912, it had not up to that point won widespread acceptance. It was not until the mid–1950s that Runcorn and his colleagues published convincing evidence for its existence.

Advocates of continental drift argued that the direction of magnetization within rocks from different continents would align if only the land masses were oriented differently. However, this suggestion was not immediately embraced by most scientists, partly because a physical mechanism to explain continental drift had yet to be found. By the early 1960s, though, Runcorn had proposed that, under very high temperature and pressure, rocks beneath the Earth's cold, outer shell—the lithosphere—might gradually "creep," or flow. The resulting upward transfer of heat by convection currents could be the force that moved continents. This idea contributed to the modern theory of plate tectonics, which posits that the Earth's shell is divided into a number of rigid plates floating on a viscous underlayer.

In 1956 Runcorn had accepted a post as professor and head of the physics department at King's College, part of the University of Durham. Seven years later, King's College became the University of Newcastle upon Tyne, and Runcorn was appointed head of the school of physics there, a position which he held until 1988. During this period, Runcorn also was a visiting scientist or professor at several institutions around the world, including the University of California, Los Angeles and Berkeley; Dominion Observatory, Ottawa; the California Institute of Technology; the University of Miami; the Lunar Science Institute, Houston; the University of Texas, Galveston; and the University of Queensland, Australia.

Proposes New Ideas on Lunar Magnetism

By the late 1960s, Runcorn's attention had turned toward the moon. At the time, the moon was generally presumed to be a dead body. As early as 1962, though, Runcorn had suggested that the moon, too, might be subject to the forces of convection—an idea that was initially rejected by most scientists.

However, examination of lunar samples brought back by the Apollo missions showed that some of them were magnetized, which implied that they had been exposed to magnetic fields while they were forming. Runcorn and his colleagues concluded that the moon had probably once possessed its own strong magnetic field, generated within an iron core.

Not only that, but this magnetic field seemed to have pointed in different directions at different times in lunar history. When Runcorn and his co-workers calculated the strengths and directions of this ancient magnetism, they found evidence of polar wandering. More recently, Runcorn has proposed that the wandering could have been caused by the same impacts that created large basins near the moon's equator. According to this hypothesis, the force of the impacts could have shifted the moon's entire surface, so that regions once near the poles might have been relocated closer to the equator. However, attempts to confirm this notion have so far proved inconclusive.

Runcorn's remarkable skill as a theorist has been recognized on numerous occasions. In 1989 he assumed an endowed chair in the natural sciences at the University of Alaska in Fairbanks. He has also been granted honorary degrees from universities in Utrecht, Netherlands; Ghent, Belgium; Paris; and Bergen, Norway. Among the many prestigious awards he has received are the Napier Shaw Prize of Britain's Royal Meteorological Society in 1959, the John Adams Fleming Medal of the American Geophysical Union in 1983, the Gold Medal of Britain's Royal Astronomical Society in 1984, and the Wegener Medal of the European Union of Geosciences in 1987.

In addition, Runcorn has been elected a fellow or member of such respected associations as the British Royal Society, the American Physical Society, the European Geophysical Society, the Royal Netherlands Academy of Science, the Indian National Science Academy, the Royal Norwegian Academy of Science and Letters, the Pontifical Academy of Science, and Academia Europaea. Although he spends fall semesters in Alaska, during the rest of the year, he can usually be found in his laboratory at Imperial College in London.

Runcorn, who never married, is an aficionado of sports and the arts. Among his favorite pastimes is rugby, which he enjoyed as a participant until he was past fifty and as a spectator thereafter. In a letter to Linda Wasmer Smith, Runcorn noted that he is also an avid fan of "squash rackets and swimming, . . . visiting art galleries, seeing opera and ballet, reading history and politics, hiking in the country, and seeing architecture in my travels." Thus his leisure preferences, like his scientific interests, are both eclectic and intense.

SELECTED WRITINGS BY RUNCORN:

Books

(Editor) *Methods and Techniques in Geophysics,* Volumes 1 and 2, Interscience, 1960 and 1966.
(Editor) *Continental Drift,* Academic, 1962.
(Editor) *Mantle of the Earth and Terrestrial Planets,* Interscience, 1967.
(Editor) *Magnetism and the Cosmos,* Oliver & Boyd, 1967.

Periodicals

"The Moon's Deceptive Tranquillity," *New Scientist,* October 21, 1982, pp. 174–180.
"The Moon's Ancient Magnetism," *Scientific American,* Volume 257, 1987, pp. 60–68.

SOURCES:

Books

A Biographical Encyclopedia of Scientists, Volume 2, Facts on File, 1981, p. 693.
McGraw-Hill Modern Scientists and Engineers, Volume 3, 1980, pp. 50–51.

Other

Runcorn, Stanley Keith, letters to Linda Wasmer Smith written on January 5 and February 3, 1994.

—*Sketch by Linda Wasmer Smith*

Ernst Ruska
1906-1988
German physicist

The inventor of the electron microscope, Ernst Ruska, combined an academic career in physics and electrical engineering with work in private industry at several of Germany's top electrical corporations. He was associated with the Siemens Company from 1937 to 1955, where he helped mass produce the electron microscope, the invention for which he was awarded the 1986 Nobel Prize in physics. The Nobel Prize Committee called Ruska's electron microscope one of the most important inventions of the twentieth century. The benefits of electron microscopy to the field of biology and medicine allow scientists to study such structures as viruses and protein molecules. Technical fields such as electronics have also found new uses for Ruska's invention: improved versions of the electron microscope became instrumental in the fabrication of computer chips.

Ruska was born in Heidelberg, Germany, on December 25, 1906. He was the fifth child of Julius Ferdinand Ruska, an Asian studies professor, and Elisabeth (Merx) Ruska. After receiving his under-graduate education in the physical sciences from the Technical University of Munich and the Technical University of Berlin, he was certified as an electrical engineer in 1931. He then went on to study under Max Knoll at Berlin, and received his doctorate in electrical engineering in 1933. During this period he and Knoll created an early version of the electron microscope, and Ruska concurrently was employed by the Fernseh Corporation in Berlin, where he worked to develop television tube technology. He left Fernseh to join Siemens as an electrical engineer, and at the same time accepted a position as a lecturer at the Technical University of Berlin. His ability to work in both academic and corporate milieus continued through his time at Siemens, and expanded when in 1954 he became a member of the Max Planck Society. In 1957 he was appointed director of the Society's Institute of Electron Microscopy, and in 1959, he accepted the Technical University of Berlin's invitation to become professor of electron optics and electron microscopy. He remained an active contributor to his field until his retirement in 1972.

Inventing a Better Way to See

Prior to Ruska's invention of the electron microscope in 1931, the field of microscopy was limited by the inability of existing microscopes to see features smaller than the wavelength of visible light. Because the wavelength of light is about two thousand times larger than an atom, the mysteries of the atomic world were virtually closed to scientists until Ruska's breakthrough using electron wavelengths as the resolution medium. When the electron microscope was perfected, microscope magnification increased from approximately two thousand to one million times.

The French physicist, **Louis Victor de Broglie**, was the first to propose that subatomic particles, such as electrons, had wavelike characteristics, and that the greater the energy exhibited by the particle, the shorter its wavelength would be. De Broglie's theory was confirmed in 1927 by Bell Laboratory researchers. The conception that it was possible to construct a microscope that used electrons instead of light was realized in the late 1920s when Ruska was able to build a short-focus magnetic lens using a magnetic coil. A prototype of the electron microscope was then developed in 1931 by Ruska and Max Knoll at the

Technical University in Berlin. Although it was less powerful than contemporary optical microscopes, the prototype laid the groundwork for a more powerful version, which Ruska developed in 1933. That version was ten times stronger than existing light microscopes. Ruska subsequently worked with the Siemens Company to produce for the commercial market an electron microscope with a resolution to one hundred angstroms (by contrast, modern electron microscopes have a resolution to one angstrom, or one ten-billionth of a meter).

Ruska's microscope—called a transmission microscope—captures on a fluorescent screen an image made by a focused beam of electrons passing through a thin slice of metalized material. The image can be photographed. In 1981 **Gerd Binnig** and **Heinrich Rohrer** took Ruska's concept further by using a beam of electrons to scan the surface of a specimen (rather than to penetrate it). A recording of the current generated by the intermingling of electrons emitted from both the beam and specimen is used to build a contour map of the surface. The function of this "scanning electron microscope" complements, rather than competes against, the transmission microscope, and its inventors shared the 1986 Nobel Prize in physics with Ruska.

In 1937 Ruska married Irmela Ruth Geigis, and the couple had two sons and a daughter. In addition to the Nobel Prize, Ruska's work was honored with the Senckenberg Prize of the University of Frankfurt am Main in 1939, the Lasker Award in 1960, and the Duddell Medal and Prize of the Institute of Physics in London in 1975, among other awards. He also held honorary doctorates from the University of Kiev, the University of Modena, the Free University of Berlin, and the University of Toronto. Ruska died in West Berlin on May 30, 1988.

SELECTED WRITINGS BY RUSKA:

Books

The Early Development of Electron Lenses and Electron Microscopy, translated by Thomas Mulvey, S. Hirzel, 1980.

SOURCES:

Periodicals

Browne, Malcolm W., "Ernst Ruska, a German Nobel Winner, Dies at 81," *New York Times,* May 31, 1988, p. D14.
Lemonick, Michael D., "Lives of Spirit and Dedication," *Time,* October 27, 1986, pp. 67–68.

Monastersky, R., "Physics: Tiny World Garners Grand Laurels," *Science News,* Volume 130, October 25, 1986, pp. 262–263.

Sullivan, Walter, "Microscope Designs Bring the Nobel Prize to Three Europeans," *New York Times,* October 16, 1986, pp. A1; B18.

Time, June 13, 1988, p. 45.

—*Sketch by Jane Stewart Cook*

Bertrand Russell

Bertrand Russell
1872-1970
English mathematician and philosopher

A seminal figure in twentieth-century mathematical logic and philosophy, Bertrand Russell produced more than seventy books and pamphlets on topics ranging from mathematics and logic to philosophy, religion, and politics. He valued reason, clarity, fearlessness, and independence of judgment, and held the conviction that it was the duty of the educated and privileged classes to lead. Having protested against Britain's participation in World War I and against the development of nuclear weapons, Russell was imprisoned twice for his convictions. In writing his own obituary, he described himself as a man of unusual principles, who was always prepared to live up to them.

Bertrand Arthur William Russell was born on May 18, 1872, in Ravenscroft, Trelleck, Monmouthshire, England. His family tree can be traced back to John Russell, a favorite courtier of Henry VIII. His grandfather, Lord John Russell, served as Prime Minister under Queen Victoria. Bertrand Russell's father, Lord Amberley, served in Parliament briefly, but was defeated because of his rejection of Christianity and his advocacy of voting rights for women and birth control. His mother was Kate Stanley, the daughter of a Liberal politician. Orphaned before the age of five, Russell was raised by his paternal grandmother, a Scotch Presbyterian with strong moral standards who gave duty and virtue greater priority than love and affection. His grandmother did not have confidence in the moral and religious environment at boarding schools, so, after briefly attending a local kindergarten, he was taught by a series of governesses and tutors. Later he wrote in his *Autobiography* that he had been influenced by his grandmother's fearlessness, her public spirit, her contempt for convention, and her indifference to the opinion of the majority. On his twelfth birthday she gave him a Bible in which she had written her favorite texts, including "Thou shalt not follow a multitude to do evil." It was due to her influence, he felt, that in later life he was not afraid to champion unpopular causes.

Intrigued by Euclid

When Russell was eleven, his brother Frank began to teach him Euclidean geometry. As he recounts in his *Autobiography,* "This was one of the great events of my life, as dazzling as first love. I had not imagined that there was anything so delicious in the world." Russell was greatly disappointed, however, to find out that Euclid started with axioms which were not proved but were simply accepted. Russell refused to accept the axioms unless his brother could give a good reason for them. When his brother told him that they couldn't continue unless he accepted the axioms, Russell relented, but with reluctance and doubt about the foundations of mathematics. That doubt remained with him and determined the course of much of his later work in mathematics.

At fifteen, Bertrand left home to take a training course to prepare for the scholarship examination at Trinity College, Cambridge. Lonely and miserable, he considered suicide but rejected the idea because, as he later said, he wanted to learn more mathematics. He kept a secret diary, written using letters from the Greek alphabet, in which he questioned the religious ideas he had been taught. After a year and a half, he took the Trinity College examination and won a scholarship. One of the scholarship examiners was

Alfred North Whitehead. Apparently impressed with Russell's ability, Whitehead arranged for him to meet several students who soon became his close friends. He was invited to join a group, "The Apostles," which met weekly for intense discussions of philosophy and history. His chief interest and chief source of happiness, he said, was mathematics; he received a first class degree in mathematics in 1893. He found, however, that his work in preparing for the exams had led him to think of mathematics as a set of tricks and ingenious devices, too much like a crossword puzzle; this disillusioned him. Hoping to find some reason for supposing mathematics to be true, he turned to philosophy. He studied the philosophy of idealism, which was popular in Cambridge at the time, concluding that time, space and matter are all illusions and the world resides in the mind of the beholder. He took the Moral Science examination in 1894 and received an honors degree.

At seventeen, Russell had fallen in love with Alys Pearsall Smith, an American from a wealthy Philadelphia Quaker family, and after graduation they became engaged. His grandmother did not approve. Hoping he would become interested in politics and lose interest in Alys, she arranged for him to become an attaché at the British Embassy in Paris. He found his work at the Embassy boring, and upon his return three months later, he and Alys were married.

In 1895, Russell wrote a dissertation on the foundations of geometry, which won him a fellowship at Trinity College and enabled him to travel and study for six years. He and Alys went to Berlin to study the German Socialist movement and the writings of Karl Marx. During his travels, he formulated a plan to write a series of books on the philosophy of the sciences, starting with mathematics and ending with biology, growing gradually more concrete, and a second series of books on social and political questions, working to more abstract issues. During his long life, he managed to fulfill much of this plan. As a result, according to biographer Ronald Clark, no other Englishman of the twentieth century was to gain such high regard in both academic and non-academic worlds.

Russell returned to London in 1896 and lectured on his experiences to students of the London School of Economics and the Fabian Society, publishing his studies as *German Social Democracy,* the first of his numerous books and pamphlets. In this publication he demonstrated his ability to investigate a subject quickly and then present it in clear and convincing language. He and Alys traveled to the United States, where they visited Alys's friend, the poet Walt Whitman. Russell lectured on non-Euclidean geometry at Bryn Mawr College, where Alys had been a student, and at Johns Hopkins University. In 1900, he was asked to lecture on German mathematician Gottfried Wilhelm Leibniz at Cambridge. He wanted to show that mathematical truths did not depend on the mathematician's point of view. He re-examined the philosophy of idealism and abandoned it, concluding that matter, space and time really did exist. He published his views in *A Critical Exposition of the Philosophy of Leibniz.*

Seeks Basic Principles of Mathematics and Logic

Russell then started work on an ambitious task—devising a structure which would allow both the simplest laws of logic and the most complex mathematical theorems to be developed from a small number of basic ideas. If this could be done, then the axioms which mathematicians accepted would no longer be needed, and both logic and mathematics would be part of a single system. At a conference in Paris in 1900, he met **Giuseppe Peano**, whose book on symbolic logic held that mathematics was merely a highly developed form of logic. Russell became interested in the possibility of analyzing the fundamental notions of mathematics, such as order and cardinal numbers, using Peano's approach. He published *The Principles of Mathematics* in 1903; its fundamental thesis was that mathematics and logic are identical.

Applying logic to basic mathematical concepts and working with **Georg Cantor**'s proof that a class of all classes cannot exist, Russell formulated his famous paradox concerning classes that are members of themselves—such as the class of classes. According to Russell's paradox, it is impossible to answer the question of whether the class containing all classes that are not members of themselves is a member of itself—for if it is a member of itself, then it does not meet the terms of the class; and if it is not, then it does. (This is the same kind of paradox as is found in the statement "Everything I say is a lie.") In developing this Theory of Types, however, Russell realized the absurdity of asking whether a class can be a member of itself. He concluded that if classes belong to a particular type, and if they consist of homogenous members, then a class cannot be a member of itself. In planning *The Principles of Mathematics,* an exposition of his ideas on mathematics and logic, Russell decided on two volumes, the first containing explanations of his claims and the second containing mathematical proofs. His former teacher, Alfred Whitehead, had been working on similar problems. Consequently, the two scholars decided to collaborate on the second part of the task. For nearly a decade they worked together, often sharing the same house, sending each other drafts and revising each other's work. The result, *Principia Mathematica,* was a separate work published in three volumes, the last in 1913. Before it was completed, Russell was elected to the Royal Society, of which Whitehead was already a member.

Russell was persuaded to run for Parliament in 1907 as a supporter of voting rights for women; he lost the election. Appointed a lecturer in logic and the principles of mathematics at Trinity College in 1910, he published a short introduction to philosophy, *The Problems of Philosophy,* in 1912, and *Our Knowledge of the External World* in 1914. Invited to Cambridge, Massachusetts, to give the Lowell Lectures and a course at Harvard University in 1914, he also lectured in New York, Chicago, and Ann Arbor, Michigan.

Imprisoned for Opposing World War I

Russell was an outspoken critic of England's participation in World War I. He worked with the No-Conscription Fellowship to protest the drafting of young men into the army. In 1916 he gave a series of lectures in London which were published as *Principles of Social Reconstruction.* They were also published in the United States as *Why Men Fight: A Method of Abolishing the International Duel.* He was invited to give a lecture series at Harvard based on the book, but he was denied a passport because he had been convicted of writing a leaflet criticizing the imprisonment of a young conscientious objector. As a result of his conviction, he was dismissed from his lectureship at Trinity College. He wrote an open letter to Woodrow Wilson, the President of the United States, urging him to seek a negotiated peace rather than go to war. Since Russell's mail was being intercepted by the British government, he sent the letter with a young American woman. The story made the headlines in the *New York Times.*

Russell wrote articles for *The Tribunal,* published by the No-Conscription Fellowship. In one article, he predicted that the consequences of the war would include widespread famine and the presence of American soldiers capable of intimidating striking workers. He was charged with making statements likely to prejudice Britain's relations with the United States and was sentenced to six months in prison. Before his imprisonment, he wrote *Roads to Freedom: Socialism, Anarchism and Syndicalism.* While in prison he wrote *Introduction to Mathematical Philosophy,* which explained the ideas of *The Principles of Mathematics* and *Principia Mathematica* in relatively simple terms.

In 1920, Russell visited Russia, where he was disappointed with the results of the 1917 revolution, and China, where he lectured at the National University of Peking. The following year, Russell divorced his wife Alys and married Dora Black. His son John Conrad was born, and in 1922 his daughter Katharine Jane was born. In 1927 he and Dora established Beacon Hill School for their children and others. He traveled to the United States for lecture tours in 1924, 1927, 1929 and 1931, speaking on political and social issues. He divorced Dora in 1935 and married Patricia Spence the following year. A son, Conrad Sebastian Robert, was born in 1937.

Russell lived in the United States during World War II, from 1938 to 1944, lecturing at the University of Chicago, the University of California at Los Angeles, Bryn Mawr, Princeton, and the Barnes Foundation at Merion, Pennsylvania. He was invited to teach at New York City College, but the invitation was revoked due to objections to his atheism and unconventional personal morality. He continued to publish works on philosophy, logic, politics, economics, religion, morality and education. In 1944, he returned to Trinity College, where he had been offered a fellowship. He published *A History of Western Philosophy,* participated in radio broadcasts in England, and lectured in Norway and Australia. He was awarded the Order of Merit by the King in 1949 and the Nobel Prize for Literature in 1950. At the age of 80, he divorced Patricia Spence and married Edith Finch.

Acutely aware of the dangers of nuclear war, Russell served as the first president of the Campaign for Nuclear Disarmament in 1958, and as president of the Committee of 100 in 1960. As a member of the Committee of 100, he encouraged demonstrations against the British government's nuclear arms policies; for this he was sentenced to two months in prison, which was reduced to one week for health reasons. In his ninth decade, Russell established the Bertrand Russell Peace Foundation, published his *Autobiography,* appealed on behalf of political prisoners in several countries, protested nuclear weapons testing, criticized the war in Vietnam, and established the War Crimes Tribunal. He died on February 2, 1970, at the age of 98.

SELECTED WRITINGS BY RUSSELL:

Books

German Social Democracy, Longmans, Green, 1896.

An Essay on the Foundations of Geometry, Cambridge University Press, 1897.

A Critical Exposition of the Philosophy of Leibniz, Cambridge University Press, 1900.

The Principles of Mathematics, Cambridge University Press, 1903.

(With Alfred North Whitehead) *Principia Mathematica,* 3 volumes, Cambridge University Press, 1910, 1912, 1913.

Our Knowledge of the External World as a Field for Scientific Method in Philosophy, Allen & Unwin, 1914.

Principles of Social Reconstruction, Allen & Unwin, 1916.

Roads to Freedom: Socialism, Anarchism and Syndicalism, Allen & Unwin, 1918.

Introduction to Mathematical Philosophy, Allen & Unwin, 1919.

A History of Western Philosophy, Simon & Schus-
　　ter, 1945.
The Autobiography of Bertrand Russell, three vol-
　　umes, Little, Brown, 1967, 1968, 1969.

SOURCES:

Books

Ayer, A. J., *Bertrand Russell,* Viking, 1972.
Clark, Ronald, *Bertrand Russell and His World,*
　　Thames & Hudson, 1981.
Gottschalk, Herbert, *Bertrand Russell,* translated
　　by Edward Fitzgerald, Roy Publishers, 1965.
Schilpp, Paul Arthur, editor, *The Philosophy of
　　Bertrand Russell,* The Library of Living Phi-
　　losophers, 1946.

—Sketch by C. D. Lord

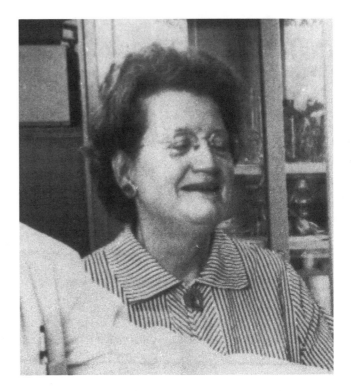

Elizabeth Shull Russell

Elizabeth Shull Russell
1913-
American geneticist

The Roscoe B. Jackson Laboratory in scenic Bar
Harbor, Maine, has been the professional home
of geneticist Elizabeth Shull Russell since the late
1930s. For the last five decades it has also been the
birthplace of millions of laboratory mice which have
been meticulously bred and characterized by Russell
and the center's staff. Through her efforts, laboratory
mice populations—which include dozens of strains
exhibiting particular characteristics that make them
desirable for research—are available to scientists
worldwide. Russell has also used the mice for her own
ongoing research in mammalian genetics and the
study of such conditions as hereditary anemias,
muscular dystrophy, cancer and aging.

Russell was born on May 1, 1913, in Ann Arbor,
Michigan. Her mother, Margaret Jeffrey Buckley,
held a master's degree in zoology and was a teacher at
Grinnell College in Iowa during an era when few
women even attended college. Her father, Aaron
Franklin Shull, was a zoologist and geneticist who
taught at the University of Michigan. Both the
Buckleys and the Shulls had scientists in their families. Elizabeth's uncle on her mother's side was a
physicist, and on her father's side there was a
geneticist, a plant physiologist and a botanical artist.
Her parents met in 1908 when both attended a

summer course at the laboratory in Cold Spring
Harbor on Long Island, New York. It seemed quite
natural that Russell became interested in the plants
and animals in her surroundings; as a girl she
carefully catalogued every flowering plant near their
summer home.

Entering the University of Michigan at the age of
sixteen, Russell graduated in 1933 with a degree in
zoology. This was during the midst of the Great
Depression, however, and few jobs were available
teaching science. Upon hearing of a scholarship
program at Columbia University, her father convinced her to participate in it. Russell's coursework at
Columbia included genetics, which was to prove her
greatest interest. She became influenced by a paper
written by **Sewall Wright** of the University of
Chicago, entitled "Physiological and Evolutionary
Theories of Dominance." He proposed that the
specific way in which characteristics are inherited
must be from either the nucleic acids or proteins on
the chromosomes (geneticists now know that inheritance is controlled by the nucleic acid DNA). Upon
receiving her master's degree, Russell went to the
University of Chicago where she obtained an assistantship and did further graduate work under Wright.
Her doctoral thesis explored the effect of genes in the
pigmentation of guinea pigs.

Russell received her Ph.D. at Chicago in 1937
and married a fellow graduate student, William L.
Russell. They moved to Bar Harbor, Maine, when he
was appointed to a position at the Roscoe B. Jackson

Memorial Laboratory. As was the general practice of most institutions at the time, only one member of a family could be employed by the laboratory, so Elizabeth Russell was invited to work as an independent investigator, which she did from 1937 to 1946.

Works with Mice at the Jackson Laboratory

While pursuing her research, Russell spent much of her time at the laboratory working with precollege, college and graduate students that came to Jackson each summer. That first summer of 1937 she had twelve summer students. As several other members of the Jackson family were also named Elizabeth, she soon became known as Tibby, a name that stuck. Over the next several years, the Russells started a family. They would eventually have three sons and a daughter together.

Although Russell had begun her investigations into how a gene controls characteristics by using fruit flies, during the 1940s she helped build up a population of laboratory mice that could be used in researching many more genetic questions. She characterized each strain, whether it be by coat color or the presence of a hereditary disease. With great precision Russell managed the genetically controlled inbred populations, and in 1946 she officially became a member of the research staff. The following year, she and her husband divorced. Russell—with four young children—now pursued her career in earnest even as the lab was starting to appreciate her great potential as a researcher.

In October, 1947, a devastating fire spread across Bar Harbor, destroying the Jackson Laboratory. Almost one hundred thousand laboratory mice perished—animals which had been carefully bred by Russell and others. In the years following, however, the team helped to once again build up the mouse population.

One day in 1951, while studying the source of mouse skin pigmentation, Russell looked in a cage and observed a most unusual mouse, a female that was dragging its feet in a peculiar way. The mouse was not injured. It appeared that it was born with some kind of muscular defect and Russell named it "Funnyfoot." By breeding Funnyfoot's brothers and sisters, the same trait cropped up in subsequent generations, leading the team to conclude that Funnyfoot and her related offspring had a genetic disease similar in some ways to muscular dystrophy in humans. This particular fact became of great interest to other researchers working on muscular dystrophy. At once, scientists flooded the lab with requests for mice with the funnyfoot trait. There was a big problem, however—the funnyfoot females were unable to reproduce and the mice died young.

Russell devised a plan for breeding more funnyfoot mice, transplanting the ovaries of funnyfoot females into those of normal females without the characteristic. The ovaries contained egg cells (ova) in which the chromosomes carried the faulty gene. When the normal females mated, many funnyfoot offspring were produced, which were then sent to researchers. Alongside the cages of funnyfoot mice were many other strains that were meticulously bred by Russell and her team. Each group of mice and its ancestry were clearly labeled and recorded. Some strains, for instance, had hereditary diseases like anemia, while others had characteristics that made them sterile or prone to tumors. Other mice were to be used for research on blood disease, the immune system, the endocrine system, diabetes, nutrition, or aging.

Assumes the Directorship of the Jackson Laboratory

By 1953, Russell was named staff scientific director at the Jackson Laboratory. The following year she organized a conference at the laboratory where—for the first time—scientists from around the globe were invited to contribute what they were studying about mammalian genetics and its relationship to cancer. The conference was a success and in 1957 Russell became senior staff scientist. The following year Russell was awarded a Guggenheim Fellowship to review what was currently known about mammalian physiological genetics; the grant provided time and money to compile all the current research in one place, resulting in reference material useful to scientists the world over.

During her directorship, Russell's responsibilities were twofold—to provide the research mice that helped support the lab financially and to work on her areas of interest. One very important area of research at the lab under Russell involved studying blood cells of mice, especially the cells which provide the immune response (the ability to fight off invading foreign substances). This research became very important in an era in which there were a growing number of organ transplants. These mice were used in experiments that determined when tissue is accepted or rejected by an organism.

Russell also took an avid interest in blood hemoglobin—a substance which carries oxygen to all parts of a mammal's body—and was especially curious about how the hemoglobins develop. A mammal fetus inside its mother (including humans) has hemoglobin from a very early stage; after birth, however, that hemoglobin changes both its structure and the site of its production. Some of Russell's work concerned the processes of these developmental changes.

Other research topics Russell investigated include different kinds of cancers, blood diseases, and the process of aging. She has written or collaborated on over a hundred scientific papers and several books. Since 1978, Russell has been senior staff scientist emeritus. Throughout her long active career, Russell's role has also been one of mentor to many of the students that have come through the Jackson Laboratory, either as permanent staff working together on biochemistry and microbiology or the many summer graduate students that come from all over the world.

Russell has been made a member of the American Academy of Arts and Sciences and the National Academy of Sciences. During the 1970s she was an active member of the Academy's Council, acting to edit and evaluate scientific papers. She was also a member of the Genetics Society of America, becoming its vice president in 1974 and president from 1975 to 1976. In 1983 she was made a member of the American Philosophical Society. Russell holds an honorary degree from Ricker College and was a trustee of the University of Maine and the College of the Atlantic. Because of her work on the aging of mice she was asked to be a member of the advisory council to the National Institute of Aging. By attending discussion groups at the laboratory, she continues to closely monitor trends in genetics research.

SELECTED WRITINGS BY RUSSELL:

Periodicals

"A Quantitative Study of Genetic Effects on Guinea Pig Coat Colors," *Genetics,* Volume 24, 1939, pp. 332–353.

"A Comparison of Benign and Malignant Tumors in Drosophila Melanogaster," *Journal of Experimental Zoology,* Volume 34, 1940, pp. 363–385.

(With C. M. Snow, L. M. Murray and J. P. Cormier) "The Bone Marrow in Inherited Macrocytic Anemia in the House Mouse," *Acta Haematologica,* Volume 12, 1953, pp. 247–259.

"Symposium of Twenty-Five Years of Progress in Mammalian Genetics and Cancer, Roscoe B. Jackson Memorial Laboratory, June 27–30, 1954," *Journal of the National Cancer Institute,* Volume 15, 1954, pp. 551–851.

(With others) "Characterization and Genetic Studies of Microcytic Anemia in House Mouse," *Blood,* Volume 35, 1970, pp. 838–850.

(With D. E. Harrison) "Fetal Liver Erythropoiesis and Yolk Sac Cells," *Science,* Volume 177, 1972, p. 187.

(With J. B. Whitney) "Linkage of Genes for Adult Alpha-Globin and Embryonic Alpha-Like Globin Chains," *Proceedings of the National Academy of Sciences USA,* Volume 77, 1980, pp. 1087–90.

"A History of Mouse Genetics," *Annual Review of Genetics,* Volume 19, 1985, pp. 1–28.

Other

A complete bibliography is on file at the Joan Staats Library at the Roscoe B. Jackson Laboratory in Bar Harbor, Maine.

SOURCES:

Books

Noble, Iris, *Contemporary Women Scientists of America,* Messner, 1979, pp. 123–137.

Other

Russell, Elizabeth Shull, telephone interview with Barbara A. Branca conducted February 18, 1994.

—*Sketch by Barbara A. Branca*

Frederick Stratten Russell
1897-1984
English marine biologist

Marine biologist Frederick Stratten Russell linked the distribution of planktonic organisms to water masses and the intensity of light in the seas off the British Isles. His work helped explain the long-term changes in the ecosystem of the English Channel. Russell was fascinated by the larval stages of fishes and the life histories of certain types of jellyfish, which he studied in great detail. He wrote and illustrated several books on his findings. Colleagues J. H. S. Baxter, A. J. Southward, and C. Maurice Yonge characterized Russell as possessing "an old world courtesy" as well as "great personal charm and friendliness."

The youngest son of William and Lucy Binfield Russell, he was born on November 3, 1897, in Bridport, England, on the coast of the English Channel. Russell attended university at Cambridge and planned to study medicine at Gonville and Caius College. But after World War I broke out, he left school to serve in the Royal Naval Air Service in France from 1916 to 1918. He served with distinction, earning the Distinguished Service Cross, the Distinguished Flying Cross, and the Croix de Guerre. After the war he returned to school, earning his degree in 1922.

That year, Russell was assigned to the Egyptian government to study the eggs and larvae of marine fishes. Before embarking on his trip to Egypt, Russell went to the laboratory of the Marine Biological Association in Plymouth, where he studied the early stages in the life histories of fish with R. S. Clark and E. Ford. There, Russell's lifelong interest in marine biology was sparked. When Russell returned from Egypt in 1924 he joined the Plymouth laboratory as a staff member. He continued to study fish larvae and other plankton. Using a special net that allowed him to filter large columns of water, Russell collected plankton, noting their vertical distributions. He built on this initial data over the next fifty years, observing how the composition of the species changed seasonally and over the long term.

Detailed Studies of Plankton and Jellyfish

Russell's work gained international attention when he showed that the depth at which fish plankton were found was related to the intensity of light in the water. He used photoelectric cells to measure the light, finding that the plankton moved up and down the water column in a daily cycle. Seasonal variations in light intensity also affected the migrations. In 1928, C. Maurice Yonge, with whom Russell had co-authored the book *The Seas,* led the Great Barrier Reef Expedition to Australia. Russell and his wife, Gweneth, joined the one-year expedition. Russell compared the distribution of plankton in tropical waters there with that of more temperate regions.

After returning to Plymouth, Russell studied in detail the biology of the torpedo-shaped marine worm, *Sagitta.* Finding that the abundance of different species of *Sagitta* varied from year to year, he traced the cause to the movement of water masses in the English Channel and the North Sea. For example, one species preferred the warmer Atlantic water masses to the Arctic water masses. Russell was able to use *Sagitta* as an indicator species, since other planktonic organisms associated with them. His work helped explain long-term changes in the English Channel ecosystem, including the varying abundance of herring. With a colleague, W. J. Rees, Russell began to study another indicator species, a type of jellyfish, *medusae.* Little was known about its early life stages. Russell and Rees raised *medusae* in captivity, studying the early hydroid stages. In 1938, he was elected a fellow of the Royal Society of London.

The outbreak of World War II interrupted Russell's work on a massive text on the *medusae* that was to contain nearly a thousand illustrations. Russell left Plymouth in 1940 to serve as an intelligence officer for the Royal Air Force. Returned to the Marine Biological Laboratory as director in 1945, he supervised the growth of the laboratory after the war. He also completed his text on the *medusae,* struggling to

remember the finer details of his research before it had been interrupted by the war. The first volume of the book, called *The Medusae of the British Isles,* was finally published in 1953. Russell then devoted more time to different types of jellyfish, including the large *Scyphomedusae.* He also studied a red jellyfish from the Bay of Biscay that gave birth to live young. Russell named it *Stygiomedusa fabulosa.* Russell's studies led to his being honored with the Gold Medal of the Linnean Society in 1961. He was knighted in 1965, the same year he retired.

Continuing his studies even in retirement, at age 78 Russell published a definitive work, *The Eggs and Planktonic Stages of British Marine Fishes,* in which he described in detail the development of fish eggs and larvae. In his later years, after his wife Gweneth passed away in 1978, Russell moved from Plymouth to live near his son in Reading. Frederick Stratten Russell died on June 5, 1984. He had left his influence on the *Journal of the Marine Biological Association,* which he had edited for twenty years, from 1945 to 1965. He had also been the founding editor of the journal *Advances in Marine Biology,* and had participated in its editing and publishing until shortly before his death.

SELECTED WRITINGS BY RUSSELL:

Books

(With C. M. Yonge) *The Seas: Our Knowledge of Life in the Sea and How It Is Gained,* Frederick Warne, 1928.
The Medusae of the British Isles, 2 volumes, Cambridge University Press, 1953, 1970.
The Eggs and Planktonic Stages of British Marine Fishes, Academic Press, 1976.

SOURCES:

Periodicals

Blaxter, J. H. S., A. J. Southward and C. M. Yonge, "Sir Frederick Russell, 1897–1984," *Advances in Marine Biology,* Volume 21, 1984, pp. vii-ix.
Times (London), June 6, 1984.

—*Sketch by Miyoko Chu*

Henry Norris Russell
1877-1957
American astronomer and astrophysicist

Henry Norris Russell was an American astronomer and astrophysicist remembered primarily for his work on the origin and evolution of stars and for his publication in 1913 of what would come to be known as the Hertzsprung-Russell diagram, which plots stars' absolute magnitude, or intrinsic brightness, against their spectral type. During his long career Russell published hundreds of scientific papers covering a wide range of subjects. He made significant contributions to the study of eclipsing binary stars (two stars that revolve around a common center of gravity), inventing ways to measure their size and orbits. He was also involved with the study of stellar and solar composition, the origins of the planets and comets, and the characteristics of planetary atmospheres.

Russell was born on October 25, 1877, in Oyster Bay, New York, where his father, the Reverend Alexander G. Russell, was a Presbyterian minister of Scots-Canadian stock. His mother, Eliza Norris, was born in Brazil where her father served as United States consul. Russell was educated at home until the age of twelve. He was in competent hands: his mother and maternal grandmother were both talented mathematicians, the latter having won a mathematical prize on her graduation in 1840 from Rutgers Female Institute in New York, and the former having come first in a "ladies class" in mathematics given by professors of the University of Edinburgh. Russell took a precocious interest in astronomy at age five after being shown the transit of Venus by his parents. The family moved to his mother's hometown of Princeton, New Jersey, in 1889. Russell was enrolled in the Princeton Preparatory School, and in due course, Princeton University, from which he graduated in 1897 *insigne cum laude*-the highest honor ever obtained by a Princeton graduate. He was awarded his Ph.D. in 1899 for research into methods of discovering the orbits of binary stars. By the time of his graduation, he had produced several other papers on a variety of topics.

Works as Research Student at Cambridge

Shortly after he completed his thesis, Russell's health faltered and he spent most of 1900 recuperating. By late 1901, he was well enough to return to Princeton. The following year he left the United States for England, where he had been accepted into King's College, Cambridge, as an advanced student for three years. He worked first at the Cavendish

Henry Norris Russell

Laboratory, and later with Arthur R. Hinks as a research assistant at the Cambridge Observatory on a grant from the Carnegie Institute. They developed a means of measuring stellar parallax, which allows astronomers to determine the distance of the stars, using photography. Their work was interrupted in September, 1904, when Russell once again was stricken with serious illness. It was left to Hinks to complete the observations and later send the results to Russell at Princeton for measurement. There Russell became an instructor in astronomy and continued making his own observations of the stellar magnitudes and the color indices of the sun, moon, planets, satellites, and a few asteroids.

Russell married Lucy May Cole on November 24, 1908, and they had four children: Lucy May, Elizabeth Hoxie, Henry Norris, and Emma Margaret. Russell was made assistant professor of astronomy at Princeton in 1908, a full professor in 1911, and director of the Princeton University Observatory in 1912, a post he held until 1947. In 1912 Russell published the first recorded analysis of the variation of the light received from eclipsing binary stars; later he would provide important insights into the importance of the periastron, or the point of a star's orbit nearest to the center around which it revolves, in understanding the internal structure of eclipsing binary stars. He also began working with astronomers from Harvard and Yale on a project to determine the positions of the moon.

Work Provides New Insights into Stellar Evolution

In 1913 Russell made observations of stars' color, brightness, and spectral class that called into question the prevailing theory of stellar evolution, which posited consecutive stages of stellar development from hot (blue) through cool (red). He noted that there seemed to be two types of red stars of greatly differing magnitudes. (Danish astronomer **Ejnar Hertzsprung** had published similar findings almost ten years earlier, but his work did not receive recognition at the time; Russell adopted Hertzsprung's terms "dwarf" and "giant" for the two types of red stars.) To produce what became known as the Hertzsprung-Russell diagram, Russell gathered data for hundreds of stars and plotted their absolute visual magnitude (which measures stars' intrinsic luminosity or brightness, as opposed to their apparent brightness) against their spectral class (which is dependent on temperature). Most of the stars thus plotted fell into a section of the diagram known as the "main sequence," which ran from the top left to the bottom right of the chart. Some very bright but cool stars, however, fell above the main-sequence red stars; Russell reasoned that the two types of red stars represented the first and last stages of the life of stars. The configuration of the diagram prompted Russell to propose a new theory of stellar evolution, in which stars move along the main sequence, either contracting as they heat up or expanding as they cool down, Although this theory was eventually found inadequate to explain the great complexity of stellar development, it was an influential starting point for much research to follow.

From June 1918 until the beginning of 1919, Russell worked as a consulting and experimental engineer at the Bureau of Aircraft Production of the Army Aviation Service. He was involved in studying problems associated with aircraft navigation. In carrying out his research, he often had to travel in open airplanes at heights of up to 16,000 feet. Afterward, Russell returned to Princeton to continue his research into the solar spectrum. Soon he was in a position to identify and measure the various chemical elements in the solar atmosphere.

In 1921 Russell made an analysis of radioactive data that led him to make a determination of the age of the earth's crust as between two and eight thousand million years old. Later the same year, he made his first visit to the Mount Wilson Observatory in California. Soon afterward he became one of its research associates, and he worked there for about two months a year for the next twenty years. His work at Mount Wilson centered on radiation and spectrum analysis and yielded important insights into the solar and stellar spectra. Between 1925 and 1930 he produced twenty papers on line spectra of the elements. In 1927, Russell was appointed to the C. A. Young Research Professorship.

Jointly Publishes Astronomy Textbook

Between 1928 and 1931, Russell continued working apace. He was jointly responsible for the Russell-Dugan-Stewart two-volume textbook on astronomy, which redefined the discipline and revolutionized its teaching. He also published a series of papers, contributed an article to *Encyclopedia Britannica* on stellar evolution, and delivered the Terry Lectures on religion at Yale, which he published as *Fate and Freedom*. During the 1930s he devoted himself to spectroscopic research. In 1933 he delivered the Halley Lecture at Oxford, in which he laid out his theories concerning the composition of the stars. He also explained the rules governing the changes of intensity of different elements along the main sequence, and of atoms of the same element at different stages of ionization. Russell's classic book, *The Solar System and Its Origin,* was published to wide acclaim in 1935, and has become a standard authority on the subject.

Much of Russell's enormous body of scientific work was produced in collaboration with other astronomers and astrophysicists. Among over twenty scientists with whom he worked, his closest colleague was **Dr. Charlotte E. Moore Sitterly**. Russell was also associated with many distinguished scientific academies during his career, including the American Astronomical Society, of which he was president from 1934 to 1937; the National Academy of Sciences; the American Association for the Advancement of Science, of which he was president in 1933; the Royal Society, of which he was a foreign member; and the Academies of Rome, Brussels, and Paris, of which he was a correspondent. He also served as president of the commissions of the International Astronomical Union on stellar spectroscopy and on the constitution of stars. Russell received numerous awards and distinctions, including honorary degrees from the following universities: Dartmouth, Louvain, Harvard, Chicago, and Michoacan (Mexico). He was presented with the Draper, Bruce, Rumford, Franklin, Janssen, and Royal Astronomer Society gold medals, and with the Lalande Prize. In 1946, the American Astronomical Society established the annual Henry Norris Russell lectureship in his honor. In 1946, he delivered the first Henry Norris Russell lecture at Radcliffe College, sponsored by the American Astronomy Society. His discussion centered on the difficulty of determining the orbits of eclipsing binary stars.

After he retired, Russell worked at the Harvard and Lick observatories. He also devoted time to his other interests: poetry, geology, archeology, botany, and travel. He continued to pursue scientific work and published the results of his research almost until the day he died. After Russell's death on February 18, 1957, in Princeton, Colonel F. J. M. Stratton, writing in *Biographical Memoirs of Fellows of the Royal Society,* described him thus: "A man of overflowing energy, never sparing himself in his own work or in assisting the researches of others, he was the most eminent and versatile theoretical astrophysicist in the United States if not in the world." **Harlow Shapley** wrote in *Biographical Memoirs of the National Academy of Sciences,* "the word *genius* more rightly applies to him than to any other American astronomer of these or earlier times."

SELECTED WRITINGS BY RUSSELL:

Books

Fate and Freedom, Yale University Press, 1927.
The Solar System and Its Origin, Macmillan, 1935.
(With C. E. Moore) *The Masses of the Stars, with a General Catalog of Dynamical Parallaxes,* Astrophysical Journal Monograph, 1940.

Periodicals

"The Density of the Variable Stars of the Algol Type," *Astrophysical Journal,* Volume 10, 1899, pp. 315–318.
"The General Perturbations of the Major Axis of Eros, by the Action of Mars," *Astronomical Journal,* Volume 21, 1900, pp. 25–28.
"On the Origin of Binary Stars," *Astrophysical Journal,* Volume 31, 1910, pp. 185–207.
"On the Determination of the Orbital Elements of Eclipsing Variable Stars," *Astrophysical Journal,* Volume 35, 1912, pp. 315–340.
"A Superior Limit to the Age of the Earth's Crust," *Proceedings of the Royal Society,* Volume 99A, 1921, pp. 84–86.
"On the Composition of the Sun's Atmosphere," *Astrophysical Journal,* Volume 70, 1929, pp. 11–82.
"Notes on the Constitution of the Stars," *Monthly Notices of the Royal Astronomical Society,* Volume 91, 1931, pp. 951–966.

SOURCES:

Books

Biographical Memoirs of Fellows of the Royal Society, Volume 3, Royal Society (London), 1957, pp. 173–191.
Biographical Memoirs of the National Academy of Sciences, Volume 32, 1958, pp. 354–378.
Kaler, James B., *Stars,* Scientific American Library, 1992.
Williams, Henry Smith, *Great Astronomers,* Simon & Schuster, 1930, p. 444.

—*Sketch by Avril McDonald*

Loris Shano Russell
1904-
American-born Canadian paleontologist

In addition to extensive teaching experience and museum administration, Loris Shano Russell has published more than one hundred papers based on extensive fieldwork in the western United States and Canada. During his long career he proposed several novel theories in geology as well as in dinosaur and early mammalian studies. More importantly for paleontology, Russell developed a methodology that combines findings in stratigraphy—the study of the composition of rock layers and how they form—with fossil records to produce a much broader picture of ancient ecologies than had been previously attempted. After World War II, Russell's interest in museum work led him to accept leading positions at the National Museum of Canada and the Royal Ontario Museum.

Russell was born in Brooklyn, New York, on April 21, 1904, to Milan Winslow, a noted calligrapher, and Matilda Shano Russell, who later became involved in mission work for the Salvation Army. The family moved to Alberta, Canada, and as a boy Russell went to public schools in Calgary, in the foothills of the Canadian Rockies. Russell's interest in zoology and geology began early, and the Calgary area—rich in fossils of early mammals—gave him plenty of opportunities to indulge his interests. Calgary was only one hundred miles from Red Deer, which contained some of the richest Cretaceous fossil beds in the world. (The Cretaceous period is known as the age in which dinosaurs became extinct, about 120 million years ago). Before he went to the University of Alberta in Edmonton in the early 1920s as an undergraduate, Russell had already collected numerous specimens of invertebrate and vertebrate fossils, carefully labeled with locations and largely accurate identifications.

At the University of Alberta, Russell wrote a series of papers based on this collection which correctly demonstrated the similarity of groups of fossils in Alberta and Montana. In 1927 he went on to Princeton University, where he received his master's degree in paleontology in 1929 and his doctoral degree in 1930. The subject of Russell's thesis dealt with the actual boundary between the Cretaceous period and the Tertiary (the dawn of the age of mammals, which began seventy million years ago) in the rock formations of Alberta. Combining the fossil evidence with geologic data, Russell upset some widely held notions about the dating of several key geologic events of that period. He showed that one in particular, the Laramide revolution—which saw the major uplift of the Rockies—occurred much later than was previously assumed.

In 1930 Russell joined the Geological Survey of Canada. During seven years of field work with the Geological Survey, he was able to get very detailed mappings of rock formations and layers to amplify the subject of his thesis. Parts of North America had been covered by sea during the Cretaceous period, and Russell found that the sea had spread quickly and had withdrawn in fits and starts, contradicting the standard model that the sea had spread slowly and subsided evenly. In southwestern Saskatchewan, he found and described the most recent marine animal life on the Canadian plains. Before anyone else, Russell tried to reconcile fossil records of Cretaceous and Tertiary mussels with the classifications assigned to contemporary specimens.

Russell joined the University of Toronto in 1937 as assistant professor in paleontology and assistant director of the Royal Ontario Museum of Paleontology, although his tenure there was interrupted during World War II for three years of military service. In 1950 he became the chief zoologist of the National Museum of Canada at Ottawa. Russell decided in 1956 to accept the directorship of the museum's Natural History Branch, permitting him oversight of the fossils available there. Later that year, he found himself heading the entire National Museum. In that role, Russell saw fit to enlarge the biological and anthropological research performed by the museum. In 1963, running into opposition to his plans for the Canadian centenary, he left the National Museum and returned to the University of Toronto to stay, this time taking the positions of professor in the geology department and chief biologist at the Royal Ontario Museum.

Proposes Revolutionary Theory on Dinosaur Anatomy

During Russell's involvement with the Royal Ontario and National museums, he continued his fieldwork and wrote many articles on dinosaur anatomy. Russell was among the first vertebrate paleontologists to notice that the bone structure of dinosaurs resembles more closely that of birds than of reptiles. These and other observations led Russell to publish a paper in 1965 in the *Journal of Paleontology* speculating that dinosaurs were warm-blooded but not insulated by fur or feathers, which might account in part for their extinction. At the time the paper did not garner much attention in academic circles. However, paleontologist Robert Bakkertook many of Russell's theories on dinosaurs and combined them with his own in the book *The Dinosaur Heresies,* which kindled considerable debate.

The heart of Russell's work exists in his analysis of the evolution of mammals at the beginning of the

Tertiary period. He discovered new mammals from that time in British Columbia and Saskatchewan while greatly expanding on what was already known about early Tertiary mammals in western Canada. Russell considered the fossil-bearing rock formations of the central mountain states of the United States and the Canadian provinces of Alberta and Saskatchewan to be vital resources not only for the richness of the fossils but for the clarity of the rock layers' sequence. He found that this clarity greatly helped to put the fossils in their proper time frames.

Russell married Grace Evelyn Le Feuvre on June 11, 1938. They had no children. Throughout his life, Russell enjoyed working in the field and clearly gathered his inspiration there. Yet he was a gifted administrator, as his numerous museum appointments attest. Russell helped the Canadian museum system take a commanding lead in the field of vertebrate paleontology. He received many awards, among them the Willett G. Miller medal in 1959 from the Royal Society of Canada, to which he was elected a fellow in 1936. He was president of the Society of Vertebrate Paleontology from 1958 to 1959 and also president of the Canadian Museums Association from 1961 to 1963.

SELECTED WRITINGS BY RUSSELL:

Books

The Cretaceous Reptile Champsosaurus natator, National Museum of Canada, 1956.
Mammal Teeth from the St. Mary River Formation (Upper Cretaceous) at Scabby Butte, Alberta, National Museum of Canada, 1962.
Fauna and Correlation of the Ravenscrag Formation (Paleocene) of Southwestern Saskatchewan, Royal Ontario Museum, 1974.

Periodicals

"Body Temperature of Dinosaurs and Its Relationships to Their Extinction," *Journal of Paleontology,* May, 1965, pp. 497–501.

SOURCES:

Books

McGraw-Hill Modern Men of Science, Volume 2, McGraw, 1968, pp. 465–466.

Periodicals

Dolphin, Ric, "Bones of Contention," *Maclean's,* December 5, 1988, pp. 57–58.

Other

Russell, Loris Shano, telephone interview with
Hovey Brock conducted September 29, 1993.

—*Sketch by Hovey Brock*

Ernest Rutherford
1871-1937
New Zealand-born English physicist

Ernest Rutherford

Ernest Rutherford's explanation of radioactivity earned him the 1908 Nobel Prize in chemistry, but his most renowned achievement was his classic demonstration that the atom consists of a small, dense nucleus surrounded by orbiting electrons. He also demonstrated the transmutation of one element into another by splitting the atom. His direction of laboratories in Canada and Great Britain led to such triumphs as the discovery of the neutron and helped to launch high-energy, or particle, physics, which concentrates on the constitution, properties, and interactions of elementary particles of matter.

Rutherford was born the fourth of twelve children on August 30, 1871, to James and Martha Thompson Rutherford on the South Island of New Zealand near the village of Spring Grove. Both parents had arrived in New Zealand as children, not long after Great Britain annexed the territory into the Commonwealth in 1840. Rutherford's father, of Scottish descent, logged, cultivated flax, worked in construction, and pursued other endeavors with a mechanical inventiveness inherited from his wheelwright father, George. Martha Rutherford was a schoolteacher of English descent.

Rutherford's early success in school earned him a scholarship to Nelson College, a secondary school in a village on the north end of New Zealand's South Island. He then received a scholarship to Canterbury College at Christchurch, New Zealand, where he earned his bachelor of arts degree in 1892. He continued studying at Canterbury, earning a master of arts degree with honors in mathematics and mathematical physics in 1893 and a bachelor of science degree in 1894. In New Zealand, Rutherford met Mary Newton, the woman who would become his wife in 1900. She was the daughter of the woman who provided Rutherford with lodging while he studied at Canterbury. Rutherford and his wife had one daughter, Eileen (1901–1930), who married Ralph Fowler, a laboratory assistant of Rutherford's in the 1920s and 1930s.

While working toward his bachelor of science degree, Rutherford researched the effects of electromagnetic waves, produced by rapidly alternating electrical currents, on the magnetization of iron. He observed that, contrary to contemporary expectations, iron did magnetize in high-frequency electromagnetic fields. Conversely, he also showed that electromagnetic waves could demagnetize magnetized iron needles. On the basis of this observation, Rutherford devised a device for picking up electromagnetic waves produced at a distance. Italian physicist **Guglielmo Marconi** would later parlay the same principles into the development of wireless telegraphy, or radio.

These experiments earned Rutherford a scholarship in 1895 derived from profits from London's Great Exhibition of 1851. Rutherford attended Trinity College at Cambridge University to work under the direction of English physicist **J. J. Thomson** at the Cavendish Laboratory as the university's first research student. The laboratory had been established in 1871 for research in experimental physics and was first led by electromagnetism pioneer James Clerk Maxwell. Rutherford's demonstration of his electromagnetic detector greatly impressed Thomson and other scientists at the Cavendish almost immediately.

Thomson invited Rutherford in 1896 to assist him in studies of the effects of X rays, which had been discovered in 1895 by **Wilhelm Conrad Röntgen**, on the electrical properties of gases. Thomson and Rutherford demonstrated that X rays broke gas molecules into electrically and positively charged ions, making the gas electrically conductive. This work brought Rutherford widespread recognition in the British scientific community for the first time.

Forges Understanding of Radioactivity

In 1897, Rutherford took up the study of radioactivity, the phenomenon discovered almost accidentally by French physicist **Henri Becquerel** in 1896. He began by studying the radioactive emissions of uranium, systematically wrapping uranium in successive layers of aluminum foil to observe the penetrating ability of these emissions. He concluded that uranium emitted two distinct types of radiation: a less penetrating type, which he called "alpha," and a more penetrating type, "beta." He also later observed what was described by French physicist Paul Villard as "gamma" radiation, the most penetrating type of all.

Not assured of a professorship at Cambridge, Rutherford applied for and was appointed Second MacDonald Professor of Physics at McGill University in Montreal, Canada, in 1898. McGill University appealed to Rutherford especially because it had perhaps the best-equipped laboratory in North America, if not the world, at the time. At McGill, Rutherford turned from studying uranium to thorium, another radioactive element. Although thorium emits alpha and beta radiation as does uranium, emission patterns for thorium substances seemed erratic. Rutherford determined in 1899 that an emanation, or new radioactive substance, was being produced. He also observed that the radioactivity of the emanation gradually decreased geometrically with time, an occurrence now known as the half-life of a radioactive substance, which is a measurement of the time it takes for half of a substance to decay. In 1901, Rutherford forged a partnership with **Frederick Soddy**, an Oxford chemistry demonstrator based at McGill who first encountered Rutherford in a debate on the existence of subatomic particles. Rutherford wanted Soddy to help him study the thorium emanations and to explain curious observations of radioactive substances noticed in Europe by Becquerel and by Sir William Crookes, who discovered thallium. Both had isolated the active parts of uranium from an apparently inert part. However, Becquerel also observed that the active part soon lost its activity, while the inert remainder regained its activity.

Rutherford and Soddy isolated the active part of radioactive thorium, which they named thorium-X, from the apparently-inert parent thorium. They charted how thorium-X gradually lost its radioactivity while the original thorium regained its activity, illustrating that thorium-X had its own distinctive half-life, which was much shorter than the half-life of thorium. Soddy tried to get thorium-X to interact

chemically with other reagents without success. From these observations, Rutherford and Soddy put together the modern understanding of radioactivity in 1903. Thorium-X was a product of the disintegration or decay of thorium. In nature, radioactive elements and their products decay simultaneously. However, when the product is separated out, it continues to decay but is not replenished by decaying thorium atoms, so its radioactivity falls off. Meanwhile, the inert parent thorium eventually regains its radioactivity as it generates new radioactive products. Rutherford's explanation of radioactivity at the atomic level is what caused a sensation in scientific circles. He explained that radioactivity—alpha, beta, and gamma radiation—was the physical manifestation of this disintegration, the pieces of the thorium atom that were released as it decayed. In other words, thorium was steadily being transformed, or transmuted, into a new element that was lower in atomic number. It was this work that earned Rutherford the 1908 Nobel Prize in chemistry.

Rutherford received, and turned down, offers to teach at Yale and Columbia Universities in the United States. He became a Fellow of the Royal Society in 1903 and received the Rumford Medal in 1904. His books on radioactivity became standard textbooks on the subject for years and he was a popular speaker. He attracted a number of talented associates at McGill, the most famous of whom was **Otto Hahn**, a German physicist who would, with Austrian physicist **Lise Meitner**, demonstrate the fissioning of uranium in 1939.

In 1904, Rutherford was the first to suggest that radioactive elements with extremely long half-lives might provide a source of energy for sustaining the heat of the Earth's interior. This would supply a means for estimating the age of the Earth in the billions of years, allowing plenty of time for evolution by natural selection to proceed along lines outlined by the naturalist Charles Darwin in 1859.

Determines Atomic Structure and Splits Atom

In 1906, Sir Arthur Schuster offered Rutherford his chair as professor of physics at Manchester University in Great Britain. Eager to return to what was then the center of the scientific world, Rutherford accepted the position in 1907. Rutherford was again blessed at Manchester with a well-equipped laboratory and talented associates from around the world, such as **Hans Geiger**, who would develop the radioactivity counter; Charles Darwin, grandson of the famous naturalist; and physicists **Niels Bohr**, Ernest Marsden, and **H. G. J. Moseley**.

Rutherford proceeded with his study of radioactive emissions, particularly the high-energy alpha particles. His research was slowed at first when a sample of radium, his favorite alpha source, was sent by the Radium Institute of the Austrian Academy of Sciences in Vienna to a rival, **William Ramsay**, discoverer of the noble gases. Rutherford had to request and await another sample from the Institute before he could proceed in earnest with his work.

Rutherford wanted to determine precisely the nature of the alpha particles. In 1903, at McGill, he had succeeded in deflecting alpha particles in electric and magnetic fields, proving they had a positive charge. He was certain that the relatively massive particle must be equivalent to helium nuclei, which consist of two protons. At Manchester in 1908, Rutherford and his colleagues proved experimentally through spectroscopic means that the alpha particles were indeed nuclei of helium atoms.

In 1908, Rutherford and Geiger devised a method for counting alpha particles precisely. Alpha particles were fired into a nearly evacuated tube with a strong electric field. The resulting ionizing effect in the gas could be detected by an electrometer, a device that measures electric charge in a gas. The alpha particles could then be detected visually as well as they struck a zinc sulfide screen to cause an identifiable flash or scintillation. Geiger would build upon this technique in developing the electric radiation counter that bears his name.

In 1909, Rutherford had instructed Marsden to study the scattering of alpha particles at large angles. Marsden observed that when alpha particles were fired at gold foil, a significant number of particles were deflected at unusually large angles; some particles were even reflected backward. Metals with a larger atomic number (such as lead) reflected back even more particles. It was not until late in 1910 that Rutherford postulated from this evidence the modern concept of the atom, which he announced early in 1911. He surmised that the atom did not resemble a "plum pudding" of positively charged nuclear particles with electrons embedded within like raisins, as suggested by Thomson. Instead, Rutherford suggested that the atom consisted of a very small, dense nucleus surrounded by orbiting electrons. Geiger and Marsden provided the mathematics to support the theory and Bohr linked this concept with quantum theory to produce the model of the atom employed today. After World War I broke out in 1914, Rutherford was called upon to serve in the British Navy's Board of Invention and Research. His main area of research for the Board was in devising a method for detecting German U-boats at sea. His work established principles applied later in the development of sonar.

The work on alpha particle scattering continued during the war. Marsden observed in 1914 that alpha particles fired into hydrogen gas produced anomalous numbers of scintillations. Rutherford first concluded that the scintillations were being caused by hydrogen nuclei. However, Rutherford later observed the same effect when alpha particles were fired into nitrogen. After a long series of experiments to exclude all possible explanations, in 1919 Rutherford determined that the alpha particles were splitting the nitrogen atoms and that the extraneous hydrogen atoms were remnants of that split. Nitrogen was thus transmuted into another element. In 1925, English physicist **Paul Maynard Stewart Blackett** used the cloud chamber apparatus devised by Scottish physicist **C. T. R. Wilson** to verify Rutherford's observation and to show that the atom split after it had absorbed the alpha particle.

Directs the Cavendish Laboratory

In 1919, Rutherford was persuaded to succeed Thomson as director of the Cavendish Laboratory at Cambridge, a post he would hold until his death. Rutherford directed the Cavendish during its most fruitful research period in its history. English atomic physicist **John D. Cockcroft** and Irish experimental physicist **Ernest Walton** constructed the world's first particle accelerator in 1932 and demonstrated the transmutation of elements by artificial means. Also in the early 1930s, English physicist **James Chadwick** confirmed the existence of the neutron, which Rutherford had predicted at least a decade earlier. Rutherford, with Chadwick, continued to bombard and split light elements with alpha particles. With Marcus Oliphant and Paul Harteck, Rutherford, in 1934, bombarded deuterium with deuterons (deuterium nuclei), achieving the first fusion reaction and production of tritium.

Rutherford was involved significantly in national and international politics during this period, albeit not for himself but for the sake of science. He worked with the civilian Department of Scientific and Industrial Research (DSIR) to obtain grants for his scientific team and served as president of the British Association for the Advancement of Science from 1925 to 1930. Beginning in 1933, Rutherford served as president of the Academic Assistance Council, established to assist refugee Jewish scientists fleeing the advance of Nazi Germany. When the Soviet Union prevented Russian physicist **Pyotr Kapitsa**, a promising Cavendish scientist, from returning to Great Britain from the Soviet Union in 1934, Rutherford launched an ultimately futile effort to convince the Soviets to release him. Rutherford maintained close relations through correspondence with leading scientists in Europe, North America, Australia, and New Zealand. Despite his preference for experiment, Rutherford corresponded with Bohr, German physicist **Max Planck**, American physicist **Albert Einstein** and other theoretical physicists transforming physics with relativity and quantum mechanics. He also remained close to his mother in New Zealand, exchanging letters with her frequently until her death in 1935.

In his long and distinguished career, Rutherford's most prestigious award, aside from his Nobel Prize, may have been the Order of Merit that he received from King George V in 1925. The Order of Merit is Britain's highest civilian honor. Rutherford was knighted in 1914 and made a peer (Baron Rutherford of Nelson or Lord Rutherford) in 1931. He died from complications after surgery on a strangulated hernia on October 19, 1937, in Cambridge. His cremated remains were buried near the graves of Isaac Newton and Charles Darwin at Westminster Abbey in London.

SELECTED WRITINGS BY RUTHERFORD:

Books

Radio-Activity, Cambridge University Press, 1904, second edition, 1905.
Radioactive Transformations, Scribner, 1906.
Radioactive Substances and Their Radiations, Cambridge University Press, 1913.
(With James Chadwick and C. D. Ellis) *Radiations from Radioactive Substances,* G. P. Putnam, 1930.
Chadwick, James, editor, *Collected Papers of Lord Rutherford of Nelson,* three volumes, 1962–65.
Badash, Lawrence, editor, *Rutherford and Boltwood: Letters on Radioactivity,* 1969.

SOURCES:

Books

Dictionary of Scientific Biography, Volume 12, Scribner, 1975.
Eve, Arthur Stewart, *Rutherford,* Macmillan, 1939.
Wilson, David, *Rutherford: Simple Genius,* MIT Press, 1983.
World of Scientific Discovery, Gale, 1994.

—*Sketch by Michael Boersma*

Leopold Ružička
1887-1976
Croatian-born Swiss chemist

Leopold Ružička worked in what he referred to as the "borderland" between bio-organic chemistry and biochemistry. His studies of odorous natural products led to his discovery of carbon rings with many more carbon atoms than had been originally thought possible. His research also contributed important information on how living things biosynthesize some steroids and sex hormones. For this work he shared the 1939 Nobel Prize in chemistry.

Leopold Stephen Ružička was born on September 13, 1887, to Stjepan and Amalija (Sever) Ružička. He was the first of two boys. They lived at first in Vukovar in Eastern Croatia (later part of Yugoslavia). His father, a cooper, died when Ružička was about four years old, and the family then moved to Osijek to live with relatives. Ružička attended elementary and high school in Osijek, where he received a classical education (Latin and Greek), and was initially determined to enter the Catholic priesthood. As a teenager, he changed his interests to chemistry, and upon graduation began to look for graduate schools in Germany and Switzerland. He eventually settled on the *Technische Hochschule* in Karlsruhe, Germany, choosing it over the Swiss Federal Institute of Technology (Eidgenossische Technische Hochschule, or ETH) in Zurich, because it provided more flexibility in courses and did not require an entrance examination in descriptive geometry.

Ružička obtained his doctorate in only four years, under the direction of **Hermann Staudinger** at Karlsruhe. He then assisted Staudinger in research on the natural products in the *Chrysanthemum* species; these chemicals, called pyrethrins, were of particular interest as insecticides. In September of 1912, they both moved to ETH, where Ružička had originally considered studying, when Staudinger replaced **Richard Willstätter** as professor of organic and inorganic chemistry. Reflecting on these events later in his life, Ružička wrote in *Annual Review of Biochemistry,* "The fact that I went to Karlsruhe for my training was a very important factor in my life. If I had taken my doctorate degree with Willstätter I should have gone to Germany with him in 1912, and two years later Germany was at war.... That war ended in 1918 with the destruction of the Habsburg empire and the beginning of bad times in Germany." Instead, he had established sufficient residency in Zurich by 1917 to obtain Swiss citizenship, and avoided the devastation caused during World War I.

In 1916, Ružička started his own research program, supported financially by a Geneva perfume company. (His position at ETH carried no salary until 1925, two years after he was named a professor.) The University of Utrecht, in the Netherlands, offered him a job as an organic chemistry professor in 1926. After three years there, he went back to Zurich to take on the job of directing ETH. During much of his career he was also supported financially by the Rockefeller Foundation.

Ružička studied various organic compounds early in his career, but in 1921 his most fruitful work began—on the structure and synthesis of several natural compounds important to the fragrance industry. (His collaborations with the Swiss pharmaceutical and perfume industries was to continue throughout his working life.) Before Ružička's discoveries, chemists thought that ring structures containing more than eight carbons would be unstable, because no one had been able to synthesize large rings. Ružička's research on muscone (obtained from the male musk deer) and civetone (from both male and female civet cats), however, indicated rings with as many as seventeen carbons—a huge number. He was able to synthesize some of these very large rings with new procedures developed by his research group.

Another line of research dealt with isoprene. Biochemists are interested in how living things biosynthesize large molecules; they had known for some time that isoprene is one of nature's favorite building blocks. Ružička found many more large biochemicals that were constructed from isoprene units, and he formulated a rule of thumb called the "isoprene rule" for predicting biosynthesis based on this starting material. Ružička also synthesized testosterone and androsterone , the male sex hormones. In recognition of these successes he was awarded the Nobel Prize in chemistry in 1939, which he shared with **Adolf Butenandt**.

Ružička conducted research in an era when instrumentation was primitive by contemporary standards. The elucidation of molecular structure, therefore, depended entirely upon the observation of chemical reactions and the purification of reaction products. In this process an unknown compound would be exposed to various well-characterized reagents; if it reacted to give certain products, the chemist knew that the original molecule contained particular arrangements of atoms. (Ružička, for example, frequently used dehydrogenation—the removal of hydrogen atoms—to gain information about molecular structure.) Once these arrangements had been identified, the chemist would attempt to synthesize the original compound, and then compare the original and the synthetic. If they matched, that was taken as good evidence that the perceived structure was at least partly correct. This time-consuming, "wet" chemistry often gave ambiguous results, and polite arguments frequently occurred in scientific literature as the chemistry community debated the structure of a complicated new molecule. Often old rules had to give way when new discoveries were made. In his Nobel lecture, Ružička said, "Experience has shown that there is no rule governing the architecture of natural compounds which is valid without exception, and which would enable us to dispense with the need to test its validity accurately for every new compound to be examined."

Ružička married Anna Housmann in 1912; they were divorced in 1950. In 1951, he married Gertrud Acklin. He was an avid gardener and collector of paintings, so much so that he once said his chemistry had suffered as a result of his hobbies. He established an important collection of Dutch and Flemish Masters of the seventeenth century, as well as an art library on that general period, which he later gave to the Zurich art museum. During World War II, he worked to secure the escape of several Jewish scientists from the Nazis, and founded the Swiss-Yugoslav Relief Society. He was instrumental in providing refuge in Switzerland to the future Nobel Laureate **Vladimir Prelog**, who succeeded Ružička as the director of ETH when the latter retired in 1957. Ružička died on September 26, 1976.

SELECTED WRITINGS BY RUŽIČKA:

Books

"In the Borderland between Bioorganic Chemistry and Biochemistry," in *Annual Review of Biochemistry,* Volume 42, 1973, pp. 1–20.

SOURCES:

Books

Nobel Prize Winners, H. W. Wilson, 1987.
Nobel Prize Winners in Chemistry: 1901–1961, revised edition, Abelard-Schuman, 1963, p. 171.

                                          —*Sketch by Gail B.C. Marsella*

Martin Ryle
1918-1984
English radio astronomer

The 1974 Nobel Prize for physics, awarded to Martin Ryle and **Antony Hewish**, was the first to be given to astronomers. The award was granted in recognition of their pioneering research in radio astrophysics. Ryle in particular was recognized for his development of the aperture synthesis technique, a method by which computer technology is used to overcome some fundamental problems in the construction of radio telescopes. By using this technique Ryle was able to make a number of important discoveries, including the nature of radio stars and the origins of radio scintillation.

Ryle was born in Brighton, England, on September 27, 1918. The Ryle name was well-known and highly respected in England: Martin Ryle 's father, John A. Ryle, was a physician, director of Oxford University's Institute of Social Medicine, and the first professor of social medicine at the university; and an uncle, Gilbert Ryle, was a philosopher. Martin's mother was the former Miriam Scully. Ryle attended Bradfield College and Christ Church at Oxford University, eventually earning first-class honors in the latter's school of natural sciences.

War Research Leads to a Career in Radio Astronomy

Ryle's graduation from Oxford in 1939 coincided with the beginning of World War II in Europe; instead of heading for graduate school, he was assigned to work in the government's Telecommunications Research Establishment (later renamed the Royal Radar Establishment). His primary assignment there was the development of countermeasures for enemy radar. Ryle also made contact with his future colleague, Antony Hewish, during his war-related research. At the war's conclusion Ryle returned to Cambridge, where he had worked briefly before being assigned to the Telecommunications Research Establishment. Like many of his colleagues, Ryle was convinced that the new science of radar could be applied to observational astronomy. Early working conditions were primitive, to be sure, with Ryle's earliest instrument being a captured German radar dish, but progress was made rapidly.

Develops Basic Techniques of Radio Astronomy

The science of radio astronomy had been established largely through the efforts of American engineer **Karl Guthe Jansky** in the early 1930s. Jansky had detected the presence of very short radio waves coming from distant parts of the universe, and had recognized the possibility that such radio waves might carry information about astronomical bodies in much the same way that light waves do. Jansky's hopes for a new field of radio astronomy were disputed by many astronomers who doubted the importance of his discoveries. However, as research continued—especially with the improved instruments and techniques available from war research—those doubts began to fade. By the late 1940s, Ryle and his colleagues were ready to attack the fundamental questions of radio astronomy.

The first challenge was simply to construct a map of the radio-emitting sources in the sky. In his first survey of the heavens, completed in 1950, Ryle identified fifty radio sources; a second survey, conducted five years later, found almost 2,000 sources. During these surveys, Ryle and his colleagues made another important discovery: they located a radio source in the constellation Cygnus, 500 million light years away. The ability to detect an object that distant meant that radio telescopes had the ability to see very far back into the history of the universe. They were, therefore, valuable tools in the science of cosmology, the study of the universe's creation.

As Ryle extended his search for radio sources, he was forced to deal with a difficult technical problem. The resolving power of any telescope (its ability to separate two nearby objects in the sky) depends on the wavelength of the radiation detected. Since the wavelength of radio waves is much longer than that of light waves, a radio telescope must be many times larger than a light telescope of comparable resolving power. In fact, the telescopes Ryle and other radio astronomers needed for their work could easily have been hundreds or thousands of meters in diameter.

Ryle's solution for this problem was conceptually simple and elegant. He designed a number of telescope parts that could be moved from place to place. He located these sections first in one region of his phantom giant telescope, aimed that at the sky, and took pictures. He then moved the sections to another region of the giant phantom telescope and took more pictures. He continued this process until the sections had been placed over a very large total area, one comparable in size to the desired, if unbuildable, giant telescope. Finally, in order to place the sections in precisely the right places and properly correlate all the individual pictures, Ryle tied the sections into a master computer. The computer then generated the kind of radio picture of the sky that would have been obtained by a single very large radio telescope. It was primarily for the design of this aperture synthesis telescope that Ryle was awarded a share of the 1974 Nobel Prize in physics.

Ryle held a variety of teaching, research and administrative positions at Cambridge until his retirement in 1982. During that time he accumulated a number of honors and awards, including the Hughes Medal of the Royal Society in 1954, the Gold Medal of the Royal Astronomical Society in 1964, the Henry Draper Medal of the United States National Academy of Sciences in 1965, and the Royal Medal of the Royal Society in 1973. He was knighted in 1966.

Ryle was married in 1947 to Ella Rowena Palmer, a nurse and physiotherapist. During the last decade of his life he became particularly interested in the role of renewable energy in the world's future and argued strongly for the development of wind power in Great Britain. He died of lung cancer in Cambridge on October 16, 1984.

SELECTED WRITINGS BY RYLE:

Periodicals

"The New Cambridge Radio Telescope," *Nature*, May 12, 1962, pp. 517–18.

"High Resolution Observations of the Radio Sources in Cygnus and Cassiopeia," *Nature,* March 27, 1965, pp. 1259–62.

SOURCES:

Books

A Biographical Encyclopedia of Scientists, Facts on File, 1981, p. 700.
McGraw-Hill Modern Scientists and Engineers, McGraw, 1980, pp. 57–59.
Nobel Prize Winners, H. W. Wilson, 1987, pp. 902–904.

Weber, Robert L., *Pioneers of Science: Nobel Prize Winners in Physics,* American Institute of Physics, 1980, pp. 237–238.

Periodicals

Findlay, John W., "The 1974 Nobel Prize in Physics," *Science,* November 15, 1974, pp. 620–21.
"Radioastronomers Ryle and Hewish Win Nobel Physics Prize," *Physics Today,* December, 1974, p. 77.

—*Sketch by David E. Newton*